1989

HISTORY OF POLITICAL PHILOSOPHY

HISTORY
OF
POLITICAL
PHILOSOPHY

Third Edition

EDITED BY

LEO STRAUSS

AND

JOSEPH CROPSEY

THE UNIVERSITY OF CHICAGO PRESS
Chicago and London

LEO STRAUSS (1899–1973) was the Robert Maynard Hutchins Distinguished Service Professor in Political Science at the University of Chicago. His many books include *Natural Right and History*, *Persecution and the Art of Writing*, *Thoughts on Machiavelli*, and *The Political Philosophy of Hobbes*.

JOSEPH CROPSEY is Distinguished Service Professor in Political Science at the University of Chicago. He is the author of *Polity and Economy* and *Political Philosophy and the Issues of Politics*, and the editor of *Ancients and Moderns* and *Hobbes's Dialogue between a Philosopher and a Student of the Common Laws of England*.

The University of Chicago Press, Chicago 60637
The University of Chicago Press, Ltd., London

96 95 94 93 92 91 90 89 88 87   5 4 3 2 1

Library of Congress Cataloging in Publication Data

History of political philosophy.

  Includes bibliographies and index.
    1. Political science—History.
I. Strauss, Leo.   II. Cropsey, Joseph.
JA81.H58   1987   320′.01   86-30775
ISBN 0-226-77708-1
ISBN 0-226-77710-3 (pbk.)

CONTENTS

v

vii

PREFACE
TO THE
THIRD EDITION

The second edition of this work appeared in 1972, the year before the death of Leo Strauss. In the intervening time, a new generation has approached or reached maturity, and the decision to issue a new edition has afforded the opportunity to include their work in this volume, and at the same time to widen the scope of the book in important particulars. Present for the first time are chapters on Thucydides and Xenophon, for which no explanation will be needed. Present also are chapters on Husserl and Heidegger, for which some explanation might be needed; and a statement on Leo Strauss, for which considerable explanation might be needed.

When, in the Preface to the first edition, we referred to the inclusion of chapters on the Muslim and Jewish medievals and on Descartes as open to question, we had in mind of course that the thinkers involved are not primarily political philosophers. Of Husserl and Heidegger the same will be said, as it will be said of phenomenology and existentialism that they are not political philosophy. Yet one has only to think of the 1960s and the "radicalism" of the times to be reminded of the impact that existentialism however transformed had on a public consciousness. Nor can it be forgotten that Heidegger's philosophizing either permitted, prepared, or induced—still a matter for controversy—his participation, long or short, in a nefarious politics. Perhaps always, perhaps emphatically in our times, politics in some derivative and uncertain way responds to the human contemplation of mankind's powers, horizons, and goals and haltingly gives effect to the emergent visions through the institutions of government. I trust that a knowledge of the work of Husserl and Heidegger will help to deepen a student's comprehension not only of the politics of the twentieth century but of political possibilities in principle.

The chapters on Aristotle, on Burke, and on Bentham and James Mill are new to this edition. Replacement was the result either of the withdrawal of the original chapter by its author or of a desire to broaden the authorship of the volume by the inclusion of the work of rising or risen scholars.

The inclusion of the Epilogue on Leo Strauss—of an essay on one of the editors of the book, withal deceased—does indeed demand an explanation. I have called for this addition to the volume because it is now quite clear that Strauss has taken his place as a thinker in the tradition of political philosophy, on a plane not now knowable but of sufficient elevation to have made him interesting and controversial in many places. I am confident that the essay will prove valuable to those who seek a sympathetic, scrupulous presentation of a difficult and widely studied *oêuvre*, a presentation that is not neutral but is nevertheless objective.

I cannot know or claim that any of the decisions that have led to the differences between this and the previous edition would have met with the senior editor's approval. I hope that this edition will be received as continuing the intention of those versions that have found favor in the past.

JOSEPH CROPSEY
Chicago, 1986

PREFACE
TO THE
SECOND EDITION

Continuing interest in the approach to the teaching of political philosophy that is presented in this book has afforded the occasion to publish a second edition. The present text differs from the previous one in containing a chapter on Kant, new chapters on Augustine, Thomas Aquinas, and Machiavelli, and in revision of important details in the chapters on Descartes and Locke. Changes have been made in a few other places, but they are minor.

L.S.
J.C.

PREFACE
TO THE
FIRST EDITION

This book is intended primarily to introduce undergraduate students of political science to political philosophy. The authors and editors have done their best to take political philosophy seriously, assuming throughout that the teachings of the great political philosophers are important not only historically, as phenomena about which we must learn if we wish to understand societies of the present and the past, but also as phenomena from which we must learn if we wish to understand those societies. We believe that the questions raised by the political philosophers of the past are alive in our own society, if only in the way that questions can be alive which, in the main, are tacitly or unwittingly answered. We have written, further, in the belief that in order to understand any society, to analyze it with any depth, the analyst must himself be exposed to these enduring questions and be swayed by them.

This book is addressed to those who for whatever reason believe that students of political science must have some understanding of the philosophic treatment of the abiding questions; to those who do not believe that political science is scientific as chemistry and physics are—subjects from which their own history is excluded. That the great majority of the profession concurs in the view that the history of political philosophy is a proper part of political science we take to be proved by the very common practice of offering courses on this subject matter.

We tender this book to the public in full awareness that it is not a perfect historical study. It is not even a perfect textbook. It is imperfect of its kind, as we freely acknowledge, because for one thing it is not the work of one hand. If the hand could be found that is moved by a single mind with the necessary grasp of the literature, that hand would write, if it found time, a more coherent, more uniform book, certainly a more comprehensive book—and we will ourselves adopt it when it appears. On the other hand, it must be allowed that the reader of a collaborative work is to some extent compensated for these shortcomings by the variety of viewpoints, talents, and backgrounds that inform the parts of the volume.

We are convinced that even the most excellent textbook could serve only a limited purpose. When a student has mastered the very best secondary account of an author's teaching, he possesses an opinion of that teaching, a hearsay rather than knowledge of it. If the hearsay is accurate, then the student has right opinion; otherwise wrong opinion, but in neither case the knowledge that transcends opinion. We would be under the profoundest possible delusion if we saw nothing paradoxical in inculcating opinion about what is meant to transcend opinion. We do not believe that this textbook or any other can be more than a help or a guide to students who, while they read it, are at the same time emphatically directed to the original texts.

We have had to decide to include certain authors and subjects and to omit others. In doing so we have not meant to prejudge the issue as to what part of political philosophy is alive or deserves to be alive. Surely an argument could be made for the inclusion of Dante, Bodin, Thomas More, and Harrington, and for the exclusion of the Muslim and Jewish medievals and of Descartes, for example. The amount of space devoted to each author could also be questioned, as could our abstaining from the practice of mentioning writers' names for the sole purpose of bringing them before the student's eye. We will not bore the reader with a repetition of the anthologist's prayer for the remission of sins. Everyone knows that there cannot be a book like this without decisions and there cannot be a decision without a question as to its rightness. The most we will assert is that we believe we could defend our deeds.

                                                            L.S.
                                                            J.C.

Note: At the end of most chapters, a reading suggestion is given, divided into two parts. The part designated as A contains the works or selections that in our opinion are indispensable to the student's understanding, while the list headed B contains important additional material that can be assigned if time permits.

INTRODUCTION

Today "political philosophy" has become almost synonymous with "ideology," not to say "myth." It surely is understood in contradistinction to "political science." The distinction between political philosophy and political science is a consequence of the fundamental distinction between philosophy and science. Even this fundamental distinction is of relatively recent origin. Traditionally, philosophy and science were not distinguished: natural science was one of the most important parts of philosophy. The great intellectual revolution of the seventeenth century which brought to light modern natural science was a revolution of a new philosophy *or* science against traditional (chiefly Aristotelian) philosophy *or* science. But the new philosophy or science was only partly successful. The most successful part of the new philosophy or science was the new natural science. By virtue of its victory, the new natural science became more and more independent of philosophy, at least apparently, and even, as it were, became an authority for philosophy. In this way the distinction between philosophy and science became generally accepted, and eventually also the distinction between political philosophy and political science as a kind of natural science of political things. Traditionally, however, political philosophy and political science were the same.

Political philosophy is not the same as political thought in general. Political thought is coeval with political life. Political philosophy, however, emerged within a particular political life, in Greece, in that past of which we have written records. According to the traditional view, the Athenian Socrates (469–399 B.C.) was the founder of political philosophy. Socrates was the teacher of Plato, who in his turn was the teacher of Aristotle. The political works of Plato and Aristotle are the oldest works devoted to political philosophy which have come down to us. The kind of political philosophy which was originated by Socrates is called classical political philosophy. Classical political philosophy was the predominant political philosophy until the emergence of modern political philosophy in the sixteenth and seventeenth centuries. Modern political philosophy came into being through the conscious break with the principles established by Socrates. By the same token classical political philosophy is not limited to the political teaching of Plato and Aristotle and their schools; it includes also the political teaching of the Stoics as well as the political teachings of the church fathers and the Scholastics, in so far as these teachings are not based exclusively on Divine revelation. The traditional view according to which Socrates was the founder of political philosophy is in need of some qualifications, or rather explanations; yet it is less misleading than any alternative view.

Socrates surely was not the first philosopher. This means that political philosophy was preceded by philosophy. The first philosophers are called by Aristotle "those who discourse on nature"; he distinguishes them from those "who discourse on the gods." The primary theme of philosophy, then, is "nature." What is nature? The first Greek whose work has come down to us, Homer himself, mentions "nature" only a single time; this first mention of "nature" gives us a most important hint as to what the Greek philosophers understood by "nature." In the tenth book of the *Odyssey*, Odysseus tells of what befell him on the island of the sorceress-goddess Circe. Circe had transformed many of his comrades into swine and locked them in sties. On his way to Circe's house to rescue his poor comrades, Odysseus is met by the god Hermes who wishes to preserve him. He promises Odysseus an egregious herb which will make him safe against Circe's evil arts. Hermes "drew a herb from the earth and showed me its *nature*. Black at the root it was, like milk its blossom; and the gods call it moly. Hard is it to dig for mortal men, but the gods can do everything." Yet the gods' ability to dig the herb with ease would be of no avail if they did not know the nature of the herb—its looks and its power—in the first place. The gods are thus omnipotent because they are, not indeed omniscient, but the knowers of the natures of the things—of natures which they have not made. "Nature" means here the character of a thing, or of a kind of thing, the way in which a thing or a kind of thing looks and acts, and the thing, or the kind of thing, is taken not to have been made by gods or men. If we were entitled to take a poetic utterance literally, we could say that the first man we know who spoke of nature was the

Wily Odysseus who had seen the towns of many men and had thus come to know how much the thoughts of men differ from town to town or from tribe to tribe.

It seems that the Greek word for nature (*physis*) means primarily "growth" and therefore also that into which a thing grows, the term of the growth, the character a thing has when its growth is completed, when it can do what only the fully grown thing of the kind in question can do or do well. Things like shoes or chairs do not "grow" but are "made": they are not "by nature" but "by art." On the other hand, there are things which are "by nature" without having "grown" and even without having come into being in any way. They are said to be "by nature" because they have not been made and because they are the "first things," out of which or through which all other natural things have come into being. The atoms to which the philosopher Democritus traced everything are by nature in the last sense.

Nature, however understood, is not known by nature. Nature had to be discovered. The Hebrew Bible, for example, does not have a word for nature. The equivalent in biblical Hebrew of "nature" is something like "way" or "custom." Prior to the discovery of nature, men knew that each thing or kind of thing has its "way" or its "custom"—its form of "regular behavior." There is a way or custom of fire, of dogs, of women, of madmen, of human beings: fire burns, dogs bark and wag their tails, women ovulate, madmen rave, human beings can speak. Yet there are also ways or customs of the various human tribes (Egyptians, Persians, Spartans, Moabites, Amalekites, and so on). Through the discovery of nature the radical difference between these two kinds of "ways" or "customs" came to the center of attention. The discovery of nature led to the splitting up of "way" or "custom" into "nature" (*physis*) on the one hand and "convention" or "law" (*nomos*) on the other. For instance, that human beings can speak is natural, but that this particular tribe uses this particular language is due to convention. The distinction implies that the natural is prior to the conventional. The distinction between nature and convention is fundamental for classical political philosophy and even for most of modern political philosophy, as can be seen most simply from the distinction between natural right and positive right.

Once nature was discovered and understood primarily in contradistinction to law or convention, it became possible and necessary to raise this question: Are the political things natural, and if they are, to what extent? The very question implied that the laws are not natural. But obedience to the laws was generally considered to be justice. Hence one was compelled to wonder whether justice is merely conventional or whether there are things which are by nature just. Are even the laws merely conventional or do they have their roots in nature? Must the laws not be "according to nature," and especially according to the nature of man, if they are to be good? The laws are the foundation or the work of the political community: is the political community by nature? In the attempts to answer these questions it was presupposed that there are things which are by nature good for man as man. The precise question therefore concerns the relation of what is by nature good for man, on the one hand, to justice or right on the other. The simple alternative is this: all right is conventional or there is some natural right. Both opposed answers were given and developed prior to Socrates. For a variety of reasons it is not helpful to present here a summary of what can be known of these pre-Socratic doctrines. We shall get some notion of the conventionalist view (the view that all right is conventional) when we turn to Plato's *Republic,* which contains a summary of that view. As for the opposite view, it must suffice here to say that it was developed by Socrates and classical political philosophy in general much beyond the earlier views.

What then is meant by the assertion that Socrates was the founder of political philosophy? Socrates did not write any books. According to the most ancient reports, he turned away from the study of the divine or natural things and directed his inquiries entirely to the human things, *i.e.,* the just things, the noble things, and the things good for man as man; he always conversed about "what is pious, what is impious, what is noble, what is base, what is just, what is unjust, what is sobriety, what is madness, what is courage, what is cowardice, what is the city, what is the statesman, what is rule over men, what is a man able to rule over men," and similar things.[1] It seems that Socrates was induced to turn away from the study of the divine or natural things by his piety. The gods do not approve of man's trying to seek out what they do not wish to reveal, especially the things in heaven and beneath the earth. A pious man will therefore investigate only the things left to men's investigation, *i.e.,* the human things. Socrates pursued his investigations by means of conversations. This means that he started from generally held opinions. Among the generally held opinions the most authoritative ones are those sanctioned by the city and its laws—by the most solemn convention. But the generally held opinions contradict one another. It therefore becomes necessary to transcend the whole sphere of the generally held opinions, or of opinion as such, in the direction of knowledge. Since even the most authoritative opinions are only opinions, even Socrates was compelled to go the way from convention or law to nature, to ascend from law to nature. But now it appears more clearly than ever before that opinion, convention, or law, contains truth, or is not arbitrary, or is in a sense natural. One may say that the law, the human law, thus proves to point to a divine or natural law as its origin. This implies, however, that the human law, precisely because it is not identical with the divine or natural law, is not unqualifiedly true or just: only natural right, justice itself, the "idea" or "form" of justice, is unqualifiedly just. Nevertheless, the human law, the law of the city, is unqualifiedly obligatory for the men subject to it provided they have the right to emigrate with their property, *i.e.,* provided their subjection to the laws of their city was voluntary.[2]

The precise reason why Socrates became the founder of political philosophy appears when one considers the character of the questions with which he dealt in his conversations. He raised the question "What is . . . ?" regarding everything. This question is meant to bring to light the nature of the kind of thing in question, that is, the form or the character of the thing. Socrates presupposed that knowledge of the whole is, above all, knowledge of the character, the form, the "essential" character of every part of the whole, as distinguished from knowledge of that out of which or through which the whole may have come into being. If the whole consists of essentially different parts, it is at least possible that the political things (or the human things) are essentially different from the nonpolitical things—that the political things form a class by themselves and therefore can be studied by themselves. Socrates, it seems, took the primary meaning of "nature" more seriously than any of his predecessors: he realized that "nature" is primarily "form" or "idea." If this is true, he did not simply turn away from the study of the natural things, but originated a new kind of the study of the natural things—a kind of study in which, for example, the nature or idea of justice, or natural right, and surely the nature of the human soul or man, is more important than, for example, the nature of the sun.

One cannot understand the nature of man if one does not understand the nature of human society. Socrates as well as Plato and Aristotle assumed that the most perfect form of human society is the *polis.* The *polis* is today frequently taken to be the Greek city-state. But for the classical political philosophers it was accidental that the *polis* was more common among Greeks than among non-Greeks. One would then have to say that the theme of classical political philosophy was, not the Greek city-state, but the city-state. This presupposes, however, that the city-state is one particular form of "the state." It presupposes therefore the concept of the state as comprising the city-state among other forms of the state. Yet classical political philosophy lacked the concept of "the state." When people speak today of "the state," they ordinarily understand "state" in contradistinction to "society." This distinction is alien to classical political philosophy. It is not sufficient to say that *polis* (city) comprises both state and society, for the concept "city" antedates the distinction between state and society; therefore one does not understand "the city" by saying the city comprises state and society. The modern equivalent to "the city" on the level of the citizen's understanding is "the country." For when a man says, for example, that "the country is in danger," he also has not yet made a distinction between state and society. The reason why the classical political philosophers were chiefly concerned with the city was not that they were ignorant of other forms of societies in general and of political societies in particular. They knew the tribe (the nation) as well as such structures as the Persian Empire. They were chiefly concerned with the city because they preferred the city to those other forms of political society. The grounds of this preference may be said to have been these: tribes are not capable of a high civilization, and very large societies cannot be free societies. Let us remember that the authors of the *Federalist Papers* were still under a compulsion to prove that it is possible for a large society to be republican or free. Let us also remember that the authors of the *Federalist Papers* signed themselves "Publius": republicanism points back to classical antiquity and therefore also to classical political philosophy.

NOTES

1. Xenophon *Memorabilia* I. 1. 11–16.
2. Plato *Crito* 51^{d-e}.

THUCYDIDES

c. 460 – *c.* 400 B.C.

Thucydides is the author of a single book, *The War of the Peloponnesians and the Athenians.*[1] He is not generally thought of as a political philosopher, and for obvious and weighty reasons. Not only does he never use the term "political philosophy," but he doesn't address, at least not explicitly, its universal questions. Though he tells us what he regarded as the best Athenian regime during his lifetime, he never speaks of the best regime simply; and though he praises several men for their excellence, he never discusses the best or most excellent way of life as such.[2] Moreover, he presents the results of his "quest for the truth" (I 20.3) as an account of a single political event, the twenty-seven-year war through which the Spartans and their allies brought down the Athenian empire. For these reasons, one is inclined to classify him as a historian. Yet unlike his predecessor Herodotus, Thucydides never uses the word "history." Nor, in fact, is his theme limited to the one particular war. He claims that his study of it will be useful for those who seek clarity, not only about the war, but more generally about the past, and even about the future, which in his view will again resemble the past that he has brought to light. Accordingly, he dares to call his work "a possession for all time" (I 22.4). Since, therefore, he sees his theme as a particular event that reveals the comprehensive and permanent truth, at least about human affairs, his focusing on that one event does not entitle us to regard him simply as a historian. Yet it is still hard to think of a man who says so little about universals, who, indeed, hardly even discusses his own claim for his work's universal significance, as a philosopher or a political philosopher. Perhaps it is best, then, instead of attempting to classify his thought, to turn to a closer look at the book's most distinctive features.

7

Thucydides' opening sentence tells us that he began to write about the Peloponnesian War from its outset, since he expected it to be a great one and the most noteworthy war there had ever been. He adds that the war did prove to be the "greatest motion," or change, that had ever occurred, at least among the Greeks. To support his claim, he observes that the antagonists were at a peak of wealth and power and also that the war was unequaled in the sufferings it occasioned (I 1.1–2, 23.1–2). But Thucydides does not restrict himself to these initial arguments to persuade us of the war's greatness or importance. More immediately compelling is the impact of the work as a whole, with its austere but vivid narrative that makes us witnesses to the actions and the sufferings it records. We feel the war's greatness because we feel its presence. This feeling is heightened still further through Thucydides' inclusion of political speeches, in direct discourse, by the participants themselves. We seem to hear the speakers as they argue in the name of justice or call upon the gods, as they appeal to the love of freedom or of imperial glory, and as they warn of the terrible consequences of mistaken policies. These speeches indeed make the war seem present to us. But, still more importantly, they speak to our own moral and political concerns, and they call upon us to respond to the war, as the antagonists themselves did, in their light. The order of the accompanying narrative, and its choice of emphases, are also designed to appeal to these concerns. And it is primarily in this way, by fostering our own moral and political concerns, that Thucydides makes us receptive to his claim for the war's greatness and its universal significance.

The speeches in Thucydides' book, with their moral seriousness and their urgency, call upon us to take sides for or against them, and yet every reader must be struck by the contrast between the outspokenness of these speeches and Thucydides' own reticence. He does, to be sure, make some explicit judgments. But for the most part he does not tell us what he would have us think of the warring cities and their leaders, or of the many speeches and actions that he relates. Now this silence does not mean that he is indifferent, or that he no longer responds to men and events, as he encourages us to do, with approval and disapproval. It shows, rather, that he is a skillful political educator. For the moral seriousness that he fosters in us remains immature, it does not sufficiently help us to promote the well-being of our communities, which it necessarily wants to promote, unless it is guided by or culminates in political wisdom. And since political wisdom is primarily good judgment about unprecedented, particular situations, it is not so much a subject matter to be taught as a skill to be developed through practice. Accordingly, instead of telling us whether or not he approves of a given policy,

Thucydides asks us to make our own judgments, and then to subject them to the testing that the war provides. He thus lets us hear speeches in the assemblies both for and against some course of action, and like the assemblymen we must take our own stand, one way or the other, without explicit guidance. Only subsequently, and in stages, as in political life itself, do we learn the aftermath of the actions that were in fact taken; and even then it is primarily up to us to weigh their true influence and to make the appropriate inferences as to their wisdom. To be sure, Thucydides' selection and ordering of narrative details, along with his explicit judgments, whose weight is all the greater for their rarity, help us to find our bearings in these reflections, to such a degree in fact that his translator Hobbes could say that "the narration itself doth secretly instruct the reader, and more effectually than can possibly be done by precept."[3] But these helps become fruitful only when we accept the book's challenge to take positions of our own and to learn from our own mistakes. Indeed, an introductory statement such as this one would be worse than useless if it were to convey the impression of being a way to avoid this labor.

Now it is true, as we have already noted, that Thucydides' reticence extends not merely to particular questions, such as those regarding policy, but also, and especially, to universal ones, and this despite the fact that the speakers in his book make many and contradictory claims about the most important of these matters. But here too, we shall see, his reserve is not a sign of indifference but, rather, an important element in his education of his readers. For mistaken positions with regard to universal questions can result in a pattern of erroneous particular judgments, and Thucydides' narrative helps his attentive readers to notice, and thereby to overcome, some of these deep-seated sources of error. In addition, the arguments themselves by which the various speakers support their universal claims often contain inconsistencies, which reveal difficulties in the speakers' own positions. If we think through these difficulties, as our own concern with the matters at issue compels us to do, they point in the direction of a more adequate understanding. On occasion, Thucydides does indicate his own answers to these universal questions, in part by criticizing the mistaken views of some of the leaders in the war. But even in these cases, where he explicitly guides our thinking, he first encourages us to take our own positions, which may well differ from his, and to approach his perspective through our own experience with the book. Moreover, his explicit judgments are always incomplete, and they raise further questions, which we must answer on our own.

After his brief introductory account of the emergence and growth of

Greek civilization, Thucydides begins his narrative of the war itself by looking at its causes. In his view the truest cause, though it was least manifest in speech, was that the Athenians, by becoming great and thus arousing fear, compelled the Spartans to go to war. But he adds that he will also record the causes, or rather—as we may also translate the same Greek word—accusations, that were openly spoken (I 23.5–6; cf. I 88). Indeed, Thucydides seems to devote far more attention to these openly spoken causes than to the one he regards as truest. This impression is somewhat misleading, however, since these open accusations concerned instances of the very growth of Athenian power that Thucydides saw as the war's truest cause. But the main justification for his procedure is that it helps us to feel the impact of the war's beginnings as they actually appeared, openly and in public. If these appearances should be decep- tive, as indeed Thucydides says they were, his presentation encourages us to confirm this fact for ourselves rather than simply accepting it on his authority. Moreover, it is only by beginning from these simplest appear- ances that we can properly appreciate the primary theme of Thucydides' study of the war, namely justice, or justice in its relation to compulsion.

The first accusation of the war was an accusation against Athens by Corinth, a naval power like Athens itself and an important member of the Spartan or Peloponnesian alliance. The Corinthians charged that Athens, by helping the Corinthian colony Corcyra in a sea battle against them, had violated the truce that bound the Spartan and Athenian al- liances (I 55.2; cf. I 44). The Athenians had recently entered into a de- fensive alliance with Corcyra, which was threatened by war with Cor- inth, despite Corinthian warnings that this would provoke a general war, for they believed that the war was coming in any event, and they didn't want to allow Corcyra, with its large navy, to come under Cor- inthian control. Corcyra's location on the coastal route to Italy and Sicily was also a factor in the Athenians' decision, though we are not told whether this impressed them more from a defensive or an offensive point of view. Soon after this first collision with Corinth there arose the occa- sion for a second Corinthian charge against Athens, to which the Athe- nians responded with a countercharge of their own. The sea battle against Corcyra had ended disappointingly for Corinth, and the Athe- nians feared that the Corinthians would retaliate by persuading Poti- daea, a city they had colonized but which was now an ally of Athens, to revolt from the Athenian alliance. Accordingly, Athens ordered the Poti- daeans to tear down one of their walls, to give them hostages, and to expel their Corinthian magistrates. The Potidaeans, however, refused these demands, which prompted them instead to carry out the revolt that the Corinthians had indeed been urging, and that Sparta had also encouraged by promising to invade Athenian territory if Athens should attack them. The Corinthians sent an army to help defend Potidaea; and when the Athenians in turn dispatched a large attacking force, there was another battle in which Athenians and Corinthians, despite the general truce, fought against one another. When the Athenians, who were the victors in this battle, proceeded to lay siege to Potidaea, Corinth accused Athens of besieging its colony, with Corinthian troops inside. The Athenians, for their part, charged Corinth with having brought about the rebellion of one of their tribute-paying allies and with having fought openly on its side (I, 66).

Soon after the siege had begun at Potidaea, the Corinthians summoned their allies to Sparta, where they accused the Athenians of having broken the truce and of doing injustice to the Peloponnese. The Spartans themselves invited the allies to make their allegations of Athenian injustice before a Spartan assembly, and we learn that a number of cities had charges of their own against Athens. The Corinthian speech at this assembly, which Thucydides presents in its entirety, argues that Athenian actions at Corcyra and Potidaea are merely the most recent instances of a long-continued policy designed to enslave all of Greece. Many cities, the Corinthians say, have already been enslaved by Athens, and now even Sparta's allies are being plotted against and deprived of their freedom. To help convey a sense of the danger to Greece, the Corinthians give a description of the bold, resourceful, and acquisitive Athenian character, a description that they summarize by saying that the Athenians "are of such a nature as neither to have rest themselves nor to allow it to the other human beings" (I 70.9). The Corinthians conclude by urging the Spartans to invade Attica before it is too late to help Potidaea and the other cities. Later, the final speaker at this assembly, a Spartan ephor, also urges his fellow citizens not to betray their allies to the Athenian aggressors. The Spartan assembly then resolved, overwhelmingly, that the Athenians had broken the truce and were committing injustice, and they prepared to ask the allies to declare war against them in common (I 87.2–4). It appears, then, that the cause of the war was Athenian injustices, and the threat of future injustices, against the Greeks and, in particular, against Sparta's allies. And this impression was shared, Thucydides tells us, by the great preponderance of the Greek world, whose sympathies at the beginning of the war inclined toward Sparta, especially since it claimed to be engaging in a war of liberation (II 8.4–5). Even the god at Delphi promised the Spartans that he would assist them, whether called or uncalled, thus suggesting that the Spartan war effort was to be in the service of punishing Athenian injustice (I 118.3; cf. II 54.4–5).

Thucydides has already told us, however, that Sparta's decision to go to war, and to try to crush Athenian power, was prompted less by the allies' accusations against Athens than by its own fear. Moreover, his narrative of the fifty-year interval between the Persian and Peloponnesian Wars tends to support this claim, at least to the extent that it shows Sparta's failure seriously to oppose the emergence and rapid growth of an Athenian empire (I 89.1–118.2). In keeping with this, the Corinthian speech at Sparta is at least as much a complaint about Spartan indifference as it is an accusation against Athens, and the Corinthians even threaten to desert the alliance if Sparta should continue to do nothing. Especially in the light of this threat, it does seem to be more a fear of losing their allies than a desire to protect them, let alone to save the rest of Greece from Athenian tyranny, that brings about the change from the Spartans' habitual reluctance to go to war. And this impression will be confirmed by subsequent Spartan behavior during the war—in particular, by their treatment of Plataea and their agreement with Athens to accept the Peace of Nicias. Yet however little of generosity there may have been in Sparta's motives for declaring war, Athenian aggression would still appear to have been responsible for its outbreak.

The case against Athens is weaker than it appears, though, in at least one respect. Though the Corinthians and the Spartans accused the Athenians of having violated the truce between them, this aspect of their argument seems to have been quite unsound. The Athenians' defensive alliance with Corcyra, however provocative, was not clearly forbidden under the truce; and even the Corinthians never claimed that Athenian harshness toward Potidaea was in violation of it. Moreover, the Athenians offered, in conformity with the truce, to submit all controversies to binding arbitration, which the Spartans neither offered nor accepted. The Athenian leader Pericles relied largely on these facts to persuade the Athenians not to yield to last-minute Spartan ultimatums (I 78.4, 140.2, 144.2). Even the Spartan king Archidamus, who opposed the war in the Spartan assembly, acknowledged that it was unlawful to go to war against a city that offered arbitration; and he warned that Sparta, if it did declare a war, would be regarded as having begun it. Later, in fact, when the war was going badly for them, the Spartans themselves came to believe that by their refusal of arbitration, and other such offenses, they had been guilty of first breaking the truce and thus starting the war (I 81.5; VII 18.2; cf. IV 20.2).

Thucydides, however, does not endorse this Spartan belief in their own guilt, nor the exoneration of Athens that it implies. According to him, we recall, the Athenians "compelled" the Spartans to go to war because of the fear that their growing power inspired in them. Though the Spartans' truest motive for waging war hardly deserves our praise, neither can they be blamed for having broken the truce, since they were compelled to do so (cf. IV 98.5–6). Their fear of Athens left them with no reasonable alternative, or so at least they had strong cause to believe. And we return, then, to our first impression that Athens, rather than Sparta, was guilty of having brought on the war.

Athens's guilt is perhaps brought into still sharper focus by the manner in which the Athenians responded to the accusations against them. Some Athenians, for example, who happened to be in Sparta on other public business when they heard of the Corinthians' and the others' charges against Athens, asked for and received permission to address the assembly on their city's behalf. They spoke, not to defend themselves against the allies' charges, as if the Spartans were judges in a court of law, but to dissuade the Spartans from a hasty decision to go to war. The core of their argument, however, was the claim that they didn't deserve to be so hated for their empire, and that it was not unreasonable, or perhaps not unfair, for them to possess it. To support this claim, they argue that they were compelled to establish the empire and to expand it, in the first place by fear, and then also by honor, and later also by benefit—compulsions they later speak of together as "the greatest things." But if actions done for the sake of honor and benefit, as well as those done from fear, can be regarded as compulsory, and excused on that account, is there anything that is forbidden? In its way, then, the Athenians' defense of their empire is indeed no defense, since it attacks the very presupposition of all accusation, namely, that there is voluntary wrongdoing. The Athenians add that they are not the first to yield to the temptation of empire, but that it has always been established for the weaker to be kept down by the stronger, and that no one with a chance to acquire something by force has ever yet been dissuaded by the argument from justice. These Athenians seem to have believed that the shocking bluntness of their argument would intimidate the Spartans, since only a powerful city would dare to say such things, and that they would thereby deter Sparta from war. They do, however, go on to claim that they rule more justly than their power requires, or than others in their place would do; and they also warn the Spartans not to violate the truce between them but to resolve their differences through arbitration. Now, as these concessions of sorts to justice may perhaps suggest, the Athenians were not so powerful as to force Sparta to tolerate their empire, and all that they were doing to increase it, through fear of that power alone; and yet they admitted openly that justice would never restrain them from seeking such power in the future. It is hardly surprising, then, that this speech failed to avert the war, for it reveals clearly what it was about Athens that so angered and frightened the Spartan alliance (I 72–78).

The argument for empire that these Athenians gave at Sparta was repeated on a number of occasions by Athenian spokesmen during the war. Pericles, under whose leadership the Athenians entered the war, later tells them, when they are beginning to grow weary of it, that their empire is "like a tyranny, which is believed to be unjust to take, but which is dangerous to let go" (II 63.2–3). He also holds out to them the prospect of all but limitless advantages from the empire, and he urges them to defend it, despite the hatred it arouses, for the sake of the honor it brings them, and especially for the sake of ever-remembered glory in the future (II 62.1–3, 64.3–6). Much later in the war, this imperialistic thesis is repeated by Athenian ambassadors from an armed force that is already present at the small and independent island of Melos, who are trying to persuade the Melian leaders to submit voluntarily to their rule. These ambassadors don't even pretend to justify Athens's empire, or its decision to subdue Melos, because, as they claim to know, justice has no place in human reckoning unless there is an equal power to compel on both sides (V 89). And when the Melian leaders keep refusing to yield, in their trust that good fortune from the divine will sustain them, since they stand "free from sin against men who are not just," the Athenians reply as follows:

As for good will from the divine, neither do we suppose that we will fall short. For we are neither claiming as our right nor are we doing anything outside of human belief with regard to the divine or human wish with regard to themselves. For we think, on the basis of opinion, regarding the divine, and on the clear basis of a permanent compulsion of nature, regarding the human, that wherever they have the might, they rule. And we neither laid down the law nor are we the first to have used it as laid down, but we received it in existence and we will leave it behind us in existence forever; and we use it in the knowledge that both you and others, if you came to have the same power as we have, would do it too. (V 105.1–2)

This dialogue between the Athenian ambassadors and the Melian leaders is the most notorious passage in Thucydides. Yet the Athenians' statements at Melos are merely a fuller disclosure and clarification of what had long been the central thought of Athenian imperialism, and as such they offer the most powerful inducement for us to see the war as a war against Athenian injustice.

If we look at the war from this anti-Athenian perspective, we are prepared to notice, and to be moved by, the two most dramatic juxtapositions in Thucydides' work, and also to see the work as having a unified theme. Pericles' Funeral Oration, in which he celebrates the beauty of Athenian power and even boasts that the Athenians have established everlasting memorials everywhere of bad things as well as good ones, is immediately followed by a horrible and devastating plague at

Athens (II 34–54). And the Melian dialogue—which shocks all the more because the Athenians, having failed to persuade the Melians, later slaughtered their adult men and enslaved the women and children—is immediately followed by the Sicilian expedition, in which Athenian ambition finally went too far and which ended in a disaster that all but sealed Athens's eventual doom. Thucydides thus invites us to think of both the plague and the Sicilian disaster, along with the ultimate defeat of Athens in the war, as the destined punishments for its insolence and injustice (cf. I 23.3–6).

Thucydides himself, however, seems not to have shared this interpretation of the war as a divine or cosmic punishment of Athens. Though he refuses to speculate on the causes of the plague, he tells us that it was also widespread in Africa and Asia before coming to Athens, and he all but ridicules the credulity of those who thought it had been foretold by an ancient oracle (II 48, 54.1–3; cf. V 26.3–4). As for the Sicilian expedition, Thucydides says that in spite of its immoderation it could have succeeded with better leadership and more support from home for the army (II 65.11; cf. VI 15.3–4). Moreover, since the narrative breaks off some six years before the end of the war, with the Athenians having recently established a superior regime and having just won an important naval victory, which restored their confidence that they could still prevail against Sparta, we are led to wonder whether the war's final outcome was in any sense destined.

But even apart from the question of what caused the Athenian sufferings, the more one reads Thucydides, the less one feels that Athens's suffering was fitting or deserved. And, more generally, our first response to the book as a whole is not satisfaction at justice having been done, but is far more likely to be a feeling of sadness. This sadness arises, in large measure at least, from a growing sense that the defeat of Athens is not the victory of justice, but that justice itself is among the chief victims of the war. Whether or not we are attentive to the fact that Athens's defeat came too late to save the Melians and the other helpless victims of Athenian power, we cannot help noticing that the victorious Spartans became, if they had not always been, at least as oppressive as the Athenians. For instance, it was the Spartans and their allies who attacked Plataea, in spite of the oath they had sworn, in honor of Plataean heroism in the Persian War, to protect Plataea's independence and although Plataea had been compelled to ally itself with Athens by Sparta's own indifference to the threat from nearby Thebes. And after besieging the city, the Spartans killed all the Plataeans who surrendered, not because they believed the savage accusations against them by the Thebans, but just about entirely, as Thucydides says, in order to gratify the Thebans, whom they regarded as beneficial to them in the present war (III 68; cf. II 71–74; III 55.1). Later, in order to recover a mere three hundred prisoners, including a hundred or so from their first families, the Spartans agreed to the so-called Peace of Nicias, in which they betrayed, among many others, the cities that had relied on the generous promises of the Spartan leader Brasidas to revolt from Athens.[4] And these are only two of the many examples that confirm what the Athenian ambassadors at Melos had said about the Spartans, that in their relations with others they most transparently hold that whatever is advantageous is just (and that whatever is pleasant is noble) (V 105.4). Yet it is not merely the Spartans and the Athenians whose behavior gives evidence of the weakness of justice in the war. To take only one telling example, in his extensive catalogue of the many cities and nations that fought against Sicily or for it, Thucydides says of all of them in general that they didn't take sides because of justice or kinship so much as because of advantage or else from compulsion (VII 57.1 ff.).

Men disregarded, moreover, the apparent restraining power of law or justice even when such behavior served no interest of their own, except perhaps to satisfy an immediate passion. This we can at least understand during the plague at Athens, when the imminence of death freed men from all restraint coming from fear of gods or from any law of human beings, and people also thought it fitting to reap their profits quickly, and with a view to pleasure, since they regarded their lives and their property alike as ephemeral (II 53). It is harder to understand, however, the bloodthirsty Thracian mercenaries who slaughtered, on their way home from Athens, the men, the women, the children, and even the beasts in the small town of Mycalessus. This was a calamity, Thucydides tells us, as worthy of being lamented, given its size, as anything that happened in the war (VII 29.4–5, 30.3). And, most horrible of all, there is Thucydides' account of the civil war in Corcyra and of the civil wars that subsequently convulsed all of Greece. The cause of these uprisings was the desire to rule, rooted in acquisitiveness and the love of honor, but after a time the violence seemed to take on a life of its own. Revenge was in greater esteem than not to have suffered oneself, and its scope was limited not by justice and the advantage of the city, but only by the immediate pleasure of whichever faction had the upper hand. The citizens who remained neutral, moreover, were killed by the partisans on both sides, whether because they didn't join with them or else from envy that they might survive (III 82).

This saddening spectacle of the powerlessness of justice in the face of selfishness and violence is not merely a feature of the Peloponnesian War. Thucydides shows, by his account of ancient times, both in Greece and in Sicily, and by his description of the emerging powers in Macedonia and Thrace, that the fate of justice in this war had been its fate before, and that it was so elsewhere (I 2–17; II 97–99; VI 2–5). Above all, he tells us that harsh things such as those that happened in the cities during the civil wars have happened before and always are going to happen in the future, for as long as the same nature of human beings exists (III 82.2). This uncompromising statement about human nature is Thucydides' clearest echo of his opening promise to reveal the comprehensive and permanent truth about human affairs. And, indeed, the most obvious lesson of the work as a whole, for statesmen and others alike, is the sobering one that as long as our species remains, we must reckon on a human nature that will again and again, when given the chance, overpower the fragile restraints of law and justice. Thucydides does not say, however, that everyone became equally depraved as a result of the civil wars. And it is true that the Spartans, for example, unlike the Athenians, had not exploited their supremacy in Greece to establish an empire, and that they became, in Thucydides' words, prosperous and moderate at the same time, as did the Chians. But it is also true, as Thucydides later tells us, that the Spartans and the Chians surpassed all other cities in the number of their slaves (VIII 24.4, 40.2). In other words, the Spartans' moderation, such as it was, in foreign affairs was rooted in their fear of a slave revolt. Their behavior does not contradict the general rule of the powerlessness of law and justice in themselves, and so it does little to relieve the sadness with which we first respond to Thucydides' work as a whole.

For the Athenians, however, who claimed before the war began that no one had ever yet been dissuaded from acquisition by considerations of justice, what we have loosely called the weakness of justice in the war would have been less the cause for sadness than a further confirmation of their fundamental thesis that the stronger must always subdue the weaker. The Athenians endorsed this thesis, and thus rejected the dedication to virtue as it had traditionally been understood (II 63.2; V 101), on the grounds that such virtue was incompatible with man's natural and compelling desires for some security, for honor, and for benefit. Now we may think that the Athenians were too quick to excuse the past behavior of the powerful, as well as their own behavior, in terms of natural compulsion; for even if those with the power to acquire or to rule have always done so, it doesn't follow from this that they were compelled to. But the Athenians did not rely on this inadequate evidence for their argument. To see this most clearly, we must look again at what the Athenian ambassadors said in the Melian dialogue, where their great superiority in power encouraged them to be most outspoken. The Athenians intend to add Melos to their empire, and they tell the Melian leaders that they shouldn't expect to dissuade them by arguing that they have done Athens no injustice. For the Melian leaders themselves, as the Athenians assert, also know that justice is decided, in human speech or reckoning, on the basis of an equal power to compel, while the superior do what they can, or what is possible, and the weak yield (V 89). The Melians think, as they indicate in their response, that they are being forbidden to speak of justice, and ordered to limit themselves to considerations of interest, if they want the Athenians to listen to them. Yet they misunderstand the Athenians, who mean instead that there is no justice, and hence no possibility to speak truly of it, and no need to forbid such speech, in any situation where the good of the one party is incompatible with that of the other. For aren't we all compelled, if we are sensible, to pursue our own good? After all, doesn't the argument of justice itself acknowledge that this good is a compulsory power, by claiming that it is in our own interest, at least in the long run or in the truest sense, to be always just? The Melians, at any rate, later in the dialogue when they accuse the Athenians of not being just, also warn that Athens will not succeed in subduing them, since they, who are free from sin, will be aided by fortune from the divine as well as by their kinsmen the Spartans (V 104). Indeed, the claim that justice is always in one's own best interest is contained in the very notion of justice, since we think of justice as the common good, and the common good would include one's own. The Melians themselves, in fact, in their first attempt to argue on the basis of interest rather than of justice, also argue, at least implicitly, from this notion of justice. For what they say is that it is useful for the Athenians, who may some day be in danger themselves, not to dissolve "the common good," but to let fairness and justice be of service to the one in danger and to allow him some benefit from arguments that are not fully precise (V 90). The Athenians, however, are able to show that it is not in their own interest to allow the Melians to remain independent. More generally, the Athenian thesis recognizes that a common good or, rather, a coincidence of interests cannot always be found in every situation among men. Moreover, it asserts that in cases where this coincidence cannot be found, we are compelled, once we understand the situation, to pursue our own good as distinct from that of the others; for it is costly to us not to, and even the counterargument on behalf of justice must ultimately admit that no true justice could oppose the power of our natural wish for our good.[5] Furthermore, if we are compelled, for the reasons indicated, to pursue our own good, we are also compelled to pursue whatever we believe to be our own good, though it is indeed costly to us to misjudge what it truly is. Now the Athenians thought that it was good for them to acquire and expand their empire, even at the risk of war with Sparta, and it is ultimately for this reason alone that they acknowledged no guilt for doing so.

One is tempted to reject this entire Athenian argument, especially because its utterance by the ambassadors at Melos is followed by the butchery of the Melian citizens. But this would be an inadequate response, and not merely because the killings, and even the ambassadors' own threats of these killings if the Melians should refuse to submit, were not necessary or appropriate consequences of the argument itself. It may well be true that the Athenian argument contributed to their willingness to acquire and maintain an empire. But it is also true of the Athenians, or at least of the best among their leaders, that they showed an extraordinary concern to be worthy of their imperial rule, and to be noble. Indeed, despite appearances to the contrary, their imperialistic thesis itself is in large measure the result of their concern with justice and with nobility, for it is these concerns that required them to give to themselves a defense of their empire, and a defense without the usual hypocrisies. Furthermore, it appeared to the Athenians that to accept their defense of empire, and of selfishness, was not necessarily to repudiate what is truly highest or most noble. It may well, then, become a matter of serious interest to us to see on what grounds the Athenians believed they were noble or, more broadly, superior, and to examine whether their view of themselves was true.

The Athenians speak of their superiority, and especially their superiority as individuals to the citizens of other cities, in a number of ways. The Athenians at Sparta, in defending their empire, combine the argument from compulsion, which would equally excuse any other ruling power, with the claim that they in particular are worthy to rule, largely on the grounds, it seems, of their superior intelligence and zeal. The Athenian speakers do not pretend, of course, that these excellences, which had contributed so greatly to the Greek victory in the Persian War, are still in the service of Greek freedom, if indeed they ever were. But they nevertheless treat them as a title to their empire, or at least as grounds for deserving less hatred for it (I 73.2–74.4; 75.1; 76.2). What the Athenians say at Sparta is further elaborated in Pericles' Funeral Oration, in which he speaks of the Athenian people as lovers of beauty and of wisdom. Moreover, he praises the Athenians for their willingness to be brave in battle, without their needing to rely on long and arduous training, and more generally for their active involvement in political life, a life which does not require, in Athens, the neglect of private concerns but, rather, completes the graceful development of the many-sided individual's highest powers. According to Pericles, Athenian power is the achievement of such an outstanding citizenry that only Athens allows its subject cities no room to make the reproach that they are not ruled by worthy men (II 37–41).

That the Athenians have freely chosen to use their intelligence and their other gifts on behalf of the city, as they are also ready to risk their lives for it, is a crucial aspect of their view of themselves as being noble. Pericles can arouse their patriotic zeal by asking them to consider not through calculation alone the well-known benefits that come from resisting one's enemies, but rather to behold the power of the city and to become lovers of it, and to be ready as its lovers to emulate the fallen soldiers who gave to it the most noble offering of their virtue (II 43.1). Pericles uses the word "noble," or "beautiful," in referring to the soldiers' deaths because he regards their dedication to Athens as having transcended mere calculation or selfishness. Similarly, when he implicitly claims that Athens itself is so beautiful or noble as to inspire erotic love, he does so not merely on the grounds of its power but also because of what he sees as its superiority, even in foreign relations, to selfish calculation. This does not mean that he believes Athenian policy is guided by considerations of justice; to repeat, he boasts that Athens has everywhere established everlasting memorials of evils as well as goods. But Pericles does say that the Athenians are the only ones who benefit others more from a fearless trust in their own liberality than from calculations of advantage (II 40.5, 41.4). And even when he speaks of everlasting memorials of evils and goods, he has in mind the evils that Athens has suffered as well as the harm it has done to others. Precisely the unlimitedness of Athens's ultimate ambitions, and its willingness to suffer greatly for the greatest ends, is evidence for Pericles of its noble superiority to mere calculations of profit and loss. Especially as individuals in their relation to the city, but even as a city in relation to others—or at least so it seemed in their own eyes—the Athenians gave freely of themselves for noble and great ends. And in this connection, we should not forget that the Athenian ambassadors at Sparta had spoken of their city's praiseworthy restraint in the use of its power over its subjects, a restraint that Athens had practiced even though this seemed to be encouraging complaints and thus making it more difficult to rule (I 76.3–77.5).

Because they regarded themselves as being noble, and worthy to rule, the Athenians also regarded the honor or glory that they anticipated from their empire not merely as a great good for themselves but also as something greater. Pericles had said to them that they were well advised to pursue a boundless empire, in spite of the hatred this aroused, on the grounds that the hatred would be short-lived whereas the empire's brilliance and its future glory would be left behind in memory forever.

But he went on to add that this glory would be something noble, by which he meant, in part, a reflection of their noble superiority to narrow or merely calculating selfishness (II 64.5–6). In keeping with the Athenians' attitude toward honor or glory, when their ambassadors at Sparta spoke of the "greatest things" that compelled them to acquire and expand their empire, they spoke of honor as being distinct from, and apparently irreducible to, mere benefit (I 75.3, 76.2). It is true that Alcibiades later spoke of his own desire for honor as an aspect of his desire for benefit. But even in his case, as Thucydides makes clear, he sought honor not merely as the greatest or most pleasant benefit, but as his noble reward for noble deeds, for deeds that, in his eyes, were both of intrinsic greatness and of benefit to the city as a whole (VI 16.1–3, 16.5–6; cf. VI 15.2).

That the Athenians were outstandingly noble or admirable was not merely their own claim about themselves. Even the hostile Corinthians, in order to warn their Spartan allies of the danger from Athens, had to praise the Athenian manner, and they said, among other things, that the Athenians "use their bodies, which are most alien to them, for the sake of the city, and their intelligence, which is most their own, in order to do something on its behalf" (I 70.6). Now it is true that the Corinthians had an incentive to exaggerate the degree of Athenian zeal, just as Pericles and the other Athenian spokesmen had their own incentives for exaggeration in their praise of Athens' beauty and its glory. But the truth about the Athenians, as it becomes manifest from their deeds, is in some ways even more beautiful than Pericles' splendid, but clearly boastful, speeches would have led us to believe. Early in the war, for example, Phormio's two naval victories against vastly greater Peloponnesian fleets in the Gulf of Corinth were brilliant testimony to his daring and intelligent leadership and to the zealous initiative of the Athenian sailors (II 83–92). We later see a manifestation of democracy at its best when Demosthenes, at a time when he wasn't even an officer, boldly proposed to fortify Pylos, on the Peloponnesian mainland, and prevailed with the Athenian troops to do so, simply because they didn't want to remain idle there while waiting for favorable winds. This action, which was followed by further instances of Demosthenes' skill and of Athenian valor, led to the previously unheard-of surrender of three hundred Spartans and thus allowed Athens to end the first phase of the war on favorable terms (IV 2.4–5.2; cf. IV 6–41).

The finer side of Athenian democracy is also evident in the aftermath of a rebellion at Mytilene, which Athens had crushed after a lengthy siege. Although the Athenians had initially resolved upon the death penalty for all the male citizens, and had even sent a ship to convey these orders, the next day they had a change of heart. They reflected that it had been a savage decree and a great one, *i.e.,* an excessive one, to destroy the entire city, and not just those who had been responsible for the rebellion. Accordingly, they held a second assembly that very day, at which they determined not to kill the great majority of the Mytileneans. A second ship was sent out at once, and, thanks in part to the eagerness of its oarsmen and the reluctance of those on the first ship, the new orders arrived in time to save Mytilene from annihilation. The Athenians' change of heart on this occasion is an unparalleled example, at least during the war, of an entire people showing mildness of character. The Athenians knew better than to believe Cleon's argument in the assembly that justice demanded the punishment of all Mytilene. The same sensitivity to justice and nobility that led the Athenians to defend their empire, and to do so with such freedom from hypocrisy, was also at the root of their remarkably moderate and relatively decent behavior toward Mytilene (III 36, 49).

The most splendid instance, however, of Athenian nobility is the one in which Athens showed itself at its most immoderate, namely, the expedition against Sicily. To add Sicily to its empire had long been an Athenian dream, a dream that Pericles himself had nourished by telling the Athenians of the limitless possibilities from their supremacy over the sea. Yet Pericles also warned against trying to expand the empire during the war with Sparta, and he would presumably have opposed the Sicilian expedition, had he lived, as being recklessly premature. Pericles' vision of Athens was of a city that loved the noble, but with thrift or economy, whereas the Sicilian expedition was lavishly expensive and an unprecedented risk. Still, Pericles himself would have had to admit that there is something especially beautiful, even if it is not the beauty of health, in this very unsparingness. All the Athenians alike, according to Thucydides, fell in love with the Sicilian expedition. The erotic love that Pericles had merely asked for from the Athenian community took hold of it in fact on the eve of the Sicilian campaign.[6] And the men in the prime of life were inspired, not by a desire for wealth or power, or even glory, but "by a longing for the faraway sight and contemplation" (VI 24.3). Nor should we entirely disregard, as a mere pretence, the Athenians' statements that their aim in Sicily was to help their kinsmen the Leontines and their Egestaean allies (VI 6.1, 18.1–2, 19.1). Furthermore, when the initial expedition had met with grave reverses, and the Peloponnesians were also causing distress at home by occupying a fort near Athens, the Athenians not only persevered in Sicily but sent a second fleet almost as large as the first. No one, Thucydides tells us, could have believed beforehand that such tenacity was even possible. And even after

Athens's terrible defeat in Sicily, it showed a resiliency in pursuing the war with Sparta that astonished the entire Greek world.[7] Sparta was indeed more moderate in prosperity than Athens. But no other city even rivaled Athens, as we see above all in the Sicilian campaign and its aftermath, for the grandeur of its ambition and for its strength in adversity.

The Sicilian campaign ended in failure. Yet Pericles had told the Athenians years earlier that they would be famous in the future for having ruled the greatest of Greek empires, even if they should fail in their immediate war aims. Failure, he implied, was always possible, since, as he went on to say, all things by nature also decline (II 64.3). Indeed, Pericles' enlightened awareness that everything must eventually decline seems to have helped nourish his belief that the Athenians were well advised to pursue ever-remembered glory as the greatest good (II 64.5–6 and context). We also recall that Pericles celebrated everlasting memorials even of Athenian failures. Yet it is hard to celebrate Athens's defeat in the Sicilian campaign, even though this was the most memorable and in some ways the noblest of Athens's failures; and one cannot help but feel that here, at least, the pursuit of imperial glory was ill advised and not worth its terrible price. For not only do we feel the greatness of the army's sufferings, but also we see an ugliness in Athens that comes to light as being the cause of its defeat. Despite Athens's amazing perseverance in a bold campaign that Thucydides himself regarded as feasible, the entire army at Sicily was destroyed because of the nearsighted pursuit of private interests, or what appeared to be private interests, at the expense of the public.

In his eulogy of Pericles, Thucydides attributes the Athenians' defeat in the war, and at Sicily in particular, to private ambitions for honor and gain, ambitions that were no longer restrained, after Pericles' death, by the intelligent and public-spirited guidance of the leading citizen (II 65.7–12). There was no longer the harmony between the leaders' private ambitions and the public good that had been characteristic of Athens under Pericles. This analysis reminds one of Nicias' charge, in his attempt to dissuade the Athenians from the Sicilian campaign, that his fellow commander Alcibiades was urging it from entirely selfish motives (VI 12.2). Now one might say, in Alcibiades' defense, that his private ambition for honor and wealth from the Sicilian expedition was in full harmony with the wishes of the Athenian assembly. But one must add that the people's wishes, as expressed in the assembly, were no true measure of the city's interests, and not merely because of their ignorance of those interests.

That even the Athenian people subordinated the public good to a kind of private interest becomes evident above all in their savage response to mutilations of the Hermes statues, which occurred while the departure for Sicily was being prepared. The Athenians believed that these mutilations were an ill omen for the expedition and also, though it was hardly plausible, that they were done as part of a conspiracy against the people (VI 27). Some of the Athenians may have believed they deserved to fail in Sicily, or to be conspired against by tyrannical individuals, as a punishment for being a tyrannical city. At all events, their morbid fear of oligarchic or tyrannical conspiracies fueled what was, for them, an uncharacteristic passion to avenge offenses against the gods. They arrested many respectable men and even killed some of them merely because they had been accused. They even recalled Alcibiades from his command in Sicily to face the capital charge of having profaned the mystery rites—this too, they claimed, in connection with a conspiracy against the people (VI 53, 60.1–61.1). Now there were reasons, to be sure, to suspect Alcibiades of having tyrannical ambitions; and he betrayed Athens to Sparta after he had fled from prosecution. Yet he was Athens's most capable general, and his dismissal from the Athenian command, together with the able counsel that he gave to Sparta, led directly to Athens's failure in Sicily. The Athenian people or, more precisely, the class of mostly poor Athenians who called themselves the whole community were so eager to conquer Sicily that those of their fellow citizens who opposed the campaign were afraid to raise their hands against it. And these Athenians were not deterred from the expedition by what they themselves regarded as an ill omen. Yet these same Athenians cared so little for the army's safety or even the city's survival in the war, as compared to their own rule within the city, that they tried to condemn their most capable general to death for an impiety that he may or may not have committed. As for the danger that success in Sicily might help Alcibiades to become a tyrant in the future, this is a risk that the Athenian democracy would have had to accept as a price for conquering Sicily. Moreover, Thucydides indicates, in an apparent digression, that the earlier Athenian tyrants had practiced "virtue and intelligence" throughout most of their rule, and that they upheld most of the customary laws, including especially the sacred observances (VI 54.4–6; cf VI 24.4). This behavior is in striking contrast, of course, to that of the populace, who were then in the grip of a foolish partisanship and whose actions were all the more heedless because they believed, apparently, that their chief concern was for the whole city and for the gods. In accordance with all this, Thucydides concludes not that it was Alcibiades but, rather, the many among the Athenians, each of whom was privately annoyed at his practices, who brought about the city's fall (VI 15.3–4; cf. II 65.8–10).

After Alcibiades' dismissal from Sicily, one of the two remaining Athenian generals was Nicias, a moderate and pious man who had opposed the expedition but whose loyalty, at any rate, the Athenians believed they could trust. Thucydides shows his own sympathy for Nicias by commenting, on the occasion of his surrender and his death at the hands of the Syracusans, that "he deserved least among the Greeks, during my time, to come to this degree of misfortune because of his full devotion to virtue as established by custom" (VII 86.5). This remark, however, may surprise some readers, since Thucydides' account has already indicated that Nicias' own weaknesses of character and judgment played a large part in Athens's defeat. Let us look, then, at some of the ways in which Nicias contributed to Athens's failure, and we will then be in a better position to explain the apparent inconsistency between Thucydides' narrative and his explicit judgment. Nicias' hope against hope to prevent the expedition, which the Athenians had already resolved upon, together with his wish to sail as safely as possible, if he were to be compelled to go, led him to advise the Athenians to send a much larger force than they were intending. His tactics failed to prevent the expedition, but he did succeed in convincing the Athenians to send this larger army. Indeed, it was only after his advice had made them confident of the expedition's safety that they fell in love with it. The reluctant Nicias' concern for safety, and for the safety of his reputation as a successful general, was thus directly responsible for the size of the Athenians' stake in Sicily as well as for their enthusiasm (VI 19.2, 24–26). Yet the gravest, and most revealing, of Nicias' mistakes occurred much later in the campaign, when even with Demosthenes' reinforcements the Athenians failed to capture Syracuse. The ships and their crews were steadily deteriorating, the enemy was gathering strength, and it should have been clear that the Athenians ought to return home at once, while their naval superiority still allowed them to do so. But Nicias was unwilling to return to Athens without orders from home, on the grounds, as he said, that the Athenians, including most of the soldiers who were then clamoring to return, would convict the generals of having been bribed by the enemy. "Knowing the natures, [he said], of the Athenians he preferred to risk perishing, if he must, at the hands of his enemies, and privately, rather than to perish on a shameful charge and unjustly at the hands of the Athenians" (VII 48.4). Nicias had good reason, given the democracy's suspiciousness of its own leaders, to fear banishment, and perhaps even death, if he had returned home with the army. Yet the fact remains that his choice to die "privately" in Sicily led directly to the army's ruin and cost the lives of thousands of his troops. One might say, in partial defense of Nicias, that he still believed there was a chance to capture Syracuse, and that when the arrival of fresh enemy troops persuaded him that he had been mistaken, he agreed to lead the army home. But then, when an eclipse of the moon so troubled the majority of the Athenians that they urged, or ordered, the generals to postpone the departure, Nicias said that he wouldn't even consider deliberating about how to depart until the "thrice nine days" prescribed by the soothsayers had passed. "For he was somewhat excessively attached," observes Thucydides, "to divination and the like" (VII 50.4). Nicias may well have believed that the fleet's best hopes for safety, and not merely his own, required them to remain at Syracuse for the prescribed period; but it is hard to excuse a general for giving in to such superstitious fears and hopes. Because of this foolish delay, the Athenian army lost its final opportunity to return home safely. After a final naval defeat, in their desperate attempt to break out of the Syracusan harbor, the Athenians were so overwhelmed by the greatness of their present evils that it didn't even occur to them, not even to the pious Nicias, to ask for the return of the corpses of their dead comrades.[8] Tearfully, and with much self-reproach, the fleeing Athenians also abandoned their wounded comrades, but the army was nevertheless unable to save itself. In the light of this narrative, we are prepared to notice that when Thucydides says of Nicias that his misfortune was so undeserved, he says that this was because of his devotion to "virtue as established by custom," that is to say, conventional virtue, as distinct from virtue simply. Though Nicias' devotion to conventional virtue helped make him a highly decent man and one whom the Athenians could trust in most ordinary circumstances, both he and also virtue, as he understood it, were unequal to the extreme test of the Sicilian campaign. Nicias was fully devoted to conventional virtue; at all events, he never willingly did any harm to his fatherland. Yet conventional virtue is an unreliable thing, for it is dependent upon, and in part guided by, hopes that have no other support than the belief in conventional virtue itself. Nicias' devotion to conventional virtue was at the root of his trustful hope that he, or at least his good name, could have the security that this same devotion led him to think he deserved (cf. V 16.1). And yet this blind hope for personal security was largely responsible, we know, for his own death and his city's disaster.

The Sicilian campaign was a grave mistake. Athens's prospects for success, or even for the army's safe return, were dependent on its power to reconcile private and public interest, and yet the expedition stretched the city too far beyond the limits of this power. Admittedly, the Athenians might have succeeded in Sicily if they had had better luck—for instance, if there had been no mutilation of the Hermes statues. But the attempt was nevertheless immoderate and unwise. And, more importantly, the tremendous costs of the expedition, along with the disharmony within the city that it brought so clearly to light, may help us toward a more sober view of Athenian imperialism altogether. For had we not ourselves been deceived by the charm that deceived the Athenians, we might already have seen that their imperialism was flawed from the beginning by a fundamental lack of wisdom. The Athenians, and the best among their leaders, devoted themselves to building a great and noble empire. Since, however, they thought of themselves as being noble, they could not help feeling the weight of the accusations against them for presuming to rule over others against their will. Accordingly, they felt obliged to defend their empire against these accusations, and they did so by arguing that they, like all men, were compelled by nature to be selfish, or to put their own good before all other considerations. On the other hand, since they thought of their empire, and of themselves, as being noble, they accepted certain risks and hardships in connection with their rule that would seem to have been at odds with their own self-interest. Now it must have troubled them to do this, for in view of their own argument for empire, these additional risks and hardships would appear to have been senseless sacrifices. But the Athenians apparently regarded them less as sacrifices than as a price worth paying, on the grounds that all of their sufferings in connection with the pursuit of empire would be more than compensated for by the reward of everlasting glory. Yet in this thought they were mistaken. For what they "experienced" with regard to glory, or with regard to the prospect of it in the future, was colored by their belief that glory was not merely a good but also something noble, that is to say, an acknowledgment of their superiority to mere self-interest and of their willingness, on occasion, to sacrifice. In other words, they had not squarely faced their own argument in defense of empire, for this argument leaves no room for superiority to self-interest, or for anything more important than one's own good. And had they truly accepted this argument, they would not have been moved, or not in the same way, by the prospect of glory, and they would hardly have felt that their sufferings in its pursuit would be so sufficiently and lastingly repaid. Long before the disaster in Sicily, then, the Athenians and their best leaders were already led astray by their failure to understand themselves and the object of their longing.

The Athenian argument, rightly understood, teaches that there can be no nobility that would be superior to self-interest. One might therefore be tempted to draw the disturbing conclusion that the wisest of all Athenians in Thucydides' account were the ambassadors at Melos, whose vindication of the rule of the stronger was least colored by any continuing or explicit concern for nobility. Yet this conclusion would be false, and not merely because the ambassadors' brutal attempt to destroy the innocence of the Melians made them if anything more determined not to submit to Athenian rule. For there is one Athenian speaker who shows a considerably deeper understanding of the Athenian argument. This Athenian is Diodotus, a remarkable man of whom we know nothing from other sources, and who appears only once in Thucydides' narrative. Although he seems not to have been a political man, his single intervention in Athens's political life was highly skillful. He succeeded in helping Athens to maintain its empire, and to maintain it by means of relatively humane treatment of a subject ally. Moreover, his speech is characterized by a gentleness, and even serenity, that are unparalleled within Thucydides' work and that seem to mirror these qualities in Thucydides himself.

Diodotus spoke at the assembly, to which we have already referred, where the Athenians were reconsidering their decree to kill all the men of Mytilene, and he urged them to rescind that decree. His task was a difficult one, even though the assembly had been convened in response to a change of heart among the people, since Cleon, who at that time had by far the most influence over them, had spoken before him and had opposed any change. Cleon had argued strongly that justice and Athenian interest alike required the severest punishment of the rebellious Mytileneans. But, of more immediate concern to Diodotus, Cleon had attacked the Athenians' habit of often reconsidering their own decisions. He had attributed this habit not at all to concern for the public good, but mostly to the speakers' wish to appear wiser than the laws and to display their intelligence in regard to public affairs, since these are held to be the greatest of matters. Anyone, said Cleon, who would speak against the previous day's decree must be moved to do so by his vanity as an orator, or perhaps also by bribes (III 38.2–3, 37.3–4). In the face of these attacks, Diodotus begins, as he must, by defending the propriety of frequent deliberation about the city's affairs, which he too calls "the greatest things." And he warns especially that the city is harmed when speakers accuse one another of being corrupted by money, since fear then deprives it of counselors. A city would do best, he says, if the kind of citizens who made such accusations were not permitted to speak. And in "the moderate city," he continues, an unsuccessful speaker would never even be dishonored, let alone accused of injustice and punished. In such a moderate city, apparently, all those who addressed the assembly would be so wholly free of private ambition that they would not feel dishonored by a failure to persuade. Yet Diodotus is well aware that the Athenian democracy, like any actual city, is necessarily suspicious of its speakers' private motives, and that the city's interest sometimes even requires this vigilance. Since he understands these facts of political life, he disregards his utopian standard of "the moderate city" and tries to dishonor Cleon, whom he accuses of either being stupid or else speaking from some private motive of his own. Yet Athenian suspiciousness is such, especially in the wake of Cleon's accusations, that Diodotus must go still much further in order to gain a hearing for his argument. For the Athenians, he says boldly, are so envious that they would reject what is manifestly the best advice for the city if they suspected a speaker of giving this good advice for the sake of gain. A speaker, therefore, who wants to lead the city for its good must first overcome its suspicions of him, and this task is apparently impossible by straightforward means alone. For Diodotus concludes that even a speaker who wants to say what is better must lie to the multitude in order to be trusted, and that it is impossible to benefit the city—and the city alone—without deceiving it (III 42–43). With remarkable frankness, Diodotus tells the Athenians that he will deceive them. And this admission leaves us with the following questions. Why is it impossible to earn the city's trust without lying to it? And how, precisely, does Diodotus lie?

Diodotus' lie would appear to be his claim that he will not even consider the question of justice, *i.e.*, whether the Mytileneans were unjust, but only that of whether it is in Athens's interest to kill them all. It is true that the bulk of his argument against these killings is a hardheaded analysis in terms of Athenian self-interest; yet one feels that he is not so simply heartless as he pretends. Moreover, he does not, as we shall see, wholly disregard considerations of justice. Diodotus begins by claiming that even the most severe punishments cannot deter all rebellions, and that Athens should therefore be prepared to try to end any rebellion that does occur with as little cost as possible. Athens can do this, he says, by exploiting the division of classes among the rebels and by giving the multitude the prospect of leniency for themselves if they should willingly hand over the city, as the multitude within Mytilene had done, more or less, once they had received heavy arms. But then, surprisingly, Diodotus adds that it would now be unjust to kill the multitude, as distinct from the oligarchs, at Mytilene, since they had been the Athenians' benefactors.[9] So in spite of his original claim, Diodotus does argue explicitly in terms of justice. Moreover, there is much in his speech that has subtly been leading up to this argument from justice. For in order to show that it is impossible to deter rebellions, Diodotus says that all men by nature, both privately and publicly, commit transgressions, and that no law or threat of punishment will restrain them from this. In other words, we are all compelled, by our natural passions together with our hopes, to try to acquire the objects of our strongest desires (III 45). And since we are compelled to do this, however foolish our hopes for success may be, our mistakes or transgressions are involuntary; and even Cleon had admitted that involuntary crimes deserve pardon. Now Diodotus, for good reasons, does not explicitly draw the conclusion that all criminals deserve pardon: among other things, he does not oppose putting the alleged ringleaders of the rebellion on trial. But by speaking of the compulsoriness of transgression, he puts the Athenians in a forgiving mood, and he reawakens and even deepens the mild temper with which they had begun the day's assembly. In this way he makes them receptive to his contention that to kill the multitude of the Mytileneans would be unjust.

If Diodotus' deception, however, is his pretence to disregard justice, the question arises of why he didn't say, more straightforwardly, that justice (or humanity) and the Athenians' self-interest alike require that they not kill the multitude of the Mytileneans. But the fact is that it would have been ill advised of him to say this. Especially because Cleon's speech had put the Athenians in an angry mood, an open argument against the justice of these killings would have pained them, and it would have made them suspect some weakness in his argument from interest. And, more importantly, they would have suspected him of knowingly betraying the city's interests, under the pretext of justice or humanity but in fact, as Cleon had charged, because of some private interest of his own. Since the city is so excessively distrustful of those citizens who address it, Diodotus must try to win its trust, and he does this by appearing to be wholly unconcerned with justice, at least to the extent that it is a notion distinct from the city's interest. In accordance with this, he also says several times that the city's concerns, and in particular its freedom and its rule over others, are "the greatest things." [10] By appearing to regard the city's interests, or its freedom and its empire, as immeasurably more important than justice and, indeed, as the most important of all concerns, Diodotus succeeds in making himself trusted. And this success is dependent, of course, upon lying and deception.

But Diodotus' deceptiveness extends still further than we have yet acknowledged, for he has deceived us into thinking that his hidden concern is primarily the concern for justice. To see that this is so, we must look again at his statement of what we have been calling the Athenian argument for empire. Diodotus had said that all men, both privately and publicly, are of such a nature as to transgress, and that no law will ever restrain them from transgression. But since Diodotus knows this fact about our nature, law or justice cannot be his chief concern, not even in those circumstances where keeping agreements regarding justice is useful. He points, however, to what is his chief concern by explicitly applying the Athenian argument to men in private, or to individuals, something that no other speaker in Thucydides ever does. In other words, he is the only speaker who clearly indicates that the primacy of the good is in fact the primacy of the individual's good, as distinct from that of the city. Just as there is nothing greater, *i.e.,* more important, than the good, there is nothing more important to the individual than what is good, or bad, for himself. The Athenians' suspicions, then, that their speakers are moved chiefly by private self-interest turn out to be well grounded, at least in the case of Diodotus. Now it is true that Diodotus' private interest as an Athenian, and even his educated humanity, both prompt him to try to be useful to Athens by persuading it to rescind a harsh and ill-advised decree. But the Athenians would not have honored him with their approval if they had understood his motives. Whether from their fear of tyranny or, as Diodotus himself has suggested, simply from envy of another's greater good, the Athenians would not have accepted his useful advice unless he had convinced them that their city's concerns were, for him, "the greatest things." And since he doesn't believe that they are the greatest things, he is compelled to lie.

Though Diodotus indicates clearly that the ultimate good is the good of the individual, as distinct from that of the city, he says little more about its character. Given his critique, however, of the city's claim that its concerns are "the greatest things," it does not seem possible that he could have been satisfied with the rewards from political life alone. Indeed, the very fact that we know so little about this politically gifted man might suggest that he did not regard rule over others, or its fruits, as the ultimate good of the individual. But apart from his statement about the necessity for deliberation before action, he conceals his positive thoughts about that good. In this respect, as in others, Diodotus is akin to Thucydides himself, for Thucydides also, as we have noted, is silent about the question of the best way of life. Or is he? Doesn't Thucydides' whole work, rather, direct us toward his own way of life—above all, his "quest for the truth" and his writing of "a possession for all time" (I 20.3, 22.4)—as the best life for man? The only mention of philosophy in Thucydides' work is in Pericles' Funeral Oration. Pericles praises the Athenians for philosophizing "without softness," by which he apparently means without retreating from political life. And he also speaks emphatically of the superior dignity of the active or political life to the life of leisure. [11] But Pericles fails to understand that the Athenians' "philosophizing" goes together with a kind of softness of its own. For men, or at least the most capable men, are compelled by the very seriousness of their moral and political concerns to question the truth of their most cherished convictions, and ultimately to turn toward philosophy as their supreme good. It was Thucydides who had the strength of mind to accept this compulsion and to think it through until he understood it clearly. And from this understanding he gained still further strength. For only from the perspective that he thus attained could he continue to look at political life, including its great horrors as well as its beauties, with such calm clarity, while also acting upon it, through his writing, with such balance and humanity.

NOTES

1. Unless otherwise indicated, all references are to this work. Translations from the Greek are my own.

I am especially indebted to two papers by Christopher Bruell: "Thucydides' View of Athenian Imperialism," *American Political Science Review*, LXVIII, No. 1 (March 1974), 11–17; and "Thucydides and Perikles," *St. John's Review*, XXXII, No. 3. (Summer 1981), 24–29.

2. VIII 97.2; IV 81.2; VI 54.5; VII 86.5; VIII 68.1.

3. Richard Schlatter, ed., *Hobbes' Thucydides* (New Brunswick: Rutgers University Press, 1975), 18.

4. Compare V 18.5–8 and 32.1

with IV 86.1, 114.3–4, 120.3. See also IV 81.2, 108.6–7, 117; and V 14.3–15.1.

5. Consider V 25.3. Contrast, however, VII 57.1.

6. VI 24.3; cf. I 143.5–144.1; II 62.2, 65.7, and also 40.1.

7. VIII 1–2, 24.5; cf. VII 28.3 and 42.2.

8. VII 72.2; cf. VII 75.3 and contrast IV 44.5–6.

9. Compare III 47.3 (and 46.5–6) with III 44.

10. III 42.1, 43.4, 45.6; cf. III 37.4 and 40.3.

11. II 40.1, 40.2, 63.2–3, 64.4–5; cf. II 41.4.

READING

Thucydides, *The War of the Peloponnesians and the Athenians*.

PLATO

427–347 B.C.

Thirty-five dialogues and thirteen letters have come down to us as
Platonic writings, not all of which are now regarded as genuine. Some
scholars go so far as to doubt that any of the letters is genuine. In order
not to encumber our presentation with polemics, we shall disregard the
letters altogether. We must then say that Plato never speaks to us in his
own name, for in his dialogues only his characters speak. Strictly, there
is then no Platonic teaching; at most there is the teaching of the men
who are the chief characters in his dialogues. Why Plato proceeded in
this manner is not easy to say. Perhaps he was doubtful whether there
can be a philosophic teaching proper. Perhaps he, too, thought like his
master Socrates that philosophy is in the last analysis knowledge of
ignorance. Socrates is indeed the chief character in most of the Platonic
dialogues. One could say that Plato's dialogues as a whole are less the
presentation of a teaching than a monument to the life of Socrates—
to the core of his life: they all show how Socrates engaged in his most
important work, the awakening of his fellow men and the attempting
to guide them toward the good life which he himself was living. Still,
Socrates is not always the chief character in Plato's dialogues; in a
few he does hardly more than listen while others speak, and in one
dialogue (the *Laws*) he is not even present. We mention these strange
facts because they show how difficult it is to speak of Plato's teaching.

All Platonic dialogues refer more or less directly to the political
question. Yet there are only three dialogues which indicate by their
very titles that they are devoted to political philosophy: the *Republic*,
the *Statesman*, and the *Laws*. The political teaching of Plato is accessible to us chiefly through these three works.

THE REPUBLIC

In the *Republic,* Socrates discusses the nature of justice with a fairly large number of people. The conversation about this general theme takes place, of course, in a particular setting: in a particular place, at a particular time, with men each of whom has his particular age, character, abilities, position in society, and appearance. While the place of the conversation is made quite clear to us, the time, *i.e.,* the year, is not. Hence we lack certain knowledge of the political circumstances in which this conversation about the principles of politics takes place. We may assume, however, that it takes place in an era of political decay of Athens, that at any rate Socrates and the chief interlocutors (the brothers Glaukon and Adeimantos) were greatly concerned with that decay and thinking of the restoration of political health. Certain it is that Socrates makes very radical proposals of "reform" without encountering serious resistance. But there are also a few indications in the *Republic* to the effect that the longed-for reformation is not likely to succeed on the political plane or that the only possible reformation is that of the individual man.

The conversation opens with Socrates' addressing a question to the oldest man present, Kephalos, who is respectable on account of his piety as well as his wealth. Socrates' question is a model of propriety. It gives Kephalos an opportunity to speak of everything good which he possesses, to display his happiness, as it were, and it concerns the only subject about which Socrates could conceivably learn something from him: about how it feels to be very old. In the course of his answer Kephalos comes to speak of injustice and justice. He seems to imply that justice is identical with telling the truth and paying back what one has received from anyone. Socrates shows him that telling the truth and returning another man's property are not always just. At this point Kephalos' son and heir, Polemarchos, rising in defense of his father's opinion, takes the place of his father in the conversation. But the opinion which he defends is not exactly the same as his father's; if we may make use of a joke of Socrates', Polemarchos inherits only half, and perhaps even less than a half, of his father's intellectual property. Polemarchos no longer maintains that telling the truth is essential to justice. Without knowing it, he thus lays down one of the principles of the *Republic.* As appears later in the work, in a well-ordered society it is necessary that one tell untruths of a certain kind to children and even to the adult subjects.[1] This example reveals the character of the discussion which occurs in the first book of the *Republic,* where Socrates refutes a number of false opinions about justice. This negative or destructive work, however, contains within itself the constructive assertions of the bulk of the *Republic*. Let us consider from this point of view the three opinions on justice discussed in the first book.

Kephalos' opinion as taken up by Polemarchos (after his father had left to perform an act of piety) is to the effect that justice consists in returning deposits. More generally stated, Kephalos holds that justice consists in returning, leaving, or giving to everyone what belongs to him. But he also holds that justice is good, *i.e.,* salutary, not only to the giver but also to the receiver. Now it is obvious that in some cases giving to a man what belongs to him is harmful to him. Not all men make a good or wise use of what belongs to them, of their property. If we judge very strictly, we might be driven to say that very few people make a wise use of their property. If justice is to be salutary, we might be compelled to demand that everyone should own only what is "fitting" for him, what is good for him, and for as long as it is good for him. In brief, we might be compelled to demand the abolition of private property or the introduction of communism. To the extent to which there is a connection between private property and the family, we would even be compelled to demand abolition of the family or the introduction of absolute communism, *i.e.,* of communism not only regarding property but regarding women and children as well. Above all, extremely few people will be able to determine wisely which things and which amounts of them are good for the use of each individual— or at any rate for each individual who counts; only men of exceptional wisdom are able to do this. We would then be compelled to demand that society be ruled by simply wise men, by philosophers in the strict sense, wielding absolute power. The refutation of Kephalos' view of justice thus contains the proof of the necessity of absolute communism in the sense defined, as well as of the absolute rule of the philosophers. This proof, it is hardly necessary to say, is based on the disregard of, or the abstraction from, a number of most relevant things; it is "abstract" in the extreme. If we wish to understand the *Republic,* we must find out what these disregarded things are and why they are disregarded. The *Republic* itself, carefully read, supplies the answers to these questions.

Before going any further, we must dispose of a misunderstanding which is at present very common. The theses of the *Republic* summarized in the two preceding paragraphs clearly show that Plato, or at any rate Socrates, was not a liberal democrat. They also suffice to show that Plato was not a Communist in the sense of Marx, or a Fascist:

Marxist communism and fascism are incompatible with the rule of philosophers, whereas the scheme of the *Republic* stands or falls by the rule of philosophers. But let us hasten back to the *Republic*.

Whereas the first opinion on justice was only implied by Kephalos and stated by Socrates, the second opinion is stated by Polemarchos, although not without Socrates' assistance. Furthermore, Kephalos' opinion is linked in his mind with the view that injustice is bad because it is punished by the gods after death. This view forms no part of Polemarchos' opinion. He is confronted with the contradiction between the two opinions according to which justice must be salutary to the receiver and justice consists in giving to each what belongs to him. Polemarchos overcomes the contradiction by dropping the second opinion. He also modifies the first. Justice, he says, consists in helping one's friends and harming one's enemies. Justice thus understood would seem to be unqualifiedly good for the giver and for those receivers who are good to the giver. This difficulty, however, arises: If justice is taken to be giving to others what belongs to them, the only thing which the just man must know is what belongs to anyone with whom he has any dealing; this knowledge is supplied by the law, which in principle can be easily known by mere listening. But if the just man must give to his friends what is good for them, he himself must judge; he himself must be able correctly to distinguish friends from enemies; he himself must know what is good for each of his friends. Justice must include knowledge of a high order. To say the least, justice must be an art comparable to medicine, the art which knows and produces what is good for human bodies. Polemarchos is unable to identify the knowledge or the art which goes with justice or which is justice. He is therefore unable to show how justice can be salutary. The discussion points to the view that justice is the art which gives to each man what is good for his soul, *i.e.*, that justice is identical with, or at least inseparable from, philosophy, the medicine of the soul. It points to the view that there cannot be justice among men unless the philosophers rule. But Socrates does not yet state this view. Instead he makes clear to Polemarchos that the just man will help just men rather than his "friends," and he will harm no one. He does not say that the just man will help everyone. Perhaps he means that there are human beings whom he cannot benefit. But he surely also means something more. Polemarchos' thesis may be taken to reflect a most potent opinion regarding justice—the opinion according to which justice means public-spiritedness, full dedication to one's city as a particular society which as such is potentially the enemy of other cities. Justice so understood is patriotism, and consists indeed in helping one's friends, *i.e.*, one's fellow citizens, and harming one's enemies, *i.e.*, foreigners. Justice thus understood cannot be entirely dispensed with in any city however just, for even the most just city is a city, a particular or closed or exclusive society. Therefore Socrates himself demands later in the dialogue that the guardians of the city be by nature friendly to their own people and harsh or nasty to strangers.[2] He also demands that the citizens of the just city cease to regard all human beings as their brothers and limit the feelings and actions of fraternity to their fellow citizens alone.[3] The opinion of Polemarchos properly understood is the only one among the generally known views of justice discussed in the first book of the *Republic* which is entirely preserved in the positive or constructive part of the *Republic*. This opinion, to repeat, is to the effect that justice is full dedication to the common good; it demands that man withhold nothing of his own from his city; it demands therefore by itself—*i.e.*, if we abstract from all other considerations—absolute communism.

The third and last opinion discussed in the first book of the *Republic* is the one maintained by Thrasymachos. He is the only speaker in the work who exhibits anger and behaves discourteously and even savagely. He is highly indignant over the result of Socrates' conversation with Polemarchos. He seems to be particularly shocked by Socrates' contention that it is not good for oneself to harm anyone or that justice is never harmful to anyone. It is most important, both for the understanding of the *Republic* and generally, that we do not behave toward Thrasymachos as Thrasymachos behaves, *i.e.*, angrily, fanatically, or savagely. If we look then at Thrasymachos' indignation without indignation, we must admit that his violent reaction is to some extent a revolt of common sense. Since the city as city is a society which from time to time must wage war, and war is inseparable from harming innocent people,[4] the unqualified condemnation of harming human beings would be tantamount to the condemnation of even the justest city. Apart from this, it seems to be entirely fitting that the most savage man present should maintain a most savage thesis on justice. Thrasymachos contends that justice is the advantage of the stronger. Still, this thesis proves to be only the consequence of an opinion which is not only not manifestly savage but is even highly respectable. According to that opinion, the just is the same as the lawful or legal, *i.e.*, what the customs or laws of the city prescribe. Yet this opinion implies that there is nothing higher to which one can appeal from the man-made laws or conventions. This is the opinion now known by the name of "legal positivism," but in its origin it is not academic; it is the opinion on which all political societies tend to act. If the just is identical with the

legal, the source of justice is the will of the legislator. The legislator in
each city is the regime—the man or body of men that rules the city:
the tyrant, the common people, the men of excellence, and so on.
According to Thrasymachos, each regime lays down the laws with a
view to its own preservation and well-being, in a word, to its own
advantage and to nothing else. From this it follows that obedience to
the laws or justice is not necessarily advantageous to the ruled and may
even be bad for them. And as for the rulers, justice simply does not
exist: they lay down the laws with exclusive concern for their own
advantage.

Let us concede for a moment that Thrasymachos' view of law and
of rulers is correct. The rulers surely may make mistakes. They may command actions which are in fact disadvantageous to themselves and
advantageous to the ruled. In that case the just or law-abiding subjects
will in fact do what is disadvantageous to the rulers and advantageous
to the subjects. When this difficulty is pointed out to him by Socrates,
Thrasymachos declares after some hesitation that the rulers are not
rulers if and when they make mistakes: the ruler in the strict sense is
infallible, just as the artisan in the strict sense is infallible. It is this
Thrasymachean notion of "the artisan in the strict sense" which Socrates uses with great felicity against Thrasymachos. For the artisan in
the strict sense proves to be concerned, not with his own advantage,
but with the advantage of the others whom he serves: the shoemaker
makes shoes for others and only accidentally for himself; the physician
prescribes things to his patients with a view to their advantage; hence
if ruling is, as Thrasymachos admitted, something like an art, the
ruler serves the ruled, i.e., rules for the advantage of the ruled. The
artisan in the strict sense is infallible, i.e., does his job well, and he is
only concerned with the well-being of others. This, however, means
that art strictly understood is justice—justice in deed, and not merely
in intention as law-abidingness is. "Art is justice"—this proposition reflects the Socratic assertion that virtue is knowledge. The suggestion
emerging from Socrates' discussion with Thrasymachos leads to the
conclusion that the just city will be an association where everyone is
an artisan in the strict sense, a city of craftsmen or artificers, of men
(and women) each of whom has a single job which he does well and
with full dedication, i.e., without minding his own advantage and only
for the good of others or for the common good. This conclusion
pervades the whole teaching of the *Republic*. The city constructed there
as a model is based on the principle of "one man one job." The soldiers
in it are "artificers" of the freedom of the city; the philosophers in it
are "artificers" of the whole common virtue; there is an "artificer" of

heaven; even God is presented as an artisan—as the artificer even of the
eternal ideas.[5] It is because citizenship in the just city is craftsmanship
of one kind or another, and the seat of craftsmanship or art is in the
soul and not in the body, that the difference between the two sexes
loses its importance, or the equality of the two sexes is established.[6]

Thrasymachos could have avoided his downfall if he had left
matters at the common-sense view according to which rulers are of
course fallible, or if he had said that all laws are framed by the rulers
with a view to their apparent (and not necessarily true) advantage.
Since he is not a noble man, we are entitled to suspect that he chose
the alternative which proved fatal to him with a view to his own
advantage. Thrasymachos was a famous teacher of rhetoric, the art of
persuasion. (Hence, incidentally, he is the only man possessing an art
who speaks in the *Republic*.) The art of persuasion is necessary for
persuading rulers and especially ruling assemblies, at least ostensibly,
of their true advantage. Even the rulers themselves need the art of
persuasion in order to persuade their subjects that the laws, which are
framed with exclusive regard to the benefit of the rulers, serve the benefit of the subjects. Thrasymachos' own art stands or falls by the view
that prudence is of the utmost importance for ruling. The clearest
expression of this view is the proposition that the ruler who makes
mistakes is no longer a ruler at all.

Thrasymachos' downfall is caused not by a stringent refutation of his view of justice nor by an accidental slip on his part but by
the conflict between his depreciation of justice or his indifference to
justice and the implication of his art: there is some truth in the view
that art is justice. One could say—and as a matter of fact Thrasymachos
himself says—that Socrates' conclusion, namely, that no ruler or other
artisan ever considers his own advantage, is very simple-minded:
Socrates seems to be a babe in the woods. As regards the artisans proper,
they of course consider the compensation which they receive for their
work. It may be true that to the extent to which the physician is concerned with what is characteristically called his honorarium, he does
not exercise the art of the physician but the art of money-making; but
since what is true of the physician is true of the shoemaker and any
other craftsman as well, one would have to say that the only universal
art, the art accompanying all arts, the art of arts, is the art of money-
making; one must therefore further say that serving others or being
just becomes good for the artisan only through his practicing the art
of money-making, or that no one is just for the sake of justice, or that
no one likes justice as such. But the most devastating argument against
Socrates' reasoning is supplied by the arts which are manifestly con-

cerned with the most ruthless and calculating exploitation of the ruled by the rulers. Such an art is the art of the shepherd—the art wisely chosen by Thrasymachos in order to destroy Socrates' argument, especially since kings and other rulers have been compared to shepherds since the oldest times. The shepherd is surely concerned with the well-being of his flock—so that the sheep will supply men with the juiciest lamb chops. As Thrasymachos puts it, the shepherds are exclusively concerned with the good of the owners and of themselves.[7] But there is obviously a difference between the owners and the shepherds: the juiciest lamb chops are for the owner and not for the shepherd, unless the shepherd is dishonest. Now, the position of Thrasymachos or of any man of his kind with regard to both rulers and ruled is precisely that of the shepherd with regard to both the owners and the sheep: Thrasymachos can securely derive benefit from the assistance which he gives to the rulers (regardless of whether they are tyrants, common people, or men of excellence) only if he is loyal to them, if he does his job for them well, if he keeps his part of the bargain, if he is just. Contrary to his assertion, he must grant that a man's justice is salutary, not only to others and especially to the rulers, but also to himself. It is partly because he has become aware of this necessity that he changes his manners so remarkably in the last part of the first book. What is true of the helpers of rulers is true of the rulers themselves and all other human beings (including tyrants and gangsters) who need the help of other men in their enterprises however unjust: no association can last if its members do not practice justice among themselves.[8] This, however, amounts to an admission that justice may be a mere means, if an indispensable means, for injustice—for the exploitation of outsiders. Above all, it does not dispose of the possibility that the city is a community held together by collective selfishness and nothing else, or that there is no fundamental difference between the city and a gang of robbers. These and similar difficulties explain why Socrates regards his refutation of Thrasymachos as insufficient: he says at its conclusion that he has tried to show that justice is good without having made clear what justice is.

The adequate defense or praise of justice presupposes not only knowledge of what justice is, but also an adequate attack on justice. At the beginning of the second book, Glaukon attempts to present such an attack; he claims that he restates Thrasymachos' thesis, in which he does not believe, with greater vigor than Thrasymachos had done. Glaukon also takes it for granted that the just is the same as the legal or conventional, but he attempts to show how convention emerges out of nature. By nature each man is concerned only with his own good and wholly unconcerned with any other man's good to the point that he has no hesitation whatever about harming his fellows. Since everyone acts accordingly, they all bring about a situation which is unbearable for most of them; the majority, *i.e.,* the weaklings, figure out that every one of them would be better off if they agreed among themselves as to what each of them may or may not do. What they agree upon is not stated by Glaukon, but part of it can easily be guessed: they will agree that no one may violate the life and limb, the honor, the liberty, and the property of any of the associates, *i.e.,* the fellow citizens, and that everyone must do his best to protect his associates against outsiders. Both the abstention from such violations and the service of protection are in no way desirable in themselves but only necessary evils, yet lesser evils than universal insecurity. But what is true of the majority is not true of "the real man" who can take care of himself and who is better off if he does not submit to law or convention. Yet even the others do violence to their nature by submitting to law and justice: they submit to it only from fear of the consequences of the failure to submit, *i.e.,* from fear of punishment of one kind or another, not voluntarily and gladly. Therefore every man would prefer injustice to justice if he could be sure of escaping detection: justice is preferable to injustice only with a view to possible detection, to one's becoming known as just to others, *i.e.,* to good repute or other rewards. Therefore since, as Glaukon hopes, justice is choiceworthy for its own sake, he demands from Socrates a proof that the life of the just man is preferable to that of the unjust man even if the just man is thought to be unjust in the extreme and suffers all kinds of punishment or is in the depth of misery, and the unjust man is thought to be of consummate justice and receives all kinds of reward or is at the peak of happiness: the height of injustice, *i.e.,* of the conduct according to nature, is the tacit exploitation of law or convention for one's own benefit alone, the conduct of the supremely shrewd and manly tyrant. In the discussion with Thrasymachos, the issue had become blurred by the suggestion that there is a kinship between justice and art. Glaukon makes the issue manifest by comparing the perfectly unjust man to the perfect artisan, whereas he conceives of the perfectly just man as a simple man who has no quality other than justice. With a view to the teaching of the *Republic* as a whole, one is tempted to say that Glaukon understands pure justice in the light of pure fortitude; his perfectly just man reminds one of the unknown soldier who undergoes the most painful and most humiliating death for no other purpose whatsoever except in order to die bravely and without any prospect of his noble deed ever becoming known to anyone.

Glaukon's demand on Socrates is strongly supported by Adeimantos. It becomes clear from Adeimantos' speech that Glaukon's view
according to which justice is choiceworthy entirely for its own sake is
altogether novel, for in the traditional view justice was regarded as
choiceworthy chiefly, if not exclusively, because of the divine rewards
for justice and the divine punishments for injustice, and various other
consequences. Adeimantos' long speech differs from Glaukon's because
it brings out the fact that if justice is to be choiceworthy for its own
sake, it must be easy or pleasant.[9] Glaukon's and Adeimantos' demands
establish the standard by which one must judge Socrates' praise of
justice; they force one to investigate whether or to what extent Socrates has proved in the *Republic* that justice is choiceworthy for its own
sake or pleasant or even by itself sufficient to make a man perfectly
happy in the midst of what is ordinarily believed to be the most extreme misery.

In order to defend the cause of justice, Socrates turns to founding,
together with Glaukon and Adeimantos, a city in speech. The reason
why this procedure is necessary can be stated as follows. Justice is
believed to be law-abidingness or the firm will to give to everyone what
belongs to him, *i.e.*, what belongs to him according to law; yet justice
is also believed to be good or salutary; but obedience to the laws or
giving to everyone what belongs to him according to law is not unqualifiedly salutary since the laws may be bad; justice will be simply
salutary only when the laws are good, and this requires that the regime
from which the laws flow is good: justice will be fully salutary only
in a good city. Socrates' procedure implies, furthermore, that he knows
of no actual city which is good; this is the reason why he is compelled
to found a good city. He justifies his turning to the city by the consideration that justice can be detected more easily in the city than in the
human individual because the former is larger than the latter; he thus
implies that there is a parallelism between the city and the human
individual or, more precisely, between the city and the soul of the
human individual. This means that the parallelism between the city
and the human individual is based upon a certain abstraction from
the human body. To the extent to which there is a parallelism between
the city and the human individual or his soul, the city is at least
similar to a natural being. Yet that parallelism is not complete. While
the city and the individual seem equally to be able to be just, it is not
certain that they can be equally happy (cf. the beginning of the fourth
book). The distinction between the justice of the individual and his
happiness was prepared by Glaukon's demand on Socrates that justice
should be praised regardless of whether or not it has any extraneous

attractions. It is also prepared by the common opinion according to which justice requires complete dedication of the individual to the common good.

The founding of the good city takes place in three stages: the healthy city or the city of pigs, the purified city or the city of the armed camp, and the City of Beauty or the city ruled by philosophers.

The founding of the city is preceded by the remark that the city has its origin in human need: every human being, just or unjust, is in need of many things, and at least for this reason in need of other human beings. The healthy city satisfies properly the primary needs, the needs of the body. The proper satisfaction requires that each man exercise only one art. This means that everyone does almost all his work for others but also that the others work for him. All will exchange with one another their own products as their own products: there will be private property; by working for the advantage of others everyone works for his own advantage. The reason why everyone will exercise only one art is that men differ from one another by nature, *i.e.,* different men are gifted for different arts. Since everyone will exercise that art for which he is by nature fitted, the burden will be easier on everyone. The healthy city is a happy city: it knows no poverty, no coercion or government, no war and eating of animals. It is happy in such a way that every member of it is happy: it does not need government because there is perfect harmony between everyone's service and his reward; no one encroaches on anyone else. It does not need government because everyone chooses by himself the art for which he is best fitted; there is no disharmony between natural gifts and preferences. There is also no disharmony between what is good for the individual (his choosing the art for which he is best fitted by nature) and what is good for the city: nature has so arranged things that there is no surplus of blacksmiths or deficit of shoemakers. The healthy city is happy because it is just, and it is just because it is happy; in the healthy city, justice is easy or pleasant and free from any tincture of self-sacrifice. It is just without anyone's concerning himself with its justice; it is just by nature. Nevertheless, it is found wanting. It is impossible for the same reason that anarchism in general is impossible. Anarchism would be possible if men could remain innocent, but it is of the essence of innocence that it is easily lost; men can be just only through knowledge, and men cannot acquire knowledge without effort and without antagonism. Differently stated, while the healthy city is just in a sense, it lacks virtue or excellence: such justice as it possesses is not virtue. Virtue is impossible without toil, effort, or repression of the evil in oneself. The healthy city is a city in which evil is only dormant. Death is mentioned only when the transition from the healthy city to the next stage has already begun.[10] The healthy city is called a city of pigs not by Socrates but by Glaukon. Glaukon does not quite know what he says. Literally speaking, the healthy city is a city without pigs.[11]

Before the purified city can emerge or rather be established, the healthy city must have decayed. Its decay is brought about by the emancipation of the desire for unnecessary things, *i.e.,* for things which are not necessary for the well-being or health of the body. Thus the luxurious or feverish city emerges, the city characterized by the striving for the unlimited acquisition of wealth. One can expect that in such a city the individuals will no longer exercise the single art for which each is meant by nature but any art or combination of arts which is most lucrative, or that there will no longer be a strict correspondence between service and reward: hence there will be dissatisfaction and conflicts and therefore need for government which will restore justice; hence there will be need for something else which also was entirely absent from the healthy city, *i.e.,* education at least of the rulers, and more particularly education to justice. There will certainly be need for additional territory and hence there will be war, war of aggression. Building on the principle "one man one art," Socrates demands that the army consist of men who have no art other than that of warriors. It appears that the art of the warriors or of the guardians is by far superior to the other arts. Hitherto it looked as if all arts were of equal rank and the only universal art, or the only art accompanying all arts, was the art of money-making.[12] Now we receive the first glimpse of the true order of arts. That order is hierarchic; the universal art is the highest art, the art directing all other arts, which as such cannot be practiced by the practitioners of arts other than the highest. This art of arts will prove to be philosophy. For the time being we are told only that the warrior must have a nature resembling the nature of that philosophic beast, the dog. For the warriors must be spirited and hence irascible and harsh on the one hand and gentle on the other, since they must be harsh toward strangers and gentle to their fellow citizens. They must have a disinterested liking for their fellow citizens and a disinterested dislike for foreigners. The men possessing such special natures need in addition a special education. With a view to their work they need training in the art of war. But this is not the education with which Socrates is chiefly concerned. They will be by nature the best fighters and the only ones armed and trained in arms: they will inevitably be the sole possessors of political power. Besides, the age of innocence having gone, evil is rampant in the city and therefore also in the warriors. The education which the warriors more than anyone else need is therefore above all education in civic virtue. That education is "music" education, education especially through poetry and music. Not all poetry and music is apt to make men good citizens in general and good warriors or guardians in particular. Therefore the poetry and music not conducive to this moral-political end must be banished from the city. Socrates is very far from demanding that Homer and Sophocles should be replaced by the makers of edifying trash; the poetry which he demands for the good city must be genuinely poetic. He demands particularly that the gods be presented as models of human excellence, *i.e.,* of the kind of human excellence to which the guardians can and must aspire. The rulers will be taken from among the elite of the guardians. Yet the prescribed education, however excellent and effective, is not sufficient if it is not buttressed by the right kind of institutions, *i.e.,* by absolute communism or by the completest possible abolition of privacy: everyone may enter everyone else's dwelling at will. As reward for their service to the craftsmen proper, the guardians do not receive money of any kind but only a sufficient amount of food, and, we may suppose, of the other necessities.

Let us see in what way the good city as hitherto described reveals that justice is good or even attractive for its own sake. That justice, or the observing of the just proportion between service and reward, between working for others and one's own advantage, is necessary was shown in the discussion with Thrasymachos by the example of the gang of robbers. The education of the guardians as agreed upon between Socrates and Adeimantos is not education to justice.[13] It is education to courage and moderation. The music education in particular, as distinguished from the gymnastic education, is education to moderation, and this means to love of the beautiful, *i.e.,* of what is by nature attractive in itself. Justice in the narrow and strict sense may be said to flow from moderation or from the proper combination of moderation and courage. Socrates thus silently makes clear the difference between the gang of robbers and the good city: the essential difference consists in the fact that the armed and ruling part of the good city is animated by love of the beautiful, by the love of everything praiseworthy and graceful. The difference is not to be sought in the fact that the good city is guided in its relations to other cities, Greek or barbarian, by considerations of justice: the size of the territory of the good city is determined by that city's own moderate needs and by nothing else.[14] The difficulty appears perhaps more clearly from what Socrates says when speaking of the rulers. In addition to the other required qualities, the rulers must have the quality of caring for the city or loving the city; but a man is

most likely to love that whose interest he believes to be identical with
his own interest or whose happiness he believes to be the condition of
his own happiness. The love here mentioned is not obviously disinterested in the sense that the ruler loves the city, or his serving the city,
for its own sake. This may explain why Socrates demands that the
rulers be honored both while they live and after their death.[15] At any
rate the highest degree of caring for the city and for one another will
not be forthcoming unless everyone is brought to believe in the falsehood that all fellow citizens, and only they, are brothers.[16] To say the
least, the harmony between self-interest and the interest of the city,
which was lost with the decay of the healthy city, has not yet been restored. No wonder then that at the beginning of the fourth book
Adeimantos expresses his dissatisfaction with the condition of the soldiers in the city of the armed camp. Read within the context of the
whole argument, Socrates' reply is to this effect: Only as a member of
a happy city can a man be happy; only within these limits can a man,
or any other part of the city, be happy; complete dedication to the
happy city is justice. It remains to be seen whether complete dedication
to the happy city is, or can be, happiness of the individual.

After the founding of the good city is in the main completed, Socrates and his friends turn to seeking where in it justice and injustice
are, and whether the man who is to be happy must possess justice or
injustice.[17] They look first for the three virtues other than justice (wisdom, courage, and moderation). In the city which is founded according to nature, wisdom resides in the rulers and in the rulers alone, for
the wise men are by nature the smallest part of any city, and it would
not be good for the city if they were not the only ones at its helm. In
the good city, courage resides in the warrior class, for political courage,
as distinguished from brutish fearlessness, arises only through education
in those by nature fitted for it. Moderation on the other hand is to be
found in all parts of the good city. In the present context, moderation
does not mean exactly what it meant when the education of the warriors was discussed but rather the control of what is by nature worse
by that which is by nature better—that control through which the
whole is in harmony. In other words, moderation is the agreement
of the naturally superior and inferior as to which of the two ought to
rule in the city. Since controlling and being controlled differ, one must
assume that the moderation of the rulers is not identical with the
moderation of the ruled. While Socrates and Glaukon found the three
virtues mentioned in the good city with ease, it is difficult to find
justice in it because, as Socrates says, justice is so obvious in it. Justice
consists in everyone's doing the one thing pertaining to the city for

which his nature is best fitted or, simply, in everyone's minding his own business: it is by virtue of justice thus understood that the other three virtues are virtues.[18] More precisely, a city is just if each of its three parts (the money-makers, the warriors, and the rulers) does its own work and only its own work.[19] Justice is then, like moderation and unlike wisdom and courage, not a preserve of a single part but required of every part. Hence justice, like moderation, has a different character in each of the three classes. One must assume, for instance, that the justice of the wise rulers is affected by their wisdom and the justice of the money-makers is affected by their lack of wisdom, for if even the courage of the warriors is only political or civic courage, and not courage pure and simple,[20] it stands to reason that their justice too—to say nothing of the justice of the money-makers—will not be justice pure and simple. In order to discover justice pure and simple, it then becomes necessary to consider justice in the individual man. This consideration would be easiest if justice in the individual were identical with justice in the city; this would require that the individual or rather his soul consist of the same three kinds of "natures" as the city. A very provisional consideration of the soul seems to establish this requirement: the soul contains desire, spiritedness or anger,[21] and reason, just as the city consists of the money-makers, the warriors, and the rulers. Hence we may conclude that a man is just if each of these three parts of his soul does its own work and only its own work, *i.e.,* if his soul is in a state of health. But if justice is health of the soul, and conversely injustice is disease of the soul, it is obvious that justice is good and injustice is bad, regardless of whether or not one is known to be just or unjust.[22] A man is just if the rational part in him is wise and rules,[23] and if the spirited part, being the subject and ally of the rational part, assists it in controlling the multitude of desires which almost inevitably become desires for more and ever more money. This means, however, that only the man in whom wisdom rules the two other parts, *i.e.,* only the wise man, can be truly just.[24] No wonder then that the just man eventually proves to be identical with the philosopher.[25] The money-makers and the warriors are not truly just even in the just city because their justice derives exclusively from habituation of one kind or another as distinguished from philosophy; hence in the deepest recesses of their souls they long for tyranny, *i.e.,* for complete injustice.[26] We see then how right Socrates was when he expected to find injustice in the good city.[27] This is not to deny of course that as members of the good city the nonphilosophers will act much more justly than they would as members of inferior cities.

The justice of those who are not wise appears in a different light when justice in the city is being considered, on the one hand, and justice in the soul on the other. This fact shows that the parallelism between the city and the soul is defective. This parallelism requires that, just as in the city the warriors occupy a higher rank than the money-makers, so in the soul spiritedness occupy a higher rank than desire. It is very plausible that those who uphold the city against foreign and domestic enemies and who have received a music education deserve higher respect than those who lack public responsibility as well as a music education. But it is much less plausible that spiritedness as such should deserve higher respect than desire as such. It is true that "spiritedness" includes a large variety of phenomena ranging from the most noble indignation about injustice, turpitude, and meanness down to the anger of a spoiled child who resents being deprived of anything that he desires, however bad. But the same is also true of "desire": one kind of desire is *eros,* which ranges in its healthy forms from the longing for immortality via offspring through the longing for immortality via immortal fame to the longing for immortality via participation by knowledge in the things which are unchangeable in every respect. The assertion that spiritedness is higher in rank than desire as such is then questionable. Let us never forget that while there is a philosophic *eros,* there is no philosophic spiritedness;[28] or in other words that Thrasymachos is much more visibly spiritedness incarnate than desire incarnate. The assertion in question is based on a deliberate abstraction from *eros*—an abstraction characteristic of the *Republic.*

This abstraction shows itself most strikingly in two facts: when Socrates mentions the fundamental needs which give rise to human society, he is silent about the need for procreation, and when he describes the tyrant, Injustice incarnate, he presents him as *Eros* incarnate.[29] In the thematic discussion of the respective rank of spiritedness and desire, he is silent about *eros.*[30] It seems that there is a tension between *eros* and the city and hence between *eros* and justice: only through the depreciation of *eros* can the city come into its own. *Eros* obeys its own laws, not the laws of the city however good; in the good city, *eros* is simply subjected to what the city requires. The good city requires that all love of one's own—all spontaneous love of one's own parents, one's own children, one's own friends and beloved—be sacrificed to the common love of the common. As far as possible, the love of one's own must be abolished except as it is love of the city as this particular city, as one's own city. As far as possible, patriotism takes the place of *eros,* and patriotism has a closer kinship to spiritedness, eagerness to fight, "waspishness," anger, and indignation than to *eros.*

While it is harmful to one's soul to jump at Plato's throat because he is not a liberal democrat, it is also bad to blur the difference between Platonism and liberal democracy, for the premises "Plato is admirable" and "liberal democracy is admirable" do not legitimately lead to the conclusion that Plato was a liberal democrat. The founding of the good city started from the fact that men are by nature different, and this proved to mean that men are by nature of unequal rank. They are unequal particularly with regard to their ability to acquire virtue. The inequality which is due to nature is increased and deepened by the different kinds of education or habituation and the different ways of life (communistic or noncommunistic) which the different parts of the good city enjoy. As a result, the good city comes to resemble a caste society. A Platonic character who hears an account of the good city of the *Republic* is reminded by it of the caste system established in ancient Egypt, although it is quite clear that in Egypt the rulers were priests and not philosophers.[31] Certainly in the good city of the *Republic,* not descent but in the first place everyone's own natural gifts determine to which class he belongs. But this leads to a difficulty. The members of the upper class, which lives communistically, are not supposed to know who their natural parents are, for they are supposed to regard all men and women belonging to the older generation as their parents. On the other hand, the gifted children of the noncommunist lower class are to be transferred to the upper class (and vice versa); since their superior gifts are not necessarily recognizable at the moment of their birth, they are likely to come to know their natural parents and even to become attached to them; this would seem to unfit them for transfer to the upper class. There are two ways in which this difficulty can be removed. The first is to extend absolute communism to the lower class; and, considering the connection between way of life and education, also to extend music education to that class.[32] According to Aristotle,[33] Socrates has left it undecided whether in the good city absolute communism is limited to the upper class or extends also to the lower class. To leave this question undecided would be in agreement with Socrates' professed low opinion of the importance of the lower class.[34] Still, there can be only little doubt that Socrates wishes to limit both communism and music education to the upper class.[35] Therefore, in order to remove the difficulty mentioned, he can hardly avoid making an individual's membership in the upper or lower class hereditary and thus violating one of the most elementary principles of justice. Apart from this, one may wonder whether a perfectly clear line between those gifted and those not gifted for the profession of warriors can be drawn, hence whether a perfectly just assignment of individuals to the upper or lower class is possible, and hence whether the good city can be perfectly just.[36] But be this as it may, if communism is limited to the upper class, there will be privacy both in the money-making class and among the philosophers as philosophers, for there may very well be only a single philosopher in the city and surely never a herd: the warriors are the only class which is entirely political or public or entirely dedicated to the city; the warriors alone present therefore the clearest case of the just life in one sense of the word "just."

It is necessary to understand the reason why communism is limited to the upper class or what the natural obstacle to communism is. That which is by nature private or a man's own is the body and only the body.[37] The needs or desires of the body induce men to extend the sphere of the private, of what is each man's own, as far as they can. This most powerful striving is countered by music education which brings about moderation, *i.e.,* a most severe training of the soul of which, it seems, only a minority of men is capable. Yet this kind of education does not extirpate the natural desire of each for things or human beings of his own: the warriors will not accept absolute communism if they are not subject to the philosophers. It thus becomes clear that the striving for one's own is countered ultimately only by philosophy, by the quest for the truth which as such cannot be anyone's private possession. Whereas the private par excellence is the body, the common par excellence is the mind, the pure mind rather than the soul in general. The superiority of communism to noncommunism as taught in the *Republic* is intelligible only as a reflection of the superiority of philosophy to nonphilosophy. This clearly contradicts the result of the preceding paragraph. The contradiction can and must be resolved by the distinction between two meanings of justice. This distinction cannot become clear before one has understood the teaching of the *Republic* regarding the relation of philosophy and the city. We must therefore make a new beginning.

At the end of the fourth book, it looks as if Socrates had completed the task which Glaukon and Adeimantos had imposed on him, for he had shown that justice as health of the soul is desirable not only because of its consequences but above all for its own sake. But then, at the beginning of the fifth book, we are suddenly confronted by a new start, by the repetition of a scene which had occurred at the very beginning. Both at the very beginning and at the beginning of the fifth book (and nowhere else), Socrates' companions make a decision, nay, take a vote, and Socrates who had no share in the decision obeys it.[38] Socrates' companions behave in both cases like a city (an assembly of the citizens), if the smallest possible city.[39] But there is this decisive difference between the two scenes: whereas Thrasymachos was absent from the first scene, he has become a member of the city in the second scene. It could seem that the foundation of the good city requires that Thrasymachos be converted into one of its citizens.

At the beginning of the fifth book Socrates' companions force him to take up the subject of communism in regard to women and children. They do not object to the proposal itself in the way in which Adeimantos had objected to the communism regarding property at the beginning of the fourth book, for even Adeimantos is no longer the same man he was at that time. They only wish to know the precise manner in which the communism regarding women and children is to be managed. Socrates replaces that question by these more incisive questions: (1) Is that communism possible? (2) Is it desirable? It appears that the communism regarding women is the consequence or presupposition of the equality of the two sexes concerning the work they must do: the city cannot afford to lose half of its adult population from its working and fighting force, and there is no essential difference between men and women regarding natural gifts for the various arts. The demand for equality of the two sexes requires a complete upheaval of custom, an upheaval which is here presented less as shocking than as laughable; the demand is justified on the ground that only the useful is fair or noble and that only what is bad, *i.e.,* against nature, is laughable: the customary difference of conduct between the two sexes is rejected as being against nature, and the revolutionary change is meant to bring about the order according to nature.[40] For justice requires that every human being should practice the art for which he or she is fitted by nature, regardless of what custom or convention may dictate. Socrates shows first that the equality of the two sexes is possible, *i.e.,* in agreement with the nature of the two sexes as their nature appears when viewed with regard to aptitude for the practice of the various arts, and then he shows that it is desirable. In proving this possibility, he explicitly abstracts from the difference between the two sexes in regard to procreation.[41] This means that the argument of the *Republic* as a whole, according to which the city is a community of male and female artisans, abstracts to the highest degree possible from the highest activity essential to the city which takes place "by nature" and not "by art."

Socrates then turns to the communism regarding women and children and shows that it is desirable because it will make the city more "one," and hence more perfect, than a city consisting of separate families would be: the city should be as similar as possible to a single human being or to a single living body, *i.e.,* to a natural being.[42] At this point we understand somewhat better why Socrates started his discussion of justice by assuming an important parallelism between the city and the individual: he was thinking ahead of the greatest possible unity of the city. The abolition of the family does not mean of course the introduction of license or promiscuity; it means the most severe regulation of sexual intercourse from the point of view of what is useful for the city or what is required for the common good. The consideration of the useful, one might say, supersedes the consideration of the holy or sacred:[43] human males and females are to be coupled with exclusive regard to the production of the best offspring, in the spirit in which the breeders of dogs, birds, and horses proceed; the claims of *eros* are simply silenced. The new order naturally affects the customary prohibitions against incest, the most sacred rules of customary justice.[44] In the new scheme, no one will know any more his natural parents, children, brothers, and sisters, but everyone will *regard* all men of the older generation as his fathers and mothers, of his own generation as his brothers and sisters, and of the younger generation as his children.[45] This means, however, that the city constructed according to nature lives in a most important respect more according to convention than according to nature. For this reason we are disappointed to see that while Socrates takes up the question of whether communism regarding women and children is possible, he drops it immediately.[46] Since the institution under consideration is indispensable for the good city, Socrates thus leaves open the question of the possibility of the good city, *i.e.*, of the just city, as such. And this happens to his listeners and to the readers of the *Republic* after they have made the greatest sacrifices—such as the sacrifice of *eros* as well as of the family—for the sake of the just city.

Socrates is not for long allowed to escape from his awesome duty to answer the question regarding the possibility of the just city. The manly Glaukon compels him to face that question. Perhaps we should say that by apparently escaping to the subject of war—a subject both easier in itself and more attractive to Glaukon than the communism of women and children—yet treating that subject according to the stern demands of justice and thus depriving it of much of its attractiveness, he compels Glaukon to compel him to return to the fundamental question. Be this as it may, the question to which Socrates and Glaukon return is not the same one which they left. The question which they left was whether the good city is possible in the sense that it is in agreement with human nature. The question to which they return is whether the good city is possible in the sense that it can be brought into being by the transformation of an actual city.[47] The latter question might be thought to presuppose the affirmative answer to the first question, but this is not quite correct. As we learn now, our whole effort to discover what justice is (so that we would be enabled to see how it is related to happiness) was a quest for "justice itself" as a "pattern." By seeking for justice itself as a pattern we implied that the just man and the just city will not be perfectly just but will indeed approximate justice itself with particular closeness;[48] only justice itself is perfectly just.[49] This implies that not even the characteristic institutions of the just city (absolute communism, equality of the sexes, and the rule of the philosophers) are simply just. Now justice itself is not "possible" in the sense that it is capable of coming into being, because it "is" always without being capable of undergoing any change whatever. Justice is an "idea" or "form," one of many "ideas." Ideas are the only things which strictly speaking "are," *i.e.,* are without any admixture of nonbeing, because they are beyond all becoming, and whatever is becoming is between being and nonbeing. Since the ideas are the only things which are beyond all change, they are in a sense the cause of all change and all changeable things. For example, the idea of justice is the cause for anything (human beings, cities, laws, commands, actions) becoming just. They are self-subsisting beings which subsist always. They are of utmost splendor. For instance, the idea of justice is perfectly just. But their splendor escapes the eyes of the body. The ideas are "visible" only to the eye of the mind, and the mind as mind perceives nothing but ideas. Yet, as is indicated by the facts that there are many ideas and that the mind which perceives the ideas is radically different from the ideas themselves, there must be something higher than the ideas: "the good" or "the idea of the good" which is in a sense the cause of all ideas as well as of the mind perceiving them.[50] It is only through perception of "the good" on the part of the human beings who are by nature equipped for perceiving it that the good city can come into being and subsist for a while.

The doctrine of ideas which Socrates expounds to Glaukon is very hard to understand; to begin with it is utterly incredible, not to say that it appears to be fantastic. Hitherto we have been given to understand that justice is fundamentally a certain character of the human soul, or of the city, *i.e.,* something which is not self-subsisting. Now we are asked to believe that it is self-subsisting, being at home as it were in an entirely different place than human beings and everything else that participates in justice.[51] No one has ever succeeded in giving a satisfactory or clear account of this doctrine of ideas. It is possible, however, to define rather precisely the central difficulty. "Idea" means primarily the looks or shape of a thing; it means then a kind or class of things which are united by the fact that they all possess the same "looks," *i.e.,* the same character and power, or the same "nature"; therewith it means the class-character or the nature of the things belonging to the class in question: the "idea" of a thing is that which we mean by trying to find out the "what" or the "nature" of a thing or a class of things (see the Introduction). The connection between "idea" and "nature" appears in the *Republic* from the facts that "the idea of justice" is called "that which is just by nature," and that the ideas in contradistinction to the things which are not ideas or to the sensibly perceived things are said to be "in nature."[52] This does not explain, however, why the ideas are presented as "separated" from the things which are what they are by participating in an idea or, in other words, why "dogness" (the class character of dogs) should be "the true dog." It seems that two kinds of phenomena lend support to Socrates' assertion. In the first place the mathematical things as such can never be found among sensible things: no line drawn on sand or paper is a line as meant by the mathematician. Secondly and above all, what we mean by justice and kindred things is not as such, in its purity or perfection, necessarily found in human beings or societies; it rather seems that what is meant by justice transcends everything which men can ever achieve; precisely the justest men were and are the ones most aware of the shortcomings of their justice. Socrates seems to say that what is patently true of mathematical things and of the virtues is true universally: there is an idea of the bed or the table just as of the circle and of justice. Now while it is obviously reasonable to say that a perfect circle or perfect justice transcends everything which can ever be seen, it is hard to say that the perfect bed is something on which no man can ever rest. However this may be, Glaukon and Adeimantos accept this doctrine of ideas with relative ease, with greater ease than absolute communism. This paradoxical fact does not strike us with sufficient force because we somehow believe that these able young men study philosophy under Professor Socrates and have heard him expound the doctrine of ideas on innumerable occasions, if we do not believe that the *Republic* is a philosophic treatise addressed to readers familiar with more elementary (or "earlier") dialogues. Yet Plato addresses the readers of the *Republic* only through the medium of Socrates' conversation with Glaukon and the other interlocutors in the *Republic,* and Plato as the author of the *Republic* does not suggest that Glaukon—to say nothing of Adeimantos and the rest—has seriously studied the doctrine of ideas.[53] Yet while Glaukon and Adeimantos cannot be credited with a genuine understanding of the doctrine of ideas, they have heard, and in a way they know, that there are gods like *Dike* or Right,[54] and *Nike* or

Victory who is not this or that victory or this or that statue of Nike but a self-subsisting being which is the cause of every victory and which is of unbelievable splendor. More generally, they know that there are gods—self-subsisting beings which are the causes of everything good, which are of unbelievable splendor, and which cannot be apprehended by the senses since they never change their "form." [55] This is not to deny that there is a profound difference between the gods as understood in the "theology"[56] of the *Republic* and the ideas, or that in the *Republic* the gods are in a way replaced by the ideas. It is merely to assert that those who accept that theology and draw all conclusions from it are likely to arrive at the doctrine of ideas.

We must now return to the question of the possibility of the just city. We have learned that justice itself is not "possible" in the sense that anything which comes into being can ever be perfectly just. We learn immediately afterward that not only justice itself but also the just city is not "possible" in the sense indicated. This does not mean that the just city as meant and as sketched in the *Republic* is an idea like "justice itself," and still less that it is an "ideal": "ideal" is not a Platonic term. The just city is not a self-subsisting being like the idea of justice, located so to speak in a superheavenly place. Its status is rather like that of a painting of a perfectly beautiful human being, *i.e.,* it is only by virtue of the painter's painting; more precisely, the just city is only "in speech": it "is" only by virtue of having been figured out with a view to justice itself or to what is by nature right on the one hand and the human all-too-human on the other. Although the just city is decidedly of lower rank than justice itself, even the just city as a pattern is not capable of coming into being as it has been blueprinted; only approximations to it can be expected in cities which are in deed and not merely in speech.[57] What this means is not clear. Does it mean that the best feasible solution will be a compromise so that we must become reconciled to a certain degree of private property (*e.g.,* that we must permit every warrior to keep his shoes and the like as long as he lives) and a certain degree of inequality of the sexes (*e.g.,* that certain military and administrative functions will remain the preserve of the male warriors)? There is no reason to suppose that this is what Socrates meant. In the light of the succeeding part of the conversation, the following suggestion would seem to be more plausible. The assertion according to which the just city cannot come into being as blueprinted is provisional, or prepares the assertion that the just city, while capable of coming into being, is very unlikely to come into being. At any rate, immediately after having declared that only an approximation to the good city can reasonably be expected, Socrates raises the question, what feasible change in the actual cities will be the necessary and sufficient condition of their transformation into good cities? His answer is, the "coincidence" of political power and philosophy: the philosophers must rule as kings, or the kings must genuinely and adequately philosophize. As we have shown in our summary of the first book of the *Republic,* this answer is not altogether surprising. If justice is less the giving or leaving to each what the law assigns to him than the giving or leaving to each what is good for his soul, but what is good for his soul is the virtues, it follows that no one can be truly just who does not know "the virtues themselves," or generally the ideas, or who is not a philosopher.

By answering the question of how the good city is possible, Socrates introduces philosophy as a theme of the *Republic.* This means that in the *Republic,* philosophy is not introduced as the end of man, the end for which man should live, but as a means for realizing the just city, the city as armed camp which is characterized by absolute communism and equality of the sexes in the upper class, the class of warriors. Since the rule of philosophers is not introduced as an ingredient of the just city but only as a means for its realization, Aristotle is justified in disregarding this institution in his critical analysis of the *Republic (Politics* II). At any rate, Socrates succeeds in reducing the question of the possibility of the just city to the question of the possibility of the coincidence of philosophy and political power. That such a coincidence should be possible is to begin with most incredible: everyone can see that the philosophers are useless if not even harmful in politics. Socrates, who had some experiences of his own with the city of Athens—experiences to be crowned by his capital punishment—regards this accusation of the philosophers as well-founded, although in need of deeper exploration. He traces the antagonism of the cities toward the philosophers primarily to the cities: the present cities, *i.e.,* the cities not ruled by philosophers, are like assemblies of madmen which corrupt most of those fit to become philosophers, and on which those who have succeeded against all odds in becoming philosophers rightly turn their back in disgust. But Socrates is far from absolving the philosophers altogether. Only a radical change on the part of both the cities and the philosophers can bring about that harmony between them for which they seem to be meant by nature. The change consists precisely in this: that the cities cease to be unwilling to be ruled by philosophers and the philosophers cease to be unwilling to rule the cities. This coincidence of philosophy and political power is very difficult to achieve, very improbable, but not impossible. To bring about the needed change on the part of the city, of the nonphilosophers or the multitude, the right kind of persuasion is necessary and sufficient. The right kind of persuasion is supplied by the art of persuasion, the art of Thrasymachos directed by the philosopher and in the service of philosophy. No wonder then that in our context Socrates declares that he and Thrasymachos have just become friends. The multitude of the nonphilosophers is good-natured and therefore persuadable by the philosophers.[58] But if this is so, why did not the philosophers of old, to say nothing of Socrates himself, succeed in persuading the multitude of the supremacy of philosophy and the philosophers and thus bring about the rule of philosophers and therewith the salvation and the happiness of their cities? Strange as it may sound, in this part of the argument it appears to be easier to persuade the multitude to accept the rule of the philosophers than to persuade the philosophers to rule the multitude: the philosophers cannot be persuaded, they can only be compelled to rule the cities.[59] Only the nonphilosophers could compel the philosophers to take care of the cities. But, given the prejudice against the philosophers, this compulsion will not be forthcoming if the philosophers do not in the first place persuade the nonphilosophers to compel the philosophers to rule over them, and this persuasion will not be forthcoming, given the philosophers' unwillingness to rule. We arrive then at the conclusion that the just city is not possible because of the philosophers' unwillingness to rule.

Why are the philosophers unwilling to rule? Being dominated by the desire for knowledge as the one thing needful, or knowing that philosophy is the most pleasant and blessed possession, the philosophers have no leisure for looking down at human affairs, let alone for taking care of them.[60] The philosophers believe that while still alive they are already firmly settled, far away from their cities, in the Isles of the Blessed.[61] Hence only compulsion could induce them to take part in political life in the just city, *i.e.,* in the city which regards the proper upbringing of the philosophers as its most important task. Having perceived the truly grand, the human things appear to the philosophers to be paltry. The very justice of the philosophers—their abstaining from wronging their fellow human beings—flows from contempt for the things for which the nonphilosophers hotly contest.[62] They know that the life not dedicated to philosophy and therefore in particular the political life is like life in a cave, so much so that the city can be identified with the Cave.[63] The cave dwellers (*i.e.,* the non-philosophers) see only the shadows of artifacts.[64] That is to say, whatever they perceive they understand in the light of their opinions, sanctified by the fiat of legislators, regarding the just and noble things, *i.e.,* of conventional opinions, and they do not know that these their most cherished convictions possess no higher status than that of opinions. For if even the best city stands or falls by a fundamental falsehood, although a noble falsehood, it can be expected that the opinions on which the imperfect cities rest or in which they believe, will not be true. Precisely the best of the nonphilosophers, the good citizens, are passionately attached to these opinions and therefore violently opposed to philosophy,[65] which is the attempt to go beyond opinion toward knowledge: the multitude is not as persuadable by the philosophers as we sanguinely assumed in an earlier round of the argument. This is the true reason why the coincidence of philosophy and political power is, to say the least, extremely improbable: philosophy and the city tend away from one another in opposite directions.

The difficulty of overcoming the natural tension between the city and the philosophers is indicated by Socrates' turning from the question of whether the just city is "possible" in the sense of being conformable to human nature to the question of whether the just city is "possible" in the sense of being capable of being brought to light by the transformation of an actual city. The first question, understood in contradistinction to the second, points to the question whether the just city could not come into being through the settling together of men who had been wholly unassociated before. It is to this question that Socrates tacitly gives a negative answer by turning to the question of whether the just city could be brought into being by the transformation of an actual city. The good city cannot be brought to light out of human beings who have not yet undergone any human discipline, out of "primitives" or "stupid animals" or "savages" gentle or cruel; its potential members must already have acquired the rudiments of civilized life. The long process through which primitive men become civilized men cannot be the work of the founder or legislator of the good city but is presupposed by him.[66] But on the other hand, if the potential good city must be an old city, its citizens will have been thoroughly molded by their city's imperfect laws or customs, hallowed by old age, and will have become passionately attached to them. Socrates is therefore compelled to revise his original suggestion according to which the rule of philosophers is the necessary and sufficient condition of the coming into being of the just city. Whereas he had originally suggested that the good city will come into being if the philosophers become kings, he finally suggests that the good city will come into being if, when the philosophers have become kings, they expel everyone older than ten from the city, *i.e.,* separate the children completely from their parents and their parents' ways and bring them up in the entirely novel ways of the good city.[67] By taking over a city, the philosophers make sure that their subjects will not be savages; by expelling everyone older than ten, they make sure that their subjects will not be enslaved by traditional civility. The solution is elegant. It leaves one wondering, however, how the philosophers can compel everyone older than ten to obey submissively the expulsion decree, since they cannot yet have trained a warrior class absolutely obedient to them. This is not to deny that Socrates could persuade many fine young men, and even some old ones, to believe that the multitude could be, not indeed compelled, but persuaded by the philosophers to leave their city and their children and to live in the fields so that justice will be done.

The part of the *Republic* which deals with philosophy is the most important part of the book. Accordingly, it transmits the answer to the question regarding justice to the extent to which that answer is given in the *Republic*. The explicit answer to the question of what justice is had been rather vague: justice consists in each part of the city or of the soul "doing the work for which it is by nature best fitted" or in a "kind" of doing that work; a part is just if it does its work or minds its own business "in a certain manner." The vagueness is removed if one replaces "in a certain manner" by "in the best manner" or "well": justice consists in each part doing its work well.[68] Hence the just man is the man in whom each part of the soul does its work well. Since the highest part of the soul is reason, and since this part cannot do its work well if the two other parts too do not do their work well, only the philosopher can be truly just. But the work which the philosopher does well is intrinsically attractive and in fact the most pleasant work, wholly regardless of its consequences.[69] Hence only in philosophy do justice and happiness coincide. In other words, the philosopher is the only individual who is just in the sense in which the good city is just: he is self-sufficient, truly free, or his life is as little devoted to the service of other individuals as the life of the city is devoted to the service of other cities. But the philosopher in the good city is just also in the sense that he serves his fellow men, his fellow citizens, his city, or that he obeys the law. That is to say, the philosopher is just also in the sense in which all members of the just city, and in a way all just members of any city, regardless of whether they are philosophers or nonphilosophers, are just. Yet justice in this second sense is not intrinsically attractive or choiceworthy for its own sake, but is good only with a view to its consequences, or is not noble but necessary: the philosopher serves his city, even the good city, not, as he seeks the truth, from natural inclination, from *eros,* but under compulsion.[70] It is hardly necessary to add that compulsion does not cease to be compulsion if it is self-compulsion. According to a notion of justice which is more common than that suggested by Socrates' definition, justice consists in not harming others; justice thus understood proves to be in the highest case merely a concomitant of the philosopher's greatness of soul. But if justice is taken in the larger sense according to which it consists in giving to each what is good for his soul, one must distinguish between the cases in which this giving is intrinsically attractive to the giver (these will be the cases of potential philosophers) and those in which it is merely a duty or compulsory. This distinction, incidentally, under-lies the difference between the voluntary conversations of Socrates (the conversations which he spontaneously seeks) and the compulsory ones (those which he cannot with propriety avoid). This clear distinction between the justice which is choiceworthy for its own sake, wholly regardless of its consequences, and identical with philosophy, and the justice which is merely necessary and identical in the highest case with the political activity of the philosopher is rendered possible by the abstraction from *eros* which is characteristic of the *Republic*. For one might well say that there is no reason why the philosopher should not engage in political activity out of that kind of love of one's own which is patriotism.[71]

By the end of the seventh book justice has come to sight fully. Socrates has in fact performed the duty laid upon him by Glaukon and Adeimantos to show that justice properly understood is choiceworthy for its own sake regardless of its consequences and therefore that justice is unqualifiedly preferable to injustice. Nevertheless the conversation continues, for it seems that our clear grasp of justice does not include a clear grasp of injustice but must be supplemented by a clear grasp of the wholly unjust city and the wholly unjust man: only after we have seen the wholly unjust city and the wholly unjust man with the same clarity with which we have seen the wholly just city and the wholly just man will we be able to judge whether we ought to follow Socrates' friend Thrasymachos, who chooses injustice, or Socrates him-self, who chooses justice.[72] This in its turn requires that the fiction of the possibility of the just city be maintained. As a matter of fact, the *Republic* never abandons the fiction that the just city as a society of human beings, as distinguished from a society of gods or sons of gods, is possible.[73] When Socrates turns to the study of injustice, it even becomes necessary for him to reaffirm this fiction with greater force than ever before. The unjust city will be uglier and more condemnable in proportion as the just city will be more possible. But the possibility of the just city will remain doubtful if the just city was never actual. Accordingly Socrates now asserts that the just city was once actual.

More precisely, he makes the Muses assert it or rather imply it. The assertion that the just city was once actual is, as one might say, a mythical assertion which agrees with the mythical premise that the best is the oldest. Socrates asserts then through the mouth of the Muses that the good city was actual in the beginning, prior to the emergence of the inferior kinds of cities;[74] the inferior cities are decayed forms of the good city, soiled fragments of the pure city which was entire; hence the nearer in time a kind of inferior city is to the just city the better it is, or vice versa. It is more proper to speak of the good and inferior regimes than of the good and inferior cities (observe the transition from "cities" to "regimes" in 543^d–544^a). "Regime" is our translation of the Greek *politeia*. The book which we call *Republic* is in Greek entitled *Politeia*. *Politeia* is commonly translated by "constitution." The term designates the form of government understood as the form of the city, *i.e.,* as that which gives the city its character by determining the end which the city in question pursues or what it looks up to as the highest, and simultaneously the kind of men who rule the city. For instance, oligarchy is the kind of regime in which the rich rule and therefore admiration for wealth and for the acquisition of wealth animates the city as a whole, and democracy is the kind of regime in which all free men rule and therefore freedom is the end which the city pursues. According to Socrates, there are five kinds of regime: (1) kingdom or aristocracy, the rule of the best man or the best men, that is directed toward goodness or virtue, the regime of the just city; (2) timocracy, the rule of lovers of honor or of the ambitious men which is directed toward superiority or victory; (3) oligarchy or the rule of the rich in which wealth is most highly esteemed; (4) democracy, the rule of free men in which freedom is most highly esteemed; (5) tyranny, the rule of the completely unjust man in which unqualified and unashamed injustice holds sway. The descending order of the five kinds of regime is modeled on Hesiod's descending order of the five races of men: the races of gold, of silver, of bronze, the divine race of heroes, the race of iron.[75] We see at once that the Platonic equivalent of Hesiod's divine race of heroes is democracy. We shall soon see the reason for this seemingly strange correspondence.

The *Republic* is based on the assumption that there is a strict parallelism between the city and the soul. Accordingly Socrates asserts that, just as there are five kinds of regime, so there are five kinds of characters of men, the timocratic man, for instance, corresponding to timocracy. The distinction which for a short while was popular in present-day political science between the authoritarian and the demo-

cratic "personalities," as corresponding to the distinction between
authoritarian and democratic societies, was a dim and crude reflection
of Socrates' distinction between the royal or aristocratic, the timocratic,
the oligarchic, the democratic, and the tyrannical soul or man, as corresponding to the aristocratic, timocratic, oligarchic, democratic, and
tyrannical regimes. In this connection it should be mentioned that in
describing the regimes, Socrates does not speak of "ideologies" belonging
to them; he is concerned with the character of each kind of regime
and with the end which it manifestly and explicitly pursues, as well
as with the political justification of the end in question in contradistinction to any transpolitical justification stemming from cosmology,
theology, metaphysics, philosophy of history, myth, and the like. In his
study of the inferior regimes Socrates examines in each case first the
regime and then the corresponding individual or soul. He presents
both the regime and the corresponding individual as coming into being out of the preceding one. We shall consider here only his account
of democracy, both because this subject is most important to citizens
of a democracy and because of its intrinsic importance. Democracy
arises from oligarchy, which in its turn arises from timocracy, the rule
of the insufficiently musical warriors who are characterized by the
supremacy of spiritedness. Oligarchy is the first regime in which desire
is supreme. In oligarchy the ruling desire is that for wealth or money,
or unlimited acquisitiveness. The oligarchic man is thrifty and industrious, controls all his desires other than the desire for money, lacks
education, and possesses a superficial honesty derivative from the
crudest self-interest. Oligarchy must give to each the unqualified right
to dispose of his property as he sees fit. It thus renders inevitable the
emergence of "drones," *i.e.,* of members of the ruling class who are
either burdened with debt or already bankrupt and hence disfranchised
—of beggars who hanker after their squandered fortune and hope to
restore their fortune and political power through a change of regime
("Catilinarian existences"). Besides, the correct oligarchs themselves,
being both rich and unconcerned with virtue and honor, render themselves and especially their sons fat, spoiled, and soft. They thus become
despised by the lean and tough poor. Democracy comes into being
when the poor, having become aware of their superiority to the rich
and perhaps being led by some drones who act as traitors to their
class and possess the skills which ordinarily only members of a ruling
class possess, make themselves at an opportune moment masters of the
city by defeating the rich, killing and exiling a part of them, and
permitting the rest to live with them in the possession of full citizen
rights. Democracy itself is characterized by freedom, which includes

the right to say and do whatever one wishes: everyone can follow the way of life which pleases him most. Hence democracy is the regime which fosters the greatest variety: every way of life, every regime can be found in it. Hence, we must add, democracy is the only regime other than the best in which the philosopher can lead his peculiar way of life without being disturbed: it is for this reason that with some exaggeration one can compare democracy to Hesiod's age of the divine race of heroes which comes closer to the golden age than any other. Certainly in a democracy the citizen who is a philosopher is under no compulsion to participate in political life or to hold office.[76] One is thus led to wonder why Socrates did not assign to democracy the highest place among the inferior regimes, or rather the highest place simply, seeing that the best regime is not possible. One could say that he showed his preference for democracy "by deed": by spending his whole life in democratic Athens, by fighting for her in her wars, and by dying in obedience to her laws. However this may be, he surely did not prefer democracy to all other regimes "in speech." The reason is that, being a just man, he thought of the well-being not merely of the philosophers but of the nonphilosophers as well, and he held that democracy is not designed for inducing the nonphilosophers to attempt to become as good as they possibly can, for the end of democracy is not virtue but freedom, *i.e.*, the freedom to live either nobly or basely according to one's liking. Therefore he assigns to democracy a rank even lower than to oligarchy, since oligarchy requires some kind of restraint whereas democracy, as he presents it, abhors every kind of restraint. One could say that adapting himself to his subject matter, Socrates abandons all restraint when speaking of the regime which loathes restraint. In a democracy, he asserts, no one is compelled to rule or to be ruled if he does not like it; he can live in peace while his city is at war; capital punishment does not have the slightest consequence for the condemned man: he is not even jailed; the order of rulers and ruled is completely reversed: the father behaves as if he were a boy and the son has neither respect nor fear of the father, the teacher fears his pupils while the pupils pay no attention to the teacher, and there is complete equality of the sexes; even horses and donkeys no longer step aside when encountering human beings. Plato writes as if the Athenian democracy had not carried out Socrates' execution, and Socrates speaks as if the Athenian democracy had not engaged in an orgy of bloody persecution of guilty and innocent alike when the Hermes statues were mutilated at the beginning of the Sicilian expedition.[77] Socrates' exaggeration of the licentious mildness of democracy is matched by an almost equally strong exaggeration of the intemperance of democratic man. He could indeed not avoid the latter exaggeration if he did not wish to deviate in the case of democracy from the procedure which he follows in his discussion of the inferior regimes. That procedure consists in understanding the man corresponding to an inferior regime as the son of a father corresponding to the preceding regime. Hence democratic man had to be presented as the son of an oligarchic father, as the degenerate son of a wealthy father who is concerned with nothing but making money: the democratic man is the drone, the fat, soft, and prodigal playboy, the lotus-eater who, assigning a kind of equality to equal and unequal things, lives one day in complete surrender to his lowest desires and the next ascetically, or who, according to Karl Marx's ideal, "goes hunting in the morning, fishes in the afternoon, raises cattle in the evening, devotes himself to philosophy after dinner," *i.e.,* does at every moment what he happens to like at that moment: the democratic man is not the lean, tough and thrifty craftsman or peasant who has a single job.[78] Socrates' deliberately exaggerated blame of democracy becomes intelligible to some extent once one considers its immediate addressee, the austere Adeimantos, who is not a friend of laughter and who had been the addressee of the austere discussion of poetry in the section on the education of the warriors: by his exaggerated blame of democracy Socrates lends words to Adeimantos' "dream" of democracy.[79] One must also not forget that the sanguine account of the multitude which was provisionally required in order to prove the harmony between the city and philosophy is in need of being redressed; the exaggerated blame of democracy reminds us with greater force than was ever before used of the disharmony between philosophy and the people.[80]

After Socrates had brought to light the entirely unjust regime and the entirely unjust man and then compared the life of the entirely unjust man with that of the perfectly just man, it became clear beyond the shadow of a doubt that justice is preferable to injustice. Nevertheless the conversation continues. Socrates suddenly returns to the question of poetry, to a question which had already been answered at great length when he discussed the education of the warriors. We must try to understand this apparently sudden return. In an explicit digression from the discussion of tyranny, Socrates had noted that the poets praise tyrants and are honored by tyrants (and also by democracy), whereas they are not honored by the three better regimes.[81] Tyranny and democracy are characterized by surrender to the sensual desires, including the most lawless ones. The tyrant is *Eros* incarnate, and the poets sing the praise of *Eros*. They pay very great attention and homage precisely to that phenomenon from which Socrates abstracts in the *Re-*

public to the best of his powers. The poets therefore foster injustice. So does Thrasymachos. But just as Socrates, in spite of this, could be a friend of Thrasymachos, so there is no reason why he could not be a friend of the poets and especially of Homer. Perhaps Socrates needs the poets in order to restore, on another occasion, the dignity of *Eros*: the *Banquet,* the only Platonic dialogue in which Socrates is shown to converse with poets, is devoted entirely to *Eros*.

The foundation for the return to poetry was laid at the very beginning of the discussion of the inferior regimes and of the inferior souls. The transition from the best regime to the inferior regimes was explicitly ascribed to the Muses speaking "tragically," and the transition from the best man to the inferior men has in fact a somewhat "comical" touch[82]: poetry takes the lead when the descent from the highest theme—justice understood as philosophy—begins. The return to poetry, which is preceded by the account of the inferior regimes and the inferior souls, is followed by a discussion of "the greatest rewards for virtue," *i.e.,* the rewards not inherent in justice or philosophy itself.[83] The return to poetry constitutes the center of that part of the *Republic* in which the conversation descends from the highest theme. This cannot be surprising, for philosophy as quest for the truth is the highest activity of man, and poetry is not concerned with the truth.

In the first discussion of poetry, which preceded by a long time the introduction of philosophy as a theme, poetry's unconcern with the truth was its chief recommendation, for at that time it was untruth that was needed.[84] The most excellent poets were expelled from the just city, not because they teach untruth, but because they teach the wrong kind of untruth. But in the meantime it has become clear that only the life of the philosophizing man in so far as he philosophizes is the just life, and that that life, so far from needing untruth, utterly rejects it.[85] The progress from the city, even the best city, to the philosopher requires, it seems. a progress from the qualified acceptance of poetry to its unqualified rejection.

In the light of philosophy, poetry reveals itself to be the imitation of imitations of the truth, *i.e.,* of the ideas. The contemplation of the ideas is the activity of the philosopher, the imitation of the ideas is the activity of the ordinary artisan, and the imitation of the works of artisans is the activity of poets and other "imitative" artisans. To begin with, Socrates presents the order of rank in these terms: the maker of the ideas (*e.g.,* of the idea of the bed) is the God, the maker of the imitation (of the bed which can be used) is the artisan, and the maker of the imitation of the imitation (of the painting of a bed) is the imitative artisan. Later on he restates the order of rank in these terms:

first the user, then the artisan, and finally the imitative artisan. The idea of the bed originates in the user who determines the "form" of the bed with a view to the end for which it is to be used. The user is then the one who possesses the highest or most authoritative knowledge: the highest knowledge is not that possessed by any artisans as such at all; the poet who stands at the opposite pole from the user does not possess any knowledge, not even right opinion.[86] In order to understand this seemingly outrageous indictment of poetry one must first identify the artisan whose work the poet imitates. The poets' themes are above all the human things referring to virtue and vice; the poets see the human things in the light of virtue, but the virtue toward which they look is an imperfect and even distorted image of virtue.[87] The artisan whom the poet imitates is the nonphilosophic legislator who is an imperfect imitator of virtue itself.[88] In particular, justice as understood by the city is necessarily the work of the legislator, for the just as understood by the city is the legal. No one expressed Socrates' suggestion more clearly than Nietzsche, who said that "the poets were always the valets of some morality. . . ."[89] But according to the French saying, for a valet there is no hero: Are the artists and in particular the poets not aware of the secret weakness of their heroes? This is indeed the case according to Socrates. The poets bring to light, for instance, the full force of the grief which a man feels for the loss of someone dear to him—of a feeling to which a respectable man would not give adequate utterance except when he is alone, because its adequate utterance in the presence of others is not becoming and lawful: the poets bring to light that in our nature which the law forcibly restrains.[90] If this is so, if the poets are perhaps the men who understand best the nature of the passions which the law restrains, they are very far from being merely the servants of the legislators; they are also the men from whom the prudent legislator will learn. The genuine "quarrel between philosophy and poetry"[91] concerns, from the philosopher's point of view, not the worth of poetry as such, but the order of rank of philosophy and poetry. According to Socrates, poetry is legitimate only as ministerial to the "user" par excellence, to the king who is the philosopher, and not as autonomous. For autonomous poetry presents human life as autonomous, i.e., as not directed toward the philosophic life, and therefore it never presents the philosophic life itself except in its comical distortion; hence autonomous poetry is necessarily either tragedy or comedy since the nonphilosophic life understood as autonomous has either no way out of its fundamental difficulty or only an inept one. But ministerial poetry presents the nonphilosophic life as ministerial to the philosophic life and therefore, above all, it presents the philosophic life itself.[92] The greatest example of ministerial poetry is the Platonic dialogue.

The *Republic* concludes with a discussion of the greatest rewards for justice and the greatest punishments for injustice. The discussion consists of three parts: (1) proof of the immortality of the soul; (2) the divine and human rewards and punishments for men while they are alive; (3) the rewards and punishments after death. The central part is silent about the philosophers: rewards for justice and punishments for injustice during life are needed for the nonphilosophers whose justice does not have the intrinsic attractiveness which the justice of the philosophers has. The account of the rewards and punishments after death is given in the form of a myth. The myth is not baseless, since it is based on the proof of the immortality of the souls. The soul cannot be immortal if it is composed of many things unless the composition is most perfect. But the soul as we know it from our experience lacks that perfect harmony. In order to find the truth, one would have to recover by reasoning the original or true nature of the soul.[93] This reasoning is not achieved in the *Republic*. That is to say, Socrates proves the immortality of the soul without having brought to light the nature of the soul. The situation at the end of the *Republic* corresponds precisely to the situation at the end of the first book of the *Republic* where Socrates makes clear that he has proved that justice is salutary without knowing the "what" or nature of justice. The discussion following the first book does bring to light the nature of justice as the right order of the soul, yet how can one know the right order of the soul if one does not know the nature of the soul? Let us remember here also the fact that the parallelism between soul and city, which is the premise of the doctrine of the soul stated in the *Republic,* is evidently questionable and even untenable. The *Republic* cannot bring to light the nature of the soul because it abstracts from *eros* and from the body. If we are genuinely concerned with finding out precisely what justice is, we must take "another longer way around" in our study of the soul than the way which is taken in the *Republic*.[94] This does not mean that what we learn from the *Republic* about justice is not true or is altogether provisional. The teaching of the *Republic* regarding justice, although not complete, can yet be true in so far as the nature of justice depends decisively on the nature of the city—for even the transpolitical cannot be understood as such except if the city is understood—and the city is completely intelligible because its limits can be made perfectly manifest: to see these limits, one need not have answered the question regarding the whole; it is sufficient to have raised the question regarding the whole. The *Republic* then indeed makes clear what justice is. However, as Cicero has observed, the *Republic* does not bring to light the best possible regime but rather the nature of political things—the nature of the city.[95] Socrates makes clear in the *Republic* what character the city would have to have in order to satisfy the highest needs of man. By letting us see that the city constructed in accordance with this requirement is not possible, he lets us see the essential limits, the nature, of the city.

THE STATESMAN

The *Statesman* is preceded by the *Sophist,* which in its turn is preceded by the *Theaitetos.* The *Theaitetos* presents a conversation between Socrates and the young mathematician Theaitetos which takes place in the presence of the mature and renowned mathematician Theodoros, as well as of Theaitetos' young companion named Socrates, and which is meant to make clear what knowledge or science is. The conversation does not lead to a positive result: Socrates by himself only knows that he does not know, and Theaitetos is not like Glaukon or Adeimantos who can be assisted by Socrates (or can assist him) in bringing forth a positive teaching. On the day following Socrates' conversation with Theaitetos, Socrates again meets with Theodoros, the younger Socrates, and Theaitetos, but this time there is also present a nameless philosopher designated only as a stranger from Elea. Socrates asks the stranger whether his fellows regard the sophist, the statesman, and the philosopher as one and the same or as two or as three. It could seem that the question regarding the identity or nonidentity of the sophist, the statesman, and the philosopher takes the place of the question, or is a more articulate version of the question, What is knowledge? The stranger replies that his fellows regard the sophist, the statesman or king, and the philosopher as different from one another. The fact that the philosopher is not identical with the king was recognized in the central thesis of the *Republic,* according to which the coincidence of philosophy and kingship is the condition for the salvation of cities and indeed of the human race: identical things do not have to coincide. But the *Republic* did not make sufficiently clear the cognitive status of kingship or statesmanship. From the *Republic* we can easily receive the impression that the knowledge required of the philosopher-king consists of two heterogeneous parts: the purely philosophic knowledge of the ideas which culminates in the vision of the idea of the good, on the one hand, and the merely political experience which does not have the status of knowledge at all but which enables one to find one's way in the Cave and to discern the shadows on its walls, on the other. But the indispensable supplement to philosophic knowledge also seemed to be a kind of art or science.⁹⁶ The Eleatic stranger seems to take the second and higher view of the nonphilosophic awareness peculiar to the statesman. Yet in the dialogues *Sophist* and *Statesman* he makes clear the nature of the sophist and of the statesman, *i.e.,* the difference between the sophist and the statesman, without making clear the difference between the statesman and the philosopher. We are promised by Theodoros that the Eleatic stranger will also expound (in a sequel to the *Statesman*) what the philosopher is, but Plato does not keep his Theodoros' promise. Do we then understand what the philosopher is once we have understood what the sophist and the statesman are? Is statesmanship not, as it appeared from the *Republic,* a mere supplement to philosophy, but an ingredient of philosophy? That is to say, is statesmanship, the art or knowledge peculiar to the statesman, far from being merely the awareness necessary for finding one's way in the Cave and far from being itself independent of the vision of the idea of the good, a condition or rather an ingredient of the vision of the idea of the good? If it were so, then "politics" would be much more important according to the *Statesman* than it is according to the *Republic.* Surely the conversation about the king or statesman takes place when Socrates is already accused of a capital crime for the commission of which he was shortly thereafter condemned and executed (see the end of the *Theaitetos*): the city seems to be much more powerfully present in the *Statesman* than in the *Republic,* where the antagonist of Socrates, Thrasymachos, only plays the city. On the other hand, however, whereas in the *Republic* Socrates founds a city, if only in speech, with the help of two brothers who are passionately concerned with justice and the city, in the *Statesman* Socrates listens silently to a nameless stranger (a man lacking political responsibility) bringing to light what the statesman is in the cool atmosphere of mathematics: the concern with finding out what the statesman is seems to be philosophic rather than political.⁹⁷ The *Statesman* seems to be much more sober than the *Republic.*

We may say that the *Statesman* is more scientific than the *Republic.* By "science" Plato understands the highest form of knowledge or rather the only kind of awareness which deserves to be called knowledge. He calls that form of knowledge "dialectics." "Dialectics" means primarily the art of conversation and then the highest form of that art, that art as practiced by Socrates, that art of conversation which is meant to bring to light the "what's" of things, or the ideas. Dialectics is then the knowledge of the ideas—a knowledge which makes no use whatever of sense experience: it moves from idea to idea until it has exhausted the whole realm of the ideas, for each idea is a part and therefore points to other ideas.[98] In its completed form dialectics would descend from the highest idea, the idea ruling the realm of ideas, step by step to the lowest ideas. The movement proceeds "step by step," *i.e.,* it follows the articulation, the natural division of the ideas. The *Statesman* as well as the *Sophist* presents an imitation of dialectics thus understood; both are meant to give an inkling of dialectics thus understood; the imitation which they present is playful. Yet the play is not mere play. If the movement from idea to idea without recourse to sense experience should be impossible, if in other words the *Republic* should be utopian not only in what it states about the city at its best but also in what it says about philosophy or dialectics at its best, dialectics at its best, not being possible, will not be serious. The dialectics which is possible will remain dependent on experience.[99] There is a connection between this feature of the *Statesman* and the fact that the ideas as treated in the *Statesman* are classes or comprise all individuals "participating" in the idea in question and therefore do not subsist independently of the individuals or "beyond" them. However this may be, in the *Statesman* the Eleatic stranger tries to bring to light the nature of the statesman by descending from "art" or "knowledge" step by step to the art of the statesman or by dividing "art" step by step until he arrives at the art of the statesman. For a number of reasons we cannot here follow his "methodical" procedure.

Shortly after the beginning of the conversation, the Eleatic stranger makes young Socrates agree to what one may call the abolition of the distinction between the public and the private. He achieves this result in two steps. Since statesmanship or kingship is essentially a kind of knowledge, it is of no importance whether the man possessing that knowledge is clothed in the vestments of high office by virtue of having been elected, for example, or whether he lives in a private station. Second, there is no essential difference between the city and the household and hence between the statesman or king on the one hand and the householder or master (*i.e.,* the master of slaves) on the other. Law and freedom, the characteristically political phenomena, which are inseparable from one another, are disposed of at the very beginning because statesmanship is understood as a kind of knowledge or art, or because abstraction is made from that which distinguishes the political from the arts. The Eleatic stranger abstracts here from the fact that sheer bodily force is a necessary ingredient of the rule of men over men. This abstraction is partly justified by the fact that statesmanship or kingship is a cognitive rather than a manual (or brachial) art. It is, however, not simply cognitive like arithmetic; it is an art which gives commands to human beings. But all arts which give commands do so for the sake of the coming into being of something. Some of these arts give commands for the sake of the coming into being of living beings or animals, *i.e.,* they are concerned with the breeding and nurture of animals. The kingly art is a kind of this genus of art. For the proper understanding of the kingly art it does not suffice to divide the genus "animal" into the species "brutes" and "men." This distinction is as arbitrary as the distinction of the human race into Greeks and barbarians, as distinguished from the distinction into men and women; it is not a natural distinction but a distinction originating in pride.[100] The stranger's training of young Socrates in dialectics or in the art of dividing kinds or ideas or classes goes hand in hand with training in modesty or moderation. According to the stranger's division of the species of animals, man's nearest kin is even lower than it is according to Darwin's doctrine of the origin of the species. But what Darwin meant seriously and literally, the stranger means playfully.[101] Man must learn to see the lowliness of his estate in order to turn from the human to the divine, *i.e.,* in order to be truly human.

The division of "art" leads to the result that the art of the statesman is the art concerned with the breeding and nurture of, or with the caring for, herds of the kind of animal called man. This result is manifestly insufficient, for there are many arts—*e.g.,* medicine and matchmaking—which claim as justly to be concerned with a caring for human herds as does the political art. The error was due to the fact that the human herd was taken to be a herd of the same kind as the herds of other animals. But human herds are a very special kind of herd: the bipartition of "animal" into brutes and men originates not merely in pride. The error is removed by a myth. According to the myth now told in its fullness for the first time, there is once a time (the age of Kronos) when the god guides the whole and then a time (the age of Zeus) when the god lets the whole move by its own motion. In the age of Kronos the god ruled and took care of the animals by assigning the different species of animals to the rule and care of different gods who acted like shepherds and thus secured universal peace and affluence: there were no political societies, no private property, and no families. This does not necessarily mean that men lived happily in the age of Kronos; only if they used the then available peace and affluence for philosophizing can they be said to have lived happily. At any rate, in the present age the god does not take care of man: in the present age there is no divine providence; men must take care of themselves. Bereft of divine care, the world abounds with disorder and injustice; men must establish order and justice as well as they can, with the understanding that in this age of scarcity, communism, and hence also absolute communism, is impossible. The *Statesman* may be said to bring into the open what the *Republic* had left unsaid, namely, the impossibility of the best regime presented in the *Republic.*

The myth of the *Statesman* is meant to explain the error committed by the Eleatic stranger and young Socrates in the initial definition of the *Statesman:* by looking for a single art of caring for human herds they were unwittingly looking toward the age of Kronos or toward divine caring; with the disappearance of divine caring, *i.e.,* of a caring by beings which in the eyes of everyone are superior to men, it became inevitable that every art or every man should believe itself or himself to be as much entitled to rule as every other art or every other man,[102] or that at least many arts should become competitors of the kingly art. The inevitable first consequence of the transition from the age of Kronos to the age of Zeus was the delusion that all arts and all men are equal. The mistake consisted in assuming that the kingly art is devoted to the total caring for human herds (which total caring would include the feeding and mating of the ruled) and not to a partial or limited caring. In other words, the mistake consisted in the disregard of the fact that in the case of all arts of herding other than the human art of herding human beings, the herder belongs to a different species than the members of the herd. We must then divide the whole "caring for herds" into two parts: caring for herds in which the herder belongs to the same species as the members of the herd and caring for herds in which the herder belongs to a different species than the members of the herd (human herders of brutes and divine herders of human beings). We must next divide the first of these two kinds into parts, so that we can discover which partial herding of herds in which the herder belongs to the same species as the members of the herd is the kingly art. Let us assume that the partial caring sought is "ruling cities." Ruling cities is naturally divided into ruling not willed by the ruled (ruling by sheer force) and ruling willed by the ruled; the former is tyrannical, and the latter is kingly. Here we receive the first glimpse of freedom as the specifically political theme. But at the very moment in which the stranger alludes to this difficulty, he turns away from it. He finds the whole previous procedure unsatisfactory.

The method which proves to be helpful, where the division of classes and into classes as well as the myth have failed, is the use of an example. The stranger illustrates the usefulness of examples by an example. The example is meant to illustrate man's situation in regard to knowledge—to the phenomenon which is the guiding theme of the trilogy *Theaitetos-Sophist-Statesman.* The example chosen is children's knowledge of reading. Starting from knowledge of the letters (the "elements"), they proceed step by step to the knowledge of the shortest and easiest syllables (the combination of "elements"), and then to the knowledge of long and difficult ones. Knowledge of the whole is not possible if it is not similar to the art of reading: knowledge of the elements must be available, the elements must be fairly small in number, and not all elements must be combinable.[103] But can we say that we possess knowledge of the "elements" of the whole or that we can ever start from an absolute beginning? Did we in the *Statesman* begin from an adequate understanding of "art" or "knowledge"? Is it not true that while we necessarily long for knowledge of the whole, we are condemned to rest satisfied with partial knowledge of parts of the whole and hence never truly to transcend the sphere of opinion? Is therefore philosophy, and hence human life, not necessarily Sisyphean? Could this be the reason why the demand for freedom is not so evidently sound as many present-day lovers of freedom believe on the basis of very similar thoughts? (Perhaps this could induce one to consider Dostoyevsky's *Grand Inquisitor* in the light of Plato's *Statesman*.) After having compelled us to raise these and kindred questions, the stranger turns to his example, which is meant to throw light, not on knowledge in general or on philosophy as such, but on the kingly art. The example chosen by him is the art of weaving: he illustrates the political art by an emphatically domestic art and not by such "outgoing" arts as herding and piloting; he illustrates the most virile art by a characteristically feminine art. In order to find out what weaving is, one must divide "art," but divide it differently than they divided it at first. The analysis of the art of weaving which is made on the basis of the new division enables the stranger to elucidate art in general and the kingly art in particular before he applies explicitly the result of that analysis to the kingly art. Perhaps the most important point made in this context is the distinction between two kinds of the art of measurement: one kind which considers the greater and less in relation to one another, and another kind which considers the greater and less (now understood as excess and defect) in relation to the mean or, say, the fitting, or something similar. All arts, and especially the kingly art, make their measurements with a view to the right mean or the fitting, *i.e.,* they are not mathematical.

By explicitly applying to the kingly art the results of his analysis of the art of weaving, the stranger is enabled to make clear the relation of the kingly art to all other arts and especially to those arts which claim with some show of justice to compete with the kingly art for the rule of the city. The most successful and clever competitors are those outstanding sophists who pretend to possess the kingly art, and these are the rulers of cities, *i.e.,* the rulers lacking the kingly or statesmanly art, or practically all political rulers that were, are, and will be. Of this kind of political rule there are three sorts: the rule of one, the rule of a few, and the rule of many; but each of these three kinds is divided into two parts with a view to the difference between violence and voluntariness or between lawfulness and lawlessness; thus monarchy is distinguished from tyranny, and aristocracy from oligarchy, whereas the name of democracy is applied to the rule of the multitude regardless of whether the multitude of the poor rules over the rich with the consent of the rich and in strict obedience to the laws or with violence and more or less lawlessly. (The distinction of regimes sketched by the stranger is almost identical with the distinction developed by Aristotle in the third book of his *Politics;* but consider the difference.) None of these regimes bases its claim on the knowledge or art of the rulers, *i.e.,* on the only claim which is unqualifiedly legitimate. It follows that the claims based on the willingness of the subjects (on consent or freedom) and on lawfulness are dubious. This judgment is defended with reference to the example of the other arts and especially of medicine. A physician is a physician whether he cures us with our will or against our will, whether he cuts us, burns us, or inflicts upon us any other pain, and whether he acts in accordance with written rules or without them; he is a physician if his ruling redounds to the benefit of our bodies. Correspondingly, the only regime which is correct or which is truly a regime is that in which the possessors of the kingly art rule, regardless of whether they rule according to laws or without laws and whether the ruled consent to their rule or not, provided their rule redounds to the benefit of the body politic; it does not make any difference whether they achieve this end by killing some or banishing them and thus reduce the bulk of the city or by bringing in citizens from abroad and thus increase its bulk.

Young Socrates, who is not shocked by what the stranger says about killing and banishing, is rather shocked by the suggestion that rule without laws (absolute rule) can be legitimate. To understand fully the response of young Socrates, one must pay attention to the fact that the stranger does not make a distinction between human laws and natural laws. The stranger turns the incipient indignation of young Socrates into a desire on the latter's part for discussion. Rule of law is inferior to the rule of living intelligence because laws, owing to their generality, cannot determine wisely what is right and proper in all circumstances given the infinite variety of circumstances: only the wise man on the spot could correctly decide what is right and proper in the circumstances. Nevertheless laws are necessary. The few wise men cannot sit beside each of the many unwise men and tell him exactly what it is becoming for him to do. The few wise men are almost always absent from the innumerable unwise men. All laws, written or unwritten, are poor substitutes but indispensable substitutes for the individual rulings by wise men. They are crude rules of thumb which are sufficient for the large majority of cases: they treat human beings as if they were members of a herd. The freezing of crude rules of thumb into sacred, inviolable, unchangeable prescriptions which would be rejected by everyone as ridiculous if done in the sciences and the arts is a necessity in the ordering of human affairs; this necessity is the proximate cause of the ineradicable difference between the political and the suprapolitical spheres. But the main objection to laws is not that they are not susceptible of being individualized but that they are assumed to be binding on the wise man, on the man possessing the kingly art.[104] Yet even this objection is not entirely valid. As the stranger explains through images,[105] the wise man is subjected to the laws, whose justice and wisdom is inferior to his, because the unwise men cannot help distrusting the wise man, and this distrust is not entirely indefensible given the fact that they cannot understand him. They cannot believe that a wise man who would deserve to rule as a true king without laws would be willing and able to rule over them. The ultimate reason for their unbelief is the fact that no human being has that manifest superiority, in the first place regarding the body and then regarding the soul, which would induce everybody to submit to his rule without any hesitation and without any reserve.[106] The unwise men cannot help making themselves the judges of the wise man. No wonder then that the wise men are unwilling to rule over them. The unwise men must even demand of the wise man that he regard the law as simply authoritative, i.e., that he not even doubt that the established laws are perfectly just and wise; if he fails to do so, he will become guilty of corrupting the young, a capital offense; they must forbid free inquiry regarding the most important subjects. All these implications of the rule of laws must be accepted, since the only feasible alternative is the lawless rule of selfish men. The wise man must bow to the law which is inferior to him in wisdom and justice, not only in deed but in speech as well. (Here we cannot help wondering whether there are no limits to the wise man's subjection to the laws. The Platonic illustrations are these: Socrates obeyed without flinching the law which commanded him to die because of his alleged corruption of the young; yet he would not have obeyed a law formally forbidding him the pursuit of philosophy. Read the *Apology of Socrates* together with the *Crito*.) The rule of law is preferable to the lawless rule of unwise men since laws, however bad, are in one way or another the outcome of some reasoning. This observation permits the ranking of the incorrect regimes, *i.e.,* of all regimes other than the absolute rule of the true king or statesman. Law-abiding democracy is inferior to the law-abiding rule of the few (aristocracy) and to the law-abiding rule of one (monarchy), but lawless democracy is superior to the lawless rule of a few (oligarchy) and to the lawless rule of one (tyranny). "Lawless" does not mean here the complete absence of any laws or customs. It means the habitual disregard of the laws by the government and especially of those laws which are meant to restrain the power of the government: a government which can change every law or is "sovereign" is lawless. From the sequel it appears that, according to the stranger, even in the city ruled by the true king there will be laws (the true king is the true legislator), but that the true king, in contradistinction to all other rulers, may justly change the laws or act against the laws. In the absence of the true king, the stranger would probably be satisfied if the city were ruled by a code of laws framed by a wise man, one which can be changed by the unwise rulers only in extreme cases.

After the true kingly art has been separated from all other arts, it remains for the stranger to determine the peculiar work of the king. Here the example of the art of weaving takes on decisive importance. The king's work resembles a web. According to the popular view all parts of virtue are simply in harmony with one another. In fact, however, there is a tension between them. Above all, there is a tension between courage or manliness and moderation, gentleness, or concern with the seemly. This tension explains the tension and even hostility between the preponderantly manly and the preponderantly gentle human beings. The true king's task is to weave together these opposite kinds of human beings, for the people in the city who are completely unable to become either manly or moderate cannot become citizens at all. An important part of the kingly weaving together consists in intermarrying the children of preponderantly manly families and those of preponderantly gentle families. The human king must then approximate the divine shepherd by enlarging the art of ruling cities strictly understood so as to include in it the art of mating or matchmaking. The matchmaking practiced by the king is akin to the matchmaking practiced by Socrates,[107] which means that it is not identical with the latter.

If we were to succeed in understanding the kinship between the king's matchmaking and Socrates' matchmaking, we would have made some progress toward the understanding of the kinship between the king and the philosopher. This much can be said safely: While it is possible and even necessary to speak of "the human herd" when trying to define the king, the philosopher has nothing to do with "herds."

The *Statesman* belongs to a trilogy whose theme is knowledge. For Plato, knowledge proper or striving for knowledge proper is philosophy. Philosophy is striving for knowledge of the whole, for contemplation of the whole. The whole consists of parts; knowledge of the whole is knowledge of all parts of the whole as parts of the whole. Philosophy is the highest human activity, and man is an excellent, perhaps the most excellent, part of the whole. The whole is not a whole without man, without man's being whole or complete. But man becomes whole not without his own effort, and this effort presupposes knowledge of a particular kind: knowledge which is not contemplative or theoretical but prescriptive or commanding[108] or practical. The *Statesman* presents itself as a theoretical discussion of practical knowledge. In contradistinction to the *Statesman,* the *Republic* leads up from practical or political life to philosophy, to the theoretical life; the *Republic* presents a practical discussion of theory: it shows to men concerned with the solution of the human problem that that solution consists in the theoretical life; the knowledge which the *Republic* sets forth is prescriptive or commanding. The theoretical discussion of the highest practical knowledge (the kingly art) in the *Statesman,* merely by setting forth the character of the kingly art, takes on a commanding character: it sets forth what the ruler ought to do. While the distinction of theoretical and practical knowledge is necessary, their separation is impossible. (Consider from this point of view the description of the theoretical life in the *Theaitetos* 173^b–177^c.) The kingly art is one of the arts directly concerned with making men whole or entire. The most obvious indication of every human being's incompleteness and at the same time of the manner in which it can be completed is the distinction of the human race into the two sexes: just as the union of men and women, the primary goal of *eros,* makes "man" self-sufficient for the perpetuity, not to say sempiternity, of the human species, all other kinds of incompleteness to be found in men are completed in the species, in the "idea," of man. The whole human race, and not any part of it, is self-sufficient as a part of the whole, and not as the master or conqueror of the whole. It is perhaps for this reason that the *Statesman* ends with a praise of a certain kind of matchmaking.

The Laws

The *Republic* and the *Statesman* transcend the city in different but kindred ways. They show first how the city would have to transform itself if it wishes to maintain its claim to supremacy in the face of philosophy. They show then that the city is incapable of undergoing this transformation. The *Republic* shows silently that the ordinary city—*i.e.,* the city which is not communistic and which is the association of the fathers rather than of the artisans—is the only city that is possible. The *Statesman* shows explicitly the necessity of the rule of laws. The *Republic* and the *Statesman* reveal, each in its own way, the essential limitation and therewith the essential character of the city. They thus lay the foundation for answering the question of the best political order, the best order of the city compatible with the nature of man. But they do not set forth that best possible order. This task is left for the *Laws*. We may then say that the *Laws* is the only political work proper of Plato. It is the only Platonic dialogue from which Socrates is absent. The characters of the *Laws* are old men of long political experience: a nameless Athenian stranger, the Cretan Kleinias, and the Spartan Megillos. The Athenian stranger occupies the place ordinarily occupied in the Platonic dialogues by Socrates. The conversation takes place far away from Athens, on the island of Crete, while the three old men walk from the city of Knossos to the cave of Zeus.

Our first impression is that the Athenian stranger has gone to Crete in order to discover the truth about those Greek laws which in one respect were the most renowned, for the Cretan laws were believed to have had their origin in Zeus, the highest god. The Cretan laws were akin to the Spartan laws, which were even more renowned than the Cretan laws and were traced to Apollo. At the suggestion of the Athenian, the three men converse about laws and regimes. The Athenian learns from the Cretan that the Cretan legislator has framed all his laws with a view to war: by nature every city is at all times in a state of undeclared war with every other city; victory in war, and hence war, is the condition for all blessings. The Athenian easily convinces the Cretan that the Cretan laws aim at the wrong end: the end is not war but peace. For if victory in war is the condition of all blessings, war is not the end: the blessings themselves belong to peace. Hence the virtue of war, courage, is the lowest part of virtue, inferior to moderation and above all to justice and wisdom. Once we have seen the natural order of the virtues, we know the highest principle of legislation, for that legislation must be concerned with virtue, with the excellence of the human soul, rather than with any other goods is easily granted by the Cretan gentleman Kleinias who is assured by the Athenian that the possession of virtue is necessarily followed by the possession of health, beauty, strength, and wealth.[109] It appears that both the Spartan and the Cretan legislators, convinced as they were that the end of the city is war and not peace, provided well for the education of their subjects or fellows to courage, to self-control regarding pains and fears, by making them taste the greatest pains and fears; but they did not provide at all for education to moderation, to self-control regarding pleasures, by making them taste the greatest pleasures. In fact, if we can trust Megillos, at any rate the Spartan legislator discouraged the enjoyment of pleasure altogether.[110] The Spartan and Cretan legislators surely forbade the pleasures of drinking —pleasures freely indulged in by the Athenians. The Athenian contends that drinking, even drunkenness, properly practiced is conducive to moderation, the twin virtue of courage. In order to be properly practiced, drinking must be done in common, i.e., in a sense in public so that it can be supervised. Drinking, even drunkenness, will be salutary if the drinkers are ruled by the right kind of man. For a man to be a commander of a ship it is not sufficient that he possess the art or science of sailing; he must also be free from seasickness.[111] Art or knowledge is likewise not sufficient for ruling a banquet. Art is not sufficient for ruling any association and in particular the city. The banquet is a more fitting simile of the city than is the ship ("the ship of state"), for just as the banqueteers are drunk from wine, the citizens are drunk from fears, hopes, desires, and aversions and are therefore in need of being ruled by a man who is sober. Since banquets are illegal in Sparta and Crete but legal in Athens, the Athenian is compelled to justify an Athenian institution. The justification is a long speech, and long speeches were Athenian rather than Spartan and Cretan. The Athenian is then compelled to justify an Athenian institution in an Athenian manner. He is compelled to transform his non-Athenian interlocutors to some extent into Athenians. Only in this way can he correct their erroneous views about laws and therewith eventually their laws themselves. From this we understand better the character of the *Laws* as a whole. In the *Republic*[112] the Spartan and Cretan regimes were used as examples of timocracy, the kind of regime inferior only to the best regime but by far superior to democracy, i.e., the kind of regime which prevailed in Athens during most of Socrates' (and Plato's) lifetime. In the *Laws* the Athenian stranger attempts to correct timocracy, i.e., to change it into the best possible regime which is somehow in between timocracy and the best regime of the *Republic*. That

best possible regime will prove to be very similar to "the ancestral regime," the predemocratic regime, of Athens.

The Cretan and Spartan laws were found to be faulty because they
did not permit their subjects to taste the greatest pleasures. But can
drinking be said to afford the greatest pleasures, even the greatest
sensual pleasures? Yet the Athenian had in mind those greatest pleasures which people can enjoy in public and to which they must be exposed in order to learn to control them. The pleasures of banquets are
drinking and singing. In order to justify banquets one must therefore
discuss also singing, music, and hence education as a whole:[113] the
music pleasures are the greatest pleasures which people can enjoy in
public and which they must learn to control by being exposed to them.
The Spartan and Cretan laws suffer then from the great defect that
they do not at all, or at least not sufficiently, expose their subjects to
the music pleasures.[114] The reason for this is that these two societies are
not towns but armed camps, a kind of herd: in Sparta and Crete even
those youths who are by nature fit to be educated as individuals by
private teachers are brought up merely as members of a herd. In other
words, the Spartans and Cretans know only how to sing in choruses:
they do not know the most beautiful song, the most noble music.[115]
In the *Republic* the city of the armed camp, a greatly improved Sparta,
was transcended by the City of Beauty, the city in which philosophy, the
highest Muse, is duly honored. In the *Laws,* where the best possible
regime is presented, this transcending does not take place. The city
of the *Laws* is, however, not a city of the armed camp in any sense.
Yet it has certain features in common with the city of the armed camp
of the *Republic.* Just as in the *Republic,* music education proves to be
education toward moderation, and such education proves to require the
supervision of musicians and poets by the true statesman or legislator.
Yet while in the *Republic* education to moderation proves to culminate
in the love of the beautiful, in the *Laws* moderation rather takes on
the colors of sense of shame or of reverence. Education is surely education to virtue, to the virtue of the citizen or to the virtue of man.[116]

The virtue of man is primarily the proper posture toward pleasures
and pains or the proper control of pleasures and pains; the proper
control is the control effected by right reasoning. If the result of
reasoning is adopted by the city, that result becomes law; law which
deserves the name is the dictate of right reasoning primarily regarding
pleasures and pains. The kinship but not identity of right reasoning and
good laws corresponds to the kinship but not identity of the good man
and the good citizen. In order to learn to control the ordinary pleasures
and pains, the citizens must be exposed from their childhood to the

pleasures afforded by poetry and the other imitative arts which in turn
must be controlled by good or wise laws, by laws which therefore ought
never to be changed; the desire for innovation so natural to poetry and
the other imitative arts must be suppressed as much as possible; the
means for achieving this is the consecration of the correct after it has
come to light. The perfect legislator will persuade or compel the poets
to teach that justice goes with pleasure and injustice with pain. The
perfect legislator will demand that this manifestly salutary doctrine
be taught even if it were not true.[117] This doctrine takes the place
of the theology of the second book of the *Republic*. In the *Republic*
the salutary teaching regarding the relation of justice and pleasure or
happiness could not be discussed in the context of the education of
the nonphilosophers because the *Republic* did not presuppose, as the
Laws does, that the interlocutors of the chief character know what
justice is.[118] The whole conversation regarding education and therewith also about the ends or principles of legislation is subsumed by the
Athenian stranger under the theme "wine" and even "drunkenness"
because the improvement of old laws can safely be entrusted only
to well-bred old men who as such are averse to every change and who,
in order to become willing to change the old laws, must undergo some
rejuvenation like the one produced by the drinking of wine.

Only after having determined the end which political life is meant
to serve (education and virtue), does the stranger turn to the beginning
of political life or the genesis of the city in order to discover the cause
of political change and in particular of the change of regimes. There
have been many beginnings of political life because there have been
many destructions of almost all men through floods, plagues, and similar calamities bringing with them the destruction of all arts and tools;
only a few human beings survived on mountaintops or in other privileged places; it took many generations until they dared to descend to
the lowlands, and during those generations the last recollection of the
arts vanished. The condition out of which all cities and regimes, all
arts and laws, all vice and virtue emerged is men's lack of all these
things; the "out of which" something emerges is one kind of cause of
the thing in question; the primary lack of what we may call civilization
would seem to be the cause of all political change.[119] If man had had
a perfect beginning, there would have been no cause for change, and
the imperfection of his beginning is bound to have effects in all stages,
however perfect, of his civilization. The stranger shows that this is the
case by following the changes which human life underwent from
the beginnings when men apparently were virtuous because they were,
not indeed wise, but simple-minded or innocent yet in fact savage,

until the destruction of the original settlement of Sparta and her sister cities Messene and Argos. He only alludes with delicacy to the Spartans' despotic subjugation of the Messenians. He summarizes the result of his inquiry by enumerating the generally accepted and effective titles to rule. It is the contradiction among the titles or the claims to them which explains the change of regimes. It appears that the title to rule based on wisdom, while the highest, is only one among seven. Among the others we find the title or claim of the master to rule over his slaves, of the stronger to rule over the weaker, and of those chosen by lot to rule over those not so chosen.[120] Wisdom is not a sufficient title; a viable regime presupposes a blend of the claim based on wisdom with the claims based on the other kinds of superiority; perhaps the proper or wise blend of some of the other titles can act as a substitute for the title deriving from wisdom. The Athenian stranger does not abstract, as the Eleatic stranger does, from bodily force as a necessary ingredient of the rule of man over man. The viable regime must be mixed. The Spartan regime is mixed. But is it mixed wisely? In order to answer this question one must first see the ingredients of the right mixture in isolation. These are monarchy, of which Persia offers the outstanding example, and democracy, of which Athens offers the most outstanding example.[121] Monarchy by itself stands for the absolute rule of the wise man or of the master; democracy stands for freedom. The right mixture is that of wisdom and freedom, of wisdom and consent, of the rule of wise laws framed by a wise legislator and administered by the best members of the city and of the rule of the common people.

After the end as well as the general character of the best possible regime have been made clear, Kleinias reveals that the present conversation is of direct use to him. The Cretans plan to found a colony, and they have commissioned him together with others to take care of the project and in particular to frame laws for the colony as they see fit; they may even select foreign laws if they appear to them to be superior to the Cretan laws. The people to be settled come from Crete and from the Peloponnesos: they do not come from one and the same city. If they came from the same city, with the same language and the same laws and the same sacred rites and beliefs, they could not easily be persuaded to accept institutions different from those of their home city. On the other hand, heterogeneity of the population of a future city causes dissensions.[122] In the present case the heterogeneity seems to be sufficient to make possible considerable change for the better, *i.e.,* the establishment of the best possible regime, and yet not too great to prevent fusion. We have here the viable alternative to the expulsion of

everyone older than ten which would be required for the establishment
of the best regime of the *Republic*. The traditions which the various
groups of settlers bring with them will be modified rather than
eradicated. Thanks to the good fortune which brought about the
presence in Crete of the Athenian stranger while the sending out of
the colony is in preparation, there is a fair chance that the traditions
will be modified wisely. All the greater care must be taken that the new
order established under the guidance of the wise man will not be
changed afterward by less wise men: it ought to be exposed to change
as little as possible, for any change of a wise order seems to be a change
for the worse. At any rate without the chance presence of the Athenian
stranger in Crete there would be no prospect of wise legislation for the
new city. This makes us understand the stranger's assertion that not
human beings but chance legislates: most laws are as it were dictated
by calamities. Still, some room is left for the legislative art. Or, inverse-
ly, the possessor of the legislative art is helpless without good fortune,
for which he can only pray. The most favorable circumstance for which
the legislator would pray is that the city for which he is to frame laws
be ruled by a young tyrant whose nature is in some respects the same
as that of the philosopher except that he does not have to be graceful
or witty, a lover of the truth, and just; his lack of justice (the fact that
he is prompted by desire for his own power and glory alone) does
not do harm if he is willing to listen to the wise legislator. Given this
condition—given a coincidence of the greatest power with wisdom
through the cooperation of the tyrant with the wise legislator—the
legislator will effect the quickest and most profound change for the
better in the habits of the citizens. But since the city to be founded is
to undergo as little change as possible, it is perhaps more important to
realize that the regime most difficult to change is oligarchy, the regime
which occupies the central place in the order of regimes presented in
the *Republic*.[123] Surely, the city to be founded must not be tyrannically
ruled. The best regime is that in which a god or demon rules as in the
age of Kronos, the golden age. The nearest imitation of divine rule is
the rule of laws. But the laws in their turn depend on the man or men
who can lay down and enforce the laws, *i.e.*, the regime (monarchy,
tyranny, oligarchy, aristocracy, democracy). In the case of each of
these regimes a section of the city rules the rest, and therefore it rules
the city with a view to a sectional interest, not to the common interest.[124] We know already the solution to this difficulty: the regime
must be mixed as it was in a way in Sparta and Crete,[125] and it must
adopt a code framed by a wise legislator.

The wise legislator will not limit himself to giving simple commands accompanied by sanctions, *i.e.,* threats of punishment. This is the way for guiding slaves, not free men. He will preface the laws with preambles or preludes setting forth the reasons of the laws. Yet different kinds of reasons are needed for persuading different kinds of men, and the multiplicity of reasons may be confusing and thus endanger the simplicity of obedience. The legislator must then possess the art of saying simultaneously different things to different kinds of citizens in such a way that the legislator's speech will effect in all cases the same simple result: obedience to his laws. In acquiring this art he will be greatly helped by the poets.[126] Laws must be twofold; they must consist of the "unmixed law," the bald statement of what ought to be done or forborne "or else," *i.e.,* the "tyrannical prescription," and the prelude to the law which gently persuades by appealing to reason.[127] The proper mixture of coercion and persuasion, of "tyranny" and "democracy,"[128] of wisdom and consent, proves everywhere to be the character of wise political arrangements.

The laws require a general prelude—an exhortation to honor the various beings which deserve honor in their proper order. Since the rule of laws is an imitation of divine rule, honor must be given first and above everything else to the gods, next to the other superhuman beings, then to the ancestors, then to one's father and mother. Everyone must also honor his soul but next to the gods. The order of rank between honoring one's soul and honoring one's parents is not made entirely clear. Honoring one's soul means acquiring the various virtues without which no one can be a good citizen. The general exhortation culminates in the proof that the virtuous life is more pleasant than the life of vice. Before the founder of the new colony can begin with the legislation proper, he must take two measures of the utmost importance. In the first place he must effect a kind of purge of the potential citizens: only the right kind of settlers must be admitted to the new colony. Second, the land must be distributed among those admitted to citizenship. There will then be no communism. Whatever advantages communism might have, it is not feasible if the legislator does not himself exercise tyrannical rule,[129] whereas in the present case not even the cooperation of the legislator with a tyrant is contemplated. Nevertheless, the land must remain the property of the whole city; no citizen will be the absolute owner of the land allotted to him. The land will be divided into allotments which must never be changed by selling, buying, or in any other way, and this will be achieved if every landowner must leave his entire allotment to a single son; the other sons must try to marry heiresses; to prevent the excess of the male citizen population beyond the number of the originally established allotments, recourse must be had to birth control and in the extreme case to the sending out of colonies. There must not be gold and silver in the city and as little money-making as possible. It is impossible that there should be equality of property, but there ought to be an upper limit to what a citizen can own: the richest citizen must be permitted to own no more than four times what the poorest citizens own, *i.e.*, the allotment of land including house and slaves. It is impossible to disregard the inequality of property in the distribution of political power. The citizen body will be divided into four classes according to the amount of property owned. The land assigned to each citizen must be sufficient to enable him to serve the city in war as a knight or as a hoplite. In other words, citizenship is limited to knights and hoplites. The regime seems to be what Aristotle calls a polity—a democracy limited by a considerable property qualification. But this is not correct, as appears particularly from the laws concerning membership in the Council and election to the Council. The Council is what we would call the executive part of the government; each twelfth of the Council is to govern for a month. The Council is to consist of four equally large groups, the first group being chosen from the highest property class, the second group being chosen from the second highest property class, and so on. All citizens have the same voting power, but whereas all citizens are obliged to vote for councillors from the highest property class, only the citizens of the two highest property classes are obliged to vote for councillors from the lowest property class. These arrangements are obviously meant to favor the wealthy; the regime is meant to be a mean between monarchy and democracy[130] or, more precisely, a mean more oligarchic or aristocratic than a polity. Similar privileges are granted to the wealthy also as regards power in the Assembly and the holding of the most honorable offices. It is, however, not wealth as wealth which is favored: no craftsman or trader, however wealthy, can be a citizen. Only those can be citizens who have the leisure to devote themselves to the practice of citizen virtue.

The most conspicuous part of the legislation proper concerns impiety, which is of course treated within the context of the penal law. The fundamental impiety is atheism or the denial of the existence of gods. Since a good law will not merely punish crimes or appeal to fear but will also appeal to reason, the Athenian stranger is compelled to demonstrate the existence of gods and, since gods who do not care for men's justice, who do not reward the just and punish the unjust, are not sufficient for the city, he must demonstrate divine providence as well. The *Laws* is the only Platonic work which contains such a demonstration. It is the only Platonic work which begins with "A god." One might say that it is Plato's most pious work, and that it is for this reason that he strikes therein at the root of impiety, *i.e.,* at the opinion that there are no gods. The Athenian stranger takes up the question regarding the gods, although it was not even raised in Crete or in Sparta; it was, however, raised in Athens.[131] Kleinias strongly favors the demonstration recommended by the Athenian on the ground that it would constitute the finest and best prelude to the whole code. The Athenian cannot refute the atheists before he has stated their assertions. It appears that they assert that body is prior to soul or mind, or that soul or mind is derivative from body and, consequently, that nothing is by nature just or unjust, or that all right originates in convention. The refutation of them consists in the proof that soul is prior to body, which proof implies that there is natural right. The punishments for impiety differ according to the different kinds of impiety. It is not clear what punishment, if any, is inflicted on the atheist who is a just man; he is surely less severely punished than, for instance, the man who practices forensic rhetoric for the sake of gain. Even in cases of the other kinds of impiety, capital punishment will be extremely rare. We mention these facts because their insufficient consideration might induce ignorant people to scold Plato for his alleged lack of liberalism. We do not here describe such people as ignorant because they believe that liberalism calls for unqualified toleration of the teaching of all opinions however dangerous or degrading. We call them ignorant because they do not see how extraordinarily liberal Plato is according to their own standards, which cannot possibly be "absolute." The standards generally recognized in Plato's time are best illustrated by the practice of Athens, a city highly renowned for her liberality and gentleness. In Athens Socrates was punished with death because he was held not to believe in the existence of the gods worshipped by the city of Athens—of gods whose existence was known only from hearsay. In the city of the *Laws* the belief in gods is demanded only to the extent to which it is supported by demonstration; and in addition, those who are not convinced by the demonstration but are just men will not be condemned to death.

The stability of the order sketched by the Athenian stranger seems to be guaranteed as far as the stability of any political order can be: it is guaranteed by obedience on the part of the large majority of citizens to wise laws which are as unchangeable as possible, by an obedience that results chiefly from education to virtue, from the formation of character. Still, laws are only second best: no law can be as wise as the decision of a truly wise man on the spot. Provision must

therefore be made for, as it were, infinite progress in improving the
laws in the interest of increasing improvement of the political order,
as well as of counteracting the decay of the laws. Legislation must then
be an unending process; at each time there must be living legislators.
Laws should be changed only with the utmost caution, only in the case
of universally admitted necessity. The later legislators must aim at the
same commanding end as the original legislator: the excellence of the
souls of the members of the city.[132] To prevent change of laws, intercourse of the citizens with foreigners must be closely supervised. No
citizen shall go abroad for a private purpose. But citizens of high
reputation and more than fifty years old who desire to see how other
men live and especially to converse with outstanding men from whom
they can learn something about the improvement of the laws are
encouraged to do so.[133] Yet all these and similar measures do not suffice for the salvation of the laws and the regime; the firm foundation
is still lacking. That firm foundation can only be supplied by a Nocturnal Council consisting of the most outstanding old citizens and select
younger citizens of thirty years and older. The Nocturnal Council is
to be for the city what the mind is for the human individual. To perform its function its members must possess above everything else the
most adequate knowledge possible of the single end at which all
political action directly or indirectly aims. This end is virtue. Virtue is
meant to be one, yet it is also many; there are four kinds of virtue,
and at least two of them—wisdom and courage (or spiritedness)—are
radically different from one another.[134] How then can there be a single
end of the city? The Nocturnal Council cannot perform its function
if it cannot answer this question, or, more generally and perhaps more
precisely stated, the Nocturnal Council must include at least some men
who know what the virtues themselves are or who know the ideas of
the various virtues as well as what unites them, so that all together
can justly be called "virtue" in the singular: is "virtue," the single end
of the city, one or a whole or both or something else? They also must
know, as far as is humanly possible, the truth about the gods. Solid
reverence for the gods arises only from knowledge of the soul as well
as of the movements of the stars. Only men who combine this knowledge with the popular or vulgar virtues can be adequate rulers of the
city: one ought to hand over the city for rule to the Nocturnal Council
if it comes into being. Plato brings the regime of the *Laws* around by
degrees to the regime of the *Republic*.[135] Having arrived at the end of
the *Laws,* we must return to the beginning of the *Republic*.

NOTES

1. Plato *Republic* 377 ff., 389[b-c], 414[b]–415[d], 459[c-d].
2. *Ibid.*, 375[b]–376[c].
3. *Ibid.*, 414[d-e].
4. *Ibid.*, 471[a-b].
5. *Ibid.*, 395[c]; 500[d]; 530[a]; 507[c], 597.
6. *Ibid.*, 454[c]–455[a]; cf. 452[a].
7. *Ibid.*, 343[b].
8. *Ibid.*, 351[c]–352[a].
9. Cf. *ibid.*, 364[a, c-d], 365[c] with 357[b] and 358[a].
10. *Ibid.*, 372[d].
11. *Ibid.*, 370[d-e], 373[c].
12. *Ibid.*, 342[a-b], 346[c].
13. *Ibid.*, 392[a-c].
14. *Ibid.*, 423[b]; cf. also 398[a] and 422[d].
15. *Ibid.*, 414[a], 465[d]–466[c]; cf. 346[e] ff.
16. *Ibid.*, 415[b].
17. *Ibid.*, 427[d].
18. *Ibid.*, 433[a-b].
19. *Ibid.*, 434[c].
20. *Ibid.*, 430[c]; cf. *Phaedo* 82[a].
21. *Republic* 441[a-c].
22. *Ibid.*, 444[d]–445[b].
23. *Ibid.*, 441[e].
24. Cf. *ibid.*, 442[c].
25. *Ibid.*, 580[d]–583[b].
26. *Ibid.*, 619[b-d].
27. *Ibid.*, 427[d].
28. Cf. *ibid.*, 366[c].
29. *Ibid.*, 573[b-e], 574[e]–575[a].
30. Cf. *ibid.*, 439[d].
31. *Timaeus* 24[a-b].
32. *Republic* 401[b-c], 421[e]–422[d], 460[a], 543[a].
33. *Politics* 1264[a] 13–17.
34. *Republic* 421[a], 434[a].
35. *Ibid.*, 415[e], 431[b-c], 456[d].
36. Reconsider *ibid.*, 427[d].
37. *Ibid.*, 464[d]; cf. *Laws* 739[c].
38. Cf. *Republic* 449[b]–450[a] with 327[b]–328[b].
39. Cf. *ibid.*, 369[d].
40. *Ibid.*, 455[d-e], 456[b-c].
41. *Ibid.*, 455[c-e].
42. *Ibid.*, 462[c-d], 464[b].

43. Cf. *ibid.*, 458[e].
44. Cf. *ibid.*, 461[b-e].
45. *Ibid.*, 463[c].
46. *Ibid.*, 466[d].
47. *Ibid.*, 473[b-c].
48. *Ibid.*, 472[b-c].
49. *Ibid.*, 479[a]; cf. 538[c] ff.
50. *Ibid.*, 517[c].
51. Cf. *ibid.*, 509[b]–510[a].
52. *Ibid.*, 501[b]; 597[b-d].
53. Cf. *ibid.*, 507[a-c] with 596[a] and 532[c-d], contrast with *Phaedo* 65[d] and 74[a-b].
54. *Republic* 536[b]; cf. 487[a].
55. Cf. *ibid.*, 379[a-b] and 380[d] ff.
56. *Ibid.*, 379[a].
57. *Ibid.*, 472[c]–473[a]; cf. 500[c]–501[c] with 484[c-d] and 592[b].
58. *Ibid.*, 498[c]–502[a].
59. *Ibid.*, 499[b-c], 500[d], 520[a-d], 521[b], 539[e].
60. *Ibid.*, 485[a], 501[b-c], 517[c].
61. *Ibid.*, 519[c].
62. *Ibid.*, 486[a-b].
63. *Ibid.*, 539[e].
64. *Ibid.*, 514[b]–515[c].
65. *Ibid.*, 517[a].
66. Cf. *ibid.*, 376[e].
67. *Ibid.*, 540[d]–541[a]; cf. 499[b], 501[a,e].
68. *Ibid.*, 433[a-b] and 443[d]; cf. Aristotle *Nicomachean Ethics* 1098[a] 7–12.
69. *Republic* 583[a].
70. *Ibid.*, 519[e]–520[b]; 540[b,e].
71. Consider *Apology of Socrates* 30[a].
72. *Republic* 545[a-b]; cf. 498[c-d].
73. *Laws* 739[b-e].
74. Cf. *Republic* 547[b].
75. Cf. *ibid.*, 546[e]–547[a] and Hesiod *Works and Days* 106 ff.
76. *Republic* 557[d-e].
77. See Thucydides VI. 27–29 and 53–61.
78. Cf. *Republic* 564[c]–565[a] and 575[c].
79. Cf. *ibid.*, 563[d] with 389[a].
80. Cf. *ibid.*, 577[c-d] with 428[d-e] and 422[a,c].

81. *Ibid.*, 568^{a-d}.
82. *Ibid.*, 545^{d-e}, 549^{c-e}.
83. *Ibid.*, 608^{c}, 614^{a}.
84. *Ibid.*, 377^{a}.
85. *Ibid.*, 485^{c-d}.
86. *Ibid.*, 601^{c}–602^{a}.
87. *Ibid.*, 598^{e}, 599^{c-e}, 600^{e}.
88. Cf. *ibid.*, 501^{a}.
89. *The Gay Science,* No. 1.
90. *Republic* 603^{e}–604^{a}, 606^{a,c}, 607^{a}.
91. *Ibid.*, 607^{b}.
92. Cf. *ibid.*, 604^{e}.
93. *Ibid.*, 611^{b}–612^{a}.
94. *Ibid.*, 504^{b}, 506^{d}.
95. Cicero *Republic* II.52.
96. Cf. Plato *Republic* 484^{d} and 539^{e} with 501^{a-c}.
97. Cf. *Statesman* 285^{d}.
98. *Republic* 511^{a-d}, 531^{a}–533^{d}, 537^{c}.
99. Cf. *Statesman* 264^{c}.
100. *Ibid.*, 262^{c}–263^{d}, 266^{d}.
101. Cf. *ibid.*, 271^{e}, 272^{b-c}.
102. *Ibid.*, 274^{e}–275^{c}.
103. Cf. *Sophist* 252^{d-e}.
104. *Statesman* 295^{b-c}.
105. *Ibid.*, 297^{a} ff.
106. *Ibid.*, 301^{c-e}.
107. Cf. *Theaitetos* 151^{b}.
108. *Statesman* 260^{a-b}.

109. *Laws* 631^{b-d}; cf. 829^{a-b}.
110. *Ibid.*, 636^{e}.
111. *Ibid.*, 639^{b-c}.
112. *Republic* 544^{c}.
113. *Laws* 642^{a}.
114. Cf. *ibid.*, 673^{a-c}.
115. *Ibid.*, 666^{e}–667^{b}.
116. *Ibid.*, 643^{c}, 659^{d-e}; 653^{a-b}.
117. *Ibid.*, 660^{e}–664^{b}.
118. *Republic* 392^{a-c}.
119. *Laws* 676^{a,c}, 678^{a}.
120. *Ibid.*, 690^{a-d}.
121. *Ibid.*, 693^{d}.
122. *Ibid.*, 707^{e}–708^{d}.
123. Cf. *ibid.*, 708^{e}–712^{a} with *Republic* 487^{a}.
124. *Laws* 713^{c}–715^{b}.
125. *Ibid.*, 712^{c-e}.
126. *Ibid.*, 719^{b}–720^{e}.
127. *Ibid.*, 722^{e}–723^{a}; cf. 808^{d-e}.
128. Cf. Aristotle *Politics* 1266^{a} 1–3.
129. *Laws* 739^{a}–740^{a}.
130. *Ibid.*, 756^{b-e}.
131. *Ibid.*, 886; cf. 891^{b}.
132. *Ibid.*, 769^{a}–771^{a}, 772^{a-d}, 875^{c-d}.
133. *Ibid.*, 949^{e} ff.
134. *Ibid.*, 963^{e}.
135. Aristotle *Politics* 1265^{a} 1–4.

READINGS

A. Plato. *Republic.*
B. Plato. *Laws.*

XENOPHON

c. 430 − c. 354 B.C.

Of the companions of Socrates who wrote about him, only Plato and Xenophon left works which have come down to us more or less intact. But whereas Plato's writings are, so to speak, entirely Socratic, Xenophon's four Socratic writings (*Memorabilia, Oeconomicus, Symposium,* and *Apology of Socrates*) fill only one of the five volumes of the complete edition of his works. The reader is thus faced with the task, which has no counterpart in the study of Plato, of understanding the place of Xenophon's Socratic writings in the larger context of his work as a whole.

Xenophon's longest work by far, the *Cyropaedia* (Education of Cyrus), is a treatment of the education and career of the founder of the Persian empire, who is in Xenophon's presentation an exemplary practitioner of the royal art of ruling. His next longest work, the *Hellenica* (Greek Affairs), is devoted to the noteworthy political and military doings of the Greeks during Xenophon's lifetime. Beginning roughly where Thucydides' history breaks off, it is sometimes regarded in its early portions as a continuation and completion of that history. The *Cyroanabasis* (Ascent of Cyrus), or *Anabasis,* as it is generally called, is largely an account of the outstanding event of Xenophon's own political career, his leading back to Greece and safety of the bulk of the "ten thousand" Greek mercenaries who had accompanied a younger Cyrus into the heart of the Persian empire in support of his attempt to overthrow his brother, the Persian king. The Greeks had become isolated there after Cyrus was killed in battle and his other troops deserted to the king. The remaining non-Socratic works traditionally ascribed to Xenophon consist of shorter writings. They comprise a eulogy of Agesilaus, a Spartan king known personally to Xenophon; a dialogue on tyranny between the tyrant Hiero and the poet Simonides; and treatises on the Spartan and Athenian constitutions, on Athenian revenues, and on the arts of the cavalry commander, of horsemanship, and of hunting with dogs.

Xenophon, who lived himself for a time as lord of a country estate, [1] has told us something about the tastes and opinions of a Greek gentleman—for example, his admiration for the royal art of ruling on the one hand [2] and for Spartan-style republicanism on the other [3]—as well as about the country or rural basis of many of the gentleman's activities, with its heavy demand for the use of horses and dogs. [4] It is tempting to conclude that his writings as a whole not only reflect such a taste but are intended to appeal to it, above all. This temptation may be strengthened when we observe, as we are bound to do, another difference between Xenophon's writings and Plato's. The solemn, moving, quasi-tragic tones of the Platonic dialogues are hardly to be found in Xenophon. In their place, we find an apparently lighthearted simplicity enlivened and graced often, if not always, by humor. Xenophon is a writer capable of presenting the problem of justice in the guise of a story of two boys, a large one with a small coat and a small one with a large coat. [5] He seems to have fled high seriousness as eagerly as, and more successfully than, Bertie Wooster (that latter-day gentleman of P. G. Wodehouse's invention) fled entanglements with women "steeped to the gills in serious purpose" and bent on improving his mind.

There may be some considerable truth to this first impression of what inspired Xenophon and of the audience he wished to address. But it fails to clarify the context in which his Socratic writings must be understood. Indeed, it leaves no place for those writings. For, as Xenophon demonstrates in his most extensive treatment of the gentlemanly life and character, the gentleman as such has no interest in Socrates, [6] while Xenophon is preoccupied with him. This is shown not only by his Socratic writings proper but also by the appearance of Socrates and related themes in each of his other major works. [7] We come closer then to doing justice to both aspects of Xenophon's work—Socratic and non-Socratic—and to bringing to light their possible unity, by suggesting that Xenophon may have been one who pursued the Socratic *question* of the best way of life without ever coming to accept completely the Socratic *answer* that that way of life is the philosophic one.

This suggestion derives some support from the consideration that Xenophon—while calling frequent attention to his own relationship with Socrates, in sharp contrast to Plato, going so far as to call the chief of his Socratic writings "Memorabilia" or "Recollections," *his* recollections of Socrates—in the only two episodes he chooses to recount from their friendship gives more evidence of resistance to Socrates' teaching and advice than of acceptance.[8] If Xenophon's levity stands in the way of our adopting it, by causing us to wonder whether anyone who wrote in the way he did could have concerned himself with the question of the best way of life, we can recall Plato's own indications that the taste for tragedy, which he was so much more willing than Xenophon to indulge, is a questionable one.[9] But even if our suggestion will have to be revised or qualified on the basis of our study of Xenophon's works, it has the merit of permitting us to begin that study by helping us to discern the order in which the most important of them stand toward one another.

In the *Cyropaedia,* Xenophon presents his thoughts on the character of the perfect ruler and on the political way of life at its peak. The Socratic writings, led by the *Memorabilia,* are devoted to the philosopher par excellence and the philosophic way of life as Xenophon had observed it firsthand in the pursuits of Socrates. "Cyrus" and "Socrates" apparently represent the two alternatives which most impressed him, constituting the poles between which, he thought, all other human possibilities (for example, the quasi-public life of the gentleman) are to be found and by reference to which they are to be understood. In the *Anabasis,* the two poles are brought together as Xenophon, the student of Socrates, leaves Socrates against the latter's advice to join a campaign being organized by a new Cyrus.

CYROPAEDIA

The accomplishments of the elder Cyrus were due partly to his birth (family), partly to his nature, and partly to his education.[10] If he had not had a certain nature (outstanding natural abilities accompanied by the inclination to use them in a certain way),[11] he could not have conceived his great plans or carried them out. If he had not been born into two royal lines—his father was king of Persia, his mother's father king of Media—his opportunities would have been limited in such a way as to affect the character of his accomplishments.[12] But leaving these matters to one side for the moment, we will begin from a consideration of his education, as Xenophon's title bids us to do.

"He was educated in the Persian laws." Xenophon's account does not seriously claim to be historical. According to it, the Persia in which Cyrus was raised, the Persia whose armies he led to the conquest of Asia and in whose name he founded an empire, was a rather small republic or what we would call a constitutional monarchy. It was, moreover, a model republic along Spartan lines, an improved Sparta. If Xenophon admired Sparta, he must have admired still more this "Persia." Publicly educating its youth, as Sparta did, instilling in them continence and obedience as well as military skills, Persia suppressed Sparta's education to thievery in favor of an education to justice.[13] Like the cities praised by Plato and Aristotle, Xenophon's Persia regarded as its laws' most important task the formation of the character of its citizens: it wished to make them such as not even to desire to commit any wicked or shameful deed.[14] And, like those other highly regarded cities, it was an aristocracy, since the country's fidelity to its laws' high purpose depended on political authority remaining firmly in the hands of those and only those who had completed the course of education thought to accomplish that purpose.[15] In other words, with the quasi-exception of his playful suggestion that the desirable political arrangements are not merely objects of future prayer or wish but actually existed at some time in the past, Xenophon's presentation of Persia follows the lines more familiar to us in Plato and Aristotle. And to the extent that Cyrus' success and that of his Persians was due to the formation they received from the Persian laws,[16] the *Cyropaedia* as a whole stands as a sort of tribute to those laws and to the Persian regime which maintained them.

But Cyrus' education in the broad sense of the term took place not just in Persia but also in Media at the court of his grandfather, a typical oriental despot presiding over a country of a very different sort from Persia.[17] In accord with this, Cyrus' success amounted to political change, indeed change on a vast scale, for Persia. The Persian empire he founded had little in common with the old Persia, which it effectively replaced, relegating it to the status of a smallish province—however much, for sound political reasons, Cyrus wished to stress the similarity between old and new orders rather than the differences.[18] And Xenophon appears to present Cyrus' transformation of Persia no less sympathetically than he presented the old Persia that Cyrus transformed. Moreover, the changes brought about by Cyrus could hardly have taken place, or been defended by him, if there had not been grave defects in old Persia. In presenting Cyrus' career, Xenophon could not help calling attention to those defects. This means, however, that he was forced to stress what Plato and Aristotle allowed themselves only to hint at: the defects of classical republicanism in its highest or most exalted form. He thus took an important step in the direction of Machiavelli's much less sympathetic critique, a favor Machiavelli acknowledged in many appreciative remarks.[19]

To return to Cyrus' Median education, he passed his thirteenth through fifteenth or sixteenth years at his grandfather's court, finding there things both to like and to dislike. For example, he was pleased with the Median style of dress and adornment, which far surpassed the Persian in richness and splendor,[20] and he took extreme delight in learning horseback riding.[21] But he disliked the Median indulgence in fancy

food—which made the process of satisfying hunger unnecessarily complicated and time-consuming [22]—and in intoxicating drink, if only because it made the king himself as well as his retainers forget the deference
they owed him. [23] While Cyrus was highly critical of the conduct of the
Median monarchs, at least in retrospect, [24] even as a boy he may have had
some awareness that absolute monarchy is not without its advantages. [25]
And at that time or later on, he formed the opinion that his comrades
back in Persia would be attracted as he was by "Median" opportunities
for wealth and distinction unavailable to them in the incomparably more
austere Persian republic.

When Cyrus was probably still only in his middle to late twenties
(but already considered in Persia one of the mature men), a combination of forces brought together and led by the king of Assyria began to
threaten Media (now ruled by Cyrus' uncle Cyaxares). The threat to Media was at the same time a threat to Persia, since its alliance with its
neighbor had surely been one of the rocks on which Persian independence had been maintained hitherto. The Persian government decided,
therefore, in response to a request by Cyaxares, to send a force of thirty-
one thousand Persians to help defend its ally. It also acceded to Cyaxares'
wish in selecting Cyrus, who still had many friends in Media from his
stay there of ten or more years before, to command this force. Cyrus was,
as he said, "not unwilling" to accept the assignment. This was the opening he must have been waiting for. But to see the forethought, daring,
and inventiveness, the patience, determination, and perseverance which
are among the elements of great political leadership, we have only to
consider the distance between what Cyrus was authorized by this commission to do and what he intended to do, and between the resources it
provided him with and those his larger project required.

Cyrus was indeed heir to the Persian throne; but even as king he
would have had no independent authority other than to conduct sacrifices on the country's behalf. [26] His lawful authority consisted then entirely in the military command he had been appointed to. That is, it
depended entirely on the (revocable) decision of the Persian government.
Now, given the size and character of the force he was entrusted with and
the occasion for its being sent, that government must have had in mind
his engaging in nothing more than a limited and defensive war. And
only such a war would have been truly compatible with the desire to
maintain the unique Persian way of life, which required close mutual
supervision on the part of citizens familiar with one another through
daily contact. [27] Such a way of life would have been difficult, not to say
impossible, to maintain in a "greater Persia" which might result from

the attempt to absorb foreign conquests, and it would have been almost equally threatened by the multiple and prolonged absences from Persia which the governing of conquered territory as subject provinces would have required. Yet Cyrus intended not merely to help Persia's ally and thus contribute to the defense of Persia but to conquer all of the countries opposed to Persia and to incorporate them, together with others, into the greater Persia he envisioned. He had no intention, moreover, of turning these conquests over to the Persian government, whose limited kingship he would someday hold. Rather he was determined to govern them himself from the outset (that is, in his father's lifetime) as absolute, and not constitutionally limited, king.

While taking the steps necessary to accomplish these things, Cyrus would have to disregard the wishes, and perhaps even the orders,[28] of the Persian government until such time as he could present them with either an irresistible temptation[29] or a fait accompli[30] or some combination of the two. His military aims alone would require a vast army, of which his original Persian force could furnish at most the core—and even that only if he could assure himself of the army's assent to projects he was not entitled to require them to undertake. He would have to secure its assent as well to a very substantial reorganization aimed at compensating for deficiency in numbers by increased capacity to fight. Allies, in addition to the Medes, would have to be found who would be willing, whether consciously or unconsciously, to toil and take risks for Persian supremacy and their own subordination; while the Medes themselves (not to mention Cyrus' uncle Cyaxares) would have to be brought to acknowledge the supremacy of their hitherto equal or even inferior ally. Finally, Cyrus' own Persian comrades-in-arms, many of whom were his political equals—collectively indeed his superiors—would have to be brought to recognize the desirability or necessity of granting him an unchecked authority, of bowing to him as Persians had never bowed to another human being.[31]

The army Cyrus had been given consisted of a thousand "peers"— that is, those who had completed the Persian education and were accordingly admitted to full citizenship rights—and thirty thousand commoners. (This was out of a total of one hundred and twenty thousand Persians.)[32] The strictly military significance of this proportion lay in the fact that only the peers were equipped and prepared for fighting at close quarters. This was the sort of fighting which generally Greeks rather than non-Greeks excelled in and which enabled numerically inferior armies to defeat considerably larger ones prepared only for skirmishing or fighting at a distance. But there was also a political significance to the division within Cyrus' army. At home in Persia, the whole class of the so-called peers was small in number, and yet it ruled over the much more numerous commoners, who had no share in civic rights.[33] Presumably, the peers' monopoly on the most effective sort of fighting contributed to the ease with which they were able to maintain their ascendancy; and we can assume therefore that in sending an army out of Persia the home authorities took care to maintain both within the army and among the Persians left at home a numerical ratio between the classes which they considered to be politically safe.[34] Even so, they must have considered the army they had given Cyrus equal to the (defensive) task that had been assigned to it. Or, if they had any doubts on that score, they had made the political decision to run a somewhat greater risk from their foreign foes rather than to put dangerous weapons into the hands of potential domestic ones.

Cyrus assessed his army's situation somewhat differently. He was unconcerned, to say the least, to preserve the political balance either within the army or at home, but very concerned that the small size of the army's most effective branch rendered it unfit for the tasks he had in mind for it. The obvious military solution was to give heavy weapons to the commoners (weapons to be paid for by the frightened Cyaxares)[35] and to induce them, by the promise of equal treatment in the future, to join the ranks of the fighters-at-close-quarters. The commoners could be counted on to jump at the chance to improve their status and lot in life; but opposition was to be expected from the peers within the army. Unlike the authorities at home, they were on the spot and would have to be informed immediately and even consulted as to any such change; and they would not be unaware of its domestic political implications. So before even broaching the subject of rearming the commoners, Cyrus addressed himself to the peers who had been chosen to accompany him.[36]

In this, the first of his many political speeches, he speaks to them of the practices they have inherited from their ancestors and of their own situation. According to Cyrus, they are now in a position to avoid their ancestors' mistake of failing to put those worthy practices to any use: "I have observed that our forefathers were no worse than we are: they too persevered in practicing what are held to be deeds of virtue. But what good thing they acquired through being men of this sort, either for the Persian commonwealth or themselves, this I am no longer able to see." Cyrus tacitly treats the preservation of the Persian regime and the Persian way of life as worthless. The good things he has in mind are precisely those which Persia does not provide: "much wealth, much happiness, and great honors" for oneself and one's country. This is the reason why the war, which was seen by the Persian authorities only as a threat to be put down as quickly as possible, is seen by Cyrus as an opportunity—an opportunity to make use of the qualities so long cultivated by the Persians which equip them in body and prepare them in soul for military supremacy:

Since we know of ourselves that, starting from childhood, we have been practitioners of the noble and good deeds, let us proceed against the enemies, whom I know with certainty to be like amateurs in a contest against us. . . . Let us then set out boldly, also because the reputation of unjustly desiring things belonging to others is removed from us. For it is the enemies who are now advancing and initiating unjust blows, while our friends call on us as allies. What is more just than defending oneself, or more noble than helping one's friends?

Xenophon has no need to indicate here the reaction of the peers who heard this speech: the whole rest of the book is the indication. The peers, with perhaps an occasional exception,[37] acquiesced not only in Cyrus' rearming of the commoners but in his many other steps, and they did so despite the grave political consequences of each step by itself and all of them taken together. The reason is not that they were so foolish as to have no awareness of those consequences. It is to be found in the effect on them of Cyrus' speech. Their hearts, and therefore also their minds, were no longer set on a return home, to their ancestral way of life, but on partaking of the great prospects Cyrus' words had opened their eyes to.

The rearming of the commoners followed in short order. Having prepared the peers in advance in the manner shown, Cyrus had merely to point out to them the advisability of such a step from a strictly military point of view.[38] In order to understand the way in which he[39] put the proposal to the commoners however, we must revert to an earlier passage, where Xenophon casts light on "the whole regime of the Persians."[40] It turns out that none of the Persians is excluded by law from a share in honors and offices or what we have called civic rights; rather, all are permitted to send their children to the public schools of justice. But only those parents who can afford to support their children without requiring them to work do in fact send them. And only those men who have been educated in the public schools and have passed successfully on to and through the other stages of training (these too requiring leisure from gainful pursuits) can participate in honors and offices. What this situation of legal equality and factual inequality tells us is that the distinction between the classes in aristocratic Persia rested upon a basis which the aristocrats themselves were not willing to defend openly as such: namely, inherited wealth. As for the commoners, we can be sure that they regarded their exclusion from political equality, and their hard lot generally, as undeserved.[41] Cyrus therefore spoke to them as follows:

Men of Persia, you were both born and raised in the same country as we [peers] were; you have bodies no worse than ours, and it befits you to have souls no worse than ours. Yet, though you are men of this sort, in the fatherland you did not share equally with us, excluded not by us but by the necessity of providing your daily provisions. Now, on the other hand, it will be my concern, with the gods, that you have those; but you, if you want, can take up arms such as we have, undertake with us the same risks, and, if something noble and good comes of that, be deemed worthy of the like rewards.[42]

In this way, thirty thousand new peers were created, regarding their elevation as due to Cyrus alone or above all, with all that that meant both for Cyrus' relations with the (newly endangered) old peers within the army and for the prospect of the army's ever being reabsorbed into old Persia.

The reform of the army was then completed by two further steps. First, by a general consent (orchestrated by Cyrus) the principle was adopted to give rewards (including promotions of course) according to merit, with Cyrus to be the judge of that merit.[43] This was necessary not only for the sake of invigorating the army through incentives but also to provide a new basis for distinction and hierarchy in place of the old discredited one. Hierarchy would be as necessary in the new order as in the old. In addition, on his own authority Cyrus ordered that those expelled from the ranks as unworthy be replaced by the best human beings available, whether or not these were fellow citizens, "just as in the case of horses you seek those which are best in preference to those of the fatherland."[44]

Needless to say, Cyrus turned to the tasks of enlarging his army with allies and of preparing the subordination of the allies to the Persians and to him personally, as well as to the military tasks proper, with the same energy and ability he revealed in reorganizing his army. Moreover, he was greatly aided in drawing human beings to him by his manifest decency and considerateness, fairness and generosity, loyalty and dependability.[45] These qualities, joined with his great military skill (which brought him an immediate reputation once he had a chance to display it in action), made a powerfully attractive combination. But we will pass by all of this activity, enjoyable as it is to read of it in Xenophon's account, to continue our consideration of the political seeds planted by Cyrus in his reorganization of the Persian army and the fruit they bore in the Persian empire he founded.

His efforts can be seen by now to have rested on a profound understanding or, at least, a remarkable intuitive grasp of the limitations of "Persia," that is, of classical aristocracy. He knew, for example, that the loyalty it demanded, like that for any particular, nonuniversal society, rested on an arbitrary division of mankind into fellow citizens (friends) and strangers (enemies actual or potential). (Compare Plato's analysis in the *Republic* of the defects of justice understood as helping friends and harming enemies.) He knew likewise that the class hierarchy without which, in the premodern condition of material scarcity, the unique Persian system of public education could not have been supported, rested not on merit or natural capacity but on the indefensible criterion of inherited wealth. (In the *Republic,* Plato was able to remove this stain from classical aristocracy only by the extreme expedient of abolishing the family.) These defects of the old order were to be removed in the new by the creation of a universal (and therefore all-inclusive) empire and by making positions of wealth, honor, and responsibility within it depend upon merit alone.

Above all, Cyrus knew or sensed the weakness of that attachment to virtue and virtuous deeds as ends in themselves which the old Persian education prided itself on producing, an attachment on which the preference for old Persia and its way of life depended. To speak now only of the attachment itself and not of the virtue that was its object, it was not truly the result of education in the strict sense of the word. Rather, it had been beaten into the Persian peers both literally[46] and figuratively (through praise and blame).[47] And an attachment so produced is vulnerable to temptation. (Compare what Plato suggests, in the myth of Er which concludes the *Republic,* by his tale of the choice of lives.) Still, in providing that temptation, in suggesting to the peers that they no longer pursue what they take to be virtue for its own sake but rather for its rewards, Cyrus would appear to be more of a corrupter than a reformer. (We note in passing that this may be the only way in which he resembles Xenophon's other hero, the alleged corrupter of the young.) And by presenting Cyrus' revolution favorably, Xenophon seems to extend his sympathy to the peers' corruption. The question of how Xenophon did view that corruption is a part, if the most important part, of the question of his final judgment on Cyrus' new order as a whole.

In what amounts to a preface to the work,[48] Xenophon tells us that he turned his attention to Cyrus after reflecting on the frequency with which democracies, monarchies, oligarchies, and above all tyrannies are overthrown and reaching the conclusion that it is exceedingly difficult, not to say impossible, for human beings to rule successfully over other human beings. This conclusion seemed to be refuted by the career of Cyrus, which demonstrated that it is neither difficult nor impossible to rule over human beings, provided that one knows how to do it. Cyrus appeared to have solved the political problem. Yet in his conclusion to the *Cyropaedia*, [49] Xenophon admits and even stresses that Cyrus' empire began to fall prey to strife and decay immediately upon his death. The reason is not merely that Cyrus' successors, lacking his great qualities, were unable to maintain the institutions he had established. [50] It is also to be found in flaws in those institutions themselves.

We will leave aside the facts that Cyrus' new founding was to a considerable extent merely a "reshuffling of the deck," with the formerly ruling tribes now reduced to slavery in service to the new masters; that the resultant ill will made necessary the maintenance of an immense military establishment and a large personal guard for Cyrus, [51] a virtually omnipresent, if informal, internal spying network, [52] and the use in addition of various "bewitching" techniques to hold the ruled in awe as well as fear; [53] that the individual "merit" rewarded so lavishly by Cyrus was sometimes difficult to distinguish from loyalty to him and willingness to serve his merely personal aims; [54] and that the rewards thus received were revocable at any time at Cyrus' pleasure. [55] It is more important for our present purpose to note that the greatest danger to his throne Cyrus judged to come from the very friends he had most rewarded. [56] The significance of this may be seen from the fact that these friends were for the most part the same peers whose acquisitiveness (in all its aspects) Cyrus had emancipated by his suggestion that they replace the pursuit of virtue for its own sake with pursuit of it for its rewards. More generally, the combination that Cyrus tried to effect between the Persian education and continence on the one hand and Median dress and luxury on the other, [57] while temporarily invigorating, was in the long run and even in the short run destructive of the law-bred qualities, the habits of mind, on which not only Cyrus' military enterprise depended but the capacity of any country to defend itself must in part depend. [58] Hence the progressive deterioration in quality of Cyrus' army even as its size and overall military capacity increased. [59] Nor could the education of the new nobility, instituted by Cyrus at the gates of his palace, supply the missing heart, dedication to virtue for its own sake, which Cyrus had excised from the old Persian education—for all of its superficial similarity to the latter and for all of its success in producing a surface orderliness and mutual respect. [60]

On the basis of these and other similar considerations, we can hardly avoid the conclusion that Xenophon thought the thesis about Cyrus put forward in his preface was refuted rather than sustained by his elaboration of Cyrus' career. He must after all have regarded the *Cyropaedia* as a whole as an endorsement of the old "Persian" laws and regime rather than of their transformation by Cyrus, if an endorsement suitably qualified in light of the defects of the old order brought out in the work. But why, in that case, did he present Cyrus' transformation in such a way as to make it attractive to us, at least on a first and even on a second impression? Did he merely wish to purge us of a dangerous temptation after first eliciting our affinity for it? Or are we now running the risk of repeating our error, this time by moving too far in the opposite direction from our earlier erroneous view? Does the truth about Cyrus, does Xenophon's own view of Cyrus, lie somewhere between these extremes? We are assisted in answering this question, or at least in coming to appreciate the point of view from which Xenophon made his final assessment, by considering two conversations that he presents between the young Cyrus and his parents.

Cyrus never consulted his parents about his larger project, and it is fairly safe to say that neither of them would have approved of it if asked in advance—which is not the same thing as yielding gracefully after the fact or making the best of a fait accompli.[61] But, to judge at least from the conversations referred to, the grounds of disapproval would have been different in the two cases. Cyrus' mother spoke with Cyrus in Media, when he was still a boy, about the difference between Median and Persian justice.[62] She speaks in tones that make unmistakably clear her opinion as to the superiority of the latter, a preference Cyrus would prove not to share.[63] Cyrus' father spoke with Cyrus as he set out again for Media, this time to assume his fateful command. He speaks of Cyrus' own situation, raising the question of what it means to undertake to rule other human beings:

Have you forgotten, son, the conclusions reached in the reckoning you and I once made: that it is a sufficient and noble deed for a man if he is able to exercise such care that he himself attains a tested nobility and goodness and that he has, for himself and his household, the daily requisite provisions? But, this being a big [enough] task, to know how to lead other human beings so that they will have all the daily provisions in abundance and so that they will all be such as they should be, that appeared to us then to be an astonishing thing. Yes, by Zeus, father, I remember your saying this; and to me too it seemed a monstrously big task to rule nobly. And even now I am of the same opinion when I consider the matter by examining ruling itself. But whenever, looking at other human beings, I recognize what sort [are able to] continue in rule and what sort of competitors we will have, it seems to me to be very shameful to cower before beings of that sort and not be willing to enter the competition against them. . . . But mark you, son, there are some things where the competition is not with human beings but with the tasks themselves, over which it is not easy to establish a sure superiority.[64]

Cyrus, as opposed to his father, apparently did not regard becoming noble and good oneself, as distinct from ruling other, as a great task. His eagerness to rule others, too, implies his belief that he had already accomplished that much or, at least, already knew quite well what it means to be noble and good. His father, whose remarks throughout the conversation remind us of Socrates, was clearly not so sure. Therefore the father was on Cyrus' *own* behalf more hesitant than Cyrus himself about the advisability of Cyrus' assuming political (or military) responsibility. And it is open to us to wonder whether some later indications of Xenophon as to the inner poverty—against a background of unlimited external splendor and success—of the life of Cyrus as king are not meant to suggest the consequences of his ignoring his father's advice.[65] Surely Xenophon never says of his Cyrus, as he said once of Socrates, "He seemed to me to be himself blessedly happy."[66]

We can now return once more to the question of Xenophon's view of Cyrus' corruption of the peers. We have already remarked, if only by way of a joke, that the fact that Cyrus was a corrupter gives him something in common with Socrates. We are now in a position to see that there was a germ of truth to that remark. For the implicit criticism that his father makes of Cyrus could have been made of virtually any one of the peers educated in old Persia. The peers were convinced that their education was sufficient to make them good;[67] and, in that conviction, they would turn their attention at the "proper" age from their own development to the conduct of public affairs, just as Cyrus was to do. In fact, they were even inferior to Cyrus insofar as he was somewhat more aware than they that what they regarded as virtue was insufficient. Viewed in this light, Cyrus' corruption of the peers, his calling their virtue into question, can be seen as a liberation. And, given the prohibition in old Persia of teaching in the Socratic manner,[68] it may have been the only sort of liberation possible there. Nevertheless, it was surely an incomplete, even an abortive liberation, as such a public effort was bound to be. It earns such sympathy as it receives only by being a dim reflection of the Socratic "corruption" of a few Athenian and foreign youths. That is, it serves to remind us of the question of what a Socratic education consists in.

Xenophon has led us to suspect that Cyrus himself lacked an education of this highest kind. But if, contrary to our earlier expectation, what is most important to know about Cyrus is not the education he received but the one he lacked, what did Xenophon mean to suggest by his title "Cyropaedia" (Education of Cyrus)? Or is it no more than a fit companion to "Cyroanabasis" (Ascent of Cyrus), which refers to the "ascent" or journey up-country that the younger Cyrus did not complete? "Cyropaedia" would thus refer to the education the elder Cyrus did not complete, or call attention to the point at which his education stopped.

MEMORABILIA

As has already been mentioned, there are a number of pointers in the *Cyropaedia* to Socrates, as well as to Xenophon's Socratic writings. The conversation between Cyrus and his father—which among other things includes mention of a teacher who taught justice in the Socratic manner—is one of these. Later on, mention is made of the killing by the Armenian king of his son's teacher, a "sophist" whom the father accused of corrupting the son, that is, of alienating his affection or admiration for his father.[69] We hear also of the dealings of Croesus with the Delphic oracle and Apollo, a god whose displeasure Croesus earned by doubting his veracity.[70] We are perhaps most clearly invited or instructed to compare Cyrus and Socrates by the parallel stories of Panthea and Theodote. When Cyrus was urged by the friend to whom he had entrusted her care to have a look at Panthea, an extremely beautiful captive queen, Cyrus refused out of fear that her beauty would make him so desirous of continuing to look at her that he would neglect what he had to do.[71] When Socrates, on the other hand, was informed of the presence in town of Theodote, a woman whose beauty, according to Socrates' informant, was too great for words to describe, Socrates replied, "Then we must go have a look, for it is not possible for those who [merely] hear to learn what is too great for words to describe."[72] There was no danger of Socrates' being kept from his daily activity by desire to continue to look at Theodote.

The most obvious difference between Cyrus and Socrates is that Socrates never sought or held high political office. At first glance, this difference might not appear to be a very significant one. The reason is that Socrates, as he admitted and even claimed, was a teacher of politics. (To mention only a few pieces of evidence: it was as a teacher of politics, according to the *Memorabilia,* that his two most notorious students, Critias and Alcibiades, sought Socrates out and consorted with him,[73] and that he presented himself to the individual whose education at his hands is given the most attention in the book;[74] in addition, another considerable portion of the book is devoted to Socrates' conversations with actual or would-be political or military leaders.)[75] A critic or rival of Socrates, who wished to steal away his students, once asked him whether his presumed belief that he made others capable of engaging in politics was not discredited by his own abstaining from politics, an abstention hardly in accord with the claim to understanding or knowledge. In his response, Socrates refused to admit that he abstained from politics: "Would I engage in politics more by doing so myself or by taking care that as many as possible be capable of doing so?"[76] Perhaps then he merely pursued by other means the same sort of goal Cyrus pursued, that is, an equally public goal. But did Socrates share the assumption of his critic that anyone who understands politics would want to put that knowledge to use by engaging in politics? And did the education by which he may have made some others more capable of engaging in politics also lead them to wish (or allow them to continue to wish) to do so?

According to Xenophon, Socrates wanted his companions to come to accept what he approved of[77]—which would have been fully possible only in the case of his best students. One of the signs by which he thought he could recognize the youths with the best natures, the ones he most wished to consort with, was their desire to learn everything required for nobly directing a political community.[78] (It is only in the section of the *Memorabilia* devoted to Socrates' conversations with actual or would-be political or military leaders that Xenophon mentions Plato, whom he implicitly but clearly identifies in the context as the student Socrates was most interested in.)[79] Xenophon tells us also that Socrates approached different sorts of youths in different ways, that he adapted his approach to the sort of nature he was dealing with.[80] Presumably then his approach to those with the best natures took into account their noble ambition; and this by itself would have been reason enough for Socratic education to introduce itself to them as an education to politics. The question of where they were led from the political starting point is still a pertinent one, therefore. What is the consequence of Socratic education—the education he acquired himself and that he supplied to some others or prepared them to acquire?

Xenophon presents the Socratic education most fully in the last book of the *Memorabilia*. It is true that he presents it as Socrates had adapted it for the sake of Euthydemus, a youth of an extremely unpromising nature.[81] But by allowing for this, while considering what even the best students have in common with Euthydemus, we may learn something from this presentation of Socrates' teaching, and perhaps especially from the presentation of its beginning. The best students have in common with Euthydemus in the first place a longing for that virtue "through which human beings become capable of engaging in politics . . . and able to rule," that is, for "the noblest virtue and the greatest art," which is called the "royal art." In the second place, since their ambition is a noble one, they share with him a conviction that one cannot become good in these things without being just.[82] Socrates would apparently begin his serious instruction by appealing to that ambition or longing and that conviction. It follows that a knowledge of justice is a prerequisite of fundamental importance to political understanding and political action. But does the youth being addressed possess this knowledge? It is unlikely that the better natures will share Euthydemus' easygoing assumption that it is a simple matter to know what justice is, or, therefore, have anything approaching his naive confidence that he does know it. But will they be entirely free of the belief that they know what justice is? And will their opinions as to what justice is be any more able to withstand Socrates' criticism than Euthydemus' were? [83]

Once this point in a conversation with Socrates has been reached, it is clear to Socrates' better students that nothing could be more important than to investigate what justice is, and to do so with the help of the one who has already performed the invaluable service of revealing the always present, but hitherto unrecognized, need for such an investigation. All thought of engaging in political activity must be postponed until that task is accomplished. But will it be accomplished in any finite period of time? It almost goes without saying that the account of justice given by Socrates in the context of the education of Euthydemus is not fully satisfactory. [84] But is any other Socratic account in Xenophon (or in Plato) fully satisfactory either? Xenophon's Socrates [85] as well as Plato's [86] was notorious for never ceasing, that is, never finishing his investigation of what justice is. The consequence is that the activity of investigation, which was to be merely preliminary to that of engaging in politics, replaces it instead. What pretended to be an education to politics, a means, becomes the end.

The account just sketched of what might have led Socrates or some of his students to turn from a political life to the philosophic life admittedly raises more questions than it answers. One might even find that it constitutes as much a case against philosophy as one for it. For if philosophic investigation is unable to supply an answer to the question of what justice is, why would anyone who feels in his bones the deep and even urgent need for an answer be willing to spend his life in that investigation? But perhaps the Socratic answer to the question is available but not openly expressed, and perhaps in that answer, and in the answers to the apparently related questions of self-knowledge and the good, [87] lies a fuller account of the reasons for the superiority—if such it be—of the philosophic life to the political life. For the sake of Euthydemus, who never objected to an inadequate or defective argument, Socrates saw fit to provide a suitably simplified version or approximation of his views; [88] we are not told by Xenophon what Socrates did at this stage in the case of the best natures. We do not know therefore whether it was not part of his treatment to awaken them to certain fundamental dilemmas which he refused to solve on their behalf, to pose certain questions which he left it to them to answer. [89] What we do know, the rock we have to fall back on in our perplexity, is only this: that an obstacle, which can be called the problem of justice, stands in the way of a reasonable or noble satisfaction with the political life, at least temporarily; and that in seeking to remove it, as we must, we almost inevitably come in contact with another life, which claims to be superior to the political life. As a result, our task becomes not only to find out what justice is but to find out what philosophy is and to look into its claim to constitute the best answer to the question of how to live.

The *Memorabilia* ("Recollections") as a whole is Xenophon's account of his exposure to that other way of life in the person of Socrates. The recollections were written and brought out under something of a cloud. Their hero had been put to death by his fellow Athenians after being convicted on the dual charge of impiety and corrupting the young. In order to begin to see how this fact might have affected Xenophon's manner of writing them, we must make an effort to free ourselves, at least for a moment, from the situation today, when almost no one regards Socrates as having been guilty of a capital crime. Socrates, it is now widely believed, was innocent of the things he was charged with, or, even if he was not entirely innocent, the things he was charged with are not and should not have been treated as crimes.

We must make this effort despite the fact that Xenophon himself, insofar as he was a defender of Socrates' innocence of the charges, is partly responsible for our situation. When Xenophon wrote, general opinion on the question of Socrates' innocence or guilt must still have been mixed. If most of the immediate addressees of his work, those most interested in Socrates, were likely to have been convinced of his innocence, they almost surely had friends or relatives who were not. Nor were the primary addressees necessarily in possession of arguments by which they could have satisfied the doubters—and thus defended the respectability of their own interest in Socrates. It was for Xenophon, therefore, to supply such arguments, not only for his own sake but also for others, actual or potential Socratics. It was necessary for his recollections, as for Plato's dialogues, to take the form of a defense of Socrates. Now there have always been some for whom Xenophon's evidence carries more weight than Plato's: according to Thomas Jefferson, for example, "Of Socrates we have nothing genuine but in the Memorabilia of Xenophon." [90] Xenophon must accordingly share with Plato the credit or responsibility for the great success such defenses have had, a success which has helped to form the current view.

Unless we make the effort referred to, we approach his work under the influence of that view, hence in a particular way. We take for granted its thesis of Socrates' innocence and thus take no special notice of the arrangement and use of arguments and examples by which Xenophon endeavors to support that thesis. We are blind to the artfulness underlying his apparently straightforward discussion because we are no longer aware, as even Socrates' partisans would have been in Xenophon's time, of the strength of the case against Socrates. As a result, we are not sufficiently attentive to the indications Xenophon gives of the sacrifices he had to make in combating that case, of the distortions he had to admit into his account of Socrates in order to make the view that is currently accepted as true prevail.

For example, in the lengthy second chapter of the work, where Xenophon takes up the corruption charge, he quotes a number of specific allegations made against Socrates by his accuser.[91] In each case, the attack is followed by Xenophon's defense of Socrates on the matter in question. Since the defense is clearly meant to dispose of the attack, the impression is given that the specific allegations were entirely unfounded. But, as Xenophon surely knew, his responses did not always meet the attacks head-on or vanquish them in their entirety.

According to the first of these allegations, Socrates made his companions look down upon the established laws and the established (democratic) regime by remarks such as his criticism of the lot as a method of choosing officeholders; and he made his companions violent. To the twofold attack, Xenophon responds that Socrates certainly did not make his companions violent. Even this assertion seems to be cast in doubt by the fact mentioned next by the accuser, that the notoriously violent Critias and Alcibiades had been among those associating with Socrates. Xenophon does not seek to defend the actions of Critias and Alcibiades; nor does he deny their association with Socrates. He simply says that Socrates, with some success, did what he could to make them moderate, while they were under his influence; and that if they turned out badly later on, Socrates is no more to be blamed for this than, say, a decent father whose child turns out badly after leaving home. This is all very well, but it fails to answer the crucial question of whether—given precisely his limited influence on their characters, whose future tendencies were not invisible—Socrates should have supplied Critias and Alcibiades with tools in the form of a political education.

According to the third allegation of the accuser, Socrates taught disrespect for fathers both by persuading his companions that he would make them wiser than their fathers and by an argument to the effect that it was lawful for the more ignorant person to be placed in confinement by the wiser one. Xenophon's denial touches only the point regarding confinement. The fourth allegation therefore repeats the accusation as to Socrates' effect on respect for fathers and extends it to relatives in general and to friends. Here even Xenophon admits, in the course of his response, that Socrates said the things he is alleged to have said about fathers and other relatives as well as friends: some loss of respect for relatives and even friends, as such, seems to be the unavoidable consequence of heightened respect for those who know the needful things and are able to explain them. The final allegation of the accuser states that Socrates made a mischievous use of certain passages in the most highly reputed poets, interpreting, for example, a line from Hesiod to mean that one should abstain from no unjust or shameful deed but do even such things for the sake of gain. Xenophon's response speaks of Socrates' standard as the beneficial or the good; it says nothing about his views on the noble and just.[92]

Once we have become aware of the way in which the *Memorabilia* is written, we are forced to wonder how that manner of writing might have affected the picture of Socratic philosophizing as a whole which it presents. At first glance, Xenophon seems to deny that Socrates ever engaged in what we can call natural philosophy: "Nor did he converse, in the way most of the others did, about the nature of all things, investigating the state of what is called by the sophists the cosmos and by what necessities each of the heavenly things comes into being."[93] Rather, he "was always conversing about the human things, investigating what is pious, what impious, what is noble, what base, what is just, what unjust, what is moderation, what madness, what is courage, what cowardice, what is a state, what a statesman, what is rule of human beings, what a fit ruler of human beings, and about the other things as to which he considered those who knew them to be noble and good, and those ignorant of them to be justly called slavish."[94] But there are other indications, both in the *Memorabilia* itself and in other of the Socratic writings, that Socrates did engage in natural philosophy. On one occasion, Socrates refers to his reputation as a natural philosopher, without objecting to it.[95] He seems to have identified wisdom (which he called the greatest good) with the science of *all* the beings.[96] And he never ceased investigating what *each* of the beings is, perhaps in part through reading and studying the writings of the wise men of old.[97] There is nothing to suggest that the beings in question did not include the heavenly beings, or the writings the works of the so-called pre-Socratic philosophers. In fact, Xenophon indicates quite clearly that Socrates was familiar with the doctrines of those philosophers, mentioning Anaxagoras in particular by name.[98] Even the passages that formed our first impression prove on reexamination to be more qualified than they appeared to be at first. Socrates did not converse about the nature of all things "in the way most of the others did": he may have done so in a different way. He was always conversing about the human things "and about the other things" the knowledge of which he considered to be essential to nobility and goodness (gentlemanship): knowledge of things other than the human things is evidently essential to gentlemanship in the Socratic sense. These two passages occur in the first chapter of the *Memorabilia,* the chapter in which Xenophon takes up the impiety charge. Perhaps his defense of Socrates on that charge *required* a denial of some sort that Socrates engaged in natural philosophy.[99]

To see as clearly as possible why this might have been the case, we must consider what it meant to engage in natural philosophy—both for Socrates himself and for the pre-Socratics whose manner of engaging in it he departed from and criticized. Xenophon guides us toward this consideration by his account of Socrates' criticism of his predecessors.

Socrates criticized his predecessors' doctrines about the nature of all things for their implausibility: "some of them are of the opinion that being is one alone, others that beings are unlimited in multitude; some that everything is always in motion, others that nothing is ever moved; some that everything comes into being and perishes, others that nothing ever comes into being or perishes."[100] Beyond that, he regarded the matters they attempted to elucidate as undiscoverable for human beings.[101] He cannot have meant by this that reason is unable to cast any light at all on the matters in question—the implausible doctrines themselves point to plausible ones (the means between the opposed extremes). He must rather have had in mind that to be in possession even of very plausible doctrines is not yet to have knowledge of those matters. Socrates' own philosophic activity would then have been distinguished from that of at least many of his predecessors by being guided by a greater awareness of its limits.

This is already implied in Xenophon's description of that activity as the attempt to discover what each of the beings is. The aspect of nature we have most access to is the "what," the perceptible character of each of the beings, rather than their unchanging causes (causes which neither come into being nor perish). The perceptible character of each being is always the character of a group or class of beings.[102] As such, it is most visible in speech. In fact, classification, the separating of things into classes or kinds,[103] underlies our speech, our capacity to speak. According to Socrates, "conversing" (*to dialegesthai*) was given its name from the practice of those who come together to deliberate in common by separating (*to dialegein*) matters according to their kinds.[104] We might be tempted to think that knowledge of unchanging classes or kinds or species could simply take the place of knowledge of the unchanging causes. But this would be to ignore the manifest dependence of classes of beings on the existence of those (individual) beings. Xenophon's Socrates never speaks of separately existing "ideas": the classes or kinds are not separate from their members; the characters are always characters of the things possessing them. It is true that the characters are causes of those things, setting limits to them. They share this responsibility, however, with something other than them, something for which they are not responsible and whose existence and nature are guaranteed neither by them nor by anything else we know of. (Socrates may point to this shared responsibility when he calls attention to the dissimilar behavior of things possessing the same perceptible character.) [105] As a result, we cannot know, though we may suspect, that some classes are permanent.

The deepest implication of Socrates' criticism of his philosophic predecessors becomes clear only when we consider more precisely what it was the pre-Socratics were trying to do. They had attempted to discover not merely the state of the cosmos but "the necessities" by which each of the heavenly things comes into being or "the way the god contrives each of the heavenly things" understood as the way he *must* contrive them. [106] Needless to say, they understood the reign of necessity to extend to earthly matters as well. Human prudence and folly, as well as chance, derive from the fundamental necessity and are limited by it. Their most basic contention, the inspiration of the doctrines by which they sought to elaborate and vindicate that contention, was that not just anything can come into being or come to pass but only what accords with or is permitted by the nature of the fundamental cause or causes. But if the fundamental causes are undiscoverable, must one not regard this contention as merely plausible? Yet could Socrates, either as a philosopher or as a human being, leave it an open question whether "just anything" can come to pass?

To spell this out a bit, Socrates may have known of no evidence that would support such a position, that would challenge the philosophers' basic contention. On the contrary, that contention may have been supported by all of the evidence available to him. But while he might reasonably have placed considerable weight on this fact, he would still have had to take into account the assertions of those who do claim to be aware of contrary evidence. The use of divination, for example, implies the claim that a meaningful connection may exist between two events (a sneeze and the future salvation of an army, to take one example from among many in Xenophon's *Anabasis*) that does not stem from the events themselves, the deliberate action of human beings, or chance. [107] Or, to refer to divine punishment for certain misdeeds, as Xenophon does very emphatically in the midst of his *Hellenica,* is to suggest that those deeds had consequences not stemming naturally, so to speak, from the deeds themselves. [108] In particular, it is to deny the validity of the suggestion which seems to be conveyed by the beginning and the ending of the *Hellenica:* that human affairs are drawn out of their usual confusion only when, and so long as, they are directed by human prudence in the form of a competent leader at the helm.[109] Whatever his own view on this question, Xenophon was surely aware of the difficulty confronting his Socrates. To repeat, Socrates may have known of no evidence casting doubt on the basic contention or premise (as distinct from particular doctrines) of his philosophic predecessors. He would have been unable, therefore, to *accept* claims that such evidence exists, claims contradicting what he could see and feel. But neither could he *prove* such claims to be false.

How then did Socrates proceed in this situation? The foregoing may hope to have shown why it was necessary for Xenophon to address this question. Yet his answer to it remains elusive. It is perhaps the most deeply hidden part of his account in the Socratic writings of the philosophic life represented by Socrates.

ANABASIS

We have already mentioned the fact that it was Socrates and not Cyrus whom Xenophon called supremely happy. His account of the Socratic life, in the *Memorabilia* and the other Socratic writings, is thus an account of the actualization of the highest human possibility known to him. Nevertheless, as we have also seen, Xenophon himself did not follow the example of Socrates, at least not in every respect. He left Socrates to join the expedition being organized by the younger Cyrus. And, as he makes clear and even stresses, he did this against Socrates' advice. But this departure from Socrates and the Socratic path does not necessarily signify a profound disagreement. It may signify no more than that Xenophon did not feel himself fully able to follow Socrates' example to the letter. Rather than attempt the impossible and thus be forced to settle for a spuriously exact and therefore somewhat ridiculous imitation,[110] he may have chosen to follow or imitate Socrates more freely, in a manner suited to his own inclinations and abilities. As becomes clear from a reading of his deeds and speeches in the *Anabasis*, Xenophon's inclinations were largely toward politics, and his political ability was of a very high order.

But would this not imply an acceptance on Xenophon's part of a way of life that—in the form in which it had been pursued by its representative par excellence, the elder Cyrus—he clearly rejected? It is tempting to seek to avoid this difficulty by suggesting that Xenophon came to his criticism of the elder Cyrus only after, and perhaps as a result of, his association with the younger one and his own experience of political life. But this suggestion is disposed of by the consideration that his decisive criticism of Cyrus (the one brought out in Cyrus' conversation with his father) was supplied to Xenophon in advance, not by his reflections on Cyrus or politics proper, but by the Socratic education he had already received prior to his entry into politics. We are forced to wonder, therefore, whether Xenophon did not understand and pursue the political life in a somewhat different manner than the elder Cyrus had, or whether there is not a middle course between Socrates and Cyrus which is an eminently fit one to travel. The *Anabasis* seems to have been given the task of demonstrating that this is the case. The foil it furnishes for understanding the differences between Xenophon and the elder Cyrus is the younger Cyrus.

Xenophon calls attention to the similarity, amounting almost to identity, of the two Cyruses by having his Socrates once playfully treat them as the same person.[111] According to both the *Anabasis* and the *Oeconomicus,* the younger Cyrus was the most able political figure to emerge in Persia since the elder Cyrus.[112] Nevertheless, there were several respects in which they were dissimilar. First, the younger Cyrus was an erotic man. At any rate, he had two mistresses, one of whom is said to have been both wise and beautiful, and he is said on a certain occasion to have had sexual relations with a visiting queen.[113] Nothing of this sort is ever mentioned with regard to the elder Cyrus, who was willing to forgo the sight of the beautiful Panthea, made an eminently sensible political marriage (perhaps to an elderly aunt), and was described by his closest Persian associate as a cold king.[114] There may be a connection between this difference and another. Whereas the elder Cyrus, once he reached maturity, never took risks that were not more or less required by his pursuit of empire, the younger Cyrus, catching sight of his brother the king in the midst of their decisive battle, let himself go and immediately attacked him although his own guard was then dispersed—an act which cost him at the same time his life and his all but achieved victory.[115] One might compare this particularly with the elder Cyrus' coolness and caution in connection with the capture of Babylon and the killing of his chief enemy, the king of Assyria.[116] It is true that unlike some of his principal allies the elder Cyrus had not personally suffered any injustice at the hands of the Assyrian, while the younger Cyrus had been grievously wronged by his brother.[117] But this observation does not so much remove the difference between the two that we are discussing as point to what may be its underlying cause. Just as he was more erotic than the elder Cyrus, the younger one may also have been more moved by considerations of justice. It took a wrong to make him act in accord with the ambition he undoubtedly shared with the elder (which is a different matter from finding a justification or pretext for acts one already intended to take for entirely different reasons).[118]

Since the younger Cyrus was known to Xenophon partly from the latter's personal experience,[119] one can say that he was the material out of which Xenophon created *his* Cyrus, the Cyrus of the *Cyropaedia*. The elder Cyrus is an idealized or perfected version of the younger one. In accord with this, the differences between the two first come to sight as defects in the younger, at least from a political point of view. Whether even from this point of view they are always defects can be finally determined only by considering the alternative represented by Xenophon.

Xenophon shared the traits that distinguished the younger Cyrus from his more illustrious predecessor. Like him (and also like his Socrates), he was an erotic man.[120] And he was, to judge at least from the attention his writings give to the problem of justice, no less concerned with justice. But he lacked the younger Cyrus' rashness or defects of judgment. In particular, he never let zeal to avenge a wrong overcome his prudence, even for a moment. To state this point in a manner more Thucydidean than Xenophontic, he knew that the existence of an injustice does not guarantee that the attempt to provide due retribution will meet with success; that our situation may be such as to require us simply to bear an unavenged wrong.[121] At the time of his leading the Greek force that had belonged to the younger Cyrus back to Greece, and indeed for the larger part of Xenophon's adult life, such wrongs were more likely than not to have been committed by Spartan hands. For Sparta's defeat of Athens in the twenty-seven-year Peloponnesian War had replaced the balance of power between the two great powers, which had prevailed in Greece for upwards of seventy-five years, with undisputed Spartan ascendancy.[122] And as Xenophon shows in both the *Anabasis* and the *Hellenica*—without departing from his customary restraint but with perfect clarity—the Spartan rule was in general distinguished by neither wisdom nor gentleness. As a political leader, Xenophon was forced to adapt himself to this situation and to induce those he led to do so. Among the most impressive passages in the *Anabasis* are the speeches in which he instructs his fellow Greeks on the necessity of compliance with certain Spartan demands that are far from just or reasonable and, in general, on the necessity of accommodating themselves to "those who now rule Greece."[123] Readers who are at all sensitive to how harsh political necessity can occasionally be may also find in Xenophon the writer, in his treatment of the Spartans, a model of how to proceed under like circumstances. He applauded and thus encouraged what was good, while pointing out without rancor or bitterness what was bad, to the extent that it was prudent and useful to do so. To return to what distinguished him from the elder and younger Cyruses, the high qualities which in the case of the two Persians (that is, barbarians) could be prevented from doing political harm only by being suppressed, or excised from the soul, could safely thrive in Xenophon, who had had the benefit of a Socratic education, an education that those qualities among others fitted him to receive.

The result was not only his ability to match the elder Cyrus on the plane of cool political calculation, hindered neither by the eros he had nor by the misguided zeal he lacked, but also the grace and dignity his whole stance toward politics derived from an inner freedom not shared by Cyrus. Xenophon too was "ambitious": he was tempted by the prospect of becoming sole commander of Cyrus' Greek army, and he aspired to become founder of a new Greek city on the shores of the Black Sea.[124] But whereas Cyrus wanted his praises to be sung by all human beings, Xenophon was concerned primarily with honor from his friends.[125] Unlike Cyrus, he was not as eager for praise from incompetent judges as from competent ones. This difference helps us to understand his equanimity in the face of the most varied political fortunes: for example, the dignity and wit with which he defended himself when confronted with ingratitude and baseless hostility on the part of the very men whose lives he had saved.[126] It helps us also to understand his ability to leave political life to return to a private life. When there was some good to be done by his leadership both for himself and for others, or some pressing need, he acted with supreme determination and ingenuity to accomplish the task or meet the need. When no more could be done, at least by him—that is, when there was nothing useful to accomplish—he stepped aside. But then his education had not left him entirely unequipped for leading a private life. Country retirement, while lacking the immediate challenges to heart and mind presented by politics at their peak, would have appealed to him as allowing more leisure for contemplation and writing—especially since that contemplation might embrace, as we know from the *Anabasis* that it did, his own political experiences among other things. For a man like Xenophon, the contemplative reliving of experiences was sure to be a deepening of them. It could thus have been looked forward to as promising a more profound enjoyment than the original experiences themselves, and one less mixed with pain.

NOTES

1. *Anabasis* V 3.7–13.

2. *Oeconomicus* 21.10; 4.4; 13.5.

3. *Memorabilia* III 5.15–16. The testimony comes from the son of the great Pericles, author of Athens's anti-Spartan policy.

4. *Oeconomicus* 5 and 11.

5. *Cyropaedia* I 3.16–17.

6. The *Oeconomicus* includes the report of an extensive conversation between Socrates and a perfect gentleman, which culminates in a comparison of

their two ways of life. The conversation is brought about by Socrates, and all of the questions which animate it proceed from him and serve his desire to learn about the gentleman.

7. *Anabasis* III 1.4–8; *Hellenica* I 7.15 and context (compare *Memorabilia* I 1.17–18 and IV 4.1–2); *Cyropaedia* I 6.31–34; III 1.14, and 1.38–40; VII 2.15–25.

8. *Memorabilia* I 3.8–13; *Anabasis* III 1.4–8.

9. See, for example, *Laws* 658ᵈ2–4 and *Meno* 76ᵉ3–7. See Shaftesbury's *Characteristics,* I, 167 and 309 (Indianapolis: Bobbs-Merrill, 1964), for the view of one who preferred Xenophon to Plato on this ground.

10. *Cyropaedia* I 1.6.

11. *Ibid.,* I 2.1, 3.1–3, 4.24.

12. The comparative mildness of his rule depended in part on the claim to legitimacy, which he was always at pains to maintain, afforded by his birth. Consider especially VIII 5.17–20, 5.26, 5.28, and VII 5.37 ff.

13. *Ibid.,* I 2.6 ff.; compare *Constitution of the Spartans* 2.6 ff. as well as *Anabasis* IV 6.14.

14. *Cyropaedia* I 2.2–3.

15. *Ibid.,* I 2.15.

16. Consider, among other passages, *ibid.,* I 1.6, 2.2, 3.1, 5.7–13; II 1.3; III 3.50–55, 3.70; IV 2.38–46, 5.1–4, 5.54; V 2.15–20; VII 5.70; VIII 8.15.

17. Compare *ibid.,* I 2.2 with 3.1, 3.13–18, 4.1, 4.25, and 5.1

18. *Ibid.,* VII 5.85.

19. For reference to the *Cyropaedia* in particular, see *Prince* 14 and 16, and *Discourses* II 13; III 20, 22, and 39.

20. *Cyropaedia* I 3.2–3; compare VIII 1.40–41 and 3.1–14.

21. *Ibid.,* I 3.3, 3.15, 4.4–5; compare IV 3 and VIII 3.16 and 3.25.

22. *Ibid.,* I 3.4; compare I 5.12; IV 2.38–47, 5.1–7; V 2.14–21, 3.34–35; VI 2.25–29; but also VIII 2.1–7.

23. *Ibid.,* I 3.10–11; compare VIII 4.9–15.

24. *Ibid.,* I 6.8; compare 3.18.

25. Consider *ibid.,* I 3.16–18 with VIII 1.22, and Aristotle, *Politics* 1269ᵃ8–12, 1286ᵃ9–16.

26. *Cyropaedia* VIII 5.26; compare I 3.18.

27. *Ibid.,* I 2.3–5.

28. Consider *ibid.,* VI 1.4.

29. *Ibid.,* IV 5.16.

30. *Ibid.,* VIII 5.

31. Compare *ibid.,* I 3.18 with VII 5.37 ff., VIII 1.1–5, and especially 3.13–14; compare *Anabasis* III 2.13.

32. *Cyropaedia* I 2.15.

33. *Ibid.,* II 1.3

34. Consider the fact that the additional force sent to Cyrus by the Persian authorities, when they decided to comply with his request for reinforcements, was composed of forty thousand commoners and no peers: V 5.3.

35. *Cyropaedia* II 1.2–10.

36. *Ibid.,* I 5.7–14.

37. Consider the remarks of Aglaitadas (a man of whom we hear nothing further) at II 2.11–16.

38. *Cyropaedia* II 1.10–12.

39. It was due to the suggestion of a helpful peer, apparently acting on his own initiative, that Cyrus himself was the one who presented the arms to the commoners: II 1.12–14. This is the first of many such "helps" Cyrus received in the course of his rise. Needless to say, those who showed such initiative were not forgotten: see VIII 4.11 and context.

40. *Cyropaedia* I 2.15.

41. Consider *ibid.,* II 1.19; compare VII 5.67.

42. *Ibid.,* II 1.15 ff.

43. *Ibid.,* II 2.17–21, 3.1–16.

44. *Ibid.,* II 2.26; compare I 6.27–34.

45. In speaking of Cyrus' manifest qualities, we do not mean to deny what

Machiavelli delights to point out, that the judicious use of qualities of a different sort was almost equally necessary to Cyrus' success. (See note 19 above.) Xenophon, too, of course, lets us see those other qualities and their importance to Cyrus, though only in a manner consistent with the principle he enunciates in the *Anabasis* (V 8.26), that "it is noble as well as just and pious, and more pleasant, to remember (or mention) the good things rather than the bad." That is, he did not entirely forgo the pleasure of mentioning the bad things.

46. *Cyropaedia* I 2.6–7, 3.16–17.
47. *Ibid.,* I 2.12, 6.20.
48. *Ibid.,* I 1.
49. *Ibid.,* VIII 8.
50. *Ibid.,* VIII 1.6–8.
51. *Ibid.,* VII 5.58–70.
52. *Ibid.,* VIII 2.10–12.
53. *Ibid.,* VIII 1.40–42, 3.1–24.
54. *Ibid.,* VIII 4.3–5, 4.9–12.
55. *Ibid.,* VIII 1.16–20 and 2.15–19.
56. *Ibid.,* VIII 1.45–48, 2.26–28, 4.3; compare V 2.7–12.
57. *Ibid.,* VIII 8.15.
58. Compare *ibid.,* III 3.51–55 with I 5.7–10.
59. This is revealed especially in the increased reliance on technical innovations and in the changing role of the rearguard officers. Compare III 3.41–42 with VI 3.27; and see VI 1.27–30, 1.50–55, and VII 1.33–35.
60. *Ibid.,* VII 5.85–86; VIII 1.10–12, 1.16–33. Of the products of this education, Xenophon says, "Seeing them there [at the palace gates] you would have thought that they really lived with a view to what is noble."
61. *Cyropaedia* VIII 5.22–28; compare VI 1.4.
62. *Ibid.,* I 3.18 and context.
63. Compare *ibid.,* VIII 5.24.
64. *Ibid.,* I 6.7–9 and context.
65. Xenophon has little to say about the life of Cyrus once his conquests are completed: see VIII 6.19–7.2. One

might compare here the sort of dinner parties that formed around Cyrus (VIII 4) with the sort that formed around Socrates (Xenophon's *Symposium* as a whole). One might also consider the prominence the *Cyropaedia* gives to eros and the "two souls" theme, that is, to the question of what constitutes the harmony or health of the soul: see V 1.2–18; VI 1.31–51, 3.34–37, 4.2–11; VII 1.15–18, 1.29–32, and 3.2–16; compare VIII 2.20–21 and 7.6.
66. *Memorabilia* I 6.14.
67. *Cyropaedia* I 2.15; compare 2.5.
68. *Ibid.,* I 6.31–33; compare *Memorabilia* IV 2.11–20.
69. *Cyropaedia* III 1.14 and 1.38–40; compare *Memorabilia* I 2.49–55.
70. *Cyropaedia* VII 2.15–29; compare *Apology of Socrates* 14–15 as well as Plato, *Apology of Socrates* 21ᵇ3–ᶜ2.
71. *Cyropaedia* V 1.2–8 ff.
72. *Memorabilia* III 11.1 ff.
73. *Ibid.,* I 2.12–48.
74. *Ibid.,* IV 2.1–7.
75. *Ibid.,* III 1–7.
76. *Ibid.,* I 6.15, 6.1
77. *Ibid.,* I 2.8.
78. *Ibid.,* IV 1.2.
79. *Ibid.,* III 6.1.
80. *Ibid.,* IV 1.3.
81. He belongs to the most foolish of the classes described in IV 1.
82. *Memorabilia* IV 2.11; compare IV 1.2.
83. Consider *ibid.,* IV 2.12–20.
84. *Ibid.,* IV. 4; compare especially I 2.40–46.
85. *Symposium* 4.1; compare *Memorabilia* I 1.16; IV 4.5, 8.4.
86. See the *Clitophon* as a whole; also *Republic* 354ᵇ⁻ᶜ and 368ᵇ4–ᶜ3, 435ᶜ 8–ᵈ5 (and context) and 611ᵃ10–612ᵃ6.
87. *Memorabilia* IV 2.21–36; compare the topics taken up in III 9.
88. *Ibid.,* IV 2.40 ff.; compare IV 6.13–15.
89. Compare *ibid.,* III 11.14 (and context) and II 6.28.
90. Letter to William Short in *The*

Life and Selected Writings of Thomas Jefferson (New York: Modern Library, 1944), 694.

91. *Memorabilia* I 2.9, 2.12, 2.49, 2.51–52, 2.56, and 2.58.

92. Compare Plato, *Hipparchus,* as well as *Memorabilia* I 2.54.

93. *Memorabilia* I 1.11; for the use of the term "natural philosophy" compare "inquiry concerning nature," Plato, *Phaedo* 96ª8.

94. *Memorabilia,* I 1.16.

95. *Oeconomicus* 11.3; compare *Symposium* 6.6–7.4.

96. *Memorabilia* IV 5.6, 6.7.

97. *Ibid.,* IV 6.1; I 6.14.

98. *Ibid.,* I 1.14; IV 7.5–7.

99. Consider *ibid.,* IV 7.6 and *Symposium* 6.6–8 as well as Plato, *Laws* 966ᶜ4–967ª8 and *Apology of Socrates* 18ᵇ6–ᶜ3.

100. *Memorabilia* I 1.14; compare IV 7.6–7.

101. *Ibid.,* I 1.13 and IV 7.6.

102. *Ibid.,* IV 6.

103. *Ibid.,* IV 5.11 and *Oeconomicus* 9.6 ff.

104. *Memorabilia* IV 5.12.

105. *Symposium* 7.4.

106. *Memorabilia* I 1.11 and IV 7.6.

107. *Anabasis* III 2.9; compare *Memorabilia* I 1.3–4; IV 7.10; I 1.6–9, 1.19.

108. *Hellenica* V 4.1; compare *Anabasis* II 6.21–29.

109. *Hellenica* I 1.1–15; VII 5.26–27.

110. Consider Xenophon's portrait of Antisthenes in the *Symposium.*

111. *Oeconomicus* 4.16–18.

112. *Anabasis* I 9.1; *Oeconomicus* 4.18.

113. *Anabasis* I 10.2–3, 2.12.

114. *Cyropaedia* V 1.2–18; VIII 5.28, 4.22.

115. *Anabasis* I 8.21–29.

116. *Cyropaedia* VII 5.20–34.

117. *Anabasis* I 1.1–4; compare *Cyropaedia* IV 6.2 ff.; V 2.27 f., 4.35 f.

118. Compare *Cyropaedia* I 5.7–13, VII 5.72–73 and 5.76–77.

119. *Anabasis* III 1.8–9; I 9.1.

120. *Anabasis* VII 3.20; V 3.10; *Memorabilia* I 3.8–15; compare *Symposium* 8.2 as well as *Memorabilia* II 6.28.

121. Thucydides, *The Peloponnesian War* IV 62.4; compare *Anabasis* V 1.15 and II 6.21–29 in light of V 8.26; compare *Cyropaedia* V 4.35.

122. Sparta had supposedly fought the war to free the Greek cities from actual or impending "enslavement" by the Athenian empire. (See, for example, Thucydides, *The Peloponnesian War,* II 8.4.) Toward the beginning of his *Hellenica,* Xenophon tells us that after Athens's final defeat, her "long walls" were torn down to the music of flute girls and with the general expectation that that day would be the beginning of freedom for Greece (II 2.23). The rest of the *Hellenica* shows how mistaken that expectation was.

123. *Anabasis* VI 6.8–16 and VII 1.25–31; compare III 2.37 and VI 1.26–28.

124. *Ibid.,* VI 1.19–21; V 6.15–16 (compare VI 4.1–8).

125. *Cyropaedia* III 2.31; *Anabasis* VI 1.20.

126. *Anabasis* VII 6.11 ff.; compare V 7.5 ff. and 8.2 ff.

READINGS

A. Xenophon, *Cyropaedia* and *Memorabilia.*
B. Xenophon, *Anabasis.*

ARISTOTLE

384 – 322 B.C.

Aristotle was born in the town of Stagira, in the Chalcidic peninsula of northern Greece. His father was the personal physician of Amyntas III of Macedon, and a close association with the Macedonian royal house and its political fortunes was to shape importantly both Aristotle's own career and the history of the philosophical school which he founded. As a young man, Aristotle was sent to Athens to pursue his education. There he encountered Plato, and he remained a member of the Academy until the end of Plato's life. After a period during which he is said (though the story may be apocryphal) to have acted as tutor to Alexander the Great, Aristotle returned to Athens and established his own school, the Lyceum, dedicated to research and teaching in every area of human knowledge. Following the death of Alexander and the subsequent rebellion of the Greek cities against Macedonian hegemony, Aristotle was forced to leave Athens once again—as he is supposed to have remarked, lest the Athenians sin a second time against philosophy. He died shortly thereafter.

Of the vast number of works ascribed to Aristotle in antiquity, only a portion survives today. Following the lead of his teacher, Aristotle apparently composed dialogues intended for a general audience, many of them on political subjects; except for a few fragmentary citations, nothing remains of these. The surviving works are principally treatises which are thought to have been prepared in connection with Aristotle's research and teaching activities. Aristotle's political teaching is available to us primarily in the *Politics* and the *Nicomachean Ethics*. Two other treatises, the *Eudemian Ethics* and the *Magna Moralia,* cover much of the same ground as the *Nicomachean Ethics,* but are of lesser interest; the relationship between these three works remains highly uncertain. Mention should also be made of the *Rhetoric,* which contains a unique discussion of political psychology as well as important reflections on the relationship between rhetoric and politics, and the *Constitution of Athens,* the only surviving example of a collection of constitutional histories of Greek cities compiled by Aristotle and his pupils.

Aristotle's writings tend to be approached generally as straight-forward attempts to present a purely scientific or theoretical account of their subject matter. Yet it is far from clear that the ethical and political treatises can be safely viewed in this light. Aristotle indicates that there is a fundamental difference between "theoretical" sciences, which are pursued for the sake of knowledge, and "practical" sciences, which are pursued principally for the sake of the benefits deriving from them. Politics is for Aristotle the "practical" science par excellence. It is necessary at the outset to understand the scope and intention of practical or political science as Aristotle conceives it, both for the sake of a proper appreciation of the literary character of Aristotle's ethical and political writings and in order to grasp the problematic role in Aristotle's thought of political philosophy as such.

THEORY AND PRACTICE

While the distinction between theoretical and practical science is nowhere systematically developed by Aristotle, it would appear that these modes of knowledge differ fundamentally in their method and the intellectual faculty they engage as well as in their objects and purpose. The objects of theoretical science are things not subject to change, or things of which the principle of change lies in themselves; its method is analysis of the principles or causes of these things; its purpose is demonstrative knowledge; and its faculty is the scientific or theoretical portion of the rational part of the soul. The theoretical sciences recognized by Aristotle include metaphysics or theology, mathematics, physics, biology, and psychology. Practical science, by contrast, is concerned exclusively with man, or with man in his capacity as a self-conscious being or a source of "action" (*praxis*); because or to the extent that it depends on human volition, human action is essentially subject to change. The purpose of practical science is not knowledge but the betterment of action; its proper faculty is the calculative or practical segment of the rational part of the soul, or what Aristotle terms "practical wisdom" or "prudence" (*phronēsis*).[1] As for the method of practical science, Aristotle appears to conceive it as a mode of analysis designed less to discover the principles or causes than to articulate the phenomena of human action—in large part, through a dialectical examination and refinement of men's opinions concerning those phenomena.[2]

Aristotle's frequent reliance throughout his political writings on dialectical argumentation—that is, on a quasi-conversational mode of inquiry that begins from premises embedded in common opinion—reveals a kinship in spirit if not form with the Platonic dialogue. Like Plato and the Platonic Socrates, Aristotle locates the proper beginning point of political philosophy in the language and opinions of ordinary men. He does not proceed by deduction from immutable principles of human nature; nor does he attempt to establish a logically rigorous technical vocabulary that is remote from actual political life. Part of the reason for this lies in Aristotle's insistence that the same precision is not to be sought in the practical or political sphere as in the theoretical sciences. Human things are inherently variable, and to approach them in the spirit of the physicist or mathematician seeking to discover universal laws is to distort fundamentally the relevant phenomena. The kind of reasoning that is appropriate in dealing with political matters is closer to the practical or prudential reasoning of the ordinary citizen, rooted as it is in the particulars of everyday experience, than to the deductive reasoning of the scientist or philosopher. These considerations, it may be added, go some way toward refuting the view commonly held today that Aristotle's political science is invalidated by its association with an outmoded teleological or metaphysical natural science.

But Aristotle's procedure also reflects his understanding of the purpose of practical science. Precisely because it is in the service of action, practical science must be centrally concerned with the presentation of its subject in a way that will engage the opinions and affect the behavior of ordinary political men. Aristotle's practical science is directed not to philosophers or students of philosophy, or not principally to them, but to political men. More precisely, it is directed to educated political men who are actual or potential wielders of political power or, in the best case, to the "legislator" who creates the constitutional framework within which all political action occurs.[3]

This is not to say that Aristotle's practical science is entirely unrelated to his theoretical science. In several passages, Aristotle indicates that "theoretical philosophy" will have a place in his political writings wherever it is proper to the inquiry,[4] and he makes frequent use of assumptions deriving from theoretical psychology in particular. Equally clear, however, is Aristotle's reluctance to establish practical science on a visibly theoretical foundation. This is at least partly due to his feeling that political men are unduly susceptible to the influence of theoretical arguments about politics put forward by intellectuals—he appears to think primarily of the sophists—who lack all practical understanding or capacity (*EE* 1.6.1217ª1–6). To the extent that the prudence of political men is constantly threatened by unsound theoretical arguments or opinions, practical science would appear to stand in some need of theoretical science; but this very fact underlines the importance of safeguarding the autonomy of the practical sphere.

On the one occasion when he uses the term "political philosophy,"[5] Aristotle does so in a way that suggests that it is foreign to the inquiry he undertakes in the existing ethical and political writings. Aristotle appears to understand the inquiry of the *Politics* and the *Nicomachean Ethics* as a form of "political expertise" or "political science" (*politikē*). But does this mean that Aristotle recognizes "political philosophy" as a distinct discipline independent of "political science"?

At first sight, one is tempted to suppose that Aristotle denies altogether the possibility of a theoretical political philosophy, given his view of the variability of human things and the impossibility of precision in the study of them. On the other hand, it is obviously incorrect to see in Aristotle's approach a foreshadowing of the modern distinction between nature as the realm of necessity and human affairs as the realm of history or freedom. It is true that Aristotle distinguishes between the natural and the human things.[6] But this distinction is itself theoretically imprecise, because man remains, for Aristotle, emphatically a part of nature, or because he possesses a "nature" which displays significant regularities amid the flux of human affairs. That the principles or causes of human action are susceptible of theoretical treatment in some sense would seem to follow. Accordingly, the possibility must at least be considered that Aristotle's political writings are in their own way as radically ironic as those of Plato—that they deliberately withhold Aristotle's final or most fundamental reflections on man.

The most extensive treatment of the scope of practical or political science occurs in the sixth book of the *Nicomachean Ethics*. There Aristotle indicates that practical science is in a sense coextensive with both political science and prudence. Practical or political science in this broad sense has three branches: ethics, or the science of character; economics, or the science of household management; and political science in its narrower and more familiar sense, the science of governing the political community. It is of critical importance to recognize that ethics forms an integral part of political science in its broad sense, and that Aristotle's ethical writings are evidently conceived not as independent treatises but as prolegomena to a study of politics. Any discussion of Aristotelian political science would therefore be incomplete without extended attention to the teaching of the ethical treatises and the relationship of that teaching to the *Politics*.

HAPPINESS, VIRTUE, AND GENTLEMANSHIP

"Every art and inquiry, and similarly every action and intentional choice, is held to aim at some good." The very first sentence of the *Nicomachean Ethics* reflects Aristotle's concern to establish the scope and dignity of political science. Just as all our actions aim ultimately at a determinate end, which is desired for its own sake rather than for the sake of anything beyond itself, so the various arts and sciences can be understood as being ultimately subordinate to a single master science, which encompasses the comprehensive human good. But this master science is evidently political expertise or political science (*politikē*). For it is political expertise that "makes a determination as to which sciences are needed in cities, which are to be learned by which sorts of persons, and up to what point; and we see that even the capacities most held in honor are subordinate to it, such as generalship, household management, and rhetoric. Since it uses the other sciences, and since it legislates as to what should be done and what avoided, its end would encompass those of the others, and this would be the human good" (*NE* 1.2. 1094ᵃ28–ᵇ7). The dignity of political expertise is reflected as much in the authority it exercises over all forms of human knowledge, it seems, as in its role in legislation. That a concern for the human good inevitably involves consideration of law and the city is initially taken for granted by Aristotle: even if the good of the individual and the good of the city are the same, that of the city is evidently greater, nobler, or more complete. "These are the things aimed at by our inquiry, which is thus a sort of political expertise" (*NE* 1.2. 1094ᵇ7–11). The good, or the good life, for men individually and for the political community is the overarching theme of Aristotelian political science.

Aristotle begins his inquiry by pursuing the question of the nature of the comprehensive human good. He has little difficulty identifying this good as well-being or "happiness" (*eudaimonia*). When it comes to specifying the content of happiness, however, it appears that there is disagreement, both among ordinary people and between ordinary people and "the wise" (intellectuals or philosophers); indeed, there are people who identify happiness with different things at different times, according to their preoccupation of the moment. Yet Aristotle does not draw the conclusion, characteristic of modern liberal thought, that happiness (as distinct from the instruments or conditions of happiness) is therefore fundamentally subjective or resistant to politically useful definition. Aristotle is satisfied that there is in fact a large measure of agreement as to the nature of happiness, and that the disagreements regarding it are non-arbitrary reflections of fundamental aspects of the human condition. For Aristotle, there are essentially three ways of life available to human beings: the life of pleasure, the political life, and the theoretical or philosophical life. A life centering on the pleasures of the body is the life led by most men—by many of those favored by fortune as well as by ordinary persons. Men of a more "refined" sort, on the other hand, hold honor to be the end of life and seek it through the display of their virtue in political action. Finally, a few men pursue the pleasures deriving from pure intellectual activity (*NE* 1.4. 1095ª 14–26).

Contrary to what one might expect, Aristotle does not undertake to adjudicate this dispute. He merely dismisses the claim of the life of pleasure; and he proceeds to elaborate a definition of happiness which seems deliberately intended to blur the difference between the political and the theoretical life. This is entirely characteristic of Aristotle's approach: shortly before, he had indicated that his proper auditor is a person well brought up in his habits and not dominated by passion (*NE* 1.3. 1095ª2– 11). In effect, Aristotle adopts the perspective of political or practical men, or of men of this sort who are "refined" as a result of their upbringing and education.

It would be a mistake to conclude that the approach is therefore a closed or circular one, or that Aristotle simply identifies himself with the perspective of the educated or upper-class Greek. Apart from the distinct suggestion that his auditor is apt to be more concerned for the honor to be won in political life than for the virtue that merits it, Aristotle by no means ignores the alternatives of pleasure and philosophy, which emerge as major themes in the later books of the treatise. Indeed, the structure of the *Nicomachean Ethics* as a whole may be said to have the character of an ascent from the perspective of ordinary political or practical men to a perspective informed by philosophy, which is presented in Book X as a pursuit decisively superior to the pursuits of the practical life (*NE* 10.7–9).

In seeking a definition of happiness that will command broad agreement, Aristotle steps back momentarily from the commonly expressed opinions regarding happiness to the more general and theoretical issue of the nature of man and his proper work or function (*ergon*). What is distinctive about man is his rational soul, in the double form of an element that possesses reason or thinks and an element that is obedient to reason. The proper function of man is therefore the putting-to-work or activity (*energeia*) of the soul in accordance with reason, or rather the most excellent form of such activity. Happiness or the human good can be defined, then, as activity of the soul in accordance with excellence or virtue (*aretē*) and, if there are several virtues, in accordance with the best and most perfect (*NE* 1.6.1097^{b}22–98^{a}18).

Aristotle denies emphatically that there is a conflict between happiness so defined and pleasure: those who habitually perform virtuous or noble actions take pleasure in doing so, for such actions are pleasant by nature. Nevertheless, the link between virtue and happiness is qualified in several important respects. Aristotle admits that it is difficult or impossible to act virtuously or to attain happiness without a modicum of "external goods." These include not only some amount of wealth, friends, and political power, but also children, good birth, and even good looks: "a man who is very ugly in appearance or ill-born or who lives by himself and has no children is not apt to be particularly happy, and perhaps still less someone whose children and friends are thoroughly vicious or were good but have died" (*NE* 1.8.1099^{b}3–6). Aristotle wrestles at length with the question whether a good man exposed to extreme suffering can in any sense be considered happy, and he acknowledges the common view that in the final analysis happiness is the plaything of fortune or a gift of the gods (*NE* 1.9.1099^{b}9– 1100^{a}9). While he rejects such notions, Aristotle is clearly alive to those aspects of the human situation that necessarily limit any individual or collective effort to secure happiness. He appears to find no merit in an alternative that would concentrate on securing the material conditions of happiness in preference to fostering the virtues that are constitutive of happiness as he understands it. At least part of the reason for this would seem to lie in Aristotle's conviction (shared by all political thinkers of classical antiquity) that wealth is less important as an external condition of happiness than human relationships, which are critically dependent on virtue. This conviction in turn reflects Aristotle's fundamental view that man is by nature a social or political animal.

Just as the human soul is divided between a rational element and an element capable of obeying reason, so virtue or excellence is twofold. To the rational part of the soul belong the intellectual virtues, which are acquired (to the extent that they are acquired) principally through speech or teaching. To the nonrational part—the part of the soul that is the locus of passion or emotion—belong the moral or ethical virtues, the virtues associated with "character" (*ēthos*). According to Aristotle, the moral virtues come to be in men neither by nature nor contrary to nature: men have a natural potential to develop them, but actually doing so requires habituation. The moral virtues are similar to the arts in the way they are acquired, for men learn to become good by performing good actions, just as a carpenter learns his trade by practicing it (*NE* 1.13–2.1). As will be seen, the requirement for habituation in the actions of virtue lends a great importance in Aristotle's eyes to education, and to its proper management by the political authorities.

Aristotle's complex presentation of the characteristics and types of moral virtue cannot be followed here in detail; but several points should particularly be noted. First, while moral virtue may be said to involve reason, it is not something essentially rational. It is, rather, a characteristic attitude or disposition toward emotions and the actions that flow from them. According to Aristotle's formal definition, virtue is a disposition involving intentional choice and directed toward observance of a "mean" between vicious extremes. This mean cannot be precisely defined in the abstract but is determined by reason in accordance with the particular circumstances of the case. The role of reason in moral action is, then, largely if not purely an instrumental one. Although moral action, in order to be truly moral, must be a result of choice, the choice in question is not assumed to involve a process of rational calculation of the advantages and liabilities of acting morally. Rather, as Aristotle repeatedly emphasizes, it is of the essence of moral behavior that the actions of virtue be performed for their own sake rather than for the sake of their consequences. It is thus a fundamental error to ascribe to Aristotle what would today be called a "utilitarian" conception of morality. The good man is not guided in all his actions by a calculation that honesty is the best policy or that every virtuous deed contributes to his own happiness.

Aristotle's general view is well illustrated by his treatment of the virtue of courage (*NE* 3.6–9), which is a test case for any utilitarian understanding of morality. The courageous man is one who habitually chooses the mean between cowardice and rashness, particularly in situations involving the risk of sudden death in battle. Aristotle distinguishes carefully, however, between the man who performs courageous deeds for their own sake and one who does so solely out of regard for the opinions of his fellow citizens—that is, out of a sense of shame and a desire for honor; courage of this sort is only "political courage," not courage simply. He also refuses to recognize as genuine courage the actions of a man motivated primarily by anger or a spirited temper. What is most striking, however, is Aristotle's failure in the course of his analysis even to allude to the requirement of preservation of the city or to the motive of patriotism. Nothing is so revealing, it may be added, of the critical difference between Aristotle's conception of civic virtue and that of the tradition of modern republicanism.

Aristotle's intention emerges with particular clarity in a passage in the *Eudemian Ethics*. He there distinguishes between two sorts of virtuous men, the "good man" (*agathos*), who acts virtuously for the sake of acquiring the naturally good things of life (*i.e.,* primarily wealth and honors), and the "noble and good man" (*kaloskagathos*), who performs the actions of virtue for their own sake, or because they are noble. To the first category, it appears, belong the Spartans, the most conspicuous exemplars of virtue for most Greeks (*EE* 8.1.1248^{b}8–49^{a}17). In an earlier passage of the same work, Aristotle indicates that the majority of "political men" are "good men" in this sense, while denying their right to be called such: "for the political man is one who chooses to perform fine actions for their own sake, but the majority of them take up this sort of life for profit and personal aggrandizement" (*EE* 1.5.1216^{a}23–27). It would appear that Aristotle's conception of moral virtue, so far from merely ratifying contemporary opinions, is intended in some measure as a deliberate challenge to them.

The term used by Aristotle to designate the man of moral and political virtue in the strict sense is borrowed from contemporary political discourse, where it carried a strongly aristocratic flavor; it is probably best translated "gentleman." Aristotle does not employ the term in a narrowly political sense, but the political reality to which it refers is highly relevant for understanding properly the rhetorical strategy as well as much of the specific argumentation of the ethical and political treatises. Nothing so clearly reveals Aristotle's view of the strengths and limitations of aristocratic morality as his incomparable description, in Book IV of the *Nicomachean Ethics,* of the virtues of "magnificence" (*megaloprepeia*) and "greatness of soul" (*megalopsychia*), the virtues dealing respectively with great wealth and great honors (*NE* 4.2–3). In spite of the presumed rarity of the type, the great-souled man is a critical element in Aristotle's overall analysis, both because of his potential political role and because of what he reveals about the nature of moral virtue simply. From the standpoint of the city, the great-souled man is invaluable by the fact that he is capable of rendering the greatest services, yet is satisfied to see his virtue rewarded with honor alone, not to say that he is finally somewhat disdainful of the honor the city has it in its power to bestow. For similar reasons, however, such men tend to maintain an uneasy detachment from the city, and under certain circumstances can even become a menace to it, as the examples of Achilles and Alcibiades suffice to show. From the standpoint of morality, it appears that greatness of soul in a sense encompasses all the virtues: the great-souled man performs the actions of the virtues in the fullness of his pride, or because he disdains the goods or pleasures for the sake of which men act basely. Greatness of soul, Aristotle concludes, "is thus, as it were, the crown of the virtues; it magnifies them and cannot exist without them"; it thus presupposes at the same time as it perfects the quality of gentlemanship.

JUSTICE AND FRIENDSHIP

If greatness of soul may be said to constitute the peak of moral virtue from the point of view of the individual, justice constitutes the peak of moral virtue from the point of view of the city. In its most general sense, justice is what produces and preserves happiness for the political community, and hence is virtually identical with law-abidingness, since the laws aim to secure the common good of the city by making pronouncements regarding every sphere of human life. Because, or to the extent that, the laws enjoin the actions of all the virtues, justice is complete or perfect virtue, insofar as virtue is exercised in relation to other men (*NE* 5.1.1129ª3–30ª1).

If, as it seems, greatness of soul is a quality that stands in some tension with the requirements of the city, justice in Aristotle's presentation does not satisfy in an obvious way the requirements of the individual. In sharp contrast to the procedure of Plato in the *Republic*, Aristotle does not probe the weak points in the common understanding of justice, or attempt to demonstrate that justice—which, as he admits, "alone of the virtues is held to be the good of another" (*NE* 5.1.1130ª3–4)—is in fact choiceworthy for its own sake. But Aristotle's decision to respect the ambiguities that surround the common understanding of justice involves by the same token a certain depreciation of justice as a motive for political action and an element of political analysis.

If justice in its most general sense is nothing other than the disposition to perform the acts of the virtues in obedience to the laws of the city, justice in its precise or partial sense is the disposition to give or take only a fair or equal (*ison*) share of good things. Aristotle distinguishes between a number of senses of justice so understood (*NE* 5.2–5). The first kind of justice is that exercised in the distribution of honors, wealth, or anything else that can be divided among members of a political community. Justice of this sort is based not on arithmetical equality but on an equality of ratios between persons and goods; just distribution involves the assignment of equal shares to equal persons and unequal shares to unequal persons. As Aristotle indicates, however, distributive justice is essentially controversial because the discrimination between persons on the basis of merit is a political matter, with different regimes giving greater weight to the claims to merit of the wealthy, the virtuous, and the freeborn. Aristotle makes no effort to resolve these substantive controversies here; the subject will be addressed in the *Politics*.

The second kind of justice is that involving transactions, which Aristotle terms "corrective." Justice in this sense abstracts from persons and applies a simple arithmetic equality to the persons and goods involved; it extends not only to voluntary transactions such as contracts, but to involuntary or criminal actions such as theft or murder. Generally speaking, however, corrective justice also involves an important element of discrimination—the role played by a judge or jury in legal cases.

Aristotle also discusses at some length a third sort of justice, which he calls "reciprocity" (*to antipeponthos*). Justice in this sense appears to encompass both simple retaliation for injuries received and the exchange of benefits or goods. Although its precise relation to corrective justice is obscure, reciprocal justice seems to be conceived by Aristotle as a more primitive form of justice, one not requiring the prudential discrimination of a political official or judge; indeed, reciprocity appears to be the original or primary form of justice underpinning every sort of human association.

Aristotle makes clear, however, that justice in the fullest sense exists only in a community of relatively free and equal men whose relations are regulated by law. The virtue of justice is something that is characteristic of the city, and adjudication is an institution that belongs to and in a sense defines the city.[7] It is with this in mind that one must approach the notoriously controversial discussion in Book V of the *Nicomachean Ethics* of natural justice or natural right (*to physei dikaion*) (*NE* 5.7.1134^{b}18–35^{a}5). According to Aristotle, political justice is divided into what is just by nature and what is just by law or convention (*nomos*). Aristotle registers his disagreement with the sophistic view that, because all just things are subject to variation or change, justice exists only by convention; in his view, while it is indeed true that the just things like all human things are subject to change, there are nevertheless things just by nature. Unfortunately, Aristotle fails to give a single example of something just by nature. But he does provide several important clues. A similar distinction, he asserts, fits other matters as well: "by nature the right hand is stronger, and yet it is possible for any man to become ambidextrous." And he compares the conventionally just to measures for grain that vary from city to city, remarking that such things are no more the same everywhere than are political regimes, "yet there is only one regime that is by nature the best everywhere."

Interpretation of this passage has been heavily influenced by the attempt of Thomas Aquinas and subsequent Christian thinkers to assimilate Aristotle's view to the doctrine of natural law. Yet Aristotle gives little encouragement to the notion that there are unchangeable first principles of justice which serve, in however remote a fashion, as a guide to actual practice. It would seem rather that Aristotle conceives natural justice less as a ceiling than as a floor, less as an aspiration than as a base from which to aspire. Natural justice would seem to stand in the same relation to the best political order that right-handedness stands to ambidexterity: both are necessary but not sufficient conditions of excellence.

The standard of excellence for society is provided, rather, by "the regime that is by nature the best everywhere"—a regime, however, which cannot and should not be implemented everywhere because of the irreducible variability of human things. Aristotle seems to indicate that natural justice is to be sought instead in the most elementary (though equally variable) requirements of the city, the preservation of its regime and observance of its laws.

Some corroboration of this line of interpretation is provided by Aristotle's subsequent discussion of the relation between justice and "equity" (*NE* 5.10). Justice in the form of the legally just is insufficient as a guide to practice because law as such has a generality which guarantees that it will fall short in some number of instances. Equity is the virtue which corrects the defective generality of law through careful attention to the particulars which evidently affect in decisive fashion the justice of the outcome of individual actions. Aristotle makes clear that none of this is an argument against the necessity of law. Yet it certainly raises a question about the simple justice of law and law-abidingness. What is most striking, however, is Aristotle's failure to ground equity in any notion of a higher law or in principles of natural justice. The exercise of equity is, it would seem, analogous to if not an aspect of the prudence of political men or citizens acting in a particular case.

But it is impossible to grasp the full extent of Aristotle's depreciation of justice without taking into account his views concerning friendship. The discussion of friendship in Books VIII and IX of the *Nicomachean Ethics* is the longest treatment of a single issue in the entire work, and it is one of the most distinctive features of Aristotle's ethical teaching. In the language of Aristotle and his contemporaries, "friendship" (*philia*) refers to a wider range of phenomena than do equivalent terms today. It encompasses not only the attachment of friends but the love of husband and wife, the affection of parents and children, and the fellow feeling between persons belonging to a variety of private associations, citizens of the same city, and (in certain circumstances) human beings simply. Aristotle can thus plausibly argue that friendship

seems to hold cities together, and legislators seem to pay more serious attention to it than to justice. For concord seems to be something similar to friendship, and this is what they particularly aim at, while attempting to drive out its enemy, factional conflict. And when men are friends they have no need of justice, but when they are just they need friendship in addition; and of just things what is particularly just is held to be something involving friendship. (*NE* 8.1.1155ª22–28)

The political significance of friendship consists fundamentally in its mitigation of men's attachment to their private interests in favor of a spontaneous sharing with others of external goods. "The things of friends are common," according to the Greek proverb. Friendship can thus act as a powerful reinforcement of the community of interest which forms the basis of every human association.

Somewhat surprisingly, however, Aristotle's analysis is less concerned with friendship in its more directly political forms than with friendship in the highest sense. For Aristotle, friendship in general can be distinguished according to whether its primary motive is utility, pleasure, or virtue. The most perfect form of friendship is the friendship of good men based on virtue. Friendship in this sense, which encompasses pleasure as well as utility, achieves the most perfect identification of one's own good with the good of friends. Aristotle admits that such friendships are relatively rare. But the significance of the phenomenon emerges on a broader consideration of Aristotle's argument. Friendship may be said to resolve, to the extent that it can be resolved on the plane of moral-political action, the antinomy of morality understood as the perfection of individual virtue and morality understood as justice. Of the great-souled man, Aristotle says that "he is incapable of living with a view to another, except for a friend" (NE 4.3.1124^{b}31−25^{a}1). Friendship affords the great-souled man the satisfaction of his need for honor and community without compromising his attachment to virtue. Differently stated, it shows that the way of life of the gentleman is not, finally, inherently tragic.

PRUDENCE, STATESMANSHIP, AND POLITICAL SCIENCE

The discussion of justice in Book V of the *Nicomachean Ethics* concludes Aristotle's account of moral virtue proper. The next several books may be said to be devoted to various aspects of the question of the relationship between moral virtue and knowledge. In Book VI, he turns to a consideration of the intellectual virtues, above all prudence or practical wisdom. In Book VII, "making another beginning," he takes up the problem of lack of self-control or moral weakness (*akrasia*)—that is, the incapacity to act in accordance with one's knowledge or moral choice owing to the influence of passion. Both discussions retrospectively complicate the analysis of moral virtue in the earlier books, and point to the inadequacy of moral virtue as such—that is, the habitual disposition to moral virtue—as a guarantor of moral behavior in society.

Prudence or practical wisdom (*phronēsis*) is for Aristotle the virtue proper to the deliberating or calculative portion of the rational part of the soul. While prudence is an intellectual virtue, it is at the same time an integral aspect of moral action and cannot exist without moral virtue.

Prudence is not to be confused with mere cleverness or cunning. The task of prudence is not to secure one's own good as such but, rather, to devise appropriate means for securing the ends posited by the moral virtues. This also implies that prudence does not deal only, or indeed primarily, with universals: the primary concern of prudence is to adapt the universals reflected in the moral virtues to the particular circumstances in which moral action must take place. Hence prudence is highly dependent on experience. For this reason, Aristotle notes, the young may become expert in mathematics or geometry, but necessarily lack prudence as a result of their limited experience of life (*NE* 6.5, 7–8, 13).

Aristotle's discussion of the relationship between prudence and political expertise or statesmanship is fundamental for our purposes. Although conceding some correctness to the common view that prudence is concerned with the good of the individual, Aristotle asserts that political expertise is a form of prudence. It appears that the prudence of the political man or statesman has two distinct varieties, an architectonic "legislative" prudence, and a more "practical and deliberative" prudence which is concerned with the particulars of day-to-day politics; this "political" prudence itself takes two forms, deliberative and judicial (*NE* 6.8.1141ᵇ23–33). Aristotle thus implies that the statesman in the true sense is one who combines moral virtue with practical intelligence, experience, and knowledge of the particular characteristics of his city or people.

Yet is there not also a more strictly intellectual component of political expertise? Aristotle returns to this question at the very end of the *Nicomachean Ethics*. There are, it seems, two sorts of claimants to a knowledge of political things: the actual practitioners of politics, and "sophists" who profess to teach the political art. Yet the practitioners of politics neither speak nor write about these matters, and they seem incapable of making their own sons or friends expert in politics; hence it would seem that their own success is owing to natural capacity and experience rather than to knowledge. As for the sophists, for the most part they do not even know what sort of thing political expertise is or with what subjects it deals, for otherwise they would not have considered it identical or even inferior to rhetoric, nor thought it easy to legislate by collecting the most famous laws (*NE* 10.9.1180ᵇ28–81ᵃ19). Somewhat earlier, Aristotle had indicated that "speeches" that exhort to virtue are by themselves insufficient to lead men toward gentlemanship: only the combination of reason and compulsion represented by law can provide an adequate framework for the habituation to virtuous action which they require not only in youth but throughout life (*NE* 10.9.1179ᵇ4–80ᵃ22). The sophists, as it seems, overestimate the power

of speech or reason by itself to affect men's behavior. The same fundamental error is reflected in their approach to legislation. The sophists believe legislation is easy because they think the strength of law lies in its
rationality, or that good laws are equally suitable for any city. For Aristotle, by contrast, "law has no strength with respect to obedience apart
from habit, and this is not created except over a period of time" (*P*
2.8.1269ª20–22). But this means that the critical consideration is not
the laws of a city so much as its enduring political culture or character—
above all, its sociopolitical makeup and manner of governance, or what
Aristotle calls its "regime" (*politeia*). Accordingly, Aristotle continues,
"since our predecessors have left unexplored what concerns legislation, it
is perhaps best if we investigate it ourselves, and in general therefore
concerning the regime" (*NE* 10.9.1181ᵇ12–14).

The chief contribution that Aristotelian political science can make
to the practice of statesmanship lies, then, in the area of "legislation." It
is necessary to grasp the full bearing of this claim, as it is of fundamental
importance for understanding the specific character of Aristotle's *Politics*.
The term "legislation" is not used loosely as a synonym for statesmanship
simply. As indicated by the distinction Aristotle draws in Book VI between "legislative" and "political" prudence, statesmanship or political
expertise in what may be called its operational sense requires knowledge
of a range of matters of practical political significance. In a passage in the
Rhetoric, Aristotle identifies five key areas of political deliberation: revenues and expenditures, war and peace, defense of the territory, imports
and exports, and legislation. Concerning the last of these he makes the
following remark: "the preservation of the city lies in its laws, so it is
necessary to know how many kinds of regimes there are, which are advantageous to each sort of city, and through what things they are naturally apt to be destroyed—both of things proper to the regimes and of
their opposites."[8] The statesman requires some familiarity with (sub-
stituting modern terminology for Aristotle's expressions) trade, finance,
defense and foreign policy; but this familiarity may be acquired, it
would seem, essentially through experience. This is evidently not true,
or not to the same degree, in the case of legislation or, more generally, of
the legal and customary institutions and practices that define a city's regime. As the *Politics* itself will amply confirm, Aristotelian political science is above all the science of regimes.

Why this should be so is not immediately clear, but at least a provisional answer may be suggested. In the first place, and perhaps most
importantly, the statesman is necessarily a creature of a particular time
and place; regardless of the extent of his knowledge of other cities and
other forms of political organization, this knowledge is likely to be in-

complete and secondhand. The statesman tends to take for granted the naturalness and permanence of the regime that is here and now, and is insufficiently sensitive to apparently insignificant developments that, over time, can dramatically affect the political makeup of a city and thereby its governing arrangements.[9] Moreover, the statesman is likely to have attachments to his city and regime—which is to say, to a particular party or governing class—that are less than fully rational. Aristotle's own political science presupposes, by contrast, a systematic comparative study of regimes and their evolution over time. And Aristotle occupies a vantage point essentially transcending the partisanship of political life. In all of this, it may be added, what would appear to be an inherent disability of philosophy—its detachment from the city—is converted into the basis for a claim on the city's gratitude.

Aristotle's implicit justification of philosophy before the bar of the city recalls the explicit apology for philosophy undertaken by Plato or the Platonic Socrates. It has often been remarked that Aristotle's assertion that "our predecessors have left unexplored what concerns legislation" conspicuously fails to make an exception for Aristotle's predecessor and teacher. Indeed, the remark seems perverse unless the precise meaning Aristotle assigns to the term "legislation" is kept in mind. In his brief critique of Plato's *Laws* in the *Politics,* Aristotle notes that the *Laws* has little to say about the actual character of the regime it presents as the most practical political order (*P* 2.6.1264[b]42–65[a]1). The question of the nature and types of regime is certainly massively present in Plato's *Republic.* But the preoccupation of the *Republic* is a best regime whose realization Plato admits to be highly unlikely if not impossible, while the *Laws,* which is more concerned with what is practicable, makes little attempt to analyze the varieties of cities and regimes. Whatever Aristotle's final view of Platonic political philosophy, he seems to consider it inadequate in failing to provide in a generally accessible form the knowledge most needful for practicing statesmen.

The essential difference between Aristotelian political science and Platonic political philosophy is nowhere more clearly visible than in the first two books of the *Politics.* It is in Book I that Aristotle takes up the most fundamental or theoretical questions concerning the nature of the city and of man; in Book II, he sets out to expose the inadequacies of previous theoretical accounts of the best regime—not least the Platonic treatments of this subject—as well as the limitations of the actual regimes generally considered best. He does so, however, not for the sake of greater theoretical clarity concerning these matters, but in order to remove the most formidable intellectual obstacles to a proper understanding of the requirements of political practice.

THE CITY AND MAN

The beginning of the *Politics* closely parallels the beginning of the *Nicomachean Ethics:*

Since we see that every city is some sort of partnership, and that every partnership is constituted for the sake of some good (for everyone does everything for the sake of what is held to be good), it is clear that all partnerships aim at some good, and that the partnership that is most authoritative of all and embraces all the others does so particularly, and aims at the most authoritative good of all. This is what is called the city or the political partnership.

The "city" (*polis*) is a kind of partnership, association, or community (*koinōnia*), that is, a group of persons who share or hold certain things in common. That there is a single kind of partnership that is more authoritative than others and embraces their particular ends or aims is assumed by Aristotle on the basis of the discussion that opens the *Nicomachean Ethics,* as is the identity of the authoritative good that characterizes the political partnership. Aristotle's view must be distinguished from the familiar view that the "state" acts merely as an instrument of the variety of private associations that constitute "society." It would be wrong to suppose, however, that for Aristotle "society" in its various manifestations is therefore merely a servant of the "state." The very distinction between "state" and "society" is foreign to Aristotle's way of thinking: the city cannot be identified with the state or a form of the state, and the "authoritative" quality Aristotle imputes to it has nothing to do with the juridical "sovereignty" that is essential to the modern conception of the state. Rather, it derives entirely from the circumstance that the city, and only the city, is comprehensively concerned with the comprehensive human good.

The nonidentity of the city and the state is further apparent in the immediate sequel. Aristotle proceeds to criticize the view—developed in the writings of both Plato and Xenophon—that political rule or political expertise is essentially the same as the expertise involved in kingship, household management, and the rule of a master over slaves. The city as a form of human association differs essentially not only from the subpolitical associations of persons in the household, but even from the rule of a king over a tribe or people (*ethnos*). Aristotle shows little interest in analyzing the political arrangements of contemporary tribal societies or empires, or distinguishing them from "kingship" understood as a regime of the *polis;* but is is important to keep in mind their deliberate exclusion from the *Politics.* The city is distinguished from kingship proper above all by the fact that the city is or tends to be a partnership of human beings who are free and equal and "differing in kind"—that is to say, characterized by a high degree of economic specialization (*P* 2.2.1261ᵃ22–34). This combination of political freedom and the arts is of the essence of the city as Aristotle conceives it. [10]

Plato's confusion of political with other forms of rule is closely related to what Aristotle regards as another fundamental error, the defense of communism offered by Socrates in the *Republic* (*P* 2.2–5): both reveal a failure to appreciate the differentiation of persons that is characteristic of the city. At first sight, a city whose citizens share in all things, or in those things which typically cause division among them, would seem superior to a city characterized by less complete forms of sharing. Yet, Aristotle argues, to achieve unity through the abolition of marriage and common ownership of property is both impossible and undesirable. Far from strengthening "friendship" among the citizens, abolishing marriage would dilute it by eliminating the primary attachments of the family; and the communizing of property would destroy the legitimate pleasure men take in what is their own as well as the virtue of liberality, without in any way eliminating the causes of conflict over material goods. The city cannot and should not seek to replicate the unity of interest that characterizes the relationships of family members and friends. Rather, the city in its irreducible diversity "should be made one and common through education" or through the combined influence of "habits, philosophy, and laws" (*P* 2.5.1263ᵇ35–40). It is the ultimate irony of Aristotle's treatment of Plato that he upbraids the author of the *Republic* for a neglect of "philosophy." But this remark is at once playful and highly revealing of Aristotle's intention: as will appear shortly, what is at issue is something quite other than philosophy in the strict sense of the term.

In attempting to elucidate the specific character of the city, Aristotle turns to an analysis of the elements of which the city is composed and the manner of their development (1.2.1252ᵃ25–53ᵃ39). There are two forms of association which make up the household: the relationship between husband and wife, and that between master and slave, reflecting respectively the natural necessities of reproduction and preservation. (That slavery represents a natural relationship between ruler and ruled is here asserted by Aristotle; this view will shortly be restated at length and suitably qualified.) The household in general is a partnership serving the needs of daily life. The first form of partnership arising for the satisfaction of nondaily needs is the village, the result of a union of several households. The city is the complete or perfect partnership that emerges from the union of several villages, and the first to achieve self-sufficiency. While the impulse that gives rise to the city is apparently not essentially different from that leading to the formation of the household and the village, the city proves to be essentially different from these partnerships: as Aristotle puts it, "while coming into being for the sake of living, it exists for the sake of living well." Since the first partnerships are natural, however, it would appear that the city too is natural, and that man is by nature a political animal.

Aristotle's famous dictum that man is by nature a political animal must be understood in the larger context of his defense of the naturalness of the city. Aristotle does not mean to say that men engage continuously in political activity or would wish to do so. On the contrary, he emphasizes elsewhere the inclination of the majority of men to attend to their private affairs (P 6.4.1318ᵇ6–27), and acknowledges that in an important sense man is by nature more a "conjugal" than a political animal, inasmuch as the household is "prior to and more necessary than the city, and childbearing more common among the animals."[11] Man is a political animal in the first instance in the sense that human beings, like certain kinds of animals, everywhere congregate in groups larger than the household, and "strive to live together even when they have no need of assistance from one another" (P 3.6.1278ᵇ19–20). In another sense, however, "man is much more a political animal than any kind of bee or any herd animal," for man alone among the animals possesses speech or reason. As Aristotle explains, speech or reason (*logos*) "serves to reveal the advantageous and the harmful, and hence also the just and the unjust"; man alone among the animals "has a perception of good and bad and just and unjust and other things of this sort; and partnership in these things is what makes a household and a city" (P 1.2.1253ᵃ8–18). It is a mistake to regard the city as constituted merely by the sharing of external goods among its members: the city is a partnership constituted in the decisive respect by the sharing of a certain perception of the good or right way of life. Man is the political animal par excellence because he is the rational and moral animal.

Aristotle contrasts his view of the nature of the city with an alternative understanding, which strikingly resembles the theory of modern liberalism. According to this understanding, the city is a sort of alliance among its members for preventing injustice and facilitating economic exchange, with law a mere "compact" and (in a phrase Aristotle attributes to the sophist Lycophron) "a guarantor among one another of the just things." For Aristotle, on the other hand, anyone concerned for the good order of a city "must give careful attention to political virtue and vice"; "virtue must be a care for every city, or at least every one to which the term applies truly and not merely in a manner of speaking."

To repeat, the city must be understood as existing for the sake not of living but of living well, nobly, or happily (P 3.9.1280ª24–81ª6).

Only in the city, then, does man fulfill his potential for happiness understood as the life of action in accordance with virtue; and because the city is essential to the fulfillment of man's natural potential, the city itself is preeminently natural. One must be cautious, however, in ascribing to Aristotle any simple view of the city as a natural organism. "There is in everyone by nature an impulse toward this sort of partnership," Aristotle remarks; "yet the one who first constituted a city is responsible for the greatest of goods." Cities do not simply grow; they are founded by the discontinuous acts of particular men. This is so because there are aspects of humanity which are resistant to the city and its purposes. "Just as man is the best of the animals when completed, when separated from law and adjudication he is the worst of all. For injustice is harshest when it is furnished with arms; and man is born naturally possessing arms for the use of prudence and virtue, which are nevertheless very susceptible to being used for their opposites" (P 1.2.1253ª29–37). As is suggested by his reference in this context to man's unique potential for cannibalism and incest, Aristotle is fully aware of man's capacity for evil—that is, for transgressing sacred restraints that are recognized as such. For the same reason, he is alive to the fragility of law and the need for an admixture of force or compulsion in every city.

Aristotle's defense of the naturalness of the city must be seen as a response to a powerful contemporary opinion according to which the city is contrary to nature and rests in the last analysis on force. This sophistic argument (familiar above all from Plato's *Republic* and *Gorgias*) finds its strongest support in the phenomenon of slavery. Accordingly, Aristotle is particularly concerned to combat the view that slavery is simply unnatural. Interpreters have generally paid insufficient attention to the rhetorical purpose of Aristotle's discussion of slavery (P 1.5–7) and to the studied ambiguities of his argument. Aristotle concedes that there is such a thing as conventional slavery—that is, slavery originating in conquest in war. When he defines the slave by nature as one who is as different from other men as soul from body or man from beast, who is capable only of bodily labor, and who shares in reason only to the extent of perceiving and obeying it, one can only sensibly conclude that Aristotle means to indicate that the natural slave is something less than a normal human being, and hence that slavery as a social institution is essentially conventional. This appears to be confirmed by Aristotle's expressed willingness to see all of the slaves of his best regime promised their freedom as a reward for cooperative behavior, as well as by his remark that the virtue required of slaves is greater than that required of free laborers.[12] It may be added that Aristotle's apparent interest in grounding slavery on a superiority of the master's virtue rather than on mere force makes excellent sense as a strategy for humanizing the contemporary practice of slavery.

CITIZENSHIP AND THE REGIME

At the beginning of Book III of the *Politics*, Aristotle makes a new beginning in the argument and takes up the fundamental question of the nature of regimes. He begins with a discussion of the nature of citizenship, proceeding thereafter to a discussion of the basic types of regimes, the differences between them, and their relative claims to political justice. The treatment of kingship and law which immediately follows develops further the broad theme of the nature of political rule.

Aristotle introduces the question of citizenship as a way of understanding the relationship between city and regime. The identity of the city derives most obviously from those who are acknowledged to be its "citizens" (*politai*). Yet what qualifies a person for citizenship is not altogether clear. The "political and offhand definitions" generally in use tend to rest on the citizenship of an individual's parents or ancestors, but such definitions are obviously inadequate when large numbers of persons are added to or expelled from the citizen body in times of revolution. Generally speaking, a citizen may be defined as one who shares in decision making or rule, whether by the actual holding of office or by enjoying the right to vote in public assemblies or juries. In the final analysis, citizenship is a function of the regime: persons who are citizens in a democracy are not necessarily such in an oligarchy. Accordingly, the identity of the city is ultimately determined by the type of regime it has, rather than by factors such as geography or nationality.

Aristotle next addresses the question of the relation between the good citizen and the good man (*P* 3.4). The basic function of the good citizen is the preservation of the political partnership; but since it is the regime that fundamentally constitutes this partnership, the virtue of the citizen is necessarily relative to the regime. Moreover, since the city is made up of persons differing qualitatively in their occupations, the virtue of all the citizens is not the same. Is there, then, some case in which the virtue of the citizen coincides with the virtue of the man who is good without qualification? The case in question is that of the good citizen who is at the same time a ruler, for only the ruler possesses the "prudence" that is necessary for virtue in the full sense. In order to avoid misunderstanding, Aristotle makes clear that the regimes or types of rule that belong to the city are characterized by a blurring of the distinction between ruler and ruled: political rule proper consists in citizens "ruling and being ruled in turn," and the virtues required for rule in the city are generally acquired through the experience of being ruled. This is not the case, however, for the virtue of prudence, "the only virtue peculiar to the ruler." Aristotle's argument appears to imply the existence of a class or type of political men who "rule" in a stronger or more precise sense than ordinary citizens and therefore require a training in prudence beyond what is available through the experience of ordinary political life.

"The regime is an arrangement of a city with respect to its offices, particularly the one that has authority over all matters. For what has authority in the city is everywhere the governing body, and the governing body *is* the regime" (*P* 3.6.1278ᵇ8–12). As Aristotle makes clear at the outset of his discussion, while the regime is in the first instance an institutional arrangement, the regime cannot be properly understood in institutional terms alone. The regime reflects more fundamental political realities—the relationships of authority and subordination between the different groups that make up the city. For all practical purposes, the politically dominant class—the "governing body" (*politeuma*)—*is* the regime. While this is by no means Aristotle's last word on the subject of the relation between institutions and groups or classes, it is the indispensable starting point for an adequate understanding of his analysis, and it reveals an important affinity between Aristotle's thought and Marxism as well as modern political sociology.

Aristotle's analysis of regimes is presented initially in a schematic and, as is soon apparent, highly simplified form. All regimes have as their governing element either one, few, or many persons; and their aim is either the common good of the city as a whole or the private advantage of the rulers. There are, then, six basic types of regime. Kingship is the correct form of one-man or monarchic rule, tyranny the deviant form; rule of the few takes the form either of aristocracy—so called "either because the best persons are ruling, or because they are ruling with a view to what is best for the city and for those who participate in it"—or oligarchy; and rule of the multitude in its deviant form is democracy, while the correct form is called by the term common to all regimes, "polity" (*politeia*).

Aristotle makes clear at once, however, that the basis for the distinction between regimes is not simply numbers. The essential difference between democracy and oligarchy is not the size of the ruling element but, rather, wealth or its absence: oligarchy is rule of the wealthy, who also generally happen to be few, and democracy the rule of the poor, who are generally the majority. The difference is fundamental because it rests on essentially differing ways of life and conceptions of political justice. Oligarchs and democrats agree on the principle of distributive justice— that equal persons should receive equal things—but they disagree as to what constitutes equality in persons. The former believe that inequality in wealth justifies unequal treatment generally, the latter that equality in freedom requires equal treatment in all respects. It should be noted that the many do not rest their claim to political justice simply on their status as human beings or free men: the equality embodied in the democrats' claim reflects an equality of risk in defense of the city from its enemies. This claim to justice in the name of "military virtue" is particularly clear in the case of polity, where the right to bear heavy arms is virtually the definition of the governing body (P 3.7.1279^{b}1−4). Indeed, it would seem to be above all the city's military requirements that explain its tendency to be a partnership of free and equal persons; and they explain at least in part its tendency to develop in the direction of popular rule (P 4.13.1297^{b}2−28).

Aristotle reminds us that the claims of the component groups in the city to political justice are most properly judged in terms of their respective contribution to the end of the city. The difficulty is that the politically most powerful groups in the city—the many and the wealthy few—have a much stronger claim to contributing to the means of happiness or virtue than to happiness or virtue as such. Does this mean, then, that authority in the city can be justly claimed by the "respectable" element—that is, by gentlemen who are bred to virtue? Aristotle does not deny the strength of their claim; he simply asserts that the exclusive rule of such men would deprive all other claimants of the honors or prerogatives they regard as their due. He thus appears to suggest that the participation in rule of the other claimants is a matter of expedience rather than right. In the immediate sequel, however, Aristotle states at greater length the case for the claim of the many, and in so doing shows that there is an important sense in which the many are able to dispute the claim of the gentlemen on its own grounds. While none of the many individually may be fully excellent, Aristotle argues, it may happen that the sum of the virtues of mind and character present in many individuals overbalances the collective virtue of a few excellent men, just as a dinner to which many contribute may be better than one prepared by a single person, or works of music and poetry may be more reliably judged by many than by a few. The examples suggest the tentative character of this defense; and Aristotle makes clear that the argument does not apply to every sort of multitude, or to participation in the highest offices, where individual virtue is at a premium. Nevertheless, Aristotle is at pains to rebut the (characteristically Platonic) depreciation of the political competence of the many by way of an analogy with the arts: the many are competent to judge the effects of policies devised by others, just as the user of a house can claim to be as good or even a better judge of it than the architect (*P* 3.11).

Aristotle's qualified defense of democracy or rule of the people must be understood in the context of his approach to the general problem of political justice. The groups that typically contest for power in the city all have claims to political justice that are valid in some degree; yet because men are bad judges in their own case, they are constantly tempted to absolutize these claims at the expense of the claims of others. At first sight, there seems no easy way to resolve this conflict between claims which appear to be fundamentally incommensurable. Yet it turns out that they may be seen as commensurable in a certain way. While it may be impossible to decide whether or to what extent the contributions of wealth or of virtue are more necessary to the city, it is possible to compare the wealth of the oligarchs with the wealth of the gentlemen, the many, or a single individual, just as the virtue of the gentlemen may be set beside the virtue of the many or of one outstanding man. But the very act of considering political justice in this perspective induces moderation in the claims of each group, since it may well happen that a particular group is outmatched in terms of its own claim by another group taken as a whole or several groups taken collectively, or is subject to plausible challenge by one of its own number (*P* 3.12–13).

What Aristotle provides cannot be said to be a theoretical solution to the problem of distributive justice. Indeed, there is reason to doubt that he regards the problem as one that is susceptible to solution at the theoretical level. The diverse groups that constitute the city fulfill functions that are equally necessary in the sense that it is impossible to assign an abstract priority to one or the other of them. The city cannot exist at all without bodies to come to its defense; it cannot exist as a civilized community without the leisure that wealth creates; and it cannot exist as a city in the full sense without virtue. In this sense, all of the key groups in the city do have an absolute claim to political justice. Aristotle seeks not to adjudicate these claims so much as to encourage a practical accommodation among them based on a recognition of the worth of competing claims and competing groups.

One of the striking features of Aristotle's analysis of political justice is his emphasis on the outstanding individual, or "the one best man," who appears as virtually equivalent in political importance to a group or class. In view of his concern to mitigate the conflict among competing claims to rule, it is surprising that Aristotle shows himself sympathetic to the democratic practice of ostracism of politically powerful individuals; indeed, he goes so far as to assert that ostracism in deviant regimes both serves the private interest of the ruling element and is just (*P* 3.13.1284ᵇ23–25). Although he does not say so explicitly, the reason would seem to be that such men pose a fundamental threat to political rule as such. All the more puzzling, then, that Aristotle should make an exception for the individual who is outstanding in virtue, or whose virtue is altogether disproportionate to the contribution of the other citizens: the only just thing is for all to obey such a man and make him a "permanent king" in their city.

With this remark, Aristotle turns to a systematic consideration of the subject of kingship (*P* 3.14–17). Much of this discussion is devoted to an examination of the question whether it is more advantageous to be ruled by the best man or by the best laws. Aristotle gives full weight, as in his treatment of equity in the *Nicomachean Ethics,* to the deficient particularity of law. What decides the issue in favor of the rule of law, however, is its freedom from passion. One might have thought that the best man is by definition one in whom passion is mastered by virtue, but this is not necessarily the case: "spiritedness [*thymos*] perverts rulers and the best men," Aristotle notes, echoing an important Platonic theme (*P* 3.16.1287ᵃ30–31). Even men of outstanding virtue are flawed, as it seems, by the malign operation of a passion or complex of passions which acts at the same time as a vital source of support for their virtue. Aristotle points again, if unobtrusively, to the problematic relationship between gentlemanship in its highest form and the requirements of the city. It would seem to be this thought that explains the unexpected turn Aristotle's argument eventually takes: the alternative to kingship is finally not so much the rule of law as the rule of a number of excellent men who are collectively less vulnerable to the distempers of spiritedness— that is to say, aristocracy. While Aristotle is willing to acknowledge kingship as an appropriate regime for certain kinds of societies, he makes clear that kingship belongs to the earliest epoch of the city. As regards his hesitation on the subject of ostracism, one may hazard the suggestion that it reflects Aristotle's reluctance to sanction the principle that moral excellence or nobility must be wholly subordinate to the requirements of political justice.

THE VARIETIES OF REGIMES

The fullest statement of the program underlying Aristotle's detailed analysis of the varieties of regimes in the remainder of the *Politics* occurs at the beginning of Book IV. Aristotle begins by comparing the science of regimes to the art of the gymnastic trainer, who needs to concern himself not only with the kind of training that is best for the best sort of physique but also with the kinds that are best or acceptable for a range of imperfect physiques. Similarly, it belongs to the science of regimes, not only to consider the absolutely best regime, but to examine the kinds of regimes that are best for particular sorts of cities, and the kind that is at the same time the best and the most suitable or acceptable for most cities. Most of those who have expressed views on the regime err, Aristotle says, by neglecting what is truly useful, the study of the less perfect but more attainable regimes, and concentrating their attention either on a best regime that is beyond the reach of most cities or on a regime such as the Spartan, which while more attainable is hardly typical of existing regimes. Instead, "one ought to introduce an arrangement of such a sort that they will easily be persuaded and be able to participate in it by the fact that it arises directly out of those that exist, since to reform a regime is no less a task than to institute one from the beginning" (P 4.1.1289ª1–4). Aristotle's central interest in the reform of existing regimes is critical to understanding his overall approach. Contrary to a common view that the analysis of existing regimes in *Politics* IV–VI is motivated by an interest in scientific classification and is fundamentally indifferent to questions of relative rank or value among regimes, the analysis is guided from the beginning by the thought that the actualization of the best regime or the best possible regime, while indeed devoutly to be wished, is likely to come about through incremental change within the framework of existing laws and political ideas rather than through the promulgation of radical utopian schemes.

There are a number of regimes, Aristotle reminds us, because there are a number of parts in any city. The most important and universal parts are the bulk of the people and the wealthy few; consequently, it is frequently held that there are in effect only two kinds of regime, democracy and oligarchy. In addition to rich and poor, however, some cities have a politically significant "middling element"—that is, a middle class. Moreover, rich and poor are far from uniform in their makeup: the poor may include farmers, artisans, and laborers (and within these groups particular occupations may predominate), each with a way of life differing substantially in its political implications; and similar differences characterize the wealthy and the gentlemen. Differences in the size or exclusiveness of the governing body, the role accorded other elements in the city, and the relative importance of law as opposed to personal rule also contribute to the shaping of distinct subtypes of regimes. For example, Aristotle recognizes a subtype of oligarchy which he calls "rule of the powerful" (*dynasteia*), a regime characterized by the personal rule of a small number of wealthy persons; and he distinguishes between those forms of democracy that rest on the political power of the farming class and the rule of law and the radical democracy characteristic of Athens in its classical phase, in which the urban laboring classes, supported by state revenues, rule in disregard of law. Not only are the differences between such regime subtypes of the utmost political importance; they are sometimes greater in key respects than the differences separating the types of regimes themselves. Thus a moderate democracy may have more in common, for example, with a moderate oligarchy than it does with a radical democracy. When the regime subtypes are taken into account, the varieties of regime appear more nearly as points on a single continuum than as politically or ideologically exclusive types. This is, indeed, central to Aristotle's intention: a certain blurring of the boundaries between regimes is essential if a strategy of incremental regime reform is to succeed.

Aristotle may justly be considered the originator of the notion of the "mixed regime," which was to exert a powerful influence on political thought and practice well into modern times. It is usual to discuss Aristotle's notion of the mixed regime in the context of his treatment of the regime he calls polity. Properly speaking, however, the mixed regime in the *Politics* is less a specific regime type than a reflection of the strategy which informs Aristotle's approach to the construction and preservation of regimes generally. The central practical task Aristotle sets himself in the *Politics* is to blunt if not eliminate the political conflict between rich and poor. Polity, which Aristotle describes initially as a "mixture of oligarchy and democracy," provides one sort of solution to this conflict. But Aristotle also experiments with the possibilities of reform within the framework of oligarchy or democracy as such; moreover, he treats as a form of mixed regime not only polity but aristocracy in a weak sense of that term—a regime in which virtue is honored and gentlemen play a politically significant role but share power with the wealthy and the people (P 4.7. 1293^{b}1–20).

Aristotle's description of polity as a mixture of oligarchy and democracy is intended to modify the initial account of Book III where polity is presented simply as the correct or public-spirited form of democracy. Polities can lean either toward democracy or toward oligarchy; those of the latter sort are generally called aristocracies, through a common confusion of the way of life of the rich with the way of life of gentlemen. At all events, it is the mark of a well-mixed polity that it can be spoken of indifferently as either democracy or oligarchy (just as the Spartan regime is often described as a democracy as well as an oligarchy or aristocracy), and that it commands the allegiance not merely of a majority but of every group in the city (P 4.8–9).

A characteristic feature of Aristotle's political teaching, and one of the greatest interest from the point of view of present-day political analysis, is the role he assigns to the "middling element" in the city in mediating the struggle between rich and poor. It is not sufficient to identify the mixed regime generally as the regime that is best or most acceptable for most cities. Because the regime is in the last analysis not merely a certain arrangement of offices but a way of life for the city as a whole, it would seem that regimes that attempt to reconcile the interests of powerful and disparate groups through institutional means alone are bound to be in some sense artificial constructs and thus constantly subject to political instability. But what if one could construct such a regime around a group that would itself act to bridge the sociopolitical and ideological differences that nurture instability?

This appears to be the thought underlying Aristotle's remarkable and unexpected praise of the middle class and its potential political role (*P* 4.11). There appears to be a link betwen virtue understood as the mean between extremes and a middling or mean condition with respect to possessions. Those who own a moderate amount of property are more inclined to behave reasonably than the extremely rich or the extremely poor: "the former sort tend to become arrogant and base on a grand scale, the latter malicious and base in petty ways; and acts of injustice are committed either through arrogance or through malice." The middling element is least inclined either to avoid ruling or to wish to rule, both of which are harmful for cities; at the same time, it is well equipped for either ruling or being ruled. By contrast, those who are raised in luxury never become habituated to being ruled, while the poor tend to be overly humble or slavish. "What comes into being, then, is a city not of free persons but of slaves and masters, the ones consumed by envy, the others by contempt. Nothing is further removed from friendship and from a political partnership." Such a relationship of rich and poor leads to factional conflict, and drives the regime in the direction either of narrow oligarchy or—given the incompetence of the poor themselves in ruling—tyranny. Where the middling element is strong, on the other hand, factional conflict is kept to a minimum, and the regime is more stable and durable.

It is important to consider this argument in its proper perspective. Aristotle admits that the middle class is small in many cities, that its political role is frequently circumscribed rather than enhanced by the struggle of rich and poor, and that international circumstances—in particular, the rivalry of Athens and Sparta—have tended further to discourage such a role. Moreover, it would be wrong to suppose that Aristotle looks to the middle class as a reliable source of support for political virtue. Aristotle makes clear that the regime he is seeking does not presuppose "virtue of the sort that is beyond private persons" or the education that would inculcate it: the middling sort is characterized not so much by the possession of virtue as by the absence of vice, and by external circumstances favorable to the acquisition of virtue. Part of the reason for Aristotle's apparent enthusiasm for the middle class, on the other hand, may well be that he considers it a breeding ground for a kind of virtue or gentlemanship that is less ambiguously in the service of the city than virtue or gentlemanship of the conventionally aristocratic type.

The remainder of Book IV and the two succeeding books are taken up with an extended treatment of political institutions, the causes of factional conflict (*stasis*) and political change or revolution (*metabolē*), and the methods of instituting and preserving regimes. In their stark realism and sure grasp of the preoccupations of day-to-day politics, these pages have few parallels in the literature of political theory; at the same time, they enrich and deepen the analysis of regime types sketched in the earlier books. Particularly striking is Aristotle's willingness to provide advice on the preservation of existing regimes not only to the politicians of imperfect democracies and oligarchies, but even to tyrants (*P* 5.10–11). This testifies at once to Aristotle's singular flexibility, the modesty of his expectations from politics, and his confidence in the possibilities of reform. While in no way indicating that the subjects of a tyrant are under a moral or legal obligation to obey him or to refrain from attempting to overthrow him, Aristotle appears to accept that there are circumstances in which change in a regime of this sort is not feasible; hence any mitigation of the severities of the tyrant's rule must depend on convincing him that the preservation of his regime demands as much.

Also of great interest is the light cast by this material on Aristotle's view of the psychology of political men. In spite of the emphasis he gives to the class basis of political conflict, Aristotle accords surprisingly slight importance to the role of economic motives in politics. He repeatedly stresses that the struggle between rich and poor is at bottom a contest not over property as such but over rival conceptions of justice; and he has much to say about the frequently decisive role played in factional conflict and revolution by passions such as anger, arrogance, fear, contempt, and love of honor. His treatment is particularly revealing of the psychology of aristocratic and oligarchic elites, and convincingly illustrates the frequently dramatic political consequences that can flow from individual virtue or its absence.

THE BEST REGIME

Aristotle's analysis of regimes encompasses, as has been seen, not only a variety of imperfect regimes but also the regime that is simply best for man. But what place can such a regime have in an emphatically practical science of politics? Is Aristotle's discussion of the best regime in the final two books of the *Politics* not after all (as many have supposed) a kind of vestige of his Platonic heritage, with little organic connection to the argument of the more practical books of the *Politics* if not of the work as a whole?

The first answer to the question of the utility of the best regime is that the best regime represents nothing more than an attempt to make explicit the assumptions and choices that underlie any reform of existing regimes. That the best regime presupposes a rare combination of circumstances (or for that matter may never actually have existed) is immaterial; the only requirement is that it respect those limitations that are inherent in the human condition. The best regime so understood provides, not indeed criteria for judging the legitimacy of existing regimes, but a model or goal for all political change.

The difficulty with such an explanation is that there remains in Aristotle a disjunction—by no means so marked as in the case of Plato's *Republic,* but nevertheless significant—between the best regime and virtually all other contemporary regimes. Aristotle's best regime rests on a form of social and economic organization which appears to have existed in the Greek world only in Sparta and a few other places—one comprising a single class of citizens who enjoy complete leisure for political and military activity, and an unfree or semifree class of agricultural laborers. When Aristotle addresses the general question of political justice and its implications for regime reform, however, he appears to assume as the norm for cities a sizable body of free citizens engaged in economic activities. Not only does the best regime not seem to function as a model for such cities; one could argue that it actually works in the opposite direction by calling into question the legitimacy of the political claim of the popular element and thus encouraging its disenfranchisement.

In spite of the fact that the best regime is not discussed in explicit connection with the earlier schematic analysis of regime types, there can be little doubt that the best regime is understood by Aristotle as a form of aristocracy. It is aristocracy in the strong sense of that term: the undiluted rule of a governing body that is publicly dedicated to the pursuit of virtue. If Aristotle seems strangely silent concerning the political arrangements of the best regime, it is precisely because the best regime does not face the normal political conflicts characterizing regimes that consist of heterogeneous groups of free citizens. The central problem of the best regime is not the accommodation of partial and incompatible claims to political justice but, rather, education in virtue, which is what sustains the best claim to political justice.

The discussion of the best regime in the final books of the *Politics*
may be said to serve two specific practical purposes. First, Aristotle is
mindful (following the example of Plato in the *Laws*) of the possibilities
offered by the foundation of new cities in remote areas of the Greek
world. The elaborate treatment he provides (*P* 7.4–12) of questions
such as the size of the city, its situation and plan, and the qualities of its
inhabitants must be understood in this light. Second, Aristotle's treatment of the education and way of life of the citizens of the best regime is
intended to supply practical guidance for leisured aristocrats or potential
aristocrats in existing cities. In Book II, Aristotle goes to some lengths
to point out the defects in the way of life of the aristocratic classes in
those cities—notably, Sparta and Carthage—which are reputed to be
the best governed. The best regime of the final books of the *Politics* is
intended above all to offer an alternative model of the aristocratic way of
life for those whose political ideas have been formed by the examples of
these impressive yet flawed societies.

A critical defect emphasized by Aristotle in his analysis of both
Sparta and Carthage is the preoccupation of their governing classes with
wealth. In Sparta, wealth is secretly coveted in spite of the austerity of
the laws (which among other things prohibited the holding of gold and
silver by individuals)—partly because the laws themselves inadvertently
foster large differences in wealth through defective arrangements regarding the inheritance of landed property, partly because of a utilitarian bias
in Spartan education. In Carthage, on the other hand, with its commercial traditions, wealth is openly honored, and considered a prerequisite
for the holding of office. Aristotle insists to the contrary that "where
virtue is not honored above all, there cannot be a securely aristocratic
regime" (*P* 2.11.1273ª41–ᵇ1). The solution proposed by Aristotle is
not, however, simply a variation on Spartan austerity. Aristotle certainly
rejects the Carthaginian alternative of a nobility whose wealth is based
on trade in favor of a landed nobility of the Spartan type. As appears
above all from the extended treatment of moneymaking or "business"
(*chrēmatistikē*) in Book I, he is convinced that the emancipation of economic activity from the natural limitations of an agricultural way of life
is bound to give a dangerous impetus to men's desires for external goods.
At the same time, however, he sees no merit in the deliberate encouragement of private or public poverty, and recognizes fully the need for trade
and money. While it is not desirable for the best city to be itself a port,
Aristotle favors a location close to the sea; this not only facilitates trade
but permits the development of naval power (*P* 7.6). But any city capable of supporting a fleet requires substantial revenues. As regards the
role of private wealth, Aristotle indicates that a moderate amount of
property is most desirable, while the evils associated with wealth are to

be mitigated by encouraging the common use of wealth through the institution of common meals, the setting aside of lands to support the public treasury, and an education in the virtues of moderation and liberality.

The brief treatment of the question of the size of the best city (*P* 7.4) reveals a characteristic aspect of Aristotle's teaching. In the common view, the best city is the largest city—a view that appears to rest on a concern that the city be militarily as strong as possible. Aristotle rejects such an idea on the grounds that it is impossible for a large city to be well governed. This is so in the first place simply because it is difficult to control large numbers of persons ("Who will be general of an overly excessive number, or who will be herald, unless he has the voice of Stentor?"). More fundamentally, however, it reflects the impairment of critical political functions that results from a lack of personal knowledge of individuals: both adjudication and the distribution of offices according to merit require the citizens to be familiar with one another's qualities. Aristotle concludes that the optimum size of the city can be defined as the greatest possible number with a view to self-sufficiency that is at the same time "readily surveyable."

Because of the importance this question assumes in the break with classical political philosophy initiated by Machiavelli, it is essential that Aristotle's position not be misunderstood. As has been seen, Aristotle is by no means insensitive to the city's fundamental requirement for security. But he denies that security can be guaranteed in the last analysis only by expansion: the examples of Athens and Sparta suffice to show that empire is at least as likely to ruin a city as inadequate military resources (cf. *P* 7.14.1333^{b}4–25). In any event, a small city is not without effective strategies for its defense. Aristotle suggests four such strategies, which can often be pursued simultaneously and are mutually reinforcing: superior training of troops in courage and military skills; fortifications; offensive naval power; and alliances. Particularly noteworthy is the last, for Aristotle in fact holds open the possibility that the best city may choose or be compelled to act in a "hegemonial and political" role with respect to other cities [13]—in the manner of Athens and Sparta in their preimperial phases. Yet Aristotle is reluctant to place too much emphasis on such a possibility. As will be seen shortly, this reflects his awareness of the central importance of the external orientation or foreign policy of the best city for the way of life of the city as a whole.

EDUCATION, CULTURE, AND THE BEST WAY OF LIFE

At the beginning of Book VII, in introducing the subject of the best regime, Aristotle turns aside to consider at some length the question of

the best way of life for individuals and cities. This passage is of fundamental importance for understanding not only the purpose and significance of the discussion of education and culture which concludes the
Politics as we have it, but the character of Aristotle's political teaching
generally.

It is not immediately clear why Aristotle returns to a question one
might think had been settled in the ethical writings. Aristotle begins by
reiterating his argument that happiness is to be identified with the life of
virtue or, more precisely, of "virtue and prudence and action in accordance with these," and he asserts that what is true of individuals must
also be true of the city as a whole. It appears, however, that a question
can be raised as to whether the happiness or virtue of the city and the
individual are one and the same. For, Aristotle tells us,

there is a dispute among those who agree that the most choiceworthy way of
life is that accompanied by virtue as to whether the political and active way
of life is choiceworthy, or rather that which is divorced from all external
things—that involving some sort of study, for example—which some assert is the only philosophic way of life. For it is evident that these two ways
of life are the ones intentionally chosen by those human beings who are most
ambitious with a view to virtue, both in former times and at the present; the
two I mean are the political and the philosophic. (*P* 7.2.1324ª25–32)

There are two issues which demand attention in this connection:
whether the better way of life is one of active participation in the political
life of the city or, rather, one characteristic of a foreigner; and which
regime and which orientation (*diathesis*) of the city are to be deemed
best. But it is the latter question—the question of the foreign policy of
the best regime—that occupies the foreground of Aristotle's discussion.
According to Aristotle,

There are some who consider rule over one's neighbors, if undertaken after
the fashion of a master, to be accompanied by injustice of the greatest sort,
and if in political fashion, not to involve injustice but to be an impediment
to one's own well-being. Others hold opinions that are virtually the opposite of these. They believe that the active and political way of life is the
only one for a man, and that in the case of each sort of virtue there is no more
room for action on the part of private individuals than on the part of those
who are active with respect to common matters and engage in politics. This
is the conception some of them have; but others assert that the mode of
regime involving mastery and tyranny is the only happy one. Indeed, among
some this is the defining principle of the regime and the laws—that they
exercise mastery over their neighbors. (*P* 7.2.1324ª36–ᵇ4)

Aristotle makes clear that he has in mind Sparta in particular as the para-
digm of the city oriented toward war, conquest, and the domination of

foreigners. There appear to be two alternatives to the Spartan orientation: noninvolvement in the affairs of other cities, or an "active and political" orientation involving, at the extreme, leadership or "political"
rule over allied cities. The alternative modes of participation in political
life by individuals are closely parallel. Individuals may withdraw from
politics like the foreigner or philosopher, participate in politics in "political" fashion by ruling and being ruled in turn, or attempt to exercise
mastery or tyrannical rule over their fellow citizens.

In fact, however, this parallelism is somewhat misleading, and the
discrepancy points to the problem with which Aristotle is chiefly concerned. No one considers mastery or tyranny a respectable way of life for
individuals within the city. But it seems that most people suppose there
is no difference between mastery and political rule when it comes to foreigners, and "are not ashamed to train to do in relation to others what
they deny is just or advantageous for themselves." This would seem to be
the view even of those (or some of those) who believe that the "active and
political way of life is the only one for a man"—that is, for the man who
is interested in performing noble deeds and winning honor. In other
words, there would appear to be an inherent instability in the idea of rule
itself such that even respectable men tend to conceive that "having authority over all is best." The impulse to rule in this fashion naturally
seeks an outlet in the domination of foreigners; but it is also an ever-
present danger within the city itself—and indulgence of the impulse
abroad is likely to have repercussions at home, as the example of Sparta
again demonstrates (P 7. 14. 1333^{b}26–36).

In order to appreciate the apparently tortuous logic of the argument
as Aristotle develops it, one must not be misled by his appeal to the
philosophic life. The intention of the discussion is not to adjudicate the
respective claims of the political and philosophic ways of life for the individual. In the tenth book of the *Nicomachean Ethics,* Aristotle makes
quite clear that the philosophic way of life is superior for those who are
capable of it; but he gives no indication that this fact by itself has direct
political consequences. In the present context, Aristotle is interested in
the philosophic life only as a model or analogy for phenomena of political significance. In particular, he raises the alternative of noninvolvement in political life on the part of individuals only or primarily because
this alternative is one that had a certain political standing. Just as some
aristocrats favored a life of political activity, others, holding that there is
"more room for action on the part of private individuals" [14] in performing virtuous deeds, kept aloof from any involvement in politics—a
stance particularly in favor among aristocrats living in democratic regimes like Athens, where demagogues competed for popular favor and
the threat of judicial expropriation was real. Such persons may be

supposed to have been well represented among Aristotle's immediate audience.

What is Aristotle's solution to this dilemma? Because he is unwilling to countenance the secession of virtuous men from politics, Aristotle concludes formally that the best way of life for city and individual alike is the practical or active life. But because he is equally concerned to moderate the tendency inherent in political life or political men to seek rule for its own sake or without limits, he undertakes to redefine the practical or active life in such a way as to alter fundamentally the orientation of the best city. The active way of life, he now argues, is not necessarily in relation to others, just as thoughts are not active only when they are for the sake of some further result, "but rather much more those that are complete in themselves, and the sort of study and ways of thinking that are for their own sake." Indeed, it seems that "not even cities that are situated by themselves and intentionally choose to live in this way are necessarily inactive," any more than individuals; "for otherwise the god and the entire universe could hardly be in a fine condition, since they have no external actions beyond those that are proper to themselves" (*P* 7.3.1325ᵇ16–29).

At a later point in Book VII, Aristotle returns to and elaborates these themes. The citizens of the best regime must be able to discharge the business of politics and to go to war, but it is more important that they be able to remain at peace and be at leisure. For just as war is for the sake of peace, so occupation is for the sake of leisure, the necessary or useful for the sake of the noble. No more than economic activity is political or military activity by itself the end of the best life: men engage in politics in the last analysis for the same reason they engage in other practical activities, in order to secure leisure and the things that are enjoyed in leisure. Happiness in the truest sense belongs not with occupation but with leisure (cf. *NE* 10.7.1177ᵃ4–15). Accordingly, the best regime depends on the presence of a variety of virtues. Courage and endurance are needed in support of the activities of politics and war; moderation and justice are required alike in occupation and leisure, though they are particularly useful for times of peace and leisure, since "war compels men to be just and moderate, but the enjoyment of peace and good fortune tends to make them arrogant." But these virtues are evidently not sufficient, for Aristotle adds that the best regime will also require, with a view to leisure alone, "philosophy" (*P* 7.15.1344ᵃ11–34).

Does Aristotle, then, finally "bring the regime around" (to quote his own criticism of Plato's *Laws*) to the rule of philosopher-kings as sketched in Plato's *Republic?* Such a conclusion cannot be sustained. Aristotle goes to considerable lengths to demonstrate that the best way of life for men generally is the practical or political life; and there is nothing in the education elaborated in the final books of the *Politics* to suggest that Aristotle assumes a capacity for philosophy in the citizen body of the best regime or some part of it.[15] In fact, Aristotle appears to have held that philosophy is not only not necessary for but a positive impediment to kingly rulers, as distinguished from an openness to advice and persuasion from those who genuinely philosophize.[16] There is no reason to believe that Aristotle regarded the rule of philosophers as a serious political possibility. When he speaks of "philosophy" in this context, then, what he appears to have in mind is not philosophy in the sense of theoretical speculation, but a broader sense of the term, of which "culture" is a tolerable approximation. When in Book II Aristotle criticizes Plato for relying on an institutionalized system of communism to ensure the unity and happiness of the regime of the *Republic* rather than on "education," which is to say "habit, philosophy, and laws" (*P* 2.5.1263^{b}37–40), he does not forget that Plato himself had relied on philosophy rather than on institutions as such. What he means to suggest is that Plato should have relied less on philosophy in the strict sense than on philosophy in the broad sense. Philosophy in this latter sense consists above all in the leisured cultivation of music and poetry.

The complex (and evidently incomplete) discussion of education and culture which occupies the remainder of the *Politics* cannot be treated adequately here. In order to understand this discussion, it is essential to appreciate the rhetorical dilemma Aristotle faced in attempting to make palatable to his proud and hard-headed interlocuters an argument which might seem merely sentimental or, worse, condescending. In presenting the leisured enjoyment of literature and the arts as the end of the best life, Aristotle is careful to appeal to traditional authorities and to emphasize the nonutilitarian character of the activity in question. On closer inspection, however, it appears that Aristotle also wants to make the case that education—moral or intellectual—is not entirely a matter for the young, or that the cultured enjoyment of mature men should serve at the same time as a kind of education in virtue. That the aristocrats of the best regime stand in need of such an education might be thought to be excluded by definition. Yet not even "great-souled" men, as Aristotle reminds us in this context (*P* 7.7.1328^{a}7–8), are altogether immune to destructive passions associated with the spirited part of the soul; and Aristotle has given us to understand that education in the higher form of virtue which he calls "prudence" may have requirements peculiar to itself. It is not possible to do more than allude to the indications Aristotle provides that the principal vehicle of education so understood is a tragic poetry designed to effect a catharsis of the passions of the soul

(*P* 8.7.1342ª10–15). In this as in other respects, Aristotle attempts to improve on the teaching of Plato only the better to fulfill its fundamental intention.

NOTES

1. *Metaphysics* E.1.1025ᵇ18–28; *Topics* 6.6.145ª15–18; *Nicomachean Ethics* (hereafter *NE*) 6.2.1139ª26–ᵇ4, 4.1140ª1–23.

2. *NE* 1.3.1094ᵇ11–27, 4.1095ª 30–ᵇ13, 7.1098ª26–ᵇ8; *Eudemian Ethics* (hereafter *EE*) 1.5–6.1216ᵇ 11–17ª18.

3. See particularly *NE* 10.9.

4. Consider particularly *EE* 1.1.1214ª9–14.

5. *Politics* (hereafter *P*) 3.12.1282ᵇ 14–23.

6. Consider *NE* 10.9.1181ᵇ15.

7. *NE* 5.6.1134ᵇ23–ᵇ18; cf. *P* 1.2.1253ª29–39.

8. *Rhetoric* 1.4.1359ᵇ19–23.

9. Consider *P* 5.7.1307ᵇ1–19, 8.1307ᵇ29–38.

10. Consider also in this connection *P* 7.7.

11. *NE* 8.12.1162ª16–19; cf. *EE* 1242ª21–26.

12. *P* 7.10.1330ª31–33, 1.13. 1259ᵇ33–60ª7.

13. *P* 7.6.1327ª40–ᵇ6; cf. 14.1333 ᵇ36–34ª2.

14. *P* 7.2.1324ª41–ᵇ2; cf. *NE* 10.8.1179ª6–8.

15. Consider *P* 7.14.1333ª27–30.

16. Aristotle, fr. 647 Rose (cited in Themistius, *Orations* 8.128 Dindorf).

READINGS

A. Aristotle. *Nicomachean Ethics*, Books I, III–V, X.
    Aristotle. *Politics*, Books I–IV, VII.
B. Aristotle. *Nicomachean Ethics*, Books II, VI–IX.
    Aristotle. *Politics*, Books V–VI, VIII.

MARCUS TULLIUS CICERO

106–43 B.C.

Few of those who have sought to present a systematic account of the development of political philosophy have attached great importance to Cicero's political thought. He has traditionally been regarded as one of that series of less inspired and less inspiring Greek and Roman thinkers who followed in the wake of Plato and Aristotle. Considered a dilettante rather than a serious student of philosophy, his thought has generally been judged eclectic and felt to be characterized neither by any great consistency of doctrine nor depth of understanding. His specifically political works, the *Republic* and the *Laws,* have been regarded as little more than ambitious attempts to justify the ideals and practices of a moribund aristocratic order. His value to later students is thought to lie less in what he himself has to say about the substantive questions of political philosophy than in the detailed account he gives of the doctrines of the several schools of Greek philosophy active in his own day, and of the adaptation of those doctrines to the radically different political and intellectual environment of Rome. His special talent is thought to have rested in the skill with which he synthesized the diverse and often conflicting teachings of these schools, thus making them available in a form congenial to the Roman taste and adequate to satisfy the demands of the practical Roman mind.

Such an assessment contains a measure of truth. It fails, however, to give serious consideration to Cicero's method or to his purpose in treating philosophical materials in the manner in which he did, to say nothing of the substance of his thought. It falls short, therefore, of that understanding essential to an adequate analysis.

A statesman and a serious student of philosophy, Cicero sought in

his writings to place his considerable talent and experience as a rhetorician in the service of philosophy, in the service of what he suggested
was "the richest, the most bounteous, and the most exalted gift of the
immortal gods to humanity."[1] His task, as he conceived it, was to introduce philosophy into Rome. By philosophy he meant not the dogmatic
teachings of this or that particular school but a way of life. The task
was not simple. Philosophy is always regarded with "suspicion and
dislike" by the majority of men, and particularly by those whose taste
runs to the practical rather than the speculative.[2] It is particularly suspect if its origins are thought to be foreign. The normal difficulty of introducing that which at all times runs counter to popular taste and
thought was thus compounded for Cicero by the fact that the teaching
was of Greek origin. The necessity for Cicero to tread lightly on Roman sensibilities and to supply a convincing justification for the existence of philosophy in Rome cannot be ignored if one hopes to appreciate the degree of circumspection with which he felt compelled to
approach this task.

Throughout his works Cicero professes to be an Academic Skeptic,
a member of that philosophic school whose origins lay in the Platonic
Academy but which in his own time stressed as its fundamental thesis
the impossibility of absolute knowledge. Man as man, the Skeptics
asserted, is limited to opinions of that which is more or less probable.
Although man may seek to attain a higher degree of probability by
examining, as Socrates did, the relative merits of all opinions, he will
never at any point in his inquiry be assured of absolute certainty. He
must act, if he chooses to act, with the understanding that the principles
which guide his action remain problematic.[3]

While skepticism and the suspension of final judgment which it
entails may be philosophically tenable, if such views are taken seriously
and developed to their logical extreme by the mass of men, the outcome
may well be politically disastrous. The thought, for example, that the
commonly accepted standard of what is just and unjust lacks, and must
always lack, a fully rational or defensible basis may not unduly disturb
the theoretician. It may, however, if clearly impressed upon the mind
of the populace, so shake popular confidence in the validity of such a
standard that faithful adherence to it, or to any standard resting on
such a tenuous and fundamentally arbitrary base, appears foolish. Such
an understanding may lead to a widespread questioning of the truth
even of those principles which are perhaps essential to the existence of
the political order, e.g., that the common good should be preferred by
the citizens to their private good.

Cicero was well aware of the potentially unsettling effect skepticism, and perhaps philosophy as such, must have on the city, *i.e.,* the political community. The stark and undiluted truth, the philosophic truth, may shake the very foundations of a given political order. Unlike some of the less perceptive members of his school, Cicero could not view this possibility with equanimity. He was aware of the ultimate dependence of philosophy on the city, and thus of the necessity for philosophy, if it was to survive, to concern itself with the development of a healthy political order. Only within such an order could philosophy exist. The philosopher, if this be true, must be guided by some understanding of the needs of the city and of the practical consequences of his teachings. He must not risk the chaos that might follow a systematic and ruthless public examination of the principles underlying and guiding a particular order, even an order which strikes him as radically defective, without having given some thought to the alternatives. A defective government, a government which falls far short of the best, may be better than no government at all. The philosopher must begin, then, with an understanding of what is possible as well as what is desirable, and direct his efforts, in turn, to the improvement of the health of a given political order, rather than to its destruction.

Cicero's decision to use the dialogue as the vehicle for his teaching springs in part from this reflection on the relation of philosophy to the city and in part from his preference, as a Skeptic and an admirer of Plato ("the wisest and . . . most learned man whom Greece has produced" [4]), for the Socratic method. The decision was dictated, he asserts in the *Tusculan Disputations,* by a desire to "conceal his own opinions, to relieve others from error and in every disputation to look for the most probable solution." [5] The dialogue lends itself to the presentation and examination of conflicting opinions. It permits the writer to focus attention on the relative merits of the positions being examined while at the same time suggesting, rather than revealing, the content and direction of his own thought. The form of the dialogue permits the writer to guide the discussion, but places the burden of following the argument to its conclusion upon the reader.

Cicero also saw, as Plato had before him, the possibilities of the dialogue as a work of art, a work so constructed that each element, *e.g.,* the place, the time, and the actions and speeches of the characters, has a part to play in advancing the inquiry. [6] Only careful readers will detect the significance of these additional touches and be led, in turn, to see that the salutary teachings which lie on the surface and are easily grasped by even the casual reader do not exhaust the content of the teaching, that they are at best partial truths. By means of the dialogue, Cicero seeks to emphasize what is politically salutary while at the same time concealing from the eyes of all except serious students those more comprehensive truths which may render political life difficult or impossible for the mass of men. He seeks in this way to fulfill his responsibility both to philosophy and to the political order.

The substance of Cicero's specifically political teaching is contained in two dialogues, the *Republic* and the *Laws*. Each dialogue purports to record an earlier conversation among Romans about political things. In the *Republic,* the conversation allegedly reported by Cicero took place during a Roman holiday in the year 129 B.C., some seventy years prior to the writing of the dialogue. The conversation is one of three days' duration among men belonging to the Scipionic circle, a group whose members combined achievements as Roman statesmen with an interest in philosophy. The *Republic* consists of six books, two devoted to each day's conversation. Cicero appears, and thus speaks in his own name, only as the writer of the preface attached to the first, third, and fifth books. The *Laws* serves to record a much more recent conversation, and one of a single day's duration, among Cicero, his brother Quintus, and Atticus, an Epicurean friend. It is generally thought that the *Laws* also contained, or was to contain, six books, but only the greater part of the first three books remains available to us; the rest of the manuscript has been lost.

Time has been no kinder to the manuscript of the *Republic.* With the exception of the portion devoted to Scipio's dream and a number of quotations scattered through the works of writers familiar with the original, *e.g.,* Augustine, the text of the *Republic* was lost for more than seven centuries. Only fragments, perhaps one-third of the complete work, remained when a copy of the manuscript was discovered in the Vatican Library in 1820. In view of the fragmentary character of the texts of both the *Republic* and the *Laws,* and particularly of the former, any account of Cicero's political thought must remain provisional in important respects.

The fundamental question to which Cicero addresses himself in these two works is that which guided classical political philosophy as a whole: What is the best political order? The *Republic,* the more philosophic of the two dialogues, is directed to answering this question, the *Laws* to sketching the legal and institutional framework of such a regime. The answer to the central question, of course, presupposes some reflection on a number of related questions, although the reflections themselves may not be included in the more popular and consequently less exhaustive works.

One such related question, that of the right life for man, is taken up in the introduction to the first book of the *Republic.* The question is, Which is superior—the active life, *i.e.,* the practical or political life, the life of the statesman; or the contemplative life, *i.e.,* the philosophic life? Cicero's interest in this issue is not simply theoretical, but is stimulated by the growing tendency, encouraged among the Romans by certain philosophers, especially the Epicureans, to denigrate the political sphere and to withdraw from participation in political matters. "We must free ourselves," Epicurus had argued, "from the prison of affairs and politics." Cicero's concern for the fate of the commonwealth dictated that his opening remarks in the *Republic* be directed to the practical end of defending the political life. To this end he examines the common arguments in favor of withdrawal and, while conceding to them a degree of truth, suggests that they can be assigned little weight when viewed in the light of the individual's responsibility both to this city and to his own nature and in the light of the glories to be won within the public sphere. Moreover, he argues, it is absurd to suppose that virtue can exist in a vacuum:

. . . the existence of virtue depends entirely upon its use; and its noblest use is the government of the state, and the realization in fact, not in words, of those very things that the philosophers, in their corners, are continually dinning in our ears.[7]

The man who has both discovered the principles of virtue and compelled others to live in accordance with them, *i.e.,* the statesman, must be deemed far superior, even in wisdom, to those who perhaps speculate about such questions but abstain from any direct participation in political affairs. Cicero's position at this point appears unambiguous: the practical life is to be preferred to the contemplative life. Despite the fervor with which Cicero advances this opinion, however, there are some indications that he does not regard the issue as settled. His praise in the prologue has not been unqualified: the life of the statesman, while "deserving of praise" and "conducive to fame," is neither a completely happy one nor one chosen simply for its own sake. It is soon made clear that necessity and a sense of duty underlie its selection.

The provisional character of this first opinion is emphasized by the fact that the question is immediately reopened as soon as the dialogue proper begins. Asked in the opening scene to give his opinion on the report that a second sun has been observed in the heavens, Scipio, the chief character in the dialogue, expresses a preference for what he calls the Socratic position in regard to such matters, a position which avoids speculative questions on the assumption that they are "either too difficult for the human understanding to fathom or else . . . of no importance whatever to human life."[8] Within a short time, however,

Scipio has been led to abandon this position. He concedes not only his own interest in speculative studies and the immediate relevance, perhaps necessity, of such knowledge for the man of action, but even admits the utter inadequacy of his earlier emphasis on practical or earthly considerations:

Who in truth would consider anyone richer than the man who lacks nothing that his nature requires, or more powerful than one who gains all he strives for, or happier than one who is set free from all perturbation of mind, or more secure in his wealth than one who possesses only what, as the saying goes, he can carry away with him out of a shipwreck? What power, moreover, what office, what kingdom can be preferable to the state of one who despises all human possessions, considers them inferior to wisdom, and never meditates on any subject that is not eternal and divine?[9]

Both here and in the account of his dream, with which the *Republic* ends, Scipio seems to leave little doubt of his own preference for the philosophic rather than the active life as the life of human excellence. Political life, the dream implies, is a duty to be undertaken by man while he lives on earth. Power and glory, the earthly rewards which are showered on the statesman, the rewards of which Cicero spoke in such glowing terms in the prologue to the first book, are seen to be both ephemeral and, in the last analysis, meaningless. The true compensation for the statesman's sacrifices is the heavenly reward, *i.e.,* the eternal life of happiness and contemplation, granted him after death.

But there is still another position to be considered. The most desirable life, Scipio suggests at another point in the *Republic,* is neither the simply contemplative nor the simply active life but that which represents a "union of experience in the management of great affairs with the study and mastery of those other arts," *i.e.,* the life of a statesman whose horizons have been enlarged by philosophy.[10] Although Cicero is not without ambiguity on this entire question, there is reason to doubt that this intermediate position constitutes his final opinion. He has suggested earlier the potential incompatibility of the two pursuits. The history of Greece and Rome provides few examples of those who have in fact combined the two pursuits with any degree of success. Why, then, does he introduce this third possibility?

Cicero's initial task is the restoration of the primacy of the political sphere. This restoration is guided, however, by an awareness of the limitations of the political or active life. He seeks to convey some sense of these limitations to those among his readers who are potential philosophers, and thus to show them the ultimate supremacy of the philosophic life. At the same time, he seeks to warn them that the philosopher, in spite of these limitations, must concern himself, directly or indirectly, with the fate of the commonwealth. What is theoretically higher, he suggests, may have to give way at times to what is necessary, to what is of immediate and urgent concern to most men.

For, in truth, our country has not given us birth and education without expecting to receive some sustenance, as it were, from us in return; nor has it been merely to serve our convenience that she has granted to our leisure a safe refuge and for our moments of repose a calm retreat.[11]

The philosopher must be prepared at certain times to abandon his concern with "eternal and divine" subjects and to place his particular talents at the service of the commonwealth. The third possibility is introduced not only to emphasize this dual responsibility but to offer a model for the many whose talents or inclinations do not lie in the direction of the philosophic life, but who nevertheless will have important political functions. Such men are well advised to seek that life which approximates the best although it necessarily falls short of it, the life of action illuminated by philosophy.

Only after some light has been thrown on the question of the right life for man is Laelius, a participant who believes theoretical knowledge to be impossible or at least irrelevant to the human situation, allowed to introduce the question of the best regime. The subsequent discussion moves along two lines: (1) an attempt to settle the question in speech, *i.e.,* to investigate the nature of political things and thus the nature of the best regime, on a theoretical level; and (2) an attempt to illustrate in deed, by using as an empirical example the Roman republic as it existed some years prior to their own time, what speech, *i.e.,* reason, has been trying to make clear.

The emphasis placed upon this dual approach has occasionally inspired the charge that Cicero's work is little more than a rationalization of an earlier Roman regime. Such an understanding neglects at the very beginning his explicit assertion that the inquiry is directed to the discovery of universally valid political principles, principles designed to "promote the firm foundation of States, the strengthening of cities, and the curing of the ills of peoples." [12] "We are composing laws not for the Roman people in particular," he asserts in the *Laws,* "but for all virtuous and stable nations." [13] The presence or absence of an empirical example does not affect the possibility of such an inquiry.

As for my using our own state as a pattern, I did so, not to help me to define the best constitution (for that could be done without using any pattern at all), but in order to show, by illustrations from the actual history of the greatest state of all, what it was that reason and speech were striving to make clear.[14]

Those who charge Cicero with seeking only to restore the republican constitution of an earlier age also ignore the suggestion, implicit in both the *Republic* and the *Laws,* that even when it was at its peak the Roman republic, the model, fell short of the ideal discovered in speech. The code of laws outlined by Cicero in the *Laws,* the code of that best state discovered in speech, is not identical with that of the Roman republic at any time in its history. The participants in the *Laws,* Quintus emphasizes, are not "simply rehearsing the actual laws of Rome, but restoring old laws which have been lost, or else originating new ones." [15] The specific deviations from what was historically the case are those dictated by reason, the ultimate standard of law and justice. The composite of old and new which results represents his attempt to bridge the gap between the popular or prephilosophic tendency to identify the good with the old, *i.e.,* the ancestral or traditional, and the philosophic identification of the good with the natural, *i.e.,* that which is dictated by reason. By bringing reason to bear on the existing code rather than beginning afresh, Cicero seeks to preserve an essential sense of continuity with the past and thus the sense of respect for the traditional which normally exists in the political community.

There are, of course, certain practical reasons for the use of an empirical model. Cicero's inquiry, which is Greek in both method and conclusions, must be given a Roman character if it is to prove congenial to the Roman palate. His task is thus rendered simpler and his demonstration more convincing if, instead of the "shadowy commonwealth of the imagination" with which Plato is said to have dealt,[16] he can illustrate his understanding of the nature of political things with a concrete example, and not simply any example, but the Roman example.

The inquiry proper begins with Scipio's statement of the essential characteristics of a commonwealth:

A commonwealth is the affair of a people. But a people is not any collection of human beings brought together in any sort of way, but an assemblage of people in large numbers associated in an agreement with respect to justice and a partnership for the common good.[17]

This association ceases to be a commonwealth when it ceases to be guided by the ends—justice and the common good—for which it exists.

Scipio asserts that the commonwealth is natural in so far as it is essential to the achievement of a happy and virtuous life. It comes into being not, as some philosophers have suggested, because of any weaknesses of human nature but because of a "certain social spirit which nature has implanted in man." [18] Man is not a "solitary or unsocial creature"; he is driven by his very nature to seek the companionship of his fellows. The government of the commonwealth is no less natural, for without some such arrangement "existence is impossible for a household, a city, a nation, the whole human race, nature and the universe itself." [19] When properly constituted, this government will reflect the hierarchical principle coextensive with the whole of nature, the lower being subordinate in each case to that which is higher.

The character of the commonwealth is ultimately determined by the "arrangements in regard to magistrates," i.e., by the form of government.[20] The three simple forms are kingship, aristocracy, and democracy. The first of these, the rule of one, is characterized by affection: "the name of king seems like that of father to us";[21] the second, the rule of the best, by counsel or wisdom; the third, the rule of all, by liberty. Although kingship is judged the best and democracy the worst of the simple forms, each of the three may offer a decent and even stable government so long as injustice and greed do not destroy the original bond of the association. Unfortunately, each of the simple forms contains within itself not only certain defects but even the seeds of its own destruction:

In kingships the subjects have too small a share in the administration of justice and in deliberation; and in aristocracies the masses can hardly have their share of liberty, since they are entirely excluded from deliberation for the commonweal and from power; and when all the power is in the people's hands, even though they exercise it with justice and moderation, yet the resulting equality itself is inequitable, since it allows no distinctions in rank.[22]

Before each lies its depraved counterpart—tyranny, oligarchy, mob rule —and history serves as a record of the inevitable tendency of each to degenerate into its opposite and the latter in turn to be replaced at some future time by still another form.

Thus the ruling power of the state, like a ball, is snatched from kings by tyrants, from tyrants by aristocrats or the people, and from them again by an oligarchical faction or a tyrant, so that no single form of government ever maintains itself very long.[23]

While it is questionable whether even the enlightened statesman can interrupt this "natural motion and circular course" permanently, there is a way in which he can at least delay the movement. This lies in the creation of a moderate and balanced regime, a regime which incorporates a judicious mixture of the institutions and principles of each of the simple regimes and exhibits in turn an "even balance of rights, duties and functions." [24] Cicero's thought on this point had been anticipated by a number of earlier writers, including Plato and Aristotle, but his immediate guide in the matter of the mixed regime was the Greek historian Polybius (205–123 B.C.). Polybius, seeking an explanation for the extremely rapid, almost unprecedented expansion of Roman power, suggested that the key lay in the mixed character of the Roman constitution, a mixture so successful "that it was impossible even for a native to pronounce with certainty whether the whole system was aristocratic, democratic, or monarchical." [25]

For if one fixed one's eyes on the power of the consuls, the constitution seemed completely monarchical and royal; if on that of the senate it seemed again to be aristocratic; and when one looked at the power of the masses, it seemed clearly to be a democracy.[26]

The mixed constitution made it possible to avoid the defects inherent in each of the simple forms. It prevented an undue concentration of power and provided a system of checks and balances. Within such a framework, Cicero suggested, "the magistrates have enough power, the counsels of the eminent citizens enough influence, and the people enough liberty." [27]

If examined carefully, however, the mixed regime proves to be in the most important respects an aristocracy. The arrangements are designed to ensure that the aristocracy, and thus the element of wisdom or counsel, is assigned the decisive role.[28] While a measure of power is to be vested in the people, it is expected that the actual authority will remain with the Senate, for liberty is to be "granted in such a manner that the people [are] induced by many excellent provisions to yield to the authority of the nobles." [29] The success of this "balanced and harmonious constitution" rests in large measure on the continued existence of an aristocracy possessing the particular qualities described by Cicero in the *Laws*. The aristocracy, he suggests there, must be "free from dishonor" and "a model for the rest of the citizens." [30] The example presented by this order is decisive for the over-all health of the commonwealth:

For it is not so mischievous that men of high position do evil—though that is bad enough in itself—as it is that these men have so many imitators.

For, if you will turn your thoughts back to our early history, you will see that the character of our most prominent men has been reproduced in the whole State; whatever change took place in the lives of the prominent men has also taken place in the whole people.[31]

If the quality of the aristocracy is allowed to degenerate, it is extremely unlikely that the regime will manage to survive for any great length of time. It will certainly prove incapable, given such a deterioration, of achieving the end for which it exists, the cultivation of virtue in the citizens.

This exposition of the theoretical principles underlying the mixed regime is followed by Scipio's account of the development and internal composition of the earlier Roman republic—the practical illustration he promised earlier. The scene is set for such a historical treatment by Scipio's reference at the beginning of the discussion to a statement once made by Cato. The latter, a noted Roman statesman of an earlier age, had traced the superiority of the republic to the fact that it was "based upon the genius, not of one man, but of many; . . . founded, not in one generation, but in a long period of several centuries and many ages of men." [32] It rested upon the collective wisdom and experience of many generations of men. Its institutions and practices had demonstrated their merit by passing the severest practical test, the test of time.

Cato's thesis reminds one immediately of that advanced at a much later date by the English statesman Edmund Burke. The superiority of the British Constitution, Burke was to argue, lay in the fact that it was not the product of fabrication or conscious planning. It had not been "formed upon a regular plan or with any unity of design" but had developed "in a great length of time, and by a great variety of accidents"; the parts had "gradually, and almost insensibly, accommodated themselves to each other." [33] Its perfection represents the culmination of a natural process, of a process of slow, continuous, and almost unconscious growth.[34]

Burke's understanding represents a radical departure from the position of the classical thinkers. The latter had taken it for granted that the best regime would be the product of reason and conscious planning. There is evidence that Cicero himself is closer to the classics than to Burke on this point. The basic difference between Cicero and the earlier Greek thinkers does not appear to spring from a disagreement in regard to the principle—the superiority of planning to accident—but from one in regard to the question whether the better plan is more likely to result from the efforts of a single wise man or

those of a series of wise men. Cicero did not simply reject the possibility that the best state could be the product of the wisdom of a single
founder. He agrees with Polybius as to the accomplishments of
Lycurgus, the Spartan lawgiver, and he concludes his account of the
contributions of Romulus to the development of the mature Roman
order in the following vein:

Do you not perceive, then, that by the wisdom of a single man a new
people was not simply brought into being and then left like an infant
crying in its cradle, but was left already full-grown and almost in the
maturity of manhood?[35]

But such pre-eminently wise men are rare. It is more sensible to plan
on the basis of what is more likely to be the case. It is more likely
that there will be a series of fairly able men, each of whom can be
expected to apply some of the lessons of experience to the task of
gradually improving the regime.

The historical account itself deserves careful examination, for it
does not appear to be free from irony. History, Cicero assures us in
the *Laws,* is distinguished from poetry by its reference to truth
rather than fancy. There are a number of suggestions throughout the
Republic that Scipio's account of the Roman origins falls short of this
standard. We are regaled at one point with the tale of the deification
of Romulus, and we are assured that the tale must be true for it was
accepted as true by the men of Romulus' time—a time, we are told, of
culture and learning, a time when men were "quick to mock at and
reject with scorn that which could not possibly have happened."[36] To
support this last assertion, Cicero presents some examples of the intellectual heights to which the men of this age of culture and learning
had risen. But the examples are only of the state of learning in Greece;
no examples are given that would allow the reader to make a judgment about the presence or absence of a similar cultivation in Rome.
We are left to draw our own conclusions. Shortly thereafter, as if to
guide our conclusions, Scipio refers to those allegedly cultured and
learned ancestors as simple rustics; and we learn that far from being
skeptical about such tales, they were willing to accept the one concerning Romulus on the authority of an "untutored peasant." Moreover, when the matter is raised in a different connection in the *Laws,*
Cicero does not hesitate to brand the tale a fable.

Scipio's presentation is not meant to be simple history, but rather
is designed to offer an idealized picture of the Roman past, a judicious
mixture of fact and fancy. It is designed to demonstrate to the citizens
the wisdom and justice of the Roman origins, to show them the firm

foundations upon which this Roman example of the best regime rests. The presentation is in its essence a deliberate example of the Platonic "noble lie." While it necessarily falls short of the philosophic truth, such a salutary account of the foundations of the commonwealth may be essential to the cohesion and very existence of the political society. The statesman's task, Cicero would have us understand, rests not in the wholesale destruction of these traditional, if unphilosophic, myths, but in placing the partial truth that they may contain at the service of those policies which reason informs him are conducive to the good of the commonwealth.

Scipio's historical presentation also serves to suggest the provisional sense in which the mixed regime is actually *the* best regime. His account indicates that the Roman decline began in fact with the transformation of kingship into tyranny. The mixed regime is not introduced until some time after this decline has begun. The unqualifiedly best regime for Cicero, as for classical thought generally, is that in which wisdom has an absolute right to rule: the absolute rule of the wise (the true aristocracy) and ultimately the absolute rule of the one man pre-eminent in wisdom and virtue (the true kingship) is the most desirable form of government. The rule of and by wisdom was possible under the early Roman kings, but this was to prove true only so long as the kingship retained its distinctive character. Its character in turn depended on the existence of a succession of good and wise kings, and thus on chance rather than planning. In view of this, kingship proves in practice to be the least stable of the simple regimes, "the first and most certain" to decay;[37] and in fact it required, as Cicero emphasizes, only the excesses of a single king, Tarquinius, to render the very title of king obnoxious to the Roman people.[38]

Scipio's account indicates that the "excellent constitution" established by Romulus and maintained by the Romans for over two hundred years began to wither with this transformation of kingship into tyranny. The subsequent history of Rome is written in terms of a series of more or less successful attempts to control the forces unleashed by this transformation. The mixed regime comes to sight as one such attempt to satisfy the popular thirst for liberty while recapturing, at the same time, a place for the wisdom and virtue characteristic of kingship. Cicero warns us in the *Laws* that the task of the statesman is to "determine not merely what [is] best but also what [is] necessary." [39] One test of his political skill is the extent to which he understands the dictates of necessity and succeeds in operating within the range of possibilities that necessity permits him. Where the absolute rule of the wise is impossible, the mixed regime allows statesmen to attempt to secure popular consent to the rule of wisdom, and thus to achieve that approximation of the best which is conceivable for most societies. The mixed regime incorporates the attributes of what we have come to call the "rule of law." It seeks to embody the precepts of a wise founder in the fundamental laws of the state, and then to insure that the subsequent administration or completion of these laws will be placed in the hands of those least likely to deviate from them and most likely to execute them in accord with the spirit permeating them. The essential elements of this basic code and the attributes of the governing class are sketched in some detail by Cicero in the *Laws*.

The particular strength of such a regime lies in its relative stability; yet, in so far as it seeks to bridge the chasm between wisdom and popular consent, it rests on a precarious foundation. Such a regime is not always easy to achieve and, once achieved, it is hard to maintain for any length of time. Even this second best, this approximation of the simply best may not be possible for all peoples or at all times.

From this analysis of the best regime the discussion shifts to a consideration of the assertion that injustice rather than justice necessarily underlies the successful conduct of the affairs of any state. Although he disclaims any belief in the arguments, Philus, another Academic Skeptic, consents to state the case for injustice as it had been presented by Carneades (214–129 B.C.), an earlier Academic Skeptic. His presentation advances from two main premises: (1) justice is conventional rather than natural; (2) justice is folly.

If justice were natural, he suggests at the beginning of his argument, then, like man's sense of what is hot and cold, it would be the same thing to all men, always and everywhere. In fact, man's conception of what justice entails varies not only from nation to nation but even from one age to another within a single city. Justice is not natural but rather the product of human society, and, more specifically, the product of this or that human society. It rests not on nature but utility; it is not desired for its own sake but only on the basis of calculation. It has no stability; its content depends only on the circumstances. It springs in large measure from man's fear that without such arrangements he, in his weakness, would always be exposed to the depredations of others, particularly of those stronger than himself.

The second and more fundamental strand of the argument presented by Philus begins with the tentative acceptance of the premise earlier denied: there is in fact a common understanding among men regarding the basic dictates of justice. To observe these faithfully, however, is to run counter to human nature, for the dictates of justice are seldom identical with those of wisdom and self-interest.

Wisdom urges us to increase our resources, to multiply our wealth, to extend our boundaries; . . . to rule over as many subjects as possible, to enjoy pleasures, to become rich, to be rulers and masters; justice, on the other hand, instructs us to spare all men, to consider the interests of the whole human race, to give everyone his due, and not to touch sacred or public property, or that which belongs to others.[40]

If this is true, justice cannot be simply natural, for neither man nor the political community can reasonably be expected to select a course of action which, while just, is at the same time the height of folly. Had Rome, Philus asserts, complied with the strict demands of justice in every instance it would not now be an empire but still a poverty-stricken village. Wisdom counsels that it is the appearance rather than the substance of justice which is to be sought, for then one may benefit from the advantages stemming from a reputation for justice while avoiding the misfortunes that may accompany a too strict compliance with its demands.

The case for justice has been entrusted to Laelius, the oldest and most conservative of the group. Unfortunately, only fragments remain of Laelius' statement. The most important of these is that in which he outlines his conception, *i.e.,* the Stoic conception, of natural law.

True law is right reason in agreement with nature; it is of universal application, unchanging and everlasting; it summons to duty by its commands, and averts from wrongdoing by its prohibitions. And it does not lay its commands or prohibitions upon good men in vain, though neither have any effect on the wicked. It is a sin to try to alter this law, nor is it allowable to attempt to repeal any part of it, and it is impossible to abolish it entirely. We cannot be freed from its obligations by senate or people, and we need not look outside ourselves for an expounder or interpreter of it. And there will not be different laws at Rome and at Athens, or different laws now and in the future, but one eternal and unchangeable law will be valid for all nations and all times, and there will be one master and ruler, that is, God, over us all, for he is the author of this law, its promulgator, and its enforcing judge.[41]

While not enforced or strictly enforceable by any human agent, the commands of this law cannot be ignored with impunity. The individual who deviates from them denies what is best in his own nature and suffers in turn the mental torment stemming from self-contempt and conscience. A similar failure upon the part of the commonwealth,

Laelius suggests, will eventually result in its destruction. To Philus' contention that the paths of justice and wisdom necessarily diverge, Laelius opposes the assertion that to do what is just will always prove to be the wisest and most rewarding course of action.

Although the position advanced by Laelius is usually thought to be also that of Cicero, there is reason to believe that Cicero regards both the strict moralism of Laelius and what one is tempted to call the Machiavellianism of Philus as fundamentally inadequate. While it is far better in practice that the state seek to be guided by the strict demands of justice rather than by the conception that such standards are arbitrary and ultimately meaningless, it may be impossible for even the best of states to do more than approximate the standard of perfect justice. This is one of the lessons Scipio sought to teach in the course of offering an account of the Roman past in the second book of the *Republic*. Even the past of this regime, the regime which Scipio presents as the best regime, was not free of injustice; even the Romans, "the most just of men" according to Philus, were not above plunder and murder. Cicero's conclusion is fundamentally the same as Plato's: the perfectly just regime probably lies outside the range of human possibilities. Its demands are too severe. The wise statesman, while seeking to be guided in his practice by such standards, will begin with the understanding that there is little likelihood, given the nature of man and the political community, that they can or will be realized fully in any state.

This conception of the limitations intrinsic to political life runs through much of Cicero's thought. It is particularly noticeable in those sections of the *Laws* in which he explores, this time in his own name, the question of justice and the question of the status and character of natural law. The inquiry in the *Laws* is stimulated by the desire to prepare a code suited to the mixed regime, the regime of which he had spoken in the *Republic*. The preparation of the positive law that will go to make up such a code presupposes, however, a much fuller, essentially philosophic, investigation of a number of other questions.

For we must explain the nature of Justice, and this must be sought for in the nature of man; we must also consider the laws by which states ought to be governed; then we must deal with the enactments and decrees of nations which are already formulated and put in writing; and among these the civil law, as it is called, of the Roman people will not fail to find a place.[42]

The first book of the *Laws* is devoted to such an inquiry. The inquiry yields much the same Stoic understanding of man and the universe as that underlying Laelius' position in the *Republic*.[43] Man, the one natural creature possessing a rational soul and sharing the divine faculty of reason with the gods, exists in a rational and ordered universe. By virtue of his unique possession, reason, he may discern and adjust himself to the comprehensive rational order. So far as he achieves this, so far as reason serves as his guiding and ruling element, he fulfills his nature to the highest degree, and he shares both law and justice with the gods. Since reason is the common possession of all men, this highest life, the life "according to nature," is accessible, at least in theory, to all men: "there is no human being of any race who, if he finds a guide, cannot attain to virtue." [44]

Cicero's teaching in the *Laws* thus seems in harmony with the Stoic position developed by Laelius in the *Republic*. Whether this is simply the case, however, remains open to question. Cicero's comments on natural law, for example, are prefaced in the *Laws* by the statement that he is not certain of their truth, although they seem to him "usually and mostly" right.[45] At another point he begs the members of his own school, the Academic Skeptics, not to examine his argument too closely, for if they "should attack what we think we have constructed so beautifully, it would play too great havoc with it." [46] Cicero has good reason to be concerned, for the fundamentally Stoic teaching which he propounds as his own in the *Laws* rests in part on an understanding of divine providence and an anthropocentric teleology which he himself had examined and rejected in two other works—*On the Nature of the Gods* and *On Divination*.

It is reasonable to suggest that this apparent inconsistency has its roots in the fact that the teaching in the *Laws* is addressed not to philosophers but primarily to all decent and honorable men. The immediate task is a practical one: "to promote the firm foundation of states, the strengthening of cities, and the curing of the ills of peoples." [47]

For that reason I want to be especially careful not to lay down first principles that have not been wisely considered and thoroughly investigated. Of course I cannot expect that they will be universally accepted, for that is impossible; but I do look for the approval of all who believe that everything which is right and honourable is to be desired for its own sake, and that nothing whatever is to be counted a good unless it is praiseworthy in itself, or at least that nothing should be considered a great good unless it can rightly be praised for its own sake.[48]

The arguments advanced in support of these principles and to a considerable extent the principles themselves are selected with a view to the appeal that they would have to such men, not simply, or primarily, with a view to theoretical certainty. If Cicero's purpose is kept in mind, then it becomes possible to understand Atticus' unqualified acceptance in the *Laws* of the teachings concerning theology and the primacy of religion in the state.[49] It is perfectly proper for Atticus, in his capacity as a Roman citizen, to assent to these politically salutary teachings, although as an Epicurean philosopher he could not have granted their theoretical soundness. Atticus and Cicero share an understanding of the importance of such teachings to the "firm foundation of states." The Stoic principles, even though inadequate on a theoretical level, are admirably suited to the achievement of this important end.

A further indication of Cicero's own position, and of the severe qualifications with which he adopts that of the Stoics, is reflected in his own treatment of the natural law. Laelius, in arguing the case for justice, had had no difficulty in reconciling the practices of the Roman past with the strict demands of justice embodied in the natural law; moreover, he did not doubt that the precepts of the natural law were fully accessible to everyone. Scipio's historical account leaves little doubt that Cicero did not share this sanguine view of the Roman past; nor, as has been suggested earlier, did he accept the premise essential to such a view, *i.e.,* that the strict demands of justice can be perfectly compatible with those of civil society. Finally, he was not at all certain that everyone is equally equipped to acquire a full understanding of the natural law and equally equipped to be guided by it. While all men may in principle acquire the wisdom and virtue requisite to the life of human excellence, the life according to nature, the life guided by fully developed reason, few in fact do so. Few find that guide of whom he had spoken earlier; most succumb quite easily to "bad habits and false beliefs," to the attractions of pleasure and vice.[50] If this is so, then it is entirely possible that the full demands of natural law are incompatible with the needs and claims of human society as we know it. In the *Republic,* for example, Cicero suggests that the law of the wise, *i.e.,* the unmitigated natural law, would assign property rights simply on the basis of the ability to use the property well.[51] Such a principle would be impossible to implement in civil society as we know it. The lesson is clear: the unmitigated and pure natural law may be inapplicable to the normal human situation. The natural law to which the activities of men and states are normally to be referred must be a diluted version of this true law, one whose standards are necessarily lower.

A similar understanding is present in Cicero's discussion of the rules of personal conduct or action in *De Officiis*. It is soon made clear that the standard being discussed there is that which should govern the conduct of the nonwise rather than the wise man.[52] While adequate to guide the lives of most men, it is inferior to that higher standard, the standard of nature itself, which guides the actions of the wise man. The definition of natural law which Cicero propounds at several points in the *Laws* also possesses this twofold character. In the second book, for example, he speaks of the natural law in the following vein:

I find that it has been the opinion of the wisest men that Law is not a product of human thought, nor is it any enactment of peoples, but something eternal which rules the whole universe by its wisdom in command and prohibition. Thus they have been accustomed to say that Law is the primal and ultimate mind of God, whose reason directs all things either by compulsion or restraint. Wherefore that law which the gods have given to the human race has been justly praised; for it is the reason and mind of a wise lawgiver applied to command and prohibition.[53]

The eternal law which rules the universe and exists in the "primal and ultimate mind of God," the law which both Cicero and Laelius have referred to elsewhere as "the highest reason inherent in nature," [54] is not simply or necessarily identical with the second and lower form of law, "the reason and mind of a wise lawgiver applied to command and prohibition." The latter is derivative from and based on the former but reflects an understanding of the lower standards which are a necessary part of political life. "The essential nature of the commonwealth often defeats reason." [55] The wise legislator and statesman will thus temper the demands of pure justice and pure reason, as Cicero does in composing the code suited to his "best" state in the *Laws,* so that they become compatible with the requirements of civil society. It should be noted, of course, that this understanding does not force Cicero to embrace the position advanced by Philus: that justice, because its specific substantive demands are not always and everywhere the same, is fundamentally arbitrary, that it is not natural but conventional. The substance of human justice, although concerned with the particular and dependent on a variety of contingent circumstances, is not, for Cicero, simply arbitrary. The standards remain, even though their complete realization, given the nature of man and the nature of political society, is extremely unlikely. They continue to serve as guides to human action, and one should always seek to approximate them as nearly as possible.

The *Laws* illuminates the question of the status of the active or political life with which the inquiry in the *Republic* began. Cicero's inquiry in these two books is directed to an understanding of the nature of political things. He has sought, as Plato had done before him, to pursue this larger inquiry by setting forth the nature of the best political order. One product of the investigation is the understanding of the limitations intrinsic to political life. Both reason and justice must somehow be diluted to meet the needs of the practical or political life. Those who are in a position to make a choice between the two ways of life, the active and the contemplative, must be aware of this fact.

NOTES

1. Reprinted by permission of the publishers from "The Loeb Classical Library," Marcus Tullius Cicero, *Laws*, trans. C. W. Keyes (Cambridge, Mass.: Harvard University Press, 1928), I. 58; *Tusculan Disputations*, trans. J. E. King ("Loeb Classical Library" [Cambridge, Mass.: Harvard University Press, 1927]) I. 1–8.

2. *Tusculan Disputations* I. 1–5; II. 4; IV. 5–6.

3. The doctrines of this school are considered in detail in E. Zeller, *The Stoics, Epicureans and Sceptics* (London: Longmans, Green, 1870); and Edwyn Bevan, *Stoics and Sceptics* (Cambridge: W. Heffer and Sons, 1959).

4. *Laws* II. 39.

5. *Tusculan Disputations* V. 11.

6. Paul Friedlander, *Plato; An Introduction* (London: Routledge and Kegan Paul, 1958), pp. 154–70.

7. Reprinted by permission of the publishers from "The Loeb Classical Library," Cicero, *Republic*, trans. C. W. Keyes (Cambridge, Mass.: Harvard University Press, 1928) I. 2.

8. *Ibid.*, I. 15.

9. *Ibid.*, I. 28.

10. *Ibid.*, III. 4–6.

11. *Ibid.*, I. 8.

12. *Laws* I. 37.

13. *Laws* II. 35.

14. *Republic* II. 66.

15. *Laws* III. 37.

16. *Republic* II. 52.

17. *Ibid.*, I. 39.

18. *Ibid.*

19. *Laws* III. **3.**

20. *Ibid.*, III. **5.**

21. *Republic* I. 54.

22. *Ibid.*, I. 43.

23. *Ibid.*, I. 68.

24. *Ibid.*, I. 69; II. 57, 69.

25. *The Histories*, trans. W. R. Paton ("Loeb Classical Library" [Cambridge, Mass.: Harvard University Press, 1927]), VI. 11.11.

26. *Ibid.*, VI. 11.12.

27. *Republic* II. 57–58.

28. *Laws* II. 30; III. 24–25, **28, 38.**

29. *Ibid.*, III. 25.

30. *Ibid.*, III. 30.

31. *Ibid.*, III. 31.

32. *Republic* II. 2.

33. *The Works of Edmund Burke* (London: "Bohn's Standard Library"), II, 554; V, 253–54.

34. *Ibid.*, II. 307–8.

35. *Republic* II. 21.

36. *Ibid.*, II. 19.

37. *Ibid.*, I. 65.

38. *Ibid.*, II. 52.

39. *Laws* III. 26.

40. *Republic* III. 24.

41. *Ibid.*, III. 33.

42. *Laws* I. 17.

43. For details in regard to the Stoic teaching see E. Vernon Arnold, *Roman*

Stoicism (Cambridge: Cambridge University Press, 1911).

44. *Laws* I. 30.
45. *Ibid.*, I. 19.
46. *Ibid.*, I. 39.
47. *Ibid.*, I. 37.
48. *Ibid.*

49. *Ibid.*, II. 15–69.
50. *Ibid.*, I. 29–34, 47.
51. *Republic* I. 27.
52. *De Officiis* I. 7–8; III. 11–17.
53. *Laws* II. 8.
54. *Republic* III. 33; *Laws* I. 18.
55. *Republic* II. 57.

READINGS

A. Cicero. *Republic.* Bks I, VI.
   Cicero. *Laws.* Bk I.
B. Cicero. *Republic.*
   Cicero. *Laws.*
   Cicero. *Offices.* Bks I, III.

ST. AUGUSTINE

354–430

St. Augustine is the first author to deal more or less comprehensively with the subject of civil society in the light of the new situation created by the emergence of revealed religion and its encounter with philosophy in the Greco-Roman world. As a Roman he inherited and restated for his own time the political philosophy inaugurated by Plato and adapted to the Latin world by Cicero, and as a Christian he modified that philosophy to suit the requirements of the faith. He thus appears if not as the originator at least as the foremost exponent in ancient times of a new tradition of political thought characterized by its attempt to fuse or reconcile elements derived from two originally independent and hitherto unrelated sources, the Bible and classical philosophy.

Augustine writes first and foremost as a theologian and not as a philosopher. He rarely refers to himself as a philosopher and he never undertook a methodical treatment of political phenomena in the light of reason and experience alone. His highest principles are drawn not from reason but from Sacred Scripture, whose authority he never questions and which he regards as the final source of truth concerning man in general and political man in particular. However, to the extent to which the choice of his position rests on a prior consideration of the most important alternative to that position, it presupposes an understanding of political philosophy or of political things as they appear to unaided human reason.

In the investigation of such philosophic matters Christians had enjoyed almost from the outset a larger measure of freedom than their Jewish or, later, their Muslim counterparts; for, unlike either Judaism or Islam, the other two great religions of the Western world, Christianity did not reject philosophy as an alien or merely tolerate it but sought early to enlist its support, making room for philosophy within the walls of Christendom, where it continued to thrive with varying degrees of ecclesiastical approval and supervision. Accordingly, Augustine acknowledges in man a capacity to know which precedes the faith. This knowledge, obtained without the help of Revelation, is the invention and the proper preserve of the pagan philosophers. It has since been superseded by faith as the supreme norm and guide of life, but it has not been nullified or rendered superfluous by it. Even after the final manifestation of the divine truth in New Testament times, God, the author of Revelation, not only does not forbid but positively enjoins the use of reason to acquire human knowledge. It would be foolish to think that he hates in us "that very quality by which he has raised us above the beasts." [1] The knowledge arrived at in this manner remains inadequate, but it is valid in its own right and is ultimately willed by God as an aid to the faith. Augustine compares it to the objects of gold and silver surreptitiously taken and claimed as a rightful possession by the Israelites at the time of the departure from Egypt. [2]

More specifically, philosophy serves the faith both in itself and in its relation to nonbelievers. It complements divine revelation by supplying knowledge and guidance in areas concerning which Revelation is either silent or incomplete. Even in matters about which Revelation does speak, philosophy may be used as a tool to gain a fuller understanding of the divinely inspired truth; just as the necessarily imperfect human knowledge points toward faith as its fulfillment, so faith seeks a more perfect grasp of its own principles through the use of reason. [3] Furthermore, although the New Testament is primarily concerned with man's eternal destiny, it has much to say about the condition of rulers and subjects and, in general, about the manner in which men are called upon to live in the city; for it is by his actions in this life that man merits the blessedness of eternal life. Since the spheres of the spiritual and of the temporal constantly intersect and impinge on each other, it becomes necessary to correlate them, and any attempt to do so presupposes a knowledge not only of Revelation but of philosophy as well. Finally, dealing as it does with truths that are in principle accessible to all men, philosophy provides a common ground on which believers and nonbelievers can meet. Only by means of philosophy is the Christian able to make his position intelligible to outsiders and, if need be, to combat with their own weapons the objections that they raise against it. [4] All such objections are thereby made to serve a useful purpose in that they stimulate greater efforts on behalf of the faith and help ward off the complacency engendered by the tranquil possession of a God-given truth.

It is hardly surprising then to find that, despite their avowedly theological character, Augustine's works include numerous considerations of a strictly philosophic nature. By extracting these considerations from their native context, one might be able to reconstruct and expound methodically what could properly be regarded as Augustine's political philosophy. However, since Augustine himself, unlike Aquinas, does not look upon philosophy as a self-contained and, in its own realm, independent discipline, or since he does not in fact deal with philosophy and theology as separate sciences, it seems preferable to respect the unity of his thought and to present his views on political matters as a single, coherent whole governed by theological principles.

Augustine is, at least on the basis of extant texts, the most voluminous writer of the ancient world. His most extensive work, and his single most important political work, is the *City of God*. The *City of God,* however, does not limit itself to politics, nor does it encompass all of Augustine's most pertinent thoughts on this subject. For a thematic discussion of justice and law, one must turn above all to the treatise *On Free Will,* and for his position on the vexed question of the use of secular power to repress heresy, to the works against the Donatists. Specific mention should also be made of *Letters* 91 and 138, addressed to the pagan Nectarius and to Marcellinus respectively, which provide a lucid defense of Augustine's views on patriotism and citizenship. There are, needless to say, numerous other works in which political considerations play a significant if subsidiary role.

The largely polemical nature of these works, dictated with rare exceptions by the circumstances of a running controversy with pagans and heretics (especially Manichees, Donatists, and Pelagians), render their interpretation difficult at times. In addition, there is evidence that Augustine shared with his predecessors, both pagan and Christian, the view that the whole truth in matters of supreme moment can be safeguarded only if its investigation is accompanied by a prudent reserve in the expression of that truth.[5] The difficulty inherent in the highest truths precludes their being made easily available to all indiscriminately. Not only error but truth itself can be harmful, inasmuch as men are not all equally well disposed toward it or sufficiently prepared to receive it. Experience had already taught that if philosophy could be used to buttress the faith, it might under less favorable circumstances prove a positive hindrance to it. Many of the major heresies of the first centuries could be traced back to the well-intentioned but misguided recourse to philosophic doctrines on the part of heterodox writers; and there was always the possibility that, by reasserting its claim to supremacy, philosophy would once again transform itself into an enemy and a rival of the faith. The simple presence of philosophy within the fold constituted a latent but abiding threat to Christian orthodoxy and cautioned against the premature exposure of young or foolish minds to its teachings. "He who dares to embark rashly and without order upon the study of those questions," observes Augustine, "will become not studious but curious, not learned but credulous, not prudent but unbelieving." [6]

Augustine attempts to forestall these dangers by writing in such a way as to satisfy the legitimate curiosity of the worthier and more demanding student without prejudice to the faith of the less well-informed or less perspicacious reader for whom a nonscientific presentation of dogma is all that is needed or possible.[7] His major works are for the most part addressed both to Christians who seek a deeper knowledge of the divinely revealed truth and to interested pagans who might find in them an added incentive to embrace the faith. These works may be said to constitute at once a philosophic defense of the faith, whose reasonableness they emphasize, and a theological defense of philosophy, for which they provide a justification on the basis of Sacred Scripture. They explore the similarities and differences between philosophy and revealed truth for the express purpose of establishing the substantial harmony of the two, as well as the ultimate superiority of the latter over the former. They are designed to make the student who has already progressed in the knowledge of the faith more fully aware of the implications of his beliefs, and at the same time they strive to remove any obstacle that could stand in the way of an intelligent acceptance of the revealed truth on the part of the nonbeliever. In consequence, they discuss openly the points of actual or potential agreement between philosophy and Revelation, and often only hint at those points on which any such reconciliation is plainly impossible. To that extent, they make use of what Augustine himself calls "the art of concealing the truth." [8] In order to be fully understood, they require that one take into account not only the author's explicit statements on a given matter but the issues that these statements raise tacitly or implicitly. It should be added that, whereas some of the earlier Church Fathers like Clement of Alexandria and Origen defended the use of noble lies in the common interest, Augustine denounces all lies, salutary or otherwise, as intrinsically evil and, following a precedent that he alleges to have been set by Christ, admits only of indirect forms of concealment, such as omissions and brevity of speech. As he is careful to point out in his treatise *Against Lies,*

To hide the truth is not the same thing as to utter a lie. Every liar writes to conceal the truth, but not everyone who conceals the truth is a liar; for we often conceal the truth not only by lying but by remaining silent.... It is therefore permissible for a speaker and an exponent or preacher of eternal truths, or even for someone who discusses or pronounces upon temporal matters pertaining to the edification of religion and piety, to conceal at an opportune moment anything that may seem advisable to conceal; but it is never permissible to lie and hence to conceal by means of lies.[9]

Augustine regarded Plato as the greatest of the pagan philosophers and as the philosopher whose thought most closely approximated that of Christianity.[10] He even goes so far as to speak of him as the philosopher who would have become a Christian if he had lived in Christian times.[11] However, his primary source of information concerning Plato's political philosophy is not Plato himself, to whose dialogues he had only limited access, but Cicero's Roman and stoicized version of that philosophy as it is found in Cicero's *Republic* and *Laws* and to a lesser extent in such other works as the treatises *On the Nature of the Gods* and *On Divination*. In the form in which it presents itself, Augustine's political thought is thus more directly Ciceronian than Platonic in content and expression. Unfortunately, both the *Republic* and the *Laws* of Cicero have come down to us in a mutilated state. Of the six books that they originally comprised, less than half survive in each case. Notwithstanding the difficulty caused by this lacuna, it is apparent that Augustine's thought differs from that of his pagan master on three important and closely related points: the notion of virtue, monotheism, and the dichotomy between religion and politics.

THE NATURE OF CIVIL SOCIETY: CHRISTIAN VERSUS PAGAN VIRTUE

The core of Augustine's political doctrine may be said to be his teaching concerning virtue, a teaching that has its roots in both the philosophic and biblical traditions. Man is by nature a social animal, who alone has been endowed with speech, by means of which he is able to communicate and enter into various relationships with other men. It is only by associating with his fellow men and forming with them a political community that man attains his perfection. Even in the state of innocence men would have sought one another's company and would have tended together toward the final goal of human existence.

The virtue that characterizes the citizen as citizen and orders all citizens to the end or common good of the city is justice. Justice is the cornerstone of civil society. Upon it depend the unity and nobility of any human society. By regulating the relations among men it preserves peace, the intrinsic common good of society and the precondition of all the other benefits that society procures. Without peace, the "tranquility order," [12] no society can prosper or even subsist. Quoting Cicero with approval, Augustine defines civil society or the commonwealth as "an assemblage (of men) associated by a common acknowledgement of right and by a community of interests." [13] He explains "right" by "justice" rather than by "law," and he insists that no commonwealth can be administered without justice, for where there is no justice there is no right and vice versa.

In all this Augustine follows closely the classical tradition and stresses its substantial agreement with Sacred Scripture. His chief objection to the pagan philosophers concerns not so much their doctrine of the naturalness of civil society and the need for justice within it as their inability to bring about a just society. The philosophers are the first to grant that their model of the best and most desirable city is one which has its existence in speech and private discussions only and not one which is capable of being realized in deed. They point to justice as the healthy condition of cities, but they are powerless to secure its performance. [14] There is no denying that the proposals that the philosophers make in the interest of society and for its improvement deserve the highest praise; but their proposals as practical measures fail signally, inasmuch as the obvious and inescapable wickedness of most men precludes such proposals being implemented in the political community at large. The locus par excellence of justice is the city; yet justice is seldom and perhaps never found to exist in it. By the philosophers' own admission, actual cities are characterized by injustice rather than by justice. In order to vindicate for them the title of cities in the true sense of the word, one would have to omit from Cicero's definition any reference to justice or virtue. Existing cities are assemblages of rational beings bound together not by "a common acknowledgement of right" but by "a common agreement as to the objects of their love," regardless of the quality of that love or the goodness or badness of its objects. [15] The whole argument may be accurately summed up as follows: By asserting the eminent desirability of perfect human justice and at the same time its practical impossibility, philosophy discloses its own inherent limitations; it thus proclaims at least implicitly the need to supplement human justice by a higher and more genuine form of justice. It is important to note that the case against political philosophy does not proceed from revealed premises, which nonbelievers would have been free to reject, or for that matter from premises foreign to the classical scheme. Its strength derives entirely from the fact that it appeals directly to a principle which was indigenous to the thought of Augustine's adversaries and which they were compelled to accept, even if they questioned the conclusion that he purports to draw from it.

Augustine's critique of the classical tradition resembles in many ways that of the early modern political thinkers, beginning with Machiavelli, who likewise took issue with that tradition on the grounds of its ineffectualness and impracticality. But in contradistinction to Machiavelli and his followers, Augustine does not seek to enhance the efficacy of his teaching by lowering the goals and standards of human activity. If anything, his own demands are even more stringent than the most stringent demands of the pagan philosophers. Classical political philosophy has failed, not because—by its stubborn refusal to take into account the all too deplorably human character of man's behavior —it makes unreasonable demands on human nature, but because it did not know and hence could not apply the proper remedy to man's congenital weakness.

Following a procedure that is more typical of Plato than of Aristotle, who generally prefers to.deal with moral matters on their own level and without explicit reference to their metaphysical presuppositions, Augustine attempts to deduce the standards of human behavior from theoretical or premoral principles. His moral order is expressly rooted in a natural order established by speculative reason. Justice in the highest sense prescribes the right ordering of all things according to reason. This order requires the universal and complete subordination of the lower to the higher both within man and outside of him. It exists when the body is ruled by the soul, when the lower appetites are ruled by reason, and when reason itself is ruled by God. The same hierarchy is or should be observed in society as a whole and is encountered when virtuous subjects obey wise rulers, whose minds are in turn subject to the divine law.[16] Such is the harmony which would have prevailed if man had persevered in the state of original justice. In that state men would have benefited from all the advantages of society without any of its inconveniences. They would not have been subjected against their will to other men and, instead of vying with one another for the possession of earthly goods, they would have shared all things equitably in perfect amity and freedom.

Sacred Scripture teaches that this harmony was disrupted by sin. Through sin man's lust and overweening desire to assert his dominion over his fellow men have been unleashed. The present economy is marked by the anarchy of man's lower appetites and an invincible tendency to place one's selfish interests above the common good of society. It is a state of permanent revolt, which has its source in man's initial revolt against God. The prototype of this revolt is original sin, the sin committed by Adam and transmitted in a mysterious way to all his descendents. As a result, the freedom that man once enjoyed in the pursuit of the good has yielded to oppression and coercion. Coercion is apparent in the most typical institutions of civil society, such as private property, slavery, and government itself, all of which are necessitated and explained by man's present inability to live according to the dictates of reason.[17] The very existence of these institutions is a consequence and a permanent reminder of man's fallen condition. None was part of the original plan of creation and all of them are desirable only as a means of inhibiting man's proneness to evil. The private ownership of temporal goods both gratifies and curbs man's innate and unquenchable greed. By excluding other men from the possession of the same goods, it removes the external conditions and hence the possibility of unlimited acquisition; but it does not cure the inner desire for it. The same is true of slavery and of all other forms of the domination of man by man. Even civil society as we know it is a punishment for sin. If it can be called natural at all, it is only in reference to man's fallen nature. Like private property, it too is willed by God as a further means of checking his insatiable lust to dominate. All rule is inseparable from coercion and is despotic to that degree. The whole of political society becomes punitive and remedial in nature and purpose. Its role is essentially a negative one, that of castigating wrongdoers and of restraining evil among men by the use of force.

Justice is neither the work nor the common lot of fallen man. Even the good that is proportionate to his rational nature eludes him for the most part. The remedy to this situation is not to be found among the proper resources of human nature. Man's salvation, including his political salvation, accrues to him, not from philosophy, as Plato had intimated, but from God. Divine grace rather than human justice is the bond of society and the true source of happiness.[18] But by definition this grace is given gratuitously; it can be received by man but it is not merited by him, for man's merits are themselves the effect and not the principle of the grace conferred. In the actual state of humanity, the task of securing the good life devolves specifically upon the church as the divinely instituted and visible instrument of God's grace. The scope of civil society is drastically limited in comparison with that assigned to it by classical philosophy. At best, civil society can by its repressive action maintain relative peace among men and in this fashion insure the minimal conditions under which the church is able to exercise its teaching and saving ministry. Of itself it is incapable of leading to virtue.

Augustine's verdict concerning the fundamentally defective character of human justice is corroborated and further clarified by his analysis of law in Book I of the treatise *On Free Will*. Augustine begins by distinguishing clearly between the eternal law, which is the supreme norm of justice, and the temporal or human law, which adapts the common principles of the eternal law to the changing needs of particular societies. The eternal law is defined very generally as the law "in virtue of which it is just that all things be perfectly ordered," and is identified with the will or wisdom of God directing all things to their proper end.[19] It constitutes the universal font of justice and righteousness, and from it flows whatever is just or good in other laws. God himself has impressed this law upon the human mind. All are capable of knowing it and owe obedience to it at all times. It is also by virtue of the eternal law that the good are rewarded and the wicked punished. Finally, the eternal law is always and everywhere the same and suffers no exceptions.

As opposed to the eternal law, which is totally immutable, the temporal law can, without injustice, vary according to circumstances of time and place.[20] As a law, it is edicted for the common good and is necessarily a just law; for a law that is not just is not a law.[21] Yet a temporal law may differ from and even be contrary to other temporal laws. If, for example, the majority of the citizens of a given city were virtuous and dedicated to the public good, democracy would be a requirement of justice and a law enjoining that the magistrates of that city be chosen by the people would be a just law. By the same token, in a corrupt city a law stipulating that only a man who is virtuous and capable of directing others to virtue should be appointed to office would likewise be a just law. Although mutually exclusive, both laws derive their justice from the eternal law, according to which it is always proper that honors should be distributed by virtuous men rather than by wicked men; for neither compulsion, nor chance, nor any emergency will ever render unjust the equitable distribution of goods within the city.[22] This variable temporal law is precisely what distinguishes one city from another and lends to each its unity and specific character. Cities and peoples are nothing else but associations of human beings living under and bound by a single temporal law.[23]

If the temporal law is a just law, it is also in many ways an imperfect law. It exists, not primarily for the sake of the virtuous, who strive of their own accord toward eternal goods and are subject only to the eternal law, but for the sake of the imperfect, who covet temporal goods and act justly only when compelled to do so by a human law.[24] To the extent to which it takes into account, as it must, the needs and claims of morally inferior men, it represents an adjustment between what is most desirable in itself and what is possible at any given moment, permitting lesser evils for the unique purpose of averting greater and more flagrant ones.[25] Its efficacy stems directly from man's attachment to earthly goods. It is solely because men are the slaves of these earthly goods that the law has any power over them. Thus, according to strict justice, only the man who uses wealth rightly is entitled to its possession. In the interest of peace and as a concession to human weakness, however, the temporal law sanctions the private ownership of material goods, regardless of the use that is made of them by the owner. At the same time, by threatening to deprive unjust men of the goods they already possess as a punishment for their transgressions, it acts as a deterrent to further injustices and safeguards what may be considered an approximation to the equitable assignment of temporal goods.[26] The most that can be said in behalf of temporal law is that it shrewdly takes advantage of man's perversity to bring about and maintain a limited measure of justice in society. For this reason alone it remains indispensable, but the justice that it embodies is no more than an image or a dilution of perfect justice.

Even within its own sphere, and despite its restricted goals, the temporal law often fails to achieve the end for which it was instituted. In the first place, it is not unreasonable to suppose that men commit many injustices which go undetected and therefore unpunished. Say that someone has entrusted a large sum of money to a friend and dies suddenly without having had a chance to claim his deposit. Assuming that no one else is aware of the transaction, what is to prevent the trustee, if he should so desire, from appropriating the money instead of returning it to the lawful heir?[27] Secondly, even when a crime is known to have been perpetrated, it is often impossible to identify the criminal. Wise and good judges are easily mistaken. Despite all their precautions to insure the proper administration of justice, they unwittingly sentence innocent men to death. In the hope of ascertaining the truth, they will occasionally resort to torture; but torture frequently does little more than involve innocent persons in suffering without leading to the discovery of the guilty party. In a dramatic way it, too, reveals to what degree human justice is shrouded in darkness.[28] Lastly and most importantly, the temporal law only prescribes and forbids external acts. It does not extend to the hidden motives of these acts, and it is even less concerned with purely internal acts, such as the desire to commit murder or adultery.[29] For that reason, if for no other, it cannot be said to instill virtue. Genuine virtue requires that one not only perform just acts but that he perform them for the right motive. It implies on the part of the doer a desire for the good commanded by the law. It therefore presupposes that one has renounced the inordinate love of worldly goods and has ordered his passions to the good of reason. Mere compliance with the temporal law is no guarantee of moral goodness, for one can abide by the law and still act for a purely egoistic or utilitarian motive. The law, for example, permits the killing of an unjust aggressor in self-defense. In so doing, it aims at the common good and is itself entirely free from passion. But the man who avails himself of the liberty thus granted to him could easily be gratifying a selfish desire for personal revenge; in which case his act, although externally just, would be morally blameworthy. It is true that by demanding just acts of everyone the temporal law predisposes men to the acquisition of virtue. But it can go no further. It therefore needs to be complemented by a "higher and more secret law," [30] namely, the eternal law, which encompasses all of man's acts, including his internal acts, and which alone is capable of producing virtue and not merely its appearance.

Thus far Augustine's treatment of this whole question parallels closely that of Cicero's *Laws* and even bears many textual resemblances to it. The similarity ceases the moment we come to the issue of divine providence, with which in Augustine's mind the notion of an eternal law is intrinsically bound up. The distance that separates the two authors on this point is partly manifested by the difference in terminology between them. Both Cicero and Augustine distinguish the eternal or natural law from the temporal or human law; but whereas Cicero habitually speaks of the former as the "natural law," Augustine shows a marked preference for the expression, the "eternal law." This eternal law not only points to what men should do or should avoid if they wish to be happy or good, it issues commands and prohibitions. It must therefore be accompanied by appropriate sanctions, for otherwise it would be ineffectual, and all the more so as it embraces the internal acts of the will, of which other human beings are not competent judges. Since it is obvious from experience that innocent men often suffer unjustly and that the misdeeds of wicked men are not always punished here on earth, the eternal law cannot be conceived without an afterlife in which wrongs are righted and the perfect order of justice is restored. It implies the existence of a just, provident, and all-knowing God, who rewards and punishes everyone according to his just deserts. Being eternal and all-perfect, God is subject to change neither in his being nor in his actions. He cannot acquire new knowledge and must know in advance as it were all the actions to be accomplished by men in the course of time and even their most secret thoughts.

This doctrine of divine sanctions was fraught from the start with considerable theoretical difficulties. If we assume that God knows all things before they come into being, it necessarily follows that men will always act in conformity with that divine knowledge; but under these conditions it is hard to see how they could be thought to remain free. One would thus appear to be faced with a choice between two alternatives, neither of which is acceptable from the standpoint of political society. One can assert that men are free and deny that God has any knowledge of the crimes committed against the eternal law or the just deeds executed in accordance with it; but then the eternal law is left without a guarantor and is thereby deprived of any means by which it could effectively restrain potential wrongdoers and promote virtuous habits. Or else one can assert divine foreknowledge and deny free will; but in that case men can no longer be held accountable for their actions, laws lose their raison d'être, exhortation becomes futile, praise and blame are revealed to be meaningless, and there ceases to be any justice whatever in the apportionment of rewards for the good and punishments for the wicked; in short, the whole economy of human life is subverted.[31]

According to Augustine's interpretation, Cicero attempted to fight his way out of this dilemma by openly professing and privately disavowing the doctrine of divine prescience. In the very public discussion of the treatise *On the Nature of the Gods,* he sides with the pious Lucilius Balbus, who defends the gods, against the atheist Cotta, who attacks them; but in his less popular work *On Divination,* he states with approval and expounds in his own name the very theory that he feigns to reject in the former treatise. By this subterfuge, he cleverly avoided undermining the salutary belief of the multitude in divine rewards and punishments without committing himself to a teaching which the learned find incompatible with human freedom and with which in any event they can easily dispense, since they need no such inducements in order to behave justly. Thus, concludes Augustine, "wishing to make men free, he makes them sacrilegious." [32]

Against Cicero, Augustine asserts both that God knows all things before they come to pass and that men do by their free will whatever they know and sense to be done by them only because they will it. Far from destroying free choice, God's knowledge actually founds it. The answer to the question as to how these two perfections may be reconciled lies in the supreme efficacy of the divine will. God knows all things because he knows their causes; and he knows their causes because his will extends to all of them, conferring upon each the power not only to act but to act in conformity with its proper mode. Natural causes exercise a necessary causality and voluntary causes a free one. Just as there is no power in natural causes that is not already contained in God, the author of nature, and is not bestowed by him, so there is nothing in man's will that is not already found in God, the creator of that will, and cannot be known by him. Otherwise one would have to postulate the existence in creatures of certain perfections that are absent from God, the universal source of all perfection. What is true of natural and voluntary causes is also true of fortuitous causes or chance. Chance is not just a name for the absence of a cause. What men call chance is really, for Augustine, a latent cause attributable either to God or to the separate substances. A problem could still be raised in regard to evil, which cannot be traced back to God as to its cause. But the fact that God does not cause sin in no way derogates from his perfection, since a sinful act, as sinful, is an imperfection explainable only in terms of deficient causality.[33] Nor does it presuppose that God must remain ignorant of the sins that men commit. If God knows what men can and will do, he also knows what they should do and will fail to do. It is true of course that men's deeds are performed in time and thus belong either to the past, the present, or the future. But even this does not prevent God from knowing them immutably. Standing as he does above time and outside of it, God knows everything from all eternity by means of a knowledge that is not measured by things but is itself the measure of all things and their perfection.

Having said this much, Augustine is fully aware of the obscurity that continues to surround our knowledge of the divine essence and its operations. His explanation may leave many questions unanswered, but, on purely rational grounds, he finds it no more difficult to accept than Cicero's, and it has in his eyes the advantage of making it possible for men not only to "live well" but to "believe well." [34]

Augustine's views on human justice and law underlie and motivate his judgment concerning the societies of the past and above all his judgment concerning Rome, the last of the great empires and the epitome of the pagan world's most brilliant political achievements.[35] The groundwork for his lengthy discussion of this subject was again laid in part by Cicero. Instead of founding a perfect city in speech, as Plato had done, Cicero sought to reawaken interest in the political life by turning to the example of the old Roman republic. In accordance with this more traditional and more practical approach, he was led to magnify the past glories of his fellow countrymen. Augustine, on the other hand, sets out to unmask their vices. These vices are nowhere more conspicuous than in Rome's dealings with other nations. Because there is no internal justice in the city, there is no external justice either; for a city that is not at peace with itself cannot be at peace with its neighbors. The so-called kingdoms of this world are hardly more than gigantic larcenies. They differ from robber gangs not by the removal of covetousness but by the magnitude of their crimes and the impunity with which they commit them. From the essential viewpoint of justice, what Alexander does on a grand scale and with a huge fleet is no better than what a pirate does on a much smaller scale and with a lone vessel.[36] Even republican Rome, for which Augustine professes a much greater regard than for the Rome of imperial days, is included in the common reprobation that engulfs all earthly cities. Rome "was never a republic because true justice and law never had a place in it." [37] The corresponding section of the *City of God* presents itself as an attempt to restore, against the embellishments of the Roman philosophers and historians, what Augustine regards as a true and faithful picture of ancient Rome.

To diagnose the character of any people one has only to consult the object of its love.[38] The old Romans were not just, and their city was not a true city, because the object of their passion was not virtue. No doubt the Romans were more worthy of admiration than any of the nations they subdued. The goal for which they toiled was by no means a vile one. It extolled courage and placed self-sacrifice and devotion to one's country above the amenities of a quiet and comfortable existence.[39] But it was nonetheless a purely earthly goal. The efforts expended in its pursuit bore the mark of greatness but not of virtue. Rome, the mistress of the world, was herself dominated by the lust to conquer. Her great men were at best outstanding citizens of a bad city. Most of them did not even possess genuinely political virtues. Their determination to excel was fed not by a desire to serve their countrymen but by the thirst for personal glory. Being practiced for what was ultimately a selfish motive, their reputedly heroic virtues were in fact little more than resplendent vices.[40] To the degree to which the Romans renounced pleasure and the gratification of their lower appetites, they were entitled to some reward. God granted this reward when he allowed Rome to assert her supremacy over all other nations.[41] Thus, in extending her conquests to the limits of the civilized world, Rome was able to fulfill her deepest aspirations and attain the end implied in all earthly ambition, universal domination. But the argument stops here. In opposition to a long-standing and at the time still powerful tradition of Christian apologetics, Augustine is apparently unwilling to concede that the Roman empire was assigned a special role in the economy of salvation and that, by bringing the whole world into one fellowship of government and laws, it even remotely prepared the way for Christianity, the one true and universal religion.[42]

Augustine's polemic against Rome is all the more striking as it comes from one who is obviously impressed by the spectacle of Rome's former greatness. Livy's account of the glorious deeds of the Scaevolas and Scipios, of Regulus and Fabricius, still fired his imagination, and he takes particular delight in relating their exploits.[43] Admirable as they may be by other standards, these exploits nevertheless belong to an irretrievable past whose memory awakens a certain sadness in the mind of the beholder but which Christianity has doomed once and for all. Christ, the sun of righteousness, has eclipsed the brightest beacons of the ancient world. His advent has destroyed forever the stage on which the pagan hero could move. True heroism is Christian heroism, but it is no longer the same type of heroism. Its newness is evinced by the fact that our "heroes" are called "martyrs" or witnesses rather than "heroes." [44] Henceforth, the accomplishments of the most noble Romans serve only two purposes: they reveal, along with the depths of human greed, the ephemeral and ultimately self-annihilating character of any purely human achievement; and they remind Christians that, if the Romans were willing to undergo such hardships for the sake of earthly gain, they themselves should be prepared to make even greater sacrifices for the sake of an eternal reward.[45]

By his devastating attack on pagan virtue, Augustine is more than anyone else responsible for the disparagement of Rome which became the hallmark of any discussion of Roman politics in the Christian world. The magnitude of his accomplishment can perhaps best be conveyed by saying that, almost singlehandedly, he imposed a new image of Rome which, from that moment forward, preempted in the minds of statesmen and political writers alike the image elaborated by the Roman historians and particularly by Livy, the trumpet of Rome's eternal greatness. Not until the Renaissance do we find a fresh attempt to recapture, beneath the massive and relentless indictments of the *City of God,* the spirit of pagan Rome and its distinctive way of life.

MONOTHEISM AND THE PROBLEM OF CIVIL RELIGION

According to Augustine, the real reason for which the classical scheme is unable to make men virtuous and is convicted by its own standards is not that it is irreligious but that it is intrinsically linked to a false conception of the divinity. This falseness is most clearly revealed in pagan polytheism. Much of what Augustine wrote on the subject of civil society, including the whole first part of the *City of God,* is in effect little more than a long and detailed criticism of pagan mythology.

Following Varro, Augustine divides all of pagan theology into three basic forms: mythical, natural or philosophic, and civil or political.[46] Mythical theology is the theology of the poets. It appeals directly to the multitude and its many gods and goddesses are revered for the sake of the temporal goods or material advantages that men hope to obtain from them in this life. Natural theology is the theology of the philosophers and is monotheistic. It rests on a true notion of God and as such it is vastly superior to both mythical and civil theology; but it remains inaccessible to all save a few exceptionally gifted and learned individuals and is therefore incapable of exerting a beneficial influence on society as a whole. Civil theology, as the name indicates, is the official theology of the city. It differs from natural theology in that it is polytheistic, and from mythical theology in that it prescribes the worship of the pagan gods on account of the life after death and not of this life. It is the theology that all citizens and especially priests are expected to know and administer. It teaches what god or gods each man may suitably worship and what sacred rites and sacrifices he may suitably carry out. Although civil theology imposes the cult of false gods, it is nevertheless more tolerable than mythical theology, for it is concerned with the good of the soul rather than that of the body and aspires to make men better by favoring the development of the political virtues.

The most authoritative exponent of Roman civil theology is Varro, to whom Augustine, quoting Cicero, constantly refers as a most acute and learned man.[47] Augustine's method consists in using Varro as a witness against himself to prove the inadequacy of civil theology. Varro defended civil theology not because it was true but because it was useful. He himself did not accept it and did not take its gods seriously. He insinuated as much by the fact that he distinguished clearly between civil theology and natural theology. The same conclusion is borne out by an analysis of his *Antiquities,* where the treatment of human things precedes that of divine things. By adopting this arrangement, Varro let it be understood that the gods of the city did not exist independently of man but were themselves the products of the human mind. This, says Augustine, is the secret of his book. In that subtle manner Varro signified his unwillingness to give priority to error over truth. If he had been dealing with the truly divine or with the divine nature in its entirety, which he regarded as superior to human nature, he would not have hesitated to reverse the order. As it is, he merely expressed a laudable preference for men over the institutions of men or, in his own words, for the painter over the painting.[48]

Varro's views in this matter were no different from those of other pagan philosophers and particularly of Seneca. Because philosophy had made him free, Seneca did not refrain from attacking civil theology in his writings; but like Varro he continued to feign respect for its sacred rites and tenets. By conforming in deed if not always in speech with the prescriptions of that theology, he showed himself to be fully aware of the fact that he was doing what the law commanded and not what was pleasing to the gods. He, too, no less than Varro, was forced into the awkward position of having to perform what he condemned or of having to worship what he decried.[49]

Varro himself was more guarded in his speech than Seneca. Out of a noble regard for the weakness of lesser minds, he did not dare censure civil theology directly and was content to reveal its censurable character by exhibiting its resemblance to mythical theology.[50] His discussion of civil theology is itself civil or political.[51] It takes into consideration, more than Seneca had done, the practical necessity of accommodating oneself to the opinions and prejudices of the multitude or, what amounts to the same thing, the practical impossibility of establishing a political order based entirely on reason or nature. Had Varro been able to found a new city, he would have written according to nature; but as he was dealing with an old one, he could only follow its customs.[52] Being the result of a compromise between nature and convention, his civil theology may be said to occupy an intermediary position between mythical theology, which demands too little of most men, and natural theology, which demands too much of them.[53] Its level is that of the citizen as citizen and it represents the only feasible means of obtaining from the majority of citizens the highest degree of virtue of which they are capable without divine grace.

If Varro felt obliged for practical or political reasons to respect outwardly Rome's civil theology, he had no such qualms about its mythical or poetic theology, with which he found fault freely and which he rejected as both unworthy of the divine nature and incompatible with human dignity. By propagating lies about the gods and depicting their conduct as unseemly and base, the poets not only commit an injustice toward them, they encourage the same immorality among men and do more than anyone else to corrupt their manners.[54] Varro himself was in full agreement with the philosophers in calling for the expulsion of poets from any well-ordered city. Unfortunately, the city with which he was concerned was far from perfect. It not only tolerated the presence of poets in its midst, it was actually dependent upon them for its survival. Poets are both the products of civil society and its creators. The morality that they profess is neither identical with the old morality nor totally different from it.[55] Insofar as their mythology overlaps that of civil theology, it must be regarded as an integral part of the city. In the final analysis, it enshrines and perpetuates the same falsehoods.

Paradoxically enough, mythical theology often proves just as helpful to the city when it departs from its traditional beliefs as when it faithfully reflects them. Poets amuse the public and excel at flattering its taste. The object of their fables is for the most part the pleasant as opposed to the useful or the noble. To that extent, their works belong to the realm of the playful rather than that of serious things. The private and vicarious enjoyment that most men derive from their performances helps to compensate for the inevitable shortcomings of the political life and provides a salutary release from the tensions that it generates. All appearances to the contrary notwithstanding, poets are not revolutionaries. Their action is at bottom a conservative one, to the point that even their innovations contribute in a roundabout way to the stability of civil society. The mere fact that the city cannot dispense with such services may be taken as further proof of its own limitations and of its radical inability to solve its problems by purely human means.

Civil theology is not only akin to mythical theology; insofar as it shares in reason, it also draws near to natural theology. Many of its teachings may be regarded as a popular or prephilosophic expression of some genuinely philosophic truth.[56] They can often be justified in terms of nature and have in fact been explained in that fashion by the pagan philosophers. For example, there is nothing to prevent one from looking upon Jupiter, the ruler of the gods, as a poetic synonym for justice, the queen of the social virtues. But there are obvious limits to these interpretations. Pagan mythology, even in its official form, can never be fully rationalized. For that reason its hold on the minds of people is weakened by the progress of science and by the unavoidable though not always salutary diffusion of knowledge. Resting as it does on a foundation of plausible lies, it cannot maintain itself indefinitely. Seen in that light, polytheism appears as both necessary to civil society and inconsistent with its highest development. One could phrase the argument in slightly different terms by saying that the worth of any society is measured by its ability to promote the good of the intellect; but to the degree to which society is successful in achieving that goal it tends to undermine its own basis. Herein lies the fallacy of the pagan scheme. By an inner necessity and quite independently of the external influence of Christianity, the crude polytheism of the pagan city must sooner or later become purified by transforming itself into monotheism.

It should not be inferred from what has been said that Augustine accepts without any reservations the monotheistic doctrine of the natural theologians. For one thing, the pagan philosophers do not all share the same conception of the divinity. Some of them, Varro included, identified the human soul or its rational part with the divine nature, thereby converting man into a god instead of making of him a servant of God.[57] Such a doctrine confuses the creature with its creator and is highly questionable from a rational standpoint, inasmuch as the mutability of the human mind cannot be reconciled with the absolute perfection of the supreme being. Only those philosophers who distinguish clearly between God and the soul or between the creator and his creation have reached the truth about God. The most outstanding among them was Plato.[58] Just how Plato arrived at this knowledge is a question that remains open. Augustine leaves it at saying that St. Paul himself asserts the possibility of a genuine knowledge of God among the pagans.[59] Aside from the fact that philosophers sometimes err in their teaching concerning God, however, there is still one crucial element which separates them from Christianity, and that is their refusal to accept Christ as mediator and redeemer. As a seeker after independent knowledge, the philosopher is basically proud and refuses to owe his salvation to anyone but himself. His whole endeavor is motivated in the final accounting by self-praise and self-admiration.[60] On that basis it is perhaps true to say that the philosopher is the man who comes closest to Christianity and at the same time the one who remains furthest away from it.

The Two Cities and the Dichotomy Between Religion and Politics

Augustine's attack on pagan religion culminates in what may be regarded as his most distinctive contribution to the problem of civil
society, the doctrine of the two cities. Humanity, as we know it, is
divided into many cities and nations, each one of which is clearly
differentiated from all the others by its laws, its manners, its rites, its
language, and its general way of life. But more fundamentally, Sacred
Scripture distinguishes only two kinds of societies, to which all men
of all times belong, the city of God and the earthly city.[61] It is only by
analogy, however, that these societies are called cities. The city of God
is not a separate city, existing side by side with other cities and founded
on a divine law, after the manner of the Jewish theocracy or the
earthly basileia of Constantine and his followers. Both the city of God
and the earthly city extend beyond the borders of individual cities and
neither one is to be identified with any particular city or kingdom.[62]
The distinction between them corresponds to the distinction between
virtue and vice, with the implication that true virtue is Christian virtue.
What establishes a person as a member of one or the other of these
two cities is not the race or nation that he might claim as his own but
the end that he pursues and to which he ultimately subordinates all of
his actions.[63] The city of God is none other than the community of the
followers of Christ and the worshippers of the true God. It is made up
entirely of godly men and its whole life may be described as one of
pious acquiescence in the word of God. In it and in it alone is true
justice to be found. Because its pattern is laid in heaven and because its
perfect state is achieved only in afterlife, the city of God is sometimes
called the heavenly city; but insofar as, by adhering to Christ, men
now have the possibility of leading truly virtuous lives, it already exists
here on earth. For the same reason it is not to be confused with Plato's
ideal city, which has no existence other than in thought and word.

In contrast to the heavenly city, the earthly city is guided by self-
love and lives according to what Scripture calls the flesh.[64] The term
"flesh" in the present context is not to be taken in its narrow sense, as
referring only to the body and to bodily pleasures. In its biblical usage
it is synonymous with natural man and embraces all of man's actions
and desires to the extent to which they are not ordered to God as to
their supreme end. It applies not only to the voluptuary, who places
his highest good in pleasure, but to all those who indulge in vice and
even to the wise man insofar as his quest for wisdom is actuated by a
false love of self rather than by love of the truth. In its widest and
most comprehensive sense, the earthly city is characterized by its affec-

tation of total independence and self-sufficiency,[65] and presents itself as the very antithesis of the life of obedience ("the mother and guardian of the virtues")[66] and of reverent submission to God. Its ancestor is the unrepentant and unredeemed Cain, and its rebellion against God renews in its own fashion the sin of disobedience that Adam committed when he first transgressed the divine command.[67]

Although Augustine occasionally equates the city of God with the church,[68] it is clear from some of his other statements that not everyone who is officially a member of the visible church belongs to it; and conversely, many persons who do not profess the Christian faith are, without their knowing it, members of the same holy city. Actually, anyone dedicated to the pursuit of truth and virtue may be said to be implicitly a citizen of the city of God, and anyone who abandons virtue for vice is ipso facto excluded from it. What is more, any human attempt to discriminate, except in an abstract way, between the two cities is rendered precarious by the fact that it is impossible to know with any degree of finality whether or not a man is genuinely virtuous. One can observe and narrate the actions of another person, but he cannot attain the inner core from which they proceed.[69] Even the man who performs virtuous actions has no way of determining with absolute certitude to what extent he is acting out of virtue, inasmuch as he may easily be deluded as to the nature of his motives. These motives pertain not just to the secret of the human heart, which one could reveal if he chose to do so, but to the secret intention of the heart, which remains obscure to everyone, including the agent himself. In this life, therefore, the two cities are for all practical purposes inextricably mixed, like the wheat and tares of the parable, which are allowed to grow together and must await the time of harvest before they can be separated.[70]

The fact remains that it is only as a member of the city of God and by virtue of his relationship to an order that transcends the political sphere that one has any possibility of attaining the peace and happiness to which all men, even the most wicked, aspire.[71] This does not mean that the city of God has done away with the need for civil society. Its purpose is not to replace civil society but to supplement it by providing, over and above the benefits conferred by it, the means of achieving a goal that is higher than any to which civil society can lead. Civil society itself continues to be indispensable in that it procures and administers the temporal or material goods which men need here on earth and which may be used as instruments to promote the good of the soul.[72] Hence citizenship in the city of God does not abrogate but preserves and complements citizenship in a temporal society. What is typical of Augustine's position is very precisely the twin citizenship by which one is enrolled as a member of the city of God without ceasing to order his temporal life within the framework of civil society and according to its norms. To the extent to which this position removes from the jurisdiction of the city and reserves for a higher authority an essential part of man's life, it represents a departure from the classical tradition, but insofar as it claims to provide the solution, sought in vain by the pagan philosophers, to the problem of human living, it may be viewed as a prolongation and fulfillment of that tradition.

The sharp distinction that Augustine draws between the spheres of ecclesiastical and civil authority raises the general question of their relationship and immediately suggests the possibility of a conflict between them. In the best instance, the conflict is resolved by the coincidence of Christian wisdom and political power. This is the situation that obtains when a Christian accedes to office and exercises his authority in accordance with Christian principles and for the common good of his subjects. It is explicitly envisaged by Augustine in Book V, chapter 24 of the *City of God,* which may be read as a mirror of Christian princes.[73] Such a situation leads to a restoration of the unity of the city on the plane of Christianity and is eminently desirable from the point of view of man's spiritual and temporal welfare; but there is never any assurance that it will come about, or if it should, that it will endure for any great length of time. Nothing in Augustine's works indicates that he anticipated the permanent triumph of the city of God on earth through the definitive reconciliation of the spiritual and temporal powers.

Beyond the broad statements that set apart and define the domains of the spiritual and the temporal and their respective jurisdictions, one does not find in Augustine a detailed theory of church and state similar to the ones elaborated, allegedly on the basis of his principles, during the centuries that followed. Given the highly contingent and unpredictable circumstances of the church's existence in the world, it is doubtful whether Augustine ever seriously considered the possibility of articulating in any but the most general way the nature of the relations between these two societies.

There is, however, one point on which he was led to take a definite stand and which deserves to be mentioned, if only because of its historical importance, namely, the appeal to the so-called secular arm to repress heretics and schismatics. The occasion was the Donatist controversy, whose roots went back to the third century and which had paralyzed the church in North Africa throughout much of the fourth century. Augustine began by advocating persuasion as the proper means of securing the return of the dissenters to the Catholic fold and was firmly opposed to any intervention on the part of the temporal authority in a matter that could be regarded at first as purely ecclesiastical. Events soon showed that more drastic measures were needed if order was to be restored, especially since the schism had in time assumed the aspect of a nationalist movement whose rapid growth was fanned by the perennial resentment of Roman supremacy among the native African population. The peculiar intractability of Donatists, their continued agitating, and the methods of terrorism to which they frequently resorted, had made of them a persistent threat not only to the religious unity but to the social stability of the North African provinces. Reluctantly and only after having exhausted all other resources, Augustine agreed to turn the matter over to the local civil authorities. His decision to sanction the use of force appears to have been dictated in large measure by the political nature of the case rather than by theological arguments. In making this decision Augustine asserted his conviction that no one should be constrained to accept the faith against his own will. He carefully distinguished between the Donatists who had willfully embraced the schism and those who sought the truth in good faith and were Donatists only because they were born of Donatist parents.[74] He further cautioned against excessive severity in punishing offenders and stipulated that penalties should be mitigated in favor of anyone who could be prevailed upon to abjure his errors. Unfortunately his action established a precedent whose consequences far exceeded anything that he himself appears to have foreseen. What was, for him, a mere concession to necessity or at most an emergency measure designed to cope with a specific situation was later invoked as a general principle to justify the church's reprisals against heretics and apostates. If such is the case, Augustine may be partly to blame for the religious persecution of the Middle Ages, which came to be looked upon as a prime example of the inhumanity fostered by the undue exaltation of moral standards and became the object of one of the principal criticisms leveled at the church throughout the modern period.

CHRISTIANITY AND PATRIOTISM

On purely political grounds, Augustine's solution to the problem of civil society was exposed to one major objection, of which he himself was fully aware and with which he was repeatedly forced to come to grips. Christianity had staked its claim to superiority on its ability to make men better and, in the eyes of nonbelievers, it could be said to stand or fall by that claim. To the impartial observer, however, it was by no means evident that Christianity had succeeded where pagan political philosophy had failed or that its diffusion had been attended by a marked improvement in human affairs. If anything, the social and political disorders that had long plagued Rome both from within and from without had seemingly increased rather than decreased, despite the fact that Christianity, once persecuted and then tolerated, had become under Theodosius the official religion of the empire. "Is it not true," asks Augustine, "that since the coming of Christ the state of human affairs has been worse than it was before and that human affairs were once much more fortunate than they are now?" [75] An open clash between Christians and pagans had already occurred in 382 when Gratian ordered the Altar of Victory removed from the Senate, over the opposition of the pagan faction, led by Symmachus, who contended that any substantial deviation from the traditional cult and practice of Rome would sooner or later prove detrimental to the empire. The fall of Rome at the hands of Alaric and the Goths in 410 brought the whole issue to a dramatic climax. The Christians were promptly blamed for the disaster and the old charge that Christianity was inimical to the well-being of society gained widespread currency among the pagan population. It was precisely to answer this accusation that Augustine undertook to write the *City of God*.[76] Rome, so the argument ran, owed her greatness to the favor of her gods. By forsaking these gods for a new religion, she had incurred their wrath and deprived herself of their protection.

Thus crudely stated, the argument could be countered by showing that all Roman history since the beginning had been marked by endless wars and civil strife and that, since these social evils antedated Christianity, they could not reasonably be laid at its door. It is obvious, however, that this popular polemic against Christianity only partially revealed the true problem, which was political rather than religious in character. Behind the common belief in tutelary deities lay the more serious allegation that Christianity had brought about a decline in civic virtue and could with every appearance of sound reason be held at least indirectly responsible for the deteriorating political fortunes of the empire. By enlisting men in the service of a "higher and more noble country," [77] it divided the city and weakened the unconditional claim that it makes on the allegiance of its citizens. The dual citizenship that it imposed on its followers inevitably led to a devaluation of the whole political order and rendered more difficult, if not impossible, the full measure of dedication to the city and its regime. As Augustine himself remarks, "so far as the life of mortals is concerned, which is spent and ended in a few days, what does it matter under whose rule a man is going to die, as long as those who govern do not force him to impiety and iniquity?" [78] Worse still, many of the most characteristic teachings of the new faith seemed to conflict openly with the sacred duties and rights of citizenship. Its doctrine of the brotherhood of all men and of their equality before God, as well as its precepts enjoining the love of one's enemies and the forgiveness of offenses, all tended at first glance to undermine the military strength of the city and to rob it of its most powerful means of defense against external foes. In the minds of Augustine's contemporaries, the danger was far from illusory. Faced with the apparent and almost tragic impossibility of reconciling Christianity with loyalty to one's country, some of Augustine's own friends had for many years refused baptism even after having been instructed in the faith. [79]

One could of course point to a similar depreciation of the purely political in classical philosophy, which placed man's happiness or highest good in the theoretical or philosophic life rather than in the life of dutiful citizenship. But philosophy was addressed to a natural elite and not to all men. By its very essence it was destined to remain the preserve of a small number of wellborn and well-bred natures. Hence there was little danger of its ever becoming a political force in the same sense as Christianity or of its having the same direct and immediate impact on the life of the city.

Augustine's answer to this general objection blends in typical fashion arguments drawn both from scriptural and from philosophic sources. It consists in saying, in substance, that Christianity does not destroy patriotism but reinforces it by making of it a religious duty. The Old Testament prophets and the New Testament writers alike command obedience to civil authority and to the laws of the city. To resist these laws is to defy God's own ordinance, inasmuch as civil society is intended by God himself as a remedy for evil and is used by him as an instrument of mercy in the midst of a sinful world, as St. Paul teaches in chapter 13 of the Letter to the Romans to which Augustine constantly refers in this connection. This being the case, one cannot justifiably allege the service of God as a reason for shunning one's civic responsibilities or refusing submission to one's temporal rulers. Indeed, Christianity is to be understood above all as a faith rather than as a divinely revealed law governing all of one's actions and opinions and called upon to replace the human laws under which men live. It is compatible with any political regime and, in temporal matters, it does not impose a way of life of its own, different from that of other citizens of the same city. Its universality is such that it can accommodate itself without difficulty to the most diverse customs and practices. The only practices to which it is opposed are the ones that reason itself denounces as vicious or immoral. By censuring these practices and by urging its adherents to abstain from them, it actually serves the best interests of the city. Its very judgment concerning the essential limitations of civil society does not, anymore than that of the pagan philosophers, entail a repudiation of that society. For all its manifest imperfections, civil society is still the greatest good of its kind that men possess. Its aim is or should be earthly peace, which Christians also seek. In the pursuit of this common goal, Christians and non-Christians can be united and live together as citizens of the same city.[80]

Furthermore, any depreciation of the fatherland, if one can really speak of a depreciation, is amply compensated for by the fact that Christianity demands and very often obtains from its followers a higher degree of morality and virtue. It thus helps to counteract vice and corruption, which are the true causes of the weakness and decline of cities and nations. Hence,

let those who say that the doctrine of Christ is incompatible with the well-being of the commonwealth give us an army of soldiers such as the doctrine of Christ requires them to be; let them give us such subjects, such husbands and wives, such parents and children, such masters and servants, such kings, such judges, in fine, even such tax-payers and tax-gatherers as the Christian religion has taught that men should be; and then let them dare to say that it is adverse to the well-being of the commonwealth. Rather, let them no longer hesitate to confess that this doctrine, if it were obeyed, would be the salvation of the commonwealth.[81]

Finally, it is unfair to assert without further qualification that Christianity breeds contempt for military valor. The New Testament does not order soldiers to surrender their arms but rather commends them for their righteousness and virtue.[82] The injunction to requite evil with good concerns not so much external actions as the inward disposition with which these actions are to be performed. It seeks to insure that war, if it must be waged, will be carried out with a benevolent design and without undue harshness. Men are compelled at all times to do what is most likely to benefit their fellow men. In some instances, peace and the correction of wrongdoers are more readily and more perfectly achieved by forgiveness than by castigation; whereas in other instances, one would only confirm the wicked in their evil ways by giving free reign to injustice and allowing crimes to go unpunished.[83] What Christianity reproves is not war but the evils of war, such as the love of violence, revengeful cruelty, fierce and implacable hatreds, wild resistance, and the lust for power. By yielding to these evils, men lose a good that is far more precious than any of the earthly goods an enemy could take from them. Instead of increasing the number of the good, they merely add themselves to the number of the wicked.[84] Just wars are therefore permissible, but they must be undertaken only out of necessity and for the sake of peace. The decision to wage such a war rests with the monarch or ruler, to whom is entrusted the welfare of the community as a whole. As for the simple soldier, his duty is to obey orders. He himself is not answerable for the crimes that may be committed in cases where it is not clear whether the orders are just or unjust.[85]

Although Augustine agrees that there would be less strife among men if everyone shared the same faith,[86] he never regarded universal peace as a goal that could be attained in this life; nor for that matter did he draw from this monotheism the conclusion that all men should be united politically so as to form a single world society. The only passage in which the question is explicitly taken up presents the happiest condition of mankind, and the one most conducive to virtue, as that wherein small cities or small kingdoms exist side by side in neighborly concord.[87] Even that condition, however, will never be fully or permanently realized. Whether men like it or not, war is inevitable. The wicked wage war on the just because they want to, and the just wage war on the wicked because they have to. In either case, independent cities and small kingdoms eventually give way to large kingdoms established through the conquest of the weaker by the stronger. The best that can be hoped for in practice is that the just cause will triumph over the unjust one; for nothing is more injurious to everyone, including evildoers themselves, than that the latter should prosper and use their prosperity to oppress the good.[88]

Augustine's remarks to that effect are directed not so much against his pagan critics as they are against his coreligionists and, in some cases, his own disciples. Many prominent Christian writers of that period— Eusebius, Ambrose, Prudentius, and Orosius among them—had interpreted in a literal or temporal sense certain Old Testament prophecies relating to the blessings of the messianic age and had predicted an era of unprecedented peace and prosperity under the auspices of Christianity and as a direct outcome of its emergence as a world religion uniting all men in the cult of the true God. Some of these writers had gone on to compare the Christian persecutions, somewhat arbitrarily set at ten, to the ten plagues of Egypt and had inferred from this parallel that the church would no longer have to endure similar hardships until the great persecution of the end-time announced by Sacred Scripture. To the Christian was promised the best of both worlds; for, according to the proposed interpretation, not only did Christianity hold out the prospect of eternal bliss in heaven, it also provided the answer to man's most urgent problem here on earth.

Augustine dismisses all such interpretations as ingenious but unfounded in Scripture and contrary to its teaching.[89] He does not deny that human art and industry have made "wonderful and stupefying advances" in the course of time, but he is quick to add that this material and intellectual progress is not necessarily accompanied by a corresponding increase in moral goodness; for if these inventions have benefited man, they can also be used to destroy him.[90] He further rejects outright the view that evils will disappear or even diminish as time goes on. God, being all-powerful, could of course do away with evil altogether, but not without the loss of a greater good for mankind. In their own way the evils that he permits contribute to man's spiritual advancement. They serve as a test for the just and a punishment for the wicked. They likewise insure that God will be loved for himself and not just for the material advantages accruing to men as a consequence of their good deeds; and by imposing on man the necessity of overcoming these evils both within and outside of himself, they enable him to reach an ever higher level of virtue and moral perfection.[91]

More generally, the evils of human existence are themselves part of an overall plan that God pursues among men. To that extent they may be said to be rational; but their rationality surpasses human reason. Beyond the simple fact, recorded by Sacred Scripture, that history takes its course not in cycles but along a straight line,[92] that it advances through successive stages toward a preestablished goal, and that with the coming of Christ it has entered into its final phase,[93] there is little or nothing to reveal the inner meaning or purpose of human events. To the earthly observer, these events retain their fundamental obscurity even once they have occurred. Considered in its totality, the life of earthly societies appears, not as an orderly progression (*procursus*) toward a determinate end, but as a simple process (*excursus*) by which the two cities run out their earthly existence, with its characteristic mixture of successes and failures but no guarantee of salvation in this world;[94] for "only in heaven has been promised that which on earth we seek." [95]

Christianity, as Augustine understands it, does indeed provide a solution to the problem of human society, but the solution is not one that is attained or attainable in and through human society. Like that of the classical philosophers, albeit in a different way, it remains essentially transpolitical.

NOTES

1. *Epist.* 120. 1, 3; cf. *Sermo* 43.3, 4.

2. *De Doctr. Christ.*, II. 60–61; cf. *De Div. Quaest. 83*, Qu. 53.2; *Confessions*, VII. 9, 15.

3. *On Free Will*, I. 2, 4; I. 3, 6; II. 2, 6; *Sermo* 43.7, 9.

4. Cf. *Epist.* 120. 1, 4; *De Gen. ad Litt.*, I. 41.

5. Cf. *City of God*, VIII. 4; *Contra Acad.*, II. 4, 10; II. 10, 24; III. 7, 14; III. 17, 38; III. 20, 43; *Epist.* 118.3, 16 and 20; 118.4, 33.

6. *De Ordine*, II. 5, 17; cf. *ibid.*, I. 11, 31.

7. Cf. *De Doctr. Christ.*, IV. 9, 23; *Epist.* 137.1, 3 and 5, 18; *Epist.* 118.1, 1 *et passim*.

8. *Epist.* 1.1.

9. *Contra Mend.*, X. 23; cf. *De Mend.*, X. 17.

10. Cf. *City of God*, VIII. 4; VIII. 5; VIII. 9.

11. Compare *De Vera Relig.*, IV. 6–7 and *Contra Acad.*, III. 17, 37.

12. *City of God*, XIX. 13.

13. *Ibid.*, XIX. 21; cf. II. 21.

14. Cf. *Epist.* 91.3–4.

15. *City of God*, XIX. 24.

16. Cf. *City of God*, XIX. 21; *Contra Faust. Man.*, XXII. 27.

17. Cf. *City of God*, XIX. 15.

18. *Epist.* 137.5, 17.

19. *On Free Will*, I. 6, 15.

20. *Ibid.*, 1.15, 31; cf. *De Vera Relig.*, XXX. 58.

21. *On Free Will*, I. 5, 11.

22. *Ibid.*, I. 6, 14–15.

23. *Ibid.*, I. 7, 16.

24. *Ibid.*, I. 5, 12.

25. *Ibid.*, I. 5, 12.

26. *Ibid.*, I. 15, 32; cf. *Epist.* 153.6, 26; *Sermo* 50.2, 4.

27. Cf. *En. in Psal.* 57.2.

28. Cf. *City of God*, XIX. 6.

29. *On Free Will*, I. 3, 8.

30. *Ibid.*, I. 5, 13.

31. Cf. *City of God*, V, 9 and 10.

32. *Ibid.*, V. 9.

33. Cf. *ibid.*, XII. 6–8.

34. *Ibid.*, V. 10.

35. Cf. *ibid.*, V. 12.

36. *Ibid.*, IV. 4.

37. *Ibid.*, II. 21.

38. *Ibid.*, XIX. 24; cf. II. 21.

39. *Ibid.*, V. 13 and 14.

40. *Ibid.*, V. 12; cf. XIX. 25.

41. *Ibid.*, V. 15.

42. *Ibid.*, XVIII. 22.

43. Cf. *ibid.*, II. 29.

44. *Ibid.*, X. 21; cf. V. 14.

45. Cf. *ibid.*, V. 16–18; *Epist.* 138.3, 17.

46. *City of God*, VI. 5; cf. *ibid.*, IV. 27.

47. *Ibid.*, IV. 1; IV. 31; VI. 2; VI. 6; VI. 8; VI. 9; VII. 28.

48. *Ibid.*, VI. 4.

49. *Ibid.*, VI. 10.

50. *Ibid.*, VI. 7; VI. 8; VI. 10.

51. *Ibid.*, III. 4; VI. 2; VII. 17; VII. 23.

52. *Ibid.*, VI. 4; cf. IV. 31 and VI. 2.

53. *Ibid.*, VI. 6.

54. *Ibid.*, VI. 7.

55. *Ibid.*, VI. 8.

56. *Ibid.*, VI. 8; cf. *Epist.* 91.5.

57. *City of God*, IV. 31; VII. 5; VII. 6; VIII. 1; VIII. 5.

58. *Ibid.*, VIII. 4; VIII. 10–12.

59. *Ibid.*, VIII. 12; cf. XVIII. 41 *in fine*.

60. *Ibid.*, V. 20; cf. *Epist.* 155.1, 2.

61. *City of God*, XIV. 1; XIV. 4.

62. *Ibid.*, XVIII. 2; XX. 11.

63. *Ibid.*, XIV. 28; cf. *De Gen. ad Litt.*, XI. 15.

64. Cf. *City of God*, XIV. 2 and 4.

65. *Ibid.*, XIV. 13 and 15.

66. *Ibid.*, XIV. 12.

67. *Ibid.*, XIV. 14.

68. E.g., *City of God*, VIII. 24; XIII. 16; XVI. 2.

69. Cf. *De Ordine*, II. 10, 29.

70. *City of God*, XX. 9; cf. *ibid.*, I. 35; XI. 1; XVIII. 49; *Ad Donat. post Coll.*, VIII. 11; *Contra Duas Epist. Petil.*, II. 21, 46.

71. Cf. *City of God*, XIX. 12.

72. *Ibid.*, XIX. 17.

73. See also *City of God*, V. 19.

74. *Contra Duas Epist. Petil.*, II. 83, 184; *Epist.* 43.1, 1.

75. *En. in Psal.* 136.9.

76. Cf. *Retractationes*, II. 43, 1; *City of God*, I. 1.

77. *Epist.* 91.1.

78. *City of God*, V. 17.

79. Cf. *Epist.* 151.14 and 136.2.

80. *City of God*, XIX. 17; XV. 4.

81. *Epist.* 138.2, 15; cf. *Epist.* 137.5, 20 and *Epist.* 91.3.

82. *Epist.* 189.4; *Contra Faust. Man.*, XXII. 75.

83. Cf. *Epist.* 138.2, 13–14.

84. Cf. *Contra Faust. Man.*, XXII. 74; *Epist.* 138.2, 12.

85. *Contra Faust. Man.*, XXII. 75.

86. *Epist.* 189.5.

87. *City of God*, IV. 15.

88. *Ibid.*, IV. 3; XIX. 7.

89. *Ibid.*, XVIII. 52.

90. *Ibid.*, XXII. 24.

91. *Ibid.*, I. 29; XXII. 22 and 23.

92. Cf., *ibid.*, XII. 11–21.

93. Cf. *De Catech. Rud.*, XXII. 39; *DeGen. contra Man.*, I. 23–24; *City of God*, XXII. 30 *in fine*.

94. See Augustine's letter to Firmus, C. Lambot, ed., *Revue Benedictine* 51 (1939), p. 212. Also *City of God*, XV. 21; XIX. 5; *Retractationes*, II. 43.2.

95. *En. in Psal.* 48.6.

READINGS

A. St. Augustine, *The City of God*. Trans. Marcus Dods. New York: Modern Library, 1950. Bk XIX.

St. Augustine, *Letters* 91 and 138. Ph. Schaff, ed., *A Select Library of the Nicene and Post-Nicene Fathers of the Christian Church*, Vol. I: *The Confessions and Letters of St. Augustine*. Grand Rapids: Eerdmans, 1956.

B. St. Augustine, *The City of God*, Bks II. 21–22; IV–VIII; XIV. 1–4; 11–15; 28.

St. Augustine, *On Free Will*. Trans. John H. S. Burleigh. *The Library of Christian Classics*, Vol. VI: *Augustine, Earlier Writings*. Philadelphia: The Westminster Press, 1953. Bk I.

ALFARABI

circa 870–950

Alfarabi (al-Fārābī) was the first philosopher who sought to confront, to relate, and as far as possible to harmonize classical political philosophy with Islam—a religion that was revealed through a prophet-legislator (Muhammad) in the form of a divine law, that organizes its followers into a political community, and that provides for their beliefs as well as for the principles and detailed rules of their conduct. Unlike Cicero he had to face and solve the problem of introducing classical political philosophy into a radically different cultural atmosphere; unlike Augustine he did not have a relatively free sphere of this-worldly life in the organization of which classical political philosophy could apply unchallenged, but had to face and solve the problem of the conflicting claims of political philosophy and religion over the whole of man's life.

The importance of Alfarabi's place in the history of political philosophy consists in his recovery of the classical tradition and in making it intelligible within the new context provided by the revealed religions. His best-known writings are political works concerned with the political regimes and the attainment of happiness through political life. They present the problem of the harmony between philosophy and Islam in a new perspective—that of the relation between the best regime, in particular as Plato had understood it, and the divine law of Islam. His position in Islamic philosophy corresponds to that of Socrates or Plato in Greek philosophy in so far as their chief concern may be said to be the relation between philosophy and the city. He was the founder of a tradition that looked to him, and through him to Plato and Aristotle, for a philosophic approach to the study and understanding of political and religious phenomena. His works inspired men like Avicenna, Averroes, and Maimonides. They admired him as their "second teacher" after Aristotle, and he was the only postclassical thinker whose authority commanded their respect alongside that of the ancients.

DIVINE AND POLITICAL SCIENCE

There are a number of striking resemblances between many of the fundamental features of Islam and the good regime envisaged by classical political philosophy in general, and by Plato in the *Laws* in particular. Both begin with a god as the ultimate cause of legislation and consider correct beliefs about divine beings and the world of nature as essential for the constitution of a good political regime. In both, these beliefs should reflect an adequate image of the cosmos, make accessible to the citizens at large (and in a form they can grasp) the truth about divine things and about the highest principles of the world, be conducive to virtuous action, and form part of the equipment necessary for the attainment of ultimate happiness. Both consider the functions of the founder and legislator, and after him of his successors in the leadership of the community, of absolutely central importance for its organization and preservation. Both are concerned with the giving and the preserving of divine laws. Both are opposed to the view that mind or soul is derivative from body or is itself bodily—a view that undermines human virtue and communal life—and to the timorous piety that condemns man to despair of the possibility of ever understanding the rational meaning of the beliefs he is called upon to accept or of the activities he is called upon to perform. Both direct the eyes of the citizens to a happiness beyond their worldly concerns. Finally, both relegate the art of the jurist and that of the apologetic theologian to the secondary position of preserving the intention of the founder and of his law, and of erecting a shield against attacks.[1]

Alfarabi's important political works (*The Virtuous City, The Virtuous Religion,* and *The Political Regime*) are a meeting ground between Islam and classical political philosophy where these affinities, and not possible differences or conflicts, occupy the foreground. By laying the stress on such affinities, and by encouraging or even forcing both Islam and philosophy each to take a step in the direction of the other, he intends to make visible the common elements in both and to encourage and guide his Muslim reader to understand the characteristic features of classical political philosophy. This is revealed first of all in the very style of these works and in the way in which they are composed. Stylistically, they bear as much resemblance to legal codes as to philosophic treatises. They consist mainly of positive statements about the attributes of God, the order of the world, the place of man within it, and how a good society is to be organized and led. Following a pattern common to Plato's *Laws* and the Koran, many of these statements are preceded by preludes preparing the way to the promulgation of sound laws for regulating the conduct of rulers and prescribing the beliefs and the actions of the citizens. Although not philosophic or political treatises or specific legal promulgation, in the strict sense, these works contain the results of philosophic and political investigations presented in a practically useful way—as a basis for formulating a plan to order a good political regime. They are works whose form and intention could be readily understood by a Muslim reader committed to the acceptance of a true view of the world at large and to obedience to laws that promote virtue and lead to ultimate happiness. But they also conform to the intention of classical political philosophy in that they aim at presenting a rational and persuasive account of the world, couched in terms understandable to the citizens. They perform an important practical task in so far as they indicate by their appearance the possibility of a rational understanding that does not destroy, but preserves and explains, the beliefs and actions prescribed by the revealed law; and they achieve a preparatory task inasmuch as they indicate the direction in which such a rational understanding can be sought.

Alfarabi's political works form a new genre of writing in Islamic political literature. With habitual caution, he discreetly abstains from directly quoting, expounding, or even referring to the Koran, Muhammad, or specifically Islamic religious issues. Yet the first impressions that Alfarabi's works leave on his readers are unmistakable: the author intends to enable his coreligionists, and indeed all communicants of revealed religions, to see the wide area of harmony that exists between their divine law and the practical intention of classical political philosophy. These readers could now see in their divine law a practical fulfillment of the doctrines of the most prominent wise men of antiquity. They could turn to the study of these philosophers, not merely for the limited purpose of defending their own beliefs and practices, or the negative purpose of assuring themselves that rational understanding is powerless before the higher authority of revelation and the divine law, but for rising above the slavish state of blind believers and for penetrating into the secret intentions of revelation and the divine law—to enlighten themselves, through the understanding of the most respectable tradition of human wisdom, about the wisdom of their religion. Alfarabi gives them in these works the possibility of gaining a new attitude toward the study of the works of Plato and Aristotle. He encourages them to cease considering these philosophers as the originators of a foreign tradition that might undermine their beliefs and social virtues, a tradition that they ought to study with a view to refuting and combating it. He makes them see that this tradition belongs to them no less than to the Greeks, and that they must make it their own because it is concerned with matters closest to their minds and hearts. They are made to hope for a fuller understanding of their highest political and religious concern—the things that constitute the essence of their religion and their way of life, distinguish them from their heathen ancestors, and give them their unique claim to superiority over other communities.

The Virtuous Regime

The central theme of Alfarabi's political writings is the virtuous regime, the political order whose guiding principle is the realization of human excellence or virtue. He conceives of human or political science as the inquiry into man in so far as he is distinguished from other natural beings and from divine beings, seeking to understand his specific nature, what constitutes his perfection, and the way through which he can attain it. Unlike other animals man is not rendered perfect merely through the natural principles present in him, and unlike divine beings he is not eternally perfect but needs to achieve his perfection through the activity proceeding from rational understanding, deliberation, and choosing among the various alternatives suggested to him by reason. The initial presence of the power of rational knowledge, and of the choice connected with it, is man's first or natural perfection, the perfection he is born with and does not choose. Beyond this, reason and choice are present in man to use for realizing his end or the ultimate perfection possible for his nature. This ultimate perfection is identical with the supreme happiness available to him. "Happiness is the good desired for itself, it is never desired to achieve by it something else, and there is nothing greater beyond it that man can achieve." [2]

Yet happiness cannot be achieved without being first known, and without performing certain orderly (bodily and intellectual) activities useful or leading to the achievement of perfection. These are the noble activities. The distinction between noble and base activities is thus guided by the distinction between what is useful for, and what obstructs, perfection and happiness. To perform an activity well, with ease, and in an orderly fashion requires the formation of character and the development of habits that make such activities possible. "The forms and states of character from which these [noble] activities emanate are the virtues; they are not goods for their own sake but goods only for the sake of happiness." [3] The distinction between virtue and vice presupposes knowledge of what human perfection or happiness is as well as the distinction between noble and base activities.

The virtuous regime can be defined as the regime in which men come together and cooperate with the aim of becoming virtuous, performing noble activities, and attaining happiness. It is distinguished by the presence in it of knowledge of man's ultimate perfection, the distinction between the noble and the base and between the virtues and the vices, and the concerted effort of the rulers and the citizens to teach and learn these things, and to develop the virtuous forms or states of character from which emerge the noble activities useful for achieving happiness.

The attainment of happiness means the perfection of that power of the human soul that is specific to man, of his reason. This in turn requires disciplining the lower desires to cooperate with and aid reason to perform its proper activity and also acquiring the highest arts and sciences. Such discipline and learning can be accomplished only by the rare few who possess the best natural endowments and who are also fortunate to live under conditions in which the requisite virtues can be developed and noble activities performed. The rest of men can only attain some degree of this perfection; and the extent to which they can attain that degree of perfection of which they are capable is decisively influenced by the kind of political regime in which they live and the education they receive. Nevertheless, all the citizens of the virtuous regime must have some common notions about the world, man, and political life. But they will differ with regard to the character of this knowledge, and hence with regard to their share of perfection or happiness. They can be divided broadly into the following three classes: (1) The wise or the philosophers who know the nature of things by means of demonstrative proofs and by their own insights. (2) The followers of these who know the nature of things by means of the demonstrations presented by the philosophers, and who trust the insight and accept the judgment of the philosophers. (3) The rest of the citizens, the many, who know things by means of similitudes, some more and others less adequate, depending on their rank as citizens. These classes or ranks must be ordered by the ruler who should also organize the education of the citizens, assign to them their specialized duties, give their laws, and command them in war. He is to seek, by persuasion and compulsion, to develop in everyone the virtues of which he is capable and to order the citizens hierarchically so that each class can attain the perfection of which it is capable and yet serve the class above it. It is in this manner that the city becomes a whole similar to the cosmos, and its members cooperate toward attaining happiness.

The virtuous regime is a nonhereditary monarchical or an aristocratic regime in which the best rule, with the rest of the citizens divided into groups that (depending on their rank) are ruled and in turn rule—until one arrives at the lowest group that is ruled only. The sole criterion for the rank of a citizen is the character of the virtue of which he is capable and that he is able to develop through his participation in the regime and obedience to its laws. Like the regime itself, its citizens are virtuous, first, because they possess, or follow those who possess, correct similitudes of the knowledge of divine and natural beings, human perfection or happiness, and the principles of the regime designed to help man attain this happiness; and, second, because they act in accordance with this knowledge in that their character is formed with a view to performing the activities conducive to happiness.

Once the main features of the virtuous regime are clarified, the understanding of the main features and the classification of all other regimes become relatively simple. Alfarabi divides them into three broad types. (1) The regimes whose citizens have had no occasion to acquire any knowledge at all about divine and natural beings or about perfection and happiness. These are the *ignorant* regimes. Their citizens pursue lower ends, good or bad, in complete oblivion of true happiness. (2) The regimes whose citizens possess the knowledge of these things but do not act according to their requirements. These are the *wicked* or *immoral* regimes. Their citizens have the same views as those of the virtuous regime; yet their desires do not serve the rational part in them but turn them away to pursue the lower ends pursued in ignorant regimes. (3) The regimes whose citizens have acquired certain opinions about these things, but false or corrupt opinions, that is, opinions that claim to be about divine and natural beings and about true happiness, while in fact they are not. The similitudes presented to such citizens are, consequently, false and corrupt, and so also are the activities prescribed for them. These are the regimes that have been led astray or the *erring* regimes. The citizens of such regimes do not possess true knowledge or correct similitudes, and they, too, pursue the lower ends of the ignorant regimes. The regimes in error may have been founded as such. This is the case with the regimes "whose supreme ruler was one who was under an illusion that he was receiving revelation without having done so, and with regard to which he had employed misrepresentations, deceptions, and delusions." [4] But they may also have been originally virtuous regimes that had been changed through the introduction of false or corrupt views and practices.

All these types of regimes are opposed to the virtuous regime because they lack its guiding principle, which is true knowledge and virtue or the formation of character leading to activities conducive to true happiness. Instead, the character of the citizens is formed with a view to attaining one or more of the lower ends. These ends are given by Alfarabi as six, and each of the general types mentioned above can be subdivided according to the end that dominates in it. (1) The regime of *necessity* (or the *indispensable* regime) in which the aim of the citizens is confined to the bare necessities of life. (2) The *vile* regime (oligarchy) in which the ultimate aim of the citizens is wealth and prosperity for their own sakes. (3) The *base* regime the purpose of whose citizens is the enjoyment of sensory or imaginary pleasures. (4) The regime of *honor* (timocracy) whose citizens aim at being honored, praised, and glorified by others. (5) The regime of *domination* (tyranny) whose citizens aim at overpowering and subjecting others. (6) The regime of *corporate association* (democracy) the main purpose of whose citizens is being free to do what they wish.

The Philosopher-King and the Prophet-Legislator

To combine divine and political science is to emphasize the political importance of sound beliefs about divine beings and about the principles of the world. We saw that both Islam and classical political philosophy are in agreement concerning this issue. Muslims believed that the primary justification of their existence as a distinct community was the revelation of the truth about divine things to Muhammad, and that, had he not come to them with his message, they would have continued to live in misery and uncertainty about their well-being in this world and the next. It was also because of such considerations that Plato thought that kings must become philosophers or philosophers kings. Once the quest for the best regime arrives at the necessity of combining divine and political science, it becomes necessary that the ruler should combine the craft of ruling with that of prophecy or of philosophy. The ruler-prophet or the ruler-philosopher is the human being who offers the solution to the question of the realization of the best regime, and the functions of the ruler-prophet and of the ruler-philosopher appear in this respect to be identical.

Alfarabi begins his discussion of the supreme ruler with the emphasis on the common function of the ruler-philosopher and the ruler-prophet as rulers who are the link between the divine beings above and the citizens who do not have direct access to knowledge of these beings. He is the teacher and guide "who makes known" to the citizens what happiness is, who "arouses in them the determination" to do the things necessary for attaining it, and "who does not need to be ruled by a man in anything at all." [5] He must possess knowledge, not need any other man to guide him, have excellent comprehension of everything that must be done, be excellent in guiding all others in what he knows, have the ability to make others perform the functions for which they are fit, and have the ability to determine and define the work to be done by others and to direct such work toward happiness. These qualities evidently require the best natural endowments, but also the fullest development of the rational faculty. (According to Aristotelian psychology as Alfarabi presents it in his political works, the perfection of the rational faculty consists of its correspondence to, or "union" with, the Active Intellect.) The supreme ruler must be a man who actualizes his rational faculty or who is in union with the Active Intellect.

This man is the true prince according to the ancients; he is the one of whom it ought to be said that he receives revelation. For man receives revelation only when he attains this rank—that is, when there is no longer an intermediary between him and the Active Intellect. . . . Now because the Active Intellect emanates from the being of the First Cause [God], it can for this reason be said that it is the First Cause that brings about the revelation to this man through the mediation of the Active Intellect. The rule of this man is the supreme rule; all other human rulerships are inferior to it and are derived from it.[6]

This supreme ruler is the source of all power and knowledge in the regime, and it is through him that the citizens learn what they ought to know and to do. As God or the First Cause of the world directs everything else, and as everything else is directed toward Him, "the case ought to be the same in the virtuous city: in an orderly fashion, all of its parts ought to follow in their activities in the footsteps of the purpose of its supreme ruler." [7] He possesses unlimited powers and cannot be subjected to any human being or political regime or laws. He has the power to confirm or abrogate previous divine laws, to enact new ones, and "to change a law he had legislated at one time for another if he deems it better to do so." [8] He alone has the power to order the classes of people in the regime and assign to them their ranks. And it is he who offers them what they need to know.

For most people, this knowledge has to take the form of an imaginative representation of the truth rather than a rational conception of it. This is because most people are not endowed, or cannot be trained to know divine things in themselves, but can only understand their imitations, which should be made to fit their power of understanding and their special conditions and experience as members of a particular regime. Religion is such a set of imaginative representations in the form of a divine law, legislated for a particular group of men, and necessitated by the incapacity of most men to conceive things rationally and their need to believe in the imitations of divine beings, and of happiness and perfection, as presented to them by the founder of their regime. The founder must then not only present a rational or conceptual account of happiness and the divine principles to the few, but also adequately represent or imitate these same things for the many. All the citizens are to accept and preserve that with which he entrusts them: "the ones who follow after happiness as they cognize it and accept the [divine] principles as they cognize them are the *wise men;* and the ones in whose souls these things are found in the form of images, and who accept them and follow after them as such, are the *believers.*" [9]

Thus far Alfarabi identifies the ruler-prophet and the ruler-philosopher. They are both supreme rulers absolutely, and both have absolute authority with regard to legislating beliefs and actions. Both acquire this authority in virtue of the perfection of their rational faculty, and both receive revelation from God through the agency of the Active Intellect. Wherein, then, does the ruler-prophet differ from the ruler-philosopher?

The first and primary qualification that the ruler of the virtuous regime must possess is a special kind of knowledge of divine and human things. Now, man possesses three faculties for knowledge: sensation, imagination, and reason (both theoretical and practical), and these develop in him in that order. Imagination has three functions: (1) It acts as a reservoir of sensible impressions after the disappearance of the objects of sensation. (2) It combines sensible impressions to form a complex sensible image. (3) It produces *imitations.* It has the capacity to imitate all nonsensible things (human desires, temperament, passions) through sensible impressions or certain combinations of them. When later the rational faculty develops, and man begins to grasp the character, essence, or form of natural and divine beings, the faculty of imagination receives and imitates these rational forms also, that is, it *represents* them in the form of sensible impressions. In this respect, imagination is subordinate to the rational faculty and depends on it for the "originals" that it imitates; it has no direct access to the essence of natural and divine beings. Further, the limitations that it fabricates are not all good copies: some may be more true and nearer to the originals, others defective in some respects, and still others extremely false or misleading copies. Finally, only the rational faculty that grasps the originals themselves can judge the degree of the truth of these copies and of their likeness to the originals. The rational faculty is the only faculty that has access to the knowledge of divine or spiritual beings, and it must exercise strict control to insure that the copies offered by the imaginative faculty are good or fair imitations. It may happen in rare cases that this imaginative faculty is so powerful and perfect that it overwhelms all the other faculties, and proceeds directly to receive or form images of divine beings. This rare case is the case of prophecy:

It is not impossible that man, when his imaginative power reaches utmost perfection, should receive in his waking hours from the Active Intellect . . . the *imitations* of separate [immaterial] intelligibles and all other noble [sacred] beings, and to view them. By virtue of the intelligibles he had received, he will thus have [the power of] prophecy about divine things. This, then, is the most perfect stage reached by the power of imagination and the most perfect stage at which man arrives by virtue of his imaginative power.[10]

The description of the nature of prophecy thus leads to the distinction between the faculty of imagination and the rational faculty. It explains the possibility of prophecy as the perfection of the faculty of imagination, and that imagination can almost dispense with the rational faculty and receive the images of divine beings directly and without the latter's mediation. There are two powers by means of which man can communicate with the Active Intellect: his imagination and his rational faculty or his intellect. When he communicates with it by means of his imagination, he is "a prophet who warns about what will happen and who informs about what is taking place now"; while when he communicates with it by means of his rational faculty he is "a wise man, a philosopher, and has complete intelligence." [11]

It would appear then that the ruler-prophet and the ruler-philosopher both can be said to possess the qualification of knowledge required for being the supreme ruler of the virtuous city; or that two kinds of equally virtuous regimes are possible, one ruled by a prophet without philosophy and the other ruled by the philosopher without prophecy. Yet in his political writings Alfarabi does not even consider the possibility of a virtuous regime ruled by a prophet who does not possess a developed rational faculty. The distinction between prophecy and philosophy is a psychological distinction, and it is useful for understanding the nature of prophecy and philosophy respectively. But in discussing the quality of knowledge required by the supreme ruler, Alfarabi is explicit in demanding the perfection of both faculties: the supreme ruler is not called a perfect prophet or a perfect philosopher, but a "perfect human being." To begin with the philosopher, even his philosophy or the wisdom he is seeking remains incomplete so long as he does not possess perfect mastery in imitating the rational or theoretical knowledge in his possession in order to teach it to the young or to present it to the multitude. This lack becomes an essential defect when he is faced with the task of governing a city and educating it. His very quality as philosopher (that is, as one who devotes himself to theoretical knowledge irrespective of its use in, or relation to, the city) disqualifies him as a ruler. He cannot be a *ruler*-philosopher without the power of imagination of which the prophet is the most accomplished representative.

As to the prophet, while his imaginative power seems to make him particularly fit for ruling, the workings of his imagination do not enjoy the benefit of rational control: he lacks the constant check of the degree of truthfulness or verisimilitude of the imitations produced by his powerful imagination, a function that only the rational faculty can perform. The best ruler for the virtuous city must therefore be a ruler-philosopher-prophet. Alfarabi does not say whether Muhammad the prophet was also a philosopher, but he requires the combination of prophecy and philosophy, or the exercise of the imaginative and the rational powers, in the supreme ruler of the virtuous city. Philosophy or wisdom is indispensable for ruling a virtuous city. "If it should happen at any time that wisdom has no share in ruling, and [the ruling authority] fulfilled all other conditions, the virtuous city remains without a prince, the ruler who takes care of the business of this city will not be a prince, and the city will be exposed to perdition. Thus if it does not happen that there should exist a wise man to associate with him, then after a time the city will surely perish." [12]

Law and Living Wisdom

Wisdom or philosophy is an indispensable condition for the founding and survival of the virtuous city. Prophecy, on the other hand, is indispensable for founding a virtuous city but not for its survival. In enumerating the qualities of the supreme ruler or the founder of the virtuous city, Alfarabi stipulates the coincidence of excellent rational and prophetic faculties. This requirement is imposed by the composition of the virtuous city as a political community, that is, the fact that it must be made up of two broad groups: (1) the few who are philosophers or can be addressed through philosophy, and who can be taught the theoretical sciences and hence the true character of divine and natural beings as they are; (2) the many who (because they lack the necessary natural endowments or have no time for sufficient training) are not philosophers, who live by opinion and persuasion, and for whom the ruler must imitate these beings by means of similitudes and symbols.

While the few can be made to grasp rationally the meaning of human happiness and perfection and the rational basis or justification of the virtuous activities that lead to man's ultimate end, the many are incapable of such understanding and have to be taught to perform these activities by persuasion and compulsion, that is, by explanations that could be understood by all the citizens regardless of their rational capacity, and by prescribed rewards and punishments of an immediate tangible kind. The supreme ruler teaches the few in his capacity as philosopher, and he presents similitudes and prescribes rewards and punishments for the many in his capacity as prophet. To be believed and practiced by the many, these similitudes and prescriptions should be formulated by the prophet, and accepted by the citizens, as true, fixed, and permanent; that is, the citizens should expect definite rewards and punishments for belief and unbelief, and for obedience and disobedience. The prophetic faculty culminates, then, in laying down laws concerning both the beliefs and the practices of the many, and the prophet who assumes this function becomes a prophet-legislator. The rational faculty, in contrast, culminates in teaching the theoretical sciences to the few. In his summary of Plato's *Laws,* Alfarabi also understood Plato to say that these virtuous few "have no need for fixed practices and laws at all; nevertheless they are very happy. Laws and fixed practices are needed only for those who are morally crooked." [13]

It is only as viewed by the subjects that laws are fixed and are of unquestionable divine authority. We saw that the supreme ruler of the virtuous regime is the master and not the servant of the law. Not only is he not ruled by any man, he is also not ruled by the law. He is the cause of the law, he creates it, and he abrogates and changes it as he sees fit. He possesses this authority because of his wisdom and his capacity to decide what is best for the common good under given conditions; and conditions can arise under which the changing of the law is not only salutary but indispensable for the survival of the virtuous regime. In so doing he must be extremely cautious not to disturb the faith of the citizens in their laws, and should consider the adverse effect that change has on attachment to the law. He must make a careful appraisal of the advantage of changing the law as against the disadvantage of change as such. Thus he must possess, not only the authority to change laws whenever necessary, but also the craft of minimizing the danger of change to the well-being of the regime. But once he sees that changing the law is necessary and takes the proper precautions, there is no question as to his authority to change the law. Therefore, so long as he lives, the rational faculty rules supreme and laws are preserved or changed in the light of his judgment as philosopher.

It is this coincidence of philosophy and prophecy in the person of the ruler that insures the survival of the virtuous regime. As long as rulers who possess these qualities succeed each other without interruption, the same situation obtains.

The successor will be the one who will decide about what was left undecided by his predecessor. And not this alone. He may change a great deal of what his predecessor had legislated and make a different decision about it when he knows this to be best in his own time—not because his predecessor had committed a mistake but because his predecessor decided upon it according to what was best in his own time, and the successor decides according to what is best for a later time. Were his predecessor to observe [the new conditions] he would have changed [his own law] also.[14]

The coincidence of philosophy and prophecy is extremely rare, and chance may not always favor the virtuous regime with the availability of a man who possesses all the necessary natural endowments and whose training proves successful. Thus the question arises as to whether the virtuous city can survive in the absence of a man with all the qualifications required in the supreme ruler, and particularly those of philosophy and prophecy. Granting that the best possible arrangement demands the existence of all these qualifications in one man who must rule, can the regime originated by such a ruler survive at all in his absence? The only qualification that Alfarabi is willing to drop in *The Virtuous City* is prophecy, and then only if provisions are made for the presence of proper substitutes for prophetic legislation. These substitutes consist of (1) the body of laws and customs established by the "true princes," and (2) a combination of new qualities in the ruler that make him proficient in the "art of jurisprudence," that is, knowledge of the laws and customs of his predecessors, willingness on his part to follow these laws and customs rather than change them, the capacity to apply them to new conditions by the "deduction" of new decisions from, or the "discovery" of new applications for, established laws and customs, and the capacity to meet every new situation (for which no specific decisions are available) through understanding the *intention* of previous legislators rather than by the legislation of new laws or by any formal change of old ones. So far as the law is concerned, this new ruler is a jurist-legislator rather than a prophet-legislator. He must, however, possess all the other qualities, including wisdom or philosophy, that enable him to discern and promote the common good of his regime at the particular period during which he rules.

In the event that no single human being should exist who possesses all these qualifications, then Alfarabi suggests a third possibility: a philosopher and one other man (who possesses the rest of the qualities, except philosophy) should rule jointly. Were even this to prove unobtainable, he suggests finally a joint rule of a number of men possessing these qualifications severally. This joint rule does not, however, affect the presence of the required qualifications but only their presence in the *same* man. Thus the only qualification whose very presence may be dispensed with is prophecy. The substitutes for prophecy are the preservation of old laws and the capacity to discover new applications for old laws. To promote the common good and preserve the regime under new conditions as these emerge, neither the coincidence of philosophy and prophecy in the same man, nor the coincidence of philosophy and jurisprudence, proves to be an indispensable condition. It is sufficient to have philosophy in the person of a philosopher who rules jointly with another man or a group of men who possess, among other things, the capacity to put old laws to new uses. Unlike prophecy, philosophy cannot be dispensed with, and nothing can take its place. Unlike the absence of prophecy, the absence of philosophy is fatal to the existence of the virtuous regime. There is no substitute for living wisdom.

War and the Limitations of Law

In addition to philosophy and prophecy (or else proficiency in the art of jurisprudence), there is a third and indispensable qualification that must be present in the ruler of the virtuous regime or in one of the group that rule it jointly: that is, daring and warlike virtue. This qualification is required for carrying out the ruler's responsibility as the supreme educator of all the citizens, that is, to form and improve their moral character. Since not all men can be convinced, or aroused to perform virtuous activities, by means of persuasive and passionate speeches, the method of persuasion or consent is not sufficient. As the father does with his children and the schoolteacher with the young, so the ruler has to use force and compulsion with those who, out of nature or habit, cannot be educated or persuaded to obey the law spontaneously. Hence the ruler needs to employ two groups of educators: a group that educates the citizens by persuasion and by means of arguments; and a warlike group to compel the lazy, the wicked, and the incorrigible to obey the laws by force. The supreme ruler, or the rulers, should lead, direct, and supervise the activities of both groups. To command the second group, he or they should possess a daring nature and excel in the art of war.

The nature and the extent of the compulsion and force to be applied within a certain regime depend on the character of the citizens: the more virtuous they are, the less need there is to apply force. But there are cases where the ruler may have to conquer a whole city and force it to accept his virtuous or divine law, or where the use of force would considerably shorten the time required to establish his law while the issue of persuasion is too uncertain and its prospects too remote. Compulsion is legitimate inside the regime with regard to those citizens who are of intractable natures or bad habits, and with respect to a whole city as a prelude to the establishment of a new divine law where it is lacking. Physical force, overpowering, or war is a "fundamental element" of the law and one of the basic "preludes" for establishing it. Alfarabi seems to favor not only defensive war but offensive war also; and he speaks of the war conducted by the ruler of the virtuous regime as a just war and of his warlike purpose as a virtuous purpose.

Further, while like Plato and Aristotle, Alfarabi considers the "city" the first or smallest unit that constitutes a political whole and in which man can attain his political perfection, unlike them he does not seem to consider the city also the largest possible unit in which a virtuous regime can be expected to flourish. Instead, he speaks of three "perfect" human associations: the largest in size is the association of all men in the entire inhabited world; the intermediate is the association of a nation in a portion of the inhabited world; and the smallest is the association of the inhabitants of a city in a portion of the land inhabited by a nation. If we combine his teaching about just or virtuous war and conquest with the idea of a perfect human association extending over the entire inhabited world, we can be led to the conclusion that Alfarabi deliberately modified the teachings of Plato and Aristotle on an important issue with the intention of supplying a rational justification for the Islamic concept of holy war whose aim was to propagate the divine law everywhere on earth;[15] that he favored a war of civilization whereby a more advanced nation justifies the conquest of more backward nations; or that he preached the idea of a universal or a world state. These conclusions must now be examined in the light of Alfarabi's views on war and the character of the law.

He mentions two extreme views regarding war. The first is the view that to overpower and dominate others is the natural state of man and that war is therefore the only universally just course of conduct. The second is that the natural state of man is universal peace and peaceful coexistence is therefore the only just course of conduct. This latter view can in turn have the corollary that only in defensive war, war forced upon one by the unnatural conduct of a warlike enemy, is there a just cause for taking up arms. These are according to him the views of the inhabitants of the "ignorant and erring cities" that are opposed to the virtuous regime.[16] They give rise to two types of regimes, "tyrannies" and "peace-loving regimes." The latter are not considered sufficiently important; and their view, though mistaken, is evidently not dangerous. At any rate, he does not list them as a main subdivision of the regimes opposing the virtuous regime which is partly due to the fact that, unlike war, peace is not one of the main "ends" pursued by men but a means to other ends, such as pleasure or gain.

War, conquest, the overpowering and enslaving of others, and tyranny over them, is, in contrast, one of the supreme ends pursued by men. It gives rise to the "tyrannical regime" in which men associate with each other, practice warlike activities, frame their laws, and order their regime with the main purpose of enslaving each other or other regimes. They do not enslave and kill to attain other ends, but to satisfy a supreme end common to all of them, "the love of tyranny." Indeed, the bad regimes pursuing other ends, such as wealth, honor, or pleasure, are in many cases transformed into tyrannies when these other ends are attained. The satisfaction of these desires seems to free the citizens of bad regimes to pursue the highest evil of "ignorant and erring" regimes, that is, the view that "tyranny is the good." War as an end in itself is for Alfarabi the supreme vice that can have no place in the regime whose end is the supreme virtue.

Having made use of the advantages of war and compulsion to establish his divine law and to suppress the wicked and the incorrigible, the ruler of the virtuous regime must return to promote friendship among the citizens and to the peaceful work of persuasion and free consent. To persuade the majority of citizens, he has to produce similitudes of divine and natural beings, and of virtue and happiness, that are adequate in respect of their proximity to the original forms of these things, but that are also adequate with respect to those who are to be persuaded by them. The similitudes should bear some relation to the nature, past experience, and habits of the citizens. Unlike the business of war, peaceful persuasion requires the legislator to make concessions to the character of the ruled, the degree of their preparation for virtuous laws, differences among them, and the extent to which the citizens can be improved. These are prelegal conditions that he does not create but must presuppose and that he cannot change except to a limited extent and then only gradually.

Further, the legislator cannot produce similitudes and utilize persuasive methods designed to meet the peculiar nature and habits of each individual citizen; the law cannot treat each man as a case by himself. General beliefs and practices must be prescribed for all the citizens and must correspond to their distinctive character as a group. Now, what is adequate for one group and hence just with regard to them may be inadequate for another group and hence unjust with regard to them. To legislate for all men with respect to "human nature" or what they all have in common will mean being unjust to most if not to all men. Therefore, if it is the case that the inhabited world is divided into nations and cities, and this division is based not on arbitrary but on natural distinctions or distinctions that are somehow related to nature, such distinctions could form the limits within which general beliefs and practices that are both effective and just could be prescribed.

Alfarabi qualifies his statement about the three perfect associations (the city, the nation, and the association of all men in the entire inhabited world) with the observation that the association of all men in the entire inhabited world is divided into nations. "Nations are distinguished from each other by two natural things—natural make-up and natural character—and by something that is composite (it is conventional but has a basis in natural things), namely, language." [17] These distinctions are the product of geographical differences among the various parts of the earth (temperature, foodstuff, and so on) that in turn influence the temperament of their inhabitants. But although they constitute the nation as a natural unit, these natural national similarities are not a sufficient political bond for the sake of which the members of a nation should like each other or dislike other nations. The proper objects of like and dislike are the perfections or the virtues, and these are not given by nature but by the Active Intellect, by science, and by legislation. The nation is in turn divided into cities or city-states that are distinguished by their regimes and laws.

Only the city is likened by Alfarabi to the perfect living body. The organs of the living body do not simply cooperate toward a common end; they have different ranks, each of which is perfect when it performs its proper function (be that a subordinate or a superior one), and all of which are ruled by the most perfect organ. Applied to the nation and the association of all men in the entire inhabited world, this similitude would require the subordination of cities to each other, and of nations to each other, according to their degree of perfection. Yet

Alfarabi never speaks of such subordination as being legitimate except within a single city; and the cities opposed to the virtuous city are not investigated with a view to being subordinated to a virtuous city but to being transformed into such a city. A virtuous nation is not a group of cities ruled by a virtuous or perfect city, but the nation "*all* of whose cities *cooperate* regarding the things by which happiness is attained"; and the association of all men in the entire inhabited world is virtuous "only when the nations in it *cooperate* to achieve happiness." [18] The virtuous community of all men presupposes virtuous nations, and the virtuous nation in turn presupposes virtuous cities.

The consideration of the specific character and function of the prophetic faculty and of the divine law points to the conclusion that religion should be particularly sensitive to the limitations imposed by the natural and conventional differences among nations and cities. If a religion or divine law is not spurious, obscurantist, or fanatic, it does not promote but suppresses and transcends the ends pursued in ignorant regimes (including tyranny), and substitutes for them the end that can be pursued only through the belief in adequate or salutary similitudes of divine and natural beings, and through commands and prohibitions that promote virtue and happiness among a particular group ready for its message. It must therefore abandon the end of the tyrannical regime whose aim is absolute and universal tyranny and restrict the use of force to the extent to which it is necessary to establish a new regime and suppress the wicked and the incorrigible inside that regime. Otherwise, it will be forced to legislate beliefs and practices that can be accepted and performed by all men, that is, to lower its standards to conform to the natural capacity of the overwhelming majority of men rather than uphold the ones that help a relatively good city or nation to achieve true virtue or happiness. The alternative aim of promoting virtue or happiness among the best or the elect in every city and nation is ruled out because this is not the proper function of religion but of philosophy. We recall Alfarabi's distinction between the functions of prophecy and philosophy in the virtuous regime. The few who are endowed with rare natures and are given proper training are offered, not similitudes, but theoretical knowledge of the divine and natural beings themselves, and of virtue and happiness, while the beliefs and practices legislated in the divine law aim at the many.

Now, the natural and quasi-natural distinctions among cities and nations need not form a barrier against the transmission of theoretical knowledge. Such knowledge presupposes the presence of a tradition of theoretical inquiry and of rare individuals; but once these conditions are fulfilled, it can be freely transplanted from one city to another and from one nation to another. The universal community of the superior men of every city and nation or of the uncrowned kings of humanity is not a community of believers in a particular set of dogmas. It is the community of lovers of the one and true wisdom. By its very nature, according to Alfarabi, a religion cannot provide the basis for such a community. Religion arises because of the incapacity of the many to understand the true character of beings and of human happiness. It remedies this situation by presenting them with similitudes that take into account the limitations of their understanding and their natural and conventional characteristics as a distinct group. Also, because the true principles of nature and true political principles are invariable, they are inflexible and cannot themselves be adjusted to the degree of understanding and the particular character of a distinctive political group. Similitudes, in contrast, may be adjusted for this purpose because they can be nearer to, or remote from, reality. In addition, there can be a number of good similitudes of the same reality. These similitudes are all good or virtuous if they succeed in making the members of the particular political groups for which they are designed good or virtuous. "Consequently, there may be a number of virtuous nations and a number of virtuous cities whose religions are different." [19] Alfarabi's approach to religion leads to a philosophic science of divine laws. By presenting divine laws, jurisprudence, and theology as parts of political science, he points to the possibility of a neutral discussion of all religions or "sects" [20] and of the features common to them all.

DEMOCRACY AND THE VIRTUOUS REGIME

Of the six regimes opposed to the virtuous regime, the first and the last, that is, the regimes of necessity and democracy, occupy the privileged position of supplying the most solid and the best starting point for the establishment of the virtuous regime and for the rule of virtuous men. The regime of necessity (as the counterpart of the city of the pigs in Plato's *Republic*) offers the opportunity for introducing a virtuous regime among citizens who are not as yet corrupted by the love of money or honor, by indulgence in pleasures, or by the desire for glory. But since all of these exist in democracy, it is not clear at first sight what contribution democracy could make to the virtuous regime.

Following Plato's description (*Republic* VIII), Alfarabi sets down the first principle of democracy (that is, of pure democracy, or of extreme democracy, as Aristotle calls it) as freedom, and he calls the democratic regime also the "free" regime. Freedom means the ability of everyone to pursue anything he desires, and that he should be left alone to do anything he chooses in the pursuit of his desires. The second principle is equality, which means that no man is superior to another in anything at all. These two principles define the basis of authority, the relation between the ruler and the ruled, and the attitude of the citizens to each other. Authority is justified only on the basis of the preservation and promotion of freedom and equality. Whatever the accomplishments of the ruler, he rules only by the will of the citizens, however unaccomplished he or they may be: he must follow their wishes and cater to their whims. The citizens honor only those who lead them to freedom and to the achievement of whatever makes possible the enjoyment of their desires, and those who preserve that freedom and make it possible for them to enjoy their different and conflicting desires, and who defend them against external enemies. If such men can perform these functions and still remain themselves content with the bare necessities of life, then they are considered virtuous and are obeyed. The rest of the rulers are functionaries who perform services for which they receive adequate honors or financial remunerations; and the citizens who pay them for these services consider themselves, because of this, superior to these rulers whom they support. Such also is the case of those whom the public lets rule either because it takes a fancy to them or because it wants to reward them for a service rendered by their ancestors. Despite these differences, a close investigation of the democratic regime shows that, ultimately, there are really no rulers and ruled; there is one supreme will, which is that of the citizens; and the rulers are instruments serving the desires and wishes of the citizens.

Unlike the other five regimes, there is no single or dominating end desired or wished for by the citizens of the democratic regime. They form innumerable groups, similar and dissimilar, with a variety of characters, interests, aims, and desires. So far as ends are concerned, democracy is a composite regime: various groups, aiming at the ends characterizing the other regimes, exist side by side and pursue different ways of life; they form a conglomeration in which the different parts are interwoven with each other; and they are free to fulfill their distinct aims independently or in cooperation with others.

Because the democratic regime makes possible, preserves, protects, and promotes every kind of desire, all kinds of men come to admire it and consider it as the happy way of life. They come to love democracy and to love to live in it. A great number migrate to it from different nations, and residents and foreigners meet, mix, and intermarry. The result is the greatest possible diversity of natural character, upbringing, education, and ways of life; yet every type of man is encouraged, or allowed, to achieve what he desires as far as his capacity admits. A fully developed democratic regime presents a colorful spectacle of infinite diversity and luxury.

But this means that, of all the regimes opposed to the virtuous regime, the democratic regime contains the greatest amount and variety of good and evil things; and the more it expands and becomes perfect, the more the goodness and the evil it contains. It will therefore also contain a number of the parts of the virtuous city. Alfarabi mentions in particular the possibility of the rise of virtuous men, and of the presence of wise men, rhetoricians, and poets (that is, men who deal with demonstrative science, persuasion, and imitation) in all kinds of things. If the regime of necessity contributes citizens uncorrupted by unessential desires and pleasures, the democratic regime, most of whose citizens are corrupted by luxury, offers the highly developed sciences and arts essential for the establishment of the virtuous regime. And in the absence of the virtuous regime in which these sciences and arts have the best opportunity to develop in the right direction, the democratic regime is the only regime that provides ample opportunity for their development and allows the philosopher to pursue his desire with relative freedom.

NOTES

All of the citations in these notes refer to the Arabic texts. Some of the works referred to have been translated into English. The translations, which reproduce the pagination of the Arabic texts, are given in the list of Readings at the end of this chapter. Translations of quotations within the chapter have been made by the author.

1. Alfarabi, *The Enumeration of the Sciences*, ed. Osman Amine (2nd ed.; Cairo: Dār al-Fikr al-'Arabī, 1949), v; *The Virtuous Religion*, MS, Leiden, Cod. Or. No. 1002, fols. 53v–54v.

2. *The Virtuous City*, ed. Fr. Dieterici (Leiden: Brill, 1895), p. 46; cf. *The Political Regime* (Hyderabad: Dā'irat al-Ma'ārif al-'Uthmāniyyah, 1345 A. H.), pp. 42–45, 48.

3. *Virtuous City*, p. 46; cf. *Political Regime*, pp. 43–44.

4. *Virtuous City*, p. 63; cf. *Political Regime*, p. 74.

5. *Political Regime*, pp. 48–49.

6. *Ibid.*, pp. 49–50.

7. *Virtuous City*, pp. 56–57; cf. *Political Regime*, pp. 53–54.

8. *Political Regime*, pp. 50–51.

9. *Ibid.*, p. 56.

10. *Virtuous City*, p. 52.

11. *Ibid.*, pp. 58–59.

12. *Ibid.*, p. 61.

13. *Plato's Laws*, ed. Franciscus Gabrieli (London: Warburg Institute, 1952), p. 41.

14. *Virtuous Religion*, fol. 54r.

15. See below, pp. 240ff.

16. *Virtuous City*, pp. 75–80.

17. *Political Regime*, p. 40.

18. *Virtuous City*, p. 54.

19. *Political Regime*, p. 56; *Virtuous City*, p. 70.

20. See below, p. 229.

READINGS

A. Alfarabi. *The Political Regime,* in *Medieval Political Philosophy*. Ed. Ralph
    Lerner and Muhsin Mahdi. New York: The Free Press, 1963. Selection 2,
    pp. 39–76.
    Alfarabi. *The Enumeration of the Sciences,* in *ibid.,* Selection 1, chap. v.
B. Alfarabi. *Plato's Laws,* in *ibid.,* Selection 4. Introduction and Discourses I–II.
    Alfarabi. *The Attainment of Happiness,* in *Alfarabi's Philosophy of Plato
    and Aristotle*. Trans. Muhsin Mahdi. New York: The Free Press, 1962.
    Part I.
    Alfarabi. *The Philosophy of Plato,* in *ibid.,* part II.

MOSES MAIMONIDES

1135–1204

A discussion of medieval Jewish political philosophy might appear to
suffer from a serious, perhaps hopeless, difficulty. Is there any reason to
assume that the subject matter exists? Little in the present-day historical
literature suggests that it does. When the medieval Jewish philosophers
appear at all in current histories, they do so mainly for their antiquarian
interest, as links in a chain of the transmission of ideas. This neglect
is even more pronounced in the histories of political thought; medieval
Jewish writers appear to be regarded as irrelevant. It would not be difficult to find some plausible reason for this neglect: a people that for more
than a millennium was unable to lead an autonomous political life and
that for the most part was firmly excluded from governance and administration is not a likely source of independent political reflection.
Yet for all its plausibility, this assumption is false; the fact remains
that problems that we can recognize as falling within the province of
political philosophy *are* discussed in the writings of medieval Jews.
Speculation about political things has never been a preserve open only
to statesmen and full citizens.

We can go further in trying to understand why medieval Jews concerned themselves with political philosophy. To begin with, the Diaspora, or dispersion of the Jews, was regarded by the Jews themselves
as an abnormal situation at least as early as the time of Philo (d. A.D.
54). In traditional, nonpolitical terms, exile was seen as a divinely ordained punishment for the people's iniquity. Just as certainly as sinfulness had led to the destruction of the Jewish commonwealth, so would
repentance lead to its restoration. *When* this abnormal situation might
come to an end, no one could ascertain, but *that* it would cease was not

to be doubted. To this extent, at least, reflection on political things was not regarded as an utterly arid exercise. A more powerful impetus to speculation of this sort was to be found in the concern of Jewish scholars with the Torah and the Talmud. Unlike Christian scholasticism, medieval Jewish political philosophy developed in the context of a divine revelation that assumed the form of law rather than dogma or faith. That law, as any reader of the Pentateuch can observe, aims at prescribing and regulating, down to the smallest detail, the conduct and beliefs of an entire community. The crucial consideration is not merely that political matters figure large in both Torah and Talmud; even more significant as a stimulus to political inquiry and as a partial determinant of the manner in which that inquiry was carried on is the *legal* character of those writings. At least for these reasons, men were led to consider political things at a time when there was little in everyday life to suggest the utility or propriety of such speculation.

However, another difficulty, no less perplexing, arises when we turn to the writings of the medieval Jewish scholars. They do not appear to have written political treatises as such, and there is not even much in the way of sustained thematic treatment of political matters. Typically, medieval Jewish political philosophy emerges from a discussion of some other subject: the interpretation of the Bible, the principal features of the divine law, the meanings of certain biblical terms, the systematic restatement of talmudic legislation, the defense of Judaism. The reason for this has already been indicated: the very circumstances we have mentioned, which, among others, led certain Jewish scholars to political philosophy, also affected the manner in which they philosophized or in which they presented their teachings. The non-thematic presentation of their political philosophy stems in part from the necessity for Jewish philosophers (like their Muslim counterparts) to justify their philosophic activity before the tribunal of the revealed law. None would have dared to begin a work with the question that opens the *Summa Theologica:* "Whether, besides the philosophical disciplines, any further doctrine is required?"

In Judaism, even more than in Islam, the case for philosophy had to be made and won before one could philosophize in public. Stated differently, that which commonly is said to be the principal concern of medieval political philosophy—demonstrating the harmony between the revealed teaching and the Aristotelian teaching—presupposes the legitimacy of philosophizing. As is clear from the chapter on Alfarabi, establishing the legitimacy of philosophic pursuits requires arguments that derive from neither the revealed teaching nor the Aristotelian teaching. The first necessity was to understand the revealed law in a way that allowed for—even required—philosophy. As far as Judaism is concerned, the decisive work in this task was done by Moses ben Maimon (Maimonides). His predominance in medieval Jewish philosophy is such that one can, without gross injustice to the others, view his teaching as the core and take note of other Jewish thinkers where they elaborate upon, or deviate from, his political teaching in some significant way. In considering his political teaching, it is well to remind oneself that philosophy by no means forms the core of the Jewish religion. Philosophy appeared rather late in Judaism and never achieved a status that made it unqualifiedly acceptable. However, in accord with the plan of this work, the present discussion will limit itself to political philosophy proper.

If one is to discuss the objects and character of law, one must proceed from an understanding of the beings for whose sake a law is made. Maimonides proceeds accordingly; in his *Guide of the Perplexed,* he examines the need for law before presenting his thematic discussion of law. Of all the species, it is man and man alone who is strictly speaking a political animal. There are indeed animals that we justly call social, but none of the animals other than man requires reflection or foresight in order to survive. If man were left to lead the life of the beasts, he would perish immediately; by themselves, his animal faculties would fall far short of what is required for his survival. It is only through his rational faculty, by means of which he exercises thought and foresight, that man can accomplish what is needed for self-preservation. Food, shelter, clothing—all require the application of some art to the raw materials of nature in order to make them fit for use by man. Since the arts, in turn, presuppose the use of tools and the existence of men skilled in their use, it follows that man's survival depends upon the division of labor and upon an orderly social arrangement under which each individual can devote himself to some particular occupation, secure in the knowledge that his contribution to the preservation of his fellows is requited by their contributions toward his preservation.[1]

Men's need to live in an organized society is increased further by the uniquely great variety prevailing among them, for the range of differences in conduct is so extreme that two individual men might appear to belong to two different species. In the face of such variety, men would not be able to live together without the supervision and control of someone who restrains and moderates individual excesses. Just as society appears to be required by man's nature, so does the perfection of that

society require a ruler "who gauges the actions of the individuals, perfecting that which is deficient and reducing that which is excessive, and
who prescribes actions and moral habits for all of them to practice
always in the same way, until the natural diversity is hidden by the
many points of conventional accord, and so the society becomes well-
ordered." The means by which this natural variety is made to vanish
is law. This law, said by Maimonides to "have a basis in what is natural"
although not being natural, must be examined in greater detail.[2]

The very circumstances that call forth law necessitate its concern
with both actions and opinions. But there is a multiplicity of laws,
human and divine, and this fact alone—saying nothing of their mutually exclusive character—requires that we be able to distinguish the
one kind of law from the other. Considering the possible objects of
legislation, Maimonides finds that they correspond to the twofold perfectibility of human beings: perfection of the body and perfection of
the soul. A law might be concerned solely with establishing good order
within the city. It would seek to prevent wrongdoing on the part of the
citizens by restraining and directing their actions; it would seek to
abolish injustice and to secure public tranquillity; it would seek to inculcate certain moral qualities in the population—qualities that facilitate peaceful social life; it would seek to enable men to attain happiness
or, more precisely, to attain what the lawgiver imagines to be happiness.
The sole object of such a law is the well-being of the body. Its complete
preoccupation with the good order of the city is matched by its utter
indifference to the kind of opinions prevailing in that city (as long as
these are compatible with peaceful civil life). Maimonides calls such
a law a *nomos*.[3]

In contrast, a law might seek to promote both perfections of man:
like the *nomos* it would prescribe the measures required for a decent
social life, thereby enabling men not only to preserve themselves, but
to live in the very best bodily state. Going beyond this, it would seek
to promote a corresponding perfection of the soul by inculcating correct
opinions in everyone according to his individual capacity. This concern
with the welfare of the soul (as well as that of the body), this effort
to develop each man's understanding of everything that exists as far
as is possible, is the distinguishing feature of a divinely revealed
law.[4]

Summarily stated, Maimonides distinguishes between a *nomos*
whose object is imaginary happiness and a divine law whose object is
true happiness. But the very possibility of securing this nobler aim—
that is, perfecting men's souls by helping them to acquire correct opinions—is contingent upon the attainment of the well-being of the body.

Inferior though they may be in dignity, the needs of the body (and, by extension, the decent ordering of society, which makes it possible for those needs to be met), have priority in time. Political welfare is the indispensable precondition of man's ultimate perfection.[5]

For Maimonides, the ultimate perfection of man is far removed from any concern with the body. Those subjects that figure so large in any legislative code—human actions and moral qualities—form no part of it. Man's perfection consists rather in his obtaining correct opinions, opinions to which he is led by speculation and that he establishes as true by means of the theoretical sciences. Law occupies a position of crucial importance, for its prescriptions order men's lives in a way that permits them to pursue their ultimate perfection. Once social life is made possible, men can turn to that private activity through which alone they can reach their proper end. In a sense it is true that the law or the study of the law is "a small thing." But in another sense it is "the great good" that the deity has caused to overflow onto the world. All the actions prescribed by the divine law, be they acts of worship or useful moral habits, are intended to regulate men's social relations. Maimonides notes repeatedly that prescriptions of this sort do not partake of the dignity of the highest end of man, but are merely preparations, albeit necessary ones, for the attainment of that end.[6]

The importance of law is in no way diminished by this view. Indeed one could say that for Maimonides the highest form of revelation is highest in virtue of its legal character. God had made His will manifest to men both before and after Moses, but the prophecies of the other men differed radically from that of Moses. The difference is so great, the one was so far superior to the others, that Maimonides declares that the term "prophet" cannot be applied with the same meaning to both. The detailed discussion of the superiority of Moses' prophecy is reserved for Maimonides' legal works, the *Commentary on the Mishnah* and the *Code;* it is only alluded to in the *Guide.*[7]

Nevertheless, his intention in the *Guide* does lead Maimonides on at least two occasions further to distinguish Moses' prophecy from that of the other prophets. The earlier prophets, for example Abraham or Noah, were addressed by God with sole regard to their private affairs; the end in view was the perfection of themselves and of their descendants. While Abraham did in fact address other men as well, his call to them was composed of eloquent speeches and speculative proofs by which he hoped to instruct men in the truth he had grasped. In short, what Abraham received from God did not have the form of law; his efforts at persuasion lacked the means of compulsion. The essentially private character of all prophecy before Moses meant that there was no explicit attempt on the part of those prophets to fashion or to improve a social and political order. The fundamental distinction between the Mosaic and pre-Mosaic prophecies is precisely this: what was given to Moses had the form of law. No one of his known predecessors ever came before the people and said, "God has sent me to you and has commanded me to say to you such and such things; He has forbidden you to do this and has commanded you to do that." While the prophets prior to Moses instructed the people, their call to the people did not take the form of divine legislation; the prophets who followed Moses were concerned principally with inducing the people to observe his law. Moses' distinction and the mark of his superiority to the prophets who preceded and succeeded him consist in his being the only legislating prophet.[8]

From this it follows that the Mosaic law is the only divine law or at any rate the only perfect divine law, although some men may continue to prophesy and to apprehend truths concerning God and the angels. Similarly it follows for Maimonides that this divine law of Moses is unchanging and unchangeable. In its character as law, it pays no heed to the isolated or rare case; it cannot concern itself with the unique human being who suffers because of the generality of the law. Indeed, as we have already noted, it is a part of the purpose of law to obscure the natural diversity of men by imposing a kind of conventional harmony that makes for civic peace. Law ought to be absolute and universal in its prescriptions and prohibitions, even though what the law requires is fitting only in the majority of cases and even though times and circumstances change. To deny this principle and to attempt to pattern legislation after medicine, where due account is taken of the particular traits of the individual, would entail the corruption of the whole fabric of the law.

Unlike Alfarabi, whom he regarded as second only to Aristotle among the philosophers, Maimonides does not explicitly discuss the possibility of the rule of living wisdom in the place of fixed written laws. Where circumstances require it, precautionary regulations may be laid down by the Great Court of Law, embodying the judgment of the men of knowledge of a given period; such regulations take the form of permanent additions to the divine law. In the extreme case, prescriptions or prohibitions of the divine law may be suspended temporarily by the Great Court of Law. But aside from these exceptions, no one can effect any change in the divine law; that law remains intact and unalterable, the unique and perfect example of its kind.[9]

This conclusion of Maimonides is explicitly denied by Joseph Albo (d. 1444). In his *Book of Roots,* wherein he distinguishes the various types of law and examines the principles of divine law, Albo notes that there have been a number of divine laws. He cites as examples the laws of Adam, Noah, Abraham, and Moses, with the clear implication that this list may not be exhaustive. For much the same reason that one *nomos* would not be appropriate for all men in the world, one divine law would similarly be unsuitable for all men everywhere. Human temperaments differ radically due to heredity and habitat, and these differences, in turn, entail different customs and conventions. Upon analysis, the divine laws will disclose certain fundamental principles shared by all of them—indicative of the unity of the giver of those laws —and, at the same time, great differences in their detailed prescriptions —reflecting the heterogeneity of the recipients of those laws. Divinely revealed laws may coexist at any given moment, although differing in the scope and rigor of their regulations. The law of Noah and the law of Moses, for example, are equally divine; they both lead to human happiness, albeit to different degrees. The fact that one divine law is superseded by another divine law for a particular people argues no defect or change in the giver and is in no way evidence that true opinions change. What has changed is the character of the recipients. Like a physician or teacher who knows that what is proper at one moment will not suffice forever, God gives a divine law only with a view to preparing men for a more difficult regimen. The succession of divine laws in the world has effected great changes in what is permitted to men and what is forbidden them; these changes have been made to accord with the changing times and with changing human character.[10]

Albo sees no reason for thinking that this alteration in the divine law may not occur again, permitting some things that now are forbidden. Not only does he deny that there is any evidence for Maimonides' contention that immutability is a root of the Mosaic law, but he denies that there is any evidence or any necessity for regarding divine law in general or the Mosaic law in particular as fundamentally beyond change or repeal. It is safe to leave it at saying that belief in the genuineness of Moses' mission implies the belief that the Mosaic law will not be altered or superseded by another divine law brought by another prophet.[11]

Jewish political philosophy, like that of Islam, attached very great importance to prophecy. Unlike Thomas Aquinas, whose discussions of prophecy make no mention of legislation,[12] Maimonides regards the prophet as performing the decisive political function. Belief in the divine law unconditionally presupposes belief in prophecy,

"for if there is no prophet, there can be no divine law." This may be
stated in another manner: since human survival depends on the existence of society, and since society rests on a harmony that must be
imposed upon contrary human temperaments, divine wisdom has endowed certain human individuals with the faculty of ruling. Included
in this order of men who have the capacity of governing others are
certain ranks of the prophets. In its more perfect manifestations, the
prophet's inspiration serves a public or political, rather than a private,
purpose. Tentatively, that purpose may be said to be the improvement
of a social order.[13] After reviewing Maimonides' definition of prophecy,
we shall return to examine the relation between the objects of the
divine law and the object of the highest form of prophecy.

Maimonides' teaching concerning prophecy is identical with that
of the Islamic philosophers in almost all major respects. He himself
distinguishes three opinions with regard to prophecy that are held by
those who admit the existence of the deity. The first is that held by the
vulgar, be they pagans or Jews: God chooses whomever He wishes and
transforms him into a prophet. According to this view, the only preconditions of prophecy are a certain goodness and sound morality. The
second opinion is identified by Maimonides as being that of the philosophers: prophecy is the natural outcome of an individual's realizing in
himself the highest perfection that is potential in the entire human
species. If a superior man has attained perfection in his rational and
moral qualities and in his imaginative faculty, and if he has undergone
the proper preparation, he necessarily must become a prophet. The third
is "the opinion of our Law": like the second opinion, it asserts that "the
natural thing is that everyone who is fit by his natural disposition and
who trains himself in his education and study will become a prophet."
According to Maimonides, natural equipment and training are the
necessary, but not—as they are according to the philosophers—the sufficient, condition for prophecy: a man may be fit and prepared for
prophecy and yet *miraculously* not become a prophet.

Prophecy is defined as an overflow from God toward a man's rational faculty and thereafter toward his imaginative faculty. To receive
this divine emanation, a man must have attained the ultimate perfection possible for the human species of reason, morals, and imagination.
His intellect is perfected through study of the speculative sciences; his
imagination must be perfect in its original natural disposition—a natural defect here cannot be remedied; his morals are perfected through
a conscious and habitual preoccupation with noble and divine things
and through freeing his thoughts from any desire for bodily pleasures

and for domination over others. One who has attained these perfections is the highest kind of man. No greater perfection can exist in the human species; a prophet, as such, is superior to the wisest philosopher.[14]

Before proceeding with Maimonides' discussion of prophecy, it is necessary to trace the relation between this threefold perfection and the prophet's function. The belief in the divine law presupposes the belief in prophecy because the revelation of that law occurs through the instrumentality of the prophet. The divine law, as we have seen, aims at securing two great ends: the well-being of the body and the well-being of the soul or, in other words, the decent ordering of society and the acquisition of correct opinions and true knowledge through speculation. The divine law is addressed to a large number of men, but they are unequal in their capacities to understand and to be perfected; the divine law must somehow speak to a great variety of human types and must somehow be appropriate for a great variety of human conditions.

These difficulties are resolved through the characteristics of the divine messenger or prophet who brings the divine law to men. Because of the perfection of his intellect, the prophet has direct knowledge of speculative truths. Unlike the philosophers, he need have no recourse to premises and inferences in order to comprehend. More than this, the prophet is able to comprehend directly and immediately what non-prophetic men cannot attain fully or at all. Man as man is limited to direct knowledge of the sensible world about him. Thus, for example, while Aristotle's teaching concerning this sublunar world is correct in all respects, his teaching concerning the upper world, the world beyond the lunar sphere, the world of God and the angels, is not perfectly correct. Here only the prophet has direct knowledge. The prophet, then, is superior to the philosopher in the very point in which the philosopher is superior to all nonphilosophic men.[15]

Moral perfection, which Maimonides lists as another precondition of prophecy, is connected most directly to the prophet's intellectual superiority; for while the desire for speculative knowledge and its attainment up to a point are not dependent upon moral perfection, the preoccupation with sensual pleasures distracts a man's thoughts from the upper world. The prophet distinguishes himself from other men by his complete preoccupation with divine things. "Interested only in the knowledge of the deity and in reflection on His works and on what ought to be believed with regard to that," a perfect man of this sort "will see only God and His angels." [16] More than any other man, the prophet is completely concerned with understanding everything that exists.

By virtue of the perfection of his intellect, the prophet is the teacher of all men. But all men cannot be taught in the same way; they are not equally capable of receiving from the prophet those speculative truths that he has apprehended with regard to God and the angels. Indeed, the overwhelming knowledge that the prophet has achieved would confuse and bewilder all but the most perfect intellects. That knowledge, or at least its general conclusions, must somehow be presented to men, particularly to nonphilosophic men, in a form that they can grasp. By means of his perfect imagination, which, through his intellect, has received a divine emanation, the prophet is able to represent these speculative truths metaphorically. This metaphoric presentation of theoretical knowledge derives from the prophet's practical understanding.

Maimonides interprets the verse of Proverbs, "A word fitly spoken is like apples of gold in settings of silver," in the light of this analysis of prophecy. He explains the verse as follows: a saying uttered with a view to two meanings is like an apple of gold overlaid with silver filigree work having very small holes. Its external meaning ought to be as beautiful as silver, while its internal meaning ought to be still more beautiful, being in comparison to the exterior as gold is to silver. Its external meaning ought to give some indication of what is to be found within, though the inattentive observer will mistake it for "an apple of silver." If one considers the parables with which the speeches of the prophets abound, they are seen to have both an external meaning and an internal meaning. "The external meaning contains wisdom that is useful in many respects, among which is the welfare of human societies. . . . Their internal meaning contains wisdom that is useful for beliefs concerned with the truth as it is." That intellectual perfection which qualifies a prophet to be a teacher of all men finds correspondence in that perfection of his imagination which qualifies him to be a leader of men. The prophet is a man with perfect theoretical and practical understanding.[17]

This doctrine may be restated as follows: as a result of his perfect intellect and perfect imagination, the prophet unites in himself the traits of men who have attained perfection in only one or the other faculty. The divine emanation affects only the rational faculty in the case of the men of science who are engaged in speculation. It affects only the imaginative faculty in the case of the class of men who govern political communities—legislators, soothsayers, and the like. As the former class embodies theoretical understanding, so the latter represents practical understanding. In receiving a divine overflow that affects both his perfect intellect and his perfect imagination, the prophet becomes at one and the same time a philosopher and a statesman and a legislator and a soothsayer. More precisely, the union of both perfections enables the prophet to surpass any one of these non-prophetic men. As the bringer of the divine law, the prophet becomes *the* teacher of men, hence of philosophers as well; he becomes *the* leader of men, hence of the rulers of political communities as well.

It is with a particular view to this political function of prophecy that Maimonides speaks of the prophet's need to have highly developed faculties of courage and divination. His "ascent" to knowledge of divine things is followed by a "descent with whatever decree the prophet has been informed of—with a view to governing and teaching the people of the earth." By virtue of his superiority, the prophet is obliged to prophesy—that is, to instruct men in practical affairs or in speculative matters. Unable to resist the divine overflow that moves them, the prophets find themselves exposed to grave dangers from the unjust and disobedient people to whom they address their call. Courage, therefore, is an indispensable prerequisite for all prophets. When present in its most highly developed form, "the lone individual, having only his staff, went boldly to the great king in order to save a religious community from the burden of slavery, and had no fear or dread because it was said to him: 'I will be with thee.' " [18] We have already mentioned Maimonides' discussion of man as a political animal. That which requires society likewise requires law to govern that society. That certain human individuals possess the faculty of ruling is a token of divine wisdom in perpetuating the species. In the first rank of those whom Maimonides mentions as possessing this faculty is the prophet or bringer of the *nomos*. These men proclaim the law; the enforcement of the proclaimed law is the province of the king. It is thus that the prophet emerges not only as divine messenger, but as lawgiver and founder of a political society.[19] To explore further this role of the prophet, we must turn to Maimonides' discussion of the law given by that "lone individual," Moses.

In a statement on political science occurring in his *Treatise on the Art of Logic,* Maimonides, after noting that the philosophers have written many books on political science, says: "In these times, all this— I mean the regimes and the *nomoi*—has been dispensed with, and men are governed by divine commands." In saying this, he suggests that the practical teaching of the philosophers in matters having to do with politics is now superfluous; he makes no such inference with respect to the philosophers' works on ethics and political philosophy. The change that has rendered the philosophers' practical political teaching superfluous "in these times" is the predominance of revealed religion. His statement suggests the decisive political importance of divine law. Maimonides' discussion of the Mosaic law in the *Guide of the Perplexed* supports this interpretation. The divine law seeks to secure the welfare of both body and soul. In aiming at these objectives, the Mosaic law treats of political matters—of matters having to do with the governance of men—extensively, precisely, and in detail; but of speculative matters, the Torah speaks in a summary fashion. In other words, since the Torah is the repository of all necessary information having to do with the governance of the household and the governance of the city, there is no need to turn to the works of the philosophers for guidance here. It is only as the Torah treats summarily those correct opinions through which men may attain their ultimate perfection, that individuals who are equipped to do so need direct their attention to the theoretical sciences.[20] The decisive point is that Maimonides regards the law given by the highest prophet as absolutely superior to the philosopher's law. The city founded by the philosophers and governed by their law is inferior to the city founded by a prophet and governed by his law, for the philosopher-legislator is inferior to the prophet-legislator.

Earlier, when discussing the relation between the objects of revelation and the object of prophecy, we tentatively concluded that the prophet's purpose was to improve a social order. That statement may now be seen to be insufficient. The divine law aims to lead men to correct opinions about God and the angels, but it does this in the main by presenting conclusions. Its principal effort is directed at establishing a certain kind of political community. If one reflects on the actions of the Patriarchs and of Moses, it becomes clear that "the end of their efforts during their life was to bring about a religious community that would know and worship God." The object of revelation, "the great good" that God causes to come forth upon the sublunar world, is the founding of a perfect religious community. This object can be attained only if the minds and actions of all men can be reached by that revelation. If the divine purpose is to be realized, the revelation must take the form of law—a perfect law that serves as the constitution, so to speak, of the perfect nation. Moreover, the revelation must be presented in a manner that all people—including the young and women—can understand. That is why "the Torah speaks in accordance with the language of the children of man." That is why a man of the utmost perfection of intellect and imagination is needed to proclaim the perfect law. The highest form of prophecy is legislative, and Moses is the greatest prophet because his prophecy is the only genuine legislative prophecy. The greatest prophet is the founder and lawgiver of the perfect city.[21]

It is typical of Maimonides' teaching that it places greater emphasis upon political considerations than upon miraculous explanations. This tendency is evident not only in his teaching concerning prophecy, but also in his discussions of two related themes—kingship and the Messianic age—in his legal *Code*. The *Code's* Hebrew title, *Mishneh Torah* (Repetition of the Torah), is the phrase by which tradition has designated the fifth book of the Bible. The book of Deuteronomy restates, and adds to, the legislation of the preceding three books; it concerns itself with the needs of a people no longer wandering in the desert and shielded and cared for by extraordinary divine providence, but rather inhabiting their own land and faced with problems arising out of agriculture, domestic strife, and foreign aggression. Maimonides' *Code* has a similar character; in it he restates the laws of the Torah and of the Talmud without limiting himself to those laws that are applicable to life in the Diaspora. Maimonides' *Mishneh Torah,* like Moses', is concerned with the practical needs of an actual state, that is, the Jewish state prior to the Diaspora and after the coming of the Messiah.

Kingship in Israel is obligatory; it is a necessity sanctioned, indeed commanded, by the divine law. According to Maimonides, the principal reason for appointing a king is that he "execute judgment and wage war." War is intimately connected with kingship; of the twenty-three commandments discussed in the section of the *Code* entitled "Laws concerning Kings and their Wars," all but five deal with some aspect of military law, while the chapters devoted to the remaining five commandments, governing the choice and mode of life of the king, all allude to war more or less openly. After subduing those nations against whom the Bible makes war obligatory, the king is free to wage "permissive war . . . against the other nations in order to enlarge the boundary of Israel and to increase his greatness and fame." The king also has a sweeping power of judgment, unlike the courts of law, which are hedged in by procedural safeguards in capital cases. Where an extreme situation requires it, he may put to death many offenders in a single day, then hang them for display for as long as he pleases, "to lay down fear."

Notwithstanding these prerogatives of office, the king remains subordinate to the law and therewith subordinate to the lawgiver and to the interpreters of that law. His function is ancillary to that of the prophet or lawgiver; the king compels people to observe the divine law or *nomos* established by these men. The fear and awe that he inspires and the deterrents that he has at his command are in the service of the judges. In a number of ways, Maimonides suggests very strongly that the king is not in fact the first man of the commonwealth. He explicitly states that the king is subject to the law and hence to the courts of law. He draws attention to the king's subservience to the spoken word of God, to God's command as spoken by the prophet. Indeed, even the greatest kings—those who, like David and Solomon, were inspired to speak of governmental and divine matters—even they have reached only the stepping-stones leading to prophecy. The greatest kings are below the prophets.[22]

Maimonides' analysis of kingship as a political and military institution is considerably qualified by Isaac Abravanel (1437–1508). Similarly, he rejects Maimonides' view of the prophet as philosopher-statesman. Drawing upon Seneca's *Ninetieth Epistle,* Abravanel builds his argument upon fundamentally antipolitical premises. For him, political society as such is an artificiality. The founding of cities, the institution of private property, the subdivision of the human race into nations—all are products of rebellion against the natural and divine order. In the beginning, men lived in a state of innocence in the fields; all enjoyed nature's goods in common; men lived in a state of liberty and equality. Abravanel sees a parallel to this natural state in the life of the Children of Israel during their wanderings in the desert—that is to say, in a life marked by a continual miraculous protection by God. Political life represents a revolt against God. Not surprisingly, Abravanel, almost alone among the medieval Jewish commentators, denies that the Bible (in Deut. 17:14 f.) made kingship mandatory in Israel. He maintains that kingship is a transgression, that in the very act of investing a man with a royal title the people "were abandoning the rule of the Lord"; "the sin lay in their rejection of the divine kingdom and in choosing the human kingdom." The best that can be said for kingship is that the divine law permitted it, recognizing it as an act of the evil urge in man and making allowance for this human weakness.

Despite his adverse judgment on the utility and propriety of monarchy, Abravanel holds that the proper government of the Jewish nation culminates in monarchic rule. He views that government as having been composed of what in Christian doctrine is known as the two swords, temporal and spiritual; each of these governments in turn contained democratic, aristocratic, and monarchic elements. At the head of the temporal mixed regime stands a man like Moses; "Moses . . . was the first king to reign over Israel." At the head of the spiritual government stands a prophet. The predominant elements of the Jewish state, in Abravanel's account, are the priests and the prophets. Though the prophet is a ruler, he is not, properly speaking, political. The greatest prophet, Moses, had to be taught by a Gentile who was not a prophet (Jethro) how to organize the administration of justice. This suggests that for Abravanel the rule of the prophet is not properly a consideration of political philosophy, as it is for Maimonides. For Abravanel prophecy, being a divine gift, is supernatural; the prophet is superpolitical. By borrowing heavily from the Christian scholastic writers, and particularly from those of extreme papalist views, Abravanel comes to conclusions that are radically at odds with those of Maimonides concerning the ideal form of government. In place of a leader who embodies the traits of both a philosopher and a king, Abravanel considers the ideal ruler to be a priest-king.[23]

The sobriety of Maimonides' teaching regarding the Messiah stands in striking contrast both to the legendary themes with which the preceding Jewish tradition had occupied itself and to the passionate speculation about the miracles to be wrought that characterizes Abravanel's Messianic writings. It is noteworthy that the thematic discussion of the Messiah is located in the concluding chapters of the fourteenth and final section of the *Code,* which deals with laws concerning kings and their wars. Maimonides' fundamental thesis is that the Messianic age is distinguished from the present only by the change in the political status of the Jewish people. "Let it not be imagined that in the days of the Messiah any thing in the world will change its way or there will be any innovation in creation. The world will go on in its accustomed way. . . ." The nonmiraculous character of Messianic times is emphasized by Maimonides in several ways. In this part of the *Code,* the Messiah appears to be first and foremost a king; not once is he here referred to as "prophet." Speaking of Bar Kokhba, the leader of the Jewish revolt against the Romans in A.D. 132, Maimonides calls him "the king" who was regarded as "the King Messiah." Only when Bar Kokhba was killed did the Jewish sages realize that they had erred in so regarding him. Maimonides makes no mention here of any claim Bar Kokhba might have on the grounds of ability to prophesy, and he explicitly denies that any miraculous deeds are required to authenticate the Messiah. The question rather is reduced to one of political and military success: Maimonides' Messiah is a warlike liberator whose primary task is to break Israel's shackles and to restore the ancient political order.

The tendency of Maimonides' teaching is to oppose the traditional notion of the Messiah as a miracle-working prophet and the more fantastic speculations concerning the Messianic age. How far Maimonides went in giving a political interpretation of the future and past fate of the Jewish people can be seen in his letter to the rabbis of southern France showing the cause of the Jews' loss of their kingdom and their subsequent dispersion. According to the traditional view, exile is a divinely inflicted punishment of a sin. That sin was understood to be idolatry or, in its common manifestation, astrology. The Jews, at the time of their kingdom, were preoccupied with astrology. "They erred and were drawn after [such subjects,] imagining them to be celebrated science and to be of great utility. They did not busy themselves with the art of war or with the conquest of lands, but imagined that those studies would help them. Therefore the prophets called them fools and dolts. And truly fools they were, for they walked after confused things that do not profit." Maimonides does not here teach that astrology is a transgression of the divine law to be punished by direct intervention of God. He rather suggests that folly brings its own punishment. By devoting their time and energies to useless confusion, the ancient Jews prepared their own downfall. Maimonides' account of the future restoration of the Jewish state is informed by this analysis of its downfall. The warlike liberator who receives the title "King Messiah" is known by his acts—political and military acts—and confirmed by his successes —political and military victories. In brief, the Messiah is a successful Bar Kokhba or, more precisely, a son of David: a general rather than a prophet.

Political success, however, is not an end in itself; it is in the service of something higher. In proportion as Maimonides regards the means to the higher end as being natural or within human power, he attaches importance to reason and politics. The evils that beset this life flow from men's "purposes, desires, opinions, and beliefs," and all of these derive from some fundamental ignorance. The vision of universal peace in Isaiah 11 is contingent upon a true knowledge of God: "For through cognition of the truth, enmity and hatred are removed. . . ." The "days of the Messiah" will differ from the present in that the Jews will return to their ancestral homeland with the aid of a successful military leader, and men will cease injuring one another out of ignorance. These two changes are related, for one of the tasks of the conquering Messiah is to "prepare the whole world to serve the Lord with one accord." The Messiah shows the world the true way, but not by means of miracles; he fights the battles of the Lord—and wins. Messianic times are indeed an object of hope, yet the goal that will then have been achieved is not the highest end of man, but rather the establishment of certain political preconditions of that end; political action in general is in the service of "the world to come." The restoration of political rule to Israel means that those laws intimately tied to the life of the people in Palestine can once again be observed; freed from tyrannical oppression, the Jews can devote themselves to the undisturbed study of the Torah and its wisdom. As a result, the way is prepared for the total final reward, "the ultimate good": life in "the world to come." Maimonides here connects "the world to come" with the immortality of the soul that follows as a matter of course from a life devoted to learning and piety. The possibility of attaining the ultimate good appears as a consequence of political success.[24]

It is noteworthy that medieval Jewish political philosophy speaks little, if at all, about natural law. But the problem that is indicated by the term "natural law" is dealt with, generally in the form of the question, Are there rational laws, as distinguished from revealed laws? The Jewish *locus classicus* of this distinction is in the *Book of Doctrines and Beliefs* by Saadya Gaon (892–928). Saadya speaks at first of a class of divine commandments whose necessity is dictated by reason. Such rational divine laws may be classified as enjoining divine worship, prohibiting idolatry, and forbidding acts of injustice. The approval and disapproval of the specific actions that are the objects of these laws are implanted in our reason; thus speculation provides independent confirmation of their necessity. The categorical dictates of the revealed laws, on the other hand, have no such independent verification. Apparently repeating his discussion, Saadya then speaks of rational laws that are suggested by wisdom. This second discussion presents a simplified account of the social utility of the rational laws. These laws are now said to be the prevention of homicide, the prohibition of adultery, the prohibition of theft, and the injunction to speak the truth. Reason is neutral or silent about such matters as religious festivals or the prohibition against eating certain foods or of marriage within certain degrees of kinship. However, most of the revealed laws have some evident practical usefulness. According to Saadya, prophetic revelation is needed to establish both classes of law, rational as well as revealed. While reason by itself is sufficient to formulate the rational commandments, it is unable to establish all the concrete details of legislation. Thus, for example, "reason deems it right that every crime be punished according to its measure, but does not define its measure." Revelation is needed to settle such details; without it men would never agree on anything beyond the general principles.[25]

In his discussion of this problem, Maimonides not only takes a stand against Saadya's teaching or a part of it, but also to a degree separates himself from the traditional orthodox view. In the letter referred to above, Maimonides states that in the *Guide* he has given clear reasons for all the biblical commandments. He silently rejects the orthodox view that it is a good thing that the Bible does not state the reasons underlying its commandments; full obedience, according to traditional religion, requires the acceptance of a commandment without knowing or seeking the reason for it. Yet in suggesting that every commandment has its reason and that its reason is within the grasp of the human intellect, Maimonides still is very far from admitting the possibility of rational commandments. He notes that the prohibitions against action that is generally regarded as evil, such as bloodshed, theft, ingratitude, and contempt for parents, are called "commandments" by the Jewish sages. "Some of our later sages"—he has Saadya, among others, in mind—"who suffered from the disease of the Mutakallimūn [Muslim dialectical theologians] called them rational commandments."

What then is the status of the moral principles? In his *Treatise on the Art of Logic,* Maimonides describes as merely conventional or generally accepted the assertions that uncovering the private parts is base and that generously compensating a benefactor is noble. In the *Guide of the Perplexed,* he asserts that only the first two commandments of the Decalogue—those proclaiming the existence and the unity of God—are knowable by human speculation alone. The remaining commandments have no rational basis; they belong to the class of generally accepted opinions and those adopted in virtue of tradition. At one point Maimonides says that what is innate in man prescribes good actions and condemns bad ones; man is rewarded or punished accordingly, quite irrespective of the specific commands of a prophet. But this is not to say that such prescriptions and prohibitions are rational. By virtue of his intellect, man knows only the distinction between truth and falsehood. The distinction between the noble and the base—moral principle— belongs to the class of things generally accepted as known, but not to the class of things cognized by the intellect. It is only the latter that remain immutably true. The principles of morality, on the other hand, are at best only probable; Maimonides suggests that the status of the moral virtues is derived from their importance in maintaining the peace of the world. Moral virtue also is required for man's ultimate perfection, that is, theoretical understanding, since a preoccupation with the pleasures of the senses or a desire for domination over others would be a barrier to such perfection. But it is primarily with a view to their political function that Maimonides understands the moral virtues. His stigmatization as "diseased" of those who affirmed the existence of rational commandments, and his studied efforts to point to the political function and conventional character of moral principle constitute a tacit denial that natural law is, strictly speaking, rational.[26]

Yehudah Halevi (1085–1141), is, among Jewish writers, perhaps the most outstanding critic of the philosophers. His positive teaching is based entirely on revelation; here, however, discussion is limited solely to what he says about the philosophers. In his dialogue, the *Kuzari*, he affirms the existence of rational *nomoi*, but the end result of his argument is something considerably different from the natural law of, say, Thomas Aquinas. Halevi designates by the one term, "rational *nomoi*," both the human codes of the pagans (as, for example, Plato's *Laws*), and the indispensable framework of any code—manmade or divine. More precisely, he identifies that part of the philosopher's code which governs the philosopher's social conduct toward nonphilosophers, on the one hand, with that body of rules which prescribes the minimal morality needed for even the lowest form of communal life, on the other; and he calls both rational *nomoi*. By means of this identification of the two, Halevi suggests that the governmental parts of the philosopher's code are but means to the higher end of speculation and accordingly are not to be understood as categorical rules, but rather as prudent rules of conduct that are valid for the most part. Similarly, he suggests that the indispensable framework of every code (or, as one might say, natural law), lacks absolute validity and universality. He further suggests in this manner that a natural law or moral code that applies equally to philosophers living in political society and to a band of robbers is neither absolutely binding upon men nor truly rational.[27]

Halevi's and Maimonides' rejection of the notion of a rational natural law is presented with greater forthrightness by Joseph Albo. Although Albo speaks explicitly of a natural law, his description of it is closer to that of Hobbes than to that of Aquinas. In content, Albo's natural law resembles Saadya's second formulation of the rational laws: it embodies that minimum of social control without which men would be unable to live together. Albo's natural law is concerned with a rudimentary justice that keeps men from theft, robbery, and murder. It is a law unconcerned with what is noble and silent about divine worship. Albo's natural law corresponds crudely to the second Table of the Decalogue if one disregards the tenth commandment. Like Halevi's rational *nomoi*, it is directed solely toward the perfection of the body. Albo suggests that this natural law is not absolutely necessary for man because it is not absolutely necessary for man to live in political society; moreover, he suggests that the validity of this natural law depends upon its establishment by some human individual. By pointing to the possibility of life outside the city, Albo casts some doubt on the obligatory character of natural law. By further distinguishing the purpose of this natural law from the perfection that is proper to man, Albo in effect denies that natural law is, strictly speaking, natural.[28] This point, on which the Muslim and Jewish medieval political philosophers agreed, was restated for the Christian world by Marsilius of Padua.

NOTES

1. Moses Maimonides, *Guide of the Perplexed*, I 72; III 27.

2. *Ibid.*, II 40.

3. *Ibid.*, II 40; III 27.

4. *Ibid.*, II 39–40; III 27.

5. *Ibid.*, III 27.

6. *Ibid.*, III 27–28, 54; *Code, Yesodei ha-Torah*, iv.13.

7. *Guide*, II 35. (Cf. *Commentary on the Mishnah, Sanhedrin* X, Introduction, article 7, and *Code, Yesodei ha-Torah*, vii.6.)

8. *Guide*, I 63; II 39; *Code, De'oth*, i.7.

9. *Guide*, II 39–40; III 34, 41, 46.

10. Joseph Albo, *Book of Roots*, I 4, 25; III 13–14.

11. *Roots*, III 14–16 (cf. 19).

12. Cf., *e.g.*, *Summa contra Gentiles*, iii.154.

13. *Guide*, II 37, 40; III 45.

14. *Ibid.*, II 32, 36 (cf. 23).

15. *Ibid.*, II 22, 38 (cf. I Introduction).

16. *Ibid.*, II 36.

17. *Ibid.*, I Introduction; III 28.

18. *Ibid.*, I 15; II 37–38, 45.

19. *Ibid.*, II 40.

20. *Ibid.*, III 27–28, 51, 54; *Treatise on the Art of Logic*, xiv.

21. *Guide*, I 33; III 51; *Code, Yesodei ha-Torah*, iv.13.

22. *Guide*, II 40, 45; III 41; *Code, Melakhim*, i.1, 8; iii.1–7, 10; iv.10; v.1.

23. Commentary on Gen. 11:1 ff., Exod. 18:13 ff., Deut. 17:14 f., I Sam. 8:6 ff., I Kings 1 and 3.

24. *Guide*, III 11; *Code, Teshubah*, ix; *Melakhim*, xi.1, 3–4; xii.1, 4; *Letter on Astrology*.

25. Saadya Gaon, *Book of Doctrines and Beliefs*, III 2–3.

26. *Guide*, I 2; II 33, 36; III 17; *Logic*, viii; *Eight Chapters*, iv, vi. (Cf. *Guide*, II 40; III 27–28, 46.)

27. *Kuzari*, II 48; III 7; IV 19.

28. *Roots*, I 5, 7; III 7, 26.

READINGS

A. Maimonides, Moses. *Guide of the Perplexed*, in *Medieval Political Philosophy*. Ed. Ralph Lerner and Muhsin Mahdi. New York: The Free Press, 1963. Selection 12. Part I, chap. 71; Part II, chaps. 32, 36–40, 45; Part III, chaps. 27–28, 34.

B. Maimonides, Moses. *Treatise on the Art of Logic*, in *ibid.* Selection 11. Chap. xiv.

Maimonides, Moses. *Letter on Astrology*, in *ibid.* Selection 13.

Albo, Joseph. *Book of Roots*, in *ibid.* Selection 14. Bk. I, chaps. 5–10.

Abravanel, Isaac. *Commentary on the Bible*, in *ibid.* Selection 15. Gen. 11:1–9; Exod. 18:13–27; Deut. 17:14–15; I Sam. 8:4–7; I Kings 3:10–12.

ST. THOMAS AQUINAS

1225–1274

Thomas Aquinas occupies a unique position in the history of political thought as the most illustrious of all Christian Aristotelians. His literary career coincides roughly with the full impact and in some instances with the initial recovery of Aristotle's works in the Western world. Both the *Politics* and the complete text of the *Ethics* in particular were first translated into Latin during his own lifetime. Through his detailed commentaries on virtually all of Aristotle's major treatises and the extensive use that he makes of Aristotelian materials in his theological works, Aquinas did more than anyone else to establish Aristotle as the leading philosophical authority in the Christian West. His own political philosophy is best understood as a modification of Aristotle's political philosophy in the light of Christian revelation or more precisely as an attempt to integrate Aristotle with an earlier tradition of Western political thought represented by the Church Fathers and their medieval followers and compounded for the most part of elements taken from the Bible, Platonic-Stoic philosophy, and Roman law.

Aquinas's endeavor to reinterpret Aristotle on the basis of the Christian faith and to reform Christian theology in terms of Aristotelian philosophy may be compared with that of the Islamic and Jewish philosophers of the Middle Ages, who also regarded Aristotle as the greatest of the pagan philosophers and who were faced with a similar problem of harmonizing Greek philosophy and revealed religion. With these Islamic and Jewish philosophers, Aquinas shared a common heritage which included the *Organon*, the *Metaphysics*, the *Physics* along with various other treatises of natural philosophy, and the *Nicomachean Ethics*. Like them, he was indebted to Aristotle for the distinction between speculative science and practical science as well as for the division of practical science into ethics, economics, and politics. But whereas Aquinas's natural philosophy, his ethics, and his political philosophy were all inspired by Aristotle, political philosophy in Islam and in the Jewish communities living in Islamic countries was based largely on the *Republic* and the *Laws* of Plato. Both of these works had been translated into Arabic at least as early as the tenth century but did not become available in the West until the fifteenth century. Alfarabi wrote commentaries on the *Republic* and the *Laws* and Averroes wrote a commentary on the *Republic*. No Arabic or Jewish commentary is known to have been written on Aristotle's *Politics* during the Middle Ages, while no fewer than seven commentaries were written on it by Christian authors from the time of the first Latin version of the text (ca. 1260) to the end of the thirteenth century.

It is possible and even likely that this first and most obvious difference between the Christian and the Judaeo-Arabic traditions was due to factors other than the mere historical accident of the availability or unavailability of the literary sources in question either in the Latin or the Arabic world. The evidence at hand suggests that the *Politics* of Aristotle had been rendered into Arabic at an early date and, in any event, its contents were known to the Islamic and Jewish philosophers through excerpts from that work as well as through the *Nicomachean Ethics* and other works of Aristotle. Likewise, the existence and part of the substance of the *Republic* and the *Laws* were familiar to the Western authors from Aristotle's *Politics* and from earlier Roman and Christian adaptations or discussions of those works by such writers as Cicero and Augustine. Yet, contrary to what was usually done in similar cases, no effort appears to have been made by either group to obtain copies or translations of the missing texts. On the strength of that and related evidence it is not unreasonable to suppose that the use of the *Politics* by the Christian authors, and of the *Republic* and the *Laws* by the Arabic and Jewish philosophers, was at least partially the result of a deliberate choice dictated by the circumstances of the political life in these different religious communities.

We know from Alfarabi that his own works were motivated by the concern to introduce philosophy into a society from which it was absent or to restore it once it had become obscured or destroyed.[1] The specific situation to which these works address themselves called for a public defense of philosophy or its justification before the tribunal of commonly accepted opinion and religious belief. It imposed or invited an approach to the study of politics which comes to terms with or attempts to surmount the native hostility of the political and religious establishment toward any science that questions and, by so doing, threatens to undermine its foundations. It thus presented a definite kinship with the situation confronted by Plato, whose philosophy was itself developed within a predominantly political context.

Unlike Alfarabi and his successors, Aquinas was rarely forced to contend with an antiphilosophic bias on the part of the ecclesiastical authorities. As a Christian he could simply assume philosophy without becoming publicly involved in any argument for or against it. Not only was philosophy already accredited in the West and officially sanctioned by Canon Law but a knowledge of it was required of all students of theology. It is typical of the Christian society of the Middle Ages, in contrast to the Islamic and Jewish communities, that its churchmen were also schoolmen. In Aquinas's works it is rather theology which is justified before the bar of reason or philosophy. The first article of his best known work, the *Summa Theologiae,* does not ask whether the study of philosophy is permissible and desirable but whether besides the philosophic disciplines another science, namely sacred doctrine, is necessary. Equally revealing from the same point of view is the fact that the reasons which Maimonides had invoked to justify the concealing of philosophic truths from the multitude could be used by Aquinas to show instead why, in addition to supernatural truths, God has seen fit to reveal certain natural truths or truths that are accessible to human reason and experience alone.[2] This unique state of affairs appears to have engendered a preference for Aristotle's *Politics,* which presupposes a larger measure of agreement between philosophy and the city and hence a greater openness to philosophy on the part of the city than Plato's *Republic.* The canonical status which philosophy enjoyed in the Christian world helps to explain at the same time why Aquinas was able to discard as unnecessary or irrelevant the esotericism common to much of the ancient philosophic tradition and purposely affected by many of the Church Fathers with whose works he was acquainted.[3]

It is impossible, however, to account fully for the decidedly Platonic character of Judaeo-Arabic political thought and the decidedly Aristotelian character of Christian political thought simply by adverting to the fact that philosophy was generally accepted in Christian society while it was often frowned upon or rejected by the Islamic and Jewish communities of the Middle Ages. One must still ask how philosophy came to be received by Christianity in the first place and why the Aristotelianism of Aquinas and his disciples eventually replaced the Platonism of the Fathers as the traditional form of Christian theology. The clue to this deeper problem is to be sought ultimately in the difference between Christianity and either Islam or Judaism as religious and political societies. The most distinctive feature of Islam and Judaism is that they both present themselves first and foremost as divinely revealed Laws or as all-inclusive social orders, regulating every segment of men's private and public lives and precluding from the outset any sphere of activity in which reason could operate independently of the divine Law. Christianity on the other hand first comes to sight as a faith or as a sacred doctrine, demanding adherence to a set of fundamental beliefs but otherwise leaving its followers at liberty to organize their social and political lives in accordance with norms and principles that are not specifically religious. This basic difference goes hand in hand with the difference that one notes in regard to the order of the sacred sciences within each religious community. The highest science in Islam and Judaism was jurisprudence (*fiqh*), upon which devolved the all-important task of interpreting, applying, and adapting the prescriptions of the divine law and to which dialectical theology (*kalam*) was always clearly subordinated. The highest science in Christianity was theology, whose prestige far exceeded any that was ever accorded to theological speculation in the Jewish and Arabic traditions. The same essential difference led to the further consequence that Christian society, and it alone, was ruled by two distinct powers and two distinct codes of law, one ecclesiastical or canonical and the other civil, each with its own sphere of competence and each relatively free in principle from interference on the part of the other. To the first belonged the care of directing men to their supernatural end; to the second, that of directing them to their earthly or temporal end. The upshot was that one was usually able to study political phenomena in the light of reason alone without directly challenging the established religious authority or running the risk of an open confrontation with it. As a result, such specific issues as the origin of divine and human laws, the relation between the two, and the communication of divine laws through the medium of prophecy or revelation, which, as Avicenna observes,[4] are discussed as political themes by Plato but not by Aristotle, were no longer seen to be as pertinent to the Christian philosophers as they had been to their Muslim and Jewish counterparts. In short, the very structure of Christian society, with its clear-cut distinction between the spiritual and temporal spheres, bore an obvious affinity with the restricted and somewhat independent manner in which political matters are treated in Aristotle's *Politics*.

The remarks that have been made thus far concerning the general characteristics of political philosophy within the Judaeo-Arabic and the Christian traditions point to a final problem which was of paramount importance to both groups, that of the relation between philosophy and revealed religion. Aquinas's solution to this problem purports to do full justice to the claims of reason as well as those of Revelation. It differs from that of the majority of the Muslim philosophers, who, while outwardly proclaiming the supremacy of the Law, regarded philosophy as the perfect science and the sole judge of the truth of Revelation; and it likewise differs from that of Augustine and his other Christian predecessors, who tend to discuss all human problems in the light of man's final end as it is known through Revelation and in whose works the mundane sciences, to the extent to which they are cultivated, form part of an integrated whole or single wisdom illumined by Faith. Aquinas begins by distinguishing clearly between the domains of faith and of reason or between philosophy and theology, each of which is conceived as a complete and independent science.[5] The first proceeds under the light of naturally known and self-evident principles and represents the perfection of man's understanding of the natural order of the universe. It culminates in metaphysics or first philosophy, which remains supreme in its own realm and is not dethroned by theology as the queen of the human sciences. Even without divine grace nature is complete in itself and possesses its own intrinsic perfection in that it has within itself that by means of which it is capable of attaining its end or returning to its principle. Theology on the other hand offers a comprehensive account of the beginning and end of all things as they appear in the light of divine Revelation. Its premises are derived from the faith and it makes use of such philosophic doctrines as may be relevant to its purpose, not indeed as principles, but as instruments in its methodical investigation of the content of Revelation.

Far from destroying nature, divine grace presupposes it and perfects it by elevating it to an end that is higher than any to which it could aspire by its own means. Hence between the truths of Revelation and the knowledge acquired by the sole use of reason and experience there is a distinction but there can be no fundamental disagreement. The preestablished harmony between the two orders is founded theoretically on the assumption that God, the revealer of divine truth, is also the author of nature.[6] Any discrepancy between the Bible and the teachings of the philosophers is traceable to the imperfection of the human mind which has either misinterpreted the datum of Revelation or erred in its quest for natural truth. The human soul is the weakest of the intellectual substances. All of man's knowledge originates with the senses and is obtained by abstraction from sensible things. As such it involves a multiplicity of concepts and necessarily exhibits a fragmented and discursive character. What differentiates man as a knowing being is "reason" as distinguished from "intellect" or the fact that he does not grasp the truth intuitively and all at once but arrives at it gradually through a complex rational process by means of which the mind passes in orderly fashion from the known to the unknown.[7] Because of individual differences stemming from their bodily nature, men do not all possess the same intellectual endowments and are not all equally well disposed with respect to the attainment of knowledge.[8] Neither is there any assurance that the more gifted among them will ordinarily have at their disposal the leisure or the means to devote themselves entirely to the pursuit of the truth. Moreover, although moral evil, to which man is invariably prone, does not directly impair his reasoning faculty or diminish his capacity to learn, it renders the acquisition of science extrinsically more arduous by the disorder that it provokes in his appetite.[9] Given the intrinsic limitations of the human mind and the external obstacles with which it must struggle in its search for knowledge, it is not surprising that even philosophers should lapse into error and disagree among themselves. To the extent to which they fall short of the truth, their teachings are occasionally at odds with the Faith; but the fact remains that reason itself cannot demonstrate the impossibility of Revelation, any more than it can prove its real possibility. The most that can be said from Aquinas's point of view is that the arguments adduced by philosophers against divine Revelation as a whole or any part thereof never offer any evidence such that the mind is compelled to assent to them.[10]

Although Aquinas looked upon Aristotelian philosophy as the most perfect expression of natural truth and as the philosophy which was most congruent with the truth of Christianity, he was fully able to coordinate that philosophy with the Christian Faith only by transforming it both in content and in spirit. For present purposes the precise nature of that transformation is perhaps best illustrated by the fact that, whereas Aristotle never speaks of natural law but only of natural right, Aquinas has generally come to be regarded as the classic exponent of the natural law theory in the Western world.

CHRISTIANITY AND POLITICS: THE NATURE OF THE POLITICAL REGIME

The cornerstone of Aquinas's political philosophy is the Aristotelian notion of nature. More than all other animals man is a political and social being.[11] Civil society is natural to him, not as something given by nature, but as something to which he is inclined by nature and which is necessary for the perfection of his rational nature. Man, nature's most remarkable product, is brought into the world more helpless and destitute than any other animal—unshod, unclad, and unarmed. Instead, nature has furnished him with reason, speech, and hands, with which he is eventually able to provide for himself and meet his needs as they arise.[12] It is beyond the capacity of one individual, however, to obtain all that is required for his livelihood. In order to subsist during the years that precede the development of reason and the acquisition of manual skills, as well as to live more conveniently in later years, man is necessarily reliant on the help that he receives from other men.

The first society to which he belongs and without which he could not live, let alone live well, is the family, whose specific purpose is to procure the necessities of life and thus guarantee the preservation of both the individual and the species. The various associations that it comprises—that of male and female, of parents and children, of master and slave—are all directed to the same end. The science or art that has as its object the proper management of the family is economics or household governance, which deals primarily with the acquisition and administration of such staples and commodities as are used or consumed by the members of the household.

But the family alone cannot supply all the material goods that man needs for his sustenance and his protection, nor is it capable of leading all of its members to the perfection of virtue. Paternal injunctions, which rely for their effectiveness on the natural love between father and son, normally suffice to insure that generous-minded youths will behave decently but are of limited use in the case of base souls, over whom persuasion has little or no power and who need to be coerced by fear of punishment.[13] The truly self-sufficient human association, the only one capable of securing the conditions of virtue and satisfying all of man's earthly needs and aspirations, is the city. The city is the most perfect work of practical reason. Although less natural from the point of view of its form than the family, as is evidenced by the fact that its structure exhibits a greater variety from one society to another than that of the family, it is nevertheless ordered to a higher and more comprehensive end. As a perfect society it encompasses all the other associations that human beings are capable of forming, including the family, whose end it subordinates to its own, which is the complete human good.[14] Only within the framework of civil society can man attain the fullness of life, so much so that the man who leads a solitary life away from the company of his fellow men either falls short of human perfection like a beast or has already exceeded that perfection and achieved a state of godlike self-sufficiency.[15]

Like the human body to which it is frequently compared, the city is made up of a multiplicity of heterogeneous parts, each one of which has its own special work or function. Since the individual part is often animated by passions and desires that do not coincide with those of other parts, it is essential that in a city there be a single authority whose proper task is to look after the good of the whole and to maintain order and unity among its various components. Political authority is the determining element of the city or its "form," as Aristotle had called it by analogy with the doctrine of matter and form as the constituent principles of natural beings. A city without a regime is like a body without a soul: to the extent to which one can even speak of it, it is a city in name only. Accordingly, if the city is natural, political authority, which is indispensable to it, is also natural, as opposed to slavery, which, for Aquinas and the Christian tradition before him, is rooted not in man's nature as such but in man's fallen nature.[16] Political authority differs from slavery in that it constitutes the rule of free men over free men and has as its object the good of all the citizens, who as free men exist for their own sakes. The slave on the other hand exists for the sake of another and hence is not ruled for his own good but for the good of the master.

It follows from what has been said that the city is more than the sum of its parts and its overall end more than the sum of the particular interests of its members. To be sure, that end is not different from the end of the single man; but since the single man depends on the city for his full development, the end of the city assumes the nature of a common good, that is to say, of a good which, while numerically one, is yet shared by every citizen of that city.[17] Just as the whole is more important than the part and prior to it as that to which the part is ordered and without which it could not exist, so the city is prior to the individual in the order of final causality and its good is higher in dignity and "more divine" than that of each man taken by himself.[18] It is paradoxical at first sight but not inconsistent to say with Aquinas that the common good of the city is itself the proper good, though obviously not the private good, of the individual citizen.[19] As a proper good it is the object of an inclination which is stronger than that which impels a citizen to seek his private good. Thus, in the event of a conflict between the common good and the private good, the former naturally takes precedence over the latter. This explains why in cases of extreme necessity a man will spontaneously sacrifice himself for the city in the same way that he will sacrifice a hand for the good of the whole body.[20]

The common good and the end of political authority is in the first instance peace or the harmony of the different parts that combine to make up the city.[21] Peace exists when each part is adjusted to the whole and functions with reasonable smoothness within it. But this fundamental unity, together with the ability to counteract the forces that threaten to destroy it, represents only the minimal condition under which the city can subsist. It is the lowest and not the highest goal to which its energies may be devoted. Over and beyond mere survival, the city has as its purpose the promotion of the good life or virtue among its citizens.[22] Experience reveals that singly and collectively men are attracted to a variety of goods, such as wealth, honor, freedom or virtue, some of which are obviously more noble than others. The goal or goals which a given city actually pursues are determined in largest measure by the men who have the decisive say in that city and thereby constitute its regime. The regime in this sense is none other than the way of life of a city with particular reference to the manner in which political power is distributed within it.[23] What distinguishes one city from another and confers upon it its specific nobility or greatness is precisely the regime by which it is governed. The best regime or the question of who should rule in the city thus emerges as the central theme of political philosophy.

Since men differ from one another in many ways but most notably with respect to their capacity for knowledge and virtue,[24] and since by nature the inferior is subordinated to the superior, it stands to reason that the best man should rule over the others and that ruling offices should be distributed according to virtue. In and of itself the most desirable regime, both on the ground of unity and of the nobility of the end to which it is dedicated, is kingship or the unconditional rule of a single wise man for the sake of virtue. But if absolute monarchy is theoretically the best of the just regimes, it is also the one that is fraught with the greatest dangers. Because of the vast powers vested in him, the king, unless he happens to be an unusually virtuous man, may become corrupted and his rule may easily degenerate into tyranny, which, all other things being equal, is the worst of all rules since by its very nature it stands furthest from the common good.[25] Moreover, virtue is not as easily recognized by most people as other more obvious though less genuine qualities such as wealth or noble birth. It is a matter of common observation that politically wise and virtuous men are not always and perhaps not generally acknowledged to be such by other men, the majority of whom have little real knowledge of wisdom or virtue.[26] Nor is it permissible to assume that the unwise multitude could readily be persuaded to accept a perfectly virtuous man as their sole ruler since the interests in which he may be expected to govern would presumably run counter to their own less noble interests. The unity of the city, if nothing else, requires that the conflicting claims of the various elements within it be taken into consideration and reconciled within the limits of possibility. In all or virtually all cases, the demands of wisdom and excellence must be combined with those of consent. This means that for concrete purposes the best regime is the so-called mixed regime or the regime which blends in harmonious fashion the best features of monarchy, aristocracy, and polity. In support of this typically classical solution Aquinas could point to a sacred precedent, that of the ancient Hebrew polity, where the authority of Moses and his successors was balanced by that of a group of Elders chosen from the people at large.[27]

The stability and efficacy of this regime, or for that matter of any regime, is best secured by the rule of law, which becomes most of the time a practical necessity because of the habitual scarcity of wise men and the abuses to which the rule by decree is inherently exposed. Since wise men are never very numerous, it is easier to find a few who are capable of framing good laws than to find many who are capable of judging in individual cases. Legislators also have more time to deliberate and are in a better position to take into account all the different facets of a problem than the man who is faced with the constant necessity of making decisions on the spot. Finally, their judgment is less likely to become clouded by their personal involvement in the issues upon which they are required to pronounce themselves, inasmuch as laws are proposed universally and regard future events.[28] Laws are the privileged instrument of politics and stand in relation to the works of man as universals to particulars. It is through them more than through any other agency that the ruler promotes justice and moral goodness among the citizens. Moral virtue is acquired precisely by the repetition of those acts which the law prescribes or by habitual living and education under good laws.[29] Hence the importance of legislation, which assumes an architectonic character and constitutes the most important act of the political art.[30] It remains that laws are enacted, enforced and, whenever necessary, amended by men. In a word, they are themselves the products of the regime in which they originate. We are thus led back to the notion of the regime as the fundamental political phenomenon and the guiding theme of political philosophy.

Up to this point Aquinas's political philosophy would appear to be in substantial harmony with that of Aristotle from which it is ostensibly derived. Closer examination nevertheless reveals that in taking over Aristotle's concept of the political nature of man and of human living, Aquinas has modified it profoundly under the influence of Christianity and Stoicism and as a consequence of the high degree of clarity and certitude that attaches to the notion of God as a lawgiver in both of these traditions. Human excellence is no longer defined or circumscribed by the conditions of the political life. Through knowledge of the natural law man accedes directly to the common order of reason, over and above the political order to which he belongs as a citizen of a particular society. By sharing in that law he finds himself, along with all other intelligent beings, a member of a universal community or cosmopolis ruled by divine providence and whose justice is vastly superior to that of any human regime. The dissociation implied in such a view between the best human regime and the perfect social order is further accentuated by the Christian and Thomistic teaching according to which the entire natural order is in turn subject to the order of grace or divine law. Hence the simply best regime is not, as it was for Aristotle, the work of man or of practical reason guided by philosophy. It is synonymous with the kingdom of God and is actual or attainable at all times through God's saving grace. Civil society ceases to be uniquely responsible for the totality of moral virtue and is itself judged by a higher standard to which human actions must conform universally. It becomes part of a broader whole embracing all men and all cities and is by that very fact deprived of its privileged status as the sole horizon limiting the scope of man's moral activity, setting the goals to which he may aspire, and determining the basic order of his priorities.[31]

The transpolitical character of the Thomistic doctrine is revealed, among other ways, by the manner in which Aquinas divides moral and political science. The *Commentary on the Ethics* goes out of its way to point out that the unity of the family or of the city is not an organic unity but a unity of order only and hence that the individual members of these societies retain a sphere of action that is different from that of the whole. From this observation Aquinas draws the conclusion that ethics, economics, and politics constitute not one science composed of three parts but three separate and specifically distinct sciences, thereby investing both ethics and economics with an autonomy that they do not possess in the Aristotelian arrangement.[32] This teaching finds a significant parallel in Aquinas's discussion of natural right which forms part of his treatise on particular justice and follows the tradition of Ulpian and the Roman lawyers, who treated natural right as a division of private right, rather than that of Aristotle, where the question of natural right is taken up entirely within the context of legal justice.[33] In discussing the virtuous citizen's readiness to give up his life for his country, Aquinas observes that such an act would be the object of a natural inclination if man were by nature a part of the society for which he sacrifices himself.[34] We are given to understand by this remark that man's relationship to a particular civil society, as distinct from other civil societies, is not simply natural but acquired. Although Aquinas agrees with Aristotle that the man who cuts himself off from society and the affairs of his fellow men is either more than human or less than human, his example of the superior person whose perfection exceeds the bounds of civil society is not that of the philosopher, which is presumably what Aristotle had in mind, but that of St. Anthony, a third-century hermit notorious among other things for his opposition to philosophy.[35] Finally, to cite only one other example, Aquinas interprets Aristotle's statement to the effect that moral virtue is relative to the regime as referring to the relative goodness of man as a citizen and not to his absolute goodness as a man. The latter is said to be inseparable from practical wisdom, whose first principles are naturally known and understood by everyone independently of the political regime.[36] Under these circumstances the notion of the best regime as the primary and indispensable condition of the happiness of individuals and cities loses its supreme importance, as does political philosophy itself, upon whose guidance the best regime is dependent for its actualization.

MORAL VIRTUE AND THE NATURAL LAW

Both the theoretical basis and the practical implications of the Thomistic position are clearly discernible in Aquinas's treatment of the moral virtues. That treatment may be described as an attempt to set forth how man should act in the light of what he is or of his rational nature. As such it appeals directly to principles which are not indigenous to moral science but rather are borrowed from natural science to which they properly belong.[37] It thus assumes on the part of the reader a determinate understanding of man's nature and of his natural end as they are apprehended by the speculative intellect. Generally speaking, it presents a more doctrinal or more strictly deductive aspect than that of Aristotle.

The difference between the two authors is already evident to some extent from Aquinas's *Commentary on the Ethics*. In Books Two to Five of the *Ethics,* Aristotle had simply listed eleven moral virtues with no precise indication as to the reason for the order in which they are presented and little or no effort to relate these virtues to the human soul and its different parts. His discussion remains exclusively on the plane of moral virtue and confines itself to an elucidation of moral phenomena as these appear to decent or honest men as distinguished from philosophers. Its typical addressee is the "gentleman" or the man of good moral habits and opinions who takes decency for granted and does not have to be convinced of the intrinsic superiority of the moral life over the immoral life. Its avowed aim is to clarify and articulate what the wellborn and well-bred man already knows in a confused way and accepts on the basis of his own experience and upbringing but without any real awareness of its theoretical presuppositions. In accordance with this eminently practical purpose, it eschews any express reference to the speculative premises in which morality is ultimately grounded but whose knowledge is only remotely helpful to the person who is more concerned with the actual practice of virtue than with a thorough grasp of its foundations in human nature. Just as one can be a good carpenter without having studied the science of geometry, so one can be a good man without having engaged in a scientific study of human acts. Simply put, the question that the discussion as a whole raises is, What is a good man? and not, Why should one be a good man? The answer that it provides to that question draws its chief support from the evidence that morality achieves in the mind of the man for whom moral goodness has become so to speak a second nature, and not from such knowledge as may be obtained through a philosophic investigation of man as a natural being. The whole account culminates in a description of magnanimity and justice, the two general virtues which epitomize or define man's perfection as an individual and as a social being respectively.

Aquinas's interpretation of the corresponding sections of the *Ethics* goes beyond what is either explicitly stated or implicitly contained in the text by bringing to light the reasons that purportedly justify Aristotle's method of procedure. Courage and moderation have as their proper matter what Aquinas calls the primary passions, such as anger and lust. Then come the virtues connected with the secondary passions, which may relate either to external goods and evils or to external actions. To the first group belong liberality and munificence, which regulate the use of wealth; the virtues relating to honor, of which the principal is magnanimity; and mildness. To the second group belong friendliness, straightforwardness, and urbane wittiness. These in turn are followed by justice, which has as its subject matter the external actions themselves, as opposed to the internal passions with which all of the preceding virtues are concerned. The order in which these virtues are taken up by Aristotle would find its rationale in the fact that the primary passions, dealing as they do with the goods that are directly related to the preservation of life or the evils that menace its destruction, take precedence over the secondary passions, which are concerned with less vital goods, as well as in the fact that, since actions originate in the passions, the treatment of the latter understandably precedes that of the former.[38] One wonders, however, to what extent Aquinas's "scientific" explanation, regardless of its intrinsic merits, respects the tenor of Aristotle's text. The distinction that it establishes between primary and secondary passions leads for one thing to a greater valuation of courage and moderation at the expense of other more spectacular but less necessary and less common virtues, such as munificence and magnanimity, which may be taken to be one of the major focuses of Aristotle's discussion of the moral life. What is more, the proposed interpretation injects into the discussion an analytic principle that is foreign, if not to Aristotle's thought, at least to the peculiar manner in which moral matters are approached in the *Ethics*.

The same conclusion is borne out in even more striking fashion by Aquinas's treatise on moral virtue in the *Summa Theologiae,* where the Aristotelian classification is abandoned altogether in favor of a modified Platonic-Stoic framework which reduces all the moral virtues to the four so-called cardinal virtues of moderation, courage, justice, and prudence.[39] Each of these virtues is linked to one or the other of the powers of the soul which it determines and whose operations it perfects. Moderation has as its subject the appetitive or concupiscible part, into which it introduces the order of reason principally by imposing the appropriate restraints on man's desire for the pleasures associated with the senses of touch and taste. Courage is the virtue that rectifies the spirited or irascible part and enables man to overcome the fears that might otherwise deter him from the pursuit of the rational good. Justice is to be found in the will and regulates every aspect of man's dealings with other men. By all three of these virtues man is properly ordered to his natural end or the good dictated by reason. But in addition to tending toward the right end, one must also be able to deliberate about, choose, and prescribe the means that are conducive to it. Such is the role of prudence, which is an intellectual virtue insofar as it has reason as its subject, but which is also included among the moral virtues insofar as its proper exercise is contingent on the rectification of the appetite by the three preceding virtues.

All the other moral virtues are grouped under one or the other of these four general virtues either as subjective parts, potential parts, or integral parts. The subjective parts are the various species into which a given virtue may be divided according to the matter with which it deals. The prudence of the ruler, for instance, excels that of the simple subject and differs specifically from it in that it extends to the common good of the entire city or realm; yet both fulfill the definition of prudence, of which they constitute two distinct and complete forms.[40] The potential parts are those virtues which deal with some secondary act or matter of the principal virtue and hence do not contain in themselves the full essence or power of that virtue, as is the case, for example, with liberality and friendliness, whose matter, while not coextensive with that of justice, nevertheless falls within the same general purview since it has to do with the right ordering of one's relations with other men.[41] The integral parts are not complete virtues in themselves but represent the various elements that contribute to the formation of a complete virtue. Thus, memory, inventiveness, caution, circumspection, and the like are all necessary components of a single perfect act of prudence.[42] In this manner there is gradually constituted a catalogue of moral virtues that is both exhaustive and clearly rooted in a theoretical analysis of the nature and parts of the human soul.

We shall grasp the larger significance of Aquinas's analytic procedure if we turn to a consideration of the particular difficulty raised by the Aristotelian doctrine of moral virtue as a mean between two extremes.[43] Since human actions may deviate from the norm of reason either by excess or defect, virtuous or rational behavior requires that both extremes be avoided and that the right mean be observed at all times. For the most part the mean in question is relative to the subject or the agent and can be ascertained only with reference to the individual circumstances of a given action, including the agent himself. Reason tells us, for example, that food and drink are necessary for life, but it cannot specify in any but the most general way how much this or that man should eat and drink. What is too much for one man may not be enough for another and vice versa; what is proper under certain circumstances or at a certain time may be improper and morally reprehensible at other moments and under a different set of circumstances. One can easily imagine a situation in which virtue itself might counsel that one act in a manner that is contrary to the prevailing or generally approved standards of conduct. A question immediately arises, however, as to the principle in the light of which a decision of this kind is to be made. It is characteristic of Aristotle's empirical approach that his discussion of this problem does not allude to any norm outside the sphere of morality or to any transmoral end to which one might turn in order to justify occasional departures from the common rule. The *Ethics* does state expressly that the mean of reason is the mean such as a prudent man, who is, as it were, a law unto himself, would determine it. But although this solution may be deemed adequate for purposes of action, it obviously leaves something to be desired from a theoretical point of view and actually begs the question since it does little more than suggest that the right mean is the mean as established by a prudent man, who is himself defined as a person who habitually chooses the right mean.[44]

One runs into the same difficulty if one examines Aristotle's doctrine of practical truth. Practical truth in the full sense of the expression, or as referred to action in a specific situation, is not solely a matter of knowledge. It requires that one take into account not only the nature of a given act but the various circumstances that surround it as well. But these circumstances are numberless and literally impossible to assess. If, in order to act virtuously, one were obliged to know all the relevant circumstances of his actions, one would never be able to move or to refrain from moving. It follows that a practical or prudential judgment may be objectively wrong and yet morally right. A person who, by mistake and without any negligence on his part, serves the wrong medicine to a patient performs a morally good act even though serious harm may result from it. Indeed, even if it were possible, a complete and accurate evaluation of the objective facts of a concrete situation would still not suffice to guarantee the moral character of one's action. True virtue demands that one pursue the good according to the mode of the good and not only according to the mode of thought. It implies on the part of the agent an habitual desire for the good as it appears and is known to him. The questions that solicit the attention of a moral man are not questions that can be raised in a purely objective and detached manner; they are inseparable from the questioner, and the answers to them defy analysis in terms of reason alone. Stated in slightly different words, the truth of the practical judgment is measured by the mind's conformity with the rectified appetite, as opposed to the truth of the speculative judgment, which is measured by the mind's conformity with what is or with its object. But if this is so, the whole argument, as Aquinas rightly points out, would again appear to be circular: truth or right reason in practical matters is contingent on the agreement of a particular action with the rectified appetite, which is itself determined by the fact that it agrees with right reason.[45]

Aquinas's attempt to solve this twofold problem again makes explicit what was at best only implied by Aristotle. Although adumbrated in the *Commentary on the Ethics,* it finds its most detailed and complete expression in the famous treatise on law of the *Summa Theologiae.*[46] Its originality is suggested by the fact that this treatise does not have its equivalent in Aristotle and relies for the bulk of its substance on the earlier natural law theories of Cicero and Augustine. Briefly, it consists in showing that, while it is true that the choice of the means to the end is the work of reason, the end that man pursues as a moral being is already assigned to him by nature and precontained in his innate desire for that end. Nature is to be understood precisely as the intrinsic principle of a determinate and necessary inclination or, as Aquinas defines it elsewhere, a sharing in the divine art by which even nonrational beings are made to act in a manner that conforms with reason.[47] Since man is himself a natural being, there is in him, prior to any deliberation, an inclination of his whole being toward the end or ends to which, like all other natural beings, he is uniformly ordered. Thus, as a substance, he naturally seeks his own preservation; as an animal, he shares with other animals a natural desire for the procreation and education of children; and as a rational being, he is naturally inclined toward such specifically human goods as the political life and the knowledge of the truth.[48]

Precisely because he is endowed with reason man participates more perfectly than all other natural beings in the order of divine providence. Through the knowledge that he has of his end and of the natural inclinations that reveal its existence, he is immediately aware of the general principles that govern his conduct. As dictates of practical reason these principles constitute a "law," promulgated by nature itself, which enables him to discriminate between right and wrong and serves as the infallible criterium of the goodness or badness of his actions.[49] Its most universal precepts form the object of a special habitus which Aquinas calls conscience or, more properly, synderesis, and which parallels the habitus of the first and self-evident premises from which all demonstrations proceed in the speculative order.[50]

The sole use of the words "conscience" (*suneidêsis*) and "synderesis," which do not occur in Aristotle but rather in the later Greek and early Christian traditions through which they were handed down to the authors of the Middle Ages, is already symptomatic of the non-Aristotelian flavor of the Thomistic teaching on this subject. There is more, however. Since they are considered to be laws in the strict and proper sense of the term, the moral principles in question take on a compulsory character that they did not have for Aristotle and the philosophic tradition generally. For the natural law not only recommends or discourages certain actions as intrinsically noble or base, it commands or forbids them under pain of retribution if not in this life at least in the next. It thus clearly presupposes both the personal immortality of the human soul and the existence of an all-knowing and all-powerful God who rules the world with wisdom and equity and in whose eyes all individual human actions are either meritorious or deserving of punishment.[51] Any violation of its precepts betrays more than a departure from reason or a simple lack of taste; it bears the mark of an offense against God, the giver and guarantor of the natural law, who, in addition to the loss of those internal goods, such as happiness and virtue, of which the sinner deprives himself, inflicts external sanctions in accordance with the gravity of the misdeed.[52] Within this context man's whole moral life acquires a distinctively new orientation; it ceases to be understood solely in terms of human completeness or fulfillment and becomes in the final instance a matter of willing and grateful compliance with a divinely authorized and unconditionally binding law.

It should be promptly added that the natural law supplies only the most general standards of human behavior or the unshakable foundation on which man's knowledge of the moral order rests. It represents the first but by no means the sufficient rule of reason among men. Only its highest principles are known to everyone without exception, and even they are usually too broad to be of immediate use in guiding one's actions. It therefore needs to be supplemented by another law which is arrived at through human effort and industry and which for that reason is called the human law. The precepts of the human law are themselves derived from the natural law either by way of specific determinations of a general rule or of conclusions from indemonstrable principles. The natural law, for example, prescribes that God should be honored and worshipped; but divine worship implies the performance of certain acts or rites which may vary according to time and place and which must be specified by human reason. Likewise, from the general principle that one should refrain from hurting others, reason infers that one should not murder, steal, or commit adultery.[53]

Needless to say, these principles do not all carry the same evidence or induce the same necessity. In most cases their universality is limited by the "deformity" or the extreme contingency of the matter with which they deal, no less than by the relative imperfection and instability of human nature. Human actions always involve particulars and their morality is likely to be affected by any one of the innumerable circumstances by which they are attended. Justice ordinarily requires that a borrowed or deposited object be returned to its owner, but this does not mean that one is morally bound to deliver a shipment of arms to a person who intends to betray his country. Moreover, not all men are capable of the same degree of virtue or moral perfection, whether it be by reason of age, natural disposition, or previously acquired habits. A moral principle that makes impossible and hence unreasonable demands on a particular subject or group of subjects must be altered to fit the situation to which it is applied.[54] The more particular the principle, the more variable and less certain it becomes. For that reason moral science, unlike natural science, offers little certitude and must be content with setting forth the truth roughly and in outline.[55]

The decisive question, then, and the real issue between Aquinas and Aristotle, is not whether moral principles are subject to change but whether there are *any* moral principles from which one is never allowed to deviate and which retain their obligatory character even in the most extreme situations. Whereas Aristotle plainly states that all of natural right is variable,[56] Aquinas distinguishes between the common or primary precepts of the natural law, with which all men must comply at all times, and its proper or secondary precepts, which are subject to variations imposed by circumstances. The former differ from the latter both by their higher degree of knowability and their greater proximity to man's natural end. Such is the case with the prescriptions against murder, adultery, and theft, which suffer no human exceptions and from which God alone, as the author of the natural law, can dispense in certain instances, as he did when he ordered Abraham to kill his son Isaac. To this category of universally valid laws belong all the precepts of the Decalogue, including the prescriptions against idolatry and the taking of the Lord's name in vain, which, unlike the ceremonial and judicial precepts of the Old Testament, have not been abrogated by the New Law.[57]

The same distinction between primary and secondary precepts is taken for granted in Aquinas's handling of the controverted issue of the justifiability or excusableness of immoral actions performed under duress. Aristotle had left the matter at saying somewhat inconclusively that there are "perhaps" some odious acts to which one should not consent even at the price of death after the most fearful sufferings and had ended his discussion with the equally ambiguous statement that "praise and blame are bestowed on those who yield to compulsion and those who do not."[58] In his commentary on that passage, Averroes explains Aristotle's assertion as relating to the fact that the man who succumbs to force may be blamed in one place but

not in another, as if to suggest that, when a person is physically or
morally tortured beyond the limits of ordinary human endurance,
the distinction between right and wrong actions becomes by and
large a matter of positive law.[59] Aquinas, on the other hand, interprets
the word "perhaps" in its rhetorical rather than its literal sense. He
states emphatically that certain actions are to be condemned altogether and cities in support of this view the example of St.
Lawrence, who underwent death by fire rather than sacrifice to
idols. Accordingly, he takes Aristotle's concluding remark to mean,
not that the victim of compulsion may sometimes be excused or
simply pitied, as Aristotle had intimated, but that he can never
escape blame or censure.[60]

Since the law that prohibits such actions embodies the intention
of the legislator as well as the common good of society to which
that intention is primarily directed, it can never be laid aside on the
ground that the legislator himself would have allowed it to be transgressed in the name of a higher law if he had been cognizant of the
unforeseen circumstances that render its observance undesirable in a
particular situation.[61] The most general principles of the natural law
are thus directly applicable to human society and do not have to be
diluted in order to become operative. The very possibility that the
common good or the preservation of society should at times compel
one to act in a manner contrary to these principles is eliminated
once and for all. Between the requirements of justice and those of
civil society there is a fundamental and necessary harmony. The
perfect social order exists or is capable of existing in deed and not
only in speech. Justice in the absolute sense is not only approximated
by civil justice, it actually coincides with it. By the same token man's
perfection as an individual turns out to be identical with his perfection as a citizen.[62]

As a consequence, both civil justice and courage, the two virtues
most closely connected with the welfare of the city, acquire a new
and more noble status. The issue between justice and magnanimity
is decided in favor of justice, which emerges as unqualifiedly the
highest of the moral virtues.[63] For the same reason Aquinas is able
to remove the ambiguity inherent in Aristotle's treatment of courage
and to speak unequivocally of courage as that virtue which is concerned above all with the death that one faces in defending one's
country.[64] The harmonious solution that he proposes to the problem
of civil society likewise does away with the need for noble lies, and
all the more so as the false but salutary belief in the gods of the city
is replaced by the acceptance of the one true God, which becomes

itself a requirement of the natural law. Wisdom can henceforth rule without recourse to falsehood. The previously noted absence of any real esotericism in Aquinas's political teaching is explained not solely by the rehabilitation of philosophy in the Christian world but more radically by the reconciliation which the Thomistic position postulates between the demands of justice and those of civil society.

That reconciliation meets with one of its clearest illustrations in Aquinas's reinterpretation of Aristotle's doctrine of legal slavery. In accordance with Roman law and the principles of the *jus gentium,* Aquinas defends not only the necessity but the justice of that practice, which he presents as beneficial to both conqueror and conquered, since it spares the life of the latter and secures for the former the services of a subject population.[65] On this point his teaching is again at variance with that of Aristotle, who looks upon the bondage of men who are not slaves by nature as a necessary evil justified by the higher and more pressing demands of society as a whole and hence as another indication of the irremediably defective and self-contradictory character of human justice on the plane of civil society.

BIBLICAL FAITH AND PHILOSOPHY

Aquinas's natural law doctrine constitutes a prime example on the moral and political level of the Thomistic synthesis between biblical faith and Aristotelian philosophy. As a law of *nature,* the natural law shares in reason and cannot be reduced exclusively to the will of God. The actions that it commands or forbids are intrinsically good or bad; they are not good or bad simply as a result of their being commanded or forbidden by God. As a *law,* however, it also contains an explicit reference to God's will, to which it owes its moving force. It thus stands midway between the natural right doctrine of the nonreligious philosophic tradition on the one hand and the strict voluntarism of the nonphilosophic religious tradition on the other. It is distinguished from the latter in that it defines law as essentially an act of reason rather than of the will, and it differs from the former in that it conceives of God not only as the final cause of the universe or the unmoved mover who moves all things by the attraction that he exerts on them but as a lawgiver and an efficient cause who produces the world out of nothing and by his ordinances actively directs all creatures to their appointed end. The key point in this regard, and the one on which the quarrel between philosophy and revealed religion would seem to turn, reveals itself in the last analysis as the opposition between the biblical doctrine of creation and the philosophic doctrine of the eternity of the world.

Aquinas strives to bridge the gap from one position to the other, not by ascribing to the pagan philosopher the notion of divine creation, as some of Aristotle's earlier commentators had done, but by contending that the reasons advanced by Aristotle in favor of the eternity of the world are at best only probable. His argument generally tends to follow Aristotle's *Topics,* where the eternity of the world is presented as a dialectical problem or as belonging to the class of problems that reason cannot solve, rather than the treatise *On the Heaven,* which treats the same problem from a scientific point of view and leaves little doubt concerning Aristotle's final position on the matter.[66] If the view that the world is eternal can neither be proved nor disproved by natural reason, the teaching of Revelation cannot be held to be in direct contradiction with that of philosophy. The conflict between the two teachings is further attenuated and partially blurred by Aquinas's rejection of the disjuncture between the eternity of the world and its creation by God; for, according to Aquinas, even if the world were eternal, it would still have its source in God's free will.[67] What the doctrine of creation essentially implies in the end is not the coming into being of the world (and concomitantly of time itself) at a given moment in the past, however near or remote, but the radical contingency of all beings other than God and their complete dependence upon God for their existence. It finds its metaphysical expression in the typically Thomistic doctrine of the real distinction between essence and existence in all beings outside of God.[68]

It is none the less true that by attributing efficient causality to God, Aquinas is compelled to preserve or restore the distinction between God's intellect and God's will. Although that distinction is to be regarded as a distinction of reason and not in any way a real distinction, it still has the effect of giving greater prominence to God's will than the Aristotelian doctrine of God as pure intellect or as the thought that thinks only itself. This conclusion is reinforced by the reasons that Aquinas puts forward to explain why, assuming the theoretical possibility of an eternal creation, God produced the world "in time" rather than from all eternity: the noneternity of the world makes it more apparent that all things owe their origin to God; it dispels any remaining doubt concerning the fact that God does not create out of necessity but through an act of his free will; and lastly, it manifests with abundant clarity God's infinite power, inasmuch as creation implies a total gift of being, of which God alone, who possesses the fullness of being, is capable.[69] The far-reaching import of such a doctrine may be glimpsed, however partially and inadequately, through the one-sided emphasis which came to be placed on will and power in modern philosophic and political thought.

Even if one were to accept Aquinas's interpretation and grant that Aristotle's teaching is not incompatible with Christian dogma, a question could still be raised as to whether, by inserting Aristotle's moral and political views into a theological framework or by complementing them with a teaching based on Revelation, Aquinas has not profoundly altered their original character. The issue of the difference between the two authors is not completely disposed of by Aquinas's occasional suggestion that Aristotle deals primarily with man's happiness in this life whereas Christianity is preoccupied above all with man's happiness in the life to come, for the simple reason that Aristotle treats the happiness of this life as the only happiness and maintains an unbroken silence on the crucial subject of the personal immortality of the soul.[70] The change in outlook effected by adding an otherworldly dimension to Aristotelian speculation is not less important for being less conspicuous. To sense that change one has only to reflect, for example, on what happens to magnanimity when it is coupled with humility—a virtue nowhere to be found in Aristotle—or on what happens to courage when life on earth is considered within the larger perspective of man's eternal destiny; for, surely, the Christian who looks forward to a heavenly reward in the event of death on the battlefield is not animated by sentiments identical to those of the heroic citizen who has no such assurance and who realizes that, by exposing his life for a noble cause, he risks the ultimate and irreparable loss of everything that men hold dear.

Formulated in broadest terms, the basic problem has to do not so much with the agreement or disagreement between the content of Revelation and the teachings of philosophy as with the contrast between faith and philosophy viewed as the grounds of total and essentially divergent ways of life. One cannot be guided at one and the same time by two different and equally authoritative norms. The acceptance of the supremacy of the life of faith or of devout response to a divinely revealed word necessarily entails the destruction of philosophy in its original sense or, what amounts to the same thing, the replacement of the natural order composed of philosophers and nonphilosophers by a supernatural order based on the more fundamental distinction between true believers and nonbelievers. When all is said and done, the gulf that separates the learned Aquinas from the learned Aristotle is infinitely wider than that which separates the learned Aquinas from the simple but pious Anthony.

The foregoing analysis suggests the true nature of the revolution initiated by Aquinas in Christian theology. Contrary to what has often been said, Aquinas did not baptize Aristotle. If anything, he declared invalid the baptism conferred upon him by his early commentators and denied him admission to full citizenship in the City of God. Instead, by casting his philosophy in the role of a handmaid, he made him a slave or servant of that City. In the light of Aquinas's own moral principles, that treatment was not unjust since, in return for his contribution to Christian theology, Aristotle received, if not the gift of grace, at least the grace to live. The proof is that, whereas he was eventually banished from Islam and Judaism, he found a permanent home in the Christian West. The place of honor that he came to occupy in the Christian tradition as the representative par excellence of the most glorious achievements of natural reason bears eloquent witness to the novelty and daring of Aquinas's enterprise.

The success of that enterprise, it should be added, was never complete or unchallenged. Because of its boldness, Aquinas ran afoul of the two most powerful (although numerically unequal) groups in the West. He aroused the antagonism of the traditional theologians, who resented the intrusion of an unregenerate pagan in the Christian fold and reproached Aquinas with having sundered the unity of Christian wisdom; and he incurred the wrath of the newly emancipated philosophers (the so-called Latin Averroists), who objected to the enslavement of the very philosophy that they could credit with having made them free. The delicate balance that he was able to establish between the extremes of faith and reason was disrupted less than three centuries later by two revolutionary developments of which he would have disapproved but which he remotely prepared or facilitated. One is Luther's repudiation of the "Aristotelian Church" in the name of an allegedly purer and less worldly form of Christianity. The other is Machiavelli's repudiation of both Aristotle and the Church in the name of an ideal which was neither classical nor Christian but emphatically modern.

NOTES

1. Alfarabi, *The Attainment of Happiness*, 63.

2. *Summa Contra Gentiles*, I. 4; *Summa Theologiae*, I, qu. 1, a. 1; I–II, qu. 99, a. 2, ad 2ᵐ; *De Veritate*, qu. 14, a. 10. Maimonides, *Guide of the Perplexed*, I. 34.

3. *In Lib. de Divinis Nominibus*, Proemium, 2. Cf. *In Boethium de Trinitate*, qu. 2, a. 4; *Summa Theologiae*, III, qu. 42, a. 3.

4. Avicenna, *On the Divisions of the Rational Sciences*, in R. Lerner and M. Mahdi, eds., *Medieval Political Philosophy: a Sourcebook*, New York, 1963, p. 97.

5. *Summa Contra Gentiles*, II. 4; *Summa Theologiae*, I, qu. 1, a. 6–7.

6. *Summa Contra Gentiles*, I. 7; *De Veritate*, qu. 14, a. 10, ad 7ᵐ and ad 9ᵐ.

7. *Summa Theologiae*, I, qu. 85, a. 3; *Summa Contra Gentiles*, II. 98; *Commentary on the Posterior Analytics*, Proemium, n. 4.

8. *Summa Theologiae*, I, qu. 76, a. 5; *Quaest. Disp. de Anima*, a. 8; *De Malo*, qu. 5, a. 5; *In II Sent.*, Dist. I, qu. 2, a. 5.

9. *Summa Theologiae*, I–II, qu. 85, a. 1–2.

10. *Summa Contra Gentiles*, I. 9.

11. *On Kingship*, I. 1, [4].

12. *On Kingship*, I. 1, [5]; *Summa Theologiae*, I, qu. 76, a. 5, ad 4ᵐ.

13. *Summa Theologiae*, I–II, qu. 95, a. 1; *Commentary on the Ethics*, I, Lect. 1, n. 4; X, Lect. 14, n. 2139–42.

14. *Summa Theologiae*, I–II, qu. 90, a. 3, ad 3ᵐ.

15. *Commentary on the Politics*, I, Lect. 1, n. 39; *Commentary on the Ethics*, I, Lect. 1, n. 4.

16. *Summa Theologiae*, I, qu. 96, a. 3–4; qu. 92, a. 1, ad 2ᵐ; *On Kingship*, I. 1, [9–10].

17. *In IV Sent.*, Dist. 49, qu. 1, a. 1, qu. 1, sol. 1, ad 3ᵐ.

18. *Summa Contra Gentiles*, III. 17. Cf. *Commentary on the Ethics*, I, Lect. 2, n. 30.

19. *Summa Contra Gentiles*, III. 24; *Summa Theologiae*, II–II, qu. 47, a. 10, ad 2ᵐ.

20. *Summa Theologiae*, I, qu. 60, a. 5; *Quodlibetum*, I, qu. 4, a. 8.

21. *On Kingship*, I, 2, [17]; *Summa Theologiae*, I, qu. 103, a. 3; *Summa Contra Gentiles*, IV. 76, 4; *Commentary on the Ethics*, III, Lect. 8, n. 474.

22. *On Kingship*, II. 3, [106]; II. 4, [117–8]; *Commentary on the Ethics*, I, Lect. 1, n. 4.

23. *Commentary on the Politics*, II, Lect. 6, n. 226; Lect. 17, n. 341.

24. *Summa Theologiae*, I, qu. 96, a. 3.

25. *On Kingship*, I. 2–3; *Summa Theologiae*, I–II, qu. 105, a. 1, ad 2ᵐ.

26. *Commentary on the Politics*, II, Lect. 5, n. 212.

27. *Summa Theologiae*, I–II, qu. 105, a. 1; *On Kingship*, I. 6, [42].

28. *Summa Theologiae*, I–II, qu. 95, a. 1, ad 2ᵐ.

29. *Commentary on the Ethics*, X, Lect. 14; II, Lect. 1, n. 251; *Summa Theologiae*, I–II, qu. 92, a. 1.

30. *Commentary on the Ethics*, VI, Lect. 7, n. 1197; X, Lect. 16, n. 2165.

31. *Summa Theologiae*, I–II, qu. 72, a. 4. Cf. I–II, qu. 21, a. 4, ad 3ᵐ; qu. 91, a. 1; *On Kingship*, II. 1, [94]; *De Perfectione Vitae Spiritualis*, 13.

32. *Commentary on the Ethics*, I, Lect. 1, n. 5–6; VI, Lect. 7, n. 1200; *Summa Theologiae*, II–II, qu. 47, a. 11, s. c.

33. *Summa Theologiae*, II–II, qu. 57.

34. *Summa Theologiae*, I, qu. 60, a. 5.

35. *Commentary on the Politics,* I, Lect. 1, n. 35. Athanasius, *Life of Anthony,* 72ff.

36. *Commentary on the Politics,* I, Lect. 3, n. 376. Cf. *Summa Theologiae,* I–II, qu. 92, a. 1, corp. and ad 4ᵐ; I–II, qu. 58, a. 4.

37. Cf. *Summa Theologiae,* I, qu. 60, a. 5.

38. *Commentary on the Ethics,* III, Lect. 14, n. 528.

39. Cf. *Summa Theologiae,* I–II, qu. 61.

40. *Summa Theologiae,* II–II, qu. 47, a. 11; qu. 48, a. 1; qu. 50, a. 1–2.

41. *Summa Theologiae,* II–II, qu. 80, a. 1.

42. *Summa Theologiae,* II–II, qu. 49.

43. Cf. Aristotle, *Ethics,* II. 6.

44. Aristotle, *Ethics,* II. 6, 1107ᵃ1.

45. *Commentary on the Ethics,* VI, Lect. 2, n. 1131. Cf. *Summa Theologiae,* I, qu. 1, a. 6, ad 2ᵐ; qu. 14, a. 16; Aristotle, *Ethics,* X. 5, 1176ᵃ4ff.

46. *Summa Theologiae,* I–II, qu. 90–108.

47. *Commentary on the Physics,* II, Lect. 1 and Lect. 14, n. 268; *Commentary on the Ethics,* I, Lect. 1, n. 11. Cf. *Commentary on the Metaphysics,* V, Lect. 5.

48. *Summa Theologiae,* I–II, qu. 94, a. 2.

49. *Summa Theologiae,* I–II, qu. 91, a. 2.

50. *Summa Theologiae,* I, qu. 79, a. 12–13; I–II, qu. 19, a. 5–6; *De Veritate,* qu. 16; *In II Sent.,* Dist. 24, qu. 2, a. 3. The use of the word synderesis (*suntêresis,* literally, "conservation") in this context may have been due initially to a faulty transcription of *suneidêsis* ("conscience") in a widely circulated passage of St. Jerome's *Commentary on Ezechiel* (I, 4).

51. *Summa Theologiae,* I–II, qu. 18, a. 9; qu. 21, a. 4; qu. 96, a. 4; qu. 98, a. 5; qu. 99, a. 1 and 5; qu. 100, a. 2.

52. *Summa Theologiae,* I–II, qu. 71, a. 6, ad 5ᵐ; *Summa Contra Gentiles,* IV. 140.

53. *Summa Theologiae,* I–II, qu. 95, a. 1–2; qu. 91, a. 2, ad 2ᵐ.

54. *Summa Theologiae,* I–II, qu. 94, a. 4; qu. 96, a. 2; II–II, qu. 57, a. 2, ad 1ᵐ.

55. *Commentary on the Ethics,* I, Lect. 3, n. 35; II, Lect. 2, n. 258–9.

56. Aristotle, *Ethics,* V. 7, 1134ᵇ25ff.

57. *Summa Theologiae,* I–II, qu. 94, a. 5, ad 2ᵐ; qu. 97, a. 4, ad 3ᵐ; qu. 99, a. 3, ad 2ᵐ and a. 4; qu. 100, a. 8, ad 3ᵐ; Suppl., qu. 65, a. 1. Cf. also I–II, qu. 100, a. 1 and qu. 104, a. 1, ad 3ᵐ, where the duty to love and worship God or the injunctions against idolatry and the taking of the Lord's name in vain, while part of the natural law, are said to owe their certitude not to human reason alone but to human reason instructed by God or informed by faith.

58. Aristotle, *Ethics,* III. 1, 1110ᵇ24–33.

59. Averroes, *In Moralia Nicomachia Expositio,* Venice, 1562, p. 31 I.

60. *Commentary on the Ethics,* III, Lect. 2, n. 395–7.

61. *Summa Theologiae,* I–II, qu. 100, a. 8.

62. *Commentary on the Ethics,* V, Lect. 11, n. 1003; *Summa Theologiae,* I–II, qu. 92, a. 1, ad 3ᵐ.

63. *Summa Theologiae,* I–II, qu. 66, a. 4; II–II, qu. 58, a. 12.

64. *Commentary on the Ethics,* III, Lect. 14, n. 537.

65. *Commentary on the Politics,* I, Lect. 4, n. 75 and 79.

66. *Summa Theologiae,* I, qu. 46, esp. a. 1; *Summa Contra Gentiles,* II. 30–38. Aristotle, *Topics,* I. 11, 104ᵇ 16; *On the Heaven,* I. 2–4 and 10–12; III, 2.

67. *Summa Theologiae,* I, qu. 46, a. 2, corp. and ad 1ᵐ.

68. *Summa Theologiae,* I, qu. 3, a. 4; *Summa Contra Gentiles,* I. 22.

69. *Summa Contra Gentiles,* II. 38, 15.

70. *Commentary on the Ethics,* I, Lect. 4, n. 4; III, Lect. 18, n. 588–590;

Commentary on the Politics, II, Lect. 1, n. 170. Cf. *Summa Contra Gentiles,* III. 48.

READINGS

Aquinas never wrote a treatise dealing exclusively and comprehensively with the subject of politics. His teaching on these and directly related matters is to be found above all in the sections on law and on moral virtue of the *Summa Theologiae* and in parallel passages of the *Summa Contra Gentiles* and other theological works. They are expounded methodically, albeit from a restricted point of view, in the short treatise *On Kingship,* written at the request of the King of Cyprus. Finally, they may be gleaned in somewhat more incidental fashion from his commentaries on the *Ethics* and on the first two and a half books of the *Politics* of Aristotle. (It should be noted that the rest of the commentary on the *Politics* in the manuscript tradition and the printed editions of that work was written, not by Aquinas himself, but by his disciple, Peter of Auvergne.)

The *Summa Theologiae,* or *Summa Theologica,* as it is sometimes called, is not a treatise in the ordinary sense of the word, after the manner of Aristotle's treatises, let us say. Because its method of procedure is generally unfamiliar to the modern reader, a few words of explanation in regard to it may be in order. The work as a whole is divided into three parts. The First Part has as its overall theme God and creation. Part Two contains an exposé of Aquinas's moral theology and is itself divided into two parts: the first is devoted to a treatment of man's final end and of the principles of human actions in general, whether intrinsic (the virtues and vices) or extrinsic (law, grace); the second treats mainly of the virtues and vices in particular. Part Three deals on the whole with Christ and the sacraments or with the way through which, in the actual economy of salvation, man returns to God. Each of these three parts is divided into a series of questions and each question into a series of articles which adhere uniformly to the pattern of the so-called "disputed question." The individual articles are given a title in the form of a question, which is immediately followed by an enumeration of the most important or most relevant objections to the thesis defended in the article. Aquinas then states his own position with the support of an acknowledged authority, such as a quotation from Scripture, the Church Fathers, Aristotle, or Cicero, and proceeds to establish that position by means of theological or philosophical arguments in the body of the article. The article ends with a point-by-point answer to the objections raised at the outset.

Aquinas's commentaries on Aristotle belong to a literary form known in the Middle Ages as the *commentarium ad litteram* or literal commentary, as distinguished from the simple paraphrases or glosses commonly employed by his Latin predecessors. They are characterized by the extreme care as well as the sympathy with which the text of Aristotle is scrutinized. The subject matter of each work and the mode of procedure to be adopted in dealing with it are indicated either in a preface or at the beginning of the commentary itself.

Aquinas then divides and subdivides the text of Aristotle for the purpose of revealing its overall structure along with the relation of each part to its immediate context and to the whole. The commentary follows the order of the books into which Aristotle's treatises are traditionally divided and breaks them down into smaller segments of varying length, each one of which forms the object of a single *lectio* or lesson. Finally, each unit of thought or ultimate subdivision within these segments is explicated briefly or in greater detail, as the circumstances of the case demand.

The general aim of the commentary is to intepret Aristotle's text accurately and objectively, not to add to it or develop from it an original philosophic teaching. Whenever needed, the commentary clarifies the meaning of the most important words and gives their Latin equivalents. It indicates in relation to each specific point the precise nature of the argument used by Aristotle. In some instances, it supplies the reasons which tacitly underlie his statements or makes explicit what was only implicit in the original text. On rare occasions, it calls attention to the difference between Aristotle's teaching and that of the Bible. Any difficulties, ambiguities, or apparent contradictions in the text are elucidated by means of plausible hypotheses based on principles which are those of Aristotle himself and which are preferably taken from the same work. To what extent Aquinas's interpretations remain faithful at all times not only to the letter but to the spirit of Aristotle is, not unexpectedly, a question that has given rise to considerable debate among scholars. Whatever the answer to that question, it cannot be denied that, both individually and collectively, his commentaries reveal an extraordinary grasp and mastery of the entire corpus of Aristotle's works.

A. Thomas Aquinas. *On Kingship to the King of Cyprus*. Translated by Gerald B. Phelan and revised by I. Th. Eschmann. Toronto: The Pontifical Institute of Mediaeval Studies, 1949. Book I.

Thomas Aquinas. *Summa Theologica*. Literally Translated by the Fathers of the English Dominican Province. 3 Vols. New York: Benziger Brothers, 1947. I–II, qu. 90–97; qu. 100; qu. 105, a. 1 (from the treatise on law). II–II, qu. 47 and 50 (from the treatise on prudence). II–II, qu. 57–58 (from the treatise on right and justice).

Thomas Aquinas. *On the Truth of the Catholic Faith (Summa Contra Gentiles)*. Newly Translated, with an Introduction, by Anton C. Pegis. Garden City: Image Books, 1955. Book I, Chap. 1–7.

B. Thomas Aquinas. *Commentary on the Nicomachean Ethics*. Translated by C. I. Litzinger. Chicago: Henry Regnery Company, 1964. Book I, Lect. 1–3; Book IV, Lect. 8–11; Book V; Book VI, Lect. 7; Book X, Lect. 9–16.

Thomas Aquinas. *Commentary on the Politics of Aristotle*. Proemium; Book I, Lect. 1; Book III, Lect. 1–6. *Medieval Political Philosophy: A Sourcebook*. Edited by R. Lerner and M. Mahdi, with the collaboration of E. L. Fortin. New York: The Free Press, 1963, pp. 298–334.

MARSILIUS OF PADUA

circa 1275–1342

Marsilius, whose chief work is entitled *Defender of the Peace* (1324), was a Christian Aristotelian. But both his Christianity and his Aristotelianism differ profoundly from the beliefs of the most celebrated Christian Aristotelian, Thomas Aquinas. Marsilius lives as it were in another world than Thomas. In the whole *Defender* he refers to Thomas only once, but even then, when he claims to quote Thomas, he in fact quotes only the statement of another authoritative Christian writer which Thomas had inserted with that writer's name[1] in a compilation he had made. Thomas had accepted the traditional ecclesiastical polity of the Roman Church. Marsilius admits that the Christian priesthood is divinely established as distinct from the Christian laity, both being part of the Christian order; but he denies that the ecclesiastical hierarchy is divinely established. According to him all Christian priests are essentially equal in all respects as far as divine right is concerned. He also denies that any priest, even if he be bishop or pope, has by divine right any of the following powers: the power to command or to coerce; the power to decide whether and how coercion is to be exercised against apostates and heretics, be they subjects or princes; and the power to determine in a legally binding way what is orthodox and what is heretical. But we cannot go into Marsilius' doctrine of the Church although it was of the greatest political importance, especially during the Reformation, for that doctrine belongs to political theology rather than to political philosophy. By following this distinction, we do not distort Marsilius' teaching, for he himself distinguishes throughout his work the political teaching which is "demonstrated" by "human demonstration" from the political teaching which is revealed by God immediately or mediately and is

therefore accepted by simple faith as distinguished from reason.[2] This is
not to deny that the principle of his doctrine regarding the Christian
priesthood supplies the key to almost all the difficulties in which his
work abounds, for that principle explains his only explicit deviation
from the teaching of Aristotle.

As regards the principles of political philosophy, Marsilius presents
himself as a strict follower of Aristotle, "the divine philosopher" or
"the pagan sage."[3] He explicitly agrees with Aristotle regarding the
purpose of the commonwealth: the commonwealth exists for the sake of
the good life, and the good life consists in being engaged in the activity
becoming a free man, *i.e.,* in the exercise of the virtues of the practical
as well as of the speculative soul. While practical or civic felicity
"seems to be" the end of human acts, in fact the activity of the metaphysician is more perfect than the activity of the prince who is the active
or political man par excellence.[4] Marsilius explicitly agrees with Aristotle
in regarding the purpose of the commonwealth as the ground for the
other kinds of causes (material, formal, and moving) of the commonwealth and of its parts. He explicitly agrees with him in very many
other points. He has only one reservation against Aristotle: Aristotle did
not know one very grave disease of civil society, an "evil thing, the
common enemy of the human race" which must be eradicated. This
ignorance does not derogate from Aristotle's supreme wisdom. Aristotle did not know the "pestilence" in question because he could not
know it, for it was the accidental consequence of a miracle and it could
have been even less foreseen by the wisest man than the miracle itself.
The miracle was the Christian revelation, and the grave disease arose
from the claims, in no way supported by Scripture, of the Christian
hierarchy—claims which culminate in the notion of papal plenitude
of power. Marsilius declares that this is the only political disease with
which he will deal, since the others have been properly dealt with by
Aristotle.[5] One ought therefore not even to expect to find a complete
presentation of political philosophy in the *Defender*. The work comes
to sight as a kind of appendix to that part of Aristotle's *Politics* which
may be said to deal with the diseases of civil society.

Yet Aristotle's unawareness of a single, if unusually grave, disease
of civil society is only the reverse side of his fundamental error: he was
a pagan. That error affects his political philosophy immediately only
in one point, however, in the teaching regarding the priesthood. He did
not know the true Christian priesthood but only the false pagan priest-
hoods. This does not mean that his teaching regarding the priesthood
is entirely wrong. On the contrary, within political philosophy that
teaching is in the main correct. He saw clearly that the priesthood

forms a necessary part of the commonwealth, even a noble part, but cannot be the ruling part: priests cannot have the power to rule or to judge. He also saw clearly that it cannot be left entirely to the individuals whether they become priests or not; the number as well as the qualifications of the priests, and in particular the admission of foreigners to priesthood in the commonwealth, is subject to the decision of the government of the commonwealth. The Christian revelation does not contradict this demonstrated teaching,[6] since revelation is indeed above reason but not against reason. Nor is this all. Aristotle did not indeed know the true ground of the priesthood which can only be divine revelation. But if not Aristotle, at any rate other philosophers (who, as philosophers, did not believe in another life) devised or accepted allegedly divine laws accompanied with sanctions in another life, because they held that such sanctions would induce the nonphilosophers to avoid the vices and to cultivate the virtues in this life. Christianity is a truly divine law and the Christian faith in punishments and rewards after death is the true faith; on the basis of the Christian faith one may then indeed say that the commonwealth is directed toward both this-worldly felicity and otherworldly bliss. But since the otherworldly end cannot be known or demonstrated, political philosophy must conceive of that end as a postulated means for promoting the this-worldly end. Besides, while Christianity is exclusively or chiefly concerned with the other life, it too makes men's fate in the other world dependent on how they lived in this world, and it too contends that the belief in punishments and rewards after death is also politically salutary.[7] The reasoning of the pagan philosophers is then true, and therefore may be said to form a part of the demonstrated political teaching. At any rate, that reasoning leads to the philosophic concept, accepted by Marsilius, of the "sect" as a society constituted by belief in a peculiar divine law or by a peculiar religion; that concept embraces equally all allegedly and all truly divine laws, for the truth of the true religion escapes philosophy as philosophy. This religiously neutral concept of the sect is an essential part of Marsilian political science, just as it had been of Alfarabi's political science.[8] It leads to the rational concept of the priesthood according to which the priests are essentially teachers and not rulers or judges: the essential function of the priests in any divine law is to teach a salutary doctrine concerning the afterlife or, more generally, to teach the divine law in which their society happens to believe. The priests are the only teachers who as teachers form a part of the commonwealth.[9] According to Aristotle's *Politics*, the priests form indeed one of the six parts of the commonwealth, but their function does not consist in teaching. Marsilius' deviation from Aristotle to this point is, however, not based on a misunderstanding; he deviates from the letter rather than from the spirit of his master. By asserting that the priesthood is the only part of the commonwealth which is essentially dedicated to teaching, Marsilius draws our attention to the most important fact that, according to Aristotle, the philosophers, so far from being the ruling part of the best commonwealth, as they are according to Plato, are not even as such a part of any commonwealth, for the end of the commonwealth as commonwealth is not speculative perfection: cities and nations do not philosophize.

The fact that the pagan philosophers in general and Aristotle in particular elaborated the rational teaching regarding the priesthood does not mean that Aristotle's whole teaching on this subject is true. According to Aristotle, the action of the priest is less noble or perfect than the action of the ruler, but in "the law of the Christians," and only in that law, the action of the priest is the most perfect of all. According to Aristotle, only old men of the upper class ought to be priests, another point which is denied by Christianity. Finally, according to Aristotle, the priests are simply citizens, but, since the Christian priests ought to imitate Christ and hence to live in Evangelical poverty and humility, it would appear that they must not have anything to do with the things that are Caesar's.[10]

The diseases of the commonwealth which Aristotle had discussed endanger this or that kind of government or render good government impossible. But in Marsilius' opinion the disease with which the *Defender* is concerned renders any government impossible, for it destroys the unity of the government and of the legal order, or it brings about permanent anarchy since it consists in the belief that the Christian is subject in this world to two governments (the spiritual and the temporal) which are bound to conflict. That disease endangers not only the good life or the fruits of peace, for the sake of which the commonwealth exists, but mere life or mere peace which is merely the condition—although the necessary condition—for the realization of the true end of the commonwealth. From this we see how appropriate the title of Marsilius' work is: the work is a defender, not of faith, but of peace, and of nothing but peace—not, to repeat, because peace is the highest good or the only political good but because, being a tract for the time, the work is chiefly concerned with the disease of the time. This is the reason why Marsilius apparently lowers his sights. Thus he abstracts from the question concerning the best regime without in any way denying its importance: any regime is better than anarchy. Thus he is more concerned with mere law, with law as law, than with good laws or the best laws, and with mere government than with the best government.

Thus he is satisfied with mere consent as the criterion of legitimacy as distinguished from the level of consent. Aristotle had as it were provided against Marsilius' predicament. When Marsilius in effect says that the law as law need not be good or just whereas the perfect law must be just, he is in entire agreement with Aristotle's remark that a ruler is no less a ruler because he rules unjustly, or with the usage of Aristotle and indeed of common sense which entitles us to speak of bad or unjust laws; to say nothing of the fact that when Aristotle opposes slavery by nature to slavery by law, he certainly does not mean by law a just law. When Marsilius frequently or mostly abstracts from the fact that the commonwealth is ordered toward virtue, he acts in entire agreement with Aristotle's observation that almost all cities are not concerned with virtue—an observation which does not prevent Aristotle from calling those bad cities "cities." [11]

Marsilius' sole reservation against Aristotle was the immediate consequence of the fact that Aristotle was a pagan. It concerned political philosophy or the rational political teaching only accidentally. Still, according to Aristotle, the best polity is the rule of gentlemen who rule their city, a fairly small society, and are enabled to do so because they are men of wealth. How can such men be thought to be rulers in a Christian society where they would have to rule Christian priests and hence the Church? For in a Christian society the activity of the priest is more noble than that of the ruler. Furthermore, the Church is universal. Finally, the best men in Christendom, *i.e.,* the best Christians, must live in Evangelical poverty. This was the problem which Marsilius believed he had to solve and that he had solved.

The problem of how to reconcile the Aristotelian principle (the men dedicated to the most noble practical activity ought to rule in their own right) with the Christian principle (the activity of the priest is more noble than that of the gentleman) could seem to have been solved in the clearest and simplest manner by the doctrine of papal plenitude of power. Marsilius avoids that conclusion within the confines of political philosophy by teaching that in every commonwealth, the fundamental political authority is not the government or the ruling part but the human legislator, and that the human legislator is the people, the whole body of the citizens. To express this in the language of Rousseau, Marsilius asserts that the only legitimate sovereign is the people but that the sovereign is to be distinguished from the government. He thus succeeds in subordinating the Christian priests to the Christian laity, the Christian aristocracy to the Christian *populus* or *demos*. But in taking these steps he seems to deviate flagrantly from the teaching of his revered master who may be said to have identified the sovereign with the government and, above all, to have preferred the sovereignty or government of the gentlemen (aristocracy) to the sovereignty or government of the people (democracy).

Marsilius does not dispose of the difficulty by accepting Aristotle's assertions according to which democracy or the rule of the vulgar is a bad regime, and the farmers, artisans and money-makers, who constitute the vulgar, are not in the strictest sense parts of the commonwealth. He rather increases the difficulty by ascribing to Aristotle himself the following teaching: the legislative power must be entirely in the hands of the whole citizen body; the government ought to be elected by the whole citizen body and ought to be responsible to it; the government must rule in strict adherence to the laws and if it transgresses a law it is liable to punishment by the whole citizen body. This teaching ascribed to Aristotle is much more democratic than Aristotle's authentic teaching: in the whole body of the citizens, as Marsilius understands it, the vulgar must play a very great, not to say a decisive role. The reasoning in favor of the vulgar by which Marsilius supports his teaching is indeed almost identical with the argument in favor of democracy which Aristotle had reported and considered in the course of his ascent from the defective regimes to aristocracy (or kingship). And Marsilius does not tire of explicitly quoting Aristotle in this context, although not without strange misinterpretations. Still stranger is his complete silence in this context about Aristotle's antidemocratic argument. He reports the antidemocratic argument but omits any reference to Aristotle. He quotes only one authority for the antipopulist position: the saying of the wise king Solomon according to which "the number of the fools is infinite." Marsilius had not quoted any biblical passage in his populist reasoning; he thus perplexes us for a moment by making us think that the Bible, or at any rate Solomon, might favor aristocracy. Yet he disposes of this possibility by suggesting that the sage meant perhaps by the fools the infidels who, however wise in the worldly sciences, are nevertheless absolutely foolish, since, according to Paul, the wisdom of this world is foolishness with God. For from this it follows that the faithful man, and hence all the more the faithful multitude, is truly wise and hence perfectly competent to make laws and to elect kings or magistrates.

There is at least one other remark of Marsilius which shows that his belief in the competence of the people at large originated in his concern, not with authority as such, but with authority in Christendom. He says in effect that the necessity of giving the multitude power to legislate and to elect officials is less evident than the necessity of entrusting the multitude with the power to elect priests and remove them from their priestly offices; for error in the election of a priest can lead to eternal

death and to very great harm in this life. That harm consists in the
seduction of women during the secret conversations in the course of
which they confess their sins to a priest. It is obvious that the simplest
citizen, and surely therefore the faithful multitude, is as able to judge
the trustworthiness of any individual priest in such matters as the most
learned men could be; and the simple multitude might even be better
informed in such respects than the learned. Marsilius also suggests that
the whole body of all the faithful which is guided in its deliberations by
the Holy Spirit, as distinguished from the whole body of citizens as
mere citizens, is infallible.[12] By far the most important argument for
popular government, however, is supplied by the example of the Church
in its purest form, in which there were not yet Christian princes, and
the Church consisted exclusively of priests and a multitude of such laymen as were subjects. Precisely in that epoch "Church" meant only the
whole body of the faithful, and thus all Christians were ecclesiastics.
Hence the traditional distinction between the people and the clergy
must be radically revised in favor of the people. In accordance with the
practice of the early Church, the election to all priestly offices belongs
to the whole multitude of the faithful. This reasoning is not weakened
but strengthened by the fact that in the very early Church the multitude
was uncivilized and inexperienced: if even then the bishops were frequently elected by the multitude, this procedure is all the more appropriate after the faith has taken root in both subjects and princes.[13]

Let us return to the confines of political philosophy and consider
Marsilius' doctrine of the human legislator somewhat more closely.
He devotes two whole chapters out of fifty-two to the statement, the
proofs, and the defense of that doctrine. He advances three proofs to
which he adds a fourth, but that fourth proof is, as he says, hardly more
than a summary of the first three. (1) The legislative power ought to
belong to those from whom alone the best laws can emerge, but this is
the whole citizen body; one reason is that no one harms himself knowingly and hence, we may add, when each thinks of his interest, no one's
interest will be neglected or the interest of all will be duly provided for.
(2) The legislative power ought to belong only to those who can best
guarantee that the laws made will be observed, but this is the whole
citizen body, for each citizen observes better a law, even if it is not good,
"which he seems to have imposed on himself"; the reason for this is
that every citizen not only is a free man, *i.e.,* not subject to a master, but
desires to be a free man. We may note that this argument causes a difficulty which Marsilius never discussed regarding the God-given and
hence not even apparently self-imposed law. (3) What can benefit and
harm each, and hence all, ought to be known and heard by all so that

all and each can attain the benefit and repel the harm. The defense of the doctrine is stated in three arguments which are in the main taken from the populist reasoning reported by Aristotle. In the second of the latter group of arguments, Marsilius illustrates the danger of entrusting legislative power to a few or to one by referring to the oligarchic or tyrannical character of the canon law.[14] Marsilius' populist thesis thus appears to be derived from his anticlericalism.

Marsilius ascribes the fundamental political power, the power of the human legislator, not simply to the whole citizen body but to "the whole citizen body or its stronger or superior part." By the stronger or superior part he certainly does not mean the unqualified majority. The stronger or superior part, which as it were replaces the whole citizen body, must be understood in terms of both number and quality, so that the vulgar may not be entirely at the mercy of the better people nor the latter entirely at the mercy of the former. The arrangement sketched by Marsilius might be called a "polity"—a mean between oligarchy and democracy—were it not for the fact that "polity" is a form of government, while Marsilius speaks of the sovereign as distinguished from the government. Furthermore, whereas in a democracy, in Aristotle's sense, the common people participate fully in deliberation and jurisdiction, Marsilius reserves these functions for the government or the ruling part as distinguished from the whole citizen body or its stronger or superior part.[15] Above all, as Marsilius already discloses in the chapters explicitly devoted to the definition of the human legislator, the human legislator may delegate his legislative power to one or to several men. Marsilius thus allows the sovereignty of the people to remain entirely dormant. In the same breath in which he proclaims the transcendent virtue of everyone's actually participating in legislation, he dismisses that participation as irrelevant. One must go further and say that he retracts the very principle of popular sovereignty. He compares the position of the ruling part in the body politic to that of the heart in the human body: it is that part which molds the other parts of the body politic. But if this is so, the ruling part is not derivative from a pre-existing sovereign, the human legislator, or the people, *i.e.,* the whole which consists of all parts of the body politic in their proper proportion, but is rather the cause of the alleged sovereign. In accordance with this Marsilius compares the position of the ruling part in the commonwealth to that of the prime mover in the universe, *i.e.,* of the Aristotelian God who surely is not subject to laws made by the other parts of the universe. In a word, Marsilius returns to the Aristotelian view according to which the human legislator (the sovereign) is identical with the ruling part (the government) or according to which the stronger or superior part is identical with the ruling part; for in every stable political order, the ruling part, whether it consists of one man or a few or the many, is as a matter of course the stronger or superior part. Marsilius even explicitly identifies the ruler with the legislator, e.g., by calling the Roman emperors legislators. He does not leave it at saying that the human legislator can give the ruler "plenitude of power." He goes so far as to say that the ruler owes his position to "the human legislator or any other human will": the ruler may owe his position to his own will.[16]

If the ruling part is the legislator it cannot be simply subject to the law. Even in a republic, where no individual is the legislator and hence somehow above the law, it is sometimes necessary for an individual magistrate to act illegally in order to save the republic, as Cicero did when quenching the Catilinian conspiracy. When Marsilius suggests that the ruler is subject only to the divine law, we must not forget that according to him the divine law is not as such knowable to human reason nor does it as such have coercive power in this world. Furthermore, if the ruling part (the government) is the legislator (the sovereign), the government is not subject to punishment in case of misconduct for the same reason for which the sovereign people in the populist hypothesis is not subject to punishment.[17] To sum up, in spite of its dogmatic tone, Marsilius' populist teaching proves to be, if in a different way, as provisional or as tentative as the democratic argument in Aristotle's *Politics*.

The characteristic of the *Defender of the Peace* viewed as a treatise of political philosophy is that it very emphatically sets forth and literally at the same time retracts the doctrine of popular sovereignty. What is the meaning of this striking contradiction concerning the very foundation of political society? What is the meaning of Marsilius' vacillation between populism and what one may call monarchic absolutism? One could say that he takes the side of the people when the people is understood in contradistinction to the clergy and to nothing else, and that he takes the side of the Roman emperors, ancient or medieval, against the popes. In other words, the contradiction disappears once one assumes, as some scholars have done, that the *Defender* is inspired by nothing but anticlericalism. He needed for his anticlerical argument a populist basis because he had to appeal from the accepted opinions regarding the Church to the New Testament. The New Testament, while giving strong support to the demand for submission to absolute monarchs or to despots, does not give support to Marsilius' suggestion that the secular Christian rulers alone as distinguished from the priests ought to rule the Church in everything affecting men's fate in this world (punishment of heretics and apostates, excommunication, property, and so on); but the New Testament apparently gives some support to the view that decisions in such matters rest with the whole body of the faithful as distinguished from the priests alone. Marsilius' "whole body of the citizens" is merely the philosophic or rational counterpart of "the whole body of the faithful," and he needs such a counterpart in order to provide his anticlericalism with the broadest possible basis: both reason and revelation speak against the rule of priests. This explanation implies that the fundamental self-contradiction which is characteristic of the *Defender* is the conscious outcome of a conscious strategy. Both the explanation and its implication are defensible, yet they do not account for certain features of Marsilius' populist teaching or for the essential character of strategies like the one justly ascribed to Marsilius. They fail to account for the latter because it is not sufficient to conceive of Marsilius as a perhaps skillful but rather unscrupulous politician or advocate.

To find a way out of the difficulty, let us consider a Marsilian doctrine which is not affected by either political theology or antitheological preoccupations, his doctrine of monarchy or kingship. He says that kingship is "perhaps" the best form of government, but he makes it his business to discuss the question as to whether hereditary or elective monarchy is preferable. He devotes to this subject only one chapter, but that chapter is longer than the two chapters taken together which are apparently meant to establish popular sovereignty. He decides in favor of elective monarchy strictly understood, *i.e.,* of a monarchy in which each monarch, and not a monarch and his descendants, is elected. This decision might have recommended him to the pope but with greater likelihood to the German emperor, who was at that time engaged in a bitter fight with the pope and who soon became Marsilius' protector; it would not have recommended him to the French king, for instance.[18] Yet it was necessary for the success of his venture—the venture aiming at the eradication of papal plenitude of power and everything reminding of it —to obtain the good will of all secular princes. It can therefore be assumed that his preference for elective monarchy over hereditary monarchy belongs to his final or serious political teaching. He certainly never contradicts this preference as he contradicts the doctrine of popular sovereignty. His argument in favor of elective kingship can be reduced to a single consideration. The most important quality of the ruler is prudence, for the infinite variety of human affairs does not permit an adequate regulation by laws, and prudence does not come by inheritance. Prudence, *i.e.,* practical wisdom in contradistinction to mere cleverness, is not separable from moral virtue and vice versa. Prudence is also and especially required for the making of good and just laws. While prudence is then of the utmost importance, it is rare; nature generated only a part of the human race apt for prudence, and still fewer men actualize that potentiality. The foregoing consideration does not imply that hereditary kingship is illegitimate; it merely means that hereditary kingship is as such inferior to elective kingship. Hereditary kingship may even be preferable to elective kingship in most countries at all times and in all countries at the beginning of their political life, when all men are still uncivilized. For in most countries at all times and in all countries at the beginning or in their decay, prudence is as it were at best the preserve of a single family and there are therefore no prudent electors. Elective kingship is superior to hereditary kingship because the former is suitable to a perfect and civilized commonwealth, whereas the latter is suitable to a still imperfect or irremediably uncivilized society.[19]

Now, this very consideration leads to the conclusion that to a perfect or civilized commonwealth the rule of a number of prudent men, i.e., aristocracy, is still more suitable than even elective monarchy, for there is no reason why, if there exists in a commonwealth a number of prudent men, as will be the case in a perfect commonwealth, all except one should always be deprived of the highest honor; those unjustly deprived of their fair share in government would justly engage in sedition. Marsilius devotes a whole chapter to the proof that the indispensable unity of government is in no way impaired if the government consists of a number of men instead of one man. Not only hereditary kingship but kingship as such is proper only at times and in places where there is an extreme paucity of men who are fit to rule a commonwealth as, e.g., perhaps in Rome at the end of the republic. Monarchy is the proper kind of government in the household rather than in the perfect civil society. That aristocracy as distinguished from kingship is possible only under the most favorable conditions, and hence very rarely, in no way contradicts the fact that it is the most natural regime. If the priests were as they ought to be, Marsilius argues, the general council of the Church could consist only of priests, for the most important requirement for participation in such an assembly is thorough knowledge of the divine law, i.e., the highest form of wisdom; but the priests are not as they ought to be. This amounts to saying that in principle aristocracy or the rule of the wise is preferable; only because the Church is no longer an aristocracy but, as Marsilius never tires of repeating, is now an oligarchy, is it in need of correction by the best part of the laity; and the laity is, in the Church, the popular element. Within his populist argument Marsilius indicates that the devising and examining of the laws is the proper business of the prudent men; the other members of society are of little use in this matter and would only be disturbed in the performance of their necessary work if they were called upon to do more than to act as "formal" ratifiers. Such popular ratification of the laws would indeed seem to be desirable, since it is likely to make the populace more willing to obey the laws.[20]

Marsilius' very vacillation between populism and absolute monarchy may be said to point to aristocracy as the right mean between these two faulty extremes. What speaks in favor of the legislative power of absolute kings redounds also to the benefit of a sovereign-government which consists of the prudent men of a city each of whom owes his position to cooptation by his peers rather than to popular election; and what speaks in favor of the legislative power of "the stronger or superior part of the whole citizen body" redounds to the benefit of what is in truth the stronger or superior part in every city which is not either too young or small or else too old or large for political excellence, namely, the most prudent and virtuous citizens. Marsilius abstains from arguing in favor of kingship while he argues emphatically in favor of popular sovereignty: the regime which he favors is somewhat closer, not indeed to democracy but to the "polity" than to kingship. At the same time his populist argument points, through its glaring defects for instance, from the "polity" to an aristocracy which is acceptable to the populace not only because of the inherent qualities of a genuine aristocracy as the rule of the most prudent and virtuous citizens, but also because it respects the susceptibilities of the populace. Marsilius presented the argument for aristocracy in the most subdued form because that argument did not provide a sufficiently broad basis for the anticlerical policy which he regarded as by far the most urgent task for his age. In addition, the argument in favor of aristocracy would have redounded in the opinion of the majority of his contemporaries to the benefit of the clergy, for if political power is shown to belong by right to the wisest, it would seem to follow that it belongs less to those wise in human wisdom than to those wise in divine wisdom.

The strategy which Marsilius employed can then be explained by the political impossibility which amounted to a physical impossibility of airing the fundamental political issue. He could have an easy conscience in proceeding as he did because he was satisfied that a government of priests was impossible or undesirable. For according to him the New Testament not only does not authorize government by priests, especially in secular matters, but positively forbids it. In the Christian law, and only in the Christian law, the action of the

priest as priest is the most perfect of all. But this action requires a
spirit and a way of life which are incompatible with rulership, for it
requires contempt for the world and the utmost humility. Christ excluded himself and the apostles from worldly rule in every form.
Paul forbade every priest to become entangled in any secular matter
whatever, since no one can serve two masters. The New Testament
recognizes in the strongest terms the duty of obedience to the human
government "which beareth not the sword in vain," not so much for
the defense of the fatherland as for executing wrath upon the evildoers, and the New Testament traces to sinful pride the view that
bad rulers or masters may be disobeyed. Christian slaves are not permitted to demand that they be set free after six years' servitude as
the Hebrew slaves are, for the Old Testament law in question acquires
in Christianity a purely mystical meaning. Humility and contempt for
the world can then go together perfectly with sincere obedience to
worldly masters. Still, within the confines of political philosophy,
Marsilius must put the accents somewhat differently than the highest
Christian authorities had done. He almost goes so far as to defend
the pagan rulers against the saying of Christ that they "lord it over"
their subjects. According to Paul, only those that are "contemptible"
in the Church, *i.e.,* those who possess wisdom in things which are
not spiritual, ought to be judges in worldly matters. The demands of
the Sermon on the Mount cannot be reconciled with the status and
the duties of governors and their lay subjects.[21] The perfect Christian
community was the community of Christ and the apostles in which
there was community of goods; but that community was imperfect
in other respects since it was meant to become universal and yet no
provision was made for its unity in the future when it would have
become a large society; it could become perfect only through the acts
of Christian princes. One is tempted to express Marsilius' thought by
saying that it was nature which perfected grace rather than grace
which perfected nature. He even goes so far as to indicate that there is
an opposition between human government and divine providence,
the former rewarding in this world the just and the doers of good
deeds and the latter inflicting suffering on them in this world.[22]
Marsilius indicates the peculiarity of the Christian law by saying that
belief in God's future judgment—*i.e.,* a belief which Christianity
shares with all other religions—would induce the Christian priests not
to defraud the poor, while belief in the Christian religion would induce the Christian priests to live in poverty. Evangelical poverty is
indeed according to him the inevitable concomitant of radical con-

tempt for this world or of radical humility. Within the confines of human reason, however, wealth, just as honor, comes to sight as something good since it is required for the exercise of moral virtue. But according to the Christian teaching, voluntary poverty is so far required for perfection that those who do not live in voluntary poverty are bad Christians. In spite of this, Marsilius can complain that the popes did not show proper gratitude for having been raised by the Roman emperors from extreme poverty to abundance of temporal goods. He appears to assume that Christian morality and the worldly morality of the gentleman contradict one another or that revelation is not simply above reason but against reason. This may be one reason why he regarded the New Testament law as especially difficult to fulfill.[23]

Marsilius has sometimes been celebrated as a defender of religious freedom. Yet he does not go beyond raising the question as to whether it is permitted to coerce heretics or infidels, while stating in the same context that he does not wish to say that such coercion is inappropriate. He does deny that such coercion can be exercised in this world on the basis of divine law. For according to Marsilius, no divine law has as such any coercive power in this world unless by virtue of a human law which makes it a crime to transgress the divine law in question. In addition, according to the Christian divine law which of course condemns heresy and infidelity and buttresses that condemnation by the threat of punishment in the other life, a man who is coerced into belief is not truly a believer; besides, Christian priests have not been given by Christ any coercive power. In spite of this, the Christian human legislator, not as Christian but as human legislator, may use coercion against heretics and infidels in this world. This right can be illustrated by the following parallel. The Christian divine law forbids drunkenness but does not as such require that coercion be used in this world against drunkards, yet it does not forbid the human legislator to prohibit drunkenness under penalties in this world. Similarly, the human legislator may enforce religious sobriety, *i.e.,* orthodoxy. Whether or not he does so will depend on his judgment on heresy, for instance. He may be guided by the biblical comparison of heresy to fornication and hence permit heresy as he permits fornication, although fornication, too, is forbidden by the Christian divine law. Or he may be guided by the biblical comparison of heresy to leprosy and hence take coercive action against heretics in compliance with the advice of experts (the priests), just as he takes coercive action against lepers in compliance with the advice of experts (the physicians). He may also be guided by the facts that the New Testament surely permits excommunication and that excommunication is bound to affect the excommunicated in this life.[24]

But apart from any theological consideration, *i.e.,* from any consideration peculiar to the Christian divine law, it is clear that if belief in divine judgment in the other world is conducive to virtuous conduct in this world, as even pagan philosophers admitted, it is not inappropriate for the human legislator to protect that belief and its corollaries by forbidding speech which may subvert that belief. This conclusion is not contradicted by Marsilius' teaching that human government is concerned only with "transeunt" as distinguished from "immanent" acts. According to that distinction (which may have been suggested to Marsilius by a passage in Isaac Israeli's *Book of Definitions*), those acts of our cognitive and appetitive powers are immanent which, like thoughts and desires, remain within the agent and are not performed by means of any of the locally moved members of the body, while the other acts of those powers are transeunt. In other words, human government is concerned only with acts the commission of which can be proved even if he who committed the act in question denies having committed it. From this it follows that speeches are transeunt acts. Since subversive speeches of the kind indicated may do harm to others and to the community as a whole, their prohibition clearly falls, according to Marsilius, within the jurisdiction of the human legislator.[25] Marsilius surely did not preach freedom from religion.

Any divine law would lose much of its value if everyone subject to it were free to understand its promises and threats as he pleases. The Christian divine law in particular, with its emphasis on faith as the necessary condition for eternal salvation, would have been given in vain, it would have been given for men's eternal perdition, if Christ had not provided that the one true meaning of his divine law is accessible to all Christians. The indispensable unity of faith is provided in a legally binding manner by the universal or catholic Church, *i.e.,* by the whole body of the faithful, in so far as it is the faithful human legislator who authorizes the general councils and gives their decisions coercive power. This provision causes no difficulty when there is a single human legislator of Christian faith whose jurisdiction extends over the whole world. Such a legislator was, according to an opinion adopted by Marsilius, the Roman people or derivatively the Roman emperor. Marsilius tries to preserve this dignity for the Roman emperors of his age. But he cannot conceal from himself or from his readers the fact that there existed in his time a number of faithful human legislators who did not recognize a superior or who were independent of one another. There was then no longer a guarantee of the unity of faith except within the borders of individual independent realms or commonwealths. Hence Marsilius regards it as advisable that the various Christian sovereigns should agree in recognizing the bishop of Rome as "the universal pastor," but in his opinion they are not obliged to do so.[26]

Yet, as he points out, a universal pastor or universal bishop is less necessary than a universal prince, for a universal prince is obviously more capable of keeping the faithful in the unity of faith than a universal bishop could be. As a Christian Marsilius seems then to be compelled, given his premises, to demand that political society be universal strictly speaking—and not only in pretense, or by courtesy, as the Roman empire was even at the peak of its power—so that it can discharge its duties to the Christian faith. He seems to be compelled, that is, to abandon the very last trace of his doctrine of popular sovereignty or of the Aristotelian preference for aristocracy which that doctrine partly represents; for neither democracy nor aristocracy as understood by Marsilius and Aristotle is feasible in any but fairly small societies. Yet in spite or because of all this, Marsilius denies that a universal prince is necessary. For Scripture does not demand a universal secular empire. Still less does reason demand it: peace among men is sufficiently guaranteed—we may understand this to mean that peace is guaranteed in the only possible way—if there exists unity of government within the particular commonwealths or kingdoms. In his only thematic discussion of the question concerning the desirability of a "world state," Marsilius refuses to decide it. He alludes to the difficulties obstructing world government which are caused by distance and by the lack of communication between the various parts of the world, as well as by the differences of languages and the extreme differences of customs. He refers to the view according to which all these things which separate men might be due to a heavenly cause, i.e., to nature which incites men, by means of these divisive things, to wars in order to prevent overpopulation. Marsilius makes it clear that, were it not for wars and epidemics, overpopulation would be inevitable if the human kind had no beginning and will have no end, i.e., if there is "eternal generation" or if the visible universe is eternal.[27] The Aristotelian doctrine of the eternity of the visible universe is irreconcilable with the biblical doctrine of the creation of the world. The Aristotelian doctrine of eternal generation is irreconcilable with the biblical doctrine that there was "a first man," with a doctrine which is the premise of the biblical doctrines that our first parents fell and that therefore man is in need of redemption. Marsilius does not declare that the Aristotelian doctrine is true. Nor does he declare that it is untrue because it contradicts the most fundamental and the most manifest doctrines of the Bible. The reader can therefore only guess whether Marsilius was a believer or an unbeliever until he considers Marsilius' discussion, presented in the thirty-eighth chapter of the *Defender* (II 19), of the question concerning the ground of the belief in the truth of the Bible.

Within the confines of political philosophy, Marsilius' tacit opposition to Thomas Aquinas shows itself most obviously in his teaching regarding natural law or natural right. Marsilius denies that there is a natural law properly so called. He presupposes that reason knows no other legislator than man and hence that all laws properly so called are human laws: reason is indeed capable of discerning what is honorable, what is just, and what is of advantage to society. But such insights are not as such laws. Besides, they are not accessible to all men and hence not admitted by all nations; for this reason they cannot be called natural. There are indeed certain rules regarding what is honorable or just which are admitted in all regions and are in addition enforced almost everywhere; these rules can therefore metaphorically be called natural rights. In spite of their being universally or generally admitted, they are not strictly speaking natural, for they are not dictated by right reason. What is universally admitted is not rational, and what is rational is not universally admitted. Among the rules which can metaphorically be called "natural rights" Marsilius mentions the rule that human offspring must be reared by the parents up to a certain time; he may have regarded this rule as not unqualifiedly rational since Aristotle had held that no deformed child should be reared. More generally, if wars are by nature necessary in order to prevent overpopulation, the distinction between just and unjust wars loses much of its force, and this grave qualification of the rules of justice cannot but impair the rationality of those rules of justice which are universally or generally admitted to obtain within the commonwealth. In other words, the universally admitted rules of right are not rational since there exists a natural necessity to transgress them or since man does not possess freedom of will to the extent to which both common opinion and the teaching of revelation assert it.[28]

One can understand Marsilius' denial of natural law best if one starts from the fact that he implicitly denies the existence of first principles of practical reason. The cognitive status of the first principles of action in Aristotle's *Ethics* is obscure. One way of removing this obscurity—the way preferred by Averroes and Dante—is to conceive of the first principles of action and therefore also of politics as supplied by theoretical reason or natural science: it is natural science which makes clear what the end of man is. Let the end of man be the perfection of his mind, *i.e.,* the actual thought of the metaphysician as metaphysician. The individual human being who is capable of pursuing this end will then deliberate as to how, given his circumstances, he can reach this end. This deliberation—an act of practical reason—will in many points differ from individual to individual, but there are certain universal rules of conduct with which all men must comply who wish to become perfect as men of speculation. Those rules are, however, not universal strictly speaking since only a minority of men is by nature capable of the contemplative life. But there is also an end which all men are able to pursue; this is the perfection of their bodies. This lower or first perfection requires among other things security in and through political society. Here a profound ambiguity enters: political society is required, although in different ways, for the sake of both man's first and his ultimate (theoretical) perfection. However this may be, political society in its turn requires a variety of "parts" (farmers, artisans, moneyed men, soldiers, priests, governors, or judges) and a certain order of these parts. It requires for its well-being that the legislators and the governors or judges possess prudence and if not all at any rate some of the moral virtues, especially justice. In agreement with Aristotle's procedure in the *Politics,* Marsilius deduces the necessity of those virtues from the purpose of civil society, and the necessity of that purpose from the end or ends of man. That is to say, deviating from the procedure which Aristotle had followed in his *Ethics* for educative or practical reasons, Marsilius does not take those virtues as ultimates, as choiceworthy for their own sake. It is because Marsilius treats prudence and the moral virtues less as choiceworthy for their own sake than as subservient to the two natural ends indicated that his political science is more obviously and more emphatically "demonstrative" than Aristotle's political science.[29]

Marsilius says much less than Aristotle even in his *Politics* about the highest end which is natural to man. For the reasons indicated above he lowered his sights. His doctrine of the commonwealth is reminiscent of the suggestion in Plato's *Republic* according to which the city of pigs is the true city. His doctrine of the human law is reminiscent of Maimonides' suggestion according to which the human law serves no higher goal than the perfection of man's body, whereas the divine law brings about the perfection of both the body and the mind.[30] But Maimonides held that the divine law is essentially rational and not, as it is according to Thomas, suprarational. One may say that Marsilius combines Maimonides' view of the human law with Thomas' view of the divine law and thus arrives, within the confines of political philosophy, at the conclusion that the only law properly so called is the human law which is directed toward the well-being of the body. Marsilius was driven to take this view to some extent by his anticlericalism. When antitheological passion induced a thinker to take the extreme step of questioning the supremacy of contemplation, political philosophy broke with the classical tradition, and especially with Aristotle, and took on an entirely new character. The thinker in question was Machiavelli.

NOTES

1. Marsilius of Padua, *The Defender of the Peace*, trans. with an introduction by Alan Gewirth (New York: Columbia University Press, 1956), II. 13.24 (= 169th paragraph of Dictio II).

2. *Ibid.*, I. 9.2.

3. *Ibid.*, I. 11.2 beginning and 16.15 end.

4. *Ibid.*, I. 4.1; 1.7; II. 30.4 end (cf. I. 6.9 first paragraph).

5. *Ibid.*, I. 1.3–5, 7; 19.3 and 8–13.

6. *Ibid.*, I. 5.1; 15.10; 19.12 end. II. 1.4; 8.9 toward the end; 30.5 (paragraph 2).

7. *Ibid.*, I. 4.3–4; 5.11; 10.3.

8. *Ibid.*, I. 5.2, 3, 13; 10.3. II. 8.4 end. (But cf. the derogatory meaning of "sect" in II. 16.17.) See above, p. 178.

9. *Ibid.*, I. 5.12; 19.4 (102, 22, ed. Previté-Orton) and 5 beginning. II. 6.10 end; 10.6; 20.13. Note that Marsilius does not quote Deut. 33:10.

10. *Ibid.*, I. 5.1, 13. II. 13–14; 24.1 end; 30.4 (paragraph 1 end).

11. *Ibid.*, I. 1.1; 8.4; 10.4–5; 15.1; 17. II. 4.5; 8.9; 28 end. *Politics* 1255^b 13–15; 1276^a 1–3; 1282^b 7–13; 1324^b 7–9; 1333^b 5ff. *EN* 1180^a 24–35.

12. *Defender*, I. 5.1, 13; 8.3; 11 (esp. 11.6); 12.3, 4; 13.1, 3, 4. II. 17.10–12; 21.3 and 9 end. *Politics* 1281^a 40ff. (esp. 1281^b 23–25).

13. *Defender*, II. 2.3; 15.8; 16.1 and 9 beginning; 17.5, 7–8, 10; 28.3, 17.

14. *Ibid.*, I. 12–13. II. 23.9, 13 beginning; 24.11; 26.19; 28.29.

15. *Ibid.*, I. 5.1, 7; 8.1; 12.4. II. 2.8; 4.8; 8.7.

16. *Ibid.*, I. 4.4 (13, 20); 8.5; 10.2; 12.3; 13 end; 14 heading and end; 15.5–6; 16.21; 17.9. II. 5.4 (149 bottom); 8.6; 21.2; 30.4 (485, 19–21—one of the two central paragraphs of the chapter). III. 2.13. *Defensor Minor*, chap. 3 beginning. *Politics* 1296^b 14–16.

17. *Defender*, I. 14.3; 15.4; 26.13. Cf. II. 3.15 and 30.6.

18. *Ibid.*, I. 9.5–7; 15.3 end; 16. II. 24.2.

19. *Ibid.*, I. 7.1; 9.4–7, 10; 11.3 (42, 14–15); 14.2–7, 10; 15.1; 16. 11–24 (esp. 16.17).

20. *Ibid.*, I. 2.2; 3.4; 9.10; 11.5 end; 12.2; 13.8; 14.9; 16.19, 21, 23; 17. II. 20.2 end and 13–14; cf. II. 3.15 with 30.6. Gewirth, *loc. cit.*, I, 254. The use of *regnum* suggested in I. 2 makes one expect a more monarchistic tendency than Marsilius actually has.

21. *Ibid.*, I. 10.3; 12.2. II. 4.13; 5.1–2, 4–5, 8 (paragraph 1); 9.10, 12; 11.2, 7; 28.24 (462, 9); 30.4 paragraph 1 end.

22. *Ibid.*, II. 4.6; 13.28; 17.7–8; 22.1 beginning, 15–16; 24.4; 27.2 (426 paragraph 2). Gewirth, *loc. cit.*, I, 81.

23. *Ibid.*, I. 6.3, 6; 15.21; 16. II. 11.4; 13.16, 23 end–24; 26.12 beginning.

24. *Ibid.*, I. 10.3–7. II. 5.6, 7 (154,

23–26 and 157, 28); 6.11–13; 8.8; 9.2–5; 10.3, 7, 9; 13.2 end.

25. *Ibid.*, I. 5.4, 7. II. 2.4 (3); 8.5; 9.11; 10.4, 9; 17.8 toward the end. Gewirth, *loc. cit.*, I, 284. See also above, pp. 174ff.

26. I. 19.10. II. 13.28; 17.2; 18.8 (paragraphs 1–2 and end); 19.1–3; 20.1–2; 21.11, 13; 22.6, 8, 10; 24.9, 12; 25.4–

6, 9, 15–18; 28.27; 30.8. *Defensor Minor*, chaps 7 and 12.

27. *Defender*, I. 17.10. II. 28.15.

28. *Ibid.*, I. 10.3–7; 12.2–3; 14.4; 15.6 end; 19.13. II. 8.3; 12.7–8.

29. *Ibid.*, I. 6–9; 11.3; 14.2, 6–7. Dante, *De Monarchia*, I. 14.

30. *Republic* 372e 6–7; *Guide of the Perplexed*, II. 40 and III. 27.

READINGS

A. Marsilius of Padua. *The Defender of the Peace*. Trans. with an introduction by Alan Gewirth. New York: Harper-Torch Books, 1967. Discourse I, chaps. i–xiii; Discourse II, chap. xii, secs. 3–12.

B. Marsilius of Padua. *The Defender of the Peace*. Discourse I, chaps xiv–xix; Discourse II, chaps viii, xii, secs 1, 2, 13–33, and xix.

NICCOLO MACHIAVELLI

1469–1527

Men often speak of virtue without using the word but saying instead "the quality of life" or "the great society" or "ethical" or even "square." But do we know what virtue is? Socrates arrived at the conclusion that it is the greatest good for a human being to make everyday speeches about virtue—apparently without ever finding a completely satisfactory definition of it. However, if we seek the most elaborate and least ambiguous answer to this truly vital question, we shall turn to Aristotle's *Ethics*. There we read among other things that there is a virtue of the first order called magnanimity—the habit of claiming high honors for oneself with the understanding that one is worthy of them. We also read there that sense of shame is not a virtue: sense of shame is becoming for the young who, due to their immaturity, cannot help making mistakes, but not for mature and well-bred men who simply always do the right and proper thing. Wonderful as all this is—we have received a very different message from a very different quarter. When the prophet Isaiah received his vocation, he was overpowered by the sense of his unworthiness: "I am a man of unclean lips amidst a people of unclean lips." This amounts to an implicit condemnation of magnanimity and an implicit vindication of the sense of shame. The reason is given in the context: "holy, holy, holy is the lord of hosts." There is no holy god for Aristotle and the Greeks generally. Who is right, the Greeks or the Jews? Athens or Jerusalem? And how to proceed in order to find out who is right? Must we not admit that human wisdom is unable to settle this question and that every answer is based on an act of faith? But does this not constitute the complete and final defeat of Athens? For a philosophy based on faith is no longer philosophy. Perhaps it was this unresolved conflict which has prevented Western thought from ever coming to rest. Perhaps it is this conflict which is at the bottom of a kind of thought which is philosophic indeed but no longer Greek: modern philosophy. It is in trying to understand modern philosophy that we come across Machiavelli.

Machiavelli is the only political thinker whose name has come into common use for designating a kind of politics, which exists and will continue to exist independently of his influence, a politics guided exclusively by considerations of expediency, which uses all means, fair or foul, iron or poison, for achieving its ends—its end being the aggrandizement of one's country or fatherland—but also using the fatherland in the service of the self-aggrandizement of the politician or statesman or one's party. But if this phenomenon is as old as political society itself, why is it called after Machiavelli who thought or wrote only a short while ago, about 500 years ago? Machiavelli was the first publicly to defend it in books with his name on the title pages. Machiavelli made it publicly defensible. This means that his achievement, detestable or admirable, cannot be understood in terms of politics itself, or of the history of politics—say, in terms of the Italian Renaissance—but only in terms of political thought, of political philosophy, of the history of political philosophy.

Machiavelli appears to have broken with all preceding political philosophers. There is weighty evidence in support of this view. Yet his largest political work ostensibly seeks to bring about the rebirth of the ancient Roman Republic; far from being a radical innovator, Machiavelli is a restorer of something old and forgotten.

To find our bearings let us first cast a glance at two post-Machiavellian thinkers, Hobbes and Spinoza. Hobbes regarded his political philosophy as wholly new. More than that, he denied that there existed prior to his work any political philosophy or political science worthy of the name. He regarded himself as the founder of the true political philosophy, as the true founder of political philosophy. He knew of course that a political doctrine claiming to be true had existed since Socrates. But this doctrine was, according to Hobbes, a dream rather than science. He considered Socrates and his successors to be anarchists in that they permitted an appeal from the law of the land, the positive law, to a higher law, the natural law; they thus fostered a disorder utterly incompatible with civil society. According to Hobbes, on the other hand, the higher law, the natural law, commands so to speak one and only one thing: unqualified obedience to the sovereign power. It would not be difficult to show that this line of reasoning is contradicted by Hobbes' own teaching; at any rate it does not go to the roots of the matter. Hobbes' serious objection to all earlier political philosophy comes out most clearly in this statement: "They that have written of justice and policy in general, do all invade each other and themselves, with contradiction. To reduce this doctrine to the rules and infallibility of reason, there is no way but first to put such principles down for a foundation, as passion not mistrusting may not seek to displace; and afterwards to build thereon the truth of cases in the law of nature (which hitherto had been built in the air) by degrees, till the whole be inexpugnable." The rationality of the political teaching consists in its being acceptable to passion, in its being agreeable to passion. The passion that must be the basis of the rational political teaching is fear of violent death. At first glance there seems to be an alternative to it, the passion of generosity, that is, "a glory, or pride in appearing not to need to break (one's word)"—but this "is a generosity too rarely found to be presumed on, especially in the pursuers of wealth, command or sensual pleasure; which are the greatest part of mankind." Hobbes attempts to build on the most common ground, on a ground that is admittedly low but has the advantage of being solid, whereas the traditional teaching was built on air. On this new basis, accordingly, the status of morality must be lowered; morality is nothing but fear-inspired peaceableness. The moral law or the natural law is understood as derivative from the right of nature, the right of self-preservation; the fundamental moral fact is a right, not a duty. This new spirit became the spirit of the modern era, including our own age. That spirit was preserved despite the important modifications that Hobbes' doctrine underwent at the hands of his great successors. Locke enlarged self-preservation to comfortable self-preservation and thus laid the theoretical foundation for the acquisitive society. Against the traditional view, according to which a just society is a society in which just men rule, Kant asserted: "Hard as it may sound, the problem of establishing the state [the just social order] is soluble even for a nation of devils, provided they have sense," that is, provided they are shrewd calculators. We discern this thought within the teachings of Marx, for the proletarians from whom he expects so much are surely not angels. Now although the revolution effected by Hobbes was decisively prepared by Machiavelli, Hobbes does not refer to Machiavelli. This fact requires further examination.

Hobbes is in a way a teacher of Spinoza. Nevertheless Spinoza opens his *Political Treatise* with an attack on *the* philosophers. The philosophers, he says, treat the passions as vices. By ridiculing or deploring the passions, they praise and evince their belief in a nonexistent human nature; they conceive of men not as they are but as they would wish them to be. Hence their political teaching is wholly useless. Quite different is the case of the *politici*. They have learned from experience that there will be vices as long as there are human beings. Hence their political teaching is very valuable, and Spinoza is building his teaching on theirs. The greatest of these *politici* is the most penetrating Florentine, Machiavelli. It is Machiavelli's more subdued attack on traditional political philosophy that Spinoza takes over bodily and translates into the less reserved language of Hobbes. As for the sentence, "There will be vices as long as there will be human beings," Spinoza has tacitly borrowed it from Tacitus; in Spinoza's mouth it amounts to an unqualified rejection of the belief in a Messianic age; the coming of the Messianic age would require divine intervention or a miracle, but according to Spinoza miracles are impossible.

Spinoza's introduction to his *Political Treatise* is obviously modeled on the 15th chapter of Machiavelli's *Prince*. There Machiavelli says:

Since I know that many have written (on how princes should rule), I fear that by writing about it I will be held to be presumptuous by departing, especially in discussing such a subject, from the others. But since it is my intention to write something useful for him who understands, it has seemed to me to be more appropriate to go straight to the effective truth of the matter rather than to the imagination thereof. For many have imagined republics and principalities that have never been seen nor are known truly to exist. There is so great a distance between how one lives and how one ought to live that he who rejects what people do in favor of what one ought to do, brings about his ruin rather than his preservation; for a man who wishes to do in every matter what is good, will be ruined among so many who are not good. Hence it is necessary for a prince who wishes to maintain himself, to learn to be able not to be good, or use goodness and abstain from using it according to the commands of circumstances.

One arrives at imagined kingdoms or republics if one takes one's bearings by how man ought to live, by virtue. The classical philosophers did just that. They thus arrived at the best regimes of the *Republic* and the *Politics*. But when speaking of imagined kingdoms, Machiavelli thinks not only of the philosophers; he also thinks of the kingdom of God which from his point of view is a conceit of visionaries for, as his pupil Spinoza said, justice rules only where just men rule. But to stay with the philosophers, they regarded the actualization of the best regime as possible, but extremely improbable. According to Plato its actualization literally depends on a coincidence, a most unlikely coincidence, the coincidence of philosophy and political power. The actualization of the best regime depends on chance, on *Fortuna,* that is, on something which is essentially beyond human control. According to Machiavelli, however, *Fortuna* is a woman who as such must be hit and beaten to be kept under; *Fortuna* can be vanquished by the right kind of man. There is a connection between this posture toward *Fortuna* and the orientation by how many do live: by lowering the standards of political excellence one guarantees the actualization of the only kind of political order that in principle is possible. In post-Machiavellian parlance: the ideal of the right kind necessarily becomes actual; the ideal and the actual necessarily converge. This way of thinking has had an amazing success; if someone maintains today that there is no guarantee for the actualization of the ideal, he must fear to be called a cynic.

Machiavelli is not concerned with how men do live merely in order to describe it; his intention is rather, on the basis of knowledge of how men do live, to teach princes how they ought to rule and even how they ought to live. Accordingly he rewrites, as it were, Aristotle's *Ethics*. To some extent he admits that the traditional teaching is true: men are obliged to live virtuously in the Aristotelian sense. But he denies that living virtuously is living happily or leads to happiness. "If liberality is used in the manner in which you are obliged to use it, it hurts you; for if you use it virtuously and as one ought to use it," the prince will ruin himself and will be compelled to rule his subjects oppressively in order to get the necessary money. Miserliness, the opposite of liberality, is "one of the vices that enable a prince to rule." A prince ought to be liberal, however, with the property of others, for this increases his reputation. Similar considerations apply to compassion and its opposite, cruelty. This leads Machiavelli to the question of whether it is better for a prince to be loved rather than to be feared or vice versa. It is difficult to be both loved and feared. Since one must therefore choose, one ought to choose being feared rather than being loved, for whether one is loved depends on others, while being feared depends on oneself. But one must avoid becoming hated; the prince will avoid becoming hated if he abstains from the property and the women of his subjects—especially from their property, which men so love that they resent less the murder of their father than the loss of their patrimony. In war the reputation for cruelty does not do any harm. The greatest example is Hannibal who was always implicitly obeyed by his soldiers and never had to contend with mutinies either after victories or after defeats. "This could not arise from anything but his inhuman cruelty which, together with his innumerable virtues, made him always venerable and terrible in the eyes of his soldiers, and without which cruelty his other virtues would not have sufficed. Not

very considerately do the writers on the one hand admire his action
and on the other condemn the main cause of the same." We note that
inhuman cruelty is one of Hannibal's virtues. Another example of
cruelty "well used" is supplied by Cesare Borgia's pacification of the
Romagna. In order to pacify that country, he put at its head Ramirro
d'Orco, "a man of cruelty and dispatch," and gave him the fullest
power. Ramirro succeeded in no time, acquiring the greatest reputation. But then Cesare thought that such an excessive power was no
longer necessary and might make him hated; he knew that the rigorous measures taken by Ramirro had caused some hatred. Cesare wished
therefore to show that if any cruelty had been committed, it was not
his doing but arose from the harsh nature of his subordinate. Therefore he had him put one morning in two pieces on the Piazza of the
chief town, with a piece of wood and a bloody knife at his side. The
ferocity of this sight induced in the populace a state of satisfaction and
stupor.

Machiavelli's new "ought" demands then the judicious and vigorous use of both virtue and vice according to the requirements of the
circumstances. The judicious alternation of virtue and vice is virtue
(*virtù*) in his meaning of the word. He amuses himself and, I believe,
some of his readers by using the word "virtue" in both the traditional
sense and his sense. Occasionally he makes a distinction between *virtù*
and *bontà*. That distinction was in a way prepared by Cicero who says
that men are called "good" on account of their modesty, temperance,
and above all, justice and keeping of faith, as distinguished from courage and wisdom. The Ciceronian distinction within the virtues in its
turn reminds us of Plato's *Republic* in which temperance and justice
are presented as virtues required of all, whereas courage and wisdom
are required only of some. Machiavelli's distinction between goodness
and other virtues tends to become an opposition between goodness and
virtue: while virtue is required of rulers and soldiers, goodness is required, or characteristic, of the populace engaged in peaceful occupations; goodness comes to mean something like fear-bred obedience to
the government, or even vileness.

In quite a few passages of the *Prince,* Machiavelli speaks of morality in the way in which decent men have spoken of it at all times. He
resolves the contradiction in the 19th chapter, in which he discusses the
Roman emperors who came after the philosopher-emperor Marcus
Aurelius up to Maximinus. The high point is his discussion of the
emperor Severus. Severus belonged to those emperors who were most
cruel and rapacious. Yet in him was so great virtue that he could
always reign with felicity, for he knew well how to use the person of

the fox and the lion—which natures a prince must imitate. A new prince in a new principality cannot imitate the actions of the good emperor Marcus Aurelius, nor is it necessary for him to follow those of Severus; but he ought to take from Severus those portions that are necessary for founding his state and from Marcus those that are appropriate and glorious for preserving a state already firmly established. The chief theme of the *Prince* is the wholly new prince in a wholly new state, that is, the founder. And the model for the founder as founder is the extremely clever criminal Severus. This means that justice is precisely not, as Augustine had said, the *fundamentum regnorum;* the foundation of justice is injustice; the foundation of morality is immorality; the foundation of legitimacy is illegitimacy or revolution; the foundation of freedom is tyranny. At the beginning there is Terror, not Harmony, or Love—but there is of course a great difference between Terror for its own sake, for the sake of its perpetuation, and Terror that limits itself to laying the foundation for the degree of humanity and freedom that is compatible with the human condition. But this distinction is at best hinted at in the *Prince*.

The comforting message of the *Prince* is given in the last chapter, which is an exhortation addressed to one Italian prince, Lorenzo de'-Medici, to take Italy and to liberate her from the barbarians, that is, the French, the Spaniards, and the Germans. Machiavelli tells Lorenzo that the liberation of Italy is not very difficult. One of the reasons he gives is that "extraordinary events without example that have been induced by God, are seen: the sea has divided itself, the cloud has led you on your way, the stone has poured out water, manna has rained." The events without example do have an example: the miracles following Israel's liberation from Egyptian bondage. What Machiavelli seems to suggest is that Italy is the promised land for Lorenzo. But there is one difficulty: Moses, who led Israel out of the house of bondage towards the promised land, did not reach that land; he died at its borders. Machiavelli thus darkly prophesied that Lorenzo would not liberate Italy, one reason being that he lacked the extraordinary *virtù* needed for bringing that great work to its consummation. But there is more to the extraordinary events without example of which nothing is known other than what Machiavelli asserts about them. All these extraordinary events occurred before the revelation on Sinai. What Machiavelli prophesies is, then, that a new revelation, a revelation of a new Decalogue is imminent. The bringer of that revelation is of course not that mediocrity Lorenzo, but a new Moses. That new Moses is Machiavelli himself, and the new Decalogue is the wholly new teaching on the wholly new prince in a wholly new state. It is true that

Moses was an armed prophet and that Machiavelli belongs to the unarmed ones who necessarily come to ruin. In order to find the solution
of this difficulty one must turn to the other great work of Machiavelli,
the *Discourses on the First Ten Books of Livy.*

Yet if one turns from the *Prince* to the *Discourses* in order to find
the solution to the difficulties not solved in the *Prince,* one goes from
the frying pan into the fire. For the *Discourses* is much more difficult
to understand than the *Prince.* It is impossible to show this without at
first inducing in the reader a certain bewilderment; but such bewilderment is the beginning of understanding.

Let us begin at the very beginning, the Epistles Dedicatory. The
Prince is dedicated to Machiavelli's master, Lorenzo de'Medici. Machiavelli who presents himself as a man of the lowest condition, as living
in a low place is so overwhelmed by his master's grandeur that he regards the *Prince,* although it is his most cherished possession, as unworthy of the presence of Lorenzo. He recommends his work by the
observation that it is a small volume which the addressee can understand in the shortest time, although it embodies everything that the
author has come to know and understand in very many years and
under great perils. The *Discourses* is dedicated to two young friends of
Machiavelli who have compelled him to write that book. At the same
time the book is a token of Machiavelli's gratitude for the benefits he
has received from his two friends. He had dedicated the *Prince* to his
master in the hope that he would receive favors from him. And he
does not know whether Lorenzo will pay any attention to the *Prince*—
whether he would not be more pleased with receiving a horse of exceptional beauty. In accordance with all this he disparages in the
Epistle Dedicatory to the *Discourses* the custom that he had complied
with in the Epistle Dedicatory to the *Prince*—the custom of dedicating
one's works to princes: the *Discourses* is dedicated not to princes but to
men who deserve to be princes. Whether Lorenzo deserves to be a
prince remains a question.

These differences between the two books can be illustrated by the
fact that in the *Prince* Machiavelli avoids certain terms that he uses in
the *Discourses.* The *Prince* fails to mention the conscience, the common good, tyrants (that is, the distinction between kings and tyrants),
and heaven; also in the *Prince* "we" never means "we Christians." One
might mention here that Machiavelli refers in neither work to the distinction between this world and the next, or between this life and the
next; nor does he mention in either work the devil or hell; above all,
he never mentions in either work the soul.

Now let us come to the text of the *Discourses.* What is the *Dis-*

courses about? What kind of book is it? There is no such difficulty regarding the *Prince*. The *Prince* is a mirror of princes, and mirrors of
princes were a traditional genre. In accordance with this, all chapter
headings of the *Prince* are in Latin. This is not to deny but rather to
underline the fact that the *Prince* transmits a revolutionary teaching in
a traditional guise. But this traditional guise is missing in the *Discourses*. None of its chapter headings is in Latin although the work
deals with an ancient and traditional subject: with ancient Rome.
Furthermore, the *Prince* is tolerably easy to understand because it has a
tolerably clear plan. The plan of the *Discourses,* however, is extremely
obscure, so much so that one is tempted to wonder whether it has any
plan. In addition, the *Discourses* presents itself as devoted to the first
ten books of Livy. Livy's first ten books lead from the beginnings of
Rome to the time immediately preceding the first Punic war, that is,
up to the peak of the uncorrupted Roman Republic, and prior to
Roman conquests outside of the Italian mainland. But Machiavelli
deals in the *Discourses* to some extent with the whole of Roman history as covered by Livy's work: Livy's work consists of 142 books and
the *Discourses* consists of 142 chapters. Livy's work leads up to the time
of the emperor Augustus, that is, the beginnings of Christianity. At
any rate, the *Discourses,* more than four times as extensive as the
Prince, seems to be much more comprehensive than the *Prince*. Machiavelli explicitly excludes only one subject from treatment in the *Discourses:* "How dangerous it is to make oneself the head of a new thing
that concerns many, and how difficult it is to handle it and to consummate it and after its consummation to maintain it would be too long
and exalted a matter to discuss; I shall reserve it therefore for a more
appropriate place." Yet it is precisely this long and exalted matter that
Machiavelli explicitly discusses in the *Prince:* "One must consider that
nothing is more difficult to handle, nor more doubtful of success, nor
more dangerous to manage than to make oneself the head of the introduction of new orders." It is true that Machiavelli does not speak here
of "maintaining." Such maintaining, as we learn from the *Discourses,*
is best done by the people, while the introduction of new modes and
orders is best done by princes. From this one may draw the conclusion
that the characteristic subject of the *Discourses,* as distinguished from
the *Prince,* is the people—a conclusion by no means absurd but quite
insufficient for one's even beginning to understand the work.

The character of the *Discourses* may be further illustrated with
two examples of another kind of difficulty. In II 13, Machiavelli asserts
and in a manner proves that one rises from a low or abject position to
an exalted one through fraud rather than through force. This is what

the Roman Republic did in its beginnings. Before speaking of the
Roman Republic, however, Machiavelli speaks of four princes who
rose from a low or abject position to a high one. He speaks most extensively of Cyrus, the founder of the Persian empire. The example of
Cyrus is the central one. Cyrus rose to power by deceiving the king of
Media, his uncle. But if he was, to begin with, the nephew of the king
of Media, how can he be said to have risen from a low or abject position? To drive home his point, Machiavelli mentions next Giovan
Galeazzo who through fraud took away the state and the power from
Bernabò, his uncle. Galeazzo too was then to begin with the nephew
of a ruling prince and cannot be said to have risen from a low or
abject position. What, then, does Machiavelli indicate by speaking in
such a riddling way? III 48: when one sees an enemy commit a great
mistake, one must believe that there is fraud beneath; this is said in the
heading of the chapter; in the text Machiavelli goes further and says
"there will always be fraud beneath it." Yet immediately afterward, in
the central example, Machiavelli shows that the Romans once committed a great mistake through demoralization, that is, not fraudu-
lently.

How is one to deal with the difficulties that confront us in the *Discourses?* Let us return to the title: Discourses on the First Ten Books
of Livy. The title is not literally correct but it is safe to say that the
work consists primarily of Discourses on the First Ten Books of Livy.
We have noted furthermore that the *Discourses* lacks a clear plan: perhaps the plan will become visible if we take seriously the fact that the
work is devoted to Livy; perhaps Machiavelli follows Livy by following
the Livian order. Again this is not simply true, but it is true if it is in-
telligently understood: Machiavelli's use and nonuse of Livy is the key
to the understanding of the work. There are various ways in which
Machiavelli uses Livy: sometimes he makes tacit use of a Livian story,
sometimes he refers to "this text," sometimes he mentions Livy by
name, sometimes he quotes him (in Latin) not mentioning or mentioning his name. Machiavelli's use of and nonuse of Livy may be
illustrated by the facts that he does not quote Livy in the first ten
chapters, that he quotes him in the following five chapters and again
fails to quote him in the following 24 chapters. Understanding the
reasons behind these facts is the key to the understanding of the *Discourses.*

I cannot treat this matter conclusively within the space at my disposal, but will deal with it through a selection of the following five
chapters or quasi-chapters: I proem, II proem, II 1, I 26 and II 5.

In the proem to I, Machiavelli lets us know that he has discovered

new modes and orders, that he has taken a road that was never trod-
den by anyone before. He compares his achievement to the discovery
of unknown waters and lands: he presents himself as the Columbus of
the moral-political world. What prompted him was the natural desire
that he always had, to do those things that in his opinion bring about
the common benefit of each. Therefore he bravely faces the dangers
that he knows lie in wait for him. What are these dangers? In the case
of the discovery of unknown seas and lands, the danger consists in
seeking them; once you have found the unknown lands and have returned home, you are safe. In the case of the discovery of new modes
and orders, however, the danger consists in finding them, that is, in
making them publicly known. For, as we have heard from Machiavelli, it is dangerous to make oneself the head of something new which
affects many.

To our great surprise, Machiavelli identifies immediately afterwards the new modes and orders with those of antiquity: his discovery
is only a rediscovery. He refers to the contemporary concern with fragments of ancient statues, which are held in high honor and used as
models by contemporary sculptors. It is all the more surprising that no
one thinks of imitating the most virtuous actions of ancient kingdoms
and republics, with the deplorable result that no trace of ancient
virtue remains. The present-day lawyers learn their craft from the ancient lawyers. The present-day physicians base their judgements on the
experience of the ancient physicians. It is therefore all the more surprising that in political and military matters the present-day princes
and republics do not have recourse to the examples of the ancients.
This results not so much from the weakness into which the present-
day religion has led the world or from the evil that ambitious leisure
has done to many Christian countries and cities, as from insufficient
understanding of the histories and especially that of Livy. As a consequence, Machiavelli's contemporaries believe that the imitation of the
ancients is not only difficult but impossible. Yet this is plainly absurd:
the natural order, including the nature of man, is the same as in antiquity.

We understand now why the discovery of new modes and orders,
which is only the rediscovery of the ancient modes and orders, is
dangerous. That rediscovery which leads up to the demands that the
virtue of the ancients be imitated by present-day men, runs counter to
the present-day religion: it is that religion which teaches that the
imitation of ancient virtue is impossible, that it is morally impossible, for the virtues of the pagans are only resplendent vices. What
Machiavelli will have to achieve in the *Discourses* is not merely the

presentation, but the re-habilitation, of ancient virtue against the Christian critique. This does not dispose of the difficulty that the discovery of new modes and orders is only the re-discovery of the ancient modes and orders.

This much, however, is clear. Machiavelli cannot take for granted the superiority of the ancients; he must establish it. Therefore he must first find a ground common to the admirers and the detractors of antiquity. That common ground is the veneration of the ancient, be it biblical or pagan. He starts from the tacit premise that the good is the old and hence that the best is the oldest. He is thus led first to ancient Egypt, which flourished in the most ancient antiquity. But this does not help very much because too little is known of ancient Egypt. Machiavelli settles, therefore, for that oldest which is sufficiently known and at the same time his own: ancient Rome. Yet ancient Rome is not evidently admirable in every important respect. A strong case can be made, and had been made, for the superiority of Sparta to Rome. Machiavelli must therefore establish the authority of ancient Rome. The general manner in which he does this reminds one of the manner in which theologians formerly established the authority of the Bible against unbelievers. But ancient Rome is not a book like the Bible. Yet by establishing the authority of ancient Rome, Machiavelli establishes the authority of its chief historian, of Livy, and therewith of the book. Livy's history is Machiavelli's Bible. From this it follows that Machiavelli cannot begin to use Livy before he has established the authority of Rome.

He begins to quote Livy in the section on the Roman religion (I 11–15). In the preceding chapter he had contrasted Caesar as the founder of a tyranny with Romulus as the founder of a free city. The glory of Caesar is due to the writers who celebrated him because their judgement was corrupted by his extraordinary success, the foundation of the rule of the emperors; the emperors did not permit writers to speak freely of Caesar. Yet the free writers knew how to circumvent that restriction: they blamed Catilina, Caesar's luckless prefiguration, and they celebrated Brutus, Caesar's enemy. But not all emperors were bad. The times of the emperors from Nerva to Marcus Aurelius were the golden times when everyone could hold and defend any opinion he pleased: golden are the times when thought and expression of thought are not restricted by authority. Those remarks form in effect the introduction to Machiavelli's treatment of the Roman religion. He there treats the pagan religion as at least equal as religion to the biblical religion. The principle of all religion is authority, that is, precisely that which Machiavelli had questioned immediately before. But for the ruling class of ancient Rome, religion was not an authority; they used religion for their political purposes, and they did this in the most admirable manner. The praise of the religion of ancient Rome implies, and more than implies a critique of the religion of modern Rome. Machiavelli praises the religion of ancient Rome for the same reason for which the free writers who were subject to the authority of the Caesars praised Brutus: he could not openly blame the authority of Christianity to which he was subject. Hence if Livy's history is Machiavelli's Bible, it is his anti-Bible.

After he has established the authority of ancient Rome and shown its superiority to the moderns by many examples, he begins to intimate the defects from which it suffered. Only from this point on is Livy, as distinguished from Rome—that is, a book—his sole authority. Yet shortly before the end of Book One, he openly questions the opinion of all writers, including Livy, on a matter of the greatest importance. He thus leads us step by step to the realization of why the old modes and orders which he has rediscovered, are new: 1) The modes and orders of ancient Rome were established under the pressure of circumstances, by trial and error, without a coherent plan, without understanding of their reasons; Machiavelli supplies the reasons and is therefore able to correct some of the old modes and orders. 2) The spirit that animated the old modes and orders was veneration for tradition, for authority, the spirit of piety, while Machiavelli is animated by an altogether different spirit. The progress of the argument in Book One is indicated most clearly. While Book One begins with the highest praise of the most ancient antiquity, it ends with the expression "very young": many Romans celebrated their triumphs *giovanissimi*.

We are thus prepared for understanding the proem of Book Two. There Machiavelli openly questions the prejudice in favor of the ancient times: "men praise always the ancient times and accuse the present, but not always with reason." In truth the world has always been the same; the quantity of good and evil is always the same. What changes is the different countries and nations, which have times of virtue and times of degeneracy. In antiquity virtue resided at first in Assyria and finally in Rome. After the destruction of the Roman Empire virtue revived only in some parts of it, especially in Turkey. So that someone born in our time in Greece who has not become a Turk reasonably blames the present and praises antiquity. Accordingly, Machiavelli is perfectly justified in praising the times of the ancient Romans and blaming his own time: no trace of ancient virtue is left in Rome and in Italy. Therefore he exhorts the young to imitate the ancient Romans whenever fortune gives them the opportunity to do so, that is, to do what he was prevented from doing by the malignity of the times and of fortune.

The message of the proem to Book Two could seem to be rather meager, at least as compared with that of the proem to Book One. This is due to the fact that the proem to Book One is the introduction to the whole work, while the proem to Book Two is the introduction only to Book Two and more particularly to the early chapters of Book Two. There Machiavelli first takes issue with an opinion of Plutarch, whom he calls a weighty author—he never applies this epithet to Livy —an opinion also shared by Livy and even by the Roman people themselves: the opinion that the Romans acquired their empire through fortune rather than through virtue. Prior to the Roman conquest, the whole of Europe was inhabited by three peoples who defended their freedom obstinately and who governed themselves freely, that is, as republics. Hence Rome needed excessive virtue to conquer them. How then does it come about that in those ancient times those peoples were greater lovers of freedom than they are today? According to Machiavelli, this is ultimately due to the difference between the ancient religion and our religion. Our religion has placed the highest good in humility, abjectness, and the disparagement of the human things, whereas the ancient religion has placed the highest good in greatness of mind, strength of the body, and in all other things apt to make men most strong. But the disarmament of the world and of heaven itself is ultimately due to the destruction of the Roman Empire, of all republican life. Apart from her excessive virtue, the second reason for Rome's greatness was her liberal admission of foreigners to citizenship. But such a policy exposes a state to great dangers, as the Athenians and especially the Spartans knew who feared that the admixture of new inhabitants would corrupt the ancient customs. Owing to the Roman policy, many men who never knew republican life and did not care for it, that is, many orientals, became Roman citizens. The Roman conquest of the East thus completed what her conquest of the West had begun. And thus it came about that the Roman Republic was, on the one hand, the direct opposite of the Christian republic, and, on the other hand, the cause of the Christian republic and even the model for it.

Book Three has no proem but its first chapter performs the function of a proem. By this slight irregularity Machiavelli underlines the fact that the number of chapters of the *Discourses* equals the number of books of Livy's history, and Livy's history, as we noted before, extends from the origin of Rome until the time of the emergence of Christianity. The heading of the first chapter of Book Three reads as follows: "If one wishes that a sect or a republic live long, one must bring it back frequently to its beginning." While the heading speaks only of sects and republics, the chapter itself deals with republics, sects, and kingdoms; sects, that is, religions, occupy the center. All things of the world have a limit to their course—a limit set by heaven. But they reach that limit only if they are kept in order, and this means if they are frequently brought back to their beginnings; for in their beginnings they must have had some goodness, otherwise they would not have gained their first reputation and increase. Machiavelli proves his thesis first regarding republics, by the example of Rome's regaining new life and new virtue after her defeat by the Gauls: Rome then resumed the observance of religion and justice, that is, of the old orders, especially those of religion, through the neglect of which she had suffered disaster. The recovery of ancient virtue consists of the reimposition of the terror and fear that had made men good at the beginning. Machiavelli thus explains what his concern with the recovery of ancient modes and orders means fundamentally: men were good at the beginning, not because of innocence but because they were gripped by terror and fear—by the initial and radical terror and fear; at the beginning there is not Love but Terror; Machiavelli's wholly new teaching is based on this alleged insight (which anticipates Hobbes' doctrine of the state of nature). Machiavelli turns then to the discussion of sects; he illustrates his thesis by the example of "our religion": "If our religion had not been brought back to its beginning or principle by St. Francis and St. Dominic, it would have become completely extinguished, for by poverty and the example of Christ they brought that religion back into the minds of men where it was already extinguished; and these new orders were so potent that they are the reason why the immorality of the prelates and of the heads of the religion do not ruin our religion; for the Franciscans and the Dominicans live still in poverty and have so great credit with the peoples through confession and preachings that they convince the peoples that it is evil to speak evil of evil and that it is good to live in obedience to the prelates, and if the prelates sin, to leave them for punishment to God. Thus the prelates do the worst they can, for they do not fear the punishment that they do not see and in which they do not believe. That innovation therefore has maintained, and maintains, that religion." Here the return to the beginning was achieved by the introduction of new orders. Machiavelli doubtless says this here because he did not think that the Franciscan and Dominican reforms amounted to a simple restoration of primitive Christianity, for those reforms left intact the Christian hierarchy. But the introduction of new orders is necessary also in republics, as Machiavelli emphasizes in the concluding chapter of the *Discourses:* the restoration of the ancient modes and orders is in all cases, including that of Machiavelli himself, the introduction of new modes and orders. Nevertheless there is a great difference between the Franciscan and Dominican renovation and republican renovations: republican renovations subject the whole republic, including the leading man, to the initial terror and fear precisely because they resist evil—because they punish evil visibly and hence credibly. The Christian command or counsel not to resist evil is based on the premise that the beginning or principle is love. That command or counsel can only lead to the utmost disorder or else to evasion. The premise, however, turns into its extreme opposite.

We have seen that the number of chapters of the *Discourses* is meaningful and has been deliberately chosen. We may thus be induced to wonder whether the number of chapters of the *Prince* is not also meaningful. The *Prince* consists of 26 chapters. Twenty-six is the numerical value of the letters of the sacred name of God in Hebrew, of the Tetragrammaton. But did Machiavelli know of this? I do not know. Twenty-six equals 2 times 13. Thirteen is now and for quite sometime has been considered an unlucky number, but in former times it was also and even primarily considered a lucky number. So "twice 13" might mean both good luck and bad luck, and hence altogether: luck, *fortuna*. A case can be made for the view that Machiavelli's theology can be expressed by the formula *Deus sive fortuna* (as distinguished from Spinoza's *Deus sive natura*)—that is, that God is fortuna as supposed to be subject to human influence (imprecation). But to establish this would require an argument "too long and too exalted" for the present occasion. Let us therefore see whether we cannot get some help from looking at the 26th chapter of the *Discourses*. The heading of the chapter reads as follows: "A new prince, in a city or country taken by him, must make everything new." The subject of the chapter is then the new prince in a new state, that is, the most exalted subject of the *Prince*. At the end of the preceding chapter Machiavelli had said: he who wishes to establish an absolute power, which the writers call tyranny, must renew everything. The subject of our chapter is then tyranny, but the term "tyranny" never occurs in that chapter: "tyranny" is avoided in the 26th chapter of the *Discourses* just as it is avoided in the *Prince,* which consists of 26 chapters. The lesson of the chapter itself is this: a new prince who wishes to establish absolute power in his state must make everything new; he must establish new magistracies, with new names, new authorities and new men; he must make the rich poor and the poor rich, as David did when he became king: *qui esurientes implevit bonis, et divites dimisit inanes.* In sum, he must not leave anything in his country untouched, and there must not be any rank or wealth that its possessors do not recognize as owing to the prince. The modes that he must use are most cruel and inimical, not only to every Christian life, but even to every humane one; so that everyone must prefer to live as a private man rather than as a king with so great a ruin of human beings." The Latin quotation that occurs in this chapter is translated in the Revised Version as follows: "He hath filled the hungry with good things; and the rich he hath sent empty away." The quotation forms part of the Magnificat, the Virgin Mary's prayer of thanks after she had heard from the angel Gabriel that she would bring forth a son to be called Jesus; he that "hath filled the hungry with good things, and sent the rich empty away" is none other than God himself. In the context of this chapter this means that God is a tyrant, and that king David who made the rich poor and the poor rich, was a Godly king, a king who walked in the ways of the Lord because he proceeded in the tyrannical way. We must note that this is the sole New Testament quotation occurring in the *Discourses* or in the *Prince*. And that sole New Testament quotation is used for expressing a most horrible blasphemy. Someone might say in defense of Machiavelli that the blasphemy is not expressly uttered but only implied. But this defense, far from helping Machiavelli, makes his case worse, and for this reason: When a man openly utters or vomits a blasphemy, all good men shudder and turn away from him, or punish him according to his deserts; the sin is entirely his. But a concealed blasphemy is so insidious, not only because it protects the blasphemer against punishment by due process of law, but above all because it practically compels the hearer or reader to think the blasphemy by himself and thus to become an accomplice of the blasphemer. Machiavelli thus establishes a kind of intimacy with his readers par excellence, whom he calls "the young," by inducing them to think forbidden or criminal thoughts. Such an intimacy seems also to be established by every prosecutor or judge who, in order to convict the criminal, must think criminal thoughts, but that intimacy is abhorred by the criminal. Machiavelli, how-

ever, intends it and desires it. This is an important part of his
education of the young or, to use the time-honored expression, of
his corruption of the young.

If space permitted it, we might profitably consider the other
chapters of the *Discourses* whose numbers are multiples of 13. I
shall consider only one of them: Book Two, chapter 5. The heading of this chapter runs as follows: "That the change of sects and
languages together with floods and plagues destroys the memory
of things." Machiavelli begins this chapter by taking issue with
certain philosophers by stating an objection to their contention. The
philosophers in question say that the world is eternal. Machiavelli
"believes" that one could reply to them as follows: if the world
were as old as they contend, it would be reasonable that there would
be memory of more than 5,000 years (that is, the memory we have
thanks to the Bible). Machiavelli opposes Aristotle in the name
of the Bible. But he continues: one could make that rejoinder if one
did not see that the memories of times are destroyed by various
causes, partly originated in human beings, partly originated in heaven.
Machiavelli refuted then an alleged refutation of Aristotle, of the
best-known anti-biblical argument of the Aristotelians. He continues
as follows: the causes originating in human beings are the changes
of sects and of language. For when a new sect, that is, a new
religion arises, its first concern is, in order to acquire reputation,
to extinguish the old religion; and when those who establish the
orders of the new sects are of a different language, they destroy
the old sect easily. One realizes this by considering the procedure
used by the Christian sect against the gentile sect; the former has
ruined all orders, all ceremonies of the latter, and destroyed every
memory of that ancient theology. It is true that it has not succeeded
in completely destroying the knowledge of the things done by the
excellent men among the gentiles and this was due to the fact
that it preserved the Latin language, which the Christians were
forced to use in writing their new law. For had they been able to
write that law in a new language, there would be no record whatever of the things of the past. One has only to read of the proceedings of St. Gregory and the other heads of the Christian religion
in order to see with how great an obstinacy they persecuted all
ancient memories by burning the works of the poets and of the
historians, by ruining the images and spoiling every other sign
of antiquity; if they had joined to that persecution a new language,
everything would have been forgotten in the shortest time. Through

these extraordinary overstatements Machiavelli sketches the background of his own work, in particular of his recovery of his
cherished Livy, the largest part of whose history has been lost
owing to "the malignity of the times" (I 2). Furthermore, he here
silently contrasts the conduct of the Christians with that of the
Muslims whose new law was written in a new language. The
difference between the Christians and the Muslims is not that the
Christians had a greater respect for pagan antiquity than the Muslims,
but that the Christians did not conquer the Western Roman empire
as the Muslims conquered the Eastern, and were therefore forced
to adopt the Latin language and therefore to some extent to preserve
the literature of pagan Rome, and thereby preserve their mortal
enemy. Shortly thereafter Machiavelli says that these sects change
two or three times in 5,000 or 6,000 years. He thus determines the
life span of Christianity; the maximum would be 3,000 years, the
minimum 1,666 years. This means that Christianity might come to
an end about 150 years after the *Discourses* were written. Machiavelli
was not the first to engage in speculations of this kind (cf. Gemistos
Plethon who was much more sanguine or apprehensive than
Machiavelli).

The most important point, however, that Machiavelli makes
through this statement is that all religions, including Christianity,
are of human, not heavenly origin. The changes of heavenly origin
that destroy the memory of things are plagues, hunger, and floods:
the heavenly is the natural; the supra-natural is human.

The substance of what Machiavelli says or suggests regarding
religion is not original. As is indicated by his use of the term "sect"
for religion, he goes in the ways of Averroism, that is, of those
medieval Aristotelians who as philosophers refused to make any
concessions to revealed religion. While the substance of Machiavelli's
religious teaching is not original, his manner of setting it forth is
very ingenious. He recognizes in fact no theology but civil theology,
theology serving the state and to be used or not used by the state,
as circumstances suggest. He indicates that religions can be dispensed
with if there is a strong and able monarch. This implies indeed that
religion is indispensable in republics.

The moral-political teaching of the *Discourses* is fundamentally
the same as that of the *Prince* but with one important difference:
the *Discourses* state powerfully the case for republics while also
instructing potential tyrants in how to destroy republican life. Yet
there can hardly be any doubt that Machiavelli preferred republics
to monarchies, tyrannical or nontyrannical. He loathed oppression

which is not in the service of the well-being of the people and hence of effective government, especially of impartial and unsqueamish punitive justice. He was a generous man, while knowing very well that what passes for generosity in political life is most of the time nothing but shrewd calculation, which as such deserves to be commended. In the *Discourses* he has expressed his preference most clearly by his praise of M. Furius Camillus. Camillus had been highly praised by Livy as the second Romulus, the second founder of Rome, a most conscientious practitioner of religious observances; he even speaks of him as the greatest of all *imperatores* but he probably means by this the greatest of all commanders up to Camillus' time. Machiavelli, however, calls Camillus "the most prudent of all Roman captains"; he praises him for both his "goodness" and his "virtue," his humanity and integrity, as good and wise—in a word, as a most excellent man. He has in mind particularly his equanimity, the fact that he had the same state of mind in good and in evil fortune, when he saved Rome from the Gauls and thus earned immortal glory and when he was condemned to exile. Machiavelli traces Camillus' superiority to the whims of fortune to his superior knowledge of the world. In spite of his extraordinary merits Camillus was condemned to exile. Why he was so condemned, Machiavelli discusses in a special chapter (III 23). On the basis of Livy he enumerates three reasons. But, if I am not mistaken, Livy never mentions these three reasons together as causes of Camillus' exile. In fact Machiavelli follows here not Livy but Plutarch. But he makes this characteristic change: he assigns the central place to the fact that in his triumph Camillus had his triumphal chariot drawn by four white horses; therefore the people said that through pride he had wished to equal the sun-god or, as Plutarch has it, Jupiter (Livy says: Jupiter et sol). I believe that this rather shocking act of *superbia* was in Machiavelli's eyes a sign of Camillus' magnanimity.

Camillus' very pride shows, as Machiavelli surely knew, that there is a greatness beyond Camillus' greatness. After all, Camillus was not a founder or discoverer of new modes and orders. To state this somewhat differently, Camillus was a Roman of the highest dignity and, as Machiavelli has shown most obviously by his comedy *La Mandragola,* human life requires also levity. He there praises Magnifico Lorenzo de'Medici for having combined gravity and levity in a quasi-impossible combination—a combination that Machiavelli regarded as commendable because in changing from gravity to levity or vice versa, one imitates nature, which is changeable.

One cannot help wondering how one ought to judge reasonably

of Machiavelli's teaching as a whole. The simplest way to answer this question would seem to be the following. The writer to whom Machiavelli refers and deferred most frequently, with the obvious exception of Livy, is Xenophon. But he refers to only two of Xenophon's writings: *The Education of Cyrus* and the *Hiero;* he takes no notice of Xenophon's Socratic writings, that is, of the other pole of Xenophon's moral universe: Socrates. Half of Xenophon, in Xenophon's view the better half, is suppressed by Machiavelli. One can safely say that there is no moral or political phenomenon that Machiavelli knew or for whose discovery he is famous that was not perfectly known to Xenophon, to say nothing of Plato or Aristotle. It is true that in Machiavelli everything appears in a new light, but this is due, not to an enlargement of the horizon, but to a narrowing of it. Many modern discoveries regarding man have this character.

Machiavelli has often been compared with the Sophists. Machiavelli says nothing of the Sophists or of the men commonly known as Sophists. Yet he says something on this subject, if indirectly, in his *Life of Castruccio Castracani,* a very charming little work, containing an idealized description of a fourteenth century condottiere or tyrant. At the end of that work he records a number of witty sayings said or listened to by Castruccio. Almost all those sayings have been borrowed by Machiavelli from Diogenes Laertius' *Lives of the Famous Philosophers.* Machiavelli changes the sayings in some cases in order to make them suitable to Castruccio. In Diogenes, an ancient philosopher is recorded as having said that he would wish to die like Socrates; Machiavelli makes this Castruccio's saying, yet he would wish to die like Caesar. Most of the sayings recorded in the *Castruccio* stem from Aristippus and Diogenes the Cynic. The references to Aristippus and Diogenes—men not classified as Sophists—could profitably guide us if we are interested in the question of what scholars call Machiavelli's "sources."

Toward the end of the *Nicomachean Ethics* Aristotle speaks of what one may call the political philosophy of the Sophists. His chief point is that the Sophists identified or almost identified politics with rhetoric. In other words, the Sophists believed or tended to believe in the omnipotence of speech. Machiavelli surely cannot be accused of that error. Xenophon speaks of his friend Proxenos, who commanded a contingent in Cyrus's expedition against the king of Persia and who was a pupil of the most famous rhetorician, Gorgias. Xenophon says that Proxenos was an honest man and capable to command gentlemen but could not fill his soldiers with

fear of him; he was unable to punish those who were not gentlemen or even to rebuke them. But Xenophon, who was a pupil of
Socrates, proved to be a most successful commander precisely because
he could manage both gentlemen and nongentlemen. Xenophon,
the pupil of Socrates, was under no delusion about the sternness
and harshness of politics, about that ingredient of politics which
transcends speech. In this important respect Machiavelli and Socrates
make a common front against the Sophists.

READINGS

A. Machiavelli, Niccolo. *The Prince.*
B. Machiavelli, Niccolo. *Discourses on the First Ten Books of Titus Livius.*

MARTIN LUTHER

1483–1546

JOHN CALVIN

1509–1564

The great Reformers Martin Luther and John Calvin thought of themselves not as philosophers or politicians, but first and last as theologians and students of the Word of God. Accordingly, we should not expect to find them presenting a comprehensive political philosophy or a general theory of politics, for they did not see this as the task to which they were called. But the Reformation of the Church demanded the formulation of a general *theological* position, and this inevitably included some central affirmations about politics and political philosophy. And, willy-nilly, both Reformers were called upon to give much concrete political advice in practical situations and even to involve themselves in political activity in which their political opinions were elaborated and put to the test. They see their political affirmations as flowing directly from their theological premises and as derived from the same source, Holy Scripture. Their political teaching can only be understood properly in the light of their theology, for it was never meant to be viewed in isolation.

Their prime concern with politics is to define its proper sphere and place this in relation to its context. But it is impossible to mark out the frontier between theology and political philosophy without saying a great deal about both; and although Luther and Calvin take biblical theology as their standpoint, inevitably they are involved in saying much about the nature and function of politics. They discuss such subjects as the place of secular government in relation to God's scheme of salvation; the connection between sin and temporal authority; the relationships of divine law, natural law, and positive law; the multitudinous implications of the Christian doctrine of man; Church and State; the limits of political power; the mutual duties of ruler and subjects; and so on. In short, most of the great questions of political philosophy are at least touched upon, if only sometimes to show which tools—reason, tradition, experience, conscience, or Holy Scripture—are appropriate to the treatment of a particular problem.

Luther and Calvin are at opposite poles as far as mood and expression are concerned. Luther is flamboyant, vivid, impulsive, immensely readable, frequently exaggerating his true position or contradicting what he said elsewhere in order to put over a point forcefully. He wrote no one comprehensive exposition of his theology, and his political teaching must be culled from "tracts for the times," theological treatises, commentaries, sermons, and even hymns. In spite of some glaring surface contradictions and exaggerations, there is a profound underlying unity and coherence in his thought; his theology of politics is very carefully worked out and is, on the whole, consistent even if sometimes misleadingly articulated. Calvin is more restrained, dry, lucid, and systematic in his writing. His *Institutes of the Christian Religion,* first written when he was only twenty-five, but revised and expanded in successive editions up to 1559, is one of the greatest and most influential works of systematic theology of all time. In its final form it is the definitive statement of his theology, although much detail may be added from his voluminous sermons, lectures, commentaries, and correspondence.

In spite of certain significant theological and political differences, Luther and Calvin have broad general agreement. They accept the same authorities, adopt much the same method, and the structure and most of the conclusions of their thought are sufficiently similar to entitle us to treat them together, pointing out differences as they occur.

A. The Basis of a Theology of Politics
1. Justification by Faith

The root and core of all reformed theology is the doctrine of justification by faith alone. All that is distinctive in the teaching of Luther and the Reformation may be traced back to a conviction of the radical perversity of man and his total alienation from God because of the immensity of his sin, together with a rejection of the currently accepted solutions to the problem of forgiveness and reconciliation. The Reformers went far beyond mere denunciation of the more obvious abuses of the indulgence system, and denied the very terms in which the problem of sin and redemption was being posed in the Roman Church.

Both Luther and Calvin believe in the total depravity of man. By this they do not mean that nothing that man can do can possibly be "good" in the generally accepted sense of the term, but rather that even what are, in the eyes of men, "good works" are pathetically and totally inadequate when measured against the standard of the righteousness which God requires of His servants. The evil that we do is the normal expression of our corrupted human nature and our own responsibility; but any good that we may do is God working through us, a gift of God's free grace for which we cannot claim merit. It is ridiculous to think of pleading our good works before Almighty God because they are hopelessly trivial in view of the condemnation of our sin which divine justice demands; they themselves are, without exception, stained with our corruption and wickedness; and besides, in so far as they are good, the goodness is God's and not our own. All men stand equally under the condemnation of God. "Even saints," wrote Calvin, "cannot perform one work which, if judged on its merits, is not deserving of condemnation." [1] Forgiveness and peace with God cannot be won or earned by anything man can do for himself.

The Reformers break with the medieval tradition not only in their more radical statement of the problem of sin and man's fallen condition, but also in the solution they present. We are justified before God, they claimed, not by works, or by the merits of the saints dispensed through indulgences, but *sola fide,* by faith alone. And faith is a gift of God, not something that man can create for himself. This does not mean simply that man must accept certain doctrinal statements, but rather that his only resource when faced by the judgment of God is to admit his total helplessness and the complete justice of the condemnation passed on him, and then, laying all his sin on Christ and relying on His work, to approach the throne of Grace clothed in the "alien holiness" [2] of Christ Himself. Our justification is an unmerited, gratuitous gift, to which any achievements of our own are simply irrelevant. The only righteousness of men which does not dissolve in the presence of God is the "passive righteousness" which is freely given with faith by God.

2. *The Authority of Scripture*

In arguing thus, Luther and Calvin find themselves returning to the teaching of St. Paul and St. Augustine and rejecting virtually the whole of medieval theology as Pelagian, that is, believing that man can in some sense earn his salvation by his own efforts. This break with scholasticism on the issue of justification is the starting point of Reformed theological thought. Luther is diverging from the whole medieval theological tradition when, as early as 1517, he can write: "It is false to state that the will can by nature conform to correct precept. . . . One must concede that the will is not free to strive towards whatever is declared good. . . . Man is by nature unable to want God to be God. Indeed, he himself wants to be God, and does not want God to be God." [3]

This leads him directly to the more academic issue: "Virtually the whole *Ethics* of Aristotle is the worst enemy of Grace. . . . No syllogistic form is valid when applied to divine terms. . . . The whole Aristotle is to theology as darkness to light." [4]

The failure to take the fallenness of man's condition with adequate seriousness, argued Luther, had led theologians to place undue reliance on reason. The true distinction and contrast between revelation and reason, theology and philosophy, had been lost in, for example, the Thomist synthesis. Reason had been regarded, at least in some of its operations, as exempt from the full effects of the Fall, and nature and Grace had been made complementary, thus evading the problem that the only nature we can know is fallen nature, nature in constant rebellion against Grace. The redemption of nature requires the restoration of its uncorrupted condition, not its fulfillment by the addition of a "supernature." Luther shows substantial agreement on the relation of reason and revelation with Ockham and the Nominalists, but finally rejects them, too, as Pelagians who "have not only darkened the Gospel, but have taken it clean away, and buried Christ utterly," [5] as the result of an unscriptural view of man's potentialities.

If reason can provide no proper tool for the treatment of issues of divinity, what is left of theology? Is the Queen of the Sciences to disappear, leaving behind her nothing but a formless pietism? The answer of the Reformers was unequivocal: the sole criterion of theological truth must be the revealed Word of God as expressed through the Holy Scriptures of the Old and New Testaments. Only thus can theology escape undue reliance on fallen nature or corrupted reason. Neither the tradition of the Church nor human philosophizing is to stand against Scripture. Reformed theology is to be *biblical* theology, basically nothing other than the exposition of the clear teaching of Scripture. Calvin, for instance, said of his *Institutes* that they were intended to be simply "the sum of what we find God wishes to teach us in His Word." [6] The authority of Scripture is self-authenticating, for it "exhibits as clear evidence of its truth as white and black things do of their colour, or sweet and bitter things do of their taste," [7] and this authority is further guaranteed to the individual believer by the working of the Holy Spirit in his heart. It is the clear sense of Scripture which is apparent to any fair-minded man, not any allegorical or spiritualized interpretation, which is the supreme rule of life and doctrine. The Reformers accuse their opponents not only of introducing alien authorities into theology in addition to Scripture and of subordinating the Word of God to the judgment of the Church, but also of refusing to be bound to its plain sense, and instead treating the Bible "as if it were a nose of wax, to be pulled around at will." [8] Rightly understood, the Reformers claim, the whole of the Bible shows itself to be a unity of witness to the revelation of God in Christ, free of obscurities and ambiguities.[9]

There is a distinction between Luther and Calvin in their doctrine of Scripture, but it is one which is nowhere formulated explicitly, and it can only be gathered in general terms from their differing approaches to exegesis. When Luther seeks to find a rule of life in Scripture he tends to understand this negatively: Scripture sets the limits within which positive guidance must be sought from reason, tradition, or history. The main concern of Scripture is to call men to salvation in Christ, but as far as life in this world is concerned it operates largely negatively, and requires to be supplemented in order to obtain an adequate ethic. Calvin, on the other hand, looks to Scripture for an unequivocally positive pattern of life and action. Where Luther sees Scripture as pointing to a relationship to Christ which may be expressed in many ways of life, Calvin tends to look for the one, immutable rule of Christian obedience. This distinction in the doctrine of Scripture is, however, far from absolute and must not be overemphasized. Much the same difference is to be found more clearly expressed in the different approaches of the two Reformers to the question of the "uses of the Law" (q.v.). Nevertheless, this disagreement is probably one of the sources of the greater radicalism of Calvin's concern with the form and workings of Church and State, and of the greater deference which Luther pays in these matters to reason and tradition.

If for no other reason than that the Bible contains a multitude of passages which are concerned with politics, it is obvious that Luther and Calvin, as biblical theologians, must have political doctrine in which they expound the teaching of Scripture on government, obedience, and so on, and relate this to the problems of the day. Neither Luther nor Calvin makes any claim to being an original thinker. They think of themselves simply as *witnesses* to the truth which is available to all men in Holy Scripture. As they see it, their business is simply to take the passages relevant to any issue and explicate, correlate, and expound such passages in relation to the needs of the moment. In matters of politics and Church government the most pressing need is the recovery of the old, true, and apostolic orderings, and in this the Bible is the only guide.

3. Justification and Ethics

It has often been argued that the doctrine of justification by faith alone with its denial of the validity before God of human judgments of worth makes impossible any serious consideration of ethics and politics. If in the last analysis (that is, in the presence of God) good works can have no merit, why be good? Has not the whole basis of morality been in fact destroyed?

Not so, but far otherwise, is the answer of the Reformers. When a man knows himself to be justified by faith alone, his faith necessarily "becomes active in love" to his neighbor. "We do not become righteous by doing righteous deeds, but having been made righteous, we do righteous deeds." [10] The Reformers never understand faith as mere passive assent to a series of propositions.

Therefore, when some say that good works are forbidden when we preach faith alone it is as if I said to a sick man: "If you had health, you would have the use of all your limbs, but without health the works of all your limbs are nothing"; and he wanted to infer that I had forbidden the work of all his limbs; whereas on the contrary I meant that he must first have health, which will work all the works of all the members. So faith also must be in all works the master workman or captain, or they are nothing at all. [11]

The works of the faithful man are of special value because they are disinterested; he serves God and his neighbor for their own sakes, not because he hopes to win salvation for himself thereby.

And ethical standards are not abrogated. Although they are irrelevant to the question of salvation, they are nevertheless given and laid down by God for a purpose, and there is another sphere—the world— in which their proper validity remains totally unimpaired. The righteousness of those who are justified is, in Luther's phrase, a "passive righteousness," something with which we are endowed, but cannot earn. But there is also an active righteousness, no less necessary, and commanded by God, but confined, as it were, to the sphere of this world.

The justified man is accepted by God in Christ *as* righteous, but it is important to remember that this does not make him sinless or morally perfect in the eyes of men, although justification, to be sure, always struggles to express itself in acts of love. The Christian—and the Christian statesman—lives in two kingdoms, in both of which he must serve God, albeit in different ways. To a fuller consideration of the Reformers' teaching on these "two kingdoms" we must now turn, as it is central to their political thought.

B. THE TWO KINGDOMS
1. The Dual Citizenship of Man

Man is a subject in two kingdoms, according to Calvin and Luther.

Let us observe that in man government is two-fold: the one spiritual, by which the conscience is trained to piety and divine worship; the other civil, by which the individual is instructed in those duties which as men and citizens we are bound to perform. To these two forms are commonly given the not inappropriate names of spiritual and temporal jurisdiction, intimating that the former species has reference to the life of the soul, while the latter relates to matters of the present life, not only to food and clothing, but to the enacting of laws which require a man to live among his fellows purely, honourably, and moderately. The former has its seat within the soul, the latter only regulates the external conduct. We call the one the spiritual, the other the temporal kingdom.[12]

Man, in short, belongs both to earth and to heaven, to the temporal and the eternal, subject to the secular law and recipient of the eternal Gospel, a being capable both of reason and of faith. In the spiritual kingdom he is wholly free, in the temporal kingdom he is totally in bondage. He is both a member of the Church, the eternal Body of Christ, and subject to the temporal authority of secular magistrates and laws. He is instructed in the temporal realm largely by reason, tradition, and the authority of the great minds of the past, and in the spiritual realm by the Word of God as recorded in Holy Scripture.

The clear distinction of these two realms is one of the primary and continuing tasks of theology, but it is far from being an easy one. The two kingdoms are not simply the Church and the State, as many medieval thinkers had suggested. Failure to distinguish, or the placing of a wrong division, leads to confusion and disaster in both realms, as we shall see in more detail. "Whoso then can judge rightly between the law and the Gospel, let him thank God, and know that he is a right divine." [13]

2. The Relation of the Two Kingdoms

While the two kingdoms must be clearly distinguished, we are not to think that they bear no relation to each other, or are wholly independent and self-sufficient. Just as Scotland and England were, between 1603 and 1707 (except for the Cromwellian period), united in the person of the crown while retaining their separate governments, so the spiritual and temporal kingdoms, although distinct from each other, have the same sovereign. Both are God's kingdoms, both expressions of His care and concern for men. In a sense we might say that they are complementary, although we must be careful to show what we mean by this in order to avoid confusion with medieval ideas which the Reformers disowned. God gives His good gifts both through the prince and the preacher, and each in his own way points toward heaven. Spiritual government leads us to love God; temporal government leads us to serve our neighbors. But love to God and service to one's fellows are ultimately so conjoined that it is impossible to do the one without at the same time also doing the other. Both law and Gospel, reason and faith, State and Church, philosophy and Scripture are necessary for life in this world. In spite of what often seems to be conflict and disharmony, we know that the two kingdoms belong together and are complementary.[14] But this union will only be fully realized at the consummation of all things, when the two will become one, and meanwhile the distinction must be maintained with care if dangerous confusion is to be avoided. "Now these two, as we have divided them, are always to be viewed apart from each other. When the one is considered, we should call off our minds and not allow them to think of the other." [15] The frontier between the two kingdoms is a division within every man. Properly considered, the two governments operate for the main part in different territories, by different means, and for different ends, and accordingly the question of the superiority of one to the other cannot sensibly be raised. They must and do cooperate, it is true, but only in such a way as not to confuse their separation and equality under God.

But it is far from easy to maintain the proper distinction, for "the Devil never stops cooking and brewing these two kingdoms into each other" [16] in order to bring chaos and disaster to earth. He acts either through human presumption or human idealism. On the one hand the secular power may seek to control the Church and dictate what is to be believed and taught; or the pope may seek to assert that all earthly authority flows through him. "Such people," says Luther, "want to be God themselves, and not to serve Him or remain subordinate to Him." [17] Law and Gospel may be confused together either by the "murdering and thieving bands of peasants" who undermine lawful authority as such, or by the pope who "hath not only mixed the law with the Gospel, but who of the Gospel hath made mere laws, yea and such as are ceremonial only. He hath also confounded and mixed political and ecclesiastical matters together; which is a devilish and hellish confusion." [18] On the other hand there are naively idealistic Christians who attempt to introduce the Gospel into spheres in which only law is appropriate—the religious enthusiasts and fanatics, notably the Anabaptists, who cannot see the bountiful hand of God in the temporal world, and so attempt to absorb the secular into the spiritual for the most laudable of reasons. They, too, are mistaken and are, albeit unwittingly, agents of the devil's confusion:

A man who would venture to govern an entire community, or the world, with the Gospel would be like a shepherd who should place in one fold wolves, lions, eagles, and sheep together and say, "Help yourselves, and be good and peaceful among yourselves; the fold is open, there is plenty of food; have no fear of dogs or clubs." The sheep, forsooth, would keep the peace and would allow themselves to be fed and governed in peace, but they would not live long.[19]

Working through the presumptuous and the naive, the devil has his way:

The people, the bishops, and the entire papacy ought to look after the Gospel and after souls. But they must rule in worldly affairs instead, wage war, and seek after temporal wealth, which in their shrewdness they are happy to do. Again, secular monarchs ought to look after their administration; but instead of that they must stand in Church, listening to Mass, and be altogether spiritual. Thus even now they are dabbling in matters of the Gospel and, following the pope's example, are forbidding what God has commanded, as, for instance, both kinds in the Sacrament, Christian freedom, and marriage. The results of this virtue are usually in evidence at the imperial diets too; thus the essential matters are postponed, or often simply omitted.[20]

One must, however, add that Luther himself from time to time transgresses his own conviction, as when he argues that " if every man had faith we would need no more laws," thereby "transferring the doctrine of the Gospel concerning spiritual liberty to civil order" illegitimately, by pretending that the man of faith can be wholly independent of secular government in this world.[21]

3. Church and State[22]

The two kingdoms are not identical with Church and State, but political government belongs wholly to the temporal realm, and it is created "for the purposes of this transitory life" only.[23] While it may show man his need of forgiveness, it cannot mediate justification, as can the Church. Nevertheless, it is in a fallen world a necessary institution, created by God as an instrument of His will and drawing its authority directly from Him, not by way of pope, Church, or people. In this the Reformers agree with medieval antipapalist theorists such as Wyclif, and with Marsilius and Ockham, except in so far as these thinkers spoke of popular sovereignty. Temporal government, for the Reformers as for the medieval antipapalists, has a very real dignity. Luther feels that in this emphasis he is restoring something long lost by the medieval confusion of the two kingdoms, so that he can write: "I might boast that, since the Apostles' time, the temporal sword and temporal government have never been so clearly described or so highly praised as by me." [24]

The term "Church" is somewhat ambiguous. It may be used to refer to the "Church Visible," that is, the empirically discernible body of baptized persons organized together for worship, instruction, and fellowship and subordinated to religious authorities; a group which contains many who are not, in fact, of God's Elect, and which may even exclude some of the Elect from its membership; a body which is manifestly imperfect and changeable. Or it may refer to the "Church Invisible," the eternal Body of Christ to which only the Elect, those who are justified by faith, belong, the true composition of which is known only to God. The Church Invisible is incorruptible, everlasting, and identical with the communion of saints. Both Reformers followed Wyclif and Marsilius in denying that the Church should be thought of as the hierarchy or priesthood. All Christians belong to the spiritual estate, and the ministry or priesthood is simply a particular function within the corporate priesthood of the whole body of believers.[25]

While both Luther and Calvin insist strenuously on the mutual independence of Church and State, it is important to realize that they mean rather different things by this. Luther, like Wyclif and Hus before him, lays greater stress on the invisibility of the Church, and is not overly concerned with its worldly independence except in relation to doctrine, preaching, and the sacraments. The secular government may organize the external polity of the Church as seems most convenient to it; it may do as it wills with the property of the Church; and the temporal authorities, if Christian, may even be recognized as "bishops" with authority over the external affairs of the visible Church, apart from the three matters mentioned above.[26]

Calvin, on the other hand, lays far greater stress on the "visibility" of the Church.[27] For him the true form of Church organization as well as true doctrine is to be found in Scripture, which also gives positive guidance for the outward behavior of Christian men. Control over outward morality cannot be surrendered entirely to the State; the Church must also exercise her discipline, with her own peculiar sanctions (notably excommunication), over her members, and even if they be governors or rulers in the secular realm, as Christians they are subject to the discipline of the Church. Discipline and polity are for Calvin the essential "sinews" of the Church, and belong to the essence of the Faith. Both Church and State are concerned with the maintenance of external morality, but they proceed in different ways appropriate to their different natures.[28] For Luther discipline and polity are matters of indifference as far as the realm of salvation is concerned.

We see, then, that Luther and Calvin both insist on the independence of Church and State, but they draw the division between these two "hierarchies" at very different points. The disputed territory covers most of the worldly functioning of the Church, and notably the form of external Church organization. For Luther, little binding guidance as to the government of the Church is to be found in Scripture, and he is willing to accept much that is traditional or seems expedient in the circumstances. For Calvin, Church polity must be conformable to Scripture, and neither tradition nor the temporal government is to be allowed to have authority in this matter. Now, if this disputed area is surrendered to the State, as by Luther, it becomes increasingly difficult for the Church to maintain its own autonomy (or rather, theonomy) at all, even within what Luther recognized as the proper sphere of the Church. And if it be granted to the latter, as by Calvin, the Church is constantly tempted to extend the sphere of "discipline" in such a way as to assert its superiority to, and authority over, the State.

In theory, if not always in practice, both these temptations are rejected by the Reformers. Although they differ in the delimitation of the two spheres, they agree that they are separate and not to be confused. But this does not mean that Church and State should not cooperate. Each is aided in its own proper work by the existence and support of the other. "The civil order is necessary for the well-being of the Church," wrote Calvin as the heading for the chapter on civil government in the first edition of the *Institutes,* and, on the other hand, the existence of a pure Church is advantageous to the State, for "all have confessed that no State can be successfully established unless piety be its first care." [29] Church and State are like the twins of Hippocrates: when one is sick the other sickens, too, and only together can they be in health.[30]

   We may fill in some of the details of the cooperation of Church and State by looking at the functions which Luther and Calvin each attribute to the spiritual and temporal powers respectively. For both Reformers the temporal government is concerned not simply with the maintenance of social life and external morality, but also is charged with responsibility for the maintenance of the true worship and service of God. The State is entitled, and indeed obliged, if necessary to purge and reform the Church in accordance with the Word of God, restoring to it the form of the true Church, an essential part of which, it must be remembered, is the Church's independence of, and distinctness from, the secular power. This may appear to be a denial of the separation of Church and State, but two points should be noted: in the first place, the interference by the secular power in the proper realm of the Church (however this realm may be defined) is an emergency action and not a regular feature, and, in the second place, the temporal authority is only entitled to intervene in order to restore to the Church New Testament Christianity. The "godly prince" is bound to restore to the Church the form and function which it has in Holy Scripture. Otherwise his intervention is totally illegitimate. The proper and normal relation of Church and State is one of mutual support and encouragement between two equals.

   The State then, has a dual function. It has duties both toward the civil community and toward the Church. Both Luther and Calvin see government as primarily a "dyke against sin" or "a remedy to vices." Luther is somewhat reluctant, as a theologian, to say much about how the State should restrain evil except in the most general terms, but Calvin does not hesitate to go into considerable detail: temporal government exists "to adapt our conduct to human society, to form our manners to civil justice, to conciliate us to each other, to cherish common peace and tranquility." [31] It must care for the poor, it must erect schools and pay the teachers, it must take care of the universities, and so on.[32]

   With regard to the visible Church, the State should provide material support for pastors and the worship of the Christian community; it should "foster and maintain the external worship of God, defend sound doctrine and the condition of the Church." It must take care that "no idolatry, no blasphemy against the name of God, no calumnies against His truth, nor other offences to religion break out and be disseminated among the people . . . in short, that a public form of religion may exist among men." [33] But the State has no arbitrary power or right to decide what is "sound doctrine" or the true Church. In such matters it must be bound by the clear teaching of the Word of God. But even if the teaching of Holy Scripture were as unambiguous as Calvin believed, it is difficult to argue that at the practical level he succeeds in maintaining the distinction of Church and State as clearly as, on his own premises, he ought.

It has always been difficult to separate with clarity the spheres of Church and State, and Luther and Calvin, as we have seen, do not entirely agree on this issue. Both, however, restrict the Church far more closely than had been the medieval pattern, and this they do on the ground that only so can the Church *be* the Church, and the State have the dignity and authority which are rightly its. They will have nothing to do either with a doctrine of the "two swords" or with any kind of caeseropapism. There can be only one sword, and that belongs to the secular government alone. Spiritual government denies its own nature if it usurps the proper function of the secular government, and the reverse is also true. In a profound sense Church and State together compose one unity, in as much as both are expressions of the sovereignty of God, but it is a disastrous mistake to attempt to realize this unity prematurely. Church and State should collaborate, it is true, but only as "separate but equal" servants of God.

4. Theology and Politics

Theology and secular learning, like Church and State, are to be limited to their proper spheres. Neither theology nor philosophy is now the Queen of the Sciences, but each is a "queen" within the confines of its own field. The theologian can make no pretension to being an authority on everything; he must recognize his competence as limited. "Why should I teach a tailor how to make a suit?" asks Luther. "He knows it himself. I shall only tell him how to do his work well in a Christian manner. The same is true of the prince. I shall only tell him he should act like a Christian." [34]

Theology is concerned with matters of faith, and its authority is Holy Scripture which in no sense sets out to be a politicians' (any more than a tailors') textbook. "In the apostolical writings we are not to look for a distinct exposition of those matters, their object being not to form a civil polity, but to establish the spiritual kingdom of Christ." [35]

Nevertheless, the theologian must tell the politician "he should act like a Christian," and Holy Scripture has a great deal to say about the behavior of rulers. Neither Luther nor Calvin had much hesitation in advising and rebuking rulers, often in the most forthright of terms. The limitation they place upon theology seems to be this: theology can offer no foolproof guidance through all the dilemmas of political life, no universally valid blueprint of the ideal society, and the theologian as such has no special qualification for the exercise of political power. Such matters can never be more than peripheral to theology. Theology cannot displace either the art or the science of politics. Political philosophy cannot be absorbed into theology any more than the State can be absorbed into the Church. There should, however, be something of a dialogue, if only to insure that neither oversteps its bounds. Let political philosophy never suggest that it can "penetrate to the heavenly kingdom of God," nor theology that it can rule the kingdom of this world.

If the political guidance to be received from theology and Holy Scripture is necessarily limited and inadequate, where are we to turn for guidance? Political activity, we are told, is based upon reason rather than revelation. As Luther puts it:

God made the secular government subject to reason because it is to have no jurisdiction over the welfare of souls or things of eternal value, but only over bodily and temporal goods, which God places under man's dominion. For this reason, nothing is taught in the Gospel about how it is to be maintained and regulated, except that the Gospel bids people honour it and not oppose it. Therefore the heathen can speak and teach about this very well, as they have done. And, to tell the truth, they are far more skilful in such matters than the Christians. . . . Whoever wants to learn and become wise in secular government, let him read the heathen books and writings.[36]

If we desire guidance in politics we must turn not so much to Scripture as to experience, reason generalizing on it, history sacred and profane, tradition, and philosophy. The very Aristotle whom Luther had labelled "this damned, conceited, rascally heathen" when considering his influence on theology,[37] becomes a most reputable authority when the question at issue is one of politics.

I am convinced that God gave and preserved such heathen books as those of the poets and the histories, like Homer, Demosthenes, Cicero, Livy, and afterwards the fine old jurists . . . that the heathen and godless, too, might have their prophets, apostles, and theologians or preachers for their secular government. . . . Thus they had Homer, Aristotle, Cicero, Ulpian, and others, even as the people of God had their Moses, Elijah, Isaiah, and others; and their emperors, kings, and princes, like Alexander, Augustus, etc., were their Davids and Solomons.[38]

But the ability to rule well is not simply the result of study of the right books and examples. Reason and political judgment are not dispersed equally among men. Ruling is a specialized craft for which preeminent gifts are required, for it is not simply a matter of following rules and principles. Very few are the truly original political innovators, the *viri heroici;* the average politician is compelled simply to "patch and darn and help himself with the laws, sayings, and examples of the heroes as they are recorded in books." [39]

C. What is Man?

1. Corruption . . .

Man, as we have already seen, is a fallen being. Created originally in the image of God, he rebelled against his Maker, and by the Fall this image has been radically distorted and changed out of all recognition. Man, the creature of God who was destined to enjoy perpetual fellowship with his Creator, has become estranged and alienated. Where order should be, disorder is now found, where harmony, strife. Since the Fall man has belonged to two kingdoms, not one, and in both the baneful consequences of corruption and sin can be traced.

Holding such views the Reformers are justly suspicious of "the great darkness of philosophers who have looked for a building in a ruin, and fit arrangement in disorder." [40] A theory of human nature derived from empirical observation cannot but project a radically false picture, based as it is upon the fallen man who "by [corrupted] nature has neither correct precept nor good will." [41] And a rational a priori doctrine of human nature would be in no better case, for it is involved in the corruption and limitation of human reason. Reason and observation can tell us many interesting and useful facts, but they are totally incapable of constructing a valid teleology. They can by themselves tell us nothing of value about the origin and destiny of man. They can describe the "ruin" and even instruct us in how to keep it in repair (and this is an important and useful function), but only revelation can describe the finished edifice and superintend the restoration.

But what do we mean when we say that reason is corrupted? Calvin joins issue with the philosophers who, he says,

generally maintain that reason dwells in the mind like a lamp, throwing light on all its counsels and, like a queen, governing the will—that it is so pervaded with divine light as to be able to consult for the best, and so endued with vigour as to be able perfectly to command; and, on the contrary, sense is dull and short-sighted grovelling among inferior objects, and never rising to true vision; that the appetite, when it obeys reason, and does not allow itself to be subjected by sense is borne to the study of virtue, holds a straight course, becomes transformed into will; but that when enslaved by sense, is corrupted and depraved so as to degenerate into lust.[42]

This position is to be rejected for two reasons, both largely based on the detailed picture of human depravity discerned by Christian experience. On the one hand, although reason is very often correct in general statements, it is normally subtly perverted by pride and selfishness in the particular advice it gives and, on the other hand, there is in fallen man a constant battle between reason and will: "The good that I would, that I do not; but the evil that I would not, that I do." The will is enslaved and at enmity with right reason; the reason aims high, but is quickly diverted into futility. Rejecting thus "the common dogma that man was corrupted only in the sensual part of his nature, that reason remained entire and will was scarcely impaired," [43] Calvin returns to Scriptural doctrine and the teaching of St. Augustine.

Nevertheless, "to charge the intellect with perpetual blindness so as to leave it no intelligence of any description whatever is repugnant not only to the Word of God, but to common experience." [44] While human reason is not to be relied upon in theology and is an inadequate guide in the sphere of salvation and in such matters "fails before it reaches its goal, forthwith falling away into vanity," [45] yet it has its proper place, and yields important results when concerned with "inferior objects," that is, the affairs of the secular realm. As examples of these, Calvin noticed "matter of politics and economics, all mechanical arts and liberal studies." [46]

Calvin then makes the somewhat surprising claim that "since man is by nature a social animal, he is disposed from natural instinct to cherish and preserve society, and accordingly we see that the minds of all men have impressions of civil order and honesty." [47] By this Calvin seems to argue that sociable instincts are one of the vestiges of the image of God, man's true nature, which are left to him. Man's total

depravity before the throne of God does not mean that God has taken
from him all resources for living in the temporal kingdom. Nevertheless, fallen man cannot be relied upon to use aright even the measure
of reason and sociable instincts which has been left to him.

2 .... Coercion

Since man is alienated from, and hostile to, God he requires restraint
if life in this world is to be possible. The pride and self-centeredness
which cut man off from God are at the same time the roots of strife
and hostility and alienation among men. Were man's reason, conscience,
and will in harmony, education and enlightenment would be enough,
and there would be no need of coercion. But since fallen man knows
little about God or justice or goodness, and since he refuses even to
follow the light that remains for him, restraint must be made the
necessary basis of social life. All men, even justified men, are sinners
who must in the earthly kingdom be forced to obey. Obedience to authority is, as we shall see in some detail, in itself a good, and the only
foundation on which stable social and political life may be built. Man,
in his pristine innocence, required no government; but fallen man must
be harnessed and forced into outward conformity with the necessary
rules of social living, for "if he is not governed, he excels in ferocity by
far all savage beasts." [48] Coercion is at one and the same time a curb on
sin, a constant reminder of the divine nature of the moral law, and the
means whereby God in His mercy provides for man the great blessing
of peaceful social life.

D. Authority and its Limits

1. The State as the Servant of God

Luther and Calvin fight on three fronts when attempting to delimit
and describe the secular government. In the first place they must oppose the fanatics such as the Anabaptists who deny that there is any
place for civil government at all and who emancipate Christians from
any obligations whatsoever toward the secular power. In the second
place, they must refute the claims of the papacy to absorb secular power
into the Church. Finally, they must curb the pretensions of those rulers
whom "God Almighty has made mad. They actually think they have
the power to do and command their subjects to do whatever they
please . . . they presumptuously set themselves in God's place, lord it

over men's conscience and faith, and put the Holy Spirit to school according to their mad brains." [49]

Against the Anabaptist view, Calvin and Luther prove theologically the *necessity* of civil government, as we have seen. Against the pope, they must prove the autonomy under God of the State. And against the presumptuous princes they must show the autonomy under God of the Church.

We have already seen something of the two Reformers' arguments for the necessity, the limits, and the independence of temporal government. God's sovereignty in the world is total. The necessity for temporal government is correlative to the necessity that God's Will should be observed among sinful men; its limits are defined by the fact that political authority is *delegated* authority, subordinate to, and dependent on, the sovereignty of God; its worldly autonomy arises from its direct dependence on the Will of God. In short, all political power flows from God and is to serve Him: "There is no power but of God: the powers that be are ordained of God .... He [the Ruler] is the minister of God." (Romans 13:1, 4) "We must firmly establish secular law and the sword, that no one may doubt that it is in the world by God's will and ordinance." [50] The origin of secular government lies in God's merciful will in shielding man from the full consequences of his disobedience, and not in human need. Its authority is a delegated authority from God and not from the people. In the thought of Luther and Calvin there is absolutely no room for any kind of social contract or notion of popular sovereignty. Secular government is an ordinance of God for the welfare of men in a fallen world. It must never under any circumstances be thought of as a human "device of government," or as in any way based on consent. It must answer for the use of its power always to God, and never simply to the people. [51]

The State, then, is "God's servant and workman" on earth. It is put there to express God's care for men, to punish the evil and protect the good, and for the well-being of the Church. [52] Coercion and restraint are not in themselves the be-all and end-all of temporal government. It exists to make possible for man the nearest approximation to the "good life" which is possible in a fallen world. We may say that it serves man, but it would be highly misleading to say it is man's servant. From man's point of view it is entitled to all respect, for "next to the preaching office [it] is the highest service of God and the most useful office on earth." [53] It may even be called *divine,* for rulers, both Luther and Calvin suggest, are sometimes even called in Scripture "gods" (*e.g.,* in Psalm 82).

2. Forms of Government

The question of the form and structure which secular government should assume as the servant of God lies on the delicate frontier between theology and political philosophy, and both Calvin and Luther show signs of uneasiness when they feel obliged to speak on the subject. Obviously certain theological and biblical insights are relevant, and indeed necessary, for the treatment of this question, but it is also obvious that other criteria apart from the Scriptures are also properly operative. The clarity of the division between theology and philosophy becomes blurred by the tension between the Reformers' denial of their competence as theologians in this field, and their clear conviction that, again as theologians, they have an indispensable contribution to make to the discussion.

The legitimacy even of asking what is the best form of government worried Calvin in particular. The authorities under which we live are God's servants, ordained by Him, and this makes it presumptuous to raise the question of their right. The fact that they are there proves that they are installed in office by God and therefore entitled to respect and obedience. The raising of abstract questions of right is quite improper for the private citizen. And the canny empiricism of both Reformers comes out clearly when they question the value of rational speculation on this issue. The answer depends on circumstances. And, although government as such is an indispensable good, the various forms of government have within themselves so many possibilities for good and evil that it is virtually impossible to say which is the best.

This subject is really a peripheral one for the Reformers. Government of some kind is essential for social living, and good government can bring many temporal blessings to men. But even the cruellest of pagan tyrannies is powerless to extinguish the flame of faith.[54] Nevertheless, both Reformers go beyond giving advice to rulers as to how they should behave as Christians, and bring theological insights to bear on the problem of what is the best form of State. They stop short of constructing an ideal state, partly because they do not see this as a theologian's—or a private citizen's—function, partly because they are suspicious that such a project is presumptuous and tends to a glorification of the State in itself and a disregard of its transitory and limited function. The doctrine of the perversity of man is the principal contribution of theology in this field, and it acts as a curb on any kind of utopianism. But the detailed consequences which Luther and Calvin draw from this principle are radically different.

Luther sees the corruption of human nature as inevitably magnified in a collectivity, and accordingly as a powerful argument in favor of monarchic rule:

If wrong is to be suffered, it is better to suffer it from the rulers than that the rulers suffer it from their subjects. For the mob has no moderation, and knows none, and in every individual there stick more than five tyrants. Now, it is better to suffer wrong from one tyrant, that is, from the ruler, than from unnumbered tyrants, that is, from the mob.[55]

Luther does not really distinguish between democracy and mob rule, which he sees as the negation of all orderly government. The mob can never be either Christian or truly reasonable. Faith, justice, and reason may belong to individuals, but never to the mob, which carries everything to excess. Monarchy allows the possibility of rule by a Christian, just, and reasonable prince, but even the tyranny and unreasoning savagery of a bad prince cannot be as bad as the rule of the mob. Respect for, and obedience to, the secular authority is a prerequisite of stable social life, but cannot survive in the atmosphere of democracy. Monarchy is the best form of government, but not necessarily absolute monarchy, for Luther does not hesitate to place moral and religious limits on the exercise of political power, and is quite prepared to acknowledge the value of constitutional checks on the monarch on the pattern of the Imperial Diet vis-à-vis the Emperor.[56]

From the principle of the depravity of man, Calvin draws as his first conclusion that rulers must be ruled, or in other words, that there should be some system of "checks and balances." Accordingly, while he admits that all forms of government have weaknesses and are liable to perversion, he strongly prefers some kind of aristocratic rule, either based on popular franchise or not, because "owing to the vices or defects of men it is safer and more tolerable when several bear rule, that they may thus mutually resist, instruct, and admonish each other, and should any one be disposed to go too far, the others are censors and masters to curb his excess." [57] Checks and balances in the exercise of political power, operating *within* the government, are not seen by Calvin as in any way derogating from the sovereignty of God; indeed they are a constant curb on the rulers' inherent tendency toward presumption against God and tyranny over men.

Liberty and a republican constitution are great goods. But they are gifts of God and we may not demand them or set about obtaining them for ourselves. The Christian is to be no utopian revolutionary. Calvin values popular election—with safeguards against excess. Election is a feature of the properly ordered Church and also a great privilege and responsibility when it is extended into the realm of secular government.

But in neither case does Calvin idolize democracy, and he has no use for notions of popular sovereignty. In the Church a properly conducted election can do no more than recognize God's prior calling of an individual to a particular ministry, and in the State the elective process is likewise the simple recognition that God has raised up a suitable person for a post. The power and authority flow from God and not the electors, and an elected magistrate is entitled to no less obedience and respect than a hereditary sovereign.[58] Liberty and the right to elect one's rulers are good, but not of ultimate importance for, as Calvin insistently reminds us, "It matters not what your condition among men, nor under what laws you live, since in them the Kingdom of Christ does not at all exist." [59]

3. "Let Every Soul be Subject unto the Higher Powers"

Since the political authority is God's servant and representative, by being obedient to it we are being obedient to God Himself: "Men ought to obey rulers as His officers and be subject to them with all fear and reverence, as to God Himself." [60] Even a bad magistrate, even a tyrant, must be obeyed. The prince's right to obedience is not conditional on his fulfillment of his duties toward his subjects as in Ockham and Marsilius, nor yet is it dependent on his standing before God, whose steward he is, as in Wyclif. We owe our rulers not only our obedience, but also our prayers and, let it be noted, our frank criticism if this is necessary.[61] This duty of obedience is clearly laid down in Holy Scripture, as in Romans 13: "Let every soul be subject unto the higher powers. . . . Whosoever therefore resisteth the power, resisteth the ordinance of God: and they that resist shall receive to themselves damnation. . . . Ye must needs be subject, not only for wrath, but also for conscience' sake."

This clear and unequivocal command of God expressed in Holy Writ is seen as in itself a completely adequate ground for the obligation of obedience. But many subordinate reasons are cited by Luther and Calvin to show that here God's Will coincides with the good of man. No government can be totally bad, and any government, however corrupt, is better than no government at all: "The form of civil government, whatever deformity and corruption it may have, is always better than the absence of princely authority." [62] Just as the misbehavior of one of the parties in a particular case does not justify the upsetting of the institution of marriage, so the misbehavior of the prince does not justify rebellion, which is interpreted as an attack on government as such. Secondly, each people receives the government it deserves: a good ruler expresses God's graciousness, a tyrant His wrath. We ought to be grateful for good government, but no tyranny can express a greater judgment than our sins deserve. Thirdly,

to suffer wrong destroys no man's soul, nay, it improves the soul, though it inflicts loss upon the body and property; but to do wrong [e.g. to resist] that destroys the soul, although it should gain all the world's wealth. . . . For the temporal power can do no harm, since it has nothing to do with preaching and faith and the first three Commandments." [63]

Obedience to an unjust ruler may be a cross we must bear in this world. To repay evil with evil would, *for a private citizen,* be to disobey God, and harm his own soul. Resistance involves the unauthorized usurpation of God's power of judgment and condemnation, and is accordingly illegitimate (cf. sec. F2–3 below). Finally, in obedience lies the necessary basis of all stable social life. Luther is not abashed to point even to the Tartars and the Persians as examples of how much a deeply engrained habit of obedience contributes to the making of strong and healthy societies.

But in spite of all, the Christian can laugh in the face of the tyrant even as he obeys him, for "we know that if our earthly house of this tabernacle were dissolved, we have a building of God, an house not made with hands, eternal in the heavens" (II Corinthians 5:1), or as Luther expressed it in one of his great hymns:

> God's Word, for all their craft and force,
> One moment will not linger,
> But spite of Hell, shall have its course;
> 'Tis written by His finger.
> And though they take my life,
> Goods, honour, children, wife,
> Yet is their profit small,
> These things shall vanish all:
> The City of God remaineth.[64]

4. "We Ought to Obey God Rather than Men"

The Reformers' doctrine of obedience must not be understood simply as the exposition of Romans 13; to balance things and avoid distorting the witness of Scripture we must pay heed also to passages such as Peter's words before the council: "We ought to obey God rather than men" (Acts 5:29). The question of when we may, or must, disobey the "higher powers" is an important one, since disobedience to constituted authority is no light matter, as we have seen. The decision cannot be left to the whimsy or selfish judgment of the individual. Injustice, tyranny, and oppression are in themselves no excuse for disobedience. Nor are we entitled to disobey because obedience will cause suffering for us. Nevertheless, "we are subject to the men who rule over us, *but only in the Lord*. If they command anything against *Him* let us not pay the least regard to it." [65] We are not justified in breaking the clear command of God in order to be obedient to men.

In working out the implications of this position it is important not to forget the distinction between the two kingdoms. A magistrate who refused to convict a criminal on the ground that Christ said, "Judge not that ye be not judged," would not be obeying God rather than men; he would simply be confusing the Gospel with the law. He would, in fact, be being disobedient to God's law of love expressed in the form proper to his situation. But Luther gives two specific examples of circumstances in which disobedience would be permitted. The first is when we are called upon to commit an act of clear injustice against others:

Thus, if a prince desired to go to war, and his cause was manifestly unrighteous, we should not follow nor help him at all; since God has commanded that we should not kill our neighbour nor do him injustice. Likewise, if he bade us bear false witness, steal, lie or deceive, and the like. Here we ought to give up goods, honour, body, and life, that God's commandments may stand.[66]

We are to suffer injustice without complaint, but on no account to become partners in it; and the standard to be applied to determine what is just is the divine and natural law which is best expounded in Scripture, and applied by the reason and conscience to individual cases. The second case of justifiable disobedience is when the secular powers step out of their proper realm and presume to prescribe matters of belief and worship contrary to God's Word, thus claiming to "lord it over man's conscience and faith, and put the Holy Spirit to school according to their mad brains." [67] In such a case we should "pay not the least regard to it." And once again it should be noted that the criterion for justifiable disobedience is not simply the individual's personal conscience and pious feelings. These must not be trusted unless rooted in the Word of God.

But while disobedience is allowable, and indeed obligatory, in such situations, violent *resistance* never is. To resist with the sword would be to confuse the two kingdoms, presuming that the spiritual realm can justifiably assume the sword which belongs properly only to the temporal kingdom. In the absence of any doctrine of social contract, popular sovereignty, or government by consent, there is no basis for subjects to attempt to change governments by violence. Commands of the temporal ruler which clearly contravene the Word of God are in themselves illegitimate, but not even a concatenation of such acts destroys the authority of the government as such and justifies rebellion, or even the threat of force, as Calvin consistently and categorically pointed out in his letters to the persecuted French Protestants. Disobedience refers to particular commands; resistance is aimed at the overthrow of authority.

What, then is a Christian to do when faced by a government which constantly attempts to compel him to disobey the Word of God, and persecutes him for his scruples? Three possibilities are open to him. In the first place, if disobedience involves great suffering, it may be possible to fly to another, less tyrannical state, following the injunction of Matthew 10:23: "If they persecute you in this city, fly ye into another." Secondly, if flight is, for one reason or another, inadvisable or impossible, one must simply suffer, refusing both to obey the illegitimate commands and to disobey God by violently resisting the secular authority. In the third place, Luther and Calvin each leave open a small loophole which seems to provide a conditional justification of resistance in certain clearly defined circumstances. Luther, at least in late life, was prepared to admit that positive imperial law made it possible to envisage legitimate resistance to the emperor on the part of the electoral princes in a number of cases. And Calvin makes much the same point:

Now, if there are any who today are elected magistrates appointed to moderate the licentiousness of princes (like the Ephors who were at one time set over against the Spartan Kings, or the Tribunes of the People against the Roman Consuls, or the Demarchs against the Senate of the Athenians— and possibly it is the same power which the Three Estates employ today in every realm whenever they meet as an assembly of notables), then I am so far from forbidding them to withstand in their official capacity the fierce licentiousness of Princes, that if they connive helplessly in the Princes' oppression and baiting of the more lowly citizens, I would declare them guilty of criminal breach of faith because they deceitfully betray the liberty of the people, of which they know themselves the divinely appointed guardians.[68]

This short passage, destined to have fateful consequences in the later development of Calvinist political thought, must be clearly understood. The subordinate magistrates are a part of the civil government, but even if elected, are not in any sense the representatives of popular sovereignty. Their authority, like that of the prince, comes from God, and to fail to use it for its intended purpose of securing the common

good, even when this involves resisting the monarch, is to be disobedient
to God and invite His judgment. The question of whether the people
at large are entitled to support by force the subordinate magistrates, or
the estates, against the monarch is simply unasked. Calvin would find
this a very tricky question to answer.

Those who suffer patiently under an unjust tyrant should remember
that God is his judge, and he cannot escape God's condemnation. How
this judgment is expressed will be shown in section F.

5. Toleration

It is impossible to discover in the writings of Luther a consistent approach to the question of toleration and religious liberty. Even if we
may justifiably say that his thought develops, in general, from a reasonable toleration of dissent in his earlier period to a vehement espousal of
persecution in the latter part of his life, he still bristles with contradictions and it is impossible to interpret the majority of his statements on
this issue as more than impulsive and often thoughtless responses to
particular situations.[69]

Luther denies the right of the papists to persecute him, and at the
same time rejoices in being persecuted, as this is a necessary mark of the
true Church: "I am not terrified because many of the great persecute
and hate me. Rather, I am consoled and strengthened, since in all the
Scriptures the persecutors and haters have commonly been wrong,
and the persecuted right. The majority always supports the lie, and
the minority the truth." [70] And yet later, when the majority was behind
him, this principle was discarded and Luther had no hesitation in advocating in the most violent terms the persecution of dissident individuals like Carlstadt and Münzer, or groups like the rebellious peasants,
the Anabaptists, and the Jews. In the early period he spoke much of the
need to leave the Word free to accomplish its own work, and of the
impossibility of enforced faith, and on this ground advocated general
toleration in the conviction that the truth would win out. The toleration
of heresy, he thought, could sharpen rather than weaken faith: "The
Spirit wrote that the Jebusites and Canaanites should be left in the land
of promise to give the Israelites exercise in war. . . . This refers to the
heretic." [71] And toleration should be extended even to Jews.[72]

His attitude toward Jews, Romanists, and the dissident sects hard-
ened rapidly, and his justifications of persecution are multifarious and
often contradictory. In *A Treatise of Good Works* (1520) he lays it down
that a prince is an example to the people, for the simple folk will be-

lieve as he does. It is therefore his duty to believe and maintain the true religion, and he has no power to decide what the true religion is.[73] In the *Commentary on Psalm 86* (1530) he discusses which heretics should be persecuted and concludes that the secular power should punish those who, on religious grounds, deny the dignity and authority of civil government and also those who deny doctrines which are found clearly in Scripture and are accepted throughout Christendom, for this is blasphemy. As to conflict between Lutherans and Romanists, Luther invites the secular ruler to judge between them on the basis of Scripture and bid the unscriptural party simply to keep silence.[74] But often Luther is far more all-inclusive and bloodthirsty in his demands for the punishment of his opponents. Sometimes he speaks of the death penalty for papists and Anabaptists, sometimes he thinks banishment sufficient. But in any case the Word should be supported by the sword of the civil magistrate. Some of Luther's utterances may be dismissed as obvious rhetorical exaggerations, but it would be more than difficult to argue that in this matter he does not create an "infernal confusion" between the two kingdoms he so clearly differentiated elsewhere.

Calvin's position is much more stable than that of Luther. It is the duty of the Christian magistrate to proceed against heresy even if it is not overtly seditious or blasphemous. The magistrate is God's lieutenant or deputy and accordingly must maintain the honor of God by all means in his power. For heresy is in itself an offense against Christian society, and as a direct assault on the honor of God it is more heinous than the worst offense committed by one man against another. The stamping out of heresy is demanded not only by natural law (as an attempt to undermine society) and Roman law (specifically in the measures against Donatists and Manichees included in the Code of Justinian) but is a specific requirement of Holy Scripture, for "God makes plain that the false prophet is to be stoned without mercy. We are to crush beneath our heel all affections of nature when His honor is involved." [75]

From the persecution of the saints at the hands of ungodly rulers neither Calvin nor Luther drew the conclusion that a godly prince should tolerate all manner of opinions. In their thought there is no trace of the relativism or indifference which is often the basis of toleration. Nor is their doctrine of the two kingdoms another way of stating the modern concept of the separation of Church and State. The truth is known, and its preservation against the assaults of skepticism is a matter of life and death with which both Church and State, each in its proper manner, must concern themselves. No compromise is possible when the truth itself is at stake.

E. Law

Luther and Calvin recognize three modes of law: the divine law given directly by God in revelation; the natural law, which is available to, and binding upon, all men; and positive law, duly enacted and enforced by the proper secular authority. We will discuss each in turn.

1. The Law of God

The divine law is eternal, unchangeable, and absolute. It is the supreme and objective standard against which all human actions should be judged, expressed concisely in the Decalogue and elaborated elsewhere in Holy Scripture. It is given by God, according to Luther, for two purposes (known technically as the "uses" of the law), and to these Calvin adds a third. In the first place, since it reveals the righteousness of God and His demands on man, it convicts of sin and points to the need of forgiveness. The law, in this its "theological use," acts as a kind of mirror showing each man himself as he really is in his depravity and sinfulness, and eliminating the false self-understandings based on pride. In the second place, the law serves to restrain sinners from open evil and procure the "forced and extorted righteousness necessary for the good of society." In the third place (and here Calvin and Luther part company), for believers "it is the best instrument for enabling them daily to learn with greater truth and certainty what the will of the Lord is which they aspire to follow, and to confirm them in this knowledge." [76]

Are all the legal prescriptions found in Scripture to be reckoned divine law binding upon man? Luther and Calvin, like most other Christian thinkers, but in opposition to certain extreme sectarians, distinguish between time-bound and eternal divine law. Luther and Calvin have no hesitation in pronouncing the ceremonial law and most of the detailed economic and social legislation to be found in the Old Testament to belong to the former category and therefore to be obsolete. The ceremonial and ritual law has been abrogated by the Work of Christ (as the Epistle to the Hebrews argues), and there is no obligation on us to attempt to reproduce the polity or legal code of old Israel in modern times. These are certainly useful and instructive as examples of social and political arrangements agreeable to God, but they are conditioned by time and environment and are now simply not applicable. We have here a special instance of a social and economic system from which much may be learned, but which was never meant to be slavishly copied. It should be regarded, with much of the rest of the Bible, as a kind of commentary on the Decalogue. General guidance on such matters as the relation of Church and State may be found in both Old and New Testaments, and in this sense the Bible is the source of the "old orders" which must be recovered. And as to the external form of the Church, where Luther finds the structure of the New Testament Church as, at least in large part, time-bound, Calvin looks to the Apostolic Church as described in the Bible as a detailed pattern of the true form of the Church. Obviously in these matters, external criteria are being applied to Scripture in order to decide what is time-bound and what is absolute.

Both Reformers reject emphatically any "two-standard" conception of the law, such as had become accepted in the medieval Church: "There are not various rules of life, but one perpetual and inflexible rule." [77] All men are called to perfection, and all men stand under the judgment of the law. The old distinction between laws which are binding on all men, or all Christians, and counsels of perfection which guide the "religious," the athletes of the Spirit, is cast aside. The call to perfection lies at the heart of the law, but down the ages it had been clouded over, primarily by a misunderstanding of justification which assumed that salvation was possible simply by obedience to a series of outward regulations. Accordingly Christ is seen as the best expounder of the divine law since He "restored it to its integrity by maintaining and purifying it when obscured by the falsehood and defiled by the leaven of the Pharisees." [78] But to assert the unity and universality of the law is not to deny that particular obligations vary in relation to function: confusion has often arisen from the attempt to universalize standards which are in fact only appropriate in the exercise of a particular function in society. The same specific obligations are not binding upon a man in all his various official and private capacities. As a statesman or an executioner a man may be called upon to perform actions which would be wrong and improper for him acting as a father or a private citizen. The moral teaching of Jesus, by and large, deals with private morality and was not meant to be applied otherwise. But the varying functional standards through which God's law is expressed only apparently conflict, for love is the "queen and mistress" of all laws, and in specific situations all law must be tested by the rule of charity, for this is at the heart of all true law.

The divine law is a call to perfection and godliness; but perfection is quite unattainable by fallen man, and accordingly the law must point beyond itself to the forgiveness and atonement offered in the Gospel.

2. *The Law of Nature*

The natural law is, for both Luther and Calvin, ultimately identical with the divine law. Unlike Aquinas and most of the Scholastics, the Reformers never speak of natural law as perfected or complemented by a "supernatural" law. There is only one law, even if it may be looked at from various points of view. The law has a "spiritual use" (to convict of sin and point toward the Gospel) and a "civil use" (to curb public immorality), and for Calvin also a third use among the redeemed, but the law itself is always one and unchanged.

But the relation of the divine law and the law of nature *as we know it,* is not one of simple identity. It is important to notice that by the term "nature" in this context is meant the uncorrupted, ordered nature of man and the world before the Fall. Objectively considered, the law of nature is the law of God, absolute, unconditional, and binding on all men. Unlike the revealed law of God which was given to a particular people, the law of nature is in principle knowable by all men. It is

the true and eternal rule of righteousness presented to the men of all nations and all times, who would frame their lives conformably with the Will of God.[79] For although the Gentiles did not receive the written law of Moses, yet they received the spiritual law which is impressed upon all, both Jews and Gentiles, to which also all are under obligation.[80]

But since corruption extends not only to man's will but also to his reason and conscience, his understanding of the natural law is impaired. Accordingly there is a difference, even sometimes a conflict, between the divine law and the natural law as understood and interpreted by fallen man. Sin and corruption show themselves in man's constant attempts to revise and alter the law of nature in order to make it less contrary to his fallen will and desires. Sin obscures and darkens his comprehension of the law of nature, so that the divine law is revealed to remove the evasions introduced by man's fallen nature.

This is true of both "tables" of the law. With regard to the first table, the measure of the natural law available to fallen man teaches him simply that he ought to worship and serve God, but what this involves, *how* he is to serve God and who the true God is, he can now find only in the revealed divine law. With regard to the second table, a good example of the way in which the divine law expands, clarifies, and purifies the adulterated or stunted natural law is provided by the question of obedience:

Every man of understanding deems it most absurd to submit to unjust and tyrannical domination, provided it can by any means be thrown off, and there is but one opinion prevailing among men, that it is the part of an abject and servile mind to bear it patiently, the part of an honourable and high-spirited mind to rise up against it. Indeed, the revenge of injuries is not regarded by philosophers as a vice. But the Lord, condemning this too lofty spirit, prescribes to His people that patience which mankind deem infamous.[81]

Pride has perverted the subjective natural law so that authoritatively promulgated divine law has become the necessary means to the restoration of the objective and absolute law of nature.

How is the law of nature to be discovered and applied in specific situations? The law is not innate in man as such, but is an external objective standard set up by God, discoverable, at least in part, by the use of reason or, in Calvin, reason and conscience cooperating. Some men may be more reasonable than others, but it is never a simple business to find the natural law. Its discovery requires careful thought and consideration of all the issues, for "the noble gem called natural law and reason is a rare thing among the children of men."[82]

3. The Law of the State

The law of the state has as its purpose simply the maintenance of outward conformity with morality, and the discipline necessary for social life. It is related, it is true, to the divine-natural law, but is not directly deducible from it. The divine-natural law sets, as it were, the limits within which free play is given to the statesman to ordain such laws as may seem fit in the light of the circumstances and political necessities. Reason—fallen reason—must produce such legislation as the conditions seem to require without conflicting with the law of God. "But if it is true that each nation has been left at liberty to enact the laws which it judges to be beneficial, still these are always to be tested by the law of love, so that while they vary in form, they must proceed on the same principle."[83]

Positive law must be obeyed, even when it is patently far from perfect, save in extreme situations such as those discussed in section D 4. Luther, while maintaining this obligation of obedience, has a manly contempt for mere positive law—it is "sick law" as against the "healthy law" of nature. Its inescapable rigidity makes civil law inadequate:

Whatever is done with nature's power succeeds very smoothly without any [positive] law; in fact it overrides all the laws. But if nature is missing and things must be done according to laws, that amounts to mere beggary and patch-work; and no more is achieved than is inherent in diseased nature. It is as if I set up a general rule that for a meal one should eat two rolls and drink a small glass of wine. If a healthy man comes to the table, he may well consume four or six rolls and drink a decanter or two of wine; thus he requires more than the law stipulates. But if a sick person comes to the table, he will eat half a roll and drink three spoonfuls of wine. Thus he will observe no more of such a law than his sick condition permits, or he will die if he has to observe this law.[84]

Lawmaking is a tricky and unsatisfactory business, and very few are the men who are adequately equipped to legislate, so: "Here one must patch and darn, and help oneself with the laws, sayings, and examples of the heroes as they are recorded in books. Thus we must continue to be disciples of those speechless masters we call books. Yet we never do as well as it is written there; we crawl after it and cling to it as to a bench or to a cane."[85]

It follows that legislation is a specialized and skilled craft in the details of which the theologian as such has no special competence. This principle, together with the Reformers' rejection of the Canon Law, leads to some radical consequences in Luther:

What is the proper procedure for us nowadays in matters of marriage and divorce? I have said that this should be left to the lawyers and be made subject to secular government. For marriage is a rather secular and outward thing, having to do with wife and children, house and home, and with other matters which belong to the realm of government, all of which have been completely subjected to reason (Genesis 1.28). Therefore we should not tamper with what the government and wise men decide and prescribe on the basis of the laws and of reason. Christ is not functioning here (Matthew 5.31–32) as a lawyer or governor, to set down or prescribe any regulation for outward conduct.[86]

F. Politics as a Vocation

1. Man and his Calling

All men have two types of callings from God. On the one hand, all men, though sinners, are called to salvation, into God's eternal kingdom. As regards salvation, all men are equal, all equally requiring God's free forgiveness. But as regards life in this world, equality disappears and is replaced by order and rank, and men find themselves in various "stations" or "vocations" in which they are required to serve God by serving their neighbor. Luther and Calvin both reject any possibility of a "religious" vocation in which service to God may be isolated from service to one's fellows. Each man has a variety of different functions in society which are to be seen as divine vocations. One man, for example, may have the vocations of husband, father, farmer, and citizen, each with its specific duties and obligations. In each, vocation acts as a curb on man's selfishness, forcing him to look outward and care for his fellows as well as himself. God's care for mankind is largely expressed through His placing of men in vocations, in each of which they are enticed into caring for their fellows and become, whether knowingly or not, "masks" or "veils" of God Himself, the instruments of His love.

Now, while vocations are in themselves good, men may and often do abuse their vocations by failing to do the appropriate duties or doing them improperly. Again, great confusion and disorder are caused if vocations are not kept distinct and separate. It would be quite wrong, for instance, for a magistrate to be as sharp and strict in his private relations as he is required to be when acting in his judicial capacity. Nor should we, spurred by ambition or love of novelty, abandon a vocation in which we find ourselves for another. This is presumption, and it is only at our peril that we neglect the duties which God has placed at our hand in order to seek something different. This teaching safeguards the stability of society and curbs sinful ambition, but it must not be allowed to conflict with the fact that God Himself often calls men to new functions, and *His* call must never be disregarded: "In everything the call of the Lord is the foundation and beginning of right action." [87]

The vocation of the statesman is a divine calling which is to have especial honor among men. Like any other man in *his* vocation, the statesman is God's "mask" or "veil," but he is entitled to peculiar honor because he is in a special sense the deputy of God. As far as men are concerned, in political life he stands in God's place.

Now, it is true that individual men are bound to obey the injunctions of the law. But God, whose nature is love, is not bound by this law, and often His love is expressed in ways which appear contrary to the law which is binding upon private individuals. Through vocation God frequently obliges men to do actions which appear to be contrary to the law, but are in fact, at a different level, expressions of the law of love. This is very apparent in the vocation of politics, where the statesman is obliged, in seeming contradiction both to law and Gospel, to resort on occasions to force, coercion, and violence. But: "The hand that wields this sword and slays with it is then no more man's hand but God's, who hangs, tortures, beheads, slays, and fights. All these are His works and His judgments." [88] And:

The Law of the Lord forbids to kill; but that murder may not go un-punished, the Lawgiver Himself puts the sword into the hands of His ministers. . . . Therefore it is easy to conclude that in this respect they are not subject to the common law, by which, although the Lord ties the hands of all men, still He ties not His justice which He exercises by the hands of magistrates—just as when a prince forbids all his subjects to beat or hurt any one, he nevertheless prohibits not his officers from executing the justice which he has specially committed to them.[89]

It is important to notice that this distinction between private and "vocational" moralities does not imply that they are not intimately re-lated and connected. The statesman is not emancipated from the full rigor of the call to perfection as far as his private life is concerned, nor is he given *carte blanche* for his official actions. In both, albeit sometimes in different and seemingly discordant ways, he must express the love and justice of God.

2. The Judgment of God

The statesman, although he may be a "god" in the realm of politics as far as other men are concerned, entitled to obedience, respect, and honor, is in the eyes of God simply another sinful man. His authority and his dignity are borrowed and do not really belong to him at all, but to God. He is in a position of special temptation to assume that the gifts with which he has been entrusted are his own to be used as he may please, and he finds it difficult not to deny his dependence on, and subjection to, God. But should he become presumptuous, "he is not worthy to be compared to a louse or a maggot or any other vermin—for lice are still creatures of God, while he is a villain who was appointed by God His lieutenant but constantly mocks and forgets his sovereign Lord." [90]

How is God's judgment on the presumptuous—and that means, as far as men are concerned, unjust and tyrannical—ruler expressed? While it is certain that he will be judged in eternity, it is also true that God's judgment is expressed within history. Luther characteristically oversimplifies his true position when he argues that "it always happens, and always has happened that those who begin war unnecessarily are beaten" [91] for he admits elsewhere that God's judgment is not expressed in such simple terms. But nevertheless, retribution does come within history and, for example "tyrants run the risk that, by God's decree, their subjects may rise up . . . and slay them or drive them out." [92] This *fact* is not to be understood as in any sense a *justification* of resistance. Those who rebel are thereby guilty before God. But "the instrumentality of the wicked" can be "employed by God while He continues free from every taint." [93] If all his subjects were faithful Christians, the ruler need fear no insurrection; but since it is impossible for this to be so, he is wise to beware of the wrath of God expressed through the violence of the godless. The workings of God's Providence do not depend on the faithfulness of men. Or God may perhaps raise up foreign rulers and nations to subject the unrighteous prince:

Thus He tamed the power of Tyre by the Egyptians; the insolence of the Egyptians by the Assyrians; the ferocity of the Assyrians by the Chaldeans; the confidence of Babylon by the Medes and Persians, Cyrus having previously subdued the Medes, while the ingratitude of the Kings of Judah and Israel, and their impious contumacy after all his kindness, he subdued and punished —at one time by the Assyrians, at another by the Babylonians. [94]

Or God may curb the tyrant by the subordinate magistrates, as we have seen, or by a "Hero."

3. The Hero

Politics, according to Luther, is normally a matter of "patching and darning." Understandably, sooner or later the garment will wear out and require renewal. The last stage of decay is usually insufferable tyranny and oppression and the agent of renewal, the destroyer of the old garment and the tailor of the new is called a *Wündermann* or *vir heroicus*. Although it is presumptuous for private individuals to attempt to overthrow established authority or refashion the state, God entrusts to certain individuals at certain times this special vocation. Examples of such men cited are Samson, David, Jehoida, Cyrus, Themistocles, Alexander the Great, Augustus, and Naaman—all, perhaps significantly, non-Christians.

The hero receives his commission directly from God, who constantly instructs and guides him:

When David wanted to beat Goliath, they wanted to teach him; they put armour on him and equipped him. Yes, Sir. But David could not wear this armour. He had another master in mind, and he slew Goliath before he could know how he was to do it. For he was no apprentice either, trained in this craft; he was a master, trained for it by God Himself. [95]

The hero is not subject to the laws and rules which are binding on ordinary men, or even on ordinary rulers. He may lead a rebellion, and the people may justly follow him. He is endowed with rare gifts of reason and is privy to the counsels of God, so that he may even override the law, or at least improve it, for he is himself "the living law." Under his regime tyranny is destroyed, everything improves, and a new era is inaugurated. But he is no pattern for ordinary folk, and woe betide the man who, without a special calling from God, attempts to ape the hero.

The hero of Luther cannot justifiably be compared with the superman of Nietzsche, nor yet with the hero of Carlyle. His freedom from law and his powers of innovation and restoration flow, not from himself, but from God's choice of him, and his direct dependence on God. The glory, the worship, the power, and the sovereignty belong to God and not to him. His pre-eminent gifts are indeed *gifts,* and should not be held to imply any freedom from the taint of original sin. As proof of this, Luther points out that most of the heroes, their work finished, come to bad ends, having finally yielded to the sin of presumption.

Calvin, refusing to take as gloomy a view as Luther of the potentialities of secular government, sees the hero simply as a "Providential Deliverer" from oppression. Renewal is not his primary function, for this is a perfectly normal aspect of political activity. Since politics is not simply a matter of "patching and darning," no special God-sent tailor is required for the making of a new garment.

NOTES

Abbreviations:
WA—Weimarer Ausgabe of the Works of Martin Luther.
PE—Philadelphia Edition of *The Works of Martin Luther.* 6 vols. in English. Philadelphia: A. J. Holman Company, 1915–32.
AE—American Edition of Luther's Works. Ed. Jaroslav Pelikan and Helmut T. Lehman. 55 volumes in process of publication by Concordia Publishing House, St. Louis, and Muhlenberg Press, Philadelphia.
CR—Corpus Reformatorum, in which Calvin's works edited by Baum, Cunitz, and Reuss comprise 59 volumes. Brunswick, 1863–1900.
Ins.—Calvin, *Institutes of the Christian Religion.* Citations, unless otherwise stated, are from the translation of Henry Beveridge. London: James Clarke & Co., 1949.

1. John Calvin, *Ins.,* III. xiv. 9.
2. Martin Luther, *Commentary on Galatians,* ed. P. S. Watson (London:

James Clarke & Co., 1953), pp. 39, etc.
3. Luther, *Disputation against*

Scholastic Theology, Clauses 6, 10, 17, *AE*, XXXI, 4 ff.

4. *Ibid.*, Clauses 41, 47, 50.

5. Luther, *Galatians*, p. 130.

6. Calvin, Preface to the French edition of the *Institutes*.

7. Calvin, *Ins.*, I. vii. 2.

8. Luther, *PE*, I, 367.

9. Luther, *The Bondage of the Will*, trans. J. I. Packer and D. R. Johnston (London: James Clarke & Co., 1957), pp. 70–74.

10. Luther, *Disputation against Scholastic Theology*, Clause 40, *AE*, XXXI, 4 ff.

11. Luther, *A Treatise of Good Works*, *PE*, I, 199.

12. Calvin, *Ins.*, III. xix. 15.

13. Luther, *Galatians*, p. 122.

14. Calvin, *Ins.*, IV. xx. 2.

15. *Ibid.*, III. xix. 15.

16. Luther, *Commentary on Psalm 101*, *AE*, XIII, 194.

17. *Ibid.*, p. 195.

18. Luther, *Galatians*, p. 123.

19. Luther, *Secular Authority: to what extent it should be obeyed*, *PE*, III, 237.

20. Luther, *Psalm 101*, *AE*, XIII, 174.

21. Luther, *Of Good Works*, *PE*, I, 199; Calvin, *Ins.*, III. xix. 15.

22. The term "the State" is used here, and throughout this chapter, simply as a synonym of "the civil government."

23. Calvin, *Sermon 1 Tim. 6:13–16*, *CR*, LIII, 618.

24. Luther, *Whether Soldiers, too, can be Saved*, *PE*, V, 35.

25. Wyclif, *Select English Works*, ed. Arnold, III, 447; *Tractatus de Ecclesia*, ed. Loserth, *passim;* Calvin, *Prefatory Address of the Institutes to the King of France,* sec. 6, etc.; Luther, *To the Christian Nobility of the German Nation, PE*, II, 61 ff.

26. Luther, *To the Christian Nobility of the German Nation*, p. 68.

27. Calvin, *Ins.*, IV, i. 7.

28. *Ibid.*, xi. 1, 3; **xii.**

29. *Ibid.*, xx. 9.

30. Calvin, *Homilies on 1 Samuel 38, CR*, XXIX, 659.

31. Calvin, *Ins.*, IV. xx. 2.

32. Calvin, *Letter to the King of England, CR*, XIV, 40.

33. Calvin, *Commentary on Isaiah, CR*, XXXVII, 211; *Ins.*, IV. xx. 2, 3.

34. Luther, *WA*, 10.iii. 380.10.

35. Calvin, *Ins.*, IV. xx. 12.

36. Luther, *Psalm 101*, *AE*, XIII, 198.

37. Luther, *To the Christian Nobility of the German Nation, PE*, II, 146.

38. Luther, *Psalm 101*, *AE*, XIII, 199.

39. *Ibid.*, p. 164.

40. Calvin, *Ins.*, I. xv. 8.

41. Luther, *Disputation against Scholastic Theology*, Clause 34, *AE*, XXXI, 4 ff.

42. Calvin, *Ins.*, II. ii. 2.

43. *Ibid.*, 4.

44. *Ibid.*, 12.

45. *Ibid.*

46. *Ibid.*, 13.

47. *Ibid.* Cf. Luther, *Galatians*, p. 490.

48. Calvin, *CR*, XXX, 487.

49. Luther, *On Secular Authority, PE*, III, 230.

50. *Ibid.*, p. 231.

51. Calvin, *Commentary on Romans* (Edinburgh: Calvin Translation Society, 1844, 1849), on 13:4.

52. Luther, *On Secular Authority, PE*, III, 245. Calvin, *Ins.*, IV. xx. 2, 3.

53. Luther, *Commentary on Psalm 82, AE*, XIII, 51. Cf. *Ins.*, IV. xx. 25.

54. Calvin, *Ins.*, IV. xx. 8; *Romans 13:1–3; Commentary on 1 Peter* (Edinburgh: Calvin Translation Society, 1855), on 2:13–14. Luther, *A Treatise of Good Works, PE*, I, 263–64.

55. Luther, *Whether Soldiers, too, can be Saved, PE*, V, 45.

56. *Ibid.*, pp. 45, 48, 50; *On Secular Authority, PE*, III, 237; *Psalm 101, AE*, XIII, 160–61.

57. Calvin, *Ins.*, IV. xx. 8. Cf. *Sermons on Deuteronomy*, *CR*, XXVII, 453–60.

58. Calvin, *Ins.*, IV. iii. 13–15.

59. *Ibid.*, xx. 1.

60. Luther, *Psalm 82*, *AE*, XIII, 44.

61. Luther, *WA*, LII, 189; Calvin, *Commentary on Psalm 82*, on vs. 2.

62. Calvin, *Commentary on 1 Peter*, on 2:14.

63. Luther, *A Treatise of Good Works*, *PE*, I, 263.

64. Luther, "Ein'feste Burg," trans. Thomas Carlyle.

65. Calvin, *Ins.*, IV. xx. 32. (Italics supplied.)

66. Luther, *Of Good Works*, *PE*, I, 271.

67. Luther, *On Secular Authority*, *PE*, III, 230.

68. Calvin, *Ins.*, IV. xx. 31 (trans. D. F.)

69. The Reformers' attitudes to toleration are expounded and discussed with great penetration and balance in the works of R. H. Bainton, in particular in his article on "The Development and Consistency of Luther's Attitude to Religious Liberty," *The Harvard Theological Review*, vol. XXII, no. 2; in the Introduction to his edition of Castellio's *Concerning Heretics* (New York: Columbia University Press, 1935); and in his books *The Travail of Religious Liberty* (London: Lutterworth Press, 1953) and *Hunted Heretic: The Life and Death of Michael Servetus, 1511–1553* (Boston: Beacon Press, 1953). The paragraphs which follow rely much on these works, from which several citations have been borrowed.

70. *WA*, 7.317 (1521).

71. *WA*, 1.624 f. (1518).

72. *WA*, 2.336 (1523).

73. *PE*, I, 265 (1520).

74. *AE*, XIII, 61 ff.

75. Calvin, *Commentary on Deuteronomy*, chap. xiii.

76. Luther, *Galatians*, pp. 297 ff; Calvin, *Ins.*, II. vii. 8–12.

77. Calvin, *Ins.*, II. vii. 13.

78. *Ibid.*, viii. 7.

79. *Ibid.*, IV. xx. 15.

80. Luther, *Romerbrief*, 37.15 f.

81. Calvin, *Ins.*, II. ii. 24.

82. Luther, *Psalm 101*, *AE*, XIII, 161.

83. Calvin, *Ins.*, IV. xx. 16.

84. Luther, *Psalm 101*, *AE*, XIII, 163.

85. *Ibid.*, p. 164.

86. Luther, *Commentary on the Sermon on the Mount*, *AE*, XXI, 93.

87. Calvin, *Ins.*, III. x. 6. Cf. *Commentary on the Harmony of the Gospels* (Edinburgh: Calvin Translation Society, 1845–46) under Matt. 22:21 and Luther, *Whether Soldiers, too, can be Saved*, *PE*, V, 34; *Commentary on the Sermon on the Mount*, *AE*, XXI, 23.

88. Luther, *Whether Soldiers, too, can be Saved*, *PE*, V, 36.

89. Calvin, *Ins.*, IV. xx. 10. From the word "Therefore" this citation is found only in the French from the edition of 1541.

90. *CR*, XLI, 395.

91. Luther, *Whether Soldiers, too, can be Saved*, *PE*, V, 37.

92. *Ibid.*, p. 48.

93. Calvin, Heading of *Ins.*, I. xviii.

94. *Ibid.*, IV. xx. 30.

95. Luther, *Psalm 101*, *AE*, XIII, 156.

READINGS

A. Luther, Martin. *Commentary on Psalm 101*, vol. XIII, pp. 146 ff., of the American Edition of *Luther's Works*. Ed. Jaroslav Pelikan and Helmut

T. Lehmann. St. Louis: Concordia Publishing House, and Philadelphia: Muhlenburg Press, 1956—.

Calvin, John. *Institutes of the Christian Religion*. Ed. J. T. McNeill. Trans. F. L. Battles. *"Library of Christian Classics."* Philadelphia: Westminster Press, 1959. II. ii. 1–4, 12–16, 22–24; III. xix. 15; IV. xx.

B. Luther, Martin. *The Open Letter to the Christian Nobility of the German Nation. The Works of Martin Luther.* 6 vols. Philadelphia: A. J. Holman Company, 1915–32. Vol. II, pp. 61 ff.

Luther, Martin. *Secular Authority: To what Extent it Should be Obeyed*, in *ibid.*, vol. III, pp. 223 ff.

Luther, Martin. *Whether Soldiers, too, can be Saved*, in *ibid.*, vol. V, pp. 32 ff.

Calvin, John. *Institutes*. I. xv. 4, 6–8; IV. x. 1–12; xi.

Calvin, John. *Commentary on Romans*. Edinburgh: Calvin Translation Society, 1844, 1849. On Romans 13.1–5.

Calvin, John. *Commentary on the Harmony of the Gospels*. Edinburgh: Calvin Translation Society, 1845–46. On Matt. 5:31; Matt. 22:21; Matt. 26: 52–56.

RICHARD HOOKER

1553–1600

Hooker's great work, *The Laws of Ecclesiastical Polity,* was conceived as an extended attack on the position of the Calvinistic Puritans of his day. But we should notice that this Puritan position was in many somewhat inconsistent ways different from that of Calvin himself. The Puritans in England, the Huguenots in France, and Knox and his followers in Scotland all claimed to be disciples of Calvin and attributed high authority to his writings. But in fact they altered much of their master's system of doctrine, especially his political teaching, and by emphasizing certain aspects, neglecting others, and introducing alien concepts, they produced a distinct and far less consistent political theology.

The heart of their innovation lay in a thoroughgoing disparagement of the validity of human reason even in the spheres which Calvin had recognized as proper to it, together with the assertion of the exclusive authority and total adequacy of Holy Scripture as the guide in *all* things. John Knox, for instance, showed in his *The First Blast of the Trumpet against the Monstrous Regiment of Women* (1558) no embarrassment at defending almost entirely with Scriptural arguments the strictly political and legal proposition that no woman may hold political power.[1] And the English Puritans suggested as a principle for the guidance of Parliament "that nothing be done in this or any other thing, but that which you have the express warrant of God's Word for."[2] Such statements remove all limits to the scope of scriptural authority and leave the autonomous reason without place or function. As a result of this innovation, the understanding of what Scripture is undergoes a change. It is no longer simply the record of God's mighty acts to which faith clings, the raw material of dogma, the guide to the imitation of

Christ, the herald of salvation, the "earthen vessel" in which God's treasure is to be found. Now it is looked upon as a totally infallible and adequate compend of moral and political guidance, a textbook in which the statesman discovers how to rule and the philosopher how to escape the delusions of corrupted reason. The considerable degree of critical acumen with which Luther and Calvin had approached Scripture almost disappears and is replaced with a new kind of bibliolatry.

This change made theocratic claims almost inevitable. The Church is the guardian of God's Word, and it is the duty of the ministers to preach it. And since this Word is the only sure guide in politics, as in everything else, kings and magistrates should submit themselves to the guidance of the Church and its ministers in all things. Thomas Cartwright, the Puritan divine against whose works so much of *The Laws of Ecclesiastical Polity* is directed, was further then he knew from the teaching of his master, Calvin, when he wrote that kings should "throw down their crowns before" the Church "and lick the dust from off her feet." [3]

But it was the question of resistance which brought the conflict between Calvin and his successors into the open. Calvin's far from unequivocal suggestion that the "subordinate magistrates" might curb the power of kings,[4] although based more on constitutional law than scriptural authority, became the banner which the radical Calvinists nailed to their mast. The *Vindiciae contra Tyrannos,* written by an unknown French Huguenot in the last quarter of the sixteenth century, asserted that even if only *one* magistrate were prepared to resist one of those kings who "toss the poor people like tennis-balls," it was the duty of all Christian subjects to take to arms to overthrow the tyrant. In defence of the right, and indeed obligation, of resistance, the author of the *Vindiciae* argues that the Old Testament shows political society to be based on two covenants or contracts, the one between God, the king, and the people, constituting a "People of God," the other between the king and the people by the terms of which the people promise to obey and the king to rule justly. The Bible, the *Vindiciae* claims, shows sovereignty to be vested by God in the people and only delegated by them to the monarch and magistrates. On similar premises Knox, writing to his followers in Scotland, had asserted emphatically the duty of revolt against an ungodly prince and appealed even to the commons to disown the tyrant. Old philosophical ideas such as popular sovereignty and contract which had been commonplaces in the Middle Ages, but rejected by the Reformers, were now reappearing in a new, ostensibly biblical, guise. Holy Scripture and Calvin were still the avowed authorities, but now the tone and terminology were often far different.

The godly were now called not so much to suffering and passive obedience as to the creation everywhere of Christian commonwealths on
earth despite all difficulties and opposition.

It was against such biblical radicalism that Hooker launched his
powerful counterattack. He might have appealed to Calvin against the
Calvinists, and indeed he does so on occasion,[5] but he was not a Calvinist of any sort and was not interested simply in scoring debating points.
For him the authority of Calvin was not final. Nor could he enter controversy on the basis of a shared understanding of the authority of
Scripture, for he could not admit that "in Scripture all things needful
to be done must needs be contained."[6] Much of what he wished to say
concerned matters in which Scripture alone was not, he claimed, the
sole authority. In matters of ecclesiastical and civil government, for
instance, there must be an appeal to reason for "there is as yet no way
known how to determine of things disputed without the use of natural
reason,"[7] and even Christ used to exercise His reason in argument. In
the natural sphere at least, reason and the great "reasoners" of the past
must have a proper authority. Accordingly, Hooker finds himself able
to invoke freely against his opponents the authorities of antiquity, notably the Fathers and the Scholastics, particularly Aquinas. Since the
Puritans had chosen to argue, they could not escape from reason by
pleading the absolute authority of Scripture or faith.[8]

The Laws of Ecclesiastical Polity is a long work in eight books
covering an immense field. The first five books were published during
Hooker's lifetime, but the remaining three had to wait for publication
until the middle of the next century. The authenticity of these three
books is now beyond doubt, although Book VI as we have it is just a
fragment.[9] Stylistically the *Ecclesiastical Polity* is a masterpiece of prose,
and it is probably the first great work of philosophy and theology to be
written in English. If its original intention is polemical, it yet ranks as an
important work of political philosophy since it rises above immediate
conflicts to abiding matters of principle.

In Book I Hooker, relying heavily on the authority of Thomas
Aquinas, expounds the metaphysical basis of his thought. It is not
misleading to suggest that he gives to metaphysics the place which the
Reformers had given to dogmatics in their political thought. The world,
he holds, is an ordered cosmos in which everything works toward an
end proper to it. Every end is itself a means toward some further end,
except the final end, the *summum bonum,* God, who is good in Himself,
and cannot be a means to any further good. This cosmos is governed by
law, which is defined as "a directive rule unto goodness of operation,"[10]
given by a superior. But "the being of God is a kind of law in His work-

ing; for that perfection which God is giveth perfection to that He doth." [11] The law laid down by God for Himself and all other things is the eternal law, and from it all other laws flow.[12] This eternal law is not an expression of an *arbitrary* will of God but is reasonable, for reason is inherent in the Godhead.[13] Thus Hooker rejects at the very start the voluntarism of the Nominalists and Reformers. Reason lies at the heart of things and is always directed toward goodness, since goodness is of the essence of God.[14] The acts and edicts of God are always both good and reasonable, and this "reasonable goodness" of God expresses itself through the various laws which bind all created things and are derived from the eternal law. These laws take different forms in relation to the beings and operations over which they have force. Natural law binds all created things. Celestial law has reference to angels. The law of reason obliges all rational creatures, who are bound also by the divine law which is known through revelation. Human law is law enacted by men and derived from rational or divine law. All these derived laws together comprise a "Second Law Eternal." Some may be broken, and thence springs evil which, however, cannot change the cosmos into a chaos, for evil and sin are at least permitted by God, and may be said to fall under the first law eternal, God's unchanging purpose.[15]

Man, like all other created things, necessarily seeks his perfection. All men pursue goodness since evil cannot be desired as such.[16] The perfection which man seeks takes a threefold form: "sensual" (or physical), intellectual, and spiritual.[17] Each mode of perfection is desired naturally by man, but spiritual perfection, the beatific vision which is the crown of man's striving, is attainable only by supernatural means provided by God to remedy the damage caused by the Fall.[18] Nature and supernature are two complementary orders to which man belongs. Accordingly his perfection must be both natural and supernatural.

How does man know what his perfection is? The good is known by means of reason,[19] or general acceptance, that is, the reason of many.[20] By following reason we are in fact following the commands of God. It is the will rather than the reason of man which is corrupted by sin, for reason points clearly to a perfection which fallen man finds himself unable to achieve by himself. Nature can take him so far, but supernatural assistance is necessary if true bliss is to be attained.

Man, then, is bound by a number of different laws. As a sensual or physical organism he operates in accordance with the same kind of law that binds all created things; as an intelligent being, he is bound by the law of reason; as an eternal soul he is bound by supernatural law. And within this basic scheme, Hooker sees many subdivisions and mixed modes of law. Man's many functions have each their proper law, and there are many different authorities which may impose laws in various spheres. There is supernatural law, moral law, political law, ecclesiastical law, and the law of nations, each produced by a different legislator.[21] All these laws are fundamentally God's laws and arise from the eternal law, but the authority to enact some of them is delegated by God to men or societies, while in others God Himself remains both legislator and enforcer.

Within this system of laws we must distinguish the mutable from the immutable. The eternal law is unchanging, and it is the direct expression of the reason and will of God. Again the "laws" which are the formulations of the great dogmatic truths of the Christian faith are eternal. If we wish to know whether a law may be altered, we must consider in each case the end to which it is directed.

The Jewish ceremonial law is abrogated, for instance, because the purpose of the sacrificial system was fulfilled by the coming of Christ. Thus even some laws laid down by God are mutable.[22] Some matters are indifferent, and are subjected entirely to human legislators; others are the subjects of immutable divine or natural laws. As regards laws made by men, change is always possible, either to increase their effectiveness in achieving a desired end, or to lay them aside when a specific end is achieved or no longer desired. But the changing of law is always dangerous and unsettling, only to be approached with great caution even if it is sometimes necessary.[23] In both the making and the changing of laws, the eternal law must be the guide.[24]

The immediate controversial edge of this analysis of law was the criticism it offered to the extreme Puritan position that there is only one true law, that of God, which is to be found clearly stated in Scripture, and which governs the whole life of man. On this thesis depended all the radical Puritan claims which offended the conservatism of Hooker. The fundamental purpose of Scripture, he claimed, is to teach supernatural duties, and for this end it is entirely sufficient.[25] But the natural and supernatural order complement each other. The achievement of bliss depends on the fulfillment both of natural and of supernatural duties. The former are discovered primarily by reason, but the latter, as a result of the Fall, are beyond reason's scope. Accordingly natural reason and Scripture "both jointly and not severally either of them be so complete that unto everlasting felicity we need not the knowledge of anything more." [26] This is not to deny that there is much in Scripture that is in fact concerned with natural rather than supernatural duties, nor yet that Scripture may often correct faulty reasoning, but simply to state emphatically that the possession of Scripture does not free us from the arduous process of reasoning to discover our duties in moral and

political matters.²⁷ The perfection of Scripture is relative to its supernatural purpose, and it is misleading to seek in it alone an absolute,
political, ecclesiastical, or moral ideal, or to treat it as the final authority
in every trivial decision. Such a procedure in fact degrades Scripture
and blinds a man to its proper sense.²⁸ Scripture presupposes rather than
replaces natural and rational laws.

Men are by nature free and equal, but a life that is not social is a
brutish existence in which man cannot advance toward perfection.²⁹
Accordingly men have a natural inclination to society. Social life is
founded on this inclination and on a social contract, "an order expressly or secretly agreed upon touching the manner of their union in
living together." The maintenance of society demands government, the
function of which is to curb strife, restrain evil, and harmonize the conflicting interests of men.³⁰ But government has as its purpose not simply the maintenance of social life by means of coercion; it also concerns
itself with the search for the *summum bonum.*" Thus Hooker looks
on political organization not only as the remedy for human sinfulness,
a consequence of the Fall, but also as a condition of human perfection
(in the Christian rather than Aristotelian sense).³¹ On this issue he
stands both in the classical and Christian traditions. Both reason's
knowledge of man's nature and the knowledge of his depravity stemming from revelation show the necessity of the state. Government, like
society, is based on a contract,³² and most legitimate political power
arises from consent, although this may take several forms. A man may
consent personally and explicitly; he may give his assent through properly appointed representatives; or consent may be assumed from traditional usage.³³ But although consent is the best basis for political power,
all political power need not be rooted in consent. A conqueror, for instance, has power over those he has subjected, limited solely by the law
of God and the law of nations. And there are men who are specially
called by God and exercise power by pure divine right.³⁴ But power
which in the beginning was based on conquest or divine right may, in
the course of time, become freely accepted so that in reality if not in
origin it becomes government by consent.³⁵ Whatever the origin of political power, those who govern are God's lieutenants, and their authority, even if delegated from the people, is His.³⁶

Normally, then, political power belongs to the people and is entrusted to the government by contract and consent. This is by far the
best form of power.³⁷ Such power is limited either by the terms of the
original "pact of submission," or, if these are not known or have fallen
into desuetude, simply by what has become traditionally acceptable in
the society.³⁸ The legitimate acts of the civil authorities are the acts of

the whole community, and express what we might be inclined to call a general will. It ill befits citizens or factions to seek exemption from what are in fact their own actions.[39]

Human nature being what it is, seeking perfection and yet corrupted and blinded by sin, some kind of government is necessary. But there are many kinds of government, and nature "leaveth the choice as a thing arbitrary." [40] Hooker's deep respect for whatever is established and traditional restrains him from talking much of the best form of government. The best is hardly to be attained, and rash attempts to achieve it often do more harm than good. It is no trivial thing to tamper with the established order.[41] Hooker has his preferences, to be sure: by and large he is satisfied with the Elizabethan Settlement both of politics and religion. He thought a properly limited monarchy, allied to a church ruled by bishops, both governing by consent, to be the best possible arrangement, but he hesitated to suggest that this arrangement should be imposed elsewhere or in different circumstances.[42]

Much of the *Ecclesiastical Polity* is devoted to an important discussion of the relations of Church and State. The principles of ecclesiastical government, like those of civil, are to be found out by reason. Against Cartwright's claim that "the discipline of Christ's Church that is necessary for all times is delivered by Christ and set down in the Holy Scriptures. . . . [It] is to be fetched from thence and thence alone. And that which resteth upon other foundations ought to be esteemed unlawful and counterfeit," [43] Hooker affirms categorically that matters of church polity, unlike matters of dogma, must be decided simply by reason guided, it is true, by the law of nature and without infringing scriptural prohibitions. The Scriptures allow a large field of variation, and are quite inadequate if looked upon as a guide in specific issues of polity.[44]

Church and State cannot rigidly be separated, thought Hooker. Religion assists and encourages both subjects and rulers in the exercise of their respective functions. It is the spring of justice and harmony.[45] Religion—almost any religion—is politically useful, but it is not adequate to think of religion simply as a political device, or to suggest, with Machiavelli, that that religion is best which is most useful for the achievement of certain political ends.[46] Nevertheless, the Christian religion is both the true religion and also ultimately the most politically useful, as it curbs the selfish ambitions of statesmen and the rebellious restlessness of subjects. Since the State is a condition of man's reaching his perfection, and this perfection culminates in the supernatural, "in all Commonwealths things spiritual above temporal ought to be provided for." [47] In nations where Christians are in a minority, the Church is inevitably separate from the State, for citizenship does not imply churchmanship. But in "Christian Commonwealths" Church and State have the same "substance," the whole body of the people, but they are to be looked on as different "accidents" or functions.[48] Church and State stand to each other in much the same relation as faith and reason. The Church complements the State, and together they guide man toward his supernatural destiny. The State is concerned with the good life of man, but this necessarily involves that the State should have a concern for the Church and for true religion.

At this point agreement with Aquinas ceases. In Church as in State, Hooker argues, sovereignty in all matters which are not the subjects of direct divine revelation belongs to the whole body of members. He is as emphatic as Wyclif or Luther in denying that authority in the Church belongs simply, by divine right, to the pope or the hierarchy. Power over external religious matters is vested in the whole body of the faithful, although it may well be delegated by them to one or a few men. In Church as in State, government is by consent.[49] In a Christian commonwealth the social contract whereby power is entrusted to the political authorities is also understood religiously so that it is common and quite natural for supreme power in ecclesiastical as in civil matters to be granted to the same person or persons. Holy Scripture does not, as the Puritans and Calvin himself thought, condemn such an arrangement. The idea of a Christian commonwealth is unknown to the New Testament, while in the Old we find ecclesiastical and civil power united in Israel.[50]

Hooker's teaching on the relationship of Church and State raises the question of toleration in a peculiarly awkward form. His conception of the visible Church is a "comprehensive" one and he is unwilling to assert that heretics and papists are, even if misled, outside the Church in an ultimate sense.[51] Matters absolutely essential to salvation are, for the main part, virtually self-evident, and most disputes among Christians concern doctrines which are, to a greater or a lesser extent, indifferent to salvation.[52] But the State, as we have seen, cannot be aloof from matters of religion, although its concern is inevitably primarily with outward observance and profession. It cannot make true by edict a doctrine which was false before, although it can create a duty where none existed before. Human laws cannot force a man to believe, although they can and do force men to act *as if* they believed. Human laws oblige only outwardly, yet in many circumstances it is inconvenient for public unity that certain opinions should be expressed or acted upon. The civil authorities should have a care for the maintenance of true religion, but they have no right to decide what pure religion is, and in any case religious opinions are unenforceable. Within the Church, therefore, a considerable degree of doctrinal diversity is inevitable and should be tolerated. But, on the other hand, the civil authorities are charged with the maintenance of a stable social order, harmony and unity in Church and State. They cannot tolerate actions which are subversive of these things, disputes which split society into warring factions, or the expression of opinions which are likely to incite people to illegal or antisocial actions. Private opinions and feelings cannot be controlled and therefore must be tolerated. But in so far as opinions and feelings are publicly expressed or give rise to action, they fall within the proper scope of human law, and toleration must be limited by consideration of the common good.[53] The "judicious" Hooker disliked all religious persecution, but unconditional toleration seemed to him a political and theological impossibility.

NOTES

1. In Laing's edition of the *Works*, Edinburgh, 1846, vol. IV.

2. *The First Admonition to Parliament*, in *Puritan Manifestoes*, ed. Frere and Douglas (London, 1907). Quoted in A. P. D'Entreves, *The Medieval Contribution to Political Thought* (Oxford: Oxford University Press, 1939), p. 104.

3. In his *Replye to an Answere* (1573).

4. Calvin, *Institutes*, IV. xx. 31.

5. *E.g.*, Richard Hooker, *The Laws of Ecclesiastical Polity*, Preface, iii. 4.

6. *Laws*, II. viii. 5. Cf. III. vii. 2.

7. *Ibid.*, III. viii. 17.

8. *Ibid.*, II. iv. 7; vii. 4.

9. On the authenticity of bks VI–VIII see R. A. Houk, *Hooker's Ecclesiastical Polity, Book VIII* (New York: Columbia University Press, 1931), and C. J. Sisson, *The Judicious Marriage of Mr. Hooker and the Birth of the Laws of Ecclesiastical Polity* (Cambridge: Cambridge University Press, 1940).

10. *Laws*, I. viii. 4.

11. *Ibid.*, ii. 2.

12. *Ibid.*, 4, 6; iii. 4.

13. *Ibid.*, ii. 4, 5; iii. 4.

14. *Ibid.*, ii. 4; xi. 2.

15. *Ibid.*, iii. 1.

16. *Ibid.*, viii. 1; vii. 6.

17. *Ibid.*, xi. 4.

18. *Ibid.*, xii. 1, 3; xv. 2.

19. *Ibid.*, viii. 1.

20. *Ibid.*, vii. 3.

21. *Ibid.*, xvi. 5.

22. *Ibid.*, II. x. 4; I. xv. 1.

23. *Ibid.*, IV. xiv. 1.

24. *Ibid.*, I. xvi. 2; IV, xiv. 1, 2; V. vii. 1.

25. *Ibid.*, I. xiv. 1; II. viii. 5.

26. *Ibid.*, I. xiv. 5.

27. *Ibid.*, xiii. 2; II. viii. 5.

28. *Ibid.*, I. xv. 4; II. viii. 6.

29. *Ibid.*, I. x. 1.

30. *Ibid.* and VIII. ii. 18.

31. *Ibid.*, VIII. ii. 18.

32. *Ibid.*, I. x. 3.

33. *Ibid.*, 8; VIII. ii. 9; vi. 8.

34. *Ibid.*, VIII. ii. 5.

35. *Ibid.*, 11.

36. *Ibid.*, 6.

37. *Ibid.*, 5, 9; I. x. 3.

38. *Ibid.*, VIII. ii. 11.

39. *Ibid.*, Preface. v. 2.

40. *Ibid.,* I. x. 5; cf. III. ii. 1.
41. *Ibid.,* V. ix. 1–2; IV. xiv. 1–2; V. vii. 1, 3.
42. *Ibid.,* III. xi. 16.
43. Thomas Cartwright and others, *A Directory of Church Government,* opening sentences.
44. *Laws,* III. ix. 1–2.
45. *Ibid.,* V. i. 2.
46. *Ibid.,* ii. 3–4.

47. *Ibid.,* VIII. i. 4; iii. 2; V. lxxvi. 4.
48. *Ibid.,* VIII. i. 5.
49. *Ibid.,* i. 8.
50. *Ibid.,* 1, 5, 14, 18; iii. 2, 6; iv. 9.
51. *Ibid.,* III. i. 10–11; *Sermon on Justification.*
52. *Laws,* Preface. iii. 2.
53. *Ibid.,* VIII. vi. 5; V. lxii. 15; lxviii. 7.

READINGS

A. Hooker, Richard. *The Laws of Ecclesiastical Polity,* in *Hooker's Works.* Ed. John Keble. Rev. R. W. Church and Francis Paget. 7th ed. 3 vols. Oxford: Oxford University Press, 1888. Bk I, chaps ii–v, viii, x–xii, xv–xvi; bk V, chaps i–ii; bk. VIII, chaps i–iii.
B. Hooker, Richard. *The Laws of Ecclesiastical Polity.* Preface, bks I, II, chaps vii–viii, bk VIII.

FRANCIS BACON

1561–1626

To Francis Bacon, Baron Verulam, Viscount St. Albans, no worldly thing was more important, or more worth penetrating, than the problem of political philosophy, the nature of the best "state or mould of a commonwealth." [1] More precisely, the most precious thing on earth was a result of the meeting of the mind of man with the nature of things. That meeting would truly take place when the mind of man could subdue nature so as to force out of nature the most nearly perfect human thing, the commonwealth which Bacon outlined in the *New Atlantis*. Although the *New Atlantis* is Bacon's most important political work, we can see its importance only if we realize that political things meant to him much more than is usually granted. To be convinced of that, one must understand Bacon's express practice of using old words and phrases to describe new things. [2]

Bacon denies, for example, that there is such a thing as "fifth essence." The "fifth essence" is a term that had been applied to an element in the stars and the celestial regions, different from the four known elements: water, earth, air, and fire. This view of heaven, which can be traced to Aristotle, is treated with great scorn by Bacon, who calls Aristotle's heaven a "fantastic heaven." Yet, in a dialogue called *Advertisement touching an Holy War,* one of Bacon's characters suggests that the Socrates of the dialogue, a man named Eupolis, may be the "fifth essence." "Eupolis" means the "good city," or, perhaps more clearly, the "well-governed country." What Bacon denies to the heavens, a fifth element or essence, he seems to grant to the well-governed country. His real quarrel with Aristotle, then, is not that Aristotle suggested something fantastic, but that he looked for the fantastic in the wrong place.

The truly fantastic is to be found in man's political world, the world of man's creation.[3]

There is another old expression, "final cause," that Bacon uses to describe something new. The final cause is the end for which things exist, and Bacon said that the search for final causes had corrupted natural philosophy. He treats that search as scornfully as he treats the search for the "fifth essence." Yet Bacon does not scorn when he grants that the search for final causes may be legitimate when relating to the "human things." Full understanding of that search leads to the notion that man is that in which the world centers, "with respect to final causes." Certainly to discuss final causes as comprehensible only in the human things, presumably the man-made things, is to change radically the meaning of final causes. The final cause, that for which all things exist, is the things which man makes, and the best thing that man can make is the best commonwealth, the commonwealth of the New Atlantis, the happy land, the land of all earthly things worthiest of knowledge. That thing, however, does not exist, except in Bacon's mind, and is his construction in principle. It remains for mankind to construct it in practice.[4]

The dependence of the highest things upon human construction is a sign of the elevation of the man-made, the artificial, over the natural. Bacon's natural philosophy was materialist and was akin to that ancient materialism, especially the materialism of Democritus, which he acknowledged as his intellectual heritage.[5] Few of those who have followed him, however, have acknowledged his own acknowledgment, except Shaftesbury.[6] Although the materialist and atheist teaching of Democritus naturally led to a denial of the fruitfulness of any search for final causes, it could not of itself lead to the creation of human or political final causes. As a materialism Bacon's is altogether novel in that it defines a possible supreme human end, albeit an end affected with what we now call utopianism. The Baconian formulation, although novel, was influenced by the work of two political philosophers who preceded him, Machiavelli and Giordano Bruno.

Bacon appeared to accept Machiavelli's formulation that political philosophy ought to concentrate on what men do and not on what they ought to do. Like Machiavelli, he took as his starting point the extreme situation. Bacon believed that nature was at its truest and most intelligible when "vexed" and "tortured" by experiments, just as Machiavelli saw the origins of the good political order in extremes, in violence and crime. Men are made up of desires, and out of those desires states and commonwealths have their origins. Man has a mind, and with that mind he may subdue nature, but only by submitting to it and by understanding it at its most irregular, in marvels or miracles. Submission to nature enables man to conquer nature. Man himself has no natural goal or end: the cosmos is alien and incomprehensible. The guide to all things is in the appetite that is in all things to take in and to expel. Like Machiavelli, Bacon was a hedonist, but a hedonist who rejected the apolitical conclusions of classical hedonism.[7]

When Machiavelli speaks of concentration on what men do rather than what they ought to do, however, he contrasts his own procedure with that of the creators of imaginary commonwealths. Bacon, while commending this statement of Machiavelli, was himself the creator of an imaginary commonwealth. The significance of this fact emerges when we realize that, much as Bacon was indebted to Machiavelli for his starting point, the course his political thought took was quite a different one. The fact that Bacon's most important political works are neither works about the nature of the prince nor discourses on an ancient historian, but that one (*Wisdom of the Ancients*) is an analysis of ancient myths and the other (*New Atlantis*) a refutation of a Platonic myth, tells us something of Bacon's difference from Machiavelli. Before we see the importance of these myths, however, we must recognize that, at the very point of inception, in the very scheme of Bacon's plan, there is a difference from Machiavelli. The importance of fame or glory, the end for which the selfish perform unselfish acts, is, for Machiavelli, overwhelming. Bacon, however, apparently wavers between the love of fame or of wisdom as the highest passion and fame or wisdom as the highest good. That wavering is only apparent, however, for those who wish true fame achieve it only as lovers of wisdom.

It is as if Bacon had said to Machiavelli that the things for which men are most grateful are not the feats of heroes or even the actions of the founders of commonwealths. The things that have made men grateful are those which have most "relieved man's estate" (a Baconian phrase), *i.e.,* inventions. It is true that in the popular essays Bacon refers to the founders of states and commonwealths as the first "marshalls of sovereign honour," but in more recondite places he points out that the ancients made inventors gods, while they made heroes only demigods. Moreover, if such honor has not always been forthcoming, it is because there have been very few inventors, and their work was largely accidental. In this respect, the beasts had done better than men. Small wonder that he borrowed much of the symbolism of the *New Atlantis* from the ancient religion of Egypt, hinting, at least, at what a more forthright Bruno had said quite openly, though perhaps less effectively. Egypt, which to Christians stood for the darkness of the material world, was an object of great admiration, where beasts who made inventions were accorded their due. In Bacon's own utopia, moreover, the statues are for the inventors, not for heroes.[8]

A practical aim of Bacon's teaching is to promote inventions. The ancient suspicion of technological progress is replaced by something like faith in technological progress. Faith in technological progress would issue in inventions, the creation of which requires a new method, the method of Bacon's *Novum Organum,* in principle the method of modern natural science.[9] Politically what was required was a veritable "New Model Army" of Baconian followers who were prepared to experiment and had faith, not only in their scientific results, but also in the political beneficence of their scientific results. Bacon's teaching demanded a following, just as Machiavelli's did, but it was a different kind of following. It was not an army of statesmen but an army of inventors. There was no conclusive reason to believe that Bacon's followers would understand his teaching. That they do so was not even necessary. The old distinction between philosophers and nonphilosophers was to be replaced by a new, threefold distinction between philosophers, experts, and the public. A teaching which issues in inventions demands a large group of experts or technicians, people who, because of shared experience and what is now called collective research, can help to make man's lot easier. Such people would not have to know the truth about the cosmos or about man. They would not really have to understand Bacon's political philosophy, but only the methods by which inventions could be made. They would, of course, have to be subordinate to those who understood which inventions truly would contribute to the relief of man's estate, since inventions can also be destructive. Bacon had his own techniques for preventing destructive inventions from triumphing over constructive ones. That such protective techniques do not exist today need not obfuscate Bacon's superior judgment in adopting them. The inventors themselves had to be men skilled in method. Therefore Bacon's emphasis on method marks a departure from the political philosophy of Machiavelli. Without denying the loftiness of statesmanship, Bacon suggests that the methods which he presents can become methods for all human invention, including political invention. Although Bacon does not say that statesmanship will be easier when aided by modern invention, the conclusion follows from the assurance that the method of the *Novum Organum* can be applied to all human knowledge.[10]

In order for inventions to multiply, Bacon had to convince the powerful that inventions were politically innocent. He made a distinction between the pure knowledge of nature and the "proud knowledge of good and evil," and tried to protect his own knowledge not only from the consequences of the doctrine of the Fall, but also from persecution.[11] Yet it is clear that, if there is a passage from Bacon's scientific method to all human knowledge, in all its branches, there must be inventions that are not politically innocent. Ultimately the pure knowledge of nature affects and must affect the proud knowledge of good and evil. Yet, when applications are made to kings and patrons, applicants must speak with great care lest kings and patrons understand the revolutionary character of their proposals. The very fact that Bacon regarded his teaching as issuing in inventions meant that that teaching must have a large following, and that that following must have a large public approval. Not so much to protect himself as to protect his teaching, Bacon hesitated to spell out his political philosophy. To some extent he could not spell it out, for, while there were some things that he considered settled, such as the rightness of his method, there were other things that could not be known until the inventions that were to be made actually succeeded in relieving man's estate. For example, Bacon set great store by the future of medicine, not only for health but also for longevity. If human life could be free of natural death, and he certainly hinted at that possibility, the scarcely predictable consequences of that freedom would force some reservations regarding any final political teaching.[12]

There were certain things about the final political teaching that Bacon did claim to know. One was that the scientific method, issuing in inventions, compelled a view of history quite different from that of Machiavelli. For this view, Bacon seems to have been indebted to Giordano Bruno, a philosopher whom he rarely mentions. The act which brings fame to the hero is time-bound, whatever may be said of the fame itself. The hero helps his country, and the country may rise and fall. Inventions, on the contrary, belong to mankind and remain with mankind. They transcend what was called the eternal recurrence, and Bacon, following Bruno, considered it his duty to refute the assertion of eternal recurrence. The doctrine of eternal recurrence referred to the cycle of birth, growth, decay, and death, and referred to that cycle in plants and seasons, as in human life and in states and commonwealths. All human things were seen as transient, and that view, which sees the green of spring come and go, was held by Bacon to be "natural." Though it was natural, it was incorrect. It was the principal source of man's despair of the future. Among the reasons for hope for the future Bacon lists, with particular emphasis, the abandonment of man's natural acceptance of recurrence. The cycles do not follow their course, and the great age of modernity, Bacon's own age, is greater than the great age of antiquity.[13]

The idea that the greatness of modernity must defy the cycles that have dominated historical thought is an idea of which Giordano Bruno was aware, and from which he took comfort, apparently, during his days of persecution. Bruno spoke of the fruits of modern science, and he believed that his discovery of the infinite universe would aid substantially in gathering those fruits. In a famous fable, men blinded by the human ineptitude to grasp the divine are cured of that blindness and have a greater clairvoyance regarding human change than they had had before. Good and evil may still alternate, but, because of Bruno's new science, each good will be a little better than the last good, and each evil a little less than the last evil. Thus Bruno contrasts his own teaching, which brings tolerance in matters of opinion, precisely because it brings unity in matters of science, with the exploits of Columbus and his followers, who insist on imposing their own beliefs on others. Bruno hoped to find a way out of the ineluctable force of human change.[14] In seeking that way, Bacon was his disciple.

While Bruno believed, however, that in order to transcend recurrent changes in the human things it would be necessary to shock men and to destroy the power of the Christian Aristotelians who dominated the schools, Bacon believed that civil peace alone could bring scientific progress and, therefore, political progress. Thus he compared himself to a certain miller who prayed for "peace among the willows, for when the windmill wrought, the water-mill was less customed." [15] The operation of the windmill, in Bacon's figure of speech, religious controversy, was cheaper and easier than the operation of the water mill, which stood for the advancement of science. Bacon saw that progress required conjoint experience and collective research, which in turn required well-stocked institutions of learning, which themselves required civil peace. To promote it he taught what may be called a provisional political philosophy. He does not use the term "provisional morality" later used by Descartes, but he advocates a moral and political way that is certainly calculated to serve men until they reach the island utopia of the New Atlantis.

That political way is provisional both practically and theoretically. In the former respect, of course, there is nothing new about it. Political philosophers have always realized that men had to live in their own societies, and those might not be the best possible societies. Bacon's view was novel in that he denied the possibility of imagining the best political order before great progress had been made in conquering nature. That progress would enable men to know what they might wish for, i.e., it would reveal to them how far they might reach out in envisioning the good for man. Bacon, standing at the fountainhead of the scientific revolution, thus had to profess ignorance of the final good for man.[16] He claimed to know enough, however, from the alien character of the cosmos and the possibility of conquering nature by means of his improved method, to be sure that men could learn what to wish, and that it would be generally good. While he had some vision of his own utopia, much of his work is concerned with the state or commonwealth that would lead man to that utopia. Knowing how much civil and religious conflict would disturb science, Bacon sought to join freedom with custom or tradition. His provisional teaching may therefore be characterized as conservative, and issuing in the maintenance and extension of three institutions: crown, church, and empire.

Concerning the first two, little need be said. Bacon was a monarchist because monarchy existed, because it gave private men time from politics for philosophy and science, and because it was convenient to write under a monarch to whom Bacon's writing "resembled the peace of God; it passeth understanding." What passes understanding also passes censorship, and, if a monarch is no brighter than James I, monarchy may well consort with freedom. Whether Bacon was a true monarchist, who thought as highly of the prerogative as he pretended, is by no means certain. As to his Anglicanism, Bacon saw that the Anglican Church was that of the *politiques* in Britain, the people who wished to put down religious controversy and unite the nations. He saw its leadership as less intolerant than that of either the Puritans or the Catholics, and thus he held it to have settled religious controversies "for all time." There is, of course, a deeper reason for his adherence. Obviously a man who sees "final causes" and "fifth essences" as related only to the things that man creates must see his own teaching as divorced from theology. Bacon's very plea that the knowledge of nature might bypass the Fall, for it was not the knowledge of nature that was condemned by the Fall, but the proud knowledge of good and evil, would naturally lead him away from religious controversy. That church which permitted the separation of philosophy from theology would be regarded by Bacon as the Christian church which was closest to the true church. He saw that separation in the Anglican rather than the Roman Church, for the power of the Scholastics to dominate learning was, he thought, very great. He also tried, however, to make the Church of England more tolerant. He was spared the necessity of joining in Bruno's complaint that learning was dominated by the "vulgar" because he believed that in Britain the problem had been solved.[17]

Bacon's imperialism is somewhat more complex. While both his monarchism and his Anglicanism may be regarded as cautious, his imperialism was bold. It is perhaps the sole evidence in his provisional teaching for his own Machiavellian statement that the middle way, useful in all other pursuits, is baneful in politics. To Bacon, to amplify the bounds of empire was a duty, a duty that had been neglected in political philosophy prior to his own. What such a concept of duty does to traditional political principles is not hard to imagine. A duty of imperialism implies that the best societies are not small cities but great empires. It places values upon "greatness," not only in terms of power but also in terms of size. Nations with growing populations, like Britain, had a better opportunity for greatness than nations with small populations, populations that could not maintain their empires, like Spain. The fulfillment of such a duty would demand conduct rather aggressive than just, and valor itself would become the virtue of warfare, regardless of the justice of the war. Indeed, the search for the just war, a problem so meaningful to the Schoolmen and to Bacon's contemporary, Grotius, takes on quite a different meaning in Bacon, when he characterizes an apprehensive war (or what is popularly called a "preventive war") as a defensive and just war. Any war against any nation that is bent on conquest (like Turkey or Spain) would then be a just war because it would be a quarrel on apprehension of war. In other words, if nation A is to do its duty by amplifying its empire, nation B, observing that amplification, will be doing its duty by going to war against nation A. Perhaps this is the Baconian form of the "state of nature" doctrine among sovereigns, and, in a state of nature, action is selfish and the solution imperialist. The very concept of the just war seems to fall before the imperialist solution to the problem.[18]

When Bacon says that the problem of the extension of empire is neglected in political philosophy, we may justly ask why he seems to overlook its treatment in Machiavelli. Machiavelli approved of warlike actions and imperial goals, and the historical precedent that he most emphatically holds up for emulation by founders of modes and orders is warlike and imperial Rome. Yet Bacon did consider the study and discussion of the duty of amplifying empire a neglected study. It is not altogether easy to see why. The one clear difference between the imperialism of Bacon and that of Machiavelli relates to the importance of naval power. Bacon's imperialism is emphatically a naval imperialism, as that of Machiavelli is not. That seems rather a small difference, hardly justifying Bacon's claim to be the first to regard imperialism as a civic duty. We must remember, however, that the kind of people who could bring about a successful naval imperialism were, around 1600, "new men." They were the kind of people who could follow the advice which Bacon scattered so freely in his *Advancement of Learning* to learn how to get along in the world, to practice the arts of rhetoric and business management, and the courtier's art. They were the people who could bring the comforts and luxuries from the far corners of the world to the London shops. They were the men who were not ashamed to exact usury, which Bacon defended. They were those who could think of imperialism rather in terms of economic gain than in terms of despotic power. They were the true representatives of the spirit of capitalism, to which Bacon, at least as much as Calvin and perhaps more, contributed.

Bacon's imperialism was, in a sense, a link between his provisional teaching and his definitive teaching because, alone among the props of his provisional teaching, it offered the way for the new man. It was directed less to kings, lords, and clerics than to merchants. Bacon's aggressive society was a society peopled by those who would be guided by his architecture of fortune, by recommendations on how to get along in the world, a study which he considered neglected in earlier political writings. Such people were to be the bulwark of the new naval imperialism. They were to man the ship to take mankind to the New Atlantis. That ship was primarily a British ship, and Bacon saw the achievement of his utopia chiefly as a British achievement. Britain was ripe for the just war. She had the most warlike breed of men. The kingdom of heaven was like a mustard seed, a small seed, from which a great tree would grow. Bacon's idea of imperialism was one that he compared with that mustard seed. From the little seed that was Britain would grow a great empire.[19]

We should do less than justice to Bacon, however, in imagining that his imperialism was a narrow design for one nation. Its aggressive quality was designed for something much more important than British imperialism, namely, for the rule of mankind over nature. This quality may well have been the link between provisional and definitive teaching. That definitive teaching was only partly complete in Bacon's own writing, but it was expected to transcend both place and time. The transcendence takes us back to the problem of the old myths. The *Wisdom of the Ancients* (*De Sapientia Veterum*) is a collection of ancient fables, with Bacon's own interpretations. That Bacon considered it a very important writing is indicated by his statement in the Preface that even in his own time anyone who had a new truth to bring forth would have to bring it forth in just such a manner. While pretending to interpret old myths or fables, Bacon is really presenting his own teaching as far as the structure of the myth permitted invention. Old fables are held to be a commerce between earliest antiquity, which is buried in oblivion, except for what the Bible tells us, and the historical things. This link between the historical things and the first things is, however, something more, for, as the biblical comparison indicates, it is a link between the divine things and the human things. As the only divinity which can be understood is the man-made divinity, however, the old fables are presented as the way to divinity through the study and the conquest of nature.

Whether the pre-Homeric authors of the fables thought of them as Bacon did, saw, for example, the wooing of Juno as the search for political understanding, the quest for Eurydice as philosophic quest, or the riddles of the Sphinx as the source of the Baconian distinction between the kingdom over nature and the kingdom over man, does not really matter. In distinction to biblical tales, these tales represent a more natural way of looking at man and the world, and suggest that, if it had not been for Aristotle and Christianity, it might not have been necessary to wait for Bacon until man could create the society which conquered nature. Bacon follows Bruno in saying that the present age is "antiquity," the old age of the world, where men know more than those who were called the ancients.[20]

The myth of greatest importance to Bacon, however, is one partly of his own creation, partly a refutation of a Platonic myth, and is found in the *New Atlantis.* This work is a description of an island utopia in the Pacific, and it is formally incomplete. It ends, rather abruptly, at the end of a description of the institution called Solomon's House, which is the most important and most powerful institution in the land, an academy of scientists. Some writers have concluded that Bacon got tired of the work and did not bother to finish it. He did bother, however, to translate it into Latin, "for the benefit of other lands," and while that would not have been so great a chore for Bacon as for some, he would have done it only if he thought the work had some merit. Bacon left a number of incomplete works unpublished. The *New Atlantis* was not one of them. The work is, moreover, intended as a refutation of a Platonic dialogue, the *Critias,* which is also formally incomplete. When we understand just why the *New Atlantis* is formally unfinished, we shall have taken a stride toward understanding it.

The *New Atlantis* differs radically from some of the island utopias which preceded it, like More's *Utopia.* Discovery of the latter was said to depend on chance, and people could not be told where to find it. The travellers to the New Atlantis also depended on chance, but once they spotted the island it was easy of access, and the land was seen from evening to morning, just as the children of Israel knew in the evening that the Lord had brought them out from Egypt, and in the morning they should see the glory of the Lord. That Bacon intended the New Atlantis to mean the Promised Land is quite clear. He calls it a "happy

land," a "blessed land," a "land of angels." He says that, in the language
of the natives, it is called "Bensalem," which means the Perfect Son.
Bacon's imagery of the sea, moreover, signifies the triumph of navigation and therefore of science. Unlike Shakespeare's *Tempest,* or *Pericles,*
in which the most important sea images are characterized by storms, in
the *New Atlantis* the travellers find their way to the island in a calm
sea. The imagery is comparable to that suggested by the phrase "peace
among the willows." So much the modern utopia demanded.

The story of Atlantis, an island somewhere in the west, as it comes
to us in Plato, is the story of a technological paradise. The people of
Atlantis, corrupted by luxury, fought against an old Athens (nine
thousand years old when Solon was supposed to have told the story),
were defeated, and the armies did not return. Later the island was punished by Zeus with extermination and remained a shoal rendering navigation impossible. Unlike Atlantis, which was destroyed by an earth-
quake, never to revive, the old Athens perished in a flood, the people of
the mountain surviving and later constructing another Athens. Bacon
deliberately turns Plato's myth upside down. He admits that the old
Atlantis was destroyed, but by a flood, suggesting that there, too, mountain folk survived and later built the Inca and Aztec civilizations. The
New Atlantis, like the old Athens, defeated an Atlantic army, but
treated it more humanely than the Athenians and allowed it to return
home. The New Atlantis, moreover, survived a flood. It had something
which the old Athens did not have, a means of surviving floods. It had
Baconian science, and with the aid of Baconian science, it was able to
transcend the vicissitudes of time. By vicissitudes, Bacon referred to both
natural catastrophe and political decay. The New Atlantis is a trans-
historical regime, and Bacon uses it to deny the view, shared even by
Machiavelli, that societies come and go. Bensalem does not come and
go. Its very age contests the Christian view of the age of the world which
prevailed in Bacon's own time, *i.e.,* less than six thousand years.

Upon their arrival at the island, the travellers are first warned,
though they approach Bensalem in sickness and want, that they must
not land. After a very mild inquisition into their customs, however,
they are permitted to land and remain on shore. They are introduced
to the strange island by a Christian priest, who is the Governor of
Strangers' House. He discusses the miracle which brought the Bible to
Bensalem and the ways by which Bensalem, unknown to Europe,
knows about Europe. By means of secret expeditions, Bensalem learns
the things about Europe that seem to them worth knowing: the inventions and progress in the sciences. The governor also tells the travellers
of the past when the famous monarch of Bensalem, King Solomona,

founded the establishment called Solomon's House. The travellers meet a Jewish merchant named Joabin, who is clearly higher in the hierarchy of Bensalem than the Christian priest. Joabin explains to them the most important festival of Bensalem, called the feast of the Tirsan, or father of the family, and favorably contrasts the marriage customs of Bensalem with those of Europe. He ushers in a still more important functionary, one of the Fathers of Solomon's House. This functionary is dressed in robes worthy of the high priest in the Old Testament, rides in a splendid chariot, and blesses the people in a manner reminiscent of Christ, or of the pope. He also consents to talk with one of the travellers, and the narrator of the tale himself is chosen for this honor. The official tells of the organization and the functions of Solomon's House, clearly the ruling body of the island, and gives the narrator permission to publish for the benefit of others.

The story of Bensalem is not without dramatic quality. The island is hardly affected by what the travellers do, but the travellers, in the course of the narrative, undergo great change. They come upon an island, blessed but inhospitable, which saves them but does not welcome them. They wonder whether they will see Europe again, but when they are given permission to stay, and when they learn of the conversion of Bensalem to Christianity, they want to remain. Yet they are not ready to stay, and the discussion of the festivals and of the role and rule of Solomon's House represents a kind of initiation. They are toughened up for a life in utopia. In the course of the acclimation of the travellers, or what may more properly be called their conversion, the leadership passes from the captain of their ship or "principal man" of the company to the narrator, who is clearly the most learned man on board. Their notion of rule must approach that which prevails in Bensalem itself before the travellers are ready to become citizens of Bensalem. The change appears to be the process whereby Western and Christian society is transformed into universal society. The names, the images of Bensalem are drawn from a variety of sources. While the journey itself is a journey to the west, the images are predominantly Eastern and are drawn from Palestine, Egypt, Persia.

By suggesting that one may go eastward by journeying westward, Bacon suggests that vicissitudes of space as well as of time may be transcended by the well-governed regime. The authenticity of the miracle which brought the Bible to the city of Renfusa ("of the nature of sheep") in Bensalem before it was brought to the West is attested by a member of Solomon's House. His claim to judge rests on his knowledge of natural philosophy, and the biblical teaching is accepted only so far as it accords with the universal teaching of natural philosophy. What follows politically is the virtually absolute power of the scientific fraternity, the academy of Solomon's House.

The exercise of the collegiate power required, however, the support of an ally. Solomon's House could decide which inventions might be given to the state and which might not. We today well know, as Bacon foresaw, that a science which seeks to "imitate the thunderbolt" must have some protection as to its use and abuse.[21] Society itself would have to have certain safeguards. These are of two kinds: the safeguard of the collegiate power, which, by deciding which inventions might be revealed, limits public knowledge; and the safeguard of paternal power, which enforces virtue. We might call these the safeguard of public ignorance and the safeguard of public spirit. As for the latter, Bacon's *New Atlantis* seems to suggest a certain civil religion, a festival of which is the feast of the Tirsan. The Tirsan is the father of a family, having thirty living descendants over the age of three. His feast is a mixture of pagan feasts, but it differs from the ordinary celebration of abundance because it is a reward for longevity as well as fertility. Its symbols are suggestive of Osiris and Isis, Egyptian divinities. It brings about the union of piety, or reverence for age, and nature, or reverence for fertility and abundance. The Tirsan himself is awarded not only honors but also powers. Bacon places great stress on the monogamous character of Bensalem, calling it "Virgin of the World," once a designation of Isis, but otherwise incomprehensible in an utopia famous for fertility. Its significance lies in the severe character of the Tirsan's feast, as well as the other festivals of Bensalem. Bacon elsewhere distinguishes between the "affections," which are natural to all men, and the "perturbed affections," which are what he calls passions. Since the feast of the Tirsan glorifies the unperturbed affections, it is a celebration not only of age and fertility but also of virtue. Its rewards are rewards given by the real rulers of Bensalem, the Fellows of Solomon's House, to those whose pleasures are faithful and simple.

The political importance of the feast of the Tirsan lies in the union of old, patriarchal power with new, vigorous science. The civil religion, adding piety to science, renders secure the rule of science; at the same time, the rulers had to secure the civil religion by the works of science. Progress would convince men of the value of virtue. If all men are guided by affections, but those affections which contribute to the good life are the ones which leave the mind free of perturbation, then the best life is the philosophical life, the life most free of perturbation, and especially of the most powerful source of perturbation, namely, superstition. In that view Bacon followed Lucretius, but he went further in trying to construct a society in which the citizens generally might be relatively free from perturbation. Their freedom would rest, however, not on knowledge but on illusion.

While Bacon claimed that his science would go far to "level men's minds," he also made it clear that he could be understood by all only in terms of "works." All men would never really understand Baconian science.[22]

While paternal power is definitely subordinate to collegiate power, it appears to replace royal power. It is the "state," not the "king," which gives the travellers leave to remain in Bensalem, and Elizabeth I objected to the use of the word "state." Kings are mentioned in the *New Atlantis*, but the rule of those kings withers. Those who rule achieve or approach the forms of immortality recognized as possible by Bacon— the Tirsan achieves the immortality that belongs with regeneration and approaches corporeal immortality that transcends death. The Fellows of Solomon's House may achieve the immortality that comes from fame. The latter are a very restricted body, representing a small fraction of the populace. When the travellers are told that one of the Fathers of Solomon's House is to visit the city where they are staying, they are also told that the populace of the city have not seen one of those fathers for twelve years. While recruitment is not according to birth, and membership in the ruling group is, in that sense, democratic, the gap between ruler and citizen is enormous. There are, apparently, thirty-six fathers and fellows. Bacon was so sure of agreement on the part of the fellows as to scientific truth and its proper utility that he did not propose an odd number of members of the house or try to make a majority always possible.

What would prevent one member of the ruling group from trying to seize power, from giving the dangerous inventions to the state? What would prevent the people from demanding them in a national crisis? Bacon tells us little of that. There is an element of faith in the construction of his utopia, as there is generally in modern utopian thought, a faith that a threefold distinction between philosophers, experts, and the wider public may be preserved. Preservation of that distinction presupposes that experts will look up to philosophers and will be guided by them, or that knowledge will remain subordinate to wisdom. Under such conditions men would not indurate the brain to propagate communism or split the atom to destroy worlds, for knowledge would be kept in the service of the good of man. To know the good of man might require more knowledge of the affections than Bacon possessed; but he claimed to know at least the ways of life that the society of Bensalem would protect and secure.

We should now understand more clearly the attempted refutation of Plato. The *Critias* ends abruptly as Zeus calls the gods together to speak to them in a place where they could see all the world of becoming. He had called them to punish Atlantis, and his unwritten speech presumably would deal with that punishment and with the destruction of Atlantis. Bacon's work also ends with a speech, but the speech is given. It is not about the destruction of something that becomes and passes away, but about how to avoid destruction. It is not given by Zeus, but the man who gives it is almost divine. He blesses the people in a Christlike or papal manner, his fellowship has the power of "natural divination," and he looks upon mankind with pity. He and his predecessors have established a commonwealth, where they also see but transcend the world of becoming. He knows the secrets of Zeus, and he may tell them. Some things, however, he does not tell because he cannot, for natural philosophy can issue fully into political philosophy only when man has discovered how to imitate the thunderbolt.

The means by which the Fellows of Solomon's House see the world of becoming are presented in the form of freedom to travel. Bensalem is actually a closed society. Travel restrictions are adopted which correspond rather closely with those found in Plato's *Laws*. Capricious travel, so necessary in order to reach the New Atlantis, is banned from that society once one arrives. As in the *Laws,* contact with imperfection could corrupt even Bensalem. Travel then is restricted to the highest and the wisest, in this case called "Merchants of Light." While Platonic travellers seek the "divinely guided men" who may grow up in corrupt countries as well as uncorrupted ones, the Baconian travellers seek light. That suggests, of course, that European science, a science which to Bacon depended on chance, may have something to teach a science which depends on a systematic mastery over nature. Only the wisest, however, may see and choose the benefits of accidental science. As Bensalem tends to become a universal society, deliberate science will have taken all it could from accidental science, and the dangers of external corruption will be eliminated.

What then would happen to the mercantile and imperialist spirit of Bacon's provisional teaching? While Bensalem is opulent, it is a hospitable society which keeps rather a leisurely pace. Through the mingling of youthful science and old society, it is able to temper its luxury with simplicity and obedience. Such a society is not one which we usually associate with the supremacy of commerce and bears little resemblance to hungry, commercial Britain. It seems that the spirit of commerce, and, indeed, the spirit of imperialism, are no longer needed with the fruition of Baconian science. Science would furnish the luxury associated with commerce, and the universality of Bensalem would render the aggressive spirit of imperialism unnecessary.

Bensalem is a peaceful society. While Bacon certainly had no superstitions, he pretends to copy not warlike Rome, as Machiavelli did, but a more peaceful civil religion, that of the Egyptian Osiris. Bensalem, moreover, apparently has not been at war for many years, since it seems to have known the rest of the world simply through its Merchants of Light. The king whose forces once defeated the old Atlantis was named Altabin, which suggests in its Latin source that he was twice lofty. He permitted his enemies to return home with a promise never to fight against the New Atlantis again, a promise which Machiavelli would have thought mad, and which Bacon seems at least to have considered foolish. He was lofty for his statesmanship and for his humanity. After Altabin, and with the establishment of Solomon's House, rulers arose who were thrice lofty, suggested by the mythical figure of Hermes Trismegistus (thrice lofty). They were lofty also because of wisdom. Under their rule the armament of Bensalem prospered, including even unquenchable fires, more violent cannons, imitations of the flight of birds, and ships that go under the water. Whatever has since been done with these dire instruments, there is no indication that the rulers of Bensalem used them. They had them because Bensalem, with its alien civil religion and its hedonistic utopia, would have needed mighty defenses in a hostile world. But Bensalem seems to have fought no wars since Altabin.

What happens to the warlike spirit can best be seen by referring to two other treatments of the problem. One is found in Bacon's discussion of the myth of Perseus in the *Wisdom of the Ancients*. The fable is said to deal with war, but Bacon's treatment is entirely devoted to a crusade and says nothing of merely defensive war. In fact, the interpretation of the fable appears to be the description of a Christian crusade and of a countercrusade or defensive war by the opponents of Christianity. The war is less a real war than a campaign of proselytism, ending with a victory over the minds of men. Probably more important than the treatment of this fable is the dialogue on the *Holy War*, which is, like the *New Atlantis*, formally incomplete. The dialogue begins with a discussion of war against infidels and whether such a war is a just war, and ends with recommendations for war against the "unnatural." The skeptic in the dialogue, a courtier named Pollio, suggests that if the interlocutors really want to have a holy war, they must organize it as a crusade and find a pope named Urban to conduct it, as an Urban conducted the First Crusade. The name "Urban" refers to the Latin word for city but came to mean not merely any city, but the best city, Rome. The name of the Socrates of the dialogue, "Eupolis," also refers to the best city (but Greek, not Roman). The crusade which Bacon advocated, the only holy war which he could really support, was the crusade conducted by the best city, or the well-governed country, whether it be called Eupolis or Bensalem. The possibility that such a holy war might actually be armed conflict is not precluded, but the holy war is primarily a crusade for emancipating the world from the obscurantist traditions.

The holy war, moreover, solves the problem raised several times in the *Wisdom of the Ancients:* the problem of the relation between natural and political philosophy. Orpheus journeyed to hell to regain his wife, Eurydice. He rescued her but looked upon her prematurely as he was leading her to the light. He then turned to the beasts and stones, eschewing the company of women, and subdued the forest with his lyre. At this he was successful, until the Thracian women drowned out his music with their rebellious din and killed him. Orpheus, Bacon says, was a man "wonderful and wholly divine." He was a "complete philosopher." Complete philosophy meant, to Bacon, natural and political philosophy. The powers of darkness represented nature, and, but for his impatience, Orpheus would have mastered nature and rescued Eurydice, who represents the things for which philosophy cares. His failure to do so brought melancholy, an affection not suitable to philosophy. Even in his melancholy, however, Orpheus subdued other alien forces, beasts and stones, as men found states and commonwealths. The subjugation, however, was temporary, as states founded without the completion of natural philosophy must be temporary. The din of the Thracian women was too strong for Orpheus. The Thracian women were followers of Dionysus, and they represented not only frenzy, but primarily religious frenzy. This was the most violent of the passions, and the one most likely to destroy the commonwealth.

What would have happened if Orpheus had not been impatient? He would have kept Eurydice, but would he still have subdued the beasts and stones? And would he have needed to compete with the Thracian women? In the fable there are three alien forces, and they stand for nature (the infernal powers), man (beasts and stones), and the religious rites that men have created (the Thracian women). The first two might be subdued; the third would have to be destroyed. Eurydice, whom the philosopher loves, must also stand for mankind, however. The road Orpheus takes leads, through contemplation, to the darkest and most recondite of nature's secrets. Then it leads back to the light, taking humanity with it. There is a certain ambiguity in the suggestion that there are two imitations of mankind in the fable, but Bacon did not invent the fable and had to take it as he found it. Clearly, if Eurydice stands for the things for which philosophy cares, as he says, then she stands for final causes, and these can be related only to humanity in Bacon's teaching.

The science of politics, Bacon says elsewhere, is a secret science, not only because it is hard to know, but because it is not fit to utter. That means that while the knowledge is only difficult the teaching is also, in a sense, shameful. The reason that political knowledge is shameful is that it may be destructive of much that men hold dear if it is not communicated with care and circumspection. Thus in another fable Bacon speaks of nakedness as meaning political secrets, and in the *New Atlantis* the nakedness of the prospective bride and groom may be understood as relating shame to politics. Here Bacon refers to Orpheus' care for his own wife. With her return he would win (or rule) mankind. It would not then be possible for the flutes of the Thracian women to drown out his lyre. In other words, once the mastery of nature, a universal goal, had been achieved, the universal society might be created, and man could have his utopia.

Yet the melancholy of Orpheus is not necessarily merely the result of his despair. We are told that the Father of Solomon's House had eyes as if he pitied man. And in another work, the *Refutation of Philosophies,* the philosopher, lecturing before an international congress, also had eyes of pity for man.[23] Why should that be necessary inside utopia? Bacon seems to have seen something that not all of his successors have seen. Mankind could, he believed, be free of old religious superstitions. But new civil institutions would have to be put in their place, and only a very few men would be really free, because very few men could be really wise. The universality of human affections, by which philosophy must steer its course, does not lead, in Bacon's thought, to the inference of natural equality. There may be much value in the relief of man's estate, in the lessening of illness and poverty. Yet one must still pity man, whose lot is miserable, for there is something more important that man cannot have, perhaps happiness, perhaps wisdom, perhaps God.

NOTES

1. Cf. opening of Francis Bacon, *Instauratio Magna* with *New Atlantis,* ed. A. B. Gough (Oxford: Blackwell, 1915), p. 13.

2. *Advancement of Learning,* II.vii.2 (paragraphing according to 5th Oxford edition, ed. W. A. Wright [Oxford: Oxford University Press, 1900]).

3. *Descriptio Globi Intellectualis,* in *Works,* ed. J. Spedding, R. L. Ellis, and D. D. Heath (Boston: Little, Brown, 1861—), VII, 313; *Holy War, Works,* XIII, 191 ff.

4. *Novum Organum,* I.48 and II.2; *Redargutio, Works,* VII, 52; esp. "Prometheus," in *De Sapientia Veterum (The Wisdom of the Ancients), Works,* XIII, 44 ff.

5. See especially *Cogitationes de Natura Rerum* and *Principiis atque Originibus, Works,* V, 203 ff. and 289 ff. See also the fables of "Cupid" and "Coelum," in *De Sap. Vet.*

6. Cf. Shaftesbury, *Characteristics,* Miscellany II. 2 (1732 ed., III, 69).

7. *Works,* II, 254; III, 31, 45, 77; VI, 327; IX, 211; XII, 119, 213, 275, 318; XIII, 124, 222. See also the fable of "Sphinx," in *De Sap. Vet.*

8. *Essays,* 55, "Honour and Reputation." (All essays are numbered according to the last edition edited by Bacon personally. He changed the numbering from earlier editions.) See also *Works,* VI, 145; "Prometheus," in *De Sap. Vet.; New Atlantis, passim; Novum Organum,* I.129.

9. Alfred N. Whitehead, *Science in the Modern World* (New York: Macmillan, 1925), pp. 60 ff.

10. *Novum Organum,* I. 79, 80, 120 ff.; *New Atlantis, passim.*

11. See *Advancement of Learning,* I.

12. See especially *Historia Vitae et Mortis, Works,* III, 331–502.

13. See Bruno, *On the Infinite Universe and Worlds* (a translation is printed in Dorothea W. Singer, *Giordano Bruno, His Life and Thought* [New York: Henry Schuman, 1950], pp. 243–45, 283, 285 ff.); *Opere Italiane,* ed. G. Gentile [Bari: Laterza, 1925–27], I, 24 ff.; II, 23, 86; *Eroici Furori* (in Michel's edition, with French translation, *Des Fureurs Héroïques* [Paris,

1954], 114, 205–7, 311). Bacon, *Novum Organum,* I. 84, 92.

14. For the nine blind men see *Eroici Furori,* pp. 415 ff.; for passage on Columbus see *Cena de la Ceneri* in *Opere Italiane,* I, 24.

15. "Peace among the willows" comes from Bacon's letter of October 10, 1609, to Toby Matthew, to whom Bacon was sending a part of the *Instauratio Magna.* It is conceivable that the letter bears on the intention of that work. The letter can be found in various collections of Bacon's writings.

16. Probably the strongest statements of our ignorance of what to wish are in the *Redargutio, Works,* VII. See also *Novum Organum,* I. 70, 117, 120–22.

17. See especially Essays 3, 17, 18; *Advancement of Learning,* II (Oxford ed.); J. Spedding, *Life and Letters of Lord Bacon,* prints the *Advertisement touching the Establishment of the Church of England,* which Bacon did not publish, I, 74 ff. See also letters at I, 48; III, 48–50; V, 373.

18. See Essay 29 and *True Greatness of the Kingdom of Britain, Works,* XIII, 231 ff. For imperialism as a duty, see the Latin translation of Essay 29 in *De Augmentis Scientiarum, Works,* III, 120; also see the piece about the Spanish war in *Life and Letters,* VIII, 483. *Holy War* is in *Works,* XIII, 191 ff. The statement about the middle way is from *De Sap. Vet.,* "Icarus."

19. See, in general, the discussion of the architecture of fortune, in *Advancement of Learning,* II. xxiii. See also Essays 34, 36, 41 and the citations in n. 18.

20. *De Sap. Vet., Works,* XII, 427 ff. and XIII, 1 ff.

21. The phrase comes from the *Redargutio, Works,* VII, 93.

22. Cf. *Novum Organum,* I. 122 with I. 128.

23. *Works,* VII, 59.

READINGS

A. Bacon, Francis. *New Atlantis.*
    Bacon, Francis. *Wisdom of the Ancients.* Preface, Fables 11 "Orpheus," 16
    "Juno's Suitor," 26 "Prometheus."
    Bacon, Francis. Essay 29 "Of the True Greatness of Kingdoms and Estates."
B. Bacon, Francis. *Wisdom of the Ancients.* Fables 1 "Cassandra," 5 "Styx,"
    7 "Perseus," 10 "Acteon and Pentheus," 6 "Pan," 12 "Coelum," 22
    "Nemesis," 24 "Dionysus," 28 "Sphinx."
    Bacon, Francis. *History of the Reign of Henry VII.*
    Bacon, Francis. *Advertisement touching an Holy War.*
    Bacon, Francis. *Of the True Greatness of Britain.*
    Bacon, Francis. Essays 6 "Simulation and Dissimulation," 10 "Love," 11 "Of
    Great Place," 13 "Goodness and Goodness of Nature," 14 "Nobility,"
    16 "Atheism," 17 "Superstition," 19 "Empire," 41 "Usury," 51 "Fac-
    tions," 55 "Honour and Reputation," 58 "Vicissitude of Things."
    Bacon, Francis. *Advancement of Learning,* in *Selected Writings.* New York:
    Modern Library, 1955. Bk II, pp. 345–78, section on "Civil Knowledge."

HUGO GROTIUS

1583–1645

Hugo Grotius was a citizen of Holland. A veritable prodigy of learning as well as a man of action, Grotius was diplomat, lawyer, magistrate, scholar, and teacher; but essentially he was a jurist. He regarded his greatest work, the *De Jure Belli ac Pacis* (1625) or *The Law of War and Peace,* as a legal treatise rather than as a treatise in political theory; and he explicitly distinguished his intention as that of a jurist from Aristotle's intention in the *Politics* as that of a political scientist.[1]

Grotius' work is not, however, simply a treatise on positive law. Nor is it—in spite of its title—limited to the treatment of the law of war and peace, which is to say to international law as we know it today. On the contrary, it is, as its subtitle indicates, a general treatise on "the law of nature and of nations" (*jus naturae et gentium*), and on the main points of "public law" (*jus publicum*). And although it is true that Grotius focuses upon the law of war and peace, he constantly places that particular branch of jurisprudence within the framework of a general juristic analysis of law and government.

So far as the history of political theory is concerned then, Grotius' work is of importance because, in the first place, it is an excellent example of a juristic as opposed to a specifically philosophic or theological teaching on politics; and in the second place it is a superb specimen of the numerous treatises on natural public law which were written by jurists and theologians in western Europe from the sixteenth through the eighteenth century. (Other important examples of such works are *On Laws and God as Legislator* (1612), by the Spanish Jesuit Francisco Suárez; *On the Law of Nature and Nations* (1672), by the German jurist Samuel Pufendorf; and *The Law of Nations* (1758), by the Swiss

diplomat Emmerich de Vattel.) The practical importance of such
works may be gauged by the fact that Grotius, Pufendorf, Vattel, and
others were authorities for statesmen and lawyers, including the founding fathers of the United States.

The idea that man is by nature a rational and social animal is the
central principle of Grotius' treatise. The work begins with a restatement of the centuries-old struggle between classical conventionalism
and classical natural right. Grotius assigns the task of pleading the case
for conventionalism to Carneades, who was head of the later Academy
at Athens. Carneades is made by Grotius to argue that men have imposed laws on themselves only for reasons of expediency and self-pro-
tection; that such laws necessarily vary from place to place; that there
is no law of nature, strictly speaking, because all men are impelled by
their natural desires toward ends which are advantageous ultimately
only to themselves; and that, consequently, there is no justice which
is natural to man. To this doctrine, which was also accepted by the Epicureans, Grotius opposes what is basically a Stoic doctrine. That is, he
begins by accepting the proposition that men are, in the beginning of
their lives, impelled by natural desire merely to preserve their own being,
as distinguished from being impelled by pleasure or pain. But he denies
that this desire constitutes the definitive quality of man. Indeed, for
Grotius the original desire to preserve one's natural constitution is in
effect an instinctive or unconscious attempt to realize one's full nature:
to grow and to develop as a rational being. The rational faculty, which
defines man because it decisively distinguishes him from all the other
animals, is more excellent and more natural than are any of the original
natural desires. And it is the rational faculty, in turn, which perceives
that justice is a virtue, a good in and for itself, apart from any considerations of self-interest or expediency. Thus men are naturally impelled
to seek society with others; they naturally come to possess speech and
reason; and they naturally are inclined to behave justly, even though it
is true that many men in fact do not always follow their true nature.[2]

It is in relation to this central conception of man as a rational and
social animal that right and political society are understood by Grotius.
Right (*jus*), in its primary meaning, is that which is just. Right thus
understood has, according to Grotius, a negative rather than a positive
meaning: it is that which is not unjust. What is unjust is anything that
is in conflict with the nature of society between beings endowed with
reason. Thus for Grotius, who quotes Cicero and Seneca to support
his statement, men act justly only when they act in conformity with
their natural attraction to and desire for society. For example, since
to steal what belongs to others is destructive of all trust, and therefore

of society, to steal is against the natural order to which man belongs.

A second meaning of right is a quality of or belonging to persons, and usually refers to the rightful power to have or to do something. Kinds of rights are liberty or power over oneself, the power of a master over a slave, the power of a father over his son, and power over property. The rights, in each case, are in fact objective laws which define how the power in question may be exercised; and in some cases, the law of nature itself specifies the right. For example, the law of nature permits a person to kill a robber escaping with stolen property, if the property cannot be otherwise recovered. But it is important to notice that by making this second sense of right pertain specifically to the abstract "person" (*persona*), Grotius was believed by several of his contemporary jurists to have departed significantly from the traditional or Roman sense of the term "right" (*jus*). And it has been argued, in recent years, that Grotius' second definition of right is a precursor of the strictly modern idea of subjective "rights," which holds that the person possesses intrinsic "rights" simply as a human being and not as embodying certain objective qualities such as those of the ruler, the father, or the landowner. Even so, however, it must also be said that Grotius goes only a short distance toward the full idea of subjective rights; the specifically philosophic statement of that idea, and therefore of individualism as we know it in the modern age, begins with Thomas Hobbes, whose first major work, the *De Cive,* was published less than two decades after Grotius' work.

The third meaning of right is law, that is, a rule of action which obliges to what is correct and which carries with it some sanction.

Having defined three senses of *jus* or right, Grotius next divides right in the sense of law into two kinds: natural and volitional. The first kind, the law of nature (*jus naturale*), is defined in relation to the essential nature of man as "a dictate of right reason which points out that an act, according as it is or is not in conformity with rational nature, has in it a quality of moral baseness or moral necessity; and that in consequence, such an act is either forbidden or enjoined by the author of nature, God." [3] But lest we think, because of the last clause, that the law of nature itself depends simply on God's will, Grotius states in the Prolegomena that the law of nature would be valid even if there is no God or if the affairs of men are of no concern to Him. This statement— which Grotius, it should be noted, instantly acknowledges as blasphemous—constitutes an indication that a desacralization of natural law is conceivable to Grotius without thereby necessarily destroying its essential validity as a rule of reason to reasonable creatures. But even this cautious statement, because it suggests the possibility of the inde-

pendence of natural law from both revealed and natural theology, was
interpreted by a number of Grotius' contemporaries as marking a decided break with medieval and classical doctrines. The point we are
mainly concerned with here is that Grotius' suggestion of the possibility
of a secularized natural law which would still be fully binding on man
was, at the beginning of the seventeenth century, very controversial
although not unique. The doctrine of the dependence of man and the
political order on the divine order was still, for most jurists as well as
theologians, the essence of natural law.

Grotius offers two proofs of the existence of the law of nature. The
first is a priori, that is, the demonstration of the necessary agreement
of an act or a thing with the rational and social nature of man. This
proof, although very difficult, is the basis of certain knowledge of what
men are bound to by their intrinsic nature, for such a proof proceeds
strictly by reasoning about that nature. The second proof is a posteriori,
that is, it proceeds by supplying evidence of that which is believed by
all nations, or at least by learned men from all civilized nations, to be
binding on all men. In developing this general line of proof Grotius
quotes Cicero to the effect that "the agreement of all nations upon a
matter ought to be considered a law of nature" and Aristotle to the
effect that "in order to find what is natural we must look among those
things which according to nature are in a sound condition, not among
those that are corrupt." [4] Furthermore, in developing the a posteriori
line of proof for particular principles of the law of nature, Grotius cites
scores of examples and arguments taken from the writings of ancient
philosophers, historians, poets, rhetoricians, and theologians, as well as
from the Bible. In so doing, Grotius bases his own argument on the idea
of the *consensus gentium,* or agreement of peoples; for, as he argues,
when so many learned and wise men, who also happen to represent
different nations, such as the Jews, the Greeks, the Romans, and so on,
affirm the same principles as being true or certain, it must be due to the
operation of a "universal cause." That cause must be either a correct
conclusion drawn from the principles of nature themselves by these
learned men, or else the common consent of civilized mankind. In
either case, such evidence serves to confirm that which is in principle
discoverable, via the a priori proof, concerning the nature of man, law,
and political society.

The second kind of law is volitional. It is divided into human and
divine law. Human volitional law is of three kinds. First is the law
which is not directly dependent on the civil power; it is less comprehensive than the municipal or civil law and comprises the commands
of a father, a master, and all similar commands. Second is the municipal

or civil law (*jus civile*), which emanates from the civil power and which therefore regulates the relations of men and things within a particular political society. Third is the law of nations (*jus gentium*), which receives its obligatory force from the will of all or of many nations. The law of nations is distinguished from the law of nature not by subject matter but by reason of its being changeable, whereas the law of nature is unchangeable, and by reason of its being based on will and not simply on what is discerned by reason as being in accordance with the rational and social nature of man. These distinctions and their importance may be understood by taking an example: the question of the responsibility for actions. Grotius states that according to the strict law of nature no person is responsible for another's acts, except in the limited case where one person inherits the property of another. Nevertheless, the law of nations—that is, the law developed by the will of all or many nations—has modified this strict principle to the effect that all the subjects of a political society are responsible for the debts of the ruler, and their possessions are considered to have a charge against them to fulfill his obligations. The reason Grotius gives is that unless this concession is made, rulers, because they alone would then be responsible for their acts, would be encouraged to licentious actions since they are practically immune from having their own property seized as repayment. And on the other side, those to whom debts are owed by the ruler would thus unjustly be deprived of redress—unless, that is, a charge may be levied against the property of his subjects.

In contrast to his exceedingly elaborate and detailed analysis and definition of the nature and the kinds of law, Grotius' treatment of more specifically political phenomena, such as the nature and origins of political society or the nature and exercise of political power, is very sketchy, and it relies heavily on the authority of philosophers, historians, jurists, and so on. For example, when Grotius defines municipal law (*jus civile*), he indicates that it emanates from the civil power (*potestas civilis*), that the civil power is that power which rules over the civil order or state (*civitas*), and that the civil order is "a complete association [*civitas coetus perfectus*], joined together for the enjoyment of rights and for the common interest." [5] Later, when he provides a slightly more extended treatment of the civil power, Grotius is content, so far as the meaning or purpose of the civil order or state is concerned, to refer the reader to his proposition that the civil order is a "perfect association [*perfectus coetus*]." [6] But he provides practically no independent argument as to what precisely is meant by this and why this should be so. The reason seems to be first, that Grotius, as a jurist, is less concerned with such questions than with questions concerning the char-

acter of law, above all in its *relation* to the operations of the civil power;
and second, that he simply accepts two general classical ideas: (1) that
only within the civil order can man fully realize the potentiality of his
rational and social nature; and (2) that ruling, as such, is as necessary
and natural to the civil body as is the rule of reason necessary and natural
over the human body.

The latter point is shown strikingly well by the way in which
Grotius treats the civil power and its parts: he relies essentially on the
concepts and the distinctions of Aristotle, as provided in the *Politics* and
the *Ethics*. Thus Grotius says that the civil power has three aspects or
branches. The first branch is concerned with the general framing of
laws, both secular and religious, and is called "architectonic," for it
embodies the overarching and directive aspect of the civil power.[7] The
second branch concerns the particular interests of the society which are
public in nature. Such interests are the making of war, peace, and
treaties; the levying of taxes; and the exercising of the right of eminent
domain over the property of private citizens. Of this branch Grotius
says that Aristotle calls it the "political" branch, properly speaking, or
the branch which "deliberates" about specific policies and the framing
of specific decrees. The third branch of the civil power concerns the
private interests of the citizens and the possible controversies which may
arise among them. Its function, as contrasted to framing general laws
or deliberating concerning particular public policies, is to adjudicate
conflicts of private interests by the public authority. It therefore is called
the "judicial" branch.

Grotius concept of the nature and locus of the supreme power
(*summa potestas*) in the civil order also links him to the classical tradition and separates him from the modern idea of "sovereignty," as the
latter emerges in the writings of men such as Hobbes. Although supreme
power is defined initially as that power whose actions are not subject to
the legal control of another and cannot therefore be rendered void by
the operation of another human will, it is also true that every political
society, and therefore its supreme power, is subject to the limitations set
by the law of nature and the law of nations. As Grotius puts it, the
mother of municipal law is that obligation which arises from consent;
but since the obligation arising from consent derives its force from the
law of nature, above all that part of the law of nature which dictates
that men live in civil society and be guided by the rules of justice, nature
itself may be considered the "great-grandmother" of municipal law.
He also says that they are in error who argue that the standard of justice
which is applicable in the case of individuals is inapplicable to a nation
or a ruler. Such a view is only a particular application of a false doctrine

of law, which fails to see that law is not founded simply on expediency but on natural justice as well.[8]

Although it is true that in the case of most states it is the benefit or good of those who are governed which is the primary consideration in judging whether the supreme power is properly constituted, this does not mean that the supreme power ultimately resides in the governed or that there is a relation of mutual dependence between rulers and ruled. On the contrary, in a monarchy, for example, the possession of the supreme power means in essence the possession of rights and powers which are intrinsic to the ruling function. It is of course quite possible that the king may misconstrue those rights and misuse those powers. But Grotius vigorously opposes the conclusion that the people thereby automatically has a right to assume the supreme power or to dethrone the ruler. Thus the general right to revolution does not exist, strictly speaking: the end of civil society being public tranquility, this end necessarily takes precedence even over the right to protect oneself against the abuse of power by the ruler. Consequently, the waywardness of the supreme power is usually to be borne, even though one ought not, if at all possible, to do acts which are against the law of nature even if they are commanded by the supreme power. And here Grotius, typically, reverts to the authority of antiquity when he quotes Cicero, who says, "To me, peace on any terms between citizens seems more advantageous than civil war." [9]

Grotius constantly seeks to make a distinction between the nature of the supreme power in itself and the absolute possession of it. Thus in some cases, and above all in the case of absolute hereditary monarchy, the supreme power is held with full proprietary right. This means that when a people so ruled is transferred from one monarch to another there is not, strictly speaking, a transfer of the individuals but of the perpetual right of governing them in their totality as a people. But in other cases—in fact, perhaps the majority of cases—the supreme power is not held absolutely. Such is the case of a king who has the supreme power because it was conferred on him by the will of the people. Even in such a case, however, the actual *exercise* of the supreme power, once granted, is plenary.

The supreme power is in principle a unity, or is indivisible, and consists of the parts enumerated above as constituting the three branches of civil power. In fact, however, there are numerous historical examples in which the supreme power is divided. A notable example would be Rome under the emperors, where it happened that one emperor administered the East, another the West, and even that three emperors governed the whole empire in three divisions. A different type of division may occur when a people, in choosing a king, reserves to itself certain powers and confers others on the king absolutely. Thus in the time of Probus at Rome, the senate confirmed the laws made by the emperors, took cognizance of appeals, appointed proconsuls, and assigned military officers to the consuls. Still a third type of division is cited from the account given in Plato's *Laws* where, because the Heraclids had founded Argos, Messene, and Sparta, the kings of these states were bound to govern within the provisions of the laws which had been previously laid down.

Finally, Grotius generally follows Aristotle's idea that the civil order or state changes when the supreme power changes from one kind to another, as when there is a change from aristocracy to democracy, or democracy to monarchy; but he distinguishes this "political" issue from the juristic one of how the laws and the government are related to one another with respect to the definition of supreme power.

We have now to glance briefly at Grotius' application of the general principles set forth above to the question of just war, which is the main theme in his doctrine of international law.

The crucial question is whether war can ever truly be just. To this Grotius replies in the affirmative, arguing from the general principles of the nature of man and society, and buttressing these principles by exhaustive and exhausting citations from history, both sacred and secular, from the *jus gentium,* and from divine volitional law (that is, the Bible). The gist of his argument is that not all use of force is prohibited by natural and volitional law, but only that use of force which is in conflict with the principles of society, that is, which attempts to take away the rights or possessions of another. Thus war may be waged justly, but only to achieve or to re-establish the natural end of man, which is peace or the condition of tranquil social life, and not for personal or collective self-aggrandizement. But this kind of definition of the scope of just as opposed to unjust war is too general to serve effectively as a guide. Grotius must, therefore, set forth with his usual detail the various categories of just and unjust war.

As for just wars, they fall into two general categories: those waged in defense of self and property, and those waged to prosecute injuries and to inflict deserved punishment. The treatment of the first category requires Grotius to enter into a very elaborate discussion of the origin and types of property, for it is only by knowing what belongs to whom that one can decide when a war is just. The treatment of the second category requires him to set forth the nature of pacts, contracts, and promises, for it is only by knowing what is owed to whom that one can decide when a war is just with respect to such matters.

As an illustration of Grotius' doctrine on just war it is instructive to consider his argument concerning the application of the law of nature to cases where a particular ruler has not been directly injured by the depredations of another ruler. The governing principle, says Grotius, is that rulers are free to serve the interests of human society by punishing those who "excessively violate the law of nature," even though no direct injury has been done to those who mete out the punishment. This principle he derives from the fact that those who hold the civil power are subject to no other legal power, yet are bound to observe *and to enforce* the law of nature wherever possible. He then quotes Seneca to the effect that "if a man does not attack my own country, but yet is a heavy burden to his own, and although separated from my people he afflicts his own, such debasement of mind nevertheless cuts him off from us." And he cites Aristotle's authority for the proposition that against men who are truly barbarians war is sanctioned by nature, that is, that a "war of civilization" is, in extreme circumstances, just. In adopting this position Grotius explicitly takes issue with writers of the fifteenth and sixteenth centuries, such as Francisco Victoria, who had taught that whoever metes out punishment must either have suffered injury in his own person or state, or have jurisdiction over him who is attacked.[10] The basic difference—and it is one which links Grotius more to the writers of classical antiquity than either to moderns such as Hobbes or theologians such as Victoria—is that for Grotius the power of punishing is derived not merely from civil jurisdiction but from the law of nature itself.

Grotius' work appeared, as we have noted, less than two decades prior to the *De Cive* (1642) of Thomas Hobbes. But in spite of this proximity in time, and in spite of a superficial agreement, such as the common use of the concept of the "law of nature," the fact is that Grotius still looks mainly to the classics of antiquity whereas Hobbes explicitly sets out to build anew. The basic disagreement concerns the question whether man is indeed by nature a rational and social animal; in turning to Hobbes we turn to the iconoclast who states the essence of the modern view of man and natural law.

NOTES

1. Hugo Grotius, *The Law of War and Peace*, Prolegomena, 57; II.ix.8.

2. *Ibid.*, Prolegomena, 3–10, 16–30; I.ii.50.

3. *Ibid.*, i.10.

4. *Ibid.*, 12.

5. *Ibid.*, 14.

6. *Ibid.*, iii.7.

7. Cf. Aristotle *Ethics* VI. viii, which Grotius cites.

8. *The Law of War and Peace,*
Prolegomena, 15–23.

9. *Ibid.,* I. iv.19.
10. *Ibid.,* II.xx.40.

READINGS

The best text of *The Law of War and Peace* is the translation of Grotius' work prepared as part of the series titled, "Classics of International Law," sponsored by the Carnegie Endowment for International Peace. The translation, by Francis W. Kelsey, is complete and was published in 1925 by the Clarendon Press, Oxford.

A. Grotius, Hugo. *The Law of War and Peace.* Prolegomena, secs 1, 2, 5–22, 28, 30, 39–42, 45–50, 57–58; bk I, chap. i, secs 1–13; chap. ii, sec. 1; chap. iii, sec. 5, par. 7–sec. 7, sec. 8, pars 1–6, 13–14, sec. 9, secs 13–14, sec. 16, par. 1, sec. 17, sec. 24; chap. iv, sec. 1, par. 3, sec. 2, par. 1, sec. 7, pars 1–2.

B. Grotius Hugo. *The Law of War and Peace.* Prolegomena; bk 1, chap. i; chap. ii, secs 1–4, 6; chap. iii, secs 1–9, 13–17, 24; chap. iv; bk II, chap. i, sec. 1, pars 1–2, secs 2–3, sec. 11, sec. 17; chap. ii, secs 1–2; chap. iii, secs 1–4; chap. v, secs 1–5, 7–9, 27–29; chap. viii, sec. 1; chap. x, sec. 1; chap. xi, secs 1–3; chap. xii, secs 7–12; chap. xiv, secs 1–6, 9; chap. xv, secs 1–3; chap. xx, secs 1–4, 18, 40, 48; chap. xxii, secs 1–3, 11; bk III, chap. i, secs 1–3; chap. ii, secs 1–2; chap. iii, secs 1, 4, 6.

THOMAS HOBBES

1588–1679

Hobbes presented his political philosophy thematically in three books, *The Elements of Law* (1640), *De Cive* (*The Citizen,* 1642), and *Leviathan* (1651). The most manifest differences among the books concern the development and elaboration of theological doctrine in the later books.

Hobbes's intention can be seen as twofold: (1) to put moral and political philosophy, for the first time, on a scientific basis; (2) to contribute to the establishment of civic peace and amity and to the disposing of mankind toward fulfilling their civic duties. These two intentions, theoretical and practical, were in Hobbes's mind closely connected. This latter intention, the civic or civilizing intention, identified Hobbes with the tradition of political philosophy that he associated with the names of Socrates, Plato, Aristotle, Plutarch, and Cicero. The entire tradition, according to Hobbes, had failed, however, both in its quest for truth and in its inability to lead men toward peace. Hobbes's emphatic break with the tradition was decisively prepared by Machiavelli and, following Machiavelli, Bacon. The classics failed, according to Machiavelli, because they aimed too high. Because they based their political doctrines on considerations of man's highest aspirations, the life of virtue and the society dedicated to the promotion of virtue, they rendered themselves ineffective; as Bacon said, they made "imaginary laws for imaginary commonwealths." Machiavelli's "realism" consists in a conscious lowering of the standards of political life, taking as goals of political life not the perfection of man but those lower goals actually pursued by most men and most societies most of the time. Political schemes framed in accordance with men's lower but more powerful motives are much more likely to be realized than the utopias of the classics. However, unlike Machiavelli, Hobbes elaborated a code of moral or natural law, natural law as a morally binding law, determining the purposes of civil society. But, following Machiavelli's "realism," he separated his doctrine of the natural law from the idea of the perfection of man.[1] He attempted to deduce the natural law from what is most powerful in most men most of the time: not reason, but passion. Because of what he regarded as his discovery of the true roots of human behavior, his knowledge of human nature, and his scientific way of proceeding, Hobbes believed that he had succeeded where all others had failed, that he was the first true political philosopher. In accordance with these convictions he recommended that his books be established in the universities as authoritative and continually attacked the doctrines of Aristotle, "whose opinions are at this day and in these parts of greater authority than any other human writings," as both subversive and false.[2]

For Hobbes, scientific knowledge meant mathematical knowledge, or geometrical knowledge. Hitherto, he wrote, geometry has been the only science that has attained indisputable conclusions. The term geometry was sometimes used by Hobbes to refer to all the mathematical sciences, the study of motion and force, mathematical physics, as well as the study of geometrical figures. Philosophy, or science, proceeds in either of two ways: (1) with the compositive method, or "synthetically," by reasoning from the first and generating causes of all things to their apparent effects, or (2) with the resolutive method, or "analytically," by reasoning from apparent effects, or facts, to possible causes of their generation. The first principles of all things are defined by Hobbes as body, or matter, and motion, or change of place: "every part of the Universe, is Body; and that which is not Body, is no part of the Universe: and because the Universe is All, that which is no part of it is Nothing. . . ." In accordance with the synthetic or geometrical mode of proceeding one would begin with the laws of physics in general, from them deduce the passions, the causes of the behavior of individual men, and from the passions deduce the laws of social and political life. However, it is by means of the analytic method, the analysis of sense experience, that one arrives at adequate definitions of the first principles themselves.

The analytic method is especially important for political philosophy. For Hobbes expected the moral and civil science which he elaborated to be able to be convincing not only to natural philosophers, but also to any man "that pretends but reason enough to govern his private family." This expectation is reasonable because the facts upon which his analysis is based are known to all normal men by experience. Hobbes invites his reader to test the truth of what he wrote by looking into himself and considering whether what Hobbes says about the passions, thoughts, and natural inclinations of mankind apply to him; then by learning to "read" and know himself, through the similitude of passions and situations he will be able to read the passions and thoughts of all other men. Although his conception of scientific method influenced Hobbes's formulations, presentation, and analysis of human experience, he indicates that it is not to his conception of science but to his understanding of common prescientific experience that we are to look in order to determine the truth and importance of his political philosophy. He suggests that the adequacy and correctness of his judgments of, or insights into, what are the fundamental human experiences can be considered and understood independently of his physics.[3]

Human behavior, according to Hobbes, is to be understood primarily in terms of a mechanistic psychology of the passions,[4] those forces in man, which, so to speak, push him from behind; it is not to be understood in terms of those things which could be thought of as attracting man from in front, the ends of man, or what for Hobbes would be the objects of the passions. The objects of the passions, Hobbes says, vary with each man's constitution and education and are too easy to disguise. Furthermore, good and evil, the words with which men characterize the objects of their desires and aversions, are strictly relative to the man using the words, "there being nothing simply and absolutely so; nor any common Rule of Good and Evil, to be taken from the nature of the objects themselves. . . ." What men really mean when they say something is good is that it pleases them. Yet it is true that as the passions issue in actions, men are guided by their imaginations and their opinions of what is good and evil; but the thoughts do not control the passions; on the contrary, "for the Thoughts are to the Desires, as Scouts, and Spies, to range abroad, and find the way to the Things Desired." [5]

Hobbes was in agreement with the tradition, stemming from Socrates and including Thomas Aquinas, that the goals and character of moral and political life should be determined by reference to nature, especially human nature. However, he determined the way in which nature sets the standards for politics very differently than did the tradition, namely, through the construction of a theory of "the state of nature." The theory of the state of nature, deduced, Hobbes says, from the passions of man, is one way of dealing with the old psychological problem, a problem of decisive importance for political philosophy: Is man by nature social and political? Hobbes denies that man is nat-

urally social and political.[6] The grounds of this denial are made evident
by the theory of the state of nature, that prepolitical condition in which
men live without civil government, or without a common power over
them to keep them in fear.

If man is not by nature social and political, then all civil societies
must have grown out of presocial and prepolitical states of nature, *i.e.,*
the state of nature must have existed among the progenitors of all
men now living in civil society. Hobbes did not believe that there ever
was such a state all over the world, but, he said, in many places of
America "at this day," during civil wars, and between independent
sovereigns such a state actually exists. The historical question, however,
is not very important for Hobbes. The state of nature is deduced from
the passions of man; it is meant to reveal and clarify what it is about
man's natural inclinations that we must know in order to form the right
kind of political order. It serves primarily to determine the reasons, the
purposes, or the ends for the sake of which men form political societies.
These ends being known, the political problem becomes one of how to
organize man and society in order to realize the ends most effectively.

What would the condition of mankind be if there were no civil
society? How would men be related to each other? First of all, Hobbes
argues, men are much more equal both in faculties of body and mind
than has hitherto been recognized. The most important equality is the
equal ability all men have to kill each other. This is most important because the most important concern of men is their own self-preservation.
Self-preservation, in turn, is most important because fear, the fear of violent death, is the most powerful passion. Equality of ability leads to
equality of hopes and to competition among men, among all who desire
the same things. This natural enmity is intensified by the diffidence, or
distrust, men without government have for each other as they anticipate
how each would like to deprive all others of whatever goods (including
life) they have, so that each is led to think of subjugating all the rest until
there is no power left capable of threatening his security. Contrary to
what is said "in the Books of the old Moral Philosophers," Hobbes says,
happiness, or felicity, consists in a continual progress of the desire from
one object to another. Since this is so, what men seek constantly is some
means of securing the way to their future desires. Men seek not only to
procure, but also to be insured of a contented life for themselves "So
that," Hobbes says, "in the first place, I put for a general inclination of
all mankind, a perpetual and restless desire of power after power, that
ceaseth only in death." [7]

The problem of civil life is further complicated by the presence
in our nature of the love of glory, or pride, or vanity. All pleasures which

are not bodily, or sensual, pleasures Hobbes calls pleasures of the mind. All pleasures of the mind are directly or indirectly derived from "glorying." Glorying is based upon the good opinions a man receives or has of himself or of his power. The opinions are always based upon comparisons with others. Every man desires to have others value him as he values himself, and consequently, upon signs of contempt and undervaluing, he becomes quite ready to destroy those who slight him. Even when men gather for pleasure and recreation they seek it mostly through those things which stir laughter. And laughter, Hobbes says, is caused by sudden glory, being pleased by some sudden act of one's own, "or by the apprehension of some deformed thing in another, by comparison whereof they suddenly applaud themselves." This bleak picture is not relieved by any reference to a sense of honor or nobility. Honor and dishonor, properly understood, according to Hobbes, have nothing to do with justice or injustice. Honor is nothing else than an acknowledgment or opinion of someone's power, *i.e.,* superiority, especially one's power to help or harm ourselves. Even reverence is defined by Hobbes as the conception we have of another being who, having the power to do good or hurt to ourselves, does not have the will to do us hurt. The emphasis is not upon admiration or love, but fear.

These three great natural causes of quarrels among men, competition, distrust, and glory, make the state of nature really a state of war, "and such a war, as is of every man, against every man." In such a state,

men live without other security, than what their own strength, and their own invention shall furnish them withal. In such condition there is no place for industry; because the fruit thereof is uncertain: and consequently no culture of the earth, no navigation, nor use of the commodities that may be imported by sea; no commodious building; no instruments of moving and removing such things as require much force; no knowledge of the face of the earth; no account of time; no arts; no letters; no society; and which is worst of all, continual fear, and danger of violent death; and the life of man solitary, poor, nasty, brutish, and short.[8]

Furthermore, there is no appeal to justice in the state of nature; nothing there can be unjust, for justice and injustice are such only in terms of some preceding law and there is no law outside of civil society. In short, man is not by nature social; on the contrary, nature dissociates man. The state of civil society, then, is radically conventional. This does not mean that there are not present in men certain natural impulses or forces that drive them toward civil life. It does mean that the antisocial forces are as natural as, and, when unmitigated by convention even more powerful than, the forces promoting civil life. Instead of serving as a direct guide to human goodness, nature indicates what man has to run away from. The only redeeming thing about the state of nature is the possibility of getting out of it. With Hobbes we are already in an atmosphere congenial to the idea of the conquest of nature.

Fear of death, desire for comfort, and hope of obtaining it through their industry incline men to peace. Reason, working along with these passions of fear, desire, and hope, suggests rules for peaceful living together. By comparing these passions with the three great natural causes of human enmity, we see that fear of death and desire for comfort are present both among the inclinations toward peace and among the causes of enmity; vanity, or the desire for glory is absent from the former group.[9] The task of reason then is to devise means of redirecting and intensifying the fear of death and the desire for comfort, so as to overpower and cancel out the destructive effects of the desire for glory, or pride. By understanding human nature mechanistically, we become capable of manipulating and finally, Hobbes seems to hope, conquering it. Hobbes calls these rules of reason Laws of Nature, the Moral Law, and sometimes the dictates of reason. In using these names he admits he is bowing to traditional usage, for him the rules are merely conclusions or theorems concerning what conduces to self-preservation. Properly speaking, only commands of the civil sovereign are laws. These rules, however, in so far as they are commanded by God in the Scriptures, may be called laws.

All the laws of nature and all social and political duties or obligations are derived from and subordinate to the right of nature, the individual's right to self-preservation. To the extent that modern liberalism teaches that all social and political obligations are derived from and are in the service of the individual rights of man, Hobbes may be regarded as the founder of modern liberalism. Social, moral, and political rules and institutions in the service of individual rights can be expected to be much more effective than the utopian schemes of Plato and Aristotle. For the individual rights themselves are derived from the most powerful selfish passions and desires of men, the desire for comfortable living and, most powerful of all, because it is the fear of what is worst of all, the fear of violent death, the passion underlying the right to self-preservation. Because the rights are backed up by the passions, they can be, in a sense, self-enforcing. As the foundations of the traditional doctrines of moral restraint and contempt for selfishness become discredited, the way is opened for a new legitimation or sanctification of human selfishness.

The right of nature is the blameless liberty to do or refrain from doing whatever one can to preserve one's life.[10] The right to an end also

implies a right to the means to that end. Because men differ in intelligence and prudence, some understand the requirements of preservation
better than others. Yet these intellectual differences are not decisive for
Hobbes. Regardless of his intelligence, no man, Hobbes argues, is sufficiently interested in the preservation of others; hence in the state of
nature, each man must be the sole judge of the means necessary to his
own preservation. Therefore, each man has a natural right to whatever
means he judges conduce to his preservation. In the universal enmity of
the state of nature, anything not under a man's own power can be regarded as a danger to his preservation, and therefore there is nothing
which cannot be regarded as a means to his preservation. Hence, in this
state "every man has a right to everything." No man is secure in such
a state. The laws of nature, as distinguished from the rights of nature, are
precepts of reason which instruct men as to what they ought to do to
avoid the perils to their own self-preservation that follow equally from
their natural rights and from their irrational desires.

For the securing of their own self-preservation, the first and fundamental law of nature enjoins men to seek peace and to defend themselves
against those from whom peace cannot be obtained. All the rest of the
moral law, the laws of nature, is directed toward establishing the conditions of peace. The first law of nature derived from the fundamental
law is that each man ought to be willing to divest himself of his right
to all things when others are also willing, and ought to be satisfied with
just as much liberty against other men as he allows other men against
himself. This mutual laying down of rights is accomplished by what
has come to be known as the social contract. Civil society is constituted
by the social contract, wherein each one of a multitude of men obliges
himself, by contract with each of the rest, not to resist the commands of
that man or council that they have recognized as their sovereign. Each
man contracts only with a view to what is good for himself, and above
all with a view to the security and preservation of his life. Therefore it
cannot be presumed that any man has contracted away those rights
whose loss would defeat the purpose of all contracts. No one, for instance, can be regarded as having laid down his right to resist anyone
who attempts to deprive him of his life.

When a man has by contract or covenant given away or renounced
any right, he is obliged or bound not to hinder those to whom he
granted or abandoned that right from enjoying the benefit of it. In other
words, according to the next law of nature, men should perform their
covenants. If this principle did not hold, society itself would dissolve.
This principle, fidelity to contracts, according to Hobbes, is the basis of
all justice and injustice; for where no covenant has preceded, no rights

have been relinquished or transferred, and each man has a right to everything. Thus injustice, or injury, is nothing other than the non-performance of covenants, exercising a right that one has already legally relinquished. All genuine legislation then becomes a form of self-legis-lation, and injury is like a self-contradiction, willing to do that which one has already willed not to do.[11] All duties and obligations to others derive from covenants. But covenants, contracts where one or both of the parties promise to perform in the future, depend upon trust. There is no trust and no valid covenant where there is a reasonable fear of non-performance on either side. There is then no trust in the state of nature. Therefore, before it is correct to use the terms just or unjust, there must be some coercive power, the sovereign, which can compel all contractors equally to perform their covenants. The sovereign must see to it that terror of punishment is a greater force than the lure of any benefit which could be expected from a breach of covenant. No moral force is appealed to in order to establish conditions of trust; once again fear is the passion to be relied upon. According to Hobbes, intelligent calculation of self-interest is all that is required to make a man just. The fact that he acts under compulsion does not make him less just, for self-interest is the only basis of morality. One consequence of this kind of reasoning is a broad-ening of the traditional notion of a just war. For Hobbes, as for Bacon, the intention to rectify a previous injury is not necessary to justify war; the subjective criterion, fear of a neighboring nation's strength, is suffi-cient.

Hobbes addressed himself directly to Aristotle's idea of distributive justice. The doctrine that some men by nature are more worthy to com-mand and others more worthy to serve is the foundation of Aristotle's political science, Hobbes wrote. The doctrine is false because in the state of nature all men are equal, the inequality found now among men has been introduced by the civil laws. Furthermore, the doctrine is danger-ous because it contributes to pride. Distributive justice properly conceived is the justice of an arbitrator and consists not in distributing to each in proportion to his virtues and vices, but in treating all as equal. For, Hobbes said, if nature made men equal, that equality ought to be acknowledged. Even if nature made them unequal, men will always consider themselves equal and thus will enter into conditions of peace only on equal terms. Therefore, for the sake of peace, such equality ought to be admitted, even if it does not exist. Hence it is a law of nature that all men should acknowledge each other as equal by nature. The natural differences between men are then either nonexist-ent or politically irrelevant. One purpose dominates Hobbes's discussion of the laws of nature: to make men sociable and peaceable, and accordingly to end or reduce to a mimimum the friction, resentment, and hostility generated among men by pride, partiality, and excessive self-love in general. Among the laws of nature are rules for the arbitration of controversies and for the impartial distribution of disputed property. Ingratitude is forbidden. Expressions of hatred, contempt, or disesteem, even by judges for convicted criminals, are not to be allowed. Lest one think that not all men are able to comprehend all these laws of nature, Hobbes asserts that they can all be comprehended, even by those who are too neglectful or too busy to learn them, through the rule: Do not do unto others what you would not have them do unto you.[12] The moral law is not directed toward the perfection of our natures. Aristotle was wrong about virtue and vice. Because his opinions were merely the opinions received during his own times and still received by most unlearned men, Hobbes said, they were not likely to be very accurate.[13] Virtue, if it means anything more than a man's power, is the habit of doing what tends to our own self-preservation, and to its fundamental condition, peace; vice is the contrary.

The essential defect of the laws of nature, the dictates of reason, is that they bind men in their consciences only, and the actions and wills of men are determined not by conscience or reason but by fear of punishment and hope of reward. There is fear of invisible powers, God or gods, in the state of nature, but this fear is not powerful enough.[14] What is needed, according to Hobbes, is the establishment of conditions that really make it safe to obey the laws of nature, otherwise one who obeys such rules only puts himself at the mercy of those who do not obey. In short, civil or political government, visible powers, are required. Security requires first of all the cooperation of many men, a multitude large and powerful enough both to make the breaking of covenants and invasion of each other's rights very dangerous, and to provide defense against foreign enemies. There is no set limit to the size of a civil society. The size should be great enough to deter any enemy from risking war, and therefore depends upon the size of the enemy. These requirements and the antisocial elements in man's nature indicate that the unity achieved through consent, many wills agreeing in one object, one common good, is not sufficient to bind men together. Political society, or the commonwealth, requires a real unity, or union.

This union, like justice and injustice, is defined by Hobbes in legal terms. The commonwealth must be constituted as one legal person by a great multitude of men, each of whom covenants with all the others to regard the will of this legal, civil, or artificial person as his own will. This legal person, the sovereign, "is" the commonwealth. In practical terms this means that every subject should regard all actions of the sovereign power as actions of his own, all legislation by the sovereign as his own self-legislation. In fact, the sovereign power, the power of representing and commanding the wills of all, can be vested in one man or in a council. Hobbes was the first to define the commonwealth as a "person." He found this necessary for the following reasons. Since the only legitimate obligation is ultimately self-obligation, the freedom of man in the state of nature must survive, in some form, in his subjection to the government; "there being no obligation on any man, which ariseth not from some act of his own; for all men equally, are by nature free." [15] This is accomplished through the legal fictions that the sovereign is a "person" with a will that can represent the wills of all his subjects, and that the sovereign's legislation is self-legislation of the subject. Through such a union the powers and faculties of every subject can be brought to contribute fully to the maintenance of peace and the common defense.

The social contract has two parts: (1) a covenant of each member of the future civil body with each of the others to acknowledge as sovereign whatever man or assembly of men a majority of their number agrees upon; (2) the vote determining who or what is to be the sovereign. All those who are not parties to the contract remain in the state of war and are, therefore, enemies of the rest.

The validity of the covenant is in no way affected by whether it was entered into under duress, fear of death and violence, or not. The body politic, Hobbes says, can be founded "naturally" as well as through institution. All paternal and despotic government arises in the first way, through fear of the sovereign himself, e.g., when he is a conqueror in war; all government by institution arises through mutual fear of the individuals. Fear is the motive in both cases. Both foundations are equally legitimate: there is no difference, as far as right is concerned, between foundation by conquest and foundation by institution. In the acquisition of sovereignty by conquest, it makes no difference whether the war was a just war or not. Since no one can really transfer his strength and faculties to another, the social contract in fact obliges all not to resist the will of the sovereign power. That all citizens have not explicitly entered into such a covenant is obvious; but anyone who lives in a commonwealth accepting the protection of the government, the sovereign, is to be regarded as having tacitly entered into the covenant. Apparently, for Hobbes, that exactness in political life which corresponds to mathematical exactness in theoretical matters is legal exactness. And just as controversies are put to rest in mathematics, so evidently he hoped that the political controversies that had always disturbed the peace of the political world could be put to rest by an exact deduction, from the social contract, of the rights and duties of sovereign and subject.

The social contract is binding only when the end for the sake of which it is entered into, security, is realized. Obedience is exchanged for protection. Not that men can ever be made completely safe from injury by others. It is sufficient for each citizen to know that anyone who intends to injure him has more to fear from punishment by the sovereign than he has to gain from his crime.

The first right of the sovereign is the right to punish or the right to wield the police power. This follows from the fundamental renunciation of the right of resistance agreed to by all the citizens. No subject can be freed from his subjection by claiming that the sovereign has committed a breach of covenant, for the sovereign has made no covenant with any subject, the subjects have covenanted only among themselves. Since the sovereign has not covenanted with anyone, he alone retains the right to all things that all men had in the state of nature. Consequently he can neither injure anyone nor commit injustice, since injustice, or injury, in the strict or legal sense is nothing but nonfulfillment of covenant, assuming a right which one has already convenanted away. Furthermore, since the sovereign represents the will of each of the subjects, anyone accusing the sovereign of injury is accusing himself, and to do injustice to oneself is impossible. Hence the sovereign cannot justly be punished in any way by his subjects. The right to make war and peace, which includes the right to levy taxes and to compel citizens to take up arms for their country's defense, is also annexed to the sovereign, for these rights must be in the hands of the same power that can punish those who will not obey.

The legislative power must also be in the sovereign's hands for the same reason: men will not obey the commands of those they have no reason to fear. The power of the sword, the punitive power, and the legislative power must be in the same hands. The civil laws of each commonwealth are nothing else than the commands of the civil sovereign. They prescribe what goods a man may enjoy, *i.e.,* they define what is and what is not private property. They determine what actions a man may do without being molested by his fellows, *i.e.,* they prescribe what is good, evil, just, unjust, honest, and dishonest. They contribute to peace by attempting to determine all controversial questions before controversy arises.

The judicial power, for the same reason as the legislative power, is also committed to the sovereign. Because the sovereign must be able to determine the means of discharging his functions, the executive power, and the power of appointing all counselors, ministers, magistrates and officers, also is invested in him. Furthermore, because all voluntary actions of men depend upon their wills and their wills upon their opinions of the good and evil, or reward and punishment, they will receive from acting or omitting to act, the sovereign is to be judge of all doctrines and opinions which may be delivered to the citizens. The criterion of censorship is what doctrines are conducive to and what repugnant to peace. This power of absolute censorship applies to religious opinions as well. As a matter of fact religion is defined with a view to this power by Hobbes. Both religion and superstition are defined as "fear of power invisible." The difference between them is that the former is allowed by the public authority, the latter not allowed. The opinions which, according to Hobbes, have most disturbed the peace of the Christian world, are the opinions that lead citizens to believe that they owe obedience to others besides those to whom the supreme civil authority is committed. We shall take up this subject again in our discussion of Hobbes's teaching regarding Christianity.

It is clear from this list of powers that the power of the sovereign is absolute, *i.e.*, no greater power can be conveyed by men to any man. The sovereign is not bound to obey the civil laws, for they are only his commands and he can release himself from them at his pleasure. No one can claim any property rights against him because all property is derived from the laws, *i.e.*, his will. Opposing the sovereign's will in any particular case would be opposing the ground of all property and, hence, self-defeating. When citizens are allowed to sue the supreme authority, the question cannot be whether the sovereign or his ministers had a right to do what was done, but rather what it was that the sovereign in fact willed in this matter. That absolute power is really implicit in all governments can be seen through the cases of generals who are granted absolute powers temporarily in wartimes. Only the possessor of absolute power can grant absolute power, even temporarily. And when, for example, a constitutional assembly prescribes limits to the powers of a government, the exercise of the power of limitation is itself an exercise of absolute power. The objection that such an absolute power has never been acknowledged by citizens anywhere is, as arguments from practice generally are, invalid, for practice may be faulty practice. The art of making and maintaining commonwealths consists in following certain definite rules like the rules of arithmetic and geometry. Hobbes believed himself to be the first discoverer of those rules.

There are certain rights of the subject that are unalienable, *i.e.*, that cannot be transferred or resigned by covenant. For there is no obligation of man which does not proceed from some act of his own, and every act of his own is presumed to aim at some good to himself; therefore no contract, including the social contract, should be so construed as to deprive a man of the condition of all good for himself, his life, and the means of securing it. Every man may justly disobey any command to kill or wound himself or to abstain from anything that he requires to live. The right to self-preservation remains inviolable. But are not soldiers required to sacrifice their lives in war? And is not the fear of violent death in a sense the basis of all legitimacy, and therefore a sufficient motive to justify civil disobedience? Hobbes faced this problem and concluded that to run away from battle out of fear is dishonorable and cowardly but not unjust. It is the sovereign's task to see that the fear of desertion outweighs the fear of battle. To refuse the sovereign's command to fight against an enemy is not unjust if a man finds a suitable substitute. For a condemned man to resist an executioner lawfully doing his duty is just. No man in a criminal trial is bound to testify against himself, for no covenant, including the fundamental covenant, can oblige a man to harm himself. No man is obliged, *e.g.,* to execute his own parent, or a benefactor, or to do any act that is so shameful that it would result in his being so miserable and despised that he would grow weary of his own life.[16]

It is clear that these inviolable liberties of the citizens could be extended and construed as providing standards for distinguishing good from bad sovereigns, *i.e.,* as providing citizens with standards by which they could legitimately criticize, judge, and thereby weaken the sovereign authority. If given institutional form they could lead to limited sovereignty. Hobbes tried his best to guard against the revolutionary principle inherent in all attempts to set forth the principles of government: he who sets forth principles justifying authority by that very act provides standards for justifying the alteration or abolishment of that authority when it departs from those principles. Despite these exceptions to the obligation of obedience to the sovereign, the sovereign's absolute right remains: he may rightfully punish with death any refusal or resistance, however just. If the sovereign exercises his right contrary to right reason, however, he, like every man in the state of nature, sins against the laws of nature and therefore is answerable to their author, God, for his iniquity. Furthermore, Hobbes admits, there is a certain natural punishment for negligent government, *i.e.,* rebellion.

In all matters where the laws are silent, the subject retains the right to do or forbear as he wishes. And sometimes a sovereign may prudently forbear to exercise his right, though that in no way diminishes the right. There is no valid reason for sovereigns to desire to oppress their subjects, for the strength of sovereigns is directly dependent upon the strength and well-being of their subjects. Certainly, Hobbes admitted, such absolute power can be abused, but there is no condition of human life without inconveniences. "The obligation of subjects to the sovereign, is understood to last as long, and no longer, than the power lasteth, by which he is able to protect them." [17] And there is no avoiding the fact that he that has the power to protect all also has the power to oppress all. Following the book of Job, Hobbes compared the sovereign to Leviathan, whom God called "King of the Proud." Only the greatest of earthly powers can govern the pride of man. Hobbes's *Leviathan* is also such a Leviathan in so far as it rules the minds of men and crushes and roots out the seeds of human pride.

There are three kinds of commonwealths, differing as the respective sovereign powers differ. When that power is committed to one man, the government is a monarchy; when committed to an assembly of men where every citizen has a right to vote, it is a democracy; when committed to an assembly where only a part of the citizens have a right to vote, it is an aristocracy. The ancient Greek and Roman writers also distinguished between good and bad governments. They called bad rule by one man tyranny, bad rule by the people, or many, anarchy, and bad rule of the few oligarchy. Good and bad governments were distinguished according to whether the rulers ruled primarily for the sake of the common good or common advantage, or for their own selfish advantages. These moral distinctions, according to Hobbes, are unsound. They indicate only the subjective like or dislike of those who use them. Those who dislike monarchy call it tyranny, likewise anarchy is a name for democracy disliked, oligarchy a name for aristocracy disliked. This rejection of what Hobbes calls Aristotle's distinction between governments which rule for the benefit of the subjects and those which rule for the benefit of the rulers makes the distinction between a tyrant and a legitimate monarch politically meaningless. Both subjects and rulers, Hobbes argues, share equally in the first and greatest benefits of all government, peace and defense. All suffer equally from the greatest misery, civil war and anarchy. Since the ruler's strength and power always depend upon the strength and power of his subjects, both suffer the same disadvantages if the ruler weakens the subjects by depriving them of money and goods.

A deeper ground, perhaps, for the rejection of the distinction was Hobbes's conviction that no ruler or bearer of the sovereignty could be expected not to pursue his private advantage, the advantages of family and friends, as much and even more than the public advantage. On the basis of Hobbes's reduction of good and evil to pleasure and pain and his doctrine of sovereignty, the age-old political controversies about what form of government is best become much less important. These controversies were necessarily connected with the question about what over-all purposes civil society should serve, *e.g.,* liberty, empire, or wealth. Contrary to the misleading doctrines of Aristotle and Cicero and other Greek and Roman writers, who were, according to Hobbes, prejudiced in favor of popular government, the power of the government and the liberty of the citizen in each form of government is the same. The sovereignty is absolute in every commonwealth. The goal, or purpose, of each form of government is the same, peace and security. The decisive political, or practical, questions tend to become technical or administrative questions, such as under what kind of administration of the sovereign powers peace and security are most conveniently produced.[18]

Since those who bear the sovereign authority, being men, will always be most concerned with their private interests, the public interest will be most advanced where it is more closely united with private interests. This occurs under monarchy, which is therefore the best form of government. In democracy, where each man bears some part of the sovereignty, the number of those capable of enriching and serving themselves at the expense of the public interest is at a maximum. In a monarchy there can be only one Nero, in a democracy there can be as many Neros as there are orators flattering the populace. A monarch may promote unworthy persons but often will not. In a democracy the promotion of unworthy persons cannot be avoided. For within democracy there is always keen competition between popular orators, or demagogues, and the power of each demagogue is dependent upon his power to control and dispense patronage. Those who did not endeavor to benefit and attach as many people as possible, worthy and unworthy, to their side, or faction, would soon be overwhelmed by those who did. From this it is easy to understand the chief defect of democracy, the tendency to breed factions and civil wars. An aristocracy in this regard stands somewhere between the other two forms. It becomes better the more it approaches monarchy, worse the more it approaches democracy. As far as the actual exercise of the sovereign powers is concerned, one can doubt whether democracy is really ever anything different from an aristocracy of orators or a temporary monarchy of one orator. Those who complain of lack of liberty under monarchy do not understand what they really want. For the liberties of a subject, as defined by the doctrine of sovereignty, are the same under all governments, but under a democracy the accusers of monarchy would be rulers as well as subjects. It is not liberty but dominion or power and its attendant honor that they want. The true cause of their disaffection is that monarchy deprives them of the opportunity to show off their wisdom, knowledge, and eloquence in deliberating, or seeming to deliberate, about matters of the greatest importance. The love of liberty, according to Hobbes, turns out to be only a mask for the desire for praise, for vanity.[19] Despite these criticisms and others, like irresolution from divided counsels, the difficulty of proceeding secretly, and so on, democracy has a certain privileged position within the framework based upon the idea of the state of nature and the doctrine of sovereignty. This may be seen as follows.

The institution of monarchy or aristocracy requires a previous official nomination or designation of certain particular persons as sovereign. Democracy, however, can be instituted directly by the separated individuals themselves. Hence the original or first form of all instituted government is democracy. Since all men in the state of nature are equal in rights, and all legitimate obligation is ultimately self-obligation, the first part of the social contract, in order to be binding, must be an agreement of each man with every other man to accept as sovereign that person or persons designated by a majority of all of them. This first agreement of every man with every other man constitutes the multitude as a democratic people; the act nominating the sovereign, each man having one equal vote, is a democratic act. One could say that only a democratic procedure is consistent with the equality of men in the state of nature. In accordance with a principle often enunciated by Hobbes, that whoever has the power to dispose of the sovereignty is the true sovereign, one could say that the people, as a democratic people, are the ultimate sovereign of every instituted commonwealth. Hobbes guarded against this conclusion by addressing himself to a more fundamental argument, namely, as all contracts depend upon the consent of the contractors, they may be dissolved by the same consent. Hence the people by withdrawing their consent may dissolve the government. First of all, Hobbes answers, the original contract obliges each man to all of the others, not to a majority, even an overwhelming majority. So long as one man dissents to the dissolution of the contract, no others have a right to dissolve. It cannot be imagined, Hobbes said, that all the people with no exception would combine against the supreme power. But there is a distinct obligation to the sovereign himself, for every man by agreeing to acknowledge the sovereign's acts as his own has transferred his natural right to use his powers as he sees fit to the sovereign. He cannot take away what now belongs to the supreme power without committing injustice against the sovereign.[20]

The traditional arguments for the mixed regime, or limited government, are rejected by Hobbes as being based upon an insufficient understanding of what a true union is. Where, for example, the sovereignty is supposedly divided between a monarchical executive, an aristocratic judiciary, and a popular body with power of the purse, the liberty of the subject is as much restricted as it can be under any government, so long as the three branches are in agreement. The advantage of such a division of powers would then be seen to exist in the disagreement or mutual checking of the three powers; but that disagreement, according to Hobbes, constitutes civil war and the dissolution of the government. He acknowledged that many governments have lasted a long time thinking wrongly that they were governments of this kind. But in the limited monarchies and temporary dictatorships known to history, the true sovereigns were not the monarchs but the assemblies that limited the monarchs. A genuine body politic, he argues, is constituted not by agreement, or concord, but by union, the uniting of the wills (and thereby the strength and power) of all in the will of one legal person, the sovereign.

A true monarchy, according to Hobbes, is a hereditary monarchy, for the true sovereign of an elective monarchy is the electing body. The chief difficulty for monarchies is the problem of succession, especially the problem of who is to appoint the royal successor. The present possessor of the sovereignty is to determine his successor. Hobbes works out detailed rules about what is to be understood as the will of the monarch in any case where he has not expressly indicated who shall inherit his power. He proceeds, speaking generally, from the presumption that the nearest in kinship is the nearest in affection and thereby should be understood as successor.

Hobbes defines law in terms of will, not reason. Counsel, on the other hand, bases itself on reasons, reasons deduced from the benefit to be gained by the one counseled. Counsel aims, or pretends to aim, at the good of another. But law is command, not counsel, and a command is expected to be obeyed only because it expresses the will of the one commanding. Since the object of every man's will is some good to himself, every command aims at the good of the one commanding. Law is a command addressed to one who has been obliged formerly to obey, a command from one who has already acquired a right to be obeyed. Civil law is such a command issued by the commonwealth, the sovereign. More fully, civil laws are those rules, commanded by the commonwealth to every subject through some sufficient sign of its will, which are to be used by the subjects for distinguishing right from wrong. Hobbes's political teachings, the laws of nature themselves, are merely counsel until commanded by some civil sovereign.

Custom in itself has no power to create law. Customary law derives its authority from the tacit consent of the present sovereign. The common law and the law of equity were said to be guided by the standard of right reason, a standard which, because it is considered to be independent and above all political authority, could be and was used to check and question the unreasonable actions of all civil authorities. Hobbes reinterprets the traditional understanding of the common law in such a way as to make appeals to any authority higher than the civil sovereign impossible. He agrees with the lawyers that the law can never be against reason. But whose reason, he asks? Not the reason of scholars, or wise men, or subordinate judges, but the reason of that artificial person, the commonwealth, he answers. In his discussion of the common law, Hobbes does not distinguish the reason of the commonwealth from its will. In every just decision, the judge refers to the reason which moves the reigning sovereign to make or consent to the law governing the case under consideration; the judge does not recur to the reasons that influenced the sovereign under whom the law in question was first promulgated. Hobbes's approach would seem to lead to the idea of the absolute supremacy of current statute law. The canon of the church, or ecclesiastical law, also is law only in so far as it is constituted by the civil sovereign. All laws, of course, require interpreters, *i.e.,* judges, to apply the laws to particular cases. The sovereign is the supreme interpreter of the law and constitutes all subordinate interpreters, or judges, as such.[21]

Nothing which mortals make, says Hobbes, can be immortal. Yet with the help of a very able architect, commonwealths can be so constructed as to prevent their perishing from internal disorders. Hobbes describes those forces in the nature of man which have always tended toward the dissolution of peace and civil order. Yet those forces are not to be counteracted by way of moral reform, by appeals to what had been regarded as the nobler part of man's nature. Hobbes appeals instead to enlightened self-interest and, on the basis of knowledge and manipulation of the mechanism of the passions, relies on the devising of the right kinds of institutions. There was no need for him, as there was for Aristotle, to distinguish the kinds and levels of peoples in order to determine what kind of government is suitable for each. He aimed at devising a scheme of government which was to be right for all times, peoples, and places. By building his edifice upon the lowest common denominator of human motivation, he could expect it to stand firm anywhere and everywhere. For when commonwealths "come to be dissolved, not by external violence, but intestine disorders, the fault is not in men, as they are the Matter; but as they are the Makers, and orderers of them."[22]

One great mistake is often made at the very beginning of a commonwealth when men, in order to gain a kingdom, are content with less power than is necessary for maintaining peace and defense. Then, when the public safety requires the exercise of those renounced powers, their resumption appears as an act of injustice. This, in turn, disposes large numbers of men to rebellion and connivance with foreign powers, which always welcome an opportunity to weaken their neighbors. Thus William the Conqueror's pledge not to infringe the liberty of the Church led to Thomas Beckett's defection and his enlisting the support of the pope against Henry II. And because neither the senate nor the people of Rome claimed the whole power, the seditions of the Gracchi developed, then the wars between senate and people under Marius and Sulla and Caesar and Pompey, and finally popular government itself in Rome was destroyed and the monarchy was instituted. Thus it is a breach of his duty for the sovereign to lay aside any of his rights.

Furthermore, it is a breach of his duty to allow the people to be misinformed or ignorant of the grounds of his rights. The first task in this regard is to purge the commonwealth of "the poisons of seditious doctrines." The first group of seditious doctrines proceed mainly from the words of unlearned divines, who, misconstruing Scripture, induce men to think that sanctity and natural reason cannot stand together. They teach that every private man is the judge of good and evil actions. This is true in the state of nature, but in civil society the civil law and the sovereign are the measure and the judge of good and evil.

A second doctrine repugnant to civil society states that whatever a man does against his conscience, including those things he is commanded to do by his sovereign, is sin. If the commanded act is sinful, it is the sovereign's sin and he is answerable to God for it. It is not the subject's sin. On the contrary, disobedience to the sovereign is sin. For by disobeying, the subject arrogates to himself the knowledge and judgment of good and evil, conscience and judgment being really one and the same thing. Third in order is the doctrine that faith and sanctity are not to be attained by study and reason but by supernatural inspiration or "infusion." If this doctrine is granted, Hobbes said, he cannot see why every Christian is not a prophet, obliged to take his own inspiration rather than the law of his country for the rule of his action. This doctrine, too, leads men to set themselves up as judges of good and evil. Then there is that group of "eloquent sophistries" penned by Aristotle, Plato, Cicero, Seneca, Plutarch, and the rest of those maintainers of the Greek and Roman anarchies, the "sophistries" taken over by the lawyers to serve their own interests, such as the doctrine that sovereigns are subject to their own laws; that the supreme authority may be divided; that private men have absolute rights over property which exclude interference from the sovereign; and, finally, the doctrine, also held by many divines, that tyrannicide is lawful and even laudable. This last amounts to saying, according to Hobbes, that it is lawful for men to rebel against and to murder their kings so long as they call them tyrants first. Finally, there is that doctrine rooted in the fear of darkness and ghosts, and drawn out of the "darkness of school distinctions," the doctrine of the division of civil, or temporal, power from spiritual, or ghostly, power. That the distinction has no significance and that no man can serve two masters Hobbes attempts to prove by Holy Scripture in his theological discussion.[23]

Rooting out seditious and false opinions is not enough. It is the duty of the sovereign to have the true grounds of his rights taught to the people. This meant, first of all, adopting Hobbes's books as the authoritative texts on morals and politics in the universities. Apparently Hobbes regarded his as a long-range educational project, for, he said, he was not very interested in whether his books would be adopted "at this day." Nevertheless he looked forward to his books being officially recommended by some sovereign for teaching in the universities, "the fountains of civil and moral doctrine." One should begin, he said, with young minds uncorrupted by the doctrines of Athens and Rome. Those who are properly educated, after they leave the universities as preachers, gentry, men of affairs, and lawyers, in the conduct of their everyday affairs will transmit the true grounds of civil right to the people. The difficulties in the way of teaching the people are usually overestimated, Hobbes thought. For, first of all, it is not too hard to learn what appeals to one's own selfish interests and secondly, in a judgment reminiscent of Machiavelli's estimation of the people, Hobbes remarks that the people lack the pride and ambition that obstructs the minds of the rich, the powerful, and those with a reputation for learning. In spite of his exaltation of sovereignty and monarchy, Hobbes evidently expected that some day his doctrines would be popular.[24]

There is not much said in a positive way about the good society which Hobbes looked forward to, once the conditions of peace are established. The emphasis in Hobbes is upon the extreme situations like civil war, where all law and order break down, upon the dangers to peace resulting from attempts to question and restrict the sovereign authority, upon negative standards rather than positive standards. Yet evidently he looked forward to a much milder regime than his total arming of the sovereign power would suggest. In the first place he looked forward to a nonimperialist society. This, however, is inconsistent with his doctrine that independent sovereigns and nations are necessarily in a state of nature with respect to each other and, hence, naturally obliged to do all they can to subdue or weaken their neighbors. The policies are inconsistent so long as there is no world state. However this may be, he also looked forward to a state with laws encouraging husbandry and fishing, laws against idleness and inordinate expense and consumption, and laws to encourage and honor industry, navigation, mechanics, and the mathematical sciences. Public burdens are to be distributed equally. Men are to be taxed according to what they spend or consume: frugality is to be rewarded, luxurious waste discouraged, and each man is to pay the commonwealth in proportion to the benefit he derives from its protection. There is to be equality before the law, strict penalties against corrupt judges, and easy access to courts of appeal. The safety of the people is to be the supreme law, and safety is to be understood as including all the contentments and delights of life a man can earn lawfully without hurting the commonwealth.[25]

The peace of civil society depends upon the sovereign's having the power of life and death over his subjects. If men believe that there are other powers capable of granting greater rewards than life and inflicting greater punishments than death, they will obey such powers and the authority of the sovereign will be destroyed. Eternal life and eternal torment or "eternal death" are greater goods and evils than natural life and natural death. Because, or so long as, men believe in the power of other men, acting as ministers of powers invisible, to grant them eternal bliss or eternal torment, theology, according to Hobbes, cannot be separated from political philosophy.[26] We must confine ourselves to a rough sketch of Hobbes's Christian theology, omitting the numerous passages from Holy Scripture that he cites as authorities.

Although from the Creation God has ruled over all men through the power of nature, the kingdom of God, in most places of Scripture, contrary to the interpretation of most divines, signifies a political kingdom with definite subjects, the Jews. Adam and all those living up to the Flood and Noah and his family after the Flood were commanded by God directly through His voice. The first in the kingdom of God by covenant was Abraham with whom God made a contract, offering Abraham the land of Canaan as an everlasting possession in return for his obedience and the obedience of his posterity. Thus God was instituted as the civil sovereign of the Jews. God needed to speak only to Abraham, the father, lord, and civil sovereign of his family, for the wills of all his family and seed were involved in his will. As the family and seed of Abraham received the positive commands of God from their earthly sovereign, Abraham, so in every commonwealth those with no supernatural revelation to the contrary ought to obey the laws of their own sovereign in all the external acts and professions of religion. Every sovereign, as did Abraham, has the right to punish anyone who pretends to a private revelation in order to oppose the laws. As was Abraham in his family, so only the sovereign in a Christian commonwealth can be the authoritative interpreter of the Word of God. God's contract was renewed with Isaac and Jacob, but was suspended while the Jews were under the sovereignty of Egypt.

The contract was renewed again by Moses at Mount Sinai. Since Moses could not inherit Abraham's authority, his authority was grounded in the consent of the people and their promise to obey him. Again, only Moses, as civil sovereign under God, was called up to God, not Aaron, the chief priest, nor any other priest, nor the aristocracy of seventy elders, nor the people. By Moses' throwing over the calf made by Aaron, and by Moses' control of those who prophesied in the camp, it was shown that all priests and prophets in a Christian commonwealth derive their authority from the approval and authority of the sovereign. The kingdom was a sacerdotal kingdom: Moses ruled as God's high priest and viceregent on earth. The kingdom was inherited by Aaron and then by his son Eleazar. After the death of Joshua and Eleazar it was said that there was no king in Israel. This was true only as far as the exercise of the sovereign power was concerned. The right to govern, the sovereign power, was still lodged in the high priest. The powers of the judges were extraordinary or temporary emergency powers. By deposing Samuel, the high priest, the people deposed the peculiar kingdom of God and instituted a monarchy of the usual type. Solomon's treatment of Abiathar, his dedication of the temple, and the whole of biblical history show that from the first institution of the kingdom of God until the captivity, the supreme religious authority was in the same hands as the civil sovereignty. And after the election of Saul, the priest's office was ministerial with respect to the sovereign, not magisterial. During their captivity the Jews had no commonwealth, and after their return everything was so confused and corrupted that nothing of value for state or religion can be learned from those times.

The "office of our Blessed Savior," the Messiah, wrote Hobbes, is threefold: Redeemer, Teacher, and King. Christ on earth was Redeemer and Teacher, not King. He never did anything to call into question the civil laws of the Jews or Caesar, nor gave anyone else warrant to do the same. He is to be King only after the general resurrection; the kingdom he claimed is to be in another world. He never actually commanded anyone. As Redeemer he was sacrificed to ransom men's sins, and as Teacher he counseled men about the path to salvation, *i.e.,* eternal life. The meaning of the Trinity is that the one person of God was represented at three different times and on three different occasions. Moses represented God the Father, Christ God the Son, and the apostles and

their successors, by receiving and transmitting the Holy Spirit, represented God the Holy Ghost. So long as there was no Christian commonwealth, no civil sovereign converted to Christianity, the ecclesiastical power was in the hands of the apostles and those they ordained as
ministers. They had no power of command, their office was only to instruct and advise men to believe and have faith in Christ. That Jesus is
the Christ is the sole article of faith necessary for a Christian. If commanded by an infidel sovereign to profess the contrary with one's
tongue, martyrdom is not necessary; confession is but an external thing,
a sign of obedience to the law. If commanded by the sovereign to do
actions such as worshipping false gods, which, in effect, deny the Lord,
the sin is not that of the obedient subject but of the sovereign. It is never
just for Christians, or anyone else, to attempt to depose even an infidel
or heretical king once he has been established; for that would be a violation of faith and thereby against the law of nature which is the eternal
law of God.

The first Christian emperor was Constantine, who was also the
supreme bishop of Rome, just as all Christian sovereigns are supreme
bishops in their own territories. This office adheres essentially to the
sovereignty. Hobbes educes long arguments, especially against the writings of Cardinal Bellarmine, to oppose the claims of the popes of Rome.
All priests in a Christian commonwealth are only the sovereign's ministers, deriving their authority from him, the chief priest. Where a
foreigner has authority to appoint teachers or priests, he does it only by
the authority of the sovereign in whose domains the teaching or ministry takes place. In fact, "church" as the word is used in the Bible
means nothing else than a Christian commonwealth. From all this it is
clear that the distinction between spiritual and temporal government
is false. All government in this life, both of the state and of religion, is
temporal and under the command of one civil sovereign.[27]

Hobbes says that the doctrine concerning the Kingdom of God has
so much influence on the kingdom of man that it should not be decided
by any but those that have the sovereign power. However, since his own
country is in a state of civil war, he writes, and the authority is undecided, he will set forth his own novel doctrine tentatively. The Kingdom
of God, wherein men shall enjoy eternal life, shall be a kingdom under
Christ here on earth and at the time of the general resurrection. Hell
is also on earth, and Satan is any earthly enemy of the church. The
torments of Hell signify metaphorically that grief of mind, envy,
caused by the sight of others enjoying that eternal felicity which the
tormented, because of their disbelief and disobedience, have lost. The
sinners will also have bodily pains and will die a second death. For

everlasting fire and everlasting death do not mean that the tormented will be granted everlasting life, which everlasting torments would require. What is meant is rather that the tormenting fire will burn eternally and the supply of sinners to be tormented and killed will not fail, because the sinners will eat, drink, generate, and die perpetually after the resurrection as before. In fact, under Hobbes's interpretation it becomes difficult to see how the life of sinners is in any way changed by the resurrection. Eternal death then turns out to be not so much, if at all, worse than natural death. The over-all conclusion that Hobbes evidently wanted the readers of his theology to draw was that there was really no essential difference between the Word of God as revealed in the Scriptures and the word of Hobbes set down in his political philosophy.[28]

However, one is forced to raise the question of whether Hobbes believed in the truth of his theology. He does say about God that "it is manifest we ought to attribute to him, existence: For no man can have the will to honor that which he thinks not to have any being." But the relation between truth and worship or honor is by no means unambiguous. For, he writes, "all words and actions that betoken fear to offend, or desire to please, is worship, whether these words or actions be sincere or feigned: and because they appear as signs of honoring, are ordinarily also called Honor." Because of these and many other statements, Hobbes became notorious as an atheist during his own lifetime.[29]

Perhaps the most charitable conclusion that one can draw from his theology is that in his dauntless zeal to destroy all opinions which he believed to be inimical to a proper understanding of the rights and duties of man, Hobbes showed that, for him, nothing was more sacred than the pursuit and promulgation of the philosophic truth.

NOTES

1. Thomas Hobbes, *Leviathan,* ("Everyman's Library" [New York: Dutton, 1950]), chap. xi, p. 79. Spelling has been modernized in quotations in this chapter.

2. See, *e.g., Leviathan,* chap. xxxi, end, and *The Elements of Law,* ed. Ferdinand Toennies (Cambridge: Cambridge University Press, 1928), 1.17.1.

3. *The Metaphysical System of Hobbes,* selected by Mary W. Calkins (Chicago: Open Court, 1948), *Concerning Body,* chaps. i and ii, esp. vi.7; *Leviathan,* chap. xxxiv, pp. 339–41, chap. xlvi, The Introduction, pp. 4–5; A Review, and Conclusion, p. 627. It is difficult to determine whether Hobbes conceived of his materialism as simply

true, *i.e.*, as "metaphysical," or as "methodological," *i.e.*, an assumption required for proceeding scientifically.

4. *Leviathan,* chap. vi. Cf. *Elements,* 1.7.1–1.10.11.

5. *Leviathan,* chap. vi, p. 41; chap. vii, p. 59.

6. *De Cive (The Citizen), The English Works of Thomas Hobbes,* ed. Molesworth (1839–45), vol. II, chap. i.2; see especially the note.

7. *Leviathan,* chap. xi, pp. 79–80.

8. *Ibid.,* chap. xiii, pp. 103–4.

9. *Ibid.,* chap. xiii.

10. *Elements,* 1.14.6.

11. *Ibid.,* 1.16.2; *De Cive,* chap. iii.3.

12. *Leviathan,* Chap. xiv, pp. 107–8; chap. xv, pp. 128, 130–31; chap. xxvii, p. 251; chap. xlii, pp. 435–36; chap. xxvi, pp. 231–32.

13. *Elements,* 1.17.14 and 1.13.3.

14. *Leviathan,* chap. xiv, p. 117.

15. *Ibid.,* chap. xxi, p. 183.

16. *Ibid.,* chap. xv, pp. 128–30; chap. xxi; chap. xxviii, pp. 258–59; *De Cive,* chap. vi.13.

17. *Leviathan,* chap. xxii, p. 187.

18. *De Cive,* chaps x.2 and x.16.

19. *Ibid.,* chap. x, esp. x.7, x.8, and x.15.

20. *Ibid.,* chap. vi.20.

21. For a confrontation of Hobbesian with premodern traditional jurisprudence, compare chap. xxvi, "Of Civil Laws," of the *Leviathan* with Thomas Aquinas' *Summa Theologica,* I-II, Qq. 90–97 (published by the Henry Regnery Co. as *Treatise on Law*), which Hobbes's chapter may have been written in opposition to. See also his *A Dialogue between a Philosopher and a Student of the Common Laws of England, The English Works of Thomas Hobbes,* Molesworth ed., VI.

22. *Leviathan,* chap. xxix, pp. 275–76.

23. *Ibid.,* chap. xxix.

24. *Ibid.,* chap. xxx, pp. 288–96; *De Cive,* chap. xiii.9.

25. *Leviathan,* chap. xxx, pp. 296 ff. and *De Cive,* chap. xiii, esp. xiii.14.

26. *Leviathan,* dedicatory epistle; chap. xv, end; chap. xxxviii, beginning; *De Cive,* chap. xvii.27.

27. *Leviathan,* chaps. xl–xliii. Cf. chap. xxii, pp. 189–90 and 200.

28. *Ibid.,* chaps. xxxviii and xliv.

29. *Ibid.,* chap. xxxi, p. 312; chap. xlv, p. 570; chap. xii; chap. xlv; cf. chap. xxvii, pp. 249–50; chap. xliv, pp. 558–59; and chap. xiii, p. 104; chap. xxxix, p. 406; chap. xlii, p. 435; chap. xl, p. 417; chap. xlvi, pp. 591–92.

READINGS

A. Hobbes, Thomas. *Leviathan.* Chaps xiii–xv, xvii–xviii, xxi, xxiv, xxvi–xxx, xlvi.

B. Hobbes, Thomas. *Leviathan.* Chaps vi, x–xii, xvi, xix, xx, xxii–xxiii, xxv, xxxi–xxxii, xxxv, xliii.

RENE DESCARTES

1596–1650

Descartes has long been celebrated as "the founder of modern philosophy," but never of modern political philosophy. His epochal beginning appears to stand in splendid isolation from the older modern political tradition founded by Machiavelli: he never even composed a thematic discussion of political things. This suggests that modern philosophy and modern political philosophy are separate in origin and perhaps divergent in intention. A link between Descartes and the modern political tradition is visible, however, in his relation to Francis Bacon, the first great and avowed advocate of Machiavellian politics directed to the mastery of fortune or nature in human affairs. Copying even the language of Bacon, Descartes asserted that philosophy founded in a new method and directed to "the mastery and possession of nature" would attain the greatest glory for philosophy and the greatest benefit to society. His political teaching, therefore, is mainly concerned with the paramount political necessity, the establishment of harmonious relations between philosophy or science and society, or with the "Enlightenment" version of that relationship, the ruling relationship of modern times. Accordingly, d'Alembert, a prime mover of the French Enlightenment, could declare in the *Encyclopédie* (1751) that Descartes "laid the foundations of a government more just and more happy than has ever been seen established." [1]

Descartes' political teaching is partially obscured because of the notorious caution of his manner of writing: "I have composed my philosophy in such a way as not to shock anyone, and so that it can be received everywhere, even among the Turks." [2] His caution is evident in the fact that he never published praise or blame of any political philoso-

421

phy in his own name, but only an anonymous praise of Bacon's *Great Instauration* and *New Atlantis;* whereas in private letters he accepted "the principal precept" of Machiavelli, "noticed nothing bad" in his *Discourses on Livy,* and thought Hobbes's politics in his *On the Citizen* superior to his metaphysics.[3]

Descartes' political teaching is part of "the highest and most perfect moral science" which is the end of philosophy altogether. "The whole of philosophy is like a tree, the roots of which are metaphysics," namely, knowledge of God and the human soul; "the trunk is physics, and the branches which come from the trunk are all the other sciences," but principally medicine, mechanics, and morality. "Just as it is not from the roots nor from the trunk of trees that one gathers the fruits, but only from the extremities of their branches, so the principal utility of philosophy depends on those of its parts that one can only learn last."[4] The ultimate branch is "the perfect moral science ... which, presupposing an entire knowledge of the other sciences, is the last degree of wisdom." Yet it is almost universally held that nowhere in his published or unpublished writings can one find Descartes' "perfect moral science." This difficulty is inseparable from another that arises from inspection of the tree of knowledge. Man is treated twice, once as the second metaphysical root and once as the highest branch. But in each of the published versions of his metaphysics Descartes treats first the human soul and then God. Moreover, the simile omits any reference in the "roots" to the metaphysical principle coeval with the soul, namely, corporeal substance, from which the "trunk" presumably must grow. Hence, the poetic simile of the tree of knowledge is deceptive as regards its least visible part.

We are forced then to seek for a nonpoetic argument according to which man is the beginning and end of the tree of knowledge and "the perfect moral science" its "principal utility." Only in the *Discourse on Method* (1637) does Descartes offer an account of the beginning and end of his philosophy, of all the parts and their true order. Nevertheless, this writing is customarily depreciated today because of its popular character. Yet precisely its popular rhetoric is the first sign that the *Discourse* alone treats the peculiar difficulty of Descartes' supreme goal: the "perfect moral science" will come into full existence only by an unprecedented political cooperation between philosophy and the public.

Descartes writes that he began with the opinion of his Jesuit teachers that study would yield "a clear and certain knowledge of all that is useful to life." By the criterion of utility, he examined and rejected the learning of the schools and the whole of ancient philosophy. One science alone, mathematics, he excepted; what "astonished" him was that "no loftier edifice had been built on the firm and solid foundations" of mathematics.[5] In place of that wonder at the fundamental perplexities that confront the mind that was the beginning of philosophy for the ancients, Descartes substitutes astonishment at a hitherto undreamed-of possibility of human "creativity" that will banish wonder: "I shall reveal to you secrets so simple that you will henceforward wonder at nothing in the works of our hands."[6] As contrasted with mathematics, "philosophy," which ought to supply the "foundations" of the sciences, is wholly disputable, useless, and uncertain. "Theology"—a term that Descartes uses here and everywhere to signify revealed theology exclusively—"shows the way to gain heaven," to which he "aspired as much as any other." But "revealed truths" are "above our intelligence": hence they are not clear and assured knowledge useful for life. The only moral writings he so much as mentions in his critique of the tradition are "the writings of the pagans"—they too lack foundations.[7]

Descartes opposes the goal of the classic tradition since he abandons the "speculations," or the quest for knowledge for its own sake, in favor of "useful knowledge." The justification of the rejection of the classic view appears from the treatment of the one discipline in the critique that treats of man's end. The "writings of the pagans" comprise the moral teachings of the Stoics especially, but also those of Platonic and Aristotelian political philosophy. While the pagan writings contain many "exhortations to virtue which are most useful," the "superb and magnificent palaces" of virtue are "built on sand and mud." What the pagans "called by such a beautiful name," i.e., "virtue," is "often only insensibility, or pride, or despair, or parricide."[8] Pagan virtue which claimed to be a mean, and the excellence of man, is therefore often an extreme, and an inhumane, presumptuous, poor-spirited, and even criminal extreme. As extremes the pagan virtues cannot be distinguished from the passions. "There is nothing in which the defective nature of the sciences that we have received from the ancients appears more clearly than in what they have written on the passions."[9]

Descartes replaced the distinction made by the ancients between the passions and the virtues with the distinction between good and bad passions. The basis of the ancient distinction was the view that the soul has parts, that certain parts are capable of listening to and obeying reason, and that by their means reason can establish and rule a natural hierarchy within the soul. Reason is autonomous because reason has its own proper object, or because "all men by nature desire knowledge," regardless of the utility of knowledge. Descartes rejects this view of a natural order of the soul: the ancients had not seen the acute "dependence of the mind" or reason on the passions or "on the temperament and the disposition of the organs of the body." [10]

Descartes' twofold reflection on the power of the passions and the promise of mathematics leads directly to his argument for a new method which is at the same time his primary political reflection. Since the virtues are replaced by certain passions, the "useful for life" must be understood as that which serves the ends of the passions. Among the passions, however, distinctions must be drawn between good and bad, useful and useless, noble and ignoble passions. More precisely, what is required is a comprehensive passion, or a passion that can supply a principle of order to the other passions, hence necessarily the passion capable of mastering the other passions. This most useful passion will thus be the noblest and most perfect master passion. Descartes begins his argument for method with the principle "there is less perfection in works composed of several portions, and carried out by the hands of various masters, than in those on which one [master] has worked." [11] What is made wholly by one master is wholly in the power of that master: thus he begins as the Stoics had done, with what is wholly in one's own power, without restricting this to "one's own thoughts." His principle is articulated by a series of examples of masters that culminates in reason as a form of mastery. But since it is "the will of some men using reason" that leads to perfect mastery, reason is in the service of the will, or as Descartes will later say, of the supreme passion he called "generosity."

The examples are seven: (1) the single architect of a building; (2) the single engineer of the buildings of a city; (3) the general case of the single "prudent" legislator who gives laws to a people; (4) the special case of the single divine legislator, God, who made "the ordinances" of "the state of the true religion," or of Christendom, which "must be incomparably better regulated than all the others"; (5) the special case of the single human legislator of pagan Sparta—the only human legislator ever praised by Descartes—even though many of the Spartan laws were "very strange and even contrary to good morals"; (6) the simple reasonings made naturally by a single man of "good sense"; and (7) the final, hypothetical case of a single man who had perfect use of his unaided reason from infancy, unaffected by "appetites or preceptors." [12]

The series of examples is an ascent: it ascends from lower practical arts concerning inanimate things to the highest (including the divine) practical art of legislation, and thence to the highest theoretical "mastery," the use of unaided human reason. Since all the masters are authors of "works," "work" must include the highest use of reason: mastery is neutral to the distinction between thinking and making, philosophy and technē. Philosophy is henceforth described, as previously by Bacon, as "architecture": the organic simile of "the tree of knowledge" is deceptive. The first meaning of "perfection" in the series is the unity of the "work" deriving from the singleness of the master. To this he adds a second, the magnitude of the subject matter on which the master works. Therefore, Descartes' mastery will be as comprehensive as the series, or such a theoretical mastery of the whole or nature, the object of greatest magnitude, as will also comprehend the highest practical mastery, "legislation" of the greatest magnitude. Political science, the architectonic or master art according to Aristotle, is replaced by philosophy understood as theoretical mastery, or "architecture." To unity and magnitude Descartes adds, by the final example, a third ground of perfection, namely, that source within the master from which perfect mastery proceeds: the unaided use of human reason. All three grounds take their place in the definition of that master passion that Descartes calls the highest virtue, "generosity": the sensation in oneself of "a firm and constant resolution . . . never to fail of one's own will to undertake and execute all the things [one] judges to be the best . . . which is to follow perfectly after virtue." [13] Evidently "generosity" has not the sense of "liberality" of its English counterpart.

Yet the final example is hypothetical—the master who had perfect use of his unaided reason from infancy, unaffected by "appetites or preceptors." Of himself Descartes observes that he was sufficiently free from the passions to be able to reflect, at the outset of his chief reflections in the *Discourse* and *Meditations,* because of chance rather than virtue. As for his preceptors, he speaks of "the religion" in which he had been "instructed from his infancy." He must therefore find a procedure or a method that will purge the mind of all opinions and beliefs that depend on "appetites and preceptors." Only the construction of a method, and not the natural use of natural reason, can overcome the natural disproportion between the rate of growth of the appetites or passions and that of reason. For the prejudices received from our appetites or passions beginning in childhood govern our sense perceptions and cannot be corrected by reason which naturally serves those passions. Hence all previous philosophy that began with sense perception and lacked a method for purging the mind of prejudices necessarily went astray. Method can master the natural defects or disproportions of man's nature by taking as its model mathematics, which is certain because it owes nothing to the senses or to the body. But to be the comprehensive mastery as well as to master the body, method must become comprehensive mastery of all body, *i.e.,* mathematical physics.

That Descartes' highest example of mastery, or "generosity," necessarily includes politics or "legislation" becomes fully evident from his immediately following reflection on "reformations." [14] The first rule of method demands the rejection of all opinions that are not "clear and distinct," or the "reformation" of those uncertain opinions that are the "foundations" of one's own life. As contrasted with this private "reformation," Descartes asks whether it is desirable that states and nations be reformed by a private individual, and if desirable whether it is legitimate and possible. But the opinions a private individual must necessarily doubt are also the ruling or constitutive opinions and therefore "foundations" of states.

The connection of private and public reform is peculiarly evident in that private reform of defects in "the body of the sciences" can lead, and perhaps ought to lead, to reform in "the order established in the schools" to teach the sciences, and the schools are the authoritative repository of the opinions that are the "foundations" of the "great bodies," *i.e.,* states and nations. Descartes thus agrees with the classic view that opinion is the element of society, the binding ligament that gives it unity and motion. Publication of his private reform would necessarily raise the question, therefore, of whether he intended a public reformation: again he agrees with the classics that philosophic questioning when made publicly tends to erode the element of opinion in which society lives. Moreover, the jeopardy to the foundational opinion of society is unprecedented in the case of Descartes' philosophy, because his method demands the blanket attainder of all opinion that lacks the certitude of mathematics. Yet Descartes did publish his method, even writing in a popular mode and in the vulgar tongue, and thereby indicated that he intended a public reformation.

Descartes' political intention in the *Discourse* remains obscure without at least brief clarification of the three chief features of its rhetoric. Descartes is often believed to be a political conformist because his provisional morality begins: "the first [rule] was to obey the laws and customs of my country, retaining constantly the religion in which God has given me the grace to be instructed from my infancy." [15] Apart from the provisionality of the rule, it is less often observed that in the center of the same paragraph he says that "in the corruption of our morals there are few people who wish to say all that they believe." He was "forced to add these rules" of provisional morality because otherwise "pedagogues and the like would say of him that he is without religion and faith and seeks to overthrow all that with his method." [16] This prudential character of its rhetoric blurs the meaning of the principal literary feature of the *Discourse.* Just as the argument on supreme mastery leads to "my way," the way of the individual Descartes which is unprecedented, unrepeatable, and needless of repetition, so likewise his act of publication is entirely unique. The form of the *Discourse* is therefore that of an autobiography of the first and final founder of philosophy. Its third rhetorical feature, its popularization of philosophy, becomes intelligible when one learns in what sense the founder is in need of nonphilosophers.

Descartes' act of publication is premised, firstly, on the desirability of the reform of existing states, which is evident "from their diversity alone," but ultimately on the desirability of a permanent reform of the relations of philosophy and the public. Since "diversity alone" evidences imperfection, there will be but one good regime characterized by the perfect relation of philosophy and the public. His particular criticisms of contemporary society imply the general character of the permanent reform. The prime authority for existing "foundations" breeds civil war: "the controversies of the schools, by insensibly making those who practice themselves in them more captious and obstinate, are possibly the chief causes of the heresies and dissensions that now exercise the world." [17] The entire reflection on mastery, Descartes' famous day in the "stove," begins with a reference to the "wars" in Germany and ends with a reference to the war in Holland: it is framed by the post-Reformation wars between the Catholic and Protestant powers of Europe. The "state of the true religion," or Christendom, exhibits not the unity of its founder but self-diremption.

The question of the legitimacy of public reformation by private individuals is subordinate for Descartes to that of its possibility, for the reason that "fortune" is a title to legitimate political power. He "absolutely disapproves of those turbulent temperaments who never fail to plan some new reformation, although they are not called by fortune nor by birth to the management of public affairs." [18] This unusual constriction of the bases of legitimacy to fortune and birth is still more surprising if one considers fortune as a claim to legitimacy: if fortune legitimates, then every attempt to seize power has the prospect of legitimacy, since an individual cannot know he has been "called by fortune to the management of public affairs" prior to success. Since chance or fortune set Descartes himself on the right path to the discovery of the true "foundations," his project is blessed with legitimacy from its inception. To show the legitimacy of supreme mastery Descartes must show the possibility of the total mastery of fortune. But "one must entirely reject the vulgar opinion that there is outside of us a Fortune that makes things happen or not happen." As with Machiavelli, whose stamp on Descartes' treatment of the goddess Fortuna is unmistakeable, it is nature that must be mastered. Still the immediate issue is but the difficulty of public reformation by a private man: it will be solved for Descartes by the attractive power for all men of the "fruits" of his philosophy and the strategy used to advertise them.

Once the general principles of physics are known, the "project" of Descartes becomes a "practical philosophy" "very useful for life" that can supplant the "speculative philosophy taught in the schools." By the "mastery and possession of nature" man can invent "an infinity of artifices that would enable us to enjoy, without any pain, the fruits of the earth, and all the comforts that are to be found there." [19] The fruits of the tree of knowledge will undo the consequences of the Fall in the garden, or, more precisely, will effectively deny its truth. The *Discourse* culminates then in a promise of a heaven on earth, or it imitates Bacon's writing on method, the *New Organon,* whose subtitle refers to "the kingdom of man." The science that leads to human happiness is not the traditional study of the excellence of the soul, moral and political science, and still less the "theology" that "shows the way to gain heaven," but medicine, the science of the body. "Health is without doubt the first good and the foundation of all the other goods of this life." Medicine is also the means to the prolongation of life, but above all it is the science that produces "wisdom," the ultimate fruit: "the mind depends so much on the temperament and on the disposition of the organs of the body that if it is possible to find some means which generally renders men wiser and more skillful than they have been hitherto, I believe that it is in medicine that one must search." [20]

To govern the relations between society and the philosophy that promises such fruits, Descartes asserts that there is a "law that obliges us to procure so far as it is in us, the general good of all men." [21] This law, the only categorical obligation ever asserted by Descartes, is stated but once in his writings, and no argument is ever offered for it. He declares that the law obliged him to publish his philosophy lest he "sin," but he never claimed to derive the law from "revealed truths." To account for this amazing mixture of bold assertion and resounding silence, we observe first that Descartes invoked the law only when he had discovered "general notions regarding physics": he did not regard his metaphysics, which contained what he claimed were the first demonstrative proofs of the existence of God and of his perfections, as of sufficient benevolence to the public to require publication. Indeed, immediately after expounding his metaphysics in the *Discourse* (Part IV), he turns to his physics in which he "discovered many truths more useful and more important than all [he] had learned before, or even hoped to learn." [22] In the context of the discussion of publication in the *Discourse* (Part VI), Descartes tacitly reformulates the law as a hypothetical obligation only, which binds those who desire the end or the fruits of the new philosophy to seek the means to that end. The means are the required experiments, or the exchange of experiments between qualified people, or the political conditions that will sanction and promote such an exchange. The hypothetical character of the obligation appears in Descartes' "promise" that he would "show so clearly the utility that the public could receive" from his philosophy that he "would oblige all those who desire in general the good of men, that is to say, all those who are in fact virtuous and not merely seem so, not only to communicate to me [the experiments] they have already made, but also to aid me in the search for those that remain to be made."[23]

The "good of men"—the term lacks the sense of community of "the common good"—now comprises chiefly what all men have always sought as individuals or through society, namely, the satisfaction of needs, comfort, health, and long life, and this drastically lowered view of the common good is the standard of virtue. Thus Descartes, in common with the founders of modern political philosophy, reversed the relation of virtue and the common good as understood by the classics, revising both in the process. The "law" of benevolence is doubly hypothetical in that it obliges one to seek the means only if one accepts the desirability of the end of utility, but also only if the true means, the true physics or the science of "fruits," is available. It has its locus therefore not primarily in the relations of citizens to each other or with the sovereign, but in the mutual relations of philosophy or science and society. For this reason, but even more for the additional one that philosophy or science must be the principal donor and society the beneficiary of utility, Descartes did not offer any teaching on justice or natural right. "Generosity," the highest virtue of philosophers or scientists, excludes or replaces justice because it is based on a view of the soul different from that of either the ancient or modern teachers of natural right.

Descartes' first beginning in a new method is completed by a mathematical physics that forced him to confront the status of the soul and its knowledge in the metaphysical argument most fully presented in the *Meditations* (1641). He resolves to doubt absolutely, or rather to reject absolutely, every opinion or source of opinion in the slightest degree dubious, in order to establish "foundations" for the edifice of science. In the sequel, this resounding demand for "universal doubt" is carefully restricted; in *Principles* I, No. 10, its universality is denied; Leibniz remarked that the demand to "doubt all things" is perhaps meant "to stimulate the sluggish reader through novelty." Doubt is a procedure devised to suspend our natural trust in the senses and the images that derive therefrom—part of what Descartes calls "the teaching of nature" and came to be called "the natural attitude." To test the dubitability of what does not depend on trust in images—especially mathematics which does not belong to opinion—Descartes invokes a God "who can do everything" and therefore can make false the most self-evident reasonings, that is, that the sum of two plus three is five. Since God, on this view of omnipotence, can suspend the principle of contradiction, all human reasoning would be at an end, unless the perfection of God necessarily excludes such deception. Since knowledge of God is as yet unavailable, or because God is but "an old opinion" and no solid reason for doubting, God is replaced by an "Evil Genius" who is not omnipotent and does not jeopardize mathematics nor that reasoning that is independent of trust in images.

The thought underlying the poetic fiction of the Evil Genius is prepared by the introduction of the "atheist" view that man and his thinking are the result of blind fate or chance or a continuous series of antecedent causes. The atheist view is often regarded as a more radical reason for doubting than the omnipotent and possibly evil God, because Descartes contends that the less powerful is man's "author" the greater is the likelihood of human deception. Yet this assertion concerns difference of power alone, and hence not a comparison with a possibly evil God. Since it is as repugnant to a perfect God that he sometimes may allow us to be deceived as that he always do so—and it cannot be doubted that he sometimes allows us to be deceived—the divine jeopardy to human knowing remains an acute difficulty throughout the *Meditations*. In the context of doubt, the atheist supposition serves to question the harmony of the knower and the known, which appears to imply that the whole is ruled by intelligence. But Cartesian doubt takes a step beyond the premodern rejections of a ruling intelligence by abandoning as well the trust in the harmony of the images of sense and their objects. The images may be wholly deceptive; "life is a dream" may describe the natural situation; nature, indifferent to our desire or need to know, is personified by "the Evil Genius."

More closely regarded, the natural trust in the similarity of image to thing had been rejected by the mathematical (or "nonempirical") character of the scientific concepts of extension, figure, magnitude, et cetera. Yet to assert the dissimilarity of image to thing would seem to imply the existence of things "outside the mind" with which they are compared, and knowledge of this existence would seem to depend on the image. Does not the rejection of "the similarity thesis" of "the teaching of nature" require trust in nature as regards "the existence thesis"—as Descartes sometimes suggests? Nevertheless, in the *Medita-*

tions he customarily treats them as of equal dubitability. Accordingly the existence thesis, or "the great inclination to believe" that bodies exist, must ultimately require the goodness of God as a guarantee of its acceptability. If we object that the same guarantee would seem to be available to guarantee our strong inclination to believe that things resemble our images, we nonetheless must recognize that this would contravene the demands of Cartesian science. The Evil Genius renders dubious the existence of "all external things" or the bodily, including the body of the doubter, and *a fortiori* by implication the similarity thesis. Only these two theses are doubted within the range of "universal doubt." It is logically possible to doubt the existence of the bodily, or of "matters of fact" in Hume's phrase, or of the teaching of nature, while asserting the existence of the doubter; it is even necessary to assert that existence. Hence "this proposition, I am, I exist, is necessarily true each time that I pronounce it or that I conceive it in my mind." Since the knowledge that "I am" does not depend for its truth on the knowledge of body, or on any knowledge of nature or being, it has an "epistemological" priority to any subsequent assertion of a "metaphysical" kind.

This principle is the "Archimedean point" that establishes the existence of the knowing ego within the whole, whose enmity is overcome by the mathematical physics of the mastery of nature. Only following the determination of the principle does Descartes ask what mind or thinking is: the "cogito" is therefore prior to, and independent of, any determination of the materiality or immateriality of the human mind. Descartes compromised the absolute autonomy of the thinking ego, according to most contemporary scholars, by proceeding to prove the existence of an omnipotent God who is possessed of an infinity of infinite perfections: God is therefore the first principle or cause of all things, and so of man and man's knowledge. Descartes made the difficulty of interpreting his metaphysics almost insuperable by also asserting that the finite human mind cannot know anything infinite, and by concluding therefore that "God is incomprehensible." [24] Resolution of these difficulties will vary as one agrees with most contemporary scholars that Descartes published his essential thought with complete candor, or with earlier men such as Leibniz who said, "Descartes took care not to speak so plainly [as Hobbes], but he could not help revealing his opinions in passing, with such address that he would not be understood save by those who examine profoundly these kinds of subjects." [25] However this may be, Descartes never claimed to derive from the knowledge of God any knowledge of man's duties or rights; whereas from "the infinite perfections of God" he did claim to derive "the laws of nature."

Descartes' metaphysical argument furnished him with one source of the understanding of the soul that underlies his theory of "generosity." The second source of his view of the soul is physics, or the "medicine" that treats "the machine of our body," most fully presented in his final publication, the *Passions of the Soul* (1649). According to his metaphysical argument, the free will is a function of mind or soul, an immaterial substance, separate from corporeal substance, yet able to act on corporeal substance, specifically on the human body, in a manner that Descartes admittedly did not adequately explain. This metaphysical view is reflected in the first part of the definition of generosity, which is the "knowledge" that "nothing truly pertains to [man] but this free disposition of his volitions, nor any reason why he should be praised or blamed except that he uses it well or badly." However, according to the physical argument, the heat of the heart "is the corporeal principle of all the movements" of "the machine of our body," while "the first cause" of the error of "the ancients" is the belief that "the soul gives movement to the body." Hence the metaphysical argument would repeat the ancient error. On the physical argument, thinking or consciousness is awareness of the motions of the (wholly corporeal) animal spirits, which awareness Descartes did not adequately explain; and the will is not free but acted on by the passions: "the principal effect of all the passions in men is that they incite and dispose their soul to will the things to which they prepare the body." This second or physical view is reflected in the second part of the definition of generosity, "that [man] is sensible in himself of a firm and constant resolution ... never to fail of his own will to undertake and execute all the things that he judges to be the best, which is to follow perfectly after virtue." "Resolution" Descartes understands as a species of courage which is a "certain heat or agitation" of the animal spirits that "disposes the soul powerfully to bear itself to the execution of the things that it seeks to do." This physiological view of the soul best explains why Descartes can say he speaks in the *Passions of the Soul*, whose first part treats "the whole nature of man," "as a physicist." [26] (The seventeenth-century English philosopher Henry More openly avowed the physiological interpretation of the Cartesian soul, which doctrine he called "Nullibism." [27])

However we view these alternatives, we may say that "generosity" is awareness of one's identity in the quality of one's will or resolution. The freedom of the will "in a certain measure renders us like God in making us masters of ourselves, provided that we do not through cowardice lose the rights which He gives us." [28] Since cowardice deprives man of rights, they belong to the brave or resolute, hence peculiarly to the "generous." Yet "cowardice has some use when it exempts us from taking the pains that we might be incited to take by probable reasons, if other more certain reasons, which have caused them to be judged useless, had not excited this passion." [29] Hence very certain reasons may perhaps deprive the generous of their God-given rights. However this may be, no argument nor any scriptural basis is ever offered by Descartes for the existence of these rights, nor does he ever mention them again.

The political meaning of generosity emerges by contrast with Aristotle's virtue of "magnanimity," of which generosity is a revised version, according to Descartes. Magnanimity is a cultivated habit or disposition of the soul, whereas Descartes chooses the new name "generosity" precisely because it is not cultivated but an ingenerate, or congenital, temperament at least partly physiological. Generous minds, or "strong and noble minds," have their strength from birth, or by nature, hence are "masters" by nature, a natural nobility or aristocracy. Whereas magnanimity was for Aristotle a comprehensive moral virtue and therefore distinct from and lower than theoretical virtue, generosity is Descartes' highest virtue simply: since its supreme object is "mastery of nature" through mathematical physics, the very distinction between theory and practice becomes doubtful. Magnanimity comprehends and presupposes the other virtues, hence in particular the virtue of justice, and is therefore "a kind of ornament of the [other] virtues." [30] Generosity, on the other hand, does not presuppose the other virtues, and Descartes does not mention justice as a virtue or passion; generosity is rather "the key to all the virtues." [31] Therefore, Descartes does not offer any kind of natural-right teaching. As contrasted with the ancients, the absence of any natural order of the soul precluded a natural-right teaching of the traditional type. He shared with Hobbes, the chief founder of modern natural-right doctrine, the view that reason serves the passions. In the decisive context of the comparison of man and the brutes, reason is a "universal instrument" [32]: what distinguishes man from the brutes is a unique means, not a specifically different end. But as contrasted with Hobbes, he viewed political society from the perspective of the strong or generous minds whose sense of the strength of their resolution, their strongest passion, is unique to them. Hence he rejected the egalitarian perspective of Hobbes's *On the Citizen* according to which the passion for self-preservation is the strongest passion of all men, and therefore the basis of natural rights.

Generosity is a political passion or virtue not merely because its object is that mastery of nature which is productive of goods for all men. Knowledge of generosity is the primary part of that "wisdom," or perfect moral science, that teaches man to be master of and hence to enjoy the passions, by which man "tastes the highest sweetness in this life." [33] "Epicurus was not wrong, when considering in what beatitude consists ... to say that it is pleasure in general." However, the "satisfaction and contentment" of the consciousness of one's own strength in the mastery of nature are not incompatible with the pleasure of glory accorded by others for the benevolent results of mastery: the highest philosophic and political rewards may coincide in the same soul. Descartes does not "profess to scorn glory as did the Cynics" [34] and the Epicurean tradition. The quest for glory may indeed disturb "contentment" or "repose" of mind, but glory as respect of "the people" or the vulgar for "the exterior of our actions" is also pursued for the sake of safety and hence "repose." The true glory is the recognition of other "strong and noble minds" for the benevolence of what is not visible externally, the perfect moral science or "wisdom." "It is a reason to esteem oneself to see that one is esteemed by others." [35] The primary self-esteem or generosity is accordingly enhanced by the esteem or glory that is granted for benevolence, and benevolence thus understood becomes the substitute for justice.

Descartes' "reformation" begins with the transformation of philosophy into the project of mastery of nature, of virtue into the science of the passions, and of perfect theoretical and practical virtue into the single virtuous passion of generosity. Since mastery of nature is a means to a practical end for all men, philosophy must bear a novel relation to society. The relation is a compound of a threat to the traditional foundations of society and a promise of benevolence by the fruits of mastery of nature. Yet this jeopardy is redeemed by the fact that the "universal doubt" that method demands is so far from doubting the view that the good is the useful that it is in fact based on this view, and the useful is needed by all societies always. Therefore, Descartes' project can be welcomed by all societies except those based on traditional virtue or piety, or it is relatively neutral to the differences among types of regimes. The support of the project of science by the most liberal as well as the most tyrannical regimes in modern times offers some evidence for this neutrality. For this reason primarily Descartes never articulated a view of the best regime. The convergence of the goals of philosophy and society is not destroyed by the fact that the useful sought by the generous minds is not identical with the useful sought by society. For the final wisdom of the passions, and the prize of glory, sought by the generous, demands the same means, *i.e.,* the advancement of science, that is required to achieve the useful fruits sought by society. The fundamental premise of the harmony of philosophy and society is that all men are ruled by the passions.

The common means, the advancement of science, cannot be achieved without a certain transformation, or new "legislation," of social institutions. Science will advance only if the free exchange of "experiments" or free communication is sanctioned within the borders of society, but also between societies; it will achieve its promise only if society also promotes science by the endowment of scientists with safety, income and deference. This free exchange cannot be limited to exchange of knowledge: societies, or more precisely, the political authorities, are not competent judges of knowledge. Hence society must not only sanction the competent or the scientists as judges but must sanction all communication of doctrines. Society therefore necessarily surrenders control of its opinions, *i.e.,* its "foundations," since the ruling opinions of society are necessarily affected by the free communication of doctrines. Moreover, society will be profoundly affected by "the infinity of artifices" or technology of science. Society cannot have knowledge of science but only belief in the benevolence of science. But since society had originally no acquaintance with the benevolence of science, nor its social requirements, it was necessary for Descartes, following Bacon, to "enlighten" society regarding both.

"Enlightenment" may be said to have three meanings. It is an unprecedented type of political action undertaken by the founders of modern philosophy and continued by most of their followers that forges the bond between philosophy or science and society in the common enterprise of "the mastery of nature." It may also be said to be the rhetoric employed in forging the bond, and the relationship established by it. Since the optimum condition of the progress of science demands the cooperation of the scientists of various countries, and hence freedom of communication among them, and requires as well the spread of knowledge of the conditions of the advancement of science, Enlightenment implies "open societies" linked with each other in the common enterprise of "the mastery of nature." It is necessarily antithetical to any societies, or elements in a society, that seek the autonomous cultivation and preservation of their own morality and way of life. Thus Enlightenment is by intention a universal politics, potentially of global magnitude, and the first of philosophic origin.

Because it is a compound of a promise and a threat, the Enlightenment rhetoric is divisive of society, both at the time of its inception and after its victory. Descartes indicates its promise to three kinds of men. In the *Discourse* especially he appeals to the men of "good sense" or "the public," a broad middle range of mankind that thinks itself adequately provided with "good sense," which Descartes provisionally and deceptively equates with reason. The truth underlying this flattery is that the men of good sense reason well on "matters that especially concern [them]" and regarding which errors of judgment "punish them soon afterwards":[36] their rationality is rooted in their self-interest or self-preservation in the here and now, and not what will punish them in another life. Descartes' rhetoric advertises to them that they are the beneficiaries of the project that produces "the fruits of the earth without pain," and of the social conditions of the progress of the project. They are the natural allies of the second group, the generous minds, or the scientists who build on his foundations and the *philosophes* who propagate his reformation. One may distinguish as a third group the political rulers proper who necessarily welcome Descartes' advocacy of knowledge useful for society, as well as his opposition to the political ambitions of "reformers" who believe God has given them "sufficient grace and zeal to be prophets." [37]

He invites these groups to join in common opposition against those opponents who draw their beliefs from "the ancient books, their histories and their fables." Together with "reformers" and "prophets" he places those who, believing themselves "devout" and "great friends of God," though in fact "only bigots and superstitious," have "committed the greatest crimes that can be committed by men, as betraying cities, killing princes, and exterminating entire peoples, only because they did not follow their opinions." The popular support of these zealous leaders comes from "the weak minds," a term used repeatedly by Descartes to designate those who are prone to "superstition," and whose "consciences" are agitated by "repentances and remorse," [38] the human type most opposed to "the strong and noble minds." But these latter have a remedy available, the science of the passions: "even the weakest minds could acquire a most absolute empire over all their passions if one employed enough industry to train them, and to conduct them." [39] Behind the zealous stands the authority of "the school," or scholasticism: "the monks have supplied the opportunity for all sects and heresies through their theology, that is to say, their scholasticism, which before all must be exterminated." [40] Because of this alliance of friend against foe, d'Alembert could "regard [Descartes] as a chief of conspirators who first had the courage to raise himself up against a despotic and arbitrary power."

Yet Descartes' Enlightenment rhetoric must vanquish more fundamental enemies to ensure the lasting success of his project. Not only his
"preceptors" or the books of Latin Christendom "corrupt the natural
reason," but so also do the "Greek and Latin books." [41] He made plain
that his only rivals on the plane of his endeavor, or those alone "whose
writings we possess" who sought out "the first causes and the true principles," were "Plato and Aristotle." Hence those whose "prejudices"
most oppose his project are those who have "most studied the ancient
philosophy." His rhetoric has then the function of opposing the whole
tradition of humanistic learning, which required him to oppose tradition simply. Since the view that the good is the old or the traditional
can never be fully eradicated, Enlightenment rhetoric has a permanently divisive social function. Descartes succeeded in turning the questioning of the identity of the good and the old by classic philosophy
against the classics by identifying them as the old or the tradition. The
classic tradition appeared to him, as it had to Stevin and Grotius, as a
corruption of the wisdom of the golden youth of the world in some
pre-Socratic *siècle sage*.[42] Since Descartes knew that some less than philosophically precise belief regarding the whole is required as a foundation for society, he sought to supply a substitute for tradition that
would foster the project of science. By a scientific "fable of the world,"
or by what purported to be a scientific account of the genesis of the
heavens and the earth, of the visible universe and all its phenomena, he
established the belief that science is master of the whole; and by the
promise of the progress of science toward infinite benefits he and Bacon
established the "idea of progress," or the belief that the good is the
future whose benevolence owes nothing to tradition, to nature, or to God.

It was not Descartes but Bacon who first proposed a "project" that
promised maximum benevolence to society by a universal method, and
hence inaugurated the politics of Enlightenment. Descartes following
Bacon may be said to have accepted but revised Machiavelli's earlier
fusion of the highest glory or mastery with the highest benevolence
through a political teaching devoted to the mastery of chance or nature
in human affairs. It was initially Machiavelli's "realism" that taught
that reason does not by nature seek the pure truth but serves the passions,
or that "the natural force of man's judgment" does not suffice, as Bacon
put it, and hence reason must be "equipped" with the artifact of method,
or that reason must be "conducted" by the "work" or art of method, as
Descartes said. Precisely Machiavelli's incipient critique of the impurities
of natural reason demanded that nature be remedied, or rather mastered,
by art, or by the construction of a method. Wheras Machiavelli thought

that the understanding of man must descend to include that of the beast in order to ascend to the mastery of human nature, Bacon thought that a first mastery of the human understanding itself must be gained by descending to learn from the mechanical arts so that the ascent to the mastery of all nature "be done as if by machinery." Hence on the basis of Machiavelli's "realism," Bacon attempted to surpass Machiavelli, as is especially evident in the *New Organon* (Book I, section 129). For the "endeavor to establish and extend the power and dominion of the human race itself over the universe" through a universal method is more benevolent than the teaching of political modes and orders. "The benefits of discoveries may extend to the whole race of man, civil benefits only to particular places; the latter last not beyond a few ages, the former through all time;" "civil reformations" usually begin in violence, but discoveries confer benefits without causing sorrow to any.

This argument in its entirety is a germinal part of the project of Descartes. The genealogy of Descartes' project is especially visible in the amazingly similar statements of the doctrine concerning "reformation" of political bodies by a private individual in the *Prince* (chapter vi), the *New Organon* (Book I, section 129), and the *Discourse* (Part II). According to Descartes, Bacon did not see with sufficient clarity that the new method must be mathematical to be certain or "systematic," or that it required a new mathematics and a mathematical physics and a corresponding determination of the soul. By these momentous amendments,[43] but on the foundation laid by Machiavelli, Descartes became "the founder of modern philosophy."

NOTES

1. J. d'Alembert, *Discours préliminaire de l'Encyclopédie,* ed. L. Ducros (Paris, 1930), 104.

2. R. Descartes, *Oeuvres,* ed. C. Adam and P. Tannery (Paris, 1910), V, 159. References are to this edition if the original text is not available in the Pléiade edition, *Oeuvres et Lettres,* ed. A. Bridoux (Paris, 1952).

3. A.-T. XI, 320; Pléiade 1245; A.-T. IV, 67.

4. Pléiade 566.

5. *Ibid.,* 127–128, 130.

6. *Ibid.,* 885.

7. *Ibid.,* 130.

8. *Ibid.,* 130.

9. *Ibid.,* 695.

10. *Ibid.,* 168–169.

11. *Ibid.,* 132.

12. *Ibid.,* 133–134.

13. *Ibid.,* 768–769.

14. *Ibid.,* 134–135.

15. *Ibid.,* 141.

16. A.-T. V, 178.

17. Pléiade 568.

18. *Ibid.,* 135.

19. *Ibid.,* 168.

20. *Ibid.,* 168–169.

21. *Ibid.,* 168.

22. *Ibid.,* 154.

23. *Ibid.,* 171.
24. *Ibid.,* 295, 579–580; A.-T. VII, 9.
25. G. W. Leibniz, *Philosophischer Briefwechsel,* I, 506.
26. Pléiade 768–769, 696–697, 698, 715; A.-T. XI, 326.
27. *Philosophical Writings of Henry More,* ed. F. I. MacKinnon (Oxford, Oxford University Press, 1925), 183–96. Descartes, "the prince of the nullibists," "befooling" his readers with his "jocular subtilty," contended that "incorporeal spirits" exist, "but would be found to do it only by way of an oblique and close derision of their existence, saying indeed they exist, but then hiddenly and cunningly denying it, by affirming they are no where" or "null ibi."

28. Pléiade 768.
29. *Ibid.,* 779.
30. Aristotle *Nic. Eth.* 1124a.
31. Pléiade 774.
32. *Ibid.,* 165.
33. *Ibid.,* 795.
34. *Ibid.,* 1199, 131, 792.
35. *Ibid.,* 791.
36. *Ibid.,* 131, 133.
37. *Ibid.,* 168.
38. *Ibid.,* 1244, 141–142.
39. *Ibid.,* 722
40. A.-T. V, 176.
41. Pléiade 179, 562, 564, 879, 884.
42. *Ibid.,* 560, 562, 564; A.-T. 373–376.
43. For these steps, see especially J. Klein, *Greek Mathematical Thought and the Origin of Algebra* (Cambridge & London, 1968), 197–211.

READINGS

A. Descartes, René. *Discourse on Method.* Trans. L. J. Lafleur. New York: Liberal Arts Press, 1951.
B. Descartes, René. *Meditations.* Trans. with introduction by L. J. Lafleur. New York: Liberal Arts Press, 1951.

JOHN MILTON

1608–1674

While an undergraduate at Cambridge, John Milton delivered seven Latin orations that reflect, as they might be expected to reflect considering their style and language, not only the extent of his reading of the authors of classical antiquity, but also the considerable extent to which, even as a schoolboy, he consciously accepted their authority as teachers. Later, when he dared to break the law respecting the licensing of printing and, in the same act, to advise Parliament of the necessity of its repeal, he entitled his speech, which was to become his most famous prose work, the *Areopagitica,* thus reminding his addressees of the classical example of Isocrates and the Athenian Areopagus. He sought to reform English education by patterning it after the "ancient and famous schools of Pythagoras, Plato, Isocrates, Aristotle and such others." For almost twenty years he expounded and defended a political teaching knowingly derived from the doctrines and institutions of ancient Greece and Rome.

He also insisted, however, that this was not a case of introducing something wholly alien to English tradition, of revolting in order to make a new beginning by establishing government on wholly new principles. Indeed, he argued in his most comprehensive political work, *The Ready and Easy Way to Establish a Free Commonwealth,* that it did not require "the introducement of . . . exotic models" at all; there was model enough to be found in the English past. As he had written in an early anti-episcopal tract: "There is no civil government that has been known, no not the Spartan, not the Roman, though both for this respect so much praised by the wise Polybius, more divinely and harmoniously tuned, more equally balanced as it were by the hand and scale of justice, than is [or was] the commonwealth of England: where, under a free and untutored monarch, the noblest, worthiest, and most prudent men, with full approbation, and suffrage of the people have in their power the supreme, and final determination of highest affairs." [1]

The virtue of this free commonwealth consisted in part in the fact that it had a mixed constitution; it was not a monarchy, aristocracy, or democracy, but a mixture that recognized the claim of each of these, a balance, "divinely and harmoniously tuned." The best and least barbarous commonwealths "have aimed at a certain mixture and temperament, partaking the several virtues of each other state. . . ." [2] Although he was to become an avowed enemy of monarchy, early adopting views wholly republican and therefore, in this respect, more in the spirit of his classical models than of English tradition, his attachment to the idea of the mixed constitution remained fixed throughout his political career. A politics knowingly derived from ancient Greece and Rome is a constitutional politics, and the cause of constitutional government, the cause that England was chosen by God to promote in the world of the seventeenth century, had no greater friend than John Milton. Even at the last moment before the restoration of the monarchy and with it the prelacy, when it appeared that the "good old cause" was doomed, it was Milton who insisted that the way to a free commonwealth was clear and easy: ". . . and if the people, laying aside prejudice and impatience, will seriously and calmly now consider their own good both religious and civil, their own liberty and the only means thereof . . . and will elect . . . men not addicted to a single person [i.e., a king] or house of lords, the work is done; at least the foundation firmly laid of a free Commonwealth, and good part also erected of the main structure." [3] The task here is to understand the form and purpose of this free commonwealth.

Even though he did not originate it, no name has been more closely associated with the doctrine of the mixed constitution, or more precisely in this case, mixed state, than that of the Greek historian Polybius. In his famous description of the Roman constitution, a description preceded by a somewhat enigmatic commentary on it, Polybius seems to combine the idea of the mixed constitution of Plato and Aristotle with a new idea, that of the division of power. Whereas Aristotle's was a mixture of oligarchy and democracy achieved by giving political power to the middle, and most moderate, class in an effort to achieve moderation, Polybius' Roman mixture seemingly involves elements of monarchy, aristocracy, and democracy, each wielding a part of the power of the state and each associated with a particular institution, the monarchy with the consulate, the aristocracy with the senate, and the democracy, but vaguely, with the popular assemblies. Without going into the question of Polybius' intention, we must attempt to grasp what Milton himself meant by the term. Did he mean by it, like Aristotle in the fourth book of the *Politics,* a regime that blends democracy and oligarchy so as to avoid the disadvantages of each and to combine the advantages of each, and yet possesses an undivided citizen body ultimately sovereign in all respects; or did he mean by it a regime in which the sum total of political power is divided into a monarchic, aristocratic, and democratic element?

Milton was not a mere spectator of the tremendous political events of his time, he was an active supporter of both the Parliament's cause against Charles I and, later, of Cromwell. Much of his political writing was presented in pamphlets written in haste and for immediate practical purposes, whether to defend himself and the English people or to make a final effort to prevent the restoration of the monarchy. In these circumstances it is not surprising that his views on some questions changed under the buffeting of the events of the civil war and its aftermath. One of these was his opinion of monarchy; another was his opinion of the character of the common people.

Milton was at no time a democrat, but he seems to have had a higher opinion of the political capacity of the common people in the beginning than he had later on. In 1644 in the *Areopagitica* he attacked the licensing of printing because, among other reasons, it was a reproach to the common people, assuming them unreasonably to be in "such a sick and weak estate of faith and discretion, as to be able to take nothing down but through the pipe of a licenser." But in his *Second Defense of the People of England,* a vindication of the nation for deposing, then executing Charles I, and thereby delivering the "commonwealth from a grievous domination," he drew a distinction between those valorous, magnanimous, and steadfast persons who were capable of great deeds and fidelity to a great cause, and the vulgar multitude.[4] At one point early in his political career he reproached an opponent for his use of the term "mutinous rabble," but he later used the term "rabble" himself, and meant thereby the common people who, he said, were dull and ignorant of the art of government, and fickle and excitable. Only a few men desire liberty, he said in this first *Defense of the English People,* and only a few are capable of using it: "Far the greatest part of the world prefers just masters—masters, observe, but just ones." [5] Yet in his *Second Defense* of the same English people, he also asked Cromwell to ensure that "all the citizens alike should have an equal right to be free." [6] In the light of these conflicting statements, perhaps the surest guide to his appraisal of the character of the common people is to be found in the place he assigned them in the constitution. In 1641 he spoke of political power being exercised only "with full approbation and suffrage of the people," but it was not until 1660 in *The Ready and Easy Way* that he spoke in any detail of the manner in which this consent was to be given, and here, in the context of a description of the election of members of the General Council, or legislature, it becomes quite clear that the role of the people is minimal. They exercise some power in a well-balanced state, but no one could describe that state as a democracy. Nevertheless, one of the reasons for his latter-day refusal to permit a king in his mixed state is his attachment to the principle of popular sovereignty.

Milton was not always a republican. Whereas in *Of Reformation,* written in 1641, he found it necessary in order to promote religious reform to argue that episcopacy was not the only form of church government compatible with monarchy, eight years later he said that a king may be deposed when he acts unlawfully, and even when he does not act unlawfully, because he "holds his authority of the people." The people choose kings in the first place and they may reject them: freeborn men have the "right . . . to be governed as seems to them best." [7] (But may other nations, especially a nation of barbarians or a "rabble concourse" legitimately be ruled by a king or even a despot? This is suggested in both the *First Defense* and *The Ready and Easy Way*.) Kings do not hold their titles from God, but from the people: "So that we see the title and just right of reigning or deposing, in reference to God, is found in Scripture to be all one; visible only in the people, and depending merely upon justice and demerit." [8] It is popular sovereignty that is derived from God, as he says in *Paradise Lost,* Book XII:

> . . . but Man over men
> He made not Lord; such title to himself
> Reserving, human left from human free.

Milton may have begun by supporting the monarchy, but he quickly became a republican, and an avid republican.

Popular sovereignty is, however, perfectly compatible with the acceptance of monarchy, even of hereditary monarchy, since the people may delegate the governmental power to a royal family while retaining the sovereign power to withdraw it. But by 1651, the year he published the *First Defense,* Milton had found in contemporary events sufficient practical reasons for rejecting monarchy, even in its limited sense of constitutional monarchy. His experience as an Englishman during the preceding decade had confirmed the argument he knew from the writings of Plato and Aristotle that monarchy tends to degenerate into tyranny—indeed, according to Milton, of all the forms of government monarchy is most likely to do so. Nothing written by the friends of the king could dissuade him; in fact, he became increasingly republican in the course of replying to the various promonarchical pamphlets. Finally, he could see nothing around a king but a corrupting luxury, a dissoluteness, a style of life that made the people abject, debauched the "prime gentry," and bred a servile nobility that aspired not to public service but to service as "stewards, chamberlains, ushers, grooms, even of the close-stool. . . ." Monarchy, in short, debases men's character. It is, as a student of Aristotle could be expected to argue, a form of government not suited to free men. To be ruled by a king, to commit all to his paternal care, is to act "more like boys under age than men." "How unmanly must it needs be . . . to hang all our felicity on him, all our safety, our well-being, for which if we were ought else but sluggards or babies, we need depend on none but God and our own counsels, our own active virtue and industry. . . ." [9] It was for these reasons that Milton was a republican. This does not mean, of course, that Milton refused to provide for the exercise of executive power; the mixed state provided for a magistracy, and if in 1641 this was a king, in 1660 it was a Council of State, chosen by the legislature.

It is clear that neither the people as a whole nor the king and his retinue were to exercise the decisive political power in the mixed state; this role was reserved for the "noblest, worthiest, and most prudent men," as he said in *Of Reformation*. It is also clear that these words did not refer to a titled aristocracy ruling through a house of lords, for there is no house of lords in the free commonwealth, and Milton had contempt for the idea that a title conferred nobility on its possessor. By noblest, worthiest, and most prudent men, he meant those men truly distinguished in their character and by their public service. "To these accomplished men and chosen citizens," he advised Cromwell in the latter's capacity as Lawgiver or founding father, "you doubtless might properly commit the care of our liberty. . . ." [10] He meant men for whom public service was not a means of amassing power, position, or wealth, but a sacred duty. "And what government comes nearer to this precept of Christ, than a free Commonwealth; wherein they who are greatest, are perpetual servants and drudges to the public at their own cost and charges, neglect their own affairs; yet are not elevated above their brethren; live soberly in their families, walk the streets as other men, may be spoken to freely, familiarly, friendly, without adoration." [11] Such men are likely to be found among the "middle sort," for, and once again Milton agrees with Aristotle, the "rest are most commonly diverted, on the one hand by luxury and wealth, on the other by want and poverty, from achieving excellence, and from the study of laws and government." [12]

It is clear, then, to whom Milton entrusts the decisive political power in the free commonwealth: not to a "single person" or to the people, but to a true aristocracy to be found among men of the middle class; and it is necessary now to see how he would effect this. The ablest and noblest men are to rule with the consent or, as he said in 1641, with "full approbation and suffrage" of the people, and they are to exercise their rule initially through a General Council or legislature. "For the ground and basis of every just and free government (since men have smarted so oft for committing all to one person) is a general council of ablest men, chosen by the people to consult of public affairs from time to time for the common good." Unlike the Roman republic described by Polybius, this legislative body not only makes the laws, raises and manages the public revenue and, generally, performs as a legislative body, but it also controls the army and navy. Furthermore, it elects, from among its own members as well as from outside, a Council of State, an executive body or magistracy, that carries on "particular affairs with more secrecy and expedition. . . ." Finally, there is local government, organized in every county in the land and exercising the powers of a kind of subordinate commonwealth, and especially with the full power to elect judges and administer justice.[13] Here, then, are the elements of a Polybian mixed state: monarchy, or the magistracy, embodied in the Council of State; aristocracy represented in the General Council or legislature; and democracy represented in the electoral process, specifically in the election of local officials and, more significantly, members of the General Council. These are the institutions of the free commonwealth, a state constructed with a view to striking a balance of some sort.

But what sort of balance? Is it a balance of legislative against executive against judicial, that is, a dividing up of power in order to prevent anyone or any one group from becoming too powerful? Or is it a balance of monarchy and aristocracy and democracy, the power of each being exercised through one of the constitutional institutions? There is, of course, no monarch, but there is a magistracy; there is no distinct popular assembly, but the people (or at least some of them) do vote. In what sense is this a balanced state? The answer to this question requires, at a minimum, a closer analysis of the institutional factors involved.

The ablest men rule with the consent of the people, but this consent is expressed only in the election of the General Council and of local officials. Milton weighed the possibility of balancing the General Council with a popular assembly, or some other popular institution, such as the Spartan ephors or the Roman tribunes, but he rejected it on the ground that "these remedies either little availed the people, or brought them to such a licentious and unbridled democratie, as in fine ruined themselves with their own excessive power." [14] On the basis of the experience of the Roman republic, which, he said, degenerated into the tyranny of Sulla because the people, not content to have only their tribunes, gained control over the choice of first one, then both consuls, then the censors and praetors, Milton rejected popular assemblies in favor of the democratic suffrage, or quasi-democratic suffrage, alone. His mature judgment convinced him against the possibility of balancing class against class by balancing institution against institution: the attempt to do this led either to a wholly unpopular constitution or to an unbridled democracy, and not to a balanced state.

But it appears that the suffrage is not democratic, and even if it were, the electoral machinery seems to be designed to minimize the influence of the common people. Members of the General Council are selected by a series of electoral commissions working with a list of nominees provided initially by a kind of electoral college. "Another way [to effect a balance] will be, to well-qualify and refine elections: not committing all to the noise and shouting of a rude multitude, but permitting only those of them who are rightly qualified, to nominate as many as they will; and out of that number others of a better breeding, to choose a less number more judiciously, till after a third or fourth sifting and refining of exactest choice, they only be left chosen who are the due number, and seem by most voices the worthiest." [15] The democratic element in the constitution seems especially weak, moreover, and scarcely sufficient to balance off the power of the aristocracy in the General Council, when we give due consideration to the fact that this council, the principal governing body under the constitution, is elected in perpetuity. Except upon "the death or default" of a member, there are to be no elections after the original one. He prefers a perpetual parliament (and it is only with the greatest reluctance that he concedes the unpopularity and infeasibility of this arrangement and accepts as a substitute an assembly one-third of whose members are elected annually) because the necessity to choose successive parliaments breeds commotions, novelty, change—that is, instability—especially because the newly elected legislators will initiate change merely in order to have something to do, or to appear to have something to do. Because the General

Council is both "foundation and main pillar of the whole state," to make an unnecessary change in it is to endanger the entire structure.

He was aware that this constitution would be attacked for its alleged failure to erect safeguards around the interests of the people, and he pointed out that one safeguard was to elect trustworthy men to the council, men who would exercise a just rule, and this could be done by a well-educated electorate (without regard, apparently, to the number of people comprising it). At this point it is possible to see an important difference between Milton and those political writers who taught that by such devices as a mixed state, but meaning thereby a division or balancing of power, men could build an indestructible commonwealth whose viability depended in no way upon the presence of citizens of good character. Milton's free commonwealth pretended to immortality,[16] but its excellence and durability depended on the presence of men of good character, in fact, it depended absolutely on the rule of truly virtuous men. The educating of these men could not be left to chance but must be assumed as a major public duty: "To make the people fittest to choose, and the chosen fittest to govern, will be to mend our corrupt and faulty education, to teach the people faith not without virtue, temperance, modesty, sobriety, parsimony, justice; not to admire wealth [the principle of the commercial society] or honour [the principle of monarchy] . . . to place every one his private welfare and happiness in the public peace, liberty and safety."[17] Who or what institution was to teach the people "faith not without virtue," becomes something of a problem because of his notion of the proper relation of Church and State, although, as we shall see, the apparent problem is readily resolved by his understanding of moral training and Christian liberty. Certainly it is clear from *Of Education,* with its outline of educational reform, and from the *Second Defense,* where he called upon Cromwell as Lawgiver to make "a better provision for the education and morals of youth,"[18] that the provision of moral training is a public duty. The excellence and durability of the free commonwealth, then, depended not on institutional devices, however soundly contrived, but on the character of the men comprising it. Thus, the true safeguard of the people's interest consisted not in a balance of institutions, but on their character and the character of the men governing.

Milton made one concession. "But to prevent all mistrust, the people . . . will have their several ordinary assemblies . . . in the chief towns of every county [and these will be as effective] toward the securing of their liberty, as a numerous assembly of them all formed and convened on purpose with the wariest rotation [*i.e.,* with the most frequent elections]." These local assemblies will have the power to "declare and publish their assent or dissent by deputies within a time limited sent to the Grand Council. . . ." [19] This does not mean that each county has a veto over decisions taken by the General Council, but that a majority of counties must assent to the decisions.

These are the institutions of the mixed state or free commonwealth, a form of government held by the wisest men in all ages to be the noblest and most just, "the most agreeable to all due liberty and proportioned equality," and also a form of government "plainly commended, or rather enjoined by our Saviour himself. . . ." [20] It is a form of government not only derived from the teachings of the wise men of classical antiquity and patterned on a model found in the English past, it is a form of government enjoined by Christ. But the question persists: what sort of balance does it strike? If this arrangement were meant to strike a balance between the various powers of government, executive, legislative and judicial, it is ill conceived. A moment's reflection on the method of selection of the executive is sufficient to reveal the lack of true balance and the extent to which the legislative is the decisive power. This is altogether proper, he says, because although it is important to have the executive power exercised by men not in the legislature, the legislative power is supreme.[21] Certainly if this strikes a balance between aristocracy and democracy, it does so not by establishing each class in an institutional stronghold, but rather by regulating the electoral franchise. In this respect it resembles less what is usually said to be the mixed state of Polybius than it does the polity of Aristotle, the rule of the middle class effected mainly through a moderate property qualification for voting.[22] This is intended to produce a suffrage wide enough to achieve popularity, and thereby, it is hoped, stability, but restricted in such a way as to minimize the full power of numbers, for, as Milton said, nothing is more natural than that "the less should yield to the greater: not number to number, but virtue to virtue, and counsel to counsel." [23] Monarchy finds no place in the mixture, and the only dividing up of power is to be found in the quasi-federalism, because Milton, as Plato and Aristotle before him, knew that power cannot be divided among classes. ". . . the balance therefore [would have to] be exactly so set, as to preserve and keep up due authority on either side, as well in the Senate as in the people," [24] and this is impossible. Give the people the tribunes and they end up with the consuls, censors, and praetors as well; either all this or nothing. Constitutional government is not a balance of class against class, but a mixture of aristocracy (or oligarchy) and democracy, made possible through the rule of the "middle sort." Among the "middle sort" are to be found the "most prudent men," the men most skillful and virtuous.

While it is clear that Milton was indebted to the writers of classical antiquity for his model of constitutional government, it is not altogether clear that he shared fully their understanding of the purpose of this constitution. True, Polybius had praised Lycurgus for introducing stability into Sparta, thus interrupting the "regular cycle of constitutional revolutions," and Milton had asked first Cromwell, and after Cromwell's death, General Monk, to imitate Lycurgus. It is also true that he believed that, properly established, the free commonwealth would endure forever, that is, until Christ came to establish His commonwealth. But for both the ancients and Milton stability was merely a necessary condition of the goals of political life, it was not the purpose of political life, and therefore they would agree that institutions are laid down with a view not only to stability but to this purpose. For, assuming a solution to the problem of succession, the most stable constitution might very well be the absolute rule of one man over a completely degraded population. It is when we look to the purpose of political life that Milton seems to part company with his classical authorities, and the obvious reason for this seems to be his Christianity.

Not only religious questions in general but questions of doctrine in particular were of decisive importance to Milton, so that his efforts to reform the constitution of England were at least matched by his efforts to reform the religious life of the English, and it would be difficult to say to which he assigned priority. The bishops were as great a threat to the well-ordered constitution as was the king, and a much more immediate threat than that posed by the common people. Just as the bishop of Rome did not hesitate to seize that city and make himself temporal ruler over it, so, Milton feared, the English bishops would assert a tyrannical temporal rule over England. The bishops and the entire establishment should be abolished. Not only can a Christian understand the truth of the Scriptures without the assistance of a bishop, but bishops with political power are destructive of Christian liberty. ". . . what numbers of faithful and freeborn Englishmen, and good Christians, have been constrained to forsake their dearest home, their friends and kindred, whom nothing but the wide ocean, and the savage deserts of America, could hide and shelter from the fury of the bishops." Episcopacy is a "wen" on the body of the constitution, its ceremonies and ecclesiastical courts are "leeches" that suck the revenue and riches of the country.[25] Milton wrote as many pages devoted to the reformation of these things as he did on the reformation of political things.

Yet it is difficult to separate the two in his thought, that is, to speak of political reform without reference to religious reform, and this de-

spite the fact that according to Milton himself the two powers, ecclesiastical and civil, are "totally distinct." It would not be altogether accurate
to say that he saw only one problem, that of the relation between the
ecclesiastical and the civil. Yet what was in need of reform was not the
Church alone or the State alone, but the relation between them. Thus
he advised Cromwell to "leave the church to itself, and have the prudence to relieve yourself and the magistrates from that burden, *which
is one half, and at the same time, most remote* from your own province.
. . ." [26] What he meant by this paradoxical statement can perhaps be
understood from the epistle dedicatory (addressed to Parliament) to
A Treatise of Civil Power in Ecclesiastical Causes. Here he wrote:
". . . both commonwealth and religion will at length, if ever, flourish
in Christendom, when either they who govern discern between civil and
religious, or they who so discern shall be admitted to govern." [27] Religious matters are not properly the concern of civil authority as is shown
by the outrages committed by Archbishop Laud and his coadjutors,
backed by the power of the State; on the other hand, religious matters
are properly the concern of civil authority in a negative sense: it is the
duty of the civil authority to maintain the separation. But Milton also
means more than this. He also means that Cromwell, as a Christian
lawgiver, can best promote the Christian religion—and it is his duty
to promote it—by establishing and maintaining a separation of civil and
ecclesiastical powers. His assistance is required to establish a free commonwealth, and the free commonwealth, more than any other form of
government, will promote the liberty of conscience, "which above all
other things ought to be to all men dearest and most precious. . . ." [28] It
is difficult to distinguish Milton's religious teaching from his political
teaching because his political reforms are guided by his religious doctrine, and, to a lesser extent, his religious reforms are guided by political
considerations. (His political reforms are undoubtedly laid down with
a view to Christian liberty, but there is also a civil liberty, which is independent of Christian liberty, and which is jeopardized by, among other
things, an established church. With respect to civil liberty, an established church is similar to a titled nobility, because both offer prefer-
ments on a basis other than merit, and both limit the access to position
by those whose only claim is merit.) It is his doctrine of Christianity,
and specifically his doctrine of Christian liberty, that provides the final
cause or purpose, and therefore the form, of the mixed constitution.
Liberty is the goal of political life, without regard to whether it is the
acknowledged goal of the majority of a particular people. Indeed, Milton knew that in 1660 the "inconsiderate multitude" seemed to be "mad"
for the restoration of the monarchy, with its trappings and its religion

so inimical to liberty, and that many who had once supported the cause of liberty had become "zealous backsliders." But it was neither just nor reasonable that their voices "against the main end of government should enslave the less number that would be free." Better and more just if the "able and worthy" minority were to compel the multitude, if necessary by force of arms, "to retain . . . their liberty. . . ." [29]

Milton's idea of liberty is complex, and not only because, while customarily dividing it into two parts, spiritual (or Christian) and civil liberty, in one place in the *Second Defense,* he adds a third, domestic or private liberty, and refers to the *Areopagitica* as the place where he treats not civil but this domestic liberty. It is complex because this befits the difficulties of the subject. Nowhere in his work is it reduced to a simple statement, and nothing he wrote can qualify as a treatise on the subject. The closest to it is the *Areopagitica,* but this deals, admittedly, with only one aspect of liberty. As he says in the *Second Defense,* there is, first, liberty in the sense of a means to the end, virtue: "to form and increase virtue, the most excellent thing is liberty." But in the next sentence he calls upon Cromwell to "make a better provision for the education and morals of youth," [30] a statement sufficient in itself to remind us of something we learn from the *Areopagitica* as well, that the free commonwealth is not a pluralistic society. We know, for example. that it does not tolerate "popery and open superstition," but only "neighboring differences, or rather indifferences." The citizen of the free commonwealth is assured the liberty to become virtuous, but he is not assured the liberty to define virtue in any way that happens to please him.

There is, secondly, liberty in the negative sense of liberty from government. The free commonwealth exercises no authority in ecclesiastical matters, nor, as we know, does it require the licensing of printing, thus providing a liberty of the press. The limited nature of that liberty, however, may best be seen from Milton's summary of the argument of the *Areopagitica* in his *Second Defense.* "Lastly, I wrote, after the model of a regular speech, *Areopagitica,* on the liberty of printing, that the determination of true and false, of what ought to be published and what suppressed, might not be in the hands of the few who may be charged with the inspection of books, men commonly without learning and of vulgar judgment, and by whose license and pleasure, no one is suffered to publish any thing which may be above vulgar apprehension." [31] Those "who are inclined to freedom of inquiry" have the liberty to communicate "without the private inquisition of any magisterial censor," but only at their own peril. Milton's distinction is the one made later by the common law, where the liberty of the press consisted in being able to publish without previous restraint, "and not in freedom from

censure for criminal matter when published." [32] Finally, the General
Council, in part because of the extent of the powers exercised at the local
level, promises to restrict its governing mostly to the area of foreign
affairs. This negative liberty is at least compatible with, and is probably
required by, Christian liberty, which Milton defines in part as the release, through the agency of Christ, "from the rule of law and of men."
What this means can perhaps best be understood from the following
passage in *A Treatise of Civil Power in Ecclesiastical Causes,* written
in 1659:

. . . the state of religion under the gospel is far differing from what it was
under the law: then was the state of rigor, childhood, bondage and works,
to all which force was not unbefitting; now is the state of grace, manhood,
freedom and faith; to all which belongs willingness and reason, not force:
the law was then written on tables of stone, and to be performed according to
the letter, willingly or unwillingly; the gospel, our new covenant, upon the
heart of every believer, to be interpreted only by the sense of charity and inward persuasion: the law had no distinct government or governors of church
and commonwealth, but the Priests and Levites judged in all causes not
ecclesiastical only but civil . . . which under the gospel is forbidden to all
church-ministers. . . .[33]

This passage serves to introduce liberty in its exalted sense.

Men may think they are free, they may boast they are free, and
they may indeed be free in the negative sense, but they may still be
slaves. They may be slaves in the decisive respect of being unable to use
properly the negative freedom they are given, and they are slaves if they
are ignorant of right and wrong, or if they think power consists in violence, or dignity in "pride and haughtiness." They are slaves if "un-
nerved through luxury," if controlled by their lusts and not by their
reason, if, in short, as he makes abundantly clear in the *Second Defense,*
they are not masters of themselves. Liberty from law is not enough.
"Unless your liberty be of that kind, which can neither be gotten, nor
taken away by arms; and that alone is such, which, springing from
piety, justice, temperance, in fine, from real virtue, shall take deep and
intimate root in your minds; you may be assured, there will not be
wanting one, who, even without arms, will speedily deprive you of what
it is your boast to have gained by force of arms." [34] The liberty that can
neither be won nor lost by force of arms, and the liberty on which all
other liberties depend, is Christian liberty in the full meaning of the
term. This is the liberty known only to the truly free man, and this is the
liberty that constitutes the end or goal of political life.

Such a liberty became possible only through Christ, because it was

Christ who changed man's condition from "legal to evangelical," from one of "servility toward God" and toward God's law to one in which man is permitted to exercise a faculty he shares only with God. True, this is a liberty to "serve God," but it is a liberty to serve God "according to the best light which God has planted in [one] to that purpose," [35] and what this signifies in fact is the liberty to seek the truth. Truth came into the world with Christ, "and was a perfect shape most glorious to look on," but was later scattered about in a thousand pieces. The liberty of man consists in the search for these pieces, which means the search for what is unknown by what is known. Not only is it the liberty of man that consists in this life of seeking after truth, but it is also the dignity or the virtue of man. For in all things, God directs his offers "not to an indolent credulity, but to constant diligence, and to an unwearied search after truth. . . ." [36] To actualize Christian liberty is to seek the truth within the limits of Scripture, the seeker being guided by the Holy Spirit, and to seek the truth within the limits of Scripture guided by the Holy Spirit, "which no man can know at all times to be in himself," [37] is to seek the truth within very broad limits. It is almost to seek the truth within no limits at all.

That this is so appears from the following consideration: how a Christian judges of the power of unassisted reason will depend to some extent on what he regards as the consequences of the Fall, of man's first disobedience to God. According to Milton, man indeed lost paradise by his Fall, but the acquisition of the knowledge of good and evil elevated man above the level of his previous existence to a point where he was more like God. Milton's poetic description of the expulsion from Eden is not reminiscent of the scene of anguish depicted in, for example, Masaccio's fresco.

> Some natural tears they dropped, but wiped them soon;
> The World was all before them, where to choose
> Their place of rest, and Providence their guide:
> They hand in hand with wand'ring steps and slow,
> Through Eden took their solitary way.[38]

With the coming of Christ and the release from the Mosaic law, paradise is regained, but not the paradise of Eden, for that original state of innocence is lost irrevocably. Man now knows good and evil. The world, moreover, has known Socrates, "wisest of men," and even Christ, who rejects Satan's offer of the earthly kingdom of Athens at the height of its intellectual power, knows the intellectual beauty of classical antiquity. He rejects it because it is not "true wisdom," but, "being built on nothing firm," is mere conjecture or fancy. It is possible to distinguish the life of the truly free man, seeking truth within the limits of Scripture guided by the Holy Spirit, from the life of the philosopher of pagan antiquity, but it is not easy; not many questions open to the latter are closed to Milton. Without the liberty to winnow and sift "every doctrine," he said, and to think and write about it, "according to . . . individual faith and persuasion," men are "still enslaved, not indeed, as formerly, under the divine law, but, what is worst of all, under the law of man, or to speak more truly, under a barbarous tyranny." [39] Not many pagan thinkers held the life of the intellect in higher esteem: for what is "more delightful, what more happy than those conferences of learned and most eminent men, such as divine Plato is said to have held very frequently under that famous plane tree. . . ." [40] Happiness, for this Christian, consists in friendship, and friendship consists in seeking the truth together. It is the duty of the free commonwealth to promote this, for the free commonwealth is a "place of philosophic freedom," as England was once thought to be. The purpose of political life, which determines the form of political life, exists outside or beyond political life.

The free commonwealth honors the pursuit of knowledge and educates its citizens in such a way that they are equipped to pursue knowledge and, thereby, to exercise the freedom that Christ gave them. The free commonwealth is built not only on certain institutions but on self-governing men, men who have learned to rule themselves. How many men will learn to rule themselves and to be truly free, Milton does not say, although he wants all men to have the right to try.

NOTES

1. *Of Reformation in England, The Complete Works of John Milton*, ed. F. A. Patterson (New York: Columbia University Press, 1931–38), III, i, 63. Cited hereafter as *Works*. Spelling has been modernized throughout.

2. *Ibid.*

3. *The Ready and Easy Way to Establish a Free Commonwealth, Works*, VI, 125.

4. *Works*, VIII, 3–5, 151.

5. *Defense of the English People, Works*, VII, 393, 75.

6. *Works*, VIII, 239.

7. *The Tenure of Kings and Magistrates, Works*, V, 14.

8. *Ibid.*, p. 18.

9. *Ready and Easy Way, Works*, VI, 120, 122.

10. *Second Defense, Works*, VIII, 235.

11. *Ready and Easy Way, Works*, VI, 120.

12. *Defense of the English People, Works*, VII, 393.

13. *Ready and Easy Way, Works*, VI, 125–26, 144.

14. *Ibid.*, p. 130.

15. *Ibid.*, p. 131. Milton is not specific concerning the method of election of local officials, but it appears that here, too, it is the "nobility and chief gentry"

who are to exercise effective power. *Ibid.*, p. 144.

16. "Now is the opportunity, now the very season wherein we may obtain a free commonwealth and establish it forever in the land." *Ibid.*, p. 125.

17. *Ibid.*, p. 131.

18. *Second Defense, Works*, VIII, 237.

19. *Ready and Easy Way, Works*, VI, 132, 144.

20. *Ibid.*, p. 119.

21. *Eikonoklastes, Works*, V, 132.

22. Aristotle *Politics* 1294^b 3–8.

23. *Second Defense, Works*, VIII, 153–55.

24. *Ready and Easy Way, Works*, VI, 130.

25. *Of Reformation in England, Works*, III, i, 48–49, 54.

26. *Second Defense, Works*, VIII, 235. Italics supplied.

27. *Works*, VI, 2.

28. *Ready and Easy Way, Works*, VI, 142.

29. *Ibid.*, pp. 140–41.

30. *Works*, VIII, 237.

31. *Ibid.*, pp. 133–35.

32. Blackstone, *Commentaries*, IV. xi. 13.

33. *Works*, VI, 25.

34. *Second Defense, Works*, VIII, 237–41.

35. *Ready and Easy Way, Works*, VI, 141.

36. *Christian Doctrine, Works*, XIV, 9.

37. *Treatise of Civil Power, Works*, VI, 6.

38. *Paradise Lost*, XII.

39. *Christian Doctrine, Works*, XIV, pp. 11–13.

40. *Seventh Prolusion, Works*, XII, 263–65.

READINGS

A. Milton, John. *The Ready and Easy Way to Establish a Free Commonwealth.*
   Milton, John. *A Second Defense of the People of England.*
   Milton, John. *Areopagitica.*
B. Milton, John. *Of Reformation in England.*
   Milton, John. *Of Education.*
   Milton, John. *The Tenure of Kings and Magistrates.*
   Milton, John. *A Treatise of Civil Power in Ecclesiastical Causes.*

BENEDICT SPINOZA

1632–1677

Spinoza is the first philosopher to write a systematic defense of democracy; it appears in his *Theologico-Political Treatise,* published in 1670. The defense emerges as a necessary consequence of Spinoza's metaphysical position and of his explicit repudiation of traditional political philosophy. The most detailed statement of the metaphysical foundations of political thought is contained in the *Ethics,* Spinoza's major work, a study of the fundamental structure of reality or Substance, and so of the relationship between human existence and eternal order. Spinoza's rejection of traditional political philosophy is most clearly stated in the opening pages of the *Political Treatise* and leads him to replace what he regards as the imaginary and useless conceptions of traditional philosophers by the realistic, scientific analyses of political life characteristic of such men as, above all, Machiavelli.

Spinoza's scientific metaphysics preserves to some extent that aspect of the classical political tradition according to which an eternal order underlies and regulates the merely human order. According to the classical understanding, the eternal order first becomes accessible through an analysis of this human order. But Spinoza's analysis, in keeping with his acceptance of modern scientific procedures, entails an initial disregard of the human order, so that the eternal order may become visible. Observation of political phenomena, as distinguished from order, attempts to eliminate the distortion of the merely human perspective: political phenomena are recorded and analyzed exactly as the phenomena of any other science. The human order is then "deduced" from the scientifically revealed eternal order.

The "classical" element in Spinoza's thought, we may suggest, is a revision from the Stoic viewpoint of one strand in the Socratic teaching: Spinoza continues to recognize the need for, and the possibility of, an improvement in the human order in the light of our vision of the eternal order, but he combines this recognition with a Stoic conception of the relationship between the philosopher and eternity. This results in a curious combination of Socratic "activism" and Stoic "passivity." Philosophic fulfillment comes from contemplation of the eternal order, of which man is but a part, and in terms of which his social and political concerns are illusory temptations from serenity. But serenity depends upon the successful reconstitution of the social and political, or human order.

The influence of the Stoics upon Spinoza is visible in his "metaphysical" definition of freedom, which, in accord with his determinism, seems to identify the highest form of activity as a passive resignation in the consequences of the eternal order. In the political sphere, although it is true that Spinoza preserves the aforementioned Socratic activism, he transforms it from the activity of gentlemen to the activity of scientists, or of politicians who have been decisively influenced by a scientific understanding of political affairs. The gentleman hearkening to the philosopher is replaced in the practical sphere by the scientific politician, with a corresponding change in the practical political teaching. Freedom is conceived in the practical sphere as the intelligent expression of human power. But human power is explained in terms of a general conception of power, a conception common to every existent thing. The common conception of power makes possible a method of study which is common to all things. The combination of the conception of power and the method of study in turn produces the scientific metaphysics which purports to explain the fundamental principles of reality, the principles which are common to every aspect of reality, whether human or eternal.

The new or scientific metaphysics changes the practical political teaching because it begins from a new conception of human nature. In ignoring the "merely" human perspective, scientific metaphysics explains man in terms which are common to the human and to the nonhuman. The new scientific realism takes its bearings by the common, by what the traditional philosophers would have called the base. It does so because these common elements may be mastered by its universal method: the new conception holds forth a promise of success in political dilemmas which was not available to the excessively exalted vision of the traditional philosophers. The mastery of power, itself the greatest power, proceeds in an identical manner in both the human and the nonhuman realm. Spinoza is a student of Machiavelli, who taught that Fortuna could be mastered by strong men, and even that, through the development of an effective method, man's nature (perhaps nature itself) might be changed.

Both Spinoza and Machiavelli emphasize their intention to set out on a new way which is useful because powerful, and powerful because initiated in an understanding of men as they are, not as one would wish them to be. By stripping man of his fantasies, by beginning with man as he is in the nakedness of his natural existence, the new way is lower than the old (classical and Judaeo-Christian) way, which "lost its way" by aiming too high. The heights, or freedom and virtue based upon the control of nature by human power, can be won only through the suitably low beginning. Such a beginning in turn prefigures the replacement of the old height by a new height. The new or lower height recognizes man's debased nature, which is due to the dominance of passion over reason. To reach the heights, reason must regulate passion. Passion is best regulated by the invocation of other passions: man can be regulated, in brief, only by means of those elements which are common to all men. The regulation of men is based fundamentally on the approval of those who are to be regulated. The scientific conception of power and the universal method of analysis lead us, by way of the new conception of man, to a rejection of classical aristocracy in favor of democracy.

Reason liberated from passion is science. This liberation involves a change in the classical conception of reason. Stoic passivity is transformed into an active mastery based upon the understanding of Substance. Thus man comes into conflict with traditional religion as well, for religion also counsels a resignation to the eternal order through the mediation of obedience to God's revealed word. The initial attempt by Machiavelli to free reason from traditional religion in the sphere of politics is continued by both Hobbes and Spinoza in a similar way: both try to modify the claims of religion by a radical reinterpretation of Holy Writ.

Spinoza also retains Hobbes's (and Descartes') admiration for mathematics as the model for the new reason whereby false utopias will be replaced by a scientifically regulated will to power. In the application of "mathematical" analysis to the human order, Spinoza dissolves this order into its individual atoms in such a way that natural man is strictly presocial. For both Hobbes and Spinoza, the state of nature is consequently characterized by a primacy of the individual, that is, the multiplicity of individuals, each striving to exist in so far as its power permits, constitutes the initial *datum*. Society arises when man, the intelligent individual, recognizes the advantages of union in compromise; he recognizes that society, or the man-made instrument for the satisfaction of desires, is in general an efficient augmentation of his individual power.

There is, however, an essential difference between the thought of Hobbes and Spinoza, which is at least partially explained by the difference in their metaphysical orientation. Hobbes continues in the materialist tradition. The intelligible order, although not invented by man, is a human interpretation of the sequence or pattern of motions. The scientific expression of this interpretation begins with, and is deduced from, definitions of primary movements and of the laws of thought whereby these definitions may be combined. But man is in effect a kind of motion which differs in its internal structure from other kinds of motion. Man, as the interpreter of motions, is not explained entirely in terms of nonhuman motions. The importance of man is indicated in the political sphere by the fact that, by "natural right," Hobbes means fundamentally *human* right. Since order is relative to the decision of the individual to accept common definitions, the decisive autonomy of the individual can never be totally transformed into the security of community.

For Hobbes, the individual's need for self-preservation is more primitive than, and indeed the condition of, society, philosophy, and religion. Therefore self-preservation remains even within society in a form which is common to all individuals in the state of nature. But for Spinoza, in accord with the Stoic tradition, the eternal order is prior to, and independent of, the individual, or the decisions of the individual. For Spinoza, the transition from the state of nature to the political society is in no sense, as it is in part at least for Hobbes, the creation of order or of the conditions of power. Society is rather the condition for philosophy, or for the discovery of order. Thus philosophy, rather than the autonomous passion common to all individuals, is for Spinoza the most powerful safeguard of the individual's self-preservation.

Because Hobbes preserves in society the radical autonomy of the individual, whose passionate striving to exist interferes with his success in doing so, it is necessary to counterbalance this natural and inexpugnable pluralism by a strongly centralized government. Hobbes is a monarchist for the sake of the individual; the monarch is better able than the individuals to provide a remedy for what underlies their common fear. Furthermore, a natural autonomy means that individuals are radically equal. This equality is best preserved in a community which is as homogeneous as possible, one in which factionalism is restricted if not altogether eliminated. The monarch is a symbol of the equality of the social units in the very fact of being the unification of their social will. His will, one and indissoluble, is the reflection of the will of each individual subject as equal to every other subject. Thus monarchy is the most secure, and therefore the best of regimes.

Spinoza, on the other hand, conceives of individuals as representing, from the human viewpoint, the articulation of the eternal order into a hierarchy of parts and wholes. He is therefore able to accept natural (as distinct from conventional) differences in men as politically fundamental. The inexpugnable character of these natural differences will always necessitate a variety of kinds and functions among men in society, and therefore of opinions, which cannot be destroyed in the unity of the governing power, except at the price of destroying the social order itself. Spinoza is therefore an advocate of democracy, in which, for the sake of philosophy (which guards the interests of all), freedom of speech must be permitted in order to reflect and to satisfy the natural differences in men. In so far as democracy is the embodiment of the correct philosophical teaching, it will regulate the opinions of men by means of religious, social, and political institutions, but will not insist on uniformity of opinion.

Thus, the philosopher is by nature the "highest" man, because he is most powerful and the best safeguard of the power of nonphilosophic individuals. But, in order for philosophy to be preserved, the philosopher must support the democracy (which is in fact the manifestation of his political teaching). Otherwise, when opinion is tyrannized, philosophy is destroyed by dogma and superstition. Conversely, in order for the democracy to be preserved, it must support the freedom of philosophy. The interests of philosophy and democracy coincide, when both are properly defined.

We have already observed that Spinoza's political teaching is intended to be a deduction from his analysis of Substance. As Spinoza tells us in the *Improvement of the Understanding*,[1] he wished to direct all sciences to one end. The end of the political science is therefore identical with the end of the natural or metaphysical sciences. The fundamental principles of all sciences are the properties of Substance, and therefore all sciences proceed according to the method whereby these properties are discovered. Since men are parts of, and thus determined by, Substance (Spinoza calls such parts "modes"), the laws governing their behavior may be deduced from the general laws of substantial parts or modes.

By equating "right" with "power," and "power" with the struggle of every mode to persist, Spinoza, unlike Hobbes, denies the peculiarly human character of political phenomena;[2] as we have seen, the "human" viewpoint leads to illusions. It is in the perspective of these equations that we shall have to understand the *Theologico-Political Treatise,* in which the principles of political science are formulated on the basis of an accommodation (explicitly alluded to by Spinoza) to the (illusory) assumption that man has a special status in the universe. This also explains Spinoza's detailed concern with theology in a political book, since the traditional ground for believing in man's special status, and so for the propagation and preservation of unscientific illusions, is (in his view) religion. In the same perspective, we also understand Spinoza's remark that the entire doctrine of the *Political Treatise* follows from the premise that the desire for self-preservation is necessarily universal.[3] This premise is the proximate cause of human activity, and so it functions in the scientific presentation of political philosophy as the middle term between Substance and the structure of the best forms of government.

All sciences are to be pursued by the use of the method that is applied in mathematics; in this respect, Spinoza follows the new movement in philosophy as exemplified by Descartes. Only those conclusions are acceptable which have been deduced from adequate (clear and distinct) ideas. Ideas are adequate when they express the nature of a mode, or aspect of Substance, as it is in itself, rather than as it appears to man. By analogy from mathematics, the internal structure of the mode, though deducible from the properties of the more general structure of Substance, can be understood merely as it is, as it stands forth before the light of our understanding, and not as tending, or seeming to tend, toward some end or good beyond its intrinsic "what-ness" or determinate structure.

Thus Spinoza banishes teleology from philosophy. The attempt by the philosopher to understand how things are, as they have been determined by the laws of Substance, must not be obstructed by the fact that the philosopher has himself been determined toward the "end" of understanding. In order to acquire a true understanding of reality, the philosopher must see things as they are, and not as they appear to him because of the influence of his passions on his reason. Without such an accurate understanding he cannot achieve that mastery of reality which his passions desire.

The understanding of political phenomena is consequently different from political action based upon correct understanding. There is no reason or purpose for the properties of a sphere, for example, beyond the necessity intrinsic in the idea of a sphere that, if it is to exist at all, it must exist in a specific way. The same holds true for mankind. The study of man, as a branch of philosophy, proceeds in the same way as the study of spheres, stones, or horses. As Spinoza says in the *Ethics,*

"I shall consider human actions and appetites just as if it were a question of lines, planes and solids." [4] Mathematical deduction is as appropriate to the study of man as it is to the study of stones. But stones do not engage in political activity. Man's rational nature has both a scientific and a nonscientific manner of expression. The nonscientific manner reaches its fullest development in political society, or the organization of individual power in terms of subjective feelings and desires. This subjective element is itself conditioned by man's tendency to draw a false analogy between his own purposive activity and the activities of natural things. Man reads purposes into the activities of natural things, and thereby develops religion, together with its degenerate form, superstition.

The scientific study of political phenomena requires a careful study of religion as the most decisive way in which political behavior in prescientific societies is conditioned. Similarly, a scientifically constructed appeal for radical political change must make accommodations to the existent forms of subjective, religious belief. The philosopher must study human passions and their modifications exactly as if they were properties of the atmosphere, but he must also consider the practical side of politics from the human or contingent viewpoint. This viewpoint, although present in both political treatises, predominates in the *Theologico-Political Treatise,* as is immediately obvious from the fact that it contains Spinoza's exhaustive treatment of religion, a subject which is touched on only lightly in the *Political Treatise.*[5] It is essential to notice that this difference between the two treatises is compatible with the fact that Spinoza's most complete statement of his political teaching is to be found in the *Theologico-Political Treatise,* precisely because it is a combination of theoretical and practical considerations.

For this teaching, two questions are paramount: (1) On the basis of the scientific understanding of human nature, what is the form of the best state (*optima respublica*)? (2) How may men be persuaded to change their present laws and customs in order to bring society into closer correspondence with the model of the best state? The *Theologico-Political Treatise,* and not the *Political Treatise,* is designed to persuade as well as to instruct. The main concern of the *Political Treatise* is in fact not the best state simply, but rather the more practical question of the best version of the three principal kinds of government: monarchy, aristocracy, and democracy.[6] Its consequently greater emphasis upon positive laws and institutions, together with an initial frankness about the scientific character of the aims and methods of political philosophy, makes it resemble much more closely than the *Theologico-Political*

Treatise the present-day model of a theoretical work in political science. But Spinoza is not a present-day political scientist; he considers it part of his scientific enterprise to move men toward conduct that is theoretically justified. Political philosophy is not scientific unless it is useful. Thus the most theoretical work is the one which leads men toward the theoretically correct activity.

The *Theologico-Political Treatise* is from Spinoza's viewpoint his most complete theoretical treatment of political philosophy because it is least concerned with positive laws and institutions and most concerned with the universal motivations of human behavior. In a somewhat similar sense, one may say that Plato's *Republic* is a more complete account of his political theory than the *Laws,* precisely because the *Laws* is more concerned with the details of legislation than with the nature of the human soul. But the *Theologico-Political Treatise* is much less obviously universal in its intention than is the *Republic.* For our present purposes, the "local" character of Spinoza's treatise may be explained as due to his accommodation to the pervasive influence in his time of Holy Scripture. Since men act from passion rather than from reason,[7] they can be moved to reconstruct religious beliefs, upon which political society rests, only by a modification of the prevailing passions through a judicious replacement of the objects which gratify them.

We can thus understand the religious exterior of the *Theologico-Political Treatise.* Spinoza cannot simply reject Scripture without cutting himself off from those whom he hopes to influence. The starting point of any public appeal must of necessity be the contemporary historical situation. But the ground from which the contemporary historical situation is considered itself transcends that situation. It is the ground of the philosophical comprehension of nature; in Spinoza's famous phrase, the philosopher who stands on this ground sees the historical world *sub specie aeternitatis.* The same point may be stated as follows. According to Spinoza, human nature functions in accord with intelligible and unvarying principles. When one understands thoroughly the contemporary situation, one sees that it is rooted in the human situation as such. The roots of the contemporary situation are the principles of human nature, which are not themselves altered by the variety of historical situations. The correct theoretical analysis of contemporary society and religion requires a correct theoretical analysis of society and religion as such. The fundamental political book is a *theologico-political* treatise because it is based upon the recognition that the relationship between religion and politics is not just an accident of history, but stems from man's nature.

We turn now to a more specific consideration of the two political treatises. The link between the two works is a negative one: the absence from the *Political Treatise* of an extensive discussion of religion. But Spinoza's politicization of religion, when it is not explicitly stated, can be deduced from his theory of human nature. The two treatises are compatible with each other, just as both are compatible with the *Ethics*. The precise form of Spinoza's religious views cannot be established here; but it is quite clear that he never challenges man's need for religion. One may agree with the statement that the *Ethics* as a whole constitutes Spinoza's exposition of a free man's worship. In his political writings, he makes it clear that there is a distinction between the religion of philosophers and the public religion. In the *Political Treatise,* he tells us that, although freedom of religious diversity is to be allowed among the people, this freedom is restricted to private belief and worship. But when discussing the rights of supreme authorities in general, and the form of an aristocracy in particular, Spinoza advocates a national religion, determined by the state, and therefore with uniform public rites. Throughout the treatise, he emphasizes the danger to public stability from a diversity of religious sects and modes of worship. This emphasis is characteristic of Spinoza's approach to each aspect of political legislation, and is a direct consequence of his view of human nature.

Since men are moved to act by passion rather than by reason, it would be folly to construct a state in which freedom rests merely upon a presumption of reason or good faith. The primary passions are fear of pain and hope of pleasure. Since each man desires nothing more deeply than his own self-preservation, the struggle to maximize pleasure and minimize pain makes men enemies by their very nature; to *fear* and *hope* may be added the basic passion of *hatred*. When men come together to form societies in an effort to safeguard individual existence through collective power, they do not for that reason change their natures, but continue to be creatures of passion. They continue to be motivated by fear and hope, and so the danger of hatred persists within society. For this reason, Spinoza continuously advises the need for the preservation of unity within the state. Political association is natural, but one of its principal functions is to curb man's passionate nature. This will best be done by playing upon the primacy of fear and hope. The principle of the state is the desire for self-preservation, and it is by this desire that men are to be led to obedience.

But the emphasis upon passion, both in the case of the individual and of the state, is compatible with Spinoza's claim to legislate according to reason and his belief that men are free only when they obey through reason rather than through fear. Man's right is identical with his power, and his power is limited by passion. Since passion can be controlled only by other passions, it is both rational and in the interest of freedom to construct the state on this basis. Society must rectify the condition of the prepolitical state of nature, wherein men are so divided by passion as to have almost no right at all. Freedom is life in accord with reason. In accord with the classical element in his thought, Spinoza conceives of the state as such as a direct expression of the rational order of the universe. Thus, in at least a qualified sense, it is reasonable to obey the law in society.

Society itself exists as the result of a common agreement by individuals to surrender their power to a sovereign authority for the sake of enhancing each man's power of self-preservation. Within society, the will of the sovereign authority is in effect the will of the reasonable individual. In the best society, the will of the individual is externalized in the best, or most reasonable, laws. To disobey the sovereign authority is to contradict oneself, to be unreasonable, to go contrary to one's best interests. Because of man's selfishness and passionate nature, if each citizen has the right of interpreting the laws, the state will be dissolved by self-interest. So each of us is bound in all things to the one mind of the commonwealth, even when we regard its decisions as iniquitous. Reason teaches us to acquire individual independence by surrendering it to the will of the state. Consequently, the most powerful and independent state may truly be said to be constituted according to the principles of right reason, which reveal the end that is in the interest of all men.

The need for unity, however, does not make men slaves to a monolithic tyranny. Since obedience is predicated upon self-interest, it is in the best interest of the sovereign authority to be reasonable: the state should avoid causing indignation among the people. It does not have the right to do so, for it does not have the power to do so, since an indignant populace is a threat to the sovereign authority's might. Just as the reasonable citizen will understand that his freedom is dependent upon a strong and united commonwealth, and that this strength and unity is not in itself an obstacle to his private freedom of thought and belief, so, too, will the sovereign authority in a reasonable state understand that it does wrong when it acts against the dictates of reason.

Spinoza is not here contradicting his regular assertions that passion is governed by passion rather than by reason. It is reasonable to appeal to self-interest rather than to religious or philosophical argument. The wrong act of the sovereign is one which causes its own ruin. Therefore, the sovereign authority is bound to act in such a way as to preserve fear and reverence among the populace. Although the social compact is no longer binding when it violates the general interest, Spinoza expressly says that the right to decide when it does so rests solely with the sovereign authority.[8] Only the sovereign authority has the power to know what is in the general interest. Nevertheless, this power is itself subject to the limitations of public passion. The sovereign authority acts in the general interest by transforming public passion into virtue and obedience, and this is done by means of good laws. Good laws are in the best interest of every citizen; therefore, they are reasonable, and, as reasonable, not to be feared. So the best commonwealth gains obedience, not by fear, but by reason. "That state is best where men pass their lives in concord, and the laws are preserved inviolate." [9] It should be understood that by reason, Spinoza has so far meant calculation in the interest of the individual.

The Spinozist state, then, transforms passion into the servant of reason by the rational understanding of man's passionate nature. Philosophy is the highest power for all men, even though its teaching must be presented in a form suited for the public mind. Philosophy is in the general interest: it is no exaggeration to say that the ultimate end of the state is philosophy. The title page of the *Theologico-Political Treatise* tells us that "freedom of philosophizing" is necessary for the preservation of piety and the public peace. The freedom of the citizen within the best state is the political manifestation of philosophical freedom. Within the state, there is a unity of citizen and sovereign. That unity depends upon rational institutions, which make the magistrates the political surrogates of the philosophers, just as the institutions are the public face of philosophy. As Spinoza says, "men are to be so led that they think themselves not to be led but to live by their own mind and by their own free opinion." [10]

On this basis, Spinoza rejects monarchy in favor of democracy. Democracy imitates the state of nature by limiting the right of the chief magistrates to the amount of their power. In the state of nature, there is a natural heterogeneity of human types which underlies the heterogeneity in amounts of power, and is itself the visible expression of the articulations in the structure of Substance. One man has not sufficient power to rule the state: monarchies are concealed aristocracies. The heterogeneity of the state of nature is in political terms the condition of the natural inequality of men. But this does not mean that one man (or a few men) has the right to rule his fellows. Since "right" is equivalent to "power," and the power of any single man is insufficient to rule (to preserve itself in accord with its best interests), the politically significant characteristic of the state of nature is not the superiority of one individual to another, but rather the variety of kinds.

This variety of human types can no more be suppressed than can the character of Substance itself. The desire of the individual must be reflected in the legal and institutional structure of the regime itself; otherwise individuals will not accept the identity of their will with that of the state. The democratic regime, or the synthesis of human types which remains faithful in its structure to the difference of those types, imitates the state of nature. But an imitation is not an identity. We may say that the democratic regime rationalizes the state of nature, or fulfills what is implicit in the state of nature. The variety of types in the state of nature contains an implicit rational inequality which is different from brute or physical inequality.

To take a simple example: The man who is able to dominate his neighbors by physical force in the state of nature may be unable to cope with threats to his power that transcend the realm of brute force. The man of superior physical strength is in fact less powerful than the man of greater intelligence. Nevertheless, he is powerful enough to destroy, under certain circumstances, the conditions, not just for his own survival, but for the survival of those who excel him in other ways. The rational democratic regime must balance the powers of strength and intelligence in order to preserve both. Spinoza conceives of this balance in such a way as to make his version of democracy differ considerably from that of most present-day writers. As his treatment of the scope of sovereign power indicates, Spinoza tends to emphasize the freedom of institutions rather than of individuals. He tends to conceive of institutions as the rational embodiment of checks upon the irrational power of the multitude. As a consequence, the freedom of individuals tends to be reserved for the private, rather than the public, sphere of the regime.

When Spinoza assesses the political intelligence of the multitude, he points out that, if they could moderate themselves, and suspend judgment when they are ignorant, they would be more fit to govern than to be governed. In his discussion of democracy in the *Political Treatise,* he says that the name "democracy" does not designate the number of voters, from whom the officeholders are chosen, but rather that there are laws which specifically determine who will be eligible to vote. In the very conception of democracy, the emphasis is upon institutions rather than upon individuals. According to Spinoza, the chief difference between an aristocracy and a democracy consists in this: in an aristocracy, the patrician governing council perpetuates itself by electing new members. In a democracy, all citizens are eligible to vote and hold office. But restrictions of age and property may reduce the number of citizens in the democracy's supreme council to less than are contained in the council of an aristocracy. This modification, in itself an expression of

Spinoza's conservative understanding of democracy, is the only essential difference between the two councils. When Spinoza attributes the political ignorance of the multitude to inexperience, he is not advocating individualistic liberalism, but rather the educative function of free institutions to which individuals are subordinate (and which make them truly individuals).

Spinoza's deviation from Hobbes may be summarized in the observation that he moves from the commonly understood to a subtly understood definition of self-preservation. We have followed this transition in our analysis of the way in which a subtly understood implication of the state of nature replaces a commonly understood generalization from the most explicit form of the state of nature. The transition becomes politically manifest in the rejection of an absolute monarchy in favor of a conservative (virtually aristocratic) democracy. The principle of the conservative democracy which embodies the philosophical significance of this transition is freedom of philosophy: philosophy is the subtly understood power of self-preservation.

In order to keep philosophy free, that is, powerful, we must correctly mirror in our political regime the differing kinds of human types. Since philosophy is the understanding of the structure of Substance, it cannot flourish unless it has access to this structure. This access is obtained by observation of the differing kinds of human institutions and activities; consequently, the political regime must allow for a variety of opinions, as has already been indicated. It is important to remember that the political regime has as its highest good the preservation of philosophy. For this is not at all the same as to say that the highest good is the "freedom" of the individual. The latter statement implies a lack of natural order on the basis of which individuals may be classified. Spinoza is neither a Christian, a modern liberal, nor an existentialist: freedom is for him possible only on the condition of philosophy, and so, in the fullest sense, only the philosopher is free. The free society is absolutely dependent, not on freedom of speech in the sense of anyone's speech, but on freedom of philosophical speech. This is the heart of Spinoza's "conservatism," and it is explicitly visible in the *Theologico-Political Treatise*.

Because of the various subordinate ends of this treatise (the most important being to free philosophy from religious or popular control), however, the aforementioned explicit visibility is frequently obscured and needs to be explicitly indicated. The *Theologico-Political Treatise* is a revolutionary work. On the other hand, Spinoza wishes to initiate practical changes without disrupting the order of society. His revolution is intended as a bloodless substitute for the bloody extravagances which have been caused by the triumph of superstition over religion. In order to bring a nation to change its ways one must present instructions which are intelligible to it. Spinoza accepted the traditional distinction between the minority of philosophers and the overwhelming majority of the unphilosophical multitude. The problem of speaking in the presence of the vulgar, to say nothing of the potential philosophers who are still under vulgar influences, led Spinoza to practice great caution in the midst of his daring. In the short view, his caution was largely ineffective, but, in the long run, it seems to have been surprisingly efficient, as may be estimated by considering the change in interpretations of Spinoza during the past hundred and fifty years.

Spinoza instructs his readers in the treatise *On the Improvement of the Understanding* to speak in a manner intelligible to the multitude and to accommodate themselves to the capacity of the many as much as possible. In the *Theologico-Political Treatise* he indicates that the vulgar include all those who are not at least potential philosophers; together with the vulgar are linked all those who suffer from the same passions as the vulgar.[11] Spinoza asks men of this sort not to read his book, but it is obvious that his request cannot be enforced. The book is surely addressed to the leaders of the multitude, for it is through these leaders that the multitude may itself be changed. Spinoza, commenting on the literary form of Scripture, says that, to instruct a nation (or mankind), one must "accommodate to the maximum the reasons and definitions of his teaching to the plebeian capacity, who form the greatest part of the human genus." But this is exactly the purpose of the *Theologico-Political Treatise:* to change mankind's views about religion and to teach a new political doctrine. In the most general sense, the treatise as a whole is an accommodation to the ordinary understanding, certainly in those cases about which the many are most concerned.

Of course, philosophers are free, in their private capacity, to make the needed corrections in order to see more clearly the theoretical teaching; but precisely if they have done so will they submit their public speech and actions to the laws of the republic which the theoretical teaching advocates. Thus we must distinguish between those aspects of the *Theologico-Political Treatise* which are designed to persuade the vulgar, those which express the principles of the best republic, and those which describe the republic itself. In the third case, we ought never to forget Spinoza's words in the crucial passage concerning freedom of speech and thought: "No one can act contrary to the decrees of the sovereign power and keep it safe; but in all things one may think and judge, and consequently even speak, provided that one speaks or thinks only and solely from reason, not from guile, anger or hatred, and that he does not try to introduce anything into the state solely on the authority of his decree." [12]

To obtain the best republic, one must first purify religion, for reasons which have already been discussed. Fifteen of the twenty chapters of the *Theologico-Political Treatise* are dedicated to this task. The argument of these chapters is much too complex to be more than summarized here. So long as we understand clearly the reasons for the complexity of the subject, we are justified, in an introduction to Spinoza's political thought, in restricting ourselves to his simple but crucial conception of religion and its relation to sound political principles.

For reasons of persuasion, Spinoza accepts initially the divine origins of Scripture. He moves, however, on a path from a conventional beginning to an unconventional end. Scripture must be studied in a way analogous to the study of nature. In contrast to the position of Maimonides, the principles for the interpretation of Scripture must be drawn from Scripture itself, and not from a prior philosophical position. When we approach the Bible without bias, we find that the speculative views uttered by the prophets are like the contradictory and inadequate opinions of other nonphilosophers. A scientific analysis of Scripture, based upon historical, linguistic, and biographical data and detailed study of internal contradictions and errors in the Scriptural compilations themselves, free us from the notion that the book has authority in speculative matters. But the moral teaching of Scripture is everywhere the same and easily understood. The prophets disagree on speculative matters, but they are in complete harmony as regards the Divine Law of morality. In this respect they prefigure the citizens of the best republic. The Divine Law, as the evident universal teaching of Scripture, must be the foundation of our understanding of Holy Writ.

True religion has authority solely over action; any religion which claims to exercise theoretical authority is superstition: "The end of philosophy is nothing but truth; of faith, however, as we have abundantly shown, the end is nothing other than obedience and piety." [13] Since "obedience" means obedience to God's law, the content of obedience is determined by the definition of piety. What is piety? The answer, as derived from Scripture, is clear, distinct, and simple. First, piety requires assent in a minimal number of theoretical propositions, as for example that an omnipotent God exists, upon whom our salvation depends. Second, true virtue consists entirely in love of God and neighbor. Love of God is expressed by love of one's neighbor (and by conforming to the public modes of worship). To love one's neighbor is to respect his rights. Since his rights are determined by positive law, piety not only demands that we obey the laws of the state, but consists in such obedience.

The true teaching of Scripture has been interpreted to make piety virtually identical with law-abidingness and patriotism. By restricting the authority of religion to morality (the precise rules of which are defined by the political order), Spinoza has freed reason from the dangers of superstition without destroying the beneficial results of faith. Reason and revelation are shown to agree, both with respect to the content of morality or religion, and also concerning the sense in which they are independent of each other and the sense in which they are related. The universal covenant, which replaced the special covenant between God and the Jews (and by means of which we have innate knowledge of God as the source of morality), is the religious manifestation of these innate ideas from which reason deduces the principles of morality. Finally, revelation alone provides man with the proof that salvation rests upon his obedience to these principles. Since the principles of morality are most adequately expressed, according to Spinoza's political argument, in the laws of the best regime, religion in effect furnishes proof that piety consists strictly in obedience to the right political order, and more generally to one's legally constituted government.

In the closing chapters of the *Theologico-Political Treatise* Spinoza demonstrates that the political teaching of natural reason is in harmony with revealed morality, as has just been noted. Natural reason teaches us the *jus naturale,* which pertains to every finite being. Activity originates in the struggle for self-preservation. For example, fish use the water and eat smaller fish by a natural right which is simply an expression of their determinate being. As Spinoza says, "nature, taken absolutely, has absolute right to all things it can get or do. In other words, natural right is coextensive with power." [14] Thus, in the state of nature, wrongdoing is impossible: nothing which one can do is prohibited, for all occurrences are natural. Wrongdoing becomes possible only within a society, as the violation of the law. Wrongdoing is a violation of the fundamental desire for self-preservation. That is, man is by nature a political animal, because political society is necessary for human survival and perfection. Society is created by reason and is the instrument whereby reason perfects itself. The perfection of reason is the perfection of man as such: the perfection of his power. In order to perfect his power, man is led, not merely into society, but to an effort to understand, and to actualize, the best society.

It is rational to moderate one's behavior according to circumstances. Men have a variety of natures, and this, together with the fact that so few are philosophers, requires that the best society be acccommodated to the nature of the majority. A fundamental accommodation of this sort is the recognition that all men are moved by their calculation of goods (pleasures) and evils (pains), but that few are capable of making such calculations accurately. The social compact on which the best regime is based can be preserved only by an appeal to self-interest: "everyone has by nature the right to act with guile, nor is he required to observe his pacts, unless in the hope of a greater good or in fear of a greater evil." [15] Spinoza must demonstrate, both to the few and (in a sense) to the many, that his best regime is so great a guarantor of goods as to make disobedience to it a contradiction of self-interest.

In accord with the primacy of self-interest, Spinoza formulates his preference for a democracy. The state exists for the sake of the individual, but it is for the individual's sake that he subordinates individuality to the common power. In his chapter on aristocracy in the *Political Treatise,* Spinoza says that it is right to treat all citizens as equals, because the power of each, with respect to the entire state, is negligible. The same conception of equality is applicable to democracy. Each individual cedes to the state all of his power, so that the democracy is "a collective assemblage of men which has collectively the highest right to all things within its power." Whether "from a free spirit or in fear of the highest punishment," [16] each citizen will thereafter be required to obey the sovereign authority. If all people agree to transfer all of their power to one government which expresses the will of all, then all are participating in self-government. This is nothing other than seeing to one's self-preservation. Since democracy gratifies this natural desire by being compatible with the variety of natures having a common general goal, democracy is preferable to other regimes.

One striking feature of Spinoza's democracy is that it gives to the sovereign power the right "to make whatever laws about religion that it decides." [17] Spinoza does not intend, of course, to abolish religion. He wishes, rather, to avoid subjecting the state to "the diverse judgments and passions of everyone. . . ." [18] Furthermore, when clergymen are granted political power, it tends to corrupt them, to the detriment of both Church and State. The form of the democracy must be such as to balance the need for public harmony and stability with the excellence of private freedom in speech, thought, and faith. The right of the sovereign authority to make religious legislation follows from the natural right of the state to supervise all matters concerning the self-preservation of its citizens. This right is expressed in the form of a contract according to which the sovereign power is alone responsible for the articulation of legal codes; but its actions must obviously be tempered by the danger of losing power. Spinoza discusses this question, together with the relationship between statesmen and priests, within an analysis of the first Jewish commonwealth as established by Moses.

Spinoza deduces specific political doctrines from that analysis. The first Jewish commonwealth ought by no means to be copied in its entirety, since the exclusive covenant with God upon which it was based is no longer valid. The new demands which follow from the universal covenant are symbolized by Spinoza's remark that the Jewish constitution is useless for states desiring foreign relations. The doctrines to be learned from study of the Jewish commonwealth may be summarized as follows: (1) there must be a separation of the religious and political functions; (2) speculative matters must not be referred to the Divine Law, for religion must consist in actions only; (3) the sovereign power must have entire right to decide what is lawful and what is not; (4) more harm than good ensues from a change in the form of government. The third conclusion is sufficiently important to merit an entire chapter. "Religion acquires its force as law solely from the decrees of the sovereign. God has no special kingdom among men except in so far as He reigns through temporal rulers." [19] Inner piety cannot be legislated; outer piety is manifested in justice and charity. God cannot be conceived as a lawgiver; His precepts become law only through the mediation of the duly constituted authority.

Despite the power of the sovereign to legislate as it wishes with respect to religion, Spinoza emphasizes that freedom of religious belief is necessary for the well-being of the sovereign power itself. This emphasis is in effect identical with Spinoza's defense of free speech. Suppression of thought is impossible; far better to allow discussion in most affairs than to force men into secret factionalism. Since the true end of government is liberty, men should be free to discuss even the laws, short of inciting to sedition. Freedom to discuss the laws is inseparable from freedom of religious discussion, and freedom of discussion in general is necessary for the progress of the arts and sciences. The health of philosophy depends upon such freedom. There are disadvantages to free speech, but the advantages are far more weighty. It should not be overlooked, however, that such freedom is not unrestricted. Those citizens who are most capable of speculative thought and speech will be restrained by considerations of private and public good from advocating doctrines which contradict the public laws and customs. Interest and reason thus combine to provide a balance between liberty and restraint. The test of the legitimacy of speech is thus the law. Since the law must be preserved, action must submit to the law's censorship. Censorship is both direct and indirect, depending upon the degree of understanding of the individual citizen, that is, upon his power to speak and think. Since power is equivalent to right, freedom and discretion are rendered compatible.

Jewish political virtue forms one element in Spinoza's best regime, but it is not sufficient. Its defect may be summarized in Spinoza's remark that the Jews despised philosophy, and that life for them was one long school of obedience to the elaborate law which differentiated them from all other men. Christianity, on the other hand, may be used to show that the apolitical character of religion leaves room for philosophical speculation. Philosophers and apostles alike argue rationally; the *logos* of Christianity can be compared with the *logos* of philosophy; but the law or *nomos* of Judaism cannot be. The virtue of obedience therefore suffers from an intrinsic defect which must be remedied by the possibility of philosophy. Despite his synthesis of elements of Judaism and Christianity, Spinoza is able to show that each separately, when correctly interpreted, is equivalent to his definition of the true universal religion.

We noted initially that the difference between the *Political Treatise* and the *Theologico-Political Treatise* lay in the relative silence of the former with respect to religion. It should now be clear that there is a second fundamental difference between the two treatises. The *Theologico-Political Treatise* is concerned with the political status of philosophy, as the *Political Treatise* is not. This concern is inseparable for Spinoza from a concern with religion and ultimately with superstition. The fully adequate treatment of political science is then the one which deals with the way in which philosophy must be preserved from superstitious corruptions of religion. The defense of democracy is essentially a defense of those conditions which make possible the development of philosophy. The details of Spinoza's conception of democracy, which are perhaps most fundamentally characterized by the aforementioned balance of liberty and restraint, express his understanding of the impossibility of sundering freedom from danger.

The political philosophy of Spinoza is of special interest today because it combines the acceptance of modern science with the traditional conception of the normative function of philosophy. Like Machiavelli and Hobbes, Spinoza believed that he had understood correctly man's nature, and therefore that his analysis of the political situation was the one true political teaching. Like Descartes and Hobbes, Spinoza saw no contradiction between mathematics and the mathematical mode of reasoning on the one hand, and the possibility of constructing a detailed philosophy on the other, a philosophy which would express the truth about the principles of every aspect of man's experience. In a more immediate political sense, Spinoza's version of democracy, apart from its historical importance, reminds us in a detailed and luminous manner of the difficulties which must be faced by all those who love freedom, and especially of the impossibility of preserving freedom when a love of speculation is absent.

NOTES

1. Benedict Spinoza, *Improvement of the Understanding*, in *Works*, ed. van Vloten and Land (3rd ed.; 4 vols. bound as 2; The Hague: Nijhoff, 1914.), I, 7. Quotations in this chapter have been translated by the author.

2. *Ethics* I. iii. 6–9.

3. *Political Treatise*, II. iii. 18.

4. *Ethics* I. iii. Preface.

5. *Political Treatise*, II. viii. 46.

6. *Ibid.*, p. 31.

7. *Ibid.*, ii. 4–6.

8. *Ibid.*, iv. 6.

9. *Ibid.*, v. 2.

10. *Ibid.*, x. 7.

11. *Theologico-Political Treatise*, II, v, p. 92.

12. *Ibid.*, xx, p. 306.

13. *Ibid.*, xv, p. 249.

14. *Ibid.*, xvi, p. 258.

15. *Ibid.*, p. 261.

16. *Ibid.*, p. 262.

17. *Ibid.*, p. 268.

18. *Ibid.*

19. *Ibid.*, xix, p. 295.

READINGS

A. Spinoza, Benedict. *Theologico-Political Treatise*, in *The Chief Works of Benedict Spinoza*. Trans. with an introduction by R.H.M. Elwes. New York: Dover, 1951. Preface, chaps iv, vi–vii, xii–xx.

Spinoza, Benedict. *Political Treatise*, in *ibid*. Chaps i–v, viii.

B. Spinoza, Benedict. *Theologico-Political Treatise*, in *ibid*. Chaps i–iii, v, viii–xi.

Spinoza, Benedict. *Political Treatise*, in *ibid*. Chaps vi–vii, ix–xi.

Spinoza, Benedict. *Ethics*, in *ibid*. Bk I, appendix; bk III, preface; bk IV, propositions 7, 37 (scholium 2).

Spinoza, Benedict. *Epistle 50*, in *ibid*. (to Jarig Jellis; numeration according to van Vloten's ed.).

JOHN LOCKE

1632–1704

Near the beginning of his *Two Treatises of Government,*[1] John Locke used the following words to describe the political doctrine of Sir Robert Filmer, an author with whom he strongly disagreed: "[Filmer's] system ... is no more but this: *That all government is absolute monarchy.* And the ground he builds on is this: *That no man is born free."* [2]

Locke's own political teaching may be stated in opposite terms but with similar brevity, in this way: *All government is limited in its powers and exists only by the consent of the governed.* And the ground Locke builds on is this: *All men are born free.*

The theme of human freedom characterizes those of Locke's works which are most important for an understanding of his political thought: in *A Letter Concerning Toleration* (1689), he wrote of religious freedom; in the *Two Treatises of Government* (1690), of political freedom; and in *Some Considerations of the Consequences of the Lowering of Interest and Raising the Value of Money* (1691), of economic freedom. Each of these works is an instructive examination of the principle of human freedom, but since this principle receives its fullest and most political statement in the *Two Treatises,* this chapter will be confined almost entirely to a description and analysis of that work.

Book I of the *Two Treatises* (usually referred to as the *First Treatise* or *Of Government,* and now infrequently published and seldom read) is devoted primarily to a discussion and refutation of the argument advanced by Filmer that kings rule by a divine right inherited from Adam. Book II of the *Two Treatises* (usually called the *Second Treatise* or *Of Civil Government,* and often published and read as if a separate work) begins with a brief summary of the argument of the

First Treatise; having refuted the principle of divine right, which many then considered to be the foundation of princely power, Locke acknowledged his responsibility to explain what he considered to be the true foundation of government.

Locke's inquiry begins with the great question: What is political power? To answer that question—"to understand political power right" (§4)* and to explain the "true original, extent, and end of civil government" [3]—is the major concern of the *Second Treatise.* We are first presented with a definition:

Political power, then, I take to be *a right* of making laws, with penalties of death and, consequently, all less penalties for the regulating and preserving of property, and of employing the force of the community in the execution of such laws and in the defense of the commonwealth from foreign injury, and all this only for the public good [§3].

But we are told at once that to understand this definition we must first consider "what state all men are naturally in," and that is "a state of perfect freedom" and "a state also of equality." Natural freedom derives from natural equality,

there being nothing more evident than that creatures of the same species and rank, promiscuously born to all the same advantages of nature and the use of the same faculties, should also be equal one amongst another, without subordination or subjection [§4].

But though this state of nature is a state of liberty, "yet it is not a state of license. . . . The state of nature has a law of nature to govern it which obliges everyone" (§6). The natural liberty of man is not to be understood as meaning that men are not restrained by any law, for "in all the states of created beings capable of laws, where there is no law, there is no freedom" (§57). "The natural liberty of man is . . . to have only the law of nature for his rule," "to be under no other restraint but the law of nature" (§22).

And reason, which is that law, teaches all mankind who will but consult it that, being all equal and independent, no one ought to harm another in his life, health, liberty, or possessions. . . . And being furnished with like faculties, sharing all in one community of nature, there cannot be supposed any such subordination among us that may authorize us to destroy one another, as if

---

* All references in the text of this chapter are to sections of the *Second Treatise.*

we were made for one another's uses, as the inferior ranks of creatures are for ours [§6].

Thus the dictates of the law of nature in the state of nature seem very different from what we were previously taught by Hobbes. According to Hobbes, the state of nature is a state of war "of every man against every man." But Locke does not equate the states of nature and war; he instead speaks of

the plain difference between the state of nature and the state of war which, however some men have confounded, are as far distant as a state of peace, good will, mutual assistance, and preservation, and a state of enmity, malice, violence, and mutual destruction are one from another [§19].

Our first impression of Locke's state of nature, then, is of men living together amicably, in the first ages of mankind, before the advent of civil society, enjoying natural freedom and equality in an atmosphere of peace and good will, under the beneficent rule of the law of nature.

But let us now examine in greater detail the main elements of this first impression. What is the state of nature? How peaceful is it? And what is the law of nature which governs it?

Our first observation on closer inspection is that the state of nature is not limited to the original, prepolitical condition of man. In fact, when Locke first answers the question whether the state of nature ever existed, the example he offers is not at all one of prepolitical men, but rather of men who are essentially, and to an unusual degree, political:

It is often asked as a mighty objection, where are or ever were there any men in such a state of nature? To which it may suffice as an answer at present that, since all princes and rulers of independent governments all through the world are in a state of nature, it is plain the world never was, nor ever will be, without numbers of men in that state [§14].

All princes and rulers—civilized men living in a civil relation with many other men—are in the state of nature. A subsequent example is of a Swiss and an Indian, at least one of them a man with political experience, meeting in the woods of America; of them Locke says, "they are *perfectly* in a state of nature in reference to one another" (§14, italics supplied). If, as we see, the phrase "state of nature" is sometimes not related to the condition of prepolitical man, what, then, in precise terms, is the state of nature? Locke provides this brief definition:

Men living together according to reason, without a common superior on earth with authority to judge between them, is *properly the state of nature* [§19].

The state of nature is more comprehensive than a description of the condition of man prior to the advent of civil society. It is a certain form of human relationship; its existence, when it exists, is without reference to the degree of political experience of the men in it; and it may exist at any time in the history of mankind, including the present: "wherever there are any number of men, *however associated,* that have no . . . decisive power to appeal to, there they are still in the state of nature" (§89, italics supplied).

Using the terms of the definition of the state of nature, we can derive a definition of its opposite. That would be a state of men living together *with* a common superior on earth with authority to judge between them. In other words, the opposite of the state of nature is civil society:

Those who are united into one body and have a common established law and judicature to appeal to, with authority to decide controversies between them and punish offenders, are in civil society one with another; but those who have no such common appeal, I mean on earth, are still in the state of nature. . . [§87].

This makes clearer the sense in which the state of nature and the state of war are not to be confounded. They are not identical and yet they are not opposites. Their difference lies in the fact that they are not things of the same kind. It would be as wrong to confuse the state of nature and the state of war as to confuse civil society and the state of war; such a confusion would reveal a misunderstanding of their definitions, for the definition of the state of war does not include the essential term ("a common superior") of the definitions of both the state of nature and civil society.

The words that define the state of war introduce a wholly different element, that is, the *use of force* without right, without justice, without authority. "The use of force without authority always puts him that uses it into a state of war" (§155); "it is the unjust use of force then that puts a man into the state of war with another" (§181); "whosoever uses force without right . . . puts himself into a state of war with those against whom he so uses it. . ." (§232). And, finally, "it is such force *alone*" (§207, italics supplied) which establishes the state of war; that is, the existence of the state of war does not depend on the presence or the absence of a common judge:

Want of a common judge with authority puts all men in a state of nature; force without right upon a man's person makes a state of war, *both where there is, and is not a common judge* [§19, italics supplied].

Since the use of force without right defines the state of war, its opposite, the state of peace, would be defined as the condition of men living
together where there is *no* use of force without right (or, the same
thing, where force is used only with right). Now we may state fully
the sense in which the state of nature and the state of war differ:

   1. The state of nature is characterized by the absence of a common
judge and by the absence of any law but the law of nature.

   2. Civil society, its opposite, is characterized by the presence of a
common judge with authority to enforce civil law.

Then, in addition, either within the state of nature or within civil
society:

   3. The state of war exists if force is used without right.

   4. Or the state of peace, its opposite, exists if there is no use of force
without right.

   This means that in the state of nature, and also in civil society, at
some times a state of peace may prevail and at other times a state of war,
and that however clearly we may have distinguished the state of nature
and the state of war one from another, we have not at all disposed of the
essential question: Will there be war in the state of nature?

   But before we turn to that question we must first understand how
it is that the state of war can exist within civil society, where there is a
common judge with authority to prevent the use of force without right.
As a matter of fact, just before Locke says that a state of war can exist
"both where there is, and is not, a common judge," he gives a definition
which seems to say the opposite, which seems to exclude the state of war
from civil society:

But force, or a declared design of force, upon the person of another, *where
there is no common superior on earth* to appeal to for relief, is the state of
war. . . [§19, italics supplied].

The resolution of this difficulty lies in the fact that even in civil society
the power of the civil authority cannot always be operative:

Thus a thief, whom I cannot harm but by appeal to the law for having stolen
all that I am worth, I may kill when he sets on me to rob me but of my horse
or coat, because the law, which was made for my preservation, where it cannot interpose to secure my life from present force, which if lost, is capable of
no reparation, permits me my own defense and the right of war, a liberty to
kill the aggressor, because the aggressor allows not time to appeal to our
common judge. . . [§19].

The state of war can exist within civil society only when the force of the
common judge is rendered ineffectual. It is as if the parties—even

though they be fellow citizens met on the king's highway—were for the moment in the state of nature, without a common judge to settle their differences. Thus we see that the state of war can occur in civil society only to the extent that the state of nature can occur within civil society. Speaking precisely, the state of war cannot exist where civil authority is presently and effectively enforcing the law of society. The state of war can occur only in the absence of such civil authority; the state of war can exist only in the state of nature or something temporarily approximating it. What seems to be the state of war in civil society is rather this: the state of war in the state of nature within civil society. The state of nature is "the state all men are naturally in"; civil society is a human contrivance which obscures, for the most part, the inescapable fact that the state of nature persists, at least partially, and is ineradicable. As we shall see later, Locke makes use of this concept of the recurrence of the state of nature and the state of war within civil society; it is in those terms that he asserts the right to resist the exercise of arbitrary, tyrannical power. Thus Locke is able to speak of the state of war occurring in civil society and also, without contradicting himself, to speak of "civil society being a state of peace amongst those who are of it, from whom the state of war is excluded. . ." (§212).

In the manner just described, war can indeed occur in civil society as well as in the state of nature—with, however, these decisive differences: war is more likely to begin in the state of nature than in civil society and, once begun, is also more difficult to terminate there, because force cannot give way to "the fair determination of the law" (§20), as it does in civil society.

Let us now return to consideration of the state of nature in the more limited and more revealing sense of the original, prepolitical condition of man, and let us ask once again: Will there be war in that state? Of numerous passages we might cite, perhaps these will suffice to indicate the answer to the question:

I easily grant that civil government is the proper remedy for the inconveniences of the state of nature, which must certainly be great where men may be judges in their own case, since it is easy to be imagined that he who was so unjust as to do his brother an injury will scarce be so just as to condemn himself for it [§13].

The state of nature is "not to be endured," because of "those evils which necessarily follow from men's being judges in their own cases." In the state of nature, "everyone has the executive power of the law of nature" (§13), and although the law of nature is "intelligible and plain to a rational creature and a studier of that law" (§12), "yet men, being biased by their interest as well as ignorant for want of study of it, are not apt to allow of it as a law binding to them in the application of it to their particular cases" (§124).

If the executive power of the law in any state should be in the hands of ignorant and biased men who misapply it against others and refuse its application to themselves, will the enforcement of the law in that state differ in any significant way from the use of force without right? Locke provides many similar passages to support the conclusion that the state of nature will frequently be indistinguishable from a state of war.

But this conclusion seems incompatible with the earlier description of the state of nature ("men living together according to reason"), unless we entertain the possibility that Locke was urging on his readers the very strange doctrine that reason sometimes counsels men to kill other men. The conclusion seems also to contradict the teaching of the law of nature that "no one ought to harm another in his life, health, liberty, or possessions" (§6). What then is the law of nature and what are the obligations it imposes?

The obligations of the law of nature are stated in two ways. Every man is obliged to preserve himself, and every man is obliged to preserve all mankind:

Every one, as he is bound to preserve himself and not to quit his station will-fully, so by the like reason, when his own preservation comes not in competition, ought he, as much as he can, to preserve the rest of mankind, and may not, unless it be to do justice on an offender, take away or impair the life, or what tends to the preservation of the life, the liberty, health, limb, or goods of another [§6].

We have in this passage direct, explicit statements of unselfish obliga-tions of restraint in relations with our fellow men, but, as we see, they are not without qualification. When there is no common judge, will a man's "own preservation" come often "in competition"? When it does, what then is his obligation? To what extent will he be able to act "to preserve the rest of mankind"? What considerations will guide him when he undertakes "to do justice on an offender"? By the law of nature "he is bound to preserve himself"; he also has the duty, "as much as he can, to preserve the rest of mankind." Will his two duties conflict?

Many passages indicate that there is a surprisingly close connection between self-preservation and the obligation to preserve all mankind. In example after example the execution of the duty to preserve others is coupled with the right to kill another man who threatens or might threaten one's own preservation. The aggressor against me is to be treated as one unfit to associate with human beings, as a savage beast, as, therefore, a threat to *all* mankind. It is

reasonable and just I should have a right to destroy that which threatens me with destruction; for, by the fundamental law of nature, man being to be preserved as much as possible, when all cannot be preserved, the safety of the innocent is to be preferred; and one may destroy a man who makes war upon him, or has discovered an enmity to his being, for the same reason that he may kill a wolf or a lion. . . [§16].

In this formulation there seems to be no conflict between the duty to preserve oneself and the duty to preserve all mankind as much as can be. But the possibility of misjudgment is obvious, if a man is forced to judge not only "who makes war upon him," but also who has "an enmity to his being," and, on the basis of that judgment, to destroy him. Thus a zealous effort to fulfill the obligation to preserve the rest of mankind may in practice be indistinguishable from an excessive concern for self-preservation and may itself, in the absence of other restraint, become an unprovoked threat to peace and the preservation of others.

Aggression against others is indeed a violation of the law of nature: it exposes all to increased danger; it jeopardizes preservation. If the law of nature is misunderstood, as it will be by those who do not study it, that is, by those who, driven by their strong desire for self-preservation, do not consider sufficiently the importance of the conditions of general peace for their own preservation, destruction of life will be the general result.

The connection between the law of nature and the desire for self-preservation is profound. "The first and strongest desire God planted in men, and wrought into the very principles of their nature, being that of self-preservation," [4] men are assured that in pursuing that desire they are also fulfilling their obligation to God and nature:

For the desire, strong desire of preserving his life and being, having been planted in [man] as a principle of action by God himself, reason, which was the voice of God in him, could not but teach him and assure him that, pursuing that natural inclination he had to preserve his being, he followed the will of his Maker. . . .[5]

A course of conduct which tends toward self-preservation, then, is not only in accord with reason, which is the law of nature, but it is, one may say, the very definition of reasonable behavior. In this sense, the law of nature is known to all men, and, in this sense, men cannot but follow its dictates. But in another sense, that of understanding the means by which that desire might be fulfilled, men are ignorant of the law of nature "for want of study of it," and therefore they unwittingly behave contrary to its dictates, contrary to reason, that is, contrary to their interest in their own preservation. However the law of nature may be "writ in the hearts of all mankind" (§11), in one sense, in the other there is little likelihood that men in the state of nature can know how to obey it. The law of nature is both known and not known. Men must discover and contrive the conditions that will enable them to fulfill their natural desire for self-preservation.

The source of the law of nature is thus to be found in the strongest desire of men. The law of nature has peace and preservation as its end. It will be obeyed because of the universal desire for preservation; it does not rely for enforcement on obligations to others. Although some relation to earlier teachings may be seen in this, compared to classical and medieval concepts of the law of nature it is indeed "a very strange doctrine" (§9), for this law of nature concerns itself neither with the excellence of man nor with the love of God and of man for his fellow man. Locke, it must be said, does not explicitly deny the importance of excellence or love; he simply disregards them. For that matter, he barely uses or does not use at all, in the *Second Treatise,* such words as *charity, soul, ethics, morality, virtue, noble,* or *love.* They are not essential to his explanation of the foundation of civil society. For that task he names other, more powerful and universal forces in human nature—and, above all, the strongest. It is as if he had said: I do not deny that men are often moderate and just, and that some strive for excellence; nor do I deny that some are moved by fear or love of God, and love and charity for their fellow man. I assert only that when we consider the true foundations of political society, the real origins of government, none of these is of sufficient consequence to merit mention. What counts is what is universal and powerful, what exists with controlling force within every man, what can be relied upon to govern the behavior of man.

The basis of the law of nature is that strongest desire implanted within every man. The desire for self-preservation determines how men will behave; since men are not able to behave otherwise, such behavior can never be wrong ("God and nature never allowing a man so to abandon himself as to neglect his own preservation" [§168]); men must be acknowledged to have a *right* to do what they are unable not to do. No government is securely grounded in nature which does not permit and even encourage men to act as they cannot help acting. This unvarying principle of action governs the behavior of men in varying circumstances and conditions; an understanding of it as the basis of the law of nature, therefore, is the necessary foundation of an inquiry into the nature of political power. And so when we read Locke's statement that the civil laws of political society "are only so far right as they are founded on the law of nature, by which they are to be regulated and interpreted" (§12), we must keep in mind the content of that law of nature, if we are to appreciate its political significance:

The obligations of the law of nature cease not in society but only in many cases are drawn closer and have by human laws known penalties annexed to them to enforce their observation. Thus the law of nature stands as an eternal rule to all men, legislators as well as others. The rules that they make for other men's actions must, as well as their own and other men's actions, be conformable to the law of nature, i.e., to the will of God, of which that is a declaration, and the fundamental law of nature being the preservation of mankind, no human sanction can be good or valid against it [§135].

The first impression of Locke's state of nature seems very unlike Hobbes's state of nature, as was said. But, in fact, we have discovered three significant similarities. However Locke may have distinguished the state of nature and the state of war, the state of nature is the home— and the only home—of the state of war: the state of nature is "an ill condition" "not to be endured." Secondly, the source, content, and end of the law of nature can be stated, briefly and not inaccurately, in the word *self-preservation*. And finally, Locke's teaching is not unlike Hobbes's in the assertion that "civil government is the proper remedy for the inconveniences of the state of nature."

Yet we must not lose sight of the validity of that first impression. There is, notwithstanding their similarities, a deep and significant difference in the two teachings: Locke's state of nature is *not* as violent as Hobbes's. If, as it seems, force will commonly be used without right in Locke's state of nature, it is not because of a "natural proclivity of men, to hurt each other," as Hobbes puts it; Locke does not, as Hobbes does, speak of every man as the potential murderer of every other man. The main threat to the preservation of life in the state of nature lies not in the tendencies of men to hurt each other but rather, as we shall see, in the poverty and hardship of their natural condition.

Since the defects of the state of nature differ in the two accounts, the remedies proposed by Locke and Hobbes differ accordingly. The main consequence of the crucial difference in the two accounts is the fact that the civil government Locke propounds has a character far less absolute than Hobbes's. And the most obvious sign of the difference is the very much greater attention Locke gives to the subject of property.

The beginning of Locke's discussion of property has three elements: (1) an assertion or supposition about the original divine donation of the world to man; (2) a question, stemming from the assertion or supposition, concerning the origin of private property; and (3) the promise of an answer to the question:

... 'tis very clear that God ... has given the earth to the children of men, given it to mankind in common. But this being supposed, it seems to some a very great difficulty how anyone should ever come to have a property in anything. ... I shall endeavor to show how men might come to have a property in several parts of that which God gave to mankind in common, and that without any express compact of all the commoners [§25].

In the original universal common of which Locke speaks, "nobody has originally a private dominion exclusive of the rest of mankind" (§26). Every man has an equal right to every part of what is common. This cannot mean, however, that everyone has a share in the ownership of everything; it can only mean that originally there was no ownership, there was no property. If in the universal common any man has a right to help himself to any part of the common without the consent of the others, then the others have no property, for it is the nature of property "that without a man's own consent, it cannot be taken from him" (§193). The assertion that the world was given to mankind in common means, simply, that in the beginning no one owned anything. The original universal common was a state of universal propertylessness. That is why Locke proceeds at once to the question: How did anyone "ever come to have a property in anything"?

The answer lies in this, that there was one exception to the otherwise universal common; that sole exception was the person of each man himself:

Though the earth and all inferior creatures be common to all men, yet every man has a property in his own person. This nobody has any right to but himself [§27].

Furthermore, every man owns not only his own person but also his own labor, which is the immediate extension of his person: "the labor of his body and the work of his hands, we may say, are properly his" (§27). The property which every man has in his own person and in his own labor is the original and natural property; it is the foundation of all other property in the state of nature. All other property, then, was derivative from that original, natural, and underived property.

In the earliest times there were vast uncultivated territories and very few men; there were therefore ample supplies of natural provisions fit for food—fruits and wild beasts. In this setting of abundance (and even superabundance) of provisions, the apples you gathered were yours, for you had combined what belonged only to you (your labor in gathering them) with something that belonged to no one (the apples hanging on the trees or lying on the ground). Another might contest your property in them, claiming that, by removing those apples from the common state, you had deprived him of the opportunity to take them for himself. Although this objection would otherwise be valid, it is fully overcome by a reminder of the condition of abundance, in the form of a decisive and always present qualification: whatever you remove from the natural common and mix your labor with is yours *"where there is enough and as good left in common for others"* (§27, italics supplied).

In the universal common, you come to own unowned apples simply by picking them, if there are so many more unowned apples left on and under the trees that anyone else may have as many simply by picking them himself. Another who contests your property in the picked apples is really not claiming the apples that are common. If apples alone are all he wants, there are enough and as good still left for his taking. By claiming the apples already in your possession, he is really seeking only the labor you have mixed with them—and to that labor he never had any right:

For this labor being the unquestionable property of the laborer, no man but he can have a right to what that is once joined to, at least where there is enough and as good left in common for others [§27].

Property in land is, in the original common, acquired in the same way. "As much land as a man tills, plants, improves, cultivates, and can use the product of, so much is his property" (§32). And if the objection is raised, that by thus enclosing the land he deprived another, the same rebuttal, based on the same qualification, applies:

Nor was this appropriation of any parcel of land by improving it any prejudice to any other man, since there was still enough and as good left, and more than the yet unprovided could use. So that, in effect, there was never the less left for others because of his enclosure for himself. For he that leaves as much as another can make use of does as good as take nothing at all [§33].

This property is a combination of what is private—labor—and what is common—the land. Why then does the combination of the private and the common produce a result that is wholly private?

Nor is it so strange, as perhaps before consideration it may appear, that the property of labor should be able to overbalance the community of land. For it is labor indeed that puts the difference of value on everything. . . [§40].

When there is so much land for so few people, however much one may
enclose, more than enough remains for the others: it is as if nothing
had been taken. What is taken is of little or no account; land without
labor "would scarcely be worth anything" (§43). This is another way
Locke has of stating why the combination of the private and the common results in private property: the private component, labor, constitutes almost entirely the value of the thing; the materials, the common
element, are "scarce to be reckoned in." Labor gives title to property in
the state of nature primarily because "labor makes the far greatest part of
the value of things we enjoy in this world" (§42). If the addition of my
labor made something valuable which was, without it, "almost worthless" (§43), then surely, my labor being the only thing of value in it,
it must be acknowledged that the labor made it mine.

There are two reasons why the natural provisions are, in themselves, almost worthless. The first is that an apple can provide no benefit
to a man until it is picked or in some way appropriated, nor a deer until
it is hunted and caught. The fruits and beasts, as they exist in nature,
before any addition of human effort, are useless to man. As an apple on
another continent is of no use, so it is with an apple ten feet away, until
the addition of labor.

The second reason why the natural provisions are almost worthless
is precisely their very great abundance, which would constitute a surplus supply when the number of human beings is relatively very small.
In speaking of the provisions as worthless, Locke does not mean that
they are unimportant for survival. The air we breathe and the water
we drink are vital, but where air and water are superabundant, we
would not pay for a breath or a drink. The natural materials, like anything that is present in practically unlimited abundance, could not
command a price or a barter equivalent. This seems to indicate that
Locke had in mind some early form of the law of supply and demand;
it should not surprise us, therefore, to find in his economic writings the
statement that value or price is determined by "quantity and vent"
(very roughly equivalent to supply and demand) and "no other way
in the world":

He that will justly estimate the value of any thing, must consider its
quantity in proportion to its vent, for this alone regulates the price. The
value of any thing . . . is greater, as its quantity is less in proportion to its vent.
. . . For if you alter the quantity, or vent, on either side, you presently alter
the price, but no other way in the world.

For it is not the being, adding, increasing, or diminishing of any good
quality in any commodity, that makes its price greater or less; but only as it
makes its quantity, or vent, greater or less, in proportion one to another.[6]

The original condition was an abundance of almost worthless provisions; it was not an actual plenty but only a potential plenty, to be made actual by human labor and invention. What seems at first to be a kind of paradise, a vast expanse of fertile land well stocked with "the fruits it naturally produces and beasts it feeds," all "produced by the spontaneous hand of nature" (§26), "the common mother of all" (§28), and with very "few spenders" (§31) to consume this abundance, is in fact a compound of too much of what is almost worthless and not enough of what is necessary to make it valuable—human labor. The general "penury" (§32) of the primitive state is comparable to the condition of the Indians, America's "needy and wretched inhabitants" (§37),

who are rich in land and poor in all the comforts of life; whom nature having furnished as liberally as any other people with *the materials of plenty,* i.e., a fruitful soil, apt to produce in abundance what might serve for food, raiment, and delight, yet *for want of improving it by labor* have not one-hundredth part of the conveniences we enjoy [§41, italics supplied].

Another major cause of the penury of the original common is that "the greatest part of things really useful to the life of man . . . are generally things of short duration, such as, if they are not consumed by use, will decay and perish of themselves. . ." (§46). This natural fact of spoiling was perhaps the major limitation of property in the state of nature.

Nature does severely limit property in the universal common: "As much as any one can make use of to any advantage of life before it spoils, so much he may by his labor fix a property in. Whatever is beyond this is more than his share and belongs to others" (§31). The possession of land was similarly limited:

whatsoever he tilled and reaped, laid up and made use of before it spoiled, that was his peculiar right; whatsoever he enclosed and could feed and make use of, the cattle and product was also his. But if either the grass of his enclosure rotted on the ground, or the fruit of his planting perished without gathering and laying up, this part of the earth, notwithstanding his enclosure, was still to be looked on as waste, and might be the possession of any other [§38].

Locke seems to have derived from the natural fact of spoiling a kind of rule to assure the fair distribution of goods in the universal common. The reasoning is plausible, but consideration of two questions reveals the inadequacy of that interpretation of Locke's discussion of spoiling. First, why is such a rule necessary? Second, would it be effective?

The foundation of property in the original condition, as has been explained, must be a superabundance of natural provisions. Your labor in picking an apple makes it your property if enough apples and as good are left for others. But when there is such an abundance, what need is there for a rule to limit accumulation? The quantity you take can make no difference to me, so long as you leave me enough and as good; nor would I care whether what you have taken spoils or not in your possession. If you are so foolish as to waste your labor acquiring more than you can use, you cheat yourself but you do not cheat me.

Some means of limiting accumulation is required only if there is less than a superabundance, only if what is taken leaves less than enough for others. But whether a rule based on spoiling would serve to limit accumulation even in that case depends on whether it is applied to perishable or durable goods. Suppose that a man achieves an effective local monopoly of nuts, leaving not one for others; since they might "last good for his eating a whole year" (§46), he could take that long to eat his way through his supply without any spoiling. The spoiling rule would be ineffective in limiting possession of these scarce, durable goods. It would not achieve a fair distribution of them.

Any rule limiting accumulation is unnecessary when there is a very great plenty of provisions. If, under other conditions, such a rule is necessary, one based on spoiling is ineffective in the case of durable goods. The spoiling rule can be necessary *and* effective as a means toward fair sharing only in the case of a scarcity of perishable goods. But, as we have seen, the establishment of property in the original condition, by mixing labor with the natural provisions, depends entirely on a very great abundance, one which automatically achieves the leaving of enough for others. If there is not enough for everyone, not even labor can establish a right to a part of the whole, to the exclusion of all other men. And if labor cannot establish a title to property when there is a scarcity, then nothing can. There is no other way in the original state. Title may be transferred by barter or purchase, but only labor can *begin* property. In short, if there is a scarcity of perishable provisions in the original state, there cannot be natural property. There can be only possession of what is common. The conclusion is that even when the scarce perishable thing is in your possession, any other man still has as good a claim to it as you have. In the struggle for possession which would ensue, right would be established by the might of the stronger, and it would be difficult, if not impossible, to keep more for yourself than could be quickly consumed.

The fact of spoiling does indeed limit possessions in the original state and keep every man in a state of penury. "Nothing was made by

God for man to spoil or destroy" (§31), we are told, but if all the denizens of the original universal common had become so demented as to devote their entire labor to spoiling as much as they could, the results of their combined efforts would be as nothing compared to the extensive spoiling and waste occurring throughout the vast territory "left to nature" (§37). When we consider "the plenty of natural provisions there was a long time in the world, and the few spenders" (§31), the spoiling that could not be blamed on man is appalling. The spoiling of things by the hand of man is dwarfed by the spoiling that occurs beyond his reach. Natural spoiling can be lessened only by an alteration of the prevailing conditions.

However much Locke deplored wastefulness and destruction, his discussion of spoiling does not point toward a moral rule of fair dealing with other men in the original state. It indicates, rather, the massive scale of waste under the rule of nature; it points toward the necessity of discovering some means of liberation from that harsh rule.

The third factor contributing to the penury of the earliest stage of the universal common is the lack of cultivation of the land: "land that is left wholly to nature . . . is called, as indeed it is, *waste*" (§42); the extent of this natural waste can be lessened, therefore, by the spread of agriculture. One is mistaken to think that a man deprives others by enclosing land to cultivate it for his own use. Because cultivated land is much more productive than uncultivated land, all his neighbors will benefit:

. . . I have heard it affirmed that in Spain itself a man may be permitted to plough, sow, and reap, without being disturbed, upon land he has no other title to but only his making use of it. . . . The inhabitants think themselves beholden to him who by his industry on neglected and, consequently, waste land has increased the stock of corn which they wanted [§36].

Agriculture then is a major step toward alleviating the penury of man's original condition, but it is limited in its effectiveness by the fact of spoiling. Unless there is some way for a man to dispose of his surplus crops before they spoil, he will surely grow no more than his own family can consume; if he grows more, the surplus will only rot or be taken from him by others. Thus there will be no surplus, which is the necessary basis for the improvement of man's condition, and no "increase of mankind," which is the main intention of nature.

In brief, what was needed was some invention that would make it reasonable for a man to produce more than was necessary for his own family's immediate wants, more than they could consume before it spoiled. And that invention was money, which, according to Locke, came into existence through a natural sort of progression. Men first bartered perishable foods for more durable foods, like nuts; later they traded goods for "a piece of metal, pleased with its color" (§46). Finally they arrived at an agreement that scarce but durable things, like gold and silver, would be taken in exchange for the perishable goods.

And thus came in the use of money, some lasting thing that men might keep without spoiling, and that by mutual consent men would take in exchange for the truly useful but perishable supports of life [§47].

By this invention of money, men solved the basic economic problems of their original condition—with what far-reaching political consequences we shall presently see.

It is important to understand that Locke did indeed mean that money came into use before civil society. The use of money came in "by mutual consent" (§47) that men would exchange it for perishable goods. This "tacit and voluntary consent" does not presuppose the existence of civil society; it was made "out of the bounds of society and without compact, only by putting a value on gold and silver, and tacitly agreeing in the use of money. . ." (§50). This tacit agreement could not in itself establish civil society,

for it is not every compact that puts an end to the state of nature between men, but only this one of agreeing together mutually to enter into one community and make one body politic; other promises and compacts men may make one with another and yet still be in the state of nature [§14].

Money was introduced in the natural common, but its use hastened the end of the natural common. Money so altered the conditions that it was no longer possible for men to live together without greater protection for their possessions. Money enabled men to enlarge their possessions; money made it profitable for a man to "possess more land than he himself can use the product of" (§50). Without money, a man can have no incentive to enlarge his holdings and produce a surplus, however favorable all other circumstances may be:

Where there is not something both lasting and scarce, and so valuable to be hoarded up, there men will not be apt to enlarge their possessions of land, were it never so rich, never so free for them to take [§48].

But, "find out something that hath the use and value of money amongst his neighbors, you shall see the same man will begin presently to enlarge his possessions" (§49).

Introduction of the use of money completes the reversal of all of the original economic conditions. Unowned land becomes scarce because enclosed holdings are enlarged. The increased production can support an increased population, that is, a more plentiful labor supply. The early condition, in which possession was limited to "a very moderate proportion" (§36), gives way to larger possessions. The prevailing equality of penury is replaced by an economic inequality: "as different degrees of industry were apt to give men possessions in different proportions, so this invention of money gave them the opportunity to continue and enlarge them" (§48). Locke, we see, has done more than he promised; he has not only shown the origin of private property, he has justified the inequality of possessions:

... it is plain that men have agreed to a disproportionate and unequal possession of the earth, they having, by a tacit and voluntary consent, found out a way how a man may fairly possess more land than he himself can use the product of, by receiving in exchange for the overplus, gold and silver, which may be hoarded up without injury to anyone, these metals not spoiling or decaying in the hands of the possessor. This partage of things in an inequality of private possessions, men have made practicable ... only by putting a value on gold and silver, and tacitly agreeing in the use of money [§50].

If we now consider the objection that might be most appropriately raised at this point—that an inequality of possessions is *not* fair—we are led directly to the central theme of Locke's whole political teaching: *increase*. The conditions of the first stages of the natural common were hostile to any prospects for increase in the supplies of goods men need for their comfort, convenience, and preservation. The question then was how to share the very little that could be wrested from the tight fist of nature. This meant that whoever took a little more than did his neighbors, "took more than his share and robbed others" (§46). But when some men, by invention and industry, created the new conditions for the production of plenty, there came to be very much more to share; and although the new conditions required an inequality of possessions proportionate to the "different degrees of industry" among men, no one was cheated. Those who had a smaller share of the greatly increased whole were better off than those who had earlier shared, on an equal basis, in the pitiful little of the original condition. The poorest of men in a society having agriculture and money is richer than the most fortunate in the primitive, pre-agricultural natural common. Consider the "needy and wretched" Indians in America, who do not cultivate the soil: "a *king* of a large and fruitful territory there feeds, lodges, and is clad worse than a *day-laborer* in England" (§41, italics supplied).

It is difficult to exaggerate the importance Locke ascribed to the combination of agriculture and money. As he described the problem in an early essay, nature is utterly powerless to provide the conditions in which nature's own main intention—the increase of mankind—might be fulfilled:

The inheritance of the whole of mankind is always one and the same, and it does not grow in proportion to the number of people born. Nature has provided a definite profusion of goods for the use and convenience of men, and the things brought forth have been bestowed in a definite manner and quantity deliberately; they have not been fortuitously produced nor are they increasing in proportion with men's need or avarice. . . . Whenever either the desire or the need of possession increases among men, there is no extension, then and there, of the world's limits. Victuals, clothes, adornments, riches, and all other good things of this life have been given in common; and when any man snatches for himself as much as he can, he takes away from another man's heap the amount he adds to his own, and it is impossible for anyone to grow rich except at the expense of someone else.[7]

This passage may be said to state the problem which Locke solved in the *Two Treatises*. The world remains constant; it is not within nature's power to extend its limits by even one square yard. But without such extension, how can there ever be sufficient support for the increase of mankind? And how can there be any improvement in the condition of men generally if "no gain falls to you which does not involve somebody else's loss"?[8] The answer Locke provides is shocking in its audacity. What is completely beyond the power of nature is well within the power of *any* farmer:

. . . he who appropriates land to himself by his labor does not lessen but increase the common stock of mankind. For the provisions serving to the support of human life produced by one acre of enclosed and cultivated land are (to speak much within compass) ten times more than those which are yielded by an acre of land of an equal richness lying waste in common. And therefore he that encloses land, and has a greater plenty of the conveniences of life from ten acres than he could have from a hundred left to nature, *may truly be said to give ninety acres to mankind* [§37, italics supplied].

Men, by their labor, invention, and arts, make *increase* possible, and thereby solve the economic problems that beset them in the original natural condition. But at the same time they also make the continuance of that state impossible. The original common, however dangerous and inconvenient, is tolerable when its conditions are a plenty of raw provisions, few men, lots of room, and a general equality of weakness. But the consequences of *increase* are to make unowned provisions scarcer, men more numerous, and open space harder to come by; and in this new situation there is generated a new inequality of power among men, based on the new inequality of possessions. Under these new conditions, labor can no longer give title to property or be the measure of value, and spoiling ceases to limit acquisition. Now, for the first time, there is the possibility of possessions too extensive to protect by the means available in a state of nature. The sovereignty of nature dissolves and men must institute a new form of rule of their own making to take its place. Men are "quickly driven into society" (§127) for the protection of their property.

The possessions of the "industrious and rational"—those men upon whose powers of increase the well-being of all depends—must be protected from the "fancy or covetousness of the quarrelsome and contentious" (§34). The final step in the long process of the liberation of man's powers of increase from the restraints of nature is government. "The increase of lands and the right employing of them is the great art of government," and the prince is called "godlike" who "by established laws of liberty [secures] protection and encouragement to the honest industry of mankind. . . ." [9]

And so we have seen that Locke's discussion of property is an account of the development of the original natural economic condition of men through several stages to the point where they can no longer live together without the authority and power of a common judge to protect the enlarged possessions made possible, to the benefit of all, after the introduction of money. Locke's theory of property explains the necessity for the transition from the state of nature to civil society. We have moved very far now toward an understanding of Locke's answer to the great question: What is political power?

Although Locke addresses himself to the question of the nature of political power throughout the *Two Treatises,* it must be acknowledged that his approach is quite indirect. The *First Treatise* is, in large measure, a demonstration that Filmer's patriarchal power cannot be transformed into political power; and the first half of the *Second Treatise* is mostly devoted to a description of the natural powers and the natural state of man, as opposed to his political powers and political state. It is only thereafter that Locke takes up directly and in detail the discussion of political power and political society. It remains for us, therefore, to see how Locke moves from the nonpolitical base he has established to the political consequences.

The relevance of the nonpolitical to the political is made immediately obvious in Locke's statement that "the great and chief end . . . of men's uniting into commonwealths and putting themselves under government is the preservation of their property" (§124). (Here, and in many places other than the chapter called "Of Property," Locke uses the word *property* in the comprehensive sense, which includes "life, liberty, and estate" [§87]). In the state of nature, property is "very unsafe, very unsecure" (§123), because there are lacking three things necessary to its preservation: "an established, settled, known law" (§124); a "judge with authority to determine all differences according to the established law" (§125); and the "power to back and support the sentence when right, and to give it due execution" (§126). Political society, the opposite of the state of nature, is designed to remedy these three defects. The character of political society derives from the fundamental intention to assure the preservation of property by providing a power to make law and judge controversies and a power to execute the judgments and punish offenders.

Any number of men can make a compact to leave the state of nature and "enter into society to make one people, one body politic under one supreme government" (§89). Only those who make such an express compact with one another are in political society together; those who do not join are, in relation to the society and its members, still in the state of nature.

The substance of the compact that all the members make with one another in order to form a political society is an agreement to transfer the powers that each had in the state of nature "into the hands of the community" (§87). In the state of nature, every man has two natural powers: "to do whatsoever he thinks fit for the preservation of himself and others within the permission of the law of nature" and "the power to punish the crimes committed against that law" (§128). These two natural powers of every man are "the original of the legislative and executive power of civil society" (§88). The second power, the power of punishing, every man, upon entering political society, "wholly gives up, and engages his natural force . . . to assist the executive power of the society, as the law thereof shall require" (§130). But Locke does not say that the first power, which includes judging what is necessary for preservation, is wholly transferred; he says it is given up "so far forth as the preservation of himself and the rest of that society shall require" (§129). We must be alert, therefore, for the answers to these questions: To what extent is the transfer of this power to society required? Why is this power not wholly transferred? and, What are the rights and obligations of a member of society if, as may happen, the preservation of "himself" conflicts with the preservation of "the rest of that society"?

The natural powers of men in the state of nature are transformed by compact into the political powers of civil society. These political powers are limited, however, by the purpose for which they were made. Since the purpose was to remedy the uncertainty and danger of the state of nature by providing settled laws for the protection of the property of all the members, the exercise of unlimited power is not and cannot be considered political power:

Absolute arbitrary power, or governing without settled standing laws, can neither of them consist with the ends of society and government, which men would not quit the freedom of the state of nature for, and tie themselves up under, were it not to preserve their lives, liberties, and fortunes, and by stated rules of right and property to secure their peace and quiet. It cannot be supposed that they should intend, had they a power so to do, to give to any one, or more, an absolute arbitrary power over their persons and estates. . . . This were to put themselves into a worse condition than the state of nature, wherein they had a liberty to defend their right against the injuries of others and were upon equal terms of force to maintain it. . . [§137].

Locke's insistence on the limited nature of political power reveals both his agreement and very great disagreement with Hobbes. Locke, starting from the principle of self-preservation as the rock-bottom foundation of civil society, shows again and again that absolute arbitrary power is no remedy at all for the evils of the state of nature. To be subject to the arbitrary power of an uncontrolled ruler without the right or strength to defend oneself against him is a condition far worse than the state of nature; it cannot be supposed to be that to which men consented freely, for "no rational creature can be supposed to change his condition with an intention to be worse" (§131). Therefore, Locke says, absolute monarchy is "no form of civil government at all" (§90). The great error of Hobbes is not his premise but his political conclusion that the only remedy for the state of nature is for men to make themselves subject to the unlimited power of the mighty leviathan, a conclusion which contradicts the premise that the fear of violent death or the desire for self-preservation is the first principle of human action. Locke's conclusion—limited government based on the consent of the governed—is more true to that premise than Hobbes's own conclusion.

Political society is a human invention and contrivance, but this artificial thing, once made, has a nature of its own and hence has an applicable natural law. It is "acting according to its own nature" when it is "acting for the preservation of the community" (§149), for, not surprisingly, "the first and fundamental natural law . . . is the preservation of the society" (§134). The first obvious consequence of this natural law of society is that all of the rights of its members must be consistent with the preservation of the society. No society can concede to any of its members any right that would lead to its destruction. To do so would threaten the preservation of its members, whose safety depends so much on the protection the society affords them. For this reason also, the commitment made by the members must be permanent. Once a man has become a member of a commonwealth, he "is perpetually and indispensably obliged to be and remain unalterably a subject to it, and can never be again in the liberty of the state of nature" (§121), so long as the government survives. And the power of the society must be all-inclusive, reaching to every member and all controversies under the law:

... there and there only is political society where *every one* of the members hath quitted this natural power, resigned it up into the hands of the community in *all* cases that exclude him not from appealing for protection to the law established by it. And thus *all* private judgment of *every* particular member being excluded, the community comes to be umpire by settled standing rules, indifferent and the same to *all* parties, and by men having authority from the community for the execution of those rules, decides *all* the differences that may happen between *any* members of that society concerning *any* matter of right, and punishes those offenses which *any* member hath committed against the society with such penalties as the law has established [§87, italics supplied].

The power of the community over its members seems sweeping—one might even say, unlimited. It is here that we see clearly the fundamental difficulty inherent in the attempt to develop a theory that political power is limited because it has its source in natural powers and rights. If the members of a community retain some of their natural power, relying on it rather than on the power of the community for their protection, can political society function as intended? On the other hand, if all power is put into the hands of the community, what then will remain to protect the members from possible abuses of that concentrated power?

Another natural law applicable to the body politic—and, in fact, to all bodies composed of discrete elements—might be called *the law of the greater force*. This law is the basis of Locke's doctrine of majority rule. As was said, political society is formed by the unanimous agreement of its members to make one community; but although every political society is founded on the basis of unanimity, no such unanimity can be expected in other matters. The immediate consequence of this first unanimous agreement and the impossibility of continuing unanimity is that a part of the society, the majority, will rule:

For when any number of men have, by the consent of *every* individual, made a community, they have thereby made that community one body, with a power to act as one body, which is only by the will and determination of the majority. For that which acts any community being only the consent of the individuals of it, and it being necessary to that which is one body to move one way, it is necessary the body should move that way whither the greater force carries it, which is the consent of the majority; or else it is impossible it should act or continue one body, one community, which the consent of *every* individual that united into it agreed that it should; and so *everyone* is bound by that consent to be concluded by the majority [§96, italics supplied].

The first proposition of this argument is that the greater force within any society will rule it. Locke seems to assume that the majority will be the greater force and that therefore the majority will rule. The same form of argument is advanced in Locke's discussion of conjugal society. When man and wife differ, the male, "as the abler and the stronger" (§82), will naturally rule. But on the basis of the law of the greater force, we would have to say that in the unusual but possible case of a husband who is not stronger and abler than his wife, he will not rule by nature. In the same way, in any body politic in which the majority is not the greater force, the rule will not naturally fall to it. But we know and Locke certainly knew that the majority of the people are not always the greater force in civil society, because inequalities of an economic, political, and social nature grow up under government; sometimes, therefore, one man is the greater force, as evidenced by the fact that the entire society is subject to his rule. Why then did Locke seem to assume that the majority would be the greater force?

In any body made of discrete elements, the majority will necessarily be the greater part of the whole only when all the parts are equal, and necessarily the greater force only when all are equal in force. Locke means that the majority will rule society at those times when the members are all equal or practically equal in force. We know that in the state of nature men are on "equal terms of force," while, after some time in political society, one man may become "100,000 times stronger" (§137) than other men. Locke's doctrine of majority rule, then, is that at those times when men in society are closest to the state of nature and therefore are most nearly equal in force—as, for example, when they first agree to leave the state of nature and make a community—the majority, being the greater force, will rule. "The majority [have],

upon men's first uniting into society, the whole power of the community *naturally* in them" (§132, italics supplied); we shall see that
there is another decisive time when the majority must rule, another
time when men in society are very close to if not in the state of nature,
that is, a time when society is briefly without government.

Thus far we have been following Locke's own procedure in speaking of political society without reference to any forms of government.
Locke distinguishes political society and government, but he does not
mean that political society can exist without government (except for
very brief periods on extraordinary occasions). Men join political society in order to be ruled by a settled law, and that purpose can be
accomplished only by establishing legislative and executive powers,
which is precisely how Locke expresses the act of making government.
Political society will continue only if government is formed practically
at once. Political society and government may be separable in the mind,
but they do not exist independently: political society requires government.

Political society without government can do nothing but make
government. The performance of that task requires a profound decision,
a choice of the form of government. Forms of government differ primarily according to how and into whose hands the legislative power is
placed. "The first and fundamental positive law of all commonwealths
is the establishing of the legislative power" (§134); the making of this
fundamental law or constitution—an act of political society necessarily
without government—is the great act that is naturally and necessarily
determined by the majority of society. The majority may retain the
legislative power, and then the government is a democracy; or may
entrust it to some few men, and then the government is an oligarchy;
or may put the power into the hands of one man, under one set of
terms or another, and then it is one form of monarchy or another. But
in every case, only majority consent can found the government; all
forms of government (remembering that absolute monarchy is not a
form of government), from "perfect democracy" to "hereditary monarchy" (§132), are equally founded on majority consent. Locke's doctrine of majority rule does not necessarily eventuate in a preference for
one form of government over others.

The people are the parties to the social compact, each man agreeing
with all the others to make one society. Nothing is said of a compact
between the people and the government. The powers of government
are only entrusted, without being relinquished, to those who become its
officials; they have only a fiduciary power. The supreme power to pre-

serve themselves and the society remains always with the people themselves. This power they cannot give away, "no man or society of men
having a power to deliver up their preservation, or consequently the
means of it." The people "will always have a right to preserve what they
have not a power to part with" (§149). And yet, though the people
remain the supreme power, Locke also says that when the legislative
power is established, *it* is and remains the supreme power so long as
the government continues to exist and function. Further, "this legislative is not only the supreme power of the commonwealth, but sacred
and unalterable in the hands where the community have once placed
it" (§134). To explain the apparent massive contradiction of having two
supreme powers requires recalling the distinction between society without government and society under government. The supreme power
remains always in the hands of the people, "but not as considered under
any form of government" (§149). The people exercise the supreme
power *actively* only in society without government; but when government exists, the supreme power is in the hands of the legislative, where
the people have placed it. The people and the legislative are both
supreme, but not both at the same time. Under government, the supreme power of the people is completely latent and never to be exercised until by some calamity or folly the government ceases to exist:
"this power of the people can never take place till the government be
dissolved" (§149). As long as government exists, the legislative is the
actively supreme power. But the latent power of the people persists, and
if the government should come to be dissolved, then once again there
is society without government; at such a time, the supreme power will
be wielded directly and actively by the people (meaning, of course, by
the majority) and to accomplish one purpose only: to form a new government as quickly as possible by deciding on a constitution and placing
the legislative power in new hands.

The fundamental principle of the separation of powers is clearly
expressed by Locke. In "well ordered commonwealths" the chief powers
are separated "because it may be too great a temptation to human frailty,
apt to grasp at power, for the same persons who have the power of
making laws to have also in their hands the power to execute them"
(§143). But Locke applies this principle only to the separation of the
legislative and executive functions; he speaks of the judicial as a part
of the legislative and does not urge their separation. Locke does distinguish one other political power, "the power of war and peace, leagues
and alliances" (§146). But though this power, which Locke names the
"federative" power, is distinguishable from the executive power, they

must nevertheless be placed in the same hands, "both of them requiring the force of the society for their exercise," which force cannot safely be placed "under different commands" (§148).

The legislative power is superior to the executive power, "for what can give laws to another must needs be superior to him" (§150). But,

where the legislative is not always in being, and the executive is vested in a single person who has also a share in the legislative, there that single person in a very tolerable sense may also be called supreme. . . . Having also no legislative superior to him, there being no law to be made without his consent, which cannot be expected should ever subject him to the other part of the legislative, he is properly enough, in this sense, supreme [§151].

This is not a denial that the legislative *power* is supreme, but it is a reminder that the legislative *body* need not be the supreme branch of government. This is the first indication of the surprising scope Locke concedes to the power of the person who is the executive—surprising because his doctrine of legislative supremacy seems so emphatic and unqualified.

However much the executive exists to perform the subordinate role of enforcing the law as set down by the legislators, it is necessary to add that at some times he must act without the direction of the law:

. . . the good of the society requires that several things should be left to the discretion of him that has the executive power. For the legislators not being able to foresee and provide by laws for all that may be useful to the community, the executor of the laws, having the power in his hands, has by the common law of nature a right to make use of it for the good of the society. . . [§159].

The executive may act not only without the sanction of the law, he may also make the laws "give way" (§159) to his power where blind adherence to them would be harmful, and he may even go so far as to act contrary to the law for the public good. "This power to act according to discretion for the public good, without the prescription of the law and sometimes even against it, is that which is called *prerogative*" (§160). The danger inherent in the executive's prerogative is no less obvious than the necessity for it. The prerogative has always grown most extensively in the reigns of the best princes. The people trust a good and wise prince even while he acts beyond the limits of the law, not fearing for their safety because they see that his purpose is to further their good.

Such godlike princes, indeed, had some title to arbitrary power by that argument that would prove absolute monarchy the best government, as that which God himself governs the universe by, because such kings partake of his wisdom and goodness [§166].

But even godlike princes have successors, and there is no assurance that one of them, claiming the precedent, will not make use of the enlarged prerogative to further his own private interests at the peril of the people's property and safety. "Upon this is founded that saying that the reigns of good princes have been always most dangerous to the liberties of their people" (§166).

According to this argument, what characterizes the wisest and best princes is not their obedience to and enforcement of settled law, but their service to the people. The scope of executive discretion is limited only by the proviso that it be used for the public good; "a good prince who is mindful of the trust put into his hands and careful of the good of his people cannot have too much prerogative" (§164). But since exceeding the bounds of constitutional or legal powers on the pretext of serving the people has been the constant practice of tyrants from time immemorial, "the public good" seems a dangerously vague and inadequate test of whether the prerogative is being properly used. The good prince and the tyrant are alike in that they both act outside the law and even contrary to it. The difference between them lies entirely in whether their lawlessness is beneficent or the opposite. The good prince breaks the law the better to serve the people; the tyrant uses his power "not for the good of those who are under it, but for his own private separate advantage" (§199). But is there a practical way to ascertain a ruler's intention? It is not always easy to determine whether the law has been broken, but it is certainly easier than to determine whether it has been broken for a good purpose. Has not Locke made it uncommonly difficult to distinguish the good prince from the tyrant? Locke does not seem to think so. The important thing is not how the question would be answered in theory, but how it is judged in practice; and in practice, he tells us, the determination is made "easily" (§161). But before he tells us how it is made, he tells us by whom it is made. To the question, who shall decide whether the powers of government are being used to endanger the people, Locke answers, "The people shall be judge" (§240).

The meaning of *the people shall be judge* is inextricably intertwined in Locke's argument with the people's *right to resist* tyranny; these two themes will, therefore, be considered together. The right of resistance, as asserted by Locke, must not too readily be equated with what has come to be known as a right of revolution. If we recall the fundamental natural law of society, it is clear that there can be no right to endanger the preservation of society. Revolution is a threat to the preservation of society. Whatever the right of resistance is, it must be consistent with the preservation of society.

The people shall be judge, says Locke. Of what shall they be judge? They shall be judge of whether they must actively resume the supreme power because the government has been dissolved. How did they get the right to make that judgment? They have always had it and are absolutely incapable of surrendering it. At this point Locke begins again to draw on his earlier discussion of the state of nature and the state of war and the rights that exist in them, in the following fashion. When a prince or anyone in a position of political power uses that power, contrary to the trust reposed in him by the people, to further his interests at their expense, he makes his good separate from theirs; he separates himself from their community; he puts himself outside their society, into a state of nature with them. Further, by using force against them without authority or right, he places himself in the state of war with them.

The tyrant wars on the people. By using the force they entrusted to him against them, he effectively destroys their government. He can no longer be considered their political ruler in any meaningful sense of the word *political*. The people thus have a natural right to defend themselves against his aggression, and their resistance is perfectly consistent with the preservation of society. They are defending society; it is the tyrant who has rebelled:

rebellion being an opposition, not to persons, but authority, which is founded only in the constitutions and laws of the government, those, whoever they be, who by force break through, and by force justify their violation of them, are truly and properly *rebels*. For when men, by entering into society and civil government, have excluded force and introduced laws for the preservation of property, peace, and unity amongst themselves, those who set up force again in opposition to the laws do *rebellare*—that is, bring back again the state of war—and are properly rebels. . . [§226].

Locke rarely uses the word *revolution* throughout this discussion, preferring the word *rebellion,* thus maintaining a strictly literal usage: according to his argument, there is no right to *overturn,* there is only a right to resist upon the *return of war.*

Locke's teaching on this subject is addressed to those who have political power, and above all to princes, for they are the most likely rebels; "the properest way to prevent the evil is to show them the danger and injustice of it who are under the greatest temptation to run into it" (§226). He thus reverses the usual discussion, which considers the people to be the likeliest source of revolution. Why does not Locke direct his teaching also to the people, warning them against the use of force to depose their rulers? Has not Locke simply played a trick on his readers by a clever reversal of terminology? The prince is called a rebel, and the people who try to depose him are called the defenders of society; and the whole argument rests on Locke's insistence that the people shall judge whether the government has been dissolved—an extremely intricate and technical question. And does their resort to force really mean anything more than that the people oppose the policies of their present government and wish to replace it, either with a new form or by putting it in new hands? Does not Locke's teaching foment popular revolution, inciting and justifying the people, whenever they shall be displeased, to rise up with the cry of tyranny on their lips to depose their properly appointed rulers?

Locke denies that he has provided any new ground for revolution. He has argued that there is no legal or constitutional right to do anything that endangers the preservation of society and government while the government exists. He has denied any right to resist authority where it is possible to appeal to the law: "force is to be opposed to nothing but to unjust and unlawful force" (§204). This right to resist is not a political right, but a natural right which may not be exercised so long as a duly constituted government functions.

Further, the people are not disposed to stir up trouble; they generally prefer to avoid the danger of disorder: "revolutions happen not upon every little mismanagement in public affairs. Great mistakes in the ruling part, many wrong and inconvenient laws, and all the slips of human frailty will be borne by the people without mutiny or murmur" (§225). And Locke is vehement in his condemnation of those individuals who do foment revolution against a just government; they are, he says, "guilty of the greatest crime I think a man is capable of" (§230).

But Locke's most instructive defense against the charge that he promotes the tendency to revolution is more profound than, but not unrelated to, these previously mentioned. In the state of nature, all men have the power to judge what is necessary to their preservation; this power of judging they cannot wholly give up into the hands of society. It may be called inalienable because, try as he might, it is impossible for a man to surrender his power to judge whether his life is in danger.

No oaths, no threats, no doctrines can accomplish it. In the state of nature or in civil society, there is no sort of surgery that can remove from a living man the desire for self-preservation and the consequences of it. But though this right to judge is reserved by all men "by a law *antecedent and paramount* to all positive laws of men," recognition of this right does not make "a perpetual foundation for disorder; for this operates not till the inconvenience is so great that the majority *feel* it and are weary of it and find a necessity to have it amended" (§168, italics supplied).

The three questions, of when the prerogative is improperly used, of how to distinguish the tyrant from the good prince, and of when the government is dissolved, all turn out to be the same question—Is the government threatening the people's safety? And *that* is the question of which only the people shall be judge. Locke sees no difficulty in assigning it to them, nor any possibility of assigning it elsewhere, because however difficult it may be to answer theoretically, the people answer it easily—not by reasoning but by *feeling*. Locke denies that his words influence this situation. His arguments or doctrines have no effect on the matter. "Talk . . . hinders not men from feeling" (§94). His hypothesis—in fact, anyone's hypotheses—can have no influence in such a matter; the natural forces are unaffected by doctrines,

for when the people are made miserable, . . . cry up their governors as much as you will for sons of Jupiter, let them be sacred and divine, descended or authorized from heaven, give them out for whom or what you please, the same will happen. . . . If a long train of abuses, prevarications, and artifices, all tending the same way, make the design visible to the people, and they cannot but feel what they lie under and see whither they are going, it is not to be wondered that they should then rouse themselves and endeavor to put the rule into such hands which may secure to them the ends for which government was at first erected. . . [§§224, 225].

Whether there will be resistance to the rulers depends entirely on what the people see and feel. When the great majority of the people have been made to feel that their lives are in grave danger, "how they will be hindered from resisting illegal force used against them, I cannot tell."

This is an inconvenience, I confess, that attends all governments whatsoever, when the governors have brought it to this pass to be generally suspected of their people; the most dangerous state which they can possibly put themselves in, wherein they are the less to be pitied, because it is so easy to be avoided [§209].

The prospect of the resistance of the people when they feel themselves in danger is the only effective limit on the use of the prerogative.

A wise prince understands this limit and always avoids actions that make the people suspect his intentions. When he must act without the sanction of the law and even contrary to it, he is attentive to the necessity to make his good intention so manifest that the people see and feel it. If he fails in this, and the people come to suspect him and rouse themselves to replace him, then, though he may for a time be able to maintain his place by force, his political power is gone.

When a king has dethroned himself, and put himself in a state of war with his people, what shall hinder them from prosecuting him who is no king, as they would any other man, who has put himself into a state of war with them [§239]?

The king is no king, the government is in fact dissolved, and the inequalities associated with government are nullified. The return to the use of force, the state of war, "levels the parties" (§235). At such a moment there are no political superiors and inferiors. The outcome will be determined by the greater force.

And so the argument has come full circle. Man's desire to preserve himself leads him out of the war of the state of nature and into political society. But men in political society face a new and more terrible danger, tyranny or absolute arbitrary power, the augmented power of one man or a few men who bring back a far worse war than the war in the ordinary state of nature. Under tyrannical rule, the odds against the individual are vastly multiplied and defense is almost impossible. Men have, at bottom, only the protection of their natural force and natural desire for preservation. This strongest desire, which gave rise to political society originally, is also its chief defense; when the people feel that society, their greatest safety, is threatened, they will resist those who would destroy it. Mankind's political enterprise is an unending struggle to climb out of and avoid falling back into the state of nature, with all of its fearful evils.

There are two places in the *Second Treatise* where Locke speaks of "godlike" princes. In one he speaks of the princes who are allowed the largest prerogative, who have the greatest freedom from the control of the laws. They are like God, who governs the universe as an absolute monarch, because they "partake of his wisdom and goodness" (§166). But in the earlier passage, the prince is said to be wise and godlike who rules "by established laws of liberty." Such a prince is like God as Creator, for established laws of liberty are the means of bringing about "the increase of lands," which is a kind of creation, as we have seen, although not a creation out of nothing. This increase is not only the cause of domestic prosperity but also the source of the power to preserve the society against the hostile attacks of other societies. The godlike prince whose law-abidingness brings increase "will quickly be too hard for his neighbors" (§42).

This mention of power and hostile neighbors reminds us that every society is in the state of nature with all other societies, and that power is the basis of safety. But the necessities of life in the international state of nature, especially the demands of war, require at times extraordinary actions in response to unanticipated situations that cannot be regulated by law. A powerful people, made powerful by the material increase resulting from the encouragement of the desire for comfortable preservation under the protection of established laws of liberty, must face always the possibility of battle, a situation in which citizens must be dutiful, public-spirited, and ready to sacrifice treasure and perhaps even their lives, under the discretionary command of the executive-federative power, for the defense of the society as a whole.

The fact that those princes who rule most by law and least by law are called *godlike* expresses the dilemma that cannot be fully resolved so long as society is understood to be founded on the principle of self-preservation. It remains a question, unresolved by Locke, whether the preservation of society as a whole and the preservation of the individual members can ever be made sufficiently compatible. For instance, can the preservation of society be made consistent with self-preservation in those moments of severest trial which often determine the fate of political societies? Can the principle of self-preservation provide the basis for the development of patriotism, public spirit, and especially the sense of the duty to give up wealth and even life in defense of one's country? Locke is profound and comprehensive on the reasons for founding political society, but those reasons turn out to be such that he is prevented by their very character from considering in what direction society should develop after the founding is secure. He does not supplement his fundamental principle; he does not discuss other reasons for continuing a society, after its founding, reasons which might grow up within a society that perhaps could not have existed at the time of its founding. There is no discussion, for example, of the bonds that grow up among fellow countrymen. He speaks often of societies, rarely of countries; often of the law of nature, rarely—if ever—of traditions, customs, institutions; often of rights, rarely of duties; often of "the people," rarely of peoples. When he speaks of Englishmen, he does not speak of their love of England, but of their "love of their just and natural rights."[10] What little Locke says of education in the *Two Treatises* has nothing to do with developing a sense of public duty; education is spoken of as having no purpose loftier than preparing children to take care of themselves.

There is a revealing passage in this regard, in which Locke speaks of the absolute character of martial discipline:

The preservation of the army, and in it of the whole commonwealth, requires an absolute obedience to the command of every superior officer, and it is justly death to disobey or dispute the most dangerous or unreasonable of them. . . [§139].

"The sergeant" can "command a soldier to march up to the mouth of a cannon or stand in a breach where he is almost sure to perish." "The general . . . can condemn him to death for deserting his post, or for not obeying the most desperate orders." He can hang him "for the least disobedience." And this extraordinary power of the military commander is justified "because such a blind obedience is necessary to that end for which the commander has his power, viz., the preservation of the rest. . ." (§139). The preservation of the rest of the society may explain very well the right of the general to command; but why must the soldier *obey* desperate orders? From Locke's words only one reason emerges: if he disobeys, the general may hang him. But does not the effectiveness of an army demand a better reason than that? What sort of army will that be in which the fear of punishment is the only support of discipline in combat? The question is whether Locke's soldier (unfamiliar with un-Lockean words such as *honor, gallantry, duty,* and *valor*) will fight for the sake of others when his fear of the enemy exceeds his fear of his own commanding officers. Neither in this passage nor in any other in the *Two Treatises* does Locke explain the basis for a soldier's duty to give his life for his country.

Locke's great theme was freedom and his great argument was that there is no freedom where there is no law. In man's natural condition there is no law, or at least there is no known and settled law. To be free, therefore, men must be lawmakers. But through ignorance of human nature and the society best suited to it, the results of their lawmaking efforts have too often been not to improve but to worsen their condition. The task of making mankind free requires an understanding of the nature of man.

The one most powerful force in human nature, and therefore the one most significant for political understanding, is the desire for self-preservation. It is at once the greatest obstacle to, and the greatest force for, peace among men. Properly guided, it provides assurance of safety in the midst of plenty. Ignored or defied, it causes violence, anarchy, and a fearful destruction of life and property. The task of reason, therefore, is to understand, pacify, and direct this passion constructively, always in awareness of the imminent peril should a feeling of uneasiness set it in the course of violence.

The desire for preservation can be diverted, directed, or cajoled, but there is no way to diminish or eradicate its overwhelming power. For this reason, men are not wholly governable, and the task of making mankind free under law can never be completed. The "remedy" for the evils of the state of nature never fully accomplishes its cure. Men live, partially at least, always and inescapably in the natural nonpolitical condition and always in danger of relapsing into a far worse condition, for men cannot be taught to have feelings contrary to their strongest desire. Government is powerless to change human nature; it must accommodate itself to what cannot be changed. The government that will not accommodate itself to this passion in every man must be prepared to struggle against it endlessly with force and terror. But the wise ruler will do more than accommodate himself; he will channel and guide, encourage and protect, the desire for preservation, and make of it the very foundation of law, freedom, safety, and plenty for his people.

Locke sought to free mankind from every form of absolute arbitrary power. He sought to present the true and complete account of man's making of civilization out of the almost worthless materials furnished to him. In this account, the chief force that spurs man on to his own liberation is a passion, the desire for preservation. As the reader of this volume well knows, the ancient political philosophers considered the passions arbitrary and tyrannical; they thought that the tendency of the passions is, above all, to enslave men. They taught, therefore, that a man is free only to the extent that the reason in him is able, one way or another, to subdue and rule his passions. But Locke recognized passion as the supreme power in human nature and argued that reason can do no more than serve the most powerful and universal desire and guide it to its fulfillment. Only when this ordering of things is understood and accepted as the true and natural ordering is there any prospect of success in mankind's struggle for freedom, peace, and plenty. That, above all else, is Locke's political teaching.

John Locke has been called America's philosopher, our king in the only way a philosopher has ever been king of a great nation. We, therefore, more than many other peoples in the world, have the duty and the experience to judge the rightness of his teaching.

NOTES

1. In the codicil to his last will and testament, Locke referred to the several editions of the *Two Treatises of Government* printed in his lifetime as "all very incorrect." Before he died, he had prepared at least one corrected copy, of the third printing, to be used by the publisher in the printing of any future editions. (One such copy, with marginal corrections and additions in Locke's own hand and that of his assistant, is now in the possession of Christ's College, Cambridge University.) From the edition of 1713 on, this corrected text was the basis of most printings; but, for some unknown reason, late in the nineteenth century editors returned to the text of the first edition. Many editions now in print in the United States and England follow this "very incorrect" text. The most notable exceptions are John Locke, *Two Treatises of Government* and Robert Filmer, *Patriarcha*, ed. Thomas I. Cook (New York: Hafner, 1947); John Locke, *The Second Treatise of Government*, ed. Thomas P. Peardon (New York: Liberal Arts, 1952); and John Locke, *Two Treatises of Government*, ed. Peter Laslett (Cambridge: Cambridge University Press, 1960).

All quotations from the *Two Treatises* in this chapter are from a photocopy of the Christ's College text; I have taken the liberty, however, of Americanizing the spelling and modernizing the punctuation. For those few passages in which the Christ's copy text is obscure, I have consulted Laslett's edition and its very helpful critical apparatus. Readers will find that the passages pre-sented here differ only in small ways from the texts of the three editions named above (but see n. 9, below).

2. *First Treatise*, sec. 2.

3. Title page of the *Two Treatises*.

4. *First Treatise*, sec. 88.

5. *Ibid.*, sec. 86.

6. *Some Considerations of the Lowering of Interest and Raising the Value of Money*, in *The Works of John Locke in Nine Volumes* (12th ed.; London, 1824), IV, 40–41.

7. The Latin text and English translation of this passage appear in John Locke, *Essays on the Law of Nature*, ed. W. von Leyden (Oxford: Clarendon, 1954), pp. 210 and 211; some minor revisions of the translation were provided by the senior editor of the present volume. Reprinted by permission of Oxford University Press.

8. *Ibid.*, p. 213.

9. *Second Treatise*, sec. 42. This passage is one of the most important of those added by Locke in the Christ's College copy. It does not appear in many editions now available (for reasons explained in n. 1, above) and is misprinted in several editions in which it does appear. It is erroneously printed as "the increase of lands and the right of employing of them," rather than the correct text, "the increase of lands and the right employing of them." Examination of the handwritten text leaves no doubt that the superfluous "of" is a printer's error, with what distortion of the meaning of the passage the attentive reader will readily see.

10. Preface to the *Two Treatises*.

READINGS

A. John Locke. *Second Treatise.*
B. John Locke. *First Treatise.*
   John Locke. *Some Considerations of the Consequences of the Lowering of Interest and Raising the Value of Money.*
   John Locke. *A Letter Concerning Toleration.*

MONTESQUIEU

1689–1755

Charles Secondat, Baron de Montesquieu, was born and died in France. His most famous writings are *The Persian Letters* (1721), *Considerations on the Greatness and Decline of the Romans* (1734), and *The Spirit of the Laws* (1748).

1. INTRODUCTION

Montesquieu's mature teaching must be gathered primarily from *The Spirit of the Laws,* as he himself indicates in its preface. His other writings ought therefore to be related to this one. Yet its thirty-one books seem lacking in over-all plan or coherence, from which the inference has been drawn that Montesquieu was not a systematic philosopher and had no mature teaching in the strict sense. The preface, however, contains a manifest claim that the work as a whole has a design and is based on long-meditated principle. Thus the design, and hence a systematic teaching, either does not exist, or it exists in an unapparent manner. If we are compelled to choose, we prefer assuming that the writer's clear reference to the existence of a design is more authoritative than any reader's denial that the design exists. Montesquieu strongly suggests that the design is not immediately apparent when he speaks of the need to look for it. *The Spirit of the Laws* is therefore an obscure work. One important reason for disguising unorthodox views was the possibility of reprisals by Church and State. But d'Alembert's *Eulogy of Montesquieu,* written shortly after the latter's death, explains the obscurity more broadly. According to d'Alembert, Montesquieu sought to instruct both the wise and the unwise in such a way as to keep from the unwise important truths the direct statement of which could do needless harm. Apparent disorder and obscurity were instruments of this purpose. Montesquieu himself tells us that his principles can be discovered by reflecting upon the details; our task, then, is to approach the whole and its principles through the parts and details.

The philosophy introduced in the preface and Book I has a double aim: to comprehend the diversity of human laws and mores (unwritten laws), and to assist wise government everywhere. The first is theoretical, the second practical, and their connection arises from within the problem of "law" itself. In his famous opening formulation, Montesquieu defines laws, in the most extensive sense, as the necessary relations deriving from the nature of things. Laws are relations; they exist objectively and by necessity. They "govern" the action of all things—of God on the world, of bodies on each other, and so on. This universal lawfulness is the background against which human law must be viewed. But the term "law" is equivocal: in human enactments it implies a law *maker,* a *promulgation* of the law to those who are to obey it, and law *enforcement,* with attendant sanctions. Then do laws "govern" all things in the universe exactly as they may govern human beings? The classic exposition for the affirmative had been St. Thomas Aquinas' treatment of law in the *Summa Theologica.* Human enactment or positive law was understood in terms of its connection with eternal law, natural law, and revealed law. Law, as such, was an ordinance of reason, made, promulgated, and enforced for the common good by the community's ruler. Its ultimate source was the mind of God.

Montesquieu's opening definition of law takes issue with the Thomistic tradition, first, by appearing to leave no room for the miraculous, and, second, by depicting the universality of sheer, blind necessity rather than governance rationally aimed at good. Human law, as human reason applied to man's governance,[1] seems curiously out of place in such a world. But it is precisely the extent to which human affairs are swayed by mechanical causes that Montesquieu undertakes to demonstrate. By abandoning both divine and natural teleology and indicating the limits of purposive human action as well, he hopes to establish a science of human affairs consistent with Cartesian and Newtonian physics. It is difficult to say with assurance what view of God he considered compatible with this view of law and nature.

Before there were human laws there was man. To comprehend the diversity of human laws we must visualize them emerging from man's nature as he acts within particular natural and social settings. The variety of actual settings will account for the variety of human affairs, and indeed for the histories of all nations, provided we know the general principles involved, and provided due allowance is made for exceptional individuals, for political skill, and for chance. Human science requires historical studies, and these studies form the link between theory and practice. Political practice, or statesmanship, demands that each society be understood and treated in its particularity, *i.e.,* in the light of its history. But historical particulars are intelligible only in the light of general causes, proximate and ultimate, and therefore sound historical knowledge requires theory or philosophy.[2] This is how law as "legislation" and law as "necessary relations among things" are connected.

What were men like before there were human laws, and why did such laws arise? At first men were hardly distinguishable from brutes. Lacking in language and reason, they were led by instinctive physical fears and wants to preserve themselves individually and then to associate with each other; only later could they consciously desire to remain in society. But society breeds discontents. Groups seek to become privileged in the possession of its advantages, and, encouraged now by a sense of their own strength, proceed to war upon each other. From war comes law, right, or the just (*droit*). Law arises as a means of suppressing war, whether within or among societies. Within societies, the relations between rulers and ruled (political law) and of citizen to citizen (civil law) are established in such a manner as to unite the war-torn community. The idea of the right, the just, the obligatory originates with the idea of law and does not precede it. Man does not by nature or originally have a conscience or sense of duty.

This account, derived from the second chapter of Book I, omits reference to the "anterior relations of equity" ascribed to men in the first chapter. These relations or duties preceding all positive law are peculiar in character. They enjoin a bare minimum—to obey positive laws, to be grateful for benefits received, to remain dependent on the being that has created man, and to repay evil with the same evil. Their slightness practically guarantees that they be felt by men everywhere. Yet they are not included in the account of man's nature and earliest behavior in Chapter ii. This suggests that they are brought into existence by primitive social requirements similar to those engendering law. In any case, such obligations fall far short of prescribing the fullness of justice or human good by which societies must be guided.

If man does not begin by knowing justice, neither does he have any natural end or perfection. Montesquieu explicitly denies that any particular form of government or set of laws is required by, or most in accord with, nature: "Law, in general, is human reason in so far as it

governs all the peoples of the earth; and the political and civil laws of
each nation ought only to be the particular cases in which this human
reason is applied." [3]

The laws of each nation must be related to its form of government,
its physical circumstances (*e.g.,* climate, geography) and social conditions (*e.g.,* liberty, mores, commerce, religion). And all the relations
laws have or ought to have, taken together, constitute their spirit
(*esprit*).

By this passage the classical quest for the best state, Thomistic natural law, and Lockean natural right are all rejected as guides to the
ordering of political society. Stark relativism emerges as the conclusion
of Montesquieu's introductory book. But it is not subjectivism. Montesquieu grants that a certain set of laws may *be,* not merely be thought
to be, objectively better or worse for a given people. He maintains, however, that there is an ultimately irreducible variety of norms as well as
of actual political configurations. These norms, in short, are not themselves capable of being judged in terms of what is absolutely best or
worst politically. It would follow that the study of history is more im-.
portant to the discovery of specific norms than the study of philosophy.
Yet history, as the study of facts and causes, cannot by itself yield any
norms whatsoever. How, then, are valid specific norms derived?

The Spirit of the Laws is an analysis of the different things to which
laws can be related. These things, taken up one after the other without
apparent order, occupy Books II through XXV of the work, while
Books XXVI and XXIX return to a level of generality akin to that of
Book I. Books XXVII, XXVIII, XXX, and XXXI, however, seem to be
adjuncts to the main body of the work rather than intrinsic parts, the
latter three serving to illuminate the constitution of modern France by
laying bare its historical origins.

2. FORMS OF GOVERNMENT

Montesquieu turns first to an examination of political structures, *i.e.,*
of the means for repressing social strife. Every government has both a
nature and a principle to which its laws must be related. We know its
nature when we know who rules and how; the passions that give it
motion are its principle. The main species of government are the republic (either democratic or aristocratic), monarchy, and despotism. Their
domestic and then their external affairs comprise the subject matter of
Books II through X.

Before taking up the details, several general observations are in
order. We note first that Montesquieu does much more than merely

supply information about the various forms of government as they have actually existed. He tells us that his chief objective is to construct the laws, institutions, and practices whereby each form is perfected. This by itself may be consistent with the relativism he purports to espouse. But he also compares the various forms with each other in such a manner as to point toward their ultimate comparative merit. Is this possible without some absolute standard of political good and evil?

Let us begin with the democratic republic. In a properly constituted democracy, the sovereign people will delegate authority to do what they themselves cannot do. They need to be guided in foreign affairs and the preparation of legislation by a council or senate, and can have confidence in it only if they choose it. They need magistrates but are admirable at discerning the worth of individuals for this purpose. Legislation itself, however, will be by the people directly.

Democracy does not require that all citizens be eligible for public office but that all participate in the selection of the officers. Senators and lower civil magistrates are to be chosen by lot, not vote, and from among volunteers drawn from those who are not needy: the poor are not eligible. Military and high civil magistrates are to be elected by all, again from among those who are better off. Members of the popular courts, finally, are chosen by lot from among all volunteers, rich or poor. Thus democracy is not the simple rule of the majority, nor simple rule by lot. It is a mixture. Indeed, the poor are obviously less privileged, and the well-to-do more so, than sheer numbers would admit—a fact strengthened by the implication that public offices would be left unsalaried and attendance at popular assemblies uncompelled. Democracy needs the conservatism as well as the self-support and leisure of the well-to-do. But it also needs merit, the procuring of which is aided by the use of the techniques of election and examination of candidates.

The principle of democracy is virtue. Where all participate in making laws which they must themselves obey and in choosing their own rulers from amongst themselves, a very high degree of public spiritedness or devotion to the common good is needed. Virtue, in short, is patriotism, love of the republic and the laws, and from it stem the particular citizen virtues of probity, temperance, courage, and patriotic ambition. To preserve virtue, the extremes of wealth and poverty must be avoided by setting legal minima as well as maxima to the possession of property. Virtue needs near-equality, and more than that, a relatively low general level of wealth, assuring frugality and precluding luxury. This condition must both exist and be loved. Other methods of sustaining virtue are a censorial senate of elders, elected for life to preserve the purity of mores; strong paternal powers; sumptuary laws; the public accusation of unfaithful wives; and, in general, the mutual surveillance of all in points of conduct.

Democracy can subsist only in a small city-state, the familylike cohesion of which engenders a continual preference for public over private good. Its public assemblies are not representative. But it is inconsistent with an independent clergy—*i.e.,* a state within the state—and probably only consistent with pagan religion and morality. Solon's Athens, Sparta, Carthage, the later Roman republic are all adduced in illustration of democracy. No Christian, nor for that matter nonpagan or nonancient commonwealth, is so named.

Democracy's most attractive feature is the moral greatness of its citizens. Democracy also assures its citizens a high degree of freedom and security under law. On the other hand, it must, perforce, set limits to both their greatness and freedom. Its poverty, its smallness, its restriction of privacy, its reliance on unquestioning public devotion, and the mutual surveillance of its citizens prevent the more complete development of human talents—especially in the area of philosophy and the fine arts. Democracy means intellectual and artistic mediocrity.[4] Montesquieu acknowledges a distinction between productive, commercial republics, like Athens, and military republics, like Sparta. The first choice for democracy seems to be something between the two: the citizen body should consist of farmers who both work and fight. Nevertheless, a democracy based on the commercial spirit as its principle is possible, provided its laws keep this economical temper from being destroyed by excessive wealth. Montesquieu gives the impression, however, that the health of a commercial democracy is very difficult to sustain. The brilliance of Periclean as distinguished from Solonian democracy in Athens was predicated upon extremes of wealth, moral corruption, and freedom, *i.e.,* on political decadence rather than health.

The aristocratic republic is a regime wherein only a part of the people is sovereign, as best exemplified in the early Roman republic and modern Venice. Aristocracy depends upon political and economic inequality between the sovereign nobles and the nonparticipating people. That the nobles should identify their own interest with the interest of the people, in this way most closely approximating the virtue of democracy, is rare but not impossible. The more probable principle of aristocracy, however, is a spirit of moderation in the nobles restraining them from seeking inordinate superiority over each other or the people. The laws and institutions conducive to such restraint are difficult to secure. In general, the larger the number of nobles, and the smaller and poorer the body of those without political rights, the healthier the aristocracy. Democracy can therefore be considered the perfection of aristocracy. It is characterized by a broader concern and provision for the common good than aristocracy. Its members are, on the average, more virtuous, freer, and more secure, or, from the other side, less humiliated and exploited.

We should note that Montesquieu radically alters the standards and names used in the traditional Aristotelian classification of regimes. Aristotle classified in terms of the holders of sovereign authority and the purpose of their rule. Good regimes are ruled for the common good, bad ones for the advantage of the rulers themselves. Thus a clear distinction is made between oligarchy and aristocracy, both being rule by the few. Montesquieu has only two (not four) types of republic, depending on whether the whole or part of the people rules. Each type is perfected in a certain way, and actual instances of either would bear greater or less resemblance to this perfection. But, as in Machiavelli, the clear-cut distinction between virtuously and viciously motivated regimes is no longer primary. Thus Montesquieu uses the term "aristocracy" for regimes that Aristotle would have called "oligarchies." He also calls "democracy" the regime that Aristotle would probably have called "polity," and even instances as "democracies" regimes that Aristotle considered mixed aristocracies (*e.g.,* Carthage). One might conclude that Montesquieu's revised classification has two effects: first, it casts doubt on the adequacy of classifying regimes according to the goodness of their rulers' motives; second, it elevates the worth of popular regimes, or of the popular element in mixed regimes, thereby teaching that the common good is best achieved through widespread popular participation in government. We might be led to question this by Montesquieu's high praise of the "singular institutions" of Plato's *Republic* in Book IV, but the consequence of this concession is not an adherence to the classical preference for aristocracy.

Republican government has its natural place in a small society, and the expansion in the size, power, and wealth of a republic leads necessarily to the breakdown of its spirit and institutions. This is the lesson Montesquieu drew above all from his study of Rome, in opposition to Machiavelli's favoring of Roman imperialism in the *Discourses*. But the smallness required by republics poses a crucial problem of defense. The solution to this problem on a republican basis is the confederation, whereby several republics gather together to form a larger defensive whole. The modern Dutch republic and the ancient Lycian confederation are illustrations of this device. Montesquieu seems to have regarded confederation as an association of societies, not directly of individuals, and refers to the possibility of the confederation's dissolving while its component societies remained. But he also explicitly favors—as in the

Lycian case—a highly centralized rather than loose association of the member states.

In monarchy, one person governs according to fixed and established laws. This requires that there be powers intermediate between the monarch and the people, hence the nobility, church, and cities. There must also be an independent depository or guardian of the laws, such as the French *parlements*. Together, these forces—by their privileges and independence—are able to restrain the actions of both the monarch and the people. Nevertheless, when the monarch combines the legislative and executive powers in his own person (as in France), the government inclines toward despotism. Cautiously, though clearly, Montesquieu gives evidence of regarding a balanced monarchy as one in which something like the old French Estates-General shared legislative power with the monarch.[5]

Unless monarchy has such a structure as this, it is not a stable regime. Montesquieu claims that the ancient world had no proper conception of monarchy. This conception arose out of the Germanic conquest of Rome, its two main components being an independent, hereditary, privileged nobility and representative government. The closest the ancients came to it was the monarchy of the heroic age described by Aristotle, but there the people had direct legislative power and were able, ultimately, to strip the king of his powers. Regarding the classification of monarchies, Montesquieu explicitly takes issue with Aristotle. He rejects the classical principle of classifying regimes on the basis of the intentions or virtues and vices of the rulers. To have a good monarchy it is not enough to have a good monarch. Government has a nature or constitution only if its structure does not depend on so unreliable a circumstance as an important individual's natural or nurtured moral endowment. Nevertheless, Montesquieu himself admits later that the moral character of a monarch is as vital to the liberty of his country as are its laws.

The principle of monarchy is honor, not virtue. Montesquieu is very severe in his moral criticism of the courts and principal men of monarchies everywhere. He speaks of their miserable character and of their trumpery spreading to all levels of society. Yet the object most sought in monarchies—honor, or superiority of condition and person—serves as a substitute for the incentives of virtuous action. Ambition for distinction on the part of all classes and individuals elicits conduct that redounds to the public benefit while aiming only at private or selfish good. In addition, the code of honor sets unofficial limits to the arbitrariness of king and subjects alike.

The honor-seeking criticized by Montesquieu cannot simply be identified with the activity attributed by Aristotle to the magnanimous or proud man. Monarchy's system of mores and manners is vulgarized honor, or honor that seeks to be recognized by many, that depends so much more on recognition by others, that succumbs to, rather than resists, the vices (*e.g.,* gallantry) that are popularly taken for signs of boldness. On the other hand, Montesquieu seems less willing than Aristotle to accept the mental horizon of the magnanimous man himself, in so far as that horizon is bounded mainly by self-esteem, and encourages action less out of love of the public good than out of self-esteem and the desire for the highest honors.[6]

The laws supporting honor in monarchies must grant hereditary privileges to the persons and property of the nobility. Luxury should be permitted as a means of supporting the poor, and commerce on the part of nonnobles favored. Monarchy is more inherently set on ambitious war and conquest than is the republic and naturally requires a larger territory. But immoderate expansion weakens the power of honor and encourages despotic power. In general, monarchy is less moral, less just, less stable than democracy. It must guarantee vast, hereditary inequalities. Nevertheless, it is compatible with, and even requires, a structure of written and unwritten law that protects person and property in their very inequality. As for France itself, Montesquieu never advises its turning toward either republican virtue or English liberty. Yet *The Persian Letters* reveals his awareness of the decay of the monarchy caused by royal absoluteness, aristocratic corruption, and middle-class wealth.

Despotism exists where one man rules as he wishes without law. In describing this type of government, Montesquieu usually takes his illustrations from the empires of the Near East and southern Asia, just as in *The Persian Letters* it was expedient to speak of the despotisms of Europe, theological or secular, via explicit or implicit comparisons with those of the east. Despotism makes use of a chief political steward or vizier who rules while the despot riots. Its principle is fear, aroused by the exercise of brutal force especially on the great, who otherwise would oppress the masses. In this way despotism fulfills a certain public function, but it also depends on its subjects lacking virtue, honor, and learning, for these are dangerous to the regime. It is the most inhumane, vice-ridden, and stupid of governments, yet it prevails amongst mankind. Moderate government requires special conditions and special skills and is thus achieved only with difficulty. In Asia especially, climate and geography combine to make despotism inevitable. It naturally thrives among a numerous but timid population occupying an immense territory. Then only one man ruling through force can keep the country together and prevent that only greater evil, anarchy. And in such cases despotism is intrinsically incapable of essential amelioration: its very existence depends on the permanent use of cruel and sanguinary violence.

Of the four forms of government, two republican, Montesquieu clearly regards democracy as best and despotism worst. It is more difficult to decide precisely why. To illustrate: democracy is praised more for the virtue of its citizens than for the freedom and security it affords them. Yet this virtue is called a passion or sentiment, something every citizen feels by being brought up within such a community. This means that the virtue founded on reason or understanding rather than passion, which we may call rational virtue, has no status either in democracy or in the political forms inferior to it. In short, all virtue having political significance remains on the level of passion and prejudice. But if democratic virtue is not substantively on a higher level than the desire for freedom and security, ought the political philosopher to cherish democracy primarily because of its virtue?

There is another way to the same difficulty. Politically considered, the passion of virtue is valuable because it makes for a healthy democracy. Its function is therefore instrumental to something other than itself, which is the truly desired object. A democracy might be likened to a family, in which something like collective selfishness animates its members, who identify their own with the common good. This thought is consistent with the view of human needs presented in Book I. There virtue is never presented as a natural need of the soul, desirable for its own sake in the same way that health of the body is desirable. Society originates and remains in the service of bodily needs, such as self-preservation, economic security, and sexual satisfaction. If so, the virtue as well as the liberty and equality of democracy would have to be valued as the political means by which such needs are best satisfied. We shall return later to the relation between political life and the goods of the soul.

3. POLITICAL LIBERTY

Up to this point in the analysis, no form of government with liberty as its principle has been introduced. The situation is remedied in Books XI through XIII and the last chapter of Book XIX. Modern England is the one country whose laws have liberty as their direct object. Liberty, politically speaking, is the right to do what the laws permit. It has two aspects: a balanced constitution and the citizen's sense of legal security, with the former contributing to the latter. Its first requirement is the separation of the three powers of government—legislative, executive, and

judicial—so that they rest in different hands. If any two or all are combined in the same hands, power will be too much concentrated and insufficiently checked.

Montesquieu does not divide the powers of government in exactly
the same way that Locke did. Locke had distinguished the function of
carrying on foreign policy and called it "federative," and had subsumed
both the execution of domestic laws and the trial of lawbreakers under
the heading "executive." What Montesquieu does is to join into one
power the execution of domestic laws and foreign policy, while also
granting independence to the judicial power. His purpose, in short, is
to guarantee the citizen even greater security than was possible within
Locke's system.

One must carefully distinguish between Montesquieu's and the
traditional or Aristotelian analysis of the powers of government. Aristotle speaks of the deliberative, magistrative, and judicial functions.
The first has to do with deliberating about common affairs or the most
important common affairs, such as making war and peace (and foreign
policy in general), lawmaking, judging the greatest crimes, and appointing magistrates. The magistrative pertains to the authority to issue
instructions and orders in more limited areas, such as strategy or finance.
The judicial has to do with judging offenses and adjudicating disputes
other than the greatest. It is clear from this that Aristotle included
within the deliberative sphere functions that Montesquieu would have
distributed among all three of his powers. Moreover, Aristotle thinks
of the magistrative function in terms of several independent magistracies, whereas Montesquieu conceives of the executive power essentially
as a unity. Above all, Aristotle does not make a principle of the distribution of the three powers among different men—rather the opposite,
as his deliberative function shows. The utmost in liberty, whether in
the form sought by Locke or Montesquieu, did not seem to him consistent with the needs of any healthy regime, much less with the needs
of the regime dedicated to the good life.

Political liberty in its relation to the constitution requires not only
that the three powers be separated but that they be constituted in a certain way. The judicial power should be given to *ad hoc* juries composed
of the defendant's peers, with judgments being determined as precisely
as possible by written law. The legislative power must be divided. Its
main part should go to the duly elected representatives of the whole
people, and only those in so base a condition that they are thought to
have no will of their own should lack voting rights. Those distinguished
by birth, riches, or honors ought to comprise a body of nobles who
protect their hereditary privileges by serving as the second half of the

legislature. The executive should be a monarch whose check on the legislature would consist of a veto power and whose ministers, in turn, could be examined and punished by the legislature, though he himself could not legally be removed.

Montesquieu regards the England so described as not only freer but more just and in some respects wiser than the ancient republics or his own democracy. Its first advantage is the clear-cut separation of powers and the checking mechanism built into the legislative and executive branches. The second is the representation of public opinion through one branch of the legislature, which can then proceed to discuss legislative matters and abstain from executive decisions in a manner impossible to the ancient city-state. In addition, the judicial power is less menacing and more just. Finally, the single executive—though not comparable in wisdom to a body like the Roman senate—will nevertheless possess a great amount of concentrated power and sufficient motives to wield that power vigorously. Constitutional government of this type could not be expected to work without a considerable amount of internal friction, so that some sacrifice of quality and smoothness in governmental operation is the necessary cost of liberty.

Montesquieu makes the ambiguous claim that such liberty is established in the laws of England, whether or not this liberty is actually enjoyed by the English people. Nevertheless, he clearly adheres to the logic of liberty as he understands it rather than to the actualities of mid-eighteenth-century England. If he did not draw attention to the very limited and irregular suffrage of the people and very irregular distribution of seats in the House of Commons, it was undoubtedly because he thought those actualities deficient from the viewpoint of liberty. Similarly, if he refused to describe those tendencies toward the merging of executive and legislative powers that later became known as cabinet government, it may well have been because he thought they were harmful to liberty.

The main advantage of England over that freest of ancient commonwealths, the Roman republic, is its having weakened the direct and massive power of the people and granted both nobles and commoners an almost impregnable, mutually limiting authority. But the main distinctions between what liberty meant to England and what it meant to any ancient republic are still to be seen. For it is not enough to have a proper constitution: proper laws are also necessary if the citizen is to enjoy the maximum in legal security. Here the criminal laws are crucial, having a function similar to that of the Bill of Rights in the Constitution of the United States. Montesquieu distinguishes four kinds of crimes: those against religion, against morals, against tranquility, and against security. The net result of his analysis is to make it impossible in a free state to prosecute sacrilege by legal means, or to punish moral turpitude except in sexual matters. Limitations are also set to the dangerous charge of treason, and writings should be considered criminal only when they prepare treasonable action. Finally, legal procedures and penalties must be so devised as to insure just treatment as far as possible.

Now the distance separating the republic founded on virtue and modern England begins to appear in its true dimensions. They have a basic resemblance: both are republics—a fact that England's monarchical past tends to obscure. They illustrate Montesquieu's judgment that the best of governments will have a massive popular foundation which will guarantee its concern for the common good. But England embodies individualism, each citizen being left alone to live as he pleases. Religion is a private concern of the individual; so also is the choice of his way of life. Philosophic inquiry has the privacy it needs, the arts and sciences have freedom of expression. England departs from the conformity, rigor, and inquisitiveness of democratic virtue. Far from being a requirement of modern England, virtue is even dangerous to it.

The analysis of England must be taken one step further. Its liberty is not only of actions and thoughts but of passions. To be free is mainly to follow one's appetites for money, prestige, and power.[7] England is capitalistic: the moral limits on endless competitive acquisition have been removed. The parallel in the field of ambition is party politics. England is the modern Athens—a commercial rather than a military or agricultural republic. Aided by its naval power, its imperialism is commercial rather than militaristic. But how does the spirit of commerce keep from destroying itself through excessive luxury and dissoluteness? High taxes keep men working, and frivolous expenditure is considered blameworthy, though whether on religious or business grounds is not clear. Furthermore, the extreme intensity of competition and the constant opening of new economic opportunities make dissoluteness the exception rather than the rule. Nor can the dissolute still have the influence they had within the narrower confines of the city-state. In sum, avarice and ambition constitute the moral foundations of the English system, not its deadly enemy. Each man's sense of self-interest supports his love of liberty and his patriotism.

In England the liberty of the impassioned many guarantees the liberty of the thoughtful few. Montesquieu does not deny that the vices of Englishmen deserve the bitter satire of a Juvenal, but he himself does not provide that satire. This is because the English system derives benefits for all from the vices it allows and encourages. The utmost in legal security, participation in government by all, and activity in commerce produce a citizen proud of his independence, hopeful of getting ahead, but completely blind to the fact that he is a slave to vulgar passions. England is a secularized society, interested in earthly goods. It does not need a common religion or democratic virtue to bind the community together, and thus can permit more privacy and freedom of expression than ancient Athens itself. With a novel constitutional system by which the striving for selfish interest is given permanent form, England has discovered how to postpone internal breakdown almost indefinitely.

4. Nature

The full significance of England and commerce for Montesquieu's thought can only be appreciated if one understands his conception of natural or primitive man and of the natural setting in which he first existed. The second chapter of Book I had led us to expect a historical treatment of human development out of the state of nature. This approach appears in the first passages of the third chapter, too, but then our attention is abruptly transferred from what is natural to man in the sense of "original" to what is natural in the sense of "best." In other words, we begin to think about advanced and later human things. This change of subject is carried forward in Books II through XIII, where the perfected forms of government are discussed. Books XIV through XVIII, however, are meant to satisfy the original expectation. Their subject is man's natural setting and beginning, the importance of which might explain the central location of these five books in the work as a whole. The topics treated are, first, the effects of climate on body and soul and its relation to diverse forms of slavery; second, the relation between geography and primitive human society. Material gathered from the references to primitive conditions in other books will help us complete the picture of what man was and is by nature.

Montesquieu displays the full strength of his ateleological naturalism in the first book on climate. Temperature, by influencing the human body, influences the mind and the passions. In hot climates, men are more sensible to pleasures and pains and hence more sensuous, more timid, more slothful. A cold climate has opposite effects, while the temperate zone is indeterminate. Thus are awakened dissimilar tendencies and needs, different moral possibilities, while the virtues themselves—e.g., courage, temperance, justice—vary radically with climate in their practicability and desirability. In general, the legislator's problem is to assure that at least the minimum conditions for society be met. But Montesquieu does not ask which climatic conditions produce the best human beings. As the relevant book titles indicate, he even stresses the connection between climate and human slavery, not human freedom. Climate sets natural limits to the extension of free, moderate, or non-despotic government, or, more generally, man is the subject, not the master, of climate. It is strange, therefore, that Montesquieu gives so little attention in Book XIV to temperate climates and their effects, for there is an obvious connection between these areas of indeterminacy and civilization—unless he means to indicate the rare and accidental character of that which supports the highest human things.

Given the variations caused by climate, what was the earliest human society like? Montesquieu does not speak openly about original family relations, but he suggests that they harbor some of mankind's deepest secrets. In all probability, the family as a stable unit did not exist originally but had to develop out of the condition of promiscuity. Incest prohibitions had themselves to be developed, thus providing a basis for peace and mutual care. The male ruled the family through his superior strength, and the female remained in a subordinate and even servile position. Under these conditions, polygamy was very widespread, whereas only in hot climates is it an enduring necessity, together with the institutions of the seraglio which preserve it.[8]

Primitive societies are either savage or barbarous, depending on whether, as hunters, the men remain in isolated tribes or, as herders, they are able to unite into a horde. Their loose organization permits each man considerable freedom, and the absence of money makes for near-equality of possessions and thus little exploitation. Political authority is in the hands of the strong, the sage, and the old. Wars are severe, and slave-taking a normal practice. The punishment of crime, too, is crude and cruel. Finally, religion and frequently priests already wield strong influence.

This picture of primitive man can help to clarify the true meaning of natural law. Natural law consists of those rights and duties of individuals or nations that ought to be respected everywhere because of the good they produce. In this sense natural law is natural to mankind. But it is not natural in the sense of being originally known to men or originally intended on moral grounds. It has two poles: on the one hand, the right to self-preservation and freedom of individuals and nations; on the other, the mutual obligations binding the members of the family. Only these ought to be universal among mankind. In point of fact, the various articles of natural law differ in the degree to which they are actually respected, and also in the time of their origin in human history.

On two heads Montesquieu's version of natural law went far beyond the practice of even civilized nations. Private slavery, he claims, is legitimate in only one case: that of a mild, contractual slavery within a political despotism. As for the necessity of harsh slavery, he inclines to the view that free labor can be obtained to do even the worst of jobs in even the most torrid climates. He argues against Aristotle that slavery is bad for both master and slave, and that no men are by nature born to be slaves. He also refuses to grant the claim of the Roman jurists that capture in war and indebtedness are sufficient grounds for enslavement. At the same time, however, he admits that all men have a deep-seated desire to enjoy the servile services of other men.

Montesquieu seems to have thought that the work of Christianity in ending slavery within Europe could be spread abroad with the help of cosmopolitan enlightenment and an appeal to humane sympathies. He is less sanguine about the possibility of ending warfare, even within Europe. In spite of the modern mitigation of warfare itself, and the greater lenience of peace settlements, Europe is hardly more peaceably inclined than ever and remains armed to the teeth. Montesquieu maintains that the only just war is one of self-defense, and the only just treatment of a conquered territory that which aims to preserve the conquest rather than to destroy or oppress the vanquished. Yet he is forced to admit that international relations have always been and will always be conducted on the basis of self-interest and force rather than agreements or consideration for the rights of others.[9] Decent nations neglect this fact at their own peril. The conclusion seems necessary that it will be more difficult to persuade mankind to give up war than slavery.

These examples also show that natural law, as dictates of reason for human good, to some extent calls for the restriction of self-regarding tendencies that are natural to man. Those natural laws observed everywhere (e.g., regarding the family) probably did not originate out of rational and just intent but out of some of the self-regarding passions themselves. Those natural laws which are much less observed probably constitute dictates of reason that fail to spread precisely because they lack sufficient basis in the human passions. It would appear, therefore, that man's natural or original endowment did not itself immediately provide for his becoming a moral and reflective being.

Machiavelli and Bacon had raised the question in modern times as to whether natural and social necessities, and chance, set any limits to what human knowledge, will, and power could achieve. Locke had implied that men could establish free societies on the English model everywhere: what they had a right to do—i.e., to replace old regimes of every kind with the new individualism—was capable of accomplishment. Montesquieu shares this admiration for modern freedom, and even goes beyond Locke in devising safeguards for it. But the English model is absolutely impossible in Asia and highly improbable even in most of Europe.

Asia is the natural home of every kind of slavery—private, marital, and political. Because Asia lacks a temperate zone and because the character of its natural barriers does not dispose it to form moderate-sized states, it has favored despotisms in the south, despotic conquests of the south by the north, and virtual immobility in its way of life and mores over many centuries. Opportunities for moderate government are much greater in Europe—hitherto the most interesting area of the world by far. But Montesquieu does not recommend revolutions against the old European monarchies in an attempt to imitate English liberty. This liberty is peculiar: on the one hand, it seems to depend on things easily subject to imitation, *e.g.*, the emancipation of the selfish passions and the establishment of a constitutional mechanism; yet England's insular position, its particular history, its climate all have a special kinship to its laws. Even in this case, then, Montesquieu attempts to restore to the modern position a prudent recognition of the necessity for a variety of political orders. He sets limits to what conscious human effort can achieve, but it must also be said that these limits go considerably beyond what the classics thought necessary or wise.

5. COMMERCE

We now have some conception of man's deficient natural beginnings and of the highest point he can attain, the regime of modern liberty. The two are connected by the development of commerce. Montesquieu was the first great political philosopher to consider commerce worthy of expansive empirical treatment within his major work. Of the various elements which enter the spirit of laws, it is the only one with a separate book devoted to its history or "revolutions."

In his analysis of primitive societies, Montesquieu regards the introduction of agriculture as the cause of the introduction of money. There is a constant interplay between man's needs and his knowledge: new needs encourage the searching for new knowledge, new knowledge encourages the growth of new needs. The art of agriculture implies the prior existence of numerous specialized skills and increases the need for some material to serve as a means of exchange and standard of value: money. Once the metallic form of money is invented, the opportunity for increasing inequalities among men is vastly enlarged. But internal exchange is still not international trade, and apart from conquest, the main source of a people's multiplying wealth, measured in terms of the variety and abundance of commodities, is international trade. Trade leads to riches, riches to luxury, luxury to the perfection of the arts. In his history of commerce Montesquieu mentions the poetry of Homer and draws attention to the perfection of taste and the fine arts in the ancient Greek cities. In the book on primitive societies there is no mention of poetry.

Montesquieu calls commerce the communication of peoples. In two ways this communication is connected with the civilizing of man, *i.e.,* with the reduction of barbarism. The first is through wealth and the arts, the second through philosophy. The tribe or nation that fails to participate in commerce is characterized by inbred superstition, prejudice, and ignorance, as well as by barbaric mores. Thus the original or "natural" condition of human societies is gravely defective. Commerce lays the basis for breaking out of this parochialism. It encourages the comparison of different ways of life. It makes possible the questioning of ancestral beliefs. It enables men to discover more of nature. In short, it makes possible philosophy, the coherent or conscious quest for knowledge of nature and man. It is curious that Montesquieu does not point to the philosophy of ancient Greece. Even more startling is his failure to draw attention to the great revolution in natural philosophy that he considered the most important feature of modernity. But the motto from Vergil prefixed to the first book on commerce is sufficiently indicative: "the things that mighty Atlas taught" (*Aeneid* I. 740) refers to a variety of topics within the study of nature. It was the revival of commerce that encouraged the revival of philosophy as well as the softening of European barbarism in early modern times. Commerce and knowledge together put an end to the Middle Ages.

Commerce develops by a combination of needs, inventions, and accidents. Montesquieu describes its principal varieties, its frequently awkward origins, its dependence on technology, its discovery of ways to outwit tyrants, its modern global extension, and finally its complex financial arrangements. The effects of commerce are to soften and polish barbaric mores (at the same time that it corrupts pure mores), to encourage the arts and sciences, to conduce toward peace by linking nations via their needs, and to raise standards of living. Of these, Montesquieu seems least interested in the last regarded as an end in itself. Nor is he solicitous of the merchant's profit-making: the greatest benefits of commerce are the less obvious, unintended consequences of the merchant's selfishness.

The book linking Montesquieu's discussion of natural or primitive man and his extensive discussion of commerce deals with the "general spirit" of nations. It begins by warning against the attempt to force all nations into the same mold, then proceeds to point out that moral virtues and vices are different from political virtues and vices, and ends by revealing modern England's foundation in the selfish passions of avarice and ambition. The idea that the political "virtues" required of its citizens by a defective political order might in reality be moral vices was a cornerstone of classical political philosophy: only rarely, if ever, were the good man and good citizen identical. But Montesquieu has in mind something far more disconcerting: the highest human things are brought about through the action of moral vices, and the *best* political order depends upon such vices. This understanding of human life Montesquieu learned from Machiavelli and his followers, not from the classics. The latter condemned commerce as institutionalized avarice, they had harsh words for moneylending, the regimes they favored had an agricultural, not a commercial base. But this amounted to wanting the fruits of commerce—the sciences and arts—without commerce itself. If popular or vulgar activities generate and nourish the highest activities of man, endangering them jeopardizes the higher things, which cannot endure independently. Remove commerce and travel, as in the Middle Ages, and you ruin philosophy. Philosophy is sustained by cosmopolitanism, and cosmopolitanism by commerce. Philosophy is freest in highly commercial England.

Montesquieu's view does not imply that the things produced indirectly through the actions of the multitude are, or ever can be, in complete harmony with the character of the multitude itself. Philosophy is a case in point. Can the people or societies as a whole be made philosophical? Are they capable of enlightenment in the radical sense? Montesquieu's answer is given in the book on the "general spirit" of each people. The general spirit is formed by climate, religion, the laws, political maxims, past examples, mores, manners. The spirit or mind of no nation is formed by reason. Nations live by passion and prejudice, not understanding. Enlightenment to make human life less barbaric or inhumane is possible, but even such enlightenment must be supported by an appeal to the passions, whether of self-interest or pity, and to the prejudices peculiar to the society addressed. Or again, England offers the greatest opportunity and security for philosophy and the arts, but England itself is neither philosophical nor poetic. Societies believe, whereas philosophers question, and societies protect philosophy more out of a concern for their own than for its freedom. Philosophy and society are therefore never bound in true amity. On his side, the philosopher is morally obliged to consider both the good and harmful social effects of his writings: hence the style of writing attributed to Montesquieu by d'Alembert, and its peculiar concealment of philosophy itself.

At the outset of the work, Montesquieu distinguishes between the tasks of the philosophical moralist and of the legislator.[10] For Aristotle, political aims had to be understood in terms of the quest for complete good: ethics and politics formed parts of a single study, with the former preceding the latter. For Montesquieu, however, ethics and politics have a much less direct relation, and as a legislator, he himself never systematically reveals the true or philosophical morality. Strictly speaking, the political world never is nor can be guided by this morality. For political virtues, like political vices, are all passions. If so, no nonphilosopher can be morally virtuous in any degree. But this is a more radical doctrine than that of the classics, who regarded men of popular or merely habitual virtue as animated by a very incomplete but nevertheless real knowledge of virtue. He concludes, for this and various other reasons we have seen, that man by nature is not a rational any more than he is a sociable or philanthropic being: the elements of the human soul do not naturally tend toward moral and intellectual perfection. It follows that the utopias and near-utopias of classical political philosophy are based on false premises. They judge and try to guide human nature by standards foreign to it and are utopian for this very reason. The philosophical legislator gains immeasurably in effectiveness by concealing his philosophical ethics and making prudent use of the real passions and opinions by which intellectual elites and greater multitudes can be moved. Yet his function changes therewith: before he was only an educator of philosophers and statesmen, now he is himself a political manipulator of men. The standards to which he appeals are those that the average man is best equipped by nature to understand. Their double root is self-preservation and pity. Their highest reach is political liberty, not excellence.

6. RELIGION

In Book I Montesquieu had vaguely suggested that God assisted man by a special revelation, and that man's being drawn toward the Creator (after forming an idea of Him) is the first of natural laws in importance, though not in time. As it turns out, religion is the last element of the spirit of laws to be discussed in the work. The two topics immediately preceding it—commerce and propagation—are concerned with the needs of the body. And in the book succeeding it, religion is treated in such a way as to obscure the distinction between the truly divine law of Jews and Christians on the one hand and the religious laws of gentiles on the other. It is also true that the work has little dependence on sacred history as such, though it sometimes draws examples from that history. With respect to the Christian Middle Ages, it is far more interested in the feudal than the Christian component.

Montesquieu claims, in this work, to be a political writer, not a theologian. But he also claims that the two capacities are perfectly consistent: Christianity is not only true but the greatest worldly good mankind could possess. He argues, against Bayle, that Christians make the best citizens. Yet the qualifications he attaches to the assertion make it clear that he considers the Christian counsels of perfection incompatible with political life, so that the most perfect Christian would make a very poor citizen. It is this view that engenders Montesquieu's praise of the ancient Stoic sects and the great Roman emperors, the Antonines, who were of their number. The Stoics were above all citizens, *i.e.,* not saints. And the main function of religion and civil laws is to make men good citizens and thereby to assist each society in satisfying its needs. For the truest and holiest dogmas can have very bad consequences if not linked to the principles of society, and the most false dogmas admirable consequences when so linked.

Montesquieu is critical of the social and political effects of Christianity on several counts. Christianity opposed commerce and money-lending in the Middle Ages; by fostering conventual chastity, it discouraged marriage and propagation; it was hostile everywhere to polygamy and divorce; it promoted civil disobedience in the name of a higher law; it turned Christian against Christian and Christian against non-Christian through an intolerant zeal for universality.[11] But it also had salubrious effects in restraining the schemes of despots and monarchs and assisting both the abolition of slavery and the mitigation of warfare in Europe. Montesquieu tries to correct its excesses. Unlike Locke, however, he does not make freedom of conscience a natural and universal right of man. A universal invitation to the establishment of religious diversity is not wise. One need not admit a new religion into a society if one can exclude it; but where any religion is already established, it should be tolerated.

7. CONCLUSION

The main virtue of the legislator, according to Montesquieu, must be moderation. He stresses the deliberate skill required by statecraft—its need for determining the kind of law to be applied, for understanding the network of relations comprising the spirit of laws and their connection with the complex particulars of each society.[12] Although Europe remained his main interest, he extended the purview of scientific explanation and evaluation in human affairs to all times and places. The phrase he applied to the Stoic emperors suits him even more aptly: he watched over humankind.

Montesquieu's philosophy delineates and relates the parts played by blind necessity and reasoned choice (another kind of necessity) in the formation of laws. His emphasis on the variety of political orders and the priority of particulars in statecraft derives from the classics. But he joins with Machiavelli and Locke in rejecting classical virtue as the ultimate political guide. This rejection foredoomed his effort to stem the revolutionary, universalistic tendencies of Lockean liberalism. Indeed, since liberty's portrait, unlike virtue's, must necessarily have widespread appeal, his elaborate description of English liberty itself became an instrument of that liberalism. The same rejection had another effect: by making a labyrinth of the relation between ethics and politics, it encouraged a political science that would lose interest in morality and statesmanship.

The surface of *The Spirit of the Laws* is both simple and disorderly, the interior difficult and coherent. What we have said may suffice to establish the truth of the claim that it has a design. Its systematic teaching, even its mystifying title, will continue to elude us until that design is fully understood.

NOTES

1. See quotation on pp. 471–72 below.

2. Montesquieu, *The Spirit of the Laws*, ed. Gonzague Truc (2 vols.; Paris: Collection des Classiques Garnier, n.d.), Preface.

3. *Ibid.*, I. iii. (trans. D. L.).

4. *Ibid.*, V. ii–iii.

5. *Ibid.*, XI. viii.

6. *Ibid.*, III. vi.

7. *Ibid.*, XIX. xxvii, beginning.

8. *Ibid.*, XVIII. xiii; XXVI. xiv; XVI, ii.

9. *Ibid.*, X. ii–iii; XXVI. xx.

10. *Ibid.*, I. i, end.

11. *Ibid.*, XXI. xx; XXIII. xxi; XXIV. xiii; XXV. x.

12. *Ibid.*, Preface; I. iii; XXVI, i; XXIX. i.

READINGS

A. Montesquieu. *The Spirit of the Laws*. Preface, bks I–V, XI, XII, XIX (11, 27).

B. Montesquieu. *The Spirit of the Laws*. Bks XIV, XV, XVIII, XX, XXI, XXIV, XXVI.

Montesquieu. *The Persian Letters*.

Montesquieu. *Considerations on the Greatness and Decline of the Romans*.

DAVID HUME

1711–1776

David Hume is best known as a skeptic, as an acute and thoroughgoing critic of human reason. Indeed, it is sometimes claimed that Hume's philosophy dealt the deathblow to natural right and eliminated the possibility of rational judgments of "value." Thus Hume's theory is presented as a challenge to the very existence of political philosophy, one which must be confronted. But we are faced with a paradox. Hume was himself the author of a comprehensive political doctrine, purporting to be the truth about such subjects as the laws of nature, justice, the obligation to civil obedience, and the best kind of government.

Our first subject, it appears, must be Hume's teaching concerning the foundation and authority of normative judgments. This must be prefaced by a brief consideration of his theory of the principles and operations of the understanding.

Turning his observation inward upon the human mind, Hume finds there a collection and succession of what he calls "perceptions": the taste of an apple, the idea of a triangle, a notion of justice, esteem for a prudent action, anger, and so on. A perception is whatever is present to the mind, and nothing is present to the mind but its perceptions. Indeed, the mind is nothing but a heap or bundle of perceptions.

Perceptions are of two kinds. There are *impressions,* what is in our mind "when we hear, or see, or feel, or love, or hate, or desire, or will." There are *ideas,* what is in our mind "when we reflect on a passion or an object which is not present." The difference between impressions and ideas is a difference in their degree of force and vivacity: impressions are more "strong" and "lively" than ideas.

All ideas, Hume says, are derived from impressions. Now it is true that the imagination is very free, and we can picture golden mountains and winged horses that we have never seen; but those ideas are compounded out of other ideas. And as to "simple ideas," those irreducible ideas that admit of no distinction or separation, we find that it is not in our power to imagine any which does not correspond to and represent some impression we have previously experienced. As a blind man can form no idea of purple nor a deaf man of a flute's sound, so in general, "we can never *think* of anything which we have not seen [or in some way sensed] without us or *felt* in our own minds." All our simple ideas are but images or copies of impressions.[1]

We cannot have *knowledge* in the fullest sense and absolute *certainty,* Hume says, concerning matters of fact and real existence, but only concerning "the relations of ideas." This may be explained as follows: It is laid down as an "established maxim" that whatever is conceivable is possible. Now the contrary of every assertion of matter of fact is always conceivable. I can imagine that the sun will not rise tomorrow; hence, I have no knowledge that it will. I cannot be certain that the objects before me continue to exist when I close my eyes, for it is imaginable that they do not. We cannot have knowledge of that which can be thought to be otherwise. Knowledge then can be only of that which cannot be thought to be otherwise—of that which càn be thought only as it is. For example, the contrary of the proposition, "The angles of a triangle are equal to two right angles," is not conceivable; the relation between "the angles of a triangle" and "two right angles" must be thought to be what it is. Since the realm of possibility is where the imagination is free, then necessity must be located where the imagination is bound.

The only objects of knowledge then are those relations of ideas that "depend entirely on the ideas which we compare together." We can know only what is necessarily implied in our ideas; in a sense, we can take from our ideas only what we have put into them. For example, the proposition, "Where there is no property, there is no injustice," is certain, when the idea of injustice is simply the violation of property. But this is nothing more than unpacking what we have previously packed. And Hume appears to think that even the demonstrations of mathematicians are merely more lengthy and complicated forms of this kind of extraction process. Let us also note that the objects of knowledge are the relations of ideas *considered as ideas.* By comparing ideas we can learn nothing about that which is not ideas. We can have no knowledge, strictly speaking, of the world of realities, but only of the world of ideas.[2]

The principle, "Whatever is conceivable is possible," deserves further examination. Now there are many statements, Hume says, whose contrary is conceivable but that we are nevertheless entitled to accept with complete assurance; for example, that all men shall die. Indeed, Hume regards all matters of fact as parts of a system of universal necessity.[3] What then is meant by saying that "whatever is conceivable is possible" or "not absolutely impossible" or "possible, at least in a metaphysical sense"? Moreover, why is this principle, which seems not to be self-evident, to be considered an "established maxim"?

In answer it can be said that at a certain point in the history of philosophy it began to be thought that the disorder, contradiction and ignorance that prevailed in philosophy was a disgrace, and that it should be ended and the edifice of human reason erected on a completely unshakeable foundation. But an unshakeable foundation could be assured only by allowing the utmost sway to skepticism to begin with. In order that philosophy should be indubitable it is necessary to begin by doubting all that can be doubted.

Now Hume's "established maxim" is to be understood as an instrument of this kind of preliminary skepticism. The starting point of philosophy is the determination to doubt. The area of doubt is most extensive when the area of the merely possible is most extensive. Thus arises the necessity of regulating our reasoning by this "established maxim," which widens the possible to that which it is possible to conceive, and as a consequence, restricts the necessary to what it is necessary to conceive. Indeed, the maxim might be considered to be preliminary skepticism in its most naked form: it compels us to doubt wherever we are not obliged to affirm. Whereas Descartes, in whose philosophy the necessity of universal doubt is most clearly urged, employed that "freedom of the mind" whereby "it supposes that no object is, of the existence of which it has even the slightest doubt," in Hume the mind supposes (one could say) that no object is, the existence of which it is not forced to acknowledge.

Hume's principal concern is not with that kind of reasoning that through intuition or demonstration discovers the relations of ideas, but rather with "probable reasoning," by which we discover matter of fact and real existence, and which guides us all our lives and indeed composes most of our philosophy. Now all our reasoning about matter of fact is based, he says, on the relation of cause and effect. Without causation we cannot go beyond our senses and memory; by causation we are enabled to infer the existence of objects and occurrences beyond our experience. So the discussion of probability resolves itself into an examination of causation.

Hume begins by raising "sceptical doubts" concerning cause and effect. Consider a particular instance of the inference from cause to effect. For example, we see a billiard ball moving across a table and striking another. We conclude that the second one will begin to move. What is the basis for this conclusion? It is not made known to us by reason, for it is possible to conceive of the movement not following the collision. It must then be founded on experience: we have seen balls collide and set in motion in the past. But it still remains conceivable that they might not do so in this case. The inference is then based on experience together with the assumption that the future will resemble the past. But what is the basis of this principle? Not reason; for it is conceivable that the future will not resemble the past. Experience then; but how can we learn from experience the very principle that alone makes it possible to learn from experience?

We seem to be at a dead end. But now Hume presents his "sceptical solution" of these skeptical doubts. When we have observed one event succeeding another in a number of instances, the mind gets in the habit of considering them together. So when I see one billiard ball striking another my imagination, falling into a familiar groove, is led to think of the second ball's moving. And I not only form this conception but I *believe* in it; which means simply that it feels different from ideas I do not believe in. What its feeling is like is hard to describe; the idea is conceived in a stronger, or more vivid, or firmer manner, so that it forms a part of what we call "reality," along with impressions and the ideas of the memory. In sum, "all reasonings [about causation] are nothing but the effects of custom; and custom has no influence, but by enlivening the imagination, and giving us a strong conception of any object."

Another question is considered: the idea of *cause* and its origin. We observe, for instance, one billiard ball striking another, causing it, as we say, to move. From what impression is the idea of cause derived? What we observe is that the collision of the balls and the motion of the second are contiguous events, that one occurs prior in time to the second, and finally that on repetition this conjunction of events is found to be constant. That is all. Yet there is more to the idea of causation than contiguity, priority and constant conjunction; we commonly suppose that there is a *necessary* connection between the two events. From what impression can this come? Hume answers, from nothing in the objects, but from something in the mind, namely, the feeling of being compelled or determined to pass in the imagination from cause to effect.

We mistakenly transfer this impression to the objects themselves; but in fact, necessity lies not in the objects but in ourselves.[4]

The argument that has been sketched above follows a pattern that recurs frequently in Hume's philosophy. What is accepted unquestioningly by common sense—here causation, elsewhere the existence of a world of objects not dependent on our perception of them, and elsewhere even the continued existence of a personal self—is found to have no rational basis. But it is dissolved only to be restored. Nature is too strong for reason. And an account is given of the way in which reason is overcome.[5] But the overcoming is of a dubious nature. The "sceptical doubts" are not refuted. Nor are they simply shaken off in the name of common sense, in the manner of Dr. Johnson refuting Berkeley by kicking a stone. They receive a "solution," but a "skeptical" solution. What is "restored" is not quite what has been dissolved. Thus, the inference from cause to effect is a habit; the belief in what is inferred is an inexplicable feeling; the idea of cause is a mistake.

By thus reducing causal reasoning to a matter of custom and sentiment Hume exposes himself to difficulties in attempting to distinguish and justify correct reasoning. For example, by observing a number of instances of the conjunction of objects a habit of mental transition is engendered, although they may have in reality no essential connection. We may, to use Hume's example, come to regard all Irishmen as dull, in the face of clear evidence to the contrary. This is prejudice, and the judgment must be called in to rectify the imagination. But how is this possible? Hume explains that the general rules called "prejudices" are corrected by other general rules called "rules of logic," based on observation of the nature and operations of the understanding and enabling us to distinguish the essential from the nonessential. Habit is overcome by habit. But it would seem that a habit could be overcome only by a *stronger* habit. Yet Hume says that these rules of reasoning are derived from the observation not of a greater number of instances but of the "more general and authentic operations of the understanding."[6]

Another problem: how it is that we can arrive at a judgment concerning cause and effect after only one careful experiment? The habit of making a mental transition from one object to another must, it would seem, vary in proportion to the number of instances of their conjunction we have observed, and after one instance would be slight at the most. How can habit exceed experience? Hume answers that we subsume our single experiment under the principle that similar objects in similar circumstances produce similar effects, and the habit of transition is produced artificially. The principle itself is of course habitual; the uniformity of nature is reduced to a habit of expecting in the future what we have been accustomed to in the past. It is a full and perfect habit, based on millions of experiments.[7] But, we must ask, is our experience of uniform succession perfect? And if not, then once again, how can habit exceed experience?

The problems put above may be summarized as follows: If the ground of inference is habit, then (it would appear) habit is reason enough for an inference, and inference cannot go beyond habit. Hume cannot allow these consequences. His theory is intended not only to explain the "reasoning" of animals but also to justify the methods of Newton.[8] The question is whether he does solve the problems without bringing in anything but habit and feeling.

We are now able to proceed to Hume's treatment of the foundation and authority of normative judgment. As in his discussion of causation, he begins with "sceptical doubts," which lead to the conclusion that "moral distinctions [are] not derived from reason." [9]

One line of argument is designed to show that virtue and vice are not objects of the understanding. The understanding has, Hume says, two operations: the comparison of ideas, by which it discovers the relations of objects, and the inference of matter of fact, by which it discovers their existence. So if virtue and vice can be discovered by the understanding they must consist in either *relations* or *matters of fact*.

First, Hume undertakes to show that virtue and vice cannot be relations. The ultimate object of moral approval and disapproval is a mental action in respect of external objects; for example, the passion of affection for one's children, or the volition to take somebody else's property. If moral good and evil are relations they must therefore be relations obtaining between internal actions and external objects, and capable of obtaining *only* between internal actions and external objects. For if, for example, moral good were a relation that could also apply between external objects, then irrational and inanimate objects could be morally good. Now there appears to be no relation that is so restricted. Consider, for instance, the relation of *fittingness*. A moral theory that Hume seems especially interested in refuting asserted that there are certain natural fitnesses and unfitnesses of things to one another, and that the virtue of an action lies in its fittingness to the situation. Hume's objection is that fittingness (supposing such a relation to exist) can obtain between external objects which, however, cannot be called virtuous.

Indeed, the relations that actually do exist between internal actions and external objects in instances of virtue and vice are found to exist between external objects, where they clearly do not constitute virtue and vice. Suppose, for example, a tree that grows up and chokes out the tree from whose seed it itself grew. The relations here are precisely the same as one finds in the case of a child strangling its parent. We do not regard the former case as an instance of vice; but if vice consisted in the relation it would be so.

Are virtue and vice then matters of fact? Hume bids the reader to take an example of a vicious action, murder, perhaps, and to "examine it in all lights, and see if you can find that matter of fact, or real existence, which you call *vice*. In whichever way you take it, you find only certain passions, motives, volitions and thoughts. There is no other matter of fact in the case. The vice entirely escapes you, as long as you consider the object."

Hume concludes that virtue and vice are neither relations nor matters of fact; that is, they are not objects of the understanding, and hence the sense of morality does not consist in their discovery.

Another and more prominent line of argument is summarized as follows: "Morals excite passions, and produce or prevent actions. Reason of itself is utterly impotent in this particular. The rules of morality, therefore, are not conclusions of our reason."

By the impotence of reason Hume means this: An action is the result of a propensity or an aversion to some object, and this propensity or aversion is excited (usually, at least) by the pleasure or pain given by or expected from the object. Now reason can inform us of the existence of objects and of the relations among them, but if the objects are indifferent to us, if they arouse no propensity or aversion, this information has no influence on the will. So reason *alone* cannot produce or, by the same token, prevent any action. As Hume puts it in a famous sentence, "Reason is, and ought only to be the slave of the passions, and can never pretend to any other office than to serve and obey them." Yet it is clear that reason *in conjunction with passion* may have a strong (if "oblique" and "mediate") influence on the will. It may *prompt* passion by informing it of the existence of its object. For example, I am of the opinion that behind a garden wall there is tasty fruit, and my desire for it is founded on that opinion. And reason may *direct* passion to its object, by tracing the connection of causes and effects. I may hit on the expedient of getting a ladder and climbing the wall. In such a case the part of reason may be great and even decisive. Thus, if I learn that my opinion about the existence of the fruit or the best way to get it is incorrect, my passion and volition cease. But reason's role remains a ministerial one, for it does not supply the impulse that moves us.[10]

The "calm and indolent judgments of the understanding" are then not sufficient to influence the will. And the crux of Hume's argument is that "those judgments by which we distinguish good and evil" are sufficient to influence the will. He denies that moral cognition is separable from a propensity or aversion to action. He denies, that is, that one can know what is morally good without feeling an inclination to it.

The following celebrated passage from Hume may at once be elucidated by and help to elucidate the preceding argument.

In every system of morality which I have hitherto met with, I have always remarked that the author proceeds for some time in the ordinary way of reasoning, and establishes the being of a God, or makes observations concerning human affairs; when of a sudden I am surprised to find, that instead of the usual copulations of propositions, *is*, and *is not*, I meet with no proposition that is not connected with an *ought*, or an *ought not*. This change is imperceptible; but is, however, of the last consequence. For as this *ought*, or *ought not*, expresses some new relation or affirmation, 'tis necessary that it should be observed and explained; and at the same time that a reason should be given, for what seems altogether inconceivable, how this new relation can be a deduction from others, which are entirely different from it. But as authors do not commonly use this precaution, I shall presume to recommend it to the readers: and am persuaded, that this small attention would subvert all the vulgar systems of morality, and let us see that the distinction of vice and virtue is not founded merely on the relations of objects, nor is perceived by reason.[11]

Morality, we see, is concerned with duty and obligation; the morally good is essentially what one *ought* to do. And this cannot be found out by reason. For example, consider once again the thesis that virtue consists in fittingness. In one place Hume concedes for the sake of argument that the relation of fittingness exists and is discoverable by reason. But this, he says, is not sufficient to show that it is virtue; it must be shown that there is a connection between fittingness and the will. For the morally good has the character of law; it is obligatory. That is to say, it is "forcible," it influences the will. Reason may (it is assumed) discover the fitting, but it cannot discover it as morally good. For the morally good is what we ought to do, and what we ought to do is what we are compelled or impelled to do. The only way to know compulsion is to suffer it; we can discover what influences the will only by feeling that influence.

Now this identification of the obligatory with the forcible is not self-evident. It seems to rest upon the need to make the obligatory *effectively* obligatory. Hume seems, in other words, to be following the lines laid down by Hobbes and Locke in trying to erect morals on a foundation that "the passions not mistrusting, shall not seek to displace." In the same way that Hume found the certainty of knowledge by identifying the necessary with what must necessarily be thought, so he finds the efficacy of morality by identifying the virtuous with what one is compelled to pursue. As the human imagination was made the ground of science so the human affections are made the ground of morality.

We turn now to the "sceptical solution of these sceptical doubts" concerning morality, which is that "moral distinctions are derived from a moral sense." Since virtue and vice are not discovered by reason, it follows that we distinguish them by some sentiment or impression that they excite. The vice of a vicious action "entirely escapes you, as long as you consider the object. You can never find it, till you turn your reflection into your own breast, and find a sentiment of disapprobation, which arises in you, towards this action. Here is a matter of fact, but 'tis the object of feeling, not of reason. It lies in yourself, not in the object." "Morality, therefore, is more properly felt than judged of. . . ."

More precisely, Hume asserts not merely that virtue and vice are *discovered* by sentiment, but that they are *constituted* by sentiment. It is not that virtue is approved because it is virtue, but that virtue is virtue because it is approved. When an action is said to be virtuous, nothing is meant but that it gives rise to a feeling of approbation, just as when an object is said to be the cause or effect of another, nothing is meant but that they are habitually united in the imagination.

The sight of virtue, Hume observes, is pleasing, and that of vice displeasing. He further declares that the very sentiment of moral approbation is pleasing and that of disapprobation displeasing. Indeed, he identifies the approbation and the pleasure. He denies that the approbation is an inference from the pleasure. He silently passes over the possibility that the pleasure is a consequence of the approbation. Rather, he reduces the approbation to the pleasure. "To have the sense of virtue, is nothing but to feel a satisfaction of a particular kind. . . ." We see then that the moral sense is not a distinct and peculiar faculty, and that moral sentiments are pleasures and pains.

Moral sentiments are, however, pleasures and pains of a particular kind, differing in their feeling from other pleasures and pains in the same way as, for instance, the pleasure given by a beefsteak differs from the pleasure given by a poem. These peculiar pleasures and pains (1) arise only from the consideration of the characters and actions of rational beings and (2) arise when these are considered "in general, without reference to our particular interest." Thus we may esteem an enemy for those very qualities that make him dangerous to us.

In sum, "virtue is distinguished by the pleasure, and vice by the pain, that any action, sentiment, or character gives us by the mere view or contemplation." [12]

Those qualities or characters that are esteemed as virtuous are found by Hume to be of four kinds. First, qualities that are useful to others: *e.g.,* justice, generosity, beneficence, honesty. Second, qualities that are useful to the one possessing them: *e.g.,* prudence, frugality, industry, temperance. Third, qualities that are immediately agreeable to others: *e.g.,* modesty, wit, decency. Finally, qualities that are immediately agreeable to the one possessing them: *e.g.,* a proper self-esteem, love of glory, magnanimity. It might be added that a quality may fall into more than one of these classes. For example, courage is not only *useful* to its possessor and to the public but also gives an immediate pleasure to its possessor.

In short, the objects of moral approbation are those qualities that are either immediately pleasant or productive of pleasure, either to their possessor or to others. The good is fundamentally identical with the pleasant. But it is *not* identical with one's own pleasure. In making moral judgments we do not value others for their value to ourselves. Approbation is not bestowed on qualities because they give pleasure to us but, on the contrary, because they give pleasure to others, including the one who has them. Yet, in another sense, we should note, it can be said that we approve of what pleases us, because our very approbation consists in being pleased.

Why do we approve of those "virtuous" qualities? Hume sometimes replies that we are moved by "humanity" or "benevolence." But this is not to be understood as an "original instinct" or desire for the good of others. It is the manifestation of a more general and extremely important principle of human nature: *sympathy,* or "that propensity we have to receive by communication from others their passions, sentiments, etc." It must be noted that sympathy is not the same as pity, and has no connotation of affection or good will. It is a mere conduit through which pains, pleasures, passions, and so on, are transmitted from one person to another.[13]

The object of moral approbation then is a source of pleasure; the sentiment of approbation is itself a pleasure; and the pleasantness of the sentiment is borrowed from that of the object. Thus Hume is enabled to reject what he calls the "selfish morality," and yet to avoid affirming the existence of general benevolence toward men apart from their relation to ourselves. He does this by postulating the operation of sympathy, which makes the pleasures and pains of others our own, but does so as it were mechanically, without the interposition of either good will to our fellows or calculations of self-interest.

At the bottom of Hume's denial that moral good and evil can be found out by reason is the demand that morality be in accordance with the passions, or, to use his own formulations, the identification of the obligatory with the forcible, and the insistence that moral judgments have a direct and immediate influence on the will. His own theory meets that demand. The principal motives to action are pleasure and pain; the judgments of moral approbation and disapprobation are nothing but pleasures and pains. Thus, virtue is essentially "amiable" and vice essentially "odious," and consequently desired or shunned. A moral judgment is therefore not only a sentiment of praise or blame, *i.e.,* a feeling of pleasure or pain, but also an "opinion of obligation" or a "sense of duty," *i.e.,* a propensity or aversion.

In requiring that morality be in accordance with and built upon the passions, Hume is following Hobbes and Locke. But he does not follow them in their conclusions. They represent what Hume calls the "selfish system of morals," which he criticizes severely. As Hume understood it, the basic premise of the "selfish system" is that the fundamental and ruling passion is self-interest. Hume denies this. (1) It exaggerates the power of reason. To show that such passions as friendship that appear to be disinterested are really only manifestations of self-love, philosophers must hypothesize very intricate and refined reasonings, reasonings much too intricate and refined to have in fact much influence on the passions. (2) Moreover, not all desires can be subsumed under the desire for one's own good. For example, there are affection for one's children and hatred of one's enemies and many others. These are original instincts or impulses quite as much as the desire of one's good is, and they pursue their objects independently of any consideration of advantage. (3) Indeed, far from all passions being reducible to self-interest, the action of self-interest itself presupposes the existence of other passions, at least sometimes and perhaps always or almost always. Self-interest moves us to desire a pleasing object, for instance, a beefsteak. But why does the object please? Because it gratifies some other desire, for instance, hunger. Without desires other than self-interest there would be nothing or little for self-interest to concern itself with. (4) Nor is self-interest necessarily the strongest or dominant passion. When placed in competition with some other particular passion, self-interest does not always command priority. And a man may prefer his lesser good to his greater, *knowing* it to be lesser. The desire for a lesser good may overcome the desire for one's acknowledged greater good.[14]

The "selfish morality" is based on an excessively simplified understanding of the passions. Hobbes, to take the clearest example, finds his starting point in a single passion, the fear of death or the desire for self-preservation; this is the strongest or most fundamental passion. Virtue consists in obedience to the laws of nature, which are dictates of reason for avoiding death and preserving life. Fear of death is the strongest passion because death is the greatest evil. It is presupposed that all men by natural necessity always seek what they think to be their own greatest good.

Hume, on the other hand, says that there is no such natural necessity. Passion supplies no single incontrovertible axiom to reason, and hence reason can furnish no authoritative guidance to conduct. " 'Tis not contrary to reason to prefer the destruction of the whole world to the scratching of my finger. 'Tis not contrary to reason for me to choose my total ruin, to prevent the least uneasiness of an Indian or person wholly unknown to me." [15] The standards of moral judgment are not "dictates of reason" derived from passion; they are themselves passions, *i.e.,* moral sentiments.

Moreover, since no passion is "axiomatic," a morality in accordance with the passions must be marked by breadth and complexity. Hume rejects the kind of narrowing of virtue characteristic of modern natural-law teaching; he declines to "fetter his moral sentiments by narrow systems." From the moderns Hume appeals to the ancient moralists, such as Cicero, who are "the best models." The modern natural-law teaching, in basing morality on the passions, as Hume does, failed, however, to do justice to the full range of human passions. A morality truly in accordance with the passions takes its standard from the "common and natural course" of the passions.[16]

According to Hume morality is distinguished and determined by sentiment. A character is virtuous or vicious in so far as it excites a certain pleasure or pain, and if it excites such pleasure or pain it is virtuous or vicious. It follows that, since we can never be mistaken as to our feelings of pleasure and pain, moral judgments are "perfectly infallible."

This appears to lead into a chaos of subjectivity. For the sentiments of different men differ, as do the sentiments of the same man at different times, depending on their particular situations. For example, we seldom have much affection for someone who works against our interest, even if he is acting in accordance with the general rules of morality. We receive a stronger and livelier pleasure from the common diligence of a servant than from the noblest qualities of Marcus Brutus.

Hume is, however, not a relativist. Morals are a matter of taste, but there is right and wrong taste. This is accounted for as follows: The variation in our sentiments arising from the variation in our situation makes us uncertain. Moreover we find that the sentiments of others based on their particular situations contradict our sentiments based on our particular situations. Now this contradiction and uncertainty makes it impossible for men "to converse together on any reasonable terms. . . ." In order, therefore, to communicate with one another we are obliged to seek a common and less variable point of view from which to judge the qualities of persons. The point of view we adopt is that of those who are immediately connected with those persons. For example, our affection and admiration for Brutus would, we know, be much greater than that for our servant were they equally near to us, and we dispense our esteem accordingly. In making moral judgments we overlook our present situation and even our own interest. We "correct our sentiments."

It needs to be asked how this is possible on Hume's ground. How can a sentiment arising from a real situation be overcome by a sentiment arising from a hypothetical situation? Hume in effect concedes that it is not: "The passions," he writes, "do not always follow our corrections." What is regulated by the transposition of situations is not so much our feelings as our "abstract notions" and "general pronouncements." [17] But, we must ask, does this not imply an abandonment of the principle that moral judgment is a matter of sentiment?

The problem with which we have been concerned—the status of normative judgments in Hume's philosophy—may now be approached by considering the question of the extent to which such judgments stand on a different footing from judgments about matter of fact. There are passages in which Hume indicates that they differ radically in kind. For example, he writes that reason, which gives knowledge concerning truth and falsehood, differs from taste, which is the source of moral sentiment, in that the former "discovers objects as they really stand in nature, without addition and diminution," whereas the latter "has a productive faculty, and gilding or staining all natural objects with the colors, borrowed from internal sentiment, raises in a manner a new creation." The standard of reason is "eternal and inflexible," whereas the standard of the other arises from the "frame and constitution of animals."

It is doubtful, however, that the contrast so vividly drawn will survive further examination. For if "morality is more properly felt than judged of," yet in the same way "all probable reasoning is nothing but a species of sensation. 'Tis not solely in poetry and music we must follow our taste and sentiment," but in the experimental sciences as well.[18] Virtue and vice are not matters of fact; or rather, they are *internal* matters of fact, *i.e.,* our sentiments of moral approval and disapproval. But the same is true of the connection between cause and effect. "Objects have no discoverable connection together. . . ." The causal relation is nothing in the object but something in the mind.

Hume of course attempts to supply a more secure foundation for causal reasoning than mere feeling, to distinguish prejudice and fantasy from solid reasoning and to give rules to guide the conduct of inquiry. But, as we have just seen, he undertakes a similar task for morality, to escape from the contradiction and variation of moral judgment and to determine the standard of correct taste in morality. And in both cases he encounters similar difficulties in doing so.

The "state of nature" is, in Hume's opinion, a fiction of the philosophers. But in tracing the origin of government it is permissible to begin by hypothesizing man in a "savage and solitary condition." We find that more than any other animal he is at once necessitous and weak. He needs food, clothing, and shelter. Yet he is ill-equipped by his natural abilities to obtain and secure them. Society alone can compensate for his weaknesses. By joining forces with others he is able to carry out projects for which he alone is not powerful enough; the division of labor induces greater skill in the arts; and mutual helpfulness is a shield against accident and bad fortune. Only in society can his wants be met—including the new wants that society itself engenders.

The origin of society cannot however be attributed to such calculations of advantage as these, which are far beyond the capacity of uncultivated men to make. It is due to another need with a more obvious remedy, namely, sexual desire. This draws together man and woman; parental affection continues to unite them; and a family society arises, ruled by the parents. It is in the family that men learn by experience the advantages of society and are at the same time fitted for it.

There are, however, certain factors that make society difficult to maintain. First, the passions of selfishness and confined generosity. A man commonly loves himself better than any other single person. And although the total of his affection for others is usually greater than his self-love, it is restricted mainly to his relatives and friends. Secondly, the scarcity and instability of external goods. External goods do not exist in enough quantity to satisfy everyone's needs and desires. And they may be taken from their possessor and become useful to someone else, unlike useful bodily attributes. These internal and external circumstances co-incide to produce the chief impediment to society, the "insatiable, per-petual, universal" desire of acquiring possessions for ourselves and those near to us. The other passions are more easily restrained or are not so dangerous. Vanity, for example, is a social passion, and "a bond of union among men."

We cannot expect this propensity to be controlled by our natural moral sentiments. These conform themselves to the natural course of the passions and tend to reinforce them. The remedy is an artifice found out by reason: "a convention entered into by all the members of the society to bestow stability on the possession of those external goods, and leave every one in the peaceable enjoyment of what he may acquire by his fortune and industry." This is the first law of nature: abstinence from the possessions of others.

This convention or agreement is not of the nature of a promise or contract. It is rather a common sense of common interest, arising grad-ually among men and gaining force by repeated experience of the inconvenience of transgressing it. Once it is established there arise the ideas of justice and injustice, and the ideas that follow from them, property, right, and obligation.

If the fundamental rule of justice is the stability of property, there are needed some other rules to determine what goods are the property of what persons. The most obvious rule was that of present possession, and afterwards others presented themselves: occupation, prescription, and so on. Now in operation these rules depend on chance and must often result in a disproportion between men's property and their wants and desires. Yet the fitness or suitability of property to persons can never, Hume insists, be accepted as a rule. The rules of justice are set up to end contention and discord, and nothing is more productive of conten-tion and discord than questions of fitness and suitability. To allow the adjustment of property to persons without stirring up trouble, the natural expedient is to permit the transfer of property by consent. This is the second law of nature, and grows up in much the same fashion as the first.

The third law of nature is the obligation of promises, and it arises as follows: The advantage of mutual helpfulness is obvious. If I help you

harvest now and you in turn help me harvest later, both of us are benefited. But if men were left to follow the natural course of their passions
selfishness and confined generosity would lose them the advantage. I
might help you and you not help me. Or more likely, I would decline to
help you lest you might not help me in return. A little experience shows
the remedy: Men invent a "certain form of words" called a promise,
by which a person expresses a resolution to do something and exposes
himself to the penalty of mistrust if he fails to perform.

Such is the origin of the rules of justice. The "natural obligation"
to their observance, Hume says, is self-interest. But since Hume rejects
the "selfish system of morals" he must account for their "moral obligation" on a different basis. Why is justice a virtue and injustice a vice?
The answer is that we recognize that justice is beneficial to society.
We may not always act justly. But in viewing the injustice of others we
regard it as pernicious and come to share the uneasiness of those who
will feel its bad consequences. This applies to some extent even to our
own actions. And this shared uneasiness or sympathetic pain is identical
with the sentiment of moral blame. It is reinforced by other means: the
"artifice of politicians" dispensing public praise and blame, education,
which teaches us to regard justice as honorable, and by a care for our
reputation. But all this without antecedent moral distinctions would be
in vain. In sum then, the original motive for the establishment of justice
is self-interest, but the source of its moral approbation is "a sympathy
with public interest."[19]

The advantages of society and hence of the rules of justice are great
and obvious. Yet a strict observance of them cannot be expected. For one
thing, one's interest may sometimes be better served by an act of injustice. More frequently, however, our infractions are due to our tendency to regulate our desires and wills in accordance with the appearance
of objects rather than their real value, and to prefer a lesser good near at
hand to a greater good that is more remote. We are thus apt to seize an
immediate advantage gained by an act of injustice at the expense of the
real but remote advantage to be gained from justice. The principal safeguard devised by men to prevent themselves from giving way to this
weakness is *government*. Men's natural propensity to prefer the contiguous to the remote is incurable, but it can be made harmless by
changing their circumstances and situations. Some men are made rulers,
i.e., they are placed in a position where they have an immediate interest
in the impartial administration of justice and no interest or only a re-

mote one in the contrary. The rest of men are ruled, *i.e.,* they are so constrained and restrained by the rulers that their immediate interest is in adherence to justice. As with the laws of justice, the original motive and the natural obligation to obedience to government is self-interest, and the moral obligation comes from sympathy with the public interest.

The fundamental and principal object of government is the administration of justice, *i.e.,* the protection of property and the enforcement of contracts. But they go beyond this, to undertake useful large-scale projects that individuals would be unable or unwilling to attempt. So government not only protects men as they pursue their interest but also requires them to pursue it.[20]

The duties of obedience to government and the observance of the rules of justice are called by Hume "artificial virtues," as distinguished from "natural virtues." The basis of the distinction is this: The natural virtues are those to which men are impelled by some original instinct or natural impulse, and which are given moral approbation because they are signs of such an instinct or impulse. For example, quite apart from any considerations of duty or of utility there is a natural affection of parents for their children. The artificial virtues on the other hand are not practiced because of any such propensity. On the contrary, it appears that our natural instincts if left unrestrained would lead us into all kinds of inequity and insubordination. The artificial virtues appear as laudable only after thought and reflection, for they are virtues only as a consequence of human contrivance. To take a clear example, suppose that in accordance with the terms of a will a fortune is taken from a deserving person and handed over to an undeserving one. Neither private happiness nor, at first glance, public happiness is thereby advanced. But the virtue of the act appears when it is considered as a part of a vast scheme which must be adhered to inflexibly even in such hard cases because the operation of the scheme as a whole is beneficial.

In another sense, however, the "artificial virtues" are natural. They arise necessarily out of man's situation. And they are a product of reason, which is part of man's nature as much as passion. Thus, as we have seen, Hume does not hesitate to speak of the "laws of nature."[21]

The artificial virtues are not to be regarded as contrary to the passions. They are contrary only to their "heedless and impetuous movement." Thus, government does not eradicate the propensity to prefer an immediate advantage to a remote one; it only gives it a new turn so that it destroys its own bad effects. Indeed the passions are better satisfied by being controlled and directed. In particular, acquisitiveness is much more fully gratified by being subjected to the restraints of justice than by being left to itself.[22]

Since justice and government are contrivances aimed at human benefit, it is clear that in very rare and extreme cases it is permissible to suspend their obligation. The common rule is the inflexible observance of justice and blind submission to government. But, for example, in a besieged city the rights of property may have to give way to public necessity. And, as the universal sentiment of mankind declares, when only public ruin would be the result of continued submission to government the ties of allegiance are loosened and rebellion is proper. Men's interest in that security and protection that can be afforded only by political society is at once the "original motive" to the institution of government and the "immediate sanction" of obedience to it. When rulers have become so oppressive that government no longer affords that security and protection, the sanction cannot remain in force. The effect ceases with the cause.

This admission of the right of disobedience in extraordinary emergencies raises the following difficulty: Since men are so inclined to follow "general rules" and to adhere to maxims after the reasons for them have ceased to exist, might not the "moral obligation" to obedience, derived from sympathy, survive the "natural obligation" founded on interest? Might not men be bound to obey a government that is destructive of justice? Hume says not. Our knowledge of human nature, of past history, and of present times informs us that those human imperfections that political society is set up to guard against are inherent in all men, not excluding rulers, and that we may reasonably expect them sometimes to act cruelly and unjustly, even against their immediate interest. This observation, being based on many examples, has itself the character of a general rule, and hence can serve as the basis of an exception to the general rule of obedience. Thus, it is that the general opinion of mankind thinks it no crime to resist great oppression.[23]

In the wise framing of political institutions, Hume says, "every man must be supposed a knave," *i.e.,* to be always seeking his own interest. The alternative to this supposition is to rely on the good will of rulers for the security of property and liberty; in other words, to rely on chance and to have no security at all. Good constitutions will not depend on the existence of great private virtues; they will ensure that the private interests of men, even of bad men, will be so controlled and directed as to serve and produce the public good. Such is the aim of free government, which Hume calls the "happiest" society.

The power of a free government is as great as that of any other government, but it is divided among several parts, perhaps a monarch, an hereditary aristocracy and a popular assembly, who have such checks on one another as to prevent any one from overcoming the others and gaining absolute control. Since arbitrary power is always oppressive to some extent, a free government must act according to general, equal, and previously known laws. There should be both a popular assembly and a smaller "aristocratic" senate. The senate furnishes wisdom, and it is kept honest by the other body. It is expedient for the popular assembly to be chosen in frequent elections by an electorate with a fairly high property qualification. Aristocracy is favorable to peace and order, but it tends to become oppressive. It is well to modify it with an element of democracy, so regulated as to avoid democracy's peculiar faults, such as turbulence. It is of great importance to protect the state against ecclesiastical encroachment and religious disturbances. There must be a union of the civil and ecclesiastical power and a dependence of the clergy on the civil government. Toleration of dissenting sects is necessary in order to "allay their fervor and make the civil union acquire a superiority above religious distinctions."

Liberty in the sense of free government is, Hume says, "the perfection of civil society." Yet authority is essential to its very existence, and when the two conflict, as they often do, authority should perhaps be given the preference. On the other hand, it may reasonably be said that what is essential can and will take care of itself, and needs less protection than what tends to society's perfection and is apt to be neglected or overlooked.

Despite Hume's esteem for free government, he thought that in recent times even absolute monarchy had improved so much that it met the ends of civil society almost as well as any kind of government. Modern civilized monarchies had borrowed institutions and manners from free governments and closely approached them in gentleness, stability, and the security given to property. They might improve even more.

This reflection illustrates the need for care in laying down eternal, permanent truths in politics. We should be cautious in prophecy. Likewise, we should be forbearing in historical judgment, and not, for example, blame former ages for religious intolerance, since they had no experience to show that toleration, although "paradoxical" in principle, is "salutary" in practice. We should judge of other times by the maxims prevailing in those times. To put it more generally, "the world is still too young" for it to be fully known what human nature is capable of or the effect of changes in men's "education, customs, or principles." [24]

Hume's views on politics have often been characterized as "Tory." For example, Thomas Jefferson held Hume's *History of England* responsible for undermining the principles of the free English government and spreading "universal toryism over the land." Hume would reply, of course, that what was offensive was his refusal to sacrifice historical truth to "the plaguey prejudices of Whiggism." His theoretical teaching concerning the nature, objects, and proper form of government has seemed to be very close to that of the great "Whig" philosopher, Locke. Yet if Hume was philosophically a "Whig," he was, as he put it, "a very sceptical one." This appears most obviously perhaps in his attack on the "fashionable system of politics" and the "creed" of the Whig party, the social-contract theory, and in his warning against and distrust of innovation.

The social-contract theory as Hume understood it taught that the powers of government are derived from the consent of the governed, that the obligation to obedience is based on the exchange of promises in the contract setting up government, and that subjects are released from their obligation when government becomes oppressive and thus breaks the promises made on its side. One argument against this theory is the following: The original motive of the duty to keep promises is the same as the original motive of the duty to obey rulers; promises serve our interest one way and government another. The latter duty does not then depend on the former. If promises had never been invented, government would still be necessary. Indeed, so far is government from depending on fidelity to promises that government was established in large part to enforce that fidelity.

Hume's principal objection is that the contract theory is contrary to the practice and sentiment of all mankind. He will concede that government in its first beginning must have been founded on consent. Men are very nearly equal in physical strength, and, until educated, even in mind; none could subject a multitude to his rule by force. Subjection to government could have arisen only when men voluntarily gave up their natural liberty and submitted to be ruled for the sake of peace and order. And this may be called an "original contract." But no government of which we have any record has been formed by the voluntary consent of the people; their beginnings are rather conquest or usurpation. As a rule, it is precisely when a change of government occurs that the people are least consulted.

The natural sentiments of all men contradict the contract theory. So far are rulers from regarding their authority as based on the consent of the ruled that they are inclined to treat that view of things as seditious. And the ruled usually think of themselves as born to obedience to a particular government.

So Hume opposes Locke's version of the modern natural-law teaching. But he opposes it from a position of fundamental agreement with its intention. The aim is to order political society in such a way that its ends are served by the natural action of the passions, without excessive reliance on extraordinary goodness, *i.e.,* on chance. As Hume says, "All plans of government which suppose great reformation in the manners of mankind are plainly imaginary." Now Hume's objection to the contract theory is precisely that it supposes such a reformation of manners. It overestimates the power of reason, or more precisely, it too readily assumes that men will correctly perceive and steadily follow their real interests. If they did, no government would in fact exist except on the basis of consent. But since they do not, other foundations must be admitted and allowed to be just. The contract theory, which is intended to be consonant with the passions of men, leads to conclusions that are contrary to universal experience and sentiment. For example, it denies the legitimacy of absolute monarchy, which is as "common" and "natural" a form of government as any.

The contract theory teaches that when rulers become so oppressive as no longer to provide for the security and protection of the ruled, the latter are no longer bound to submit. Hume agrees, as we have seen. But the doctrine of an original contract is not needed to reach this conclusion in theory, nor to assure it in practice. In such extreme cases men can be counted on to resist, without reference to any theory; the doctrine of passive obedience is as remote from their common sentiments as that of the social contract. The latter is, however, not only unnecessary but even pernicious. In the normal course of events the duty of the ruled is "blind submission." Yet the contract theory draws our attention from the general rule and directs it to the exceptions, exceptions we may be "but too much inclined of ourselves to embrace and extend." A voluntary allegiance is a precarious allegiance.

The bonds of allegiance ought not to be dissolved but held tight. Human society is a continuing body, gaining and losing members every moment, and hence stability in government is essential. It is necessary for the sake of peace and order that there be government and rulers. It is desirable of course that the form of government be good and that the rulers be suitable. But to make the superiority of a form of government or the suitability of a particular ruler the overriding standard is to open the door to that very strife and disorder that government is meant to exclude. Hence the claims of the established order should be given the greatest weight.[25]

Every government, Hume says, is founded on opinion. The main support of the rule of the few over the many, *i.e.,* of the weak over the strong, is the opinion that those in authority have a right to that authority. This opinion is usually the fruit of time and habit. Custom is the great guide of human life; most men never think of inquiring into the reasons for the authority of the form of government to which they have become habituated. Or, if they should, they are satisfied to be told that it has prevailed for a long time and that they are treading in the path of their forebears. "Antiquity always begets the opinion of right." That foundation of government truly in accordance with men's natural inclinations is not contract but custom.

From the above consideration it appears that there are limits to what can be done in the way of innovation and, more important, since novelty, too, has its charms, to what ought to be done. Violent innovation is never justified. To shake the authority of custom and antiquity gives it not to reason, which is an uncertain guide with little sway over man, but to every man's private interest, disguised as reason.

The wise statesman therefore "will bear a reverence to what carries the marks of age." In attempting to improve a constitution he will adapt his innovations to the "ancient fabric," so as not to disturb society. His caution may be reinforced by reflection on the limits of human foresight. Political measures have many consequences that cannot be foretold; one must be guided by experience; one must learn of errors by feeling their inconvenience when it appears. Time not only strengthens political institutions; it also perfects them.[26]

Hume begins, we see, from the most fundamental principles of the modern natural-law teaching, and draws consequences that are to a large extent like those of Locke. At the same time, and working from the same principles, he rejects important elements of Locke's teaching and becomes a strong advocate of conservatism. His political doctrine thus presents something of a paradoxical appearance and perhaps contains a certain tension, reflected in his maxim that there is "nothing of greater importance in every state than the preservation of the ancient government, especially if it be a free one." [27]

NOTES

1. David Hume, *Treatise of Human Nature*, ed. L. H. Selby-Bigge (Oxford: Clarendon, 1896), I. i. 1; *Enquiry Concerning Human Understanding*, ed. L. A. Selby-Bigge (Oxford: Clarendon, 1894), 2.

2. *Human Understanding*, 4. I. first two pars; an earlier and less satisfactory statement is in *Treatise*, I. iii. 1.

3. *Treatise*, I. iii. 11, beginning, and 12. 5.

4. *Ibid.*, 2, 3, 4, 6, 7, and 14; *Human Understanding*, 4, 5, and 7.

5. *Treatise*, I. iv. 2 and 6.

6. *Ibid.*, iii. 13.

7. *Ibid.*, 8. 13 and 14; 12. 3.

8. *Ibid.*, I. iii. 15 and 16.

9. *Ibid.*, III. i. 1; also *Enquiry Concerning the Principles of Morals*, appendix I.

10. *Treatise*, II. iii. 3.

11. *Ibid.*, III, i. 1, last par.

12. *Ibid.*, next to last par., and 2.

13. *Principles of Morals*, 10. 1. and 10. 5; *Treatise*, III. iii. 1.

14. *Principles of Morals*, appendix II; *Treatise*, II. iii. 3, last par., and 9. 8.

15. *Treatise*, II. iii. 3. 6.

16. *Ibid.*, III. ii. 1, next to last par.; cf. *Principles of Morals*, appendix IV.

17. *Treatise*, III. iii. 8 next to last par., and iii. 1. 14 ff.; *Principles of Morals*, 9. I.

18. *Principles of Morals*, appendix I, last par.; *Treatise*, III. i. 2. 1; I. iii. 8. 12.

19. *Treatise*, III. ii. 2–5; *Principles of Morals*, 3.

20. *Treatise*, III. ii. 7; *Essays*, "Of the Origin of Government"; *Principles of Morals*, 4.

21. *Treatise*, III. ii. 1.

22. *Ibid.*, 2. 13; 5. 9; 6. 1.

23. *Ibid.*, 9; *Essays*, "Of Passive Obedience."

24. *Essays*, "On the Independency of Parliament," "That Politics May Be Reduced to a Science," "Of the Origin of Government," "Idea of a Perfect Commonwealth," "Of Civil Liberty"; *History of England*, end of chap. xxiii, Appendix to the Reign of James I. On religion see *History*, beginning of chap. xxix, and chap. lxvi (1678).

25. *Essays*, "Of the Original Contract," "Of Passive Obedience," "Idea of a Perfect Commonwealth"; *Treatise*, III. ii. 8–10.

26. *Essays*, "Of the First Principles of Government," "Of the Original Contract," "Idea of a Perfect Commonwealth," first two pars, "Of the Coalition of Parties," par. 5, "Of the Rise and Progress of the Arts and Sciences," par. 25.

27. *Essays*, "Of the Liberty of the Press," par. 6.

READINGS

A. Hume, David. *Enquiry Concerning Human Understanding*. Secs 2, 3, 4, 5, 6, 7.

Hume, David. *Treatise of Human Nature*. Bk III, parts i and ii.

Hume, David. *Essays*. "Of the Origin of Government," "Of the Original Contract," "Of the First Principles of Government," "Idea of a Perfect Commonwealth." (A good selection of Hume's essays on politics is found in *David Hume's Political Essays*. Ed. Charles W. Hendel. New York: Liberal Arts Press, 1953.)

B. Hume, David. *Treatise of Human Nature*. Bk I, parts i and iii.
Hume, David. *Enquiry Concerning the Principles of Morals*. Secs 1, 3, 4, 5, 9; appendices I, II, and III.
Hume, David. *Essays*. "Of the Liberty of the Press," "That Politics May Be Reduced to a Science," "On the Independency of Parliament," "Whether the British Government Inclines More to Absolute Monarchy, or to a Republic," "Of Parties in General," "Of the Parties of Great Britain," "Of Civil Liberty," "Of the Rise and Progress of the Arts and Sciences," "Of the Balance of Power," "Of Some Remarkable Customs," "Of Passive Obedience," "Of the Coalition of Parties," "Of the Protestant Succession."

JEAN-JACQUES ROUSSEAU

1712–1778

Rousseau begins the *Social Contract* with the celebrated words: "Man was born free, and everywhere he is in chains. . . . How did this change come to pass? I do not know. What can make it legitimate? I believe I can resolve this question." With this statement he poses the political problem in its most radical form and at the same time suggests the revolutionary principle that almost all existing regimes are illegitimate. Civil society enchains man and makes him a slave to law or other men whereas he was, as man, born to freedom, to the right to behave as he pleases. What is more, civil society, as it is now constituted, has no claim on the moral adhesion of its subjects; it is unjust. Rousseau's political thought points away from the present in both directions: to man's happy freedom of the past and to the establishment of a regime in the future which can appeal to the will of those under its authority. It is the task of the philosopher to make clear what man's nature truly is and, on this basis, to define the conditions of a good political order. Rousseau's thought has an externally paradoxical character, seeming at the same time to desire contradictories—virtue and soft sentiment, political society and the state of nature, philosophy and ignorance—but it is remarkably consistent, the contradictions reflecting contradictions in the nature of things.[1] Rousseau undertook to clarify the meaning of modern theory and practice, and in so doing he brought to light radical consequences of modernity of which men were not previously aware.

Modern politics, according to Rousseau, are based on a partial understanding of man. The modern state, the Leviathan, is directed to its own preservation and, consequently, to that of its subjects. It is, hence, totally negative, taking into account only the condition of happiness, life, while forgetting happiness itself. Any political system which takes into account only one side of human existence cannot satisfy men's longing for fulfillment or call forth their full loyalty. And it is further Rousseau's argument that the modern state based on self-preservation constitutes a way of life precisely contrary to that which would make men happy. The life of the big nations is characterized by commerce and, consequently, by the distinction between rich and poor. Each man can pursue his gain within the framework laid down by the state. Money is the standard of human worth, and virtue is forgotten. Calculation of private advantage is the basis of human relations; this may not lead to perpetual war, but it destroys the foundations of trust and easy sociability and leads to selfishness and poor citizenship. But, most of all, because there is scarcity and the needs and desires of all men in society cannot be satisfied, the rich are protected and the poor oppressed. Civil society is a state of mutual interdependence among men, but the men are bad and the majority are forced to give up their own wills to work for the satisfaction of the few. And, since these few control the laws, the many do not even enjoy the protection for which they are supposed to have entered into society. The result of the oversimplified and one-sided concentration on preservation is the destruction of the good life which is the only purpose of preservation.[2]

This is the basis of Rousseau's attack on the Enlightenment. The progress of the arts and sciences was believed to be the condition, perhaps the sufficient condition, of a progress of civil society and of an increase in human happiness. Prejudice would be vanquished by learning, manners softened by the arts, nature conquered by science. Sound government could be assured by grounding it on the passions of those who take part in it. The hopes of the Enlightenment are those of modern man, according to Rousseau, and it is the picture of human society painted by the Enlightenment that is the starting point for his revolution in political thought. Rousseau not only denies that progress in the arts and sciences improves morality but asserts, on the contrary, that such progress always leads to moral corruption. The arts and sciences require an atmosphere of luxury and leisure in order to flourish. They themselves emerge, in general, from vices of the soul; at best idle curiosity is their source, and most often they come from the desire for unnecessary comforts which only weaken men and satisfy unnecessary wants. The society dominated by the arts and sciences is one full of inequality, both because the talents needed to pursue them become grounds of distinction among men, and because great sums of money are needed to support them, as well as workers to man the implements devised by those arts and sciences. Society is transformed to support the arts and the sciences and their products, and this very transformation creates a life full of vain self-regard and injustice.[3]

The first stage of Rousseau's reflection leads to admiration of the past. The situation of modern man is new, but in classical antiquity models of civil society can be found in which men were free and governed themselves. The old republic, the *polis,* above all Sparta, was the refuge of real men and provided long periods of peace, stability, and independence. Rousseau revives the quarrel between the ancients and the moderns in restating the case for the ancient city. That city was not founded on comfort, self-preservation, or science but on virtue—the science of simple souls. Virtue in the classic sense meant good citizenship and the qualities that necessarily accompany it. Only on the basis of courage, self-sacrifice, and moderation can a city in which the great majority govern themselves be founded. Rousseau is a republican; he is a republican because he believes men are naturally free and equal. Only a civil society which is a reflection of that nature can hope to make men happy. The requirements of a free society were best met by the Greek cities and Rome, although they were not perfect, and Rousseau's ultimate solution is an improvement upon them. They were small so that everyone could know everyone else and hence have both common interests and trust. They were governed by the people so that the rulers and ruled were one and the same; there were thus no fundamental differences of interest between governors and governed. The laws were of ancient date and men grew used to their heavy weight by force of long habit. The rule of law is necessary to civil society, and just laws require a stern moral code to support their burden equally; only strict mutual surveillance and habits of justice can ensure their operation. The primary consideration of the government is the virtue of the citizens. The civil society which is to function as a society must be a unity in which the individuals give up their private wishes for the sake of the whole. Society cannot be conceived of as the balance of conflicting interests if men are to be free and not the pawns of interest groups in power. Not enlightenment but severe moral education is the prerequisite of sound civil society. Rousseau's taste and his analysis of the injustice of modern society lead him back to Greece.[4]

But he is led even further. His teaching is not merely a revival of those of Plato and Aristotle. If he admires the practice of antiquity, he does not accept its theory. No political teaching can suffice which merely describes how to construct a stable order or how to make the citizens content. It must also legitimate the authority exercised by the government; it must state the grounds of the citizen's duties and rights. The central political question is always: What is justice? and this leads necessarily to the question: What is natural? For, outside the limits of the positive law, when the problem is to found or reform a regime, the only standard can be nature and, more specifically, the nature of man. And it is concerning this question that Rousseau differs from his predecessors, or, rather, he joins the moderns in their denial that man is by nature political. Following the current of modern science in general, as well as of political science, Rousseau rejects the notion that man is directed by nature toward an end, the end of political life. The city or the state is a purely human construction originating in the desire for self-preservation. As such, man is conceivable without political society, although in this later age it may have become necessary for him.

Justice, as it can be seen in nations, consists in maintaining the privileges of those in positions of power. All known states are full of inequalities of birth, wealth, and honor. These inequalities can perhaps be justified in terms of the preservation of the regime, but that does not make them more tolerable for those who do not enjoy them. The laws institute and protect these differences of rank. If there are natural inequalities, those existing in the nations do not reflect them; they are the results of human deeds and of chance. They cannot be morally binding on those oppressed by their weight.

If civil society is not natural, then one must go to a time prior to civil society to find man as he is naturally. This investigation is necessary in order to determine the origins of the state; if civil society is not natural, it is conventional; therefore, if there is to be any legitimacy in the laws of civil society, its conventions must be founded on that first nature. Rousseau makes an attempt to describe man in the *state of nature*. Other modern thinkers who agreed that civil society is conventional tried to do the same thing and to ground political right on a prepolitical natural right. But, according to Rousseau, they never succeeded in reaching the primitive state of nature. They were not radical enough in their own rejection of the naturalness of civil society. They denied that attachment to the common good and the political community are parts of human perfection, and they tried to derive the rules of politics from the individual unattached to any state. But they, in describing that individual, described in fact the man living in civil society. They were cryptoteleologists in the sense that they tried to understand man as he is naturally from the point of view of his complete development in civil society. But, if man is truly not a political and social being, then his nature must have been transformed in order for him ever to have come to the point where he could live in civil society. The earlier thinkers, in stripping man of his social nature, saw in him many characteristics which are results of communal living, for example, envy, distrust, unlimited desire for acquisition, and reason. To know the natural man requires an almost superhuman effort of the mind, for we have no contact with him, we are civilized men worn by the corrosion of civil society.

There is a road from natural man to civil man, and the passage of that road is not like that from embryo to man where the first step is directed to the last and illuminated by it. The movement is not a necessary one, so we are in need of a history of the human species. For the first time, history becomes an integral part of political theory. Man is a different being at different epochs, although for Rousseau he still has a primeval nature which dominates all transformations brought about by time. Rousseau's awareness of the disproportion between natural man and civil man, which is implied in a rejection of the naturalness of civil society, forces him to an investigation of primitive man. The other teachings which do not discover the truly natural lead only to a deeper enslavement to the vices engendered by civil society. The investigation he undertakes proceeds in two ways: the first is by means of what we would today call anthropology. The primitive, which was formerly despised as inferior and imperfect, now seems to throw light on that earlier period and hence becomes an object of serious scientific interest. But, because the so-called savages or primitives already live in societies, they are no more than signposts on the road back. More important is the second way: introspection to uncover the first and simplest movements of the human soul.

Since man is not primarily political and social, he must be divested of all qualities that are connected with life in a community if we are to understand him as he is by nature. The first and most important of these is reason. Reason depends upon speech, and speech implies social life. Hence, the definition of man can no longer be that he is a rational animal. At first one can say only that he is an animal like other animals. He roams the forest in search of nourishment. He seeks to preserve his being, but he is not a ravenous beast naturally hostile to every other member of his species as Hobbes understood him to be. Hobbes could only assert this by attributing to the first men the unlimited desires of political man. Actually this first animal-man has only the simplest needs of the sort that are usually easily satisfied. He cannot think far into the future. He is not frightened of death because he cannot conceive it; he only avoids pain. He has no need to fight his fellow creatures except when there is a scarcity of the bare necessities. He is idle by nature and stirs himself only to satisfy his natural wants. Only a being with foresight who has needs beyond the natural seeks wealth. Locke's industrious natural man is also a construction drawn from already developed society. It is in this idleness that the true pleasure of the animal is enjoyed; he senses the sweetness of his own existence. He has only two fundamental passions: the desire to preserve himself and a certain pity or sympathy for the sufferings of others of his kind. The latter prevents him from being brutal to other men when such "humaneness" does not conflict with his own preservation. He has no virtues because he needs none. One cannot say that he has morality; whatever he does, he does because it pleases him to do so. But he has a certain goodness; he does no harm.

Considered in this way, it may be said that all men are by nature equal. They have, practically speaking, only physical existences; if there are differences in strength, they have little meaning because the individuals have no contact with one another. From man's natural state can be derived no right of one man to rule another. The right of the stronger is no right, first, because the enslaved can always revolt in his turn; no moral obligation is established by a stronger man subjugating a weaker one. Second, one man could never enslave another in the state of nature because men had no need of one another, and it would be impossible to hold a slave. Nor does the family provide a source for political right because in the state of nature there is no family. The relations between man and woman are casual, and the mother instinctively takes care of the children until they are strong enough to fend for themselves; there is no authority or duty involved. The state of nature is a state of equality and independence.

There are two characteristics which distinguish man from the other animals and take the place of rationality as the defining quality of humanity. The first is freedom of the will. Man is not a being determined by his instincts; he can choose, accept, and reject. He can defy nature. And the consciousness of this liberty is the evidence of the spirituality of his soul. He is aware of his own power. The second, and least questionable characteristic of man, is his perfectibility. Man is the only being which can gradually improve its faculties and pass this improvement on to the whole species. All the superior faculties of the mind seen in civilized man are proofs of this. They are now a permanent part of the species, but they did not belong to it naturally. On the basis of these two fundamental characteristics of man, it can be said that natural man is distinguished by having almost no nature at all, by being pure potentiality. There are no ends, only possibilities. Man has no determination; he is the free animal. This constitution leads him away from his original contentment toward the misery of civil life, but it also renders him capable of mastering himself and nature.

Natural man, then, is a lazy beast, enjoying the sentiment of his own existence, concerned with his preservation and pitying the sufferings of his fellow creatures, free and perfectible. His motion toward the civilized state is a result of unforeseeable accidents which leave unalterable marks on him. He is forced into closer contact with other men by natural catastrophes. He develops speech and begins to maintain a permanent establishment with his woman and children. He is softer and his needs are now greater, but his existence is intrinsically pleasant. There are, as yet, no laws, no state, no inequality. The needs of men are not such as to make them competitors. But men have at last become dependent on one another, and the first experiences of cooperation or common ends bring to consciousness what obligation or morality might be. Man's freedom still comes first, and he can withdraw from any engagement he might have made when it is to his advantage; but he also sees the advantage in getting help from others and the necessity of doing his share if he is to receive in kind. However, he is still so independent as to be unwilling to sacrifice any of his freedom in order to guarantee the fulfillment of contracts.

In addition to the first consciousness of moral obligation, man in this new communal situation begins to practice vengeance. Because men are in daily contact with one another there is more occasion for friction; and, because there is no law, each man is judge in his own case. The natural pity which was the root of humanity in the state of nature is weakened as a result of the conflict between self-love and pity; in any such case the former always wins. But it is not these battles which cause men to form civil society; it is the foundation of private property. The founder of political society and the man who brought the greatest evils to mankind was the first who said, "This land belongs to me." The cultivation of the soil is the source of private property. Only what a man has made or that to which he has added his work can in any sense be said to belong to him. With the foundation of private property forethought also arises. When the fields and streams of themselves provided nourishment, clothing, and housing, man did not think to the future. But the farmer must do so, and the desire to increase and protect his crops both multiplies his desires and causes him to seek power.

And, further, in the foundation of private property, we have also discovered the origin of inequality. For different men have different skills and talents which enable some of them to increase their possessions. Soon all available land is enclosed, and some have more than they need, others less. Men recognize property as something real, but their own need is also something real. There is no judge between these different claims, and there is no natural law to resolve them because the situation is man-made, not natural. A state of war necessarily ensues between the haves and the have-nots.

At this stage man has developed all his powers, and he has made himself miserable. The greatest change in his nature is that formerly he lived entirely for himself within himself. Now he lives for others, not only because he is physically dependent on them but because he has learned to compare himself with them. His soul has become enslaved to other men, and this is more of a bond than his need of them to help him satisfy his desires. He seeks money and honor instead of reflecting on his real wishes. Man has become vain, and in the search to gratify that vanity there are endless sources of quarrel. Vanity (*amour-propre*) has taken the place of the original self-love (*amour de soi*); instead of physical desires which must be appeased, he is now possessed by infinite yearnings for possessions he can never use and a glory he despises as soon as it is gained.

It is now that someone among the rich, aware of the constant danger to his property and the wretched condition of the people, suggests a contract for the establishment of civil society. This clever man sees the possibility of guaranteeing his questionable right to property by the consent of other men and of maintaining peace by a mutual pact to protect each and all against aggression. The natural passion of pity has been extinguished, and the only substitute for it in the new conditions is a morality defining men's duties, backed up by a recognized authority. Nature no longer suffices. The frightful state of war makes this step necessary and ensures the acquiescence of the poor. But it is a swindle. The rich give an appearance of legitimacy to their control of their property and are able to enjoy it peacefully. The inequality which has gradually come into being is made lawful, and the oppression of the poor is maintained by public force. Hobbes is right when he says that the men who are constrained to found civil society are hostile to one another and afflicted by infinite desires. He is wrong only in asserting that this is the nature of man. There was an earlier state which defined the essential character of man's freedom and which makes it impossible for him legitimately to deliver himself over to the will of anyone else. Locke is right when he asserts that the purpose of civil society is to protect property. He also is wrong only in asserting that property is natural to man, and that the inequalities stabilized by civil society conform to real standards of justice. Every man has a natural right to preserve himself and to act in accordance with this right. Civil society has no natural ground to legitimate a command which contradicts the natural right. But all civil societies issue such commands; natural right cannot be their legitimation. Man is naturally free, and civil society takes his freedom away from him; he is dependent on the law, and the law is made in favor of the rich—at least in its origin it was meant to favor them.[5]

So the political problem is posed in the presentation of the history of its birth. Man, free by nature, needs government to organize and regulate the life in common to which he has become committed. But precisely because he has developed terrible passions which necessitate government, a just government is rendered factually difficult because the men who form the laws are under the influence of those passions, and the citizens continue to possess those passions and have every interest in altering the government for the sake of their satisfaction. Only the most severe moral education can obviate this difficulty, a moral education almost never to be found. And, from the point of view of right, civil society demands a devotion to the common good, a subordination of the individual to the whole, while man by nature is a selfish, independent animal. At any point where he senses a conflict between society and himself he is naturally and properly motivated by his selfish interest. How can civil society rightfully call upon a man to sacrifice himself for it? How can one selfish individual demand that another obey him? No contract can bind to the point of sacrificing that for which it was made, and no man willfully contracts away the freedom which is the core of his being.[6]

Civil society cannot be grounded on natural right; nature dictates only self-interest. Nature is too low to comprehend civil society; the study of nature leads to its rejection as the standard, at least for society. This was what Rousseau's predecessors had not understood, according to him. Civil society requires morality because man's natural character does not suffice to bind him, *in foro interno,* to the more stringent demands of political life, and his newly inflamed passions make him even less fit for society. A society which was based on each man's calculation of his interest would only cause those passions to develop further, for his interest is already determined by his passions, and would lead inevitably to tyranny or anarchy. Hence, since morality is not natural to man, he must create it. It is the basis for this project that Rousseau sets down in the *Social Contract;* in it he tries to resolve the problem posed by the conflict between the individual and the state, or self-interest and duty. Nothing can bind man's freedom, but civil society is bondage. The act of establishing civil society is identical with that of establishing morality or binding commitments to others. Since nature does not provide the basis for the agreement, it must be a convention. Traditionally, conventions were considered to be of a lower order than natural laws, precisely because they are man-made and changeable; conventions differ everywhere and seem to be the result of arbitrary will and chance. The man who obeys convention would seem to be the prisoner of other men. But, if man is free, his capacity to make conventions is the sign of that freedom; his will is not limited by nature. To this extent, man the maker of morality and the state is the fulfillment of the notion of man as the free, undetermined being. If the simply arbitrary character of conventions could be avoided, then one could say that a conventional civil society is at once the fulfillment of man's nature and worthy of his respect and obedience.

As Rousseau puts it in his own forceful formulations: "[The difficulty is] to find a form of association which defends and protects with all the common force the person and the goods of each associate; by which each, uniting himself to all, obeys nevertheless only himself and remains as free as before." [7] The solution is that every man give himself entirely to the community with all of his rights and property. The deposit is made with the whole, with no individual; in this way no one puts himself into the hands of another. The contract is equal, for each gives all. No one reserves any rights by which he can claim to judge of his own conduct; hence there is no source of conflict between individual and state, for the individual has contracted to accept the law as the absolute standard for his acts. The social contract forms an artificial person, the state, which has a will like the natural person; what appears necessary or desirable to that person is willed by it and what is willed by the whole is law. Law is the product of the *general will*. Each individual participates in legislation, but law is general, and the individual in his role as legislator must make laws which can conceivably be applied to all members of the community. He makes his will into law but now, as opposed to what he did in the state of nature, he must generalize his will. As legislator he can only will what all could will; as citizen he obeys what he himself willed as legislator. Although men of diverse tastes and understandings go to make up the sovereign legislative body, none can impose his will on the others unless the others could have willed it themselves. The law is produced by the will of each thinking in terms of all. The primary function of the social contract is to constitute a regime which can express the general will.

Civil society is simply the agreement among a group of men that each shall become a part of the general will and be obedient to it. As a result, each remains as free as he was before, because he obeys nothing but his transformed will. The conventional liberty of civil society satisfies the primary natural right of man—freedom. As long as the society is organized so that the laws can be made impersonally, no man can make a claim against it on the basis of natural right. Man in the state of nature had a right to all that he willed; neither the will nor the reason of other men could legitimately issue commands to him. There is no eternal reason which can and should control our actions. Each man has his own judgments based on his personal experience and affected by his particular will. This fact is reflected in the notion of the general will; man is a being who wills, and the capacity to do what he wills is the essence of freedom. Willing is, as such, independent of what is willed. The natural law, or any other rational command directed toward the common good, is a limitation on freedom drawn from a questionable source. Therefore, the general will contains no specific directives; it can determine itself to do whatsoever occurs to it; it is in itself empty; it is pure will. This is another aspect of the preservation of the natural freedom. The general will is formal, and the only thing which distinguishes it from the particular will is that it can only will what all could conceivably will. This sets some limitation on what society as a whole can do, as opposed to the complete license of nature, and Rousseau believes that these purely formal limitations are sufficient to guarantee decency, or that the generalized will is in itself moral. He considers that he has discovered the true principle of morality that others had only sensed and had tried to base on dubious and arbitrary interpretations of nature or on revealed religion. Man's freedom, which seems to be independent of, and opposed to, moral rule is the sole source of morality. With this discovery, Rousseau completes the break with the political teaching of classical antiquity begun by Machiavelli and Hobbes. His immediate predecessors had maintained the notion of natural law which limited the human freedom which they themselves taught.[8]

The movement from the natural state to the civil state produces a very great change in man. Formerly he was an amiable beast; now he has become a moral being. All of his capacities come into play, his ideas are developed and extended, and his sentiments are ennobled. In the state of nature man acted only from instinct; now he must consider his action in relation to principle so that the words *choice* and *freedom* take on a moral sense. If a man continues to act according to his private will, he can be said to degrade himself to the level of the animals. He gives up his freedom, both in the sense that he is a mere tool of his passions and in the sense that he destroys the possibility of a just society and hence puts himself in the power of others. Society is justified, therefore, in forcing him to be free, in constraining him to exercise his will in the

proper way. Education and punishment are the instruments of this constraint. But the truly human dignity emerges in the conscious choice of
the general will over the private.

The social contract constitutes the sovereign. Rousseau uses the
term "sovereign" to indicate that the source of all legitimacy is in the
people at large as opposed to the monarch or the aristocrats or any other
segment. There must be a government, and it may be monarchic, aristocratic, or democratic, but its right to rule is derived from the people
and exercised only so long as it pleases them. Since nature and revealed
religion have been set aside, only the voice of the people can establish
law; every enactment must return to them, to their will. The will of
the people is the only law. The government is obedient to the law alone,
and each citizen is constantly a member of the lawmaking body. Every
citizen finds himself in a double relation to the state, as a lawgiver, in
so far as he is a member of the sovereign, and as a subject of the law, an
individual who must obey.

Several consequences follow from the fact that the sovereign is the
only source of legitimacy. In the first place, sovereignty is inalienable.
No man or group of men can be given the right to make laws in the
place of the citizen body at large. They would be acting according to
their individual wills, and their enactments would not be binding. This
means that representative government is a bad form of government.
Others take the responsibility from the citizens, and they lose their citizen virtue as well as their freedom. If a nation is so large that the citizens
cannot hope to meet in a common body, then representation becomes
an unfortunate necessity, a necessity which weakens the expression of
the general will. If any legitimacy is to be preserved in such a case, the
representatives must be elected by local assemblies in which all citizens
meet, and the representatives must be given complete instructions. They
must have no independent judgment, and for every new question which
arises they must return to those who elected them. Otherwise there is
no general will. The general will requires constant consultation.[9] It can
be consulted only by vote, so that the system suggested by Rousseau
turns out to be majoritarian. But it is not a simple majoritarianism; the
laws can only be properly instituted if the citizens possess the virtue to
suppress their private wills. The individuals must be citizens in the
classical sense, and this requires a very severe, self-imposed morality.
Rousseau is not a libertarian in the modern sense of the word; every
man cannot live as he likes, for that would end the possibility of agreement and destroy the sources of the moral energy necessary to self-
control. Rousseau despised democracy as it is usually practiced because
it means a wild anarchy of self-interest. A formalistic insistence on the

vote of the people is meaningless without the establishment of its moral preconditions. Sparta was right in its concentration on the habits of its citizens as over against the modern laxity which leaves the private life to the individuals. The tastes and manners of the citizens affect all their judgments, and certain habits make free government altogether impossible. Rousseau re-establishes the Greek city but brings to light the true principle which motivated its insistence on austere virtue: virtue is not itself the end; it is a means to freedom.

Moreover, in addition to virtue, the expression of the general will must be guaranteed by the suppression of faction. Each citizen alone cannot hope to have his private will prevail and recognizes that if everyone voted according to his passions there would be no order. It is only when he belongs to a group large enough to influence the vote decisively that his private will overcomes his sense of the general will in seeing what he personally can gain. Thus, parties must be forbidden, and extremes of wealth and poverty must be prevented. In so far as possible, informed citizens must vote as individuals, and the result of such a vote can be considered a general will.

Rousseau was aware of the tension that exists between the stability that law requires and the constant reconsideration implied in the assembly of the people. There is no law or institution which cannot be revoked if the state is going to be governed by the actual wills of its present citizens. Every assembly must begin with the question: Does the sovereign please to preserve the present form of government?[10] But the idea that the law is a product of one's will weakens the almost religious awe that is necessary to maintain the respect for law. Old institutions and the sacredness of the law are restraints on the expression of selfish interest; the man who never conceives of the possibility of altering the established way is more likely to behave according to the commands he never questioned than the one who is accustomed to easy change. This is a difficulty never entirely resolved by Rousseau, but which he attempts to do away with by making the process of change difficult, by making the individuals who suggest it responsible for its effects, and by an education in the respect for good institutions. But the possibility of change cannot be obviated if the citizens are to be conscious of their freedom and able to judge what preserves it and what destroys it.

The sovereign is by its nature also indivisible. The notion of the general will makes it impossible for there to be a separation of powers which is anything more than a delegation for the execution of functions previously defined by the sovereign and ultimately dependent upon it. The sovereign power is a unity which cannot be divided without destroying it. No authority is anything but derivative from it.

The social contract is an agreement to form a civil society and establishes the instrument of authority—the sovereign. But the institution of this body does not give the body motion; the new society must have activities and ends; it needs laws. The character of the laws is undetermined by the contract; the contract only sets up the legitimate organ of legislation. The particular enactments can vary according to the interests of the society. The laws must, like the general will, be only general. They cannot refer to particular persons or acts. If they did, the persons involved would not partake in the general will; they would be alien to it, since their wills did not take part in forming the law. The law can establish regulations distinguishing diverse duties, honors, and classes, but it cannot say to whom these regulations should apply. It considers the citizens as a body and acts as abstract.

The laws must have sanctions imposed by men, since there are no other sources of them on earth; these sanctions must include the power of life and death in so far as the vicious need repression. Otherwise society would be of advantage to the unjust rather than the just. And there is no limitation on the scope of the law. Whatever does not touch the needs of civil society itself should be left to the citizen's free determination, but there is no means of establishing in advance what will be necessary for society's preservation. There are no reserved rights on behalf of the citizens. If there were, the citizens could withdraw from the contract at critical moments. And, since civil society entails a whole way of life, the apparently most trivial matters of private enjoyment can have a political effect. The manners of the society are of as much or more concern than the institutions of government, because manners underlie institutions and give them their force.[11]

To find a code of laws which fits a people, which is complete, and which will be obeyed is not a task for primitive men; such a code cannot arise from the mere gathering together of a group of men who constitute themselves as a sovereign. The private wills are still too dominant; they are not repressed by the habit of civil life. Practically speaking, it is only after a people has lived with its laws and habits for a long time that it can be said to be a people, a group with common interests and a general will, something more than an agglomeration. It is only afterwards that the body of the people is prepared to judge if its laws are good. But the society needs laws from the beginning if the strongest are not to take over and impose their private wills on the mass of the people and make slaves of them. Hence, for the formation of a real civil society a legislator is needed. This extraordinary man must discover the rules appropriate to the society in question, and he must force or persuade the people to accept them. He himself cannot be a member of the state, and

he has no authority; he presents the laws which must be approved ultimately by the general will. His is a labor of love from which he can win
only honor. Rousseau has in view men like Moses and Lycurgus who
established a people and along with it justice. He returns in this, too, to
a classic view in that he does not believe in piecemeal reform or in the
gradual automatic triumph of reason in politics. Conscious, statesmanlike action is necessary; the whole order must be founded at one time
according to rational plan, and only greatness can compass the task.
The greatest political task is the establishment of a regime, and nothing
can do away with the need for extraordinary virtue to accomplish it.
The very greatness of the legislator makes his success more difficult,
because he cannot be understood by those whom he wishes to convince.
He must learn the language of the vulgar, and that is chiefly the language of divine inspiration or religion. The people can be impressed
and persuaded by the accents of piety and the semblance of miracle. This
is one of the few ways to still the voice of private interest long enough
for the many to learn to appreciate the advantages of law. Religion is
used for political purposes and, in Rousseau's view, should not become
independent of political control. The religion should not contain teachings which do not conduce to the ends of the regime. Rousseau was
perfectly aware that impostors could play the role of legislator and that
the "strong man" is always a danger. But in looking to the origins of
regimes, he could see only means such as these to establish orderly and
legitimate ones. Regimes are made by men, and good ones require
great men and unusual means.[12]

Although the formal conditions of legitimacy are the same everywhere, Rousseau wanted to preserve a realm for the activity of statesmanship. He knew that politics could not be made an abstract science
as some modern theory wanted it to be. He tried to combine the clarity
and certainty of modern political science with the flexibility of the
classical art of politics. The fact of difference of circumstance means
that many nations cannot enjoy liberty and that many others can only
have a diluted form of it. A regime that could be realized everywhere
would be of such a low order that the few who can enjoy a good one
would be deprived of it without the others gaining by it. Legislation
must be made at the right moment, and a primitive people uncorrupted
by decadent habits is most eligible for it. The climate and the territory,
its extent and character, must be taken into consideration. The traditions of the people and their manners determine the range of possibilities. The fact that the general will is formal allows for these differences. There is no doctrine of natural law which limits the statesman's
activities and forces him to mitigate his judgments about what most

conduces to the common good. That there are different peoples implies that the determinations of the general will will differ. The diversity of life is preserved, but man is not left without moral guidance; in the diversity there is the unity which is everywhere the same, the general will. But there are no universal substantive commands implied in the general will; a great variety of opposed principles can legitimately be emitted by it; it can make laws which lead to widely varying styles of life and action. According to the *Social Contract* and the political philosophy underlying it, there is no one best regime or scheme of laws. Different arrangements can equally well allow for the existence of a general will in different circumstances.[13]

The general will is only the expression of a desire that something be done. The force to do it is also necessary. This necessity brings into being the distinction between the legislative and the executive, between the sovereign and the government. Since the sovereign can legitimately make laws only about general objects, the application of the laws to particular acts or persons is not of its domain and belongs rather to the government. The government receives its instructions from the general will and uses its authority to determine the acts of the citizens according to the sense of the sovereign. It is the intermediary between sovereign and individual citizen and is totally derivative. This distinction is new in Rousseau and works a fundamental break with his predecessors, especially those of classical antiquity.[14] It prefigures the distinction between state and society so important today. For the classical thinkers the arrangement of the offices—the government—was the primary consideration. The form of government determined the form of society, and with a change of government a new society would be constituted. Loyalty was not owed to the country, the people, or the society but to the government. In Rousseau's scheme the existence of the sovereign prior to the existence of government means that the latter is only a secondary phenomenon from the point of view of right and fact. The contract constitutes the society which antedates the government and maintains itself in spite of changes in the government. Hence, the most interesting object of study is the society, and loyalty is owed primarily to it rather than to the government. The primary fact of politics is not the government of men; government is a necessary evil because men need direction in the exercise of their freedom. The less government, the better, and there is a great pre-occupation with limiting the scope of the government and preventing it from contradicting the general will. Government is always viewed with suspicion, and the citizens must be careful that the exercise of its functions does not unjustly inhibit them in the exercise of their liberty. The government institutes inequalities of rank and authority which are necessary to it, but those differences do not establish real differences of worth among the citizens who are all equal. The government is always completely dependent on the will of the people and can be reduced to its original equality with them.

It is easy to see how later thinkers were able to develop on this basis such notions as "the withering away of the state" without believing that the fundamental advantages of society would be lost; and it is less shocking to think of changes in government on this basis. The older tradition taught that the establishment of government is the fundamental act in the formation of a community, and that the destruction of government is equivalent to the destruction of society. Hence, the inequality which government implies is coeval with society, and it follows that the authority of government is not derivative from the people as a whole or the general will. The superior men do not owe their superiority to the people. This difference leads in Rousseau's thought to a certain deterioration in the respectability of government and more concentration on the rights of the citizens than on the effectiveness of execution.

Government must be powerful enough to dominate the particular wills of the citizens but not powerful enough to dominate the general will or the laws. The more inhabitants a country has, the more the particular wills are powerful, and the harder it is for the individuals to identify themselves with the community. Hence the government must be more vigorous in populous lands, especially when the extent of the territory is great. The more persons sharing the authority of government, the less vigorous the government; monarchy is the most vigorous of governments and democracy the least. It follows that difference of size of nations means that different sorts of government are required. One cannot speak of the best government. The difference between democracy, aristocracy, and monarchy is one of number, and consequently of vigor. The classic notion, that the difference is one of virtue and that the choice between the three forms of regime is the decisive political act, is tacitly denied by Rousseau. As a rule, aristocracy has the fewest inconveniences. Democracy requires too much virtue, is almost no government at all, and the identification of the collective private wills with the general will is too easy. Monarchy is too concentrated and the problems of succession are too great. Aristocracy is a sort of mean between the inconveniences of the two, but it can become the worst of regimes. There are three possible sorts of aristocracy: hereditary, natural, and elective. The first is the worst sort in Rousseau's view, based as it is on wealth and conventional inequality; and its members are under the delusion that their rights are independent of the will of the people.

They have a collective interest of class which divides the community. Contradicting the whole tradition of political philosophy, Rousseau denies that a true aristocracy is a politically identifiable class.[15] In primitive societies the best-equipped to rule are chosen almost naturally, and this is an excellent solution but inadequate for more developed societies. Election is the sole legitimate mode of selecting a limited number of governors, for it guarantees that they will be in constant submission to the general will.

In this way, aristocracy becomes little more than an expression of the fact that in most societies not everyone rules so that some limited number of men must be chosen. There are no criteria of birth or wealth for the selection of those few, and the aristocracy does not represent a way of life. Rousseau, of course, tries to make provision for the selection of the truly best and to avoid demagoguery, but his notion of aristocracy is not far from our present-day notion of popular or democratic government. Above all, no classes are allowed to establish special rights for themselves and, consequently, no special way of life may be connected with their class privileges. Rousseau tries to preserve differentiation and special privilege for political talent, but the fundamental principle of political right is equality, and privilege should never become identified with the conventions of traditional aristocracy which preserves mediocrity under the guise of superiority. His thought entails a wholesale condemnation of the encouragement of the class differences which were central to classical thought.

The death of a government occurs when the particular wills substitute themselves for the general will. This can lead either to anarchy or tyranny—anarchy when the individuals go off each in his own direction, tyranny when the private will of a single man directs the government. The entire political problem is, in sum, to establish the proper relation between the particular and the general will. The transformation of man in his passage from the state of nature to the civil state and his discovery of his free capacity to will is the crucial event for him, and the first and continuing preoccupation of the statesman is to guarantee the preservation of that transformation. For this purpose the ancient city serves best: because it is small enough to permit an aristocratic government and for the citizens to share a common heritage and a common way, because the particular wills can more easily be submerged in custom, and because the statesman can control the entirety. The question of the size of a nation is not a matter of mere technical limitations as has been most often supposed in modern thought, but has to do with the nature of human possibilities. Rousseau believed that revolutions could restore conservative antiquity on new, self-conscious grounds. His thought is an amazing union of the radical, revolutionary progressivism of modernity with the discretion and restraint of antiquity.

As has been said, Rousseau began his critique of modern thought from the point of view of human happiness. A political solution which does not fulfill humanity is only an abstraction, nor can the proper place of the political be distinguished except against the background of the whole man. And that raises the question whether the solution of the *Social Contract* is as completely satisfactory as that book itself would seem to indicate. The question is whether all men, especially the best men, can find complete satisfaction within a possible civil society. That the *Social Contract* provides a basis, from Rousseau's point of view, for establishing orders in which most men can live satisfactorily when laws have become necessary for them, there is no doubt. But whether these orders can realize a perfect justice that commands the attachment of the minds and hearts of the best is not entirely clear. There are two reasons drawn from Rousseau's writings which make this question unavoidable.

The first is purely political and has to do with property. Rousseau never envisioned as universally feasible a common use of the fruits of the earth. Private property is almost inextricably bound up with civil society and attaches men to it. But private property is not natural and is always a source of inequality. Private property is the root of power in civil society, and it cannot help influencing the establishment of laws. Even in a society where there are not the extremes of wealth and poverty, the distinction exists, and the tendency is always toward aggravating these differences. A man's life is very different if he is born to poverty or wealth, and money has a great deal to do with his capacity to remove external impediments to his freedom. Society protects the rich more than the poor, and the poor have much less to lose and perhaps much to gain in the destruction of the established order. Rousseau recognizes this in being willing to weight the procedures of voting somewhat in favor of the solidly entrenched rich who have the preservation of the regime at heart, if only selfishly. As soon as the equality of persons is the basis of political right, the legitimacy of the inequality of private property becomes highly questionable. Rousseau did not believe that real equality of wealth could be maintained without constant revolution and the destruction of the advantages of political life, but his view of private property is not wholly unlike Marx's. Private property is a perpetual question mark standing after the words "legitimate civil society." [16]

But more important is the doubt raised by the investigation of man's nature and Rousseau's own life as he saw fit to describe it for the public. Man is naturally an idle animal whose real pleasure is in sentiment, especially the sentiment of his own being. The movement of time and events does not entirely efface that nature. But civil society requires effort and work; one has little time to exercise the sentiments. The good citizen wants the esteem and affection of his fellow citizens; he looks to their opinions rather than living within himself as does the savage. Above all, civil society demands virtue, and virtue is hard. Virtue means living according to principle, conscious repression of the animal and sentimental in man. Virtue is necessary for civil society, but it is unclear whether it is good in itself—whether, as for the ancients, it is the specific human perfection, desirable for itself in addition to its effect of preserving society. The natural man had a goodness which caused him to care for his fellows; this was a pleasure for him just as was the satisfaction of his personal needs. He never did anything because he had to, but because it flowed naturally from him. Rousseau makes a distinction between the moral and the good man.[17] The moral man acts from the sense of duty and has the character of the trustworthy citizen. The good man follows his natural instincts, that first nature uncorrupted by vanity; he is the sentimental friend and lover. Rousseau put himself in the class of the good men, and his *Confessions* are the revelation of the life, actions, and feelings of such a man. He is not a reliable citizen; he is useless to society. He is idle. Finally, he is a solitary walker who dreams and recovers the sense of his existence under the layers of convention that have caused it to be utterly lost. He goes away and lives in the country, alone, untouched by civil society. This is another solution to the human problem, impossible for most men who do not have the strength of soul and intellect necessary to free themselves from their dependence and to think through the false opinions of society; but it is more satisfactory and more pleasant because it is closer to that first nature.

One can say that there are two roads from the state of nature and that they do not meet, the one leading to civil society, the other to the condition of men like Rousseau. One looks forward to the future and to a transformation of man, the other longs passionately for a return to nature. There is no harmonious solution to the human problem; there are unsatisfactory alternatives at tension with one another: the statesman versus the dreamer or the poet. They are mutually exclusive. One is left with a sense of incompleteness or imperfection in Rousseau's view of human life. Civil society does not satisfy much that is deepest in man. The dreamer cannot live well with his fellows. And, in the state of nature, where this split had not occurred, man was not really man. But Rousseau resisted the temptations to which his successors succumbed. Because he was aware that man's morality was purchased at the sacrifice of his sweetest natural sentiments and is partly only a means to the preservation of the state, he did not try to absolutize that morality to the exclusion of all else that is human. He did not teach that history, for all its power, would overcome the force of man's nature. He did not believe that man could become entirely social. And he did not neglect the importance of the political to give himself up to romantic longings for the lost past. All of these possibilities are to be found in his thought, but each was given no more than its due. For this reason one feels that he presented the human problem in its variety with greater depth and breadth than any of his successors.

NOTES

1. Rousseau's awareness of the paradoxical character of his works is well illustrated in the *Letter to M. d'Alembert*, in *Politics and the Arts. Letter to M. d'Alembert on the Theatre by Jean-Jacques Rousseau*, trans. with notes and an introduction by Allan Bloom (Glencoe, Ill.: The Free Press, 1960), p. 131, n.; and in Rousseau's *Lettre à M. Beaumont*, sixth paragraph.

2. *Discourse on Political Economy*, in *The Social Contract and Discourses*, trans. with an introduction by G. D. H. Cole ("Everyman's Library" [New York: Dutton, 1950]), pp. 306–8, 323–24. This volume will be cited hereafter as Cole's Rousseau.

3. *Discourse on the Sciences and Arts*, in *Jean-Jacques Rousseau, The First and Second Discourses*, ed. by Roger D. Masters and trans. by Roger D. and Judith R. Masters (New York: St. Martin's Press, 1964). This volume will be cited hereafter as Masters' *Discourses*.

4. *The Government of Poland*, in Rousseau, *Political Writings*, trans. and ed. by Frederick Watkins (New York: Nelson, 1953), chap. ii, pp. 162 ff.; cf. *Discourse on the Origin and Founda-*

tions of Inequality among Men, in Masters' *Discourses*, pp. 78–90.

5. The preceding pages summarize the argument of the *Discourse on the Origin and Foundations of Inequality among Men*.

6. *Social Contract*, I.ii–v.

7. *Ibid.*, I.vi.

8. *Ibid.*, I.vii.

9. *Ibid.*, III.xv. Cf. *Government of Poland*, chap. vii, pp. 187–205.

10. *Social Contract*, III.xviii.

11. *Discourse on Political Economy*, p. 298, in Cole's Rousseau.

12. *Social Contract*, III.vii; cf. *Government of Poland*, chap. ii, pp. 163–65.

13. *Social Contract*, III.viii. *Letter to M. d'Alembert*, p. 66.

14. *Social Contract*, I.vii, III.i; *Discourse on Political Economy*, pp. 289–97.

15. *Discourse on the Origin and Foundations of Inequality among Men*, Masters' *Discourses*, p. 227, note(*s*) to p. 174 of the text.

16. *Ibid.*, pp. 141–42.

17. See Rousseau's *Les Rêveries du promeneur solitaire*, sixième promenade (Paris: Garnier, 1960), pp. 75–86.

READINGS

A. Rousseau, Jean-Jacques. *Discourse on the Sciences and Arts*, in *Jean-Jacques Rousseau, The First and Second Discourses*, ed. by Roger D. Masters (New York: St. Martin's Press, 1964).

Rousseau, Jean-Jacques. *Discourse on the Origin and Foundations of Inequality among Men*, in *ibid*.

Rousseau, Jean-Jacques. *Social Contract*, bks I and II.

B.   Rousseau, Jean-Jacques. *Discourse on Political Economy*.

Rousseau, Jean-Jacques. *Social Contract*, bks III and IV.

Rousseau, Jean-Jacques. "The Confession of Faith of the Savoyard Vicar," in *Emile*, bk IV.

Rousseau, Jean-Jacques. *The Government of Poland*, in *Political Writings*. Trans. and ed. F. Watkins. New York: Nelson, 1953.

Rousseau, Jean-Jacques. *Letter to M. d'Alembert on the Theatre*, in *Politics and the Arts*. Trans. with notes and an introduction by Allan Bloom. Glencoe, Ill.: The Free Press, 1960.

IMMANUEL KANT

1724–1804

PHILOSOPHY AND POLITICS

Kant has given politics a place both central and derivative in his philosophy. In his three chief works (*Critique of Pure Reason*, 1781; *Critique of Practical Reason*, 1788; *Critique of Judgment*, 1790) he speaks of politics rarely, and only by allusion except in one paragraph of the *Critique of Judgment*. Where he explicitly presents a political teaching, he does so through the medium either of a doctrine of law[1] or of philosophy of history.[2] His explicitly political writings are mostly brief and occasional. The concepts and practical proposals that they contain confirm the thought that they are essentially a means of relating to each other two already existing universes: that of the Kantian system as developed in the three *Critiques* and that of modern natural right as developed by Hobbes, Locke, and especially Rousseau. Kant sometimes transcends his masters; but even when he does so, as in his doctrine of perpetual peace through international organization, his originality lies not in the content of the proposal (borrowed in this case from projects such as those of the Abbé de St. Pierre, on which Rousseau had commented) but in the novel philosophic basis and scope that he gives it, expressing it in legal terms that claim to be independent of all experience and founding it on his moral philosophy and his philosophy of history.

Kant's political teaching may be summarized in a phrase: republican government and international organization. In more characteristically Kantian terms, it is a doctrine of the state based upon law (*Rechtstaat*) and of eternal peace. Indeed, in each of these

formulations, both terms express the same idea: that of legal constitution or of "peace through law." Within and among states, it
is a matter of passing from the state of nature which is a state of
war to the lawful state which is a state of peace. The definition of
the lawful state and, above all, of the foundations on which it rests
and the conditions that compel its coming into being are the objects
of Kant's effort so far as he is a "political" philosopher. He performs
his task by drawing on his conceptions of morality and history,
showing the dependence of peace on law and of law on reason, and
the drive in the nature of things toward a free, rational, and thus
peaceable state.

Kant's enterprise might be said to have as its point of departure the tension between science and morality, between modern
physics most systematically developed by Newton and the moral
conscience most purely expressed by Rousseau—between the universal determinism implied by the former and the freedom of will
implied by the latter. Kant seeks to resolve the problem by radicalizing it. He seeks to preserve the two terms not by reconciling them
but by giving their tension and their coexistence a theoretical basis,
namely, the articulation of the opposition between nature and freedom—between the world of phenomena and the world of noumena.
The world of phenomena is the world of things in their manifestation or appearance; the world of noumena is the world of things
as they are in themselves or as they might be known if knowledge
of them could be had without the mediation of experience. The
world of phenomena is what science can know; the world of noumena
is the realm which is opened up by morality. It is in this latter
realm that reason attains perfect freedom from the conditioning
and thus limiting effect of the natural world of things. Precisely in
this realm of unconditioned reason can men be free of every external thing, of every object of doing, making, or acquiring. Left
to them is perfect autonomy—freedom to obey a self-prescribed law
out of pure respect for the universality (or impartiality) of law itself. The complete disjunction of the empirical from the noumenal
entails an equally complete disjunction of happiness and virtue:
Happiness is the satisfaction of our empirical, natural inclinations
while virtue is obedience to the moral law. The one belongs to the
order of nature, the other to the order of freedom.

But Kant cannot leave matters at the absolute disjunction of
the two realms. An accord must be procured between virtue and
happiness so that freedom can operate within nature and nature
be receptive to moral action, even to being transformed by it. Kant

achieves this accord by raising the question, for what can man hope? and then showing that the answer lies in two directions: what can be hoped in this life (thus drawing into consideration the realm of phenomena), and what can be hoped hereafter. In order to show what we can hope in the next world, Kant elaborates the postulates of practical reason: existence of God and immortality of the soul. His discussions of law, politics, and historical teleology enable him to show what man can hope for here on earth.

Having separated the two realms of morality and nature, Kant tries to reunite them by producing intermediaries and correspondences between them. Law, history, and politics appear as the composite criterion for evaluating that reunion. The evaluation, and thus the criterion, are of singular importance, for the question of the relation between the realms of nature and morality is in fact the question of the possible existence of the two realms, the conceptions of which are the products of a freedom and a reason at work in the phenomenal world. The root of the question raised by Kant's political philosophy resides in the ambiguity of morality and politics, each in itself and the two in their mutual relation. That ambiguity makes Kant's own formula that true politics is the application of his morality acceptable only with some refinement. The difficulty arises because it is true not only that Kant's politics must be understood on the basis of his morality but his morality may be understood on the basis of his politics. Moreover, his politics must also be understood independently of his morality, and his morality, ultimately, depends radically on conditions that lie beyond politics. This ambiguity or contradiction explains both Kant's division and reunion of law and morality and his strange hesitation on the threshold of philosophy of history while apparently according it a place both decisive and tangential.

The difficulty comes into view when we turn from the Kantian system as such to its inspiration and human meaning. Kant's morality is revolutionary not only in its theoretical status and its being based on the pure form of the law rather than on any specific content, but also in the content towards which this formalism cannot help pointing, namely, the rights of man. But the notion of the rights of man—like that of autonomy on which it rests and which Kant claims to be deducing a priori—has a prehistory which is political. Kant repeatedly acknowledges Rousseau's decisive influence on his political and moral doctrines. The priority of the practical over the theoretical, of the moral over the intellectual, the superiority to the scientists or philosophers as such of simple souls obedient to the voice of duty, all proceed from the Rousseau of the *First Discourse* and of the *Profession of Faith of the Savoyard Vicar,* just as the notions of liberty as obedience to self-prescribed law and of the generalization of particular desires as guaranteeing their legality are taken ultimately from the teaching of Rousseau in the *Social Contract.* Finally, Kant's philosophy of history is oriented explicitly upon Rousseau's *Discourse on the Origin of Inequality.*

To perceive the Rousseauism of Kant's morality is to perceive immediately the political inspiration of that morality. But at the same time, Kant's radicalization of Rousseauism—his transformation of the generalization of desires or wills into the universalization of maxims—and the consequences he draws from it in his doctrine of postulates produce a morality both apolitical and inapplicable to politics. Whether Kant's morality is political, and whether it needs or depends upon politics are questions that can be asked with a view to the sources or inspiration, the content, and the application or consequences of that morality.

We cannot avoid asking also whether Kant's politics is moral, that is, whether it depends in every respect on the ethic of the practical reason. Thus, perpetual peace is held out as the supreme political good because indeed the practical reason absolutely forbids war; but peace is shown also in the manner of Hobbes and Locke as indispensable to life and property, that is, good for the sake of some end or happiness in the realm of nature or unfreedom. Also, the state of civil society has a moral content because it is the state of that respect for rights which is the basis of freedom and human dignity. But while philosophy of history appeals to the working of a good will (a moral will) for the bringing into being of the truly civil state, Kant recognizes that nature forces the progress toward that state to depend upon passion, discord, and war. Again, the idea of true republican government can occur only to a moral politician, a man who thoroughly subordinates politics to morals and for whom the attainment of eternal peace is not a merely technical but a truly moral task. At the same time, not only does republican government not presuppose perfection in its citizens, but the establishment of civil society in general is possible among devils if only they be intelligent.[3] Morality and politics thus appear sometimes to converge, sometimes to exist on different planes altogether. We may anticipate our conclusions so far as to say that what makes this problem difficult and interesting with respect to Kantianism, and Kantianism in turn with respect to political philosophy, is that from a single source arise not only the rigorous and solid foundations, but also the disjunction, of morality and politics; while the political importance of this system rests above all on its power to approximate the two to each other. It is true that the disjunction of the two worlds is more convincing than the reconciliation; the purity of the soul and the hope for its indefinite progress in another world are more essential to morality than are republican government and indefinite progress in this world toward perpetual peace; and, conversely, the problem of civil society referred more effectually to the demands of happiness and security than of morality. Yet it is also true that Kant is uniquely important not only to philosophy but to the political conscience precisely for the political consequences of his moral teaching and the moral dimension of his political teaching. He invests certain moral themes with a direct political bearing, and political themes with a sacred moral dignity. Anyone who seriously considers the basis of liberalism and democracy will discover a moral sentiment therein that is absent in Hobbes and Locke and even in Rousseau but given a theoretical support by Kant.

The question of the relation between morality and politics in Kant comes to a head in his teaching concerning respect for the dignity of man. The essential problem of Kantian politics is the nature and the philosophic and moral status of the rights of man. We turn now to that theme.

The Rights of Man

Kant's enterprise on behalf of the rights of man expresses itself in an intention to establish unconditionally a moral foundation for political liberty and equality, or to free men by enlightening them about their rights, disclosing to all of them that the freedom to legislate is the only legitimate basis for the obedience of the subject.

For a better understanding, we consider the relationship of Kant to Rousseau and Hume who, according to Kant, provided the point of departure for his philosophy and decisively motivated him to undertake such an enterprise. Kant has recorded the powerful effect that Rousseau had upon him: "I am myself by inclination a researcher. I feel in fullest measure the thirst for knowledge and the greedy desire to progress in it, as well as satisfaction at every advance. There was a time when I believed that this alone could constitute the honor of mankind, and I despised the vulgar which knows of nothing. Rousseau brought me into the right shape. That illusory distinction vanishes; I learn to respect human beings, and I should consider myself more useless than the common workingmen if I did not believe that this consideration could give a value to all others by establishing the rights of man." [4] As for Hume, Kant wrote, "I readily confess that the animadversions of David Hume were what first interrupted my dogmatic slumber many years ago and gave my investigations in speculative philosophy an entirely altered direction." [5]

Rousseau's was the affirmative inspiration upon which Kant oriented his own conception of human worth and of the task of philosophy: and that worth and that task have a direct, imperative political bearing. From Rousseau, Kant adopts the primacy of morality over philosophy, of action over contemplation, of practical over theoretical reason; the thought that the primacy of morality entails the equal worth of all men; and the thought that morality and the recognition of the rights of man substantively coincide. But the primacy of action over contemplation implies the primacy of freedom over nature; the primacy of practical reason implies the critique of theoretical reason, that is, of both science and metaphysics. Hume's skepticism had rendered questionable both science and metaphysics and thus awakened Kant from his dogmatic slumber: Kant had to disinter the true, rational foundations of science and thus to show its limitations and thus to put the rejection of (theoretical) metaphysics on a solid foundation.

Hume had maintained that the fundamental notions—necessity and causality—are validated for us by experience and convenience, not by reason. Kant accepted Hume's negative judgment on the "dogmatism" of prevailing thought, that is, his criticism of the philosophers' failure to consider the possible tenuousness of their most fundamental notions; but he rejected the positive part of Hume's doctrine, its empiricism. Kant demanded that the principles that support our understanding, especially causation, be better founded than upon mere experience, lest their necessity and their universality become unintelligible and the possibility of science, particularly mathematical physics, thus be lost.

Kant states the problem by means of the distinction between analytic and synthetic judgments. Analytic judgments are those in which the subject itself contains or implies the predicate perfectly, so that the predicate merely explicates something already said when the subject was uttered and does not produce any new knowledge. The validity of analytic judgments is therefore independent of experience; such judgments are a priori. Synthetic judgments are those in which the predicate does add something to what the thinker of the judgment can have in mind in uttering the subject itself. Judgments based on experience are necessarily synthetic; they are synthetic judgments a posteriori. But experience as such is not possible if there are not synthetic judgments a priori—judgments of apodictic necessity and universal validity, hence incapable of being validated by experience. For instance, all experience *presupposes* the principle of causality which, as Hume had shown, is not analytical and which, as Hume had failed to see, cannot be derivative from experience since it is a presupposition of all possible experience. But causality is not the only principle of this kind. There is a whole system of categories and the forms of pure intuition (space and time). The cooperation of the categories and the forms of pure intuition supplies the framework that renders possible the science of nature. Science of nature, that is, of the phenomenal world is thus not a contemplation of a reality existent outside ourselves but is rather the laying down of law to nature by ourselves, the investing of things by ourselves with that which alone we can know about them "a priori." Science of nature is fundamentally the "spontaneous" product of the understanding, as distinguished from the "receptivity" of the senses. It is the practical reason that permits us to participate in the intelligible world, to escape at the same time the passivity of mere contemplation and the empirical relativity of the phenomenal world, that world to which the theoretical reason is limited. The ascent from determinacy toward spontaneity is achieved by the discovery of the freedom of the practical reason. That freedom finds its culmination in the freedom of the moral man, or in morality proper.

The primacy of practical reason has a twofold consequence: it brings relief from the unknowability of the world as it is in itself by giving all men—equally—access to the deepest truth, which is the moral truth, and through the continuous challenging of the merely empirical world by practical reason, leads to the emancipation of men's moral and political formulations from the experience of the past. "With regard to nature, it is experience no doubt that supplies us with rules and is the source of all truth; with regard to moral laws, on the other hand, experience is, alas! but the source of illusion, and it is altogether reprehensible to derive or limit the laws of what we ought to do by our experience of what has been done." [6]

The new conception of reason moves, through the primacy of practice, to the radical distinction between the "is" and the "ought" (a distinction present in Hume but elaborated first by Kant), and thence to moral formalism and political and legal doctrinairism. The rights of man are to be known "a priori," valid and demandable universally. They can have as source and content only that radical liberty which is linked to the essence of the rational being as such. As this liberty is independent of the nature of the cosmos, of man, and of society, it cannot be defined in terms of the achievement of ends, nor applied in terms of determined or determining circumstances. The critique of theoretical reason which Hume had begun opens the way for a radical liberation of man by eliminating everything that could impose laws on liberty outside of liberty itself. It is to Rousseau's influence that Kant owes the origin and the moral and political consequences of this liberation, the true point of departure and the true destination of his enterprise.

There is an echo of this influence in the famous sentence which opens section 1 of Kant's *Fundamental Principles of the Metaphysic of Morals*: "Nothing can possibly be conceived in the world, or even out of it, which can be called good without qualification except a *good will*." The virtues themselves are not simply good, for they can be put to corrupt uses by a bad will. Morality is not for the sake of happiness or the perfection of man's nature; on the contrary, it is morality that gives value to that happiness and that perfection. Conversely, the goodness of the good will is in no way validated by the achievement of the will's desired end, nor diminished by its failure to achieve its end.

We can now begin to perceive the characteristic two-sidedness of Kant's moral and political teaching—its demand for both obedience and emancipation, for both submitting and glorying in liberty. For morality or the good will consists in acting not merely conformably to the law but out of respect for law to which it renders absolute obedience. But since that law is an expression of the subject's autonomy, it stands not for an external authority but for his own will. The good will as good in itself independently of any effect it might have, and as constituting in itself the highest good, in some measure replaces God or nature. Men who vaunt their intelligence or their happiness are depreciated; it is in the humble individual who submits to law to the utmost that man as such is raised, through goodness of will, to an unprecedented sovereignty.

This revolutionary doctrine of the priority and substance of morality has various political implications. First and most obvious, it powerfully supports the belief in human equality, disparaging the various natural and social (empirical) sources of inequality and maintaining that a man's distinction depends only on his quality as a moral being. But every man can have a good will, the one thing needful and the only thing good in itself. Hence follows the equality of all men in the decisive respect, and their absolute value, to be respected by all in each. Not only hereditary rank but every abasement of one man by or before another is an offense against the equality and autonomy of man.

The transition from the primacy of morality through the dignity of the moral subject to the equality of all men poses a difficult and important problem. Does the dignity or absolute value of the moral subject as legislator belong to all men or only to those who fulfill their duty, to man as capable of acting morally or to man as acting morally? If the former, how far ought the perfect dignity and rights of man as merely capable of doing his duty be translated into political and social equivalents?

Kant's answer to the first question is not unambiguous. In most passages of the short *Fundamental Principles of the Metaphysic of Morals,* he maintains the narrower and more rigorous stipulation in terms of man's actually behaving morally. However, in the second part of the work called *Metaphysics of Morals* (the "Doctrine of Virtue") where he is less concerned with the basis of respect than with the implications of it, the broader conception definitely prevails, and Kant stresses the claims upon others that follow from the respectability of every human being as such. But it is in this place that we find an articulation of the narrow and the broad conceptions, at least so far as men's duties toward each other are concerned. Every man is entitled to respect from every other man and in return owes all of them respect: "Humanity itself is dignity," meaning that a man cannot be treated, even by himself, as a means but always and only as an end. "His dignity (personality) consists precisely in this" and he has the obligation to recognize in practice this dignity in respect of all men. "I cannot deny a depraved man all the respect which, at least in his capacity as a man, cannot be taken away from him; and this is so even though his actions make him unworthy of it." The reproaches and the condemnations provoked by vice, deserved though they be and inseparable from one's silent contempt for the individual in question, must "never lead to complete contempt for the depraved man, nor to the denial of all moral worth in him; for he would then be supposed unable ever to improve himself, which cannot be reconciled with the idea of man who, as such, as a moral being, can never lose every inclination toward what is good." [7]

The dignity that belongs only to the moral man imposes precisely on him the duty of treating all men with a certain respect; for the dignity of the moral man in action redounds upon the species, upon all potentially moral men, possessors of an inclination to good which, wicked as they might be, distinguishes them from the beasts and assimilates them to moral man. Men are not equal in dignity, but one has the duty to treat them as though they were. The right of the individual to be treated as an equal or at least to see certain aspects of his dignity respected is not based on his being equal or respectable but on the duty to treat all men as equal or respectable. It is based less on the primacy than on the content of morality. If respect for the rights of man is based on morality, it is so because morality is defined as respect for the rights of man. The content of morality appears as a deduction (a priori) from universality as the form of morality. The line of moral formalism comes close to defining the political horizon in a conceptual world dominated by the ideas of universalization, of rational mankind as an end in itself, of the kingdom of ends, and of autonomy.

The moral worth of an action proceeds from the goodness of the will by which that action is animated, which in turn means the purity of that will—the goodness of the will in its abstraction from every empirical end. Purity of will implies purification of the will of all substantive intention, the animation of the will only by its self-respect, its respect for the formal principle of will in general, in other words respect for law as such. Duty itself means the necessity of performing an action out of respect for law. But how does the moral man find the law that is to govern every action of his life? How does a man of good will recognize his duty? Kant's criterion for the good will proves to be universalization, as Rousseau's criterion for the general will was generalization. Kant's criterion requires a man on the point of acting to ask himself whether the maxim governing his intended action (for example, "the greatness of my need justifies this departure from honesty") could become the universal law of action for all men without destroying the act itself. For example, a man needing a loan realizes that he will never be able to repay it. Should he promise to do so nonetheless? If all men would promise to repay even when knowing themselves unable to fulfill their promises, promises would become universally nugatory. His false promise, if universalized, would abolish promises —and would also abolish the very borrowing that is the aim of the promise. A self-contradicting or irrational rule cannot be the law for a rational being. It follows that a man should not make a promise that he expects not to fulfill. That a man should act only according to the criterion of his action's universalizability is called by Kant the categorical imperative—the imperative that binds categorically or universally, not merely hypothetically or with a view to certain circumstances, needs, or ends connected with the action. "Act so that the maxim of your action might be elevated by your will to be a universal law of nature." [8] There is only one categorical imperative and that is the imperative of universality. But Kant elaborates this universality by giving three alternate formulas for the categorical imperative—formulas which help reveal both the human meaning and the ground of duty.

The second formula seeks the objective principle by which the will is to determine itself. Rejecting as merely hypothetical the dictate of the subjective ends of the rational being aiming at its particular purposes, Kant demands that the will orient itself upon the categorically valid ends-in-themselves. But the only possible ends-in-themselves endowed with an objective value are rational beings as such. The supreme objective practical principle from which all the laws of the will can be deduced is, according to the second formulation of the categorical imperative, "Act so as to treat humanity, in your own person as well as everyone else's, always as an end and never as a mere means." It is this formulation of the categorical imperative that directly provides the moral basis of the political doctrine of the rights of man. The violation of the duty to respect man as an end in himself is most conspicuous in attacks on liberty and property, where the intention can only be to treat one's fellow rational beings as mere means or instruments rather than as beings themselves capable of participating in the ends of the action in question. [9]

The requirement that all men be treated as ends in themselves restricts freedom in an obvious way; but because it implies the overriding by law of all subjective ends, this formulation leads to the idea of *autonomy,* of the will laying down its law and being subject to it only as its own determination. This third principle, that of autonomy, conceives the will of each rational being as instituting a universal legislation, a conception that leads in turn to the pregnant concept of the "kingdom of ends." "Kingdom" is the systematic linkage of various rational beings by common laws, and the kingdom of ends is the conjunction of rational beings who are linked by objective laws which aim precisely at conjoining those beings both as ends and also as helpful to one another's particular purposes, that is, as means. Not only the consequences but even the formulation of Kant's principle of morality is political in nature. Duty points in the direction of order or community.

Kant stresses, indeed, the difference between the idea of an ethical community, which is internal and universal, and that of a political society, which is external and particular. Nevertheless, the ethical community has a political structure. "A rational being belongs to the kingdom of ends as a *member* of it when, prescribing universal laws to it, he is himself also subject to those laws. He belongs to it as a *ruler* in that, prescribing laws, he is not subject to an alien will.... In the kingdom of ends, it is not to the ruler that duty speaks but to each member, and to all in the same degree." [10] The kingdom of ends is a republic, based on reciprocity. The importance of reciprocity for morality cannot be exaggerated. Duty is nothing less than the practical necessity of acting according to the principle of reciprocity, which gives an expression not only to the equality of human beings in dignity but to the basis thereof in rationality. Reciprocity is the principle par excellence of interaction among rational beings, agents who adjust their relations to one another with objectivity.

The sphere of men's relations with each other, the sphere dominated by justice, which in the classical understanding was but a part of the domain of virtue, becomes for Kant coterminous with virtue altogether. At the beginning of the *Fundamental Principles of the Metaphysics of Morals,* Kant depreciates three of the four classical cardinal virtues, namely, courage, moderation, and intelligence, because they can be harmful if unaccompanied by good will. Now we can understand why he does not include the fourth, justice, in the depreciation: good will tends to be identical with justice. No one has proclaimed more forcefully than Kant the subordination of the passions to reason and, therewith, the existence in man of a vertical hierarchy. Nevertheless, as in Rousseau before him, the limiting of human desires is not achieved by Kant "vertically," by conformity to a natural hierarchy in man, but "laterally," by the reciprocal (mutual) limitation of and respect for liberties and individuals. The idea of the kingdom of ends, showing as it does that universalization is crucial for connecting autonomy and reciprocal limitation of liberty, illustrates the heavy debt owed by Kant's morality to Rousseau's politics. It shows also how far Kant's morality, in its rational formalism, goes beyond Rousseau's politics in radicalizing, on the moral level, the reciprocity of rights and duties and the primacy of both rights and duties over virtue.

This primacy is made emphatic in the *Metaphysics of Morals,* where Kant distinguishes legal duties and the duties that virtue entails, assigning distinct priority to the legal duties. Legal duties apply to external acts, which are subject to the external constraints of legislation; the duties commanded by virtue apply to the maxims behind the actions, to the internal intentions which are directed toward some end that ought to be a duty but that cannot be constrained from without. Although the duties of legality deal only with the external acts, they take precedence over the duties of virtue, though these are linked to intention and good will, because the duties of legality are themselves of the essence of morality, defining as they do the reciprocity of rights and duties in demanding that every man respect the rights of man both in others and in himself.

The legal duties specify the commands of justice: first, to respect the right of humanity in oneself by refusing to allow others to treat one as a mere means and by demanding to be treated as an end; second, to harm no one; third, for the sake of the foregoing, to enter into a society in which the property of each can be guaranteed against the others. Virtue directs men toward ends that should have the character of duties—the perfection of oneself and the happiness of others. The legal duties are definite and perfect; those imposed by virtue are broad and imperfect so far as their dictate must leave some latitude to men's free choice. The legal duties take precedence over the moral: Before attending to other men's happiness, be solicitous of their rights. Love of humanity is conditional, respect for its rights a sacred and absolute duty. Practice can be given priority without compromising morality because external prescription or legality and interior morality converge on respect for the rights of man.

Kant's attempt to deduce politics from morality presents serious difficulties. True though it be that he derives from morality the sacredness of law and the unconditional duty to respect it, it is also true that he radically separates law from morality: His legal doctrine includes within the right to freedom (the only innate right and source of every other right) the right to lie, while his moral doctrine does not countenance lying in any circumstance. Kant has developed an absolute moral duty to respect a morally neutral right, even if it is a right to immorality.

Beyond this tension between the obligatoriness and the moral neutrality of the rights of man is the more general and more radical tension between the duty to obey exterior laws and the contingent, often immoral, content of those laws. Not only is the conformity of laws to the rights of man or to the general will no guarantee of their morality, but such conformity does not even constitute the necessary condition for the subject's moral duty to obey authority. It is up to the sovereign to act in conformity with the general will; the subject is to obey the law as it stands. But then the problem of applying morality to politics becomes even more serious and leads to a new tension. The existing political laws or directives, to a considerable degree, oppose both the rights of man and the demands of morality. These laws not only authorize, they positively prescribe, acts that contravene morality. Morality therefore commands us to wish that the legislation be replaced by a political order that conforms to the rights of man and is compatible with morality itself; at the same time morality demands obedience to those immoral laws. Morality forbids fighting immorality with fraud or with force; it forbids using immoral means to aim at a moral end. Between the desired end and the permissible means a gulf is opened which seems to make it impossible to resolve the first tension, namely, that between the obligatoriness and the content of the external law.

In the Appendix of *On Perpetual Peace,* Kant deals thematically with the problem raised by the application of morality to politics. He begins with the conflict between politics and morals that is expressed in the two maxims, that of politics, "Be wise as serpents," and that of morals, "and innocent as doves;" but he does so in order to deny that this conflict causes any real difficulty. In principle, politics is simply the application of that legal doctrine whose theory is morality. Any conflict between politics and morality is to be resolved by the pure subordination of the former to the latter. "Honesty is the best policy" contains a "theory" often betrayed by practice, but the really theoretical "Honesty is better than any policy" is absolutely unassailable by any practice. Kant contrasts the "political moralist," who tries to bend morality in order to adjust it to politics, with the "moral politician," who derives his political action from his recognition of duty. Kant rejects the Machiavellian maxims of political prudence which invoke practical wisdom or experience with men—"Act, then apologize;" "Disown your doings at will;" "Divide and conquer"—in favor of the moral maxim based on knowledge of man: "Let justice prevail though the world perish for it." When politics and morality conflict, morality resolves the conflict in a way characteristic of its own essence: It depreciates the material principle or the results of the act and concentrates on the formal principle thereof.

The subject of the second part of the Appendix of *On Perpetual Peace* is the harmony between politics and morality on the basis of the supra-empirical meaning of public law or public right. Kant maintains that public right in principle absolutely requires *publicity.* The maxim of an action will require secrecy only if the publication of the maxim would expose its injustice and would thus threaten and arouse mankind. Injustice calls for secrecy; secrecy betokens injustice. As a norm for the morality of maxims and thus of actions, publishability resembles universalizability in its formalism and contrivedness. In an illustration of publicity at work, Kant shows how it precludes that repudiation of a sovereign's promises sanctioned by Machiavelli, Spinoza, and later Hegel, the repudiation supposed subservient to the sovereign's supreme duty to his own state. Practical reason establishes a priori precisely what has come to be called public diplomacy, the diplomacy of "open covenants, openly arrived at."

From discussing the criterion (publishability) of a maxim that betokens the morality of a political act flowing from that maxim, Kant goes on to seek for the positive condition under which the practical maxims will agree with right. He recognizes the need for this further effort because he understands that an actor's maxims would be publishable not only if they were just but if the actor were so irresistibly powerful that he could publish iniquitous projects with contempt for the world's responses. As we might say, publishability of the maxim is necessary but not sufficient for the morality of an act. Thus Kant proposes the general condition for the coincidence of morals and politics, the condition also for the existence of public right and a law of nations: the rule of law among men—agreement among the nations to leave the state of nature in order to abjure war. Not experience but pure reason shows the necessity of a federation of the states (for the idea proceeds from the notion of law itself) if the conjunction of morals and politics is to be achieved and political prudence given a lawful basis.

The clues that Kant offers regarding the direct application of morality to politics bring us back to the familiar difficulty: formal and universal morality demands, without showing itself to be a basis for, a certain political order; and much more rigorously, it forbids the use of means seen by Kant to be necessary for the realization of that order. The abstractness and rigidity of morality create a chasm between itself and its political applications, as much in the realm of ends as in that of means, as much in the realm of legal order (which for Kant is that of external liberty, not of moral intentions) as in the realm of political action which, even for Kant, is inevitably the realm of contingent, particular, and unpredictable situations.

PHILOSOPHY OF HISTORY

To overcome the disjunction of morality and politics is precisely the task of philosophy of history, whose duty is to point the direction of and give hope for progress toward the lawful order that would permit the decisive union. Philosophy of history must therefore reconcile the interdiction and the indispensability of immoral means; it must replace the anarchy and injustice that the human scene projects and the unpredictability accompanying freedom of will with the conception of a progress marked with both the purposiveness associated with morality and the necessity corresponding with physical determinism. Here Kant's debt to Rousseau reappears and is acknowledged in Kant's characterization of Rousseau as the Newton of the moral world. As Newton discovered the simplicity and order of a material world apparently marred by hazard, Rousseau for the first time saw beneath the multiplicity of human appearances to the depths of human nature and perceived the hidden law that justifies Providence itself.[11] Before Rousseau, Providence might have appeared to authorize a human scene in which politics ignored morality not only in the present but without hope of progressive remedy through history.

But Rousseau is the Newton of the moral world and his doctrine a justification of Providence partly for a reason that looks not to the future but to the past: The tension between savage morality and the universal moral law is resolved in the *Second Discourse*. As Kant indicates, he himself takes his departure not from man but from that civilized man at whom Rousseau arrives only after having recovered and begun with natural man. If the savages were ignorant of the moral law, it was because reason had not yet sufficiently arisen in them. The promulgation of the moral law to all mankind could then have been only miraculous; but it is Rousseau's merit to have shown on the level of history, as Newton had done on the physical level, that the wisdom and glory of God manifest themselves better in the necessity and regularity of natural laws than in any miraculous interruption of them in their course.

The essential function of philosophy of history is, however, in interpreting the past, to give hope for the future and thus to support moral action with an encouragement that it cannot do without. Kant considered that morality would lose its meaning unless mankind were progressing morally, or unless the progress of the species as well as of individuals were at least not regarded as impossible. Belief in a moral progress transmissible from generation to generation and belief in intellectual and political progress must support and help generate each other. The individual's morality, though it depends ultimately on the good will, that is, on the man himself, must be progressively prepared and rewarded by external conditions which neither seduce nor penalize virtue. It is the task of history to prepare the rise of reason and civilization, which are necessary though not sufficient for obedience to the universal moral law, and to prepare the lawful state which is demanded by morality by abolishing violence, that standing invitation to immorality. Kant does not present the historical progress of intellect, culture, and politics as a fact but rather as the indispensable practical *postulate* for the moral subject. Historical progress does not issue from moral action but is due to the operation of nature's mechanism or to Providence rather than to any human consciousness at all; Providence uses those very inclinations, vices, violence and war—the domination or abolition of which are its appointed mission. Between philosophy of history and morality there are both concord and tension, each essential, reproducing the problem brought on in Rousseau's thought by his realization of the tension between intellectual and moral progress. Philosophy of history does perhaps provide a link between morals and politics; but its own ambiguity makes it incapable of overcoming their disjunction completely.

Kant's philosophy of history, more than that of any of his successors, addresses itself to the requirements of morality. Its chief value is practical, as a guide to action. The task of theoretical reason is to show that the impossibility of progress cannot be demonstrated, certainly not by appeal to experience; and incidentally, that experience itself gives indications—if not decisive yet certainly encouraging—in favor of progress. Kant does not assert that men have a duty to believe in the attainability of the ends of progress; their duty is to act consistently with the desire for those ends as long as their unattainability is not certain. Once moral reason has laid down its absolute veto on war, for example, the question whether perpetual peace is attainable or not is replaced by our duty to act as if it is attainable, hence to establish those domestic and international institutions of republicanism that it demands. Rather than making ourselves thus the dupes of morality, it is precisely the belief that the moral law might deceive man that would prompt in us the fatal wish to abdicate reason and submit ourselves, like the beasts, to the mechanism of nature.[12] Moral reason liberates us from the dogmatism of theoretical or scientific reason.

Why, now, is the moral law made to depend, for the conservation of its value, on the possibility of a progress toward some political order, when every man's moral duty has already been united to an absolutely categorical imperative whose dictate he can obey because he must? In brief, because of the need to show (through philosophy of history) that there is concord or no essential discord between virtue and happiness, morality and nature, morality and politics, or duty and interest. It is true that Kant thus introduces into his philosophy of history and politics considerations such as happiness which are not strictly moral. It might be objected that Kantian morality as abstracted from happiness is compromised by Kant's preoccupation with reconciling morality and happiness. It must be admitted, though, that the attempt to reconcile happiness and the virtue that makes one worthy of it is, for Kantianism, less decisive on the plane of human history than on the plane of belief in another world. However, the attempt at reconciliation limits itself to supplying history with a tendency and politics with an end—the establishment of a lawful or peaceful order—rather than claiming to effect the moral education of mankind, a limited project for removing obstacles to morality only so far as they are obstacles also to civil society. In fact, even with respect to right, as the reconciliation adopts the vantage of man's species-destiny in the natural world, it deviates dually from the vantage of morality in the strict sense, which is the vantage of the individual in the noumenal world. In the first place, the moral problem presents itself every moment to every individual; at every moment he must be virtuous, therefore he can be, and the postulates of practical reason thus come decisively to bear. But then on the contrary, unlike the immortality of the individual soul, the historical progress of the species proposes an answer to the problem of virtue and happiness solely on the level of the future of the species: not only can the individual dispense with the notion of historical progress for purposes of moral behavior at the present moment, but the extraneous hope that it offers does not even affect him directly. Kant, the first great philosopher in whose work political philosophy transforms itself into philosophy of history, formulates clearly and powerfully an objection to all philosophy of history including his own. He clearly perceived that historical progress is the work of generations of men building more or less unwittingly an edifice whose perfection brings a happiness in which they of course cannot share. But Kant regards this as the unavoidable condition of rational beings who are individually mortal and immortal only as a species.

Now appears the second respect in which philosophy of history is inferior to the postulate of the soul's immortality as a guarantee of morality. Envisaging the perfection of morality being reached only indirectly through the realization of man's natural ends in society, philosophy of history rests heavily on the empirical and phenomenal—the brevity of a man's life, the immortality of the species, the very fact that there is progress, and the vulnerability of all to natural catastrophes that could bring history itself to a close. Even if satisfied, these conditions are conditions, peculiarities of human life not deducible a priori as characteristics of a rational being who enacts and obeys the moral law. Moreover, as empirical, they call for empirical confirmation. Even if, theoretically, historical progress requires in support of its practical applicability no more than a showing that its impossibility cannot be proved, Kant cannot avoid seeking positive empirical evidence in its favor: Man's gamble on the convergence of history and morality cannot be left as a mere gamble. Moral action assumes and implies hope, or a practical faith, which must produce a new way of viewing nature, experience, and history. Human experience must be susceptible to an interpretation that is more compatible with the ideal of eternal peace than is that of the mere politicians.

Thus it is that Kant turns again to that experience from which he had contemptuously recoiled, seeking therein the signs of progress toward peace, lawfulness, and morality. Any experience that indicates man's aptitude to be the author of his own progress is represented by Kant as subject to projection into the past and the future as significant of the human tendency to advance. Depending thus on a certain reading of events and interpretation of signs, philosophy of history cannot claim the necessity or rigor of either the postulates which refer to the other world or the scientific laws which refer to the world of natural determinism.

On what plane and in what dimension of human life will the signs and means of progress show themselves? Not on the level of the particular acts of men, of their interests and their motives, their wisdom cannot be counted on to unite men with a view to a rational common design. Precisely for this reason the philosopher must proceed from the planlessness of human affairs to a search for the plan of nature which is the basis of history proper.[13] Under the circumstances there are only two ways in which to conceive the advance toward the lawful republican regime and perpetual peace: Either man will freely choose that path but will follow it not by virtue of his empirical nature (for the sake of interest or happiness) but rather through duty, morality, and law-abidingness, or he will be drawn onto and along it unwittingly under the constraint of higher power. For these possibilities to become clues to the future, experience would have to contain evidence either of a moral disposition among men to overcome their inclinations and to enter a universal lawful state or of the action of a higher power which, unknown to men, deflects their actions from their particular ends toward the service of a common goal coincident with perpetual peace.

These are precisely the two aspects or facets of the Kantian philosophy of history. The first possibility reflects indeed the action of something that surpasses history, but the second constitutes philosophy of history properly speaking: history exists only so far as there is something beyond liberty and to the extent that human actions take an involuntary direction. Paradoxically, morality can advance and assert itself in nature only to the extent that men do not accomplish what they want, or that their plans betray them—in the language of Adam Smith, to the extent that they are led as by an invisible hand to promote ends that are no part of their intention. Thus it is the "end of nature" (which Kant formulates explicitly as a more prudent version of Providence) that will serve history as a lead. Practical reason and nature collaborate with and fortify one another because "nature irresistibly desires that law at last prevail. What men neglect to that end will come to pass anyhow, though not without travail." [14]

Thus philosophy of history can retort upon the practical people the charge of unrealism that they direct against the "idealism" of the moralists and utopians: What seemed like a contradiction between pious wishes and the necessities demonstrated by experience now appears as a debate between genuine but limited empirical probabilities and a necessity which is both superior to experience and already partly fulfilled in it.

Kant goes even further: It is precisely the selfish propensities in human nature that nature exploits in order to bring about those ends proposed by the venerated but impotent general will of mankind. Selfishness promotes war and acquisitiveness, but it simultaneously inspires those selfish counter-measures against aggression and cupidity that lead to a pacified, prosperous progress. Both through the course of history and in its various culminations, order emerges from conflict, peace from war, and public benefit from private vice. The political order which morality requires and which in turn is to pave the way to morality or facilitate its task is not only morally neutral but is achieved through immoral means, or would at the least be impossible without the passions and vices. [15]

Nature being interpreted teleologically, that is, morally, the end and, therefore, the meaning given by nature to history consists in the elaboration of all the dispositions of the human species. These dispositions culminate in culture, that is, in the general aptitude of man as intelligent being to make use of nature as a means and to choose freely for himself whatever ends he desires. Kant agrees with Rousseau that man is radically characterized by his freedom or, better still, by his perfectibility. He is capable of being rational before being actually rational; his culture and his intelligence develop slowly as their development wrenches him out of his animal state. And, like Rousseau, Kant maintains that such progress in culture and intelligence does not in itself constitute progress towards happiness or towards morality. When reason and instinct break apart, reason breaks also with innocence and a rupture opens between reason and man's adaptation to his animal existence. The growth of reason suggests refinements of desire by no means always wholesome, and gives man also a sense of evil and of vice while introducing prohibition, and therefore infraction, into his life. Kant refers to Rousseau and to the biblical teaching of original sin in showing the vice and misery that accompany civilization. These are compounded by the inequality that grows up among men as skills develop among them, material abundance emerges, and with it the oppression of the lower orders and the malaise of the higher.[16]

We understand now how Rousseau could persuade Kant not only of the necessity of viewing man in the historical perspective of transition from nature to civilization, but also to hesitate before seeing in this perspective any guarantee or even foundation of morality. Kant's observation, following Rousseau, about a tension between moral progress and the progress of civilization, of the sciences, the arts, and even of political institutions may be the most serious explanation for the collateral and ambiguous role of philosophy of history in Kant's thought. The idea that the human species in developing its potentialities can draw farther and farther away from virtue and from happiness, or in any case that it must set out on its way with such a separation, leads to a doubt that humanity will be consummated in this world, and to a certainty that the means of consummation are vitiated by an impurity that depreciates mankind's fulfillment in this life by comparison with the moral destiny of the individual hereafter.

Kant's conclusion is more optimistic than Rousseau's. In Rousseau there is probably an irreducible tension between the fate of the individual and that of society. In Kant—indeed in his interpretation of Rousseau—this tension must eventuate, through historical evolution itself, in a reconciliation within a certain type of society which corresponds to nature's design and man's destiny. Kant interprets the contradictions that Rousseau points out between civilization and the state of nature as contradictions between those propensities of man that are linked to his moral destination and those linked to his preservation. Luxury, inequality, and violence cannot be separated from moral progress. In drawing man away from nature, they must lead him to the society of the "social contract," to that point at which "art reaching perfection becomes nature again."[17] If Kant stigmatizes the evils of civilization as Rousseau did, he emphasizes much more than Rousseau their positive and indispensable historical role and the manner in which they must in the end overcome or transcend themselves. The "glittering misery" of culture which awakens and encourages appetites and vices must lead to the "culture of discipline" in which the will is liberated from the despotism of vicious appetite, and the ways of morality are prepared through lawfulness. Similarly, inequality conduces to the emergence of egalitarian society and war to peace. Kant of course does not exculpate the tainted means; indeed he proscribes the use of such means more uncompromisingly than any other philosopher. He is, however, willing to see a benefit in them retrospectively, and thereby shows history as overcoming the antinomy of ends and means. It is nature which somehow takes responsibility for the violence and immorality of politics, making use of the maxim "The end justifies the means" that is so strictly forbidden to individuals by practical reason. Thus, when Kant takes up such subjects as the French Revolution, rebellion against tyrants, or wars of liberation, he arrives at a troublesome dual judgment: retrospective vindication by history and unconditional condemnation by morality. Whether the historical view remains coordinate with the moral, as for Kant, or dominates it, as it will in Hegel, a promise of reconciliation between them exists where in Rousseau there is only the intimation of antinomy.

The reconciliation in question is made problematical, however, precisely by the fact that the society that makes it possible is itself the permanent product of the very appetites and vices that lie at the sources of men's objectionable behavior. Perhaps inequality and war must eventually annihilate themselves, but the same is by no means true of the egoism and hostility from which they proceed, for these are of the eternal nature of man, that nature which it is the function of history to develop and of the civil state to exploit in the interest of rights, morality, and happiness. The fundamental phenomenon out of which grow both the political problem and its solution is what was identified by Hobbes as man's natural asociality, the latent or manifest war of all against all. Kant's striking formula to describe this animosity is the "asocial sociality of men, that is, their inclination to enter society, an inclination paired however with a pervasive revulsion that continually threatens to break the society down." [18] The decisive element in the formula is asociality: Concord is merely the desire of men; discord is the prescript of nature, imposed in order to strain and thus develop the human being. Still, though it might be true that discord is nature's device for procuring eventual concord, that concord itself proves to be only a well regulated discord, at least on the legal and political level. Civil society is to the state of nature as order is to disorder and peace is to war, yet natural liberty and antagonism do and should survive in the civil state. The regime most conformable to the essence of civil society is the one which best conserves that liberty, while fostering this antagonism, achieves through the play of institutions the compatibility of each man's freedom with each other man's and the elimination of violence from antagonism.

If civil life depends on the egoistic restraint of egoism, our former question revives with new urgency: what is the relation between the social order and the morality to whose demands it is supposed to respond and for whose practice it is supposed to prepare? How does it differ from the "realistic," cynical, egoistic, or utilitarian constructions of the Machiavellian tradition? With the mediation of philosophy of history, Kant's political philosophy seems more than ever to be compounded of an abstract morality not of this world and an amoral politics too much of it.

The Legal State

Taken simply by itself, Kant's political philosophy, being essentially a legal doctrine, rejects by definition the opposition between moral education and the play of passions as alternate foundations for social life. The state is defined as the union of men under law. The state rightly so called is constituted by laws which are necessary a priori because they flow from the very concept of law. A regime can be judged by no other criteria, nor be assigned any other functions, than those proper to the lawful order as such. It is of the essence of law to stand a priori as proceeding from the practical reason and also to bear only on the external acts as those can be brought under legislation and external constraint without any regard to a man's purposes or interior motivation. Law thus provides a point of view, that is, in its abstractness and its universality, essentially neutral with respect to morality and happiness even though it may accord with either. Kant differs indeed from his predecessors in presenting morality as condemning the state of nature and commanding men to enter a lawful state in which they come under external constraint and in which alone the rights of man can be respected; and it is to morality that those rights owe their sanctity. But the sole innate right, the one upon which all others turn, is that guaranteeing every man's liberty to perform every external act that he pleases so long as he does not encroach on the same liberty in others. This external liberty is defined without regard to any internal moral limitation and it implies the rejection of every external moral limitation—every attempt by the state at moral education. Conversely, however responsible civil society might be for the preservation of its members, it must not adopt as its end their being, well being, or happiness, but may aim properly only at the preservation of the legal order itself. The universal and a priori character of law and the legal character of the political society require that the latter confine itself to the universal and hence minimum conditions for the coexistence of free men without regard to those men's empirical nature or the uses to which they will put their liberty. Moreover, there is another, more directly political basis for the disjunction between the ends of political society and the ends of its members: Individuals pursuing their diverse ends under an identical right to external liberty, the regime that would, withal benevolently, aim at prescribing to them the way to their happiness would be a paternal despotism inimical to their rights. In the same vein, the state cannot and should not attempt to constrain its citizens to act morally, for though the actions may be regulated, the intentions indispensable to the morality of those acts cannot be induced from without: I can perhaps be compelled to use certain means in order to gain a certain end, but I alone can dictate to myself the end.

It thus appears that this lawful state which must abstract from both happiness and moral duty to be based exclusively on external liberty will be that state by its nature opposed to despotism, namely, the republican state. Once it exists, this state proves to be most conducive both to men's happiness and to their morality—to their happiness because the sense of owing their fate to no one else is indispensable for men's happiness, and to their morality because conformity of men's acts to law prepares the conformity of their intentions to the moral law. It remains to be seen whether the Kantian system can succeed in enjoining the state, in the interest of external liberty, from any care for men's morals and happiness and at the same time make good its showing that the state follows from a concern with both and impels men toward both.

Kant's construction is based upon the absolute primacy of every man's innate right to external liberty (freedom from the constraint of another's will). At the same time, the practical reason affirms as its sole legal postulate the possibility of considering every external object as one's own. The innate right and the postulated possibility both require for their protection that men's external liberty be restricted. Lawful constraints on external liberty are indispensable to the conversion of mere possessions into definitive—because legal— property. Right demands that there be constraint, both of law-breakers and of those who must be forced into civil life.

The constitution of civil society is conceived as based on an original contract by which individuals join to establish a collective will to whose representative they delegate their separate powers of mutual constraint. As in Hobbes, only the chief of state may constrain others without being himself subject to constraint; but as in Rousseau, each, because joined to all, obeys only himself: The general will, source and product of the original contract, is sole sovereign and legislator, but with the understanding that the citizen body is itself that sovereign. Thus Kant can maintain, in *On Perpetual Peace,* that external liberty is not a man's freedom to do whatever he likes even within the limits of the similar freedom of others, but is rather his freedom from obeying any external laws to which he might not have consented. It follows that representative government, in which legislation is dominated by the general will, is the only legitimate government.

Kant distinguishes three political powers which are, in fact, the general will manifested in three "persons": the supreme power, or "sovereignty" in the person of the legislator; the executive power in the person of the governor; and the judicial power (securing to each his own) in the person of the judge. The test of a government's conformity to the original contract and of its representativeness and thus legitimacy is the separation of powers within it. In distinguishing the regimes, Kant replaces the traditional criterion of one, few, or many rulers in favor of looking to the manner (rooted in the action of the general will which effected the primitive transformation of the mob into a people) in which the state applies its absolute power. He emerges with the distinction between republican and despotic states. Despotism is exactly the collapsing of the legislative and executive into a single power that executes laws of its own creation, a condition exemplified in thoroughgoing democracy. On the other hand, the smaller the number of governors and the larger the representation of the people, the more perfectly the regime can approximate republicanism, in which in effect the government represents the people while the people themselves are the sovereign lawmaker.

Kant modifies this doctrine of popular sovereignty, with its obvious revolutionary implications, in ways that apparently run afoul of his distinctions between a priori and empirical and between law and morality. He declares, to begin with, that the original contract, that indispensable condition of civil society, law, and republicanism, need not be regarded as a historical fact and is, indeed, impossible except as an idea useful for impelling legislators to respect a seriously postulated general will.[19] But if the "original contract" is merely a criterion for judging regimes, so also is the general will that supposedly emerged from it. Thus an actual expression of the general will by popular vote may legitimately be replaced by monarchic legislation so long as that legislation *could* have received the approval of the general will. While republicanism is thus transforming itself into justice as the criterion of legitimacy, any government at all can be considered legitimate, at least provisionally; although it is to be understood that no substantive principle of justice is applicable but only the formal principle of universalizability: A measure is adopted rightfully by an entire people, or consistently with the general will by a governor, if there is nothing contradictory in it. This confirms the definition of right in abstraction from all moral and empirical considerations. But it is distinctly up to the ruler and not the people to judge whether the definition is being respected; the people are to obey under all circumstances.[20] The disqualification of the people from defending their inalienable rights almost guarantees some departure from strict rightfulness. This is not seriously affected by the fact that the citizens must have the right of free discussion and criticism. Hence justice must eventually depend upon the good will of the chief of state, whose power is not to be checked by any other. Kant subscribed to the modern replacement of education by institutions and of the moral regulation of the passions by their mutual limitations, but until the revolutions that he condemns on moral grounds will have installed republicanism everywhere, respect for the rights of man, deduced a priori though they be, will apparently depend on such empirical facts as the education and morality of the rulers.

This is doubtless why Kant regards the political problem as incapable of perfect solution: Man is an animal that needs a master, but the master is himself a man. The abstract solution according to which every man will be his own master, all being reciprocally masters and subjects, appears viable only (and at that precariously) when seriously modified by empirical or moral considerations that Kant struggles vainly to represent as necessary a priori and purely in the interest of lawfulness as such. More generally, he is led to justify many prudential measures which ultimately concern the prosperity of the state and the happiness of its citizens; but he strains to derive their justification from arguments that prove them necessary for the defense of the legitimate state against external enemies of the people.

ETERNAL PEACE

The same problems recur even more pointedly in Kant's most original and perhaps most decisive political teaching, namely, his doctrine of the relations among states and of perpetual peace. Here too the desire to reconcile a purely legal doctrine based on the demands of morality with the mechanism of the passions, to reconcile the ideal with the real through the morally demanded teleology of nature (the cunning of nature), leads to far-reaching concessions based on empirical considerations. In the course of shattering the neutral, abstract ground of law, the elaboration of this doctrine revives in all its difficulty and harshness the problem of the relation between morality and history.

It is precisely the uncompromising and abstract legalism of Kant's enterprise that carries it beyond the positions of Hobbes and Locke; for, conceiving the institution of the state as a mere developmental stage, Kant displaces the problem of the transition from the state of nature to the state of civil society onto the universal or cosmopolitan plane. The necessities that lead to the formation of any particular civil society are so pervasive that they affect also the relations among the societies, to the point of precluding any perfect response to those necessities on the part of the coexisting states. The same juridical postulate underlies internal and external politics, public law, the law of nations (or of the relations of states), and cosmopolitan law (of men and states as citizens of the universal city): "All men who can affect each other reciprocally should be within the purview of some civil institution," for even if only one enjoys his natural license, the state of war returns.[21] Any external danger, whether from a community or an individual, disturbs civil society's guarantee of peaceful freedom and property against violence. Individuals cannot heed their own interest, nor the command of practical reason ("there shall not be war") nor nature's plan ("complete civil unification of mankind") if the states do not follow the path from the state of nature to the lawful state. Kant, like Hobbes, maintains that the state of nature is a state of war, and that the nations are in that state in relation to each other. Again like Hobbes, he maintains that, in the natural state, the peaceableness of any given moment is only an empirical episode in the underlying state of war. The state of peace, if it is to exist, must be explicitly in-

stituted. Kant's political philosophy, because essentially legal, becomes primarily a doctrine of war and peace in which foreign policy
openly takes precedence over domestic: Particular civil constitutions
must fail to bring peace internally while external threats to peace
persist. Kant heatedly criticizes Grotius and other theorists of international law, as well as the balance-of-power school, because they
do not recognize the decisive importance of procuring lawful organization among the states.

Having maintained so much, Kant astonishes the reader of the
first part of the *Metaphysics of Morals* ("Doctrine of Law") by declaring that the organization of states must not possess sovereign
power but should be merely an alliance or federation, revocable at
will and requiring periodic renewal. It is obvious that such an
organization's ability to procure compliance or peace is questionable.
Kant's obscurity or hesitation on this point compromises two even
more fundamental concerns: Perpetual peace may be only precarious
or provisional rather than definitive; and it might in fact be a
purely unattainable ideal rather than a moral necessity or a predictable fact. Finally, the difficulties affecting a juridical conception
of international order bring us face to face again with the problematic
character of Kant's claim to have solved Rousseau's problem—does
historical progress really prepare the moral regeneration of mankind?

The difficulties that arise for Kant on the political and legal
level inhere in the nature of an international organization that
might or should stand to its component states as those states stand
to their citizens. The full effectiveness of the organization would
presuppose encroachments on the authority of the states themselves,
or even on their very standing as states. On the other hand, if the
organization's power is restricted, the states remain effectually in
the original condition of lawlessness and imminent war. The alternative consists of the universal state on the one hand and mere pact
or alliance of states on the other. Kant rejects the universal state
and seems to favor the federation or "republic of republics." It is
not clear whether the republic of republics is an unattainable ideal
useful for regulating action or a realizable goal that alone could
introduce lawfulness and meaning into politics and history.

Kant rejects the universal state for reasons that depart from
the abstractions of legality, and that depend rather upon empirical
political wisdom, morality, and philosophy of history. His objection
is that "Laws lose more and more of their force as the government
gains in extent, and a soulless despotism decays at last into anarchy

after having destroyed the germs of good." [22] The universal state would be the universal despotism and the peace that would prevail would be the peace of the tomb, uncognizant not only of liberty but of virtue, taste, and science. Moreover, the universal state must disintegrate into the smaller bodies whose interaction is the chosen instrument of nature. Kant firmly decides in favor of the difficult reconciliation of the multiplicity of states and a lawful order, although it is true that, in *Religion within the Limits of Reason Alone,* he refers to the "premature and therefore fatal fusion of states (if it occurs before men have become morally better)" thus leaving open the possibility of the universal state as the culmination of a historical progress that has moral progress as its prerequisite condition.

In his notes and published writings, Kant comments variously though not merely inconsistently on the triple question of the coercive power of the Confederation, the provisionality or perfection of the peace it might procure, and the status of the project as possible and hence obligatory or as impossible and distracting. In some statements, participation in a lawful constitution is obligatory on the states, in other statements not. In some, the states may compel their neighbors to participate in such a constitution, in others they may not. In some, the international body can coerce, in others it cannot. Sometimes the international organization is shown as persistently progressing because it is of the nature of Good to endure, once begun, as of Evil to destroy itself; but sometimes the organization is represented as being in constant danger of falling apart. Sometimes the project is presented as an unrealizable idea, sometimes as a limit approachable by indefinite asymptotic progress, and sometimes as an end attainable by the agreement of three European rulers. Kant's published writings taken by themselves reflect doubt and perhaps evolution in his thought, indicating the impossibility of a purely legal solution of the problem and the difficulty of obtaining any solution at all. The reader is referred particularly to *The Idea of a Universal History with Cosmopolitan Intent, Theory and Practice,* and *On Perpetual Peace.* His view as it emerges in the "Doctrine of Law" (in the *Metaphysics of Morals*) deserves special consideration for the issues that it raises. His argument there may be summarized as follows. (1) Eternal peace constitutes a radical and indispensable transformation of human affairs without which all possession and security are merely provisional. It requires the establishment of a universal civil constitution (*Völkerstaat*). (2) This is impracticable; a congress of states must be accepted instead. (3) As the impracticability has not been demonstrated absolutely, and morality demands eternal peace and thus the universal civil constitution, one must nevertheless adopt eternal peace as the goal to be forever approached through perpetual progress.

This argument is not free of serious difficulties. In the first place, is the profundity of the transformation introduced by eternal peace compatible with the progressive, imperceptible, and above all apparently endless evolution that leads to that transformation? Kant's doctrine appears to appeal implicitly both to the notion of the end of History and to that of perpetual progress; but the two notions are mutually contradictory.

In the second place, if entry upon a civil constitution appears for the moment as no more than a distant goal, and the institutional constraint of the passions is correspondingly remote, it follows that in the immediate present international law has, as Hegel was to say, the form of duty, of the "ought." It is the dictate of morality that the states transform themselves and their relations immediately so as to make possible a future lawful condition (or perhaps *as if* to make that condition possible). Kant had criticized existing international law, and Grotius particularly, by emphasizing that there can be no law without the lawful state and no lawful state without contract and constraint. But he himself, in his project for perpetual peace, is led to enumerate certain preliminary articles that are justified by the maxim, "So act as not to hinder the departure of states from the state of nature and the inauguration of perpetual peace." Some of those articles are for immediate application, some may be deferred for prudential reasons; but in any case it is certain that, in them, part of classic international law reappears, if with a new ultimate justification, constituting what is most concrete and most tangible in Kant's doctrine of perpetual peace and of the law of nations. In his last published work, "The Strife between the Faculties," Kant appears to place his emphasis and his hopes regarding eternal peace on the institution of essentially peaceful republican government within the states rather than on the submission of the states to a universal civil community.

Kant's arguments seem to imply that the transformation of nature and of international relations, the latter the most virulent and conspicuous testimony to the wickedness of human nature, can lead eventually to the submission of the states to a lawful constitution and to perpetual peace, which in turn must open the way to the moral regeneration of states and men. The dual question now reappears: Can moral progress be depended upon to transform history in a way conducive to law and peace? Can historical progress be depended upon to produce a universal lawful constitution and a state of peace favorable to morality? With either history or morality as the point of departure, and allowing for the apparent neutrality of the legal point of view, the question whether and how either might influence the other recurs: imperceptible progress or radical transformation?

Let us consider first what Kant regards as the concrete historical indications that nature vouchsafes eternal peace, and also what near or remote prospects are opened by that guarantee. The central theme, dictated by the problem itself and by Kant's conception of history as governed by antagonism, is the part played in history by war; but this theme is articulated with that of the progress of civilization in the age of enlightenment, and more particularly with the opposition between religion and commerce. In the first place, there are the external conditions by which nature manifests its philanthropy and by which natural teleology prepares the framework for historical theology: the devices for example, by which nature has made even the most inhospitable regions of the earth inhabitable. Secondly, it is through the mediation of warfare that nature has driven men into every corner of the world, compelling them actually to inhabit it throughout, thus making possible its progressive political unification. To the extent that men do not advance toward their moral end by the instrumentality of their freedom, they must advance under the constraints of nature; and thus, according to the third provisional disposition of nature, men are compelled, under the shadow of war, to enter upon more or less legal relations. More specifically, external war and also domestic antagonisms press in the direction of republican government as being most effective in meeting both kinds of threat. But republican government is of all forms the most conducive to peace. Therefore precisely as republicanism is diffused in the world, war tends to be suppressed. Within the international law perspective, however, presupposing as it does the independent existence of many states, nature appears as obstructing that eternal peace obtainable by the fusion of states into a universal state. Nature interferes with that fusion by procuring difference of language and of religion. These are to some extent desirable and permanent even though they entail hatred and war. This necessary evil is gradually overcome, however, by the progress of enlightenment which, collaborating with the advance of civilization and of a broad human concord, conduces to a general pacification based on liberty, equilibrium, and emulation. Supervening over all the diverse manifestations of religion must be the one universal "religion within the limits of reason alone," valid for all men and all times, the gradually emerging, pacifying product of that same enlightenment.

Rational religion could not produce unity and peace without a concurrent progress of civilization that would support them with a more solid basis in common interest. Within the large scene of natural division and coerced union among the peoples, the commercial spirit sooner or later begins to move in every nation, tending to bring harmony where the notion of cosmopolitan law could have little effect. Commerce, the medium of their common interest, is promoted by a spirit that is incompatible with war. "Of all the powers and means at the disposal of the state, the power of money is undoubtedly the surest, and the states thus find themselves constrained to assist the advance toward noble peace (not, it is true, for moral reasons) and to avert war where it threatens, by mediation, precisely as if they were joined in perpetual alliance for this purpose. ... It is thus that nature guarantees perpetual peace by the very mechanism of the human propensities." [23]

One has the sense of confronting at last the true reasons that underlie Kant's hopefulness—in large measure the reasons of his century. Religions which divide are opposed, as in the thought of Montesquieu, by commerce which unites. The internal economic development of the states and the elaboration of their external commercial relations will make war unprofitable and disastrous, respectively. Wealth replaces power as the measure of superiority. Conquest had carried mankind far along the road to unity and lawfulness, but the diversity of languages and religions had effectually stood in the way. Now commerce replaces conquest to carry on the work of unification in a way that respects that diversity and insures peace within limits compatible with it. Where war, through conquest, and morality, through education, had failed, it seemed to Kant's age as though commerce or more generally money was about to succeed.

Yet the working of commerce is intertwined with that of war, enlightenment, and morality; and the obscurities of Kantianism prevent us from discerning clearly the modes and final direction of that working. Does the economic evolution of mankind tend to the abolition of war through making warfare so brutal as to be unbearable or through the decay of warfare as contrary to the spirit and interest of the states? If Evil (the conflict of propensities) gives rise to Good (perpetual peace), does it do so through catastrophes brought on by its overwhelming power or through meliorations brought on by its debility? The former possibility points toward radical revolution and regeneration, the latter toward a gradual and indefinite process.

The most massive indication given by Kant seems to point in the former direction: Wars are becoming more frequent and deadly and above all more expensive—in brief, so catastrophic as to be impossible. Mankind will be compelled to change its course. But the turning toward the good will not have the character of a unique, inevitable, and decisive event. On the contrary, it is bound up with the progress of civilization and enlightenment, and depends in some degree on the understanding and decisions of sovereigns, which in turn depend on a basic advance in enlightenment the deferment of which casts the crucial event into an indefinite future. And even then, the originally supposed turning toward the good will not radically and decisively transform the condition of states and of man.

The perspective is one of a gradual melioration, corresponding with progress in enlightenment and culture, entailing progress if not in men's morality at least in the lawfulness of their acts which, apart from the intentions at work, will conform more and more closely to the dictate of duty. The tension between perpetual peace as eventuality and as regulative principle, between indefinite progress as a movement that never attains its goal and as one that attains it increasingly, is well expressed in the final passage of *On Perpetual Peace:* "If the realization of the regime of public lawfulness is a duty, and if there is some reason in experience for thinking it realizable though only by approaching it through an indefinite progress, the 'eternal peace' that will replace the misnamed treaty-peaces (really only truces) is not an inane idea but a task which, performed little by little, constantly approaches its end—for it is to be hoped that the intervals of equal progress will continually shrink." The notion of asymptotic progress is the most consistent with the Kantian conception of infinity as presented in the *Critique of Pure Reason.* Kant draws on the mathematicians to deny that one contradicts himself in maintaining that mankind's progress is a constant approaching of the goal and assimilation to it without ever reaching it. But in the political and historical world of man, the idea of accelerated progress toward a goal never really reached poses difficulties greater than those in the paradox of Achilles and the tortoise. The idea becomes intelligible only by virtue of various "replacements": What on one level appears as a realizable goal appears on a lower level as a regulative idea; morality is replaced by legality; the lawful state of mutually-cancelling egoisms under external constraints replaces the state of man made good by the inner compulsion of duty; the situation in which the states engage to renounce war (although it is itself a juridical condition) replaces the juridical condition in the strict sense as defined by submission of the nations to public constraint (*Völkerstaat*). And the situation in which states gain nothing from war, in which they intervene to suppress it as if they were engaged to do so but are not, is a "quasi-juridical" condition, a substitute for the lawful state in which peace is not merely probable but would be assured by submission to public authority, or at least war would be explicitly outlawed by pact.

Progress entails a growing mollification of the state of war, which however remains the essence of the relations among states and, strictly speaking, among men. A combination of education (enlightenment) and incapacity (equilibrium of forces and the costliness of war) brings the state of nature increasingly to resemble the lawful state, the state of war to resemble the state of peace; but neither the nature of societies nor that of men is truly changed, nothing is truly guaranteed, and in the end, strictly speaking, nothing is truly saved.

Perhaps nothing is saved not because it cannot be saved but because the essential and decisive step remains to be taken. History leads men to civilization, that is to say, to a manipulable arrangement within the state of war or the play of passion; it leaves men at the threshold of true peace and true legality. But perhaps this is because it leaves men on the threshold of morality which, confronting the interior debility of its adversary, will exploit the opportunity to administer the decisive stroke, introducing that genuine republican government whose concept is accessible only to the moral politician and that peace whose concept is moral. Historical reformation is to be succeeded by moral revolution. Indeed, for Kant, "revolution is necessary for the manner of thinking (*Denkungsart*) but gradual reform for the manner of feeling (*Sinnesart*)." The radical turnabout is necessary because "becoming not merely a legally but a morally good man ... cannot be achieved through gradual reform, so long as the foundation of the maxims remains impure; rather it must be achieved through a revolution in the mentality (*Gesinnung*) of the man ... ; and he can become a new man only by a kind of rebirth resembling a new creation, and a change of heart." [24]

We may infer that "nature's cunning" eventuates, through progress in culture and lawfulness, through war and commerce, in a negative triumph that consists merely in disposing of the hindrances to morality or in bringing them into a state of mutual neutralization, while its proper goals (peace and universal lawfulness) are attained only when the practical reason intervenes directly to achieve its own ends, which include those of nature but surpass them. As appears in *On Perpetual Peace,* Kant believed that evil is self-destructive and the designs of wicked men reciprocally frustrating. And he shows further that it is a matter of the active intervention, *in extremis* so to speak, of the moral intention and not merely the unconscious realization of good through evil: "When the motives of natural politics will suppress and destroy one another, that of moral politics will begin to become manifest in action and to realize the idea of eternal peace." [25]

From History to Morality

As it appears, morality on the one hand and nature or history on the other will have their effect through a collaboration rather resembling a relay. First, "nature comes to the aid of that general will founded on reason and revered by all but practically ineffectual, by insuring the mutual cancellation of the selfish propensities to such effect that, for reason itself, it is as if they did not exist." [26] But then, in the second instance, the ground having been cleared, it is morality or the practical reason that takes charge and by itself brings the task to completion; and it is "the general or universal will, given a priori, that alone determines what is lawful among men," and that can, "if we conduct our affairs with consistency, be the cause that produces the desired effect through the mechanism of nature itself and that at the same time permits the notion of law to be realized." [27]

But if the institution of the true lawful state and of eternal peace is bound to the actual intervention in history of a moral intention, in what concrete kinds of action will this intention express itself? Does the moral transformation of men lead to the decisive transformation of the institutions that the perfect equilibrium of the passions has failed to procure? Is it on the contrary the transformation of institutions which must, in the long run, lead to the moral transformation of the citizens, insuring thereby the stability of those very institutions? Or is the moral intention that manifests itself in history in fact the intention of sovereigns enlightened by philosophy who undertake simultaneously the transformation of institutions and the moral education of their subjects? In *Religion within the Limits of Reason Alone* and in the *Idea for a Universal History with Cosmopolitan Intent,* Kant presents the moral regeneration of men and their moral education by the states as necessarily antecedent to the unification of mankind. In *On Perpetual Peace,* however, he moves from the notion of moral education by the community to the thought that such education is not indispensable for the formation of republican government. In fact Kant indicates that nature accomplishes what is needful for the purpose through the selfish propensities themselves, leaving to the state the task of exploiting the natural mechanism for making good citizens of morally defective men. He uses the example of the nation of devils to argue that the founding of the state does not require the moral goodness of men. Kant drew attention to the approximation to morality that can be observed in actual states, wherein moral perfection is certainly not the decisive influence nor even intended by the law, and commented that one is not to expect a good constitution from the people's morality but rather the sound moral education of the people from the constitution.[28]

The two lines of thought can indeed be reconciled to some extent. Where the institutions were given precedence over moral transformation, the context was the domestic constitution of the state and the external constraints of law as a substitute for the internal constraints of morality proper. Where moral transformation was given precedence over the institutions, the context was the relations among states which cannot dispense with morality since they do not recognize any effectual external constraint. But there remains the paradox according to which one may expect a constitution that grows out of the mechanism of the propensities to educate a people properly: If a republican government can accomplish that, why should that not become the chief function of such a government? Can it fulfill that function regardless of the dispositions, training, and intentions of its citizens? Can it inspire with a good will a nation of devils who, forced by their selfish propensities to enter into a lawful state, would become morally good through the influence of that state?

Elsewhere, Kant mitigates this paradox, presenting as complementary the two ideas which seem to be in conflict: "The constitution of the state rests ultimately on the people's morality, which in turn cannot take root without a good constitution."[29] This could easily have been said by Plato and Aristotle. If then Kant agrees so far with the Classics, should he not accept also their presuppositions and their conclusions concerning the moral aim of politics and the politic character of morality? Stated differently, Kant's position as expressed in this passage seems to raise two questions, one practical: "Why should not the state adopt as its goal the people's morality?"

and one theoretical: "Does not the stated reciprocity between law and morality conflict with whatever is specifically Kantian in the conception of each? Is not the core of Kantianism precisely the radical disjunction of legality, which bears solely on the external actions, and morality, which bears solely on the intentions?"

The reply to the first question is to some extent contained in the second. Kant can never for a moment abandon the idea that a moral intention, a good will, cannot be introduced into us by any external command: We can be forced to perform certain acts but we cannot be forced to adopt a certain end as our own. The suggestion of political influence upon morality can be made legitimately only with a view to the attenuated, gradual, and indirect compulsions implicit in education and habituation. Can these latter not transform man's empirical nature sufficiently to favor his moral liberty? If an educator, whether the family, the state, or nature, teaches us to develop our reason and to master our instincts, do not this development and mastery, even though they began by promoting selfish ends, lead us up to the border of morality and render highly probable that final conversion of liberty that would give them a moral value? In brief, in multiplying the conduits between nature and liberty, through the notion of a liberty sprung from nature and progressively emancipating itself from it, are not nature and liberty being reunited according to the internal principles of law? That is indeed the primary function of philosophy of history according to Kant. The final problem of philosophy of history is to grasp the moral bearing of progress in culture, civilization, and lawfulness, which converges, on the level of the education of mankind, with the problem of the possibility of the moral education of the individual.

Kant's replies to the decisive question are as diverse and hesitant as are those that he gives regarding the institutional and historical conditions of peace. Perhaps the most exact formulation of his thought on the issue can be elicited from two passages, one on the effects of the lawfulness that prevails within states and the other on the level of historical teleology. In the former (*On Perpetual Peace,* Appendix I) Kant maintains that the enforced prohibitions against acting upon lawless propensities encourage a moral predilection to respect the law. In the *Critique of Judgment,* which contains the latter passage (§83), Kant wishes to show how the ultimate end of nature, viz., "culture" as meaning the aptitude freely to propose ends to oneself and to use nature as the means thereto, prepares moral liberty, the only unconditional end in itself independent of nature. For this purpose he must introduce an intermediate notion, that of the superior form of culture that he calls the *culture of discipline,* under which men master without expunging those natural desires that conduce to the ends of life, being free to give rein to them but only so far as reason itself dictates. This possibility of mastering the passions prepares that radical emancipation vis-a-vis all external proclivities that itself constitutes morality. The growth of such mastery must be understood as based upon that civilization of man that manifests itself in the refinement of taste and the elaboration of knowledge, notwithstanding the heightening of sensuality that is inseparable from the process. "The fine arts and the sciences, which render man if not morally better at least more civilized by virtue of enjoyments that are accessible to all and of the graces of society, prevail mightily against the despotism of the senses and thus prepare man for a dominion in which power will belong to the reason alone; and in the meantime, the evils that nature inflicts upon us, such as the intractable selfishness of man, summon up the energies of the soul, intensify them and strengthen them for resistance, thus revealing to us the aptitude for higher ends that is hidden within us." [30]

The crucial question that must be faced concerning the two passages, the question in which is concentrated the entire problem of Kantian philosophy of history and politics, is this: What precise meaning should be attached to such expressions as "make easier," "make susceptible to," "reveal the aptitude for," "prepare for," "prevail mightily against," "take a long step towards," and so on? What is the nature, or more precisely what is the necessity of the link between what prepares and what is prepared, between "the long step towards morality" and the "moral step" itself? The latter might necessarily imply the former, but the former does not appear necessarily to lead to the latter. Too strict a union between them would import a determinism or mechanism into the conditions of morality that would jeopardize the essential freedom of morality itself. Too stark a disjunction of them, too radical a transition from nature to freedom or from the phenomenal to the noumenal world, renders idle the entire project of philosophy of history which was precisely to attempt to bridge that gap. It is hard to see how an imperceptible transition from the premoral to the moral condition would be compatible with the radical moral choice between passions and duty that is implicit in Kant's conception of morality. What may be said with confidence, however, is that civilization and lawfulness must necessarily precede morality and that the moral decision in turn is the beginning, the *archē,* of the moral life, and cannot be replaced by the various appeals to egoism, or by discipline and legality, all of which can never be more than the submoral preparation for morality.

Philosophy of history can mitigate but it can in no way annul the absolute disjunction of evil and good, of egoism and morality, of nature and freedom. Freedom must either be or not be, and if it is, it is incompatible with the working of any automatic mechanism. The moral conversion of mankind, which can never become a theoretical certainty or mechanical necessity, cannot be regarded as the basis for a solution of the political problem. Reciprocally, the historical and juridical exploitation of the mechanism of the passions renders impossible a moral solution of the human problem.

Politics, law, and history remain for Kant in an ambiguous or unresolved relation to morality, the two sides of the relation being in a state of mutual need and mutual repulsion. Kant presents the political and juridical order as being limited to external actions yet both morally necessary and achieved by immoral means. But as we have seen, Kant does not succeed in maintaining the merely legal character of the juridical order for he reintroduces morality surreptitiously into that order. We have seen, in examining the moral bases of the rights of man and of philosophy of history, that Kant fails to demonstrate either the moral bases of those rights or the moral necessity of that philosophy. We have seen, finally, in considering the application of philosophy of history to the decisive problem of eternal peace, that immoral or Machiavellian means did not suffice to bring about such peace.

In effect, whether one looks at Kant's political doctrine, his legal doctrine, or his philosophy of history, morality is seen always to have either too much or too little to do. If a political preoccupation associated with the rights of man is central to his inspiration and particularly to the inspiration for his morality, his effectual political doctrine nonetheless remains an unstable and unsatisfying synthesis of a moral and a "realist" intention. Kant's understanding and formulations enabled him to reinterpret modern political life with a view to the crucial and neglected issue of its moral dignity, deliberately sacrificed by the tradition of Machiavelli and Hobbes; but what enabled his philosophy to achieve this gain stood in the way of a truly coherent solution. The existence of his moral doctrine forbids a solution of the political problem by means of institutions; the nature of that doctrine forbids a solution by means of education.

In the last analysis, it is the problem of moral education and moral conversion that lies at the center of Kant's difficulties, for this problem is affected by the mutual influence and intercourse passing between the two worlds, that of moral freedom and that of natural determinism, that Kant sought with great labor to preserve by keeping radically disjoined from one another. The meeting grounds that he attempts to multiply between them are insecure and problematic: Politics is not guided by natural prudence, it is simply sometimes moral and sometimes immoral; history presupposes the paradoxical notion of a teleological nature that apparently lacks ontological foundation and that collaborates historically with determinism to exploit, unknown to them, the designs of men; in other words, of a Providence which is nature called by another name and which somewhat incomprehensibly prefers the use of immoral means but which stops before man's moral freedom; law is simultaneously the expression of the mechanism of nature and of the concepts of practical reason; but what "nature and freedom joined according to the internal principles of law" eventuates in is a combination of formal principles and contingent arrangements which is so hard to apply to the relations among states that it casts doubt not only upon itself but, by implication, on the very demands of morality and the very guarantees of nature. Every one of these proposed meeting grounds between the two worlds is exposed to a criticism that would draw attention at the same time to the decisive character of the problems being posed and the sometimes extraordinarily crude or contradictory character of the solutions being offered.

Even if it be admitted, however, that Kant fails to reconcile the external and the internal, necessity and freedom, nature and morality, the evidence of physics and the testimony of conscience, it must nevertheless be considered whether there is not in each of these terms something irreducible which Kant alone has caused to emerge in all its power. The critic of Kant's political philosophy can doubtless win victories either on the field of the concrete political phenomena examined on the level appropriate to them, or by challenging the coherence of the system as a whole; but if the victories are to be decisive, the criticism should deal with the foundations of Kant's thought. The critique of Kant's political philosophy must become a critique of the *Critique of Pure Reason* and the *Critique of Practical Reason*.

NOTES

1. The political section of the first part of the *Metaphysics of Morals* entitled "Metaphysical Elements of the Doctrine of Law"; *On Perpetual Peace;* and the article "On the Common Saying: That Might Be True in Theory But It Does Not Apply in Practice." These three writings follow the tripar-

tition: public law, law of nations, and "cosmopolitan" law.

2. Especially "Idea for a Universal History with Cosmopolitan Intent"; "Conjectural Beginning of Human History"; and the second section of "Battle between the Faculties" (of philosophy and law).

3. *On Perpetual Peace*, Appendix I; First Addition.

4. Annotations to *Observations on the Sense of the Beautiful and the Sublime*, Akademie Ausgabe, vol. 20, p. 44. See also *The Philosophy of Kant*, ed. Carl J. Friedrich, p. xxii (New York: Modern Library, 1949).

5. Cf. *The Philosophy of Kant*, ed. Friedrich, p. 45.

6. *Critique of Pure Reason*, Transcendental Dialectic, book 1, sect. 1.

7. *Metaphysics of Morals*, part 2, "Doctrine of Virtue" (*Tugendlehre*), paras. 38, 39.

8. *Fundamental Principles of the Metaphysic of Morals*, section 2.

9. *Ibid.*

10. *Ibid.*

11. Annotations to *Observations on the Sense of the Beautiful and the Sublime*, Akademie Ausgabe, vol. 20, p. 58.

12. *Metaphysics of Morals*, "Doctrine of Right," conclusion.

13. "Idea for a Universal History with Cosmopolitan Intent," proem.

14. *On Perpetual Peace*, First Addition.

15. *Ibid.*

16. *Critique of Judgment*, §84.

17. "Conjectural Beginning of Human History" ("Mutmasslicher Anfang der Menschengeschichte," *Vermischte Schriften*, p. 274 Inselverlag).

18. "Idea for a Universal History with Cosmopolitan Intent," 4th Principle.

19. "On the Common Saying: That Might Be True in Theory but It Does Not Apply in Practice," conclusion.

20. *Ibid.*

21. *On Perpetual Peace*, sect. 2, note 3.

22. *Ibid.*, 1st Addition.

23. *Ibid.*

24. *Religion within the Limits of Reason Alone*, I. v.

25. Vorarbeiten zum *Ewigen Frieden* (preparatory notes for *On Perpetual Peace*) in Kant's *Gesammelte Schriften*, Akademie Ausgabe, vol. 23, p. 192.

26. *On Perpetual Peace*, 1st Addition.

27. Vorarbeiten zum *Öffentlichen Recht* (preparatory notes for *Public Law*) in Kant's *Gesammelte Schriften*, Akademie Ausgabe, vol. 23, p. 353.

28. *On Perpetual Peace*, 1st Addition.

29. Vorarbeiten zum *Ewigen Frieden*, *Gesammelte Schriften*, Akademie Ausgabe, vol. 23, p. 162.

30. *Critique of Judgment*, §83.

WILLIAM BLACKSTONE

1723–1780

Sir William Blackstone was not a political philosopher, but an English lawyer and judge. His major piece of writing is not a book on justice or even on law, but a set of *Commentaries on the Laws of England*. He was not original or inventive, but deliberately the opposite; and he often treats important and difficult questions in what seems to be an obscure or superficial way. Indeed, Blackstone is fairly widely regarded as having been contradictory or confused on important points of political philosophy. He is thought to exhibit a character that is amiable if a bit pompous; a style that is crisp and sometimes elegant; an intellect not strong in theory but capable of sound practical judgment and intrinsically bent to compromise—in short, to present himself a thorough Englishman. There is considerable ground for this view, but it is insufficient, and the reasons for its insufficiency are the reasons for giving note to Blackstone in a history of political philosophy.

When Blackstone first offered a course of lectures on the laws of England at Oxford University in 1753, he set a precedent that was intended to have a major effect on English legal and, more broadly, civic education.[1] Although the *Commentaries* are addressed to officers of every description and subjects of every order, they are aimed particularly at the lawyer and the gentleman. The lawyer was to be lifted from the confines of mere practice and directed to the elements and first principles upon which his practice was based. The gentleman was to be rescued from his dishonorable ignorance of the laws that it was his duty to safeguard, improve, and administer. In both cases what was required was academical instruction in the laws of the land which would enable the student not only to learn the outlines of the positive law but also to comprehend, and even himself to form, arguments "drawn *a priori,* from the spirit of the laws and the natural foundations of justice." [2] Blackstone invites examination of the laws of the land, their natural foundations, and the intervening "spirit of the laws." It is true that he also discusses divine law, for example, in his introductory treatment of law in general, but divine law typically makes an early and brief appearance, soon collapsing into natural law; and Blackstone makes little or no use of it in explaining, as distinguished from supporting, the laws of England. Religion does indeed have an important place under the laws of England, and Blackstone is a warm friend of the established Church; but what is relevant is the influence of the Church in making men sober, industrious, and good citizens. [3]

Blackstone's highest theme, then, deals with the relation between natural law and conventional law, as this relation presents itself to one who is a lawyer in the best and highest sense. The plan or organization of the *Commentaries* is characterized by a symmetry which contains, as a whole and in each of the parts, a movement or progression from the natural to the conventional. [4] Following an Introduction, the four volumes of the *Commentaries* are divided into two parts, each comprising two volumes or books. First are "Rights," divided into the Rights of Persons (Book I) and the Rights of Things (Book II); there follow "Wrongs," divided into Private Wrongs (Book III) and Public Wrongs (Book IV). The argument as a whole moves from individual rights to public wrongs.

The first chapter of Book I begins with what Blackstone calls the absolute rights of individuals, which are those that appertain and belong to particular men as individuals and "would belong to their persons merely in a state of nature. . . ." The "first and primary end" of human laws is to maintain and regulate these absolute rights. [5] Blackstone spends little time, however, with the natural liberty of mankind, even in this first chapter, but moves quickly to the subject of civil rights and specifically the absolute rights of Englishmen, which are treated under the familiar Lockean headings of personal security, personal liberty, and private property. The remainder and by far the bulk of Book I deals with relative rights, that is, the secondary and more artificial rights of individuals as they stand in legally established relationships to other individuals, first the public relationships of governors and governed, then the private relationships of master and servant, husband and wife, parent and child, and the like, which are consequent on civil society. Although the right of property is discussed, as has been said, in the first chapter of Book I as one of the absolute rights of individuals, Blackstone treats property in a separate and subse-

quent book, subsequent, it may be noted, even to the relations of government. The reason for this is that the natural origin of rights of
things is, compared to rights of persons, both less clear and less relevant
to civil society. It is less clear because Blackstone finds the natural origin
in occupancy or possession, and he seems to leave open the difficult question of what kind of right mere possession can be or grant; it is less relevant because, whereas natural personal rights, such as self-defense, are
more or less regulated by positive law, the natural right to acquire
property is substantially replaced or superseded by conventional rights
to hold and transfer property.[6]

"Wrongs," the subject of the second part of the *Commentaries,* are
said "for the most part [to] convey to us an idea merely negative, as
being nothing else but a privation of right."[7] The second part contains
no chapters comparable in philosophical intention to the first chapters
of Books I and II, because wrongs are defined by and derivative from
rights. The last pair of books is not, however, merely a mirror image
of the first pair. Book III describes how the law provides for the redress
of private wrongs relating to both persons and property (civil injuries),
reflecting therefore the discussion in both Book I and Book II and bringing to a conclusion, as it were, the whole subject of individual rights.
Public wrongs (crimes and misdemeanors), the subject of Book IV,
constitute that part of the law that is most artificial. Rights are the
basis of Blackstone's jurisprudence, and there are, strictly speaking, no
rights of the public but only rights of individuals. In Book IV, however, political society, which is a means to the end of protecting individual rights, is treated—as it can and must be treated for many
practical purposes—as if it were an end. That end is "the government
and tranquillity of the whole," or more simply, peace; "for peace is the
very end and foundation of civil society."[8] Without entering into detail, we may say that Blackstone's description of the several species of
crimes and misdemeanors, for example crimes against God and religion
and against the king and government, contains his negative or indirect
discussion of the kind of artificial public or common good that must
be constructed for the sake of the peaceful enjoyment of individual
rights.

"The only true and natural foundations of society," Blackstone
asserts, "are the wants and fears of individuals"[9]; but it is not Blackstone's procedure to enter into any detailed or exhaustive examination of
these wants and fears or of the natural liberty of mankind from which
he begins. Rather he hastens on (not, we may imagine, to the displeasure

of his English gentlemen and lawyers) to a discussion of civil rights, as if to define the rights of man in terms of the rights of Englishmen. The rights of Englishmen, however, are all rights *under law*. Personal liberty, to give but one example, "consists in the power of loco-motion, of changing situation, or removing one's person to whatsoever place one's own inclination may direct; without imprisonment or restraint, *unless by due course of law*." [10] But if the law were amended to permit arrest and imprisonment for indefinite periods on suspicion of executive officials, would that not constitute an abridgment of the Englishman's right of personal liberty? Putting the point more generally, Blackstone says, following Montesquieu, that in England as perhaps nowhere else, "political or civil liberty is the very end and scope of the constitution"; but he goes on to say that "this liberty, rightly understood, consists in the power of doing whatever the laws permit. . . ." [11] Blackstone seems to present a circular argument: defining good law as that which best maintains individual liberty and defining individual liberty as that which is permitted by law. This circularity or ambiguity is present throughout the *Commentaries,* not because of a defect in Blackstone's powers of reasoning or some irrational commitment to the English legal system, but because the theoretically sound argument, the argument taken from nature, tends to be practically self-defeating.

Even self-defense, "justly called the primary law of nature," is strictly confined, although "it is not, neither can it be in fact, taken away by the law of society." [12] The principle of law is "that where a crime, in itself capital, is endeavoured to be committed by force, it is lawful to repel that force by the death of the party attempting." Blackstone immediately goes on to warn that "we must not carry this doctrine to the same visionary length that Mr. Locke does; who holds, 'that all manner of force without right upon a man's person, puts him in a state of war with the aggressor; and, of consequence, that . . . he may lawfully kill him that puts him under this unnatural restraint.' " This principle may be just "in a state of uncivilized nature," but "the law of England, like that of every other well-regulated community, is too tender of the public peace, too careful of the lives of the subjects, to adopt so contentious a system; nor will suffer with impunity any crime to be *prevented* by death, unless the same, if committed, would also be *punished* by death." [13] The law of England does, however, provide an exception to this rule of justifiable homicide, and that is, in the terminology of the law, excusable homicide. Where, for example, a man protects himself from assault and in the course of the quarrel kills his assailant, he is excused from legal penalty, provided that "certain and immediate suffering would [have been] the consequence of waiting for the assistance of the law" and that "the slayer had no other possible (or, at least, probable) means of escaping from his assailant." [14] A man attacked must turn his back and flee, if he can, and later bring his assailant to court. The presumption is always in favor of the law of civil society, not the law of nature.

The maintenance of government and therefore law itself is an even more delicate case. Blackstone is often pointed to as an exponent of parliamentary sovereignty, in contrast, for example, to American ideas of limited government. In Parliament, consisting of king, lords, and commons, lies "that absolute despotic power, which must in all governments reside somewhere. . . ." Parliament can deal with matters outside the ordinary scope of law, it can remodel the succession to the crown, it can alter the established religion, it can change the constitution of the kingdom and Parliament itself. "It can, in short, do every thing that is not naturally impossible. . . ." [15] It is true that Blackstone frequently seems to assume that Parliament cannot do what it ought not to do (for example, substitute an elective for a hereditary monarchy); and he emphasizes "the true excellence of the English government, that all the parts of it form a mutual check upon each other." [16] But however great the safeguard provided in practice by the English system of mutual social and political checks, in the end Blackstone must return to the first principle of civil society, which is that Parliament, or the legislature, can do what it likes.

Is there not, however, a still more fundamental principle? "It must be owned that Mr. Locke, and other theoretical writers, have held, that 'there remains still inherent in the people a supreme power to remove or alter the legislative, when they find the legislative act contrary to the trust reposed in them. . . .'" Blackstone insists that, "however just this conclusion may be in theory"—and it *is* just in Blackstone's theory for precisely the same reasons that it is just in Locke's—"we cannot practically adopt it, nor take any *legal* steps for carrying it into execution, under any dispensation of government at present actually existing." Such a devolution of power to the people at large presumes a dissolution of government, a reduction of the people to their "original state of equality," and the repeal of all positive laws. "No human laws will therefore suppose a case, which at once must destroy all law, and compel men to build afresh upon a new foundation; nor will they make provision for so desperate an event, as must render all legal provisions ineffectual." [17] The ultimate resort to first principle, to what Blackstone calls elsewhere the "law of nature" or "the God of battles," [18] is at the foundation of law because it enforces, as no law and no internal checks can do, the limits on political authority. Yet the law cannot provide for or even suppose this ultimate resort and is, in fact, in tension with it: the maintenance of law and therefore the effective maintenance of individual rights depends upon a putting aside, as if for once and all, of the original state of lawless equality out of which civil society arose and into which it may, in desperate event, relapse. Mr. Locke and his theoretical friends are not wrong, but they may endanger the polity precisely because of their clear expression of its true foundation. "For civil liberty rightly understood, consists in protecting the rights of individuals by the united force of society: society cannot be maintained, and of course can exert no protection, without obedience to some sovereign power: and obedience is an empty name, if every individual has a right to decide how far he himself shall obey." [19] Blackstone is not fearful that his constant emphasis on law and law-abidingness will incapacitate the people for the resumption of their original right should that be necessary. Where the sovereign power becomes tyrannical and threatens desolation to the state, "mankind will not be reasoned out of the feelings of humanity; nor will sacrifice their liberty by a scrupulous adherence to those political maxims, which were originally established to preserve it." [20]

The origin of civil society, Blackstone suggests, is anarchy; its tendency, tyranny. There have been times when the rights of Englishmen were "depressed by overbearing and tyrannical princes; at others so luxuriant as even to tend to anarchy, a worse state than tyranny itself," says Blackstone, as befits a lawyer, "as any government is better than none at all." [21] But the objective is to avoid both, as the British constitution has generally done. In support of this objective, Blackstone's jurisprudence acknowledges the extremes, while resisting their pull, for either is fatal to liberty. Stated positively, Blackstone seeks to maintain between the ground and the tendency of civil society the central position of law, particularly the law as it is understood by judges and administered in their courts. In a list of five "auxiliary subordinate rights," which serve principally as "barriers" to protect the three great primary rights, Blackstone gives central place to the right of every Englishman to apply to the courts for redress of injuries. The law (not Parliament or the people at large), Blackstone says here, is in England "the supreme arbiter of every man's life, liberty, and property. . . ." In this "distinct and separate existence" of the judiciary lies "one main preservative of the public liberty; which cannot subsist long in any state, unless the administration of common justice be in some degree separated both from the legislative and also from the executive power." In particular, "were it joined with the legislative, the life, liberty, and property, of the subject would be in the hands of arbitrary judges, whose decisions would be then regulated only by their own opinions, and not by any fundamental principles of law; which, though legislators may depart from, yet judges are bound to observe." [22]

Blackstone here expresses again the principle of mutual checks, but our present concern is with his comment that there are "fundamental principles of law; which, though legislators may depart from, yet judges are bound to observe." This seems curious when we consider what may be called Blackstone's basic (though not exhaustive) definition of law: "the will of one man, or of one or more assemblies of men, to whom the supreme authority is entrusted . . . is in different states, according to their different constitutions, understood to be *law*." [23] Law is the will of the sovereign; but good law, and therefore law properly speaking, requires something more. Not only consent, for "even laws themselves, whether made with or without our consent, if they regulate and constrain our conduct in matters of mere indifference, without any good end in view, are regulations destructive of liberty. . . ." The good end in view is genuine civil liberty, which is "no other than natural liberty so far restrained by human laws (and no farther) as is necessary and expedient for the general advantage of the publick." [24] How far and in what respects the general advantage requires restraint of natural liberty is not a question that can be answered, except in a way that reformulates the question, by some general principle or rule. It is a matter of judgment. And free government depends on the maintenance within it of a central place for the judiciary, that peculiar body of men who are capable, by tradition, political position, and training, of judging well. While providing disinterested protection of the lives, liberties, and properties of the subjects, the judiciary also serves as a brake on the unwise use of parliamentary and popular authority and as a source (or at least a mouthpiece) of instruction in the true principles of civil liberty.

The fundamental principles of law to which judges must adhere, and which mitigate the view of law as the will of the sovereign, consist of or are drawn in the first place from custom. In English law, "the goodness of a custom depends upon it's [*sic*] having been used time out of mind; or, in the solemnity of our legal phrase, time whereof the memory of man runneth not to the contrary. This it is that gives it it's [*sic*] weight and authority: and of this nature are the maxims and customs which compose the common law, or *lex non scripta*, of this kingdom." When in his Introduction Blackstone turns from a discussion of the nature of law to the laws of England, he does not begin with a contracting people or a sovereign legislature but with these common laws, of which judges are the "depositaries" and "living oracles." Written laws or statutes are merely declaratory or remedial of some defect in the common laws, which are "the first ground and chief corner stone of the laws of England. . . ." [25]

In innumerable ways throughout the *Commentaries* Blackstone recognizes, strengthens, and uses the authority of the old. He is often taken for a mere patriot or conservative, even though he gives ample indication that neither his praise of what is English nor his devotion to what is old is to be taken simply at face value.[26] Certainly Blackstone does emphasize the bindingness of precedent and the deference owed by the present generation to former times. He chooses, for example, to defend on the ground of authority rather than reason and justice the decision of the lords and commons to regard James II as having merely abdicated the throne, rather than as having subverted the government and broken the original contract. While making clear his own opinion that the decision was reasonable and just, in avoiding "the wild extremes into which the visionary theories of some zealous republicans would have led them," he fears that such speculation, if carried too far, "might imply a right of dissenting or revolting from [the decision], in case we should think it to have been unjust, oppressive, or inexpedient." [27] Blackstone was as perceptive as those commentators who have pointed out that there is a defect in this argument because on Blackstone's own principles the present generation does have a right at any time to be judge of whether the contract has been broken. Blackstone's implicit argument is that if desperate circumstances arise, as they did in 1688, it must be hoped that the original right will be exercised as wisely and moderately as it was then, when the fabric of government and law was maintained while a revolution was made. But the exercise of this basic right is to be discouraged. The stability of any polity, not least a polity whose fundamental principles contain an intrinsic tendency toward instability, depends upon a widespread opinion of the bindingness of the old.

It is the duty of the judge, and the concern of Blackstone as his teacher, to articulate and maintain the integrity of the system of positive law as it stands. The reader of the *Commentaries* is frequently told of the nicety with which the old rules of law were framed, "and how closely they are connected and interwoven together, supporting, illustrating, and demonstrating one another." [28] He is cautioned that the very number and complexity of English municipal laws which vex him, whether as student or litigant, testify to the extent of the country, its commercial prosperity, and above all the liberty and property of the subjects.[29] He is reminded that every science has its terms and rules of art, the reason of which may not be immediately visible. Many of these artificial rules reflect the lawyer's preoccupation with forms and procedures, arising out of his trained understanding that if laws are cast in a certain form, promulgated in a certain way, and enforced according to certain processes, the likelihood of doing substantive justice is increased. The legal art provides the framework within which judgment is exercised and justice done. Thus, lawyer-like, Blackstone says that municipal law is "something permanent, uniform, and universal" and describes the procedure of trial by jury as "the most transcendent privilege which any subject can enjoy, or wish for. . . ."[30] But his concern with the integrity, or rationale, of the English legal system goes deeper than forms and procedures, important as they are and large a place as they inevitably occupy in an analysis of English law.

The *Commentaries* are full of intricate and seemingly endless "explanations" of the old rules of law, many of them apparently irrelevant or even in opposition to present needs and modern principles. Dizzy with the effort to comprehend the reason of a system where, for example, a brother of the half blood may never succeed as heir to the estate of his elder brother even if they have the same father,[31] the reader is likely to conclude that the old maxim of the common lawyer that "what is not reason is not law"[32] is maintained only by an unshakable determination to assert, however artificially and at whatever cost in Latin maxims and patchwork fictions, that what is English law is reason. If there is any consistent underlying principle it seems to lie in Blackstone's emphatic intention to draw his students away from "the rage of modern improvement." Yet "modern improvement" is the very foundation of the *Commentaries;* but it is essential to the modern enterprise itself that reform should wear a conservative cloak.[33] The weight and influence of the old is to be preserved and used to support the new.

We inherit an old Gothic castle, erected in the days of chivalry, but fitted up for a modern inhabitant. The moated ramparts, the embattled towers, and the trophied halls, are magnificent and venerable, but useless. The inferior apartments, now converted into rooms of convenience, are chearful and commodious, though their approaches are winding and difficult.[34]

Blackstone helps to remodel the old castle, by means of which its comfort is improved, for example by relaxing some of the old legal restrictions on commerce; but he is careful to warn against reform that might loosen some apparently useless stone or weaken some inconvenient timber and cause the whole edifice, the pleasant apartments as well as the noble shell, vital damage.

Blackstone is therefore an extremely cautious reformer, but his metaphor also has a deeper significance. Civil society consists of a set of conventional, and in a sense arbitrary, rules and regulations whose purpose is the regularization and thereby the protection of natural rights. But the effectiveness of that conventional system depends upon its becoming confounded, for many practical purposes, with nature. Too persistent inquiry into the grounds of the conventional system may reveal too clearly and widely that it *is* a conventional system and not a set of natural rules, thereby encouraging self-destructive appeals from the artificial system to its natural foundation. "It is well if the mass of mankind will obey the laws when made, without scrutinizing too nicely into the reasons of making them." [35] And of course the older and better established the laws, the less likely that their reasons will be questioned. The general tendency to "mistake for nature what we find established by long and inveterate custom" [36] can be a trap for the academic student of law, but it is absolutely indispensable to the maintenance of law.

The classic case, because the most modified or artificial of individual rights, is the right of property, and Blackstone provides two versions of its origin. In his introductory discussion of property in general, he finds the origin in sheer possession or occupancy. He then shows how men's desire to hold their property in greater security drives them by stages from a "savage state of vagrant liberty" to civil society, and to civilization, with its increasingly complex and artificial system of law establishing property rights.[37] The second version of the origin of property begins at the peak of the hierarchy rather than its base and describes a conquering general seizing lands, partitioning them among his followers, and eventually establishing a hierarchical military system.[38] English law, and English history as well, is presented here as a combination of these two developments. Thus the basic pattern of land law is feudal tenure, of which "the grand and fundamental maxim" is "that all lands were originally granted out by the sovereign, and are therefore holden, either mediately or immediately, of the crown." [39] But this fundamental maxim is a fiction; a fiction to which our ancestors consented under William only in order to establish a then generally useful military system; a fiction that later Norman lawyers made the engine of ecclesiastical tyranny; a fiction, now much modified and adapted to a commercial society, that signals the recognition that a man can most effectively preserve what is his own by consenting to regard it as the king's.

Indeed, the hereditary monarch is himself a kind of fiction, or he is an altogether artificial entity, the prime sign and example of the replacement of men's natural equality by that "due subordination of rank" that government requires.[40] While Blackstone praises the modern freedom to discuss the limits of the king's prerogative, "a topic, that in some former ages was thought too delicate and sacred to be profaned by the pen of a subject," he discusses it nevertheless with "decency and respect." "For, though a philosophical mind will consider the royal person merely as one man appointed by mutual consent to preside over many others, and will pay him that reverence and duty which the principles of society demand, yet the mass of mankind will be apt to grow insolent and refractory, if taught to consider their prince as a man of no greater perfection than themselves. The law therefore ascribes to the king . . . certain attributes of a great and transcendant [sic] nature; by which the people are led to consider him in the light of a superior being, and to pay him that awful respect, which may enable him with greater ease to carry on the business of government." [41]

Thus the merely conventional superiority of the king is widely regarded, thanks partly to certain laws and writings about law, as a natural superiority; his conventional title to the throne a natural title; his contractual right to the loyalty of his subjects a natural right. As subjects we stand in awe of the king, without considering that he is our servant; we accept our subordinate rank in society, without considering our original equality; we accept the property that the laws assign us, without considering our original right to seize what we can. In sum, we obey, without considering our right to rid ourselves of the sovereign who commands and the law he administers; for to exercise this right would be the destruction of the security of our persons, our liberty, and our property. "The moated ramparts, the embattled towers, and the trophied halls," Blackstone says, "are magnificent and venerable, but useless." It is true that the noble and chivalrous purposes that they once supported and displayed are now displaced; newer and better ends are expressed in the comfortable apartments. But these apartments cannot provide for themselves that magnificence and venerability with which their own outer walls must be reinforced if the modern edifice is to stand. The Gothic labyrinth of hierarchy and duty, to which Blackstone provides the key, is the indispensable means to the regulation and thus the preservation of human equality and individual rights.

NOTES

1. The four volumes of the *Commentaries on the Laws of England* first appeared in 1765, 1766, 1768, and 1769. The edition used here is the eighth, published in 1778 and the last published during Blackstone's lifetime; except where otherwise indicated, citations are to volume and page. The authenticity of the changes made by the editor of the ninth edition, on which many modern editions are based, is somewhat doubtful; but the differences are minor, and numerous standard editions reproduce the entire text with original pagination. The useful edition of William G. Hammond (San Francisco: Bancroft-Whitney, 1890) contains a collation of all changes in the first eight editions.

2. *Ibid.*, I, 32.

3. See *ibid.*, III, 100–103; IV, chaps iv, viii, xxviii.

4. In an early sketch of the ground covered later in the *Commentaries,* Blackstone remarks that he follows in many respects the plan of Sir Matthew Hale (*The Analysis of the Law . . . of England,* 3rd ed., 1739); but he emphasizes that he has chosen "to extract a new Method of his own, [rather] than implicitly to copy after any." *An Analysis of the Laws of England* (3rd ed., 1758), p. vii.

5. *Commentaries,* I, 123–24.

6. *Ibid.*, II, 3, 8–9, and *passim.* In Blackstone's significantly loose formulation, "The original of private property is probably founded in nature . . . : but certainly the modifications under which we at present find it, the method of conserving it in the present owner, and of translating it from man to man, are entirely derived from society. . . ." I, 138.

7. *Ibid.*, III, 2.

8. *Ibid.*, IV, 7; I, 349.

9. *Ibid.*, I, 47.

10. *Ibid.*, 134; italics supplied. For the definitions of the rights of personal security and property, see I, 129, 138.

11. *Ibid.*, 6.

12. *Ibid.*, III, 4.

13. *Ibid.*, IV, 181–82; cf. III, 168–69. Italics original. The passage here from Locke is not a direct quotation but a paraphrase. See *Second Treatise,* secs 18–19.

14. *Ibid.*, IV, 184.

15. *Ibid.*, I, 160–61.

16. *Ibid.*, I, 154–55. See I, 50–51: ". . . as the legislature of the kingdom is entrusted to three distinct powers, entirely independent of each other; first, the king; secondly, the lords spiritual and temporal, which is an aristocratical assembly of persons selected for their piety, their birth, their wisdom, their valour, or their property; and, thirdly, the house of commons, freely chosen by the people from among themselves, which makes it a kind of democracy; as this aggregate body, actuated by different springs, and attentive to different interests, composes the British parliament, and has the supreme disposal of every thing; there can no inconvenience be attempted by either of the three branches, but will be withstood by one of the other two; each branch being armed with a negative power, sufficient to repel any innovation which it shall think inexpedient or dangerous."

17. *Ibid.*, 161–62. Italics original.

18. *Ibid.*, 193.

19. *Ibid.*, 251.

20. *Ibid.*, 245.

21. *Ibid.*, 127.

22. *Ibid.*, 141, 269.

23. *Ibid.*, 52. Italics original. An obvious misprint in the text of this passage has been corrected.

24. *Ibid.*, 125–26.

25. *Ibid.*, 67, 69, 73.

26. See *ibid.*, 172, 190–91; IV, 3–5.

27. *Ibid.,* I, 212–13.
28. *Ibid.,* II, 128; cf. II, 376.
29. *Ibid.,* III, 325–27.
30. *Ibid.,* I, 44; III, 379; cf. Blackstone's discussion of equity at I, 62, 91–92; III, 429–41.
31. *Ibid.,* II, 227–33.
32. *Ibid.,* I, 70.
33. *Ibid.,* 10. For some of Blackstone's suggestions for reform, see III, 381–85 (trial by jury); IV, 235–39 (capital punishment); IV, 388–89 (corruption of blood).

34. *Ibid.,* III, 268.
35. *Ibid.,* II, 2.
36. *Ibid.,* 11.
37. *Ibid.,* 6–8.
38. *Ibid.,* 45 ff.
39. *Ibid.,* 53.
40. *Ibid.,* I, 271; cf. I, 208–9; IV, 105; and Blackstone's discussion of allegiance, I, 366–70.
41. *Ibid.,* I, 237, 241.

READINGS

A. Blackstone, William. *Commentaries on the Laws of England.* Introduction, I. i; II. i.
B. Blackstone, William. *Commentaries on the Laws of England.* I. ii, iii, vii, xii, xiv; II. iv, xiii, xiv; III. i, iii, viii, xxiii, xxvii; IV. i, iv, vi, xiv, xxviii, xxxiii.

ADAM SMITH

1723–1790

The major writing of Adam Smith is contained in two books, *Theory of Moral Sentiments* (1759) and *An Inquiry into the Nature and Causes of the Wealth of Nations* (1776). His major professional employment was to serve, for thirteen years, as Professor of Moral Philosophy in the University of Glasgow. His fame now rests upon the foundation he laid for the science of economics. In all of this there is not much of political philosophy to be seen, even allowing for the inclusion of jurisprudence in the Morals course. Smith's contribution to economics, however, has the character of a description and advocacy of the system now called liberal capitalism; and the ligaments between the economic order and the political system, close under any circumstances, are exceptionally broad and strong in the world as seen and molded by Adam Smith. The close conjunction of economics and political philosophy, even or perhaps especially if tending toward the eclipse of the latter, is a powerful fact of political philosophy; the men, like Smith, who were responsible for it would have a place in the chronicle of political philosophy on that ground alone.

Smith is of interest for his share in the deflection of political philosophy toward economics and for his famous elaboration of the principles of free enterprise or liberal capitalism. By virtue of the latter, he has earned the right to be known as an architect of our present system of society. For that title, however, he has a rival in Locke, whose writing antedated his own by roughly a century. Our thesis will be that, although Smith follows in the tradition of which Locke is a great figure, yet a distinct and important change fell upon that tradition, a change that Smith helped bring about; that to understand modern capitalism adequately, it is necessary to grasp the "Smithian" change in the Lockean tradition; and that to understand the ground of engagement between capitalism and postcapitalistic doctrines—primarily the Marxian—one must grasp the issues of capitalism in the altered form they received from Adam Smith. To state the point in barest simplicity: Smith's teaching contains that formulation of capitalist doctrine in which many of the fundamental issues are recognizably those on which postcapitalism contests the field.

It would be vastly misleading to suggest that the initiative in modifying the classic modern doctrine was Smith's. To avoid that intimation, we must cover all of what follows with a single remark on the obligation of Smith to his senior friend and compatriot, David Hume. Smith's moral philosophy, as he in effect admits, is a refinement upon Hume's which differs from it in respects that, although very significant, are not decisive.[1] A thorough study of the relation between the doctrines of Smith and Hume would disclose in full the connection between liberal capitalism and the "skeptical" or "scientific" principles upon which Hume wished to found all philosophy. The broadest conclusions that would emerge from such a study can be deduced from an examination of Smith's doctrines alone, precisely because they do reflect so deeply the influence of Hume.

Many of Smith's fundamental reflections are contained in the *Theory of Moral Sentiments,* wherein he sets forth his important understanding of nature and human nature. He does this in the course of answering the following question: What is virtue, and what makes it eligible? The premise of his answer is that, whatever virtue may turn out to be, it must have very much in common with, perhaps it must simply coincide with, that by reason of which men or their actions deserve approbation. The question, What is virtue? is never distinct from the question, What deserves approbation? Approbation and disapprobation are bestowed upon actions. The spring of any action is the sentiment (or emotion, or affection, or passion—they are synonymous) which is the motive for committing the act. Approbation of any action must ascend to the passion which truly explains the action.

The sentiment or affection of the heart from which any action proceeds, and upon which its whole virtue or vice must ultimately depend, may be considered under two different aspects, or in two different relations; first, in relation to the cause which excites it, or the motive which gives occasion to it; and secondly, in relation to the end which it proposes, or the effect which it tends to produce.

In the suitableness or unsuitableness, in the proportion or disproportion which the affection seems to bear to the cause or object which excites it, con-

sists the propriety or impropriety, the decency or ungracefulness of the consequent action.

In the beneficial or hurtful nature of the effects which the affection aims
at, or tends to produce, consists the merit or demerit of the action, the qualities
by which it is entitled to reward, or is deserving of punishment.[2]

Propriety and merit are thus the attributes of the passion behind
each action that determine the virtuousness of the action. These bear a
certain similarity to the "agreeable and useful" of Hume, but Smith
believed his own doctrine to be original in that it avoids the final reduction of all approbation to utility, which Smith rejected on the
Humean ground that "utility" is not as such recognizable by immediate
sense and feeling, but only by a sort of calculation of reason. Smith believed he had been able to ground morality on a phenomenon of the
passions alone, a belief to which the name of his book testifies. If sense
and feeling are indeed immediate—unmediated in the sense that nothing is between them and the root of the fundamental self—then there
is considerable value in bringing down the analysis of the virtues to
its true bottom in the passions. In Smith's doctrine, the clue to that reduction is in the phenomenon of Sympathy, the criterion of propriety
and merit.

Sympathy is a word used by Smith in its literal meaning, an
etymological parallel of compassion: "feeling with," or a fellow feeling.
It is a fact of which, perhaps, no further mechanical account can be
given, that the passions of one human being are transferred to another
by the force of imagination at work in the recipient. The man who
sees or merely conceives the terror, hatred, benevolence, or gratitude of
another must to some extent enter into that passion and experience it
himself, for he must imagine himself in the other's circumstances, and
therefrom everything follows. Of chief importance in the foregoing is
the qualification "to some extent." If the impartial spectator, cognizant
of what stimulated the terror, hatred, or other passion of the agent,
feels in his own breast the same measure of that passion as moved the
agent to his action, then the spectator literally sympathizes with the
agent and approves his act as consistent with "propriety." The spectator
experiences sympathetically the passion of the agent; and if he experiences it in the same degree, he further experiences the "sentiment of
approbation"—for that, too, is a passion.

Propriety, however, is not the only ground of moral virtue. Not
only the suitableness of the agent's passion to its cause, but the aim or
tendency of that passion, its effect, has a bearing on the moral quality
of the act in question. Smith refers to "the nature of the effects which
the affection aims at, or tends to produce." The "or" is disjunctive, and

we must later discuss the important difference between the effects that
the sentiment aims at and those that the act it inspires actually tends
to produce. For the present it is enough to note that when an action
falls upon some human being, it will cause him to feel gratitude or resentment because it will be either beneficial or harmful, pleasurable or
painful. If an impartial spectator, informed of all the circumstances,
would sympathize with the gratitude felt by the object human being,
then the spectator would judge the agent's act to be meritorious, and
the second condition of moral virtue would have been met. In brief: if
the actual or supposed impartial spectator should sympathize with the
passion both of the agent (propriety) and of the patient (merit), then
the agent's act may be pronounced virtuous on the basis of the spectator's feeling of approbation.

If Smith's elaboration of the sympathy mechanism did nothing
more than show how a rather strict morality could be educed from the
passions and the imagination alone, it would have a certain interest. In
fact, it points toward a much wider circle of consequences. Sympathy
cannot be separated, in Smith's formulation, from imagination. Together they define an undoubted natural sociality of man. By the exercise
of two subrational capacities, sympathy and imagination, each man is by
his nature led or compelled to transcend his very self and, without
indeed being able to feel the other man's feeling, is able and is driven
to imagine himself in the place of that other and to participate, how
vicariously is a matter of indifference, in the feelings which are the
fundamental phenomena of the other's existence. Smith, it will be recalled, wished to know not only what virtue is but what makes it
eligible. Why—in principle—do men choose to be virtuous, when to be
virtuous means to be deserving of approbation? Smith's answer is that
it is of the nature of a human being to desire the approbation and love
of his human congeners.[3] The first sentence of the *Theory of Moral
Sentiments* intimates the withdrawal that is in progress from the doctrine of the war of all against all: "How selfish soever man may be
supposed, there are evidently some principles in his nature, which
interest him in the fortune of others, and render their happiness necessary to him, though he derives nothing from it except the pleasure of
seeing it." The combination of imagination, sympathy, and the need
for the love and approbation of other men is the ground for Smith's
asseverations that nature formed man for society.[4]

Not only does Smith thus teach a natural sociality of man, but
also the natural character of the moral law. He can with ease refer to
"the natural principles of right and wrong," [5] understanding by "right"
not merely what benefits or avoids bringing harm to the agent. He can

do so because the ground of moral action and perception is the inner constitution of human nature; not in the antique sense of man's highest possibilities, it is true, but in the sense of human psychology—the instincts, sentiments, mechanisms of sympathy that are the efficient causes of human behavior. These are perfectly natural, and the sentiments of approbation are equally so; hence the principles of right and wrong are incontestably natural.

Smith's version of natural right depends very heavily upon the construct of the "impartial spectator," the imaginary being who is supposed to represent all mankind in viewing and judging each individual's actions. Judgment rendered from such a point of view implies that no man may rightly prefer himself to the extent of making exceptions from the general rule in his own behalf. "As to love our neighbour as we love ourselves is the great law of Christianity, so it is the great precept of nature to love ourselves only as we love our neighbour, or what comes to the same thing, as our neighbour is found capable of loving us." [6] Recourse to the imagined judgment of general humanity at the same time directs conscience toward the imagined surveillance maintained over each man at all times by a supposed all-seeing humanity. The constructive standard of "universal mankind" is fundamental to the version of natural right and natural sociality taught by Smith. It is also a premonition of the postcapitalistic construct of "all mankind" as the focus of right and history.

It is true that Smith taught the natural sociality of man and the natural basis of the moral law, but this modification of the modern natural law doctrine did not mean a return to antiquity. It must be repeated that natural right for Smith rests upon the primacy of the subrational part of the soul, and that natural sociality as he understood it is not an irreducible principle of man but the product of a mechanism at work. Later on, Kant was to speak of the same phenomenon as man's asocial sociality. Natural sociality in this sense does not, as it did for Aristotle, point toward political society. It rather resembles gregariousness. It is a compassion with one's fellow species-members that has everything in common with the alleged unwillingness of horses to tread upon a living body (of any species) and the distress of all animals in passing by the cadavers of their like.[7] To claim on the basis of it that man is by nature a social animal is by no means to claim equally that he is a political animal. Man is tied to humanity by the bonds of immediate sense and feeling, but he is tied to his fellow citizens as such by the weaker, superinduced, bonds of calculation or reason, derivative from considerations of utility. As we have seen, the viewpoint of moral judgment for Smith is that of "man" or universal mankind, the homo-

geneous class of species-fellows. The moral law is natural in such a sense
as to overleap the intermediate, artificial frontiers of political society
and regard primarily the natural individual and the natural species.
Under that law, the perfection of human nature is "to feel much for
others and little for ourselves, . . . to restrain our selfish, and to indulge our benevolent affections. . . ." [8]

Political society, however, is not directed toward this humane
perfection of human nature but toward the safeguard of justice very
narrowly conceived. "Mere justice is, upon most occasions, but a negative virtue, and only hinders us from hurting our neighbour. The man
who barely abstains from violating either the person, or the estate, or
the reputation of his neighbours, has surely very little positive merit."
Justice means to do "every thing which [one's] equals can with propriety force him to do, or which they can punish him for not doing." [9]
Justice, in brief, closely resembles compliance with the law of nature as
seen by Hobbes and Locke. Smith understood it so himself. He concluded the *Theory of Moral Sentiments* with a passage on natural
jurisprudence, justice, and the rules of natural equity, meaning by all
of them "a system of those principles which ought to run through, and
be the foundation of the laws of all nations." (He closes by promising
to take up this theme in a later work. His only other book is the *Wealth
of Nations*.)

We shall not sufficiently understand Smith's version of man's natural sociality if we do not grasp thoroughly the difference between man
conceived as a social animal and as a political animal.[10] It is helpful for
this purpose to consider further the problem of justice, the singularly
political virtue which might even be synonymous with obeying the
positive law. Justice, in the context of Smith's moral theory, is a defective virtue. He prepares for the exceptional treatment of justice by
dividing moral philosophy into two parts, ethics and jurisprudence, the
subject of the latter being justice. The defense of justice means the
punishment of injustice; and the punishment of injustice is based upon
the unsocial passion of resentment, the desire to return evil for evil, the
command of "the sacred and necessary law of retaliation" which "seems
to be the great law which is dictated to us by Nature." [11] Political
society is based upon a moralistic paradox, one of many we will encounter: sociality rests upon latent animosity, without which the state
could not exist.

In the second place, justice, equal to rendering another no less (or
more) than what is his due, does not command gratitude and therefore
in Smith's system is not attended with merit—or with "very little." Considering both the nature of justice and the safeguard of it, it is a de-

fective virtue in that it cannot, or almost cannot, deserve fullest approbation, on the grounds of merit as well as propriety.

In the third place, although there is a sense in which political society is natural, it is a weak sense. The national society is indeed the protector and the matrix of ourselves, our homes, our kin, our friends, and Smith does not for an instant dream of the withering away of the state. "It is by nature endeared to us." But "the love of our own nation often disposes us to view, with the most malignant jealousy and envy, the prosperity and aggrandisement of any other neighbouring nation."

The love of our own country seems not to be derived from the love of mankind. The former sentiment is altogether independent of the latter, and seems sometimes even to dispose us to act inconsistently with it. France may contain, perhaps, near three times the number of inhabitants which Great Britain contains. In the great society of mankind, therefore, the prosperity of France should appear to be an object of much greater importance than that of Great Britain. The British subject, however, who, upon that account, should prefer upon all occasions the prosperity of the former to that of the latter country, would not be thought a good citizen of Great Britain. We do not love our country merely as a part of the great society of mankind: we love it for its own sake, and independently of any such consideration.[12]

These reservations and qualifications upon political sociality deserve notice. They will appear in a swollen incarnation conjured by Marx a century later, when the replacement of political man by the species-animal reaches a climax.

It would be misleading to suggest that Smith's doctrine of man's sociality was a relapse into the Middle Ages or into antiquity. It would be more misleading to suggest that, in Smith's view, human nature is simply dominated by a natural sociality of any description. We have given attention to the mechanical or psychological bond of sympathy, at the basis of Smith's moral theory, in order to show the change in emphasis between the preparation of capitalism in Locke's doctrine and the elaboration of it in Smith's. But the theme of man's natural directedness toward preservation is not by any means made to languish by Smith. On the contrary: "self-preservation, and the propagation of the species, are the great ends which Nature seems to have proposed in the formation of all animals."[13] There is no reason to doubt that Smith meant this in all its force. We are able to gather, therefore, that if we use "altruism" and "egoism" in their literal sense, man can be described, according to Smith, as being by nature altruistic and egoistic—a species-member moved by love of self and fellow feeling with others.

It is one of the outstanding characteristics of Smith's system that sociality, withal of a certain description, and self-centered concentration upon preservation are shown as profoundly combined in a natural articulation of great strength; and this is achieved simultaneously with a rehabilitation of morality upon natural grounds: "Nature, indeed, seems to have so happily adjusted our sentiments of approbation and disapprobation, to the conveniency both of the individual and of the society, that after the strictest examination it will be found, I believe, that this is universally the case." [14] When it is borne in mind that Smith's teaching aims at the articulation of morality and preservation, and that the practical fruits of his doctrine are intended to be gathered by emancipating men, under mild government, to seek their happiness freely according to their individual desires, the accomplishment as a whole commands great respect. The reconciliation of the private good and the common good by the medium not of coercion but of freedom, on a basis of moral duty, had perhaps never been seen before.

In this wide and symmetrical edifice Smith perceived what appeared to him to be an irregularity or a class of irregularities. He observed that at certain points a disjunction develops between what man would by nature be led to approve as virtuous and what he is led by nature to approve as conducive to the preservation of society and the human species; and this notwithstanding the over-all truth of the passage quoted immediately above. It will be recalled that the elements of a virtuous act are propriety and merit, and that both rest upon a ground of sympathy. If men did not desire the sympathy of others, as well as respond to the impulse to sympathize with them, there would be no morality and no society. But the natural tendency of men is to sympathize especially with joy and good fortune; and it goes without saying that men not only desire to be sympathized with but to be sympathized with by reason of their prosperity, not their adversity. But the wish to be sympathized with on the grandest scale becomes, as a consequence, the foundation of ambition, which is the aspiration to be conspicuous, grand, and admired. To this aspiration the multitude of mankind lends itself, for it naturally sympathizes with eminence, that is, wealth and rank. But wealth and rank are not, as Smith occasionally said, necessarily conjoined with wisdom and virtue. He remarks, "This disposition to admire, and almost to worship, the rich and the powerful, and to despise or, at least, to neglect persons of poor and mean condition, though necessary both to establish and to maintain the distinction of ranks and the order of society, is, at the same time, the great and most universal cause of the corruption of our moral sentiments." [15]

Merit, we remember, is the quality of an act that the impartial spectator would pronounce worthy of gratitude. The decisive quality of such an act is the propriety of the agent's passion in committing it, his benevolent intent toward the patient, and the patient's pleasure in the benefit conferred, in consequence of which he desires to reciprocate a benefit to the agent. The conjunction is perhaps complicated, but through it all one condition stands out clearly: benefit must be conferred on the patient. Now Smith observes that there is a gap of sorts between the intention and the consummation. That gap is Chance. Because of mere chance good will miscarries, and the benevolent agent produces nothing or worse than nothing for his intended beneficiary. On other occasions the agent, intending nothing or possibly worse than nothing, happens to be the source of a benefit to the patient. Contrary to sound morality, the first agent's act goes without the approval of sympathy and the stamp of virtue while the second agent's act wins applause and gratitude. The universal tendency of men to regard the issue rather than the intention is said by Smith to be a "salutary and useful irregularity in human sentiments," for two reasons. In the first place, "to punish . . . for the affections of the heart only, where no crime has been committed, is the most insolent and barbarous tyranny." To try to live a common life while holding men culpable or laudable for their secret intentions would mean that "every court of judicature would become a real inquisition." In the second place, "Man was made for action, and to promote by the exertion of his faculties such changes in the external circumstances both of himself and others, as may seem most favorable to the happiness of all. He must not be satisfied with indolent benevolence, nor fancy himself the friend of mankind, because in his heart he wishes well to the prosperity of the world."[16] Smith goes on to speak of the utility to the world of the cognate inclination men have, to be troubled in spirit even when the ill they have wrought is wholly unintended, a subject that he illuminates with some healthy remarks upon the fallacious sense of guilt, illustrated by the "distress" of Oedipus. In sum, nature has wisely provided that our sentiments direct us toward the preservation of our kind where a conflict between preservation and either moral virtue or sound reason is brought on by the divergence of intent and issue.

Further in the same vein, Smith notes that when a man conquers fear and pain by the noble exertion of self-command, he is entitled to be compensated with a sense of his own virtue, in exchange for the relief and safety he might have had by giving way to his passions. But it is the wise provision of nature that he be only imperfectly compensated, lest he have no reason to listen to the call of fear and pain and to respond to their promptings. Fear and pain are instruments of preservation; a man or a species indifferent to them would die. The self-command that dominates them does not, as it ought not, bring with it a sense of self-esteem sufficient to outweigh the anguish of suppressing those violent passions.[17] Evidently moral virtue neither is nor ought to be simply its own reward; nor therefore can it be unqualifiedly eligible or eligible for its own sake. It must yield, according to the dictate of nature, a certain precedency to preservation.

In an important passage,[18] Smith unfolds further the paradoxy of natural morality as he conceives it. He is led to contrast "the natural course of things" with "the natural sentiments of mankind." It is in the natural course of things that industrious knaves should prosper while indolent men of honor starve, that great combinations of men should overweigh small ones, and finally that "violence and artifice prevail over sincerity and justice." The natural sentiments of man, however, are in rebellion against the natural course of things: sorrow, grief, rage, compassion for the oppressed, and at last despair of seeing the condign retribution of vice and injustice in this world—these are man's natural sentiments. The natural course of events, though, for all its offensiveness, has something weighty to recommend it. In allotting to each virtue, without favor or accommodation, the reward proper to it, nature has adopted the rule "useful and proper for rousing the industry and attention of mankind." Toil and moil happen to be indispensable to human survival, and the only way to draw them forth is by appropriate reward and punishment. The natural course of events supports the preservation of the race at the expense of precise morality; the natural sentiments of mankind are stirred by "the love of virtue, and by the abhorrence of vice and injustice." Nature is divided, but not equally divided against itself. The cause of unmitigated virtue can be heard only upon a change of venue to a jurisdiction in a world beyond nature.

Smith pursues his theme of the price in goodness and reason that must be paid to get the world's fundamental business done. He takes up the question, of much importance to his doctrine, whether the utility of actions is the basis of their being approved. If the answer were a simple affirmative, then it would follow that the principle of virtue (approbation) is rational: the calculation of usefulness. But we know that in his view the principle of virtue and approbation is not reason but sentiment and feeling, via sympathy. Yet it is evident that mankind exhibits a steady tendency toward those measures of labor and government which are the supports for the preservation of the race. Smith explains this by recurring to a delusion imposed upon men by nature, a delusion that does the work of reason better than reason could have done it. When we look upon the power or wealth in a man's possession, our minds are led in imagination to conceive the fitness of those objects to perform their respective functions. At the same time we sympathize with the imagined satisfaction of the possessors of those prizes. It is only a step from that to desiring ourselves to be happy in greatness, and thence to putting forth the immense exertions that eventuate in wealth and government. Upon consideration, it appears that we are led to pursue prosperity and power by a psychological motive, and thus to generate wealth and order among men as by-products of subjective "drives," as we would say. Moreover, and conjunctively, we act under the influence of the appetite for the means to gratification, not even for the gratification itself, when we seek after wealth and power. Both are desirable for the happiness they supposedly give their possessors. In fact, happiness is not at all or very little promoted by the possession of power and riches, those "enormous and operose machines contrived to produce a few trifling conveniencies to the body, consisting of springs the most nice and delicate, which must be kept in order with the most anxious attention, and which in spite of all our care are ready every moment to burst into pieces, and to crush in their ruins their unfortunate possessor." [19]

Smith's reason for depreciating distinction of wealth and place is of interest: "In what constitutes the real happiness of human life, [the poor and obscure] are in no respect inferior to those who would seem so much above them. In ease of the body and peace of the mind, all the different ranks of life are nearly upon a level, and the beggar, who suns himself by the side of the highway, possesses that security which kings are fighting for." [20] It is in this context that Smith announces, in the *Theory of Moral Sentiments,* the notion and the expression of the "invisible hand," very famous from its elaboration through the central argument of the *Wealth of Nations.* The passage deserves extensive quotation:

And it is well that nature imposes upon us in this manner. It is this deception which rouses and keeps in continual motion the industry of mankind. It is this which first prompted them to cultivate the ground, to build houses, to found cities and commonwealths, and to invent and improve all the sciences and arts, which ennoble and embellish human life; which have entirely changed the whole face of the globe, have turned the rude forests of nature into agreeable and fertile plains, and made the trackless and barren ocean a new fund of subsistence, and the great high road of communication to the different nations of the earth. The earth by these labours of mankind has been obliged to redouble her natural fertility, and to maintain a greater multitude of inhabitants. It is to no purpose, that the proud and unfeeling landlord views his extensive fields, and without a thought for the wants of his brethren, in imagination consumes himself the whole harvest that grows upon them. The homely and vulgar proverb, that the eye is larger than the belly, was never more fully verified than with regard to him. The capacity of his stomach bears no proportion to the immensity of his desires, and will receive no more than that of the meanest peasant. The rest he is obliged to distribute among those, who prepare, in the nicest manner, that little which he himself makes use of, among those who fit up the palace in which this little is to be consumed, among those who provide and keep in order all the different baubles and trinkets which are employed in the œconomy of greatness; all of whom thus derive from his luxury and caprice, that share of the necessaries of life, which they would in vain have expected from his humanity or his justice. The produce of the soil maintains at all times nearly that number of inhabitants which it is capable of maintaining. The rich only select from the heap what is most precious and agreeable. They consume little more than the poor, and in spite of their natural selfishness and rapacity, though they mean only their own conveniency, though the sole end which they propose from the labours of all the thousands whom they employ, be the gratification of their own vain and insatiable desires, they divide with the poor the produce of all their improvements. They are led by an invisible hand to make nearly the same distribution of the necessaries of life which would have been made, had the earth been divided into equal portions among all its inhabitants, and thus without intending it, without knowing it, advance the interest of society, and afford means to the multiplication of the species.[21]

Beyond this there is no advantage in multiplying the evidence of Smith's belief that the dominant end of nature with respect to man, namely, the prosperity of the species as a whole, is achieved by mitigations of morality and reason. Since this is a point which postcapitalistic thought was to take up polemically and against which it was to bring its ultimate, most ambitious dialectic, it deserves to be examined with some attention.

That nature's end for man is advanced by the guidance of his sentiments rather than his reason follows from the premise that the passions are more governing than the mind, and every animal persistently desires its own uninterrupted being. A man's nature is more immediately reflected in what he feels than what he thinks; moreover, the difference between the two is not the profound one anciently conceived but is rather such as can be composed by their being both subsumed under "perceptions." Smith does not employ the language of "impressions and ideas" used by Hume in the enterprise by which the operation of the mind was given a unified appearance as the distinctions among sensation, emotion, and reason were blurred. If Smith had done so, he would more explicitly have concurred in Hume's definition of the self as "that succession of related ideas and impressions, of which we have an intimate memory" and of "ideas [as] the faint images of [impressions] in thinking and reason."[22] The reduction of the self, the ego or the real man, to his actuality or to the traces of what he has actually perceived

rather than to his soul and its powers or "faculties" is part of the doctrine that rejected innate ideas and therewith all but the nominal
essences. This doctrine, with its echoes of Hobbes and Locke, is inter-
laced with the view that the lines of force along which nature produces
and communicates its motions penetrate him and govern him more
through his passions than through his reason.[23]

In any event, Smith's formulation is that nature did not leave it to
man's feeble reason to discover that and how he ought to preserve himself, but gave him sharp appetites for the means to his survival as well
as for survival itself, thus insuring him in his preservation. But it is this
same primacy of sentiment over reason, or at least the equal subsump-
tion of them both under something like perception, that is the basis for
the concessions which must be made against morality on behalf of
preservation.

It will be recalled that Smith's moral doctrine begins with approbation: the virtuous is so because it is in fact or in principle approved by
the sentiment of mankind. We now understand that a difficulty exists
because nature teaches man to approve both what conduces to morality
and what conduces to preservation. The instruction of nature is occasionally equivocal. Evidently the attempt to derive the Ought from the
Is is vexed by the fact that, although what is virtuous is actually approved, it does not follow either that everything which is approved is
virtuous or that everything which is virtuous is approved. It is from this
circumstance that the "irregularities" or concessions previously mentioned have their origin. What, then, is to be gained by the psychological or "behavioral" derivation of a natural morality? It is that by this
method, moral virtue may be deduced from the character of "man as
man," *i.e.,* in abstraction from his character as a political being and
attentive only to his character as a "natural" one. Smith's moral philosophy aims at comprehending the basis of virtue as that basis may be said
to exist in a fully actual state at every moment in "the bulk of mankind" [24] as such. That is to say, Smith's starting point is the natural
equality of men in the sense elaborated by Hobbes. The contrast with
classical antiquity throws light on the modern position. The famous
scheme of Plato's *Republic* makes a high principle of the division of
labor or distribution of functions in the political society because virtue
in one social class could not well be measured by the same rule against
which it must be measured in another class. Aristotle's *Politics* distinguishes the virtue of slaves, freemen, and men of excellence; the
Nicomachean Ethics cannot be regarded as a manual of the excellence
of the bulk of mankind. The ancient moralists coldly concentrated upon
the distinction between the politically weighty people and the entire

populace that dwelt within the frontiers. Only democracy has the merit of making possible the effacement of that distinction, and we are entitled to deem the "humanization" of moral virtue—its universalization or reference to what is actually present in "all men as men"—as the democratization of morality.

Democracy is the regime that minimizes the distinction between rulers and ruled, the fundamental political phenomenon; and in that sense it can be said that democracy or liberal democracy tends to replace political life by sociality (private lives lived in contiguity) at the same time that it diffuses political authority most widely. The abstraction of morality from the demands of political life proper is in a way impossible: political life has to be lived, and support for it must be provided in the form of economic organization, the use of force for suppressing crime and rebellion, the legitimation of conventional inequalities in the interest of order, and so on. Where morality is radically "human" or "natural" in the sense of those words that is opposed to political, the indispensable provision for political life will have the character of an inroad on morality, or an irregularity. It is not our contention that the moral basis of Smith's social doctrine is contrived to produce an abstraction from the conditions of political existence. It is rather, on the contrary, that in order to mitigate or forestall that abstraction, which his premises threaten to enforce, he must have recourse to "irregularities" of nature or exceptions to his premises.

There is hardly a better way of illustrating the elusive relation between rectitude and politics than by the following passage from Churchill's *Marlborough:*

The second debate in the Lords . . . drew from Marlborough his most memorable Parliamentary performance. It is the more remarkable because, although he had made up his mind what ought to be done and what he meant to do, his handling of the debate was at once spontaneous, dissimulating, and entirely successful. As on the battlefield, he changed his course very quickly indeed and spread a web of manœuvre before his opponents. He made candour serve the purpose of falsehood, and in the guise of reluctantly blurting out the whole truth threw his assailants into complete and baffling error. Under the impulse of an emotion which could not have been wholly assumed, he made a revelation of war policy which effectively misled not only the Opposition but the whole House, and which also played its part in misleading the foreign enemy, who were of course soon apprised of the public debate. He acted thus in the interests of right strategy and of the common cause as he conceived them. He was accustomed by the conditions under which he fought to be continually deceiving friends for their good and foes for their bane; but the speed and ease with which this particular manœuvre was conceived and accomplished in the unfamiliar atmosphere of Parliamentary debate opens to us some of the secret depths of his artful yet benevolent mind.[25]

It is apparent that dissimulation cannot be made the principle of morals; it is also apparent that morality which makes no serviceable distinction between dissimulation in a noble cause and common mendacity will end either in the precisianism that condemns it all as vice or in the latitudinarianism that peers unsuccessfully for the line between vice and virtue. Ancient moral philosophy could in this respect be described as very politic. It recognized in prudence a subtle virtue that animated the others from its seat in the mind. In palliation of the Odysseanism of the ancients' moralizing, it should be said that departure from the straitest morality was countenanced by them in the ultimate interest of something higher, for they did not conceive moral excellence to be the greatest of all excellences. The Smithian subtractions from morality cannot be in the interest of anything higher, for there is nothing higher: "The most sublime speculation of the contemplative philosopher can scarce compensate the neglect of the smallest active duty." "The man who acts solely from a regard to what is right and fit to be done, from a regard to what is the proper object of esteem and approbation, though these sentiments should never be bestowed upon him, acts from the most sublime and godlike motive which human nature is even capable of conceiving." [26] To state the case somewhat simplistically, the ancients and the moderns alike conceded something in mitigation of strict moral virtue, the ancients without repining because they had in view a higher excellence, Smith with mixed feelings because his aim could not exceed moral virtue in worth.

Smith's aim, a free, reasonable, comfortable, and tolerant life for the whole species, found its hope, its basis, and its expression in the science of economics as he to a considerable extent launched it. Anything like a detailed account of Smith's economics would be far out of place here, and we shall confine ourselves to selected themes. His teaching in the *Wealth of Nations* is above all famous for its defense of free enterprise on a broad and simple line: The welfare of the nation cannot be separated from its wealth, which he conceives in the modern mode as the annual national product. But the annual product of the nation is the sum of the annual products of the individual inhabitants. Each inhabitant has an undying interest in maximizing his own product and will do everything possible to accomplish this if left in freedom. Thus all should be accorded this freedom, and they will simultaneously maximize the aggregate product and keep each other in check by the power of competition. His renowned attack on mercantilistic capitalism—the system of invidious preference for the merchant interest—is part of his argument that the common interest is served not by differential legislative stimulation of enterprises but by allowing nature automatically to convert the individual self-interest into the good of all:

As every individual, therefore, endeavours as much as he can both to employ his capital in the support of domestic industry, and so to direct that industry that its produce may be of the greatest value; every individual necessarily labours to render the annual revenue of the society as great as he can. He generally, indeed, neither intends to promote the public interest, nor knows how much he is promoting it. By preferring the support of domestic to that of foreign industry, he intends only his own security; and by directing that industry in such a manner as its produce may be of the greatest value, he intends only his own gain, and he is in this, as in many other cases, led by an invisible hand to promote an end which was no part of his intention. Nor is it always the worse for the society that it was no part of it. By pursuing his own interest he frequently promotes that of the society more effectually than when he really intends to promote it. I have never known much good done by those who affected to trade for the public good. It is an affectation, indeed, not very common among merchants, and very few words need be employed in dissuading them from it.[27]

We have no difficulty recognizing the natural reconciliation of the individual and common interest for which the *Theory of Moral Sentiments* has prepared us. Nor are we unprepared for the moral "irregularities" that Smith conceived to be incidental to that reconciliation. They fall under two or three main heads in the argument of the *Wealth of Nations*. In the first place, the prosperity of each and all cannot be disconnected from their productivity, and their productivity rests upon the division of labor. But the division of labor inevitably stultifies the working classes, much if not the bulk of mankind. The laborer's "dexterity at his own particular trade seems . . . to be acquired at the expense of his intellectual, social, and martial virtues. But in every improved and civilized society this is the state into which the labouring poor, that is, the great body of the people, must necessarily fall, unless government takes some pains to prevent it." [28] In his discussions he tries not to exaggerate the likelihood that the government will succeed.

In the second place, a large part if not the preponderant part of the economic life of the nation must come under the regulation of the class of merchants and manufacturers. His animadversions upon them as a body of men are sometimes shockingly severe. The burden of his objection against them is that their preoccupation with gain puts them in illiberal conflict with the other orders of society and with the nation as a whole—except by inadvertence.[29] The wisdom of government is necessary to prevent their mischief, *i.e.,* their interested interference, and to give free rein only to their useful activities, *i.e.,* their productiveness. Smith was not the dogmatist that some advocates of *laissez faire* were later to become.

In the third place, the annual addition to product is believed by Smith to be generated by labor. The "exchangeable value" or price of each commodity, once land has been made private property and capital has been accumulated, "resolves itself" into wages, rent, and profit. In this way, landowners and the employers of labor "share" in the produce of labor. Smith is at pains to argue that the profits of capital are not a wage for the "supposed labour of inspection and direction," which he said is often "committed to some principal clerk." [30] He was far from attempting to conceal the contribution to output that results from the accumulation of capital. On the contrary, he dwelt upon it; but he described it as taking effect by an "improvement in the productive powers of labour." [31] In the course of his investigations into what we now call national income accounting, he certainly gave later generations some reason to regard him as holding a labor theory of value, with concomitant beliefs about distribution. As for rent, that is "a monopoly price" [32] for the use of land, by the exaction of which the owner is enabled to share in the annual product of labor. We cannot fail to notice how little trouble Smith gave himself to justify this "sharing" and this "resolving." On the contrary, by a certain invidiousness of expression ("As soon as the land of any country has all become private property, the landlords, like all other men, love to reap where they never sowed, and demand a rent even for its natural produce." [33]) he indicates a reserve as to its perfect propriety. He seems to think, it is true, that when the facts of distribution are recited, the intimation of possible inequities may be fully balanced by a statement of the broad, compensatory benefits: he speculates whether it might not be true "that the accommodation of an European prince does not always so much exceed that of an industrious and frugal peasant, as the accommodation of the latter exceeds that of many an African king, the absolute master of the lives and liberties of ten thousand naked savages." [34] But Smith manifestly did not imagine himself to be addressing the multitude of laboring poor in detailed defense of capitalism, as Marx was to address them in detailed denunciation. Smith freely hinted at his notion that something like one of his moral "irregularities" lay around the root of the distributive order, but it was much outweighed by the correlative advantages for all—and he loathed the men of "system" who would be incapable of grasping such a simple computation.

Smith did not refer to the complex of free enterprise as "capitalism" but as "the system of natural liberty," or the condition in which "things were left to follow their natural course, where there was perfect liberty."[35] Nature meant for Smith the humanly unhindered or unobstructed, and this more amply means what is not confounded by the misplaced interventions of human reason: letting nature take its course, letting men do as they are instinctively prompted to do, as far as that is compatible with "the security of the whole society."[36] It is easy to conceive and to grant that natural is in distinction to artificial, human, or constrained to obey a forecontrived design. Thus freedom is all on the side of nature, as opposed to constraint on the side of human reason. At the same time, however, nothing in the world is so unyielding and hence constraining as the necessary dictate of deaf and dumb nature, while the source of man's freedom resides in his power of reason, the origin of his various contrivances.[37] Smith's manner of confronting this difficulty is in effect to declare for the freedom of reason harnessed in the service of the more binding freedom of nature: calculation at the command of passion. Smith's doctrine is pervaded by the consequences of the fact that the superordinate element, nature conceived as the free motive of passion, is the symbol of man's unfreedom, as Kant was to emphasize so elaborately.

It is a distinguishing characteristic of Smith's doctrine and of liberal capitalism at large that they do not conceive freedom to be important primarily because it is the condition for every man's existence as an individual moral being, the ground of his self-legislating will in action or of his humanity. Liberty continued to mean for Smith what it had meant to Locke, to Aristotle, and to the long tradition of political philosophy: the condition of men under lawful governors who respect the persons and property of the governed, the latter having to consent to the arrangement in one way or another. This view of liberty is primarily political and belongs to the libertarianism of Locke, not of Rousseau. The capitalistic project is not animated by a search for methods of institutionally liberating the inner drives of every man in the interest of the moral will. It is animated by a search for methods of institutionally liberating every man's natural instinct of self-preservation in the interest of external, politically intelligible freedom and peaceful prosperous life for mankind as a whole. Therefore Smith had no difficulty in conceiving man as free while both in thrall to nature and subject to forms of law which guarantee his external freedom but can scarcely aim to be the basis of his internal emancipation from that same nature.

Smith is thus at liberty to repose his trust in a wisdom of nature that shows itself even or especially in the folly and injustice of man: the

moral hygiene that produces a multitude, in fact a race of self-legisla-
tors was not indispensable to his plan, nor was political life a species of
psychotherapy for bringing on man's subpolitical emancipation. Smith
was thus resigned to receive the benefits of civil society even if they
must be mediated by certain undoubted ills, and he was prepared to
do so indefinitely if the benefits are vast and the ills unavoidable. In
this respect he anticipated the mechanisms of philosophy of history as
it would emerge, but not its ends: good through ill and reason through
folly, but no Elysium at a rainbow's end.

It is important for us to see more exactly what Smith's doctrine
has in common with philosophy of history as that was later to develop.
There is, to begin with, his belief in a "natural progress of things toward improvement"—animated by "the uniform, constant and uninterrupted effort of every man to better his condition," bettering his
condition being understood in "the most vulgar" sense.[38] Smith illustrates this in an account of the progress of Europe from medieval
disorder to the comparative regularity of modern times. The anarchy of
old persisted because the great landed proprietors had troops of retainers
who comprised, in fact, private armies. Nothing could produce order
which did not dissolve those armies. The basis for their existence was
the fact that the grandees had abundant income in kind which, under
the primitive conditions of commerce then prevailing, they could not
dispose of by exchange or sale. They accordingly were compelled to
feed it to crowds of men who became their dependents and inevitably
their soldiers. What brought down the entire system was the enlargement of trade, which enabled the magnates to convert their produce
into money and thence into luxuries for their personal delectation
instead of into the military basis of their political power.

A revolution of the greatest importance to the public happiness, was in
this manner brought about by two different orders of people, who had not
the least intention to serve the public. To gratify the most childish vanity
was the sole motive of the great proprietors. The merchants and artificers,
much less ridiculous, acted merely from a view to their own interest, and in
pursuit of their own pedlar principle of turning a penny wherever a penny was
to be got. Neither of them had either knowledge or foresight of that great
revolution which the folly of the one, and the industry of the other, was
gradually bringing about.[39]

Smith speaks of the ascendancy of the Roman Church from the
tenth through the thirteenth century. He regards it as signalized by the
temporal power of the clergy, and that in turn as resting upon the influence of the clergy with the multitudes of men. The inferior ranks of

people were bound to the clergy by ties of interest, the multitudes depending upon a charity which was bestowed freely because, once again, the clergy had no other means of disposing of an enormous produce from their lands. When such means presented themselves, the constitution of the Catholic Church underwent a profound alteration:

Had this constitution been attacked by no other enemies but the feeble efforts of human reason, it must have endured for ever. But that immense and well-built fabric, which all the wisdom and virtue of man could never have shaken, much less overturned, was by the natural course of things, first weakened, and afterwards in part destroyed. . . .

The gradual improvements of arts, manufactures, and commerce, the same causes which destroyed the power of the great barons, destroyed in the same manner, through the greater part of Europe, the whole temporal power of the clergy.[40]

By these same instrumentalities, the species of mankind at large is drawn together, probably upward as well as onward. Smith regards the geographical discoveries as of unparalleled significance for the species: "The discovery of America, and that of a passage to the East Indies by the Cape of Good Hope, are the two greatest and most important events recorded in the history of mankind." The communication and commerce of the species as a whole was thereby in principle achieved for the first time in the memory of man, and with that epochal event came the supreme occasion for enabling all mankind reciprocally "to relieve one another's wants, to increase one another's enjoyments, and to encourage one another's industry." [41]

Smith believed that, to a large extent, nature speaks to history in the language of economics, and that the broad course of history so instructed is probably toward an easier, more cultivated, more rational and secure life for the generality of mankind. At the same time, he imagined that the advance of civilization was synchronous with the generation of a tremendous industrial mob, deprived of nearly every admirable human quality. Civilization is not an unqualified good, or more accurately, it comes at a price. This famous theme, of which Rousseau was the virtuoso, was developed by Smith with concern but without agitation. He proposed to palliate the ill with a wide system of almost gratis elementary schooling for the masses and with the encouragement of an unheard-of number of religious sects (as many as three thousand), each necessarily to be so small that every member of it would be conspicuous to the surveillance of his fellow communicants. All would maintain a vigil upon each other's morals that, far from being in any danger of flagging through lack of interest, would itself require to be moderated by febrifuges: courses of education in science and philosophy and artistic spectacles such as theater.[42] Smith repeatedly recommends the intellectual and moral state of much of industrial mankind to the most serious attention of government, not only out of philanthropy but for obvious reasons of state.

Our thesis, with a summary of which we shall now conclude, has been this: Within a short time of the completion of Locke's work, intelligent men began to reflect on and to draw out what would today be called the "moral implications" of his doctrine.[43] How far he had mitigated Hobbes's teaching of the natural ferocity of man and thereby turned political philosophy in the direction of economics has been shown above in the chapter on Locke. But the chief teaching of the modern school of natural law was not thereby impaired: nature continued univocally to mean preservation, with the supporting rights to whatever pertains thereto. Now this came to be regarded as insufficient, and the reduction of man to his affections was thought to imply that man is affected not only toward himself but toward his species. Perhaps Locke was not given enough credit for the important mitigation mentioned above, which is in this direction, but in any event the theme was made emphatic by Smith (at about the time of Rousseau's *Second Discourse*). The reduction of human life to its emotional foundations was enlarged to become the ground of duties as well as rights. It cannot be denied that those duties were consciously made to revolve about the preservation of the species; but it cannot either be denied that duties are different from rights, and the two require somehow to be reconciled with one another. In the course of reconciling the duties of moral virtue with the rights of nature, which is to say preservation, Smith had recourse to the tension between nature and the moral order derived from it, leaving the reconciliation inevitably imperfect. From this germ grew the teaching as to the moral imperfection of the natural or best order of society—the free, prosperous, and tolerant civil society. In its self-understanding, capitalism thus anticipated the chief postcapitalistic criticism of capitalism: civil society is a defective solution of the human problem.

Our second point, inseparable from the first, is that the self-understanding of capitalism also anticipated an astonishing proportion of what was to be proposed by the nineteenth century as the alternative to capitalism. We have tried to show how the direction of capitalism was toward the construction of a universal mankind, both as the ground of duty (the universal spectator) and as the ultimate beneficiary of economic progress—thus as the ultimate society. The engine of that progress was the ignoble desires and strivings of man, channeled through the economic institutions of production and distribution that opened up to him from time to time. An expectation of good through evil, reason through unreason, progress, a belief in the tendency of the interest of mankind to supersede that of particular political society, in the preponderance of economic influence on human affairs, in the primacy of labor in the process of production, in the preoccupation of civil society with the defense of property, this and more which Marxism would trumpet was present to the doctrines of capitalism in one measure and form or another, as it has been our purpose to show. A strange light is cast on Marx's theory that capitalism contains the seed of its own negation. It might perhaps be said that according to its own self-understanding, the ground of capitalism coincides to a remarkable degree with the seed bed of its own negation; but the seed itself is an alien thing, namely, philosophy of history, something that was generated not by the working of any economic institutions but by an act of human speculation.

Perhaps Smith is to be blamed for not having extracted a metaphysic from that "wisdom of nature" which he believed to guide the human process and to which he so often recurs, a metaphysic that would historicize the consummation of the whole human career. Perhaps he ought to have perceived the potency in such a metaphor as the "wisdom" of nature and gone on to postulate still higher wisdoms by which the laws of nature itself might be brought under orders. He never reached that point, however, for he did not question the belief that there is an unchanging horizon within which all change takes place, that horizon or framework being Nature.

Philosophy of history will be a subject of later chapters. For the present we may observe that when Rousseau's teaching of the malleability of human nature received its due cultivation and enlargement, it proved to be the little leaven that leavened the whole lump. The paradoxes and irregularities that liberal capitalism was willing to abide because of their origin in man's nature could not be tolerated by the nineteenth century since it no longer saw a need to tolerate them. The nature that gives rise to inconveniences must away, and itself submit to be superseded by the law of the change of nature, namely, History. It is this fissure, narrow but bottomless, that divides capitalism from communism.

NOTES

1. *Theory of Moral Sentiments,* in *The Essays of Adam Smith* (London: Alexander Murray, 1869), part VII. sec. II. chap. iii *ad fin.*, p. 271.

Comparison of such a representative passage from Hume as part V of *An Enquiry Concerning the Principles of Morals* with, for example, part I of *Theory of Moral Sentiments* will suggest the broad agreement between the two doctrines.

2. *Theory of Moral Sentiments*, I. I. iii. p. 18.

3. "The chief part of human happiness arises from the consciousness of being beloved." *Ibid.*, I. II. v. p. 40.

4. For example, *ibid.*, III. II. p. 105. Cf. above, pp. 372–75, concerning Hobbes's denial of the natural sociality of man.

5. *Theory of Moral Sentiments*, V. II. p. 177.

6. *Ibid.*, I. I. v. p. 24.

7. From Rousseau, *Discourse on the Origin of Inequality*, First Part. Readers of Rousseau's two *Discourses* will be struck by the similiarity of themes and views between them and the *Theory of Moral Sentiments*. The division of human nature between self-love and compassion, and the qualified goodness of civil society are but instances.

8. *Theory of Moral Sentiments*, I. I. v. p. 24.

9. *Ibid.*, II. II. i. p. 75.

10. The reader is urged to refer to the treatment of this subject in the chapter on Aristotle.

11. *Theory of Moral Sentiments*, II. I. ii. p. 65; II. II. i. p. 75.

12. *Ibid.*, VI. II. ii. pp. 202, 203–4.

13. *Ibid.*, II. I. v. p. 71n.

14. *Ibid.*, IV. ii. p. 166.

15. *Ibid.*, I. III. iii. pp. 56–57.

16. *Ibid.*, II. III. iii. pp. 96–98.

17. *Ibid.*, III. iii. p. 129.

18. *Ibid.*, III. v. pp. 147–49.

19. *Ibid.*, IV. i. p. 161, and throughout the book.

20. *Ibid.*, p. 163.

21. *Ibid.*, pp. 162–63.

22. Hume, *A Treatise of Human Nature*, I. I. i and II. I. ii.

23. Hume's remark is characteristically uncompromising: "[the reason] can never oppose passion in the direction of the will." *Ibid.*, II. III. Smith makes two remarks, in the form of allusions, which deny man's unique rationality: "mankind, as well as . . . all other rational creatures" (*Theory of Moral Sentiments*, III. v. p. 146) and "that great society of all sensible and intelligent beings" (*ibid.*, VI. II. iii. p. 209.)

24. *Theory of Moral Sentiments*, III. v. p. 142.

25. Winston S. Churchill, *Marlborough: His Life and Times* (4 vols in 2 bks; London: Harrap, 1947), vol. III. bk II. p. 303. Reproduced by permission of Charles Scribner's Sons and George Harrap & Co., Ltd.

26. *Theory of Moral Sentiments*, VI. II. iii. p. 210; VII. II. iv. p. 275.

27. *An Inquiry into the Nature and Causes of the Wealth of Nations* (New York: Modern Library, 1937), IV. II. p. 423.

28. *Ibid.*, V. I. iii. 2. p. 735.

29. *Ibid., e.g.*, I. conc. pp. 249–50; IV. III. ii. p. 460.

30. *Ibid.*, I. VI. pp. 48–49.

31. *Ibid.*, II. intro. p. 260. Also II. II. p. 271, etc.

32. *Ibid.*, I. XI. p. 145.

33. *Ibid.*, I. VI. p. 49.

34. *Ibid.*, I. I. p. 12. Also, Introduction and Plan of the Work, p. lviii.

35. *Ibid.*, IV. IX. p. 651; I. X. p. 99.

36. *Ibid.*, II. II. p. 308.

37. Smith commonly juxtaposes "naturally" and "necessarily," the latter often used apparently as an intensified form of the former. Cf., *e.g., ibid.*, pp. 8, 86, 357, 414, 421, 422, 591, 674, 723 and footnote, 754, 756.

38. *Ibid.*, II. III. pp. 326, 325.

39. *Ibid.*, III. IV. pp. 391–92.

40. *Ibid.*, V. I. iii. 3. p. 755.

41. *Ibid.*, III. VII. iii. p. 590; also IV. I. p. 416.

42. *Ibid.*, V. I. iii. 2. pp. 736–38; V. I. iii. 3. pp. 747–48.

43. The reader's attention should be

drawn to the work of Bernard Mandeville (*c.* 1670–1733) whose *The Fable of the Bees* (1714) had the subtitle "Private Vices, Public Benefits." Controversy raged around him, and Smith added his rebuke by dealing with him in a chapter "Of Licentious Systems" (*Theory of Moral Sentiments,* VII. II. iv), at the same time admitting that Mandeville was not mistaken in all respects.

READINGS

A. Smith, Adam. *An Inquiry into the Nature and Causes of the Wealth of Nations.* Book I, chaps i–x; chap. xi, intro. and conc.; book V, chap. i.
B. Smith, Adam. *An Inquiry into the Nature and Causes of the Wealth of Nations.* Book III; book IV, chaps i, ii, vii.

THE FEDERALIST*

1787–1788

Immediately after the 1787 federal convention Alexander Hamilton turned to the difficult task of securing New York's ratification of the proposed Constitution. As part of his strategy, he planned a series of short essays to expound the virtues of the Constitution. Hamilton secured the collaboration of John Jay and, ironically only after several others declined his invitation, of James Madison as well. *The Federalist* was published serially in groups of two and four essays in the New York City press. The essays were intended to influence the election of delegates to the state ratifying convention and, since for this election universal manhood suffrage was adopted, the essays were therefore addressed "to the People of the State of New York." But *The Federalist* was further intended to instruct and inspirit favorable delegates and to persuade or mollify unfavorable delegates to the convention. To this end, even before completion of serial publication in the press, the essays were published as a book and circulated to leading supporters of the Constitution throughout the country. Thus *The Federalist* was at once addressed to the widest electorate but also to those able and educated men who actually would determine the fate of the Constitution. It seems clear that its authors also looked beyond the immediate struggle and wrote with a view to influencing later generations by making their work the authoritative commentary on the meaning of the Constitution. While *The Federalist* was the most immediate kind of political work, a piece of campaign propaganda, it spoke also to thoughtful men then and now, with a view to the permanence of its argument.

* Alexander Hamilton (1757[5?]–1804); James Madison (1751–1836); John Jay (1745–1829).

The reading of *The Federalist* is further complicated by the fact that it was written by two men (Jay's small contribution may be disregarded here) whose individual opinions and subsequent careers radically diverged.[1] This fact has encouraged many readers to see fundamental inconsistencies in the work where they do not exist, on the presumption that a work written jointly by Hamilton and Madison must contradict itself. Like the belief that *The Federalist* was merely a propaganda piece, the belief that it was the inconsistent work of incompatible authors has depreciated *The Federalist* as a theoretical writing. But *The Federalist* presents itself as the work of one Publius who claims to supply a consistent, comprehensive, and true account of the Constitution and of the regime it was calculated to engender. As will be seen, Publius makes good his claim.

Apart from the fact that Hamilton and Madison had motive and capacity to achieve a remarkably consistent Publius, *The Federalist* has a literary character which made it possible for them to agree quite easily on much of what had to be said. *The Federalist* deals largely with factual matters. Whatever their differences, Hamilton and Madison could agree as to what the convention had done and what kind of country would be the result. Similarly they could readily agree on how to make the Constitution seem most attractive or least noxious to those they were seeking to persuade. The Federalist was a commentary on and a plea for a constitution. Its authors were therefore not *primarily* obliged to deal with the most controversial subject, namely, the standard by which they themselves deemed the Constitution good. This is, of course, not to say that Publius stays only at the surface or says only what his readers want to hear. In fact, Hamilton and Madison go very far, as Publius, in suggesting the theoretical grounds upon which a wise acceptance of the Constitution should rest. That is what makes *The Federalist* an illuminating work. But the literary character of *The Federalist* did not oblige them to push so far in the discussion as to lay bare their ultimate differences. Unfortunately, what helps explain Publius' consistency explains also why *The Federalist* falls short of those great works in which theoretical matters are pressed to their proper, that is, farthest limits.

One last observation on Publius leads directly to the teaching of *The Federalist*. We know that Hamilton took his pseudonyms seriously; they were meant to convey the character of his argument.[2] Shortly before Publius appeared, a series of essays in support of the Constitution had been initiated under the pseudonym "Caesar." It has often been thought that Hamilton was also Caesar, but scholarship has now made this seem unlikely. In any event, Caesar's first two essays were very poorly received and the series was abandoned by its author. The choice of "Publius" is especially revealing when compared with the ill-fated Caesar essays, whether the latter were written by Hamilton or not. Publius, the educated reader knew, was the Publius Valerius Publicola described in Plutarch. Publius like Caesar was a "strong man," but between them there was one enormous difference: Caesar destroyed a republic, Publius saved one. Unlike Caesar, Publius makes his contribution to the republic in a way compatible with its continued existence. He brings to its salvation qualities it cannot itself supply, but leaves it essentially intact after his efforts. Whoever wrote them, the Caesar papers had to founder. The Constitution was in fact not Caesarist, and the public to be persuaded was then profoundly hostile to a Caesarist appeal. The character of Publius on the contrary was exactly appropriate to the situation and perfectly characterized the argument of *The Federalist*. Publius, with a capacity and knowledge that the people cannot themselves supply, brings to the people the constitution that will preserve, indeed will safely found the republic.

In the first essay Publius supplies the outline of the work.

[1] *The utility of the UNION to your political prosperity*—[2] *The insufficiency of the present Confederation to preserve that Union*—[3] *The necessity of a government at least equally energetic with the one proposed, to the attainment of this object*—[4] *The conformity of the proposed Constitution to the true principles of republican government*—[5] *Its analogy to your own State constitution*—and lastly, [6] *The additional security which its adoption will afford to the preservation of that species of government, to liberty, and to property.*[3]

Publius then finds it necessary to explain the order of his work. "It may perhaps be thought superfluous to offer arguments to prove the utility of the UNION," he says, since it is thought that it "has no adversaries." Publius justifies his opening theme on the ground that there are in fact secret adversaries. But apart from this peculiar justification, it is possible to see Publius' other grounds for the organization of his work. In particular it is clear why he begins with the utility of the union. For one thing, he gets off on the right foot by beginning with a subject on which he is in accord with nearly all his readers. Further, a proper and full statement of the agreed end of union turns out, as a full statement of the end always does, to contain the clearest implications for what must be done to achieve the end. Therefore, by the time Publius has fully stated the value of union, he has introduced

all his major arguments on disputed matters in the amiable context of
the undisputed end. Rightly stated, the end of union is palpably inconsistent with the "imbecility" (*i.e.,* weakness) of the Confederation and
requires an "energetic" government. Publius wants to extort from the
"general assent to the abstract proposition" [4] that union is good and the
Confederation inadequate, acquiescence in what is necessary to sustain
the union. Publius is able to convert "general assent" into intelligent
and detailed assent by instructing his readers on what is logically
implied in their vague commitment to union. The first three branches
of Publius' work therefore make this argument: to desire union is
necessarily to despise the present Confederation and to welcome the
energetic government union needs. All that remains is to show that the
union under this energetic government, the proposed Constitution, is
satisfactorily republican. Hence Publius must teach a republican way
more fully to enjoy the "utility of Union" than hitherto thought possible.

This, as will be seen, is both Publius' most difficult political task
and his most important theoretical teaching. A closer look at the organization of the work reveals its importance. The work is actually divided
among the six "branches of the inquiry" in the following way: (1) "the
utility of Union"—14 papers; (2) "the insufficiency of the present Confederation"—8 papers; (3) the necessity of energetic government—14
papers; (4) the republicanism of the Constitution—48 papers; (5) and
(6)—1 paper. By the time he has reached the last paper, Publius claims
to have "so fully anticipated and exhausted" the last two branches that
he only brings together the appropriate arguments and concludes the
work. The book is therefore written in fact under four "heads." But
the organization may be stated still more simply. As has been seen,
the first three heads deal with one theme, the immediate political
question of what is to be done about the union—showing why it is
good, what is inadequate in the Articles of Confederation, and what
kind of government will be adequate to the end of union. The proposed
Constitution being adequate to that end, all that remains is to show that
this Constitution conforms to the *true* principles of republican government. And this is the work of the fourth, and by far the largest branch
of the inquiry. The organization of the essays stated in its simplest form
therefore is: union and republicanism. The organization of the essays
perfectly conveys *The Federalist*'s teaching. *The Federalist* teaches a
new and true republicanism which involves crucially a new view of
the problem of union.[5]

Americans were already living under republican governments, and
under a confederal union of these republics; but, in the view of *The*

Federalist, the principle of these republics and their confederal union was old and false. The Confederation was therefore necessarily foundering, and the individual republics were tending to "the mortal diseases under which popular governments have everywhere perished." [6] The Constitution contains the new and true principle of republican union which will rescue republican government in America. The proud conclusion of the famous tenth essay summarizes the teaching: "*In the extent and proper structure of the Union,* therefore, we behold a *republican* remedy for the diseases most incident to republican government." (Italics supplied.)

The Federalist is remarkable for the conjunction it achieves between discussion of the most urgent political matters and of theoretical matters. This is nowhere more evident than in the treatment of republican union. The right arrangement of union was the first political problem of the day; but what *The Federalist* has to say on this practical question is based on its most novel and important theoretical teaching. The opposition to the Constitution also rested upon a theoretical view. Indeed, one of the remarkable features of the debate over the Constitution was the extraordinary intrusion of theoretical considerations into the settlement of the practical question. The great attack on the Constitution was the charge that the new union was antirepublican. Certain features of the Constitution were regarded as specifically antirepublican, but the main thrust of the opposition resulted from the more general argument that only the state governments, not some huge central government, could be made effectively free and republican. This rested on a widely held belief, popularized in the way men understood Montesquieu, that only small countries could enjoy republican government. The reasoning that *The Federalist* had to oppose ran as follows.

Large countries necessarily turn to despotism. For one thing, large countries need despotic rule simply in consequence of largeness; political authority in the parts breaks down without more forceful government than the republican form admits. Further, large countries, usually wealthy and populous, are warlike or are made warlike by envious neighbors; the conduct of wars inevitably nurtures despotic rule. And even if large countries try to be republican, they cannot succeed. To preserve their rule, the people must be patriotic, vigilant, and informed. This requires that the people give loving attention to public things, and that the affairs of the country be on a scale commensurate with popular understanding. But in large countries the people are baffled and rendered apathetic by the complexity of public affairs, and at last become absorbed in their own pursuits. Finally, even the alert citizenry of a large republic must allow a few men actually to conduct the public business; far removed from the localities and possessed of the instruments of coercion, the trusted representatives would inevitably subvert the republican rule to their own passions and interests. Such was the traditional and strongly held view of the necessity that republics be small. It followed that such small republics could only combine for limited purposes into confederacies which respect the primacy of the member states. But its opponents regarded the Constitution not as a proper confederacy, but as "calculated ultimately to make the states one consolidated government," which is to say, one large republic; hence the Constitution was *necessarily* antirepublican. That is, the Constitution was denounced as resting on a novel and false view of republican union.

The Federalist, understandably then, asks its readers to "hearken not to the voice which petulantly tells you that the form of government recommended for your adoption is a novelty in the political world; that it has never yet had a place in the theories of the wildest projectors; that it rashly attempts what it is impossible to accomplish." [7]

While the readers are urged to hearken not, *The Federalist* does not deny the charge of novelty; on the contrary, it extols novelty as "the glory of the people of America."

Happily for America, happily, we trust for the whole human race, [the leaders of the revolution did not fear to depart from old ways but rather] pursued a new and more noble course. They accomplished a revolution which has no parallel in the annals of human society. They reared the fabrics of government which have no model on the face of the globe. They formed the design of a great Confederacy, which it is incumbent on their successors to improve and perpetuate.[8]

But one must expect, we are immediately told, some flaws in these achievements. It turns out that "they erred most in the structure of the Union." But this was to be expected because *this was the work most difficult to be executed.* (Italics supplied.) The right republican union, then, is a more difficult work to accomplish than a revolution without parallel and the creation of state governments without previous model. But the Constitution will accomplish this most difficult work. It will fulfill and therefore save "the new and more noble" way of life America has brought to the world. This "more perfect Union" rests upon the new and true republicanism which it is Publius' task to expound.

Publius states his most important claim in the conclusion of the famous tenth essay: he presents "a republican remedy for the diseases most incident to republican government." Again, Publius praises Thomas Jefferson for displaying equally "a fervent attachment to republican government and an enlightened view of the dangerous propensities against which it ought to be guarded." [9] Publius thus claims to be the wholehearted but cool-headed partisan of republicanism. But the word republican does not tell us enough about the kind of regime which Publius advocates. That is, the question immediately arises: what *kind* of republic? How may Publius' republic be fitted into the traditional distinction of three kinds of rule, by the one, few, or many? The answer is obvious: Publius espouses a *democratic* republic. Indeed, what is remarkable is the extent to which Publius gives the word republic, in the key passages, an exclusively democratic content. For example, "the republican principle . . . enables the majority to defeat [a minority faction's] sinister views by regular vote." And this must be a majority "derived from the great body of the society, not from an inconsiderable proportion, or a favored class of it." [10] While it is true that the word republic always meant the absence of monarchy and implied the importance of the whole body of citizens, it did not imply universal or nearly universal manhood suffrage: earlier usage always distinguished between aristocratic or oligarchic republics and democratic republics. But Publius' exclusively democratic idea of republicanism obliges him explicitly to deny the appellation republic to all those aristocratic and oligarchic regimes formerly so styled.[11] In short, in so far as it accepts the old threefold distinction of regimes, *The Federalist* treats its republican regime as belonging overwhelmingly to the democratic kind of rule. However much its regime departs from the character of a "pure democracy," *The Federalist* emphatically and rightly denies that the departure removes the Constitution from the class of democratic governments into the monarchical or aristocratic class.

Publius' new and true republicanism is therefore a new and true democratic teaching. For many reasons, which cannot be discussed here, the democratic character of *The Federalist,* and of the Constitution it expounded, has been obscured. This has been to miss the most important thing about *The Federalist*. It is necessary and appropriate, however, to examine one argument frequently made in support of the view that Publius' Constitution did not establish a democratic regime. In a famous passage in the tenth essay, Publius is thought himself to have radically distinguished republics from democracies, and hence himself to have withdrawn the Constitution from the democratic class. This is not quite accurate. Publius distinguishes a republic from "a *pure democracy*," [12] and that is a very different thing. By a pure democracy, Publius says he means "a society consisting of a small number of citizens, who assemble and administer the government in person." As Publius compares the two, a republic "varies from a pure democracy" only in that it is "a government in which the scheme of representation takes place." This and this alone is the distinction Publius makes. The perfect synonym for Publius' use of republic is therefore representative democracy. The principle of representation, however, introduces an impurity into the republican form from the point of view of pure democracy. But this does not mean that republics are opposed in kind to democracies; rather, republics are, so to speak, "impure" democracies.

On the crucial question of where sovereignty is lodged, namely, with the many, republics and pure democracies alike belong to a more inclusive class. The apparent difficulty raised by *The Federalist*'s distinction between republics and pure democracies is resolved when we see that this larger class or genus is what Publius calls *popular* government. And by popular government Publius means what is meant today by the term democracy. That is, Publius sees popular government as including all the forms of rule by the many, as distinguished from the various forms of rule by the few or the one. We may seek aid in understanding Publius from Madison and Hamilton individually. On the crucial question of the locus of political authority, Publius, Madison, and Hamilton all speak of a republic, democracy, and popular government interchangeably. Publius in the tenth essay speaks identically of a *republican* remedy for the disease of faction, and a remedy that will "preserve the spirit and form of *popular* government." On June 6 at the federal convention, Madison discussed the identical remedy as "the only defense against the inconveniences of *democracy* consistent with the *democratic* form of government." Hamilton styled the republic created by the Constitution a "*representative democracy*."[13] Publius must be understood, then, as having undertaken, in the fine phrase G. L. Pierson applied to Tocqueville, to "make democracy safe for the world." This is how Publius' greatest claim is to be understood. To save popular government from its "mortal diseases" while preserving both "the spirit and the form of popular government is . . . the great object . . . [of] our inquiries." Publius claims to rescue "this form of government . . . from the opprobrium under which it has so long labored," and therefore to recommend it "to the esteem and adoption of mankind."[14]

The foregoing is not intended, however, to depreciate the importance of Publius' distinction between republic and pure democracy. On the contrary, the peculiar property of a republic, that it is a *representative* democracy, is the foundation of *The Federalist*'s teaching; it "promises the cure for which we are seeking."[15] But the democratic character of *The Federalist*'s republicanism must be emphasized in order to grasp its central contention. Publius claims to cure the hitherto incurable ills of popular government, while remaining perfectly consistent with the principle of popular government, that is, lodging sovereignty with the many.

Publius helps us to see what is new in his teaching. In the fourteenth essay, which continues the assault on "the error which limits republican government to a narrow district," [16] Publius explains why men so long committed that error. What Publius now knows about republicanism was hitherto veiled from men by both the ancient and modern examples of it. The possibilities latent in the popular republican form were veiled because "most of the popular governments of antiquity were of the democratic species." While

in modern Europe, to which we owe the great principle of representation, no example is seen of a government *wholly popular,* and founded, at the same time, wholly on that principle. If Europe has the merit of discovering this great mechanical power in government, by the simple agency of which the will of the largest political body may be concentred, and its force directed to any object which the public good requires, *America* can claim the merit of making the discovery the basis of *unmixed* and *extensive* republics. It is only to be lamented that any of her citizens should wish to deprive her of the additional merit of displaying its full efficacy in the establishment of the comprehensive system now under her consideration.[17]

The ancients had many wholly popular governments but mostly of the *pure* democratic species, that is, of the direct, not the representative kind. The Europeans have partly or wholly representative governments, but none at once wholly representative and wholly of the popular kind. It has remained for America to innovate the combination: governments wholly popular and wholly based upon the representative principle. The word "unmixed" must be read in its full force. The American states were not *mixed regimes;* as wholly popular states, they had no significant admixture of aristocratical or monarchical elements. And they were not small republics as that term had been traditionally understood; they were already *extensive* republics. All that is needed, Publius concludes, is to display the "full efficacy" of the representative principle in the unmixed and still more extensive republic proposed by the Constitution. But Publius' mild speech is deceptive; as we have seen, all that remains to be done is "the work most difficult to be executed."

Publius understandably treats gently the pride and affection of his readers for their state governments. The state governments are fine, he seems to say, and the Constitution will be even finer. He says that "the valuable improvements made by the American constitutions on the popular models, both ancient and modern, cannot certainly be too much admired." [18] This sentence can be read in two ways; the amount of praise it bestows is uncertain. How does Publius actually regard the "valuable improvements" in the state government? The state governments, for all their improvements, fail utterly to solve the problem of faction which is *the* problem of popular government. The state governments will founder on this rock as all previous democracies have foundered. They will founder because they do not have a sufficient "number of citizens and extent of territory." They are "extensive republics," but not extensive enough.

The ancient popular governments obscured the possibilities latent in republicanism, we were told, because "most" of them lacked the representative principle. But something else was lacking in antiquity. Publius therefore comes back to this very question many essays later. Now he warns "that the position concerning the ignorance of the ancient governments on the subject of representation, is by no means precisely true in the latitude commonly given to it." [19] He now gives a considerable list of ancient representative institutions. True, none of the ancient republics was based wholly on the representative principle as are the American states. And this was a defect. But it was a trivial defect; they suffered from a much worse ill. "It cannot be believed, that any form of representative government could have succeeded within the narrow limits occupied by the democracies of Greece." [20] The utility of the representative principle, then, which offers "the cure for which we are seeking," depends entirely upon the size of country. Even the relatively large American states will not suffice; only a union of the magnitude and character envisaged by the Constitution will solve the problem of popular government.

"The enlightened friends to liberty" would have had to abandon the cause of republican government as "indefensible" if this new solution had not been found. The solution rests upon the "science of politics," which "like most other sciences, has received great improvement. The efficacy of various principles is now well understood, which were either not known at all, or imperfectly known to the ancients."

The regular distribution of power into distinct departments; the introduction of legislative balances and checks; the institution of courts composed of judges holding their offices during good behavior; the representation of the people in the legislature by deputies of their own election: these are wholly new discoveries, or have made their principal progress towards perfection in modern times. They are means, and powerful means, by which the excellences of republican government may be retained and its imperfections lessened or avoided. To this catalogue of circumstances that tend to the amelioration of popular systems of civil government, I shall venture, however novel it may appear to some, to add one more, on a principle which has been made the foundation of an objection to the new Constitution; I mean the ENLARGEMENT of the ORBIT within which such systems are to revolve, either in respect to the dimensions of a single State, or to the consolidation of several smaller States into one great Confederacy.[21]

Publius is thus the spokesman for the new "science of politics," the previous teachers of which he does not name, who has himself made an important addition to the science, namely the possibility of a very large republic. Further, everything in that modern science of politics is seen now in a democratic light; if the earlier teachers of the new science only tended in a democratic direction, or suggested only partly democratic regimes, Publius takes the new science of politics and enlarges upon it and uses it for the amelioration of a "wholly popular" system of civil government. Finally, through Publius, the moment has come for the new science to cease being merely a teaching and to become a great political actuality.

Publius sees the problem of representative popular government as threefold. First, there is the possibility that the people will lose control of their government, that the representative rulers will subvert the regime. Second, there is the possibility that popular majorities, through compliant representatives, will rule oppressively. Third, there is the possibility that majorities, through compliant representatives, will rule not oppressively, but foolishly, failing to do the things necessary for the strength and stability of the government.

Protecting the people is the simplest task. "The whole power of the proposed government is to be in the hands of the representatives *of the people*." [22] The actual rulers will have no warrant ultimately save as they are "the objects of popular choice." [23] This guards against subversion by the representative rulers; making the representatives wholly dependent upon the people "is the essential, and, after all, only efficacious security for the rights and privileges of the people, which is attainable in civil society." [24] Although the regime is now to be wholly popular and wholly representative, there is nothing new thus far; democracy's oldest claim is that the right of suffrage guards the society against the oppression of its rulers. The new science of politics, however, offers an additional safeguard to the rights of the people. Separation of powers, "the regular distribution of power into distinct departments," lessens the threat that the rulers will be able to concert and execute schemes of oppression. The liberty of the people generally and the rights of individuals are secured by "the improbability of . . . a mercenary and perfidious combination of the several members of government, standing on as different foundations as republican principles will well admit, and at the same time accountable to the society over which they are placed." [25] This is what was sought in separation of powers by Jefferson, who feared above all oppression of the people by their rulers. How separation of powers will supply this protection can be better understood when we see how separation of powers mitigates the other evils Publius feared.

It is not enough, Publius argues, to guard society against the oppression of the representative rulers, it is necessary also "to guard one part of the society against the injustice of the other part." [26] In plain words, the problem is to guard against "overbearing" popular majorities. This is a far greater problem than the unconstitutional treachery of representatives because "the form of popular government" permits a popular majority "to execute and mask its violence under the forms of the Constitution." [27] In this sentence Publius boldly displays the democratic nature of the regime he expounds: the many rule and therefore can legally do oppressive things. Unlike Jefferson's "elective despotism," this evil occurs, not when the representatives are unfaithful to their constituents, but when they too faithfully heed the oppressive wishes of popular majorities. The great danger Publius sees is that popular majorities will demand oppressive measures and that their elected representatives will only too readily oblige. Publius seeks to solve the problem at both levels, among the people and among their representatives. "Multiplicity" of factions is his famous answer to the problem of the oppressive majority itself. But first we must consider how separation of powers solves the problem at the level of the representatives.

Publius is aware of two other respectable ways of preventing majorities from oppressing minorities. One is to create "a will in the community independent of the majority—that is, of the society itself." [28] But this is the monarchical solution which Publius rejects. The other is exemplified in the Roman republic where the legislative authority was divided into two "distinct and independent legislatures," [29] which enabled the patrician minority constitutionally to resist the plebeian majority. This may be taken to illustrate the traditional idea of the mixed republic which is excluded in Publius' "unmixed" republic, in which "all authority . . . will be derived from and dependent on the society." [30] The problem of oppressive majorities cannot be solved in a wholly popular regime by means belonging to the monarchical or mixed regimes. Publius finds in the new science of politics, which is not necessarily democratic, a solution which can be grafted onto democracy: separation of powers. Perhaps there is even a deeper kinship between separation of powers and democracy. In any event, Publius employs separation of powers, as he does all other things in the new science, so as "to preserve the spirit and the form of popular government."

Separation of powers mitigates the evil of oppressive majorities at the level of the government. In a republic without separation of powers, where a single body of representatives performs all the functions of government, there would be nothing in the machinery of government that could stay the will of an oppressive popular majority. But this is precisely what separation of powers is designed to do: to create a distance 'twixt the majority's cup and lip. Separation of powers takes the old distinction of the legislative, executive, and judicial functions of governing and makes it a distinction of the legislative, executive, and judicial personnel. This means, then, to create some representatives who will resist the wrong desires of the people to which other representatives are supinely yielding, or which they are even demagogically arousing. When the governing power is distributed into distinct departments, it is clear which are the representatives who may resist and which are those who will yield to popular demands. "In republican government, the legislative authority necessarily predominates." [31] "The legislative department" as the sad experience of the state governments had shown, "is everywhere extending the sphere of its activity, and drawing all power into its impetuous vortex." [32] As it were, it is against the legislature that the force of separation needs especially to be directed. "The great security against a gradual concentration of the several powers in the same department, consists in giving to those who administer each department the necessary constitutional means and personal motives to resist encroachment of the others." [33]

Publius had reason to speak blandly but his meaning is clear. The executive and the judiciary must have the means and personal motives to resist the legislature. For example, "when occasions present themselves, in which the interests of the people are at variance with their inclinations"; or when the legislators, who "commonly have the people on their side," are bent on oppression, then "the Executive should be in a situation to dare to act his own opinion with vigor and decision." [34] Separation of powers creates authorities who, despite their dependence upon the people and their lack of any independent title to rule, are yet likely to resist and stay the legislature when it is yielding to the wrong demands of the populace, the constitutional master of all three branches of government.

Publius shows quite easily how the executive and the judiciary will have the "means" to stave off oppressive legislation; the veto, the president's legislative initiative, his discretion in the enforcement of the laws, judicial review, and the judges' discretion in the adjudication of individual cases, all give to the other two branches the constitutional means temporarily to void or to moderate oppressive legislation. But it is more difficult to see why the executive and the judiciary will have the "personal motives" to resist the legislature. Why will they collaborate with the legislature in good actions, without which collaboration government would be reduced to the imbecility Publius despised, and collide with the legislature in its bad actions? Publius gives us two reasons. First, "ambition must be made to counteract ambition. The interest of the man must be connected with the constitutional rights of the place." [35] If the government is properly arranged, presidents and judges will defend their offices against the legislature because their pride, love of power or fame, even avarice, will lead them to identify their self-interest with the integrity of their offices. But there is a crucial assumption here. Publius assumes that oppressive legislation necessarily or at least ordinarily derogates from the dignity of the executive and judicial offices. Publius appears to assume that oppressive legislation requires servile execution and servile adjudication; and that servile executives and judges enjoy no dignity, no power, no fame, and ultimately not even pecuniary rewards. Hence Publius expects the executive and judiciary, for reasons of private interest and passion, to resist the legislature when it is oppressive. Separation of powers supplies democracy with governors who, without the traditional motives of family distinction or wealth, simply because of the jobs they hold and their self-regarding attachment to them, will tend to rule in the best interest of the democracy.

Publius' second reason for believing that the other branches will resist oppressive legislation desired by a popular majority is also based on his assumption that oppressive legislation ordinarily derogates from the integrity of the executive and judicial offices. But he appears further to assume that presidents and judges will resist oppressive legislation, not only because of interested attachment to their offices, but also out of a decent regard for the proper fulfillment of their duties. As reasonably decent men doing a job, they will have the motives, as it were the professional motives, to resist oppressive legislation because it tends to violate the arts they serve, and to subordinate the executive and judicial offices.

This last consideration leads to an understanding of how Publius expected separation of powers to help solve the third problem of popular government, not the oppressiveness but the ineptitude of popular rule. Again, Publius is confronting the traditional criticism of popular government which was that it gave over government into the hands of the many, which is to say the unwise. The very principle of representation itself may be a step in the right direction. The effect of representation may be

to refine and enlarge the public views, by passing them through the medium of a chosen body of citizens, whose wisdom may best discern the true interest of their country, and whose patriotism and love of justice will be least likely to sacrifice it to temporary or partial considerations. . . . It may well happen that the public voice, pronounced by the representatives of the people, will be more consonant to the public good than if pronounced by the people themselves, convened for the purpose.[36]

But we know that Publius does not count much on the wisdom and courage of the legislature alone. It is those other representatives of the people, the executive and the judiciary, who are crucial to elevating the whole representation of the people. (It should be noted that much of what is said here of separation of powers applies as well to "legislative checks and balances," that is, those checks imposed by the existence of the Senate.) The executive and judiciary are elected and appointed at some remove from the immediate opinion of the people, but democratically, that is, not upon any authority outside the sovereignty of the people. They serve for longer terms and serve larger constituencies; the nature of their duties thrusts more forcefully upon them awareness of what is necessary for the interest of the whole. They come to want to do their jobs well. Separation of powers creates offices which of themselves tend to make the men who occupy them worthy of the offices.

Moreover, separation of powers aids in securing for the executive and judiciary the men most likely to acquit themselves well; that is, it influences beneficially the majority choice. Separation of powers, one can see, supplies a superb rhetorical mode to those who are concerned with the ineptitude of popular rule. Publius has the courage—and it says something about his audience that he felt he could dare—to ask the many to select for their rulers men who are their superiors in wisdom and virtue. Every people ought "to obtain for rulers men who possess most wisdom to discern, and most virtue to pursue, the common good."[37] Separation of powers gives Publius a framework within which to press the people to seek wisdom and virtue in their rulers. He can present the executive and judiciary (and the Senate) as having, so to speak, a list of job specifications, qualities which are necessary to the performance of the functions and which approximate wisdom and virtue. It is politically easier and more effective to ask the people to select the right man for the specific job, especially a people with the "commercial character of America." [38] More willing to vote for superior men when superiority is presented in the guise of job qualifications, the people are also instructed in how to choose the better men; the job specifications supply them with a kind of simple checklist to guide choice to better rather than poorer men.

Publius shows how separation of powers, legislative checks and balances, and numerous practical embellishments upon these make possible for the first time a sound popular regime, a system of popular rule which will be less oppressive and wiser in the art of government than any before. But we must now see that this achievement depends utterly upon the last item in Publius' science, the enlargement of the republican orbit.

Separation of powers is a refinement of the representative principle. It would have no place in a pure democracy. Separation guards against that "accumulation of all powers, legislative, executive, and judiciary, in the same hands, whether of one, a few, or many, and whether hereditary, self-appointed, or elective [which] may justly be pronounced the very definition of tyranny." [39] But a pure democracy, by Publius' definition, is precisely the accumulation of all powers in the hands of the many. Hence it is only in a representative democracy that the rulers can be separated into distinct departments. But just as it is not enough to have a representative democracy, so it is not enough even to have properly separated representatives. It must be remembered that Publius said that the small ancient democracies could not have been helped by "*any* form of representative government"; they fatally lacked the advantages of an extensive territory and a numerous population. The representative principle is meant to supply rulers who can govern the people better than the people can govern themselves directly. But in small republics, the representative rulers are so immediately under the scrutiny and influence of a compacted popular majority that the representatives constitute no independent presence in the regime, but are merely the tools of the majority. Hence the representative principle is useless in a small republic.[40] Nor can separation of powers save the small republic. The immediate influence there of popular majorities, sufficient to awe a single representative body, is sufficient also to make of separated departments the mere agents of popular will. Only when there is a distance between the people and their government will there be that difference between the ultimate authority of the people and the immediate authority of their representatives which is the decisive condition for the advantages supplied by the principle of both representation and separation of powers. Not even in those large republics, the states, but only in a very large republic, the union, will the representative principle and its corollary, separation of powers, work "to the amelioration of popular systems of civil government."

The representative principle, reinforced by separation of powers, is meant to deny the authority of the government to oppressive popular majorities *after* they have formed. But Publius was aware that this was not enough, even in large republics. If a majority comes to have the same oppressive passion or interest and holds to it for only four to six years, it will find the means to triumph over separation of powers, checks and balances, the not so difficult amending procedure, and all the contrivances of the Constitution. These devices were designed, and could be designed, only to stay the will of the majority. This is not to depreciate the importance of the legal barriers; they have enormous efficacy in tempering the force Publius feared. But that efficacy depends ultimately upon a prior weakening of the force applied against them, upon the majority having been deflected from its "schemes of oppression." This is why Publius calls the problem of the popular majority itself *the* problem of popular government.

Publius therefore seeks to solve the problem of the oppressive and unwise rule of popular systems by trying to deal with the popular majority itself. Again everything depends upon the novel conception of a very large republic and, as we shall see, a certain kind of very large republic. The problem is dealt with in the famous tenth essay on the problem of "violence of faction."

Publius is not concerned with the problem of faction generally; he devotes only two sentences in the whole essay to the dangers of minority factions. The real problem in popular government is majority faction, or, more precisely, *the* majority faction, *i.e.,* the great mass of the little propertied and the unpropertied. If the people is the sovereign, the many are the sovereign, and the many may desire to oppress the few; it is the many therefore from whom can come the greatest harm. Publius emphasizes one harm in particular, the harm which results from the struggle between the rich and the poor and which made the ancient democracies short-lived "spectacles of turbulence and contention." *The* problem for the friend of popular government is how to avoid the "domestic convulsion" which results when the rich and the poor, the few and the many, as is their wont, are at each others' throats. Always before in popular governments the many, armed with political power, precipitated such convulsions. The many can be diverted from this natural course, Publius says, by one of two means only.

Either the existence of the same passion or interest in a majority at the same time must be prevented, or the majority, having such co-existent passion or interest, must be rendered, by their number and local situation, unable to concert and carry into effect schemes of oppression.[41]

But "we well know that neither moral nor religious motives can be relied on" as a control if such a majority forms and concerts its action. The "circumstance principally" which will provide both defenses against oppressive majorities is the "greater number of citizens and extent of territory which may be brought within the compass" of very large republican governments.

The smaller the society, the fewer probably will be the distinct parties and interests composing it; the fewer the distinct parties and interests, the more frequently will a majority be found of the same party; and the smaller the number of individuals composing a majority, and the smaller the compass within which they are placed, the more easily will they concert and execute their plans of oppression. Extend the sphere and you take in a greater variety of parties and interests; you make it less probable that a majority of the whole will have a common motive to invade the rights of other citizens; or if such a common motive exists, it will be more difficult for all who feel it to discover their own strength, and to act in unison with each other.[42]

In a small republic the many poor come to see themselves as a single interest arrayed against the single interest of the few rich; accordingly, the politics of the small republic is the fatal politics of class struggle. That is what is important here about smallness. In the small republic, the many are divided into but a few trades and callings; further, it can be suggested, the smallness of the country makes instantly visible to anyone that these few differences among the many are trivial as compared with the massive difference between all the poor and all the rich. In a small republic, the divisions among the many are insufficient to prevent them from conceiving their lot in common and uniting in fatal struggle against the common enemy. In a large republic, however, distinctions arise among the many, sufficiently numerous and divisive to prevent the forming and concerting of such majorities. But clearly, largeness is not as such decisive; there can be large countries in which the poor are undifferentiated, poor only in a few ways. Only a certain kind of large republic holds out the prospect of the right kind of divisiveness. Publius tells us where this occurs. The properly divisive host of interests grows up "of necessity in civilized nations, and divide[s] them into different classes, actuated by different sentiments and views." Strikingly, as it does in Adam Smith, "civilized nations" means large nations devoted to the commercial life. The largeness of the large republic offers a remedy for the republican disease only if the large republic is also a modern commercial republic.

Publius' republican remedy depends entirely upon achieving the right kind of political divisions. Now Publius sees more than one source of division; for example, he clearly relies upon the presence of a "multiplicity of [religious] sects." [43] But he is well known to emphasize primarily the economic. "The possession of different *degrees* and *kinds* of property . . . [influences] the sentiments and views of the respective proprietors . . . [and produces the] division of the society into different interests and parties." Although other causes of division must not be overlooked, "the most common and durable source of factions has been the *various* and *unequal* distribution of property." (Italics supplied.) It is important to notice that in both statements Publius distinguishes two kinds of divisions which result from property: men differ according to the *amount* of property they hold, but also according to the *kind* of property they hold. The difference according to amount of property, between rich and poor, was the basis of the fatal class struggles of small republics. But Publius sees in the large commercial republic the possibility for the first time of subordinating the difference over amount of property to the difference over kind of property. In such a republic the hitherto fatal class struggle is replaced by the safe, even salutary struggle among different kinds of propertied interests. In such a republic, a man will regard it as more important to himself to further the immediate advantage of his specialized trade, or his specialized calling within a trade, than to advance the general cause of the poor or the rich. The struggle of the various interests veils the difference between the few and the many. In particular, the interest of the many as such can be fragmented into sundry narrower, more limited interests, each seeking immediate advantage. In such a republic and with such citizens, "you make it less probable that a majority of the whole will have a common motive to invade the rights of other citizens." In such a republic, popular majorities will still rule but now "among the great variety of interests, parties, and sects which it embraces, a coalition of a majority of the whole society could seldom take place on any other principles than those of justice and the general good." [44]

Publius is aware of what is involved in his novel teaching regarding the large commercial republic. His doctrine moves in directions which carry it beyond those manifestly political concerns with which we have dealt. Publius sees, as does Adam Smith, the connection between a very large area of trade and the possibility of division of labor, which in turn is so closely connected with the saving multiplicity of faction. This is why Publius so desperately seeks to preserve, render vastly more intimate, and strengthen the union. Publius also knows that his solution to the problem of popular majorities requires that the country be profoundly democratic, that is, that all men must be equally free and equally encouraged to seek their immediate gain and to associate with others in the process. There must be no rigid barriers which bar men from the pursuit of their immediate interest. Indeed, it is especially the lowly, from whom so much is to be feared, who must feel least barred from opportunity and most sanguine about their chances. Further, his solution requires a country that achieves commercial success, a wealthy country. That is, the limited and immediate gains must be real; the fragmented interests must achieve real gains from time to time, else the scheme ceases to beguile or mollify. Further, the laws, and especially the fundamental law, must look to the protection of the property of all, of the little propertied so that they may cleave to their little as their fundamental concern, and of the much propertied so as to make their property seem beyond the reach of envy. The fundamental law must also render difficult especially those most likely oppressive acts such as the states' tampering with the value of money or impairing the obligation of contracts.

And Publius is aware that his scheme involves an enormous reliance on the ceaseless striving after immediate private gains; the commercial life must be made honorable and universally practiced. Publius counts on a portion of patriotism and wisdom in the people and especially in their representative rulers. But precisely in his discussion of separation of powers, that device for securing enlightened rulers, he returns to his primary emphasis. Enlightened though they may be, it is primarily their private passions and interests that render them useful to the public. In perhaps the most remarkable and revealing single sentence of the book, Publius speaks of "this policy of supplying, by opposite and rival interests, the defect of better motives, [which] might be traced through the whole system of human affairs, private as well as public." [45] To understand fully how Publius understands "the defect of better motives," and how he seeks to make up for the defect by founding a regime in which the art of government is made commensurate with the capacity of men when their passions and interests are rightly arranged, is to understand Publius' contribution to the new "science of politics" and to understand the American republic he had so large a hand in framing.

NOTES

1. The authorship of the 85 papers has long been disputed. According to the convincing attribution of Douglass Adair, Hamilton wrote 51 papers (1, 6–

9, 11–13, 15–17, 21–36, 59–61, 65–85),
Madison 29 (10, 14, 18–20, 37–58, 62–
63), and Jay 5 (2–5, 64).

2. See the fine essay by Douglass
Adair, "A Note on Certain of Hamilton's Pseudonyms," *William and Mary
Quarterly*, third series, XII (April
1955).

3. *The Federalist*, ed. Henry Cabot
Lodge, introduction by Edward Mead
Earle (New York: Modern Library,
1941) 1, p. 6. Italics original.

4. *Federalist* 15, p. 89.

5. The organization of the essays is
perfectly revealed in *Federalist* 39
which defends the Constitution on two
grounds, that it is sufficiently republican
and sufficiently federal. That is, in this
essay, which links the two main divisions of the book and is in a sense the
central essay, the issue is stripped to its
essentials: union and republicanism.

6. *Federalist* 10, pp. 53–54.

7. *Federalist* 14, p. 84.

8. *Ibid.*, p. 85.

9. *Federalist* 49, p. 327.

10. *Federalist* 10, p. 57. *Federalist*
39, p. 244. See also *Federalist* 52, pp.
341–42: "The definition of the right of
suffrage is very justly regarded as a
fundamental article of republican government." It is "to be the same with
those of the electors of the most numerous branch of the State legislatures."
"It cannot be feared that the people of
the States will alter this part of their
constitutions in such a manner as to
abridge the rights secured to them by
the federal Constitution." The national
suffrage is made as democratic as the
very democratic suffrage in the states,
and there is no likelihood that the suffrage will become less popular.

11. *Federalist* 39, p. 243.

12. *Federalist* 10, p. 58. Italics supplied.

13. Alexander Hamilton, *Writings*,
ed. Henry Cabot Lodge (12 vols.; New
York: Putnam, 1904), II, 92. Italics
original.

14. *Federalist* 10, p. 58.

15. *Ibid.*, p. 59.

16. *Federalist* 14, p. 80.

17. *Ibid.*, p. 81. Italics supplied.

18. *Federalist* 10, p. 54.

19. *Federalist* 63, p. 412.

20. *Ibid.*, p. 413.

21. *Federalist* 9, pp. 48–49.

22. *Federalist* 28, p. 173. Italics supplied.

23. *Federalist* 57, p. 371.

24. *Federalist* 28, p. 173.

25. *Federalist* 55, p. 364.

26. *Federalist* 51, p. 339.

27. *Federalist* 10, p. 57.

28. *Federalist* 51, p. 339.

29. *Federalist* 34, pp. 203–4.

30. *Federalist* 51, p. 339.

31. *Ibid.*, p. 338.

32. *Federalist* 48, p. 322.

33. *Federalist* 51, p. 337.

34. *Federalist* 71, pp. 465–66.

35. *Federalist* 51, p. 337.

36. *Federalist* 10, p. 59.

37. *Federalist* 57, p. 370.

38. *Federalist* 11, p. 62.

39. *Federalist* 47, p. 313.

40. See also *Federalist* 10, p. 59,
where Publius notes that the "effect" of
representation "may be inverted."

41. *Federalist* 10, p. 58.

42. *Ibid.*, pp. 60–61.

43. *Federalist* 51, pp. 339–40.

44. *Ibid.*, p. 341.

45. *Ibid.*, p. 337.

READINGS

A. *The Federalist.* 1, 6, 9, 10, 14, 15, 23, 37–39, 47, 51, 63, 68, 70, 72, 78.
B. *The Federalist.* All the remaining numbers.

THOMAS PAINE

1737–1809

Thomas Paine was a brilliant pamphleteer in an age which gave full scope to his talents. Born and raised in England, he spent much of his life in America and France, where he took an active part, through his publications, in the great revolutions which swept over those countries in the late eighteenth century.

It was Paine's strength as a propagandist, though his weakness as a thinker, that he saw man and society entirely in black and white, with no shades of gray. The revolutions of his day were, for him, struggles between unmitigated good and evil. A typical child of the Enlightenment, he viewed the past as an almost unbroken reign of ignorance, superstition, and tyranny. But he felt that it was his privilege to live in "a morning of reason" when the native good will and common sense of the average man were beginning to assert themselves and would speedily make all things new.

There was a ground for Paine's confidence: "All the great laws of society are laws of nature." [1] Human reason, he believed, once freed from the impostures of political tradition and the absurdities of revealed religion, could easily apprehend the natural laws of society and government. As rational knowledge spread, governments would inevitably be reconstituted on natural principles. Then all major social problems could be solved without great difficulty. There was in Paine's thought more than a trace of what has been called "redemptive futurism" or "political messianism," the crusading faith that a revolution in the social and political order would uproot the tares of evil in man and create a new and sinless humanity. "The present age," he said, "will

hereafter merit to be called the Age of Reason, and the present generation will appear to the future as the Adam of a new world." [2]

The problem of social life, as Paine saw it, was essentially that of
founding government on right principles. Fortunately, it was a simple problem. "Notwithstanding the mystery with which the science
of government has been enveloped, for the purpose of enslaving, plun-
dering and imposing upon mankind, it is of all things the least mysterious and the most easy to be understood." [3] In regard to government,
"men have but to think and they will neither act wrong nor be misled." [4]

Underlying Paine's political philosophy was the doctrine of the
natural harmony of individual interests. "Society," he said, "is produced
by our wants and government by our wickedness." [5] Man is fitted by
Nature for society, because no man is capable of supplying his own
needs without the aid of society. These needs, and his natural social
affections, force man into society. Indeed, "man is so naturally a creature
of society, that it is almost impossible to put him out of it." [6] The
principle which forms society and holds it together, therefore, is common interest.

Common interest largely suffices for the purposes of social life.
Government correspondingly has a minimal role to play, because "society performs for itself almost every thing which is ascribed to government." All that government need do is "to supply the few cases to
which society and civilization are not conveniently competent." Social
progress therefore is in the direction of ever less government. "The more
perfect civilization is, the less occasion has it for government, because
the more does it regulate its own affairs, and govern itself." [7]

Government, as hitherto constituted, has been "the generating
cause" rather than the remedy of social disorder, of poverty and war.
The solution to the problem of government, however, is not its abolition
(an idea which Paine apparently never entertained), but its reconstitution on the right principles: "by the simple operation of constructing
government on the principles of society and the rights of man, every
difficulty retires...." The sum and substance of political philosophy, and
the one thing it is beneficial to know, is this: "*That government is
nothing more than a national association acting on the principles of
society.*" [8]

What then are the principles of society? As has already been said,
"All the great laws of society are laws of nature.... They are followed
and obeyed, because it is the interest of the parties so to do...." [9]
Government's function is to enable men to follow their own interests.
"Every man wishes to pursue his occupation, and to enjoy the fruits of

his labors and the produce of his property in peace and safety, and with the least possible expense. When these things are accomplished, all the objects for which government ought to be established are answered." [10] In short, man's security in the pursuit of his own interest is "the true design and end of government."

This security is also man's right. Paine's theory of society and government is elaborated entirely in terms of rights. He speaks of duties, too, but they consist in guaranteeing to others the same rights one vindicates for oneself. All men deserve equal protection because they come into the world equally endowed with rights. These rights are the principles on which alone a just and legitimate political order can be built. This theory, of which Paine was an influential exponent though by no means the originator, furnished the intellectual ammunition for the great revolutionary movement of the eighteenth century.

The rights of man include both natural and civil rights. In *The Rights of Man,* Paine explains the distinction between them in these terms:

Natural rights are those which appertain to man in right of his existence. Of this kind are all the intellectual rights, or rights of the mind, and also all those rights of acting as an individual for his own comfort and happiness, which are not injurious to the natural rights of others. Civil rights are those which appertain to man in right of his being a member of society. Every civil right has for its foundation some natural right pre-existing in the individual, but to the enjoyment of which his individual power is not, in all cases, sufficiently competent. Of this kind are all those which relate to security and protection.[11]

That is to say, there are natural rights "in which the *power* to execute it is as perfect in the individual as the right itself." For example, "religion is one of those rights." In the exercise of these rights the individual is self-sufficient and has no need of government. But there are other rights, equally natural, "in which, though the right is perfect in the individual, the power to execute them is defective." These rights man "deposits in the common stock of society." [12] That is, he gives up the personal enforcement of some of his natural rights and exchanges them for civil rights, so that society may the more effectively protect him in exercising his rights.

Civil power is thus a sort of joint capital "made up of the aggregate of that class of the natural rights of man, which becomes defective in the individual in point of power." [13] Men pool their right to be judges in their own cause and establish a government to exercise judgment between their conflicting claims. But the power of government is only the collected power of individuals and cannot be used to infringe the natural rights which they retain for themselves. For natural rights are the rights with which God endowed man as man at his creation; they are consequently inviolable and imprescriptible.

Paine, it is obvious, belonged to the social-compact school of political thought. But he would not hear of a compact between the people and their rulers. There was only one contractual act, by which "the *individuals themselves,* each in his own personal and sovereign right, *entered into a compact with each other* to produce a government: and this is the only mode in which governments have a right to arise, and the only principle on which they have a right to exist." [14] This compact does not create a sovereign government but a sovereign community or nation. The title of king cannot make a man a sovereign. "Sovereignty, as a matter of right, appertains to the nation only, and not to any individual; and a nation has at all times an inherent indefeasible right to abolish any form of government it finds inconvenient, and establish such as accords with its interest, disposition, and happiness." [15]

Government is never more than an agent of the people who form the nation, and the only sovereignty which Paine will recognize is popular sovereignty. Just as the natural rights of the individual are imprescriptible, so, too, the inherent sovereignty of the nation is imprescriptible. No claim to authority by the holders of power stands against the right of the people to dispossess them and change the form of government. Paine showed no genuine understanding of the doctrine of prescription in government as expounded by Edmund Burke, but he left no doubt about the vehemence with which he rejected it.

All forms of government, at least in large states where direct democracy was impossible, could be classified under two headings: "government by election and representation" and "government by hereditary succession." Hereditary government included monarchy and aristocracy, or that combination of the two which prevailed almost everywhere in Europe in the eighteenth century. Paine's opinion of it can be stated succinctly: "All hereditary government is in its nature tyranny." [16]

It was impossible, Paine said, that hereditary governments, such as had hitherto existed, "could have commenced by any other means than a total violation of every principle, sacred and moral." [17] Not only the origin but the entire history of these governments was a monstrous record of crime. Their major purpose was plunder, called by the gentler name of taxation, and one of their chief means of raising taxes was to engage in continual warfare. Since they were systems of exploitation, they had to rely on fraud, mystification, and induced ignorance to maintain themselves. "Monarchy," said Paine, "is the popery of government;

a thing kept up to amuse the ignorant, and quiet them into paying taxes." [18]

But the crimes of monarchical and aristocratic governments did not constitute their radical fault. Rather it was that hereditary government was slavery by definition, because it deprived a nation of its inherent and imprescriptible right to govern itself through its chosen representatives. Paine's conclusion was that "there is not a problem in Euclid more mathematically true than that hereditary government has not a right to exist." [19]

Representative government, on the other hand, was the only legitimate form of government, because it alone was founded on the inherent right of the nation to govern itself. But since the nation was a collection of originally independent individuals who had contracted among themselves to form a government, the ultimate right on which government was founded was the natural right of every man to govern himself. Paine drew the logical conclusion from this principle and objected to the establishment of property qualifications on the right to vote for representatives. "To take away this right," he said, "is to reduce a man to slavery, for slavery consists in being subject to the will of another, and he that has not a vote in the election of representatives is in this case." [20] Representation must be accorded to everyone on the principle of one man, one vote. In that way everyone's rights would be equally protected, and that, after all, was the whole purpose of government.

If every citizen's equal right to representation were respected, Paine professed to be indifferent about the particular form which the constitution assumed. The government would operate on the principle of majority rule, of course. The legislature, as the elected representative body, would be supreme. The executive—a term which Paine disliked—would have no function but to administer the laws made by the people through their representatives; it certainly would not act as an independent force in the state. But the best way of constructing and combining the several organs of the government was a matter of opinion and in any case was subject to revision in the light of experience.

What was essential was a republican government based upon a large and equal representation. Under such a government men would govern themselves in their own interest. Then there would be no complaints about high taxes, for only such taxes would be levied as commended themselves to the reason of the nation. Nor would a republic squander its treasure in wars, because its government would have no interest distinct from the nation's interest. The people of the nation would not of themselves be inclined to war. "Man is not the enemy of man, but through the medium of a false system of government." [21] The true system of government thus operated to reduce or abolish two major social evils, war and the poverty caused by excessive taxation and exploitation.

Paine hoped that war could be abolished or at least sharply reduced as a feature of international relations. If England would accept the principles of the French Revolution, the two nations together could reform the rest of Europe. An end to the causes of war could then be reasonably expected. "When all the governments of Europe shall be established on the representative system, nations will become acquainted, and the animosities and prejudices fomented by the intrigues and artifices of courts will cease." [22] The combined English, French, and Dutch fleets would be able to enforce a general naval disarmament and reduce navies to perhaps a tenth of their present strength. An alliance of these three powers, which the United States would gladly join, could also force the end of Spanish rule in South America and put a stop to the Algerine piracy.

The other great social evil against which Paine inveighed was poverty, which he blamed on the high taxation and other unjust policies of monarchy and aristocracy. A son of the poor himself, Paine had a sincere and passionate hatred of the poverty he saw all about him in Europe. This hatred led him to propose a strong and positive governmental program for the abolition of poverty.

Paine assumed that if government were conducted without civil or military extravagance (as it would be in a representative republic), there would be a large surplus arising from taxation at the prevailing, or even at reduced, rates. Part of this surplus could be disposed of by abolishing the poor rates, namely the tax on householders for the relief of the poor. The rest of the surplus could be used to prevent the poverty that required relief. This would be accomplished by giving the poor what today would be called marriage, maternity, and funeral grants, family allowances, old-age pensions, and a crude form of unemployment relief. Accompanying this social security plan would be a progressive tax on the income of estates, designed to redistribute property by inducing families to break up estates instead of maintaining them through the law of primogeniture. A national fund would also be raised by an inheritance tax on estates, out of which all young people would be given a modest capital to start them in life on arriving at the age of twenty-one.

It is not necessary to accuse Paine of inconsistency with his fundamental principles in making these proposals. Government, on his principles, exists only to secure individual rights. But if one emphasizes the equality of the rights to be secured, then it follows that government has a positive function to perform. Still, it is striking that Paine, who proclaimed that government was "no farther necessary than to supply the few cases to which society and civilization are not conveniently competent," should almost in the same breath have revealed himself as a prophet of the modern welfare state.

Paine, of course, was not the first or the last to minimize and maximize the function of government at one and the same time. Behind such theories there is usually the doctrine of the natural harmony of interests and of a single, sovereign popular will which embodies and expresses that harmony. Government will have much to do until the popular will is executed, over the opposition of the wicked and the ignorant, but thereafter society will largely govern itself. As Paine said, the American and French revolutions had shown "that the greatest forces that can be brought into the field of revolutions, are reason and common interest. Where these can have the opportunity of acting, opposition dies with fear, or crumbles away by conviction." [23] In other words, democratic government, when it is truly democratic and completely responsive to the will of the people, really is not government at all.

NOTES

1. *The Complete Writings of Thomas Paine*, ed. Philip S. Foner (2 vols.; New York: Citadel Press, 1945), I, 359.

2. *Ibid.*, I, 449.
3. *Ibid.*, II, 571.
4. *Ibid.*, I, 353.
5. *Ibid.*, p. 4.
6. *Ibid.*, p. 358.
7. *Ibid.*, pp. 357–58.
8. *Ibid.*, pp. 359–61. Italics original.
9. *Ibid.*, p. 359.
10. *Ibid.*, p. 388.

11. *Ibid.*, p. 275.
12. *Ibid.*, p. 276.
13. *Ibid.*
14. *Ibid.*, p. 278. Italics original.
15. *Ibid.*, p. 341.
16. *Ibid.*, p. 364.
17. *Ibid.*, p. 361.
18. *Ibid.*, p. 375.
19. *Ibid.*, II, 572.
20. *Ibid.*, p. 579.
21. *Ibid.*, I, 343.
22. *Ibid.*, p. 449.
23. *Ibid.*, p. 446.

READINGS

A. Paine, Thomas. *Rights of Man.*
B. Paine, Thomas. *Common Sense.*
　　Paine, Thomas. *Agrarian Justice.*
　　Paine, Thomas. *Dissertation on First Principles of Government.*

EDMUND BURKE

1729–1797

For almost all his adult life, Burke was a politician; for almost thirty years he was a member of the House of Commons, busy with the affairs of his party in the daily management of men and issues. His speeches, pamphlets, and books sound the grand themes of political philosophy, but not for their own sake. Burke did not primarily address other political philosophers and did not construct a system or theory in political philosophy. He spoke to the rulers and to the educated of his time, supporting "the cause of the Gentlemen," as King George III once said to him.[1] This closeness to politics has brought Burke to the notice of historians and of conservatives in our day, the former generally disapproving of him, the latter approving.

Absorbed as he was, Burke looked at public issues with almost matchless penetration. Among observers of modern politics only Tocqueville and perhaps Churchill are his rivals in seeing the meaning of events. Like Tocqueville and unlike Churchill, Burke did not enjoy the ruling view that an office of command affords. His highest office was Paymaster-General, a dignified secretaryship lacking in glory. Though the ablest in his party, prominent in debate, and influential to the point of indispensable in the management of affairs, he never sought and was never trusted with leadership. He was indeed distrusted by the leading statesmen of his time for the very energy he used in their behalf, for his eagerness to act against dangers of which only he could see and feel the full measure, and for the passion displayed in the gorgeous rhetoric they admired. "Much to admire, and nothing to agree with,"[2] was Pitt's famous sum-

This chapter appeared, in a slightly different form, as the Introduction to *Selected Letters of Edmund Burke*, ed. Harvey C. Mansfield, Jr. (Chicago: University of Chicago Press, 1984), © 1984 by The University of Chicago.

mary judgment on Burke's longer persuasions for counterrevolution against the French Revolution. And when, in 1788, it looked as though Burke's party might regain office during a regency for George III, who had gone mad, Charles Fox and his confidants omitted him from a list of leading office holders: he was too heated in counsel, too passionate in his prosecution of Warren Hastings, to seem responsible to them.

In our day historians, particularly those influenced by that master of minute investigation, Sir Lewis Namier, have taken up this distrust and faulted Burke rather than his contemporaries for it. They find him pretentious, his behavior extreme, and his words exaggerated. If Burke once spoke of foolishness in the individual, wisdom in the species, they consider Burke foolish in his own time, wise only for posterity. For to see deep into the roots of events, into the "cause of the present discontents," cannot but seem a sort of inflation as daily occurrences are put in a trend and seen as effects. Burke's attempts to invest the mundane with significance seem to make it lose its character as mundane, and while historians may find his eloquence thrilling, they also fear it and distrust him. Even his prescient understanding of the character, importance, and future of the French Revolution is obscured by the extreme partisanship to which his understanding compelled him. He loses credit for his foresight because he acted on it.

Yet Burke was a remarkable man because he was a remarkable thinker. One cannot confine his merit to his rhetoric and sum up his accomplishments as literary, while putting aside the substance of his thought as controversial or embarrassing. His words do not ring hollow; his flights of imagination are not empty abstractions. His marvelous literary skills do not excuse us from taking him seriously, which requires taking his thought seriously as political philosophy. Although he never wrote a treatise of political philosophy, there is ample reason in his political philosophy itself for his having omitted to do so. Burke's thought in a treatise would have lost the essence of his thought, and his style was suited to its substance. We would not know of Burke if it were not for his speeches and writings, and we would not know them if the substance of his thought were bombast.

If readers will grant a hearing for Burke's political philosophy, or for its possibility, then how do they come to grips with it? Burke is known today as the philosopher of "conservatism." But he has not yet shared much in the recent revival of American conservatism. Of the two schools of thought that have been identified in that revival, traditionalism and libertarianism, Burke is very much with the former. Although he favored the freeing of commerce wherever possible, contributed his *Thoughts and Details on Scarcity* (1795) to the new school of political economy, and was an admiring friend of Adam Smith, he so opposed unhampered individual freedom, theoretical systems of self-interest, and the influence of new property that he surrounded and enveloped the abstract free economy of political economists with the traditions of the British constitution. But of course these traditions—"establishments," Burke called them—are far from the provisions of the American constitution, and even farther, as we shall see, from the planned character of the American constitution. Such are the obstacles to Burke's influence in American politics today. In the late 1940s, however, Burke was discovered for American conservatism as the proponent of a theory of natural law. He was brought forward to oppose the irreligion and relativism of liberals and to provide conservatives with a theory that conceded the political advantage or necessity of religion and the bearing of circumstances on morality, but that nonetheless affirmed natural law, the will of God, as authoritative for men. Burke's frequent references to natural law, previously ignored or dismissed as rhetorical, were gathered together in a system that could be described as Thomism conservatively modernized.

Whatever one may think of the success of this system, it is striking that Burke was made the purveyor of a *theory* necessary to healthy politics. If there is one recurrent theme in Burke's letters, speeches, and writings, it is his emphasis on the moral and political evils that follow upon the intrusion of theory into political practice. It is theory as such that he rejects; his emphasis on the evils of intrusive theory is not balanced by a compensating reliance on sound theory that men would need as a guide to their politics. Sound theory, to him, would seem to be self-denying theory. Although Burke may occasionally refer to "the pretended philosophers of the hour,"[3] thus implying the existence of another sort, he is usually content to denounce philosophers, metaphysicians, and speculators as such without making a point of what might seem to be the vital distinction among them. In a famous passage in *A Letter to a Member of the National Assembly* (1791), he attacks Rousseau—"the philosopher of vanity," "a lover of his kind but a hater of his kindred" (II 535–541)— in terms no philosopher had flung at another, until a decline of decorum in this matter occurred in the nineteenth century. In that place Burke distinguishes "modern philosophers," which expresses "everything that is ignoble, savage and hard-hearted," from "the writers of sound antiquity," whom Englishmen continue to read more generally, he believes, than is now done "on the continent." But Burke does not propose that ancient authors be adopted, even remotely, as guides to show the way out of the crisis into which modern philosophers have brought all mankind. Reading them is not so much the cause as the effect of English good taste, something that is sadly lacking "on the continent."[4] If we consider Burke's hostility to the intrusion of philosophy in politics, yet recall too that Burke does not merely despair at the growing influence of philosophy, the problem of his political philosophy would seem to be to design a theory that never intrudes into practice. Our question in assessing it is: Can theory serve solely as a watchdog against theory and never be needed as guide?

The harms done by theory to sound practice had been under Burke's eye from the first. His first publication, *A Vindication of Natural Society* (1756), was a satire showing the absurd political consequences of Bolingbroke's theory; and in the early pamphlets on party, *Observations on a Late Publication Intituled 'The Present State of the Nation'* (1769) and *Thoughts on the Cause of the Present Discontents* (1770), he argued against the factious effects of a theoretical preference for "men of ability and virtue" over parties composed of gentlemen acting together publicly in mutual trust. In his speeches opposing British policy in America, he attacked the government's insistence on the rights of taxation and sovereignty without regard to consequence or circumstance as a speculative, legalistic reliance on "the virtue of paper government." For lawyers with their concern for rights and forms do not have regard to the actual exercise of formalities, substitute legal correctness for prudent policy, and seek to generalize in the manner of law—which is also that of theory (I 431, 453, 476; II 7). In a speech given in 1785, Burke was already denouncing "the speculatists of our speculating age" (III 139). But it was in the French Revolution that the evils of speculation in politics became visible in their full extent and as a whole. Burke was surprised by the outbreak of that revolution, but he had been prepared by every major concern of his previous career in politics to identify it as a philosophical revolution, the first "*complete* revolution," a "revolution in sentiments, manners and moral opinions" that reached "even to the constitution of the human mind" (II 352; III 350; V 76, 111). The French Revolution displayed and summed up all the evils of speculative politics.

These evils, as Burke sees them, may be quickly summarized. First, the French revolutionaries went to the extreme of destroying the old regime and of defeating every moderate reform short of destruction because, as theorists (or inspired by theorists), they based their reasoning on the extreme case. The universality of their theory of revolution was achieved by generalizing from the extreme case when revolution might be unavoidable. In the course of generalization, limited actions undertaken with great circumspection and compunction in the extreme case are transformed into wanton, irresponsible destructiveness in the universal case. The vaunted humanity of the revolutionaries is similarly affected. From concern for improving particular human beings, it is diluted to a humanitarian profession on behalf of the French people and of mankind which requires a ruthless sacrifice of natural affections. Since in the extreme case one may or must be selfish, no universal argument either for self-restraint or for helping others can be sustained, and so loose morals go together with hard hearts. This humanitarianism forces men down to the level of bestiality, all the while perversely claiming to free them and even to ennoble them.

Second, theorists wrongly suppose that politics is predictable. Having stated the ends of government in universal terms, they believe that the means to these ends can be put in rules equally universal, unless they put aside the question of means altogether. But means are determined by circumstances, which are "infinite and infinitely combined . . . variable, and transient." Anyone who does not take them into consideration is "metaphysically mad" (V 114). Circumstances, in turn, are determined by chance, and chance always brings new situations (I 312, 365; V 153–154, 257). Since universal ends are always refracted through new, unpredictable circumstances, Burke concludes: "Nothing universal can be rationally affirmed on any moral or political subject" (III 16).

Third, theory is simple; for the extreme and the universal case with which it is concerned is also the simple case, uncomplicated by accidents and confusions. But practice, especially political practice, is complex. It is faced with rival claims of simple justice, which it must compromise, and with claims of exceptions, which it must accommodate. And while theory is simple, it is at the same time refined. It goes beyond common experience in its attempt to exclude everything accidental. But common people cannot see beyond common experience and will distrust those who explore "the labyrinths of political theory" (III 106); refined policies that depend on the cooperation of common people will fail as a result of their confusion. Theoretical men, in addition, are as such detached from whatever is their own; if they turn to themselves, it is only to their own "case," which is merely one case among others. That is why speculation in the theoretical sense is connected to speculation in the sense of gambling; theoretical speculation is unconscious gambling with one's own stake (II 463). But practical men are as such attached to whatever is their own; their loyalty is presupposed by their responsibility. They cannot act without being partial to a group they have not chosen and cannot choose; all their choosing is in a context imposed on them by circumstance or providence. "No man examines into the defects of his title to his paternal estate, or to his established government" (II 26, 428). But the neutrality of speculators is, in political effect, a desire to have everything their own way. They do not admit their own partiality; so they do not admit anyone else's.

Next, theoretical questions are timeless and reversible; practical questions are for decision here and now and cannot be reversed. Political men are bound by dangers that are imminent, that do not permit "a long discourse, belonging to the leisure of a contemplative man" (I 323; II 552). Last, the activity of speculators is essentially private, unconcerned with or critical of common opinion; but politics rests on opinion and must respect it. If opinion be called prejudice or superstition, Burke does not hesitate to defend it. Prejudice contains "latent wisdom" which is "of ready application in the emergency"; superstition must be tolerated, "else you will deprive weak minds of a resource found necessary to the strongest" (II 359, 429–430).

In developing the evils of speculative or metaphysical politics, Burke does not trouble to discriminate good speculation from bad, or to make that difference unmistakable to his readers. He seems to mix together the faults of the theory on which the French Revolution was based—the theory of the rights of man set forth by Hobbes, Locke, and Rousseau—with the necessary defects of all theory, of which previous theorists might have been aware. Burke mentions Aristotle's objections to geometrical morality, and several times calls Aristotle to his aid;[5] but he does not use Aristotle's fundamental investigations into the nature of theory and practice. Except for the attack on Rousseau that we have mentioned, he does not consider the theoretical sources of the doctrine of the rights of man; and even his attack on Rousseau was not a theoretical consideration but was expressly confined to the use of Rousseau's theories by the French revolutionaries (II 541). In sum, he does not offer a theoretical clarification and reconstruction which would meet the revolutionaries on their own ground. Instead, he attempts to stand on the ground and stay within the realm of political practice, insofar as possible. His writings proposing action are much richer in political wisdom—hence seemingly more "theoretical"—than those of ordinary statesmen even when reminiscing; yet they are also much more circumscribed and circumstantial than treatises which are intended to interest theorists: thus, fulsome for historians, meager for philosophers. He once said: "The operation of dangerous and delusive first principles obliges us to have recourse to the true ones" (V 213)—thereby admitting the necessity of such recourse, by contrast to ordinary statesmen, and declaring his reluctance, against the habit of theorists.

Yet the "true" first principles to which Burke has recourse do not appear to be first principles. Instead of providing theoretical clarification, he asserts that direction of human affairs belongs to prudence; and instead of establishing what might be the best or legitimate state, he celebrates the genius of the British constitution. Burke's political philosophy emerges from the elaboration of these two things, prudence and the British constitution. They may not be the first, grounding principles but they are surely the principles Burke puts forward to claim our attention before all others.

Prudence, Burke says, is "the god of this lower world," since it has "the entire dominion over every exercise of power committed into its hands" (II 28). Prudence is "the first of all the virtues, as well as the supreme director of them all."[6] This means, in particular, that "practical wisdom" justly supersedes "theoretic science" whenever the two come into contention (II 306). The reason for the sovereignty of prudence is in the power of circumstances to alter every regularity and principle. "Circumstances (which with some gentlemen pass for nothing) give in reality to every political principle its distinguishing color and discriminating effect."[7] Burke emphasizes that the prudence he speaks of is a "moral prudence" or a "public and enlarged prudence" as opposed to selfish prudence, not to mention cleverness or cunning.[8] But he does not say how to be sure of the morality of prudence. If prudence is supreme, it must reign over morality; but if prudence can be either moral or selfish, it would seem to require the tutelage of morality. Aristotle, when facing this problem, was led to understand prudence as the comprehensive legislative art, and then to subordinate that to theory. Burke makes a different disposition. Instead of pursuing an inquiry into the first principles or ends of prudence, which would necessarily lead beyond prudence, he distinguishes within prudence between "rules of prudence" available to ordinary statesmen and "prudence of a higher order" (II 284; III 16; V 236). Rules of prudence are not mathematical, universal, or ideal; but they are nonetheless rules, Burke says grandly, "formed upon the known march of the ordinary providence of God," that is, visible in human experience. But as these rules are sovereign over all theoretical rights or metaphysical first principles, so higher prudence, the prudence of prudence, can suspend the rules of prudence when necessary (III 81).

This distinction within prudence, by which Burke attempts to secure the morality of prudence without subverting its sovereignty, corresponds to a distinction he draws between presumptive virtue and actual virtue: "There is no qualification for government but virtue and wisdom, actual or presumptive" (II 323). Presumptive virtue and wisdom is the lesser, probable virtue that can be presumed in well-bred gentlemen of prominent families born into situations of eminence where they are habituated to self-respect; to the "censorial inspection of the public eye"; to taking a "large view of the wide-spread and infinitely diversified combinations of men and affairs in a large society"; to having leisure to reflect; to meeting the wise and learned, as well as rich traders; to military command; to the caution of an instructor of one's fellow citizens and thus to acting as a "reconciler between God and man"; and to being employed as an administrator of law and justice (III 85–86). Actual virtue, such as Burke's own perhaps, is higher but more dubious; it must intervene when the rules of prudence fail, but it must not rule ordinarily lest society fall victim to the instability of men of ability. The idea of presumptive virtue presumes ability, not the highest but ordinarily sufficient, in men of property; at the same time it presumes at least instability, and sometimes immorality, in those who have nothing but ability and, rather than being born and bred in an elevated condition, must rise to eminence by means that may not be moral and should not be exemplary. No country can reject the service of those with actual virtue, but "the road to eminence and power, from obscure condition, ought not to be made too easy" (II 323). When that road is made too easy, too many follow it, and men of actual virtue are encouraged to display their ability rather than their virtue, and are crowded out by new men who have only cleverness and no property, as happened in the French Revolution. Actual virtue must therefore be kept subordinate ordinarily to presumptive virtue, while being allowed, after due probation, the right of intervention in an emergency, such as the French Revolution, when men of presumptive virtue are confronted with an event so astonishing that they do not know how to react.

Thus Burke solves the problem of prudence within prudence: he keeps moral prudence distinct from mere cleverness, yet maintains its sovereignty over clever theorists except for occasional interventions by higher prudence. But, to sustain this solution, the presumptions of presumptive virtue must of course hold true. They are "legitimate presumptions, which, taken as generalities, must be admitted for actual truths" (III 86). But this is not enough: actual truth must be behind what is admitted for actual truth. These presumptions are shown to be sound in Burke's admiring, not to say worshipful, analysis of the British constitution. The British constitution guarantees both the sovereignty and the morality of prudence by sustaining the presumptions necessary to ward off or subordinate the claims of higher virtue. The theory of that constitution, or *in* it, is the theory that enables prudence to remain sovereign over theory.

Burke was not the first to laugh at modern philosophers. He himself refers to "the learned academicians of Laputa and Balnibarbi" found in the pages of Swift's *Gulliver's Travels* (II 404). But when Swift had made fun of political projectors whose inventions smack of the same inappropriate extension of theory into practice that Burke described, Swift did not then turn to vaunting the beauties of the British constitution.

On the contrary, he carried his satire to that hallowed ground. Of modern political philosophers, Montesquieu is most obviously Burke's inspiration in praise of the British constitution as the model of liberty (Montesquieu's admiration of that constitution is apostrophized by Burke in a closing passage of *An Appeal from the New to the Old Whigs*, 1791 [III 113]). But Montesquieu was not so hostile to theory as Burke was, and he believed that prudence would need guidance from theory to escape from the mistaken simplicity of modern sovereignty, the inhuman ambition of religion, and the allure of ancient virtue.

Tocqueville shared Burke's opinion of the influence of theorists in the French Revolution, but the two diverge in a manner that will help introduce Burke's thoughts on the British constitution. Tocqueville's theme, in regard to the French Revolution, was democracy; and he showed how the influence of literary men and *philosophes* fed the passion for equality that characterized the Revolution. Burke's theme was the intrusion of metaphysicians, one consequence of which was a democratic leveling that "perverts the natural order of things" (II 322). Yet, whereas Burke could not believe that democracy was in accord with nature, and hence must be traced to a perversion by theorists, Tocqueville believed that democratic claims were at least partly natural to men, hence always available to be endorsed by theorists. This difference appears in utterly contrary judgments of the French constitution-makers in 1789: Burke describes these "constitution-mongers" "the wickedest and most foolish of men," and condemns them for trying vainly to make a constitution wholly anew; Tocqueville praises them for this very attempt, despite their failure.[9]

Making a constitution or founding a society was for classical political science, and even more for such modern thinkers as Machiavelli, Bacon, Hobbes, and Locke, the crux of politics where theory and practice met. At that point prudence, sovereign over practice, cannot be satisfied with temporary shifts and arrangements, and must extend itself to legislation embodying fundamental, comprehensive choices. Such legislation, in turn, must be guided by an art, ultimately by a theory, that elaborates the model for choice, which is the best, most choiceworthy regime. When prudence becomes comprehensive and makes its determinations for good—both for the best and permanently—then it must cooperate with theory and perhaps even subordinate itself. It is the ruling characteristic of Burke's political philosophy as well as the guiding theme of his politics to avoid the ground on which theory and practice converge. Founding, which prior to Burke had been considered by all political thinkers to be the essential political act, is for him a nonevent. The making of a constitution can never be "the effect of a single instantaneous regulation" (II 554). It cannot happen, and it is wrong to try to make it happen.

In complete disagreement with Tocqueville, Burke does not consider that democracy is a possible regime. The people cannot rule; they are the passive element in contrast to the "active men in the state." Though the people may be led by a vicious oligarchy of some kind, they should be led by a "true natural aristocracy," by ministers who "are not only our natural rulers, but our natural guides" (III 85; V 227). Thus, for Burke, one cannot choose between democracy and aristocracy, nor can there be a democratic or an aristocratic age, as for Tocqueville; nature has made the many incapable of governing themselves. "A perfect democracy is . . . the most shameless thing in the world" (II 365), because each person's share of responsibility is so small that he does not feel it, and because public opinion which should restrain government is in the case of democracy nothing but the people's self-approbation. Responsible government is capable of shame, perhaps more than anything else; it is rather defending what one has had to do than taking credit for what one has chosen to do. No aristocracy, any more than a democracy, can rule long or well without the sense of a power above it; the lack of this sense is what makes democracy impossible as well as shameless. Only in an attenuated sense, therefore, is any human government, even a true natural aristocracy, a kind of self-government. Government is so far from a matter of choice, of choosing a form of rule, that it is a "power out of ourselves" (II 333).

Fundamentally, government is not ruling; it is changing, reforming, balancing, or adjusting. Government is not nourished, as Aristotle thought, by claims to rule asserted by democrats and oligarchs in defense (and exaggeration) of their equality and inequality to others. The people do not claim to rule of their own accord; only when inflamed by a few do they believe they want to rule. And aristocrats, however natural, are bred to their eminence, which they accept rather than demand.

As far as Burke is from the Aristotelian sense of rule—government by human choice, art, and political science—he does not rush into theocracy and grasp at divine right in order to keep governments under control by shame. To make it certain that government has a human origin, Burke adopts the language of contract from modern theorists. But since government by contract might seem calculated, if not chosen, for convenience—in effect, a matter of arbitrary will or pleasure, not of judgment—he stresses the great differences between ordinary contracts "taken up for a little temporary interest" and the social contract that establishes the state. The latter contract is a "partnership in all science; a partnership in all art; a partnership in every virtue, and in all perfection"

(II 368). And it is a contract made between the living, the dead, and those to be born—that is, a contract not in the power of the present generation but in trust for the past and the future. The past and the future, one could say, substitute for divine law to ensure that present governments govern with a sense of shame. This does not mean, again, that present governments assume responsibility for ruling on principles established by their founders. The dead are not founders; they are silent partners who have had their say and now make their point by unspoken reproach (II 177–178; VI 21). Thus for Burke, the rights of man do not include the right to rule (II 332). The right to rule would be the right to alter rule, that is, at pleasure; but the right to alter rule at pleasure is destructive of rule. Rulers must accept limitations to their rule, yet without submitting themselves to superhuman rule. To do so, they must, for the sake of future generations, accept the authority of the past without submitting to the rule of founders. The only way to do this, Burke saw, was to attenuate the meaning of rule and make the present generation equal to the past, as is necessary to a contract. He praises the British constitution to the skies, but never its founders. The old whigs, to whom he appeals against new whigs favorable to the French Revolution, set a good example but did not lay down principles that new whigs must follow. [10] They made a revolution in 1688 only in dire necessity arising from unique circumstances (II 292, 299); so their conduct (Burke ignores the theory of John Locke, which might interpret their conduct) does not imply, much less express, a principle of revolution available for use a century later. For Burke the essence of morality is self-restraint, not choice: "Much the strongest moral obligations are such as were never the results of our option." [11] That is why morality must be understood as it is in a contract, which cannot be broken without the consent of all parties, rather than in a founding or a revolution, where the principles of choice come to light.

The founding of a constitution relies on its form. The form of a constitution must be capable of prevailing over its material and circumstances, which are bound to change over time, by embodying the end peculiar to the constitution and making that end visible to its citizens or subjects. Hence in classical political science one sometimes sees actual governments classified by their form, and imaginary governments fashioned by the improvement of the forms of actual governments, to the point where political science almost forgets the varied material of politics. For Burke, however, "the circumstances and habits of every country . . . decide upon the form of its government." [12] When circumstances change, forms change. "A state without the means of some change is without the means of its conservation" (II 295). Not a fixed form but precisely the contrary, "a principle of growth," preserves states. Constitutional forms are superseded by timely reforms, made in cool blood after the people feel a grievance but before they become aroused; and if such reforms are to be temperate, they must be left incomplete. "Whenever we improve, it is right to leave room for further improvement" (II 65). Thus even the best constitution has a principle of growth; this is its only "ruling principle . . . , a power like that which some of the philosophers have called a plastic nature." [13] Although Burke has praise for Britain's ancient constitution, he thinks it "visionary" to suppose that its ancient form could have been the same as that enjoyed today (VI 294); the constitution is ancient today insofar as it has lasted by constant adjustment, not because its forms remain as they were in ancient times.

Accordingly, Burke maintains that "manners are of more importance than laws" (V 208). Laws, which are formal decisions by governments because they have been made in accordance with its forms, depend on informal manners rather than the reverse. "In all forms of government," therefore "the people is the true legislator," since the people makes its manners. "The people are the masters"; we statesmen, Burke says, "shape their desires into perfect form" (II 121–122; VI 20). Since the people is the true legislator, not some part of the people promoting and imposing its own end, the best constitution has neither a single end nor a hierarchy of ends but the "greatest variety of ends" (V 254). To secure our natural rights is the "great and ultimate purpose of civil society"; therefore, "all forms whatsoever of government are only good as they are subservient to that purpose to which they are entirely subordinate" (VI 29). The purpose of civil society is to secure the natural rights which we exercise diversely in the "greatest variety of ends." As the best constitution is defined by rights variously exercised, it cannot be found in the "rich treasury of the fertile framers of imaginary commonwealths" (I 489); it is here and now, the British constitution. The British constitution is not perfect (for example, it is not made for offensive warfare as is required against the French revolutionary state [V 423–425]) but if it were perfect it would not have a principle of growth and then would not be best.

Since the British constitution does not have a lasting form, the order it establishes is not visible in its form, as was the order of the classical regime according to Aristotle. [14] The British constitution, then, does not have a *kind* of order (democratic or oligarchic) corresponding to one of the several forms of constitutions; rather, it has order that is of no particular kind because its parts have variety and diversity. The parts represent interests that combine or oppose one another in "that action and counteraction, which, in the natural and in the political world, from the reciprocal struggle of discordant powers, draws out the harmony of the universe." [15] Discordance does not produce social contradiction, in that strange Marxist expression so familiar to us today that holds society to the standards of logic, but it yields a harmony that owes much more to the experience of living together in liberty than to thinking alike or holding certain common principles (II 554). Such an order is complicated; indeed, one might say that it consists in complication, in never directly affirming or denying any claim of justice that would require a particular ordering of society. These claims must be compromised, but not by finding a principle that preserves what is true in each claim, as in the classical mixed regime. A safer, truer compromise will result from deflecting claims of right to matters of convenience, so that "the whole organization of government becomes a consideration of convenience." [16] A statement like this one certainly smacks of utilitarianism, and insofar as Burke gives priority to what is convenient in the sense of actual, useful, and effectual over what is formally correct, he may be said to have inspired "utilitarianism," a nineteenth-century doctrine that narrowed Burke's notion of convenience and exploited it to attack the British constitution he held dear and the rule of gentlemen he thought necessary. In keeping with the growth of constitutions, "convenience" to Burke refers not to what is truly or naturally suitable but rather, with typical British understatement, to what is "not inconvenient." Thus, the whole organization of government which must be described as "a consideration of convenience" can also be said to "balance inconveniences" (I 500).

Burke adopts that Machiavellian notion that every human good has its accompanying inconvenience, and that, consequently, all human things are in motion, [17] but he does not agree that this motion need be violent and he does not accept the calculation of convenience that Machiavelli, and utilitarians, recommend. Although constitutions must grow, they are kept from mere fluidity and from violent change by their establishments. The "establishments" of the British constitution do the work, in Burke's thought, of the constitutional forms and formalities of which he thinks so little. They supply stability and security, slowing and directing the flow of passions and ideas while gradually establishing themselves in this task; like our "institution," establishment is a verbal noun whose substance is gathered from its process. Like the familiar use of "the Establishment" today, Burke's establishments refer to informal social classes, but they differ by being plural and in the public eye. Burke's establishments are not a conspiracy united to diminish and reduce to nothing the formal rights of a people; rather, they are the social prominences that result from the actual, necessarily unequal exercise of those rights: the Church, the monied interest, the landed nobility, the

military, even the monarchy (II 106, 363, 434). These institutions are
so far from subverting liberty that they are the only means for securing
it. Burke contrasts the growth of establishments in Britain over centuries—a work not of mindless adjustment but one that "requires the
aid of more minds than one age can furnish," in which "mind must
[benignly] conspire with mind"—to the products of hasty legislators of
the French Revolution, who begin their work with science, demolishing
the old establishments and reducing the French people to "one homogeneous mass" (II 439–440, 455), and end with sheer force, replacing
the old establishments with new republics, delineated mathematically,
which promise anarchy but are held together in fact by speculation on
confiscated wealth, by the power of Paris, and by the army. Whereas
establishments keep the British constitution steady and balanced, with
an "excellence in composition" that makes a "consistent whole" of the
varied interests of a free society because it does not impose a plan (II
440), the cementing principles of the French Republic are instruments
and evidence of tyranny, because they cannot unite without revealing a
bias. Burke quotes Montesquieu's praise of the "great legislators of antiquity," who knew better than to deal with men as abstract, metaphysical entities (II 454–455), but he does not infer from the legislator's need
to consult the actual human material, as did Plato and Aristotle, that no
actual constitution can be a "consistent whole," that all must be partisan.

The constitution made steady by establishments is maintained by
the principle of property, that is, of inherited property. Each of the establishments is a property, and Burke makes it clear, even in the example of
the Church, whose high purpose is to consecrate the commonwealth and
to elevate men's wills above selfishness, that the attack of the French revolutionaries was a usurpation of property (II 132). Such property in social
eminence survives and grows not by the reason that justified its original
acquisition but by the benefits that can be seen in its present working—
benefits often discernible only by the eye of wisdom and experience,
since appearances are deceiving and the forms of free government are
compatible with the ends of arbitrary government, and vice versa (I 313;
II 397, 399). Therefore we must "venerate where we are not able presently to comprehend" (III, 114); we must regard the constitution as an
inheritance, which means (to repeat) not inherited from founders but as
if it has come to us from no beginning.

Burke illustrates "the idea of inheritance" with a "philosophic analogy." Our political system, he says, "working after the pattern of nature," is "in a just correspondence and symmetry with the order of the
world." He calls it "a permanent body composed of transitory parts,"
and he compares it to the whole of the human race, which at any given

time is never old, or middle-aged, or young, but always the same, while it moves on through decay, fall, rise, and progress (II 307). In this figure the constitution is likened to a body—the human race—which is a whole and has no form. It is not likened to an individual human body with a form, as certain medieval thinkers conceived it. Burke's analogy is generic rather than organic, so that we conceive that we inherit our constitution as we do our human nature, with no possibility of rejection. We can and must accept our opportunities and limitations without attempting to find the origin or the purpose of the whole. Burke settles his politics on a notion of property, rather than the reverse; but he manages to keep his politics free of the spirit of acquisition, indeed to keep it directed against that spirit.

What does it mean to say that the idea of inheritance works by "the method of nature"? Burke said that man's nature is intricate (II 307, 334), and his way of understanding the relationship between nature and human institutions is especially difficult for us today, who have expelled "nature" from respectable theoretical discourse. Yet he assailed the French revolutionaries for nothing more than their "unnatural" conduct, and if we need to learn what Burke thought, we cannot remain ignorant of the meaning of his attack on the French Revolution. Inheritance by the "method of nature" does not mean that we inherit our politics and constitutions from nature. Although we have a "natural sense of wrong and right,"[18] Burke does not say in the manner of Thomism that we have natural inclinations in our souls that are fulfilled in politics; the soul is not a theme of his.[19] Nor does he say with Aristotle that man is a political animal by nature, so that our political artifices would be the fulfillment of a natural potentiality. He says, instead, that "man is by his [natural] constitution a religious animal" (II 363), since atheism is against our instincts as well as our reason. We are propelled, it seems, to the recognition of a superior will in order to avoid dependence on our own arbitrary will, a recognition which is a human instinct for human good. It is not that we seek to know God, as Thomas Aquinas said. When Burke attacked the French Revolution for doing violence to our nature, he meant that it ignores or opposes the instincts we have for our own good, the natural affections for our families and neighborhoods, for "the little platoon," together with the check on such affections in our sense of justice and in our religion (II 320, 347, 410; V 255).

We do not inherit *from* nature, but we inherit the products of human making according to laws of nature. Natural rights, which Burke deprecatingly calls "metaphysic rights," do not come to us directly but, "like rays of light which pierce into a dense medium, are, by the laws of nature, refracted from their straight line" (II, 334). Taking a cue from this famous remark, we might say that for Burke laws of nature are laws of refraction. They are laws describing the ways in which men, making their own conventions, constitutions or property, imitate or follow nature as nature conducts itself without reference to humans. For example, as we have seen, men making constitutions imitate nature in finding harmony through the struggle of its discordant powers and permanence through the rise and fall of its transitory parts. "Art is man's nature," Burke says (III 86), in reproach of the modern philosophers who place the "state of nature" outside civil society. Art (not choice) is nature's special gift to humans, but the gift is not used in a manner to preserve human specialness. All society is artificial, yet all artifice is according to natural law; the gift of art must be given back to nature. One wonders whether prudence is after all sovereign for Burke, if it must operate "under that discipline of nature." [20]

The sovereign rule of prudence is also a rule *for* prudence. It is prescription, "this great fundamental part of natural law" (II 422), which describes the manner of growth of property and constitutions and lays down the method of inheritance. Strange to say, prescription before Burke was never considered to be unequivocally part of natural law, for it was not thought to be applicable in public law. [21] Burke borrowed the concept from Roman law, in which prescription gives title to property without a deed by long-continued use or takes it away despite a deed after long-continued disuse. This rule of private law was transformed by Burke into a rule of public law applicable to constitutions (not merely to the law of nations). Thus, a rule of private property becomes *the* rule for government, "the most solid of all titles, not only to property, but, which is to secure that property, to government"; "a title which is not the creature, but the master, of positive law," "the sacred rules of prescription." [22] If the problem of theory's intrusion into practice is the theme of Burke's political philosophy, prescription is his special discovery—one must say, since he could not abide the word "innovation," his grand reform (V 120). It was merely a description of the working of the British constitution, he claimed; but as theory it was certainly new. Indeed, Burke had, he said, "a very full share" in the passage of the Nullum Tempus Act of 1769, by which he attempted to establish prescription as public law in Britain. Burke made this claim proudly in his splendid self-defense against the Duke of Bedford, *A Letter to a Noble Lord,* but he did not similarly advertise the theoretical reform that justified the legal novelty (which went against the authority of Blackstone). [23] Nor did he remark that prescription became public law in 1769 not through prescription but by statute. That not merely *a* title, but the *most solid* title to property comes from long use rather than a deed implies that government, which issues deeds, is bound by long-continued practices rather than by principles. Property by prescription implies government without a founding or a theory: the best claim to rule comes not from establishing one's own claim as best but by securing the abandonment of rival claims. Yet it required a theory to show this, and, even if Burke had trod softly to introduce it, even if his theory had fit neatly the shape of fact, it cannot be denied that his theory intrudes upon the prudence of statesmen.

Prescription follows nature but improves on it. Change, Burke says, is "the most powerful law of nature. . . . All we can do, and that human wisdom can do, is to provide that the change shall proceed by insensible degrees." Nature on its own might produce great and swift change, but such change imitated in human proceedings would breed a "black and sullen discontent" in those suddenly dispossessed of influence and, on the other side, intoxicate those who had been long depressed "with a large draught of new power" (III 340). Change there must be, but men must take care that it proceed by insensible degrees. Insensible change can be legal change, because it does not call the established laws or constitution into question. Or it can legalize change; it "mellows into legality governments that were violent in their commencement" (II 435). Agreeing, as was said above, with Machiavelli that all human things are in motion, Burke denies that the motion need be violent or revolutionary. For this reason prescriptive right is not the same as historical or traditional right. Prescription takes its bearing from current use, unless property or government has been recently usurped. It is opposed to historical claims that would overthrow established power, and it is skeptical of historical research that would confirm it (VI 414).

For Burke, then, prescription is a "great fundamental part of natural law." He does not quite say it is *the* fundamental part, and he does not specify the full content of natural law in the manner of more theoretical theorists such as Aquinas or Hobbes. He is satisfied that natural law be understood as a law beyond and above human legislation; he does not require that human law be seen as application of natural law. In the debate between Cicero and Hobbes as to whether "men have a right to make what laws they please," Burke is on the side of Cicero in denying that they do. He then says that "all human laws are, properly speaking, only declaratory; they may alter the mode and application, but have no power over the substance of original justice" (VI 21–22). But since Burke has imported prescription into natural law itself, and has said little to establish the substance of original justice, it seems in effect that the mode and application, more than the substance, of natural law is to guide practice. Natural law is more means than ends because prescrip-

tion, in order to exclude violent, comprehensive change, prevents the
ends of politics from appearing in politics unrefracted by materials and
circumstances. Prescription is prudence crystallized in theory. As such it
is censor to the rest of natural law, so that natural law can speak in its own
voice only "the principle of a superior law" (VI 21; VII 99– 100, 504).
Human liberty is so far from opposed to the principle of a superior will
that it cannot survive without one. Although society is the product of a
contract among men, men cannot live freely if they are free to make a
new contract in every generation. Each generation must regard its liberties as an "entailed inheritance" (II 306), as its property precisely because
those liberties were not created by it. One may venture to conclude that
at the center of Burke's political philosophy is the British constitution,
not natural law. Natural law is the ground, but only because a constitution, made by accidents, needs a ground. However admirable it may be,
the British constitution is not, for Burke, the rational state. But the
ground of the constitution must be unseen and unfelt lest it upset the
constitution that rests on it.

Here one might object that we are forgetting the "laws of commerce," which Burke, in a passage in his *Thoughts and Details on Scarcity*
(1795), once equated, to the disgust of Karl Marx, with the "laws of
nature, and consequently the laws of God." [24] The laws of commerce, it
would seem, promote too much novel enterprise to be held accountable
to the principle of prescription (V 207, 217, 256). That is so, except
insofar as prescription welcomes and justifies private enterprise without
deeds or charters from the government. But the mobile property of merchants, together with the active abilities that create it, could be held in
check and kept in balance, Burke believed, by the establishment of
landed property and by the rule of gentlemen. With some basis in English experience, and some degree of hope, he joined together the supremacy of the landed interest, which he rightly said was recommended
by "the practical politics of antiquity" (particularly Aristotle and Cicero),
with a statement that could not be found, except as satire or disapproval,
in ancient writers: "The love of lucre, though sometimes carried to a
ridiculous, sometimes to a vicious, excess, is the grand cause of prosperity to all states" (V 313, 342). While the landed interest should be
supreme, it should not form a separate body in the nation, as in countries other than Britain; and though Burke endorsed the prejudices that
gentlemen live by, he did not accept or share the gentleman's contempt
for those who make money. He himself represented a merchants' constituency, Bristol, in Parliament from 1774 to 1780 (though not to his
voters' satisfaction); and at his own estate in Beaconsfield he was active,
as his letters attest, in the search for new methods (and greater returns)
in agriculture. [25]

However one may connect Burke's doctrine of natural law to the natural law tradition, whether he was closer to Cicero or to Locke, it must be admitted that he makes most visible, not that connection or his own allegiance within the tradition, but the peculiar features of natural law according to him. His natural law leaves sovereignty to prudence and gives prominence to circumstance; it does not demand transcendance of self-interested affections (including the love of lucre), which Burke emphatically labels "natural"; and it is more than tolerant of prejudice, it is positively hospitable to it. With a view to protecting the prejudices of gentlemen, Burke did not wish to show the British constitution in debt to philosophical tradition, though he did not hesitate to exclaim that Montesquieu, who held out that constitution to the admiration of mankind, was a man "tinctured with no national prejudice" (III 113).

"We are generally men of untaught feelings," Burke asserts of the British in a passage of the *Reflections on the Revolution in France,* congratulating his people on their imperviousness to the philosophy of enlightenment. We cherish our prejudices, he continues, "and to take more shame to ourselves, we cherish them because they are prejudices." "Our men of speculation" (one of his few approving references to this breed), instead of exploding general prejudices, use their sagacity to discover the latent wisdom in them (II 359). Prejudice is not opposed to reason but allied with it. Prejudice supplies the untaught, natural feelings that give permanence to reason, for "naked reason" is flighty; and at the same time "prejudice is of ready application in the emergency," whereas reason by itself is hesitant. Burke's frank recognition that politics is inseparable from prejudice, that society can never be rational and enlightened, reminds one of Aristotle; but his confidence that prejudice contains sufficient latent wisdom does not. For Aristotle, latent wisdom indeed exists in political opinion, but not in the uncontradicted seclusion that Burke seems to suppose. On the contrary: according to Aristotle, political opinion typically asserts itself against an opponent, present or imagined; it has the character of debate. Any observation, not to mention speculative study, of political opinion reveals differences taking the form of contradictions, especially *the* typical difference in politics between the many and the few. Burke leaves the obvious partisanship of prejudice out of account. Although he often speaks of the few and the many, he does not stress their difference of opinion, the gentleman's prejudice against the vulgar versus the people's resentment of privilege. As may be recalled, Burke does not think that every man has a natural right nor the people a natural desire to rule (II 177, 332; III 497). The people are content to let their wisdom be latent rather than to assert it, and so the aristocracy can be bred to rule without asserting its own distinctiveness.

Aristotle thought that political opinion becomes wisdom only if partisan assertions are brought out for examination, corrected for their partiality and combined with truth from their opponents. He wrote his *Politics* as if he were conducting a debate, and he implied that the statesman could improve politics despite the ineradicability of prejudice by drawing out the latent implications of a prejudice which might make it more wholesome. Burke, however, implies that the wisdom in prejudice remains wisdom only so long as it is latent; prejudice must not be disturbed, or natural feelings will be inflamed. He seems to presuppose a fundamental cooperation between gentlemen and people, liable to disruption from outside but essentially uncontentious. A "natural aristocracy" rules without asserting itself, hence without imposing itself. But even if this were possible, Burke took a risk in recommending that prejudice be left unenlightened, as if he could be sure that prejudice would never bite. He knew that "the will of the many, and their interest, must very often differ" (II 325). But he supposed that it is "out of the power of man . . . to create a prejudice . . . A king may make a nobleman but he cannot make a Gentleman." [26] The slow, natural growth of prejudice in manners and sentiments would render it harmless by habituating gentlemen and people alike to the satisfaction of their wants within the bounds of their natural affections. Philosophers and statesmen should leave prejudice to exercise its good effects uninstructed.

Yet Burke himself did not leave gentlemanly prejudice as he found it. He once said that his chief employment was the "woeful one of *flapper*," to awaken the gentlemen in his party. [27] The very conception of party that Burke elaborated in *Thoughts on the Cause of the Present Discontents* was an implication of gentlemanly prejudice used to correct gentlemanly prejudice. "So to be patriots, as not to forget we are gentlemen" was Burke's summary of his advice (I 379). Previously, in Britain and in other free countries, it had been taken for granted that a politician could not be both partisan and patriot, that open, committed partisanship could not, as a regular practice, be principled. Burke was the first to argue the contrary, that principled behavior in politicians must inevitably be partisan, and that partisanship is not only occasionally necessary in emergencies but useful and respectable in the ordinary working of the constitution. These beliefs are now held as universally and as thoughtlessly as were their contraries before Burke wrote, and, insofar as Burke was responsible for the change, his theorizing had a mighty effect. But to make this change, Burke appealed to gentlemanly prejudice: ". . . not to forget we are gentlemen." Those politicians (Burke had his eye on Lord Chatham) forget they are gentlemen who pretend to put patriotic devotion to the public ahead of all private friendship and parade their "supernatural virtue" as a demanding qualification for high office. "When I see in any of these detached gentlemen of our times the angelic purity, power, and beneficence, I shall admit them to be angels. In the mean time we are born only to be men" (I 378). One is reminded of the passage in *The Federalist* 51, which says: "If men were angels, no government would be necessary." While in *The Federalist* the nonangelic nature of man justifies tolerance of ambition, for Burke it confirms the need for gentlemanly virtue to oppose hypocritical ambition. Party is informal; yet, when made respectable, it is no longer concealed or conspiratorial. With its source in private friendship and honorable attachments, party loyalty provides a visible measure of consistency in principle; not deserting one's friends becomes the mark of a patriot. In gentlemanly party politics, Machiavellian flexibility is not required and not rewarded.

Gentlemanly virtue, for Burke, is manliness. It would not go too far to say that manliness is *the* virtue, according to Burke. It was the virtue he claimed for himself: in his progress of life, he asserted in *A Letter to a Noble Lord,* "I had no arts but manly arts." [28] And it was the virtue he set against the liberty propagated by the French revolutionaries: "I love a manly, moral, regulated liberty." [29] Manliness to Burke appears to be courage and prudence so combined that manly actions are open to public inspection without being subservient to public opinion. Having some admixture of Christian humility, manliness is not quite up to the pride of magnanimity (I, 509; II 536; III 438); but it is perhaps more effective in opposition to vanity for that reason, and also because it has the strength of a virtue that brings men together rather than elevating a few. Vanity and affected pity were the vices that Burke saw in the French doctrine of the rights of man; he tried to replace that doctrine with the "*real* rights of men," the rights of manly men who can sustain the severe virtues as well as the liberal (II 331, 418, 536, 537; V 322). In our day manliness is losing its identification as male, but after the telling denunciation of democratic softness from authorities as diverse as Tocqueville and Nietzsche, we cannot afford not to reconsider Burke's principal virtue.

Burke, the champion of gentlemanly prudence, spent his political life beyond the limits of gentlemanly prudence, looking ahead to what his party could not see, urging it on to unaccustomed activity on uncongenial ground. One should also say that he devoted himself to securing and improving the boundaries of gentlemanly prudence, to keeping out subversive speculators and refashioning constitutional practices, such as party and impeachment, that would facilitate the rule of gentlemen. Having helped to found his party—by giving it a doctrine and a soul rather than by directing it—he abandoned it after the French Revolution and then attacked it. His colleagues could not see the difference between the American Revolution and the French; they did not appreciate the uniqueness of the latter event, the most complete revolution ever known. Burke's political philosophy centers on the defense of an actual constitution rather than the construction of an imaginary one. His theme is the sufficiency—rather, the perfection—of gentlemanly prudence. But his defense of his beloved gentlemen reveals their limitations, perhaps better than any revolutionary attack. For the revolutionaries found no suitable replacement for gentlemen; nor indeed have we, though we have sought one among bureaucrats, technocrats, and democrats. One could almost define "gentlemen" by adding up everything that is lacking in bureaucrats, technocrats, and democrats. Burke's admiring view of them is clearer than that of their critics; the defects of gentlemen are to be seen in the need for his own contribution to their defence. That contribution went well beyond warning them of perils they were too dull to sense and arousing them with fine phrases. Using what he once called "the seasonable energy of a single man" (V 78), Burke tried to fortify the rule of gentlemen so as to make them less liable to subversion and attack. The result in the nineteenth century was both to fix them in place, immobile in their newly philosophical prejudice (the conservatives), and to loosen their attachments, trusting in the promise that reform would be the means of their conservation (the liberals). Somewhat unwillingly, Burke bears testimony to the necessary imperfection of politics in the very midst of his inspiring speeches and noble deeds.

NOTES

1. *The Correspondence of Edmund Burke*, ed. Thomas W. Copeland, 10 vols. (Chicago: University of Chicago Press, 1958–78), VI 239.

2. *Ibid.*, VIII 335n.

3. *The Works of Edmund Burke*, 8 vols. Bohn's British Classics (London: Bohn, 1854–89), II 430. All parenthetical text references are to this edition.

4. See also *Works*, I 501, and *Correspondence*, V 337.

5. Works, I 501; see also II 396, 454–455; V 342; VI 251; *Correspondence*, IV 36.

6. *Works*, VII 161; see III 16.

7. *Works*, II 282; see I 497.

8. *Works*, II 29, 56; V 218. Cf. Aristotle, *Nicomachean Ethics* 6.1144ª 6–37.

9. *Works*, V 317. Alexis de Tocqueville, *l'Ancien Régime et la Révolution*, 2 vols., ed. J. P. Mayer (Paris: Gallimard, 1952), I 72, 88, 193–201, 247.

10. *Works*, III 54–66; see I 375; II 293; VI 153.

11. *Works*, III 76–78. Cf. Aristotle, *Nicomachean Ethics*, 2.1106ᵇ 36–1107ª1.

12. *Works*, III 36; see II 313.

13. *Works*, II 440; see George Berkeley, *Alciphron*, III 14.

14. Aristotle, *Politics*, 3.1274^b 38–39, 1276^b5–6.

15. *Works*, II 308–309; see III 25.

16. *Works*, II 333; see III 109; VI 22.

17. Machiavelli, *Discourses on Livy*, I 6.

18. *Works*, II 354; see II 155; III 92.

19. See *Works*, II 484; III 86.

20. *Works*, III 87; see I 345; II 369; VI 21.

21. Burke's appeal to the authority of Jean Domat (*Works*, II 422) ignores Domat's refusal to apply prescription to public property; Jean Domat, *Les lois civiles dans l'ordre naturel*, III, vii, 5. A closer anticipation of Burke may be found in David Hume, *A Treatise of Human Nature*, III, ii, 3, 10; see also William Paley, *Principles of Moral and Political Philosophy* (1785), VI 2.

22. *Works*, V 137; VI 80, 146; see II 493 for Burke's statement of the revolutionaries' argument against prescription.

23. *Works*, V 137; Blackstone, *Commentaries on the Laws of England*, II 263–264.

24. *Works*, V 100; Marx, *Capital*, ch. 24, sec. 6. Marx apparently overlooked the following passage in Burke, which is more congenial to him: "Even commerce, and trade, and manufacture, the gods of our economical politicians, are themselves perhaps but creatures; and themselves but effects, which, as first causes, we choose to worship." *Works*, II 351.

25. *Correspondence*, II 165–167, for example.

26. *Correspondence*, VIII 130.

27. *Correspondence*, III 388–389.

28. *Works*, V 125; see II 128.

29. *Works*, II 282; see I 323, 370, 376, 451, 490; II 287, 308, 339, 352; III 438; V 212.

READINGS

A. Burke, Edmund. *Reflections on the Revolution in France.*
Burke, Edmund. *An Appeal from the New to the Old Whigs.*
B. Burke, Edmund. *Tracts on the Poperty Laws in Ireland.*
Burke, Edmund. *Thoughts on the Cause of the Present Discontents.*
Burke, Edmund. *Speech to the Electors of Bristol* (Nov. 3, 1774).
Burke, Edmund. *Speech on Conciliation with America.*
Burke, Edmund. *Letter to the Sheriffs of Bristol.*
Burke, Edmund. *Speech on Economical Reform.*
Burke, Edmund. *Speech on the Reform of the Representation of the Commons in Parliament* (May 7, 1782).
Burke, Edmund. *Letter to Sir Hercules Langrishe* (1792).
Burke, Edmund. *Letter to a Noble Lord.*
Burke, Edmund. *Four Letters on a Regicide Peace.*

JEREMY BENTHAM

1748–1832

JAMES MILL

1773–1836

Jeremy Bentham may be variously described as a political and legal philosopher, a social reformer, the founder of utilitarianism, and a *philosophe*. "Utilitarianism" indicates the view that whether an act is right or wrong depends on whether one believes its consequences to be good or bad. For Bentham, "good" and "bad" refer to pleasures or pains produced in the experiences of individual human beings. "*Philosophe*" refers to a category of European intellectuals of the eighteenth century, among whom Bentham enjoyed much more immediate success than in his native England. Like the *philosophes*, Bentham believed that the human condition must inevitably improve through the sheer proliferation of knowledge in the sense of encyclopedic information, coupled with abstract principles for classifying the information and putting it to work in reforming society.[1] Bentham distrusted inherited experience and features of political order defended by appeal to traditional acceptance. Reliance on past practice was, to him, a sign of ignorance.

In this view, ignorance, to Bentham, was a problem with a solution. The antidote to ignorance was to become well informed. Not surprisingly, then, Bentham rejected with scorn the notion of Socratic ignorance. The latter points to the mysterious difficulty of reaching any fixed, final understanding of the fundamental questions of how we ought to live.

According to Plato's Socrates, questions of right and wrong, good and bad, the beautiful and the ugly, must apparently ever be in dispute in political life (*Euthyphro,* 7^d). The beginning of wisdom would be always to keep in mind this sobering and limiting condition in our arguments with each other. The follower of Socrates may question the received opinions of society but not necessarily to overthrow them, since it is always possible that those opinions may be discovered to be worthy of support. Beyond that, a follower of Socrates would not disregard the commonsense argument that, if one is against the prevailing order, one ought to be willing to say what alternative one has to offer. The philosopher's task is to remind his dialectical partners of this need to consider alternatives through the not always well-received effort to find the weaknesses in arguments that have been put forward as strong. Socratic ignorance dramatizes the difficulty of harmonizing the search for wisdom with the exigencies of political decision making.

Bentham concluded that this traditional philosophic reticence was misplaced and a barrier to developing a proper science of legislation and government. Bentham thus dramatizes the difference between a Socratic philosopher and a *philosophe*. He combines the frame of mind of the *philosophe* with utilitarianism, arriving at what he takes to be the simple key that will unlock the complexities of the social universe.

It is possible to be well informed, because the universal basis of human action can be discerned in all that people do and say. Bentham wanted to translate the significance of actions into explicit calculations of the pleasures and pains attending those actions in order to advise people on the adequacy of the means they have chosen to seek happiness. Bentham ruled out assessing actions in respect to some putative objective rightness or wrongness. We cannot judge actions apart from their consequences, or independently rank the merits of the experiences people find pleasurable. Bentham rejected the efforts of the Socratic philosophers to do precisely these things, finding them to be, as it always has been found by Socrates' opponents, a spur to his impatience to get on with creating a rational social order.

This turn of mind is further illustrated in the fact that Bentham was trained in law at Oxford, but never practiced it. His knowledge of English law led him to contempt for its imprecision and "disorderliness." The English legal tradition was itself a "mystery," which could not be explained simply. Bentham's detachment from it reinforced his penchant for a science of legislation. He became an observer and a theoretician, seeking to transform and demystify the English order before settling into it. To be a theoretician in Bentham's sense was to seek to supersede, once and for all, political philosophy in the Socratic sense, to turn all unresolved mysteries into simple problems with legislative solutions. Among the vast array of his writings on a vast array of topics, his most influential work remains *An Introduction to the Principles of Morals and Legislation* (1789).[2] The gist of his position may be gathered from its arguments.

In this book, Bentham elucidates principles to guide the renovation and transformation of politics and society through scientifically designed legislation. Bentham saw himself crusading to destroy "prejudice" so as to install the critical spirit in society. Custom and tradition were to become guilty unless they could prove themselves innocent, thus emancipating humanity from the haphazard modes and customs that may have begun in inadvertence but now had become entrenched interests of a few at the expense of the rest. He saw the contemporary state of affairs as a conglomeration of conflicting, undefended principles and practices in which there was no distinguishing the irrational from the rational. English law, to employ a famous metaphor of Descartes, was like a mansion built over many eras in a hodgepodge of architectural styles, lacking elegance and proportion:

Common law, as it styles itself in England, *judiciary* law, as it might more aptly be styled every where, that fictitious composition which has no known person for its author, no known assemblage of words for its substance, forms every where the main body of the legal fabric: like that fancied ether, which, in default of sensible matter, fills up the measure of the universe. Shreds and scraps of real law, stuck on that imaginary ground, compose the furniture of every national code. What follows? That he who . . . wants an example of a complete body of law to refer to, must begin with making one.[3]

Descartes had said "that there is very often less perfection in works composed of several portions, and carried out by the hands of various masters. . . . Buildings planned and carried out by one architect alone are usually more beautiful and better proportioned than those which many have tried to put in order. . . ."[4] Since much of our existence is composed of different portions from many hands, it is not hard to see that, for the proponent of rationalist methods of design, that existence is raw material to be torn down and rebuilt from scratch. Yet, at the same time, Descartes, who, along with Francis Bacon, was the principal advocate of the modern quest for rational method, also expressed a caution about the "claim of any private individual to reform a state by altering everything, and by overturning it throughout, in order to set it right again. . . ."[5]

Descartes acknowledged the potential violence and uncertainty attending social reformation. He also admitted that custom might mitigate the faults of great bodies. Custom has "helped us to avoid, or insensibly corrected" imperfections "which mere foresight would have found it difficult to guard." Descartes concludes that "the imperfections are almost always more supportable than would be the process of removing them. . . . I cannot in any way approve of those turbulent and unrestful spirits who, being called neither by birth nor fortune to the management of public affairs, never fail to have always in their minds some new reforms. And if I thought that in this treatise there was contained the smallest justification for this folly, I should be very sorry to allow it to be published."[6]

Descartes expresses a degree of philosophic reticence which Bentham seemed bound to disregard under the assumption that the need for such restraint did not exist. When and if the difficulties of social reform should diminish, as Bentham believed he had shown to be possible, Benthamite reform could become a legitimate consequence of Cartesian method. There would no longer be a reason to be reticent given the advent of adequate modern methods to make philosophy, finally, really useful; thought and action could be brought together. Fearing the "turbulent and unrestful spirits," Descartes could resolve to walk "alone and in the twilight," being circumspect and patient in the quest for rational knowledge, paving the way for a *philosophe* without himself being one. Such caution vanished in Bentham.[7]

The ambience of philosophical caution being stripped away, the existing state of society can easily begin to seem intolerable, distasteful to the theorist gazing upon it, and ill suited to eliciting the improvement of those condemned to dwell in it. Bentham held no brief for the alternative perspective of Blackstone and of Edmund Burke.[8] Burke found beauty where Bentham saw ugliness: the beauty of an elaborated, conventional order, reflecting generations of trial and error and accomplishments legitimated by long standing. From Burke's point of view, abstract social principles were caricatures ripped out of context and then reapplied, as if they were master, to the very culture which gave to the principles whatever meaning they could actually have. From Bentham's point of view, the more data gathered, the more readily a simple model of the world could be constructed.

This difference of perspective on the English legal tradition, and on the validity of custom and tradition generally, is crucial to understanding many of the debates in modern legal and political philosophy ever since the time of Bentham and Burke. Previously, the rule of law had meant that persons could have reasonable expectations as to what the rules governing their transactions required of them. These evolved through the particular decisions of judges whose rulings were informed by customary practices in locales where they presided. The idea of a centralized source of uniform legislation, informed by a science of human nature, was absent. Bentham wanted to supply it.

In supplying it, Bentham intended to establish a general framework of social conditions which he believed would inevitably advance the well-being of the public. More astonishingly, Bentham believed that, if this were accomplished in England, a standard would be incarnated by which to reform the whole world: "Legislators who, having freed themselves from the shackles of authority, have learnt to soar above the mists of prejudice, know as well how to make laws for one country as for another."[9] He did not intend to tell individuals directly what to do; he did intend to guide their calculations in fruitful directions under laws promoting the greatest happiness of the greatest number. Bentham, to be sure, did not think one could merely dictate another's happiness. He recognized that the order designed by legislation would encourage the improvement of attitudes and procedures in relations among individuals but not seek simply to dictate personal attitudes and motives. These, he thought, would vary enormously among differing individuals and historical circumstances. Nonetheless, reforming legislation of Bentham's sort would unavoidably affect personal beliefs and habits of conduct, making it easier for some and harder for others to persist in their accustomed ways. The very principle of the greatest happiness for the greatest number implied that some happinesses would not and indeed should not be satisfied.[10]

Legislation requires judgment as to how the principles of morals and legislation fit particular historical conditions. The ability to make sound judgments, Bentham conceded, was an art as well as a science. But he believed that there are better and worse judgments—those that are rational because informed by science, and those that are irrational because governed by mere prejudice. In the realm of judgment there can always be dispute about decisions to do one thing rather than another, but there can be no disputing the superiority of the scientifically informed judgment: "prejudice and the blindest custom must be humoured; but they need not be the sole arbiters and guides. He who attacks prejudice wantonly and without necessity, and he who suffers himself to be led blindfold a slave to it, equally miss the line of reason."[11] The science of law "is, to the art of legislation, what the science of anatomy is to the art of medicine: with this difference, that the subject of it is what the artist has to work *with*, instead of being what he has to operate *upon*. Nor is the body politic less in danger from a want of acquaintance with the one science, than the body natural from ignorance in the other."[12]

One of the central meanings of the appeal to the principle of utility is revealed here. Bentham's science is universal, but it must be adapted to the historical conditions in which it is applied. Yet, at the same time, the historical conditions cannot be permitted a veto power over the application of scientific legislation. If that were to happen, then prejudice could legitimately prevail over science, or could claim an insight inaccessible to science. This tension between custom and tradition on the one hand and scientific progress on the other is at the heart of modern political debate. The opposition between conservatives and progressives is to be resolved in favor of progress by Bentham and his utilitarian followers: the scientifically informed pursuit of happiness is justified on the ground that no empirically demonstrable limit on human self-fulfillment or improvement has as yet been shown. In the tradition of Francis Bacon, Bentham believed that the work of relieving man's estate had barely begun but was the great hope for the future.

Moreover, Bentham did not think that social improvement was an arcane matter. Better food, better sanitary conditions, better education, greater equality of opportunity—these are the simple and obviously desirable conditions that constituted, for Bentham, the necessary conditions of human happiness. He believed that it is perfectly within the powers of human ingenuity to perfect social arrangements in which these desired goods will be more and more available. The power of Bentham's political philosophy depends on the degree to which his view of happiness, combined with his optimism about scientifically constructing policy to achieve it, is persuasive.

For a Benthamite, moreover, progress in the material sphere will go a long way toward producing conditions in which spiritual anxiety will dissipate. It is not obvious that this should be so if one is inclined to believe that the distinction between material and spiritual satisfaction is such that the satisfaction of one does not satisfy the other, or that they are antagonistic. Bentham, however, following a manner of thinking that can be traced back to Hobbes, sees no scientific method of stipulating spiritual satisfaction. It is not possible to make people good or happy. But it is possible to design improvements in the material conditions which otherwise may detract from the sense of well-being.

Human happiness, for Bentham, could not be determined by reference to an objective good or to natural rights such as were proclaimed in the American Declaration of Independence or in the French Declaration of the Rights of Man and Citizen.[13] The aim to achieve the greatest happiness of the greatest number does not mean that anybody's particular happiness is privileged. In fact, it is altogether likely that the principle will, in practice, lead to policies under which some ideas of happiness will be depreciated systematically, and thus the principle itself is a source of tension in Bentham's thought. Depending on the issue and one's point of view, the denial of any particular happiness may seem to be either good or bad. Elimination of slavery and sweatshops may generally be thought to be good (although not to slaveholders and profiteers); forced school busing and affirmative action in hiring may be thought to be generally bad (although not to some parents and their children or to the worker who suspects discrimination); freedom of religion will seem, to some, essential to human dignity and, to others, the road to moral decline. However individuals may judge these matters, though, a social policy contrived to promote the greatest happiness for the greatest number does not have to be justified in relation to any specific individual or group, even though it is, in principle, intended for the well-being of as many as possible. Bentham rejects the notion of absolute goods or self-evident truths because he means to defend individual self-fulfillment. Still, social engineering to improve the general well-being scientifically can reasonably take precedence over individual claims of rights.

Whether the conflict between social duties and individual desires can be resolved satisfactorily in terms of Bentham's principles is a matter for the thoughtful student to examine carefully. The point is all the more significant when it is realized that the modern liberal tradition shapes much of its political thinking in terms of striking a proper balance between interference and noninterference in the lives of citizens by means of government action. Questions of the proper scope and limits of government regulation assumed great importance. That they have become central is indicative of the powerful influence of Bentham's way of thinking.

It may be that the impact of this way of thinking rests on accepting the conflict between duties and desires as permanent: then one is never free to relax the effort to rethink and revise one's assumptions about social order. Since custom and habit are harbingers of irrational prejudice, the antidote must be sought in self-conscious application of the principle of utility to actions and legislation. If the members of society can be shaken out of their unreflective condition and taught, under the auspices of the principle of utility, to employ calculations of advantage and disadvantage, it will become clear that the vast majority are perfectly capable of self-regulation. They will show themselves to be capable of altering their conduct to remain in tune with evolving social conditions. In time, we would agree that the general principle—that human beings are equal and should be treated as equals—is true, and we would espouse the conviction that each should count for one and no more than one. For the most part, then, human beings should be and would be free to enter into voluntary contractual relations, according to their own lights.

There is no inherent limit on the use of government power for purposes of social reform in utilitarianism. But it meant to Bentham primarily the removal of arbitrary and outmoded restrictions on individuals' reliance on their own faculties in the prudent pursuit of their interests. Scientific legislation was intended to liberate in the direction of democratic individualism. It was expected to lead to what would later be called by John Stuart Mill, Bentham's philosophical godson, the spontaneously growing, improving society.

This vision of progressive order carried with it the optimistic belief that political stability does not depend on harsh restrictiveness, that human nature is neither irredeemably unruly nor capricious, that there is no special class of people naturally suited to rule. The influence of this view led to significant revisions of English criminal law in the nineteenth century. For example, the number of crimes punishable by death was greatly reduced. Bentham shifted the emphasis from punishment for doing wrong to enhancing incentives for doing right. He played a major role in the development of that modern sensibility which abhors the infliction of pain and which, when compelled to inflict it, takes the necessity as a sign of lingering imperfection in the social design. It led above all to major electoral reform, encouraging a pattern of extending more and more the right to vote.

These ideas coalesced with the ideas of economic liberalism, intellectual freedom, and religious tolerance in nineteenth-century England. Artificial barriers to trade were to be removed, restrictions on the free criticism of the government (*e.g.*, seditious libel) were to be lifted, and those previously excluded in England (Roman Catholics, atheists, Jews) were to be granted all the privileges of citizenship. Bentham envisioned a society of cooperative individualists. No one is to be treated as infallible in opinion or judgment, for one can never know that one's conception of reality corresponds to reality as such. Neither claims of absolute authority nor claims of absolute rights can be justified: "Under a government of laws, what is the motto of a good citizen? *To obey punctually: to censure freely.*" [14]

The common understanding of politics, since the time of Hobbes and Locke, has taken the balancing of liberty and authority as the central issue. Bentham thought his political science would make it possible to create a permanent symbiotic relationship between the two. Depending upon which features of his thought are emphasized, Bentham may appear to stand on one side or the other. On one hand, laws are to be scientifically designed commands of a sovereign power not restrained by a doctrine of natural rights. On the other, such commands are to be disinterested aids to help individuals find the way to their own happiness. In either emphasis there is a severity and austerity in the legislating atti-

tude. Moral and political truths "flourish not in the same soil with sentiment. They grow among thorns; and are not to be plucked, like daisies,
by infants as they run." [15]

Bentham demanded the transcendence of instinct, sentiment, unchallenged "common sense." Rather than first acquiring intimacy with
the workings of prevailing political, social, economic relations, Bentham counsels the acquisition of a method of scientific investigation
which then can be applied to the existing state of affairs. In this way one
is protected from seduction into current practices. Instead, one achieves
a cool detachment toward society and, indeed, toward oneself. One
must examine all things with an eye to the universal mechanisms that
underlie them. Only then would it be possible to control our destinies
through a program of rational reform—reform that is more than merely
the imposition of one selfish interest upon others in an endless process of
ill-informed, impulsive struggle.

Bentham's passion, from beginning to end, was to found "that system, the object of which is to rear the fabric of felicity by the hands of
reason and of law." [16] The unifying premise of his work is the principle of
utility: "that principle which approves or disapproves of every action
whatsoever, according to the tendency which it appears to have to augment or diminish the happiness of the party whose interest is in question
. . . , I say of every action whatsoever; and therefore not only of every
action of a private individual, but of every measure of government." [17]
The principle of utility is sanctioned by nature, since "nature has placed
mankind under the governance of two sovereign masters, *pain* and *pleasure*. It is for them alone to point out what we ought to do, as well as to
determine what we shall do." [18]

It is important to note that the sovereign masters, pleasure and
pain, not only determine what we actually do; they also show us what we
ought to do. The first step in becoming scientific is to become fully conscious of the "springs of action." At the same time, however, one wonders how there can be a discrepancy between what we do and what we
ought to do, given that the basis of both is the same. One answer is that,
in an unreformed political system, a partisan definition of what we
ought to do is generalized through law and policy, so that what some
selfish interests think ought to be done is imposed on all.

In other words, unreconstructed society is an aggregate of irratio-
nally and unequally related interests, each of which pursues its own calculations of what will give pleasure and what will give pain. Few persons
are consciously committed to the goal of making the greatest possible
number of others happy. Most are prone to generalize from their own

points of view about felicity or well-being. The common aspirations of humanity under nature's sovereignty are insufficiently appreciated.

But if and when there is sufficient appreciation, then mutual acknowledgment of nature, our universal sovereign, can induce a greater sense of our universal plight, and a plan to enhance the happiness of the largest number can become more appealing. The change in attitude away from a merely self-centered pursuit of happiness is rational, since humans cannot live solitary lives. In the latter condition, living directly only in relation to nature, the conflict between what we do and what we ought to do would not arise. If part of felicity consists in living in peace, security, and tranquillity of mind in the midst of others, then there has to be agreement, by no means automatic, on what we shall all accept as what we ought to do. But this obviously cannot be exclusively what I or any other would independently prefer. Given no agreed-upon, objective standard to rank the various preferences, it is necessary to discover and support those arrangements which permit the greatest number of preferences to be pursued without chaos. Such arrangements would foster conditions in which what I will to do and what I ought to will are reconciled. Then reason will have been employed to bring humanity back toward harmonious conformity to its nature. Otherwise, ill-informed, unscientific reasoning will lead us into constant conflict and anxiety. Every effort to resist ordering ourselves in this way, "every effort we can make to throw off our subjection, will serve but to demonstrate and confirm it." [19]

The principle of utility expresses simply and directly a chain of reasoning which, in its details, is complicated and lengthy. It provides a shorthand way of orienting every individual's frame of mind correctly. It reminds us that "the community is a fictitious *body,* composed of the individual persons who are considered as constituting as it were its *members.* The interest of the community then is, what?—the sum of the interests of the several members who compose it." [20]

For Bentham, all rational action is action in conformity with the principle of utility. Individuals who accept this will freely submit to prevailing laws insofar as they are formed with reference to utility (which they do not merely identify with their personal desires), and criticize them insofar as they are not: "A man may be said to be a partisan of the principle of utility, when the approbation or disapprobation he annexes to any action, or to any measure, is determined by, and proportioned to the tendency which he conceives it to have to augment or to diminish the happiness of the community." [21]

Upon reflection, the reader may still wonder, given Bentham's stipulation of the inescapable force of the principle of utility, what choices of individuals could ever be criticized for failing to conform to it. Or, where conflicting claims or proposals equally appeal to the principle of utility, how is one to decide among them? How shall we distinguish proper from improper applications of the principle?

There can be no abstract resolution of such questions. For Bentham, there is no such thing as an independently right or true rule of morality, of value, or of law. What counts has to be determined through the debate of those who are fully self-conscious in their commitment to the observance of the principle. The method of self-conscious, self-critical deliberation is essential to producing useful rules that rise above partisanship. No interests in society may be taken as expressing the best interest of the whole. No rules can exempt themselves from reassessment and revision. To some these arguments will appear to rest on an attitude of moral relativism. Bentham himself asks whether there are not "as many different standards of right and wrong as there are men? and whether even in the same man, the same thing, which is right to-day, may not (without the least change in its nature) be wrong to-morrow?" [22]

In asking these questions, Bentham wants to show that the cure of moral anarchy is not despotism but cooperative deliberation. He thought that conscious commitment to the principle of utility was the only way ultimately to achieve sustainable agreements on substance. By contrast, he thought appeals to natural rights or natural law presupposed points of substance and then tried to elicit submission to them. Because he denied the possibility of natural right or natural law, Bentham assumed that behind all appeals to them were selfish interests well or ill disguised. He thought the principle of utility would continually remind us that proposals always originate from identifiable interested persons and encourage us simultaneously to assess them with detachment in light of the greatest-happiness principle.

Agreement on the principle implies the joint search for agreement on substance. Nevertheless, the very use of the principle is paradoxical. It is intended to produce legitimate substantial agreements and simultaneously to call all substantial agreements into question: the word "right" cannot be meaningful apart from "utility." [23]

To measure right in terms of utility means measuring right with respect to one's interests, remembering that one's interests must be understood benevolently or with regard for the greatest happiness of the greatest number. Each of us must retain jurisdiction in defining our own happiness; we cannot submit ourselves to a fictitious collectivity. However, laws are required to bind us together. For example, one may be sorely tempted not to keep one's promises but may decide, nonetheless, that a rule to keep promises brings better consequences for society. One can weigh the happiness one will enjoy when self-restraint is combined with peace and order against the happiness to be expected from the unrestrained pursuit of self-interest amidst conflict and disorder. In choosing the former, a rule to govern society, one is calculating that, on the whole, it contributes to the greatest overall happiness and that one will be better off in that context.

Arriving at this conclusion, one would be saying, in effect, that one should act in a way (keeping promises) that one would like to see others act too. This sounds rather like Kant's categorical imperative. But Bentham does not say that we must will such a rule apart from having personal interests in so doing. The tension between self-interest and regard for others lies at the heart of utilitarianism and cannot be resolved by appeal to a transcendent moral duty for its own sake. From a utilitarian perspective, the Kantian principle cannot, if it is to be practically useful, exclude considering consequences. To utilitarians, consequences must be weighed whenever arguments arise among alternative possible courses of action. Whenever individuals permit each other to express opinions, or find they cannot escape them, they must argue the relative merits of differing courses of action with respect to their possible outcomes.[24]

Socrates expressed a different form of transcendent morality when he said that he had spent his life trying to be good rather than seeming to be good (*Gorgias,* 527). By this the Platonic Socrates meant that he was obliged not to decide what was right on the basis of guesses as to what consequences might follow in the temporal sequence of events. The consequences of his actions as ordinarily understood—for example, by Crito who had tried to persuade him to escape imprisonment and death—had no bearing on his duty to hold true to the philosophic life.

Moreover, in his vision of the philosopher-king, Socrates portrayed a ruler who could, through the ordering of his soul to the divine order, transmit the divine order to an earthly city. Such a soul could live in accord with the heavenly city even if it were not instituted on earth (*Republic,* 592), and thus the philosopher could pass beyond the perplexing realm of hints and intimations that is the vocation of the politician. For Socrates, then, the pursuit of wisdom is happiness, and, if happiness is a form of pleasure, it is the pleasure that sets the standard by which to judge the merits of all other purported pleasures. Here rightness is detached from utility in a vision of the ascent of the soul.

This contrasts with Bentham's utilitarian vision of immanent social improvement. Bentham considered the search for a *summum bonum* (highest good) "consummate nonsense," a quest for something supposedly better than and different from pleasure but nowhere to be found. Bentham calls Plato "the master manufacturer of nonsense" and generally dismisses the "antique sages." [25]

What excited Bentham's rage is the ancient effort to depreciate ordinary ideas of happiness as "vulgar." Such depreciation could be defended only so long as the alleged "highest good" was uncritically accepted. He thought that anyone who urges one to act against one's interest strives "to create in you an interest in so acting and to make you act according to it." [26]

Bentham's rejection of Rousseau's "general will" follows from this point also. To Bentham, a "general will" is a modern form of the ancient attempt to impose "virtue" on individuals at the expense of their own self-understood happiness. "Forcing men to be free" is, for Bentham, an impossible contradiction that arises from the failure of the social contract theory to provide an adequate foundation for the exercise of political authority.

Like David Hume, Bentham saw that social contract theory assumes a prior commitment to keeping one's promises (as in agreeing to leave the state of nature and obey a government). Thus, it is not the contract that creates promise keeping, but promise keeping that makes contracts plausible. Social contract theory expresses an attitude to government that must already have come into being long before as a habit of obedience acquired through the experience of its usefulness. Bentham straightforwardly argued that law, with its punishing sanctions, does not create freedom but inhibits it. What justifies law in so doing is that overall happiness is enhanced thereby.

Bentham expected his perspective, when universally accepted, to lead to two consequences at once: first, the number of substantial agreements would be few but solidly founded; second, many traditional restrictions inherited from what he considered antiquated religious, moral, political, and economic theories would be overthrown. For Bentham, a rational political order is one in which there is an increasingly precise distinction between what is obligatory and what is a matter of private preference. It would be seen that order need not depend on extensive legal obligations but, rather, on the assurance that what obligations there are can be defended independently of any special interests. In return for the assured conformity of citizens to the law, the range of their free choice in the moral realm could be indefinitely expanded.

But the indefinite expansion of individual freedom, if it is indeed to be compatible with order and progress, must be shown not to lead to crude selfishness and mutual antagonism. Could we enjoy reasonable assurance of mutual regard? Why should anyone care about anyone else?

As we have seen, the principle of utility operates to elicit greater awareness in each of the aspiration to happiness that is in all. The principle does not ask us to suppress the reality of our own experiences of pleasures and pains. It does not imply that there is some independent common good or interest to which our experiences are irrelevant, or to which they must be subordinated unquestioningly.

On "all occasions," Bentham asserts, one has the "purely social motive of sympathy or benevolence," and on "most occasions, the semi-social motives of love of amity and love of reputation."[27] The power of these motives will vary according to the dispositions of individuals and circumstances, and "principally according to the strength of his intellectual powers, the firmness and steadiness of his mind, the quantum of his moral sensibility, and the characters of the people he has to deal with."[28]

The fundamental aspiration to happiness in each individual is identical to the fundamental aspiration of legislation, properly understood. This aspiration does not vanish when legislation is absent, and it could be thwarted where bad legislation is imposed. Legislation should not necessarily be used to obligate us to perform beneficial actions, or to prevent actions that may be harmful.[29]

Bentham's theory tries to specify the relationship between private ethics and legal duties. The art of legislation consists in knowing when not to legislate as well as when to do so:

> The general object which all laws have, or ought to have, in common, is to augment the total happiness of the community . . . , to exclude . . . every thing that tends to subtract from that happiness . . . , to exclude mischief.
> But all punishment is mischief: all punishment in itself is evil. Upon the principle of utility . . . it ought only to be admitted in as far as it promises to exclude some greater evil.[30]

Since Bentham holds that "the dictates of utility are neither more nor less than the dictates of the most extensive and enlightened (that is *well-advised*) benevolence,"[31] it would seem to follow that the highest fulfillment of the dictates of utility would be uncoerced. Thus punishment is the last resort. Legislators should be reluctant to act. Indeed, reluctance to legislate may well be a precondition of good legislation. But when legislation is needed, it should be clear and precise, and the punishment should be swift, sure, and proportional to the offense, though not more than is necessary.[32] "Inefficacious remedies," because they cause pain without curing the evil they are designed to cure, multiply evil rather than reducing it.[33]

Since Bentham rejects appeals to eternal or immutable rules of right, the only goal for legislators should be to ensure the pleasures and the security of the people. All policies and legislation must be explicable in terms of the principle of utility. Therefore, since this principle is understandable to all, all are eligible to assess critically all legislation. Those who exercise the powers of an office of government have no other wisdom than that provided to every human being who understands the economy of sovereign nature and can absorb the lessons of experience with prevailing arrangements: "the powers of nature may operate of themselves; but neither the magistrate, nor men at large, *can* operate, nor is God in the case in question *supposed* to operate, but through the powers of nature."[34]

Bentham then provides a model of rational thinking for the legislator: the value of a pleasure or pain is directly related to its intensity, duration, certainty, immediacy, fecundity, purity, and the number of persons actually affected.

To take an exact account, then, of the general tendency of any act, by which the interests of the community are affected, proceed as follows. Begin with any one person of those whose interests seem most immediately to be affected by it. . . . Sum up all the values of all the *pleasures* on the one side, and those of all the pains on the other. . . . *Sum up* the numbers expressive of *good* tendency, which the act has, with respect to each individual, in regard to whom the tendency of it is good upon the whole . . . , again with respect to each individual, in regard to whom the tendency of it is *bad* upon the whole. Take the *balance*. . . . In all this there is nothing but what the practice of mankind, wheresoever they have a clear view of their own interest, is perfectly conformable to.[35]

Although Bentham does not insist that legislators laboriously go through this process incessantly, he does think we should always keep this model in mind, since every person has a bias in favor of some kinds of pleasures over others.

Such a political order, so Bentham assures us, will enjoy increasing self-confidence as the long-term effects of the conscious application of the principle of utility make themselves felt. This standard, the common possession of all, constitutes the common ground for discussion and debate. Society, informed by the principle, can exercise its political will, preserving and changing in a continuous process of self-development.

James Mill was Jeremy Bentham's principal disciple. He led the movement to put Bentham's ideas into practice, not least in devising an educational program to bring up his son, John Stuart Mill, to be the living embodiment of utilitarian ideals. Mill was confident that drastic parliamentary reforms were achievable without violence. He believed in the power of intellectual arguments to express and to mobilize popular discontent, thereby pressuring governments into change. *An Essay on Government,* published in 1820, is intended to be a simple, tightly argued rationale for a democratically elected, representative government that anyone could understand. Mill thought he could intensify and unify the political outlook among all segments of society excluded from political power.

Mill's essay describes the "road we must travel" to transcend the aristocratic politics that prevailed. He invokes the principle of the greatest happiness of the greatest number in order to attach it to specific goals for the future. Such general principles are "defective inasmuch as the particular ideas which they embrace are indistinctly announced, and different conceptions are by means of them raised in different minds, and even in the same mind on different occasions." [36] The right political reform will overcome these defects.

The sole task of government is to "increase to the utmost the pleasures, and diminish to the utmost the pains, which men derive from one another" (p. 8). The law of nature dictates that men must labor to survive. Scarcity leads to injury and dispute and competition for authority over each other to secure their interests. So long as there is no government committed to an equitable distribution of the "scanty materials of happiness," political power will be used to defend the rich against the laborers (pp. 48–49). The principal source of wealth is labor. If laborers cannot retain the greater proportion of what they produce, they have little incentive to work and must be coerced or enslaved. The consequence of this could only be the systematic exclusion of the many by the few from participating in the definition of the greatest happiness of the greatest number.

Government must be redesigned against this outcome. It must have the power necessary to resist special interests. Having achieved such power, however, "all the difficult questions of government relate to the means of restraining those in whose hands are lodged the powers necessary for the protection of all from making bad use of it" (p. 50). It would be a great misfortune for reform to substitute a new predator for an old one.

Mill finds, however, that the traditional forms of government—of the many, of the few, or of one—will not do. Government by the many, the democratic solution, requires the whole community to assemble. This is impractical for the very laboring population that it is supposed to protect. Even if assembly of the whole community were feasible, however, such assemblies are notorious for their volatility; they are unfit to conduct the business of government.

Government by the few, the aristocratic solution, fails as well. He-

reditary aristocracies "are deprived of the strongest motives to labor."
They are likely to be mentally defective because "intellectual powers are
the offspring of labor" (p. 53). Aristocrats are prime candidates to adopt
a predatory attitude to the people. The monarchical form is open to the
same objections: a few with power will always try to "defeat the very end
for which government exists" (p. 54).

Mill asks, rhetorically, Are we forced to the depressing conclusion
that government is necessary but that no form of government is acceptable? Might we not argue, following Hobbes, that the smaller the number of rulers, the smaller portion of the goods of the rest of us they would
demand, and, therefore, an oligarchy or monarchy would be a lesser
evil? Perhaps even a single, absolute sovereign would be a rational solution. Unfortunately, history seems to provide equal numbers of good and
bad sovereigns.

Nor is this all. An absolute sovereign must always fear rebellious-
ness in his subjects, for they are not sheep but thinking, feeling beings.
The absolute ruler will never be able to assume that the people are subservient enough. He will seek more and more assurance of control. This
happens not because the sovereign is different from others, but because
the logic of human relations would apply to anyone in the same position:

Power is a means to an end. The end is everything, without exception,
which the human being calls pleasure and the removal of pain. The grand
instrument for attaining what a man likes is the actions of other men.
Power in its most appropriate signification, therefore, means security for
the conformity between the will of one man and the acts of other men. This,
we presume, is not a proposition which will be disputed. . . . The demand,
therefore, of power over the acts of other men is really boundless . . . in the
number of persons to whom we would extend it, and boundless in its degree
over the actions of each (pp. 56–57).

Since power can become an end in itself, it does not follow that the
smaller the ruling group the less the danger of arbitrary subjection. Furthermore, while the ruler might try to maintain power by distributing
rewards that give pleasure, greater security is more likely to be sought in
the "grand instrument" of Terror (p. 59). But this feeds on itself, becoming ever more extreme and pervasive. Power tends to enslave; unlimited government must enslave those whom it was intended to serve.
Unchecked desire is unlimited desire; "actions which flow from this unlimited desire are the constituents whereof bad government is made"
(p. 63).

An alternative often proposed, and said to be illustrated by the
structure of the then existing British government, was a mixed government comprising all three of the simple forms. This supposes that the

king, the aristocracy, and the people are three separate wills, each unified in pursuing its own interest. By the science of human nature, as Mill has laid it down, each must pursue its own interest to the utmost. The possibility that two of the interests will combine against the third cannot be excluded. In fact, Mill thinks this is inevitable. Power is never equally distributed, there is no natural balance of forces. In particular, people are prone to overrate or underrate the power of each interest and to act in accordance with their misperceptions. Human affairs are incessantly changing, and there is no preventing differences of talent and fortune from showing themselves. Success creates momentum toward greater and greater disparities among interests. The doctrine of checks and balances is "visionary" and "chimerical" (p. 65).

But the surest outcome is the combination of monarchy and aristocracy against democracy: the two interests may differ, but neither wants to be swamped by the democratic power. Mill finds it inevitable that the people will be overrun unless other precautions are introduced. We approach once more the possibility that the people, whose interest is the most extensive in the community, can neither govern nor protect themselves.

The remedy can only be to create a representative body that can govern for the people under such checks as will prevent corruption of the representatives. The representative body must be permitted the power requisite to the discharge of its responsibilities; it must also "have an identity of interest with the community" (p. 67).

Practically speaking, this would mean ensuring that the power of the British House of Commons could stand up to the power of the House of Lords combined with the king's. This aspect of reform seemed to Mill uncomplicated at least in conception. More difficult is the question of how to raise up the House of Commons without making it the new wolf in place of the old.

The scheme of representation must be carefully considered. First, representatives must be members of the communities whom they represent. They must be exposed to the consequences that follow from misgovernment. Efficiency prevents reducing the power, but we can reduce the length of the representative's term of office in order to guarantee he will suffer the consequences of the decisions he takes when in office. Hereditary or life-appointment offices are to be rejected, but reelection is to be permitted (there should be rewards for faithful service and not merely penalties for displeasing action in office). But election of representatives must itself be representative of the community. This means that the franchise must be extended (although children and women are excluded on the grounds of identity of interest with fathers and husbands). Adult

males, at least forty years of age, subject to a modest property qualification, are the "natural representative of the whole population." Mill believed that this was the best approximation to a body both representative
and not too large, and enjoying few incentives to exploit minorities.
There is to be no special representation for traditional interests such as
landowners, merchants, or manufacturers. There is to be no special representation of the military or legal professions.

Would this new scheme of representative government revolutionize
the established order, destroying the monarchy and the House of Lords?
Whether they are retained or not, the basis of decision will no longer be
found in a reverence for custom or tradition. They will be kept only if
they "are important and necessary branches of good government" (p. 83).
But given Mill's own account of the logic of competing interests, how
can we expect a dispassionate assessment of these institutions? Only if
we assume as he does that the newly reformed legislative body will, in
fact, represent the interest of the whole community so that nothing that
it examines for possible reform will be judged by any other standard
than the interest of the whole community. Even if these ancient institutions were to be kept, however, their whole meaning and function
would have to change.

Mill is very clear in denying any dependency of the people on aristocratic guidance. Thus monarchy and aristocracy must be judged in
terms of their administrative utility. Furthermore, Mill is confident his
representative body can have none of the "evils by design" found in traditional aristocratic rule. He does not consider the question of the "tyranny of the majority" as do Madison in *The Federalist* (1788) and Tocqueville in *Democracy in America* (1835). Everything stands or falls on the
success of his representational reform in circumventing the natural law
of boundlessly expanding power. The new legislative power must identify and support the interest of the whole.

Mill believes this political reformation can have all the salutary
effects of the religious reformation which preceded it. The power of personal interpretation of the Bible, without priestly guidance, "has totally
altered the condition of human nature and exalted man to what may be
called a different stage of existence" (p. 88).

If this has been so in the very difficult matters of religious interpretation, will it not be much easier for each to understand his own local
interest? The political virtue is prudence, and "prudence is a more general characteristic of the people who are without the advantages of fortune than of the people who have been thoroughly subject to their cor-
ruptive operation. . . . The powers of government . . . were better
entrusted to incapables who have an interest in good government than to
incapables who have an interest in bad" (pp. 88–89).

The proportion of foolish to wise men is about the same, Mill asserts, in the aristocratic and in the democratic classes. The proportional presence of foolishness and wisdom will, therefore, not alter merely because the democracy has replaced the aristocracy in power. The middle rank of society, the portion most inclined to prudence, "are wholly included" in the democratic part of the community. Those who are below the middle rank will be subject to the influence of the middle rank. Thus there is a natural source of prudent political leadership in the democratic part:

There can be no doubt that the middle rank, which gives to science, to art, and to legislation itself their most distinguished ornaments, and is the chief source of all that has exalted, and refined human nature, is that portion of the community of which, if the basis of representation were ever so far extended, the opinion would ultimately decide. Of the people beneath them a vast majority would be sure to be guided by their advice and example (p. 90).

The middle rank will mediate between poor and rich, providing the exemplary model of right personal and political conduct.

Thus Mill's essay is a rhetorically powerful plea for electoral reform that, he promises, will bring to power that element in society most likely to identify its interests with the interests of the whole. In turn, proper interpretation of the Benthamite calculus of pleasure and pain in legislative policy will become possible.

Whether the natural laws of human competition, asserted without qualification by Mill, can be turned to advantage by means of this mechanical reform must be carefully considered. Whether the natural authority Mill claims for the middle rank will, by the logic of his own arguments, come to seem arbitrary to their constituents must also be considered. Moreover, disparities in the intensity of commitment among interests may lead not to prudent legislative action but to each interest's pressuring government for preference over its rivals, and to a brokering of interests. The conflict between the intellectual leadership necessary to legislate scientifically, and the demands of individuals and groups to liberate and develop themselves as they see fit, looms behind the self-confident arguments of *An Essay on Government*.

NOTES

1. In *Article on Utilitarianism: Long Version*, Bentham refers to the "highly celebrated work of Helvetius entitled *Sur l'esprit*. [1758] In this work, a commencement was made of the application of the principle of utility to practical uses. To the direction of human conduct, in the ordinary course of life, a

connection was formed between the idea attached to the word 'happiness', and again between the idea attached to the word 'happiness' and the ideas respectively attached to the words 'pleasure' and 'pain'. . . . Attached to the words 'utility' and 'principle of utility' were now ideas in abundance, ideas which could not but be continually present and familiar to the most inattentive, unobservant and scantily-instructed minds." Bentham goes on to discuss the importance to his thinking of Francis Bacon's *Advancement of Learning*, D'Alembert and the French Encyclopedia, Chambers' *Cyclopedia*, and Hume's political essays. Speaking of his own reputation in France, Bentham remarks, "Greater—far greater—is the honour bestowed on him in that foreign country than in his own." *Deontology together with A Table of the Springs of Action and The Article on Utilitarianism*, ed. Amnon Goldworth (Oxford: Clarendon Press, 1983). pp. 290, 311.

2. Jeremy Bentham, *An Introduction to the Principles of Morals and Legislation*, ed. J. H. Burns and H. L. A. Hart (London and New York: Methuen University Paperback edition, 1982). (Hereafter cited as *PML*.) Speaking of this work in 1829, Bentham described himself thus: "Keeping pains and pleasures all along in view in the character of the principle materials of which the structure of the human mind is composed, he undertook to frame the first inventory list that had ever been attempted to be framed in the sort of articles called Motives . . . , these motives being accompanied and explained by the several correspondent pleasures and pains: a motive being nothing but the fear of some pain . . . or the hope of a certain pleasure. . . ." *Articles on Utilitarianism*, p. 293.

3. *PML*, Preface, p. 8.

4. Descartes, "Discourse on the Method of Rightly Conducting the Reason," in *The Philosophical Works of Descartes*, trans. E. S. Haldane and G. R.

Ross (Cambridge: Cambridge University Press, 1972), vol. I, p. 87.

5. *Ibid.*, p. 89.

6. *Ibid.*, pp. 89–90

7. *Ibid.*, p. 91.

8. For Bentham's general attack on Blackstone one should consult *A Fragment on Government*, in *The Collected Works of Jeremy Bentham*, ed. John Bowring (repr. New York: Russell & Russell, 1962), Vol. I, pp. 221–295.

9. *Of the Influence of Time and Place in Matters of Legislation*, in *ibid.*, p. 180, col. B.

10. In the *Article on Utilitarianism*, Bentham recognized a problem with the phrase "of the greatest number": If you have a society of 4001 and transfer all the means of happiness to 2001, leaving 2000 with nothing (enslaved), it is obvious that the greater number has the greatest happiness and the society will be miserable. Bentham saw that the principle could be misused to rationalize the systematic persecution of groups such as Roman Catholics in Great Britain or Protestants in Ireland (p. 310). Such an outcome was in complete opposition to his intentions: "A principle, which lays down, as the only, *right* and justifiable end of Government, the greatest happiness of the greatest number—how can it be denied to be a dangerous one? dangerous to every Government, which has for its *actual* end or object, the greatest happiness of a certain *one*." *A Fragment on Government*, p. 272, explanatory footnote, col. A.

11. *Of the Influence of Time and Place in Matters of Legislation*, p. 180, col. B.

12. *PML*, Preface, p. 9; see also the Preface to the first edition of *A Fragment on Government* (1776) in *Works*, Vol. I, p. 226, col. A.

13. See *Anarchical Fallacies, being An Examination of The Declarations of Rights issued during The French Revolution*, in *Works*, Vol. II, pp. 489–534.

14. *A Fragment on Government*, p. 230, col. A.

15. *PML*, Preface, pp. 9–10.

16. *PML*, Ch. I, p. 11.
17. *PML*, Ch. I, p. 12.
18. *PML*, Ch. I, p. 11.
19. *Ibid.*
20. *PML*, Ch. I, p. 12.
21. *PML*, Ch. I, p. 13.
22. *PML*, Ch. I, p. 16.
23. *PML*, Ch. I, paragraph 4, pp. 15–16.
24. Bentham argues that we ought to keep our promises because "such is the benefit to gain, and mischief to avoid, by keeping them, as much more than compensates the mischief of so much punishment as is requisite to oblige men to it," and this is "a question of *fact,* to be decided . . . by testimony, observation, and experience." *A Fragment on Government*, p. 270, col. B.

25. *Deontology*, in *Deontology together with A Table of the Springs of Action and The Article on Utilitarianism*, pp. 134–147.
26. *A Table of the Springs of Action*, in *ibid.*, p. 26.
27. *PML*, Ch. XVII, p. 284.
28. *Ibid.*, pp. 284–85.
29. *Ibid.*
30. *PML*, Ch. XIII, p. 158.
31. *PML*, Ch. X, p. 117.
32. *PML*, Ch. XIII, *passim.*
33. *PML*, Ch. XVII, p. 288.
34. *PML*, Ch. III, p. 37.
35. *PML*, Ch. IV.
36. James Mill, *An Essay on Government*, ed. Currin Shields (New York: Liberal Arts Press, 1955), p. 47. All parenthetical text references are to this edition.

READINGS

A. Bentham, Jeremy. *An Introduction to the Principles of Morals and Legislation.* Edited by J. H. Burns and H. L. A. Hart. London and New York: Methuen University Paperback, 1982.

Mill, James, and others. *Utilitarian Logic and Politics: James Mill's 'Essay on Government,' Macaulay's 'Critique' and the Ensuing Debate.* Ed. Jack Lively and John Rees. Oxford: Oxford University Press, 1978.

B. Bentham, Jeremy. *A Fragment on Government,* in *The Collected Works of Jeremy Bentham.* Ed. John Bowring. Vol. I, pp. 221–295. Repr., New York: Russell and Russell, 1962.

Bentham, Jeremy. *Deontology together with A Table of the Springs of Action and the Article on Utilitarianism.* Ed. Amnon Goldworth. Oxford: Clarendon Press, 1983.

GEORG W. F. HEGEL

1770–1831

The most important political writings of Hegel are his *Philosophy of Right* on the one hand and some essays like those on the German Constitution (1802) and on the British Reform Bill (1830) on the other. We shall limit ourselves here to a consideration of his political philosophy proper, notwithstanding the importance of his more practical works. His philosophy of right, or rather his philosophy of the state, is to an extraordinary degree inseparable from his philosophic teaching as a whole, for his doctrine is more "systematic" than are those of most other thinkers. This becomes clear in the bare outline of his presentation. The state that Hegel describes is the work of eternal Reason as it is presented in his *Science of Logic* and the *Encyclopedia of the Philosophic Sciences,* but it is also the result of universal history as Hegel traces it in his *Lectures on the Philosophy of History*. In the last analysis, Reason and History are not separable, according to Hegel. The unfolding of Reason parallels the process of universal history, or, the historical process is fundamentally rational. Hence, Hegel does not want to construct an ideal state but to rehabilitate the real state in showing that it is rational.[1] This rehabilitation is addressed to two kinds of opponents.

Against the attitude of a moral, religious, or intellectual consciousness which attempts to take refuge in the inner life and to reject the "sound and fury" of political realities, Hegel justifies political life as such. It is only in and by the state that the individual gains his true reality, for it is only in and by it that he comes to universality. Only the state can act universally by instituting laws. Morality, which seeks universality, can be actualized only by being incarnated in institutions and manners. Manners or morals (*Sittlichkeit*) are "the life of the state in the individuals." [2] It is in his devotion to the state that the individual goes beyond his primitive spontaneous selfishness; it is the state's activity of instruction which gives him a training and an education. Hegel, with this in view, repeats the answer of a Pythagorean to a father who asked him about the best way to raise his son morally: "Make him a citizen of a state [which has] good laws." [3]

In spite of what might be thought on the basis of certain Hegelian texts, this rehabilitation of the state should not be interpreted as a deification of it. It is true enough that according to Hegel the state constitutes a "final end" for the individual who finds in it the truth of his existence, his duty, and his satisfaction, and that the state constitutes the actualization or the appearance of the divine in the external world. Still, the state's relation with the individual is essentially reciprocal; it is only a final end for the individual to the extent to which its own end is his liberty and satisfaction. Moreover, an individual soul's morality or religion has an infinite value independent of the state. In the state, the individual goes beyond the level of his private, personal thoughts and wishes, his mere existence which Hegel calls the subjective mind. Through the state he has learned to universalize his wishes, to make them into laws and to live according to them. The state is a reality not a project; it can be lived and thought. It is only through the state that the individual takes his place in the world; it is as a citizen that he learns what is reasonable in his wishes. This is the stage of the objective mind. But the "appearance" or "realization" of the "divine," that is, of the absolute or the rational, is neither constituted nor exhausted by the state. The state only introduces and makes possible the absolute mind. It is the source of art, religion, and philosophy, which in a certain way transcend the state. When Hegel speaks of the state as divine, he is only insisting that it be respected in showing that it is fundamentally informed by rationality, that, in spite of its apparent faults and contingency, it is what it should be.

Therefore Hegel must defend the rationality of the real state against the romantics who turn away from politics simply, but equally against the utopians and reformers who turn away from the real state in favor of an ideal state. The function of philosophy is not to teach the state how it ought to be but to teach men how the state ought to be understood. Philosophy cannot go beyond the reality of its time but can only reconcile itself with it in recognizing reason "as the rose in the cross of the present." [4] Philosophy's function is neither to invent nor to criticize but to bring out the positive truth with which reality is already informed.

Thus Hegel wants to show the rational in the irrational. Not only does he want to discover the necessary essence of the state behind the contingent details, but he also wishes to show that what appears irrational in the state itself works unconsciously toward the triumph of the rational, that what appears contradictory will finally be brought into harmony, that the blind play of particular passions and actions necessarily ends in the advent of the universally just and fully developed political order. Hence the bad leads to the good, the passions to reason, contradiction and conflict to synthesis and peace.

It is the state understood as a harmonious and differentiated totality that makes this synthesis possible. To express the relation between the articulated whole which is nothing without its parts and the parts which are nothing without the whole, Hegel turns to the metaphor of the organism, in particular the human body, in which each organ has its true reality only in the particular function it fulfills within the whole, and also to the metaphor of an architectural structure like a Gothic cathedral. The paradox of such an articulation is that it is the result of the play of unconscious forces. The double Hegelian undertaking ends in this paradox, and to it corresponds the idea of the "cunning of reason." The state comes to light as both a final result and a precondition. It is a result of the action of individuals and of the play of the passions but, once constituted, its structure appears as first and primary while its genesis is interpreted as a merely empirical and external fact. "The state is a final result in which the fact that it finds its origin in the operation of individuals disappears." [5] That these individuals—whether one means by this the mass of men pursuing their particular interests or the great men who perform heroic actions—are unconsciously the instruments of a plan which transcends them and often directly contradicts their conscious objectives, that the action of irrational forces constructs an architectonic edifice which is the image of eternal reason, is what is meant by the "cunning of reason" [6] which demonstrates the rationality of history. This is what permits the philosophy of history to end in political philosophy and, conversely, what permits political philosophy to transform itself into a description of the final, fully developed state.

The state is born of conflict and is, in its turn, the theater and the origin of numerous potential conflicts. This is true of the state because it is true of man himself. Man does not raise himself to the level of humanity in isolation but in a battle to the death for "recognition." He exists for himself, is conscious of himself or of his own freedom only to the extent to which he is recognized, as consciousness or freedom, by another consciousness or another freedom. Each wishes to be recognized by the other without in turn recognizing him. Each establishes himself as free, and hence as human, only to the extent to which he is able to negate his natural being for the sake of recognition, risking his life for prestige. The struggle for recognition will thus be a life-and-death struggle. For that very reason it will end in an inequality. One of the two adversaries will prefer life to prestige or freedom. Moved by his fear of violent death, he will consent to recognize the other without insisting on being recognized by him. He will submit to the other. Thus man necessarily emerges from the fight for recognition as either a master or a slave. His reality is, then, essentially social and even political, since "the struggle for recognition and the submission to a mastery is the phenomenon from which men's social life emerged and it is the beginning of states." [7]

The conflict between master and slave is prior to the state. It has the same place in Hegel's formulation that the state of nature, the opposite of the civil state, has in Hobbes's. And, as in Hobbes, it leaves its imprint on the political reality which follows. For both, the state emerges from violence; the first relationship among men is one of conflict, which puts in play the two fundamental passions, vanity (or the desire for recognition) and the fear of violent death. But the relation of the master and the slave, far from stopping at the victory of the master, engenders a dialectic which will be the driving spring of human history. The master forces the slave to work for him. Essentially idle, the master's life is summed up in the quest for recognition, for prestige and glory, through war. He does not work, he is not in direct contact with things. The slave, on the other hand, who prepares the things to satisfy the master's needs, is the one who transforms nature and himself through work. He postpones the destruction of the thing (through consumption) in preparing it by work, and he postpones the satisfaction of his own needs in working to satisfy those of the master: "work is repressed desire." [8] He works in terms of an abstract idea, a project to be realized. He forms the external world which acquires a consistency of its own and bears his mark, and he forms himself by separating himself from his instincts and by becoming an apprentice in abstract general notions, language, and thought. Thus, through the slave's work, both the world of technique and society itself on the one hand, and the world of thought, art, and religion on the other are constituted. It is therefore the attitude of work and fear of violent death, the prosaic attitude, that of the slave and of the bourgeois as opposed to the heroic and aristocratic attitude, which, just as in Hobbes, is at the foundation of Hegel's society. Moreover, whereas for classical political philosophy leisure had a higher dignity than work because their opposition reflected that between theory and practice, for Hegel, thought and the universal are on the side of work, and leisure is conceived of as essentially warlike.

But this is not compensation enough for the slave, and he is still dissatisfied, just as is the master, for neither of them has obtained the recognition he hoped for, the recognition of another free consciousness. The conflict continues, and it is the function of the state to resolve it. The reconciliation which the state must effect is two-pronged. On the one hand, the state is founded on reciprocity: its citizens recognize one another; it is the ground of the reciprocal recognition at which the master and the slave aim in vain. On the other hand, the state finds within it both the moment (or element) of work and need and that of sacrifice and war. This tension appears in the form of the opposition between "civil society" and the state, between the "bourgeois" and the "citizen." The problem of the modern state will be precisely to tolerate the two moments and to reconcile them, *i.e.,* to implement the synthesis of the aristocratic point of view and the bourgeois point of view, or, in the last analysis, of the master and the slave.

All the conflicts which are implicit in the relations of the individual, the family, the society, and the state ultimately refer back to a fundamental opposition which has its seat in the individual's will, a conflict the stakes of which are the individual's status in the state. At various levels the conflict stands forth as the opposition between the individual and the universal, the particular will and the general will, private interest and public interest, bourgeois and citizen, satisfaction of needs and sacrifice, rights and duties, passions and reason, negative inwardness and positiveness, critical consciousness and acceptance of the law, in sum, between what Hegel calls "subjective liberty" (as individual consciousness and will pursuing its particular goals) and "objective liberty" (*i.e.,* "the substantial general will"). For Hegel, the state as "concrete freedom" is the union of these two elements in so far as the individual is satisfied in recognizing the universal as law and in taking the state as end. Hegel says that "the union of the particular and the universal in the state is that upon which every thing depends." [9] This "unity of its final universal end and the particular interests of the individuals" is expressed in the fact that "they have duties to the state in proportion as they have rights against it." [10] This reciprocity of rights and duties then permits the state to constitute a "serene totality." The right of subjective liberty should be recognized in two ways: as the right of the subject's particularity to be satisfied in its needs and its well-being, and as the right of consciousness to recognize nothing of which it does not approve rationally. But particularity should adapt itself to the universal and to collective life, and critical consciousness should not endanger the existence of an authority, of a government, of an organized state.

This condition is, of course, met only by the modern state. As for the past, historical examples abound to show the dangers which had to be surmounted in order to achieve the rational state. The imperfection and ruin of the Greek world, from the political point of view, are the consequences of its misunderstanding of the principle of particularity. "The right of the subject's particularity, his right to be satisfied, or in other words the right of subjective freedom, is the pivot and centre of the difference between ancient and modern times." [11] The Greeks lived naturally and immediately for the general or the substantial, for the fatherland. "Of the Greeks we may affirm that in the first and true form of their freedom they had no conscience. Among them there reigned the habit of living for their fatherland without further reflection." [12] Hence there is no place for subjectivity in any of its forms—as the right to the satisfaction of particular needs and to well-being (the quest for them belonging only to slaves), as the right to freedom in the choice of calling and in the determination of class position, or as the right of the critical consciousness which feels the need to found its attachment to the political regime and its moral action on reason. To the contrary, the independent development of particularity or subjective freedom appears in the Greek states as a hostile principle, as a destruction of the social order. Its emergence in the ancient states is coeval with the corruption of morals, and it is the supreme cause of their decadence.[13] In the Roman Empire, individuality is recognized, but abstractly and externally. The state as an organic whole is dissolved. "All the individuals are degraded to the level of private persons, equal with one another, possessed of formal rights and the only bond . . . to hold them together is abstract insatiable self-will." [14] This is because a constitution and an organization of the concrete moral life in general, binding the master and the subjects together, were lacking.

In another form and in a very different context, the double reproach of abstractness and arbitrariness connected with the absence of organization is to be found in Hegel's allusions to France. The French Revolution represents an absolutely capital achievement, the decision to put thought or reason at the foundation of the state. It is the advent of the principle of subjective consciousness and, with it, of the principles of liberty, equality, and the rights of man and citizen. But these principles, which in themselves belong to the very essence of the modern state, are conceived in an abstract and individualistic fashion which leaves no place for organization and government, or for anything concrete. The fulfillment of this negative and destructive liberty, which wishes to suppress all differentiation and determinateness, is indefinite terror, "since any institution whatever is antagonistic to the abstract self-consciousness of equality." [15] Since the attempts at democracy in large, developed states can only lead to abstractness, and "since a government is always there," [16] revolutionary liberalism is condemned to being perpetually in opposition. After Napoleon, who had correctly understood the necessity of conciliating principles of the revolution with the authority of an organized state, French political life remained in the grip of the contradictions besetting a nation the life of which had been dominated by abstract categories: there was a perpetual opposition of statesmen to men of principle, and of government to the people.

So long as the people is not organized in and by the state, it is only a collection of particular wills and "does not know what it wills." [17] It can speak only arbitrarily, in a way harmful to all organization.

With this formalism of liberty, with this abstraction, no solid organization can be established. The particular dispositions taken by the government find themselves immediately opposed by freedom, for they are only manifestations of the particular will and hence arbitrary. The will of the many overturns the ministry and what was up to now the opposition comes on the stage as the new government. But it, inasmuch as it is now a government, has in its turn the many against it. In this way change and unrest are perpetuated.[18]

Hegel, therefore, denies that recognition of individual liberties and rights and juridical equality ought to lead to democracy.

To hold that every single person should share in deliberating and deciding on political matters of general concern on the ground that all individuals are members of the state, that its concerns are their concerns, and that it is right that what is done should be done with their knowledge and volition, is tantamount to a proposal to put the democratic element without any rational form into the organism of the state, although it is only in virtue of the possession of such a form that the state is an organism at all.[19]

The individual should be taken into political account only in so far as he occupies a definite place in that organism. The possibility for each to become a member of the governing class, juridical equality, ought not to be detrimental to social differentiation, nor ought public opinion, the possibility for each to make his voice heard by authority, do damage to the authority of the state and its competent representatives.

Thus Hegel desires a synthesis of "liberation and respect," of passion and morality, of revolutionary principles and the necessity of the political order. Historically the modern state should represent a synthesis of the *polis* (of which the unity, the citizens' mutual confidence and their attachment to the whole should be preserved) and the liberal society of political economy (of which the diversity and differentiation, the satisfaction of individual needs, the realization of the universal by the individual free will, should be preserved). Philosophically, Hegel wishes to effect a synthesis of classical (or substantial and concrete) morality and Christian-Kantian (or internal and abstract) morality, of the politics of Plato, founded on the primacy of reason and virtue, and the politics of Machiavelli, Bacon, Hobbes, and Locke, founded on the emancipation of the passions and their satisfaction.

The means of this synthesis is history. The subject and the end of history is the progressive revelation of freedom, or, what amounts to the same thing, the consciousness which the mind gains of itself through history. The mind grasps itself as being essentially constituted by its freedom, and its freedom is realized in this gaining of consciousness. Freedom is realized in the modern state because, on the one hand, the state has separated out and manifested freedom's different moments and aspects (objective liberty, subjective liberty, and so on); and, on the other, since freedom is now revealed as the essence of man, all men are in the state, and know that they are in it, as essentially free. The discovery of the true and complete essence of freedom coincides with the freedom of all. But then, if it is true that the end of history is only realized in and by the modern state, it is no less true, reciprocally, that the modern state can only be constituted when the principle on which it is founded has been revealed in its different aspects. Thus it is necessary that all men be recognized as free, that the principle of internal freedom, or of the infinite value of the individual, have made its appearance in religion, that the particularity of needs and the demand for their satisfaction have made their appearance in men's manners and morals. This revelation is only complete at the end of history, since the web of history is made of the progressive appearance of incomplete principles, each one of which manifests a new aspect of freedom but each one of which is doomed to disappear as a consequence of its very incompleteness. The developments of these particular principles are the spirits of peoples (*Volksgeiste*); they constitute concrete totalities within which the animating principle expresses itself comprehensively in religion, science, art, events, and destiny. Thus history is the history of religion, manners and morals, art, economics, and so on, at the same time as it is political history. The political constitution of a people is a result of its spirit (mind); thus it is dangerous to impose on a people a constitution constructed a priori. Political forms can only be spoken of historically; they can be judged only in relation to the extent of consciousness of freedom with which they are associated.

Fundamentally, universal history is arranged in three stages which are not three forms of government but three degrees of consciousness of freedom, ranked according to whether it is one, some, or all who know themselves to be free.

The Orientals do not know yet that mind or man as such are in themselves free; because they do not know it, they are not. They know only that one single man is free. That is why such a freedom is only caprice and barbarism. . . . This single one is hence only a despot and not a free man. It was with the Greeks that the consciousness of freedom first came to sight; that is why they were free; but they, as well as the Romans, knew only that some are free, not man as such. That even Plato and Aristotle did not know. This is why the Greeks not only had slaves, . . . but their own freedom was both closed up within narrow limits and at the same time a harsh servitude . . . of the human. Only the Germanic nations have in Christianity come to the consciousness that man as man is free, that spiritual freedom truly constitutes his nature. This consciousness appeared first in religion, in the most inward region of the mind; but to inform the world with this principle was a new task whose solution and execution exact a long and painful effort of education.[20]

It is "the application of the principle to the affairs of the world" which ultimately decides the fate of political regimes. The Greek city failed partly because it did not know the Christian principle, partly because its own principle was too simple to admit of sufficient development and diversity in society. In contrast, the modern state rests on the Protestant Christian religion and on an economically and socially differentiated society. It is only in the Christian religion that the principle of the individual's infinite worth makes its appearance.

But in order for the Christian principle to be realized in the world by means of the rational state, another spiritual revolution was required, the Reformation. It is only in the Protestant religion that Christian freedom is actualized and effects its reconciliation with the world and the state. The discovery of Christian inwardness engenders a series of oppositions: between the conscience and the world, the other world and this one, piety (which commands vows of chastity, poverty, and obedience) and terrestrial morality (which recommends marriage, work, and reasonable freedom), the clergy and the laity, the church and the state. In the Lutheran religion, however, "the reconciliation leads to the consciousness of the temporal world's capacity to contain the truth within itself." Marriage, work, industriousness, the crafts acquire a moral value. Above all, blind obedience is eliminated. In Protestantism there is no class of priests, but a universal priesthood; the individual conscience has the right to judge. This is eventually transformed into the right of the individual reason to judge. Thus the principle peculiar to Protestantism is that of the free mind: "that is the essential content of the Reformation; man decides by himself to be free." And in this way the rational state can be constituted, by leading subjective freedom to universality. But this is possible only because within religion itself truth resides henceforward in the subject as such to the exclusion of all external authority. There is no longer any difference between priests and laymen; the content of the truth is no longer exclusively reserved to a caste. "It is rather the heart, the sensitive spirituality of man, which can and ought to take possession of the truth, and this subjectivity is that of *all men*. Each must accomplish the work of reconciliation within himself." [21] This reconciliation, by abolishing the difference between the two worlds, leads to the result that, in a sense, religion is done away with while being fulfilled: Protestantism signifies both the Christianization of the *saeculum* and the secularization of Christianity. The modern state is Christian and Protestant to the extent that its principle has its source in religion. But, since that principle is nothing other than that of rational universality, it is accessible to all men as such, and the state which expresses it is secular. At all events, this state is inconceivable so long as the Reformation has not taught freedom to the peoples. If, in spite of Napoleon's activity, the modern principles have failed in the Latin countries, the reason is the Catholicism of those countries. Subjection to religion brings with it political servitude.

The other fundamental (which is, however, connected with the first) for the constitution of the rational state is economic and social differentiation founded on the liberation of individual wants and needs. The multiplication of individual circumstances and needs, competition, division of labor, make a regime founded simply on the wisdom and virtue of the rulers impossible. They make necessary the passage to the universality of law which characterizes the modern state. The rational state is far from being founded on a society without class or directed to homogeneity; rather, Hegel believes that the differences of class and wealth are not only inevitable but indispensable to the effectiveness of individual freedom and the activity of the state. There is, according to him, not yet a true state in North America because of the absence of economic and social tension.[22]

The modern state is characterized by its rational laws, but their introduction depends upon historical and social conditions in the absence of which those laws would be fragile or even pernicious. Hence Hegel exhibits a very prudent reserve in proposing concrete application of the universal principles. The manners or habits of the people must be prepared (this is the source of the importance of religion), and the transition to rationality must be made prudently in order to avoid a revolution. This is the task of governmental power, which must have a strong authority for the purpose. In his last article, devoted to the English Reform Bill of 1830 (aimed at doing away with the rotten boroughs and increasing the rationality of the English electoral system, thus promoting democratization), Hegel agrees with the theoretical inspiration of the project, which attempts to introduce in England the universal principles long since victorious on the continent, and he delivers a violent criticism of the political and social arbitrariness reigning in England as well as of its law, which is merely positive and reflects no thought. But, at the same time, Hegel criticizes the bill itself no less carefully and concurs in most of the fears of its adversaries. Although the article does not come to a conclusion, it leaves the impression that considerations of prudence led the author to decide against the Reform Bill in spite of his agreement with it in principle. The reason is that, besides the absence of a rational law, England's other great defect is the absence of a strong governmental power, the monarchy being weak and the aristocracy incompetent.

It was the action of the princes, aided by the civil servants, which permitted the introduction of rational principles in Prussia without the convulsions caused in France by the abstract spirit. In the absence of guidance and control by the firm hand of the government, in the absence of the preparation of a directing class founded on competence rather than money, tradition, or demagogy, the evolution runs the risk of being precipitate and engendering anarchy. The Prussian state is, for Hegel, the model most akin to the rational state because it represents, thanks both to the Protestant religion and the authority of the monarchy, a synthesis between the revolutionary exigencies of principles and the traditional exigencies of organization. The establishment of the modern state, then, requires three elements: rational laws, government, and sentiment or morals. Plato, according to Hegel, based his teaching on the second and third only, and neglected the first. The doctrinaire revolutionaries and liberals, on the other hand, recognize only rational laws, forgetting the importance of the government and the citizens' state of mind. The examples of France and England show, each in its own way, the dangers of the absence of a real government, just as the example of the Catholic countries, where the rational constitution is impossible, shows the political importance of religion and morals as bases for the individuals' "culture" (*Bildung*), their education to the universal, and their training as citizens of a free state.

The state is, in a sense, nothing less than the crown and the foundation of this labor of morals that raises the particular to the universal, teaching the individual to fulfill himself in giving himself to a whole. The stages of this education, or the moments of the concrete moral spirit (*Sittlichkeit*), are the family, civil society, and the state. We shall now discern the double movement already mentioned, the process by which the modern state fulfills that synthesis which is the result of the subordinate moments, founded on particularity, and of rational necessity, founded on the universal concept.

Both the family and the civil society are distinct from the state, that is, opposed to it, as particular to universal. But both have something in common with it, hence something by which they contribute to moral education in opening the individual to the universal. The family has a substantial unity: it constitutes a whole founded on the confidence of its members, an end in itself in which the individual is conscious of having his reality. It is thus the image of the state, with this difference: the unity that prevails in it is natural, immediate, felt, rather than thought or accepted rationally. Civil society, on the other hand, is an association of independent members in which the private person, as a totality of wants, is the first principle. Civil society thus represents the moment of separation and difference in which concrete morality (*Sittlichkeit*) seems to be dissolved in favor of particularity and egoism. But, at the same time, it is in civil society that thought makes its appearance in a form which is still abstract, that of understanding and formal universality. Although it represents the moment of particularity par excellence, the universal is present in it in several ways. In the first place, the reciprocal relations of individuals create a system of mutual dependence which produces a formal universality, one which is external and not willed by the individuals: the particular person, the first principle of civil society, "is essentially so related to other particular persons that each establishes himself and finds satisfaction by means of the others, and at the same time purely and simply by means of the form of universality, the second principle here." [23]

Political economy, a creation of modern times and a consequence of the liberation of individual needs, is precisely the science of this reciprocal dependency through which each, while following his particular interests, unwittingly obeys general laws. In the meantime, as a result of his relations with others, the individual, his needs, and his work undergo profound adaptation. Civil society engenders new needs which are created by it and are not natural. The necessity of orienting oneself according to others in a daily routine and in manners (clothing styles, hours of meals, and so on) raises the natural individuality of the members of civil society to the formal universality of culture. It is still a universality unconsciously obtained, but one which already transforms individuality itself. Beyond this, in civil society the universal has a direct presence, free and conscious, in the form of man's necessity to have re-

course to law and administration. The property right, engendered by
the system of needs and their reciprocal recognition, is itself recognized
in its universality in so far as authority assures its protection. It is the
sphere of the relative itself, culture, which gives birth to right.

Right means universality, willed and recognized as such; it is the
ground of the only valid equality. "It is part of culture, of thought as
consciousness of the individual in the form of universality, that I am
apprehended as a *universal* person in which all are identical. A man
counts because he is a man, not because he is Jewish, Catholic, Protestant, German, Italian, etc." [24] But this universality continues to have
the character of merely abstract right. The actualization of its unity
with the whole realm of the particular is the mission of the administration which insures that "first, . . . undisturbed safety of person and
property be attained; and secondly, that the securing of every single
person's livelihood and welfare be treated and actualized as a right
. . . ." [25] Administrative foresight, *i.e.,* the action of the state, protects the
universality in civil society's particularity in the form of external order
and of institutions which maintain and support the mass of ends and
interests in it. Hegel wishes to assure a balance between the freedom of
industry and commerce and the necessity of foresight and direction by
the state as a whole. Although the will and the interest of individuals
are the springs of action of civil society and the function of the state is
simply to "bring it back to the universal. . . . to diminish the danger of
upheavals arising from clashing interests and to abbreviate the period
in which their tension should be eased through the working of a necessity of which they themselves know nothing," [26] it is nevertheless still
the case that the principle of their organization is the opposite of liberal.
"Public social conditions are on the contrary to be regarded as all the
more perfect the less (in comparison with what is arranged publicly)
is left for an individual to do by himself as his private inclination
directs." [27]

But, within the system of needs itself, there is an aspect through
which the individual is connected to the universal in an immediate way
and acquires a definite reality. This is in the division of classes or "general groups" (*Stände*). If the family is the first basis of the state, the
Stände are the second. There are three classes, and their division is
dialectic: the agricultural class, called substantial or immediate; the
industrial class, called reflective or formal; and the class of civil servants,
called the universal class. The agricultural class is the class of "security,
consolidation, lasting satisfaction of needs" and these are "nothing but
forms of universality. . . ." It has an immediate concrete morality resting
on the family and good faith. [28] And "the universal class has in its very

definition the universal for itself as goal, as ground, as end of its activity." [29] The civil servants are by nature oriented to the state and find in its service their *raison d'être* and their satisfaction.

Hence only the intermediary class, the industrial class, is essentially oriented to the particular. This is why it is enslaved to harshness, insecurity, the struggle of needs, their indefinite multiplication and the indefinite division of labor, and the contradiction of poverty and wealth. For this reason it requires the intervention of the state. On the other hand, since "for its means of subsistence it is thrown back on work, reflection and intelligence," [30] it is essentially this class which gives the individual culture, refinement, and intellectual formation. The individual in this class is awakened to freedom by being awakened to reflection. Freedom is born in the cities, while the country is traditionally more submissive because more passive. Above all, even in this class, particularity is led to take the universal as its goal: *Sittlichkeit* is thus reintegrated in civil society. To reintegrate it is the mission of the *corporation* (in the sense of guild rather than joint-stock, limited liability business firm), which limits the contradictions in civil society by making sure that there is a common ground for poverty and wealth, employees and employers, by giving a rational consecration to the diversity and rivalry of talents and aptitudes, by protecting individuals against particular accidents, in short, by surmounting the isolation and harshness of civil life in playing the role of a second family. The corporation introduces objective morality into civil society by means of the sentiments of professional honor, for which it provides a basis, and probity, which is truly recognized and honored in it. Thus, the corporation's role is central, for in modern society probity and professional honor are the only really living forms of virtue.

Since virtue in this case merely represents the individual's adaptation to the necessities of the situation in which he happens to find himself, it can only be called probity. Virtue itself, in the sense of subjective moral reflection or in the sense of virtue's determining a particular individual character, has a place in the daily life of modern societies founded on systematization and objective universality, only in extraordinary circumstances and conflicts of duties. In primitive and ancient states, heroic virtue had its place because there was room for the action of exceptional individuals. Today, once the modern state has been constituted, the rational system replaces them. What remains of virtue in society as such is the sanctity of marriage and professional honor. That is why "after the family, the corporation constitutes the second moral root of the state, that root which is implanted in civil society." [31] The corporation reunites within itself the moments of subjective particularity and objective universality which had previously been divided in civil society. But this work of union is merely a particular aspect of what the state sets as its goal. The sphere of civil society leads, therefore, to the state.

This movement can be understood if one reflects on the relation of *Sittlichkeit,* as it is expressed in the family and civil society, to patriotism. Family sentiment, professional honor, and probity seem in normal times to substitute themselves for political virtue and patriotism. But they lead to patriotism to the extent that the security and confidence they express are founded on the state, and those who possess these sentiments should, upon becoming conscious of this fact, take the state as their object. This conversion can be seen in the definition which Hegel gives of political sentiment or patriotism.

This sentiment is principally confidence . . . and the certitude that my particular interest and my substantial interest are preserved and maintained in the interest and the ends of another (here, the state) as a consequence of its relation to me as an individual. The result of this is that properly it is not an other for me and that in this state of consciousness I am free. . . . Under the name of patriotism, the disposition to sacrifice and extraordinary actions is understood, but it is essentially the disposition of consciousness which, in ordinary situations and circumstances, leads one to consider the collective life as the basis and the goal.[32]

In order to understand the content of this civic sentiment, we must now consider the state as a rational and necessary organization. "Civic sentiment receives its particular content from the different aspects of the state's organism. . . . This organism is the political constitution." [33]

This constitution "is rational to the extent to which the state inwardly differentiates and determines its activity in itself according to the nature of the concept," *i.e.,* in such a way "that each of the powers is in itself the totality of the constitution." [34] There must indeed be differentiation of powers, but it should be organic and not mechanical. The powers should be considered neither as entirely independent, nor as reciprocally limiting one another, nor still as mutually hostile; on the contrary, they should mutually reflect one another and be determined uniquely by the idea of the whole.

The whole forms a constitutional *monarchy* founded on a corps of professional *civil servants* and provided with certain *representative* institutions. "The completion of the state in a constitutional monarchy is the work of the modern world." The object of universal history is nothing but the history of its formation, which coincides with that of "the intimate deepening of the mind of the world." Only constitutional monarchy corresponds to the fully developed idea of the state, which has freed all its moments, and to a complicated society, which has freed the powers of particularity. For example, the modern state cannot be founded on virtue, as are republics according to Montesquieu: "in a more complicated social state, when the powers of particularity are developed and freed, the virtue of heads of state is insufficient. Another form of rational law than that which manifests itself in subjective dispositions becomes necessary if the whole is to possess the force to maintain itself and accord to the developed particular forces their positive as well as negative right." [35] Speaking generally, the classical typology—monarchy, aristocracy, democracy—was only valid for a still undifferentiated society. These forms are found again as moments in constitutional monarchy: the monarch is one, a few participate in governmental power, and the multitude in general participate in legislative power. The true differentiation is not based on a quantitative distinction, however, but on the logical nature of the concept of the state. It distinguishes:

(*a*) the power to determine and establish the universal—the Legislature.
(*b*) the power to subsume the particular spheres and individual cases under the universal—the Executive;
(*c*) the power of subjectivity as the will with the power of ultimate decision—the Crown. In the Crown, the different powers are brought together in an individual unity which is thus at once the apex and the basis of the whole, i.e. of constitutional monarchy. [36]

There must be a locus of supreme decision; the sovereignty and unity of the state should be expressed in a will which determines finally. The sovereignty of the state, as will, is personality; it should be incarnated in an individual, the monarch. Since he is "in essence characterized as this individual in abstraction from all his other characteristics," [37] he should be designated in an immediately natural way: by birth. It is only by the hereditary principle that the monarch's person, which symbolizes the unity and continuity of the state, escapes from the struggles of interest and opinion which necessarily dominate an elective empire. But the prince's action itself has a certain symbolic and arbitrary character; it is, of course, he who declares war, signs laws, names his counselors, and settles their differences. But on each occasion it is the *fiat* of decision which is incumbent on him rather than the actual task of governing, and most often the latter determines the former almost necessarily. That is why "with firmly established laws and a well defined organization of the state, what has been reserved to the sole decision of the monarch ought to be considered as slight with respect to what is substantial. It must certainly be considered great good luck that a noble monarch has fallen to the lot of a people. However, this is not of so great an importance, for the force of this state is in its reason." [38]

Who, then, represents this reason and consequently exercises what is essential in power? It is the government and, in general, the universal class of civil servants, since "the government rests on the world of the civil servants [Beamtenwelt]." [39] It is this government which both prepares and applies the sovereign's decisions. It affirms the general interest even in the pursuit of particular ends. It is "in the actions of civil servants and in their training" that "one finds the point where the laws and the decisions of government come into contact with individuals and are actually made good." [40] It is in the situation of the civil servants themselves that the state's function, the synthesis of the particular and the universal, is best realized, since it is only in the accomplishment of their duty, in their service to the state, that they find the satisfaction of their particular needs. They represent the type of man who incarnates the spirit of the regime and serves as a model to the entire community. Each member of the community can, by right, become a civil servant. The universal class is open to all the citizens; this is the democratic aspect of the rational state. But it is only open subject to an objective examination of their aptitudes and their intellectual and moral formation.

It is perhaps in this sort of examination, bearing on the sciences directly related to administrative competence as well as on intellectual training and general morality so that "a dispassionate, upright, and polite demeanour becomes customary" [41] that the most important element of the Hegelian state is to be found, that state which is justly characterized as the Beamtenstaat (bureaucracy) and is as such opposed to the aristocracies of the old order founded on nobility, to the oligarchies founded on money, and to the modern democracies founded on number, public opinion, and particular interests. In the article on the English Reform Bill, Hegel deplores the absence, in both the bill and the existing state of things, "of the conditions set in Germany, even on those who have claims of birth, fortune or great property, requisite to participation in government or affairs of state in either their general or particular branches: theoretical studies, scientific training, and practical exercises and experience." [42] In England, a man need only have a certain fortune to be able to enter Parliament, which holds the real power. The result is that the rulers are a disparate collection of individuals instead of an assemblage of men competent and devoted to the state. "It is those who know, hoi aristoi, who ought to reign and not ignorance or vanity." [43] The government of civil servants is the modern form of aristocracy. The "bureaucracy," a term which first appeared in the latter half of the eighteenth century with the beginnings of the modern state and which immediately acquired a pejorative sense, is rehabilitated in Hegel's thought. He sees in it the sytematized and rationalized form (in conformity with the spirit of modern times and the necessity of the concept of the state) of the government of the best. But, at the same time, Hegel is quite careful to avoid the reproach implicit in the pejorative sense of the term "bureaucracy": that it is a tyranny of civil servants, forming a caste, obedient to the *esprit de corps,* and constituting a state within the state. Not only does the hierarchy constitute an internal means of control against arbitrariness, but, above all, the institutions of sovereignty, from above, and the rights of the corporations, from below, keep the civil servants from taking the isolated position of an aristocracy and prevent culture and talent from becoming the means of arbitrariness and domination.

The legislative power brings into being not only the monarch and the government the moments of which we have just spoken, but also a new element, the "assemblies of the orders." The role of these latter is not precisely to legislate. They do not make any essential or definitive decisions. They give voice to the subjective freedom of individuals, to the opinions and the interests of the mass, and to civil society, to the extent that these are cut off from the government. Essentially, the assemblies mediate between the prince, the government, and the people. Thanks to this mediation, the prince's power does not seem to be isolated or, consequently, to be simple domination or willfulness; nor are the particular interests of communities, corporations, and individuals isolated from one another either. Everything is done to prevent the people, as an undifferentiated mass, from participating directly in power while giving it a relationship to the state. Thus there is no direct individual vote, which would give recognition to the existence and role of the isolated and abstract individual and would give authority to the weight of number. The individual should be represented in his concrete reality, as a man endowed with certain characteristics and interests which give him a place in the social organism. The vote is cast by orders (*Stände*). The orders in the political sense (assemblies of the orders) are founded on the orders in the social sense (classes); the economic and social groups, the groups with particular interests, must be represented as such. But here, too, there must be organs of mediation; there must, within the orders, be an element essentially oriented to the intermediary function which has been assigned to them.

This is the role of the substantial class of landed proprietors who are favored because of their stability and their great independence in relation to both the state and the uncertainties of economic life. The landed proprietors themselves sit directly in the assembly while

The second section of the Estates comprises the fluctuating element in civil society. This element can enter politics only through its deputies; the multiplicity of its members is an external reason for this, but the essential reason is the specific character of this element and its activity. Since these deputies are the deputies of civil society, it follows as a direct consequence that their appointment is made by the society as a society. That is to say, in making the appointment, society is not dispersed into atomic units, collected to perform only a single and temporary act, and kept together for a moment and no longer. On the contrary, it makes the appointment as a society, articulated into associations, communities and Corporations, which, although constituted already for other purposes, acquire in this way a connexion with politics.[44]

Thus the members of the industrial class are represented through the intermediacy of the corporations. The representatives themselves participate in the spheres of interest which they represent, and should, moreover, meet certain conditions of competence which correspond to the conditions of fortune exacted of the members of the first order. The two orders sit in two distinct assemblies; the role of the first chamber can be to conciliate the second and the government. Thus a series of intermediary bodies and mediating organs serve to set aside the specter of abstract democracy and to realize a state in which liberty coincides with organization.

To what extent do they succeed? More generally, what is the result of this enterprise of conciliation between modern abstract principles and the necessities of governmental organization, which constitutes the synthesis of the rational Hegelian state? It can be said that the institutions which we have discussed guarantee a free play of liberty, equality, and fraternity (or the universality of the human person), but within very strict limits imposed by this organization of the state. Thus there is freedom in the choice of calling, in the distribution of class membership (contrary to the rule in Plato's *Republic* where it is fixed by the government, or in the Indian caste system where it is determined by birth), and in the fact that the only demands the state makes in normal times are of money in the form of taxes. From all these points of view it is the free will which should be the intermediary through which the state obtains what it needs. As for public opinion, freedom of the press, and freedom of speech and writing in general, the situation is more ambiguous. "The formal subjective freedom of individuals consists in their having and expressing their own private judgments, opinions, and recommendations on affairs of state. This freedom is collectively manifested as what is called 'public opinion'. . . ." [45] It contains external principles of justice along with prejudices, profound tendencies of reality along with subjective and contingent particular opinion. In it truth and endless error are so immediately and closely united that the serious, or universal, element cannot be discerned by or on the basis of opinion itself.[46] It should, therefore, have the occasion to manifest itself but never to make the final judgment, since it is only justified in a general and confused way, not precisely and consciously. "Hence, to be independent of it (in science as well as in life) is the first formal condition of doing anything great or rational. Great achievement is assured, however, of subsequent recognition and grateful acceptance by public opinion, which in due course will make it one of its own prejudices." [47]

The liberty of public communication (and in particular of the press), "the satisfaction of this pressing instinct to say and have said one's opinion," is also recognized but limited because of its ambiguity. It is both the expression of the principle of the infinite freedom of critical consciousness and of the arbitrariness of subjective opinion and, ultimately, an inducement to disorder and crime. To define the freedom of the press as the freedom to say and write what one pleases belongs to "the ignorant barbarousness and superficiality of representation." [48] But the indeterminateness of the matter and the form in question (Where does opinion end and infraction begin?) makes the law which limits it always imprecise; the judgment against it always appears subjective. This subjectivity and contingency in repression, which are by nature inevitable, are still indispensable. Hegel nevertheless pleads for indulgence to the extent that the state is sufficiently healthy and strong to be able to bear the expression of irresponsible opinions because they are treated with contempt. But even here it is "those who know" who are judges of the extent to which public opinion, as it is expressed in the assemblies, should or should not be followed and freedom of expression, as it is found in the press and in speech, is helpful or dangerous and should be encouraged, ignored, or repressed.

In the same way *equality* is recognized, but only as abstract equality of persons before the law. It is politically and socially expressed in the possibility of each man's becoming a member of the universal and directing class. But equality must give way to the primacy of differentiation and articulation. There is no social equality. The equalization of fortunes is a dream produced by the abstract mind. The society based on the modern economy encourages social inequalities more significant than had been known previously, and the rational state presupposes great differentiation. From the political point of view, the power of number is carefully avoided. The viewpoint of the enlightened minority ought to win out over that of the mass (*hoi polloi*) which does not know what it wants. Finally, the universality of the human person is recognized, but only to the extent that it does not bring political cosmopolitanism with it. Just as the equality of persons does not signify a homogeneous state, so also the universality of human nature does not signify the universality of the state, which always remains a particular sovereign totality excluding, by its very individuality, other sovereignties. There is, indeed, the creation of a sort of world society from an economic point of view, but it does not do away with this essential individuality of states. Speaking generally, the Hegelian synthesis brings us back to the opposition between society and the state which was its point of departure. It is a largely liberal and decentralized society, but more from an economic and social than a political point of view. To make political decisions which concern the state, one must adapt oneself to its organization.

But it is in the relation between domestic and foreign policy, in the last analysis, between peace and war, that the problem of the relation between society and state, between the particular spheres and the universal good, is posed in all its intensity and breadth. From the state's point of view there is a community between war and peace. The state affirms itself through opposition. The sovereignty which is directed within brings with it a sovereignty directed outwards; in so far as the state is above all constituted by its independence and individuality, it necessarily comprises a negative and exclusive aspect which opposes it to other autonomous individualities. The state, therefore, cannot rightfully affirm its internal authority without thereby affirming its external independence. There is not only a necessary relation but a proportional relation: the more a country is unified within under the authority of the state, the more it is able to make its independence respected from without. ". . . peoples unwilling or afraid to tolerate sovereignty at home have been subjugated from abroad, and they have struggled for their independence with the less glory and success the less they have been able previously to organize the powers of the state in home affairs." Reciprocally, "successful wars prevent internal disturbances and consolidate the state's internal power." [49]

Only a great danger or a great external undertaking permits the achievement of the sacred union of the state by silencing divisions and particular interests. Thus it becomes evident that it is in and by war that the state best reveals itself and best fulfills its function. Normal times are characterized by the free activity of the particular spheres. Each individual lives for his family and his calling. The totality intrudes only indirectly in the form of tax levies, the sole requirement exacted by the state. There is a definite predominance of society, particularity, and diversity. On the other hand, it is crisis and especially war which bring the particular spheres together in the unity of the state; it is in crises that the true nature of the state and patriotism is seen affirming itself by exacting and obtaining from the individual the sacrifice of what in times of peace seemed to constitute the essence of his existence: his family, his property, his opinions, his life. Thus war, by showing the primacy of the state over civil society and the individual in its right to demand the supreme sacrifice in order to maintain independence, refutes the liberal contractual theories of the state proposed by Hobbes, Locke, or political economy. "An entirely distorted account of the demand for this sacrifice results from regarding the state as a mere civil society and from regarding its final end as only the security of individual life and property. This security cannot possibly be obtained by the sacrifice of what is to be secured—on the contrary." [50] And, what is more, "in peace civil life continually expands; all its departments wall themselves in, and in the long run men stagnate. Their idiosyncrasies become continually more fixed and ossified." [51]

Thus, although war brings with it insecurity of property and existence, it is a healthy insecurity, connected with life and movement. Insecurity and death are necessary naturally, but in the state they become moral in being freely chosen. Mortality becomes something willed, and the negativity at its root becomes that which constitutes the moral being in its essence.

War is the state of affairs which deals in earnest with the vanity of temporal goods and concerns. . . . War has the higher significance that by its agency . . . "the [moral] health of peoples is preserved in their indifference to the stabilization of finite institutions; just as the blowing of the winds preserves the sea from the foulness which would be the result of a prolonged calm, so also corruption in nations would be the product of prolonged, let alone 'perpetual' peace." [52]

Criticizing the Kantian idea of perpetual peace insured by an association of states, Hegel remarks that "even if a number of states make themselves into a family, this group as an individual must engender an opposite and create an enemy," [53] so true is it that true politics is foreign politics and that the latter is guided by the possibility of war.

As a result, international law is extremely precarious; it is *de facto* and even *de jure* incompetent to handle the possibility and the reality of war. "International law is the result of the relations between independent states. Its content has the form of the 'ought to be,' because its realization depends upon different sovereign wills." [54] Of course, states, like individuals, exist only to the extent to which they recognize one another; this leads to the possibility of contracts and treaties which ought to be respected. "But since the sovereignty of a state is the principle of its relations to others, states are to that extent in a state of nature in relation to each other. Their rights are actualized only in their particular wills and not in a universal will with constitutional powers over them." [55] When these particular wills cannot find a ground for agreement, their conflicts can be settled only by war. International law cannot prevent war by settling the conflicts, for there is no universal authority over the states imposing itself upon them; a league of the Kantian sort presupposes the adherence and obedience of the states, which are always contingent. Nor can international law distinguish between just and unjust wars according to the violation of treaties. For every state, its particular good is the supreme law; in the name of this good it can call into question all the engagements it has made whenever they no longer correspond to its interest. The conflict between morality and politics is resolved by the concrete existence of the state and not by the abstract demands of a universal justice. But to the extent to which the good of the state is the supreme law, war remains the supreme recourse by which this law is necessarily expressed.

However, the explanation based on the plurality of independent states does not exhaust the Hegelian theory of war any more than its justification by human negativity does ". . . real wars have need of still another justification. . . ." [56] This justification comes to them from their historic mission. During history, wars and revolutions are the instruments of the universal spirit. The rise of the people which bears the Idea and the diffusion of the principle in which the universal Spirit is incarnated are effectuated by wars. But the place which Hegel gives to this justification of wars by their historical role raises a difficult problem. If the sense of war is to be found primarily in the development and diffusion of civilization, what happens once this development and diffusion have been definitively realized? Politically, is it not the case that the end of history is defined by the disappearance of wars and violent revolutions? There would seem to be a tension, if not an opposition, between the two Hegelian ideas of the necessity of war and the end of history.

Both appear to be indispensable to the construction of the rational state. Without war the state would tend to be subordinated to society, the universal to the particular, and the whole moral and political life drawn from the classics which Hegel wants to reconstruct on the foundations of modernity—courage, patriotism, civic-mindedness—would collapse. The opposition of rich and poor and the multiplicity of states would seem to guarantee the permanence of crises and wars. But could they not give a new shape to things? Above all, in a world which would continue to be dominated by oppositions, would the end of history by the solution of all contradictions still make sense? On the other hand, without the end of history and without a total reconciliation, the whole Hegelian construction of the state would lose its definitive and necessary character. As we have seen, political philosophy can coincide with the philosophy of history because the final state replaces the best regime. Both Hegel's description of the historical development and that of the rational state imply that the final state represents a synthesis which reconciles all the human possibilities and leaves no room for the incompleteness and the dissatisfaction which would produce a further development of universal history.

Hegel's texts on this question of the end of history are remarkably ambiguous. On the one hand, the sun has set; the long day of the mind is ending; humanity has reached its old age which is also its flowering; history is finished because mind has found itself by knowing itself; liberty is realized in the coincidence of its form and its content.[57] On the other hand, Hegel speaks of the problems that history will have to resolve in the time to come; he cites America as "the land of the future where the burden of world history will reveal itself, perhaps in the antagonism between North and South America" [58]; he sees in Russia "a primitive solidity" which "may bear in itself an enormous possibility of development out of its intensive nature." [59] It is only by finding a solution to these apparent contradictions concerning the problem of the end of history itself that one can decide about its relation to the problem of war.

The way to a possible solution seems indicated by the texts in which Hegel distinguishes between the historical principles and their translation into reality, between their victory as such and their manifest victory. It is indeed concrete freedom which is the final principle; it is indeed the Reformation which is its definitive instrument; Europe is the terrain where universal history, begun in Asia, is completed. With regard to the Reformation Hegel writes: "Here the new, the last standard around which the peoples rally, the banner of the free mind, is unfurled. . . . This is the banner under which we serve and which we bear. Since then and up to our own days, time has had no other work to accomplish than to inform the world with this principle. . . ." [60] But this introduction of the principle in the world is not completed, even though the principle is realized and the present world is the world of completion which has no further need of anything from without. The revolutions henceforward take place within.

The Christian world is the world of completion. The principle has been realized and thereby the end of days has come. The Idea can no longer see anything in Christianity which is unsatisfied. . . . Thus the Christian world has nothing external to it in an absolute sense but only relatively; it is an external which is, in itself, already overcome and which only needs to be shown that it has been overcome.[61]

Thus history is finished in the sense that the final principle has made its appearance. The world is virtually European or Western just as it is, in principle, Christian and Protestant. But just as there are still Catholic or non-Christian states, this spiritual victory of western Europe remains to be translated into the political reality. We have seen that, to the extent to which the Reformation represented the Christianization of the world, it also represented the secularization of Christianity. The universalization of the principle in a certain sense does away with the principle in realizing it. This is politically expressed by the fact that the true state should be founded on the Protestant religion but that citizenship in it should be open to Catholics, Jews, and others. Protestantism is the basis of the rational state and ceases to be its basis. In the same way, the Europeanization or Westernization of the world will signify the loss of western Europe's supremacy, or at least of its uniqueness as the privileged domain of the universal spirit. Hegel can, therefore, conceive that, within a world become definitively European, the rise of non-European powers like America or non-Western powers like Russia will, to the extent to which they become Europeanized, occupy the center of the historical stage without representing an original principle or introducing a new step.

We may now return to the problem of war. Hegel makes, it seems, a fundamental distinction between the peoples which have already reached the final stage of civilization and the others. Therefore, he considers wars of civilization to be legitimate, inevitable, and indispensable; this means the conquest by the civilized nations of those which have not reached the same level of development of the state. In virtue of this principle, "it is the necessary fate of the Asiatic empires to be submitted to the Europeans, and China too will some day have to adjust itself to this fate." [62] On the other hand, the fully developed states recognize each other as legitimate. They constitute a federation of states or at least a family within which the kinship or the community of manners makes possible a juridical tie that subsists during wars and that humanizes and limits them. What is more, this limitation, this transformation, ends with the withering away of war itself which, among European states, is no longer feasible. In his *Aesthetics* Hegel, with respect to the future of the epic, says:

If one wishes to get an idea of what future epics might be like compared to those of the past, one only needs to imagine living and universal American rationalism triumphing over imprisonment in an infinite process of bounding and particularization. In Europe today each people is limited by all the others and cannot alone undertake any war against the European peoples. If one wants to escape from Europe, it can only be in the direction of America.[63]

But, if Europe is the future of America, if America in its turn must come to know the rational organization of the developed state, then it too will go beyond the age of youth, of "nascent poetry," of heroism, and of war which is the age of epic. America, too, will come to "the form of general principles, duties, and laws, which are valid in themselves even without the living subjective particularity of individuals." It will go from epic poetry in which "the free individuality of the figures is given free rein," to "the simple rational prose of an ordered domestic and civil life." In short, the final state ought to conform to "a reality appropriate to prose" [64] in which abstract principles flower in the place of individual discovery, firearms in the place of heroes, the novel in the place of the epic. Europe in Hegel's time is the example of such a society. Like the epic, war in principle belongs to the past.

This, then, is the solution to which Hegel leads: war is indispensable to the rational state to the extent to which the state is distinguished from civil society. But the very realization of the fully developed state brings with it the withering away of war. Both indispensable and contrary to the developed state, it only subsists because of the existence of other states which are not yet developed. It is thanks to their relationship with the outside, with those peoples they do not recognize as states and which are not yet rationally organized and historically represent the past, that the developed modern states, which, like those nations of western Europe, can no longer fight among themselves, are able to insure their own unity and the political virtue of their citizens.

Such a solution obviously raises a great number of questions which Hegel does not answer, at least explicitly. In the first place, is it not essentially provisional? Is there in the peoples not yet converted to the rational state an "uncivilizable residue" which would make them the providential and permanent adversaries which the rational state needs? Would the Westernization of the world, the translation of the principle in reality, resemble that infinite progress which Hegel criticized in Kant? If, on the contrary, this process must be brought to its end, if the world, like Europe, must constitute "a prosaically organized society," will it not find an adversary, if necessary by forming one within itself, as Hegel insists would be the case for the society projected by Kant? Will war be reborn from the simple fact of the plurality of states and the absence of a sovereign authority? Or does this situation point toward the birth of a universal state? Or, finally, is the definitive situation that of a plurality of states among which war will have lost all normal and legitimate sense due to the reciprocal recognition of the similitude of their ways of life and manners and their community of principle, but among which it will always remain possible due to the contingency of their relations? In this last case, would not a war which was not an opposition of principles, which no longer represented historical progress, which no longer had this "other justification" which real wars need, a war which, in the extreme case, was only born of accident and, in any case, was the result of a contingency unredeemed by the necessity of history, a war contrary to the universal constitutive principle of the states which waged it, also lose the politically and morally educative function which it alone could fulfill? Even if the possibility of war continued to exist, would not civil society tend more and more to gain the advantage over the state? In short would not that decadence, that *Versumpfen des Menschen* which Hegel attributes to pacific civil society, continue and reach its end? Hegel refuses to answer; he refuses to make predictions. History has only to do with the past, and, as for philosophy, "the owl of Minerva flies only at dusk."[65]

Perhaps it is possible to say that, if Hegel wanted to make the synthesis of ancients and moderns, of pagan master and Christian slave, of ancient warrior and modern worker, of the *polis* founded on the devotion of the citizens and the society founded on the satisfaction of private persons, he ended up less with a true synthesis than with a tension between two poles or a precarious balance. It is perhaps possible to go even further and say that the balance reached tends, in the last analysis, in one direction. Taking the modern revolution and the emancipation of the passions as given, Hegel wanted on these bases to restore the political organization and the human excellence which he blames the moderns for endangering. But if it is true that his "state of civil servants" constitutes the formula which most rationally conforms to the essence of the modern state and the one which is most feasible, it is perhaps no less true to say that the reconciliation of ancients and moderns, as Hegel elaborates it in this formula and in his philosophy of history, represents in its essential elements a decisive consecration of modernity.

NOTES

1. G. W. F. Hegel, *Philosophy of Right,* trans. T. M. Knox (Oxford: Clarendon, 1942), Preface, p. 11. Unless otherwise noted, citations refer to this translation.

2. G. W. F. Hegel, *Lectures on the Philosophy of History,* trans. J. Sibree (New York: Dover, 1956), Introduction, p. 52. All citations refer to this translation.

3. *Philosophy of Right,* par. 153 (trans. P.H. and A.B.).

4. *Ibid.,* Preface, p. 12. Reprinted by permission of the Clarendon Press, Oxford.

5. *Phenomenology of Mind,* ed. Hoffmeister ("Philosophisches Bibliothek" [Hamburg: F. Meiner, 1952]), chap. vi, B, a, p. 355 (trans. P.H. and A.B.).

6. *Philosophy of Right,* Preface, p. 6; cf. par. 275, pp. 174–75; *Philosophy of History,* Introduction, p. 33.

7. *Encyclopedia of Philosophic Sciences* ("Philosophisches Bibliothek" [Hamburg: F. Meiner, 1959]), par. 433, p. 352 (trans. P.H. and A.B.).

8. *Philosophy of Mind,* ed. Hoffmeister ("Philosophisches Bibliothek" [Hamburg: F. Meiner]), chap. iv, sec. A, p. 149 (trans. P.H. and A.B.).

9. *Philosophy of Right,* par. 261, addition (trans. P.H. and A.B.).

10. *Ibid.,* p. 161.

11. *Ibid.,* par. 124, p. 84.

12. *Philosophy of History,* p. 253.

13. *Philosophy of Right,* Preface, p. 10.

14. *Ibid.,* par. 357, pp. 221–22.

15. *Ibid.,* par. 5, addition, p. 228.

16. *Philosophy of History,* p. 450.

17. *Philosophy of Right,* par. 301, p. 196.

18. *Philosophy of History,* p. 452.

19. *Philosophy of Right,* par. 308, p. 200.

20. *Philosophy of History,* p. 18.

21. *Ibid.,* part IV, sec. III, chap. i, p. 416.

22. *Ibid.,* Introduction, p. 85.

23. *Philosophy of Right,* par. 182, pp. 122–23.

24. *Ibid.,* par. 209 (trans. P.H. and A.B.).

25. *Ibid.,* par. 230, p. 146.

26. *Ibid.,* par. 236, pp. 147–48.

27. *Ibid.,* par. 242, p. 149.

28. *Ibid.,* par. 203, p. 131.

29. *Ibid.,* par. 250 (trans. P.H. and A.B.).

30. *Ibid.,* par. 204 (trans. P.H. and A.B.).

31. *Ibid.,* par. 255 (trans. P.H. and A.B.).

32. *Ibid.,* par. 268 (trans. P.H. and A.B.).

33. *Ibid.,* par. 269 (trans. P.H. and A.B.).

34. *Ibid.,* par. 272 (trans. P.H. and A.B.).

35. *Ibid.,* par. 273 (trans. P.H. and A.B.).

36. *Ibid.,* p. 176.

37. *Ibid.,* par. 280 (trans. P.H. and A.B.).

38. *Philosophy of History,* part IV, sec. III, chap. iii, p. 456.

39. *Ibid.*

40. *Philosophy of Right,* par. 295 (trans. P.H. and A.B.).

41. *Ibid.,* par. 296, p. 193.

42. "On the English Reform Bill," in *Werke,* ed. G. Lasson (Leipzig: Meiner, 1921 ff.), VII, 304 (trans. P.H. and A.B.).

43. *Philosophy of History,* p. 456.

44. *Philosophy of Right,* par. 308, p. 200.

45. *Ibid.,* par. 316, p. 204.

46. *Ibid.,* par. 317, p. 205.

47. *Ibid.,* par. 318 (trans. P.H. and A.B.).

48. *Ibid.,* par. 319 (trans. P.H. and A.B.).

49. *Ibid.,* par. 324, p. 209.

50. *Ibid.*

51. *Ibid.,* addition, p. 295.

52. *Ibid.,* p. 210.

53. *Ibid.,* addition, p. 295.

54. *Ibid.,* par. 330 (trans. P.H. and A.B.).

55. *Ibid.,* par. 333, p. 213.

56. *Ibid.,* par. 324 (trans. P.H. and A.B.).

57. *Philosophy of History,* Introduction, pp. 78 and 109.

58. *Ibid.,* p. 86.

59. Letter to Baron von Uexküll, *Briefe von und an Hegel,* ed. Hoffmeister ("Philosophisches Bibliothek"

[Hamburg: F. Meiner, 1952]), II, 298, No. 406 (trans. P.H. and A.B.).

60. *Philosophy of History,* part IV, sec. III, chap. i, p. 416.

61. *Ibid.,* p. 342.

62. *Ibid.,* part I, sec. II, p. 142.

63. *Aesthetics,* in *Hegels Sämtliche Werke,* ed. H. Glockner (Stuttgart: F. Frommann, 1927–41), III "System of Individual Arts," 3, A, a *Das Epische Allgemeine Weltzustand;* vol. III, pp. 354–55 (trans. P.H. and A.B.).

64. *Aesthetics,* p. 341 and c *Das Epos als Einheitsvolle Totalität,* p. 395 (trans. P.H. and A.B.).

65. *Philosophy of Right,* Preface (trans. P.H. and A.B.).

READINGS

A. Hegel, Georg W. F. *Philosophy of Right.* Trans. T. M. Knox. Oxford: Clarendon, 1942. Preface; Third Part.

Hegel, Georg W. F. *Philosophy of History.* Trans. J. Sibree. New York: Dover, 1956. Introduction; part II: "The Greek World"; part III, chap. ii: "Christianity"; part IV, sec. III, chap. i: "Reformation"; chap. iii: "Enlightenment and Revolution."

Hegel, Georg W. F. *Phenomenology of Mind.* Chap. iv, sec. A: "The Master and the Slave."

B. Hegel, Georg W. F. *Philosophy of Right.*

Hegel, Georg W. F. *Philosophy of History.*

Hegel, Georg W. F. "On the English Reform Bill" and "On the German Constitution," excerpts in C. J. Friedrich, ed., *The Philosophy of Hegel.* New York: Modern Library, 1953.

ALEXIS DE TOCQUEVILLE

1805–1859

The publication in 1835 of the first part of *Democracy in America* established Alexis de Tocqueville as one of the foremost analysts of the problem of democracy. Tocqueville was the first writer of modern times to undertake a comprehensive investigation of the way in which the democratic principle, equality, functions as a first cause, shaping or affecting every aspect of life within society.

Tocqueville's approach to the study of political things appears as a departure from the method of those political writers of the seventeenth and eighteenth centuries who began their inquiries with the study of man simply, irrespective of his citizenship in a particular regime. For Tocqueville, the study of politics begins with an inquiry into social condition.

Social condition is commonly the result of circumstances, sometimes of laws, oftener still of these two causes united; but when once established, it may justly be considered as itself the source of almost all the laws, the usages, and the ideas which regulate the conduct of nations; whatever it does not produce, it modifies.[1]

Tocqueville's *Democracy* is explicitly devoted to an exposition of the way in which a particular social condition, a condition of equality, has made itself felt in the political institutions of the nation, and in the customs, manners, and intellectual habits of the citizens. Social condition is the cause of a regime having its own particular characteristics. This is not to say that social condition explains everything about a society, for antecedent customs and geographical factors, among others, also play a role in shaping the regime. But in no enduring case will these secondary factors conceal or frustrate the operation of the fundamental moving principle. Social condition forms opinions, modifies passions and feelings, determines the goals pursued, the type of man admired, the language in use, and, ultimately, the character of the men it encompasses.

That social condition which is the moving principle of democratic regimes is the condition of equality. For Tocqueville, this is the "fundamental fact from which all others seem to be derived." [2] Tocqueville's political thought originates with the recognition and acceptance of the inevitable triumph of the principle of equality. Not only has the course of the last eight hundred years been purposive (leading to the triumph of equality), but, also, in analyzing the record of man's deeds, Tocqueville sees an expression of divine will. The development of equality of conditions is a providential fact.

If the men of our time should be convinced, by attentive observation and sincere reflection, that the gradual and progressive development of social equality is at once the past and the future of their history, this discovery alone would confer upon the change the sacred character of a divine decree. To attempt to check democracy would be in that case to resist the will of God; and the nations would then be constrained to make the best of the social lot awarded to them by Providence.[3]

It is evident from these remarks that Tocqueville does not regard man as constrained within the grip of a complete determinism. "Providence," he tells us, "has not created mankind entirely independent or entirely free. It is true that around every man a fatal circle is traced beyond which he cannot pass; but within the wide verge of that circle he is powerful and free." [4] Tocqueville's work appears as an admonition to men to make the best of the lot awarded them by God—men cannot determine whether conditions will or will not be equal, but theirs is the responsibility whether equality will lead to wretchedness or to greatness, to slavery or to freedom. Indeed, it is a sobering reflection upon the providential march of history that the inevitable triumph of the democratic condition might eventuate as well in a condition of human slavery as in one of human freedom. A social condition has triumphed which man could not forestall, but it rests with man's art to grasp and to turn to advantage those potentialities of the democratic condition that are conducive to freedom. To accomplish this end, Tocqueville calls for a "new science of politics," one adequate to the novel conditions occasioned by the triumph of equality.

That equality can be understood to be the principle of democratic regimes may be seen in the language of the Declaration of Independence. "All men are created equal" is therein regarded as the primary proposition or self-evident truth; the rights of life, liberty, and the pursuit of happiness as universal rights are derivative from this fundamental truth. If all men are equal, no man has by nature a superior right to take another man's life, infringe his liberty, or determine for him his way of life. The equality in question does not extend to intellectual capacity. Tocqueville acknowledges that even with the advent of the most extreme equality of conditions the inequality of intellect will remain as one of the last irksome reminders of the old regime. But the passion for equality even where there can be none will lay to rest the practical force of the classical contention that the wise should rule. Men of democratic ages will brook no privileges, no matter what their foundation.

Tocqueville's purpose in the *Democracy* is to show men how they might be both equal and free, and by not equating democracy with any institutional form associated with it—government of the people, representative government, separation of powers—Tocqueville underscores his fear that the real driving force of democracy, the passion for equality, is compatible with tyranny as well as with liberty. Tyranny may very well coexist with what appear to be democratic institutions. Unlike some of his contemporaries who believed that the gradual development of equality went hand in hand with the final destruction of the possibility of tyranny on earth, Tocqueville understood that the democratic principle was prone, if left untutored, to a despotism never before experienced. We shall return to this theme below.

In his writings, Tocqueville turns to the American regime of the 1830's, not because it necessarily embodies the principles of the best regime, but because it marks the culmination of that historical progress toward ever increasing equality. The nature of democracy thus stands revealed in Jacksonian America; the visit to America is, for Tocqueville, a confrontation with democracy itself. In emphasizing equality of conditions rather than equality simply, Tocqueville calls attention to a state of society in which the concept of equality has become actualized. It is that state of society in which men confront each other when their equality in the abstract has been made manifest to them in equal opportunities for education, in a general levelling of wealth, in the uniform assurance of political rights. Tocqueville did not regard America, or any other society, as a state in which the principle of equality had become completely actualized, but America did approximate this ideal more closely than any other regime. Like all democratic states, it was characterized by the progressive diminution of the inequalities of the "old regime."

Equality of conditions is understood, of course, in contrast to inequality of conditions, the social state of the old regime, either of France or of feudal Europe generally. Within the *Democracy,* the characteristics of the old regime continually intrude upon the argument; it is through Tocqueville's awareness of democracy's grand and, at that time, still respectable alternative that he is able to inform and to chasten the democracy destined to be triumphant. In Tocqueville's characterization of the old regime—that standard against which he seemingly measures democracy and calls it to account—we may begin to grasp the meaning of his thought. It is as if we must say that no one can understand the democratic revolution who is insensitive to the qualities Tocqueville ascribes to an aristocratic state of society: a certain elevation of mind and scorn of worldly advantages, strong convictions and honorable devotedness, refined habits and embellished manners, the cultivation of the arts and of theoretical sciences, a love of poetry, beauty, and glory, the capacity to carry on great enterprises of enduring worth. An understanding of democratic things requires an awareness of the alternatives to democracy; this necessity is not obviated by the "march of history." With this awareness in mind we are ready to turn to Tocqueville's account of democracy.

THE CHARACTER OF THE REGIME

The characteristic feature of democratic society is its atomism. The carefully prescribed codes which governed the relations of the three classes of society in aristocratic times have been overturned. The barriers separating the classes have been toppled; property has been divided and equalized; new avenues to social, intellectual, and political achievements have been opened to all. The concern of the ruling classes for those over whom they watched like shepherds over their flocks has been replaced by virtual indifference; the social and political bonds uniting men have been severed. Men confront each other as equals, each independent, each impotent. Individuals comprising such a society have, as citizens, no natural ties to one another; each being the equal of every other, no one is obliged to do the bidding of another. A major task of modern democratic society is the construction of artificial bonds to replace the ties of the Middle Ages.

According to Tocqueville, the key to the atomistic quality of democratic ages lies in the diffusion of "individualism," a disposition to reject as authoritative all obligations or articles of faith which have not been submitted to, or have not withstood the test of, personal inquiry. Each individual becomes the center of a tiny private universe consisting of himself and his immediate circle of family and friends. Wholly absorbed in the contemplation of this universe, the individual loses sight of that greater universe, society at large. The spiritual father of this "novel idea" or disposition is Descartes, whose philosophic method supplies the example and justification for submitting to the private judgment of each man all venerable objects of belief and attachment. Equality of conditions is responsible for the ready and widespread acceptance of the new disposition; in the fulfillment of its own attempts at overturning the social restraints of the Middle Ages, democracy finds a welcome ally in the Cartesian philosophy calling into question traditional beliefs. Around the issue of individualism will be seen to cluster certain propensities which together give rise to what we may call the problem of democracy. These are the passion for well-being and material comforts, a concern for one's private welfare to the exclusion of all consideration of public affairs, and an inevitable drift toward mediocrity. They make democratic man all too prone to accept or to drift into a soft despotism securing him in these pursuits and preferences. A resolution of the problem of democracy entails finding a place within democracy for liberty, for human excellence, for the re-emergence of public virtue, and for the possibility of greatness.

When individualism is linked with equality of conditions, an insatiable thirst develops for the material comforts of this world. In a society shorn of the traditional restraints and obligations—to country, to lords, to church—men strive eagerly to gratify their immediately felt and immediately intelligible desires to improve their conditions of life. Under the old regime, the disparity of wealth and material well-being was accepted as part of the natural scheme of things; moreover, the nobility of feudal Europe had managed to satisfy its desire for material comfort in such a way as to leave it free to cultivate the higher faculties. That is, the nobility were not apprehensive that such wealth as they enjoyed would momentarily be seized from them. This salutary peace of mind had been achieved through the legitimizing effect of long-standing usage and custom. With the overthrow of the feudal system, and with the dissemination of the individualistic doctrines, the need for the amelioration of the material conditions of life is seen as the legitimate expression of the natural rights of all men.

Democracy, then, must satisfy the desire for well-being, not of a few men, but of all men, and do it in such a way as to induce men to devote some part of their energies to other pursuits and to the needs of the nation at large. The problem is soluble either if there are enough material goods to satisfy everyone, so that no one need be apprehensive of not getting his share, or if democratic man can moderate his desires. Tocqueville appears to hold two conflicting views on the likelihood of

effecting a resolution of the problem. On the one hand, he appears confident that the taste for physical gratifications will be kept within
modest bounds. Democratic man will seek out the little comforts of
life: the means of rendering existence less arduous, the purchase and
planting of a few more acres of land, the enlargement of his dwelling.
Tocqueville's reproach to the principle of equality is not that it encourages men in the pursuit of unlawful or excessive gratifications, "but that
it absorbs [men] wholly in quest of those which are allowed. By these
means a kind of virtuous materialism may ultimately be established in
the world, which would not corrupt, but enervate, the soul and noise-
lessly unbend its springs of action." [5] The sudden, dramatic, and violent
upheaval against religion, morality, and property which erupted in 1789
was but a transient reaction, characteristic only of a revolutionary period; it should not be looked upon as a permanent penchant of democratic eras. Democratic man's taste for well-being is not only compatible
with morality and public order, but may not even be satisfied without
them. It may even be combined with "a species of religious morality."
Thus, although democracy may be accompanied by the neglect of what
is highest in man, at least it will solve the problem of a modest well-
being for the greatest number. This is the virtue of democracy that
Tocqueville celebrates in his famous conclusion to the second part of
the *Democracy*.

There is, however, another and less sanguine facet of the pursuit
of material comfort. All avenues to the satisfaction of the desire for well-
being have been opened, but opened equally to all—the competition is
overpowering. However much one may have, he thinks continually of
the vast store of goods which constantly eludes him; this thought "fills
him with anxiety, fear, and regret and keeps his mind in ceaseless trepi-
dation." [6] If this is so, there can be no technological solution to the problem of well-being—the desires of men increase with what they feed
upon; there can never be enough for all.

This unexpected shift from a decent materialism to a more or less
thoroughgoing pursuit of material comforts is concomitant with the rise
of a commercial spirit—commerce is seen as the most fruitful way of
facilitating the satisfaction of the taste for well-being. Commerce readily
transforms the simple desire for modest comforts into a caricature of its
former self. It comes to be regarded as itself the noblest pursuit, and be-
guiles the faculties of the men of most competence in society. Men of
superior intellect are diverted from politics to business, from public life
to private affairs. In commerce, these men find adequate outlets for their
distinctive talents, as well as freedom from the conformity and vulgarity
of political life. In fact, these men threaten to form the nucleus of a new

aristocracy: Tocqueville warns the "friends of democracy" to be wary, "for if ever a permanent inequality of conditions and aristocracy again penetrates into the world, it may be predicted that this is the gate by which they will enter." [7]

Individualism and materialism, divisive features of democracy, are offset to a degree by a general softening of manners and the growth of a spirit of compassion or human fellow-feeling. The classes of the Middle Ages had looked upon each other as beings belonging to different species, such was the difference in their manners, pursuits, and tastes. Society had been cool, uncompromising, severe. The democratic revolution succeeds in dissolving social or political obligations while bringing to the fore natural human ties. As conditions become equal, men become cognizant of their likeness to each other; this awareness evokes feelings of genuine sympathy, and an act of the imagination suffices to enable one to experience the sufferings of another. The democratic revolution discloses the natural goodness of man; he would not needlessly hurt another. We may recognize here the parallelism between Tocqueville's "democratic" man and Rousseau's "natural" man.

There is, moreover, a link between the consequences of individualism and the growth of compassion. Contrary to what might have been expected, the freedom to rely wholly upon oneself, along with emancipation from traditional restraints, does not make democratic man altogether confident and proud. His gravity reflects the seriousness of the enterprise upon which he is engaged, but his confidence is undermined by the "anxiety, fear, and regret" which accompany his condition. Confronted as he is on all sides by those who, like himself, are restlessly striving for unattainable goods, "each citizen is habitually engaged in the contemplation of a very puny object: namely himself." [8] He has no alternative but to seek the assistance of others, something he is obliged to do the more equal social conditions become.

It might appear that compassion and self-interest could combine to serve as the foundation of a social or political bond in democratic times, thus overcoming the divisive forces of individualism and the pursuit of well-being. Yet compassion and self-interest, while not necessarily opposed, are not always compatible. Tocqueville, like Rousseau before him, suggests that compassion, although a natural instinct in man, is weakened by calculation. Inasmuch as men are not disinterested, they will consult their own self-interest before looking to the welfare of others; democracy encourages this by throwing each man upon his own resources. Democratic men will come to the aid of one another if it involves no loss or injury to themselves. For the spirit of compassion to become fully effective, society would require not only a condition of equality, but also a condition of plenty, one in which there were enough material goods for all. We have already alluded to the forces at work within democracy thwarting such a possibility.

Moreover, the spirit of compassion transcends national boundaries, and, as such, operates to weaken political ties; men become indifferent to those arbitrary usages which distinguish men as citizens. Compassion is a natural instinct tending to undermine ties which are merely conventional; for Tocqueville, political society itself has just such a conventional character. The gentleness, softening of manners, and air of humanity which characterize democratic societies are apt to be felt most strongly within the family unit rather than between citizens. "Democracy," Tocqueville tells us, "loosens social ties, but tightens natural ones; it brings kindred more closely together, while it throws citizens more apart." [9]

THE PROBLEM OF DEMOCRACY

These characteristics—materialism, mediocrity, compassion, domesticity, and isolation—arising, or gathering their strength from, equality of conditions and individualism, constitute the core of Tocqueville's teaching about democracy. A regime in which their effects were not somehow mitigated, a regime in which there would be no encouragement offered for the exercise of higher human faculties, in which society itself would seem to stand still and public virtues languish—such a regime might well cause one to call into question the goodness of the Providence that promotes it.

Nor is this all. The fundamental paradox of democracy, as Tocqueville understands it, is that equality of conditions is compatible with tyranny as well as with freedom. A species of equality, at least, can coexist with the greatest inequality. Left to its own devices, democracy is actually prone to the establishment of tyranny, whether of one over all, of the many over the few, or even of all over all. To the elaboration of this paradox we must now turn.

The ruling passion of democratic ages is love of equality. This passion is itself generated out of the prevailing social condition which, as we have seen, is the fundamental source of all the passions, ideas, and manners of society. But the love of democratic man for equality overpowers every other feeling, even that for liberty. Liberty requires effort and vigilance; it is difficult to attain, and easily lost; its excesses are apparent to all, while its benefits may easily escape detection. The advantages and pleasures of equality, on the other hand, are immediately felt and require no exertion. They are accessible to all, even to those of the meanest capacity, and, "in order to taste them, nothing is required but to live." [10] But if this is true of the pleasures of equality, its short-comings may not be evident at all except perhaps to those who have not been benumbed by its delights. Equality of conditions, then, has un-leashed a passion which will not be put down; every government of the future must acknowledge its roots in this omnipotent drive. The passion of men of democratic communities for equality is "ardent, insatiable, incessant, invincible; they call for equality in freedom, and if they cannot obtain that, they still call for equality in slavery." [11]

Love for equality may express itself in either of two forms, a "manly and lawful passion for equality" which seeks to raise all to the level of the great, or a "depraved taste for equality" which strives to reduce all to the lowest common denominator. Obviously, if the former passion for equality were to prevail, the power of the objections to de-mocracy would be appreciably reduced. But the forces at work under conditions of equality offer little hope that the manly passion for equality will triumph. Men are driven to desire goods they cannot ob-tain. Equality raises in everyone hopes for the attainment of these goods, but the competition is such that each has little likelihood of realizing his ambitions. Moreover, the race to satisfy these desires is not an equal one; the victory inevitably goes to those of superior ability. All cannot be raised to the level of the great, for differences of ability originate from God, or from nature. Democracy thus awakens a consciousness of the equal right of all to the advantages of this world, but it frustrates men in the attainment of them. This frustration breeds envy and displaces respect. Man's soul is thus constantly excited, forever battered, and hopelessly wearied in the struggle; he cannot long endure such a con-dition. He seeks a solution which will satisfy his most intense desire while relieving him of the anguish to which it gives rise. Equality thus prepares man to surrender his freedom to safeguard equality itself.

To Tocqueville, this surrender of man's liberty might be made to a despot of the time-honored description, but more than likely the char-acter of the despot would assume a form entirely novel. In fact, terms like "despotism" and "tyranny" become almost inadequate to express Tocqueville's thought, and he seeks to describe rather than name the new despotism. In a society in which all are equal, independent, and impotent, one agency alone, the state, is specially prepared to accept and to supervise the surrender of freedom. Tocqueville calls attention to the increasing centralization of governments—the growth of im-mense tutelary powers which willingly assume the burden of providing for the comfort and well-being of their citizens. Democratic men will abandon their freedom to these mighty authorities in exchange for a "soft" despotism, one which "provides for their security, foresees and supplies their necessities, facilitates their pleasures, manages their principal concerns, directs their industry," and, ultimately, "spare[s] them all the care of thinking and all the trouble of living." [12] Tocqueville foresaw that such a government was not inconsistent with popular sovereignty, or at least with the forms of popular sovereignty. The people as a whole might very well console themselves with the knowledge that they themselves had chosen their own masters. Democracy originates a new form of despotism, society tyrannizing over itself.

No statement of the problem of democracy would be complete without an account of Tocqueville's description of the tyranny of the majority, of the many over the few. Tocqueville is not unaware of the pleadings of special interest groups or of the fact that the composition of a majority in a democracy frequently fluctuates. But such fluctuation takes place within the context of a settled conviction upon certain principles which are themselves unchanging—in this sense one can speak of a permanent majority within a democracy. Moreover, the apparent homogeneity of democratic society conceals from view two ineradicable sources of heterogeneity: intellect and wealth. Intellectual capacity is distributed unequally, and Tocqueville affirms that the majority of mankind lack the capacity to arrive at rational convictions. Beyond the question of capacity, the requirements of knowledge are such that men under democratic conditions will rarely have either the time, the patience, or the interest to pursue it. Tocqueville envisages no revolutionary breakthrough in the means of education, no "profusion of easy methods and cheap science" sufficient to overcome the want of time and talent. As long as the people remain the people, *i.e.,* the many, they will be obliged to earn their bread and hence lack the leisure indispensable for the cultivation of knowledge. The many, if they acknowledge these facts at all, dispute the significance of them. For the intellectual superiority of the few, they substitute a superiority derived from considerations of quantity: "The moral authority of the majority is partly based upon the notion that there is more intelligence and wisdom in a number of men united than in a single individual, and that the number of the legislators is more important than their quality." [13] The authority of the majority is such that even the minority at last assent to this assault upon the intellect. This, Tocqueville observes, marks a new phenomenon in the history of mankind. The majority not only demand conduct that conforms but strive also to make it impossible for individuals to conceive of nonconformity. To hold an opinion on an important matter contrary to that of the majority is not merely imprudent or unavailing but even dehumanizing. "The power of the majority is so absolute and irresistible that one must give up one's rights as a citizen and almost abjure one's qualities as a man if one intends to stray from the track which it prescribes." [14] The tyranny of the majority over the minds of those who are its intellectual superiors absolutizes the disposition of democracy toward mediocrity.

The tyranny of the majority over the wealthy, the propertied few, is less clear. Tocqueville certainly tries to overcome the fear of those critics of democracy who saw in the rule of the many the inevitable destruction of all property rights; in his Preface he takes care to point out that in the most advanced democratic country in the world property rights have enjoyed greater guarantees than anywhere else. Still, Tocqueville is not sanguine that the eternal struggle between the rich and the poor has been resolved by the democratic revolution—neither have all been reduced or elevated to the same level of wealth, nor has the envy of the poor toward those in better circumstances been assuaged by whatever levelling has occurred. How secure, then, are the rights of property?

According to Tocqueville, the division between the few and the many, the rich and the poor, is a permanent feature of all societies, destined to remain despite the progressive realization of equality of conditions. This is a "fixed rule" to which all communities are subject. On the other hand, the proportion of individuals within a society making up each of the three great orders—the wealthy, those of moderate means, and the poor—may vary from one society to another. Though these proportions may change, Tocqueville rejects the idea that the wealthy or the moderately wealthy may ever constitute a majority. "Universal suffrage, therefore, in point of fact does invest the poor with the government of society." [15] Moreover, he declares that it is inescapable that the ruling class be the oppressor: "It is certain that democracy annoys one part of the community and that aristocracy oppresses another." [16] Finally, Tocqueville despairs of instructing the poor to realize that it is against their own interest to impoverish the rich. He sees, then, no reason to believe that the traditional conflict between rich and poor will cease under democratic conditions, or that the one will lack the will or the opportunity to oppress the other. Since the majority are poor, and since it is they who will be sovereign, the fears of the critics of democracy are justified after all.

Yet how are we to reconcile this with statements apparently quite to the contrary in other portions of the *Democracy*? In the second part, for example, Tocqueville declares that in democratic communities the poor, instead of comprising the great majority of a nation, as they have always done hitherto, will be comparatively few in number, their place being taken by those of the new middle classes. Not only do the middle classes now constitute the majority, but they possess property, and, in fact, are the foremost defenders of the rights of property. What, then, have the rich to fear from a majority whose passions and interests are so similar to their own?

We may suggest a link between the tyranny of the majority and the new despotism. The men who surrender to this soft, comfortable tyranny are the men of the new majority who have tasted and enjoyed the first fruit of the universal pursuit of well-being. But their desires have outrun their opportunities: frightened at the prospect of losing what they have to those more able than themselves, the majority turn to the government as the only power capable of protecting their rights and goods and of restraining the ambitions of the few. The new despotism is one form the tyranny of the majority may assume. At the expense of the few, the wealthy, it secures to the many a modest enjoyment of the good things of this life; in this sense, it is not incompatible with protection of the rights of property on a limited scale.

The Resolution of the Problem

If the problem of democracy is to be resolved, the resolution must take place on the level of democracy, that is to say, the resolution must be consonant with the principle of democracy, which is equality. Any attempt to temper democracy with principles or practices from a regime alien to it is doomed to failure; not even a despot can rule under the democratic principle without making his obeisance to equality. Thus Tocqueville warns his contemporaries that the task is not one of reconstructing aristocratic society, but of making liberty proceed out of the democratic state of society and of working out "that species of greatness and happiness" appropriate to equality of conditions.

The irony of the democratic predicament is that democracy encourages men to surrender their liberty, the one thing essential to their deliverance. If individualism is responsible for the atomism of democratic society, it is freedom which, paradoxically, can re-establish a sense of political interdependence by fostering an awareness of the dependence of each individual upon every other. What is the likelihood that liberty will issue from a democratic state of society? Tocqueville's reply discloses an essential optimism at the foundation of his political thought:

Far from finding fault with equality because it inspires a spirit of independence, I praise it primarily for that very reason. I admire it because it lodges in the very depths of each man's mind and heart that indefinable feeling, the instinctive inclination for political independence, and thus prepares the remedy for the ill which it engenders.[17]

The passion for equality at any cost is confronted by a similarly engendered passion for equality in freedom. Nevertheless, these passions are of unequal strength, as we have already seen. Moreover, the passion which induces a man to turn over to government the concern for his own welfare is augmented in its effect by the omnipresent tendencies toward centralization of government. Governments grow more powerful; individuals appear more helpless than ever. Consequently, the natural passion for freedom must be supplemented by the political art, an art which Tocqueville finds has been practiced in an exemplary way by America. The American experience suggests for the resolution of the democratic problem certain "democratic expedients," such as local self-government, the separation of church and state, a free press, indirect elections, an independent judiciary, and the encouragement of associations of all descriptions. It must be recognized that Tocqueville does not simply recommend the adoption of each and every American practice. Although he admires the federal system, for example, he argues that such a complicated mechanism is wholly unsuited to the temperament and realities of European political life. More than anything else, America provides the principles, such as the principle of self-interest rightly understood, upon which a respectable democratic order might be constructed. Before turning to consider the doctrine of self-interest, the heart of Tocqueville's resolution of the problem of democracy, we must examine some aspects of the democratic expedients we have just named.

To counteract the effects of centralization, Tocqueville acknowledges the value of local freedom at the township and community level. Within the confines of this smaller whole, each citizen receives his initial training in the use of freedom. By learning to care for and to cooperate in matters within his own purview, the citizen imbibes the rudiments of public responsibility. The township is the locus of the transformation of self-interest into patriotism, at least into a species of patriotism. According to Tocqueville, free institutions, particularly those at the local level, transform essentially selfish individuals into citizens whose first consideration is the public good. Still, the importance or perhaps the relevance Tocqueville attaches to local self-government may easily be overstated. It should be noted that he nowhere gives a simple or a comprehensive formula for the determination of the affairs which properly belong to local as distinct from national authorities. Moreover, he suggests that the more complex and civilized a nation grows, the less likely it is to establish local freedom, or to tolerate the stumbling efforts of a community with no tradition of freedom.

The jury system is another of the democratic expedients Tocqueville recommends to preserve freedom and counter the individualistic tendencies of democracy. Like local freedom, it, too, impresses upon citizens a consciousness of the needs of others. Critics have remarked that Tocqueville's expectations from this source have scarcely been fulfilled, but they have generally failed to recognize that Tocqueville pinned his hopes for its success upon the availability of a body of superior judges, and that he was aware that the quality of judges as a class would diminish in proportion to the increase in their number. It is upon the qualities of such men that Tocqueville relies in his belief that the jury system will form the judgment of the people and instill in them an awareness of the requirements of justice. Tocqueville's characteristic procedure is to attempt to discover those means by which the tastes and passions of the many may be tempered and instructed; the jury system is one such means, and, in this regard, serves as a particular instance of the general and pervasive role Tocqueville expected judges and others associated with the legal profession to play in a democracy. The training lawyers, in particular, receive gives them certain tastes for order, for legal and political forms, and for the connection of ideas—tastes which distinguish them from the multitude and give an aristocratic turn to their thinking and preferences. Their spirit tends to be conservative and antidemocratic; to the extent that they come to play a prominent role in society (as they are bound to do in a society where almost every political question is transformed sooner or later into a legal issue), they will act to restrain the impulses of the many. We may note that the role of lawyers in resolving the problem of democracy is an apparent breach of the principle that such a resolution must take place on the level of democracy, but it is, after all, only a partial breach. While lawyers are marked by aristocratic tastes and habits, they retain their fundamental tie to the people by birth and interest; thus they do not constitute a distinct class.

Of all the democratic expedients, freedom of association is the foremost. Tocqueville looked upon associations as artificial substitutes for the nobility of former ages which, in virtue of its wealth and position, served as a bulwark against the encroachments of the sovereign upon the liberties of the people. Similarly, Tocqueville argues, associations protect the rights of the minority in a democracy against the tyranny of the majority. Since each individual in a democracy is independent but also impotent, it is only by associating himself with others that he may oppose his views to those of the majority. This is one "political" function of the right of association, a right which has its origin in nature. Tocqueville attaches to the proliferation of associations a dignity which is perhaps novel in political thought. Whereas earlier writers had looked upon the encouragement of parties, factions, or associations as a divisive measure in society, Tocqueville thought it absolutely essential to the well-being of democratic society. Far from contributing to the destruction of the unity of society, associations overcome the divisive propensities of democracy: in the acts accompanying the organization and operation of an association, individuals learn the art of adapting themselves to a common purpose. But the utility of associations goes far beyond any merely political considerations. Participation in political groupings engenders a taste for, and reveals the advantages of, associations for other purposes as well—educational, scientific, commercial. According to Tocqueville, learning to associate is the prerequisite for the preservation of civilization itself: "A people among whom individuals lost the power of achieving great things single-handed, without acquiring the means of producing them by united exertions, would soon relapse into barbarism." [18] Tocqueville saw in associations a means not only of mitigating the tyranny of the majority, but also of overcoming that mediocrity to which democracy was prone.

Democracy places the responsibility for government in the hands of those who, in Tocqueville's view, "will either believe they know not wherefore, or will not know what to believe." [19] Nevertheless, a democratic regime may achieve viability if a certain enlargement of view does occur; the free institutions Tocqueville recommends are designed to facilitate this. Men are to be transformed into morally conscious citizens through the operation of these democratic expedients. Individuals will cease to think only of themselves; their capacities will be enlarged through contact with great judges; their sympathy for their fellows will grow through jury service; their minds will be broadened by participation in associations. Tocqueville thought it impossible to devise a system of institutions which would ensure good government through the actions and reactions of citizens who were wholly thoughtless or driven by base motives.

The evolution of a sense of public morality out of the spirit of extreme individualism characterizing democratic ages is the theme not only of the institutions we have been discussing but of Tocqueville's work as a whole. Men will be made citizens through the operation of the principle of self-interest rightly understood. In his Introduction to the *Democracy,* Tocqueville tells us that the poor man "has adopted the doctrine of self-interest as the rule of his actions without understanding the science that puts it to use; and his selfishness is no less blind than was formerly his devotion to others." [20] Tocqueville's call for a "new science of politics" to meet the novel conditions of equality is a call for a science which would establish the principle of self-interest on a firm foundation. Of course, it is the "poor" man who is to be taught the principles of the new science, for it is he who, as a member of the majority, will govern the new society; by the same token, the principles of the new science must be commensurate with the level of his understanding.

Whatever may be the ultimate shortcomings of the doctrine of self-interest rightly understood, Tocqueville insists it is "the best suited of all philosophical theories to the wants of the men of our time," [21] and that all moralists and educators must bend every effort to impart its principles. The possibility of motivating the many by appeals to self-sacrifice or to the inherent attractiveness of virtue vanishes with the destruction of the feudal system and, with it, of the belief in authority and of the dignity of nonmaterial ends. Under conditions of equality, private interest becomes the principal if not the only spring of human action. Private interest, Tocqueville affirms, is "the only immutable point in the human heart." [22]

Tocqueville contrasts the doctrine of self-interest rightly understood with the view that man serves his fellow creatures best in serving himself. Both views appeal, ultimately, to the self-regarding instincts of man, but the latter makes no provision for the emergence of political virtues: it would only intensify the tendency toward individualism. If men are not to withdraw entirely into their own domestic circles, if public spiritedness is not to disappear altogether, men must be taught that out of an enlightened regard for themselves they need constantly assist one another and sacrifice some portion of their time and wealth to the welfare of the state or community. Men must come to see the desirability of postponing the immediate gratification of their desires in the expectation of a more certain or greater degree of satisfaction at a later time, an expectation arising from the contribution of the common welfare to their own well-being. The foundation of the public or social order rests upon enlightened selfishness: each individual accepts the view that "man serves himself in serving his fellow creatures and that his private interest is to do good." [23] Faithful to the requirements of equality, Tocqueville appeals to the self-regarding instincts of man and strives to erect upon this basis a species of public morality and of patriotism: he would make men virtuous by teaching them that what is right is also useful.

The doctrine of self-interest is one that may be thoroughly relied upon:

The principle of self-interest rightly understood is not a lofty one, but it is clear and sure. It does not aim at mighty objects, but attains without exertion all those at which it aims. As it lies within the reach of all capacities, everyone can without difficulty learn and retain it. By its admirable conformity to human weaknesses it easily obtains great dominion; nor is that dominion precarious, since the principle checks one personal interest by another, and uses, to direct the passions, the very same instrument that excites them.[24]

This succinct statement reveals Tocqueville's fundamental agreement with the presuppositions of modern political thought; despite apparent departures, Tocqueville follows in the tradition originating with Machiavelli and continued in the natural right teaching of Hobbes. The political problem of man is solved by lowering one's standards— the doctrine of self-interest rightly understood does not aim at lofty objects. The realization of such standards as are adopted is insured through the reliance upon a doctrine within the reach of the meanest capacity, hence within the reach of all. The doctrine has its roots in what is considered to be man's most powerful passion, here, the concern for individual well-being. The success of the doctrine is still further guaranteed by the device of playing one interest against another while turning over to reason the office of insuring the satisfaction of the passions. In common with most of the typically modern political philosophers, Tocqueville strives to erect his system upon what is operative in most men most of the time and, not unexpectedly, this turns out to be what is lowest rather than what is highest in man. As in Machiavelli, we take our bearings from what men are, not from what they may become. Tocqueville is no Philistine; he is not insensitive to what is highest in man. Nevertheless, we are confronted with his acquiescence in, and encouragement of, a principle of political morality whose effect is to settle a middling standard upon mankind:

If the principle of interest rightly understood were to sway the whole moral world, extraordinary virtues would doubtless be more rare; but I think that gross depravity would then also be less common. The principle of interest rightly understood perhaps prevents men from rising far above the level of mankind, but a great number of other men, who were falling far below it,

are caught and restrained by it. Observe some few individuals, they are
lowered by it; survey mankind, they are raised.[25]

We noted earlier that the resolution of the problem of democracy
must, according to Tocqueville, take place on the level of democracy.
Tocqueville accepts equality and, with it, the individualism which is
its inevitable accompaniment. Equality undermines the deference given
to those in other ages whose responsibility it was to care for the common
good; individualism turns men away from a concern for the common
welfare. The problem of democracy is to re-create a sense of public
morality on the basis of equality and individualism. The doctrine of
self-interest rightly understood constitutes Tocqueville's attempt to resolve the problem upon this basis. To rely upon self-interest rightly
understood necessitates, of course, that self-interest be *rightly* understood. Within the context of the *Democracy,* self-interest is understood
primarily in an economic sense—it is a concern with the most immediate, tangible, material signs of a man's well-being. Out of an
enlightened regard for one's own material welfare, a good other than
an economic one will emerge: patriotism or public spiritedness is the
by-product arising from the intelligent pursuit of one's own interest.
    We have so far omitted any mention of the role of religion in
mitigating the problem of democracy. At first sight, Tocqueville's
insistence upon the indispensability of religion seems to point to a
radical deficiency in the doctrine of self-interest rightly understood.
There are certain sacrifices which individuals are called upon to make
for which they cannot reasonably expect a reward in this life; moreover, whatever ingenuity may be employed to prove that virtue is useful, there are individuals upon whom such arguments fail to make any
impression. Virtue, then, must have an otherworldly support. The
solution lies in a simple extension of the principle of self-interest to
include the rewards of a future life. Tocqueville contends that the
founders of almost all religions have used the same language in advancing their cause as have moral philosophers in setting forth the
principle of self-interest: the track is the same, "only the goal is more
remote." [26] He does not deny that some religious individuals may have
been motivated by nothing other than the love of God, but he insists
that "self-interest is the principal means that religions themselves employ to govern men, and . . . that in this way they strike the multitude
and become popular." [27] Not only may self-interest be supplemented by
religion, but a species of religious feeling may itself be grounded in a
spirit of calculation.
    Tocqueville's treatment of religion is "popular" throughout. Re-

ligion is invoked not only to justify the supreme sacrifice, but also to combat both the individualism and materialism of democratic ages. Religion cannot but show men that there are goods and aspirations which transcend the experience of their senses; it thus combats the materialist teaching that everything is reducible to matter and perishes with the body. It awakens the use of man's "sublimest faculties." Religion, moreover, serves to remind men of their obligations to one another and, by so doing, withdraws men from their exclusive preoccupation with themselves. Tocqueville affirms that freedom is impossible without morality, and morality impossible without religion. Religion supplies those "dogmatic beliefs" which are the cement of society, beliefs about the nature of God, the soul, and of men's obligations to each other and to that greater whole, the state, of which they are a part. This is especially necessary in times of extreme individualism, when men are free to form and to hold their own opinions but lack the confidence to do so. In this situation, when all is in doubt and all opinions ill-defended and easily abandoned, men are prone to submit to the first demagogue who lulls their sensibilities with false promises of order and stability. General ideas about God and the human soul are therefore preservers of human freedom. But if individuals cannot determine for themselves the answers to the eternal questions; if philosophers, as Tocqueville declares, cannot supply unequivocal answers; if it is nevertheless essential to the freedom and well-being of society that there be a common core of such beliefs, then society must have recourse to religion to supply the defect. Although Tocqueville alludes to "false and very absurd" religions, he does not insist on truth or consistency in the religion which is to serve this political function; he is virtually indifferent to the particular tenets of the religion professed by this or that democratic society.[28] His recommendations thus amount to little more than the justification of simple beliefs designed to satisfy (and to keep within proper bounds) the instinctive demand of the human soul for some answer to the question of immortality.

Tocqueville's defense of the utility of religion does not lead him to advocate a state religion; on the contrary, he draws from political considerations the necessity of the separation of church and state. But unlike those who sought to sever the two in order to strengthen the political while weakening the religious order, Tocqueville argues that only by separation will the religious influence remain strong enough to exert its beneficent effects upon civil society. The salutary effect of the spirit of religion upon society in democratic ages would be jeopardized were religion, by its entry into the political realm, to implant the suggestion that its tenets were subject to majority determination. Only by relying upon the natural passion for religion which belongs to man as man, and by eschewing alliance with any particular party or state, can religion maintain its hold upon men in democratic times. Religion must remain strong, and hence separate, in order to fulfill its political function. The settlers of New England had transmitted to their descendants this precious bequest: the knowledge of the manner in which the spirit of liberty and the spirit of religion could be combined. In the political realm, all was malleable and subject to change; but

having reached the limits of the political world, the human spirit stops of itself; in fear it relinquishes the need of exploration; it even abstains from lifting the veil of the sanctuary; it bows with respect before truths which it accepts without discussion.[29]

Democracy, it seems, is impossible without such a sanctuary above and beyond democratic inquiry.

Tocqueville is acutely aware that conditions of equality impose their own limitations upon religion. If religion is to remain faithful to its political function, it must accept these limitations; it, too, must be consonant with the principle of the democratic regime and with the passions unleased by equality. It cannot hope, for example, to persuade men that the passion for self-gratification is immoral, but it may try to regulate and to moderate the drive for well-being. Religion must defer without surrendering to democratic passions. While holding fast to its essential beliefs, religion must not excite the hostility of the majority by needlessly running counter "to the ideas that generally prevail or to the permanent interests that exist in the mass of the people."[30] Tocqueville's efforts are devoted to preserving the religious sanctuary from the impious and destructive inquiry of the many.

THE JUSTIFICATION OF DEMOCRACY

Tocqueville's work has been celebrated for its objectivity, and to suggest that he undertakes to provide a justification for democracy seems contrary both to the spirit and to the letter of his work. Tocqueville attempts to grasp the propensities of democracy and turn them to advantage, but he studiously avoids stating a preference either for democracy (even in its perfected state) or for aristocracy, the regime it had succeeded or was in the process of succeeding. In the Introduction to his *Democracy,* he warns that he has not written to praise democracy or to advocate any particular form of government, nor will he even hazard a judgment whether the irresistible movement toward equality is detrimental or advantageous to mankind. And, at the conclusion of his great work, he says of aristocracy and democracy that they are like two different kinds of human beings, not susceptible of any just comparison. In this same conclusion, however, Tocqueville declares,

We may naturally believe that it is not the singular prosperity of the few, but the greater well-being of all that is most pleasing in the sight of the Creator and Preserver of men. What appears to me to be man's decline is, to His eye, advancement; what afflicts me is acceptable to Him. A state of equality is perhaps less elevated, but it is more just: and its justice constitutes its greatness and its beauty.[31]

Tocqueville rejects the classical contention that justice has as its theme the pursuit of human excellence. In common with modern political philosophers, he holds that justice is derivative from natural rights; the idea of natural rights, he tells us, is "simply that of virtue introduced into the political world." [32] The natural rights of all are, in turn, derivative from the natural equality of all men, a conclusion which escaped the greatest minds of antiquity and had to await the Christian revelation before its truth could be grasped. The inequalities characterizing the Middle Ages were founded not upon nature but upon positive law. Aristocracy itself, according to Tocqueville, is contrary to "natural equity," and cannot be established without recourse to violence. Even the rule of aristocracy is oppressive to the greatest number of people in the state, the virtue and the talents of the aristocrats notwithstanding; the aristocrats constitute a distinct group having interests typically adverse to the interests of the many. On the contrary, through the operation of a "secret tendency," the majority, though they be ignorant, can hardly help ruling in the interests of the greatest number.

Tocqueville argues, furthermore, that moral obligation derives from two sources—either from the wants and interests common to all men, or from the particular needs of a specific nation or ruling group. General notions of justice have, in every previous state of society, been overlaid with systems of morality reflecting or supporting the particular needs of that society, or of the particular ruling groups within that society, as, for example, the principles of inequality which allegedly justified the rule of the feudal aristocracy. These secondary moral codes were thus tied to special circumstances or issued from those individuals enjoying distinct privileges at certain periods of history. With the disappearance of these privileges, the moral codes to which they gave rise also disappear, and only that simple and uniform code of justice remains which is based upon the wants and the interests common to all men as men. In other words, as conditions become equal, conventional moral codes wither away, to be replaced by that natural code of morality corresponding to the natural condition of man, equality. The democratic condition is thus the only condition which does not give rise to a conventional moral code, and, in this, we may infer from Tocqueville's thought, democracy receives its justification. In its foundations, at least, democracy is in accordance with nature.

Those to whom Tocqueville's *Democracy in America* was primarily or immediately addressed were both the partisans and the critics of democracy. Tocqueville sought to moderate the passions of the former and temper the fears of the latter. The result was a statesmanlike work in which both factions could find some solace and neither too much offense, while the cause of a moderate democracy was itself advanced. Tocqueville accepted the democratic revolution, divined its weaknesses, and sought to remedy them by wholly democratic means.

NOTES

1. Alexis de Tocqueville, *Democracy in America,* the Henry Reeve text, rev. Francis Bowen, ed., with a historical essay by Phillips Bradley (2 vols.; New York: Vintage Books [Knopf], 1958), I, 48.

2. *Ibid.,* p. 3.
3. *Ibid.,* p. 7.
4. *Ibid.,* II, 352.
5. *Ibid.,* p. 141.
6. *Ibid.,* p. 145.
7. *Ibid.,* p. 171.
8. *Ibid.,* p. 82.
9. *Ibid.,* p. 208.
10. *Ibid.,* p. 102.
11. *Ibid.*
12. *Ibid.,* p. 336.
13. *Ibid.,* I, 265.
14. *Ibid.,* p. 277.

15. *Ibid.,* p. 222.
16. *Ibid.,* p. 197.
17. *Ibid.,* II, 305.
18. *Ibid.,* pp. 115–16.
19. *Ibid.,* I, 196.
20. *Ibid.,* p. 11.
21. *Ibid.,* II, 131.
22. *Ibid.,* I, 255.
23. *Ibid.,* II, 129.
24. *Ibid.,* p. 131.
25. *Ibid.*
26. *Ibid.,* p. 133.
27. *Ibid.,* p. 134.
28. See, *e.g., ibid.,* pp. 22, 154–55; I, 314.
29. *Ibid.,* I, 45.
30. *Ibid.,* II, 28.
31. *Ibid.,* p. 351.
32. *Ibid.,* I, 254.

READINGS

A. Tocqueville, Alexis de. *Democracy in America.* Vol. I, Preface, Introduction, chaps ii, iii, iv, v (61–71, 89–101), vi (102–7), viii (165–80), ix, x (181–86), xiii (206–9, 240–45), xiv, xv, xvi (281–90), xvii, xviii (433–47, 452); vol. II, bk I, chaps i, ii, v, viii, xx; bk II, chaps i, ii, iv, v, vii, viii, ix, x, xi, xiii, xiv, xix, xx; bk III, chaps i, xvii, xviii, xix, xxi; bk IV, chaps i, ii, vi, vii, viii.

B. Tocqueville, Alexis de. *The Old Régime and The French Revolution*. Trans. Stuart Gilbert. Garden City: Doubleday Anchor Books, 1955.

Tocqueville, Alexis de. *The European Revolution and Correspondence with Gobineau*. Ed. and trans. John Lukacs. Garden City: Doubleday Anchor Books, 1959.

Tocqueville, Alexis de. *The Recollections of Alexis de Tocqueville*. Trans. Alexander de Mattos. New York: Meridian Books, 1959.

JOHN STUART MILL

1806–1873

I. Method in Political Philosophy

John Stuart Mill was plunged into the problem of determining the proper method for the study of politics by the appearance of Macaulay's criticism of *Essay on Government* by his father, James Mill. Up to that time, J. S. Mill, along with other Utilitarians (or Philosophical Radicals as they called themselves), had accepted the deductive method of Bentham and James Mill as the proper one for political science. According to their conception of deductive method, the principles of political philosophy and the practical rules of political action were to be deduced from a few simple laws of human nature, *i.e.*, psychological axioms. Bentham enunciated these principles, and James Mill worked out the theory of government based on them.

Thomas Macaulay presented a brief but devastating criticism of this approach to politics.[1] He argued that the theory of human nature on which it was based was incorrect: men were guided in their action by more than the desire for their own pleasure. He thus showed that even as a deductive theory, James Mill's view was too narrow. More important, he questioned the possibility of developing a theory which would have relevance to practice from a priori first principles. What we know about politics we learn from observation and from the study of history. With observed and recorded historical events and sequences of events as our data, the fruitful procedure, Macaulay thought, was to classify and generalize in the manner advocated by Francis Bacon. These generalizations, continually tested by comparison with new facts, would constitute political knowledge, both theoretical and practical, and would lead to a science of politics far superior to the barren a priori theories of the Philosophical Radicals.

J. S. Mill was much impressed by these and other criticisms made by Macaulay.[2] However, he believed that the Utilitarians were correct in the essentials of their theory, and that the error of his father was one of form and not of content. He held the *Essay on Government* to be a polemic for parliamentary reform rather than a systematic treatise and regretted that his father did not admit this. Thus, while the essay was correct in its major conclusions, it was inadequate in its method. In his own thinking he tried to formulate a method which would do justice both to the insights of utilitarianism and to the strictures of Macaulay.

His own conclusions concerning method rest on distinguishing three kinds of deduction: direct, concrete, and inverse.[3] Thus he recognized four methods, all scientific, but applicable to different subject matters. Induction proper, or, as he called it, the "Chemical Method," establishes causal laws by comparing specifically observed cases using the canons of induction: the methods of Agreement, Difference, Concomitant Variations, and Residues. While applicable to chemistry and useful to some extent in the study of history, this approach is inapplicable to the science of politics. The direct deductive or "Geometric" method, that used by James Mill, argues by syllogistic reasoning from first principles to less general laws. This method is applicable only in those areas where there are no other causes to impede the operation of the cause being studied. It can therefore be used in mathematics, but not in mechanics or politics. The concrete deductive or "Physical" method infers the laws of effects not from one causal law, but from a number of them taken together, considering all the causes which influence the effect and compounding their laws with one another. The aggregation of causes is possible because the effect which is produced is the sum of the effects which would be produced by the causes taken singly. Simple aggregation is not operative in chemistry but is in mechanics and social science, since men remain men even when they act on or in conjunction with other men. Thus the concrete deductive method is proper for that part of social science which is concerned with determining the effect of a given cause, *e.g.,* a new law, in a given condition of society.

On the other hand, to ascertain how conditions, or states of society, themselves are determined, we must invoke the inverse deductive, or "Historical" method. The procedure here is to develop empirical laws of society on the basis of induction and then to "verify" those laws by deducing them from the a priori laws of human nature. The inductive approach in itself is not sufficient because we have too few cases to use as data. Any generalization we develop gains plausibility only by its deductive connection with a general theory. It was from Comte that Mill drew the general theory he believed to be necessary for bringing human progress itself within the scope of science. Usually, and for practical purposes, the physical method is serviceable. It breaks down when progress becomes a factor in political action, that is, when the circumstances which are the background for an action cannot be assumed to remain constant. Thus there are two branches of social science, one which supposes that conditions remain the same but that new or different factors or agencies are introduced (*e.g.,* political economy), and one which attempts to determine how it is that conditions themselves change (*i.e.,* philosophy of history). In Mill's view, no social science is complete without both branches, and the latter historical branch is basic. As will appear, both are directly applicable to political studies, the physical when considering the value of a specific legislative proposal in a particular stage of society, the historical when considering the effects of particular proposals on the progress of society to the next stage.

II. Philosophy of History

The content of Mill's philosophy of history was strongly influenced by eighteenth-century French thought, by the movement for reform in England to which he contributed, and by his study of nineteenth-century French philosophies of reform, especially those of the Saint-Simonians and Comte.[4] He believed in the possibility and desirability of social progress, but not in its inevitability. Mankind, we know from history, is capable of moving from barbarism to civilization, and this forward movement takes different forms and occurs at various paces in different societies, although, he admits, there is a certain order of human progress. By the use of the proper historical method we can determine the stages through which any people must pass in its progress, and this understanding of the pattern of historical change provides the coordinates within which it is possible to determine what steps must be taken to advance to the next stage. Thus the philosophy of history, understood as the philosophy of the progress of society, is basic for the practical science of politics and gives that science an added dimension. It is not merely necessary to know what must be done in the present situation to achieve the ends of the presently existing government in the present society. It is also necessary to know how that should be done so as to enable mankind to move to the next higher stage of civilization. Even this must be done in such a way as to pave the way for the stage of civilization beyond the next. Such a theory, it may be pointed out, is satisfactory as long as we are looking at less advanced societies from the point of view of the more advanced. We ask, What do such societies require to achieve the level of civilization that we have already reached? This is the kind of question that Mill raises about primitive societies. It is more difficult to determine what our society, a highly civilized one, requires to move on to its next stages of which we at present have no example and no clear conception. The gap in the philosophy of history is filled by the ideal derived in a deductive fashion from a theory of human nature and a theory of ethics.

When he was still a young man, Mill formulated a suggestive approach to this problem.[5] He distinguished two basic states of society: the natural and the transitional. The natural state of society was that in which those best fitted to govern were actually the governors. In the transitional state, on the other hand, individuals other than those best fitted were in power. Natural states tend to be undermined by the rise of new leaders; the struggle between them and the old leaders produces the state of transition which is eventually replaced by a new natural state. While Mill later seems to have abandoned this type of analysis, there remained a residue of it in his thinking, namely, that no state of society is satisfactory unless those who are best fitted to rule exercise the major authority in society.

Mill was also impressed by the three-stage analysis of Comte. That the intellectual development of mankind has had a theological and a metaphysical stage, and is now in a positive (or as Mill would prefer to call it experimental) stage, he thought quite correct, and his acceptance of this doctrine survived his disillusionment with Comte's later social philosophy.

If we ask Mill what is the efficient cause of social progress, we find that he has no simple answer. At each stage of civilization certain conditions may be produced which make possible the next stage; e.g., he points out that the first lesson that must be learned before any social progress is possible is the lesson of obedience. Yet the existence of the conditions of progress does not guarantee that progress will occur. The forward movement of society is actually produced by the ideas, example, and moral and intellectual leadership of superior individuals. Superior individuals have flourished chiefly under conditions of liberty, so that liberty becomes a necessary condition for progress. The argument is fairly simple: Progress depends on the emergence of new ideas; new ideas emerge only as challenges to old and accepted ideas, and then only if there is freedom to challenge the existing beliefs and to suggest alternatives. That the existing beliefs provide a basis for the stability of society Mill recognized. That the challenging of those beliefs was a threat to society he also recognized. The implicit tension between the demands of stability and the demands for reform is considered at length by Mill in his *Representative Government* (to be discussed below).

Another question that must be considered by any philosophy of history if it wishes to contribute to the study of politics is the place of the existing society in the pattern of history. Mill had no doubt that the societies of western Europe and the United States were civilized. There were also areas in the world which were uncivilized, and others at various stages of civilization below the levels achieved in western Europe. The signs of civilization are the existence of responsible government and the emergence of scientific knowledge. Mill seems to believe that the measure of a society's advance is the state of the intellect, and he seems to have little doubt that the future progress of mankind is tied to the continued development of scientific knowledge, especially in the area of social science (since he believed that the physical sciences were on the verge of becoming complete). That further progress remains to be achieved is a foundation stone of his whole system of political thinking, and that it can only be achieved deliberately through a science of society is a corollary for which he is indebted to Comte and the French Socialists.

To understand Mill's philosophy of history in its relation to his political science, one must appreciate the influence upon him of Tocqueville.[6] Mill accepted Tocqueville's thesis that the movement toward more and more democracy, that is, toward greater and greater equality of status, was almost inevitable. Like Tocqueville he felt not that this movement was in itself progress, but rather that it indicated the problem to be faced by those who wished to promote progress. Equality carried too far interferes with justice and can undermine both the liberty and the respect for intellectual and moral excellence that is the condition for further progress. It is from this analysis that Mill was led to qualify in his own theory the faith in radical democracy of the earlier Utilitarians.

III. Moral Considerations

The philosophy of history adopted by Mill required a revision of the ethical theory of utilitarianism in so far as it was applied to politics.[7] The end of the state, for the earlier Utilitarians, was the good of the individuals who composed the state, and that good was defined in hedonistic terms as the maximum of pleasure attainable with the minimum of pain. Thus government was looked upon as an agency for increasing pleasure and decreasing pain. That Mill accepted this view in principle is true without a doubt, but he found it inadequate, both in neglecting one aspect of human nature and in misunderstanding the aspects it included. The burden of Mill's argument in "Utilitarianism" is directed against the intuitionists who, he believed, claimed that the distinction between right acts and wrong acts, or between correct moral principles and incorrect ones, could be known a priori. He rejected this view and claimed that the fundamental principle of morality is known by experience, and he even goes so far as to offer a sort of inductive proof for the greatest happiness principle.

Mill revises the theory of Bentham in the course of his attempt to answer specific objections to the earlier version of utilitarianism. The objection that seemed to concern him most was that utilitarianism took a low view of human life, not distinguishing a life fit for animals from what is fit for men. In reply to this, Mill introduced a qualitative distinction among pleasures to supplement the merely quantitative distinctions of Bentham, and he traces this qualitative distinction back to ancient Epicureanism. Some pleasures, specifically the mental and spiritual ones, are in themselves superior to the bodily pleasures, regardless of quantitative or circumstantial considerations. Thus happiness would require not only a life of pleasure without pain, but the achievement of the superior pleasures even at the cost of pain and the sacrifice of the inferior pleasures.

This point is significant for Mill's political philosophy in three ways. First, it is connected with his theory of human progress. A society in which people pursue the superior pleasures is more advanced in civilization than one in which they do not. Thus the promotion of the pursuit of the higher pleasures is at the same time the promotion of the advancement of society. In the second place, the cultivation of the higher pleasures requires social freedom, so that only a free society can be truly civilized in Mill's sense. Finally, men can live together more justly and with higher human achievements to the extent that they pursue the higher pleasures rather than the lower. Thus the problem of government is partly solved by the pursuit of the higher pleasures, because those traits of character which are developed from that pursuit are the very traits of character which are necessary to achieve the best form of political organization. Science, the highest achievement of the intellectual life, requires just that objectivity and disinterestedness that man requires to be a truly moral being, and hence to be a citizen in the best type of state.

Thus, while the core of utilitarianism is present in Mill's assertion that those actions, individual or social, are right which produce the greatest happiness of the greatest number, that core has been so modified and expanded that the resultant theory has a cast different from that of original utilitarianism. Government does not exist merely to produce the maximum of that kind of pleasure which the citizens happen to prefer. Rather some types of pleasure are better than others, and the government has the responsibility for having its citizens educated to pursue the higher pleasures in place of the lower pleasures. Moral education, whether it is actually carried on by the government or by private individuals (and Mill seems to prefer the latter), is thus one of the responsibilities of the good society; and moral education must be directed at man not simply as a pleasure-seeking animal, but as "a progressive being."

Some further distinctions are important for the politically relevant portion of Mill's ethical theory. For Mill the individual is prior to the state, but not the individual as he is, rather the individual as he may become with proper education in a well-organized society. This does not mean that Mill conceives of one pattern of human life which should serve as a model for all men, but rather that there is a great variety of potentials in men, and society should provide the conditions in which each man can develop his special talents and make them available to the community. He can do this best by having the opportunity actively to use his talents. Mill sees the active life as morally superior to one of passive obedience at almost all levels of human achievement. From this it follows that the government which encourages active participation in its operation by all its citizens is better, in spite of the problems which may arise as a consequence, than one which is more orderly but encourages its citizens to be passively obedient to the commands of a ruling group, whatever the morality and justice of those commands.

IV. The End of the State

Mill commences his most extended single treatment of political philosophy, *Considerations on Representative Government,*[8] with a reworking of the old question as to whether governments exist by nature or by convention. He takes this as a question concerning the range of choice as regards forms of government. If government is entirely a matter of convention, then choice is unlimited. If governments exist entirely by nature, then no choice is possible. He rejects both positions and tries to show the element of truth in each by pointing to three conditions that any people must satisfy in order that a particular system of government may succeed among them: They must be willing to accept it, willing to do what is necessary to keep it standing, and willing to do what is necessary to enable it to fulfill its purpose. The conditions favorable to the establishing and maintaining of particular systems of government may be to some extent the result of the education of the people; and within the limits set by these conditions, the specific form of government is a matter of choice.

The choice of one form of government from among the ones whose conditions are present should be guided by an understanding of the purpose or purposes of government. After canvassing some current views on the subject, Mill finds that the most widely held view, even among the Utilitarians, is that governments exist to preserve order and to achieve progress in society. He finds this redundant since the achievement of progress presupposes order, *i.e.,* security in what has been achieved. Mill would thus be willing to say that progress is the whole end of government, but somewhat reluctantly, since saying this does not place sufficient emphasis on the equally important need to guard against the danger of retrogression. A more appropriate way to get at the requisites of a form of government is to recognize that the supposed antithesis between order and progress is merely a reflection of a deeper psychological antithesis between two types of human character, the type in which caution predominates and that in which boldness is dominant. Good government, that which achieves progress on a basis of order, requires men of both types to provide a balance, though no special provision in the constitution is necessary to assure this. All that is necessary is to be sure that neither type is systematically eliminated. What is fundamental is the qualities of the human beings over whom the government is exercised, and this is seen in two perspectives. One test of good government is the extent to which the virtue and intelligence of the people themselves are promoted. The other is the extent to which the machinery of government takes advantage of the good qualities of the populace. Thus, the end of government is to make the people better, and the means are to educate the people and to put to use the highest qualities which they have achieved.

Thus Mill's moral theory provides the basis for his political theory, and both of these are supported by his account of the stages of social progress. While Mill recognizes that the government must take care of the affairs of the community, its responsibility for developing the people is more important. The criterion of its effectiveness in the former is its efficiency, and the standards of efficiency are the same for all forms of government. The criteria of its effectiveness in the education of the people are more complicated and depend on the stage of development in which the people find themselves. Just as there is a natural order in the education of an individual, so there is a natural order in the education of a people. Easiest lessons are learned first; those which presuppose others cannot be learned until those others have been mastered.

If the precivilized condition is barbarism, obedience is the first lesson, labor is the next, and self-government is the final step. Mill sees a continuous line of development from slavery to self-government, with each stage prepared by the learning of a specific lesson, that is, by the acquiring of a new character trait on the part of the population as a whole. Apart from the business side of government, the criterion of the best form of government for any particular people is that it provide what is necessary to teach them the lesson they must learn in order to move to the next more advanced state of society, and that it not hinder them from moving on, after suitable training, to the step beyond. It is in this context that we can understand Mill's view that despotism is "a legitimate mode" of government for barbarians, if "the end be their improvement." [9] For Mill this sequence of steps implies a culmination in the best form of government altogether, one which, if the necessary conditions existed, would promote more than any other, not one form of human improvement, but all forms and degrees of it. This he says is some variety of the representative system.

V. The Argument for Representative Government

Representative government has only one rival for its place as the ideally best polity, and that is benevolent despotism.[10] After considering carefully the benefits to be derived by the absolute rule of an intellectually and morally superior individual, Mill finds several arguments decisive against its claim. One, which comes from the earlier Benthamite theory, rests on the principle that the "rights and interests of any person are only secure from being disregarded when he is able and disposed to stand up for them." In a benevolent despotism, however, the rights of individuals, those limitations on the power of others to interfere with a man's actions which can be justified on the principle of utility, are not secure because they depend on the guarantee of the despot. While specific despots may in some cases protect these rights, human nature being what it is, despotism is not reliable in that respect. Historical evidence, which shows that free people have prospered more than those under despotisms, supports this argument. The other argument goes to the root of what is distinctive in Mill's theory. Despotism requires obedience on the part of the citizen body, that is, passivity. Intellectual, practical, and moral excellence, the highest aims which the state ought to strive to cultivate among its citizens, are all the products of an active character. Thus while despotism may be suitable where a people has to learn obedience to progress to higher stages of civilization, once it has learned that lesson, it ought to be encouraged to active participation, which is possible only in a popular government. Popular government therefore appears to be the ideal polity for two reasons: It protects the rights of individuals, and it promotes their highest moral and intellectual development. However, Mill has one more step in his argument: The highest development of individuals rests also on an advanced civilization, which is only possible in a large state. Popular government is only possible in small states. The closest approximation to popular government which is feasible in large states is representative government, *i.e.,* representative democracy.

Representative government is not only the ideally best polity, all things considered, but is also a form of government that can be established in the modern world. Its existence depends on the three conditions already mentioned, together with a degree of maturity which makes possible this form of self-government. Where the people have some lesson still to learn, some other form of government will be more suitable for them, *e.g.,* they may learn obedience more easily from a military leader, or a king may teach them to overcome that spirit of locality which prevents them from joining with other localities to set up the central authority which representative government presupposes. Barring such defects as these, and they were certainly, Mill felt, not problems in the England of his time, a properly constituted representative government could do most to aid the people to achieve progress to the next stage of society.

VI. The Analysis of Representative Government

The proper constitution of a representative democracy is not a simple matter, however, and no government of Mill's time exhibited it, chiefly because the role of the representative in government had not been understood correctly. The usual error in conceiving of representative government, Mill believed, was in holding that the representatives of the people should actually govern. The functions of government, executive, legislative, and judicial, are highly skilled activities which require experienced, well-trained individuals whom the populace is not qualified to select. Thus it may be said that Mill believes in government by experts. However, every constitution has "an ultimate controlling power," and this power must in a democracy reside in the people themselves. Not being able to exercise this power themselves, the people exercise it in effect, can control the operations of government in the public interest, through periodically elected deputies. Thus, for Mill, the representatives are not the government, but act for the people to control the government.

A parliament of elected representatives would serve as the controller of the government in the interest of the people. Mill sees this parliament as chiefly a deliberative body, at once a "Committee on Grievances" and a "Congress of Opinions." Containing "a fair sample of every grade of intellect which is at all entitled to a voice in public affairs," its function would be "to indicate wants, to be an organ for popular demands, and a place of adverse discussion for all opinions relating to public matters. . . ." [11]

The point of interest here is that Mill's "Representative Democracy" is two stages removed from democracy in the literal sense of the term, rule by the people. Rule by the representatives of the people is one stage removed, and rule by experts controlled by the representatives of the people is another stage removed. Mill comes to this view not only on the basis of considerations of practicality, but on the basis of his belief that while justice requires democracy, an uncontrolled democracy can be just as much a tyranny as absolute monarchy.

The effective operation of representative democracy requires the presence of conditions not required of other systems of government. A nice balance must be preserved between the representative body and the actually governing bodies. Too strong a representative body will hinder the government from carrying out its functions. One that is too weak will be unable to control the government. The representative body might not have the mental qualifications needed for its work. Sinister interests, interests not identical with the interest of the community as a whole, may gain predominance. These latter defects tend to be present in all constitutions. They are inherent in the nature of monarchy and aristocracy, but by suitable institutions their danger may be reduced to a minimum in a representative system. Mill devoted considerable attention to designing specific arrangements for the representative democracy he favors, to enable it to overcome its possible defects.

The technique of the better monarchies and aristocracies for securing talents of a sufficiently high order for governmental functions is the establishment of a bureaucracy. But bureaucracy relapses into routine, which represses the individuality of its members and becomes a system governed by trained mediocrity. Only popular government (and Mill considers his system of representative democracy the most feasible type of popular government) keeps alive antagonistic interests in the community, and thus stimulates individual thought and initiative, enabling the man of original genius to pierce the barrier of trained mediocrity. However, the freedom produced by the representative system must be combined with trained skill. The distinction between governing and controlling, which is at the basis of Mill's system, produces the combination. The experts govern, but they are controlled by the representatives of the people.

Mill's specific proposals for the reform of existing representative government can be understood as attempts to secure the establishment of a skilled democracy. Without skill the complex problems of the government of a free society cannot be solved. Without democracy there is no security for good government, that is, for the protection of the rights of citizens. Mill finds that the current conception of democracy is based on an inadequate understanding of majority rule. If democracy means government of the whole by a majority which alone has representation, the ends of democracy are bound to be frustrated, for the minority, having no representatives, has no assurance that its rights will be protected, and the majority will be in a position to pursue its sinister interest. Mill fears, for example, that a representative body representing the interests of the working class will jeopardize the property rights of the wealthy, and thus undermine the economy of the nation. Rule by the majority in its own interest is as much a government of inequality and privilege as rule by a privileged minority in its interest. True democracy on the other hand is government of the whole by the whole equally represented. The existing system of false democracy involves both misrepresentation (of those of the majority party who opposed the candidate chosen) and nonrepresentation (of those who vote for the party which loses). The absence of an effective voice in opposition to the majority in the representative body tends to produce a mediocre and incompetent ruling group.[12]

Mill believed that Thomas Hare's scheme for personal representation provided means for giving representation to each voter. In Hare's variant of proportional representation, each voter votes for a series of candidates, marking them as his first choice, his second choice, his third choice, etc. When a sufficient number of ballots to elect is credited to a candidate, the remainder for him go to second, third, and subsequent choices so that each vote counts for someone who is elected. Every voter has at least one candidate who may be said to represent him. Mill believed that in the existing system in which a majority in a geographic district determines the representation for that district, the voters for the losing candidates are disenfranchised. Under Hare's system every vote counts. On Mill's theory of representation the elected representative had the responsibility of thinking and discussing public issues in the interest of the whole, not merely reflecting the views of his constituency. He argued against pledges on the part of candidates for office and refused to give any when he himself stood for Parliament in 1865.

While the earlier Utilitarians had assumed that the extension of the suffrage alone would guarantee that the interests of all would be defended, Mill felt that without personal representation universal suffrage would lead to the tyranny of the majority. The earlier reformers also assumed that the lower classes would choose their betters to represent them. Mill was by no means as sanguine. He believed that special measures had to be taken to prevent the views of the instructed classes from being drowned in a flood of votes from the uninstructed classes. The system of personal representation would obviate the rule of the uninstructed by enabling the instructed from all parts of the nation to pool their votes to secure the election of the candidates they preferred. But this was not enough for Mill. To give the instructed an even greater weight than their mere numbers would merit, he advocated plural voting for the professional and other classes that carried greater responsibility in the community. While personal representation has an ambiguous effect on democracy (being democratic in the sense that it gives everyone a voice, and contrary to democracy in that it increases the strength of the minorities in relation to the majority), the system of plural voting is definitely a curb on democracy and indicates the strength of Mill's conviction of the dangers of unlimited democracy. He placed his reliance on a representative body in which the interests of the two major classes in society, the working class and the upper class, were evenly balanced, on the expectation that most of the representatives would vote in accordance with their class interest, while a minority of each group, carrying the balance of power, would vote in the public interest.

VII. Theory of Liberty

The essay *On Liberty* was held by Mill to be his most carefully composed work and the one which was most likely to be of enduring value. We can appreciate why Mill felt this way and judge more adequately of the significance of the book if we consider it in the context of his philosophy of history and his theory of the state.

Believing in the progress of society from lower to higher stages of civilization, Mill saw the political culmination of this development as the emergence of a system of representative democracy. Thus he judged representative democracy to be the ideally best polity, *i.e.,* that form of government toward which mankind was progressing. Nevertheless Mill did not see the emergence of representative democracy as the emergence of utopia. Not only was there an ever-present tendency toward retrogression which society had continually to struggle against, but equally dangerous was the tendency of the most idealistic and high-minded reform movements to harden into dogmatic systems which forced conformity and thereby inhibited future progress. Just as obedience and work were the main conditions of human progress at earlier stages of man's development, so in the civilized period, obedience and industriousness having been engrained, liberty becomes the condition for subsequent progress.

Evidently Mill's theory of liberty is far from a universal doctrine which applies to all peoples at all times. Rather it is practically relevant only when society becomes more important than the state. As long as there is a recognized opposition of interest between the governors and the governed, the progress of mankind requires that men work to achieve the conditions of representative government. Once these conditions are achieved, a representative democracy can emerge in which the opposition between governors and governed disappears, for the governors then represent the interests of the governed. This condition, which makes possible the liberty of the individual, does not guarantee it. The very emancipation of society from the constraint of a government in the interests of a few creates in society itself, in the great mass of the people, a new and more dangerous threat to the liberty of the individual. In dealing with this newly emerging problem, Mill believes that he is thinking for the future. The problem of subsequent stages of progress is to prevent the individual from being oppressed by the ever more powerful and confident mass of mankind. Progress toward civilization requires curbs on individual liberty; progress in civilization requires the emancipation of the individual from those restrictions.

What is required, Mill believes, is a practical principle which will so define the area of individual liberty as not to prevent government from meeting its obligation to promote the progress of society. Mill grounds this principle in his moral theory: The only thing of ultimate value is the happiness of individuals, and individuals can best achieve their happiness in a civilized society when they are left free to pursue their own interests with their own talents as these have come to be understood and developed by them under an adequate system of education. Underlying all this is the assumption of the ultimate value of individuality, of individual development, both for the individual himself and for the future progress of society—for the individual, once the conditions of free development, namely, civilization and representative government, are achieved; for the society because the progress of civilization depends on the contributions that can be made only by individuals who think for themselves. The civilized man, for Mill, is the one who acts on what he understands, and who exerts every effort to understand. This Socratic model is not meant for the few who have the philosophic bent, but is intended as a model for all men in so far as they are capable of achieving it.

The question then arises as to the conditions under which society can progress toward this goal. The principal condition is self-restraint on the part of the individuals in society, and Mill's theory of liberty is an attempt to spell out in practical terms what that self-restraint requires. It requires as a foundation that each individual, groups of individuals, the government, and the mass of the people refrain from interfering with the thought, expression, and action of any individual. This is the basic principle of liberty.

Radical noninterference with individuals, applied abstractly and absolutely, would of course make government and an orderly society impossible. It is in effect an anarchistic principle. Mill qualifies it in its practical application by recognizing that while thought must be absolutely free, the freedom of action of individuals must be limited for the safety of society. Mill argues that the individual belongs to himself and is subject to social control only for the purpose of preventing him from harming others. The individual is sovereign over himself, and the society is sovereign over the acts of the individual that impinge on others. The thoughts of the individual are part of himself, and therefore the principle requires that society exert no control over them. (Here we must bear in mind that Mill is not talking about any collection of individuals anywhere, but about a mature body of citizens who have been educated to a sense of public responsibility. He explicitly excludes children and savages.)

The public expression of one's private thoughts might be supposed to fall into a different category, that of action. Mill admits that it does so, in some isolated cases, but generally speaking he believes that expression requires the same absolute liberty as thought for the following reasons: First, expression is so closely related to thought that the control of expression would become in effect a control on thought. Second, he asserts that the claim to the right to limit freedom of expression, that is, the claim to the right to silence the expression of opinions in society, presupposes infallibility on the part of those who make the claim. Mill's belief is that no one can legitimately claim infallibility, and hence no one can legitimately claim the right to suppress any opinion. On the contrary, society has everything to gain and nothing to lose by absolute freedom of discussion. An unpopular opinion may be true, in which case the rest of mankind can learn something from the dissident view. This would hold even if it were partly true and partly false. Even if the dissident opinion were entirely false, society would be the gainer by allowing it to be expressed. Society would be kept alert as to the grounds of its own (true) view, which would become a dead dogma if it went forever unchallenged; and the instruction of the mistaken dissident would always remain as a possibility.

Mill's approach to the problem of the limits, if any, to freedom of public discussion in society assumes, it must be recalled, a mature public carrying on its discussion in a restrained and civilized way. Those who do not live up to the rules of the game have no such rights; they must be restrained in the same way as those whose actions harm others in society. The implicit principle here is that as long as discussion remains discussion, it ought to be permitted absolute freedom; but once it passes beyond discussion to action, it ought to be treated as action. The illustrations that Mill gives of the latter, *e.g.,* telling an excited mob that corn dealers are starvers of the poor in front of the house of a corn dealer, suggest that it is not the opinion alone which determines to which category, thought or action, expressing the opinion belongs, but rather the circumstances in which the opinion is expressed.

It is generally agreed that actions cannot be as free as opinions. Actions must be limited to the extent that they result in harm to others. Mill is very careful to make sure that this rule is not made the basis for a general restriction of liberty of action. When men consent to the action by which they are harmed, that action is of no concern to society. In general, the burden of proof is on society to show that the individual's action is harmful, rather than on the individual to prove that it is harmless. Danger of harm to oneself, once one is a mature individual, is no ground for interference by government. Under that circumstance the individual may be remonstrated with, but not coerced.

The ultimate aim of social action should be "to secure to all persons complete independence and freedom of action." This includes especially freedom to gratify tastes and engage in pursuits, as well as freedom of association, all to the extent that other individuals are not harmed. By education in the self-regarding virtues the individuals in society should be encouraged to use their freedom to advance themselves morally and intellectually; if they succeed, they become suitable objects of admiration and emulation; if they fail, they become objects of distaste and perhaps even contempt. However, they are not to be interfered with by society or by government unless they fail in some social obligation which is ultimately grounded in the utilitarian principle of the greatest happiness of the greatest number. To the objection that it is difficult, if not impossible, to distinguish between that part of a person's life which concerns only himself and that part which concerns society, Mill offers a partial answer in practical terms. If the basis of the objection is that many apparently self-regarding actions do harm to others, Mill replies that to the extent that they do harm to others they should be punished. Definite damage or harm to others should be punished, but merely contingent injury (that which does not violate a specific duty) ought to be tolerated for the sake of greater freedom. In these terms Mill discusses spending income, drinking fermented beverages, sale of poisons, polygamy, gambling, and other acts which have been objects of legal restriction. He admits that there is no mechanical application of his basic principles, but insists that they are the only proper guides to correct social policy.[13]

He concludes by restating the arguments for individual initiative in preference to social control: Most things tend to be done better when done by individuals than when done by the government; individual action promotes the mental education of the individual, which governmental action does not; and increased governmental action is a threat to liberty.

While Mill does not rule out the interference of government in the economic life of the community as either impossible or undesirable in principle, he would restrict those interferences to the area of the distribution of goods, exempting the area of the production of goods as being governed by laws of nature. Though in later life he came to consider himself something of a Socialist, he also expressed fears of the extension of social control over economic life. Using individuality, liberty, and the progress of society as his standards, he recognized the advantage of "non-authoritative" governmental interference in the form of supplying advice and information and in competing with private enterprise where there was danger of monopoly. Recognizing that the organization of society on a communistic basis might raise the standard of living of the laboring classes, he did not believe that the increased standard of living would be worth the price of restrictions on liberty if these should be the outcome.[14]

NOTES

1. "Mill on Government," *Edinburgh Review*, vol. X (March, 1829). Reprinted in *The Miscellaneous Writings of Lord Macaulay* (London: Longman, Green, Longman, and Roberts, 1860), I, 282–322.

2. J. S. Mill, *Autobiography* (New York: Columbia University Press, 1924), pp. 110–13.

3. J. S. Mill, *A System of Logic* (1843), III and VI.

4. *Ibid.*, esp. VI.

5. J. S. Mill, *The Spirit of the Age* (Chicago: University of Chicago Press, 1942). These essays were originally published in 1831.

6. J. S. Mill, "M. de Tocqueville on Democracy in America," in *Disserta-*

tions and Discussions (New York: Henry Holt, 1874), II, 79–161. See also *Autobiography*, pp. 134, 141.

7. J. S. Mill, "Utilitarianism," *Fraser's Magazine* (1861). Reprinted in many editions.

8. J. S. Mill, *Considerations on Representative Government* (London, 1861). Reprinted in many editions.

9. J. S. Mill, *On Liberty* (London, 1859), i.

10. *Considerations on Representative Government*, iii.

11. *Ibid.*, v.

12. *Ibid.*, vii.

13. *On Liberty*, iii–v.

14. J. S. Mill, *Principles of Political Economy* (2 vols; London, 1848), V.

READINGS

A. Mill, John Stuart. *On Liberty*, in *Utilitarianism, Liberty, and Representative Government*. New York: Dutton, 1951.

Mill, John Stuart. *Representative Government*, in *ibid*. Chaps i–vii.

B. Mill, John Stuart. *Utilitarianism*, in *ibid*.

Mill, John Stuart. *Representative Government*, in *ibid*. Chaps viii–xviii.

Mill, John Stuart. *A System of Logic*. New York: Longmans, 1949. Bk VI.

Mill, John Stuart. *Principles of Political Economy*. Ed. W. J. Ashley. New York: Longmans, various dates. Bk V.

KARL MARX

1818–1883

Marxism presents itself as a comprehensive account of human life, and not only of human life but of nature as well. It offers an account of man's present, and of his past and future, educing its teaching from the premise that a full and final account of things is impossible except as an account of the transitoriness or endless flux of things. The definitive description of the present is given in Marx's economic writings, *i.e.,* in his critical analysis of capitalism. The account of past and future, or of the evolution of society, is given in Marx's writings on the theory of history and the relation of history to a certain notion of metaphysics. Marx's political philosophy consists of his teaching on economics and his teaching on history and metaphysics—on the present society and on the coming into being and passing away of all societies including the present.

The reader might wonder whether an economic analysis of capitalism is the same as a full account of the modern time (ignoring for the present the existence of communist countries). It is Marx's contention that the economy is the living kernel of the society, and therefore to grasp the truth about the modern economy is to understand the most potent facts about modern society. But the reader might also wonder whether a full account of society is equivalent to a full account of human life. Marxism takes the two, if society is rightly understood, to be equivalent. Marxism can thus present itself as a comprehensive explanation of the past, present, and future of man. It claims to have discovered that the economy is the true ground of society and therewith of human life. Marx's analysis of the present, *i.e.,* of capitalistic economy, is based upon his labor theory of value. His account of the transition from past to future, *i.e.,* of history, depends on his doctrine of dialectical materialism. Our description of Marx's political philosophy will therefore have this outline: (1) Dialectical materialism, or Marx's theory of history and of the priority of the economic conditions; (2) the labor theory of value and Marx's account of the capitalistic present; (3) the convergence of dialectical materialism and the labor theory of value.

In what follows we shall speak of "Marxism" and the doctrines of Marx. It should be understood that from 1844 on, Marx had as his collaborator Friedrich Engels, who gracefully and without doubt justly declared that Marx's was the genius of the movement, although he, Engels, had made his contributions to it. We shall not try in every case, even were it possible, to distinguish Engels' work from Marx's.

Marx repeatedly asserts that the study of man must concern itself with "real" men, not with men as imagined or hoped for or believed to be. Marx means by this that the foundation of social science is not a notion of some wished-for human good, or some reconstruction of pristine "natural" man, but rather empirical man as anyone could at any time observe him. Empirical man is primarily a living organism consuming food, clothing, shelter, fuel, and so on, and compelled to find or to produce those things. Men might once upon a time have survived by using materials which they simply found and gathered, but the increase in population at some point forced them to produce their necessities and thereby to become distinguished from the beasts. The singular sign of humanity is conscious production—not rationality, or political life, or the power of laughter, for example, as some have maintained. There is, to be sure, an element of unclarity in Marx's teaching on this point, since he concedes that human production differs from "production" by beasts in that the human being plans or conceives in advance the completed object of his labor while the bee or insect toils by mere instinct. In other words, only human production is characterized by rational intention, and human production could thus be said to be unique because it is the doing of the rational animal. Then, however, it would be more exact to assert that man's singular characteristic is rationality rather than productiveness; but Marx is prevented from saying so because the implications of that assertion would interfere with his materialism, which argues that man's rationality or rather "consciousness" is not fundamental but derivative. The Marxist doctrine of the primacy of production in human life rests upon the belief that it was the pressure of his needs that first forced man upward into his humanity and then continues to press him onward and upward; and that the content of his reason must be determined by conditions external to his reason, conditions which are strictly material.

In what ways, more exactly, do the material conditions determine life and thought, according to Marx? He begins by observing that, in every epoch, men have access to certain productive forces, which they apply by making use of the objects—animals, tools, machines, and so on —in which those forces are embodied. But the forces of production— say, roughly, the bare technology—compel men to adapt themselves and their institutions to the requirements of the technology. Nomads, for example, who suddenly gained access to steam power and mechanically drawn agricultural implements would be forced to give up their nomadism and to adopt instead the sedentary habits, division of labor, trading practices, and property institutions which are determined by factory production, and also to take up the practices and institutions correlate to agriculture. That this is true in a general sense is self-evident; it surely was well understood in Greek antiquity. As stated above, however, it is insufficiently comprehensive to express Marx's meaning. Marx asserts repeatedly that to a given set of forces of production there corresponds a certain "mode of production," such as the Asiatic, the ancient, the feudal, and the modern bourgeois or capitalist. According to the feudal mode of production, for example, the possessors of the means of production and the men who labored with or upon those means were connected by a personal relation of mutual responsibility; under the capitalist mode, employers and employees are, as the terms imply, users and used, free of duty to each other, with only the payment of money connecting them. With each such mode of production, there goes, as an effect, one form of social organization. A compact formulation of this view is given by Marx in his letter to P. V. Annenkov, December 28, 1846: "What is society, whatever its form may be? The product of men's reciprocal action. Are men free to choose this or that form of society for themselves? By no means. Assume a particular state of development in the productive forces of man and you will get a particular form of commerce and consumption. Assume particular stages of development in production, commerce and consumption and you will have a corresponding social structure, a corresponding organization of the family, of orders or of classes, in a word, a corresponding civil society. Presuppose a particular civil society and you will get particular political conditions which are only the official expression of civil society." This he compresses further, in *The Poverty of Philosophy* in the remark, "The hand-mill gives you society with the feudal lord; the steam-mill, society with the industrial capitalist." [1]

The conditions of production determine the prevailing property relations, meaning by the latter not the abstract definition of property, but rather who in the particular situation has access to property and who is prevented from acquiring it. Under feudalism, there were lords who possessed land and had rights to other property, and serfs who could accumulate no property. Similarly under the other social circumstances: under capitalism, employers own and accumulate, employees struggle along on the verge of destitution, owning nothing, separated from the means of production. This doctrine is directly connected with the Marxian belief that the conditions of production control distribution of income and consumption of output. They also govern exchange: if production is organized around a commonly occupied arable, for example, there will not even be exchange of the produce of the soil, only sharing. It follows also that money will be in use or not depending on the mode of production: money is not, in its present meaning or use, intrinsic to every economic situation or to economic life as such.

Marx asserts, therefore, that it is a mistake to treat consumption, distribution, exchange, money, and so on as eternal categories having an abstract, permanent content, relevance, or validity. It is one of the defects of the science of political economy, "bourgeois" economics, that it views these purely historical phenomena as fixed categories, having an objective, essential, "natural" character—things that can be understood once and for all because they exist once and for all. Not only are the "categories" historical products, but the science of those categories, namely economics, proves itself to be merely historical or transitory by mistaking the transitory for the eternally true, i.e., by believing itself to consist of laws founded in a changeless nature. Marx denounces Edmund Burke, but through Burke all economists, for his assertion that "the laws of commerce . . . are the laws of Nature, and consequently the laws of God." [2] Actually, according to Marx, the economic science of the capitalist period is given its "categories" (wages, interest, exchange, profit, and so on) by the practices prevalent under capitalistic production, and it takes up these categories without recognizing their genesis in the historical conditions. Failing to treat its material as historical and bound to pass away, it of course condemns itself to pass away when its material does so.

Marx's doctrine of the dependence of theories on the historic conditions of production takes in far more than economic theory. He asserts that all morality, philosophy, religion, and politics are the result of the conditioning of men by their environment—their manmade environment which is the expression of the mode of production. The opposite view, that man has an independent intelligence by the light of which he fashions his institutions and forms his convictions, is rejected as ideology, the Marxist term for the doctrine that thought has an independent status.[3]

Marx's materialism has been presented thus far as asserting simply that the conditions of production determine the concrete character of human life, which exists as a "superstructure" on the foundation of the more truly real material conditions. Nothing has been said, however, about the goodness or badness of the actual superstructures that have in fact arisen on the hitherto existing material foundations. Such a judgment is intrinsic to Marx's materialism, however, and to it we now turn.

All historic modes of production have had one feature in common, and that feature has in turn affected all the corresponding societies: control of the means of production has not been shared by all men, but in each age some have been owners or possessors while many more have had to give of themselves, *i.e.,* of their capacity for work (having nothing else to give), in order to have access to the instruments of production, to gain a livelihood. Thus in all previous history the act of production has brought many men into dependence upon the few. The masses have been deprived of the opportunity to become free and self-respecting men because they have always been forced into the position of cringing dependents—slaves, serfs, or proletarians—subject to men who, although private citizens or subjects like themselves, could yet arbitrarily deprive them of their living by cutting off their connection with the means of production. The dehumanization inevitably resulting from such servile dependence has been compounded by the poverty imposed upon the many by their exploiters.

Furthermore, the process of production, from its inception, had a character that Marx calls "natural" in the sense that certain natural differences among men (of physique, talent, and so on) determined the allotment of special tasks to individuals, and the relations of production were therefore determined, imposed, or involuntary, thus natural in the sense of not resulting from human choice. The prototype of all such allotments is the division of function between male and female in continuing the race. This grew into the more general form of division of labor incorporated in the family. As the forces of production were developed, the division of labor became increasingly elaborated, and the particular occupations became correspondingly restricted. As men are compelled by the conditions of production to become shepherds, plumbers, or violinists, they are deprived of the opportunity to develop to the full their human capacities by turning their minds freely in all directions. They are made into fragments of men, prevented by the stultifying division of labor from growing into whole men for whom labor would become a source of satisfaction rather than pain.

While this parcellation is going on within each man, the same process is being repeated among the men. The community comes to be composed of weavers who are set in opposition to bakers, farmers pitted against merchants, townsfolk versus country people, hand workers against brain workers—a war of all against all, fought on the field of material interest, the terms of struggle dictated by the mode of production. Finally, the fracture of society is completed by the coalescence into a class or group of classes of the few who control the means of production, and the parallel coalescence of the many dispossessed into the class or classes that work at the means of production.

The fracturing of social life may be epitomized in the existence of civil society or bourgeois society. (The German term used by Marx is *bürgerliche Gesellschaft,* which may be translated as either civil or bourgeois society.) The breakdown of the integrity of human life is symptomatized and presupposed by the split in our common existence between the political and the economic and social: "Where the political state has attained its true development, the individual leads not only in thought, in consciousness, but in reality, a double life, a heavenly and an earthly life, a life in the political community, wherein he counts as a member of the community, and a life in bourgeois society, wherein he is active as a private person, regarding other men as a means, degrading himself into a means and becoming a plaything of alien powers." [4] Civil society means for Marx an individualistic enclave in society, the realm of privacy as against community, with the understanding that community finds its corrupt expression in political society under nowprevailing conditions. Civil society, far from being synonymous with political society for Marx, is the infrapolitical cognate of political society that is an inevitable part of the capitalistic order. A simple equivalent of "civil society" in this sense is "the economy" of a capitalistic state, or even "the market." Civil society is the stratum of common life that is given its essential character by the self-assertiveness of men, one against the other, in the name of their inalienable, irreducible rights. The sanctity of those rights, thought by writers like Locke to be the ground for guaranteeing the freedom and thus the humanity of men, is rejected by Marx because he views the assertion of those rights as the source of, surely the expression of man's dehumanization. The war of Marxism against the ruling principles of Western constitutionalism must never be mistaken for a mere skirmish.

It is evident, according to Marx, that the many-sided factual negation of all community of interest under capitalism results from the private ownership of the productive resources. Production, a social act in the sense of being by and for all men, cannot be carried on humanely and rationally if the institutions of production are private, particular, and hence antisocial.

The modes of production and institutions of property that have existed hitherto have caused fragmentation and conflict within and among men. What has kept the fragments of society from flying apart? Or, more pertinently, what has prevented the many from summarily ridding themselves of the impositions of the few? According to Marx, the state power is precisely the agency devised by the oppressive few to keep the many in order. The state is the organ of class coercion, made necessary by the dividedness of society that is engendered in turn by the private control of the means of production. It goes without saying that the government does not appear in this light to the multitude of men. Marx allows that all classes collaborate in sustaining government by respecting it and its power of coercion; but this means no more than that men, because of the imperfection of their material conditions, are prepared and compelled to erect over themselves their own tyrant, their own creature that must, as it does, assert itself against them.

It was Marx's belief that while men remain in the state of constraint, of subjection to want and to one another via the process of production, they will be unable to lead fully human lives; for full humanity would require perfect emancipation from bonds of every sort. If Marx had ever used the term "state of nature" in his own name, he would have meant by it the state of man's incomplete domination of nature, the alternative to the state of freedom. While men are in bonds, as they have been under government and "civil society," they experience as part of their bondage a constraint that compels them to contribute to their own dehumanization through institutions of their own devising.

We may conclude this summary of Marx's materialism by explaining the foregoing remark, and at the same time showing how Marx conceives the state of need and the state of political society to coexist as the state of human bondage or what he calls man's alienation. Without a grasp of this element of Marxism it would be impossible to form a sufficient judgment of Marx's political philosophy as a whole.

Returning to our point of departure, we note Marx's primary observation that man is a needing being. Each man is condemned to dependence upon external things, say nature, and upon other men to help supply his needs. But in addition to being essentially needy, man is what Marx calls a species being or a social being, which does not mean simply that man must live and act in common with other men, but that man cannot realize his human possibilities except by acting upon and being acted upon by other human beings. That man knows his fellowmen to constitute a whole of which he is a part, and that he therefore associates himself with them in thought in a way which is ruled out for all subhuman animals, is part also of Marx's rather diffuse notion of man as a species-being. At any rate, it was Marx's belief that man's essential activity, production, has in all previous societies been carried on under institutions that compel men to look upon each other and upon nature itself as alien things, objects, mere means to the end of satisfying the individual's needs. Productive labor itself has always been regarded as a painful necessity because of the conditions under which it has been performed. Thus men's environment and their fellow-men have been objects of predation, and the acting men themselves, and their very own essential life-activities, have been merely instrumental, means to ends without the intrinsic worth they must have if man is to be fully human, to be at one with himself, or to overcome his "estrangement" from nature, from himself, and from the fruits of his labor. Marx's contention is no less sweeping than this: until every man simply merges himself in the whole of humanity, producing only because production is the release and cultivation of human energy, and not because production is a way of obtaining subsistence directly or through exchange by exploiting other men's neediness—not until then will men be perfectly free and the perfect, final articulation of man, society, and nature be achieved. Until that time, men will distort each other's natures by treating each other as objects, each being made thus to grow up as at odds with his species, even regarding nature itself, incidentally, not in its beauty and splendor but as a source of gain. The arrangement of the process of production within the institution of common ownership of productive resources, under the formula "From each according to his ability, to each according to his needs," is thought by Marx to be the condition for causing the absolute translation of human life onto a basis which is in the most literal sense unprecedented. Men have lived hitherto in civil society, *i.e.,* under institutions that have presupposed or positively cultivated self-interest as the principle of productive life and life itself. Marxian materialism leads up to the supersession of all civil society and its replacement by the human species as a universal brotherhood. Marxian materialism, which begins by insisting upon the need to consider empirical man, paradoxically ends in a social prescription with no empirical foundation or precedent.

It was stated above that, from the point of view of Marxism, economics or political economy is defective in that it gives an account of economic life in terms of prices, wages, costs, profit, capital, and so on as if these were transhistoric "categories," or eternal elements intrinsic to economic life under all circumstances. The now common definition of economics as the science of the allocation of scarce resources among alternative uses is a better example of what Marx objected to than most economic notions that existed in his own day. This definition implies that there is something that can be called the economic problem for all men in all stages of civilization and technology, and that the rational solution of that problem requires either genuine or simulated markets to produce certain equilibria between commodity and discommodity— a universal law resembling the generalizations of physics. Marx's denial of the truth of political economy was not only a denial that the economists had given an accurate description of free enterprise. It was a denial that the description of a particular economic arrangement was a time- lessly true description of the essence of economic life. This in turn is part of Marx's broad doctrine that in general there are no timeless essences and therefore no eternal truths which are not either trivial or purely formal. Marx's political philosophy is mingled with a theory about the nature of all things; indeed his political philosophy is to a certain extent governed by a universal scheme or "system," a doctrine that things neither have essences nor do they, as fixed things, have exist- ences, but they have histories or careers. Becoming, according to the formula, takes the place of being.

Marx followed Hegel in fact, if not in expression, in rejecting as "metaphysical" the view that there are finished "things" or "objects" which have a fixed, given, straightforward constitution. He asserted on the contrary that everything is affected by both change and relation. Thus the various species are forever evolving and the individuals come into being, grow, and then decline. The inanimate things are thrown up by natural processes and then erode, oxidize, or otherwise decay, while internally, they are, like the living beings, constantly in motion. Moreover, each thing is affected, indeed constituted, by the relation in which it stands to other things. For example, a man who is a servant is a servant only in virtue of his relation to another being who is the opposite of a servant, namely a master. The nature of a servant is not intelligible by exclusive reference to the servant himself, just as one could not understand "employee" if there were not "employers." In addition, there is an element of contradictoriness that is introduced into the constitution of perfectly motionless, unchanging things independ- ently of their relations with other things: a curved line, everywhere curved, is nevertheless straight between two points infinitesimally sepa- rated. The best example of this paradox is given not by Marx and Engels but by Democritus: "If a cone were cut by a plane parallel to the base, what ought one to think of the surfaces resulting from the section: are they equal or unequal?" [5] The easy answer is "both."

Further, the lines of distinction between classes of things are not sharp, for there are individuals at the margins that are as much of one class as of another ("plant-animals" and "sensitive plants"); and even life itself is not simply distinguishable from nonlife. The transition from life to death is not instantaneous (*e.g.,* the nails and hair continue to grow after "death"), and life proper consists of a process by which the living thing continually dies and renews itself through excretion and nutrition, so that life is inseparable from a continuous dying. It goes without saying that if life and death were in no way distinguishable, it would be impossible to distinguish living from dead material, or to say of life that it implied or presupposed or even required death; yet the Marxist position is that life as a process is not simply life, but it is also necessarily and at the same time death. Life exists as a process in virtue of a contradiction: life is both life and death. And so it is with the other "things."

All things are in flux, as Marxism asserts following Heraclitus, and all flux is motion. To understand the character of all things, it is necessary to grasp the universal law of motion, the law governing nature, human history, and thought. That law is derived from the Marxist doctrine of the essential contradictoriness of motion itself. Since the time of Zeno the Eleatic, a "proof" has existed that motion is impossible: every moving body is at each instant in one and only one place—which is the definition of being at rest. To be in motion is thus to be at rest and also not to be at rest. Each thing is, therefore, by analogy with a body in motion, equally what it "is" instantaneously and what it "is" historically, not in spite of, but in virtue of the fact that the two are contradictory.

Contradiction is fundamental to development, *i.e.,* to historical change, when change is assimilated to physical motion. Change is generated by contradiction through the mutual opposition of the two contradictory elements present in the thing in question. Consider an example given by Engels: a grain of cereal is planted, and it is annihilated as a grain while the plant grows up. As the plant develops to its own extinction, it produces many grains like the one from which it sprang. The grain is the affirmation (or "thesis"), the plant the negation (or "antithesis"), and the many grains the negation of the negation (or "synthesis"). Let us consider one more example: select any algebraic quantity, a, as the affirmation. Negate it by multiplying it by -1, to form $-a$. Negate the negation by multiplying it by itself, and the product is a^2, the affirmation on a higher level. The sequence of affirmation, negation, and negation of the negation is called the dialectic, and it is this that Marxism believes to be the universal law of nature, history, and thought. All development occurs on this pattern.

In the special case of human history and thought, a cause is assigned to the unfolding of the dialectical process. That cause is the mode of production and its mutations. Because the primary phenomenon is the material conditions of production, the Marxist doctrine of history is called dialectical materialism, to distinguish it from the idealist dialectic of Hegel which asserted the primary phenomenon to be self-dependent reason as the source of historical change. As a theory of human life, dialectical materialism asserts that the ground of all development in society and understanding is contradiction in the order of production. The most massive of such contradictions is the conflict between classes in society. By subsuming the opposition of class interests under the apparatus of the dialectic, Marxism seeks to show that the conflict cannot be resolved through compromises or mutual accommodations but only by a "negation of the negation," *i.e.*, by revolutionary changes in which the existing classes are annihilated and replaced by a synthesis "on a higher level."

An important element of Marx's political philosophy is his reconstruction of history for the purpose of showing that history has in fact been governed by the materialist dialectic. According to that reconstruction, each epoch inherits a mode of production and a complex of relations among men that is peculiarly fitted to that mode of production. Eventually a change takes place in the mode of production, brought on perhaps by a change in needs that could have been engendered by that very mode of production, and, more immediately, brought on by a fundamental discovery or invention stimulated by those needs. The new mode of production comes into being while the relations among the human beings are still those generated by the previous mode of production. The contradiction between existent social relations and the emergent mode of production, *i.e.*, the clash between the established and the embryonic dominant classes, is the source of "all collisions in history."

Marx and Engels cite a number of historical developments as evidence of this hypothesis, the most amply treated being the transition from feudal to capitalistic society, and the evolution toward postcapitalism. The former is explained by recurring to the rise of machine manufacture in the Middle Ages, first in the textile industry and then more generally. The spread of machine production broke down the structure of guildmasters with journeyman and apprentice labor, replacing it by a relation of bourgeois employers and wage-earning employees between whom no ties existed but that of the wage payment. The manufacturing mode of production was the vehicle by which the most fortunate and most active escaped serfs rose to displace the guild-masters as the owners of the new means of production, and to become the progenitors of a new class, the bourgeoisie. Opposed to them, and at the same time indispensable to them, were the proletarian laborers having nothing to live by but the wages from the sale of their labor power. As industry and commerce expanded, the scale of production increased enormously, and as it did, the relations between the owning and non-owning classes underwent a further change, an aggravation. The clash of interests between capitalists and wage-earners inevitably sharpened, for the proletarians' condition had to deteriorate because of the contradictions that are intrinsic to capitalism, contradictions that will appear when we consider Marx's critique of capitalist production. For the present it suffices to say that, according to Marx, the full development of machine production (under private ownership) requires the absolute pauperization and dehumanization of the wage-earners because of the pressures of capitalist competition. At last the wretchedness of the masses will become unbearable, and the conflict of the classes will break forth into a decisive combat—decisive because the victory of the proletariat will usher in a new age of man.

The proletarians have neither the wealth nor the wish to become the owners of the means of production *as a class*. Unlike every other insurgent class in the past, their purpose is not to take the place of their oppressors but to put an end to oppression. The means of achieving this end is to abolish the private ownership of the means of production and thus to abolish the distinction between owners and nonowners thereof, the distinction which is the condition for the division of human society into classes. Upon the dissolution of classes will necessarily ensue the end of the class struggle and the beginning of strictly human history. When that has occurred, the relations among men will have caught up with the latest great development in the mode of production; the conditions of oppression disappearing, the need for coercion will disappear as well, and the state will wither away to be replaced by the universal brotherhood of man.

Marx was well aware that his prognosis for mankind was necessarily linked to a diagnosis of prevailing conditions. He realized that he must investigate the contemporary (European) world in its essentials, which is to say in its economic character, in order to satisfy himself and others that the dialectic of materialism is actually operative in the decisive period, namely the present. It was necessary for him to demonstrate that the law of the nature of capitalism is the law of the transformation of capitalism into something radically different. His enterprise incidentally required him to show that no explanation of capitalism other than his own had grasped the essential character of capitalism, and therefore no other account, at least no other then known, could be made the basis of a prognosis for mankind. This means that ordinary political economy, which did not come to the conclusion that capitalism is self-vitiating, is in various respects unsatisfactory even as a description of how capitalism works. Marx's own economics is almost wholly "critical," devoted not to the explanation of how a socialist economy should or would be constituted but to a detailed representation of the self-contradictoriness and transitoriness of capitalist institutions, and to the inadequacy of political economy as known. The inseparability of the two criticisms is implicit in the subtitle of *Capital: A Critique of Political Economy.*

Marx's general criticism of political economy has already been mentioned. We must take up here his critical analysis of capitalism proper, and with it his more specific reflections on political economy. The title of his major economic work, *Capital,* indicates what seemed to him to be the central economic problem. Capital, according to Marx, does not mean simply the artificial means of production—equally a stone axe in the hand of a primitive, a bow in the hand of a Grecian hunter, or a power loom in nineteenth-century England. Capital is productive wealth in the peculiar form that generates profit. The prevailing system is called capitalism because the means of production, privately owned, are a source of profit to their owners the capitalists. It is very important to understand the nature of profit with perfect precision, for profit is at the heart of the prevailing social and economic order. Profit is not simply any economic surplus, such as might arise in primitive or feudal economies, any more than capital is simply productive wealth. Profit and capital are uniquely, mutually complementary.

Profit appears directly as a part of the price of a commodity, a part which the owner of the means of production, the capitalist (as Marx was not the first to call him) is able to claim. What exactly does his share consist of? How does it originate and by what right does the capitalist lay claim to it? Classical political economy had provided a certain answer, which was the point of departure for Marx's own analysis. Classical political economy had begun with the assertion that labor is the source of value, that the amount of labor embodied in a good is thus related to the amount of value in the good, and that the relative values of two goods must be in proportion to the relative amounts of labor embodied in them. The accompanying presumption is that the one who has created the value by pouring his labor into the object has the right to be the owner of his product. The classical economists agreed that, when production was carried on by individuals for themselves, using their own hands and the implements fashioned by them or owned by them, each man could claim for himself whatever he produced. But that condition ceased when, in order to carry on production, men required access to land and instruments belonging to others. Thereafter, those others had a right to share in the product. Evidently, profit (to leave aside the problem of rent) is coeval with the accumulation of productive property by some members of society.

There was, according to the classic view, a period of human life when every man could "produce" independently; and then there was—and still is—a period in which land was made subject to appropriation, and the accumulation of durable property was made feasible. In the earlier period of human life, the labor theory of value applied in its simple and direct form. In the latter period, the product of labor is shared with capitalists and landlords. Readers of the doctrines of Hobbes and Locke, but especially the latter, will be reminded of the division of all human history between a period in the state of nature and a period in the state of civil society. We are now prepared to understand more fully Marx's asseveration that classical political economy assigns to the institutions of capitalism the status of prospectively timeless, natural conditions. Classical political economy and the political philosophy to which it was linked regarded as absolutely epochal the progress of man from the prepolitical to the political condition. That same crucial change was perfected or consummated with the replacement of absolute monarchy by constitutional government, for between a subject and an arbitrary master there is only the law of nature. That crucial change in the human state was connected by classical political economy with the accumulation and protection of property in the means of production. The institutions of property thus come to parallel, and to have the same status as, civil society or civilization—political life—itself. Neither Hobbes and Locke nor the classical political economists looked beyond civil society for a further radical melioration of man's estate. It was left for Rousseau to raise the broad question of the goodness of both civil society and property, and thus to open the way for his successors to search for a horizon beyond that of civil society. Marx, in rejecting the view that property and civil society, or say political life, were the absolute condition for decent human existence in peace and prosperity, denied the natural and permanent status of "the laws of commerce." He rejected the implication of classical political economy that profit and the private ownership of the means of production are here to stay, as much as and for the same reasons that political society is here to stay.

Surely Marx did not concede that the transition from the state of nature to the state of political society was the absolutely epochal change in human life. Neither did he concede that the parallel change from the pure to the diluted application of the labor theory of value was epochal or even that it provided a valid ground for understanding the prevailing economic institutions. That a difficulty indeed existed in that mode of explanation·was noticed by Ricardo as he examined Adam Smith's theory of value and wages. Ricardo pointed out that if it were true in a simple sense that a commodity which required a day's labor for its production should be said to contain a day's-labor-worth of value, then when that commodity is exchanged for labor, it should purchase its equal in value, namely a day's labor. The brief formulation would be, labor embodied equals labor commanded, for any commodity.[6] In other words there would be no profit: a workman could be hired for a week only if his product for the week (or the full value of it) were paid him as his wage. The fact that the wage is not equal to the whole product compelled Ricardo (and Smith, incidentally) to find an alternative formulation, one that ascribed value-productivity to capital as congealed labor. Marx rejected the Ricardian and other classical explanations of profit, wages, and value because those explanations, in accounting for the difference between the labor embodied in and the labor commanded by a commodity, did not lead up to a condemnation of profit as resting upon exploitation, which Marx believed it to do. We must now consider his alternative explanation.

Marx begins by noting a problem that arises out of the exchange of goods: when one commodity is exchanged for another, a common ground is indicated between two things which appear to have nothing at all in common. Suppose a pair of shoes to be exchanged for three shirts. The shoes and the shirts are so perfectly unlike as to be incommensurable. How can the ratio of three for one, or any other ratio, ever be arrived at? To deal with the problem of commensurability, Marx recurs to, but modifies, a distinction which was traditional in political economy, the distinction between value in use and value in exchange. For the distinction use value–exchange value, regarded by political economy as fundamental, Marx substitutes use value–value. The reason for this is that he does not regard exchange as a permanent, natural institution but rather as a historic and transitory one. But exchange value is derivative from value proper, and in order to understand capitalism it is necessary to understand exchange value and therefore value simply. Returning now to the two commodities, we notice that they are absolutely unlike so far as we consider their value in use or their qualitative character, each good being designed for a certain purpose that the other could not serve. Now a shoe comes to be a shoe in virtue of having been produced by the peculiar labor of a shoemaker. A shirt is a shirt because it is the product of shirtmaking labor. The difference between shoemaking and shirtmaking labor is the source of the qualitative difference between shoes and shirts. Marx goes on to assert that, just as the two commodities can, indeed must, be looked at as if they are not only dissimilar but also have commensurable values, so the labor that produced them must be capable of being looked at not only as qualitatively differentiated labor. It must also be seen as homogeneous or undifferentiated human labor, as the generation of a certain amount of motion in a certain mass by a certain expenditure of human energy. As skills, therefore, the kinds of human labor are simply different; but as toil, all labor is the same, and is measurable in units of time, according to the length of its duration. Upon this latter fact depends the mensurability and commensurability of values. The summary formula would be, differentiated human labor produces use values and qualitative differences among commodities, while undifferentiated human labor produces value simply and quantitative commensurability among the commodities. Thus it is in their character as products of undifferentiated human labor, not as products of specific labor aimed at satisfying specific wants, that commodities have commensurable values and can enter into exchange.

It should be pointed out that the assignment of labor alone as the source of value is not demonstrated by Marx, but is asserted by him as something self-evident.[7]

The foregoing account of value provides support for Marx's definition and elaboration of the notion of a commodity. By a commodity Marx means a good which is privately produced for the sake of exchange (or sale, *i.e.,* exchange against money.) Capitalism could thus be described as a system of commodity production and, as such, based upon confusion and distortion. Rationally, the sum of all the individual labor-powers in the community is the aggregate of labor-power available to the society for the satisfaction of all its wants. If men were to live without distortion in their affairs, their labor-power would be directly applied to the satisfaction of their wants rather than to production for exchange. Because the means of production are privately owned, however, production is carried on not directly for its true purpose—the satisfaction of wants—but for the special advantage of the owners of the means of production. The social character of labor is thus mediated and distorted by the mode of production. What Adam Smith regarded as a peculiar virtue of private enterprise, namely, the voluntary performance

of a social function under the influence of a desire for private advantage, is regarded by Marx as the ground of the iniquity and instability
in the prevailing system. Why he did so conclude can be understood if
we look further at the capitalistic mode of production as Marx interpreted it.

Indispensable to capitalism are the private ownership of the means
of production and the existence of a body of men who both do not own
any means of production and are perfectly free, in the sense of being
unbound to the owners of the means of production by any personal ties
of duty or rights. In order to live, the unpropertied must therefore
engage themselves to labor at the machines and on the land of the
propertied. The propertyless in effect sell to the propertied a commodity
called labor-power—not labor. Labor-power means the ability to labor
for a given period; labor means the actual duration of the labor. For
Marx the distinction is crucial. Labor-power is a commodity, under
capitalism, and that means that it is something produced for sale and
having a value determined by the amount of labor congealed or incorporated in it. But what could be meant by the amount of labor incorporated in the capacity of a laborer to work for eight hours? The answer
is, that amount of labor that was required to produce the necessities that
must be available to the man furnishing the labor-power in question.
Somewhat more broadly, the value of a day's labor-power is determined
by the amount of labor necessary to produce the subsistence for the
laborer and his family in order to maintain the supply of labor-power
at its level, not only from day to day but from generation to generation.

Let us suppose that in order to provide all the materials of subsistence necessary to support a labor-power of eight hours, six hours of
labor must be performed. Then the value of a labor-power of eight
hours would be equal to the value of six hours' output. One would then
obtain the output of eight hours by giving for it the output of six hours.
The value generated by the employed labor-power during the two
hours of its application while it is "not paid for" is called by Marx "surplus value"; it is the basis of profit. Profit exists only because a portion
of the workingman's labor-power results in an output for which he is
not paid. Yet he is not being cheated, in a certain sense. Marx is at pains
to point out that the labor-power is bought at its full value, its value
understood as being rigidly subject to the labor theory of the value of
all commodities including labor-power itself. Thus the man is paid in
full for his labor-power but not for his labor. By this formulation Marx
believed he had solved the problem that classical political economy had
failed to clarify with consistency, the problem caused by the inequality
of the labor embodied in a product and the labor commanded by it. His

solution depends on the distinction between labor and labor-power. By this radicalization of the labor theory of value that applies it to labor-power itself, Marx was enabled to argue that a serious hidden contradiction of capitalism was brought to light: the relation between employer and employee is at one and the same time both cheating and not cheating. In the sense that it is not cheating, no one can individually be blamed: the buying and selling of labor-power are done at full value according to the rules of the market. So far as it is cheating, however, it requires rectification. Marx's conclusion is that the abuse demands the abolition of the system rather than a change of the rules within the system: "reform" could never suffice, because no mere reform could terminate the buying and selling of labor-power.

This contradiction is but the ground for many more. For example, from the proposition that profit originates in the consumption of labor-power by the capitalist, it follows that profit can be made to increase either by consuming more labor-power or by increasing the amount of labor that is produced by a given labor-power (say, approximately, increasing the output per working day). But the increase in output per day (increase in productivity) is achieved by increasing the use of machinery. Increasing the use of machinery opposes the increase in consumption of labor-power. In order to prevent the introduction of machinery from suppressing the profitable consumption of labor-power, the working day must be lengthened. Marx thus arrives at the conclusion that the introduction of machinery leads and will lead to the lengthening of the working day and to the formation of a large population of the chronically, technologically unemployed.[8] Here and elsewhere, Marx's economic analysis led him to make certain grossly incorrect predictions as to conditions in a matured capitalistic economy. Not because his power of prediction is in itself of great interest, but because so much of his revolutionary animus is vindicated by the horrors he professes to foresee in the flowering of capitalism, his mistakes of prediction come to have a singular effect on the credibility of the analysis on which they rest.

To continue. The restless struggle for profit causes the capitalistic economy and society to be in a state of endless flux. Under the lash of competition, which tends to reduce profits, capitalists must constantly revolutionize the process of production in order to cheapen it. Old skills are rendered obsolete and the average level of skill required in the work force is reduced as the motions of the artisan's hands are analyzed and copied in machinery. Since the fundamental condition of capitalist economic life is a free, propertyless work force toward which the propertied have no duty, the whole burden of technological change falls upon the wage-earners in the form of unemployment and poverty. But technological change as such is not peculiar to capitalism; only under capitalism does it become a source of misery. In a dialectical manner, Marx argues that in its abuses, capitalism serves to expose a transcapitalistic human problem that can be resolved only by the transcending of capitalism:

... Modern Industry ... through its catastrophes imposes the necessity of recognizing, as a fundamental law of production, variation of work, consequently fitness of the labourer for varied work, consequently the greatest possible development of his varied aptitudes. It becomes a question of life and death for society to adapt the mode of production to the normal functioning of this law, Modern Industry, indeed, compels society, under penalty of death, to replace the detail-worker of to-day, crippled by lifelong repetition of one and the same trivial operation, and thus reduced to the mere fragment of a man, by the fully developed individual, fit for a variety of labours, ready to face any change of production, and to whom the different social functions he performs are but so many modes of giving free scope to his own natural and acquired powers.[9]

It must be pointed out that the tendency of technological change has not in fact been to reduce the average level of skill in the work force or to lead to falling real wages and a growing "industrial reserve army of the unemployed." Nor is there any evidence anywhere in the world that modern technology can be made compatible with institutionalized jack-of-all-tradeism.

Marx takes up many more aspects of capitalistic economic life than we can deal with here. His single-minded purpose throughout is to show that in virtue of what capitalism is, in virtue of its being intrinsically contradictory, its development must be its dissolution: the more it fulfills itself and approaches its peak, the more it destroys itself and approaches its fall. He provides a remarkable summary of his understanding of the case, late in Volume I of *Capital:*

We saw in Part IV., when analysing the production of relative surplus-value: within the capitalist system all methods for raising the social productiveness of labour are brought about at the cost of the individual labourer; all means for the development of production transform themselves into means of domination over, and exploitation of, the producers; they mutilate the labourer into a fragment of a man, degrade him to the level of an appendage of a machine, destroy every remnant of charm in his work and turn it into a hated toil; they estrange him from the intellectual potentialities of the labour-process in the same proportion as science is incorporated in it as an independent power; they distort the conditions under which he works, subject him during the labour-process to a despotism the more hateful for its meanness; they transform his life-time into working-time, and drag his wife and child beneath the wheels of the Juggernaut of capital. But all methods for the production of surplus value are at the same time methods of accumulation; and every extension of accumulation becomes again a means for the development of those methods. It follows therefore that in proportion as capital accumulates, the lot of the labourer, be his payment high or low, must grow worse. The law, finally, that always equilibrates the relative surplus-population, or industrial reserve army, to the extent and energy of accumulation, this law rivets the labourer to capital more firmly than the wedges of Vulcan did Prometheus to the rock. It establishes an accumulation of misery, corresponding with accumulation of capital. Accumulation of wealth at one pole is, therefore, at the same time accumulation of misery, agony of toil, slavery, ignorance, brutality, mental degradation, at the opposite pole, *i.e.,* on the side of the class that produces its own product in the form of capital.[10]

Marx believed that when, at last, the bourgeoisie had been reduced for the most part to proletarianism by savage competition, and the proletariat had been reduced to stark poverty by the laws of accumulation and profiteering, then the uprising would occur and mankind would stand on the eve of history.[11] It is not going too far to assert that Marx's economics consists of the attempt to show how that fateful transformation is implicit in the labor theory of value as concretized in the practices of capitalism.

Whether or how far these doctrines of Marx are sound is a question of more than ordinary interest to the world. It arises in two parts: whether what Marx regarded as inevitable is so; and whether the premises of his system are acceptable. These questions we must now take up.

Marx's predictions are on two subjects—the fate of capitalism and the character of socialist society. On the former he is at great length, as we have seen, and to a large extent he predicts incorrectly. A century after he came to his conclusions, it is fair to deny that the introduction of machinery must lead to lengthening of the working day, that there must be massive, growing, technological unemployment, that the bourgeoisie must be proletarianized and the proletariat pauperized, and that socialism is the culmination of capitalism. Marx's predictions were based upon the belief that an economic order has a life and being of its own, that it resembles the articulation of inert parts, and that when it is somehow or other launched on its way, it functions mechanically, as little subject to change of direction as a bullet shot from a gun. Marx had a certain loathing for utilitarianism, but he was as prone as any utilitarian doctrinaire to liken social life to a syllogism. Logic is supremely universal, everywhere and at all times the same. It is expressive of reason, but it has nothing to learn from prudence. Marx made concessions, but absolutely insufficient ones, to such simple and undialectical influences as laws—laws to limit the length of the working day, laws to encourage or compel collective bargaining, to enact workmen's compensation, progressive income taxation, unemployment insurance, old-age benefits, laws to regulate securities exchanges, to promote full employment, to protect competition, to control the money supply, to support agriculture, to relieve the sick, to suppress the adulteration of food, to compel the young to submit to be educated, to insure savings, and a thousand other laws, not the least of which is the law that puts lawmaking under the influence of the reigning multitudes that he mistook for a pauperized proletariat. Marx was an astute journalistic observer of political things, but in his teaching he conceded nothing significant to politics, *i.e.,* to discretion, which he discounted as mere "reform." He postulated the economic man with as much narrow assurance as any political economist, if with a more brilliant rhetoric.

Marx's predictions are not only of the baleful kind. Occasionally he alludes to the character of life in the postcapitalistic epoch and gives brief sketches of the communist world. There is no way to test empirically his visions of socialism, because all existing socialist societies claim to be in a state of transition toward communism proper, and every disparity between the expectation and the reality is explained as temporary. Whether all such disparities are in truth temporary, or how many could be temporary, depends upon the soundness of the ground upon which Marx's expectations rested. We turn to that question in conclusion.

The ruling principle of Marxian socialist society is, "From each according to his ability, to each according to his needs." This is a maxim fit to serve as the fundamental law among loyal, wise, and incorruptible friends, devoted to one another with an absolutely unselfish benevolence. Among such friends, not only would no individual seek his advantage at the expense of others, but the thought of doing so would never occur to him. In this sense, duty as duty would be transcended: what the mere sense of duty dictates to a man capable of selfishness would be the most spontaneous desire of a man as member of the friendly society. His duty would not appear to him as duty. Marxian society would be a society of billions of friends warmly joined in the rarest and most sensitive union of amity.

It is imaginable that there would be a great concourse of men living together without any threat of coercion to restrain them from offending each other, but that their uncoerced sociality would reflect not goodness but utter indifference, the extinction of every animating impulse. Marx emphatically does not have this in mind: his socialists would be alive at the peak of all their powers, each abundantly active. His vision of life for the generality of mankind is what the ancient thinkers conceived as the highest possibility open to the wisest and the best—the mutual love of a few noble spirits, elevated above every petty desire, free from every trace of envy or worldly ambition, willingly sharing that invaluable good which does not pass away from its possessor when he bestows it upon another and which is multiplied when it is divided, that good being wisdom. The notion of the quintessence of justice materializing among the wise is intelligible, for wisdom excites the admiration that generates love, and wisdom is a good for which men cannot contend invidiously but only harmoniously. The conditions for rational benevolence would be fully met among the few who desire a good the pursuit of which cannot corrupt. The perfect society is the society, then, in which philosophy as the rule of life would become indistinguishable from justice, which also is the rule of life. In the perfect society, justice would administer itself, and it would therefore be perfectly pure because untainted by the need to coerce, to punish, or to deceive. The disappearance of justice into philosophy might be said to be equivalent to the disappearance of the political in the philosophic.

The perfect society could not be described except on the premise that there is such a thing as philosophy, that a few men take it to be the greatest good, that more than a few never can or will take it to be so, and that therefore it is in the nature of things that justice and political society or government will not dissolve into philosophy. Marxism dreams of the disappearance of justice and political society—not in philosophy, it goes without saying, but in rational economics, and therefore for the mass of humanity, not merely for the infinitesimal few.

The economic system that would be approved as rational by Marx would of course not be the liberal economy in which the "economic man" finds free scope for his "rationality." That rationality, which is in fact only self-interested calculation, is thought by Marx to be infected with contradiction. A self-contradicting rationality would appropriately serve as the spring of action in a system that seeks prosperity through poverty, freedom through subordination, and the common good through the emancipation of self-preference.

Pre-Marxian, or at any rate pre-Hegelian, political philosophy, both ancient and modern, was characterized by a certain moderation that allowed it to approve regimes which achieve reason through myth, freedom through coercion, or sociality through selfishness. Wayward and unreflective as men are, they may still be made amenable to social life if they can be brought under the guidance either of well-disposed men or of cunning institutions that play men's lower motives off against each other to a salutary outcome. In either case the end or outcome was conceived to be of utmost importance, apart from such considerations as whether the end is given by nature, or whether it justifies the means. How far Marx was affected by the tendency of Kant to depreciate the mere ends we cannot here consider; but it is certain that Marx repudiated the willingness of the ancient and the eagerness of the modern traditions to make peace with, though not to surrender to the weaknesses of human nature, and to be content with society consisting of men as they are. Marx dreamed of that human condition in which good ends would be sought by good men using only good means and responding to (because possessing) only good motives. The basis or presupposition of his dream was the generation of a new man, or the regeneration of man—and the instrument of regeneration would be the rational economy rightly understood.

Unexpectedly, we now see coming into view a ground of agreement between ancients and pre-Marxian moderns on this most important point: political life rests upon the imperfection of man and continues to exist because human nature rules out the elevation of all men to the level of excellence. The connection between civil government and man's imperfection is expressed by Rousseau, for example, in the form of the distinction between state and society: men can be social while uncorrupted, but in political community they prey and are preyed upon by one another.[12] At the beginning of *Common Sense,* Thomas Paine wrote, "Society is produced by our wants, and government by our wickedness; the former promotes our happiness *positively* by uniting our affections, the latter *negatively* by restraining our vices. . . . The first is a patron, the last a punisher."

Rousseau may be said to have suggested, via the doctrine of the perfectibility of man, that government may be more and more replaced by society: in the perfect freedom of self-government, coercion loses most of its sting. But Rousseau did not at all suppose the utter collapse of government into society, for he did not suppose that all men would become philosophic, nor that there is any perfect substitute for the full rationality of men that would render coercion and rhetoric of all kinds, *i.e.,* political life, dispensable. He did not, in brief, expect ordinary selfishness simply to disappear from among the generality of men.

What in Rousseau was a limited suggestion, although an emphatic one, came to be the dogmatic core of a confident prognosis, a strident propaganda, and a revolutionary incitation in Marx: the state or political order will wholly wither away, and homogeneous mankind will live socially under the rule of absolute benevolence—from each according to his ability, to each according to his needs. No longer will duty be performed incidentally to the pursuit of selfish interest. The link between duty and interest, which is to say the subordination of duty to interest, will be broken for once and all by the abolition of the categories "duty" and "interest." They will be abolished by the revision of the property relations, by the inauguration of a new economics which will bring on the full perfection of human nature via the transcendence of production for exchange.

In barest outline, Marx's radicalization of Rousseau can be said to rest upon the supersession of philosophic reason by historic reason. Philosophic reason, the intelligence of individual human beings, being unequally present among men, political society with coercion and rhetoric cannot be dispensed with if calamity is to be avoided. So the philosophic tradition believed. Marx's teaching is that there is a reason inherent in the course of history: History abhors a contradiction as profoundly as nature was ever thought to abhor a vacuum. Whether a contradiction means more than a clash of interests, we are not told. In any case, the unviability of every individual contradiction is transformed by the philosophy of history into the unviability of contradiction simply. The philosophy of history tries to communicate its confidence that contradiction must wipe itself out, working through the discontents of men afflicted with the symptoms of the contradictions that exist in society. The progressive resolution of contradictions, and the movement of man toward the condition free of contradiction deserves to be called the expression of historic reason. It supersedes or overcomes the philosophic reason, or the intelligence of individual men, not only in the obvious sense that, through the historic evolution of human nature, the unequal distribution of intelligence will cease to have political relevance. When the new breed of man is generated by the common ownership of the means of production, all the old (natural) categories of right will fall before the logic of history, and subphilosophic men will live in uncoerced and myth-free (*i.e.,* perfectly rational) society, as only the rarest of men were thought to be able to do, but even more emancipatedly than the rarest, who never had the benefit of the perfect environment. The multitudes of men will be conditioned to reach the heights by abundance of goods produced and distributed without any opposition of interest. Marx appears to believe that, if men are divided by scarcity, they would be united by abundance. We would be readier to be convinced of this if there were reason to believe that men will some day be indistinguishable from the grazing herbivores.

Marxism is famous for looking forward to the end not only of political life but also of religion. Religion is the belief in the existence of a realm of the whole where there is a rectification for every defect in the terrestrial world. Here there is death, there life. Here iniquity goes unseen or unpunished, there it is recorded and retributed; or if it is beyond human punishment, it receives divine punishment even here below. The goodness that is ignored or mocked on earth is accounted and honored in heaven. The belief that the whole is or tends to be good can be maintained even if the visible part of the whole is imperfect, by arguing that the invisible part perfectly makes up the deficiencies present to our view. We would be led far out of our way if we attempted to compare the teachings of the theological and the philosophic traditions with respect to this question; but we may observe that the ancient philosophic tradition also taught that nature as a whole is good. Yet it is not so unequivocally good as to render superfluous the coercion and rhetoric that support political life; thus the goodness of nature as a whole does not permeate all of human life. On this fundamental point there is a ground of agreement between ancient philosophy and revealed religion: for all practical purposes, the goodness of the whole, whether the whole is the sum of the natural and the supernatural, or the complex of form and matter in nature itself, cannot be translated or transformed into the goodness of man's common life. In the case of modern political philosophy, the goodness of nature as a whole was characteristically not asserted; teleology was of course rejected, and the wretchedness of the state of nature strongly argued. Nature required to be rectified, or rather to be governed; and the clue to the government of nature was to be found in the laws of nature—the laws of science and the laws of politics and economics. The belief in the possibility of conquering or governing nature perhaps opened the way to the Marxian notion that the perfection of human life is possible, and not only possible but foreseeable, in the classless society. But as has been seen, that consummation was not explicit in the teaching of pre-Marxian modern political philosophy. Not before Marx asserted the historicity of nature itself,[13] the absolute perfectibility of human nature under the influence of economic conditions, was it supposed that political life and religion must vanish and be replaced by uncoerced, rational society.

We are led, through the doctrines of Marxism, to reconsider some commonly held views. One is that there is a deep hostility between philosophy and political society because philosophy, by its unconfined questioning, eventually exposes the polity itself to the blasts of skepticism; while the body politic, suspicious of theories and prone to Philistinism, always threatens the thinking sort of men with contempt or worse.

But however well-founded the mutual suspicions might be, we observe that philosophy, certainly classical political philosophy, argues that man is by his nature political and that political society is the truly human society taking into view the characteristics of men generally. Philosophy has been thought to threaten politics; we see that in fact it defended politics, and that the anticipation of the end of political life had to await the supersession of philosophy by history—that is, by the doctrine of the emendation of Nature.

Another opinion brought under revision is that between philosophy and religion there is in principle war to the death, the one asserting the supremacy of reason, the other of faith. We have seen that philosophy can have, and did for ages have, a certain common ground with religion; both had views of nature that did not lead to the expectation of perfect society within the natural order. The theoretical discountenancing of religion in the name of an aspiration toward perfect society had to await the supersession of philosophy by history.

We might summarize by saying that the replacement of philosophy by history was the condition for the replacement of politics and religion by society and economics. This is the kernel of Marxism.

Marxism is not simply another political system, or one more ideology. It proposes nothing less than the end of the West—of political life, philosophy, and religion—as the foregoing summary indicates. Perhaps we should look forward with eager anticipation to the end of the West—but we cannot know whether we should without rationally examining the project for strangling philosophy. That rational examination is part of the philosophic quest itself. We cannot free ourselves of philosophy, if only because we must philosophize to pass judgment on philosophy. We begin to suspect the soundness of the antiphilosophic historicism of Marx. Observing its weakness prepares us to concede that history can make room for spiritually impoverished societies: the viability of Marxist nations is a sign not of the soundness of Marx's prophecy but of the unsoundness of the sanguine historicism on which he based it. We have every right to conclude that history is the opiate of the masses.

NOTES

1. Karl Marx, *The Poverty of Philosophy*, ii. 1. 2nd observation.

2. *Capital* (New York: Modern Library, n.d.), I, 834, n.l. Copyright by the Modern Library. Pagination is the same in the edition published by Charles H. Kerr & Co. The reference is to Burke's "Thoughts and Details on Scarcity."

3. Cf. Engels' *Herr Eugen Dühr-*

ing's Revolution in Science [Anti-Dühring], x. 1: ". . . ideology, the deduction of reality not from itself but from its mental image." Also Engels' *Ludwig Feuerbach*, iv. 7th par. from the end: ". . . ideology, that is, occupation with thoughts as with independent entities."

4. "On the Jewish Question," in *Selected Essays by Karl Marx*, trans. H. J. Stenning (New York: International Publishers, 1926), pp. 55–56.

5. From K. Freeman, *Ancilla to the Pre-Socratic Philosophers* (Cambridge:

Harvard University Press, 1957).

6. David Ricardo, *Principles of Political Economy and Taxation*, i. 1.

7. See, for example, *Capital*, i (p. 45).

8. *Ibid.*, IV. xv. 3 (p. 445).

9. *Ibid.*, 9 (p. 534). .

10. *Ibid.*, xv. 4 (pp. 708–9).

11. See *ibid.*, xxxii.

12. Cf. the sentence with which Montesquieu begins I. iii of *The Spirit of the Laws*.

13. See above, p. 811.

READINGS

A. Marx, Karl, and Engels, Friedrich. *The Communist Manifesto.*
    Marx, Karl, and Engels, Friedrich. *The German Ideology.* Ed. R. Pascal. New York: International Publishers, 1939. Part I.
    Marx, Karl. *Theses on Feuerbach.*
    Marx, Karl. *Capital.* New York: Modern Library, n. d. Bk I, part I, chap. i, secs 1, 2, 4.
B. Engels, Friedrich. *Ludwig Feuerbach and the Outcome of German Classical Philosophy.* Ed. C. P. Dutt. New York: International Publishers, n.d. Chap. iv "Dialectical Materialism."
    Engels, Friedrich. *Herr Eugen Dühring's Revolution in Science (Anti-Dühring).* Trans. E. Burns. Ed. C. P. Dutt. New York: International Publishers, 1935. Part I "Philosophy."

FRIEDRICH NIETZSCHE

1844–1900

The young Nietzsche thought of the philosopher as a physician of culture. His own philosophy is both a diagnosis of the sickness or crisis of his time, the nineteenth century, and the search for a cure. In his first published book, *The Birth of Tragedy* (1872), Nietzsche placed his hope in a revival of German culture through the music of Richard Wagner. His second book, *Untimely Considerations,* known in English as *Thoughts Out of Season,* consists of four essays published separately between 1873 and 1876. One of these is again a tribute to Wagner. Nietzsche soon ceased to believe in the cure he had suggested, repudiating Wagner and losing faith in the possibility of a German cultural revival. He thus entered into the second stage of his development, a stage characterized by disillusionment and a turning to Western positivism. Symbolic of this is the dedication of his third book, *Human, All-too-Human* (1879) to Voltaire.[1] Nietzsche's final position is articulated in *Thus Spoke Zarathustra* (its four parts were written and published between 1883 and 1885) and the books following it. Nietzsche, however, never repudiated but only deepened the view of his time as sick and critical, a view which is to be found in the writings of his first stage of development; and the problems he raised at this stage are problems with which he never ceased to wrestle. One is, therefore, justified in beginning an exposition of Nietzsche's political philosophy with a discussion of one of his earlier writings, the second essay of *Thoughts Out of Season.*

The title of the essay, which was published in 1874, may be translated as "Of the Use and Disadvantage of History for Life"; in English it is known as *The Use and Abuse of History.*[2] Nietzsche's thoughts are out of season because they are meant to be contrary to his time and yet with an influence upon it for the benefit of a coming time. The essay is a critique of a specific "fault and defect" of the time, historicism, which Nietzsche calls the historical movement, the historical trend, or the historical sense. He believes his time to be suffering from a "malignant historical fever." [3]

Nietzsche's critique of historicism is also his confrontation with, and criticism of, Hegel. In the latter part of the essay Nietzsche refers to a "very celebrated philosophy" and continues, "I believe there has been no dangerous turning point in the progress of German culture in this century that has not been made more dangerous by the enormous and still living influence of this Hegelian philosophy." Hegel regards contemporary man as the perfection of world history; Hegelianism establishes the sovereignty of history over other spiritual powers such as art or religion; for Hegel "the highest and final stage of the world process came together in his own Berlin existence." [4] Against Hegel's doctrine that the historical process is a rational process which in Hegel's time has ended in an absolute moment at the zenith, Nietzsche asserts that the historical process neither is nor can be finished, that the completion of history is not merely impossible but undesirable because it would lead to a degeneration of man, and that history is not a rational process but is full of blindness, madness and injustice.

It might thus appear that Nietzsche simply effects a return to a pre-Hegelian viewpoint which considers history a realm of chance rather than a dimension of meaning. However, Nietzsche's critique of historicism does not deny the validity of the essential premises of historicism, and his criticism of Hegel is based on a crucial area of agreement with Hegel, as a closer analysis of The Use and Abuse of History will show.

The essay begins with a consideration of the life of animals. Animals forget each moment as soon as it passes. To live entirely in the present, without memory of the past, means to live unhistorically. Man remembers the past and cannot escape from it; man lives historically. He also suffers from the awareness of the past and the passing of time, if only because it brings with it an awareness that man is an imperfectible imperfection. Happiness depends on the ability to forget and to surrender completely to the present. A man who could forget nothing would be a totally unhappy man, for he would see only flux and change and would have no fixed points by which to take his bearings.

On the other hand, man would not be man without a memory of the past. Moreover, it is only by developing his historical sense and by virtue of his power of turning the past to the uses of the present that man rises above other animals and becomes man. Man's problem is therefore to find that balance between remembering and forgetting which is most conducive to his life as man. The degree and limits of man's memory of the past must be fixed by the extent to which man can incorporate or absorb the past. A healthy organism is one which instinctively assimilates only as much of the past as it can digest; the rest it simply does not see. The dividing line between the historical and the unhistorical is the organism's horizon. According to Nietzsche, "This is a universal law: a living thing can only be healthy, strong and productive within a certain horizon. . . ." [5]

Man's horizon is constituted by his fundamental set of assumptions about all things, by what he considers the absolute truth which he cannot question. His historical knowledge must be surrounded by an unhistorical atmosphere of darkness which limits the historical sense of man.

The proper sphere of history lies within and under the unhistorical atmosphere which must envelop man if he is to endure. Nietzsche admits that there are uses as well as abuses of history. He speaks of three kinds of history which can serve life. *Monumental* history provides the man of action with models of greatness by its depiction of the great men and events of the past. *Antiquarian* history addresses itself to the preserving and revering element in man, imbuing him with a salutary love for tradition. It is of special benefit to less gifted peoples and races because it keeps them safe from a restless and unproductive cosmopolitanism. *Critical* history places obsolete aspects of the past before the bar of judgment and condemns them; it brings to light injustices surviving from the past so that they can be abolished in the interest of the present.

Nietzsche is, however, more concerned with the abuses than with the uses of history. He is quick to point out how easy it is to misuse each of the above-mentioned kinds of history. Monumental history's models of past greatness can be erected to hinder the emergence of present greatness. The reverence for the past which antiquarian history fosters can act to stultify the present. There is always the danger that critical history will uproot more of the past than deserves to be uprooted. Moreover, Nietzsche links the efficacy of each kind of history to its blindness to the whole truth. By paying insufficient attention to the conditions needed for the emergence of greatness, monumental history deludes one into thinking that, because greatness was possible, it is still possible, which need not be the case. In cultivating a general reverence for the past, antiquarian history is necessarily indiscriminate and praises aspects of the past which do not deserve praise. Critical history fails to realize the extent to which men are the results of the past they seek to condemn. The uses of the past for the present depend on a violation of the truth about the past: useful history cannot be scientific history.

Science and the demand that history become a science disrupt the proper relation between history and life. Historical science is motivated by the desire to know rather than the desire to serve life, and it forces on the attention of man more historical knowledge than he can properly absorb or digest. At this point history no longer serves life; it disrupts life.

Nietzsche presents the reader with a catalogue of calamities resulting from an excess of history. One of these calamities is that men, confronted with a spectacle of history so vast that it becomes meaningless for them, will come to think of themselves as *epigoni,* late arrivals on the scene for whom there is nothing whatever to do. If Hegel were right, if history were finished, modern men would indeed be *epigoni.* Hegel is wrong, but the belief that he is right makes men act as if they were *epigoni.* Men who have no further task to accomplish or men who believe there is nothing more to be done are bound to degenerate, for what is best in man is his aspiration.

But neither the assertion that the historical process is finished nor the assertion that the historical process is rational is the most fundamental assertion of historicism. Historicism asserts the overwhelming importance of history, the determination of man's life and thought by history, and the impossibility of transcending the historical process. Nietzsche accepts this assertion of the omnipotence of history, and his acceptance constitutes a crucial area of agreement with Hegel. The calamities which Nietzsche attributes to an excess of historical knowledge can be summarized by saying that an excess of historical knowledge destroys man's horizon. There is, however, no permanent horizon of man as man. Men's fundamental assumptions about things are unevident, unsupported, historically variable and historically determined. There are neither eternal things nor eternal truths; there is only flux and change, which Nietzsche calls the finality of becoming.[6] While doctrines asserting the finality of becoming are true they are also fatal. History as the science of universal becoming is true but deadly.

If human life can only thrive within a certain horizon which men believe to be the absolute truth, but which in reality is merely one of many possible horizons, then life is in need of illusions, and the truth which exposes the horizon as a *mere* horizon is deadly. There is, then, a conflict between truth and life, or between life and wisdom.

In such a conflict, according to Nietzsche, one must choose the

side of life. There can be life without wisdom, but there can be no
wisdom without life.

It is, however, impossible to accept the illusions which life demands
if they are known to be illusions. Myths are useful only so long as they
are mistaken for the truth. A man's horizon is his most comprehensive
myth, and it enables him to live because he thinks of it as the truth.
To see a horizon as horizon is to be beyond that horizon. At the very
least the continued acceptance of a discredited horizon would involve
man in a degrading self-deception, but Nietzsche is concerned with the
ennoblement of man. If there is a tension between wisdom and life, it
cannot be resolved by the preference for life. An impasse has been
reached.

Yet *The Use and Abuse of History* ends on a note of hope, asserting
a harmony between life and wisdom. After historicism's exposure of the
arbitrary character of all human horizons, man is subjected to "the
hopeless waves of an infinite skepticism"; but Nietzsche professes to
sight land: man can recover from "the malady of history." [7] Such a
recovery is only possible if historicism is proved to be untrue or at least
not completely true. Tentatively in *The Use and Abuse of History,* and
more comprehensively in his later writings, Nietzsche attempts to overcome and transcend the historicist insight; what begins as the questioning of the objective truth of historicism ends as a questioning of the
very possibility of objective truth.

The kind of history which culminates in historicism is history
which understands itself as scientific and objective. Historicism is a
theoretical assertion based upon an examination of historical phenomena. Nietzsche questions whether the historical phenomena can be
understood by objective and scientific history and historians; he questions whether history will yield its secrets to disinterested inquiry. History is made by historical actors, by great men. History-making men
are dedicated men having a commitment to a cause. They act within a
horizon of commitment, unhistorically believing the absolute validity
of their attempt. The great men of history were the great creators,
facing the future and devoting themselves to that which was to be. The
greatest creators are those who create horizons within which future men
will live. They create these horizons unconsciously and under the illusion that they are merely discovering truth. All previous horizons enveloped a belief in an absolute truth which cannot be created but which
may be discovered.

Objective history stands or falls by its fidelity to its object, by its
ability to present the past as it really was. Nietzsche quotes with ap-

proval the old maxim that like can only be understood by like. Only committed men facing the future and only creative men can understand the creations of future-directed and committed men of the past. "The language of the past is always oracular. You will only understand it as builders of the future who know the present." [8] The objective historian is not a creative man, and he does not face the future. He may establish the date of Michelangelo's birth, but only an artist can really understand Michelangelo.

The objective historian deludes himself into thinking that he does not interpret the past but only describes it. There is, however, an illusion which lurks in the very word "objectivity." Any statement about facts is an interpretation of facts. The very selection of data from an infinity of data is already an interpretation. Ultimately there is not a choice between objective and subjective history but only a choice between a noble, rich interpretation of the past and a base, impoverished interpretation of the past.

Thus Nietzsche does not deny the validity of the insight that horizons are the creations of men; he attacks historicism as a particular interpretation of that insight. He attempts to transcend the apparent deadliness of the historicist insight by interpreting it nobly. If it is a fact that the values by which men have lived have been their own creations or fictions, it is an ambiguous fact. Nietzsche moves in the direction of viewing this insight as a revelation of man's creativity and therefore of his power. Man is revealed as the animal who is able to create horizons. For the first time he can create his horizon consciously: could not a consciously created horizon be the most glorious horizon yet created by man?

Nietzsche only hints at the possibility of such a solution in *The Use and Abuse of History,* and the questions raised by those hints are not resolved in that essay. If horizons are the creations of men, can there in principle not be as many different horizons as there are men? If horizons are free projects, how is one to choose between different horizons? When these questions arise, one must turn from *The Use and Abuse of History* to the main body of his work, but with an appreciation of the importance which the historical process has for Nietzsche. In *Human, All-too-Human,* Nietzsche criticizes traditional philosophy for its lack of the historical sense.[9] The importance of the historical process is such that Nietzsche's own political philosophy can almost be said to be couched in terms of a historical analysis. Nietzsche tries to create man's horizon of the future. His creation cannot, of course, be derived, or merely derived, from history, for it is a free project. But the historicist insight into horizons as horizons, for instance, is necessarily a post-

Christian insight, as will be seen. And Nietzsche's own project is in some respects meant to be a synthesis of the best projections of the future which have occurred in history. With these considerations in mind, one may turn to Nietzsche's interpretation of man's history, which has led men to the total crisis of Nietzsche's time.

The peak of man's history was reached near the beginning of recorded history; the highest culture hitherto was that of the Greeks. To Nietzsche culture is the perfection of nature, and every culture is characterized by a unity of style which pervades all its activities. A great culture is one which abounds with great, creative men and which elevates men. In *Beyond Good and Evil* Nietzsche writes:

Every enhancement of the type "man" has so far been the work of an aristocratic society—and it will be so again and again—a society that believes in the long ladder of an order of rank ... and that needs slavery in some sense or other. Without that *pathos of distance* which grows out of the ingrained difference between strata—when the ruling caste constantly looks afar and looks down upon subjects and instruments and just as constantly practices obedience and command, keeping down and keeping at a distance —that other, more mysterious pathos could not have grown up either—the craving for an ever new widening of distances within the soul itself, the development of ever higher, rarer, more remote, further-stretching, more comprehensive states—in brief, simply the enhancement of the type "man." [10]

The pathos of distance existed in Greek society, which was a master-slave society. Nietzsche also notes with approval that the Greeks made a virtue of combat and contests; even the poets contested each other.

If Greece is the peak of recorded history, Greek tragedy is the peak of that peak. Man's fundamental experience is abysmal: he is confronted with an abyss of meaninglessness in a world that is a chaos and not a cosmos; man is a suffering animal. Optimism is a shallow reaction to man's condition, a self-deception. Pessimism may be a mere weakness of the will, but it can be a courageous confrontation of the abyss. Greek tragedy is a pessimism of strength, an affirmation and therewith a transfiguration of man's suffering.

The Greek culture Nietzsche admires is primarily pre-Socratic, just as the Greek philosophers he praises are mainly pre-Socratics, especially Heraclitus. Socrates is, to Nietzsche, the destroyer of Greek tragedy. A healthy culture is one in which men's creative instincts are maximized. Socrates is the enemy of the instinctive life, a theoretical man who is critical rather than creative, who bizarrely equates both happiness and virtue with reason, who withers nobility and the noble virtues by subjecting them to a ruthless dialectical inquiry they cannot withstand, who imposes his will on posterity so successfully that, since Socrates, rationalism has been the fate of Western man.

Socrates and Plato are an anticipation of an even greater calamity for mankind: the appearance of Christianity. Nietzsche labels Christianity as "Platonism for the people." [11] Christianity's triumph over Rome is the triumph of slave-morality over master-morality.

For Nietzsche moralities are creations, but the first creators were individuals rather than herds. Herd-morality is the first form of morality, from which both slave- and master-morality derive. However, there were always strong herds and weak herds. Strong herds impose their will on weak herds and enslave them. Master-morality is the affirmation of strength by the strong, a celebration of the vigorous and active life by those who are possessed of vigor and capable of action. The strong do not repress their instincts but glorify them. Masters are cruel but they are innocently cruel. They identify the good with the powerful, and they dismiss the weak with contempt, calling it bad.

Conversely, slave-morality is the rejection of strength by the weak. Whereas masters distinguish between good and bad, slaves distinguish between good and evil; what the master affirms as good the slave rejects as evil. Slave-morality is essentially negative, being a reaction against, and a revenge upon, the rulers and their values. Its primary concern is with evil. Good becomes a label attached to various kinds of weakness, such as humility and passivity. Eagles cannot help being eagles, and lambs cannot help being lambs, but lambs pretend—and must pretend —that their weakness is voluntary, just as the strength of the eagles is voluntary and can therefore be condemned.

Nietzsche tends to use the terms slave-morality and priest-morality interchangeably. Slave-morality is formulated by priests who are members of the ruling herd, but weak and decadent members. They make common cause with the herd: the sick minister to the sick. They develop ascetic ideals which are the revenge which weak life attempts to take on life, but this attempted revenge serves life by keeping the herd from destroying itself. *The* priestly people are the Jews, who are the inventors of Christianity. Through Christianity they connive to effect a transvaluation of all values. They succeed: humility becomes a virtue and pride a vice; master-morality is stood on its head. Christianity makes life soft by sapping its vigor. The instincts are denied their free play and forced to turn back upon themselves.

The worst effect of this transvaluation of all values is to preserve what Nietzsche calls a surplus of "defective, diseased, degenerating forms of life"; in the economy of life this preservation is necessarily at the expense of higher forms of life. It has made man a "sublime mis-carriage" who is too tame for his own good.[12]

Nietzsche conceived of his own labors as an attempt at a transvaluation of all values, but it would be a mistake to assume that he merely attempted to restore a pre-Christian master-morality. Such a restoration would be impossible because of the changes in Western man which Christianity has produced, and it would be undesirable because the changes have not all been for the worse. Nietzsche thinks of the abortion as sublime in a very serious way. Christianity has deepened man. Slave-morality spiritualizes man by sublimating his instincts until there is a possibility of their expression in ever more delicate forms. The spirit-ualization of man has produced, among other things, science, which has widened the scope of man's possible future. Furthermore, Christianity has universalized man and has made any restoration of limited goals for peoples or races obsolete. Christianity has superseded the Greeks. Nietzsche's transvaluation of values will replace the false universalism of Christianity with a true universal goal for mankind; it will transcend Christianity rather than merely destroy it.

When Nietzsche compares his own time with the great age of the Greeks or even with the eras in which Christianity produced in Euro-pean man a magnificent tension of the spirit, he finds it wanting in all decisive respects. There are almost no true individuals in the nineteenth century; even the rare true selves that do occur in such a paltry time are stunted by the time. The rule of low forms of life at the expense of higher forms is for Nietzsche the meaning of democracy. Democracy is mediocrity. There is no significant difference between democracy and socialism. Both democracy and socialism preach egalitarianism and both are the true heirs of Christianity and its slave-morality. Christianity prepares the way for egalitarianism by holding all men to be equal in decisive respects: they have, in God, a common father; and they are all sinners.

Nietzsche finds that all the governments of his day are inherently democratic. Even states which consider themselves to be monarchies take their bearings by the many and cater to them. All modern states yield to public opinion; Nietzsche equates public opinion with private lazi-ness. The rule of public opinion is the rule of sloth and laziness, breeding conformity. Modern societies are all mass societies which not only mold all men into one shape but also into a very degraded shape. The morn-ing paper replaces the morning prayer. The time prides itself on its paci-ficism: the truth is that men no longer believe in anything strongly enough to fight for it.

Nietzsche condemns both the modern state and modern society. The state is a powerful, new idol, whereas Nietzsche is concerned with the destruction of idols. The state is a mere superstructure based on the unique quality of a people, but it warps that uniqueness: the state preaches universal doctrines like the rights of man. Its shallow universalism destroys the genius of particular people; its impersonal machinery depersonalizes man.

A false quality pervades society. Success in the market place is a sign of worthlessness. One must be an actor, the opposite of a genuine self, to succeed.

Modern education no longer molds true individuals but turns out specialists. The corruption of education necessarily produces a corruption of the general level of taste. Symptomatic of this is the debasement of literary style. People cease to speak well and to write well, for excellence as such tends to be rejected.

Philosophy, too, has been affected by the total crisis of Nietzsche's time. It is tolerated only because of its impotence. It is no longer sovereign over other disciplines. It is in such a bad state that it almost deserves the disrepute in which it is held. All varieties of philosophy which Nietzsche examines he finds deficient. To begin with, they all tend to be dogmatic. Philosophies turn into philosophic systems; the will to a system is a lack of integrity. Certain varieties of philosophy continue to be instructive. One can learn from cynics the "seamy" underside of values and to appreciate the animal qualities in man; one can learn from skeptics a necessary kind of detachment, and from pessimists the necessarily great role of suffering and pain in life. In themselves, however, these philosophies offer no solution for the crisis of the time, being themselves symptoms of the crisis. Nor does science offer a solution. It possesses the rare virtue of integrity, but it is involved in the crisis: science is the last form assumed by the ascetic ideals of slave-morality. Science turns against life in the interest of truth. Its very truthfulness, however, disarms it. Science has taken to discrediting itself by revealing its own limitations.

Nietzsche has a short saying to express what is at the root of the total crisis of his time, a crisis reflected in thought and in deed, in individuals and in institutions. That saying is, "God is dead."

With Nietzsche's saying that God is dead one arrives at the core of his philosophical endeavors. In Nietzsche's greatest book, *Thus Spoke Zarathustra,* Zarathustra, who to some extent is the self-idealization of Nietzsche, asserts the death of God near the very beginning of the work.[13] He does not at first prove that God is dead but makes it, as it were, a matter of personal honor that God be dead. The belief in God has become an indecency for all men except those who have had no opportunity to hear of the death of God. Later on the meanings of the saying, its basis and its consequences, are articulated.

Nietzsche is obviously not the inventor of atheism, but his atheism is nevertheless unique and significant in various ways. First of all, Nietzsche makes no attempt to conceal his atheism but proclaims it again and again with all the eloquence at his command; many previous atheists had tended to be more reticent about their atheism. Secondly, atheism had been in the nineteenth century chiefly a preserve of the political left. Nietzsche, who abhorred the politics of the left and who envisioned a new aristocracy, may be said to have invented the atheism of the political right. Aristocracy has traditionally been associated with the preservation of religion; Nietzsche's aristocrats are to be candid atheists. Thirdly, Nietzsche's atheism is historical atheism. The saying that God is dead implies that God once existed. God existed while one could believe in God; God is dead because belief in God has become impossible.

Since Nietzsche is concerned with an analysis of *his* particular time, his teaching of the death of God refers primarily, but not exclusively, to the death of the Christian God. The speeches in Part I of *Thus Spoke Zarathustra* are to a large extent concerned with Christianity and its effects. It is part of the intention of the whole book to be an imitation and parody of the Bible. Zarathustra wants to create a true universal goal for humanity and must therefore overcome the false universal goals which already exist. Christianity and Buddhism are false universal goals, but since only Christianity is a significant force in Europe, Nietzsche devotes more attention to it. The death of the Christian God leaves European man without a universal goal but at the same time so universalized by the influence of Christianity that he is beyond any national or ethnic goal.

The death of God is the last event in the history of Christianity, but with the death of the Christian God all other gods die also. With the exposure of man's most universal horizon as mere horizon, all belief in eternal truths and beings becomes impossible. At the end of Part I of *Thus Spoke Zarathustra,* Zarathustra proclaims the death of all gods.[14] The death of God is also the death of the Platonic ideas and of metaphysics. Traditional philosophies and traditional religions have shared a belief in a true world which they distinguished from the world known by man through his senses, the apparent world. Both philosophy and religion have been other-worldly. The impossibility of the belief in God is also the impossibility of the belief in a true world, but the abolition of the true world is also the abolition of the apparent world: the world known by man through his senses and feelings and through his whole being is now the only world and not the apparent world. Or, one could say that with the death of God the apparent world becomes the true and real world.

The death of God comes about when men realize that God is their own creation. The descendants of the men who created God, men who have been radically changed by the belief in God, now murder God. The Christian God is the anchor of Christian morality. Christian morality, by making man conscious of his weakness, also made him strive to overcome that weakness. Christianity deepened and heightened man's spiritual powers. Christian morality emphasizes the desirability of truthfulness. It not only makes man a tamer but a more subtle and clever animal. The devotion to God evolves into a devotion to truth which may be called science. The strict and tender conscience which the belief in the Christian God creates finally turns against God. The Christian God is killed by intellectual probity, which is the consummation of Christian morality.

But with the death of the Christian God at the hands of Christian morality, Christian morality renders itself baseless. Christian morality cannot survive the death of God. Devotion to the truth or devotion to anything now becomes problematical: all visions and aspirations are exposed as arbitrary and unsupported. The death of God is the death not only of Christian morality but of all traditional moralities.

In *Thus Spoke Zarathustra,* Christianity is considered as a metamorphosis of man's spirit, which by the acceptance of Christianity becomes a camel. It burdens itself with moral obligations which say to the spirit, "Thou shalt." Man "burdens" himself with the mortification of his pride, with the denigration of his own wisdom, with devotion to lost causes, and with the search for truth. The camel goes into the wilderness but there a second metamorphosis occurs: the spirit of man becomes a lion. It rebels against its burdens. It slays the dragon of obligation; instead of listening to the dragon's "thou shalt" it now says, "I will." But while the lion may slay the dragon of values which precede the will of man, he cannot create new values; he is left in a desert.[15]

With the death of God man finds himself in a desert which is the total crisis of Nietzsche's time. It is obviously more than a crisis in the history of ideas. Christian morality may continue to be observed for a while, perhaps out of habit, but such a situation cannot endure. Men are progressively less able to believe in anything. There is no longer a horizon to give life meaning: the crisis is total.

The politics of the left are to Nietzsche a symptom of the total crisis and an aggravation of it, so they obviously are not a solution. What about conservatism, or the politics of the political right? Nietzsche rejects the possibility of a conservative solution on various grounds, criticizing both the specific form which German conservatism took under Bismarck and the general assumptions of conservatism.

First of all, nineteenth-century conservatism is forced to make overwhelming concessions to the democratic movement of modern times. Bismarck attempts to preserve a monarchy but at the same time is forced to introduce universal suffrage and extensive welfare legislation and thus to advance the democratic movement. The king is no longer considered the ruler but merely the first servant.

Secondly, conservatism embraces the ideals of nationalism. Nationalism is inherently a democratic phenomenon, as is shown by its outgrowth from the French Revolution. It is also an anachronism. The very concessions which all European states must make to democracy and the increasing likeness of all European cultures show that there is already a hidden European unity which cannot be denied: Nietzsche calls himself a good European. The few true individuals of the nineteenth century, like Napoleon and Goethe, were not national but European events. The superficial conflicts of European nation-states can no longer be tolerated, if only because of the threat to Europe from the sleeping giant Russia.

Thirdly, conservatism relies on the old nobility, which is decrepit. What is needed is a new nobility and a new idea of nobility.

Finally, conservatism is allied with Christianity, but, as has been seen, Nietzsche advocates a candid atheism.

One may summarize Nietzsche's view of conservatism by quoting from an aphorism in one of his late works, *The Twilight of the Idols:*

Whispered to Conservatives. What was not known formerly, what is known, or might be known, today: a reversion, a return in any sense or degree is simply not possible. . . . Today there are still parties whose dream it is that all things might walk backwards like crabs. But no one is free to be a crab. Nothing avails: one *must* go forward—step by step further into decadence (that is *my* definition of modern "progress"). One can *check* this development and thus dam up degeneration, gather it and make it more vehement and *sudden:* one can do no more.[16]

Nietzsche rejects both the politics of the right and the left as petty politics, opposing to them his rather vague concept of great politics, the politics of the future. The transvaluation of all values is also the transvaluation of all politics; Nietzsche equates the moral with the political.

The total crisis of the time must be resolved but there is absolutely no necessity for it to be resolved for the benefit of man. With the death of God man is exposed to the greatest danger: man may become utterly degraded. Both the belief in God and the fight against God improved man; with the death of God man has no more opportunity to love or to hate God. The death of God may result in man's abandonment of all striving, all aspirations, and all ideals. Such a man, motivated only by the desire for comfortable self-preservation, is called by Nietzsche the last man. The last man is the most despicable man because he is no longer able to despise himself. He neither wants to rule nor be ruled, to become rich or poor; he wants everyone to do and be the same. " 'We have invented happiness' say the last men, and they blink." [17] When Zarathustra describes the last man in order to warn men, his listeners are enthralled by the picture he draws: contemporary man is not yet the last man but his ideal is the last man.

Nihilism is a protest against the approach of the last man. The formula for nihilism is: nothing is true, everything is permitted. Since all aspirations and ideals have proved meaningless, men cannot devote themselves to a cause: they have no future to will. Nihilists will nothingness rather than to desist from willing. The ascetic ideals of Christianity, being a denial of life, can be seen as an unconscious form of nihilism. Furthermore, nihilism is a necessary consequence of modern science which destroys the validity of values. Nietzsche at times thinks of nihilism as the inescapable future of Europe; at other times he calls himself a nihilist. The creator of new values must be a destroyer of old values.

However, the death of God is not only the time of man's greatest danger but of his greatest possibility, because it makes possible the supreme creation of the values of the future. The death of God is the liberation of man from God. Previous horizons have kept man in chains; they have prevented him from being at home in this world which is the only world. Man can now be loyal to the earth, as Zarathustra admonishes him to be. The heart of the earth is gold: there is no hell. The death of God is the liberation of man from guilt: the productive innocence of the blond beast, the finest specimen of prehistoric man, can be recovered on a higher level.

The death of God is the discovery of man's creativity. Knowing that horizons are his creations, he also is more aware of his own power; if nothing is true, everything is possible. Man has become man by unconsciously projecting horizons; with the conscious projection of horizons man can become more than man.

At this point it becomes evident that Nietzsche needs a philosophical doctrine to explain man and the situation of man. Previous doctrines are discredited with the dissolution of previous horizons. The new doctrine must explain how man has become man without recourse to teleological principles; the new doctrine must be in harmony with the knowledge of the sovereignty of becoming, of man's animal origins, and of the inherent meaninglessness of all givens. Nietzsche calls this doctrine the doctrine of the will to power.

Nietzsche maintains that the will to power is the basic characteristic of all reality. The doctrine of the will to power is a wholly new philosophical doctrine. In *Thus Spoke Zarathustra* and in *Beyond Good and Evil* the presentation of the doctrine is coupled with a rejection of all previous philosophical doctrines. These share the belief in an objective truth; that belief is, according to Nietzsche, a mere prejudice. Philosophers have spoken of a will to truth and have assumed that there is a truth which can be discovered by thinking. In reality, according to Nietzsche, they have merely and unconsciously sought to imprint their interpretation on the world. The thought or reason of philosophers is inseparable from the philosopher's personality. The will to truth is only a form of something more basic, a will to overcome and to master everything, the will to power.

In *Thus Spoke Zarathustra*, the fullest exposition of the doctrine of the will to power is given in Zarathustra's speech on "Self-Overcoming." [18] Zarathustra has observed living things and has found that wherever there is life there is obedience. But obedience is always obedience to something, it is relative to commanding. This commanding must not be sought outside of life. The urge to overcome, to command, to master is not a mere characteristic of life but the core of life.

Life is will to power. A living thing is one which tries to *overcome;* it "seeks above all to *discharge* its strength." However, it does not try to overcome and discharge with any view to a given end. Nietzsche denies that the instinct of self-preservation is the cardinal instinct of an organic being. Self-preservation is merely a result of the will to power, not the purpose of life; the instinct of self-preservation is a superfluous teleological principle.

The will to power is not peculiar to human beings, though it explains how man has become man: life consists in overcoming, and some beasts have overcome their beastliness, just as some men may overcome their humanity. The beast's preying in the jungle and the artist's painting of a picture are both forms of the will to power. Finally, the doctrine of the will to power is a cosmological doctrine, explaining the character of all reality. There are no inanimate things: the doctrine refutes not only all idealistic but also all materialistic philosophies.

Nietzsche's primary emphasis, however, remains on *man's* will to power. Man is the horizon-creating animal. For Nietzsche, man has no determined nature or function; man is the animal which has not yet been defined (*festgestellt*). Man is a rope over an abyss, an interlude between what is less than man and what is more than man. The will to power explains all of man's activity, from his lowest cravings to his highest creations. Philosophy is the highest and most spiritualized form of the will to power.

Reason can then no longer be understood as being of man's essence, as traditionally it had been. Man is not primarily a thinking being. Reason and consciousness are mere surface phenomena. Man's ego is created; it is part of the total organism which is the source of reason and which reason cannot fathom. The highest things are neither accessible to reason nor communicable by reason. Beneath the ego is the self, the ground of the ego, the seat of the will to power, the source of all possible meaning. Nietzsche's concept of the self has some relation to Freud's concept of the id, and Nietzsche once called the self an "it." But Nietzsche's self, in contradistinction to Freud's id, is meant to be radically mysterious and itself a creation.

Zarathustra calls the self the body. The traditional dualism of mind and matter, of body and soul, is thus abolished; the self is also called the soul. The result is not only a less exalted notion of what had previously been thought to pertain to the soul, but a more spiritualized notion of things previously thought to pertain to the body; for instance, Zarathustra refers to blood as spirit.

The doctrine of the will to power necessarily leads to a revision of traditional notions of virtue. To Nietzsche, virtues are sublimated and transfigured passions, dedicated passions. Nietzsche compares traditional virtues with sleep because they were thought to lead to happiness understood as a state of peace and rest, and because traditionally the highest virtue is a wisdom conceived of as the contemplation of the eternal and uncreated. For Nietzsche virtue is creativity; wisdom is self-conscious creation. With Nietzsche's emphasis on the self comes an increased emphasis on self-realization and on such virtues as sincerity and integrity. Since every self is, however, unique and mysterious, there can be no comprehensive doctrine of virtues for Nietzsche: one man's virtue may be another man's vice. It may also be maintained that Nietzsche attempts to reduce notions of virtue and vice to notions of the sickness and health of the self which is the body, and these notions in turn to notions of strength and weakness.

Nietzsche is aware that the doctrine of the will to power raises difficulties. Is the doctrine of the will to power merely the expression of Nietzsche's will to power or is it an objectively true doctrine? Nietzsche can neither maintain that it is simply true nor that it is in no way more plausible than the man on the street's opinion about the character of reality. Nietzsche wrestles with this problem in various ways. Previous philosophy had understood itself as simply true. Nietzsche characterizes traditional philosophy as dogmatic philosophy. He therefore takes pains to present his own philosophy differently. The doctrine of the will to power differs from previous doctrines not only in content but in mode. Nietzsche thinks there can be no objective knowledge of reality but only perspectives of reality. At times he therefore not only admits but asserts that the doctrine of the will to power is a perspectivistic interpretation of reality, characterizing it as a hypothesis to be tested. He thinks of his own philosophy and of the philosophy of the future to which his own philosophy is a prelude as an experiment, an attempt which is also a temptation. Even if there can be only perspectives of reality, there can be more and less comprehensive perspectives. Nietzsche's perspective is the highest perspective yet attained because it embodies the insights of all previous perspectives, and because it is the first perspective aware of the law of perspectivity. Nietzsche's doctrine of the will to power, similarly, represents the first self-consciousness of the will to power; Nietzsche's philosophy is the first creative interpretation of creativity; Nietzsche has reached a peak where there is no difference between creation and contemplation. But this still means that some kind of finality has been reached. Nietzsche is both compelled to affirm and compelled to deny the objective truth of the doctrine of the will to power; the doctrine of the will to power must somehow be both an insight into the truth of things and the creation of Nietzsche's unique, created self. The arguments for the will to power in *Beyond Good and Evil* are also only Nietzsche's most private thoughts. *Thus Spoke Zarathustra* is, as its subtitle indicates, "A Book for All and No One." It is both a new Bible for all mankind and Nietzsche's most personal expression. Nietzsche can only hint to others of what he means. At best he can only demand that others become true, creative selves. Zarathustra wants no disciples. Nietzsche's teaching is a creative call to creativity and can only be understood by creative men.

There is a second difficulty. What are the limits of the will to power? Can everything be overcome? If everything can be overcome, then man will finally overcome even the conditions of inequality which, according to Nietzsche, are indispensable for the elevation of man. Finally men will indeed become *epigoni;* there will be nothing left to overcome. Nietzsche believes in a hierarchical society, in the superiority of men over women, and in the necessity for suffering. But if the will to power is all, and if all is in principle possible, why should not and why will not the difference between the sexes or the rank differences between men be abolished? Traditional political philosophy does not need to face these problems because it takes its bearings by nature. For Nietzsche man has no determined nature. There can be nature in the sense of the outside world but this nature is valueless and consists of meaningless data. One cannot live according to nature because nature dictates no course of action. To Nietzsche nature is a problem, but he cannot do without some concept of nature and a natural principle of ruling and being ruled which would guarantee hierarchy.

The gravest question of the limits of the will to power concerns the past. In principle everything can and must be willed, but can the past be willed? Nietzsche's own project of the future is based, if only nega- tively, on the past. His project is the creation of the self, but the self is also a creation of the past. Do not the passing of time and the past frus- trate the will? Nietzsche thinks of previous philosophies as the will's *reaction* to its own impotence before the passing of time, the revenge of the will to power on time by the creation of fictitious eternal beings. But his own philosophy is not negative but a liberation from the spirit of revenge. It is to be a total affirmation, even of the past. The past could only be willed and affirmed if it were shown to be also the future. If there were an eternal return of all things, then the past would also be the future. Nietzsche's doctrine of the eternal return asserts that all things have already happened an infinite number of times before and will happen an infinite number of times again, exactly as before. The doctrine of the eternal return is a moral as well as a cosmological doc- trine. If there is an eternal return, man will be aware of the awful grav- ity of all his actions, since they *will recur* an infinite number of times. Furthermore, by willing the eternal return of all things, man wills and affirms a future that will become his past; he can, so to speak, become the cause of himself. Finally, the return of all things guarantees the existence of low things and therefore of things which cannot be over- come by the will to power. By willing the eternal return the will reaches its highest peak: it overcomes itself but survives in the total affirmation of all things. Through the total affirmation of all things man can cease to be man and become superman.

The superman is Nietzsche's project of man's future. He is meant to be a fulfillment and a transcendence of the highest ideals of man which have been previously conceived. He is part poet, part philosopher, part saint. He is a poet because he is creative, but he is more than the poets of today, whom Nietzsche criticizes for lying (they falsify the meaningless given) and for failing to create new values but rather acting as the servants of traditional morality. The superman will create new values and in this respect will resemble the traditional philosopher, but his creations will be self-conscious creations. Finally, the superman will resemble the saint because his soul will contain all the depth which Christianity has given to man. The superman will be Caesar with the soul of Christ. Ultimately the Christianity which Nietzsche curses plays a larger part in the noble future of man than does the classical antiquity he praises. Zarathustra is the most pious man who never believed in God.

The superman must be willed. There is no necessity for him to emerge; he is merely a possibility of the future, as is the last man. The total crisis means only that man can no longer be man; he must rise to the superhuman or sink to the subhuman.

The superman is Nietzsche's *free* project of man's future, but its roots in the past ideals of man which it transcends save the project from being arbitrary. The superman will recapture the innocence of the blond beast on an infinitely higher, post-Christian level. The superman represents the third metamorphosis of the spirit. The nihilistic lion who can only say "I will" and who destroys old values without being able to create new ones is replaced by the child who says "I am," who affirms all, and whose creativity resembles the innocence of a child at play.

The superman as a type cannot be fully described because he will be above all a true self. Every superman will be unique. One cannot describe the values by which he will live, because each superman will give his own law unto himself. One can, however, say he will be a man who suffers much and who creates much, and that he will be a man of infinite pride and infinite delicacy. For instance, he will not turn his cheek to his enemies, not because he is brutish, but because he does not want to shame his enemies. But the exact forms his delicacy and pride will assume are necessarily undetermined.

Nietzsche's concept of the superman is thus necessarily vague and ambiguous. It is not even certain whether the superman will be a ruler. Nietzsche does speak of the planetary rule of a new nobility, and the superman is Nietzsche's new idea of nobility. At other times he speaks of the coexistence of last men and supermen: last men will live in communities that resemble ant heaps and supermen will roam the earth, but the supermen will not rule the last men and will try to avoid having any contact with them.

Nor can Nietzsche recommend a way of political action which will make the possibility of the superman a reality. There is a strong strain of radical individualism in Nietzsche. He counsels men to become true selves. He advises men to seek solitude, to flee from public life, to reject established modes of conduct and thought. From this point of view it might be maintained that the superman represents an apolitical solution to the total crisis of modernity. Nietzsche's creative call to creativity accounts in part for the predominant interpretation of Nietzsche which sees in him a teacher of true individualism. Such an interpretation, however, fails to understand the serious political consequences of a suggested apolitical solution. There is an underside to Nietzsche's advocacy of radical individualism. He teaches men to abdicate their public responsibility, to despise the pettiness of day-to-day politics, and to abstain from the ordinary duties of the citizen. There is always the danger, even from his point of view, that the worst men and not the best men will listen to this advice. Even if only the best men were to heed the advice, there would be the danger of withdrawing from the political arena the men most needed in it.

The predominant interpretation of Nietzsche is compelled also to overlook another strain in Nietzsche's writing, a strain which is overtly political. Nietzsche foresees a time of apocalyptic politics. What is more, he sees a necessity for an apocalypse and welcomes it. He looks forward to a time of great wars which will be an important part of the great politics of the future. He speaks approvingly of the need for a eugenics program; he anticipates a time when whole sectors of the earth will be devoted to man's experimentation on man; and he is in favor of the merciless extinction of inferior people and races. Nietzsche thinks of nihilism as knocking on the door of Europe. In his hatred for the degradation of man which is the last man, he advises that the door be opened to nihilism.

Part of the significance of Nietzsche's political philosophy lies in the fact that it is an implicit critique of Marxism. Nietzsche never refers to either Marx or Engels, but he was familiar with various forms of nineteenth-century socialism. Furthermore, Nietzsche, like Marx, was influenced by Hegel. One may summarize the relationship of Marxism to Nietzsche's political philosophy as follows: the Marxist realm of freedom which is to be secured by the revolution is for Nietzsche the realm of the last man, the utter degradation of man. Nietzsche thought more philosophically, more profoundly, than Marx did about what was to follow the revolution.

If Marx is inseparably linked to the growth of communism, it must be admitted that Nietzsche is linked to the emergence of fascism in the twentieth century. The relation of fascism to Nietzsche recalls the relation of the French Revolution to Rousseau. The problem of Nietzsche's connection with fascism is unfortunately not resolved by claiming, as many interpreters of Nietzsche are prone to do, that Nietzsche was no fascist, that he was a violent critic of German nationalism, and that he would have loathed Hitler. These things are undoubtedly true, and uttering them shows the absurdity of a crude identification of Nietzsche's doctrines with Hitler's ravings. Nietzsche was a man with a noble vision of man's future. His own delicacy, integrity, and courage shine through his writing. He was also free of the crude racism which was to be an important element of fascism, and he had only contempt for political anti-Semitism. But the fact remains that in various ways Nietzsche influenced fascism. Fascism may have abused the words of Nietzsche, but his words are singularly easy to abuse. Nietzsche was an extremist, and no man was more gifted than he in making an extreme view seem appealing by presenting it with great audacity and eloquence. A man who counsels men to live dangerously must expect to have dangerous men like Mussolini heed his counsel; a man who teaches that a good war justifies any cause must expect to have this teaching, which is presented half in jest but only *half* in jest, to be abused. Nietzsche praises cruelty and condemns pity without reflecting sufficiently on whether man must really be advised to be more cruel than he is, or what the effect of such a view will be on cruel men. Nietzsche was not a racist, but his writings abound with reflections on race and the possibilities of a biological rejuvenation of man. Nietzsche not only fails to advocate or teach prudence and public responsibility; he slanders prudence and public responsibility. Finally, it must again be repeated that Nietzsche is the inventor of an atheism of the political right.

Any exposition of Nietzsche's political philosophy must not only reveal the deep ambiguities, but must point to the grave consequences, of that political philosophy. Neither the revelation of ambiguity, however, nor a demonstration of grave consequences constitutes a refutation. Even if one could prove Nietzsche to be in error, one might still ponder what Nietzsche himself wrote about Schopenhauer: ". . . the errors of great men are venerable because they are more fruitful than the truths of little men. . . ." [19]

NOTES

1. The dedication appears in the first edition of the first volume of this work (Chemnitz: E. Schmeitzner, 1878). It does not appear in the English translation in *The Complete Works of Friedrich Nietzsche*, ed. Oscar Levy (Edinburgh and London: T. N. Foulis, 1910), vol. VI.

2. Trans. Adrian Collins (New York: The Liberal Arts Press, 1949).

3. *Ibid.*, pp. 3–4.

4. *Ibid.*, pp. 51–52.

5. *Ibid.*, p. 7.

6. *Ibid.*, p. 61.

7. *Ibid.*, pp. 65, 69, 73.

8. *Ibid.*, p. 41.

9. Levy, *op. cit.*, aphorism 2, pp. 14–15.

10. *Beyond Good and Evil*, Aphorism 257. Translated, with Commentary by Walter Kaufmann. New York: Vintage Books, 1966.

11. *Ibid.*, Preface, p. 3.

12. *Ibid.*, Aphorism 62, pp. 74–76.

13. See secs. 2 and 3 of "Zarathustra's Prologue," *Thus Spoke Zarathustra,* in Walter Kaufmann, ed., *The Portable Nietzsche* (New York, 1954), pp. 122–26. Copyright 1954 by the Viking Press and reprinted by their permission.

14. *Ibid.*, p. 191.

15. *Ibid.*, pp. 137–40.

16. *The Portable Nietzsche,* pp. 546–47.

17. *Thus Spoke Zarathustra,* Prologue, sec. 5, in *The Portable Nietzsche,* pp. 128–31.

18. *Ibid.*, pp. 225–28.

19. *Ibid.*, p. 30.

READINGS

A. Nietzsche, Friedrich. *The Use and Abuse of History.* New York: The Liberal Arts Press, 1949.

B. Nietzsche, Friedrich. *Beyond Good and Evil.* Translated, with Commentary by Walter Kaufmann. New York: Vintage Books, 1966.

JOHN DEWEY

1859–1952

John Dewey has been widely recognized as the foremost American philosopher of democracy of the twentieth century. His guiding intention throughout an extraordinarily long and influential career may be summarized as the attempt to further the realization of democracy in every sphere of life. Accordingly, he sought an all-embracing conception of democracy, a comprehensive formulation which he opposed to the understanding of democracy held by all preceding philosophers. Prior political philosophy, he contended, had tended to restrict its attention to such narrowly political concerns as "the state" and the various institutions of government. Dewey's fundamental objective was rather the development of a democratic philosophy designed not merely to encompass the traditional concerns of politics, but, more importantly, to provide a democratic understanding of ethics, education, logic, esthetics, and the many other fields of thought and activity with which he was concerned. Every element of his work as a whole was affected decisively by his political intention.

Dewey's philosophy is politically programmatic, which is to say that it addresses itself to what it regards as the true end of philosophy, social progress, and it concentrates its attention on the contemporary state of things rather than on any supposedly eternal, fixed conditions. Thus Dewey's rejection of traditional political philosophy springs partly from his belief that it led to little more than a sterile "consideration of the logical relationship of various ideas to one another, and away from the facts of human activity,"[1] as if those logical or rational relations were self-sufficient and themselves important. His rejection of traditional political philosophy is also partly inspired by his conviction

851

that its approach and content, governed as they were by historical conditions that no longer existed, required to be modernized.

Nevertheless, Dewey consistently refused to join the ranks of those "positivists" who rejected philosophy as simply meaningless or who insisted that man cannot deal rationally with questions of "value," but only with matters of "fact." Dewey sought to achieve fresh meaning for philosophy by making it relevant to the solution of the most pressing problems of life. He sought this goal through a thoroughgoing *Reconstruction in Philosophy,* an objective expressed most clearly in his well-known work by that title and reiterated in one form or another in virtually all of his major writings. Dewey's democratic political teaching, the primary concern of this essay, must be understood as but one aspect of this reconstruction of philosophy in the interest of democracy. We must, therefore, concern ourselves initially with certain of the fundamental objectives of this reconstruction: (1) Dewey's attempt to make philosophic investigation relevant to the solution of contemporary social problems, (2) his development of "the method of intelligence" as the chief tool for the solution of these problems, and (3) his development of a political theory based on an evolutionary understanding of man and society, an understanding which is at the root of Dewey's concept of "growth" as the ultimate human good and true measure of social justice.

1. The beginning of Dewey's reconstruction in philosophy is his contention that the genuine "problems and subjectmatter of philosophy grow out of stresses and strains in the community life in which a given form of philosophy arises." [2] It follows, in Dewey's view, that the initial task of the genuine philosopher is the identification of the most fundamental and pressing problems of *his* society. Dewey has endeavored to do just this. The subject matter of Dewey's social philosophy is decisively shaped by the observation, forcefully expressed in *Human Nature and Conduct,* that "one class of the community" has consistently attempted "to secure *its* future at the expense of another class." [3] Class divisions are understood by Dewey as symptomatic of a deeper derangement in society, the derangement between production and consumption, which persistently leads to the undermining of sound human relationships. The fervor and scope of Dewey's indictment of this aspect of modern society can be appropriately conveyed only in his own words, when he writes that mere production has been

grossly and intensely attended to. Making things is frantically accelerated; and every mechanical device used to swell the senseless bulk. As a result most

workers find no replenishment, no renewal and growth of mind, no fulfillment in work. . . . The fatuity of severing production from consumption,
from present enriching of life, is made evident by economic crises, by periods
of unemployment alternating with periods of exercise, work or "over-produc-
tion." . . . Leisure is not the nourishment of mind in work, nor a recreation;
it is a feverish hurry for diversion, excitement, display, otherwise there is no
leisure except a sodden torpor. Fatigue due for some to monotony and for
others to overstrain in maintaining the pace is inevitable. Socially, the separation of production and consumption, means and ends, is the root of the most
profound division of classes. Those who fix the "ends" for production are in
control, those who engage in isolated productive activity are the subject-class.
But if the latter are oppressed the former are not truly free.[4]

One may better understand Dewey's criticism of contemporary,
capitalist society by contrasting it, as he himself frequently does, with
the Marxist critique. He credits Marxism for its attempts to address
itself to many of the dominant problems of modern capitalist society.
He notes also that, given the debased conditions of modern society, the
"materialistic conception of history" or "economic determinism" is of
considerable pertinence. Indeed, "we are in for some kind of socialism,
call it by whatever name we please, and no matter what it will be called
when it is realized. Economic determinism is now a fact, not a theory." [5]
While granting the usefulness of particular aspects of the socialist diagnosis of the ills of capitalism, Dewey nevertheless vigorously criticizes
the Marxist prescription for a cure. Marxism's most pernicious, as well
as most revealing, error he holds to be its promulgation of "the monstrous belief that class-struggle civil war is a means of social progress,
instead of a register of the barriers to its attainment." [6] In Dewey's view,
social progress must be achieved by application of "the method of intelligence," not through Marxism's reliance on increasing tension and
strife. What Dewey regards as the underlying reason for the failure of
Marxism, and of the other twentieth-century "isms" as well, becomes
clear through consideration of the second major objective of his reconstruction in philosophy, the development of "the method of intelligence" as the chief tool for the solution of social problems.

2. Mankind's failure to achieve social justice, while understandable in past ages, is now tragically unnecessary, according to Dewey.
An instrument is now available for the effective solution of the problems which have perennially plagued mankind. This instrument is "the
method of intelligence," or "scientific method," as Dewey frequently
terms it. It is defined in *Reconstruction in Philosophy* as but "a shorthand designation for great and ever-growing methods of observation,
experiment and reflective reasoning," or again, as the threefold tech-

nique of observation of facts, construction of hypotheses, and testing of consequences.

Dewey gives chief credit for the discovery of scientific method to Francis Bacon, whom he describes as "the real founder of modern thought." The "method of intelligence," which Bacon sought to usher in, is distinguished in part from non-Baconian science by its resort to active *experimentation,* in contrast to the passive *contemplation* of nature. The traditional, contemplative approach is inadequate because "scientific principles and laws do not lie on the surface of nature. They are hidden, and must be wrested from nature by an active and elaborate technique of inquiry. . . ." Paraphrasing Bacon, Dewey contends that the true scientist "must force the apparent facts of nature into forms different to those in which they familiarly present themselves; and thus make them tell the truth about themselves, as torture may compel an unwilling witness to reveal what he has been concealing." [7] Through such *subjugation* of nature, mankind has "opened up marvelous possibilities in industry and commerce, and new social conditions conducive to invention, ingenuity, enterprise. . . ." [8] Accordingly, enormous advances have been made possible in the industrial, agricultural, and medical arts. A far happier and more abundant life has become possible for all mankind.

Why then, he is led to ask, have these seemingly boundless goods made possible by "the method of intelligence" remained largely unrealized? Why has the greater part of mankind fallen victim to new evils? How has it come to pass that the new science "has played its part in generating enslavement of men, women and children in factories. . . ." Why has it "maintained sordid slums . . . grinding poverty and luxurious wealth, brutal exploitation of nature and man in times of peace and high explosives and noxious gases in times of war"? [9]

Dewey believes that the cause for the tragic frustration of "the method of intelligence" can be traced to defects in the practice of politics. Obsolete and unjust political institutions whose origins antedate the development of Baconian science are found to have been chiefly responsible for the abortion of the benefits promised by the conquest of nature. Archaic social institutions unsuited to an epoch of scientific technology and production have persisted, a phenomenon which Dewey summarizes by the term "cultural lag." He concludes that "the new industrialism was largely the old feudalism, living in a bank instead of a castle and brandishing the check of credit instead of the sword." [10] These outmoded institutions are perpetuated and controlled by the manifestly unjust rulers of mankind: kings, aristocrats, the "possessing and acquisitive" classes of modern society, who have consistently misappropriated the benefits of science for "pecuniary ends to the profit of a few." That is, the benefits of science largely serve the interests of "a possessing and acquisitive class," whereas a *democratic* dissemination of the benefits of science "would signify that science was absorbed and distributed." [11] In short, it is only within a genuinely democratic social order that the benefits promised by the Baconian understanding of science can be effectively applied to " 'the relief of man's estate.' " [12]

Realization of the benefits of the new science requires democracy, but the requisite development of democracy depends, in turn, on application of "the method of intelligence" to social problems, on its application to human relations—political, economic, and moral. Dewey's plea for such application of scientific method is reiterated through his entire work. He is convinced that the acknowledged triumph of the natural sciences in the physical realm can and must be extended to every sphere of human existence. This hope is strongly expressed in his 1946 introduction to *The Public and its Problems:*

science bears exactly the same relation to the progress of culture as do the affairs acknowledged to be technological (like the state of invention in the case, say, of tools and machinery, or the progress reached in the arts, say, the medical) . . . . a considerable part of the remediable evils of present life are due to the state of imbalance of scientific method with respect to its application to physical facts on one side and to specifically human facts on the other side; . . . the most direct and effective way out of these evils is steady and systematic effort to develop that effective intelligence named scientific method in the case of human transactions.[13]

There are, then, according to Dewey, no insuperable difficulties involved in applying to "human and moral" problems the method "by which understanding of physical nature has been brought to its present pitch." [14] The scientific method of observation, hypothesis construction, and evaluation of consequences is applicable to the social as well as the natural sciences. Dewey does, however, take note of a complicating factor in the application of scientific method to the solution of social problems. His point, simply put, is this. The evaluation or testing of consequences in the natural sciences is facilitated by the existence of general agreement regarding objectives. For example, there is usually little disagreement about at least the immediate goals "of invention in the case . . . of tools and machinery," [15] or in the medical art. Consensus as to the goals facilitates the measurement and thus the evaluation of the consequences of introducing newly invented tools or machines. A similar argument may be made as regards the medical art, the agreed purpose of which is the maintenance or restoration of health. Consider, for example, a number of medical scientists engaged in cancer research in a large clinic. Observation of the same patients, analysis of roughly the same data, may give rise to diverse hypotheses regarding the nature and treatment of cancer. Yet the testing of the consequences of these various hypotheses presents no insuperable difficulty since there is consensus on the goals of research, namely, prevention of cancer or reduction of its incidence and ravages.

Dewey acknowledges that testing consequences proves to be considerably more difficult when one attempts to apply "the method of intelligence" to human relations, to political, economic, and moral problems, because consensus for judging consequences is notably lacking in these spheres. As he grants, "every serious political dispute turns upon the question whether a given political act is socially beneficial or harmful." [16] We are therefore forced to consider the question of how the application of scientific method to human concerns can overcome the difficulty which results from the fact that parties to human disputes have sharply divergent opinions as to what *is* socially beneficial or harmful. An example suggested by Dewey may illuminate this problem. Suppose that in a hitherto "unorganized" steel mill certain workers initiate measures to form a labor union. Their action may be motivated by certain evident facts on which there is no disagreement, *e.g.,* wage rates, hours of work, lack of worker participation in controlling conditions of labor. The very facts which lead workers to the hypothesis that union organization will prove beneficial often lead management to the opposed hypothesis. How then will application of "the method of intelligence" assist management and workers in resolving this disagreement?

Dewey's answer appears to take the following form. He calls, first of all, for a detailed statement of the specific consequences which would ensue from unionization, as well as those consequences which would follow from maintenance of the *status quo.* Unquestionably, strikingly different consequences would stem from the failure or the success of the union movement. In the event of success, there would probably be general increases in wages, changes in hours and other conditions of labor, and some reduction in the autonomy of management. In similar fashion, the consequences associated with maintenance of the *status quo* could be traced out at considerable length and in great detail. The next step required by "the method of intelligence," Dewey says, is to contrast and evaluate these differing consequences. Still, it is at precisely this point that the crucial difficulty in applying "the method of intelligence" again presents itself. Would not workers and management insist on applying different standards in evaluating consequences? Would not this disagreement, in turn, stem from sharply divergent understandings of what will contribute to their well-being or self-interest? Not necessarily, Dewey contends. Genuine application of "the method of intelligence" makes possible the evaluation of consequences by a standard which transcends the selfish interests or limited perspectives of such disputants. This higher standard he terms "growth."

The meaning of "growth" and its place in Dewey's political teaching can be understood only through consideration of his evolutionary understanding of man and society, the last aspect of his reconstruction in philosophy with which we must be concerned.

3. It was Charles Darwin who "freed the new logic" which had produced such revolutionary effects in the natural sciences "for application to mind and morals and life." [17] In an essay entitled *The Influence of Darwin on Philosophy* Dewey delineates the consequences of his understanding of evolution for his social philosophy, thereby further distinguishing it from traditional political philosophy. The latter is understood by Dewey to have been engaged in a misguided search for "fixed species and essences" within "a closed world"—a world consisting "of a limited number of fixed forms." Following Darwin, Dewey decries the notion of fixed species, especially in its application to "the nature of man." Such an understanding, he argues, reduces human life to "the monotonous traversing of a previously plotted cycle of change," a principle and prospect as little challenging as that "in virtue of which the acorn becomes the oak." [18] In opposition to this drab vision of traditional philosophy, Dewey offers the bright promise of an evolutionary understanding of human potentialities, a view which presents boundless possibilities for development, for "novel and radical deviation." From an evolutionary perspective, "change becomes significant of new possibilities and ends to be attained; it becomes prophetic of a better future." [19] Change should be "associated with progress" rather than with lapse and decline, the position he ascribes to traditional political philosophy.

Dewey further argues that general acceptance of the evolutionary perspective has been impeded by yet another of the deficiencies of traditional philosophy, its postulation of a rigid hierarchy of "fixed ends." While Dewey grants that the ethical standards that exist side by side with those ends may have been compatible with a static conception of social justice and human nature, an evolutionary understanding of man demands that they be replaced by a standard of the human good which provides for progressive change. This standard he terms "growth."

The concept of "growth" provides Dewey with a criterion of the good which is universal and at the same time compatible with an evolutionary understanding of man and society. It permits Dewey to reject the alleged absolutism and inflexibility of traditional philosophy without embracing that radical relativism which points to nihilism. Human "growth" is understood by Dewey as the progressive realization of human possibilities produced by a complex interaction between "habit" and "impulse," a formulation which he develops exhaustively in *Human Nature and Conduct,* his treatise on social psychology. The crux of his teaching on this point is that "the direction of native activity depends upon acquired habits, and yet acquired habits can be modified only by redirection of impulses." [20] Since the content of neither "habit" nor "impulse" is understood by Dewey to be determined by the fixed "nature of man," the outcome of this interaction may produce infinite human variation. Whatever the substantive content of the "habits" or "impulses," Dewey asks only that the outcome of their interaction produce "growth"—hence "growth itself is the only moral 'end.' " [21] Since Dewey eschews any substantive definitions of "growth," the standard remains always formal, thus providing a relativistic understanding of human development within a universalistic framework. For example, "growth" is said to signify the realization of an organism's full potential, the "full release," as Dewey frequently terms it, of its latent capacities. Indeed, "reality *is* the growth-process itself .... real existence is the history in its entirety." [22] With respect to man, Dewey calls for "all-around growth," by which he explains that he means "growth, or growing as developing, not only physically but intellectually and morally" as well.[23] The scope and significance of this standard is well summarized in *Reconstruction in Philosophy,* where Dewey concludes that

government, business, art, religion, all social institutions have a meaning, a purpose. That purpose is to set free and to develop the capacities of human individuals without respect to race, sex, class or economic status. . . . Democracy has many meanings, but if it has a moral meaning, it is found in resolving that the supreme test of all political institutions and industrial arrangements shall be the contribution they make to the all-around growth of every member of society.[24]

"Growth" serves as the capstone of Dewey's reconstruction in philosophy. As such, it subsumes and makes more intelligible the other aspects of this reconstruction. Thus, it is the concept of "growth" which guides philosophic investigation to those contemporary problems that require solution, for it is precisely "growth"-retarding "stresses and strains" in community life which must be eliminated through application of "the method of intelligence." Since the sweeping social reconstruction required for the sake of "growth" must be carried out to a certain extent through political means, Dewey has concerned himself primarily with those aspects of political theory which appear to bear on this objective.

Dewey's democratic political theory may, for present purposes, best be considered under two headings. In his terms, they are: (1) a modified pluralistic conception of society, and (2) the "indirect consequence" test for defining the legitimate scope of state authority.

1. *The Public and its Problems* emphasizes that human "growth" takes place primarily within associations. Man's very existence depends on associated activity, inasmuch as "each human being is born an infant. . . . immature, helpless, dependent upon the activities of others. That many of these dependent beings survive is proof that others in some measure look out for them. . . ." Human beings are associated, then, in virtue of their very structure. "They are made that way; it is 'the nature of the beast.' " [25]

Among the many associations contributing to human "growth," Dewey takes special note of the family, clan, and neighborhood, as well as schools, trade unions, business and industrial corporations, and a variety of groups and clubs designed for scientific, artistic, and athletic pursuits. These associations may be divided into two categories for purposes of investigation.

The first category includes those groupings which are characterized by relatively permanent, "face to face relationships": the family, clan, neighborhood, and even the small village. These groupings "have always been the chief agencies of nurture," or "growth," since "there is something deep within human nature itself which pulls toward settled relationships." Such "vital, steady, and deep" ties can be developed "only in an immediate community." It is here that the basic, human "dispositions are stably formed" and ideas acquired which form the very "roots of character." Dewey is led to conclude that "the local is the ultimate universal, and as near an absolute as exists." [26] It is important to note that Dewey initially excludes these immediate associations from the realm of political concerns since the "face to face relationships, have consequences which generate a community of interests, a sharing of values, too direct and vital to occasion a need for political organization." [27] Informally established customs and special measures improvised to meet emergencies as they arise are said to suffice for such regulation as may be needed within the "local community."

Those groupings which transcend the local community give rise to the need for political regulation for two reasons. First, certain associations may find themselves working at cross-purposes or locked in conflict, as in the case of the labor-management dispute cited previously. Such conflicts abound, in one form or another, in all complex societies: school and church dispute their respective spheres of influence; organizations intent on securing equal treatment for downtrodden minorities are opposed by associations seeking to preserve the *status quo*. Such conflicts lead frequently to civil strife, and, in any event, they consume energy and resources which might otherwise contribute to the "growth" of the members of the associations involved. "The method of intelligence," we will recall, demands the peaceful resolution of conflict, a "reordering," as Dewey says, of the contending associations for the common good. Since "this supervision and regulation cannot be effected by the primary groupings themselves," [28] a special agency must be created for this purpose. This agency Dewey terms the "state." Thus understood, the state is a "secondary" form of association chiefly empowered to facilitate the smooth and effective functioning of all other associations. Dewey compares this function of the state with that "of the conductor of an orchestra, who makes no music himself but who harmonizes the activities of those who in producing it are doing the things intrinsically worthwhile." [29]

It is in the necessity for harmonizing the relations of other associations that Dewey has found the initial justification for the state. He grants that the figure of the orchestra conductor "has obvious points of contact with what is known as the pluralistic conception of the state," and he finds much to recommend that position. Pluralism appears to provide a safeguard against the "totalitarianism" allegedly inherent in the dominant formulations of traditional political philosophy which are said to permit "the monopolistic absorption of all associations into The State . . . of all social values into political value." The strict pluralistic conception, by contrast, permits the state to act only "to fix conditions under which *any* form of association operates . . ." thus preventing the glorification of the state and magnification of its power. For that matter it often happens "that the state, instead of being all absorbing and inclusive, is under some circumstances the most idle and empty of social arrangements." [30] The locus of "growth" continues to be found in other associations, and this is as it should be, he concludes.

Although pluralism provides the foundations for Dewey's formal political theory, he nevertheless finds conventional pluralistic theory insufficient. Strict pluralism limits political action "to settling conflicts among other groups," thereby tending to restrict the state to the role of a mere umpire. Dewey is anxious to retain this aspect of the theory as a safeguard against totalitarianism; at the same time, he has an extremely

important and interesting reason for wanting to go beyond strict pluralistic theory. He is determined to transcend the umpire conception of
the state in order to realize the *positive* contribution which the state
may make in fostering "growth." This potential contribution of the
state is unduly restricted, Dewey argues, if the state may do no more
than fix the rules "under which *any* form of association" operates. To
be sure, there would be no difficulty if, in fact, all associations contributed to "growth," but Dewey acknowledges that such is not always the
case. The state must therefore be empowered to evaluate, even to look
behind the avowed objectives of associations in order to determine their
real intent, the factual consequences of their operation, and to undertake appropriate action.

Dewey illustrates this aspect of his theory in *Democracy and Education,* where he discusses certain characteristics of some of the less
desirable associations found in society. There are, unfortunately, associations of "men banded together in a criminal conspiracy, business aggregations that prey upon the public while serving it, political machines
held together by the interest of plunder...." [31] Now, the problem posed
by the criminal conspiracy may indeed be adequately met by conventional pluralistic theory, for it may be argued that upon the perpetration
of crime, the criminal association violates agreed conditions or breaks
"rules of the game." The "umpire-state" may accordingly suppress such
criminal activities and the associations from which they stem.

On the other hand, those "business aggregations that prey upon
the public while serving it," and "political machines" intent on selfish
gain present conventional pluralistic theory with a more serious difficulty. As long as the activities of such businessmen and politicians remain within the framework of the law, the "umpire-state" has no legitimate grounds for interference with their operations. Yet these are the
very associations which, in Dewey's view, require the most thoroughgoing, even radical, reconstruction. We may recall his reiterated castigation of the disastrous effects on men of the malpractices of modern
capitalistic industrial enterprises. It is pertinent also to take note of his
further contention that these destructive practices are sustained and
abetted by the "machine politicians," the "bosses," as he often terms
them, who have formed an alliance with business interests. Together,
they dominate contemporary public life and misdirect the activities of
the state. Characterizing this relationship in *The Public and its Problems,* Dewey finds that "the forms of associated action characteristic of
the present economic order are so massive and extensive that they determine the most significant constituents of the public and the residence of
power." Furthermore, they inevitably "reach out to grasp the agencies

of government; they are controlling factors in legislation and administration." Dewey is unwilling to permit the tenets of conventional pluralistic theory, which provide for only the "umpire" function of the state,
to stand in the way of the reformation of the rapacious business associations and political machines, for they seriously interfere with the
"growth" of the multitude of ordinary citizens. "Growth," the universal nurturing of "growth," is always Dewey's ultimate standard for political action. He therefore insists that the state must not confine itself
simply to fixing the conditions "under which *all* associations" may operate. The good state, therefore

renders the desirable associations solider and more coherent; indirectly it
clarifies their aims and purges their activities. It places a discount upon injurious groupings and renders their tenure of life precarious. In performing
these services, it gives the individual members of valued associations greater
liberty and security. It relieves them of hampering conditions which if they
had to cope with personally would absorb their energies in mere negative
struggle against evils.[32]

Dewey provides two standards by which the state may determine
whether the activities of a particular association should be fostered or
discouraged. They are precisely summarized in *Democracy and Education* as follows: "How numerous and varied are the interests which are
consciously shared? How full and free is the interplay with other forms
of association?" Dewey clarifies these standards by applying them to
such destructive associations as the criminal band, the rapacious corporation, the self-seeking political machine. Each of these associations he
finds restrictive of "growth" in that the ties which bind its members are
few. This is most apparent in the case of the criminal band, membership
in which is based on "a common interest in plunder." By the same
token, the tie that binds entrepreneurs in a rapacious business aggregation is limited chiefly to an interest in pecuniary profit. It is the narrow
quest for "spoils," rather than a broad concern with the common good
which characterizes membership in a political machine. It follows that
participation in such associations tends to isolate its members "from
other groups with respect to give and take of the values of life."[33] By
contrast, Dewey speaks glowingly of the possibilities of "growth" which
stem from membership in associations devoted to scientific and artistic
pursuits, education, social service, and the like.

The full measure and meaning of democracy cannot be realized,
Dewey adds, until a second qualification is made to conventional pluralistic theory and practice. The material conditions of life have generally
been such as to handicap severely the "growth" of a substantial part of

the citizenry, even in a country as rich as the United States. Concentrated economic power "has consistently and persistently denied effective freedom to the economically underpowered and underprivileged," [34] thereby depriving many of an opportunity for sound development. Such deprivations, as Dewey argues in *The Public and its Problems,* tend to perpetuate themselves, since the "underprivileged" have often been unable to provide their children with adequate education and the other essentials for full "growth." When such primary associations as the family are unable to provide adequate conditions for "growth," the state must accept the responsibility. Thus Dewey welcomes the "steady tendency for the education of children to be regarded as properly a state charge in spite of the fact that children are primarily the care of a family." The cooperation of the state in such matters is indispensable, since "the period in which education is possible to an effective degree is that of childhood; if this time is not taken advantage of the consequences are irreparable. The neglect can rarely be made up later." Of course, "those who are not parents are taxed" to make possible sound education for all, since it is the responsibility of the state to provide sound conditions for the maximum "growth" of everyone, regardless of economic or other handicaps.

The principle underlying this argument is elucidated by Dewey's further contention that "other dependents (such as the insane, the permanently helpless) are peculiarly" the wards of the state, for "when the parties involved in any transaction are unequal in status, the relationship is likely to be one-sided, and the interests of one party to suffer. If the consequences appear serious, especially if they seem to be irretrievable, the public brings to bear a weight that will equalize conditions." [35] The full application of this principle would obviously require extensive taxation of the wealthy in order to equalize opportunities for all citizens. It would also result in an increase in the power and complexity of state machinery as administrative agencies were created to collect such taxes and to carry out or supervise state-supported programs. The human wants and needs which require something like the democratic welfare state for their satisfaction are not to be denied by the limitations of conventional pluralistic theory, so far as Dewey is concerned.

It is in the light of this conclusion that one may better understand Dewey's insistence that the precise size and character of the state cannot be determined in any universal or a priori fashion, but must be discovered anew within the context of particular circumstances through application of "the method of intelligence." The standard for guidance must be the empirical determination of which consequences of private activity are sufficiently "serious" or "irretrievable" to warrant political intervention. This argument points to two further questions: Who, precisely, is to make this determination, and What are the criteria by which it may be determined whether the activities of a given association are conducive to sound "growth" and thereby to be fostered—or the opposite? The very great breadth, if not to say vagueness, of such criteria as "growth" or "seriousness" makes all the more relevant the question of who is to define and apply them. These questions assume even greater significance when one considers the fact that Dewey's progressive modification of pluralistic theory has extended the sphere of legitimate state activities even to those "face to face" associations which were initially said to lie outside of the political realm. In order to provide compulsory public education, protect the weak and dependent, and equalize opportunities for the "growth" of all, political authority would necessarily intrude into the affairs of even "the family, clan, neighborhood." It would seem that if such pervasive political authority were to fall into unjust hands, the threat would arise of that very "totalitarianism" which Dewey is so intent on avoiding. Dewey's awareness of this threat leads to his formulation of the "indirect-consequence" test of the legitimacy of any exercise of state authority. The test is the second major element of his formal political theory which must be considered.

2. The application of Dewey's "indirect-consequence" test may be most easily understood through an illustration. Suppose that the workers in a steel mill are attempting to organize a union. At its inception, the union movement may be limited to a few workers, who might utilize a portion of their lunch hour to "talk shop," i.e., to discuss the problems which they encounter in their work. Such discussions, even if regularized, are characterized by Dewey as "private" according to the rule that an action is private so long as its consequences "are confined, or are thought to be confined, mainly to the persons directly engaged in it. . . ."[36] As such, the discussions are of no concern to the state and may suffer no interference.

Suppose, however, that the participants in these initially private discussions decide to form a union and then take action to implement their decision. In order to achieve their goal they may bring other workers into their meetings, outside organizers may be introduced into the plant to help the cause, a strike may be precipitated in order to force recognition of the union. Should the union movement succeed, there will be extensive indirect consequences that will affect the lives of many. Increases in the cost of steel may have important effects on the operation of associated industries, rising labor costs may induce management to introduce automatic equipment, an action which would give rise to further, indirect consequences. The ramifications of all these consequences will, in one form or another, finally reach the consumers, the buying public.

Those who are seriously affected by such indirect consequences form a "public," as Dewey defines it. The "public's" welfare requires that such indirect consequences be controlled. It is for this purpose that the members of the "public" must select representatives who, in turn, will exercise political power. Dewey is little interested in the institutional details of the state. He contends that "the only statement which can be made is a purely formal one: the state is the organization of the public effected through officials for the protection of the interests shared by its members." [37]

It is apparent to Dewey that the complex, industrial society of the twentieth century gives rise to many such "publics," "for conjoint actions which have indirect, serious and enduring consequences are multitudinous beyond comparison, and each one of them crosses the others and generates its own group of persons especially affected. . . ." Given this diversity of "publics" with overlapping membership, Dewey is necessarily led to wonder whether there is any way in which "these different publics [can be brought] together in an integrated whole." [38] This question is of fundamental importance, since the terms of Dewey's theory authorize the members of each "public" to elect representatives to deal with the indirect consequences generated by particular private activities, as in the example above. This would appear to require the election of an enormous number of representatives, or the devising of a system by which one individual would be elected to represent many "publics."

Dewey does not, unfortunately, develop his doctrine of representation much beyond this point. Such further guidance as he provides is largely negative, as, for example, his argument against the idea of functional representation on the grounds that such a system affords political expression to interest groups rather than to those affected by their operation. Dewey is insistent that "political democracy" requires some system of representation, but he willingly leaves to others the task of working out the institutional forms and details of his political teaching. He does so for two reasons. First of all, he argues that political institutions must be subject to constant modification in order to give prompt expression to the endlessly changing conditions of associated life. Consequently, any attempt to fix their shape would prove to be dangerously restrictive. Second and far more fundamental is Dewey's view that it is the character of the citizen body which is virtually all-important for the achievement of the good polity. Throughout his political writings, Dewey deliberately minimizes the importance of institutional and constitutional arrangements. He thereby places almost full dependence for the achievement of the good, democratic regime upon the existence of an educated, enlightened, public-spirited, and active citizenry. Such a citizenry, he proclaims throughout his work, could bring into being a new era in democratic living, an era which, for the first time in human history, would make possible the realization of the rich and abundant potentialities of life.

A citizenry which, by contrast, is predominantly ignorant, selfish, and apathetic promises a different outcome. Dewey's "indirect-consequence" test of the limits of state authority, as well as his theory of association, have been seen to place in the hands of the "publics" and their representatives complete responsibility for determining the limits of political power and its mode of implementation. It is they who must determine whether indirect consequences are sufficiently "serious" or "extensive" to warrant political control. The misunderstanding or misapplication of such standards by "publics" swayed by passion or misguided by demagogues might obliterate the sphere of the private. Tyranny of the majority presents itself as a distinct possibility.

The only sound protection against misgovernment now and in the future lies in the development of a citizenry which is fully democratic in every respect. One of the most important instruments for producing democratic men, Dewey has consistently argued from virtually the beginning of his work, is a school system designed for the purpose. In the schools, the future citizens must be so formed that the society they will create as adults will be somewhat better than their parents' society, and each generation in its turn will repeat the process, thus engendering endless "growth." The task of the schools therefore is not simply to link the minds of the generations but to form "personalities" by the organization or method as well as by the content of instruction, and so doing to prepare and safeguard the progress of the society.

What democracy requires is men whose natures have been so democratized that they can tolerate, not to say benefit from democracy, as purified of the institutions that now contaminate it. Uncooperative men would threaten the democracy of Dewey's dream, as would men inclined to grasp coldly for wealth or power and men who do not wish to grow in every direction. Therefore, in their impressionable years children should be conditioned by life in their classrooms to strive without "competing," to study and work cooperatively in groups, and to acquire the expansive habits of self-expression that will fit them for life in ever more perfect democracy. It is well-known that the influence of Dewey upon the theory of education has been considerable.

Dewey's efforts in the field of education were consistent with his belief that all theory should be brought into the service of democracy and that all aspects of life must be democratized in practice if democracy is to be secure and progressive. From the latter it might be thought that Dewey had recurred to the traditional view of a comprehensive political order, the all-embracing political community in which there were no institutionalized strongholds of resistance against the legitimate ruling principle, but every citizen's life was guided by the laws toward the good. How far this was from being in fact Dewey's position may be seen by recalling his own judgments on traditional political philosophy. He denied the existence of a fixed, substantive good for man and asserted instead that the good is a process of "growth" and change. Moreover, he did not conceive the community as primarily political, *i.e.,* a unity determined in the fundamental respects by the "constitution." He believed rather that the influence of psychological and economic factors was decisive in forming the dispositions and thus the behavior of men. The measure of Dewey's depreciation of the political is his refusal to treat democracy as primarily a form of government; instead it is a way of life, and political or legal democracy is more in the nature of an effect, though a very important effect, than a cause of psychological and economic democratization.

Political democracy, then, stands firm only as it rests on foundations secured through a democratic reconstruction in philosophy and in every aspect of life. Dewey's awareness of the enormousness of this task was relieved by his unquestioning faith in the capacity of men everywhere to achieve the "growth" which is the indispensable concomitant of democracy. Always hopeful, he did not permit the calamities of the twentieth century to destroy his sanguine expectations for the future of mankind. His work rests always on the assurance that with the progress of the democratic reconstruction for which he calls,

we have every reason to think that whatever changes may take place in existing democratic machinery, they will be of a sort to make the interest of the public a more supreme guide and criterion of governmental activity, and to enable the public to form and manifest its purposes still more authoritatively. In this sense the cure for the ailments of democracy is more democracy.[39]

NOTES

1. John Dewey, *The Public and its Problems* (Chicago: Gateway Books, 1946), p. 9. Reprinted by permission of Holt, Rinehart and Winston, copyright 1927 by John Dewey. This work was originally published by Henry Holt and

Company in 1927. The 1946 edition, to which exclusive reference is made in this essay, is distinguished by an extensive, new introduction of considerable importance.

2. John Dewey, *Reconstruction in Philosophy* (New York: New American Library, 1950), p. 8. Reprinted by permission of the Beacon Press, copyright 1958 by Beacon Press. This work was originally published by Henry Holt and Company in 1920. An enlarged edition was published in 1948 by Beacon Press, with an important, new introduction written by Dewey. References in this chapter are to the New American Library (Mentor) edition of 1950.

3. John Dewey, *Human Nature and Conduct* (New York: Henry Holt and Company, 1944), p. 270. Reprinted by permission of Holt, Rinehart and Winston, copyright by Henry Holt and Company. No important changes appear to have been made in this work since it was published initially in 1921. References in this essay are taken from the paperback edition of 1944.

4. *Ibid.*, pp. 271–72.

5. John Dewey, *Individualism Old and New* (New York: Minton, Balch and Company, 1930), p. 119.

6. *Human Nature and Conduct*, p. 273.

7. *Reconstruction in Philosophy*, pp. 10, 46, 48.

8. *Human Nature and Conduct*, pp. 212–13.

9. *The Public and its Problems*, p. 175.

10. *Human Nature and Conduct*, p. 213.

11. *The Public and its Problems*, p. 174.

12. *Reconstruction in Philosophy*, p. 52.

13. *The Public and its Problems*, p. x.

14. *Reconstruction in Philosophy*, p. 10.

15. *The Public and its Problems*, p. x.

16. *Ibid.*, p. 15.

17. John Dewey, *The Influence of Darwin on Philosophy* (New York: Henry Holt and Company, 1910), pp. 8–9.

18. *Reconstruction in Philosophy*, pp. 62, 65.

19. *Ibid.*, p. 102; cf. *Human Nature and Conduct*, p. 284.

20. *Human Nature and Conduct*, p. 126.

21. *Reconstruction in Philosophy*, p. 141.

22. *Experience and Nature* (Urbana, Ill.: The Open Court Publishing Company, 1925), p. 275.

23. John Dewey, *Experience and Education* (New York: The Macmillan Company, 1938), p. 28.

24. *Reconstruction in Philosophy*, p. 147.

25. *The Public and its Problems*, pp. 24, 11.

26. *Ibid.*, pp. 211, 213, 214, 211, 215.

27. *Ibid.*, p. 39.

28. *Ibid.*, p. 27.

29. *Reconstruction in Philosophy*, pp. 158–59.

30. *The Public and its Problems*, pp. 73, 72, 28.

31. John Dewey, *Democracy and Education* (New York: The Macmillan Company, 1916), p. 95.

32. *The Public and its Problems*, pp. 107, 71–72.

33. *Democracy and Education*, p. 96.

34. "Authority and Social Change," printed in the Harvard tercentenary publication *Authority and the Individual* (1937), p. 178, and more readily available in *Intelligence and the Modern World, John Dewey's Philosophy*, ed. J. Ratner (New York: Modern Library, 1939), pp. 351–52.

35. *The Public and its Problems*, pp. 63, 62.

36. *Ibid.*, p. 12.

37. *Ibid.*, p. 33.

38. *Ibid.*, p. 137.

39. *Ibid.*, p. 146.

READINGS

A. Dewey, John. *The Public and Its Problems*. Chicago: Gateway Books, 1946.
     Chap. i, pp. 3–36; chap. ii, pp. 37–74; chap. vi, pp. 208–19.
    Dewey, John. *Reconstruction in Philosophy*. New York: New American
     Library, 1950. Introduction, pp. 8–28.
B. Dewey, John. *Human Nature and Conduct*. New York: Holt, 1944. Chap. iv,
     pp. 125–30; chap. vi, pp. 223–37.
    Dewey, John. *Experience and Education*. New York: Macmillan, 1938.
     Chap. iii, pp. 23–32.
    Dewey, John. *Liberalism and Social Action*. New York: Putnam, 1935. Pp.
     74–85.
    Dewey, John. *Democracy and Education*. New York: Macmillan, 1916.
     Chap. vii, pp. 94–102.

EDMUND HUSSERL

1859–1938

The student of politics may well wonder if an essay on Edmund Husserl should be included in a history of political philosophy. Surely one will not find in such an essay a rich articulation of political matters: virtues and vices, regimes and laws, prudential considerations and the knowledge of politics acquired by the statesman through long experience (*empeiria*) of its particulars. Yet the inclusion can be justified. Many hold the view that Husserl introduced a "revolution" in philosophy comparable in importance to that of Kant or even Descartes; many would argue that Husserl's work marks the end, or the beginning of the end, of modern philosophy. We must acknowledge that such judgments are made by men who are close to being Husserl's contemporaries; Husserl's significance cannot receive final assessment from us. Nonetheless, we must, as students of political philosophy, regard it as highly revealing that such a fundamental and comprehensive form of thinking, as Husserl's surely is, contains relatively little in the way of political philosophy. This absence is not due to indifference on Husserl's part (or his followers') to things that concern political man. On the contrary, Husserl's intensely ethical conception of the philosopher's aim includes the ambition to provide philosophic guidance to political reflection and action. Paradoxically, the absence of political philosophy is due to Husserl's having extremely high expectations about what is possible in the practical realm. Reflection on this state of affairs may further our understanding of what makes political philosophy possible.

To be more precise, Husserl makes the assumption that the highest way of life, that of pure theoretical inquiry, is a potential, a hidden *telos* or consummation, waiting to be realized in every human being. Husserl believes that all men can achieve the kind of autonomy characteristic of the ancient philosopher: full independence of prejudice, of distorting attachment to "one's own." Earlier philosophers—at least until Kant and Hegel—had been more cautious about harboring any assumptions or hopes of this kind. Seeing the enduring tension between the striving for the truth and the blinding attachments that make political life possible, they assumed the permanent necessity for prudence in the presentation and application of "theory" to practical life. Thus Descartes and Leibniz, although their writings on political subjects are not extensive, employ a rhetoric suited to the nonphilosophic reader that tacitly acknowledges the intractability of practical life by theoretical argument. Husserl, also not writing much on politics, is nonetheless closer to philosophers such as Marx and Nietzsche in his understanding of the relation of theoretical discourse to practical life. A certain extreme optimism in Husserlian ideals is connected, as we shall see, with suggestions that the political realm may not have a distinctive and enduring nature.

In his philosophical activity Husserl essays, in a remarkably single-minded way, to disclose the ultimate grounds of rationality, so as to rescue rationality from the falsifying interpretations of positivist and historicist modes of skepticism. The fundamental insight of Husserl, one could say, is that *all* earlier accounts of rationality have tended toward a self-undermining conclusion (wholly apparent to us in the skepticism of late modernity), insofar as they have failed to grasp that reason's essence is absolute autonomy. In order to uncover this "hidden" essence of autonomy, Husserl undertakes to examine the premises of the tradition of scientific and philosophic thought, an examination that makes evident the autonomous constructive activity of reason in the production of such premises. Thus we can no longer take the truth of such premises "for granted." For the student of politics, there are three things of immediate significance in Husserl's endeavor: (1) it proposes a notion of rationality as essentially normative and sees the task of "rescuing" rationality to be in the service of the human good; (2) it proposes critiques of positivism (or, as Husserl prefers, "psychologism") and historicism which are of course immediately relevant to political science; (3) it engages in a close examination of the inherited premises of the philosophic tradition, an examination that has provided an impetus to fundamental historical inquiries into the sense of the Greek beginnings and the early modern "foundations" of philososphy.

PHENOMENOLOGY AND THE WESTERN CRISIS

Husserl is the principal founder of the twentieth-century philosophical movement known as "phenomenology." He is not the first thinker to employ the term "phenomenology" for a kind of thinking that seeks to uncover and describe the primary "phenomena" of consciousness precisely as they appear, without the intervention of theoretical constructions. He is the first, however, to propose an ideal of a rigorously scientific phenomenology that has two salient features: (1) the science of phenomenology must be absolutely presuppositionless, *i.e.*, it must be able to "ground" any assumptions or concepts in the absolute self-evidence of the inspecting consciousness, and hence it will not take for granted the truth of any assumptions or concepts made by existing sciences (including logic), or made by ordinary experience; (2) scientific phenomenology is the true first philosophy and the foundation of all sciences, and is not merely a propaedeutic to first philosophy (as a form of "phenomenology" was for Hegel).

Not all forms of twentieth-century phenomenology are Husserlian, yet nearly all phenomenologists after Husserl owe something to his formulation of the "ideal" of phenomenology, and to his suggested programs for realizing this ideal. Most areas of intellectual life on the continent of Europe in this century have been touched by the phenomenological way of thinking. Husserl's theoretical ideal and methods are inseparable from a message to the later modern age, which has been unmistakably pertinent to the sense of a "crisis" in European civilization since 1914. The message can be put as follows: not only philosophy but our civilization as a whole can no longer take for granted the validity of the starting points and the results of established sciences. A certain account of "knowledge" taken from these sciences has become even the ordinary citizen's understanding (or prejudice) concerning knowledge. Yet that account is extremely questionable; it rests upon basic confusions and errors which eventually result in doubts about the meaning and the "value" of science and, therewith, of reason and knowledge themselves.[1] Doubts about our ability to ascribe rationally a positive "value" to reason and knowledge in Husserl's time were receiving powerful voices in such men as Nietzsche and Weber. It is Husserl's great merit to have exposed through critical and historical analysis how such doubts would inevitably arise from errors existing at the very bases of modern scientific philosophy, and to have pointed toward a way of resolving such doubts in an affirmation of reason as the ultimate good.

All of Husserl's writings and his teaching after 1900 are thus addressed to resolving the crisis in the self-understanding of the sciences in the modern West that has become, in Husserl's view, a crisis in the self-understanding of the ordinary man of his own tasks, standards, and purposes. In Husserl's view, Western man must see his life as having a *telos,* an end or purpose or meaning, based upon reason and norms derived from reason. Yet Husserl notes that many in his generation and the one following are evincing a hostility toward science and reason that is based upon the experience of the failure of science and reason to say something of weight about the questions of freedom and the meaning of life.[2] Accordingly, Europe (or the West) is threatened with the loss of its unique *telos;* it is on the verge of spiritual collapse and a "barbarian hatred of spirit." It is Husserl's sense of his own mission to avert this collapse by means of a demonstration that the failures of reason are only the failures of modern (post-Cartesian) misconstruals of reason.[3] Phenomenology thus is above all else an attempt to give reason the correct construal as the source of meaning, value, and ultimate *telos* for humanity as such, but especially for the West. For the latter has already acquired some awareness of its rational end, and the habit of regarding itself as the bearer of a special enlightenment for all humanity. But thus far in his history, Western man has had only an obscure anticipation of the true essence of reason as *autonomy:* as *giving itself* all meaning, value, and ends.

Husserl is thus one of the chief analysts of and respondents to what has been called the fact, or the threat, of nihilism. The thinking of all of his followers and students lies within the ambit of such concern: the recovery of the Western spirit in the face of imminent nihilism. Yet it must be said that many of Husserl's students and readers defected from his account of that spirit in terms of a "heroism of reason," whereby Western man's *telos* consists in the uncovering of the true essence of things and of Being by means of rational inquiry.[4] Husserl claimed that the discovery of this *telos* was first made by the Greeks in antiquity. Those students who rejected the rational view of the West's *telos* were thus required either to show that Greek antiquity pointed to, but failed to realize, another and higher *telos,* or to show that the spirit which can save the West and the world is not Greek in origin at all. The first of these efforts was made chiefly by Heidegger and is at the heart of what is now called "hermeneutical philosophy." The second effort was made by those who sought to recover the sources and power of various orthodoxies, and could only questionably retain the name "philosophy." Can some responsibility for the defection from Husserl's vision be laid at the door of Husserl himself?

The critics among Husserl's students make one criticism with one accord: whereas Husserl claims that his thinking is presuppositionless, he has nonetheless presupposed that rational inquiry is the human *telos;* his phenomenological groundings of our primary beliefs have not grounded this belief. In fairness to Husserl, one must say that he attempts fully to ground his account of the human essence as rational, in his last investigations. Such grounding is central to the turn to the life-world" as an object of inquiry. At the same time, Husserl's thinking brings him nearer to something like political philosophy, as he takes up the theme of the "life-world." We shall see that Husserl's writing is engaged on at least two occasions with a problem recognizably crucial to the whole tradition of political philosophy, that begins with Socrates: that of the relation of the philosopher to the context of practical and political life that his activity presupposes, or of the "sources" of philosophy and science in the prephilosophic and prescientific world.

We might note in advance that Husserl's way of taking up this Socratic problem is in some respects widely divergent from the original Socratic way. These divergences help to account for the defection of later phenomenologists from Husserl's stress on rationality. Whereas Husserl agrees with Socrates that reason is essential to humanity, he is unable to say that reason belongs to human nature.[5] That is, one can speak of human essence but not of human nature; man's essence consists in a rationality that realizes itself through the formation of structures of "meaning." The manner in which reason so constitutes meanings has certain invariant features, and one can thus speak of the invariant essence of reason. But the constituted meaning-structures can vary historically, and they include such crucial human features as the discovery of *theoria* in antiquity. Otherwise put, the manner in which man regards nature or, as Husserl says, "objectifies" nature, undergoes historical change; the power of reason to form new meanings is infinite and thus its power to create "history" is unlimited. "Nature" then belongs to the "historicity of spirit"; in other words, the manner in which man relates his rationality to a "surrounding world" is historically changeable.[6] It indeed is reason's unchanging essence to seek clarity about ultimate grounds, but those grounds are to be found in its own activity; how the "surrounding" or "natural" world is conceived, as something "external" to rationality, has nothing permanent about it. When one speaks of human nature, one really means to speak of reason's relation to the surrounding world (which includes the human body). Thus the discussion of human nature is generally replaced by Husserl and phenomenologists with the discussion of culture or civilization as the sphere of constituted relations between reason and the surrounding world. One can say that this replacement is possible because phenomenology is far more rationalistic than the thought of Socrates, Plato, and antiquity: it claims that humanity's *whole* essence is reason (or consciousness).

All the same, Husserl is one of the strongest critics of historicism. Yet he is a devoted critic who knows his affinity with his opponent. His critique of historicism is a crucial aspect of his attempt to rescue rationality as the Western *telos* by the achievement of rigorous science. Eventually Husserl finds that he must give historicism its due; he arrives at the view that reason, in its quest to define its own *telos,* must combine historical investigations with systematic ones.[7] The *telos* of reason, furthermore, cannot be defined except in the terms of a "philosophy of history." One can say that Husserl's political philosophy takes the form, in his last writings, of a philosophy of history.

THE CRITIQUE OF PSYCHOLOGISM

The discussion of Husserl's critique of historicism and his own later reflections on the importance of history must be prefaced by some further account of the concepts and arguments of phenomenology. Husserl began as a mathematician; his point of entry into the problems of the modern crisis was reflection upon the philosophical foundations of arithmetic and logic. In this region of inquiry he discovered the issue which opened up to him the whole realm of philosophy: the tendency of modern thought since Descartes and Locke to "psychologize" all problems of knowledge by the reduction of the mind's directedness toward "intended objects" to mere psychological attributes or states of mind. The nineteenth century had witnessed notable attempts to ground logic and arithmetic in psychological processes. Against such attempts, Husserl argued that mathematical and logical concepts are "ideal entities" and "wholes of meaning" that cannot be understood as causally produced by physical or quasi-physical events within the psyche. Such concepts (and many others, as Husserl would discover) have an irreducible "objectivity": different thinkers can grasp the same objective meaning regardless of real or apparent differences in their psychic processes, physicalistically understood. The errors of the psychological accounts of the basis of the sciences are then twofold: (1) such accounts assume that the human mind or reason can be understood in the same terms as physical objects, or in quasi-physical terms modeled upon those used to explain bodies (*e.g.,* sense data and their "laws" of dependence, association, etc.); this is the error of "naturalism"; (2) these accounts also assume, or argue, that a psychology based on such principles is the true first philosophy and the foundation of all sciences; this is the error of "psychologism." Husserl saw in psychologism a chief source of modern subjectivism, skepticism, and relativism. His critique of its principles moved from the narrower question of its harmful consequences for the account of the exact sciences, to the broader question of how to extricate the account of rationality as the giver of *norms* from psychologistic falsifications.[8]

Since psychologism presupposes naturalism, it is necessary to articulate an alternative account of the psyche as something wholly unlike "nature" as understood by modern principles (as the realm of extended body governed by causal laws). Husserl does not immediately subject that account of nature to a critique; rather, he objects to the inclusion of "psyche" within "nature" so understood. This is crucial to grasping why psyche (and hence reason) can have an "essence" but not a "nature." [9] The naturalization of the psyche is according to Husserl apparent in Descartes's regarding it as a kind of substance (parallel to, but not the same as, the bodily substance). All the same, Husserl avows his debt to Descartes; the latter opened up the world of subjectivity as a field of inquiry, when he found the common denominator for all acts of awareness in the "I think" (the *cogito*). But while Descartes discovered the universality (and foundational role) of consciousness, he did not stress that which is absolutely unique to consciousness, making it unlike anything natural: awareness is always implicated in a world of "meanings" which is present to it whenever there is consciousness. The "I think" can never be empty; it is always directed beyond itself (and beyond what is most immediately present, i.e., sensation) to an object. The relation of consciousness to its object, called "intentionality," is unlike any relation between objects or events in mere nature. The scientific account of intentionality, the essence of reason, must replace naturalistic psychology as the true first philosophy or metaphysics, [10] thereby both imitating and departing from Descartes's laying of the foundations of all knowledge in the account of consciousness.

One must see how this new account of the psychic is meant to rescue (or make fully evident for the first time) the essence of reason as giver of norms. It is often said that Husserl sought to preserve the articulation of the commonsense world as it appears to us (prior to distortions by theory). This is correct to the extent that Husserl, in opposition to modern scientific reductions of experience, insists that all appearances to consciousness have a *logos,* an immanent reason for appearing the way they appear. They are not reducible to hidden and underlying processes or substrata. This *logos* is also called "meaning"; there are structures for various kinds of meaning, which Husserl calls *eidē.* The various basic types of conscious acts (willing, desiring, remembering, imagining, etc.) have their different eidetic structures. [11] Husserl argues that the evidence of these structures (or different ways of intending meanings) must be directly intuited, in the acts themselves, wherein the kinds of objects (meanings) being sought are indeed found (or "fulfilled"). Thus the object or meaning I really intend in a certain act cannot be of a wholly different type from the one I believe I intend; thus one cannot accept the statement of a reductive psychologist that when I intend to uphold justice I am in reality only expressing repressed animal lust. The source of all evidence about our reason is "intuition," rather than inference or derivation of the rational from the nonrational (or of one type of rational act from another type).[12] It is evident then that Husserl's account of reason must entail a defense of the commonsense view of the integrity of normative thinking.

On the other hand, Husserl's account of the rational is far from being simply a justification of "commonsense realism." One is tempted to say that in defiance of commonsense realism, Husserl maintains a peculiarly radical view of the absolute autonomy of reason. One might say that he departs from "common sense" precisely insofar as he characterizes reason as normative, or law-giving, and as nothing else. The rather one-sided account of reason can be understood as arising in part from a criticism of the bases and methods of modern science, or certain versions thereof: insofar as a physicalistic psychology cannot accept the normative as an irreducible datum of psychic life, it is wholly unable to account for itself as scientific activity. All science rests on "ideal norms" of truth; inductive method is itself an ideal norm that cannot be arrived at inductively. Reason is essentially normative, through and through, for we cannot even encounter "facts" as "facts" without the presupposition of the "ideal."[13] (Thus all "meaning" is "ideal" and irreducible to the "factual.") Phenomenology, which discloses this idealizing and ideal-making structure of reason, thus can claim to be the "science of the scientific," disclosing how science is possible.

But just on this issue of the thoroughgoing "ideality" of reason, Husserl finds the commonsense view to be wanting, and to be allied to the naïveté of physicalistic psychology. Rigorous reflection upon rationality discloses that its structures have nothing at all to do with "nature" as the realm of the "existent"; reason as norm-creating is not in any way limited by the facts of existence, the mere contingency of the *a posteriori*. Thus all assumptions about existence must be suspended (not denied) if one wishes to have access to the essence of the rational. This suspension (*epochē*), which first makes possible the access of consciousness to the phenomena of experience as phenomena (without the intervention of assumptions about their "metaphysical" basis in anything existent), is the first moment of Husserl's famous "phenomenological reduction." Ordinary consciousness with its "naturalistic" attitude takes the existence of nature for granted; it tends to "objectify" or to regard all reality as "thing-like." It thus does not focus upon the phenomena as phenomena, precisely because it does not aim at rigorous analysis. Existence always eludes rigorous description, because reason cannot constitute existence; it can constitute only the ideal realm of meaning.[14] Whereas nature as the realm of the existent can be of no concern to phenomenology, nature, insofar as it has ideal meaning (*e.g.,* in scientific law) is of concern to it:

nature in that sense in fact is the product of law-giving reason. Thus to engage in phenomenology and to focus upon the pure realm of ideal meaning require a strenuous discipline of disengaging oneself from the ordinary preoccupation with nature as existing. Philosophy prior to phenomenology as rigorous science has failed to make this "radical" disengagement, and thus has always tended to "naturalize" reason; in so proceeding, it has revealed that it is merely the victim of the unexamined prejudices of "common sense." This has been evident in its tendency to regard nature as a self-sufficient whole of things existing independently of mind (as in the earliest Greek cosmology), and to regard mind as a dependent variable upon nature (or body), or as a parallel, nature-like entity.[15] In sum, one can say that Husserl's recovery of the "appearances" is most concerned with uncovering the absolute autonomy of the rational.

The Critique of Historicism

In the essay "Philosophy as Rigorous Science" (1911) Husserl makes a powerful rhetorical argument in favor of the new approach in philosophy. The fact that this is one of Husserl's most rhetorical writings indicates that it is also one of his most explicitly political; its rhetoric discloses rather than masks the deepest levels of the intentions of phenomenology. The argument again turns upon the disclosure that modern naturalistic and psychologistic thinking unwittingly undermines itself, and thus appears to undermine all of reason. When reason seems to be undermined, the consequences are disastrous for all of human life, since all of human life rests upon rational norms. Man must look to rigorous science for the satisfaction of the highest theoretical needs and of the needs for norms of an ethical, even religious, nature. The claim that science can satisfy such needs was raised in antiquity and has never been wholly abandoned, in spite of "interests" allegedly in conflict with the pursuit of free inquiry.[16] Oddly, in the present age free inquiry is its own agent of dissolution. The notions of absolute truth and ideal norms are giving way to a relativism of multiple "standpoints"; the scientific spirit is being weakened by an enervating skepticism that has no source but science itself.[17] The various forms of early modern philosophy grounding the natural sciences inaugurated these skeptical tendencies. But the naturalistic "positivism" of the eighteenth century was followed by the flowering of a much more skeptical spirit: the historicist positivism of the nineteenth century. That century alleged that the experience of history had disclosed the transience and time-bound character of all ideals; "the proof" of this thesis (*i.e.*, the "experience" offering the evidence) was nothing other than the mere "fact" of the rise and fall of all cultures and forms of spiritual life. But such positivist historicism is self-refuting; facts alone can never determine the truth of ideals; the judgment "all ideals are valid only for their age" is clearly not merely a statement of fact about the history of beliefs but is intended prescriptively as a statement about the validity of all ideals, past and future. As such it cannot be valid only for its age, and it cannot be derived from mere past experience.

The various forms of positivism are thus manifestly self-refuting. The result of this self-destruction should have been a strengthening of the scientific spirit with a return to classical ideals of absolute truth, instead of its weakening. Thus one must take note of a more seductive form of skepticism, which is winning the battle with rigorous science to be the successor to naive positivism. Husserl refers to an especially German phenomenon, the rise of *Weltanschauungsphilosophie,* the philosophy of world-views. This recognizes the independence of spiritual life from a basis in mere fact (and in so doing is akin to phenomenology), and regards all "truth" (including that of "fact") as the product of great personalities that interpret the destiny and the aspirations of humanity for their own generation and perhaps for those coming after; these interpretations are the great "world-views."[18] The scientific spirit is weakest in this form of philosophy; science is here replaced by a wisdom that is in the service of the immediate interests of life. It aims at an elevation of those interests, yet it lacks the critical standards of rigor that are needed for determining what the highest form of those interests might be. The older historicism discredited all ideals and thus served no interest of life; the enhancement of life is the burden assumed by a new historicism in scholarship and philosophy. Husserl directs his arguments against the *Lebensphilosophie* of Dilthey, who, unlike Nietzsche, attempts to incorporate the new *telos* of inquiry within relatively traditional canons of scholarship and research.

Husserl observes, prior to 1914, that "the spirit of the time is essentially anti-naturalistic and inclined to historicism" of the more radical, life-affirming sort. The exhilarating emancipation from a humanly banal science is unfortunately also an emancipation from reason itself. The "mood" of emancipation has "relative value," with respect to what it leaves behind, but it must not be forgotten that "the highest interests of human culture require a rigorously scientific philosophy."[19] The philosophy of world-views, however, proposes that "there is a human need for a unified and unifying, comprehensive and all-clarifying knowledge," and that science cannot provide that knowledge. The knowledge required exists in the form of the complete educational and spiritual formation of the individual: *Bildung.* Such formation cannot be advanced by means of propositions and doctrines, but rests upon a many-sided experience: aesthetic, religious, ethical, political, as well as scientific. *Bildung* is virtue in the fullest sense, as the habitual excellence of all powers of knowing, willing, valuing, and self-justification. A great personality having *Bildung* (for Dilthey and most Germans, this meant Goethe above all other possible prototypes) possesses the germ of this virtue or wisdom in "a rich but unconceptualized wisdom." The role of science is ancillary to this wisdom: it articulates this wisdom into the systematic world-views or philosophies that offer "the relatively most perfect answer to the riddle of life and the world." [20] The history of philosophy is the history of world-views; one learns from this history the variety of possible great human types, the creators of world-views. The essential meaning of philosophy, therefore, can be grasped only by means of interpretative "empathy" with these creators, and not through mere logic alone.

Husserl will not deny that the aims of world-view thinking are in many respects both noble and necessary; it intends to serve a necessary "teleological function" in the life of man. [21] In his view, however, the world-view philosophy relativizes all truth to the subjective standpoint of individuals, albeit the greatest individuals; it is not unlike positivism in encouraging a slavish submission to the authority of reigning "realities." [22] Whatever is highest in the great individual should be expressible as some form of universally valid ideal, not merely as the unique possession of a great soul. Husserl's objection, otherwise stated, is that world-view thinking does not maintain the distinction between "science as cultural phenomenon" and "science as valid theory," and is thus like positivism in failing to see that facts teach us nothing about the truth. [23] On the other hand, the ideal of *Bildung* has the merit of obscurely foreshadowing a true universal "idea of humanity": "Every striving human being is a 'philosopher' in the most original meaning of the word." [24] Philosophy must indeed serve the interests of life, but these are not the transient interests of a particular people or age, and they can be served only by a rigorous science that attains a universal standpoint. We are in danger of sacrificing the well-being of future generations, which rests upon the uninterrupted progress of reason, to the immediate "pressures of life, the practical need of taking a stance." World-view thinking loses sight of the "infinite goal" of science and is preoccupied with finite practical goals. The difficulty our age experiences seems to disclose that man is a complex and unstable being with two goals: "one for one's time, one for eternity." Nonetheless, rigorous science correctly understood signifies nothing other than the convergence of these two goals upon an infinite point, which the human species must approach asymptotically. [25]

Our age with its "unbearable need" for a world-view should seek out a rational world-view. At the same time, there is a clear difficulty in this proposal: public life requires "particularly significant personalities who can effect the public good in practical spheres," and their wisdom is not the impersonal and painstaking knowing of pure science. Such individuals are better served by world-views not based on rigorous science. It is then unclear in Husserl's account how the nonscientific world-views will acquire a nonrelativistic legitimation, if rigorous science is not able to legitimate them. The difficulty does not seem to be addressed by Husserl's remark that the most needful step philosophy must take at the present time is the clear separation of world-view thinking from philosophic knowledge in the genuine sense. [26]

THE LIFE-WORLD AND HISTORY

The difficulty just mentioned, and others that one can assume were brought to Husserl's attention by his critics and by the deepening moral and political crisis of the time, provoked Husserl to take up some new concerns and to give phenomenological inquiry a new direction. The most striking and fundamental of the new concerns is the reflection in Husserl's last great work, *The Crisis of European Sciences and Transcendental Phenomenology* (begun 1934 and unfinished), on the "science of the life-world." In Husserl's view, such a new science is needed to provide a more perfect grounding to all the "radical" inquiries of phenomenology (and therewith to all sciences). One can isolate the following considerations leading to the conception of such a science:

1. Phenomenology is always concerned with disclosing the unexamined and "naive" assumptions made by the sciences and earlier philosophy. It becomes evident to Husserl that the most fundamental and pervasive of the "naive" assumptions of science is not merely the existence of nature but of the "world-horizon" of man as practical being, governed by the interests of ordinary life; these crucially include man's interests in the life of the political and religious communities to which he belongs. [27] Husserl supposes that many of the most basic conceptions and concerns of man as scientist are not the products of that science but are presupposed by it; they are "constituted" within the primary experiences of ordinary life. Phenomenology must reenact or "reactivate" the primary constitutions of meaning that include the purposes of science. [28] It is still the case for Husserl that pure reason is responsible both for the original and "forgotten" constitutions, and for the reactivations. The turn to ordinary life in the "life-world" is not simply a description of the attitudes of a common sense observer; even such an observer (or espe-

cially such a one) is naively unaware of the original constitutions of his assumptions. These have occurred "anonymously," for the most part, and therefore "naively." Thus the phenomenological recovery of the basis of the life-world is not identical with the self-understanding of the life-world; the latter must first be ascertained in order to be "grounded" in yet "deeper" inquiries.

2. Husserl discovers that his phenomenological thought has hitherto been limited by a naïveté of its own; it has taken the ideal of pure theory as "given," as already constituted, and as only needing a more faithful following. That ideal itself must be "reduced"; that is, its original constitutions must be recovered. Phenomenology cannot be "presuppositionless" without such recovery. Yet the ideal of pure theory arose in a particular place at a particular time, in Greek antiquity; it arose there as a "theoretical attitude" contrasting sharply with the prevailing "mythico-religious attitude." At the time it arose as a new possibility for life, pure theory could not be taken for granted; the motives governing the first philosophers would reveal how a "transformation" of prephilosophic interests had occurred in their adoption of a new attitude. Husserl points to three significant "transformations": (a) philosophy takes the "world" as a theme, thus directing its attention to what is implicit but unnoticed by practical humanity immersed in its various interests with partial aspects of the world; (b) the attitude of theory is detached from those interests that immerse one within the world, especially the interests connected with the mythico-religious account of the world as governed by powers that affect human destiny and that humanity seeks to influence or control; this new attitude is one of "wonder" rather than one of obedience, reverence, and fearful submission or supplication; (c) the earliest philosophy is, like all true philosophy, a "universal science of the totality of what is," [29] but the first form philosophy takes is cosmology, i.e., the account of the whole as "nature," understood as an objective structure of body, independent of mind. Exploring fully the implications of these "transformations" entails undertaking historical investigations; history and systematic philosophy cannot be wholly divorced. There is some question as to what exactly Husserl hopes to find in this exploration. He can claim to find some "grounding" for philosophy in the prephilosophical world with respect to aspects (a) and (c) of the new attitude. Thus (a) shows that philosophy reveals the human capacity to turn to what is implicit but hidden in ordinary awareness of things; (c) shows that early philosophy still in some way partakes of the "naïveté" and "naturalizing" tendency of ordinary or "natural" attitudes. But can one show that the attitude of wonder (b) is a transformation of other attitudes? In any case, Husserl is correct to stress the rup-

ture that the emergence of the new attitude introduced between new "sects" guided by a newly discovered *telos* with an infinite character, and with a potential for creating a cosmopolitan community based on inquiry, and the "conservative" and ancient communities based on tradition. The new *telos,* in other words, was inevitably the source of conflicts within human life.[30] Husserl is thus unwilling to follow Heidegger in regarding pure theory as merely a "derivative" attitude that has wrongly asserted its autonomy over against the poetic-mythical traditions that provide man's primary access to Being.

3. The science of the life-world pursues the goal of clarifying and affirming pure theory as the ultimate *telos* of the West and, through the West, of humanity; in so doing, however, it must take seriously the questions of why the *telos* is not always evident, and why it becomes forgotten or obscured. To raise these questions in a serious way is to go to the sources of the great "conflict" just mentioned. For Husserl this means to examine how the natural attitude, with its naïveté and resistance to pure theory, seems to belong to the essence of reason; on the basis of his earlier account of phenomenology, such a view of reason as inherently self-concealing or self-forgetting was impossible. Thus in the essay "Philosophy as Rigorous Science" one could find no evidence that reason itself might be at the source of the conflict between rigorous science and the pressures of life, which must distort the aims of science. Husserl now makes the attempt to show that because science (rationality in its perfection) must develop historically and has conditions in history, it is also subject to distortion and forgetfulness. Husserl now thinks that the deepest problem of all philosophy is "the meaning of reason in history."[31]

4. The science of the life-world must be especially a consideration of the Western life-world. It is in this life-world that pure theory has emerged as the highest *telos* of man's being; so it is here that the problem of "history," of the ongoing struggle of man to remain faithful to this *telos* in spite of forces that compel him to "forget" it, actually unfolds. An examination of the history of Western efforts to achieve rigorous science is indispensable to the completion of the inquiry announced in (3) above, the account of reason's essence which reveals self-concealing to belong to its essence as much as disclosure of its *telos*. Holding central place in the drama of this history for Husserl is the creation of modern mathematical physics. This physics, or rather its philosophical basis, contains both the promise of the discovery of a true rigorous science, and the seed for the falsifications of science in modern forms of skepticism. We can find the roots of our present crisis in the foundational work of Galileo, Descartes, Locke, and Newton, who are followed by the great analysts of the first crisis in these foundations: Berkeley, Hume, Kant, and Hegel.

Husserl's *Crisis* is much devoted to a historical investigation of their thought, with the expectation that a hidden *telos* is working itself out in their efforts to establish a scientific philosophy.[32] In other terms, there is a design evidently unfolding in history whereby reason proceeds through error toward full clarity about its autonomy.

One must ask, however, what such a history has to do with the life-world. In the first place, Husserl offers an account of the origins of the mathematical—or, more precisely, of Greek geometry—in terms of anonymous constitutions of meaning taking place within ordinary activities in the life-world: measuring, calculating, surveying, etc.[33] Husserl shows that the precision of the mathematical derives from a process of "idealization" of ordinary perceptions; once such idealizations have been constituted, they are embodied in symbolic and notational forms that enable them to be transmitted, taught, more easily manipulated, and thus to become the basis of bodies of knowledge that are scientific. The same symbolic embodiments, however, conceal their own origins in the primary constitutions of the life-world. The premises of sciences are "sedimentations" of forgotten original meanings. The price paid for the establishment of transmissible sciences and "progress" made on the basis of beginnings that are not reenacted by later generations is an increasing superficiality, an evaporation of meaning in the ideas passed down. A body of original insights thereby becomes mere technique.[34] (A difficulty in Husserl's account lies in the notion of the anonymity of the original constitutions; it is hard to see how anonymous insight is truly insight, and how what was never truly seen by anyone can be forgotten and reenacted.)

What is true of mathematical knowledge is true of all knowledge: teaching, learning, application, validation, and further development all presuppose that original insights have become communicable, that is to say, that they have become "traditional." The traditionality of knowledge is the source of its dual character as self-forgetting and disclosing. The pressures for this creation of traditions arise from reason itself, in Husserl's account. We do not have to leave the plane of theoretical concerns in order to discover distorting pressures. (We are not reducing theoretical to extratheoretical concerns.) But we do have to take note of an aspect of theory that becomes evident only from the standpoint of the life-world: the tradition-creating character of reason.

Furthermore, pervasive in Husserl's discussion is the claim that the tradition of mathematical knowledge has played an enormous role in the distortion of Western science and philosophy and, through them, of the Western life-world. Briefly stated, it is Husserl's view that Galileo interpreted nature in terms of number in such a way as to conceal the

"idealizing" activity of reason involved in the interpreting and so to mis-
lead all later Western science into regarding his mathematicization of
nature as the *reality* of nature; this is decisive for the "naturalization" of
the realm of mind along mathematico-physical lines.[35] Mathematics to a
preeminent degree permits the merely technical and self-forgetting use
of concepts. Thus when philosophy itself becomes mathematicized, the
potential for the distortion of all the norms and ideals that must be
grounded in philosophy is very great. At the same time, Husserl suggests that the pressure to mathematicize nature comes to some extent
from the life-world itself, in the form of the various demands for the
technical mastery of nature.[36]

One can say that Husserl considerably understates the nature and
degree of the pressures arising from practical interests, concentrating almost wholly on the distortion of theory through its own exigencies, and
of the life-world through theory. It seems that this asymmetry of emphasis is related to certain fundamental assumptions underlying phenomenology that may be called "enlightenment" assumptions. The distorting
pressures arising from the life-world do not seem to be permanent or
insuperable for Husserl. He believes that "ideas are stronger than experience,"[37] and that philosophy properly assumes the role it has had in the
modern West of exercising leadership in human affairs. Modern philosophy, however, has assumed this role with false principles that ground
new prejudices; phenomenology is the kind of philosophy that can, by
contrast, "overcome the prejudices of millennia" successfully.[38] Western
history is thus seen as culminating in the prospect—which may take
humanity millennia to approach—of man's becoming fully responsible for himself, fully autonomous, abandoning "ancient habits of
thought."[39]

Behind this sanguine view of human affairs is a rather particular
version of modern enlightenment, one that emerged during the modern
age's "first crisis" in the eighteenth century. This is the view that the ills
of society and the forces standing in the way of general virtue and decency arise from theory itself. This view is clearly expressed in the Kantian subordination of merely "dialectical" speculation with its "injurious
influence" to practical reason and its basis in the "good will" of the ordinary person. Whereas such thinking seems to be taking the standpoint
of common sense or common reason, it is in fact ascribing central importance and power—for good or for evil—to the theoretical man. The
obverse side of the view that our world is corrupted principally by false
theories is the view that it will be set right by the true theories (or, perhaps, the end of all theory). A version of this thinking is certainly found
in Husserl. It has been claimed for Husserl that he takes the tremendous

step of reinstating for *doxa,* or opinion, its rights as the ground of all philosophy (in the primary constitutions of the anonymous subject) and shows the error of the Platonic elevation of *epistēmē* (knowledge) over and against *doxa.*[40] That is to say that nearly all is right with the common understanding; philosophy does not transcend it but elaborates its implicit rationality, the noble *telos* within it. Some of Husserl's successors modify this position through the rejection of the rational *telos,* but remain as phenomenologists committed to the elaboration of the "human world" that constitutes itself through the primary experiences of existence. Reflection upon this phenomenological focus should help to throw light upon the relative absence of political philosophy in phenomenology.

NOTES

1. E. Husserl, *The Crisis of European Sciences and Transcendental Phenomenology,* trans. D. Carr (Evanston: Northwestern University Press, 1970), pp. 389–395, 335–341. (Hereafter *Crisis.*)

2. *Crisis,* pars. 1, 2, 5.

3. "Philosophy and the Crisis of European Man" (the Vienna lecture of 1935), in E. Husserl, *Phenomenology and the Crisis of Philosophy,* trans. Q. Lauer (New York: Harper and Row, 1965), pp. 178–80, 191–92. (Hereafter "Philosophy.") *Crisis,* pars. 6, 2.

4. "Philosophy," p. 192.

5. *Ibid.,* p. 183 (on Socrates).

6. *Ibid.,* pp. 188–91, 154; *Crisis,* pp. 315–334.

7. *Crisis,* pp. 343–351.

8. "Philosophy as Rigorous Science," in *Phenomenology* (see n. 3 above), pp. 79–84, 98ff. (Hereafter "Rigorous Science.")

9. *Ibid.,* pp. 102, 105–106, 110; *Crisis,* p. 265 (there is no ontology "for the realm of souls").

10. *Crisis,* pars. 16–21 (on Descartes); "Rigorous Science," pp. 88–89, 116–117 (Husserl's note on the "genuine metaphysics"); "Philosophy," p. 190 (the new science that treats "every conceivable question").

11. "Rigorous Science," pp. 112 ff.

12. *Ibid.,* pp. 146–47; *Crisis,* par. 155 ff.

9, sec. c (the criticism of "indirect methods").

13. "Rigorous Science," pp. 85, 92–98; "Philosophy," pp. 185–188, 154.

14. "Rigorous Science," pp. 85–87 (the natural sciences take the existence of nature for granted); *ibid.,* pp. 116 ff. (reason does not constitute existence).

15. "Philosophy," pp. 181–82, 152–53.

16. "Rigorous Science," pp. 71–72.

17. *Ibid.,* pp. 73–75.

18. *Ibid.,* pp. 122–130.

19. *Ibid.,* pp. 71–79.

20. *Ibid.,* pp. 131–133.

21. *Ibid.,* p. 130.

22. *Ibid.,* pp. 122–123, 145.

23. *Ibid.,* pp. 124–129.

24. *Ibid.,* p. 134.

25. *Ibid.,* pp. 134–137.

26. *Ibid.,* pp. 137–144.

27. *Crisis,* pp. 317–334.

28. "Philosophy," p. 186 ("life" as condition of science); p. 150 ("life" as condition of all culture); *Crisis,* par. 9, sec. 1.

29. "Philosophy," p. 159 and pp. 158–64 *passim;* pp. 169–172.

30. *Ibid.,* pp. 160–164, 173 ff.

31. *Crisis,* par. 3; "Philosophy," pp. 155 ff.

32. "Philosophy," p. 161 (the special historicity of the West); *Crisis*, par. 14 and pars. 5–7 (the hidden *telos* of the struggles between philosophical movements, *e.g.*, skepticism and faith in reason).

33. *Crisis*, pp. 353–378 ("The Origin of Geometry"), and par. 9, sec. a.

34. *Ibid.*, pp. 366–367, and par. 9, secs. f–i; cf. pp. 373–375, for the description of sedimentation as "the a priori of history"; also "Philosophy," pp. 161 ff.

35. *Crisis*, pars. 9–10.

36. "Philosophy," p. 151; *Crisis*, pars. 8, 12.

37. "Philosophy," p. 176.

38. *Crisis*, p. 90; "Philosophy," p. 178 (on philosophy's leadership).

39. *Crisis*, pp. 264–265.

40. A. Gurwitsch, *Studies in Phenomenology and Psychology* (Evanston: Northwestern University Press, 1966), p. 447.

READINGS

A. Husserl, Edmund. "Philosophy as Rigorous Science." Trans. with introduction by Q. Lauer, in Edmund Husserl, *Phenomenology and the Crisis of Philosophy*. New York: Harper and Row, 1965.

Husserl, Edmund. "Philosophy and the Crisis of European Man," Trans. Q. Lauer, in *ibid*.

B. Husserl, Edmund. *The Crisis of European Sciences and Transcendental Phenomenology: An Introduction to Phenomenological Philosophy*. Trans. with introduction by D. Carr. Evanston: Northwestern University Press, 1970.

MARTIN HEIDEGGER

1889–1976

Martin Heidegger was the first philosopher since Plato and Aristotle seriously to consider the question of Being. Indeed, his devotion to this question has marked him out as the preeminent continental European philosopher of the twentieth century. His status as a political philosopher, however, is less clear. In his early magnum opus, *Being and Time,* Heidegger demonstrated little concern for ethics or politics and shortly thereafter rejected the suggestion that he write an ethics as emanating from a fundamental misunderstanding of his thought. Moreover, late in life he asserted that his thinking offered no help with social and political problems. Why then should he be considered in a text devoted to political philosophy?

There are two answers to this question. On the practical level, Heidegger's assertion that his thought is politically irrelevant must be understood in light of his affiliation with Nazism from 1933 to 1934. This incident bespeaks a political significance to his thought that he was later less than anxious to acknowledge. The more profound importance of his thought for ethics and politics, however, arises out of his concern with nihilism.

Nihilism has both a metaphysical and a moral meaning. Metaphysically, it means that nothing is, *i.e.,* not that there is absolutely nothing, which would be absurd, but that there is no unchanging ground, no eternal God or Being such as the Western tradition since Plato has imagined to underlie the flux of experience. Thus, the innumerable things that according to our experience so evidently "are," in fact only seem to be and are actually constantly changing, constantly becoming something other than what they are in a chaotic and utterly unpredictable way. Without some unchanging ground or foundation to this flux, however, it is difficult to see how truth, justice, and morality are possible. If there is no Being or if God is dead, as Nietzsche maintained, then there is only becoming and hence no fixed standard or eternal truth. But, if nothing is fundamentally true, then, as both Dostoevsky and Nietzsche recognized, "everything is permitted." The consequence of metaphysical nihilism is thus moral nihilism. The denial of an eternal God or Being entails the destruction of all fixed or immutable standards of good and evil or noble and base and hence the destruction of the basis for either a universal moral law or natural standards of human excellence. In this light, all standards are revealed as historically relative, as mere prejudices or ideologies serving to maintain the explicit power of some group, race, caste, or class.

This recognition of the historical relativism of all standards has two different but related consequences. On one hand it leads to the abandonment of all higher human aspirations, since nothing is ultimately of any more value than anything else and there is thus no reason to strive and sacrifice for difficult and distant goals. The result is a banal hedonism that pursues the path of least resistance and thus is guided by whatever desire happens to predominate at a given time. Concomitant with this "gentle" nihilism is a "brutal" nihilism that seeks to destroy all standards and to establish itself as the be-all and end-all of human activity. This is nihilism as the will to power that in the form of science and technology aims at the conquest of nature and in the form of a politics of power at the subjugation of mankind. In these two "practical" forms of nihilism, the most abstract and remote metaphysical doctrines come to have real and quite ominous moral, ethical, and political implications.

The world into which Heidegger was born was only beginning to become acquainted with nihilism. Indeed, late nineteenth-century Europe was generally characterized by a pervasive faith in the progress of reason and science, a faith which philosophy with a few notable exceptions shared. World War I shattered this faith, however, and gave the philosophic debate a seriousness and urgency it previously had lacked. Some attributed this disaster to the deficiencies of capitalism, some to excessive nationalism, but to many others it seemed that the philosophic presuppositions of modernity and perhaps even of the Western world as such were horribly defective, that the nihilism which Nietzsche heard knocking at the door had found its way into the heart of European civilization. Heidegger too became concerned with this problem, first only within the horizon of phenomenology, as developed by his teacher and later colleague Edmund Husserl, but increasingly within the context of the Western tradition as a whole.

Nihilism in Heidegger's view is the final consequence of a fundamental misconception of Being, of what he calls the forgetfulness of
Being. It is a peculiarity of Heidegger's thought that he ascribes the profoundest practical importance to what are apparently the most abstract
and remote theoretical considerations. On the surface, Heidegger's attempt to convince the reader that a pervasive misconception regarding
Being can, and in fact has, characterized all of Western civilization seems
absurd, since it seems highly unlikely that such an abstract metaphysical question could ever concern more than a handful of individuals.
However, this is not Heidegger's meaning. Rather he assumes that those
thinkers who have developed the basic framework within which we
think and act, those whom we might justly call law-givers in the most
fundamental sense, have misconceived Being and forgotten its original
meaning. The failure of these thinkers to recognize the truth about
Being, *i.e.,* the truth about what is most fundamental, has led in Heidegger's view to a fundamental distortion of the categories of language
and thought. This distortion not only prevents us from coming to terms
with Being or understanding its importance for our everyday lives but
also establishes a framework for thought and action that cuts man off
from authentic human understanding and activity. In this sense it renders an authentic ethical and political existence impossible and ultimately casts man into nihilism.

Heidegger locates the source of this misconception of Being in the
thought of the Greeks and especially Plato. The forgetfulness of Being
that ends in nihilism is the result of Plato's redefinition of Being as eternal presence, or what stands in place unchangingly forever. This notion
was so persuasive that it seemed to provide the definitive answer to the
question of Being, and as a result the question itself was forgotten. In Heidegger's view, however, this Platonic answer is insufficient. The forgetfulness of the question of Being that it engendered, however, subsequently
made it impossible even to recognize this insufficiency. The Platonic
conception of Being thus became the guiding premise of the Western
tradition. The ever-deepening error that this insufficient premise engenders culminates in nihilism.

But nihilism, as Heidegger understands it, is not merely a negative
phenomenon. Rather it represents two different possibilities. On one
hand, the forgetfulness of Being that ends in a denial of Being and thus a
denial of all categories and standards allows the most banal and brutal
passions to come to predominance. On the other hand, this obliteration
of categories and standards clears the horizon and makes possible an
original experience of the mystery and wonder of existence that has been
impossible since the time of Plato and Aristotle. Nihilism is thus both

the greatest ethical and political disaster and the greatest philosophical possibility in the last 2,500 years. Heidegger thus believes that nihilism contains the possibility of its own destruction and hence the possibility of mankind's salvation. This, however, remains a possibility that must be grasped and actualized and consequently can be bypassed and lost. The danger for man, as Heidegger sees it, is that he may believe nihilism is only a recent deviation from an otherwise healthy tradition that can be restored by a minor correction. It is necessary instead to recognize the irremediably nihilistic essence of the Western tradition as a whole and turn away from it altogether toward a recollection and reconsideration of the forgotten question of Being that nihilism makes possible.

Heidegger's first and greatest attempt to come to terms with the question of Being was *Being and Time.* The specific task of this work was to raise the question of the meaning of Being (*Sein*) through an analysis of human Being (*Dasein*) in terms of temporality, or, in more familiar terms, to come to an understanding of the relationship of Being and time by examining the way in which they are united in man as a historical being.

On the surface there is little indication that this project has a practical or political motive. Indeed, the work presents itself only as an attempt to recover the foundations of science. In this sense it stands within the horizon of phenomenology. A somewhat closer examination, however, reveals a fundamental continuity of the theoretical and practical. The question of Being, according to Heidegger, is the source and ground of all ontologies or orderings of beings and thus of all human understanding. In forgetting this question, man thus forgets the source of his own knowledge and loses the capacity to question in the most radical way, which is essential to both real thought and authentic freedom. Without it, man is reduced to a calculating beast concerned only with preservation and pleasure, a "last man," to use Nietzsche's terminology, for whom beauty, wisdom, and greatness are mere words. The nihilistic banality of this last man thus seems to lie behind Heidegger's concern with the foundations of science.

To come to terms with this implicit nihilism, it is necessary in Heidegger's view to overcome the forgetfulness of Being. Being, however, is not forgotten in any ordinary way. The question of Being is forgotten because Being itself is accepted as self-evident, as the most universal but also the emptiest of concepts. Being is forgotten, in other words, because people all think they know what Being is. This, in Heidegger's view, is the result of a misunderstanding of the relation of Being and time. Since Plato, Being has been understood in opposition to actual things as that which is beyond time and does not change. All actual things in this sense stand between Being and nothing. All things come to be and also pass away. In opposition to the unchanging realm of Being, actual things thus exist in the realm of becoming or time. The Western tradition in this sense is characterized by the antithesis of Being and becoming or Being and time. What has become apparent in modern times, however, is that this distinction, which lies at the heart of the categories of our understanding, prevents us from adequately grasping our concrete historical reality, what Heidegger calls the facticity of human existence. Thus, we cannot understand the truth about ourselves as historical beings because the tradition that informs our way of thinking rests upon the understanding of Being as eternal presence, which proves to be the understanding of Being in terms of a defective notion of time. What is necessary is to come to a fuller understanding of Being in terms of the deeper conception of time that has come to light as a result of the discovery of history.

Heidegger attempts to raise the question of Being and time through an investigation of man because he believes humanity stands in a special relation to Being. Man is the only being which has its own Being as a question, *i.e.,* man is the only being who is concerned about what he is to be, about his future, his possibilities of Being. There is no question for an acorn about what it will become. Accidents aside, it becomes an oak. Man, in Heidegger's view, has no such determinate end. His end and thus his future is always a question for him. In contradistinction to the acorn, he thus cannot dwell merely in the present but is continually concerned with the future. Indeed, in contradistinction to the acorn he has a future. The future of the acorn is something only for man. In this sense man is likewise the only being who is authentically historical, who is actively involved in planning and shaping his future, in making history. It is because of this conjunction of Being and time in human Being that Heidegger believes man can serve as an entrance to the question of Being itself. By examining the way in which history arises out of man's concern with the question of his Being, *i.e.,* with his undetermined end, Heidegger hopes to come to a more profound understanding of the question of Being as such, *i.e.,* of the ends not only of man but of *all* the things that are, and thus to show how time as such arises out of Being.

Heidegger attempts to open up this question of Being by means of an analysis of human Being that lays bare the basic structures of human existence, that shows not *what* man is but *how* he exists, how he is in and through time. He begins with an analysis of everyday existence that focuses on the fact that man everywhere and always finds himself thrown into a world that is characterized by a particular ontology or order of beings. Man as human Being is thus what Heidegger calls "Being-in-the-world." Man consequently finds himself *by* things and *with* others, *i.e.*, within a particular structure that determines the relations between all beings, that defines their purposes and hence their activities, that thus determines *how* man and everything else *is*. For the most part, man is simply absorbed in the prevailing order and is determined on a practical (ready-to-hand) and theoretical (present-at-hand) level by the concerns that arise within it. For the most part he is thus characterized by what Heidegger calls fallenness and exists inauthentically as "they" do, "they" being the generality of ordinary mankind. In this mode of being, man is dominated by what Heidegger calls the "they-self," which accepts the world as given and never seriously questions the prevailing order of things.

According to Heidegger, the question of Being arises for humans only when this everyday existence is called into question by an authentic confrontation with death. As Being-in-the-world, man is always directed toward the future, because his own Being is always a question for him. His Being in this sense is characterized by what Heidegger calls "care." As a futural being who cares about what will happen to him, man inevitably encounters the question of death. This is true even for man in his mode as the they-self. This self prepares for death, however, only inauthentically, grasping death only in terms of the death of others, as what happens to "one" or to "them." This inauthentic experience of death confirms and does not transcend the prevailing order of things. An authentic understanding of death requires another experience altogether. Heidegger discovers the possibility of authentically understanding death in the phenomenon of anxiety, especially as it appears in the call of conscience, which he argues is the call of one's own Being, as care for future possibilities of Being. This experience of death in anxiety liberates man from the prevailing order of beings. It is the recognition of the finitude of one's own Being and opens up the possibility for the experience of the question of Being itself.

Life is generally understood in terms of the possibilities available within a particular world or order of beings. These possibilities seem to the they-self to be given and immutable. The authentic experience of death, however, reveals these possibilities *as* possibilities, since it reveals that we cannot do everything. In this moment of vision we confront death as that which is most our own, as the ineluctable possibility that limits all of our other possibilities. We recognize that we are thrown into a determinate world that we must leave. The experience of death thus reveals the particular horizon of our world and our own personal fate within the larger destiny of those with whom we are, our people or generation. Appearing as the *question* of our own Being, death directs us toward a specific set of *answers* or possibilities. Discovering these answers or realizing these possibilities becomes the goal of our activity. The question of our Being that arises out of our authentic recognition of the inevitability of our own death thus is the source of the goal which is projected in front of us. This projected goal in Heidegger's view is the source of our future, since the authentic future is always only as we foresee it, as that which we are on the way toward. It is on the basis of this future goal or end that we then grasp the past and keep it from slipping away, for it is only on this basis that it becomes at all relevant to us. The revelation of the possibilities of our own Being in the moment of vision in the face of death thus opens up an entire world of beings.

Heidegger has not, however, thereby grasped the fundamental conjunction of Being and time. Indeed, it is understood only from the perspective of human Being, only negatively in terms of death. The goal of *Being and Time* was to understand Being and time in their own right, independently of man, but Heidegger was unable to complete the work to his own satisfaction. He had intended in the unfinished portion of the book first to raise the question of Being explicitly and then to undertake what he called the destruction of the history of ontology or what we might call the destruction of metaphysics. He had thought when he began *Being and Time* that it would be possible to circumvent the entire history of Western metaphysics and raise anew the question of Being by a direct investigation of human Being itself and on that basis to reinterpret this history. He discovered in the course of writing *Being and Time,* however, that the language and especially the philosophical terminology he had to use was derived from, and was thus fundamentally dependent upon, metaphysics. The categories within which he tried to rethink the question of Being were thus constituted in a manner that concealed the question itself, *i.e.,* in a manner that made it impossible even to grasp the question adequately. Because of this dependence upon metaphysics, Heidegger was unable to finish *Being and Time* as he had intended. The failure of *Being and Time* thus made clear to him that the destruction of metaphysics would have to precede and not follow the explicit confrontation with the question of Being.

This destruction of metaphysics is carried out in a number of later works and is basically a critique and reinterpretation of Western philosophy that traces the increasing forgetfulness of Being and thus the growth of nihilism. This is accomplished not by demonstrating internal contradictions or subliminal psychological or economic motives but by showing how each thinker accepts the prevailing notion of Being and thus leaves the guiding question of Western philosophy, the question of Being, unthought. This critique and reinterpretation, however, is not essentially negative but, rather, aims at coming to terms with Being itself, for while it demonstrates the ever deepening obliteration of Being, it also points to the emptiness of the place Being has vacated, where Being is left unthought, forgotten. In this way the destruction of metaphysics is also what Heidegger calls the history of Being, *i.e.*, the history of the misconception, forgetfulness, and what Heidegger often calls "withdrawal" of Being that constitutes the essence of Western civilization.

As we have seen, there is already an implicit critique of metaphysics in *Being and Time*. But this critique remains within the general horizon of the phenomenological concern with the ground of science that Heidegger inherited from Husserl. Heidegger's critique of the Western tradition in the years following *Being and Time* shows a deeper appreciation for the ethical and political consequences of the forgetfulness of Being or what he increasingly called nihilism. This "turn" in his thought was the result of a number of factors, but perhaps none was so important as Nazism.

Heidegger became involved with the Nazis during the early 1930s at Freiburg University.[1] In the midst of the revolution that followed Hitler's rise to power, Heidegger was asked by his colleagues to become rector of the university in order to help preserve its independence. He hoped for more than this, however, and believed that the Nazi revolution could be directed toward a more fundamental experience of human existence that could serve as the basis for a more authentic ethics and politics. In this scheme for reform and redirection, the German university in Heidegger's view would have to play a leading role and give the political movement an intellectual substance that it hitherto had lacked. Such a fundamental refounding of German life thus presupposed a refounding of the German university. It was this that Heidegger thought he might effect. The decidedly un-Nazi title of his inaugural address as rector, "The Self-Assertion of the German University," reflects such an aspiration.

Heidegger's hopes soon revealed themselves as illusions. He found himself at odds with the Nazis as a result of his resistance to the Nazification of the university and his unwillingness to dismiss Jewish faculty members, and his attempts at compromise failed to satisfy the authorities. Nor were these Heidegger's only difficulties, for the positive forces in the German university that he had hoped to unite behind him resisted his attempts at reform. His hopes for a political transformation on the basis of an antecedent academic transformation thus were shattered. Confronted with Nazi demands he was unwilling to fulfill and faculty intransigence he could not overcome, he resigned. As a result, he was viewed with growing suspicion by the regime and subjected during the

rest of the Nazi period to a variety of punitive measures including surveillance of his seminars and forced labor on military fortifications.

Whatever his aversion to Nazism, Heidegger apparently also saw
something positive in it, for in 1935 he spoke of "the inner truth and
greatness of this movement" in his lectures on the "Introduction to Metaphysics" and included this passage when they were published in 1953.
Does this mean that Heidegger was a Nazi? Heidegger tried to defend
himself against this charge in two ways. First, he argued that to alter the
text would be a historical falsification.[2] Indeed, this would have left him
open to the charge that he was trying to conceal his Nazi past. Second,
he drew attention in the 1960s to a parenthetical gloss on the offending
passage, which ran "(namely the encounter between world technology
and modern man)." It was Heidegger's contention that his serious audience understood him correctly in 1935 while the stupid and suspicious
interpreted the passage to their own satisfaction as a sign of his affection
for the regime. All intricacies of fact and speculation aside, it remains
incontrovertible that Heidegger never publicly repudiated his Nazi
utterances.

This said, what does this gloss tell us about Heidegger's understanding of Nazism? Modern man, as Heidegger understands him, is fundamentally bound up with technology. As Ernst Jünger, in Heidegger's
view, had insightfully shown in his book *The Worker,* the model for man's
Being in the contemporary technological world is the worker. It was apparently the attempt of the Nazis to give a new meaning to man as
worker that Heidegger admired and that he believed offered a possibility
for a new and more authentic ethics and politics, although how this
might be achieved he never made clear. He recognized that those in
power were too unskilled in thinking to come to grips with technology
in an adequate way but believed they might listen to those capable of
thinking more profoundly. Here he was clearly wrong and failed to appreciate the dedication of the leaders of the Nazi movement to an ideology of genocide and apocalypse.

The philosophical result of this experience for Heidegger was a new
appreciation of the power and pervasiveness of metaphysical thinking
and its connection to nihilism. Metaphysics culminated, not merely in
the "gentle" nihilism he had recognized in *Being and Time* as the banality
of the everyday world and the they-self, but also in the "brutal" nihilism
of the Nazis. His failure to complete *Being and Time* was thus bound up
with his failure to transform either the German university or the Nazi
movement. A more fundamental analysis and critique that would explain the origin of the brutal nihilism that manifested itself in Nazism
was thus necessary. Such an analysis in the first instance meant an examination of modernity.

According to Heidegger, modernity is characterized by subjectivity, *i.e.*, by the fact that in modern times man himself serves as the measure and ground of all truth. Modernity is thus also the realm of freedom, for the predominance of subjectivity frees man from the theocentric structure of traditional Christian society and establishes him on himself alone. The source of this new notion is Descartes's interpretation of man as self-consciousness, which establishes man's absolute independence as the measure of all things. Henceforth, only what can pass before the tribunal of consciousness, *i.e.*, only what can be perceived and ascertained, counts as a thing.

When man takes his stand upon himself alone, however, he loses his place in the ordered cosmos of traditional society. Modern freedom is thus bound up with an alienation that catapults man into the pursuit of security through the subordination of nature to his own will. Nature thus no longer provides guidelines for human action but is an uncertain and therefore dangerous "other" that must be mastered. It is subdued on an intellectual level by modern science, which develops a mathematical picture or model of the world and thereby reduces the world to a predictable and hence controllable object. Heidegger calls this process objectification. Modern technology then unites this new science with human labor to subdue and transform the natural world into an object suitable for human use and habitation.

The attempt to secure subjectivity and human freedom through the technological subjugation of nature fails, however, because it necessarily entails the subjugation of human nature as well and thus brings people into conflict with one another. This increasingly competitive conflict leads to the formation of ever larger and more technically organized political entities and thus in reality leads only to the subordination of all humans to the world-technological task. Conflict in modern times is thus for Heidegger not the consequence of passion, human partiality, the will to power, class antagonism, or disputes about the nature of justice but the result of the attempt to secure human freedom in the natural world through technology. Conflict is therefore also unavoidable, since what it means to be human in the modern world is to measure, master, and subdue nature, *i.e.*, to be technological. Heidegger traces this development from Descartes through Leibniz, Kant, Hegel, Schelling, and Nietzsche to the world technology of the twentieth century.[3] It is the story of the ever growing nihilism of modern thought in the journey of modern man as subject, from Cartesian self-consciousness to the Nietzschean will to power, that in Heidegger's view lies at the heart of world technology. It is likewise the story of the degeneration of man from self-conscious lord of creation to worker and mass man. Modernity culminates as Heidegger had already recognized in *Being and Time* in the complete forgetfulness of Being and the utter dehumanization of man, who himself becomes a mere raw material for a world technology that aims only at its own nihilistic self-perpetuation and growth.

Uprooted and alienated from traditional society, we moderns attempt to construct a place for ourselves in the midst of becoming with the help of history. History allows us to measure and demarcate time so that we can determine our origin and place with respect to all other things. We can thus secure ourselves from the terrifying uncertainty of an aimless becoming. This project, however, at heart attempts to make time into an object of exploitation and thus is analogous to the objectivization of space undertaken by modern natural science. It thus succeeds, however, only in severing man more completely from the metaphysical tradition that gave him a true place and meaning by joining him on some basic level to the long-forgotten question of Being. Cut off from this question entirely, man is also cut off from the direction it gives to his thought and activity. Without such direction, however, history can be interpreted in any way since there is no longer a standard of truth and reality. Man, in Heidegger's view, thus falls prey to the confusion of historicism and relativism, from which he can escape only by giving himself up to ideology, by adopting an arbitrary and irrational worldview that provides a simplified but totalistic explanation resolving all uncertainty and insecurity.

History and ideology thus only serve as two more tools in the service of the technological conquest of the earth. Indeed, they augment the competition to secure mastery and give rise to an ideological struggle that ends in world war, which in turn is the means for further securing a total mobilization and a total control of mankind that ultimately obliterates the very difference between war and peace. The end of modern subjectivity and freedom in this sense is a universal homelessness and alienation under the hegemony of an ideological totalitarianism that aims at the universal mastery and exploitation of both man and nature. Under such conditions, *homo sapiens* is reduced to *homo brutalitas*.

Heidegger describes three forms of political life at the end of modernity: Americanism, Marxism, and Nazism.[4] In his view, all three are forms of subjectivity and nihilism and thus metaphysically identical. All are characterized by the dictatorship of the public over the private, and by the predominance of natural science, economics, public policy, and technology. Americanism in his view is not liberalism or democracy but a particular form of logical positivism that serves as a handmaiden to science and technology. The reality of Americanism is the industrial complex, the central agency of economic and technological planning, which organizes the labor of the common man and extends its rule through the world market. Marxism is likewise not merely a party or world-view but is, rather, the elevation of the process of production to predominance and the consequent reduction of man to a socially produced being. Both Americanism and Marxism misconstrue human spirituality as calculative intelligence and consequently fail to grasp the necessity for the consideration of the *question* of Being. The most extreme form of this thoughtlessness is Nazism, which completes and reverses modern thought by replacing reason with instinct. Instinct is intrinsic not to the individual but to the race and is given voice by leaders, who speak for the subjectivistic racial essence. Their instincts rise above the nihilistic paralysis of reason to deed and thus give the illusion of certainty and security. Nazism, however, fails to recognize that its fundamental distinction of overman and underman is arbitrary since both have in principle been reduced to beasts.

The various forms of modern life thus represent only an institutionalization of nihilism. This, however, is not due to the defective character of modernity itself, for modernity and hence nihilism are only the final consequences of the metaphysical project that begins with the Greeks. To grasp the origin and true extent of nihilism, Heidegger maintains, it is thus necessary to examine the Greeks.

The Greek world and Western civilization as such began, in Heidegger's view, with the revelation of Being, with what he sometimes calls, using the Greek *alētheia,* "truth" or, literally, "unforgetting." [5] In this revelation Being appeared as chaos or nothingness, as the violence of the abyss that overpowered man in all its mysteriousness and opened up a new way of thinking and acting, a new world, brought new gods, a new ethics, a new politics, and a new conception of man's humanity. Man, in other words, was struck by the fundamental mystery and incomprehensibility of existence. This Heidegger holds to be the concrete experience of Being, the way in which Being appears to man. Being in this sense appeared for the Greeks as a fundamental *question.* As a question, however, it directed them toward answers and thus away from the question itself, away from Being. The pre-Socratics stood in the midst of this struggle between Being as the fundamental mystery or *question* of existence and beings as determined by categories or *answers* to this question. This struggle was carried out in art, or what Heidegger often calls language, not merely by poets but also by sculptors, architects, thinkers, and statesmen who took part in establishing the laws, customs, and institutions of the Greek world. They all confronted the mysteriousness of existence that the experience of Being evoked and constructed a new way of understanding and a new world as an answer or solution to this mystery.

The foremost creation of the Greeks was the polis. For them it was not merely the place where the business of state is conducted but the place at which gods and men take up relationship to one another, where man first recognizes his earthly mortality in opposition to a heavenly immortality. The Greeks, as Heidegger understands them, thus were able to embody an authentic understanding of death and hence of their own finitude and fate in their art, religion, and philosophy, and above all in their political institutions. It is in this sense that the polis is the source of man's humanity as human Being. Insofar as man recognizes his own mortality and fate in opposition to the immortal gods, he has a particular place or *ethos* of his own and thus becomes capable of ethics. The character of his place and thus of his ethics and politics is likewise a reflection of the particular character of the gods and man's relationship to them. The polis in this sense is always the place of the gods and is characterized in its laws and institutions by the particular pantheon that has been revealed.

This pre-Socratic experience of Being, in Heidegger's view, is fundamentally tragic. The abyss of Being that evokes wonder and thought also casts man out of the everyday order of things. Being calls everything into question, and those like Antigone, Oedipus, and Heraclitus who encounter the question of Being become "*apolis,* without city and place, alone, alien, without a way out in the midst of being as a whole, at the same time without statute and limit, without structure and order because as creators they must first ground all this."[6] In a heroic-tragic sense, cast out of ordinary life, these founders represent for the Greeks the highest human possibility.

The tragic age in which such figures have meaning and significance comes to an end with the disappearance of the revelation of Being. This world ended when the question of Being became submerged in its answers and failed to reappear as a question, *i.e.,* when in Heidegger's terms Being withdrew and was forgotten. Why this occurred is, in Heidegger's view, dark and mysterious and lies not with man but with Being itself. That it occurred is the central and decisive fact of all Western history.

This withdrawal of Being as a question began with the Sophists and culminated in the thought of Plato and Aristotle.[7] The exception to this trend was Socrates, who followed Being in its withdrawal, *i.e.,* who followed the dialectical path backward through the answers to the question of Being itself in an attempt to come to the mysterious and often contradictory beginning of thought.[8] Plato, on the contrary, turned away from the question of Being and indeed closed off the question by giving it a decisive answer. Being as he portrays it is eternal presence, the unchanging form or idea in contradistinction to the ephemeral things of the world of becoming. Being in this way disappears as a question and re-appears as the highest answer, as the Being of beings, as the immutable essence of all things. On this basis Plato, Aristotle, and the Scholastics were able to articulate an ontology or hierarchy of beings in terms of their proximity to Being itself. It is this metaphysical hierarchy that in its various transformations constitutes the structure of the Western world. The first of these transformations gave birth to Christianity and the Middle Ages, the second to the modern world. In the former, Being withdrew out of nature and into transcendence, thus undermining the ancient cosmos. The immediacy of the Being or essence of things in their natural form gave way to the notion that this form was only one of many possible creations of a transcendent and ultimately incomprehensible God, who alone truly "is" in the highest sense. Christianity itself was undermined by the withdrawal of Being, in which man replaced a disap-pearing God as the ground of all being and hence as the center of all ontology. Man as the self-conscious subject is henceforth what truly is. Insofar as man grasps himself as Being, however, Being loses its last vestiges of mystery and hence the ability to evoke wonder and thought, for man, as Descartes argues, knows himself immediately and com-pletely. Western history in this sense is determined by the original ques-tion of Being and its successive withdrawals. It is thus the history of the forgetfulness of Being as a question and the triumph of being as an an-swer. With Nietzsche's interpretation of Being as just another among many different beings, Being disappears completely, and the West, which had been guided by the concealed *question* of Being, comes to an end.

Heidegger thus turns against the Enlightenment tradition to reveal the darkling character of modern life. But he does not draw our attention to this pervasive nihilism merely to provoke despair or self-disgust but because he believes he discerns in its depths the dawning light of a new revelation of Being. To demonstrate this, however, is to show the inner concealed connection of Being and nothing. In this inquiry Heidegger takes his cue from the pre-Socratics. In particular, he sees a parallel be-tween the pre-Socratic experience of the question or abyss of Being and the contemporary experience of nihilism. Nihilism is ordinarily under-stood as the assertion that nothing is, *i.e.,* not that absolutely nothing is but that there is no ground for beings and thus no unchanging standard or order. Heidegger, for his part, wants to understand nihilism as the realization that the ground is quite literally nothing, *i.e.,* no-thing or no being. This means that the ground must be understood as something other than beings, and that means Being in its primordial sense as chaos or abyss. Nihilism is thus the dawning recognition of Being, of the fun-damental question or mysteriousness that is the source of the wonder

that evokes all thought, all categories, and therefore all order. In nihilism, Being appears as chaos or abyss and undermines all ontology and
therefore all ethics, politics, and religion. The advent of nihilism thus
signals the end of Western civilization, hence the possibility of a return
to a pre-Western perspective, and perhaps even a rapprochement of East
and West.

Nihilism, however, is not a return to the pre-Socratics and in fact
directs us away from the world they opened up. The early Greeks experienced the question of Being in Heidegger's view as the question "What is
Being?" The guiding question of Western thought is thus the what-
question. It is this question that philosophy and the sciences sought to
answer. Hence, ancient biology sought to explain *what* the different
forms of life *are, i.e.,* to discover and describe the categories or species
of things. The question of Being that appears out of nihilism, on the
contrary, is not the what-question but the how-question, which in many
ways has always been central to modern thought and is concealed, for
example, in the heart of modern science, technology, and history. Our
thinking is thus not directed toward answering the question "What is
it?" but, rather, the question "How does it work?" Modern biology is
thus not principally interested in discovering the division of nature according to genera and species but in explaining how organisms work.
Nature is consequently not understood as a beautiful cosmos to be contemplated and emulated but as a conjunction of forces or as a mechanism
that can be used to secure human preservation and prosperity. Insofar as
Being occurs as the *howness* of what is, *i.e.,* as how things are, it is incomprehensible within the categories of language that have been determined by a metaphysics that has always understood Being and beings as
things, as whats. The framework of our understanding thus precludes
the recognition of Being. Hence, as Heidegger concluded after the failure of *Being and Time,* Being necessarily remains concealed and consequently unthought and forgotten.

Fundamental to Heidegger's thought is the attempt to show the
conjunction of Being as the how of what is with history or time.[9] History (*Geschichte*) for Heidegger is not a causal series or the unfolding of
human freedom or the dialectical development of the means of production but the destiny (*Geschick*) of Being itself. Heidegger draws this notion of destiny from the Greek *moira,* "fate," "destiny," which is the dark
and mysterious source of change that establishes the horizon for beings
but itself remains beyond that horizon. *Moira* is Being itself as the fundamental question that provokes man and directs him to answers but
thus withdraws and is itself concealed by the answers and forgotten. It is
as this directing question that Being is history or destiny.

In this light, Heidegger's thought seems to be radical historicism. Hegel understood history as the dialectical development of reason to its culmination in absolute knowledge; Marx accepted this notion of the dialectical character of actuality but denied it had come to its conclusion; Nietzsche in turn denied even this dialectical rationality and asserted instead that the world was sheer becoming, governed only by the will to power and the eternal recurrence. Heidegger seems to bring this progressive development of historicism to an end with his assertion of the identity of history and Being. Such an interpretation, however, at least in part misconstrues Heidegger's thought, for he attempts to show not that Being is history but that history is the revelation of Being. He thus aims not at the historicization of Being but at the eternalization of history or time. For Heidegger, history as destiny unfolds itself forward and backward out of the revelation of Being. For whatever dark and incomprehensible reason, Being appears to man as a particular, fundamental question. This question then directs man, as we have seen, toward a particular realm of answers and thus establishes a goal or future and a past appropriate to this goal. History is then a series of unique projections of eternity upon temporality, of unique revelations of Being that are unpredictable and incommensurable with one another. Each age believes it has the truth and indeed does have the truth, since it understands in its own way what is eternal, is itself an expression of the eternal, of Being as the *how*, as the history or destiny of beings.

Heidegger suspects that modern nihilism is the advent of such a revelation of Being. It opens up the possibility for an immediate encounter with Being not only because it obliterates all the categories within which Being has been imprisoned, concealed, and forgotten but also because it obliterates all of our misconceptions about our own human Being, all notions of immortal fame, immortality of the soul, or actual biological immortality and thus makes possible again an authentic experience of our own mortality, of death as our ownmost possibility. Nihilism thus cannot be simply rejected or overcome. It is, rather, the contemporary reality and contains both the possibility of utter degradation and the possibility of salvation in a new revelation of Being. What is crucial for man is to prepare himself to receive this revelation. This does not mean rejecting the modern technical and political world which is the basis for man's contemporary human Being. Heidegger believes rather that this new revelation will lead to a fundamental reinterpretation of the relation of man and technology that will give a new meaning and significance to human existence and thus to human activity. The recognition of Being as the how of beings, as technology and history, is thus nothing other than the liberation of man to accept his own essence as human Being. The substantive character of human life and thus the shape of ethics and politics in the context of this new world, however, remain obscure and depend in Heidegger's view upon the full revelation of Being as well as the human reception and response to the question it poses. While Heidegger thus explains *how* the future will be shaped, he does not know and cannot explain *what* shape it will take.

Although man cannot overcome nihilism, he can prepare for a new revelation. Indeed, Heidegger's project is such a preparation. It involves (1) liberating man from all metaphysical categories and standards through a fundamental destructive reinterpretation of the history of Western thought; (2) fostering an authentic experience of contemporary nihilism by calling man to a resolute confrontation with death and meaninglessness; and (3) convincing man to accept his particular fate within the destiny of his people or generation made manifest in the revelation of Being.

Heidegger of course cannot guarantee that even under such circumstances Being will reveal itself, that the mysterious "essence" of existence will strike man again with all its great force, thus engendering wonder and authentic thought. The result of all the efforts and sacrifices Heidegger demands may thus be nothing. Perhaps more ominously, however, Heidegger does not explain how to distinguish an authentic revelation of Being from the projections of subliminal prejudices and passions. Indeed, his destruction of metaphysics would seem to render such a distinction impossible since it destroys all the categories on the basis of which such a distinction could be made. Similarly, his emphasis upon a new authentic existence in contradistinction to the inauthenticity of our contemporary existence leads Heidegger into an identification of Americanism, Marxism, and Nazism that dismisses the most important political issues of the twentieth century as epiphenomenal and undermines the basis for any differentiation of decent and monstrous regimes. Finally, because Heidegger is unable to foretell what shape even a genuine revelation would take, it is unclear whether the new god Heidegger believes necessary to save us would in fact be preferable to the "gentle" nihilism of the technical world. Indeed, such a god might well be a "rough beast" whose solution to "gentle" nihilism was in fact a monstrously "brutal" nihilism, which offered perversion in place of pleasure and terror in place of banality.

This perhaps offers some insight into Heidegger's attachment to Nazism and the dangers that await others on the path he marks out. Heidegger was hardly ignorant of the dangers he faced. The last line of his inaugural address as rector—"Everything great stands in the storm"— is drawn from the sixth book of Plato's *Republic,* where Socrates describes the dangers run by the philosopher who tries to take the city in hand. Heidegger saw his age as akin to that of the pre-Socratics. Both offered great opportunity but also great danger, especially for those who opened up the unsettling question of Being. Heidegger here might well have taken a lesson from the story of Oedipus, for which he shows such respect. Or perhaps we must conclude that he was all too well aware of its lesson, that the man who seeks to found a new politics on the basis of a new revelation is not merely cast out of ordinary political life but also becomes entangled in the most heinous crimes and most horrible degradations. Here Heidegger's failure ever to criticize the Nazis explicitly for their atrocities weighs heavily against both him and his thought.

Aristotle remarks that the man who lives outside the city is either a beast or a god. Heidegger may well teach us that those who pass beyond the city in their search for a new god often find themselves worshiping at the feet of the beast, that those who derive reason from revelation all too easily become entangled in the highest and most monstrous unreason. His thought and his example thus seem to lead us in opposite directions and open up anew the question of the relationship of the philosopher and the city.

NOTES

1. For the documentation on Heidegger's relation to Nazism, see his "The Self-Assertion of the German University," *Review of Metaphysics*, XXXVIII (March 1985), 467–502; "Only a God Can Save Us," in *Heidegger: The Man and Thinker*, ed. T. Sheehan (Chicago: Precedent Publishing, 1981); *An Introduction to Metaphysics* (New Haven: Yale University Press, 1959) (hereafter *IM*) and his speeches from the Nazi period in M. Friedman, ed., *The Worlds of Existentialism* (New York: Random House, 1964).

2. Günther Neske, ed., *Erinnerung an Martin Heidegger* (Pfullingen: Neske, 1977), p. 49.

3. For Heidegger's account of this development, see the following article and books by him: "The Principle of the Ground," *Man and World*, VII (1974), 207–222; *Kant and the Problem of Metaphysics* (Bloomington: Indiana University Press, 1962); *Hegel's Concept of Experience* (New York: Harper & Row, 1970); *Schelling's Treatise on the Essence of Human Freedom* (Athens: Ohio University Press, 1985); *Nietzsche*, 4 vols. (New York: Harper & Row, 1979–1987); and *The Question of Technology and Other Essays* (New York: Harper & Row, 1977).

4. For Heidegger's understanding of Americanism, Marxism, and Nazism, see *IM*, pp. 37–51, and *Vier Seminare* (Frankfurt am Main: Klostermann, 1977).

5. For Heidegger's discussion of the Greeks, see *IM; Early Greek Thinking* (New York: Harper & Row, 1975); and *Erläuterungen zu Hölderlin's Dichtung* (Frankfurt am Main: Klostermann, 1944).

6. *IM*, pp. 152–153.

7. For his discussion of Plato and Aristotle, see especially his "Plato's Doctrine of Truth," in *Philosophy in the*

Twentieth Century, ed. W. Barrett and H. D. Aiken, 4 vols. (New York: Random House, 1962), III, 251–270; and "On the Being and Conception of *Physics* in Aristotle's Physics B, 1," *Man and World,* IX (1976), 219–270.

8. Heidegger nowhere explains his separation of Socrates and Plato. In most respects he seems to follow Nietz-

sche's distinction and characterization of the two.

9. For Heidegger's discussion of history, see his "A Letter on Humanism," in *Basic Writings,* ed. D. F. Krell (New York: Harper & Row, 1977); *Nietzsche,* IV, 199–250; and *Being and Time* (New York: Harper & Row, 1962).

READINGS

A. Heidegger, Martin. *An Introduction to Metaphysics.* New Haven: Yale University Press, 1959.

Heidegger, Martin. *Being and Time.* New York: Harper & Row, 1962. "Introduction."

B. Heidegger, Martin. *Nietzsche.* 4 volumes. New York: Harper & Row, 1979–1987. Volume 4.

Heidegger, Martin. "A Letter on Humanism." In *Basic Writings,* ed. D. F. Krell. New York: Harper & Row, 1977.

Heidegger, Martin. *The Question of Technology and Other Essays.* New York: Harper & Row, 1977.

EPILOGUE

Leo Strauss and the History of
Political Philosophy

A student using this book might legitimately and naturally wonder about the approach to the teaching of political philosophy presented here. The originator of this approach was the work's senior editor, Leo Strauss. Born in Germany in 1899, he studied philosophy, mathematics, and natural science there, and attended courses by Husserl and Heidegger. After working as a researcher at an institute for Jewish studies in Berlin, he left Germany in 1932 and eventually settled in the United States, where he taught at the New School for Social Research from 1938 to 1949, the University of Chicago from 1949 to 1967, Claremont Men's College in 1968–69, and St. John's College until his death in 1973. He was an extraordinarily influential teacher; his many students include most of the contributors to this book. More important, he wrote fifteen books (the first three in his native German and then a dozen in English) interpreting a wide range of texts and authors and investigating the fundamental problems of political philosophy.

THE TURN TO THE HISTORY OF POLITICAL PHILOSOPHY

Strauss appears primarily as a historian of political philosophy. He presents his turn to that history, however, as motivated not by antiquarian curiosity about the past but by what he diagnosed as the present crisis of the West and of modernity.

Only the most apparent sign of the crisis of the West, according to Strauss, was the practical danger to its survival coming from the East—

from a Communism that, as both a form of modern Western political theory and a form of Eastern despotism, constitutes an unprecedented form of the tyranny of old.[1] The true crisis was, rather, that the West, under the influence of its highest intellectual authorities, no longer believed in itself, in its purpose, in its superiority. For Strauss understood the modern West to be constituted by a specific purpose or project: the construction of a universal society of free and equal nations of free and equal men and women enjoying universal affluence, and therefore universal justice and happiness, through science understood as the conquest of nature in the service of human power. This purpose, so familiar to us living in the century of Wilson's Fourteen Points and Roosevelt's Four Freedoms, came to characterize the West only in modernity. In contrast, premodern thinkers accepted both the plurality and the particularity of political societies and politically significant natural and conventional inequalities among human beings. They emphasized the social pursuit of virtue or salvation and the avoidance of luxury and the corruption it engenders. And they understood science as the contemplation (and technology as the imitation) of nature. The loss of belief in the new purpose was therefore specifically a crisis of modernity. And since the purpose that has come to animate the West was originated by modern political philosophy, Strauss came to the apparently strange conclusion that the general crisis of the West was fundamentally the crisis of the particular discipline of political philosophy.[2]

Strauss viewed the West's loss of certainty about its purpose not as a psychological want of willpower or as a moral lack of courage, but rather as the result of theoretical challenges. The challenges rested partly on specific doubts about the particular premises of the modern project, such as the worth of universalism, the connections between affluence and justice and happiness, and the understanding of science as the conquest of nature in the service of human power. These doubts derived in part from twentieth-century experience: of continued political divisions as a bulwark against universal tyranny; of the persistence of evil and misery in the midst of affluence; and of the dangers to both man and nature from unfettered science.[3] But, even more fundamentally, doubt about the superiority of the purpose of the West rested on late modern doctrines that denied the possibility of rational knowledge of the universal validity of any purpose or principle. Social science restricted its competence to facts as distinguished from moral and fundamental choices and principles, which it understood as "values" or irrational preferences. The doctrine Strauss called "historicism" asserted that all human thought and action are essentially dependent on historical situations, the sequence of which proves to have no rational goal or meaning. Relativism claimed that all apparent absolutes are only ideals relative to particular frames of reference. All these doctrines therefore rejected political philosophy in its original form.[4] This situation constituted a true crisis for modern political philosophy because these doctrines were the ultimate implications of the understandings of nature and history that were the presuppositions of modern political philosophy itself.

This theoretical crisis had consequences, in Strauss's view, for the practical crisis insofar as it made the wholehearted defense of the West impossible except as a matter of fanatical obscurantism.[5] The practical consequences included not only vulnerability to external danger but, more important, an internal tendency for liberal democracy, deprived of belief in the rationality of its purpose and standards, to degenerate into permissiveness or conformism and philistinism.[6] The practical problem for Strauss, therefore, was not liberal democracy itself, of which he considered himself a friend, but the need to defend it against both external and internal dangers. To show the practical need for a solution, however, is not to prove a solution to be true: Strauss never lost sight of the distinction between utility and truth. The practical need could dictate only an inquiry without a foreordained result, one conducted "without squinting at our present predicament."[7]

The crisis of the West, of modernity, and of liberal democracy was, for Strauss, most clearly exemplified by the Jewish problem, which he regarded as "the most manifest symbol of the human problem insofar as it is a social or political problem."[8] The Jewish problem reveals, in the first place, the limitations of liberalism: liberal society, constituted by universal morality rather than by religion (which it regards as private), seems to offer Jews equal membership; but, precisely because it recognizes a private sphere, it also recognizes, and can offer no guarantee against, private anti-Jewish feelings and consequent social inequality. More important, by holding up assimilation as *the* model, liberal society deprives Jews of the self-respect deriving from loyalty to their own heroic tradition, while it gives in return too often only shallow self-satisfaction and membership in a nonexistent universal human society. Yet, for all its inadequacies, this nonsolution is manifestly superior to the "solutions" resulting from the destruction of the liberal state by the anti-Jewish states of National Socialism and Communism. As for political Zionism (of which Strauss as a young man was an ardent adherent),[9] that attempted solution offers Jews assimilation not as individuals but as a people, with their own liberal secular state like those of other peoples. The otherwise empty form of that state, however, requires Jewish culture as its content. And Jewish culture in any serious sense means first and foremost Jewish faith, which, as faith or trust in God rather than in men, "must regard as blasphemous the notion of a human solution to the Jewish problem." [10]

In the second place, the Jewish problem therefore manifests a tension that transcends modernity and its crisis, the tension between human reason and divine revelation—the rival claims to human dedication represented by Athens and Jerusalem—a tension Strauss considered "the core, the nerve of Western intellectual history, Western spiritual history" and "the secret of the vitality of Western civilization." [11] Strauss denied that modern philosophy had put an end to this conflict by refuting revelation; indeed, its unsuccessful efforts to do so through transforming philosophy into systematic certainty had only blurred or destroyed that awareness of ignorance that is the philosopher's primary evidence of the need for philosophy. [12]

Strauss's response to the crisis of modernity was a study of both modern and ancient political philosophy. Since the crisis resulted from the most recent expressions of what was implied in the deepest premises of modern political philosophy, it was impossible to go forward directly and resolve it on the basis of those most recent doctrines. It was necessary instead to go back, at least provisionally, and try to recover those premises in their earlier and original forms to see whether the crisis could be overcome on their basis. To understand and question those original modern premises, it was necessary in turn to try to counterpose them to classical political philosophy, since they originally emerged partly on the basis of and partly in opposition to that now all-but-forgotten alternative. Not only the modern belief in progress but the fact-value disjunction, relativism, and historicism—the very doctrines that constituted the crisis—had prevented most modern scholars from considering the possibility that past doctrines (which were not only past but committed to the rationality of what these recent doctrines stigmatized as "absolute values") might be true. Thus they lacked the openness that is necessary for understanding. Strauss therefore doubted that adequate understandings were available of either earlier modern or ancient political philosophy; he had to engage in and encourage historical investigations that did not presume the truth of current thought or the falsehood of past thought. [13]

Strauss's inquiry into ancient and modern political teachings had to be historically as well as philosophically serious: historically serious by first inquiring into the original understandings of their authors; philosophically serious by then inquiring into their truth. This double character of Strauss's inquiry was paradoxical. Whereas historicism, in opposition to which Strauss was hoping to show again the possibility of political philosophy, takes historical inquiry into past (nonhistoricist) thought seriously but is closed to the possibility of the truth of such thought, the nonhistoricist philosophy Strauss hoped to recover did not take historical inquiries seriously. Classical political philosophy was an inquiry into the nature of political phenomena and the best or the right political order, not into the particular phenomena—statesmen and states with proper names—that concern political history, let alone into the history of political philosophy. Plato, for example, Strauss admits, had such "unconcern with, or even contempt for, the merely historical truth" that he considered the philosophic question of the best political order "infinitely more important than the historical question of what this or that individual thought of the best political order." [14]

Strauss therefore had to show how his resort to historical inquiry was necessary only because he lived in exceptionally unfavorable circumstances, and not because he was superior to the earlier thinkers, whose resort to nonhistorical inquiry was in turn a sign of their more favorable circumstances. [15] Only in this way could he hope to be open to the possible truth of the thought of the past—an openness needed, in the first place, for understanding it, and then for learning something from it that might address the present crisis.

Strauss therefore explained that while political philosophy naturally begins with the direct analysis and clarification of the opinions that surround it, the analysis and clarification of modern opinions first requires *historical* understanding of them as modifications or transformations of earlier opinions. For he understood modern opinions to be "modifications" or "transformations" not just accidentally, as opinions that happened to succeed others, but essentially—so that they can only be understood as modifications or transformations. [16] These opinions permeate the intellectual atmosphere in such a way that people are often unaware of even holding them, let alone of their historical character. This peculiar character of modern ideas is due in part to their traditional or inherited character and in part to the specifically modern belief in progress, the belief that the continually new results of science or philosophy rest on premises that have long been settled and need no longer be the subject of examination. [17] In this way, modern opinions differ from those which were the subject of the analyses of classical political philosophy, which can be understood without a further regress of historical inquiry and can be regarded at least in that respect as the "natural" opinions or starting points of philosophy. [18]

In particular, Strauss argued that his historical studies were peculiarly necessary in an age dominated by historicism. He gave several reasons for this. First, historicism, which ultimately produced the crisis of the West, can be understood and questioned best through confrontation with the nonhistoricist philosophy of the past, accessible through non-historicist historical studies.[19] Second, historicism claims to rest on "the experience of history," which is supposed to show the failure of nonhistorical political philosophy to answer definitively its own nonhistorical questions and the dependence of its transient answers on their historical situations. To question this "experience" and examine whether it can be otherwise interpreted also requires nonhistoricist historical studies.[20] Third, consistency demands that historicism be applied to itself, that the supposedly final and universal insight into the essential dependence of all human thought on transient historical situations be itself understood as essentially dependent on a transient historical situation. This self-contradictory application of historicism to itself leads ultimately to a nonhistoricist understanding—such as the one that Strauss himself sketched in *Natural Right and History*—of the genesis of historicism as perhaps only "an artificial and makeshift solution to a problem that could arise only on the basis of very questionable premises."[21] Finally, the experience of genuine historical understanding itself liberates one from the shackles of historicism; this is the "self-destruction of historicism."[22]

More generally, Strauss pointed out, historical studies are of philosophic importance only in ages of intellectual decline, when "there are good reasons for believing that we can learn something of utmost importance from the thought of the past which we cannot learn from our contemporaries."[23] Strauss's study of the history of political philosophy therefore presupposed a radical dissatisfaction with contemporary thought and a resulting interest in that earlier thought which did not start from the premises responsible for the present crisis.

THE CONDUCT OF THE HISTORY OF POLITICAL PHILOSOPHY

The distinctive reasons for Strauss's turn to the history of political philosophy dictated the distinctive characteristics of his way of studying it.

Strauss's understanding of the crisis of the West prompted him to struggle to achieve that genuine historical understanding of the thought of the past which historicism originally aimed at but was constitutionally incapable of. To try to understand past thinkers as they understood themselves required that one seek to suspend one's own questions to see their questions; that one attempt to rely as much as possible on what they say directly or indirectly, and as little as possible on extraneous information; and that one strive to use their own terms and premises and avoid using alien modern terminology and premises. For Strauss, this historical effort to understand the meaning of past thought necessarily involves the philosophic effort to take seriously the claim to truth of that thought. One must think the thought: one must question an argument's logical connections and relations to the world in order to follow it. [24]

This approach contrasts sharply not only with the history of political philosophy as conducted on the basis of the belief in progress (the faith in the superiority of the thought of the present to that of the past), but also with that conducted on the basis of relativism or historicism. To appreciate that contrast, it would be useful for students to compare this book with the most influential such textbook at the time Strauss-Cropsey first appeared—George H. Sabine's *A History of Political Theory* (1937). The original preface to Strauss-Cropsey claims to take past political philosophy seriously as a phenomenon *from* which to learn about questions still alive; the original preface to Sabine asserts that political theories can hardly be said to be true insofar as they include valuations (which distort even their factual judgments), and that they cannot step out of the relationships in which they stand to the problems, valuations, habits, and even prejudices of their times. In sharp contrast to Strauss-Cropsey, Sabine's preface avows a preference for the fact-value disjunction and an intention to write the history of Western political theory "from the point of view of this sort of social relativism." [25]

Strauss took seriously the claim to truth of past political philosophers: that means he regarded it as most urgent to "accept it as true or reject it as untrue or make a distinction or recognize my inability to decide and therefore the necessity to think or learn more than I know at present." Sophisticated scholarly attempts to treat such thinkers as reflections of their times, or to derive their thought from psychological or economic causes, were therefore distractions or distortions for him, at best appropriate only after those claims to truth had been found to be mistaken. Indeed, he preferred to understand their times, and even psychological questions and economic developments, in light of their thought. In this he exemplified his general view that "it is safer to try to understand the low in the light of the high than the high in the light of the low. In doing the latter one necessarily distorts the high, whereas in doing the former one does not deprive the low of the freedom to reveal itself fully as what it is." [26]

As in the preface to the first edition of this work, Strauss emphatically directed students to the original texts; but his emphasis on texts and thought did not amount to the absurd notion that they are self-sufficient objects of inquiry, which can be understood in isolation. He readily admitted that to understand a text of political philosophy we may need information not supplied by the author, information not easily available to every reasonable reader regardless of time and place. But he insisted that such external evidence be integrated into a framework supplied by the author. We may have to learn a terminology familiar to the author's contemporaries but no longer to us. We have to learn to see his contemporaries, his predecessors, and "the philosophic tradition" as *he* saw them; indeed, *"the* tradition and *the* continuity disappears once one begins to interpret." We have to read even a great text in its context, but we have to understand what its author understood that context to be, not insert it into some context constructed by our scholarship.[27] Strauss was especially concerned with establishing whom a book was intended to argue against and whom it was intended to persuade, but in looking at such external facts he tried to take his cues from the book itself. Strauss indeed stressed the importance of the historical situation not because the thought of a political philosopher of the past must unwittingly reflect it but because he may have deliberately adapted the expression of his thought to it.[28] Above all, Strauss insisted that to understand as well as to judge a book of political philosophy one has to look not only at the book itself but at the phenomena the book directs us to, just as political philosophy itself requires knowledge of politics.[29]

From Strauss's concern with the historical context of past political philosophy flows probably the most controversial aspect of his approach to the history of political philosophy: his suggestion that some past philosophers engaged in "exoteric writing." As indicated just above, Strauss's doubt of historicism led him to wonder whether the apparent relation between the thought of past political philosophers and their historical situations did not reveal deliberate adaptation rather than unconscious reflection. This led him to try to distinguish those parts of their political teachings which were merely desirable or necessary under their particular circumstances (their "exoteric" teachings) from what they considered to be the political truth always and everywhere (their "esoteric" teachings). It led Strauss to emphasize in particular the dialogue form in which Plato wrote, which "says different things to different people," the need to understand its arguments in the light of the dramatic setting and action, and the irony of Socrates, who is shown conversing with particular individuals, none of them his equal in wisdom.[30]

Strauss's discovery of exoteric writing was not an invention but a recovery of a previously well-known phenomenon. His concern with the Jewish problem had led him to Spinoza (the philosophic originator of both assimilationist liberal democracy and political Zionism), and thus to Maimonides, whom Spinoza seemed to take as the representative of theology, then to Farabi, whom Maimonides regarded as the greatest philosophic authority of his period, and finally to Plato and Aristotle seen in a fresh light as the teachers of Farabi and Maimonides. (Strauss differed from many other scholars in being willing to believe that medieval thinkers who took ancient writers seriously as philosophic teachers were more likely to understand their writings than were modern scholars, who regarded them only as objects of historical curiosity and who rejected their views of the relation between philosophy and society.) Farabi explained that "the wise Plato did not feel free to reveal and uncover the sciences for all men. Therefore he followed the practice of using symbols, riddles, obscurity, and difficulty, so that science would not fall into the hands of those who do not deserve it and be deformed, or into the hands of one who does not know its worth or who uses it improperly."[31] Maimonides, in the introduction to *The Guide of the Perplexed*, explained that his book contains deliberately concealed contradictions because "in speaking about very obscure matters it is necessary to conceal some parts and to disclose others. . . . This necessity requires that the discussion proceed on the basis of a certain premise, whereas in another place necessity requires that the discussion proceed on the basis of another premise contradicting the first one. . . . The author accordingly uses some device to conceal it by all means."[32] These medieval writers made explicit the kinds of writing likely to characterize all thinkers who do not believe that the truth can always be safely told to everyone.[33]

Why did some philosophers in previous ages practice such strange modes of communication? According to Strauss, "the most obvious and the crudest reason" was persecution, the danger to philosophy from society, which required philosophers to protect themselves. This danger and response are more readily appreciated in contemporary tyrannies than in contemporary liberal societies.[34] But a less obvious reason was the danger to society from philosophy. Philosophy, as the intransigent attempt to question and replace opinion with knowledge, inherently endangers society, which requires its members to act on the basis of unquestioned but necessarily questionable opinions. Philosophers must therefore practice political responsibility and respect the opinions indispensable for practical and political purposes. This danger, and the response to it, from philosophy are even harder to appreciate for societies that understand themselves to be founded on universal scientific truth, but ought to be more intelligible to social sciences that understand societies to be constituted by myths or arbitrary values.[35] Another reason for exoteric writing is the requirements of education, which must begin with the initial views of students and lead them toward the truth only "step by step" and without repelling them.[36]

Strauss knew that one cannot prove with absolute certainty either the presence or the absence of exoteric writing in a particular text, and that the dogmatic assumption of either would produce arbitrary interpretations. One must make the best judgment one can on the basis of the evidence in each case. Doubtful that interpretation could be reduced to a method and aware that his suggestion was liable to abuse, Strauss referred to that suggestion as a "method" only somewhat playfully and pointed out that the alternative methods of modern scholarship for dealing with contradictions in a text (such as attributing them to the author's development, to textual difficulties, or to unconscious psychology, let alone to simple confusion or the inherent contradictions of textuality) are even less able to achieve absolute certainty or universal agreement or to exclude perverse ingenuity. [37]

Strauss regarded his approach to the history of political philosophy as a crucial component of liberal education. He understood liberal education as an effort to philosophize primarily through listening to and trying to judge the conversation between the greatest minds, which could be done by studying the great books, thereby reminding oneself of human excellence and greatness. That reminder necessarily contributes to the well-being of the political community and fosters civic responsibility. It is especially needed and appropriate in liberal democracy, which "by giving freedom to all . . . also gives freedom to those who care for human excellence." [38]

The history of political philosophy was for Strauss an education in awareness of the fundamental and permanent problems. All that is necessary for such history to be possible is the presupposition or hypothesis, denied by historicism, of the persistence through historical change of the same fundamental problems, not any particular solution to them. [39] Strauss understood that history, as he conducted it, to help confirm the persistence of fundamental problems and even of alternative solutions. [40] Awareness of the persistence of those problems refutes historicism; indeed "in grasping these problems as problems, the human mind liberates itself from its historical limitations." [41] For Strauss, genuine awareness of the fundamental problems legitimates and even constitutes philosophy itself. [42]

MODERN POLITICAL PHILOSOPHY

Strauss emphasized the role of Machiavelli as originator of modern political philosophy. Despite the frequency of radical change and the immense variety within modernity, Strauss found a basic unity within it originated by Machiavelli and continued by his successors. That unity appears first negatively: the moderns reject classical political philosophy as unrealistic, as culminating in utopias whose actualization is admittedly highly improbable and dependent on uncontrollable chance. [43] In contrast, Machiavelli and modern political philosophy seek to make probable or even guarantee the actualization of the right order, to conquer chance and overcome the obstacles posed by nature and especially human nature. But in order to make the goal more likely of actualization they must also lower it. Whereas classical political philosophy subordinated politics to moral and, above all, intellectual virtue (as the end of man or perfection of the human soul supplied by nature), Machiavelli subordinates virtue to politics (as merely politically useful virtue), finds in the desire for glory an amoral substitute for morality, and initiates the view of philosophy as in the service of the goals of all mankind.[44]

Strauss viewed this modern "realism" not as a true discovery or enlargement of the horizon but in fact as a narrowing of the horizon. It forgets that which essentially transcends every possible human reality: eternity and the whole, or the natural inclinations of the human soul toward them.[45] Strauss accounted for this amazing narrowing as a humane, generous, and public-spirited reaction against the inhumanity (exemplified by the Inquisition) produced by the infinitely high aims of the classical tradition as transfigured by Christianity.[46] Despite or because of that reaction, he understood Machiavelli to have taken Christianity as his most important model for the transformation of the mode and function of philosophy into propaganda or enlightenment that seeks to control the general fate of human thought.[47]

The underlying unity Strauss discerned in modernity—the effort to make probable, or guarantee the actualization of, the right order—was also responsible in his view for the many transformations modernity has undergone. Just as the new political philosophy of Machiavelli sought to guarantee the actualization of the right order through rejection of a natural end of man, so the new natural science of Bacon and Descartes sought to guarantee the actualization of wisdom through foolproof method that did not depend on the natural intelligiblity of the universe.[48] Similarly, Hobbes sought to guarantee the actualization of the right order on the basis of scientific knowledge and popular enlightenment, by deducing a new version of natural law from fear of violent death as the strongest passion and from the beginnings rather than from reason and the end (*telos*) of man as did the older version. Hobbes's resulting focus on the pursuit of power, to the exclusion even of the nobility of the love of glory recognized by Machiavelli, amounted to a further contraction of the horizon.[49] Locke, in Strauss's view, took this shift of emphasis—from duties and man's end to rights and man as individual—even further, through the emancipation of productive acquisitiveness as the remedy for the niggardliness of nature.[50] Rousseau, despite or rather because of his efforts to return to nature and to restore the dignity of virtue, went further and presented the general will as the guarantee of justice that makes appeal to natural law altogether superfluous.[51] The philosophies of history of Kant, Hegel, and Marx explicitly attempted to show that the actualization of the right order is a necessary byproduct of the dialectical conflict of blind selfish passions in the historical process.[52] Finally, even Nietzsche resembled Marx in claiming that the final insight opened the way for the actualization of the final ideal characterized by the end of the rule of chance, though he asserted that its coming was a matter of choice rather than of necessity.[53]

Strauss seemed to regard these successive transformations as in a way necessitated by the original impossible effort to guarantee actualization of the right order. He seemed to regard modernity as a kind of necessary progress in consistency, or in ever-fuller understanding of the implications of the original modern principle—as well as a consequent corrosion or destruction of the premodern heritage of Western civilization.[54]

Strauss's account of the history of modern political philosophy is, however, more complicated than a simple, unidirectional progress or decline away from the classical understanding. At least at two crucial moments, there were attempts to return to premodern thought. They led, however, "consciously or unconsciously, to a much more radical form of modernity."[55] The crisis of modern natural right was initiated by Rousseau and led to the effort to derive standards from history rather than from nature; that crisis paved the way for the second or present crisis of modernity, which was initiated by Nietzsche and discredited all attempts to derive permanent standards from history. Both crises were marked by passionate and forceful critiques of previous modern thought, critiques with which Strauss seems to have generally agreed. We cannot return to the earlier forms of modern thought, according to Strauss, because "the critique of modern rationalism or of the modern belief in reason by Nietzsche cannot be dismissed or forgotten"; he even adds that this is "the deepest reason" for the present crisis.[56] Similarly, Strauss regards the most radical historicism, the thought of Heidegger, to be the culmination and "highest self-consciousness" of modern thought.[57]

Certain elements of Strauss's account of the history of modern political philosophy (such as the sense of a kind of necessary progression, the attribution of profound practical effects to profound theoretical arguments, the way in which attempted returns turn into advances, and the culmination at the end) seem to elaborate, sketch, or suggest what in the case of almost any other man would be called his philosophy of history.[58] Not only, however, is Strauss's account remote from showing the necessity of the actualization of the right order, but the sort of necessity it evokes applies only to modernity and not to human history as such, and only so long as the premises of modernity remain unquestioned.

Strauss's account of the history of political philosophy does, however, both begin and end with what might be called privileged points. Classical political philosophy saw politics "with a freshness and directness which have never been equalled" because it "belongs to the fertile moment when all political traditions were shaken, and there was not yet in existence a tradition of political philosophy." Similarly the genuine understanding of past political philosophy both is necessary in our time and "may be said to have been rendered possible by the shaking of all traditions; the crisis of our time may have the accidental advantage of enabling us to understand in an untraditional or fresh manner what was hitherto understood only in a traditional or derivative manner." [59] Heidegger's radical historicism, according to Strauss, both compels us to reconsider the most elementary premises of philosophy and, by uprooting the tradition, opens the possibility of a genuine recovery of classical philosophy. [60] Strauss's study of modernity enabled him to attempt such a recovery of classical political philosophy: to see classical political philosophy as it saw itself and no longer through the lenses of modern political philosophy.

ANCIENT AND MEDIEVAL POLITICAL PHILOSOPHY

The more Strauss progressed in unlocking the original self-understanding of the premodern philosophers, the more he "inclined" to the judgment that the human or political wisdom of the ancient thinkers, and especially of the Socratics, was decisively superior to any of the various modern alternatives. This is not to say that Strauss simply threw in his lot with the "ancients"—or their medieval disciples. One of the preeminent virtues Strauss found in the ancient and medieval rationalism inspired by Socrates was its openness and tenacity in engaging major alternative outlooks—including not only antagonistic ancient philosophic positions but, above all, the claims to divine inspiration advanced in such different ways by the Greek poets and the biblical prophets. Besides, Strauss never ceased being deeply and fruitfully challenged by his recurrent studies of each of the major modern positions. This very rethinking, however, repeatedly confirmed his basic judgment.

What are the chief elements in the superior outlook Strauss resurrected from the old books? Like Cicero, Strauss identified himself as a Platonic or Socratic "skeptic." *Skepsis* is the Socratic word for inquiry (see, *e.g.*, Plato *Gorgias* 487[e] and *Laws* 636[d]; Xenophon *Oeconomicus* vi 13). Socratic skepticism is a way of life devoted to inquiry into the most comprehensive questions regarding the human situation. Such lifelong inquiry would not be necessary or sensible if the truth about the human situation were already adequately known. Strauss understood Platonic or Socratic political philosophy to emerge out of a profound awareness of ignorance, especially as regards metaphysics and cosmology, but also as regards the human good. He claimed to have demonstrated, from the evidence of the classical texts, that Nietzsche and Heidegger were wrong in their assertions about the dogmatism of rationalism and its account of existence or being. While it is true that rationalism, in its original form, discovers in human existence an unchanging nature from which can be deduced immutable principles of right, it is not true that original rationalism grounds this discovery on a dogmatic assumption that "to be" means "to be always," or "to be intelligible," let alone "to be an object" or "to be predictable." "Socrates was so far from being committed to a specific cosmology that his knowledge was knowledge of ignorance. Knowledge of ignorance is not ignorance. It is knowledge of the elusive character of the truth, of the whole. Socrates, then, viewed man in the light of the mysterious character of the whole." [61]

Yet Socratic rationalism "is characterized by the gentle, if firm, refusal to succumb" to the "charm of humble awe," which this awareness of mystery might be thought to induce. To know that we are situated in an elusive or mysterious whole is to know something of great importance about the human situation, and even about the whole. Knowledge of ignorance in this sense can be, and for Socrates surely was, the solid foundation for a fertile exploration of the enduring elements in the human condition. The exploration lays bare the timeless questions or problems that never cease to define and set in motion human life. Socrates, as Strauss understands him, held "that we are more familiar with the situation of man as man than with the ultimate causes of that situation. We may also say that he viewed man in the light of the unchangeable ideas, i.e., of the fundamental and permanent problems." [62] Preeminent among the unchangeable ideas or problems is the problem of the nature of justice (the common good)—a question that is deepened and made more puzzling by the conflicting answers offered by the laws, human and divine, of the various political regimes. The question of justice takes precedence because justice or law comes to sight as the highest standard for judging what ought to be done, what is the right way of life, for individuals, households, and political societies. [63]

Strauss sharply distinguished what he called the "erotic" (needy, longing) or "zetetic" (searching, questing) skepticism of the Socratics from the "dogmatic" or more absolute skepticism introduced by Descartes and underlying modern science and epistemology. The Socratic awareness of ignorance does not imply that the "real world" or the "things in themselves" are unknowable, and that we can therefore know only an "apparent" world. Socratic skepticism does not involve a radical doubt (as opposed to a questioning) of common sense; it does not suppose that the articulation of the world given in our sense perception and rational discourse is an unconscious construction of our minds, and that therefore true "knowledge" (science) is possible only on the basis of conscious or consciously "creative" mental constructions. What *is* meant by Socratic skepticism is this: we possess an insight, but an incomplete insight, into the "natures," *i.e.*, the kinds or class characteristics or "ideas" of things, as perceived by the senses and expressed in ordinary speech; and we grasp, but only dimly grasp, the whole that is articulated by these natures as parts. Thus, while we can make some progress in our knowledge of nature as a whole, our knowledge in this comprehensive sense remains highly controversial. Above all, it seems unlikely that metaphysical or cosmological or psychological speculation by itself can definitively decide the most important and urgent question: whether our lives can and should be guided by human reason alone, or whether the God or gods revealed by the Scripture or the poets exist—and therefore demand from us that we follow their laws and piously seek illumination from them.[64]

Still, as Plato shows most vividly by his account of Socrates' encounter with the Delphic Oracle, and as Maimonides indicates by the very title of his chief work, *The Guide of the Perplexed,* our perplexity cannot be resolved by our simply bowing to the religious authorities. For the pronouncements and even the commandments of those authorities—be they conveyed in oracles, or scriptures, or poetic verse—are somewhat enigmatic; they require human interpretation; and the official interpreters disagree. Worst of all, there is a variety of mutually exclusive or at least antagonistic gods or purported gods and divine legal codes. The conflicts among the different divine authorities are not merely "theological" controversies; they are at the same time conflicts among competing moral-political systems or regimes, with their clashing conceptions of justice and the right way of life. The various gods or purported gods stand as the guarantors and upholders of various interpretations of the just or right way. The "theological" question (whether and which divinities exist) is therefore, as Spinoza insisted, more properly termed the "theologico-political" question; the theological question is a part of, or at any rate intertwined with, the question of justice.[65]

It had been the shameful evidence of the seemingly irreconcilable moral disagreements among the various political regimes and accompanying divine commandments that had started Socrates' intellectual predecessors on the line of thought that led them to the conclusion that all civic or popular claims about gods, justice, and nobility are imaginary or invented and merely "conventional" opinions. From the fragmentary evidence available, Strauss concluded that most of the philosophers and sophists aside from Socrates (the outstanding exception is Thucydides) had tended to brush past the apparently contradictory justifying speeches of citizens and statesmen in order to study instead their actions, especially the actions by which political orders are established. In this light, they argued, every political "community" is analyzable into those (the majority or a minority) who exploit by ruling and those who are exploited by being ruled. This universal condition of struggle and domination is a necessary consequence of the nature of the goods or pleasures men pursue through political society. It is of the essence of these goods to be either scarce (like material prosperity) or resistant to being shared (like the civic advancement of loved ones), or both (like glory). If one looks from this analysis of the deeds, and of the goals revealed in the deeds, back to the justifying speeches or beliefs— regarding the existence of a "common good" and the nobility of (and divine sanctions for) civic brotherhood and sacrifice or service to the community, these latter opinions appear to be simply the illusions by which men wittingly or unwittingly dupe the exploited and salve their own half-duped sense of shame.[66]

From all this, the sophists and their facile students may conclude that the best life, i.e., the most pleasant life, is found in manly dedication to clear-sighted, sly, and ruthless political competition. But the more thoroughgoing pre-Socratic thinkers, the genuine philosophers, point out that so long as one remains a contestant in the political arena, one stays trapped in endlessly anxious, radical dependence on large numbers of supporters and their deluded opinions expressed in honor and dishonor. The only self-sufficient, solid, painless, and consuming or inexhaustible pleasure is the pleasure of thinking and knowing. The best life by nature, as opposed to convention or imagination, is therefore the life of the philosopher, who lives with a few like-minded friends as a more or less harmless parasite on the fringes of society.[67]

Strauss devoted a large portion of his writings to an exploration of this "pre-Socratic" or "Epicurean" tradition because he was convinced that Socrates' *political* philosophizing can be understood only if it is seen as the product of a skeptical rebellion against *both* the traditional authorities *and* this original, antipolitical, philosophic critique of those authorities. Socrates characterizes his new approach as a "turn to the speeches," or as the practice of "dialectics," the art of friendly disputation. His way, as presented by Xenophon and Plato, is to attend carefully to the justifying arguments given by engaged, active citizens of different sorts—and also by their critics, the sophists and their followers. Socrates tests those arguments by bringing them into debate with one another, by cross-examining them, by unraveling their full and hidden implications. (Prudence, not to speak of other considerations, dictates that he usually conduct this inquiry not with the citizens themselves but with the most intelligent among their more open-minded sons.) His conversations reveal that the actions of men must be understood in light of the meaning given them by opinions and speeches. In that light, the harsh deeds the pre-Socratic sophists or philosophers focus on become less conclusive. Besides, even if one deemphasizes what men say, even if one accepts, provisionally, the focus of the pre-Socratics, one finds that what human beings actually do, the way they actually live together, is not as the pre-Socratics claim. [68]

In the first place, political life taken as a whole bespeaks a natural human sociability, a need to share life with others, a mutual affection and sympathy and concern that points toward a natural common good. This evidence cannot be adequately explained on the basis of selfish calculation; moreover, since human sociality expresses itself above all in potentially rational speech, it is also much richer than any mere hive or herd instinct. Of course, for this same reason human sociability remains profoundly ambiguous: Socrates is far from underestimating the ubiquity of the peculiarly human, peculiarly unlimited, competition for superiority and prestige. But shining through even this gloom, in the speeches with which men express their reasons for their actions, he discerns a higher and more important if more fragile dimension to politics. [69]

Even in the struggles with economic and military necessity that take up so much of the political agenda, men exhibit an awareness of sacred limitations on what they may do to others and for themselves in order to overcome danger and scarcity. Those limits are frequently breached; but the very fact that shame, and attempts at disguise, attend such violations is a sign of a natural inhibition in human beings. What is more, men admire not only success at enlarging mundane interests but also certain qualities of heart and mind that are deployed in achieving— but that are also seen as transcending—these beneficial results. In seeking to develop or promote these qualities as ends and not merely as means, men move beyond the constituents of happiness in the primary sense. They aspire to a leisure that would give opportunity for noble deeds of peace and for beautiful or graceful preoccupations. They revere not only war heroes and gift givers but also men—like the poets—who seem capable of giving content to such aspiration. [70]

Nor is it true that the diverse political regimes, and their concrete specifications of the aforementioned limits, traits of character, and noble leisure, are as irreconcilably contradictory as the pre-Socratic critics say. When the opposed authoritative opinions are brought into dialectical confrontation, some appear confessedly narrower, shallower, less consistent than others; some admittedly point beyond themselves or can be seen to supplement one another. As a result, one can begin to discern a rank ordering of the virtues and of the versions of each virtue, ascending from courage or the virtues of war through moderation and generosity, and thence to tasteful patronage of the arts, pride, graceful wit, truth-telling, and friendship. In its civic expression, this emergent ordering of the virtues gives a clearer and richer directedness to public education and hence to justice or the common good—understood now as the concern for the health of the souls, in addition to the well-being of the bodies, of the citizenry. The Socratic dialectic discovers that what is "right by nature," or in all times and places, comes to sight not as a code of universal rules or laws (such as what later was identified as "natural law," or "the categorical imperative") but rather as a hierarchy of goals consisting in qualities of character and in joys or satisfactions found in the exercise of those qualities.[71]

The full, sympathetic investigation of those qualities and joys lays bare the *natural* basis and power, in the human heart, of justice and nobility—and hence allows us to see with unprecedented clarity the aspects of that natural basis and power that are truly or legitimately (from every point of view) sources of wonder and puzzlement. Virtue or morality shines forth in its nobility when it involves self-sacrifice; it is this tragic dimension of virtue that evokes and establishes, more unambiguously than anything else in human experience, the belief in divine support or recognition; and yet this very evocation of a divinity that will somehow compensate for heroism testifies to the fact that virtue is also seen—in the final analysis, with greater certainty and insistence—as something that should be good for the possessor, as holding the key to personal happiness and fulfillment: how do these two contradictory aspects of virtue cohere?[72] What exactly are the grounds for human responsibility, guilt, punishment, praise and blame, given that virtue can be shown to be or require a kind of knowledge?[73] These and other puzzles, when brought home to intelligent men endowed with strength of soul, reveal that the civic virtues of action are by themselves incomplete. Precisely when taken seriously and as a whole, the moral or pious life in its intellectual deficiencies points beyond itself, to a more awakened and intransigently thoughtful life—to the philosophic life, as lived by Socrates. In other words, Socratic political philosophy culminates in a vindication of the philosophic life. Now, however, the philosophic life is conceived no longer as the socially marginal existence of thinkers scornful of politics but, rather, as the life devoted to the politically responsible examination of civic opinions as well as philosophic opinions; Socrates' *political* philosophizing deepens the city by compelling civic life to become more self-conscious about its own grandeur—but also about its own insufficiency, or qualified directedness toward philosophy.[74]

If philosophy is to be held up in this way as the surprising summit of human existence, it is incumbent upon the political philosopher to clarify much more concretely than ever before the precise nature of the genuine, as opposed to sham, philosophic way of life. This provides still another reason why the investigation of, and attack on, sophistry—in its highest and most sinuous as well as more vulgar forms—is so pervasive and dramatic a theme of the Platonic dialogues. Strauss translates this key Platonic theme into contemporary terms by stressing the enormous gulf between the genuine philosopher and the modern "intellectual"—who ranks considerably below the ancient sophist. The intellectual or sophist, as contrasted with the philosopher, "is concerned with wisdom, not for its own sake, . . . but for the sake of the honor or the prestige that attends wisdom." Strauss drew from this the discomfiting conclusion that while there are, to be sure, many who have some experience or taste of the love of truth, yet genuine philosophers, men consumed by this love, are so "extremely rare" that "it is a piece of good luck if there is a single one alive in one's time."[75]

The vindication, which is at the same time the defining with precision, of the philosophic way of life is of course only the peak of the Socratic tradition's political philosophizing. That vindication grows out of, and in turn inspires, a comprehensive reflection on the good for society as a whole. Partly, no doubt, because they pay such heed to speech (*logos,* reasoning) about justice, but also on the basis of careful observations of political life, the classics argue that the key social phenomenon is the dispute, in the political arena, over who will have the say in setting the society's highest goals—in determining the community's way of life and what that life reveres. This does not mean that the Socratics ever suppose that fundamental political disputes are carried on only in words: precisely because he took so seriously what was at stake in civic argument, Socrates taught an appreciation of the role played by passion, violence, and the threat of violence. To the extent that the fundamental dispute is settled in each society, a "regime" (*politeia*) results: "regime" means above all what type of human being rules, and is looked up to as exemplifying, and as having the right to enforce through coercion as well as authoritative exhortation, a distinctive way of life. Politics, in this supreme sense, determines the character of society more than any other factor, and hence political science is the architectonic social science. Even a "liberal" society, which allows the private sphere and the market to eclipse, in some measure, the political sphere, does so only by virtue of a specific political constitution erected by a founding political decision. The central human question then is, what is the best regime for any given society? And the answer to this question depends on some kind of answer to the more general question, what is the best regime simply—what is the standard? [76]

If the political philosopher lives the best life, in large part because he best comprehends the problematic human situation as a whole—if the philosopher, because of his single-minded concern for the pursuit of knowledge, is the most immune to temptations of money, glory, and dominion—it would seem to follow that the best regime is that in which the political philosopher rules, and assigns to each person what is best or what is due. But this "best regime" is extremely paradoxical. As Strauss shows in his chapter on Plato in this book, the *Republic* teaches both why the rule of philosophers is so urgently needed and why—once it is really thought through—it is manifestly impossible or absurd. The life of the political philosopher is a life of relentless questioning, leisured research, and cosmopolitan detachment from one's own for the sake of the universal truth. The life of the statesman demands immediate answers, noble dedication to action that produces results, and loving attachment to and an intimate knowledge of one's own people. Two distinct kinds of men and two different ways of life: each can learn or profit from the other, but they remain divided by a chasm and at some tension with one another. For the philosopher's questions and doubts and detachment tend in themselves to unsettle, to corrode, the habitual and emotional bonds that knit any healthy society together. The great practical teaching of the *Republic,* as interpreted by Strauss, is then a lesson about the limits of what we can reasonably hope for from politics—as well as a lesson about the constraints on political philosophy. There can never be a simply rational or enlightened society, in which knowledge rules, replacing mere opinion and habit. There can never be freedom of expression for the philosopher. Hence the wise philosopher must philosophize *politically.* He must learn how to employ rhetoric, oral and written, so as to carry on his liberating questioning and reach out to potential philosophers in an unobtrusive or even covert manner. But at the same time, his natural attachment to his fellowmen, as well as his knowledge of his dependence on society, impose on him additional and complex civic obligations. The philosopher must respect, even as he tries constructively to criticize and enlarge, the traditional perspective of his own and other societies. [77]

The practical upshot is that the regime the Socratic tradition favors as the best practicable, or as the guide to action, is a "mixed" republic, inclining where possible toward aristocracy. Plato's *Laws* and Aristotle's *Politics* provide models of how the political philosopher acts as an umpire, trying to arbitrate or "mix" the conflicting claims of poor majority and wealthy minority, of royal or noble families, artisans, soldiers, merchants, laborers, seamen, farmers. The goal is to devise ways the diverse classes or parties may partake in political responsibility so as to bring out the specific virtues, and repress the specific vices, of each. Yet the Socratic speaks from a perspective that looks down on all the major contenders for rule. He favors (when he can find them) the true "gentlemen" (*kaloi kagathoi*) or aristocrats, the few among the educated and leisured who try genuinely to dedicate themselves to the moral virtues and to some appreciation of the superiority of the life of the mind, even if only as pursued in reflective poetry and piety. As the Socratic dialogues repeatedly illustrate, usually with some comic effect, very few of the rich, well-born, and "well-educated" fall into such a category of true *aristoi*. In other words, the Socratics do not entertain great hopes that the few true aristocrats will play a weighty role in most republics—let alone in the despotic regimes that predominate in most places most of the time. Typically, the political voice of the Socratic will be a voice in lonely if loyal and prudent opposition: a voice that quietly but stubbornly reminds of the meaning and the question of true excellence, while calling attention to, and criticizing, the blinding prejudices and the proclivities to fanaticism in the reigning way of life. In oligarchies, the Socratics question the overemphasis on money-making; in theocracies, the slavish obedience to tradition; in military regimes, the stultifying stress on manliness; and in democracies, the leveling zeal of egalitarianism and the licentious interpretation of liberty. Every regime sees all too clearly the failings of its opponents; but it needs to be sternly reminded of the dangerous excesses that may flow from its unqualified attachment to what it regards as "obviously" right.[78]

STRAUSS'S POLITICAL TEACHING

Strauss's own teaching on politics, in the narrow sense, can best be understood as an attempt to revivify, adapt, and apply, in the dramatically new circumstances of our time, this centuries-old Socratic tradition. Having come to maturity in the unfortunate Weimar Republic, and having gratefully found in the United States a refuge and protection against Fascism, Strauss was a firm supporter and friend—but for this very reason, no flatterer—of liberal democracy.[79]

However distant liberal or mass democracy may be, in both its theory and its practice, from the civic republicanism of antiquity, liberal democracy remains a form of republicanism. It remains, that is, a form of self-government by the citizenry. It therefore continues to require, Strauss insisted, some version (an attenuated version, to be sure) of the Greco-Roman ideal of an active, proud citizenry imbued with knowledgeable respect for outstanding statesmanship. Strauss consequently deplored the influence of those thoughtlessly egalitarian historians who debunk, rather than make more intelligible, the greatness of statesmen; he vigorously opposed the prevalent tendency to belittle political history, to reduce the arguments and deeds of citizens and rulers to a merely "ideological" surface masking supposedly deeper, subpolitical economic or "social" forces; he ceaselessly challenged those among his social science colleagues who focused on what they called "behavior," and who thus treated the written opinions of judges, the deliberations of representatives, and the formation of public opinion as purely quantifiable and largely predictable "elite-group" or "mass" phenomena. He argued that these scholarly and teaching fashions not only undermined the already precarious respect for political debate and public-spirited leadership, but also falsified the empirical data, the reality of man as the political animal.[80]

Yet in trying to keep glowing the embers of the older republican citizenship and statecraft, Strauss did not succumb to any kind of nostalgic longing for the *polis* and its *vita activa,* "public space," or "sense of community." In this Strauss differed not only from various contemporary leftist and rightist critics of liberal democracy but also from Machiavelli, Rousseau, Nietzsche, and other radical modern thinkers. Strauss's overriding allegiance was to classical *philosophy,* not to the classical city or even to classical art. Strauss was too deeply penetrated by Thucydides' dissection of all that is implied in the immoderation of Pericles' funeral oration to be able to celebrate the splendors of imperialistic Athens. Partly as a result, it was not Strauss's habit to speak contemptuously of "bourgeois" individualism, or to spurn with ingratitude the unprecedented humanity, compassion, social welfare, and protection for diversity brought by the modern commercial republic. Strauss saw perhaps more clearly than anyone the disharmony in the American tradition between an older, nobler, but less influential classical or civic ideal and a new, ever more triumphant, permissive and individualistic order. But precisely for this reason he saw more clearly both the distinct virtues and the distinct vices of each component of the uneasy combination.[81]

In particular, Strauss admired the tolerance and respect for personal liberty that are the hallmarks of liberalism not only because they provide a haven for persecuted philosophy but also because they allow, if they do not encourage, the emergence of invigorating political disputation that can sometimes extend far beyond current events and controversies. There is then room within "liberalism," of the modern sort, for "liberalism" of the ancient sort. Strauss even found in modern liberalism a native place for the highest ingredient of that older liberalism—the liberalism that consists in liberation of the mind through study and debate of the alternative visions of human excellence developed in the great books. In the liberal university at its best, the ancient idea of "liberal education" continues to shine, as the crown jewel of modern liberalism—so long, that is, as the university resists the distorting pressures of democratic society's ceaseless demands for "relevance," "service to society," and the endorsement of current moral crusades and dogmas.[82]

This threat to the idea of the liberal university is endemic, Strauss argued, because it is only the most acute manifestation of a threat to authentic freedom of the mind that everywhere haunts the steps of modern liberalism: the grave fact is, the very openness of the open society contains within itself a self-destructive germ. This disease to which Strauss pointed is not the one liberals see readily and often resist nobly—the persistence and frequent resurgence of "unofficial" persecution and discrimination. More insidious and hence more corrosive is the tendency of democratic tolerance to degenerate, first into the easygoing belief that all points of view are equal (hence none really worth passionate argument, deep analysis, or stalwart defense), and then into the strident belief that anyone who argues for the superiority of a distinctive moral insight, way of life, or human type is somehow "elitist" or antidemocratic—and hence immoral. This is the syndrome that Tocqueville characterized, in an earlier manifestation, as the new, soft "tyranny of the majority": a subtle, unorganized, but all-pervasive pressure for egalitarian conformity arising from the psychologically chastened and intimidated individual's incapacity to resist the moral authority of mass "public opinion." In its most sublime expression, equality promises to every human being the opportunity to ascend to a just rank in the natural hierarchy of talents and attainments, of virtue and wisdom; but especially under the poisonous influence of the leveling moralism that disguises itself as "relativism," equality all too easily degrades itself.[83] Moreover, the problem is not alleviated, it is in fact aggravated, by the thoughtless lurch away from "relativism"; for contemporary democratic moralism in its overt form tends to overstress the virtues of a rather soft or flaccid sociability:

there exists a very dangerous tendency to identify the good man with the good sport, the cooperative fellow, the "regular guy," i.e., an overemphasis on a certain part of social virtue and a corresponding neglect of those virtues which mature, if they do not flourish, in privacy, not to say in solitude: by educating people to cooperate with each other in a friendly spirit, one does not yet educate nonconformists, people who are prepared to stand alone, to fight alone. . . . Democracy has not yet found a defense against the creeping conformism and the ever-increasing invasion of privacy which it fosters.[84]

There is, in Strauss's judgment, only one adequate response: "Liberal education is the counterpoison to mass culture . . . the ladder by which we try to ascend from mass democracy to democracy as originally meant"—i.e., "an aristocracy which has broadened into a universal aristocracy." Strauss held out no expectation that such a society could be achieved, and he in fact insisted that one not entertain distorting illusions and hopes as to its achievement; but he contended that small steps in its direction could be taken, and that to take such steps was the highest calling of liberal democracy.[85] Yet, to repeat, Strauss never tired of stressing the importance of distinguishing, especially in politics, between what is highest and what is most urgent; and what is most urgent as regards liberal democracy is not its improvement but its defense. In our aspirations to improve liberalism, Strauss argued, we must not lose our appreciation for the precious prosperity, humanity, and freedom we already possess.

Strauss found modern democracy endangered, in both its high aspirations and its urgent need for loyal defense, by contemporary social science. It was not only, as we have already explained, that the prevalent "methodologies" of social science and social scientific history necessarily induced cynicism about the very possibility of autonomous and reasonable political practice; even worse in its effects or implications was the purported distinction between "normative" and "empirical" propositions, between scientific "fact" and unscientific "value." As Strauss demonstrated in his critique of Max Weber (and also of lesser positivist thinkers), the theoretical underpinnings for this fact-value distinction were and are weak; the true, if not always acknowledged, source of the distinction's widespread acceptance is its coincidence with egalitarian relativism, the most simplistic and dogmatic but for that reason most readily available variety of democratic moralism. But this means to say that the supposedly "value-free" social science masks what is in fact a heedless endorsement, a dangerous extension or promotion, of the worst drift in democratic thinking.[86]

Against this tide, Strauss sketched the foundations of a very different political science, inspired by Aristotle's *Politics*. The impetus for this alternative political science came from reflection on the failings of the "scientific" study of politics, seen in the light of what could be learned from the history of political thought; but the actual practice of the new political science Strauss had in mind was by no means intended to be limited to historical studies. The alternative approach was to be genuinely "empirical," because derived strictly from the genuine *experience* of actual political behavior and thought. Truly empirical political scientists would start, not from an impossible "scientific" blank slate, but from "prescientific" political common sense. They would eschew scientific jargon and invented theoretical terminology, and instead follow the articulation of politics given in the practical language of engaged political men. Their study would attempt to be neither value-neutral (relativistic) nor "committed" (in the fashion of so-called "postbehavioral" efforts to muster theoretical or empirical evidence for left or right ideological programs); rooted in Socrates' conversational transcendence of common sense, a theoretically sound political science would begin from and never leave off critical engagement with the perspective of actively involved citizens arguing in defense of various persuasions. From that civic perspective, truly political science would adopt as its basic category of analysis the "regime," in the sense earlier delineated. The questions to which political scientists would direct their research, and the criteria of relevance or importance that would guide their selection and weighing of data, would be practical rather than theoretical or "scientific"; the questions and criteria of relevance would be derived very self-consciously from the burning issues and from the arguments over the regime in each country as well as from the arguments between the distinct regimes established in different countries. The aim would be not only to discover new information that would bear on the assessment of the various competing partisan positions, but also to carry the reasoning of each to its unstated or unthought conclusion, so as to illuminate and arbitrate the full implications of the nation's most basic or overarching disputes past and present. The methods and results of modern mathematics and natural science would be judiciously employed, in a strictly subordinate role. Political science would be less obsessed with trying to make predictions, on the basis of pseudo-universal laws or abstract models (it would know and admit that in politics anything other than the trivial and short-term is largely unpredictable), and would devote itself more to guiding genuine deliberation by enriching the citizenry's awareness of the range, weight, and validity of the factors and principles involved in major decisions. Sophisticated practitioners of such a political science would focus less on characteristics common to all regimes (defense, monetary policy) and more on the diverse political goals that mold and give distinctive meaning to these common things; they would cautiously ascend to man's common humanity by way of arbitration of the different and competing regimes' moral definitions of what is highest in man.[87]

This vision of a civic and empirical political science that Strauss tried to resuscitate dictates that our primary concern, as political scientists, should be the study of our own regime. This is the case because such a choice of focus expresses honestly our undeniable, primary concerns as human beings and because, recognizing this, we know we need to engage in a thorough and critical review of those concerns if we are ever to hope for any objectivity. Political scientists who are informed by Aristotle's and Strauss's stress on the regime, and the radical differences among regimes and their conflicting ways of life, are keenly aware of the awesome hold each regime has on the souls of those who grow up under it. As Plato expressed it in the most famous image of the *Republic,* each regime is a kind of cave-prison of the soul. Political scientists who come to feel this truth in their bones are stung by the knowledge of how very difficult it is even to become aware of the questionableness of one's own ingrained moral and political outlook. They know how easy it is to compound that initial blindness or distortion, by subtly and unconsciously forcing the data from earlier ages, from alien societies and regimes, into theoretical frameworks based on moral and human-behavioral assumptions appropriate only to the regime in which one was brought up. They do not trust to a supposedly neutral scientific method to produce neutral results: they know, in the first place, that the initial, basic questions political scientists ask are not generated by the method; they know, second, that no method is proof against the deep-seated moral opinions of its user; most important of all, they know that it is impossible truly to grasp or understand political phenomena, that it is impossible truly to *see* them, for what they are, without evaluating them—as just or unjust, cruel or benevolent, destructive or constructive. Aristotelean students of politics therefore move out from their own rootedness to a fruitful encounter and debate with foreign regimes, past and present. In doing so they do not act as mere "comparativists," comparing political systems as entomologists compare beehives. They engage in challenging debate, with a view to what is better and worse, more and less just. They aim at giving advice that will improve the lives of those they study, and seek to hear criticism that will improve the lives of their own fellow citizens. Like any sensible citizens who travel among or argue with foreigners in order to learn, such political scientists strive to suspend judgment, to cross-examine their own firm beliefs—not out of freedom from value judgments but as a direct consequence of the value judgment that the truth is sacred and must underlie the truly just by nature. Especially if they have been touched by the influence of the history of political philosophy, political scientists will go further than the citizen as such in this direction. Their pursuit of truth as citizens will be suffused by a sense of duty as citizens of the world: they will engage as judges and not only as enlightened contestants in the greatest of human controversies.[88]

In our age, the overriding political controversy is that between Western liberal democracy, centered in the United States, and Marxism, centered in the Soviet Union. The efforts and hopes we invest in negotiating and maintaining an uneasy peace must not divert us, Strauss insisted, from clear-sighted recognition of this essential and, for the forseeable future, continuous moral and political antagonism. Well-meaning "internationalist" attempts to downplay the significance of the conflict manifest both an ignorance of the importance of the political dimension, or the regime dimension, and a characteristically naive or apolitical belief that the leaders of profoundly different regimes nevertheless share the "reasonable" priorities, if not some version of the pacific and humane virtues, of our liberal regime. It is a principal function of political science, rightly understood, to dispel this illusion by promulgating an adequate understanding of the significance of the conflict among regimes in general and between the Marxist and liberal regimes in particular.[89]

This means that Strauss felt a special duty to engage the most thoughtful or fully articulate defenders of Marxism in searching debate. He accordingly devoted attention to more orthodox Marxists like Lukács and Macpherson; but he found the most compelling version of the Marxist conception to be that of Alexandre Kojève, the great Left-Hegelian. It was in his extensive, respectful, but uncompromising debate with Kojève that Strauss developed most fully his reflection on the deepest roots of Marxist thought. In that complex reflection we discern the following keynotes. On the strictly political or practical level, while intelligent Marxism seizes with some clarity certain inadequacies in the liberal-democratic conception of human nature (*e.g.*, the overemphasis on man as consumer, the drift toward relativism, the illusion of a value-neutral social science), the vague positive alternative that Marxism offers is, when thought through, indistinguishable from Nietzsche's nightmare vision of the future society of "Last Men."[90] Moreover, Marxism shares with its great enemy Nietzsche a gross underestimation of the value of liberal decency, compassion, civility, and lawful freedom. Worst of all, Marxism fails adequately to recognize the permanent need to devise institutional checks against the abuse of power. It is therefore no accident that Marxism as a historical reality (*i.e.*, as tested in the only test Marxism itself regards as probative) reveals itself as overwhelmingly prone to become the basis for a new and peculiarly cruel form of despotism.

On the theoretical level, or with regard to the rational self-consciousness that is humanity's distinguishing and most precious endowment, Marxism in all its forms fails to appreciate or come to terms with the most fundamental, and insuperable, contradiction permeating all social life: the disproportion between the politicized and collectivized thinking nowadays called "ideology"—a kind of "reasoning" which, even at its best, never transcends the level of dogma or "commitment"; and the radically independent philosophic questioning which at its core refuses to make any compromises whatsoever with any need or moral imperative other than the need and imperative to know the truth. True opinion—a faith, a loving dedication, a rootedness in one's own age or people that surmounts all doubts—is what all political societies, and almost all individuals, need, as the spiritual air they breathe. Genuine rationalism—rooted in knowledge of ignorance, possessed by eros for the eternal truth, in its heart longing to flee the atmosphere of the cave—can as a result never become the direct basis of any political or even cosmopolitan society.[91]

It was his unflinching recognition of this deepest of all human tensions that led Strauss to teach on so many levels the need for a moderation of our political or moral or religious expectations. "Human beings will never create a society which is free of contradictions." In compensation, as it were, Strauss invited us to taste an unfinishable but by no means fruitless quest for the truth about ourselves and the whole we inhabit. His political teaching was in the last analysis an instruction in "the sacrifices we must make so that our minds may be free." "We cannot be philosophers, but we can love philosophy"; this consists in "listening to the conversation between the great philosophers," *i.e.*, "in studying the great books." But "this conversation does not take place without our help . . . we must bring about that conversation." "The notion of the beneficence of nature or of the Good must be restored by being rethought through a return to the fundamental experiences from which it is derived. For while 'philosophy must beware of wishing to be edifying,' it is of necessity edifying." "We cannot exert our understanding without from time to time understanding something of importance; and this act of understanding may be accompanied by the understanding of understanding, by *noesis noeseos*. . . . This experience is entirely independent of whether what we understand primarily is pleasing or displeasing, fair or ugly. It leads us to realize that all evils are in a sense necessary if there is to be understanding. It enables us to accept all evils which befall us, and which may well break our hearts, in the spirit of good citizens of the city of God. . . . By becoming aware of the dignity of the mind, we realize the true ground of the dignity of man and therewith the goodness of the world, whether we understand it as created or as uncreated, which is the home of man because it is the home of the human mind."[92]

NOTES

Except where otherwise indicated, all works are by Leo Strauss.

1. "On a New Interpretation of Plato's Political Philosophy," *Social Research*, XIII, No. 3 (September 1946), 332–333; *On Tyranny* (Ithaca, N.Y.: Cornell University Press, 1968), pp. 21–22, 189–190; *The City and Man* (Chicago: University of Chicago Press, 1978), pp. 3–5 (hereafter *City*); "The Three Waves of Modernity," in *Political Philosophy: Six Essays by Leo Strauss*, ed. Hilail Gildin (Indianapolis and New York: Bobbs-Merrill and Pegasus, 1975), p. 98.

2. *Natural Right and History* (Chicago: University of Chicago Press, 1953), pp. 1–2 (hereafter *NRH*); *City*, pp. 2–4; "The Crisis of Our Time," in Harold J. Spaeth, ed., *The Predicament of Modern Politics* (Detroit: University of Detroit Press, 1964), pp. 41–45; "Three Waves of Modernity," pp. 81–82.

3. "Crisis of Our Time," pp. 42–43; *City*, pp. 5–6.

4. *City*, pp. 1, 6–7; "The Crisis of Political Philosophy," in Spaeth, ed., *Predicament of Modern Politics*, p. 91; *What Is Political Philosophy?* (Westport, Conn.: Greenwood, 1973), pp. 17–27 (hereafter *WIPP*).

5. *NRH*, p. 6.

6. *WIPP*, p. 20; "Crisis of Our Time," p. 48.

7. *NRH*, pp. 6–7; "The Mutual Influence of Theology and Philosophy, *Independent Journal of Philosophy*, III (1979), 114; *City*, p. 11.

8. *Spinoza's Critique of Religion* (New York: Schocken, 1965), p. 6.

9. "A Giving of Accounts: Jacob Klein and Leo Strauss," *The College*, XXII, No. 1 (April 1970), 2.

10. *Spinoza's Critique of Religion*, pp. 3–7; "Progress or Return? The Contemporary Crisis in Western Civilization," *Modern Judaism* I (1981), 21–22.

11. "Progress or Return?" p. 44; above, pp. 296–297.

12. *NRH*, pp. 32, 36, 71–72, 74–76; *Spinoza's Critique of Religion*, pp. 28–29, 30–31; "Mutual Influence," pp. 113–114, 116, 117–118; *Studies in Platonic Political Philosophy* (Chicago: University of Chicago Press, 1983), pp. 149–50 (hereafter *Studies*); *On Tyranny*, pp. 215–216.

13. "A New Interpretation," pp. 328–332; *WIPP*, p. 68; "On Collingwood's Philosophy of History," *Review of Metaphysics*, V, No. 4 (June 1952), 574; *NRH*, p. 33.

14. *Persecution and the Art of Writing* (Glencoe, Ill.: Free Press, 1952), pp. 157–158; "A New Interpretation," pp. 330–331, 333–334; *WIPP*, pp. 56–57, 68, 74.

15. *Persecution and the Art of Writing*, pp. 155–156; *WIPP*, p. 77.

16. *WIPP*, pp. 73–75; on modifications and transformations, see also *NRH*, pp. 76–79; *City*, p. 10; and "Three Waves of Modernity," p. 83.

17. *NRH*, p. 31; *WIPP*, pp. 27–28, 76–77, 78–79.

18. *Persecution and the Art of Writing*, pp. 155–156; *NRH*, pp. 79–80; *WIPP*, p. 75.

19. *NRH*, p. 33; *On Tyranny*, p. 24.

20. *NRH*, pp. 20–24, 31–32; *WIPP*, pp. 62–64.

21. *NRH*, pp. 24–25, 33; *WIPP*, pp. 72–77; "Collingwood's Philosophy of History," pp. 585–586.

22. *Persecution and the Art of Writing*, p. 158; *On Tyranny*, p. 27; *NRH*, p. 32.

23. "Collingwood's Philosophy of History," pp. 576, 585.

24. "A New Interpretation," pp. 328–329; *On Tyranny*, pp. 24–25; *Persecution and the Art of Writing*, p. 161; "Collingwood's Philosophy of History," pp. 574, 579–585.

25. George H. Sabine, *A History of Political Theory*, 3d ed. (New York: Holt, Rinehart and Winston, 1961),

pp. v–vi; cf. Strauss, "Crisis of Our Time," p. 51; *City*, p. 8; *WIPP*, pp. 227–228.

26. Leo Strauss to Hans-Georg Gadamer, February 26, 1961, in "Correspondence Concerning *Wahrheit und Methode*," *Independent Journal of Philosophy*, II (1978), 6; *Spinoza's Critique of Religion*, p. 2.

27. Strauss to Gadamer, February 26, 1961, p. 6; *Persecution and the Art of Writing*, pp. 159–161.

28. *WIPP*, p. 63; *Persecution and the Art of Writing*, pp. 55–56; *NRH*, pp. 198–199 n. 43.

29. "Collingwood's Philosophy of History," p. 583; *WIPP*, p. 14.

30. *WIPP*, pp. 63–64; *City*, pp. 50–62.

31. Alfarabi, *Plato's Laws*, in Ralph Lerner and Muhsin Mahdi, eds., *Medieval Political Philosophy: A Sourcebook* (Ithaca, N.Y.: Cornell University Press, 1972), pp. 84–85.

32. Moses Maimonides, *The Guide of the Perplexed*, trans. Shlomo Pines (Chicago: University of Chicago Press, 1963), pp. 18, 20.

33. See, *e.g.*, Plato's *Republic* 331ᶜ, 382ᶜ⁻ᵈ, 415ᵇ⁻ᶜ, 450ᵈ, 494ᵃ.

34. *Persecution and the Art of Writing*, pp. 17–18, 22–25; *WIPP*, pp. 93–94, 224–225.

35. *Persecution and the Art of Writing*, pp. 7–8, 33–36, 110, 182–183; *WIPP*, pp. 221–222; *NRH*, pp. 257–258, 260, 263.

36. *Persecution and the Art of Writing*, pp. 36–37; see also Maimonides, *Guide of the Perplexed*, pp. 17–18.

37. *Persecution and the Art of Writing*, pp. 26, 29–31; *WIPP*, pp. 223, 231–232; Strauss to Gadamer, February 26, 1961, pp. 5–6.

38. *Liberalism Ancient and Modern* (New York: Basic Books, 1968), pp. 6–8, 13, 15, 24.

39. *WIPP*, pp. 228–229; "Collingwood's Philosophy of History," p. 586.

40. *NRH*, pp. 23–24, 74–75;

Thoughts on Machiavelli (Chicago: University of Chicago Press, 1984), p. 14.

41. *NRH*, p. 32.

42. *NRH*, pp. 29–30, 32, 35; *On Tyranny*, p. 210.

43. *WIPP*, pp. 34–35, 40–41, 132; *NRH*, p. 139; "Three Waves of Modernity," pp. 83–85; and above, pp. 55–58, 68, 299–300.

44. *WIPP*, pp. 41–43, 49; *NRH*, p. 178; *Thoughts on Machiavelli*, pp. 294–297; "Three Waves of Modernity," pp. 85–87; *Liberalism Ancient and Modern*, pp. 19–20; above, p. 294.

45. *WIPP*, pp. 43, 51, 55; *NRH*, pp. 176, 178; *Thoughts on Machiavelli*, p. 295.

46. *WIPP*, pp. 43–44; *NRH*, pp. 177–178; above, p. 315; *Thoughts on Machiavelli*, pp. 157, 167, 185–188, 207–208.

47. *WIPP*, pp. 44–46; *Thoughts on Machiavelli*, pp. 84, 102, 118–119, 171–173, 297.

48. *NRH*, pp. 171–175; *WIPP*, p. 47; "Three Waves of Modernity," pp. 87–88.

49. *NRH*, pp. 179–180, 195–196, 199–201; *WIPP*, pp. 47–49.

50. *WIPP*, p. 49; *NRH*, pp. 248–250.

51. *WIPP*, pp. 50–52; "Three Waves of Modernity," pp. 89–93.

52. *WIPP*, pp. 53–54; "Three Waves of Modernity," pp. 91, 97; *Studies*, p. 32; *NRH*, pp. 316–319.

53. "Three Waves of Modernity," pp. 96–97; *Studies*, p. 189.

54. *WIPP*, pp. 47, 49, 50, 52, 55; "Progress or Return?" p. 30.

55. *WIPP*, p. 50; *NRH*, pp. 252–253.

56. "Three Waves of Modernity," p. 98.

57. *WIPP*, p. 55.

58. Cf. *Studies*, p. 32; *WIPP*, p. 53.

59. *WIPP*, p. 27; *City*, p. 9.

60. *NRH*, p. 31; "Giving of Accounts," p. 3; "An Unspoken Prologue

to a Public Lecture at St. John's," *The College,* XXX, No. 2 (January 1979), 31.

61. *WIPP,* pp. 11, 38–39, 248–251; *NRH,* pp. 30–32, 120–122; *Studies,* pp. 41–42, 170–171, 175, 185, 210; *Liberalism Ancient and Modern,* pp. 27, 232–234; cf. "Mutual Influence," p. 114: "The prototype of the philosopher in the classical sense was Socrates, who knew that he knew nothing, who therewith admitted that the whole is not intelligible, who merely wondered whether by saying that the whole is not intelligible we do not admit to having some understanding of the whole."

62. *WIPP,* pp. 38–40; *NRH,* pp. 23–24, 92–93, 123–124.

63. *NRH,* pp. 2–3, 81–86; *City,* pp. 19–20, 22, 25.

64. "Introduction," above, p. 5; *WIPP,* p. 116; *City,* pp. 19–21, 29, 42–43; *NRH,* pp. 73, 80, 121–124, 145–146, 163–164, 169–177, 201, 249; *Persecution and the Art of Writing,* pp. 95–98, 105–112; *Studies,* pp. 147–173, 210–211; *Socrates and Aristophanes* (New York: Basic Books, 1966), p. 313; *Spinoza's Critique of Religion,* pp. 8–9.

65. "Introduction," above, pp. 4–5; *City,* pp. 20–21; *Spinoza's Critique of Religion,* pp. 7–31, esp. 29: "The antagonism between Spinoza and Judaism, between unbelief and belief, is ultimately not theoretical but moral"—with which cf. *Persecution and the Art of Writing,* pp. 139–141.

66. *NRH,* pp. 93–113, 126; *City,* pp. 14–15.

67. *NRH,* pp. 10–12, 114–117; *City,* pp. 14–15; *Socrates and Aristophanes,* pp. 4–8, 11–53.

68. *NRH,* pp. 120–126; *City,* pp. 13–21, 53–54; *Xenophon's Socrates* (Ithaca: Cornell University Press, 1972), pp. 122–123.

69. *NRH,* pp. 129–130; *On Tyranny,* pp. 213–214.

70. *NRH,* pp. 128–135; *On Tyranny,* p. 205; *City,* pp. 34–35; *WIPP,* pp. 86, 89–90, 111.

71. *NRH,* pp. 140–143, 162–164, 193–194; *WIPP,* pp. 80–87, 89–91; *City,* pp. 31, 35–42, 44.

72. *City,* pp. 23–28, 226–231; *NRH,* pp. 128–129, 133–134; *On Tyranny,* p. 109; *Xenophon's Socratic Discourse* (Ithaca: Cornell University Press, 1970), pp. 115–122, 128–129, 133–139, 142–143, 147–150, 161–163; *Xenophon's Socrates,* pp. 59, 60–61, 63, 68, 76–77, 83, 85, 98, 121, 167. Cf. Christopher Bruell, "Strauss on Xenophon's Socrates," *Political Science Reviewer,* XIV (Fall 1984), 263–318.

73. *City,* pp. 28–29, 38–40; *Xenophon's Socratic Discourse,* pp. 165–179, 195; *The Argument and the Action of Plato's "Laws"* (Chicago: University of Chicago Press, 1975), pp. 70, 130–133; *Studies,* p. 185.

74. *City,* pp. 25–29, 37, 49; *NRH,* pp. 140–146, 149–152, 156–157; *Xenophon's Socratic Discourse,* pp. 132, 159–166, 175–176, 209; *WIPP,* pp. 29–33, 90–94; *Studies,* pp. 172–173; *Liberalism Ancient and Modern,* pp. 13–14, 19.

75. *NRH,* pp. 34, 115–117; *Liberalism Ancient and Modern,* pp. 3, 7, 53; *On Tyranny,* p. 198.

76. *City,* pp. 17, 45–49; *NRH,* pp. 135–138, 191–194; *WIPP,* pp. 33–36, 83–90.

77. *Liberalism Ancient and Modern,* pp. viii, 14–15; *Persecution and the Art of Writing,* pp. 7–37; *WIPP,* pp. 221–232.

78. *Liberalism Ancient and Modern,* pp. 14–15; *WIPP,* pp. 80–81, 85–90; *NRH,* pp. 138–143; *On Tyranny,* pp. 213–214, 219–222.

79. *Liberalism Ancient and Modern,* pp. 15, 23–25; *WIPP,* pp. 36–38, 263–264, 306–311; *On Tyranny,* p. 22; *City,* p. 11: "The return to classical political philosophy is both neces-

sary and tentative or experimental.
. . . We cannot reasonably expect that
a fresh understanding of classical political philosophy will supply us with
recipes for today's use. For the relative
success of modern political philosophy
has brought into being a kind of society
wholly unknown to the classics. . . .
Only we living today can possibly find a
solution to the problems of today. But
an adequate understanding of the principles as elaborated by the classics may
be the indispensable starting point for
an adequate analysis, to be achieved by
us, of present-day society in its peculiar
character, and for the wise application,
to be achieved by us, of these principles
to our tasks."

80. *Liberalism Ancient and Modern,*
pp. 4–5, 10, 23, 207–208, 213–
214, 216, 218–219; *WIPP,* pp. 27–
28, 78–87, 235–241.

81. *City,* pp. 22–23, 151–153,
192–195, 226–229; *Persecution and the
Art of Writing,* pp. 21, 22–37; "Introduction," above, p. 6; *Liberalism
Ancient and Modern,* pp. 15–23, esp.
p. 21.

82. *Liberalism Ancient and Modern,*
pp. vi, 3–25, 53–54, 262; *On Tyranny,* p. 27.

83. *Liberalism Ancient and Modern,*
pp. 5, 7–8, 23–25, 63–64, 262–
264, 268, 272; *NRH,* pp. 5–6.

84. *WIPP,* p. 38.

85. *Liberalism Ancient and Modern,*
pp. 4–5, 24–25; *NRH,* pp. 1–4.

86. *NRH,* pp. 1–7, 35–80; *Liberalism Ancient and Modern,* pp. 26, 28,
222–223; *WIPP,* pp. 18–24.

87. *Liberalism Ancient and Modern,*
pp. 205–215; *WIPP,* pp. 14–17,
27–29, 78–95; *NRH,* pp. 191–194;
"Social Science and Humanism," in
The State of the Social Sciences, ed.
Leonard D. White (Chicago: University of Chicago Press, 1956), pp. 416–
420.

88. *WIPP,* pp. 10–17, 21–25,
27–29, 56–57, 73–77; *NRH,* pp.
56–62; *Liberalism Ancient and Modern,*
pp. 216–223; "Social Science and Humanism," pp. 418–419.

89. *City,* pp. 4–6; *On Tyranny,*
pp. 21–22, 201–202, 222–226; *Liberalism Ancient and Modern,* pp. 24–25,
230–231, 270–271.

90. Nietzsche, *Thus Spake Zarathustra,* Prelude, sec. 5.

91. *Studies,* pp. 32–34, 229–231;
"'Relativism'," in *Relativism and the
Study of Man,* ed. H. Schoeck and J. W.
Wiggins (Princeton: Van Nostrand,
1961), pp. 145–148; *On Tyranny,*
pp. 143–226; *WIPP,* pp. 230–232.

92. *WIPP,* pp. 27–28; *Liberalism
Ancient and Modern,* pp. 7–8, 24; *Spinoza's Critique of Religion,* p. 6; *The Political Philosophy of Hobbes: Its Basis and Its
Genesis* (Chicago: University of Chicago
Press, 1952), p. xvi; *Thoughts on Machiavelli,* p. 299.

INDEX